CW00922881

Red Storm over the Balkans

Red Storm over the Balkans

The Failed Soviet Invasion of Romania, Spring 1944

David M. Glantz

University Press of Kansas

Published by the University Press of Kansas (Lawrence, Kansas 66045), which was organized by the Kansas Board of Regents and is operated and funded by Emporia State University, Fort Hays State University, Kansas State University, Pittsburg State University, the University of Kansas, and Wichita State University

Library of Congress Cataloging-in-Publication Data

Glantz, David M.
Red storm over the Balkans : the failed Soviet invasion of Romania, spring 1944 / David M. Glantz.
p. cm. — (Modern war studies)
Includes bibliographical references and index.
ISBN 0-7006-1465-6 (cloth : alk. paper)
1. World War, 1939–1945—Campaigns—Romania. I. Title.
D766.4.G63 2006
940.54'2198—dc22 2006019963

British Library Cataloguing-in-Publication Data is available.

Printed in the United States of America
10 9 8 7 6 5 4 3 2 1

The paper used in this publication meets the minimum requirements of the American National Standard for Permanence of Paper for Printed Library Materials Z39.48-1992.

Contents

Illustrations

Tables

Maps

PHOTOGRAPHS

Preface

During the course of over five months of nearly continuous fighting in the winter and spring of 1944, the Red Army's 11 operating *fronts* inflicted major defeats on three German army groups, liberated large amounts of German-occupied territory in the western Soviet Union—including virtually all of the Leningrad region [*oblast'*], most of the central and western Ukraine, and the Crimean peninsula—and made significant inroads against the *Wehrmacht*'s defenses in eastern Belorussia. While doing so, the Red Army destroyed or severely damaged at least 16 German divisions and eliminated hundreds of thousands of soldiers from the *Wehrmacht*'s order of battle, either by encirclement or sheer combat attrition, and reduced another 60 German divisions to only skeletal strength.

Whereas the *rasputitsa* [rainy season] compelled the Red Army to call a halt to its offensive operations during the springs of 1942 and 1943, this was not the case during the spring of 1944. As a result, the *Wehrmacht,* which had been able to exploit the rainy weather and mud-clogged roads to rest, refit, and regroup its forces during the spring of previous years, faced a prolonged and unremitting struggle for its very survival. Therefore, when the Red Army's winter campaign ended in May 1944, the only region where the *Wehrmacht*'s defenses held firm was in eastern Belorussia, where the beleaguered forces of its Army Group Center defended an immense salient jutting eastward, but with virtually no reserves.

Operating along the northwestern (Leningrad) axis, during January 1944 the Red Army's Leningrad and Volkhov Fronts defeated German Army Group North in the Leningrad region, finally raising the German blockade of Lenin's namesake city. Joined by the 2nd Baltic Front, the same two *fronts* then expelled Army Group North's forces from most of central and southern Leningrad *oblast'* by the end of March and, during April, commenced offensive operations to penetrate the Germans' Panther Defense Line and recapture the Baltic region, which the *Wehrmacht* had invaded and seized in June and July of 1941. Simultaneously, from January through March 1944, the Red Army's 1st Baltic, Western, and Belorussian Fronts conducted nearly continuous though often futile attacks against Army Group Center's defenses in eastern Belorussia, pressing German forces back into the fortress city of

Vitebsk, turning the army group's northern and southern flanks, and forcing it to commit its last precious reserves to contain their assaults.

Finally, operating far more effectively than their counterparts to the north, the Red Army's 1st, 2nd, 3rd, and 4th Ukrainian Fronts, joined by the new 2nd Belorussian Front during February, which were advancing along the southwestern axis in the Ukraine, liberated virtually the entire Right Bank of the Ukraine (the region west of the Dnepr River) from German Army Groups South and "A," expelled German forces from the Crimean peninsula and the city of Sevastopol', and advanced westward to the borders with Poland and Romania.* As the four *fronts* advanced westward, they shattered or seriously damaged the *Wehrmacht*'s First Panzer, Sixth, Eighth, and Seventeenth Armies.

Since the war's end, Soviet and, more recently, Russian historians have insisted that the military strategy Stalin pursued during the winter campaign of 1943–1944 required the Red Army to conduct major offensive operations against German forces defending along the northwestern (Leningrad) and the southwestern (Ukrainian) axes to the exclusion of other sectors of the front, in particular, the western (Minsk-Warsaw) axis. Furthermore, these historians claim, once the Red Army accomplished Stalin's objectives in these regions by mid-April 1944, Stalin abruptly halted further offensive operations by the Red Army and thereafter shifted his strategic focus to Belorussia and Poland, the most direct axes into the heart of Hitler's Germany, where the Red Army resumed offensive operations in the summer of 1944.

In short, these historians assert Stalin's military strategy involved concentrating the bulk of the Red Army's strength along the northwestern and southwestern strategic axes so that the army's operating *fronts* could achieve the missions the *Stavka* (High Command) assigned to them, while the *Stavka* economized on the expenditure of vital Soviet manpower and material resources. In reality, however, during the winter and spring of 1944, Stalin pursued the same "broad front" strategy he had employed since the beginning of the war, based largely on the assumption that, if the Red Army applied maximum pressure everywhere, the *Wehrmacht*'s defenses were likely to break somewhere.

* Before 1945 and during World War II, the English spelling of the country's name was "Rumania." The spelling "Romania," as used in this volume, follows current practice in English. It is also the only spelling ever used in Romania itself, since 1859, when the land came into existence as a state. The form with "o" was particularly chosen to stress the people's descendency from the ancient Romans. It was a statement the Romance-speaking population surrounded mostly by Slavic countries and then under Turkish rule wanted especially to make.

Close examination of German and Russian archival materials now indicates that this traditional explanation of the military strategy Stalin pursued during this period is incorrect. In reality, contrary to this Soviet construct, archival records prove beyond any reasonable doubt that Stalin ordered the Red Army to conduct major offensives along the entire Soviet-German front during the winter and spring of 1944. Specifically, in addition to the major offensive operations it ordered the Red Army to conduct in the Leningrad region, the Ukraine, and the Crimea during the winter, the *Stavka* also directed the Red Army to conduct large-scale offensive operations against German Army Group North's defenses in the Baltic region, as well as against German Army Group Center's defenses in eastern Belorussia. Furthermore, once the Red Army's forces liberated most of the Ukraine during the winter and early spring, in mid-April Stalin and his *Stavka* ordered the Red Army's 2nd and 3rd Ukrainian Fronts to commence a coordinated invasion of Romania, by doing so, evidencing Stalin's deliberate strategy to project Soviet military power and political influence into the Balkans so that the Soviet Union could secure a more favorable postwar settlement and division of the spoils of war with its western Allies.

Although the Red Army's invasion of Romania during April and May 1944 ultimately failed, it exacerbated the harshly negative military and political effects of the devastating defeats the *Wehrmacht* suffered in the Ukraine during the preceding winter. In addition to seriously weakening Army Group South Ukraine, the Red Army's invasion of northern Romania during the spring of 1944 also seriously damaged the fighting spirit and will of Romanian Armed Forces; undermined the morale of its soldiers, sailors, and airmen; and weakened Romanian support for the German war effort in light of Romania's previously catastrophic military losses and the loss of its northern provinces of Bessarabia and Moldavia. Tangentially, but as a consequence of the defeats it suffered in the Ukraine, the German Army occupied Hungary on 19 March 1944 to prevent its possible defection to the Allied camp.

By exploiting a wide range of existing but unexplored German archival materials and newly released Soviet archival documents, along with more fragmentary materials found in numerous Red Army unit histories and the memoirs of its wartime commanders, this study reconstructs an imposing mosaic, thereby revealing the immense scope and scale and ambitious intent of what should be termed the Red Army's first Iasi-Kishinev offensive.

Like so many other "forgotten battles" of the Soviet-German war, which encompass as much as 40 percent of the actual war record, Soviet and Russian historians have "forgotten" the Red Army's invasion of Romania during the spring of 1944 largely because the offensive failed and because this failure seemed to tarnish the luster of the Red Army's newfound and lofty fighting reputation, as well as the reputations of the senior commanders who planned and conducted the offensive.* However, while "forgetting" this military defeat helped preserve the reputations of the Red Army and some of its generals, it also insulted the memories of the thousands of Red Army soldiers and officers who participated in, perished, or otherwise suffered during its conduct and obscured the remarkable feats of those thousands of German and Romanian soldiers and officers who inflicted this signal defeat on the Red Army. It is to those soldiers that I dedicate this volume.

* Ironically, the Red Army's winter campaign of 1944 also included a successful "forgotten battle," Rokossovsky's offensive in southern Belorussia from January through March 1944, whose conduct Soviet and Russian military historians have also covered up. In this case, presumably they covered up this partially successful offensive, which will be the subject of a future volume, because it enhanced Rokossovsky's reputation to the detriment of other senior Red Army commanders, in particular, V. D. Sokolovsky, the commander of the Western Front during this period, who rose to prominence during the postwar years despite his dismal record in *front* command during wartime. See also David M. Glantz, *Forgotten Battles of the Soviet-German War (1941–1945)*, vol. 6: *The Winter Campaign (24 December 1943–April 1944) (Part Three: The Western Axis)* (Carlisle, PA: Self-published, 2004).

CHAPTER 1

Introduction

THE WINTER CAMPAIGN (DECEMBER 1943–APRIL 1944)

The Conventional Construct

As is the case with the Soviet-German War (1941–1945) as a whole, for a variety of reasons, historical studies of military operations that took place during the eight seasonal campaigns constituting this most terrible of wars remain strikingly incomplete. While it is impossible to quantify precisely how incomplete these histories are, recently released archival materials indicate that, depending on the specific campaign, these histories have overlooked, obfuscated, or, in certain extreme cases, deliberately covered up as much as 40 percent of the military operations that actually took place. No campaign illustrates this problem more succinctly than the Red Army's winter campaign of 1944 (Map 1).

By both German and Soviet definitions, the winter campaign of 1944 commenced in early January 1944, when the Red Army launched massive offensives in the Leningrad region and the Ukraine, and ended in mid-April 1944, after these and other savage offensives forced the *Wehrmacht*'s forces to withdraw from vast territories in the northwestern and southwestern Soviet Union. Within the context of this definition, both German and Russian histories of this campaign have focused almost exclusively on the Red Army's successful offensives in the Leningrad region during January and February 1944, in the Ukraine from late December through early April 1944, and in the Crimea during late March and April 1944.

Russian studies of this campaign assert that the *Stavka* (High Command) formulated strategic plans during early December 1943 aimed at expelling the *Wehrmacht*'s forces from the Leningrad region and the Ukraine during the course of the third winter of the war. Specifically, these plans required the Red Army's Leningrad and Volkhov Fronts, which were operating in the Leningrad and Novgorod regions, to drive German Army Group North's forces from the Leningrad region and liberate all Soviet territory up to the eastern borders of the Soviet Union's three Baltic republics. During the same period, the Red Army's 1st, 2nd, 3rd, and 4th Ukrainian Fronts, whose forces were operating along the Dnepr River or from bridgeheads on this river's western and southern bank, were to drive German Army Groups South's and "A's"

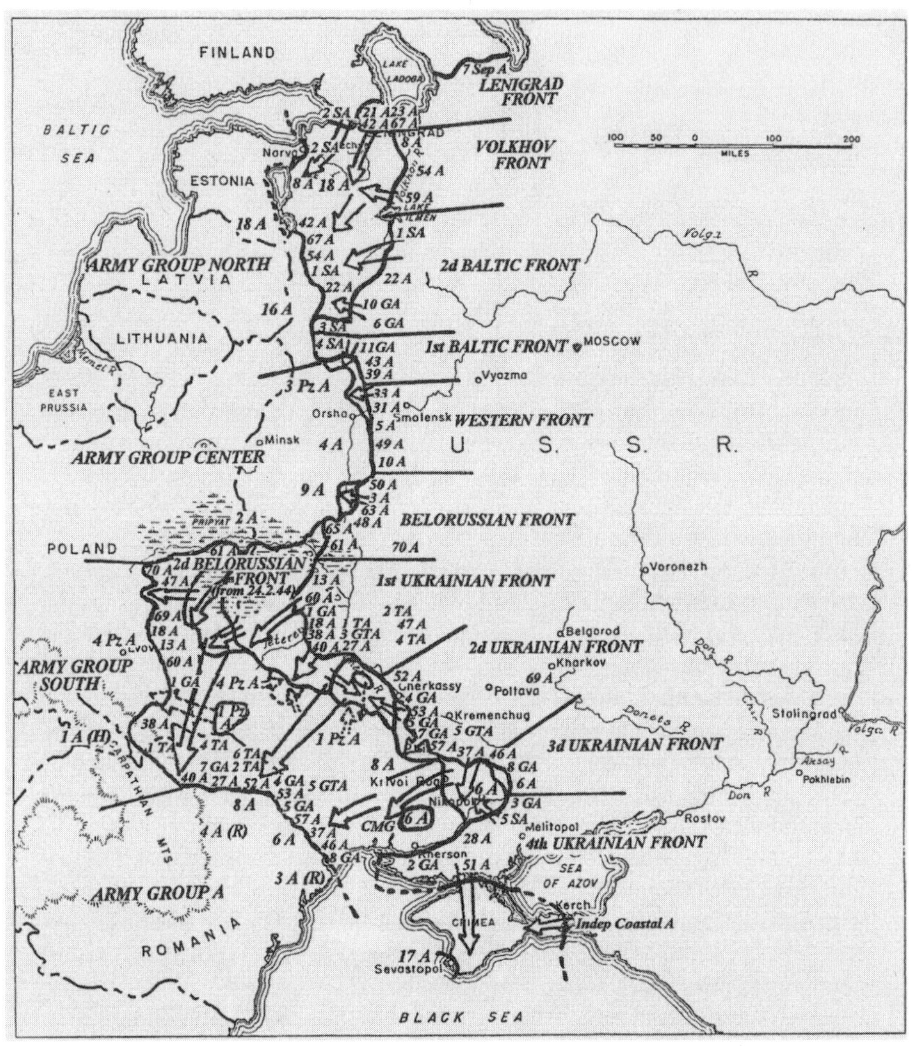

Map 1. The Red Army's winter campaign, December 1943–17 April 1944

forces from the Ukraine and the Crimea and liberate all Soviet territory east of the Polish border and north of Romanja.

These studies claim that, by conducting these two strategic offensives successfully, the *Stavka* hoped to create favorable conditions for the subsequent destruction of Army Group Center's forces in Belorussia during the ensuing summer of 1944. Although it ordered its forces to conduct strategic offensives along both the northwestern and southwestern axes, the *Stavka* supposedly accorded strategic priority to its offensives in the Ukraine, where it expected its 1st, 2nd, 3rd, and 4th Ukrainian Fronts to commence their offensive operations in staggered fashion in terms of their timing but thereafter both simultaneously and successively. This offensive pattern presumably permitted the *Stavka* to shift vital artillery and mechanized forces and weaponry from *front* to *front,* all the while concealing the full scope and true intent of these offensives.

Existing histories indicate that the first phase of the Red Army's offensive in the Ukraine, which began on 25 December 1943 and lasted through late February 1944, consisted of five major offensive operations: the 1st, 2nd, 3rd, and 4th Ukrainian Fronts conducted either singly or jointly against separate elements of Field Marshal Erich von Manstein's Army Group South and Field Marshal Ewald von Kleist's Army Group "A." Actually, the first two of these offensives, the Zhitomir-Berdichev and Kirovograd offensive operations, were continuations of previous offensive operations designed to expand the Red Army's bridgeheads across the Dnepr River.

During the first of these offensives, the Zhitomir-Berdichev offensive, Army General N. F. Vatutin's 1st Ukrainian Front attacked from its bridgehead roughly 35 miles west of Kiev on 24 December 1943 and advanced southward through Zhitomir and Berdichev to the outskirts of Army Group South's headquarters at Vinnitsa, 80 miles southwest of Kiev, where the offensive ground to a halt by 14 January 1944. Although Army Group South's Fourth and First Panzer Armies (the latter was transferred to this region on 1 January) encountered difficulties in containing this offensive, they managed to stop the deep thrust by the Red Army's 1st and 3rd Guards Tank Armies just short of their objective, Vinnitsa, by launching counterstrokes with their III, XXXXVI, and XXXXVIII Panzer Corps.

During the second offensive, the Kirovograd offensive, which Army General I. S. Konev's 2nd Ukrainian Front conducted from 5 through 16 January 1944, Konev's forces wheeled westward from its previous axis of advance toward Krivoi Rog, 65 miles south of the Dnepr River and 220 miles southeast of Kiev, and its exploiting 5th Guards Tank Army captured the city of Kirovograd, 160 miles southeast of Kiev, from Army Group South's Eighth Army. By mid-January, Vatutin's and Konev's offensives managed to pin two of the German Eighth Army's army corps into a large salient that was protruding precariously northward toward the Dnepr River north of the Ukrainian town of Korsun'-Shevchenkovskii, 100 miles southeast of Kiev, which became the target of the next Red Army offensive.

After the Red Army's first two winter offensives in the Ukraine succeeded, from 24 January through 17 February, Vatutin's and Konev's 1st and

2nd Ukrainian Fronts conducted the third Red Army offensive, the Korsun'-Shevchenkovskii offensive, a coordinated surprise offensive against the defenses of Army Group South's Eighth Army at the base and flanks of the Korsun'-Shevchenkovskii salient. During the course of several weeks of intense and difficult winter fighting, the two *fronts* that were exploiting 6th Tank and 5th Guards Tank Armies, later reinforced by the 2nd and 1st Tank Armies, encircled the Eighth Army's two defending corps and destroyed up to 30,000 *Wehrmacht* troops while fending off fierce German counterstrokes before Army Group South was able once again to stabilize its positions in new defenses south of the Dnepr River.

While the *Wehrmacht's* attention was riveted on the desperate struggle around the Korsun'-Shevchenkovskii salient, the *Stavka* ordered all four of its Ukrainian *fronts* to mount fresh coordinated assaults against Army Group South's northern and Army Group "A's" southern flanks to capitalize on the fact that the bulk of both army groups' panzer reserves were decisively engaged in the Korsun'-Shevchenkovskii region. In response, Vatutin's 1st Ukrainian Front initiated the fourth Red Army offensive in the Ukraine, an assault by his 13th and 60th Armies and 1st Guards and 6th Guards Cavalry Corps, which were deployed on his *front's* right wing, against Army Group South's exposed left flank in the Poles'e region, south of the Pripiat' Marshes and roughly 150 miles west of Kiev. During the Rovno-Lutsk offensive, which lasted from 27 January through 11 February, Vatutin's forces turned Army Group South's left flank; captured the cities of Rovno and Lutsk, 180 and 225 miles west of Kiev, respectively; and occupied favorable positions from which to conduct future operations into Army Group South's rear area.

Finally, while Vatutin's and Konev's *fronts* were savaging Army Group South's defenses in the central and western Ukraine, Army General R. Ia. Malinovsky's 3rd and Army General F. I. Tolbukhin's 4th Ukrainian Fronts conducted a joint offensive along concentric lines against the defenses of Army Group "A's" Sixth Army, which was anchored along the "great bend" of the Dnepr River in the eastern Ukraine. Malinovsky's and Tolbukhin's assaults, which were termed the Nikopol'–Krivoi Rog offensive and which lasted from 30 January through 29 February, collapsed Army Group "A's" defenses in the Nikopol' bridgehead, on the Dnepr River's southern bank, seized the salient in the Dnepr River's "great bend," and captured the vital road and railroad junction at the city of Krivoi Rog.

The five major offensives conducted by the Red Army's four Ukrainian *fronts* drove the *Wehrmacht's* forces from the entire "great bend" in the Dnepr River by the end of February 1944. Deprived of this formidable defense line, the forces of Manstein's Army Group South and Kleist's Army Group "A" now became vulnerable to complete defeat in detail in the vast interior plains of the central and western Ukraine.

While the four Ukrainian *fronts* were wreacking havoc on German defenses in the Ukraine, the *Stavka* unleashed the Red Army on fresh assaults in the Leningrad region. In this case, the *Stavka*'s destructive tools were Army General L. A. Govorov's Leningrad Front and Army General K. A. Meretskov's Volkhov Front, later joined by Army General M. M. Popov's 2nd Baltic Front. Govorov's and Meretskov's two *fronts* began their massive concerted offensive, the Leningrad-Novgorod offensive operation, on 14 January 1944; raised the blockade of Leningrad within days; and, later joined by Popov's 2nd Baltic Front, thereafter orchestrated a painfully slow advance toward the eastern borders of the Baltic region. This combined assault drove Army Group North's Eighteenth and Sixteenth Armies back to their Panther Line defenses by the end of February, where the Red Army advance collapsed from exhaustion.

According to existing accounts, the *Stavka* directed the Red Army to continue to focus its main strategic efforts in the Ukraine during early March virtually without a pause, despite crippling terrain problems caused by the spring *rasputitsa* [rainy season]. During this second phase of the *Stavka*'s strategic offensive on the so-called Right Bank of the Ukraine (the region west of the Dnepr), which began on 4 March and lasted until mid-April, the Red Army's 1st, 2nd, 3rd, and 4th Ukrainian Fronts launched five more mutually supporting offensives, employing all six of the Red Army's tank armies, and completely cleared the *Wehrmacht*'s forces from the Ukraine and the Crimea (Map 2). The *Stavka*'s priority strategic objective during this offensive was to split German Army Groups Center in Belorussia from Army Groups South and "A" in the Ukraine and to destroy the two army groups operating in the Ukraine by driving them southward and pinning them against the Black Sea or Carpathian Mountains.

The 1st Ukrainian Front, now under the personal command of Marshal of the Soviet Union G. K. Zhukov after Vatutin's death at the hands of Ukrainian partisans, began the first of these coordinated offensives, the Proskurov-Chernovtsy offensive, on 4 March. By attacking southwestward from the Shepetovka and Dubno regions, 150 and 210 miles west of Kiev, respectively, Zhukov's forces thrust deeply into Army Group South's rear and advanced toward Chernovtsy, 255 miles southwest of Kiev and just north of the Ukrainian-Romanian border. During the first stage of this offensive, Zhukov's 3rd Guards and 4th Tank Armies tore a gaping hole in the defenses of Army Group South's Fourth Panzer Army and by 7 March approached Proskurov, where Manstein's hastily redeployed III and XXXXVIII Panzer Corps finally brought their advance to a halt.

Within days, however, Zhukov regrouped his 1st Tank Army from his *front*'s left wing to its right wing and employed this fresh tank army and the 4th Tank Army to spearhead the second phase of his offensive. Attacking on

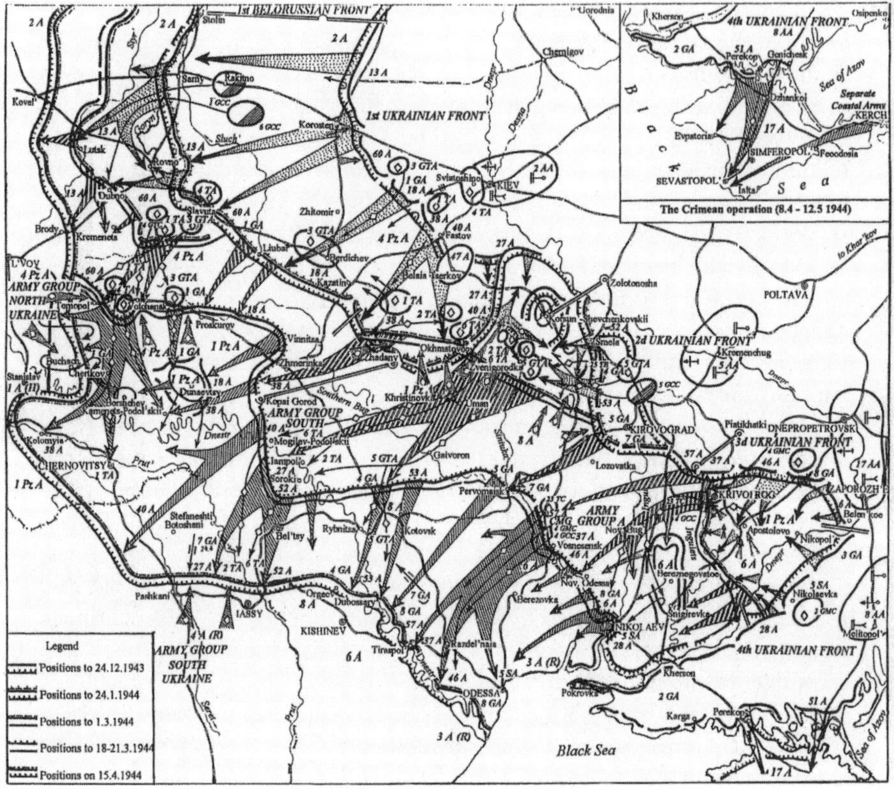

Map 2. Operations on the right bank of the Ukraine, 24 December 1943–17 April 1944

21 March, Zhukov's 1st and 4th Tank Armies once again burst into the operational depths of Manstein's Army Group and reached and crossed the Dnestr River on 27 March, encircling the bulk of the German First Panzer Army in the Kamenets-Podol'skii region, 260 miles southwest of Kiev. Continuing its headlong advance, the 1st Tank Army reached the Carpathian Mountains on 17 April, severing all communications between Manstein's army group, recently renamed Army Group North Ukraine, and the also newly renamed Army Group South Ukraine, now operating in northern Romania, now commanded by Colonel General Ferdinand Schörner, who had replaced Kleist on 31 March.

A dizzying series of strokes and counterstrokes ensued as Manstein struggled to rescue his encircled First Panzer Army, while Zhukov tried equally hard to destroy it before it escaped. After more than a week of complex and often confused seesaw fighting, Manstein finally managed to extract his beleagured panzer army westward to the relative safety of southern Poland as Zhukov's offensive collapsed in exhaustion.

The day after Zhukov's 1st Ukrainian Front commenced its offensive southward toward Proskurov, on 5 March Konev commenced the *Stavka*'s second offensive operation in the Ukraine, called the Uman'-Botoshany offensive, by unleashing his 2nd Ukrainian Front's forces in an attack toward Uman' and Vinnitsa, 120 and 130 miles south of Kiev, respectively. Spearheaded by the *front*'s 2nd Tank, 5th Guards Tank, and 6th Tank Armies, which captured the cities of Uman' and Vinnitsa on 10 March, Konev's forces advanced steadily across a broad front in tandem with Zhukov's forces to the west. Konev's exploiting forces finally reached and crossed the Dnestr River near Mogilev-Podol'skii, 180 miles southwest of Kiev, on 17 March, effectively separating Army Group North Ukraine's First Panzer Army from Army Group South Ukraine's Eighth Army to the south. Konev's forces continued their slow but steady advance through early April against skillful delaying operations by Army Group South's Eighth Army and, in spite of terrible *rasputitsa* conditions, finally approached the Romanian border in early April.

While the Red Army's six tank armies were setting the offensive pace for the 1st and 2nd Ukrainian Fronts, on 6 March Malinovsky's 3rd Ukrainian Front launched the *Stavka*'s third offensive, the Bereznegovatoe-Snigirevka offensive, along the Black Sea coast against Army Group "A," which Hitler had formed during late 1943 to defend the southern Ukraine. Although Malinovsky's forces managed to encircle Army Group "A's" Sixth Army in the Bereznegovatoe region, 230 miles southeast of Kiev, by 8 March, they failed to destroy the army, which escaped successfully westward to the Southern Bug River. Nevertheless, by severely damaging the Sixth Army, the 3rd Ukrainian Front created conditions conducive to subsequent westward advance toward the port of Odessa, on the Black Sea coast 290 miles south of Kiev.

Exploiting the victory of Malinovsky's 3rd Ukrainian Front, Tolbukhin's 4th Ukrainian Front began the *Stavka*'s fourth offensive operation, the Crimean offensive, on 8 April. After assaulting and quickly penetrating the German Seventeenth Army's defenses in the Crimea, Tolbukhin's forces bottled the beleaguered army up in the fortress port city of Sevastopol' by 16 April and forced the Germans to evacuate the city by 10 May. While Tolbukhin's forces were clearing German and Romanian forces from the Crimea, on 26 March Malinovsky's 3rd Ukrainian Front capped its victory in the southern Ukraine by commencing the *Stavka*'s fifth offensive operation in the region, the Odessa offensive. Spearheaded by a cavalry-mechanized group, Malinovsky's forces swept southwestward and southward toward the Dnestr River, pierced Army Group South Ukraine's defenses northwest of the city, and captured Odessa on 10 April, forcing its Sixth Army's three army corps to withdraw westward in considerable disorder to new defensive positions along the Dnestr River's western bank.

Official Soviet and Russian histories have consistently claimed that the Red Army's 1st Baltic, Western, and Belorussian Fronts conducted only two "limited-objective" offensives, together with several "diversionary" operations against Army Group Center's defenses in eastern Belorussia throughout the entire duration of the winter campaign. According to these accounts, the first of these "limited-objective" offensives took place between 3 February and 13 March, when Army General I. Kh. Bagramian's 1st Baltic and Army General V. D. Sokolovsky's Western Fronts assaulted the defenses of Army Group Center's Third Panzer and Fourth Armies around Vitebsk in northern Belorussia, but with only limited success. The second offensive supposedly occurred during 21–26 February, when Army General K. K. Rokossovsky's Belorussian Front struck the defenses of Army Group Center's Ninth Army at Rogachev and Zhlobin, in southern Belorussia, but only managed to capture Rogachev and seize other inconsequential bits of German-occupied territory. Thus, these histories treat both offensives as essentially designed to divert the German attention from the more strategically vital sectors to the north and south.

Therefore, chronologically by strategic axis, Soviet (Russian) and most German histories of the war assert the following major military operations took place during the winter campaign of 1943–1944:

THE NORTHWESTERN AXIS

The Leningrad and Volkhov Front's Leningrad-Novgorod Offensive (14 January–1 March 1944)

THE WESTERN AXIS

The 1st Baltic and Western Fronts' Vitebsk Offensive (3 February–13 March 1944)

The Belorussian Front's Kalinkovichi Raid (11–14 January 1944)

The Belorussian Front's Rogachev-Zhlobin Offensive (21–26 February 1944)

THE SOUTHWESTERN AXIS

The 1st Ukrainian Front's Zhitomir-Berdichev Offensive (24 December 1943–14 January 1944)

The 2nd Ukrainian Front's Kirovograd Offensive (5–16 January 1944)

The 1st and 2nd Ukrainian Fronts' Korsun'-Shevchenkovskii Offensive (Cherkassy) (24 January–17 February 1944)

The 1st Ukrainian Front's Rovno-Lutsk Offensive (27 January–11 February 1944)
The 3rd and 4th Ukrainian Fronts' Nikopol'–Krivoi Rog Offensive (30 January–29 February 1944)
The 1st Ukrainian Front's Proskurov-Chernovtsy Offensive (Kamenets-Podol'skii) (4 March–17 April 1944)
The 2nd Ukrainian Front's Uman'-Botoshany Offensive (5 March–17 April 1944)
The 3rd Ukrainian Front's Bereznegovatoe-Snigirevka Offensive (6–18 March 1944)
The 3rd Ukrainian Front's Odessa Offensive (26 March–14 April 1944)
The 4th Ukrainian Front's Crimean Offensive (8 April–12 May 1944)

Within the context of this operational construct, virtually all histories and other analytical studies of the winter campaign, Russian and German alike, adhere to two basic theories regarding how the *Stavka* conducted the campaign strategically. Advanced primarily by Soviet and Russian military historians and theorists, the first theory asserts that, when Stalin, his *Stavka,* and the Red Army General Staff formulated their campaign strategy and planned and conducted the Red Army's strategic operations during this period, they consistently adhered to a "narrow-front" strategy to achieve victory. Argued by most German historians, the second theory maintains that Hitler adopted a "stand fast" policy during this period, which affected the *Wehrmacht*'s military operations adversely. Although the first of these theories proves mythical, the second contains at least a germ of truth.

The first theory contends that Stalin and his principal military advisers adopted and tenaciously pursued a "'narrow-front" strategy throughout the entire duration of the campaign by requiring the Red Army to focus its most important offensive operations along two principal strategic axes: the northwestern axis in the Leningrad region and the southwestern axis in the Ukraine. This strategy required the Red Army to concentrate the bulk of its soldiers, weaponry, and material along these axes so that its operating *fronts* could achieve the missions assigned to them by the *Stavka,* and, while doing so, the *Stavka* could economize on the expenditure of vital manpower and material resources. Of these two strategic axes, argue these historians, the Ukrainian axis was by far the most important.

The second theory correctly asserts that Hitler began adhering to a "stand fast" strategy during the winter of 1944 to a far greater extent than previously and to such a degree that it seriously inhibited and adversely affected both current and future *Wehrmacht* military operations. Hitler indeed began transforming the "stand fast" strategy he had employed during previous years, at Stalingrad for example, to an outright *festung* [fortress] strategy, but he did so with only mixed success.

While Hitler's repeated orders for Army Group North to "stand fast" in the face of the Red Army's Leningrad-Novgorod offensive juggernaut ultimately failed to halt the Red Army's advance to the eastern borders of the Baltic states, his adoption of a *festung* strategy to defend such vital cities as Pskov and Ostrov did succeed in halting the Red Army's advance in the region along the fortified defenses of the Panther Defense Line during early March. Likewise, even though Hitler's insistence that Army Group Center convert the cities of Vitebsk, Orsha, Gomel', and others in eastern Belorussia into fortresses forestalled the army group's defeat in Belorussia during the winter of 1944, in this case it ultimately led to an even more disastrous German defeat along the periphery of the Belorussian "balcony" during Operation Bagration (the Red Army's Belorussian offensive) in the summer of 1944.

Finally, Hitler's employment of both stand fast and *festung* strategies in the Ukraine cost the *Wehrmacht* the better part of two army corps lost in the battle for the Korsun' (Cherkassy) pocket during February 1944, almost an entire panzer army in the Kamenets-Podol'skii region during April 1944, and significant forces at Sevastopol' in the Crimea also during April. However, his employment of a similar strategy in the defense of Kovel' and Brody in the western Ukraine succeeded in holding Red Army forces at bay, at least for several months, and his use of a similar strategy to defend northern Romania defeated what turned out to be a major Red Army thrust into the Balkans region.

Overwhelming archival evidence now indicates that both this operational construct of the winter campaign and the two theories associated with its conduct are patently false, largely because they overlook, ignore, or cover up other significant offensive operations the Red Army tried to conduct in Belorussia, as well as in the southern Ukraine and Romania.

The Forgotten War

By focusing almost exclusively on the successful offensive operations the Red Army conducted in the Leningrad region, the Ukraine, and the Crimea, this conventional construct of military operations during the winter campaign of 1944 ignores several major Red Army offensives that fall into two general categories: first, offensive operations the Red Army deliberately conducted to exploit previously successful strategic offensives, in particular, in the Leningrad region and the Ukraine; second, significant offensive operations, both successful and unsuccessful, which Red Army forces conducted in eastern Belorussia as a continuation of operations that had begun as early as October 1943.

Although it is quite easy, if not convenient, for historians to overlook these follow-on and continuation offensives since most of them failed and their nature and limited impact made them easy to conceal, the *Stavka's* rationale for conducting them in the first place is now quite clear. Specifically, pursuant to strategies it consistently employed earlier in the war, by 1944 the *Stavka* routinely expanded its strategic horizons and aims during the course of ongoing major Red Army offensive operations, particularly if those offensives developed successfully. It did so, first and foremost, by assigning its victorious operating *fronts* new and more ambitious missions once they accomplished their initial objectives, and it justified these expanded missions on the grounds that, since it could not determine whether or when the German defenses would collapse, it would sacrifice lucrative opportunities for even greater victories if it did not relentlessly exploit its offensive operations to the maximum.

Of course, by ordering its forces to perform these new missions, the *Stavka* always risked defeat of its overextended attacking forces by the sort of counterattack, counterstrokes, and counteroffensives it faced in the Donbas region during February and March 1943 and in the Kiev region in November and December 1943. However, by the winter of 1944, this was a risk the *Stavka* was usually willing to take, particularly if it could mask the existence of any subsequent failures by successes achieved in previous offensive operations.

Finally, the dramatic successes the Red Army recorded in the strategic offensives it conducted during 1944 and 1945 has made it far more difficult to assess accurately whether follow-on offensive operations conducted at the end of its successful major offensives were genuine attempts to exploit success, were merely attempts to improve its strategic posture for undertaking future offensive operation, or were simply designed to deceive the Germans regarding its future strategic offensive intentions.

Detailed analysis of German and Soviet (Russian) archival materials indicates that the roster of "forgotten" battles or overlooked offensive operations the Red Army conducted during the winter campaign of 1944 include at least the following:

THE NORTHWESTERN AXIS

The Leningrad Front's (8th, 54th, and 2nd Shock Armies) Narva Offensives (2–28 February, 1–16 and 17–24 March 1944)

The German Narva Counterstrokes (26 March–24 April 1944)

The 2nd Baltic Front's (1st and 3rd Shock, 6th and 10th Guards, and 22nd Armies) Pustoshka-Idritsa Offensive (12–16 January 1944)

The 2nd Baltic Front's (1st and 3rd Shock, 6th and 10th Guards, and 22nd Armies) Novosokol'niki-Idritsa Offensive (31 January–13 February 1944)

The 2nd Baltic Front's Offensive Preparations and Pursuit to the Panther Line (17 February–1 March 1944)

The Leningrad Front's (42nd and 67th Armies) Pskov-Ostrov Offensive: The Struggle for the Panther Line (2–17 March, 7–19 April 1944)
The 1st Baltic Front's (4th Shock and 6th and 11th Guards Armies) and 2nd Baltic Front's (1st and 3rd Shock, 10th Guards, and 22nd Armies) Opochka and Sebezh Offensives (1–8 March, 10–26 March, and 7–18 April 1944)

THE WESTERN AXIS

The 1st Baltic, Western, and Belorussian Fronts' Belorussian Offensive (1 January–15 March 1944)

- The 1st Baltic (4th Shock and 11th Guards Armies) and Western Fronts' (5th and 33rd Armies) Vitebsk Offensive (23 December 1943–6 January 1944)
- The 1st Baltic (4th Shock and 11th Guards Armies) and Western Fronts' (5th, 33rd, and 39th Armies) Vitebsk-Bogushevsk Offensive (8–24 January 1944)
- The 1st Baltic (4th Shock and 11th Guards Armies) and Western Fronts' (5th and 33rd Armies) Vitebsk Offensive (3–16 February 1944)
- The Western Front's (31st Army) Babinovichi Offensive (22–25 February 1944)
- The Western Front's (5th and 33rd Armies) Vitebsk Offensive (29 February–5 March 1944)
- The Western Front's (31st and 49th Armies) Orsha Offensive (5–9 March 1944)
- The Western Front's (5th and 33rd Armies) Bogushevsk Offensive (21–29 March 1944)
- The Belorussian Front's (61st and 65th Armies) Kalinkovichi-Mozyr' Offensive (6–14 January 1944)
- The Belorussian Front's (61st and 65th Armies) Ozarichi-Ptich Offensive (14–30 January 1944)
- The Belorussian Front's (48th and 65th Armies) Bobruisk (Marmovichi-Mormal') Offensive (29 January–9 March 1944)
- The Belorussian Front's (3rd and 50th Armies) Rogachev-Zhlobin Offensive (21–26 February 1944)

The 2nd Belorussian Front's (47th, 61st, and 70th Armies) Poles'e (Kovel') Offensive (15 March–5 April 1944)

THE SOUTHWESTERN AXIS

The 2nd Belorussian Front's Poles'e (Kovel') Offensive (15 March–5 April 1944)

- The 2nd Belorussian Front's Penetration Battle, Exploitation, and Encirclement of Kovel' (14–29 March 1944)

- The German Relief of Kovel' (29 March–5 April 1944)

The 1st Ukrainian Front's (13th Army) Encirclement Battle at Brody (Proskurov-Chernovtsy Offensive) (20 March–17 April 1944)

- The 13th Army's Penetration Battle, Exploitation, and Encirclement of Brody (15–26 March 1944)
- The German Relief of Brody (27 March–7 April 1944)
- The Aftermath (8–17 April 1944)

The 2nd and 3rd Ukrainian Fronts' Iasi [Iassy]-Kishinev Offensive (Tirgu Frumos and Dnestr River Bridgeheads) (8 April–6 June 1944)

- The 2nd Ukrainian Front's Advance to Tirgu Frumos, Iasi, and Dubossary (8–23 April 1944)
- The 3rd Ukrainian Front's Advance to the Dnestr River and the Bridgehead Battles (11–25 April 1944)
- The 2nd and 3rd Ukrainian Front's Iasi-Kishinev Offensive (25 April–8 May 1944)
- German Sixth Army's Counterstrokes along the Dnestr River (8–30 May 1944)
- Army Group Wöhler's Iasi Counterstroke (Operations "Sonja" and "Katja") (30 May–5 June 1944)

Archival evidence now indicates that, with the full agreement of his principal military advisers, Stalin ordered the Red Army to conduct major offensive operations across the entire extent of the Soviet-German front during the winter campaign of 1943–1944. Representing nothing less than a continuation of the "broad front" strategy he had pursued since the beginning of the war, this strategy clearly reflected Stalin's long-standing belief that the *Wehrmacht*'s defenses were likely to break somewhere along the front if the Red Army applied pressure everywhere. Therefore, in addition to ordering the Red Army to conduct offensive operations to expel *Wehrmacht* forces from the Leningrad region and the Ukraine, during the winter campaign, Stalin also ordered the Red Army to launch major assaults against the German Panther Defense Line in the Baltic region and across the entire expanse of eastern Belorussia.

However, once the Red Army's offensives against German defenses in eastern Belorussia bogged down during late February and early March, in light of its more successful offensives in the Leningrad region and the Ukraine, Stalin and the *Stavka* devoted special attention to organizing and pressing additional offensive operations by the Red Army's operating *fronts* in the Baltic region and also ordered at least two of its four *fronts* operating in the Ukraine to mount ambitious follow-on offensive operations once they successfully completed their second wave of offensives in mid-April. Specifically, in addition to ordering the Leningrad, Volkhov, and 2nd Baltic Fronts to mount heavy assaults against the Germans' Panther Line defenses, which protected the approaches to the Baltic region, in March and April, after the 2nd and 3rd Ukrainian Fronts reached the Dnestr River line in mid-April, Stalin also ordered these two *fronts* to mount a major coordinated strategic offensive deeper into Romania and the Balkans region during late April and May. The latter also signaled the beginning of Stalin's future strategy for projecting the Red Army's forces ever deeper into the Balkans region in order to secure a more favorable postwar settlement and division of the spoils of war with his Western Allies.

THE BALKAN DIMENSION: THE WAR IN SOUTHERN UKRAINE AND NORTHERN ROMANIA (APRIL–JUNE 1944)

The Conventional Construct

With a few minor exceptions, most Soviet and Russian accounts of the offensive operations the Red Army conducted in the Ukraine during the late winter and early spring of 1944 assert that the Right Bank of the Ukraine offensive operation, which the 1st, 2nd, and 3rd Ukrainian Fronts began on 3 and 4 March 1944, ended on 17 April when the forces of the three *fronts* reached the eastern border of Poland and the northern border of Romania. As such, the general offensive on the Right Bank of the Ukraine consisted of three distinct *front* offensive operations: the Proskurov-Chernovtsy offensive conducted by Zhukov's 1st Ukrainian Front from 4 March through 17 April and the Uman'-Botoshany offensive conducted by Konev's 2nd Ukrainian Front from 5 March through 17 April; the Bereznegovatoe-Snigirevka and subsequent Odessa offensives conducted by Malinovsky's 3rd Ukrainian Front from 6 through 18 March and from 26 March through 14 April, respectively; and the Crimean offensive conducted by Tolbukhin's 4th Ukrainian Front from 8 April through 12 May 1944 (Map 2).

The descriptions of the Red Army's winter campaign found in the official Soviet military encyclopedia published in eight volumes during the late 1970s and the official Russian eight-volume military encyclopedia published in the late 1990s both assert that the 2nd and 3rd Ukrainian Fronts went over to the defense in mid-April 1944 after their offensive momentum ebbed and German resistance stiffened. For example, the encyclopedia entry describing the 2nd Ukrainian Front's Uman'-Botoshany offensive operation states categorically:

> After developing their offensive from bridgeheads on the Dnestr River, the 27th and 52nd Armies, together with formations from the 2nd and 6th Tank Armies, reached the state borders of the USSR along an 85-kilometer [51-mile] front north of Iasi on 26 March. The fronts' forces

forced the Prut River from the march on the night of 28 March and began operations on Romanian territory. They reached the Carpathians [Mountains], captured the city of Botoshany [60 miles northwest of Iasi], and reached the approaches to Iasi and Kishinev by mid-April. Striving to save the southern wing of their front from complete destruction, the German-Fascist command transferred 18 divisions and three brigades to that axis. After encountering increasing enemy resistance, the 2nd Ukrainian Front's forces dug in along the lines they reached during the middle of April.[1]

Likewise, when describing the 3rd Ukrainian Front's Odessa offensive, the same encyclopedia asserts Malinovsky's *front* also went over to the defense in mid-April after it completed liberating the city of Odessa:

While continuing to pursue the enemy [after capturing Odessa], from 11 through 14 April, the fronts' forces reached the Dnestr River, captured Tiraspol' [on the Dnestr River 40 miles east of Kishinev], and, after forcing the river from the march, seized bridgeheads on its western bank. By order of the Stavka VGK, the Soviet forces went over to the defense along that line [on 14 April].[2]

Nor do other more detailed accounts of Red Army actions during this period shed any additional light on actually what occurred during combat in this region after mid-April. For example, the official Soviet six-volume *History of the Great Patriotic War*, which was published in the 1960s, reaffirms the standard official interpretation of as to when and why the 2nd and 3rd Ukrainian Fronts terminated their offensive operations in April 1944:

Confronted with the reality that his defenses on the Right Bank of the Ukraine had broken down, and the Sixth and Eighth German and Third Romanian Armies were threatened with encirclement, the enemy moved the fresh Fourth Romanian Army up to the Iassy [Iasi] region, whose main forces then occupied the most important mountain passes in the Carpathians and defenses along a line [extending] from Pascani [45 miles west of Iasi] to north of Iassy. At the same time, under pressure from the 3rd Ukrainian Front, the Sixth German Army began to retreat hurriedly from the Southern Bug River [westward] to the Dnestr. During this [retreat], six of its divisions were transferred to the Kishinev axis against the 2nd Ukrainian Front.

The 2nd Ukrainian Front's forces reached the Radauti [95 miles northwest of Iasi], Pascani, Orgeev [25 miles north of Kishinev], and Dubossary [22 miles northeast of Kishinev] line at the end of March and middle of

> April and, by order of the Supreme High Command, went over to the defense on 6 May. . . .
>
> After continuing its offensive [after capturing Odessa], the 3rd Ukrainian Front's forces occupied Tiraspol' [40 miles east of Kishinev] on 12 April and then forced the Dnestr from the march and captured bridgeheads on the opposite bank.[3]

The official Soviet 11-volume *History of the Second World War,* which was published in the late 1970s, added little more light to this otherwise sketchy description:

> Enemy resistance increased on the Iassy [Iasi] and Kishinev axes at the end of March. By this time the 2nd Ukrainian Front's forces were overextended, and, during the course of its headlong offensive in totally deplorable road conditions, its artillery and rear services lagged behind. Therefore, having halted any further advance, the front's forces dug in along the Radauti, Pascani, and Dubossary line during the middle of April. . . .
>
> Continuing its [Odessa] offensive from 11 to 14 April, the 3rd Ukrainian Front's forces reached the Dnestr River and captured bridgeheads on its western bank. Here, it encountered organized enemy resistance. Just as along the Iassy axis, the fighting for the Dnestr line was of an exceptionally prolonged nature. While conducting furious counterattacks, the enemy continued moving fresh forces into the region. The correlation of forces changed in his favor. [Therefore], on 6 May the Stavka of the Supreme High Command ordered the 2nd and 3rd Ukrainian Fronts' forces to go over to the defense along their existing lines.[4]

Nor do the memoirs of the key marshals and generals who led the Red Army during these operations add much relevant detail to these official accounts. For example, when describing his 2nd Ukrainian Front's operations during the spring of 1944, Konev simply notes: "A *Stavka* directive dated 6 May 1944 approved the transition to the defense. Thus, having entered Romanian territory along the Radauti, Orgeev, and Dubossary line, the forces of the 2nd Ukrainian Front went over to the defense at the end of March and during the first few days of April."[5]

However, several notable exceptions exist to these common accounts. Specifically, a few Russian general histories and studies of operations during this period, as well as a few memoirs of officers who served in this sector at this time, note the heavy fighting that raged in the Iasi region and along the Dnestr River during April, May, and June 1944, although most do so only within the context of German counterattacks and counterstrokes, without mentioning the *Stavka*'s or the 2nd and 3rd Ukrainian Fronts' operational, much less strategic, intentions. For example, without providing any further details about or rationale for the fighting in terms of the *Stavka*'s intent or the two *fronts'* participation, a general survey of the Red Army's contributions to the liberation of the Balkans states:

> Considering the importance of these bridgeheads [in northern Romania] for the destruction of Army Group "Northern Ukraine" and the withdrawal of Romania from the war, as well as for the liberation of the other countries in the Balkans, the Soviet command concentrated significant forces (the 40th, 27th, 52nd, and 7th Guards Armies, and also part of the 2nd and 6th Tank Armies) in the small territories of northeastern Romania.
>
> Soviet forces fought for more than four months to hold on to these bridgeheads, on some days repelling 15–20 attacks by large enemy forces supported by tanks and aircraft. The enemy suffered great losses in personnel and weapons. During the course of April alone, the forces of the 40th, 37th, and 52nd Armies destroyed 166 tanks and assault guns.
>
> Particularly fierce fighting began in May and the beginning of June. After deciding to throw our forces back across the Prut [River] [a western tributary of the Dnestr River], the German command created a powerful grouping consisting of ten divisions, including four panzer [divisions], in the Iassy [Iasi] region. The enemy went over to the offensive against the units of the 52nd and 27th Armies on 30 May after a strong artillery preparation and a massive air bombardment. . . .
>
> The enemy was not able to achieve his aims. The enemy was able to push our forces back several kilometers in some sectors, but at the cost of heavy losses. The enemy lost 27,170 soldiers and officers, more than 500 tanks and assault guns, and 266 aircraft from 30 May through 5 June. Our forces also suffered heavy losses. During the battles to hold on to liberated Romanian territory, the 52nd and 27th Armies and the 2nd and 6th Tank Armies lost 14,871 men in these days, including 2,800 killed and 11,600 wounded. The enemy destroyed 96 of our tanks and self-propelled guns and damaged 132 aircraft and 18 self-propelled guns.[6]

Although it provides precious few details concerning either the *Stavka*'s overall strategic intent or actual plans or the 2nd Ukrainian Front's involvement in the offensive, by far the most revealing memoir covering action during this period is that written by Lieutenant General V. I. Chuikov, the commander of the 3rd Ukrainian Front's 8th Guards Army who had earned lasting fame as the commander of the 62nd Army during the defense of Stalingrad in late 1942. Chuikov's unusually candid memoir provides a uniquely clear and accurate account of his army's role in the fighting during April and

May 1944. Although his account deals only with his 8th Guards Army's experiences in the fighting along the Dnestr River, even if in a backhanded way, it confirms the vital role the *Stavka* intended the 3rd Ukrainian Front to play during its planned offensive deep into Romania by describing why the *Stavka* ultimately cancelled the offensive:

> On 4 May the army received a short order from the [3rd Ukrainian] front commander. It read: "To the commander of the 8th Guards Army—prepare to conduct the main attack with your left wing toward Chimisheny [14 miles east of Kishinev] and Kostozhany [five miles south of Kishinev] to envelop Kishinev from the south. I will point out the time of the offensive personally."
>
> R. Ia. Malinovsky, the front commander, assembled all of his army commanders at a meeting in the village of Malaeshty [seven miles east of the Dnestr and ten miles north of Tiraspol'] on 6 May, during which he briefed us on the operational situation. [He said] the enemy's forces on the Right Bank of the Ukraine were beaten and their remnants were withdrawing across the Dnestr, and this created the prerequisites for an offensive toward Kishinev, to liberate Bessarabia, and to strike toward Bucharest [220 miles south of Kishinev] and Ploeshti [Ploiesti] [180 miles south of Kishinev]. We were assigned the mission to concentrate our forces. Together with our staffs, we departed to think through what needed to be done to mount so extensive an offensive.
>
> However, as early as the morning of 8 May, we received an order from the *front* commander that determined the subsequent course of events along the Dnestr right up to the month of August. The order required the *front*'s forces to go over to a firm defense.[7]

Although Chuikov carefully asserted that the *Stavka* cancelled the 3rd Ukrainian Front's May offensive because of shortages of artillery and ammunition, it is now clear it actually cancelled the offensive only because Konev's 2nd Ukrainian Front, which was supposed to conduct its main thrust southward west of Iasi, suffered a severe defeat in early May along the Tirgu Frumos and Iasi axes.

Historical Reality

German archival documents, a few German histories of the war, recently released Soviet (Russian) archival materials, and fragmentary Soviet accounts now clearly reveal that, on several occasions during April and May 1944, the *Stavka* indeed ordered its 2nd and 3rd Ukrainian Fronts to mount a major coordinated offensive with definite strategic implications into northern Romania. These materials indicate the *Stavka*'s strategic intent was nothing short of rupturing German and Romanian strategic defenses in northern Romania, propelling its forces across the Dnestr River, capturing the key cities of Iasi and Kishinev, and projecting these forces deep into Romania, perhaps as deep as Ploiesti and Bucharest.

In partial confirmation of this fact, the four-volume official Russian history of the Great Patriotic War, which was published in 1999, now provides an accurate thumbnail sketch of these operations and the *Stavka*'s strategic intent as it conducted them:

> On 2 May Konev undertook a new attempt to envelop the enemy in the Iassy [Iasi] and Kishinev regions with the armies on the 2nd Ukrainian Front's center and left wing and, in cooperation with the 3rd Ukrainian Front, destroy him and advance to the lower reaches of the Prut River. During the first day [of the offensive], the 2nd Ukrainian Front's forces achieved success and wedged up to ten kilometers [six miles] into the defenses. However, while suffering heavy losses, subsequent fighting did not result in an advance. On 6 May the Stavka ordered the front's forces to go over to a resolute defense. . . .
>
> As early as 5 April, Konev submitted his views to the Stavka regarding a new offensive operation by his front, whose aim was to envelop "the main enemy southern grouping" by Soviet forces. The operation was planned to commence on 8 April with an offensive by the 40th and 27th Armies to reach the Radauti [95 miles northwest of Iasi], Tirgu-Neamt [60 miles west of Iasi], and Bacau [52 miles southwest of Iasi] line. Thereafter, the 40th Army was to go over to the defense to protect the front's right flank. At first, the 27th Army was to conduct its main attack along the Bolotino [five miles north of the Prut River, 42 miles north of Iasi], Tirgu Frumos [28 miles west of Iasi], Roman [35 miles southwest of Iasi], and Bacau axis with the 3rd Guards Tank Corps attached. The offensive was to be supported soon after by the 7th Guards and 5th Guards Tank Armies, which were to be transferred [westward] from other sectors of the front. The missions of the 2nd Ukrainian Front's remaining armies (the 4th Guards, 53rd and 5th [Guards] Combined-Arms, and the 2nd and 6th Tank Armies) were to capture Kishinev and reach the Prut River. After approving Konev's decision on 6 April, at that time the Stavka ordered him to transfer either the 2nd or 6th Tank Armies to the right [western] bank of the Prut River for an attack toward the south along the Seret River [running north to south 35 miles west of Iasi], to transfer the 7th Guards Army's base [of operations] to the region west of Rybnitsa [on the

Dnestr 55 miles north of Kishinev], and to commit a corps of the 40th Army [southward] from Khotin [north of the Romanian border 110 miles northwest of Iasi] and employ it to reinforce the attacking units.

The 2nd Ukrainian Front had sufficient forces to fulfill its assigned missions. . . .

The offensive conducted by the forces on the 2nd Ukrainian Front's right wing was sufficiently energetic from 8 through 11 April. They forced the Seret and Zhizhia [Jijia] Rivers [50–60 miles northwest of Iasi], advanced 30–50 kilometers [18–30 miles] to the southwest and south, and approached the foothills of the Carpathians [Mountains]. The 27th Army's forces captured Tirgu Frumos [28 miles west of Iasi] on 9 April but were forced to abandon the town two days later as a result of an enemy counterattack. The forces on the *front's* left wing encountered organized resistance and were able to advance only 10–15 kilometers [six to nine miles]. The 2nd Ukrainian Front's offensive had essentially ended by 11 and 12 April, . . .

During the next several days, the 40th and 27th Armies engaged in continuous combat with counterattacking enemy forces. The 2nd Tank Army, which was committed to combat on 12 April, repelled a counterstroke by an enemy tank group in the Podu-Iloaie region [15 miles west of Iasi] in cooperation with the 27th Army. The forces on the *front's* left wing liberated Dubossary [23 miles northeast of Kishinev] and Grigoriopol' [23 miles east of Kishinev], reached the Dnestr River, and fought to expand their bridgeheads. . . .

On 18 April Konev submitted a more precise decision [plan] to the *Stavka:* to penetrate the [enemy's] defense in the 15-kilometer [9-mile] sector from Pascani to Tirgu Frumos [45–28 miles] west of Iasi, to conduct his main attack along the left bank of the Seret River toward Bacesti [28 miles southwest of Iasi], and, subsequently, to develop the offensive toward Bacau [52 miles southwest of Iasi] or Vaslui [40 miles south of Iasi]. The shock group was to consist of 15 rifle divisions from the 40th, 7th Guards, and 27th Armies and 470 to 520 tanks and self-propelled guns from the 5th Guards and 2nd Tank Armies. . . . The operation was planned to begin on 27–29 April. Simultaneously, secondary attacks were to be conducted along the Iassy [Iasi] and Kishinev axes. A 23 April directive of the *front* commander formulated even more decisive missions for the shock group [to accomplish]—that is, to capture the Bacau and Vaslui regions and to cut off the withdrawal routes of the enemy's Iasi-Kishinev region to the west. Therefore, the *front's* operational plan took on clearer contours during the last ten days of April. The 2nd Ukrainian Front's forces completed their regrouping to form a shock group in the

Tirgu-Frumos region only by the end of April, and, as a result, it had to postpone the start date for the offensive several times. . . .

The 2nd Ukrainian Front's forces launched their offensive along the secondary Iasi and Kishinev axes on 25–26 April to attract enemy reserves from the main axis. However, the German command determined our operational concept prior to the operation and, in addition, learned the exact time of our attack. It quickly transferred the SS "Death Head" [*Totenkopf* or "*T*"] Motorized Division from the Piatra region [40 miles southwest of Tirgu-Frumos] to Tirgu-Frumos and inserted it into the forward area of his defense the night before our forces began their offensive. We also conducted our artillery preparation against only open spaces. Therefore, beginning on the morning of 2 May, the armies of the *front*'s main shock group encountered strong fire resistance and their advance was extremely slow.

Four enemy panzer divisions were already operating in the 2nd Ukrainian Front's penetration sector on 3 May, and two Romanian infantry divisions were being transferred to the Roman-Bacau axis. The 7th Guards and 5th Guards Tank Armies' formations tried unsuccessfully to penetrate the second defensive belt on this and subsequent days, and the units of the 2nd Tank Army, which reached the approaches to Tirgu-Frumos without effective cooperation with the 27th Army's formations, were forced to withdraw to their jumping-off positions under the pressure of strong counterattacks. Attempts by Soviet forces to resume the offensive beginning on the morning of 5 May also did not yield any success. As a result, we withdrew both of our tank armies from combat by early the next day.

Thus, during the Tirgu-Frumos operation, the 2nd Ukrainian Front's forces tried unsuccessfully to complete a deep penetration of the enemy's defense and reach the territory between the Seret and Prut Rivers. By order of the *Stavka*, they themselves went over to the defense along their existing lines on 6 May.[8]

Regarding the operations by Malinovsky's 3rd Ukrainian Front during this same period, the new official history simply states:

The commander of the 3rd Ukrainian Front sent his proposals to Moscow regarding "the conduct of an operation after we reach the state's borders" on 12 April. Five armies were to conduct its main attack along the Tiraspol' [40 miles east of Kishinev], Komrat [50 miles south of Kishinev], and Kagul [82 miles south of Kishinev] axis, and the 8th Guards Army [was to conduct] a secondary attack along the [northern] coast of the Black Sea.

> [The front] intended to commit Cavalry-Mechanized Group Pliev to exploit its success. We planned to reach the Prut and Danube Rivers [60–80 miles deep] on the ninth or tenth day. The operation was to begin on 18–20 April, when all of the front's forces were to force the Dnestr River. Before the 5th Shock and 6th Armies concentrated in their jumping-off regions for their offensive, the 57th, 37th, and 46th Armies were to continue widening the bridgeheads on the right bank of the Dnestr. The Stavka approved Malinovsky's decision on 15 April without change.
>
> However, subsequent combat operations indicated that, by the time they reached the Dnestr, the 3rd Ukrainian Front's forces had exhausted their offensive capabilities. During this short period, they had not succeeded in refilling their reserves of ammunition, fuel, and foodstuffs or in filling out their formations and units with sufficient personnel. The several attempts the participating armies made to conduct attacks out of their bridgeheads and seize new bridgeheads led to nothing. By order of the Stavka, the 3rd Ukrainian Front went over to the defense on 6 May. The front lost 32,633 men, including 6,882 permanent [killed, captured, or missing], from 20 April up to 6 May.[9]

Despite these relatively accurate and candid but sketchy recent revelations, Russian historians have yet to produce a thorough account of the intense fighting that raged during the final stages of the Red Army's offensive on the Right Bank of the Ukraine. At least in part, this has been the case because the Red Army's two *fronts* failed to achieve their objectives and in part because these offensives demonstrate Stalin's political intent to gain a foothold in the strategically vital Balkans region long before any previous history has indicated. However, thanks to existing German archival sources, fragmentary materials from Soviet sources, and many newly released Russian archival documents, it is now possible to reconstruct these failed offensive operations in considerable detail.

CHAPTER 2

Prelude

THE SITUATION IN EARLY APRIL 1944

General

After nearly a month of continuous offensive operations, by late March 1944, the forces of the Red Army's 1st, 2nd, and 3rd Ukrainian Fronts had breached the defenses of German Army Groups South and "A" across the entire breadth of the Ukraine and advanced deep into the *Wehrmacht*'s strategic rear area along virtually every axis traversing the Ukraine from north to south and east to west. With their defenses irreparably shattered, the German *Oberkommando des Heeres* (OKH) (Army High Command), which controlled *Wehrmacht* operations in the East, was struggling to restore some semblance of a contiguous defensive front to protect the approaches to southern Poland and northern Romania.

Despite the OKH's best efforts, in cooperation with the 40th Army, which was advancing southwestward on the 2nd Ukrainian Front's extreme right wing, on 4 April the forward elements of Zhukov's 1st Ukrainian Front swept southward to capture the key road junction at the town of Khotin, situated on the Dnestr River 110 miles northwest of Iasi at the junction of the approaches to southeastern Poland and northern Romania. Only days before, Zhukov's 1st Tank Army had already lunged even father to the south and captured the city of Chernovtsy (Cernauti), located on the Prut River in northern Romania; in the process, he had isolated the German First Panzer Army of Manstein's Army Group South in a pocket around and east of the city of Kamenets-Podol'skii. In one of his last acts as the army group's commander, with a reluctant Hitler's grudging permission, Manstein ordered his First Panzer Army to break out of encirclement to the west.

The capture of Chernovtsy and Khotin by Zhukov's forces separated Manstein's shattered Army Group South operating in the western Ukraine from Schörner's Army Group "A" defending the southern Ukraine and forced the OKH to take drastic measures to reorganize its command structure along the southwestern axis to protect the approaches to both southern Poland and Romania. To cope with this crisis, the OKH reorganized Army Groups South and "A" into two new army groups, North and South Ukraine. Commanded by Field Marshal Walter Model, Manstein's successor in Army Group South, Army Group North Ukraine, which consisted of the German Fourth and First Panzer Armies and the Hungarian First Army, was responsible for rescuing the beleaguered First Panzer Army and restoring reliable defenses along the approaches to southeastern Poland. Still under Schörner's command, Army Group South Ukraine, which included the Eighth Army on former Army Group South's right wing, the Sixth Army of former Army Group "A," and the Romanian Fourth and Third Armies, was responsible for defending the approaches to northern and eastern Romania, the Dnestr and the Prut River lines, and the key port city of Odessa, which anchored German defenses on the Black Sea coast.

From the *Stavka*'s perspective, the Red Army's victories in the Ukraine during March offered dramatic new opportunities to begin mounting strategic offensives into both southeastern Poland and northern Romania. By the end of March, forces subordinate to Colonel General P. A. Kurochkin's 2nd Belorussian Front were already conducting offensive operations westward through the Poles'e region in the northwestern Ukraine toward the cities of Kovel', Brest, and Vladimir-Volynskii on the Western Bug River. On Kurochkin's southern flank, the forces of Zhukov's 1st Ukrainian Front were besieging the cities of Brody and Ternopol' in the western Ukraine, preparing to advance westward to capture the city of L'vov, and struggling to destroy the encircled First Panzer Army in the Kamenets-Podol'skii region.

In the wake of its March victories, the *Stavka* decided to exploit this unique opportunity by ordering its 2nd and 3rd Ukrainian Fronts to complete destroying the *Wehrmacht*'s forces in the southwestern Ukraine and commence a general advance deep into Romania. In addition to the Black Sea port of Odessa, the *Stavka* designated the cities of Iasi and Kishinev in Romanian Bessarabia (Moldavia) as the initial objectives of its new strategic thrust. The capture of these cities, the first of which was situated ten miles west of the Prut River 150 miles northwest of Odessa, and the second 15–25 miles west of the Dnestr River 90 miles northwest of Odessa, would prevent Axis (German and Romanian) forces from erecting viable defenses anywhere in northern Romania, thus facilitating future Red Army offensive operations toward Bucharest and Ploesti deeper into Romania and the depth of the Balkan region. The *Stavka* also believed that the capture of these cities would likely force the Romanian government to renounce its alliance with Hitler and end Romanian participation in the war.

Marshal of the Soviet Union A. M. Vasilevsky, the chief of the Red Army General Staff, who was serving as the *Stavka*'s representative to the 2nd, 3rd, and 4th Ukrainian Fronts at the time and, as such, was responsible for coordinating the three *fronts*' operations, recalled the *Stavka*'s rationale for the expanded offensive effort:

> We decided to do the following: The 1st Ukrainian Front was to advance [westward] toward L'vov and Peremyshl' and reach the Soviet state border at the Western Bug River with its right wing. Thus, this front altered its axis of advance from the southwestern axis to a strictly western axis, and it focused all of its efforts on liberating the western regions of the Ukraine. In the long term, it shifted its combat operations to the territory of southern Poland. The 3rd Guards Tank Army was urgently brought up to its full complement in order to reinforce the L'vov axis. The 1st Ukrainian Front planned to begin its general offense on 20 and 21 March. In the meantime, its left wing was to liberate the Bukovina region [in northern Romania]. As was the case before, the 2nd Ukrainian Front was assigned the mission of preventing the enemy from organizing his defenses and advancing into northern Moldavia from the southeast. Meanwhile, the shock group on its right wing was to advance through Mogilev-Podol'skii and Iampol' toward the Dnestr, while its left flank was to advance along the Kirovograd-Rybnitsa railroad line and then turn sharply southward toward Kishinev. The 2nd Ukrainian Front, as a whole, was to reach the Soviet border along the Prut River, and the 3rd Ukrainian Front was to liberate Nikolaev and Kherson from the march and then, moving parallel to the Black Sea coast, capture Tiraspol' and Odessa, advance through southern Moldavia, and reach the Soviet state border at the lower Danube [River]. To prevent Army Group "Center" from assisting its southern neighbor, the 2nd Belorussian Front was to begin an offensive toward Kovel' and Brest during the next few days.[1]

The 2nd Ukrainian Front

During the latter stages of its successful Uman'-Botoshany offensive, which took place during the last week of March, the armies subordinate to Konev's 2nd Ukrainian Front advanced southward and southwestward across a broad front extending from the approaches to Botoshany, on the Prut River 60 miles northwest of Iasi; eastward through Bel'tsy, 45 miles north of Iasi; to Rybnitsa, on the Dnestr River 80 miles northeast of Iasi; and to Kotovsk, east of the Dnestr and 65 miles north of Kishinev. The armies operating on the right wing of Konev's *front* lunged across the upper Dnestr and Prut Rivers against only weak resistance by mixed German and Romanian covering forces, while the bulk of Konev's armies, including his assigned tank armies, which were deployed in his *front*'s center and on its left wing, advanced steadily southward toward Iasi and Dubossary along a broad front but against stiffening German resistance (Map 3).

By the winter of 1944, although he was only 47 years old, Army General Ivan Stepanovich Konev had become one of the Red Army's most experienced

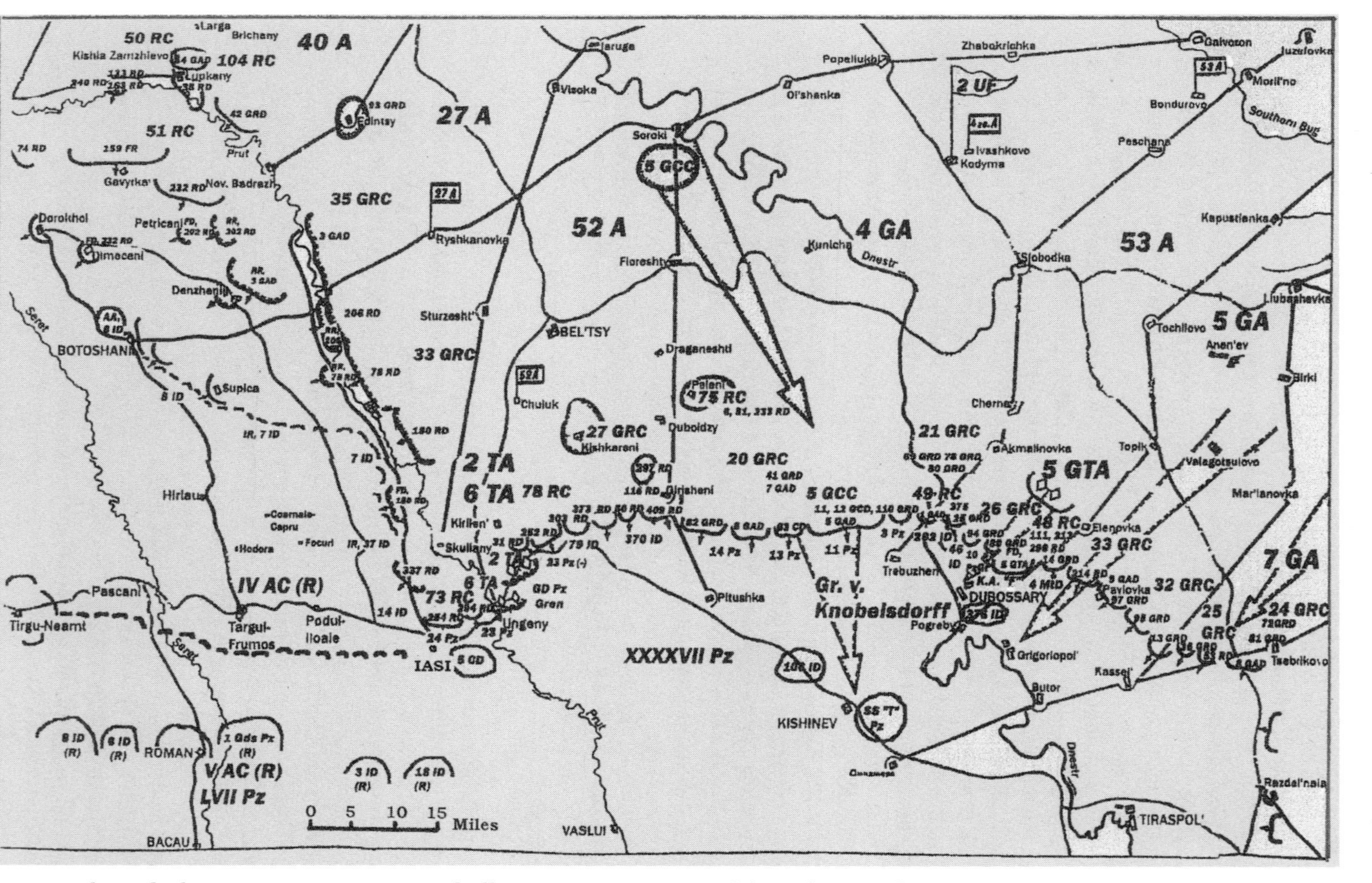

Map 3. The 2nd Ukrainian Front's situation and offensive operations, 5 April through 10 April 1944

and accomplished *front* commanders, despite many misfortunes he experienced during the first year of the war. After beginning his military career fighting in the Tsar's army during World War I, Konev joined the Red Army in 1918 and served as a commissar in an armored train, a rifle brigade, and a rifle division and in the People's Revolutionary Army in the Far East during the Russian Civil War. After war's end, Konev participated in the suppression of anti-Bolshevik uprisings in Moscow and at the naval base at Kronshtadt; later he served as a regimental and deputy divisional military commissar in the 17th Coastal Rifle Corps and 17th Rifle Division during the 1920s, in between graduating from the Course for Perfecting Red Army Command Cadre (*KUVNAS*).

During the 1930s Konev attended the Frunze Academy and rose to command a rifle division, a rifle corps, and, finally, the famed 2nd Red Banner Far Eastern Army. Although accused of disloyalty during Stalin's great purge of the Red Army's officer corps, somehow Konev avoided the tragic fate of many of his colleagues, and he was assigned, in succession, to command the Trans-Baikal and North Caucasus Military Districts during 1940 and 1941.[2] Only months before war began in June 1941, during April and May, the People's Commissariat of Defense (NKO) ordered Konev to form the 19th Army from forces stationed in his North Caucasus Military District and deploy it to the Kiev region to protect the capital of the Ukraine against any potential German invasion.

Once war began, however, the *Stavka* quickly redeployed Konev's army northward to the Smolensk region, where advancing German forces literally ground it up during the initial stages of the Battle for Smolensk and, still later, utterly destroyed its remnants in the struggle around Viaz'ma during October 1941. Escaping Stalin's wrath over his disastrous defeats, in part because Zhukov interceded on his behalf, Konev commanded the Kalinin Front successfully during the defense of Moscow and the Red Army's subsequent Moscow offensive, once again at Zhukov's side. Konev commanded the Kalinin and Western Fronts during the summer and fall of 1942, again under Zhukov's supervision, and, with Zhukov, experienced the bitterness of defeat in the ill-fated Operation Mars during November and December 1942, after which Zhukov again intervened to save Konev from disgrace.

After briefly commanding the Northwestern Front during the spring of 1943 and, on Zhukov's recommendation, the Steppe Military District during June 1943, Konev's fortunes sharply changed for the better. In addition to commanding the Steppe Front during its victory at Kursk during July and August 1943, Konev led his *front* (renamed the 2nd Ukrainian Front) during its spectacular pursuit of the *Wehrmacht*'s forces back to the Dnepr River in September and seized sizable bridgeheads across the river during October, although his forces failed to expel German forces from the Krivoi Rog region as ordered later in the year. After recording spectacular successes as a *front* commander during 1943, Konev led the 2nd Ukrainian Front to victory in the Korsun'-Shevchenkovskii and Uman'-Botoshany offensives during the winter of 1944, feats that prompted the *Stavka* to task him with leading the ensuing Red Army invasion of Romania and the Balkans.[3]

Although most of his colleagues described Konev as "emotional and hot tempered," one noted, "Personal courage and energetic initiative in difficult circumstances were characteristic of Konev as a military leader throughout the war. . . . Konev was particularly taken with military history, and, throughout his life, he regarded it as an integral component of success." Another claimed that Konev was often harsh with his subordinates, vain, and prone to jealousy of his peers.[4] Still another praised him, noting he "was swift in his decisions and actions and unrestrained with his subordinates." Although "his behavior was acceptable," at times it was "somewhat frightening for the target of his wrath. . . . However, those who fought under him all commented on his temper. Still, they did not accuse him, as they did Chuikov, of being insulting."[5]

On 1 April 1944, Konev's 2nd Ukrainian Front was a formidable force indeed (see Table 2.1 at chapter's end). Its major combat formations included seven combined-arms and three tank armies—specifically, Lieutenant General F. F. Zhmachenko's 40th Army, Lieutenant General S. G. Trofimenko's 27th Army, Lieutenant General K. A. Koroteev's 52nd Army, Lieutenant General I. V. Galanin's 4th Guards Army, Lieutenant General I. M. Managarov's 53rd Army, Lieutenant General A. S. Zhadov's 5th Guards Army, Lieutenant General M. S. Shumilov's 7th Guards Army, Lieutenant General of Tank Forces S. I. Bogdanov's 2nd Tank Army, Colonel General of Tank Forces P. A. Rotmistrov's 5th Guards Tank Army, and Lieutenant General of Tank Forces A. G. Kravchenko's 6th Tank Army. In addition, Konev retained a reserve consisting of three rifle divisions, the 5th Guards Cavalry Corps, the 7th and 8th Separate Mechanized Corps, and the 20th Separate Tank Corps and an impressive array of supporting artillery, engineer, and logistical forces.

The nucleus of Konev's *front* consisted of 48 rifle and eight airborne divisions, most of which were subordinate to 18 rifle corps, one cavalry corps with three cavalry divisions, two fortified regions, and six tank and four mechanized corps. These forces were supported by an impressive array of artillery, including two artillery penetration divisions, one artillery division, three separate artillery brigades, and seven separate artillery regiments, seven brigades and 14 regiments of tank destroyer artillery, ten separate mortar regiments, three brigades and 12 regiments of guards-mortars (*Katiusha* multiple-rocket launchers), and nine divisions and five regiments of antiaircraft artillery. Konev's infantry support armor consisted of two separate tank brigades and six separate tank regiments, one brigade and five regiments of self-propelled artillery, one regiment and one battalion of motorcycles, and five armored train battalions with a total of ten armored trains. Counting his infantry support armor, Konev's *front* fielded more than 600 tanks and self-propelled guns in early April.

To overcome the daunting terrain problems associated with traversing the Ukrainian steppes and the hills of northern Romania during the spring *rasputitsa,* as well as overcoming the German and Romanian defenses, Konev's *front* fielded six brigades and 24 engineer battalions of various types, one brigade, one regiment, and six battalions of pontoon bridges, and five flame-thrower battalions and companies. Finally, in terms of air support, Konev's 8th Air Army consisted of a total of ten bomber, fighter, and assault aviation divisions and one separate night bomber aviation regiment subordinate to four aviation corps, plus an aviation regiment to conduct reconnaissance, as well as a transport aviation regiment and a regiment detailed from the Civil Air Fleet to provide his forces with aerial resupply.

Konev was conducting his advance in late March and early April with the 40th and 27th Armies on his right wing; the 52nd and 4th Guards Armies and the 2nd and 6th Tank Armies in his center; and the 53rd, 5th Guards and 7th Guards Armies, and 5th Guards Tank Army on his left wing. By day's end on 5 April, the 40th and 27th Armies on his *front's* right had crossed the upper reaches of the Dnestr and Prut Rivers; had captured Khotin (with Zhukov's forces), Mogilev-Podol'skii, and Dorohoi; and were approaching the Tirgu Frumos and Botoshany regions west of the Prut River and 30–60 miles north-west of Iasi. The two advancing armies were encountering only light resistance offered by the Romanian IV and V Army Corps, supported by the lead elements of the German Eighth Army's LVII Panzer Corps, which had just begun deploying its main forces into the region around the city of Roman, situated 35 miles southwest of Iasi.

In the center sector of Konev's *front,* the combined forces of the 2nd and 6th Tank Armies and the 52nd and 4th Guards Armies had captured the city of Bel'tsy, west of the Dnestr River, and Rybnitsa, east of the river, and were approaching the cities of Iasi and Orgeev from the north. These armies were facing stouter resistance from the German Eighth Army's IV Army Corps (Group Mieth) and XXXXVII Panzer Corps, which were defending along a broad front between the Prut and Dnestr Rivers north of the two cities. The 2nd and 6th Tank Armies, which were spearheading the advance in this sector, proceeded with relative abandon until German forces halted them on the approaches to Iasi during late March and early April.

For example, Bogdanov's 2nd Tank Army captured Bel'tsy and Faleshty, 45 and 30 miles north of Iasi, during the last week of March and then advanced rapidly southward through Todoreshty and seized a section of the Iasi-Kishinev railroad line at Pyrlitsa, 16 miles northeast of Iasi, on 27 March; by doing this, they threatened to split apart the German Eighth Army's defenses. Reacting quickly, however, the Eighth Army orchestrated a hasty counterattack with its IV Army Corps' (Group Mieth's) 23rd Panzer and *Grossdeutschland* Panzer Grenadier Divisions, which succeeded in recapturing Pyrlitsa on 28 March, bringing the 2nd Tank Army's attack to an abrupt halt.

After the 2nd Tank Army proved unable to revive its offensive thrust northeast of Iasi, on 29 March Konev ordered Bogdanov to turn his sector over to Koroteev's 52nd Army, which had just reached the region, and regroup his tank army westward across the Prut River to the region due north of Iasi. Konev ordered Bogdanov's army "to conduct a passage of lines through the forces of the 27th Army after crossing the Prut River at Badarai [roughly 20 miles north of Iasi] and attack in the general direction of Focuri [20 miles northwest of Iasi] and Podu Iloaie [15 miles west of Iasi]. Subsequently, attack toward and capture Iasi."[6] Late on 5 April, Bogdanov's tank army was busy regrouping its sizable forces and logistical trains westward across the Prut River toward his assigned assembly areas in the Coarnele-Capru region, five miles northwest of Focuri and 15 miles northwest of Podu Iloaie.

While Bogdanov's tank army was deploying westward, the tank and motorized rifle units of Kravchenko's 6th Tank Army, which were considerably under strength because of the wear and tear of many weeks of continuous operations, reached the Prut River between the towns of Skuliany and Ungeny, 12 miles north and ten miles northeast of Iasi, respectively, on 28 March and seized several bridgeheads on the river's western bank north of Iasi. Late that day Konev ordered Kravchenko to withdraw most of his weakened tank forces to rest and refit, while the infantry and supporting troops of Koroteev's 52nd Army continued their advance toward Iasi from the north. On 29 March the lead elements of the 73rd Rifle Corps from Koroteev's army captured the village of Popricani and reached the outskirts of the village of Vulturi, six miles north of Iasi, threatening an immediate advance on the vital city.

Reacting quickly to the new threat, on 30 March the German Eighth Army's Group Mieth, which was defending the northern approaches to Iasi with a threadbare Romanian force, ordered its reserve, the German 24th Panzer and Romanian 5th Cavalry Divisions, to conduct a hastily organized but well-coordinated counterattack north of the city. This measure succeeded in halting Koroteev's advance. In response, Kravchenko, the commander of the 6th Tank Army, ordered his 5th Mechanized Corps to create a task force and commit it to combat to help Koroteev restore the situation. After fighting for several days north of Iasi in early April, the 52nd Army's infantry, supported by the 5th Mechanized Corps' task force, managed to stabilize their defensive positions south of the village of Popricani, nine miles north of Iasi.

By this time, the combat strength of both Bogdanov's 2nd and Kravchenko's 6th Tank Armies had been severely eroded by the incessant fighting, and the two tank armies numbered about 120 tanks and self-propelled guns each.

Meanwhile, on the 2nd Ukrainian Front's left wing east of the Dnestr River, the combined forces of Managarov's 53rd, Zhadov's 5th Guards, and Shumilov's 7th Guards Armies had captured Kotovsk and Pervomaisk and by 5 April were advancing southward toward the Dubossary and Grigoriopol' regions, on the eastern bank of the Dnestr River 23 and 20 miles northeast of Kishinev, respectively. Unlike their counterparts to the west, their forces encountered stronger resistance offered by the German Eighth Army's XXXX Panzer Corps, which was task-organized as Group von Knobelsdorff led by the panzer corps commander. Operating in the vanguard of the 4th Guards and 53rd Armies, Rotmistrov's 5th Guards Tank Army, whose strength was reduced to a mere handful of tanks and self-propelled guns as a result of its previous fighting, had to overcome heavy resistance in the Rybnitsa, Krasnye Okhy, and Chernaia sectors north and northeast of the city of Dubossary from 28 March through 2 April as the German Eighth Army conducted a skillful phased withdrawal southwestward toward Dubossary.

To end this stalemate and accelerate his *front*'s advance to and across the Dnestr River, on 3 April Konev ordered Rotmistrov to concentrate all of the 5th Guards Tank Army's remaining armor under the control of the tank army's 18th Tank Corps, which was commanded by Major General of Tank Forces V. I. Polozkov, and to transfer the tank corps to the western bank of the Dnestr River secretly. Once across the Dnestr, in cooperation with Lieutenant General A. G. Selivanov's 5th Guards Cavalry Corps, the task force from Polozkov's tank corps was to advance as rapidly as possible—to capture, first, the town of Orgeev, on the northern bank of the Reut River 25 miles north of Kishinev, and, later, the *front*'s ultimate prize, the city of Kishinev, the capital of Bessarabia.

Supported by riflemen from the 4th Guards Army and elements of Selivanov's cavalry corps, the task force of Polozkov's 18th Tank Corps marched westward with a meager force equipped with eight T-34 tanks and two SU-85 self-propelled guns, crossed over to the Dnestr River's western bank on 6 April, and reached the town of Kipercheny, ten miles north of Orgeev, by day's end. There it ran straight into the teeth of a strong and well-organized counterattack by Group von Knobelsdorff (the XXXX Panzer Corps), which, after heavy fighting, brought the 18th Tank Corps' assault to an abrupt halt on the northern approaches to Orgeev. Thwarted in his attempt to capture Orgeev by a coup de main, the next day Konev ordered Rotmistrov's 5th Guards Tank Army to cease its offensive and regroup its forces to the Bel'tsy region for rest and refitting.

The 3rd Ukrainian Front

After defeating the German Sixth Army in its Bereznegovatoe-Snigirevka offensive during mid- and late March, in accordance with *Stavka* orders, on 26 March Malinovsky's 3rd Ukrainian Front resumed offensive operations to capture the city of Odessa and, at the same time, reach the Dnestr River northwest of the city (Map 4).

Like his counterpart, Konev, the 46-year-old Army General Rodion Iakovlich Malinovsky's wartime career had also been marred by frequent misfortunes during 1941 and early 1942, but, like Konev, he was able to overcame these earlier failures during late 1942 and early 1943 to emerge as one of the Red Army's most reliable *front* commanders throughout the remainder of the war.

During World War I, Malinovsky had enlisted in, fought with, and deserted from a special Russian expeditionary force in France. Returning to Russia through the Far Eastern port of Vladivostok, Malinovsky joined the Red Army ranks during the chaotic fighting in the Far East, commanded at company and battalion levels during the 1920s, and graduated from the Frunze Academy during 1930. After serving a variety of command and staff positions in the cavalry forces, Malinovsky "volunteered" to serve in the International Brigade fighting in defense of the republic during the Spanish Civil War. After returning unscathed from Spain in 1938, he miraculously escaped Stalin's purges and taught at the Frunze Academy.[7]

When war began in June 1941, Malinovsky was serving as the commander of the Odessa Military District's 48th Rifle Corps. Although his forces withdrew successfully in the face of the *Wehrmacht*'s deadly onslaught during the summer and fall of 1941, Malinovsky performed credibly enough as a corps commander and, later, as commander of the Southern Front's 6th Army for Stalin to appoint him commander of the Southern Front in December 1941. Although Malinovsky's *front* took part in the partially successful Barvenkovo-Lozovaia offensive during January 1942, Malinovsky's reputation was severely tarnished by his forces' overly passive participation in the disastrous defeat at Khar'kov during May 1942, when the *Wehrmacht* completely destroyed two of his *front*'s armies.

Despite this embarrassing defeat, Stalin retained Malinovsky in command of the Southern Front throughout the summer of 1942 when the *Wehrmacht* forced his *front*'s armies to withdraw, with heavy losses, eastward to the Rostov region. In the wake of this fighting retreat, Stalin assigned him command, first, of the Don Operational Group and, later, the 66th Army, which Malinovsky led effectively during the early stages of the Battle for Stalingrad. His tenacious defense of the Don River line during September and October 1942 earned Malinovsky command of the most powerful reserve army in the *Stavka*'s reserve, the new 2nd Guards Army,

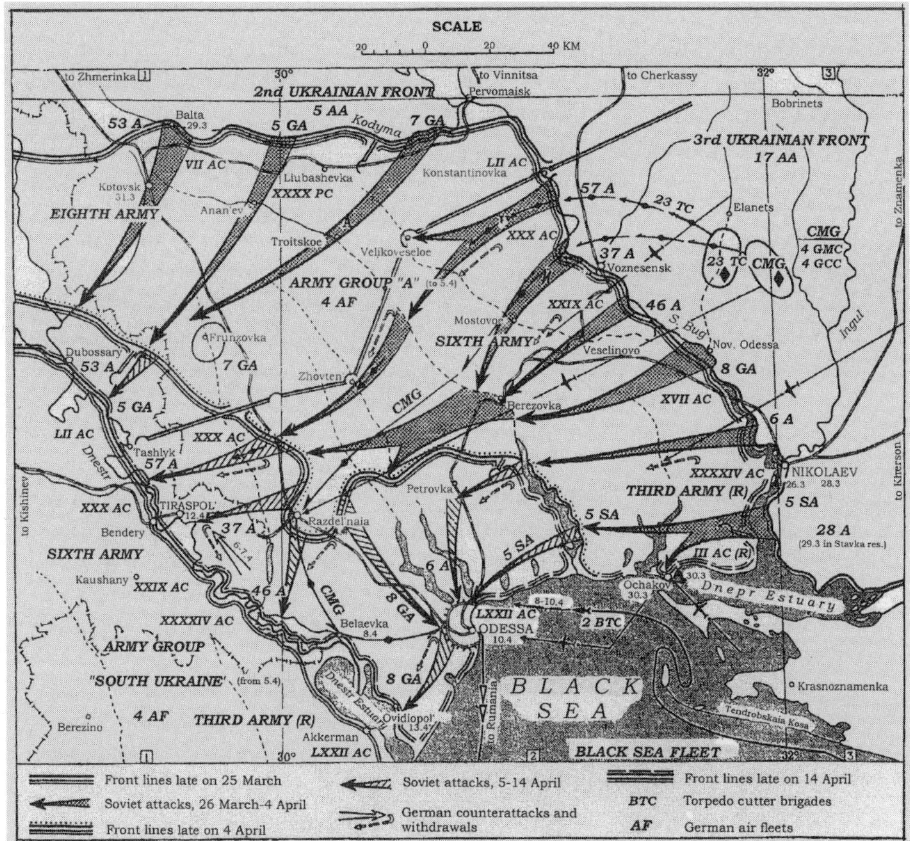

Map 4. The 3rd Ukrainian Front's operations, 26 March–14 April 1944

which the *Stavka* intended to employ to exploit its counteroffensive in the region.

During the latter stages of the Red Army's Stalingrad offensive (or counteroffensive), Malinovsky's guards army was instrumental in blocking and defeating the *Wehrmacht*'s attempts to rescue its Sixth Army from encirclement in Stalingrad. Later still, in December 1942 and January 1943, his guards army spearheaded the Stalingrad (later Southern) Front's spectacular advance through Rostov and to the Mius River. In reward for his outstanding performance during these offensives, Stalin assigned Malinovsky command of the Southern Front during February 1943 and the Southwestern Front during March. Although Malinovsky's forces failed to overcome the

Wehrmacht's formidable defenses along the Mius River during February, his *front* (renamed the 3rd Ukrainian Front) did so during the late summer of 1943, subsequently liberating the Donbas during August and September and capturing the key city of Dnepropetrovsk and seizing bridgeheads over the Dnepr River during October.

After the turn of the year, Malinovsky's *front* helped smash German defenses in the "great bend" of the Don River, capturing Krivoi Rog during January and February; organized and conducted operations in the southern Ukraine, which almost encircled the German Sixth Army; captured the key Black Sea port and naval base at Nikolaev; and cleared German forces from the region north of the Black Sea coast as far west as the approaches to Odessa during March and April. His sound record provided ample reason for the *Stavka* to assign his *front* the task of leading the march into Romania.

A thoroughly competent but not flashy commander, Malinovsky rose to become Defense Minister of the Soviet Union during the 1960s. Steady and thoughtful, he rose to *front* command largely because of his reputation as a tenacious fighter in the mold of Zhukov. In the words of one biographer, Malinovsky, "while unusually able, courageous and keenly intelligent, was also headstrong, ambitious, prone to vanity, and, at times, ruthless when the occasion warranted. Once his mind was made up, nothing could shake his determination to do things his way."[8]

On 1 April 1944, Malinovsky commanded an imposing force of six combined armies—specifically, Lieutenant General N. A. Gagen's 57th Army, Lieutenant General M. N. Sharokhin's 37th Army, Lieutenant General V. V. Glagolev's 46th Army, Colonel General V. I. Chuikov's 8th Guards Army, Lieutenant General I. T. Shlemin's 6th Army, and Colonel General V. D. Tsvetaev's 5th Shock Army (see Table 2.2 at chapter's end). As the month of March ended, these armies were deployed abreast from north to south in this sequence and were supported by both a powerful Cavalry-Mechanized Group commanded by Lieutenant General I. A. Pliev and the separate 23rd Tank Corps. Their attack frontage extended across an immense expanse along the Southern Bug River from north of the river city of Voznesensk, 100 miles north-northeast of Odessa, southward to the port of Nikolaev, on the Black Sea coast 60 miles east of Odessa.

The nucleus of Malinovsky's *front* consisted of 50 rifle divisions and one airborne division, which were subordinate to 16 rifle corps, one cavalry corps with three cavalry divisions, one fortified region, and one tank and two mechanized corps. These forces were supported by an impressive array of artillery, including two artillery penetration divisions and 16 separate artillery regiments, five brigades, 12 regiments, and one battalion of tank destroyer artillery; one separate brigade and six separate regiments of mortars; two brigades and nine regiments of guards-mortars (*Katiusha* multiple-rocket launchers); and four divisions, 19 regiments, and three separate battalions of antiaircraft artillery. Malinovsky's infantry support armor consisted of one separate tank brigade and five separate tank regiments, one separate motorized rifle brigade, six regiments of self-propelled artillery, three regiments and one battalion of motorcycles, and three armored train battalions with a total of six armored trains. Counting his infantry support armor, Konev's *front* fielded as many as 350 tanks and self-propelled guns in early April.

To overcome the daunting terrain problems, particularly the passage over the many rivers in his offensive sector, as well as the German and Romanian defenses, Konev's *front* fielded five brigades and 15 engineer battalions of various types; two brigades, two regiments, and one battalion of pontoon bridges; and three flamethrower battalions. Finally, in terms of air support, Malinovsky's 17th Air Army consisted of a total of seven bomber, fighter, and assault aviation divisions and one separate night bomber aviation regiment subordinate to two aviation corps, plus an aviation regiment to conduct reconnaissance.

Shortly after Malinovsky's *front* resumed its advance across the Southern Bug in early April, which was, in reality, a pursuit operation, by 5 April the 57th, 37th, and 46th Armies on his *front*'s right wing captured the towns of Berezovka and Zatish'e, 60–80 miles north of Odessa, and Pliev's Cavalry-Mechanized Group seized the vital railroad junction at Razdel'naia, 42 miles northwest of Odessa, which dominated all the communications routes extending eastward from the Dnestr River to the Odessa region. Hard pressed by Malinovsky's seemingly unstoppable advance, the defending German Sixth Army's LII and XXX Army Corps conducted a fighting withdrawal toward the Tiraspol' region and the Dnestr River, 20–40 miles to the west. Late on 5 April, on the left wing of Malinovsky's *front,* the 8th Guards and the 6th and 5th Shock Armies captured the Pavlinka and Stepanovka regions north of Odessa from the Sixth Army's XXIX and XXXXIV Army Corps and the Romanian III Army Corps and prepared to envelop Odessa's defenses, which were manned by the German LXXII Army Corps, from the north and southwest.

In accordance with the *Stavka*'s orders, Malinovsky allocated roughly one half of his *front*'s forces to conduct an offensive to envelop and destroy German forces in the Odessa region, a task his forces were to accomplish during the period from 26 March through 14 April. At the time, the German Sixth Army's XXIX, XXXXIV, and LXXII Army Corps, along with elements of the Romanian Third Army, were defending the city. As the ensuing Odessa offensive developed, Chuikov's 8th Guards, Shlemin's 6th, and Tsvetaev's 5th Shock Armies, supported by Pliev's Cavalry-Mechanized Group, encircled the defending German forces from the west, smashed their defenses, and captured the city by day's end on 10 April. The defeated German and Romanian forces then conducted a fighting withdrawal back to the Dnestr River, a task that required them to cut their way through a cordon of Red Army forces blocking their escape routes to safety on the Romanian side of the river.

While three of Malinovsky's armies were capturing Odessa, Gagen's 57th, Sharokhin's 37th, and Glagolev's 46th Armies, which were operating farther north and northwest of the city, continued to press the German Sixth Army's defending LII, XXX, and XVII Army Corps back toward the Dnestr River north and south of Tiraspol'. During the later stages of this offensive, which occurred from 11 through 14 April, Chuikov's 8th Guards Army and Pliev's Cavalry-Mechanized Group regrouped their forces and began advancing westward from Odessa, joining the 3rd Ukrainian Front's general advance toward the Dnestr River. By this time, Malinovsky's armies formed a left wing of a gigantic effort to pierce the Dnestr River line and envelop Kishinev from the south.

Army Group South Ukraine's Defenses

While trying to cope with this massive Red Army offensive across so broad a front, the German OKH and Army Groups South and "A" faced the daunting task of identifying and assembling sufficient forces to form a coherent defense along a continuous front, thereby protecting the northern and northeastern approaches to Romania. Hitler attempted to resolve this problem on 5 April 1944 when he reorganized Army Groups South and "A" into Army Groups North and South Ukraine, assigned Field Marshal Model to command the former and Colonel General of Mountain Troops Schörner to command the latter, and ordered Schörner to defend the approaches into Romania.

Only days before, on 26 March, Hitler and the OKH had also approved the general principle of combining both German and Romanian forces in Army Groups South and "A," even though the reliability of Romanian forces was suspect at best in the eyes of many German officers and soldiers:

> West of the Dnestr, Army Group South Ukraine was forced to make all of the use it could of the Rumanian Third and Fourth Armies. To keep the Rumanians in hand, the army group command devised an involved chain of command, which, while preserving appearances, actually subordinated Rumanian Fourth Army to Eighth Army and Rumanian Third Army to Sixth Army. Marshal Antonescu, the existence of his regime at stake, gave the alliance his desperate loyalty, but his soldiers at all levels were interested only in personal survival. Many officers had stopped wearing their German decorations. After talking with the Commanding General, Rumanian Fourth Army, on 27 March, Woehler [Wöhler] came away with the impression that the Rumanians "had no discernable desire to fight."[9]

After it was formed on 5 April, Group South Ukraine consisted of two subordinate special ad hoc army groups containing a mixture of German and Romanian formations. The first group, which was named Army Group Wöhler after the German Eighth Army's commander, Colonel General Otto Wöhler, consisted of Wöhler's Eighth Army and the newly formed Romanian Fourth Army, which was commanded by the former cavalry man, General Mihail Racovita. Group Wöhler's most important combat forces included Corps Mieth (the IV Army Corps, commanded by General Friedrich Mieth); the Romanian I, IV, and V Army Corps; the German LXXVIII, XXXX, and XXXXVII Army Corps; and the German LVII Panzer Corps. Wöhler's group was responsible for defending the northern portion of Army Group South Ukraine's defensive front, specifically, the sector extending from the city of Radauti, which was situated in the foothills of the Carpathian Mountains southwest of Chernovtsy, eastward to the Orgeev region just west of the Dnestr River and 25 miles north of Kishinev.

The second group, which was named Army Group Dumitrescu after the commander of the Third Romanian Army, General Petre Dumitrescu, consisted of the Romanian Third Army's headquarters and forces and the German Sixth Army, which was commanded by Colonel General Karl Hollidt. Group Dumitrescu's most important combat forces included the Romanian III Army Corps and the German LII, XXX, XXIX, XXXXIV, and LXVII Army Corps. Dumitrescu's group was responsible for defending the southern portion of Army Group South Ukraine's defensive front, which extended from Orgeev to the Black Sea coast northeast of Odessa.

In the first week of April, because his group's forces had become dispersed during the fighting withdrawal they conducted in late March and he had few German units at his disposal, Wöhler had no choice but to rely heavily on Romanian forces to defend his army group's overextended left wing west of Iasi.[10] On 5 April, for example, Wöhler was forced to defend his extended left wing along and forward of the Carpathian Mountains from Radauti to just west of the Botoshany region, with separate small and dispersed battalion and company groups subordinate to the relatively weak German LXXVIII Army Corps operating under the Romanian Fourth Army's control.

Further to the east and southeast, Wöhler defended the sector extending from Botoshany eastward to the Prut River, particularly the northern approaches to the towns of Tirgu-Neamt and Pascani, with the Romanian I Army Corps. This corps' 8th Infantry Division manned forward defensive positions south and southeast of Botoshany, 60 miles northwest of Iasi, and its special Divisional Group Siret and the 6th Infantry Division occupied stronger and better-prepared defensive lines just south of Pascani, 45 miles west of Iasi.

Wöhler defended the central portion of his defensive front, which extended from southeast of Botoshany to the Prut River 20 miles north of Podu Iloaie, with the Romanian IV Army Corps. Elements of this corps' 7th

Infantry Division manned forward defensive positions along a fairly broad front north of the town of Hirlau, 17 miles north of Tirgu Frumos and 40 miles northwest of Iasi, and the corps' 1st Guards Division, the remainder of its 7th Infantry Division, and its 3rd Infantry and 18th Mountain Infantry Divisions occupied stronger defensive lines at and south of the towns of Podu Iloaie and Tirgu Frumos, 15 and 30 miles west of Iasi.

Finally, Wöhler defended the eastern portion of his front, which stretched from north of Podu Iloaie 15 miles eastward to the Iasi region, where Red Army armor and rifle forces had already reached the northern approaches to the city, with the German IV Army Corps (Group Mieth). This corps was already employing the German 23rd and 24th Panzer Divisions, the German *Grossdeutschland* Panzer Grenadier Division, and the Romanian 5th Cavalry Division to parry the Red Army advance on the northern outskirts of the city.

In general, as Red Army forces accelerated their offensive and the fighting intensified during the first ten days of April, Wöhler tried to replace the Romanian forces manning his forward defenses with German forces as soon as it was feasible to do so. While doing so, he ordered most of his Romanian forces to occupy and defend the so-called Strunga Defense Line, an imposing fortified defensive line constructed by the Romanians, which consisted of multiple, well-prepared partially fortified defensive belts anchored on the low mountain range stretching roughly 48 miles from the eastern foothills of the Carpathian Mountains south of Tirgu-Neamt eastward to the Prut River south of Iasi. The main belt of the Strunga Line contained about 3,000 concrete emplacements and 36 miles of antitank ditches, principally concentrated west and east of the Seret River valley. Its main belt was manned by the 106th, 115th, and 121st Fortress Detachments, which had been formed from the 6th, 15th, and 21st Infantry Divisions, whose home bases were in the region.[11] The forward edge of the Strunga Defense Line consisted of forward outposts and lighter covering positions situated in the Tirgu-Neamt, Pascani, Tirgu Frumos, Podu Iloaie, and Iasi regions.

Given the strength and potential obstacle value of the Strunga Defense Line, both the *Stavka* and Konev's 2nd Ukrainian Fronts considered it to be one of their most important initial objectives as they formulated their strategic offensive plans.[12]

SOVIET OFFENSIVE PLANNING

The 2nd Ukrainian Front

Impatient to accelerate their offensive into northern Romania, late on 5 April, both the Red Army General Staff and the *Stavka* sent messages to Konev, inquiring about his future offensive intentions and ordering him to take advantage of the rapid advance by Zhmachenko's 40th and Trofimenko's 27th Armies across the Prut River toward Botoshany (Map 5). For his part, in a message dispatched to Konev at 1945 hours that day, Army General A. I. Antonov, 1st deputy chief of the Red Army General Staff, asked Konev to "communicate your views on the forcing [Prut River crossing] operations with the aim of capturing Iassy [Iasi] and Kishinev and your evaluation of the enemy along these axes" so that he could "report to Comrade Ivanov [Stalin]."[13]

Taking no chances that Antonov's intent be misunderstood, a few hours later the *Stavka* simply directed Konev to accelerate his offensive. Noting the "unimpeded advance by the 40th and 27th Armies' reconnaissance detachments between the Prut River and the Siret [Seret] River," Stalin ordered Konev to "advance the *front*'s right wing to the line of the Siret and Bahluiul Rivers and capture the Dorohoi, Botoshany, and Iasi regions."[14] Antonov and Stalin dispatched these messages to Konev because both were concerned over mounting German resistance north and east of Iasi and because both appreciated the clear opportunity at hand to envelop those defenses with an offensive by the 40th and 27th Armies from the west. As subsequent events indicated, Stalin's concerns were indeed well founded.

By 5 April, for example, intelligence organs subordinate to the General Staff's Main Intelligence Directorate (GRU) and the corresponding intelligence directorates (URs) in the 2nd and 3rd Ukrainian Fronts reported that the Germans had already regrouped their 3rd, 23rd, and 24th Panzer Divisions; the 46th, 79th, and 370th Infantry Divisions; and Corps Group "F," which was assessed as consisting of divisional groups from the already partially destroyed 38th, 62nd, and 123rd Infantry Divisions, from the Sixth Army in the 3rd Ukrainian Front's sector westward across the Dnestr River to the Eighth Army. From Konev's perspective, these intelligence organs assessed that this transfer of forces reflected German intent to resist the 2nd Ukrainian Front's advance strenuously, in particular its advance along the Kishinev axis.[15]

Just a few hours later, fresh combat reports indicated that several of these regrouped German panzer formations were already in action north and east of Iasi, where they were halting any further advance by Bogdanov's 2nd and Kravchenko's 6th Tank Armies. Therefore, Stalin insisted Konev provide him with his views regarding the conduct of new and expanded operations to exploit this apparent but already fleeting offensive opportunity. Konev responded by submitting a more detailed plan of action to Stalin and his *Stavka* at 2400 hours on 5 April.

Although separate German and Romanian units were defending along the Seret River on his *front*'s right wing, Konev reported that "the enemy is offering stout resistance along the Kishinev axis," where he "has reinforced

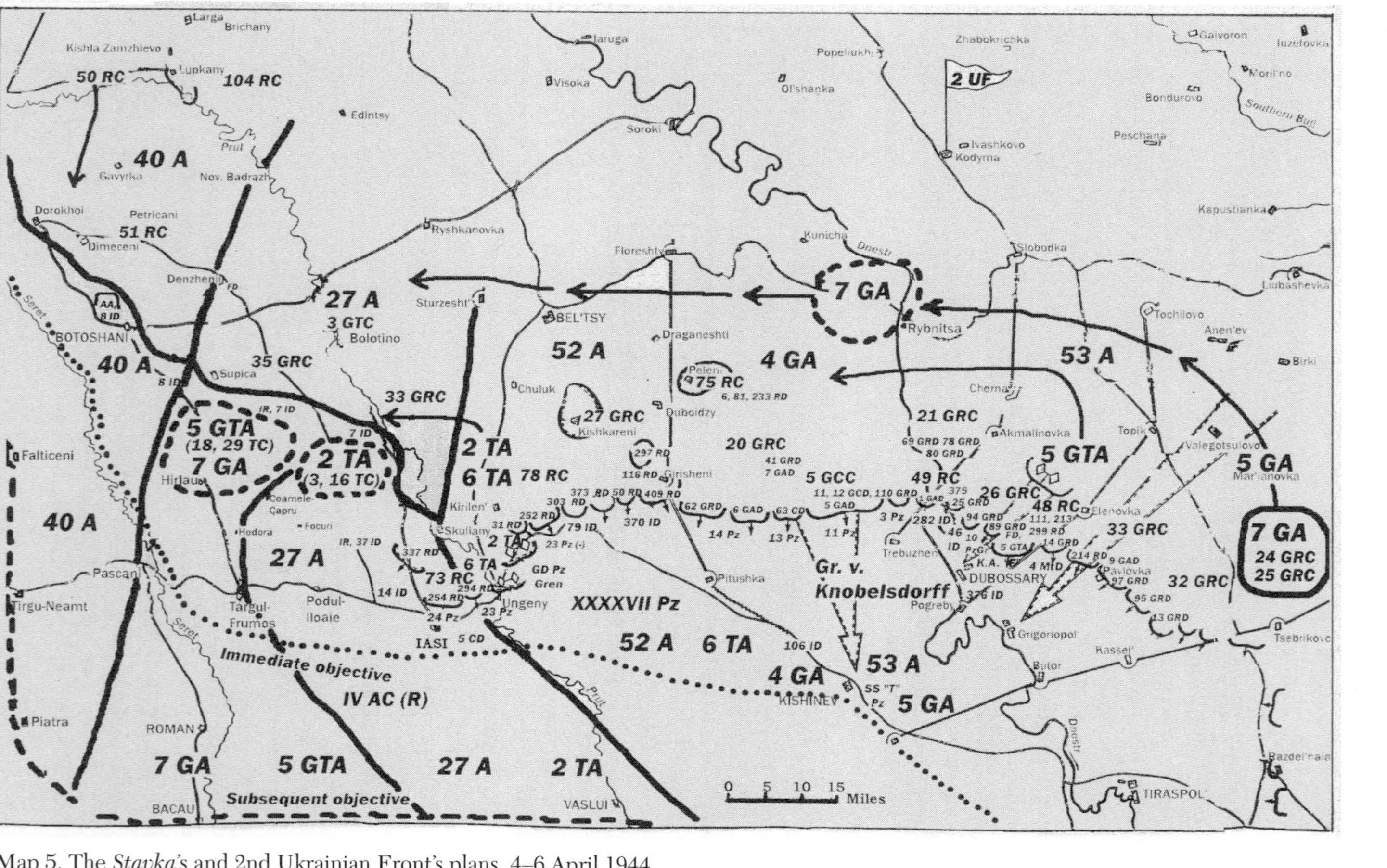

Map 5. The *Stavka's* and 2nd Ukrainian Front's plans, 4–6 April 1944

the Kishinev axis at the expense of units withdrawing from the 3rd Ukrainian Front's front," including "the 62nd, 46th, 79th, and 370th Infantry Divisions and the 3rd and 24th Panzer Divisions" and "units transferred from the left bank of the Dnestr." Concluding from prisoner-of-war reports that "the enemy is striving to organize a dense defense along the Kishinev axis," Konev proposed enveloping "the Germans' main southern grouping" by conducting "an offensive with the *front*'s right wing consisting of the 40th and 27th Armies reinforced by the 3rd Guards Tank Corps, and, subsequently, Shumilov's [7th Guards] Army."[16]

Konev's proposed plan required the 40th and 27th Armies to attack and reach the Radauti, Falticeni, Tirgu-Neamt, Piatra, and Bacau line, from 95 miles northwest of Iasi to 52 miles southwest of Iasi, after which the 40th Army was to erect a firm defense to protect the *front*'s right flank. Trofimenko's 27th Army would begin its assault southward along the Bolotino, Tirgu Frumos, Roman, and Bacau axis immediately but was to be reinforced during the course of its advance, first, by the 3rd Guards Tank Corps, and, later, by Shumilov's 7th Guards Army and Rotmistrov's 5th Guards Tank Army as soon as they were able to regroup into the region. Once regrouped, Rotmistrov's tank army was to consist of two tank corps with a total of 120 tanks. The 40th and 27th Armies were to begin their offensive on 8 April, with the immediate mission to reach the Seret River. Finally, while Konev was mounting this offensive in his center sector, the 4th Guards, 53rd, and 5th Guards and the 2nd and 6th Tank Armies on his left wing were to continue their offensive southwestward to capture the Kishinev region and reach the Prut River north and south of the city.

Therefore, the viability of Konev's proposed offensive plan was based on three basic assumptions: first, the Germans had reinforced their defenses along the Kishinev axis with forces transferred from the Sixth Army; second, the best prospects for achieving offensive success rested with an attack by the 40th and 27th Armies west of Iasi; and, third, the 3rd Guards Tank Corps, Rotmistrov's 5th Guards Tank, and Shumilov's 7th Guards Armies would be able to regroup in timely enough fashion to be able to "strengthen" Konev's offensive so that it would be able to accomplish the *Stavka*'s ambitious aims. While the first two assumptions proved essentially correct, the third was clearly suspect. Stalin indicated as much in his reply.

After receiving Konev's proposal, Stalin and his other advisers in the *Stavka* reviewed the *front* commander's plan. Although they approved Konev's general concept and intent, they ordered him to incorporate several significant changes that reflected their reservations regarding his third assumption. Specifically, in a directive issued at 2245 hours on 6 April, Stalin approved the plan but noted that "the reinforcement of Trofimenko's 27th Army with just the 3rd Guards Tank Corps for operations to the south along the Siret [Seret] River will be insufficient." Instead, Stalin ordered Konev "to transfer one tank army, either Bogdanov's [2nd] or Kravchenko's [6th], to the western bank of the Prut River, immediately."[17] Asserting, "With regard to the axis toward Kishinev, two tank armies, whether Rotmistrov's, Kravchenko's, or Bogdanov's, will be entirely sufficient," Stalin reminded Konev, "You must bear in mind that the 3rd Ukrainian Front's right wing will reach the region south of Kishinev, which will ease your capture of Kishinev." After ordering Konev to regroup Shumilov's 7th Guards Army to the region west of Rybnitsa and the Dnestr River to compensate for the shortage of forces along his *front*'s main attack axis, Stalin directed Konev "to commit the corps on the right wing of Zhmachenko's 40th Army, which were situated in and south of the Khotin region, [southward] immediately and employ them to reinforce the 40th Army's units attacking toward the Siret [Seret] River."[18]

Underscoring their belief that the 3rd Guards Tank Corps was not strong enough to spearhead the 40th and 27th Armies' offensive southward along the Seret River, Stalin and the *Stavka* ordered Konev to regroup either Bogdanov's 2nd Tank Army or Kravchenko's 6th Tank Army to new assembly areas west of the Prut River and northwest of Iasi and to employ the tank army as a mobile group to exploit the offensive operations on his *front*'s right wing. If he did so, argued Stalin, this would leave him two tank armies, Rotmistrov's 5th Guards and either Bogdanov's 2nd or Kravchenko's 6th, to spearhead the offensive against Kishinev on his *front*'s left wing. Furthermore, the *Stavka* firmly believed that these two tank armies, together with the 53rd and 5th Guards Armies on Konev's left wing and the 57th, 37th, and 46th Armies on the right wing of Malinovsky's 3rd Ukrainian Front, were sufficiently strong to pierce the Germans' defenses along the Dnestr River east of Kishinev, seize bridgeheads across the river, and exploit westward from these bridgeheads to capture the Kishinev region.

For this reason, the *Stavka* ordered Konev to begin regrouping Shumilov's 7th Guards Army from his left wing to his right so that it, too, could reinforce his offensive along the Seret River. Finally, to ensure his *front*'s successful advance southward along the Seret, the *Stavka* also instructed Konev to regroup the 40th Army's 104th Rifle Corps, which was operating on the army's extreme right wing in the Khotin region, to the 40th Army's left flank west of Tirgu-Neamt so that it could participate in the *front*'s main attack along the Seret River.[19]

The *Stavka* mandated these changes in Konev's plan in full knowledge that, after Malinovsky's forces captured Odessa, which it believed would occur by about 10 April, the 8th Guards and 5th Shock Armies of Malinovsky's *front* would also become available to participate in the offensive into Romania. With such massive forces, there was every reason for the *Stavka* to expect immediate and dramatic success.

3rd Ukrainian Front

While the *Stavka* and Konev were exchanging messages regarding the 2nd Ukrainian Front's plans for enveloping Iasi from the west and mounting an advance on Kishinev from the north, the *Stavka* ordered Malinovsky's 3rd Ukrainian Front to complete encircling the German forces defending Odessa and push the armies deployed on his *front*'s right wing westward to the Dnestr River between the cities of Grigoriopol' and Tiraspol' and the Black Sea coast.

Vasilevsky, the *Stavka*'s representative to Malinovsky's *front,* later described the situation in Malinovsky's *front* as it began its operations to capture the Odessa region:

> After forcing the Southern Bug River and seizing bridgeheads on its right [western] bank, the 3rd Ukrainian Front fought an intense battle for possession of the city and port of Nikolaev on 27 and 28 March. All three of our armies, Colonel General V. D. Tsvetaev's [5th Shock], Lieutenant General A. A. Grechkin's [28th Army], and Lieutenant General I. T. Shlemin's [6th Army], attacked the enemy's defenses from various sides, but were unable to drive all of the enemy from Nikolaev until after they conducted a night assault.
>
> The forces of Lieutenant General N. A. Gagen's [57th] Army and Lieutenant General M. H. Sharokhin's [37th] Army then advanced to the Bol'shoi Kuial'nik River [west of Nikolaev]. The 23rd Tank Corps and I. A. Pliev's Cavalry-Mechanized Group occupied jumping-off positions, preparing to conduct a dash through Razdel'naia to Tiraspol'. To deny the enemy the ability to withdraw from the Southern Bug River back across the Dnestr River, we sent up to 430 tanks and self-propelled guns from the 3rd Ukrainian Front there [to Razdel'naia], together with the Kuban' [4th Guards] cavalry corps.
>
> The sticky mud was so deep that it came almost up to the knees. We were short of men, and our ammunition had run out. Nevertheless, we continued our offensive without a pause. The 5th Shock Army captured Ochakov and the fort at Krasnyi Maiak at the mouth of the Dnepr-Bug lagoon [40 miles east of Odessa] on 30 March. The renewed downpour could not stop the successful operations by our mobile forces. Operating in advance of the combined-arms armies, A. O. Akhmanov's 23rd Tank Corps was already fighting with enemy tanks at Zhovten and Tsebrikovo [60 miles north of Odessa] on 31 March. Further to the south, after capturing Berezovka [50 miles north of Odessa], the forces of Pliev's group continued their advance toward Razdel'naia and into the Kuchurgan River valley [45 miles northwest of Odessa]. There they suffered a serious

> loss, the death of Lieutenant General of Tank Forces T. I. Tanischishin, who was the brave and experienced commander of the 4th Guards Mechanized Corps. . . . The guardsmen responded by seizing Razdel'naia. The forces of Glagolev's [46th], Chuikov's [8th Guards], Shlemin's [6th], and Tsvetaev's [5th Shock] Armies attacked Odessa from the north and the east. . . . In fact, almost the entire 3rd Ukrainian Front was directed at the liberation of Odessa.[20]

The *Stavka*'s decision to divert more than one half of the forces of Malinovsky's *front* to reduce and capture Odessa meant that, until Odessa fell, the only forces with which he could continue an advance toward the Dnestr River between Grigoriopol' and Tiraspol' were those subordinate to Gagen's 57th and Sharokhin's 37th Armies and the battle-weary 23rd Tank Corps. Therefore, while Chuikov's army enveloped Odessa from the west, Malinovsky's new plan required the forces of Glagolev's 46th Army to protect the left flank and rear of Chuikov's army as it enveloped Odessa and, while doing so, close up to the Dnestr River line and seize bridgeheads on the river's western bank only if Chuikov's attack succeeded in demolishing all German resistance northwest of Odessa. Thus, Glagolev's forces were to form a virtual outer encirclement line around the city on its western flank.

Condition of the Opposing Forces

Regardless of type of force, by late March 1944, the combat strength of virtually all of the 2nd and 3rd Ukrainian Fronts' combat, combat support, and logistical units had fallen precipitously because they had been conducting virtually continuous combat operations for nearly three months. Although both *fronts* had suffered only relatively light combat casualties during this period, the flow of personnel replacements to both *fronts* sharply decreased—in part, because the Germans implemented a "scorched earth" strategy as they withdrew by deliberately destroying all rail and road communications and, in part, because the wet weather of the *rasputitsa* crippled whatever roads remained unscathed. Therefore, to an increasing extent as they advanced, Konev's and Malinovsky's *fronts* relied heavily on local conscription, often carried out by force by both army and NKVD forces, to obtain necessary manpower to fill out their ranks.

The incessant spring rains and ubiquitous spring *rasputitsa* turned the largely macadamized or dirt road system into muddy quagmires, slowing all ground movement to a crawl and either damaging heavy weapons and equipment or forcing them to lag behind the advancing infantry. Although both *fronts* often resorted to aerial resupply to solve their most critical logistical problems, there were not enough transport aircraft available to satisfy even the basic needs of so large a combat force, particularly its insatiable appetite for fuel and ammunition. However, while the lack of trafficable roads seriously degraded the effectiveness of tank, mechanized, and, to a lesser extent, artillery forces, it increased the usefulness of horse cavalry, which could operate effectively in weather and terrain where tanks and trucks could not.

Despite the persistent problems the two Ukrainian *fronts* faced as they deliberately continued to conduct active offensive operations during March and April 1944, their decision to do so accorded them two major advantages. First, since the spring of 1944 was the first time in the war when the Red Army did not go over to the defense when the thaw and wet weather began, its continued offensive operations clearly caught the Germans by surprise. Caught "wrong-footed" and deprived of their accustomed spring respite, the Germans had no choice but to withdraw if they hoped to escape piecemeal defeat. Second, the very same weather and terrain conditions that confounded the Red Army also plagued the *Wehrmacht* by denying them their usual advantages in maneuver and mobility and by forcing them to abandon much of their damaged or bogged-down weapons and equipment.

As far as the correlation of forces between the opposing forces was concerned, despite the serious erosion of combat strength both sides had experienced, in early April the 2nd and 3rd Ukrainian Fronts outnumbered the German Eighth and Sixth Armies by a factor of well over two to one in infantry and about two to one in tanks, self-propelled guns, and artillery. For example, on 5 April Konev's *front* still fielded a total of over 500 tanks and self-propelled guns in his three tank armies and infantry support tank brigades and regiments. However, much of this armor and artillery was still bogged down on the muddy roads far to the rear and would take considerable time and effort to move forward and reassemble.

To their advantage as the Germans withdrew into northern Romania, they were able to exploit the excellent and still intact rail and road system to replace lost weaponry and replenish their supplies. In addition, although many Germans questioned their reliability, as many as 200,000 Romanian troops were available to support the defending Germans.

Table 2.1. The 2nd Ukrainian Front's Order of Battle on 1 April 1944
2nd UKRAINIAN FRONT:
Army General I. S. Konev

40th Army: LTG F. F. Zhmachenko
50th Rifle Corps: MG S. S. Martirosian
4th Guards Airborne Division
133rd Rifle Division
163rd Rifle Division
51st Rifle Corps: MG P. P. Avdeenko
42nd Guards Rifle Division
74th Rifle Division
232nd Rifle Division
104th Rifle Corps: LTG A. V. Petrushevsky
38th Rifle Division
240th Rifle Division
159th Fortified Region
1898th Self-propelled Artillery Regiment

27th Army: LTG S. G. Trofimenko
35th Guards Rifle Corps: LTG S. G. Goriachev
3rd Guards Airborne Division
93rd Guards Rifle Division
202nd Rifle Division
206th Rifle Division
33rd Rifle Corps: MG A. I. Semenov
78th Rifle Division
180th Rifle Division
337th Rifle Division
713th Self-propelled Artillery Regiment
1892nd Self-propelled Artillery Regiment

2nd Tank Army: LTGTF S. I. Bogdanov
3rd Tank Corps: LTGTF V. A. Mishulin
50th Tank Brigade
51st Tank Brigade
103rd Tank Brigade
57th Motorized Rifle Brigade
881st Self-propelled Artillery Regiment
1818th Self-propelled Artillery Regiment
1540th Heavy Self-propelled Artillery Regiment
74th Motorcycle Battalion
728th Tank Destroyer Regiment
234th Mortar Regiment
126th Guards-Mortar Battalion
121st Antiaircraft Artillery Regiment
16th Tank Corps: MGTF I. V. Dubovoi
107th Tank Brigade
109th Tank Brigade
164th Tank Brigade
15th Motorized Rifle Brigade
298th Guards Self-propelled Artillery Regiment
1441st Self-propelled Artillery Regiment
51st Motorcycle Battalion
729th Tank Destroyer Regiment
226th Mortar Regiment
89th Guards-Mortar Battalion
1721st Antiaircraft Artillery Regiment
11th Guards Tank Brigade
8th Guards Separate Tank Regiment
13th Guards Separate Tank Regiment
754th Self-propelled Artillery Regiment
1219th Self-propelled Artillery Regiment
87th Motorcycle Battalion

6th Tank Army: LTGTF A. G. Kravchenko
5th Mechanized Corps: LTGTF M. V. Volkov
2nd Mechanized Brigade
9th Mechanized Brigade
45th Mechanized Brigade
233rd Tank Brigade
697th Self-propelled Artillery Regiment
745th Self-propelled Artillery Regiment
999th Self-propelled Artillery Regiment
64th Motorcycle Battalion
458th Mortar Regiment
35th Guards-Mortar Battalion
1700th Antiaircraft Artillery Regiment
5th Guards Tank Corps: LTGTF V. M. Alekseev
20th Guards Tank Brigade
21st Guards Tank Brigade
22nd Guards Tank Brigade
6th Guards Motorized Rifle Brigade
1416th Self-propelled Artillery Regiment
1458th Self-propelled Artillery Regiment
1462nd Self-propelled Artillery Regiment
80th Motorcycle Battalion
1667th Tank Destroyer Artillery Regiment
454th Mortar Regiment
1696th Antiaircraft Artillery Regiment
6th Self-propelled Artillery Brigade
156th Separate Tank Regiment

52nd Army: LTG K. A. Koroteev
73rd Rifle Corps: MG P. F. Batitsky
31st Rifle Division
254th Rifle Division
294th Rifle Division

Table 2.1. *Continued*

78th Rifle Corps: MG G. A. Latyshev
- 252nd Rifle Division
- 303rd Rifle Division
- 373rd Rifle Division

27th Guards Rifle Corps (hq): MG E. S. Alekhin
- 116th Rifle Division
- 25th Separate Tank Regiment

4th Guards Army: LTG I. V. Galanin
- 20th Guards Rifle Corps: MG N. I. Biriukov
  - 5th Guards Airborne Division
  - 6th Guards Airborne Division
  - 7th Guards Airborne Division
  - 41st Guards Rifle Division
  - 62nd Guards Rifle Division
- 21st Guards Rifle Corps: MG P. I. Fomenko
  - 69th Guards Rifle Division
  - 78th Guards Rifle Division
  - 80th Guards Rifle Division
- 75th Rifle Corps: MG A. Z. Akimenko
  - 6th Rifle Division
  - 84th Rifle Division
  - 233rd Rifle Division

5th Air Army: ColGAv S. K. Goriunov
- 2nd Guards Bomber Aviation Corps: MGAv I. S. Polbin
  - 1st Guards Bomber Aviation Division
  - 8th Guards Bomber Aviation Division
- 1st Guards Assault Aviation Corps: LTGAv V. G. Riazanov
  - 8th Guards Assault Aviation Corps
  - 9th Guards Assault Aviation Corps
  - 12th Guards Fighter Aviation Division
- 4th Fighter Aviation Corps: MG I. D. Podgornyi
  - 294th Fighter Aviation Division
  - 302nd Fighter Aviation Division
- 7th Fighter Aviation Corps: MGAv A. V. Utin
  - 205th Fighter Aviation Division
  - 304th Fighter Aviation Division
- 312th Fighter-Bomber Aviation Division
- 511th Reconnaissance Aviation Regiment
- 95th Transport Aviation Regiment
- 85th Medical Aviation Regiment
- 714th Sep. Signal Aviation Regiment
- 18th Aviation Regiment, Civil Air Fleet
- 85th Corrective-Aviation Squadron

53rd Army: LTG I. M. Managarov
- 26th Guards Rifle Corps: MG P. A. Firsov
  - 25th Guards Rifle Division
  - 89th Guards Rifle Division
  - 94th Guards Rifle Division
- 48th Rifle Corps: MG Z. Z. Rogoznyi
  - 111th Rifle Division
  - 213th Rifle Division
  - 299th Rifle Division
- 49th Rifle Corps: MG G. N. Terent'ev
  - 1st Guards Airborne Division
  - 110th Guards Rifle Division
  - 375th Rifle Division
- 63rd Separate Antitank Rifle Battalion
- 122nd Separate Antitank Rifle Battalion
- 116th Tank Brigade
- 69th Tank Regiment (8th MC)
- 38th Separate Tank Regiment

5th Guards Tank Army: ColGTF P. A. Rotmistrov
- 5th Guards Mechanized Corps: MGTF B. M. Skvortsov
  - 10th Guards Mechanized Brigade
  - 11th Guards Mechanized Brigade
  - 12th Guards Mechanized Brigade
  - 24th Guards Tank Brigade
  - 104th Guards Self-propelled Artillery Regiment
  - 1447th Self-propelled Artillery Regiment
  - 2nd Guards Motorcycle Battalion
  - 737th Tank Destroyer Artillery Regiment
  - 285th Mortar Regiment
  - 409th Guards-Mortar Battalion
- 18th Tank Corps: MGTF V. I. Polozkov
  - 110th Tank Brigade
  - 170th Tank Brigade
  - 181st Tank Brigade
  - 32nd Motorized Rifle Brigade
  - 1438th Self-propelled Artillery Regiment
  - 78th Motorcycle Battalion
  - 1000th Tank Destroyer Artillery Regiment
  - 736th Tank Destroyer Artillery Battalion
  - 292nd Mortar Regiment
  - 106th Guards-Mortar Battalion
  - 1694th Antiaircraft Artillery Regiment
- 29th Tank Corps: LTGTF I. F. Kirichenko
  - 25th Tank Brigade
  - 31st Tank Brigade
  - 32nd Tank Brigade

Table 2.1. *Continued*

53rd Motorized Rifle Brigade
1446th Self-propelled Artillery Regiment
75th Motorcycle Battalion
108th Tank Destroyer Artillery Regiment
271st Mortar Regiment
11th Guards-Mortar Battalion
53rd Guards Separate Tank Regiment
1st Guards Motorcycle Regiment

5th Guards Army: LTG A. S. Zhadov
32nd Guards Rifle Corps: MG A. I. Rodimtsev
13th Guards Rifle Division
95th Guards Rifle Division
97th Guards Rifle Division
33rd Guards Rifle Corps: LTG N. F. Lebedenko
9th Guards Airborne Division
14th Guards Rifle Division
214th Rifle Division
123rd Separate Antitank Rifle Battalion

7th Guards Army: LTG M. S. Shumilov
24th Guards Rifle Corps: LTG N. A. Vasil'ev
8th Guards Airborne Division
72nd Guards Rifle Division
81st Guards Rifle Division
25th Guards Rifle Corps: MG G. B. Safiulin
36th Guards Rifle Division
53rd Rifle Division
3rd Separate Antitank Rifle Battalion
27th Guards Tank Brigade
34th Separate Armored Train Battalion
38th Separate Armored Train Battalion

Front Reserves
50th Rifle Division
297th Rifle Division
409th Rifle Division
5th Guards Cavalry Corps: LTG A. G. Selivanov
11th Guards Cavalry Division
12th Guards Cavalry Division
63rd Cavalry Division
60th Tank Regiment
119th Tank Regiment
1896th Self-propelled Artillery Regiment
150th Guards Tank Destroyer Regiment
5th Guards Separate Tank Destroyer Battalion
9th Guards-Mortar Regiment
72nd Guards-Mortar Battalion
585th Antiaircraft Artillery Regiment
54th Fortified Region
130th Separate Antitank Rifle Battalion
7th Mechanized Corps: MGTF F. G. Katkov
16th Mechanized Brigade
63rd Mechanized Brigade
64th Mechanized Brigade
41st Guards Tank Brigade
1440th Self-propelled Artillery Regiment
94th Motorcycle Battalion
109th Tank Destroyer Artillery Regiment
392nd Separate Tank Destroyer Battalion
614th Mortar Regiment
40th Guards-Mortar Battalion
1713th Antiaircraft Artillery Regiment
8th Mechanized Corps: MGTF A. N. Firsovich
66th Mechanized Brigade
67th Mechanized Brigade
68th Mechanized Brigade
1822nd Self-propelled Artillery Regiment
97th Motorcycle Battalion
205th Guards-Mortar Battalion
1716th Antiaircraft Artillery Regiment
20th Tank Corps: LTGTF I. G. Lazarov
8th Guards Tank Brigade
80th Tank Brigade
155th Tank Brigade
7th Guards Motorized Rifle Brigade
1895th Self-propelled Artillery Regiment
96th Motorcycle Battalion
1505th Tank Destroyer Artillery Regiment
735th Separate Tank Destroyer Battalion
291st Mortar Regiment
406th Guards-Mortar Battalion
1711th Antiaircraft Artillery Regiment
10th Separate Armored Train Battalion
25th Separate Armored Train Battalion
61st Separate Armored Train Battalion

Source: *Boevoi sostav Sovetskoi armii, Chast' 4 (Ianvar'-dekabr' 1944)* [The combat composition of the Soviet Army, Part 4 (January–December 1944)] (Moscow: Voenizdat, 1988), 106–108.

Table 2.2. The 3rd Ukrainian Front's Order of Battle on 1 April 1944
3rd UKRAINIAN FRONT:
Army General R. Ia. Malinovsky

57th Army: Lieutenant General N. A. Gagen
- 9th Rifle Corps: MG I. P. Roslyi
  - 118th Rifle Division
  - 230th Rifle Division
  - 301st Rifle Division
- 64th Rifle Corps: MG M. B. Anashkin
  - 73rd Guards Rifle Division
  - 19th Rifle Division
  - 52nd Rifle Division
- 68th Rifle Corps: MG N. N. Mul'tan
  - 93rd Rifle Division
  - 113th Rifle Division
  - 223rd Rifle Division
- 93rd Separate Antitank Rifle Battalion
- 96th Tank Brigade

37th Army: Lieutenant General M. N. Sharokhin
- 6th Guards Rifle Corps: MG G. P. Kotov
  - 20th Guards Rifle Division
  - 195th Rifle Division
- 57th Rifle Corps: MG F. A. Ostashenko
  - 58th Guards Rifle Division
  - 92nd Guards Rifle Division
  - 228th Rifle Division
- 82nd Rifle Corps: MG P. G. Kuznetsov
  - 10th Guards Airborne Division
  - 28th Guards Rifle Division
  - 188th Rifle Division
- 15th Guards Rifle Division
- 22nd Separate Armored Train Battalion

46th Army: Lieutenant General V. V. Glagolev
- 31st Guards Rifle Corps: MG A. I. Ruchkin
  - 4th Guards Rifle Division
  - 34th Guards Rifle Division
  - 40th Guards Rifle Division
- 32nd Rifle Corps: MG D. S. Zherebin
  - 60th Guards Rifle Division
  - 259th Rifle Division
  - 266th Rifle Division
- 34th Rifle Corps: MG I. S. Kosobutsky
  - 236th Rifle Division
  - 394th Rifle Division
- 353rd Rifle Division

8th Guards Army: Colonel General V.I. Chuikov
- 4th Guards Rifle Corps: LTG V. F. Glazunov
  - 35th Guards Rifle Division
  - 47th Guards Rifle Division
  - 57th Guards Rifle Division
- 28th Guards Rifle Corps: MG S. I. Morozov
  - 39th Guards Rifle Division
  - 79th Guards Rifle Division
  - 88th Guards Rifle Division

Table 2.2 *Continued*

29th Guards Rifle Corps: LTG S. A. Bobruk (LTG Ia. S. Fokanov on 13 April)
27th Guards Rifle Division
74th Guards Rifle Division
82nd Guards Rifle Division
152nd Rifle Division
5th Guards Separate Tank Regiment

6th Army: Lieutenant General I. T. Shlemin
34th Guards Rifle Corps: MG N. M. Makovchuk
59th Guards Rifle Division
61st Guards Rifle Division
243rd Rifle Division
66th Rifle Corps: MG D. A. Kupriianov
203rd Rifle Division
244th Rifle Division
333rd Rifle Division

5th Shock Army: Colonel General V. D. Tsvetaev
10th Guards Rifle Corps: MG I. A. Rubaniuk
86th Guards Rifle Division
109th Guards Rifle Division
320th Rifle Division
37th Rifle Corps: MG S. F. Gorokhov
49th Guards Rifle Division
108th Guards Rifle Division
248th Rifle Division
416th Rifle Division
295th Rifle Division
1st Guards Fortified Region

Cavalry-Mechanized Group: Lieutenant General I. A. Pliev
4th Guards Mechanized Corps: MGTF V. I. Zhdanov
13th Guards Mechanized Brigade
14th Guards Mechanized Brigade
15th Guards Mechanized Brigade
36th Guards Tank Brigade
212th Tank Regiment
292nd Guards Self-propelled Artillery Regiment
62nd Motorcycle Battalion
1512th Tank Destroyer Regiment
748th Separate Tank Destroyer Artillery Battalion
129th Guards-Mortar Battalion
4th Guards Cavalry Corps: LTG I. A. Pliev
9th Guards Cavalry Division
10th Guards Cavalry Division
30th Cavalry Division
128th Separate Tank Regiment
134th Separate Tank Regiment
151st Separate Tank Regiment
1815th Self-propelled Artillery Regiment
152nd Guards Tank Destroyer Regiment
4th Guards Separate Tank Destroyer Battalion
68th Guards-Mortar Battalion
12th Guards-Mortar Regiment
255th Antiaircraft Artillery Regiment
17th Air Army: ColGAv V. A. Sudets
1st Mixed Aviation Corps: MGAv V. I. Shevchenko
5th Guards Assault Aviation Division
288th Fighter Aviation Division

Table 2.2 *Continued*

9th Mixed Aviation Corps: LTGAv O. V. Tolstikov
- 305th Assault Aviation Division
- 306th Assault Aviation Division
- 295th Fighter Aviation Division

244th Bomber Aviation Division
262nd Fighter-Bomber Aviation Division
371st Fighter-Bomber Aviation Regiment
39th Reconnaissance Aviation Regiment
96th Corrective-Reconnaissance Aviation Regiment
282nd Sep. Signal Aviation Regiment
3rd Medical Aviation Regiment
14th Aviation Regiment, Civil Air Fleet

Front Reserves:

10th Separate Automatic Weapons Battalion
2nd Guards Mechanized Corps: LTG K. V. Sviridov
- 4th Guards Mechanized Brigade
- 5th Guards Mechanized Brigade
- 6th Guards Mechanized Brigade
- 37th Guards Tank Brigade
- 23rd Guards Tank Regiment
- 24th Guards Tank Regiment
- 25th Guards Tank Regiment
- 99th Motorcycle Battalion
- 1509th Tank Destroyer Regiment
- 744th Separate Tank Destroyer Artillery Battalion
- 408th Guards-Mortar Battalion

23rd Tank Corps: MGTF A. O. Akhmanov
- 3rd Tank Brigade
- 39th Tank Brigade
- 135th Tank Brigade
- 56th Motorized Rifle Brigade
- 1443rd Self-propelled Artillery Regiment
- 82nd Motorcycle Battalion
- 1501st Tank Destroyer Artillery Regiment
- 457th Mortar Regiment
- 442nd Guards-Mortar Battalion
- 1697th Antiaircraft Artillery Regiment

5th Guards Motorized Rifle Brigade
28th Guards Separate Tank Regiment
35th Separate Tank Regiment
43rd Separate Tank Regiment
52nd Separate Tank Regiment
398th Guards Heavy Self-propelled Artillery Regiment
864th Self-propelled Artillery Regiment
1200th Self-propelled Artillery Regiment
1201st Self-propelled Artillery Regiment
1202nd Self-propelled Artillery Regiment
1891st Self-propelled Artillery Regiment
3rd Guards Motorcycle Regiment
53rd Motorcycle Regiment
67th Motorcycle Battalion
26th Separate Armored Train Battalion
28th Separate Armored Train Battalion

CHAPTER 3

The 2nd Ukrainian Front's April Offensive (8–23 April 1944)

THE INITIAL ADVANCE ALONG THE TIRGU FRUMOS AXIS (8–12 APRIL)

Konev's Main Shock Group

The recently published four-volume Russian official history of the Soviet-German War describes the initial phase of Konev's April offensive tersely but quite accurately:

> The offensive conducted by the forces on the 2nd Ukrainian Front's right wing was sufficiently energetic from 8 through 11 April. They forced the Seret and Zhizhia [Jijia] Rivers [50–60 miles northwest of Iasi], advanced 30–50 kilometers [18–30 miles] to the southwest and south, and approached the foothills of the Carpathians [Mountains]. The 27th Army's forces captured Tirgu-Frumos [28 miles west of Iasi] on 9 April but were forced to abandon the town two days later as a result of an enemy counterattack. The forces on the front's left wing encountered organized resistance and were able to advance only 10–15 kilometers [six to nine miles]. The 2nd Ukrainian Front's offensive had practically essentially ended by 11 and 12 April.[1]

Although this source reveals for the first time that this offensive actually took place, the short paragraph it devotes to the 2nd Ukrainian Front's operations during the first two weeks of April captures neither the scale nor the scope of the mission the *Stavka* assigned to Konev's *front*, the complexity of his *front*'s ensuing offensive, or the importance the *Stavka* attached to the offensive.

On 8 April Konev designated Zhmachenko's 40th Army and Trofimenko's 27th Army as his *front*'s offensive shock group and ordered the two armies to begin a coordinated advance southward along the Tirgu Frumos axis, in close cooperation with the lead elements of Bogdanov's 2nd Tank Army. At the time, the main body of Bogdanov's army was still regrouping westward toward and across the Prut River. While Konev's shock group was advancing on Tirgu Frumos, Koroteev's 52nd Army and a portion of Kravchenko's 6th Tank Army, which were operating north of Iasi, were to conduct secondary operations along the Iasi axis in support of Konev's main effort.

The commanders of all five of Konev's armies were seasoned combat veterans, who had amassed considerable experience commanding at all levels up to army, and their armies were as battle-seasoned as their commanders. Two years older than Konev, 49-year-old Lieutenant General Fillip Fedoseevich Zhmachenko, the 40th Army's commander, had begun his military career in 1917 as a private in the Tsar's Imperial Army. After fighting for several months during World War I, he joined the Red Guards in November 1917 and the Red Army shortly thereafter, fighting on the southern and western fronts in the Russian Civil War. During the 1920s Zhmachenko served stints as a commissar in a rifle regiment and a military school and graduated from the Khar'kov Commanders' Course in 1922, the Higher Tactical School in 1923, and the "*Vystrel*'" Command Course in 1926. He then commanded a rifle regiment and rifle division during the early and mid-1930s and served as directorate chief in the Khar'kov Military District from 1937 through 1939.

When the Germans began Operation Barbarossa in June 1941, Zhmachenko was commanding the 67th Rifle Corps in the *Stavka*'s reserve. When his corps was assigned to the Western Front's 21st Army in early July with the mission of defending the Dnepr Defense Line near the city of Gomel', Zhmachenko fought with distinction, contesting the advance by Guderian's Second Panzer Group to Smolensk and later surviving encirclement by the same panzer group when it lunged southward toward Kiev during September. After escaping from the encirclement north of Kiev, Zhmachenko was appointed deputy commander of the Briansk Front's 3rd Army in late October and was serving in that capacity when the 3rd Army conducted its successful counterstroke at Elets, south of Moscow, during December 1941 and January 1942. Subsequently, he commanded the 3rd Army from May 1942 through September 1943, leading it successfully in the Orel offensive during July and August and the Briansk offensive during August.

Thereafter, the *Stavka* assigned Zhmachenko to command the Voronezh Front's 47th Army in September 1943 and, after it was renamed the 1st Ukrainian Front, the same *front*'s 40th Army in October. After the *Stavka* awarded him with the title of Hero of the Soviet Union for his skillful conduct of operations to cross the Dnepr River, Zhmachenko led the 40th Army with distinction in the Kiev, Korsun'-Shevchenkovskii, and Uman'-Botoshany offensives during the late fall and winter of 1944.[2]

On 1 April, Zhmachenko's 40th Army fielded three rifle corps, the 50th, 51st, and 104th; a total of eight rifle divisions, two of which were guards divisions; and one fortified region. The 50th Rifle Corps, which was commanded by Major General S. S. Martirosian and included the 4th Guards and the 133rd and 163rd Rifle Divisions, was deployed in the army's center. Major General P. P. Avdeenko's 51st Rifle Corps, with its 42nd Guards and 74th and 232nd Rifle Divisions, was situated on the army's left wing, and Lieutenant General A. V.

Petrushevsky's 104th Rifle Corps, which consisted of the 38th and 240th Rifle Divisions, defended the 40th Army's long right wing and flank in cooperation with the army's 159th Fortified Region. In addition, a self-propelled artillery regiment and a wide variety of artillery units supported Zhmachenko's army.

Zhmachenko's counterpart in the 27th Army, 45-year-old Lieutenant General Sergei Grigorievich Trofimenko, had commanded at the army level since March 1942. A platoon commander and deputy commander of a machine-gun command during the Russian Civil War, during the 1920s Trofimenko served as commissar in a rifle regiment, commanded a rifle battalion, and graduated from the "*Vystrel*'" Officers Course. After serving as chief of staff of a rifle division and chief of the Volga and Kiev Military Districts' operations directorates during the early and mid-1930s, Zhukov's recommendations and the effects of the purges combined to propel Trofimenko to the position of chief of staff of the Zhitomir Group of Forces during the Czech crisis of 1938, chief of staff of Kiev Special Military District's 5th Army when it participated in the invasion of eastern Poland during September 1939, and deputy chief of staff of the Karelian Front's 7th Army during the Soviet-Finnish War of 1939 and 1940. Thereafter, Trofimenko served as chief of staff of the North Caucasus Military District during 1940 and commander of the Central Asian Military District during the first half of 1941.

In the wake of the Germans' Barbarossa invasion, Trofimenko commanded the Northern Front's Medvezh'egorsk Group of Forces through March 1942, the Karelian Front's 32nd and 7th Armies from March 1942 to January 1943, and the 27th Army thereafter. Reliable but not flashy, his 27th Army spearhead Red Army offensive operations at Demiansk, Belgorod-Khar'kov, and Velikii Bukrin along the Dnepr River during 1943 and, thereafter, took a supporting role in the 1st and 2nd Ukrainian Fronts' offensives at Kiev, Korsun'-Shevchenkovskii, and Uman' during late 1943 and the winter of 1944.[3]

On 1 April, Trofimenko's 27th Army fielded both the 35th Guards and the 33rd Rifle Corps, with a total of seven rifle divisions, two of which were guards or guards airborne divisions, and two self-propelled artillery regiments. The 35th Guards Rifle Corps, which was commanded by Lieutenant General S. G. Goriachev and included the 3rd Guards Airborne, 93rd Guards, and 202nd and 206th Rifle Divisions, was deployed on the army's right wing. Major General A. I. Semenov's 33rd Rifle Corps, with the 78th, 180th, and 337th Rifle Divisions, was located on the army's left wing.

The commander of the third army spearheading the first stage of Konev's offensive along the Tirgu Frumos axis was Lieutenant General of Tank Forces Semen Il'ich Bogdanov, an accomplished senior armor officer who had commanded the 2nd Tank Army since September 1943. Fifty years old in April

1944, Bogdanov had also served in the Tsar's army during the World War but joined the Red Army in 1918. After commanding at the platoon, company, and battalion levels during the Russian Civil War, he commanded a rifle regiment and graduated from the Higher Military School in 1923 and the Higher Rifle-Tactical Course in 1930. Transferring to the Red Army's mechanized arm during the early 1930s, Bogdanov graduated from the Military Academy of Motorization and Mechanization in 1936 and commanded mechanized and light tank brigades before being assigned to command the 14th Mechanized Corps' 30th Tank Division in the Western Special Military District shortly before the Germans began their invasion in June 1941.

After surviving the destruction of his division and its parent mechanized corps in the battles along the frontiers during the first few weeks of war, Bogdanov served as chief of armored forces in the newly organized 10th Army during the Battle for Moscow. His capable performance then earned him command, in succession, of the 12th, 14th, and 6th (5th Guards) Mechanized Corps during 1942 and 1943 and the 2nd Tank Army in September 1943. After distinguishing himself as commander of the 2nd Tank Army in the Battle of Kursk during July 1943 and the Central Front's counteroffensive at Orel during July and August, Bogdanov's tank army unhinged the Germans' defenses at Sevsk during September, helping precipitate the German withdrawal to the Dnepr River. After refitting during the fall of 1943, Bogdanov's tank army spearheaded the 2nd Ukrainian Front's offensives at Korsun'-Shevchenkovskii and Uman', where he was anointed as Hero of the Soviet Union for his outstanding performance.[4]

Bogdanov's colleagues noted:

> Semen Bogdanov, the commander of the 2nd Guards Tank Army, was a man of astonishing audacity. From September 1943 onwards his army took part in nearly all of the decisive battles of the war. He displayed outstanding abilities after the war too, as head of an academy, and for nearly five years he held the post of commander of Armoured Troops of the Soviet Armed Forces. . . .
>
> General Bogdanov, as a good organizer and personally brave, was respected by German commanders as one of the best Red Army tank commanders. . . . Bogdanov was a very paladin of courage and efficiency when fighting began, moved forward on the battlefield to ensure his subordinate commanders understood their tasks and missions. Using his physical presence to motivate and inspire, he could correct problems on the spot with the ability to clearly and precisely set the mission. His presence on the battlefield from the first to the last days added an unwearied tenacity and vigor. Bogdanov exemplified the universal, great combat leader who must be up front with sword in hand. Capitalizing on enemy mistakes,

Bogdanov looked for an opponent backing up on the battlefield, and that is where he poured his armored force.[5]

The nucleus of Bogdanov's 2nd Tank Army on 1 April consisted of Lieutenant General of Tank Forces V. A. Mishulin's 3rd Tank Corps and Major General of Tank Forces I. V. Dubovoi's 16th Tank Corps, each of which was organized in the standard configuration of three tank brigades and one motorized rifle brigade, supported by a variety of self-propelled, tank destroyer, and antiaircraft artillery regiments, mortar and guards-mortar regiments and battalions, motorcycle battalions, and logistical subunits. In addition, Bogdanov's tank army included the 11th Guards Tank Brigade, commanded by Colonel B. R. Erfmeev, the 8th and 13th Guards Separate Tank Regiments, which were equipped with new I. S. Stalin–model heavy tanks, and two separate self-propelled artillery regiments. Although Mishulin and Erfmeev were appointed to their respective commands on the very eve of the offensive, the former had commanded the 4th Tank Corps from March through September 1942. Dubovoi, however, had commanded his 16th Tank Corps successfully since early December 1943.

As the armies of Konev's shock group were preparing to unleash their advance southward toward Tirgu Frumos, Army Group Wöhler and the German Eighth Army had their collective attention riveted on the heavy fighting taking place in and around the village of Popricani, nine miles north of Iasi, where a small armored force from the 5th Mechanized Corps of Kravchenko's 6th Tank Army and the 73rd Rifle Corps of Koroteev's 52nd Army were involved in a seesaw struggle with armored *kampfgruppen* [combat groups] subordinate to Group Mieth. Koroteev's army had reached the region north of Iasi during the first week of April after failing to break through the Germans' defenses along the railroad line near Pyrlitsa to the northeast.

As of 1 April, Koroteev's army fielded two rifle corps, the 73rd and 78th, with a total of seven rifle divisions, none of them guards divisions, and a separate tank regiment. The 78th Rifle Corps, which was commanded by Major General G. A. Latyshev and included the 252nd, 303rd, and 373rd Rifle Divisions, was deployed on the army's left wing in the Pyrlitsa region, and Major General P. F. Batitsky's 73rd Rifle Corps, which consisted of the 31st, 254th, and 294th Rifle Divisions, had shifted westward to assault German defenses north of Iasi, together with the small task force from the 6th Tank Army. Finally, Koroteev retained the 116th Rifle Division in his army's reserve.

A seasoned veteran, Lieutanant General Konstantin Apollonovich Koroteev himself had commanded the 52nd Army successfully since July 1943. Forty-three years old in 1944, Koroteev had begun his military service as a 15-year-old soldier in the Tsar's army during 1916 before joining the Red Army in 1918. After commanding a platoon during the Civil War, Koroteev served as a platoon and company commander during the 1920s and graduated from the Saratov Infantry and Machine Gun Course in 1920, a mid-level command course in 1924, and the "*Vystrel*'" Course in 1926. After commanding at the battalion and regimental level from 1930 through 1937, Koroteev received command of the 27th Rifle Division in 1938, which he led during the invasion of Poland in 1939 and the Soviet-Finnish War of 1939–1940.[6]

After proving his competence in division command, Koroteev served as a corps commander and, later, an inspector of infantry in the Leningrad Military District during 1940 and 1941 and was commanding a rifle corps when war began in June 1941. Based on his fine performance during the initial period of the war, the *Stavka* assigned Koroteev command of the 12th Army in October 1941 and as deputy commander of the Southern Front in April 1942. Thereafter, Koroteev commanded, in succession, the 9th, 18th, 37th, and, finally, the 52nd Armies and participated in the defense of the Caucasus region during the Battle for Stalingrad, the Donbas offensives during 1943, and the Korsun'-Shevchenkovskii and Uman'-Botoshany offensives during 1944. Known as an excellent organizer and a thoroughly competent field commander, the *Stavka* employed Koroteev as a virtual "fireman" to restore and reinvigorate combat-worn armies until his assignment to command the 52nd Army in July 1943. Although Koroteev's army had only a tangential role during the first and second stages of Konev's Iasi offensive, it would take a far more significant role when German forces went over to the offense during May and June 1944.

Although its ranks were severely depleted as a result of over three months of near constant, heavy fighting in the Ukraine, Kravchenko's 6th Tank Army was providing the 52nd Army with minimal armor support as Koroteev's forces bore down on German defenses north of Iasi. The *Stavka* had formed the 6th Tank Army in early January 1944 as the Red Army's sixth and last wartime tank army. Only 44 years old in April 1944, despite his relative youth, the tank army's first and only wartime commander, Lieutenant General of Tank Forces Andrei Grigor'evich Kravchenko, was one of the Red Army's most experienced and accomplished armor commanders.

Originally an infantryman by trade, Kravchenko had joined the Red Army in 1918 and fought through the Russian Civil War as a private and junior lieutenant. A 1923 graduate of the Poltava Infantry School where he became a close friend of future *front* commander, N. F. Vatutin, and a 1928 graduate of the Frunze Academy, Kravchenko commanded a rifle battalion and served as chief of staff of the 7th Rifle Division's 21st Rifle Regiment before transferring to the Red Army's tank and mechanized arm and becoming a tactics instructor at the army's Saratov Tank School from 1935 through May 1939. After serving short stints as chief of staff of the 61st Rifle and 173rd Motorized Rifle Divisions during 1939, the latter during the Soviet-Finnish

War, the NKO appointed Kravchenko, first in April 1940, as chief of staff of the newly formed 2nd Mechanized Corps' 16th Tank Division and, later in March 1941, as chief of staff of the 18th Mechanized Corps.

In the wake of the German invasion in June 1941, Kravchenko orchestrated the 18th Mechanized Corps' difficult retreat across the Ukraine during the summer of 1941 and commanded the 31st Tank Brigade, which fought with General Dovator's famed 2nd Guards Cavalry Corps during the equally difficult Battle for Moscow. Because of the instrumental role his brigade played during the Red Army's victory at Moscow in December, when Kravchenko's tank brigade formed the spearhead of the counterattacking 20th Army, Kravchenko's star rose precipitously in 1942. After serving as chief of staff of General M. E. Katukov's famed 1st Tank Corps from March through June 1942, the NKO assigned Kravchenko command of the 2nd Tank Corps in June and the 4th Tank Corps in October.

Under Kravchenko's command, the 4th Tank Corps earned lasting fame for its role in the encirclement of the German Sixth Army at Stalingrad and, not coincidentally, the honored designation of 5th Guard Tank Corps. Thereafter throughout 1943, Kravchenko's tank corps played a vital part in many Red Army offensive operations, including the temporary capture of Khar'kov during the winter, the successful defense of the Kursk "Bulge" in July, the Belgorod-Khar'kov offensive in August, the forcing of the Dnepr River (where it spearheaded Vatutin's Voronezh Front in the seizure of Kiev) during November, and the Zhitomir-Berdichev offensive in December 1943 and January 1944. As a reward for his outstanding performance, the NKO assigned Kravchenko command of the new 6th Tank Army in January 1944, after which he led this army with distinction during the Korsun'-Shevchenkovskii offensive during January and February 1944 and the ensuing Uman'-Botoshany offensive during March and April 1944. Under his command to war's end, Kravchenko's 6th (Guards) Tank Army spearheaded Red Army offensives in Hungary and August before leading the Trans-Baikal Front to victory over the Japanese Kwantung Army in Manchuria during August 1945.

Kravchenko's biographers uniformly praise the tank army commander's contributions to the Red Army's ultimate victory in the war:

> The heroic feats of Kravchenko's units throughout the war were accomplished with greatly improvised methods. Improvisation does not come without initiative; he was extraordinarily persevering and a master of conserving resources. Kravchenko proved to be a remarkable tank commander with unsurpassed bravery and operated forward away from his command post. Not once was he wounded. . . . Kravchenko achieved a good balance in his leadership style between commanders and his staff with a strong sense of control and demand for detail. Duty was a word

> Kravchenko understood. The brave and respected armored guard commander epitomized the old Russian warrior code: "He who comes to us with a sword shall perish by the sword."[7]

The nucleus of Kravchenko's 6th Tank Army on 1 April consisted of Lieutenant General of Tank Forces M. V. Volkov's 5th Mechanized Corps and Lieutenant General of Tank Forces V. M. Alekseev's 5th Guards Tank Corps. While the former was organized with three mechanized brigades and one tank brigade—supported by a variety of self-propelled, tank destroyer, and antiaircraft artillery regiments; mortar and guards-mortar regiments and battalions; motorcycle battalions; and logistical subunits—the latter fielded three guards tank brigades, one guards motorized rifle brigade, and similar support. Unlike most other tank armies, Kravchenko's army lacked its own separate tank brigade.

Both of Kravchenko's corps commanders were also experienced combat veterans. Volkov, who had commanded a tank brigade in late 1941 and early 1942, received command of the 5th Mechanized Corps (the former 22nd Tank Corps) in early November 1942 and subsequently led this corps through its baptism of fire along the Chir River in December and throughout the battles in the eastern Ukraine during 1943 and early 1944. Alekseev, who succeeded Kravchenko as commander of the 5th Guards Tank Corps in late January 1944, had survived the disaster at Khar'kov in May 1942 while he was commanding a tank brigade, and he commanded the 10th Tank Corps from July 1942 through October 1943. His illustrious record included service in special Mobile Group Popov in the Donbas offensive during February 1943 and a prominent role in both the Kursk defense during July and the Belgorod-Khar'kov offensive during August of that year. Thereafter, his 10th Tank Corps took part in the forcing of the Dnepr River in October and the heavy fighting around Kiev in December, after which Alekseev commanded his tank corps under the 6th Tank Army's control during the 2nd Ukrainian Front's offensive across the central and southern Ukraine during the winter of 1944.

Despite its imposing strength on paper, Kravchenko's tank army was the "weak sister" in Konev's *front* and, as a result, had only a tangential role during the *front*'s Iasi offensive. During the 52nd Army's advance on Iasi, for example, Kravchenko was forced to cannibalize tanks from his entire army in order to muster a task force of about 20–30 tanks under the 5th Mechanized Corps' control to support Koroteev's advance. However, to the benefit of Konev's main shock group, the sharp seesaw duel north of Iasi, which pitted Kravchenko's small tank force and Koroteev's infantry against Group Mieth's armored *kampfgruppen,* did distract the Germans' attentions and forces away from the more critical Tirgu Frumos sector.

The Advance to Tirgu Frumos (8–9 April)

Exploiting the 52nd Army's diversionary operations along the Iasi axis, the three armies forming Konev's shock group began their southward advance early in the morning of 8 April.[8] Advancing in the vanguard of Zhmachenko's 40th Army, Avdeenko's 51st Rifle Corps lunged southward across the Sitna River north and south of Botoshany, 60 miles northwest of Iasi, while Goriachev's 35th Guards Rifle Corps and Semenov's 33rd Rifle Corps of Trofimenko's 27th Army thrust southward across the Prut River, 10–40 miles northwest of Iasi. The rifle corps' initial mission was to reach the Tirgu-Frumos, Pascani, and Tirgu-Neamt regions, 30–60 miles west of Iasi, and capture the three towns from their Romanian defenders, if possible, by surprise. As they marched southward, all three of Zhmachenko's and Trofimenko's rifle corps had to contend with multiple rivers and streams crisscrossing their routes of advance, as well as the rough and heavily forested hilly regions stretching eastward from the foothills of the Carpathian Mountains, which were still rain soaked from the *rasputitsa*.

On the shock groups' left flank and to the rear, Mishulin's and Dubovoi's 3rd and 16th Tank Corps from Bogdanov's 2nd Tank Army, whose long columns of tanks, trucks, and motorized infantry stretched out tens of miles to the rear along the mud-clogged roads, engaged in the arduous and time-consuming process of crossing to the west bank of the Prut River northwest of Iasi.

Far to the northwest on the 2nd Ukrainian Front's and the 40th Army's extreme right wing, which rested in the eastern foothills of the Carpathian Mountains in far northwestern Romania, pursuant to Zhmachenko's orders, Petrushevsky was beginning the difficult process of regrouping the two rifle divisions of his 104th Rifle Corps from this region southeastward to the *front*'s center sector to support the advance by Avdeenko's 51st Rifle Corps. The day before, Major General M. E. Kozyr's 232nd Rifle Division from Avdeenko's corps had captured the city of Botoshany, forcing the defending Romanian 8th Infantry Division to withdraw southward toward Tirgu-Neamt with Kozyr's forces in close pursuit. While the three divisions of Avdeenko's rifle corps continued pressing southward toward Tirgu-Neamt and Pascani, Petrushevsky regrouped his rifle divisions, one after the other, into the region north and northwest of Tirgu-Neamt to protect the right flank and rear of Avdeenko's advancing corps.

Further to the east but in tandem with Avdeenko's forces, the seven rifle divisions assigned to Goriachev's and Semenov's 35th Guards and 33rd Rifle Corps of Trofimenko's 27th Army advanced steadily southward along a broken front extending eastward 45 miles from Botoshany to the Prut River and then southeastward another 20 miles along the Prut. The 3rd Guards Airborne Division of Goriachev's guards corps, flanked on the left (east) by the corps' 206th and 202nd Rifle Divisions, began its attack southward from the Supica region on 7 April, driving the Romanian 8th Infantry Division's main forces back toward the town of Hirlau, situated only 17 miles north of Tirgu Frumos. Further east along the Prut River, the 78th and 180th Rifle Divisions of Semenov's 33rd Rifle Corps, now joined by the forward detachments from the two regrouping tank corps of Bogdanov's 2nd Tank Army, pressed the Romanian 7th Infantry Division steadily back toward Tirgu Frumos. By nightfall on 7 April, the lead tanks of the forward detachment spearheading the advance of Mishulin's 3rd Tank Corps reached and captured the town of Coarnele-Capru, ten miles east of Hirlau and only 13 miles north of Tirgu Frumos.

The following day the 206th Rifle Division of Goriachev's 35th Guards Rifle Corps drove elements of the Romanian 8th Infantry Division from their defenses around Hirlau, while the same corps' 3rd Guards Airborne and 202nd Rifle Divisions, supported by forward elements of the 2nd Tank Army, closed in on Tirgu Frumos from the northeast. By this time, all that stood between the advancing Soviet forces and their initial objectives of Pascani and Tirgu Frumos were the disheveled remnants of the Romanian 8th and 7th Infantry Divisions, whose forward elements were still clinging desperately to their forward defensive positions near Belcesti, eight miles northeast of Tirgu Frumos, and Erbicani, only three miles north of Podu Iloaie.

Fortunately for the defenders, however, the Romanian Fourth Army's IV Army Corps, which was responsible for defending this sector, managed to assemble sufficient forces to man the forward defensive positions in the Strunga Defense Line, positions that extended from Tirgu-Neamt eastward south of Pascani and through Tirgu Frumos and Podu Iloaie to just south of Iasi. As a result, by the morning of 9 April, the IV Army Corps' Divisional Group Siret was in position to defend the town of Tirgu-Neamt, its 8th and 6th Infantry Divisions were manning defenses stretching from Tirgu-Neamt eastward to Pascani, and its 1st Guards and 7th Infantry Divisions were likewise defending the sector from Pascani eastward past Tirgu Frumos to Podu Iloaie. North of this line, detachments from these forces were actively fending off Soviet probing attacks of their forward defenses.

Farther to the east in the Iasi region, Group Mieth (the German IV Army Corps) had already ordered Lieutenant General Freiherr Maximilian von Edelsheim, the commander of the 24th Panzer Division, which had been defending north of Iasi, to deploy a meager force of 12 tanks and a battalion of panzer-grenadiers from his division's 21st Panzer Grenadier Regiment toward Podu Iloaie in an attempt to strike the flank of the advancing Soviet forces, whose exact composition was as yet unknown. When the 24th Panzer Division's small *kampfgruppe* reached the Rominesti and Epureni regions, six to eight miles northeast of Podu Iloaie, by day's end on 8 April, it immediately established defensive positions alongside a regiment of the Romanian 7th Infantry Division, which, hard-pressed by the advancing Soviets, had withdrawn to that region in considerable disorder.

Egged on by Konev, the three armies constituting his *front*'s main shock group continued their headlong advance early on 9 April. The concerted assault quickly overcame the Romanian IV Army Corps' forward defensive positions north of Tirgu-Neamt, Pascani, Tirgu Frumos, and Podu Iloaie and reached the outskirts of the latter, forcing the defending Romanians and the 24th Panzer Division's weak *kampfgruppe* to withdraw southward to new defenses protecting Podu Iloaie proper. This set the stage for a short but vicious seesaw struggle for the town of Tirgu Frumos, which Army Group Wöhler was determined to retain.

The First Battle of Tirgu Frumos (9–12 April)

In the vanguard of Trofimenko's 27th Army, Goriachev's 35th Guards Rifle Corps resumed its advance southward from the Hirlau region toward Tirgu Frumos at mid-morning on 9 April, with Colonel V. P. Kolesnikov's 206th Rifle Division and Colonel I. M. Khoklov's 202nd Rifle Division deployed from left to right in his first echelon (Map 6). Kolesnikov's riflemen quickly cleared the Romanian troops from Tirgu Frumos and the adjacent region and dug into defensive positions just southeast and southwest of the town. Soon after, the riflemen of Khoklov's 202nd Rifle Division, who had kept pace with Kolesnikov's advance, swept eastward north of the Hirlau-Podu Iloaie railroad line toward Belchesti and Munteni, nine and ten miles northeast of Tirgu Frumos, respectively, while the infantry of Colonel I. N. Konev's 3rd Guards Airborne and Colonel Ia. N. Bronsky's 93rd Guards Rifle Division, which were following in the corps' second echelon, hurried to reinforce the corps' forward divisions before the enemy could react.

Meanwhile, in the offensive sector of Zhmachenko's 40th Army west of Tirgu Frumos, marching rapidly southward in the vanguard of Avdeenko's 51st Rifle Corps, Major General F. A. Bobrov's 42nd Guards Rifle Division captured the town of Pascani, 14 miles west of Tirgu Frumos, from the Romanian 6th Infantry Division at midday on 9 April, just as Major General M. E. Kozyr's 232nd Rifle Division, also from Avdeenko's rifle corps, closed up against the Romanians' defenses north of Tirgu-Neamt, 17 miles to the west. At the same time, east of Tirgu Frumos, the forward detachments of Bogdanov's 2nd Tank Army, which had been dueling with the 24th Panzer Division's *kampfgruppe* north of Podu Iloaie, tried to reinforce Trofimenko's infantry fighting in the Tirgu Frumos region, but they were unable to break contact with the stubborn German defenders. This granted the defending

Romanians and Germans the breathing spell necessary to react effectively to the new threat.

React the Eighth Army did and quite promptly. Realizing the grave danger to its main defenses west of Iasi, which threatened to render its entire defense in the Iasi region untenable, at about midday on 8 April, the Eighth Army alerted the commander of the *Grossdeutschland* Panzer Grenadier Division, General Hasso von Manteuffel, to regroup his division from its previous defensive positions extending along the railroad line between Ungeny and Pyrlitsa, 10–20 miles northeast of Iasi, and regroup it westward to restore the situation in the Tirgu Frumos region. A member of Manteuffel's staff later recalled the perilous situation:

> The [Grossdeutschland] division was told to move as quickly as possible from the Pyrlitsa region to west of Jassy [Iasi], where the Russians were advancing south on a broad front against the Rumanians and where the spearhead of their attack had already crossed the Jassy-Podul-Targul-Frumos [Tirgu-Frumos] road. Details of their strength and equipment could not be obtained from the terrified Rumanians. It seemed to me that the Rumanians were greatly exaggerating.
>
> From the battle at Pyrlitsa on 8 April, the division was concentrated at Jassy, 40 kilometers [24 miles] away on the 9th, only 36 hours after being relieved and after an exhausting march over difficult roads in severe wintry conditions. It was an impressive achievement, and we feel it gives clear proof of the division's operational efficiency and the leadership of its commanders at all levels. It also meant that it must have been extremely efficient logistically.
>
> Four hours after reaching Jassy and after being continually in action for that period, the western edge of Poduluke [Podul-Iloaie or Podu-Iloaie] was reached [on the afternoon of 9 April]. The Russian threat consisted mainly of infantry with armour and artillery support.[9]

While Manteuffel was regrouping his panzer grenadier division westward past Iasi, early in the afternoon on 9 April, he dispatched the division's 52nd Assault Engineer Battalion (Pi 52) and ordered it to launch a counterattack into Tirgu Frumos from the south as soon as it reached the town. Attacking later in the day, this small force managed to seize and hold a small foothold in the southern part of the town. By this time, however, the second echelon of Goriachev's 35th Guards Rifle Corps, Colonel Konev's 3rd Guards Airborne, and Bronsky's 93rd Guards Rifle Divisions had also reached the region, and both divisions soon added their weight to Trofimenko's southward thrust.

Once his airborne division reached the region just south of Tirgu-Frumos, Konev reinforced the defenses of Kolesnikov's 206th Rifle Division

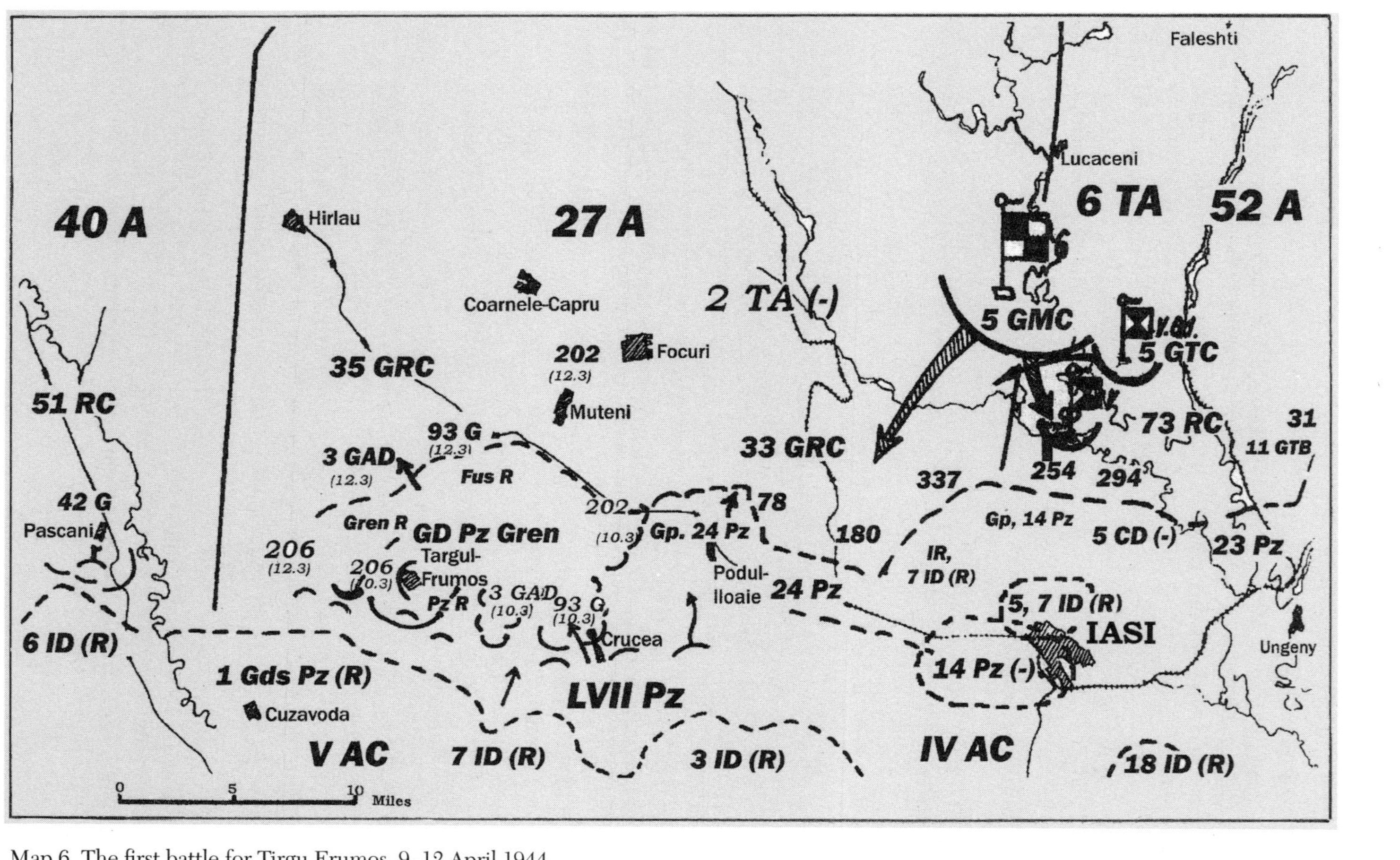

Map 6. The first battle for Tirgu Frumos, 9–12 April 1944

southeast of the town and dispatched a strong forward detachment further south to the village of Ganesti, which was situated along the road in the hills about four miles south of Tirgu Frumos and just north of the forward edge of the Strunga Defense Line's forward positions. Further to the east, Bronsky's 93rd Guards Division advanced southward from the Facuti region, five miles northeast of Tirgu Frumos, crossed the Tirgu Frumos and Iasi road just east of the town, and captured the villages of Lungani and Crucea, seven to eight miles southeast of Tirgu Frumos and two to three miles south of the railroad line from Tirgu Frumos to Podu Iloaie. Bronsky also formed a forward detachment of his own and dispatched it southward to the town of Stornesti, nine miles south of the railroad line, where it engaged the Romanian 7th Infantry Division's troops who were manning their sector of the main Strunga Defense Line.

Still further to the east, Khoklov's 202nd Rifle Division reached and captured the village of Sirca (Sarca), situated on the railroad line five miles west of Podu Iloaie, cut the road extending eastward from Tirgu Frumos to Podu Iloaie, and approached the western outskirts of Podu Iloaie, where it was halted by approaching forces from *Grossdeutschland* Panzer Grenadier Division's main body, which was just reaching the region. Making matters even worse for the defending Germans, the riflemen of Major General M. N. Mikhailov's 78th and Major General A. L. Kronik's 180th Rifle Divisions, which were marching in the vanguard of Semenov's 33rd Rifle Corps, were also bearing down on Podu Iloaie from the north.

Late in the afternoon of 9 April, Mikhailov's and Kronik's riflemen reinforced the forward detachments from the 2nd Tank Army's 3rd and 16th Tank Corps, which were already locked in a struggle north of Podu Iloaie with a *kampfgruppe* from the 24th Panzer Division. By day's end, fighting engulfed the entire sector northwest and north of Podu Iloaie from the village of Spinoasa, five miles to the northwest, to the villages of Erbicani and Totoesti, four to five miles to the north. Despite these reinforcements, however, the 27th Army's forces were unable to break through the 24th Panzer Division's defenses. All the while, in the rear area of Trofimenko's army, the main columns of Bogdanov's two tank corps were still struggling to plow their way through the virtually roadless and muddy terrain northeast of Tirgu-Frumos, too late to provide adequate support to the infantry they were supposed to support.

Thus, by nightfall on 9 April, the three rifle divisions leading the advance of the 27th Army's 35th Guards Rifle Corps captured Tirgu Frumos and carved a menacing salient three to seven miles deep into the Romanians' defense south and southeast of the town. Further east, the two forward rifle divisions of the 27th Army's 33rd Rifle Corps, supported by the forward detachments from Bogdanov's tank army, were exerting heavy pressure against the Romanian 7th Infantry Division's defenses around Podu Iloaie from the north and west, all the while anxiously awaiting the arrival of the 2nd Tank Army's main body so that they could crush the Romanians' defenses in the region. Although the situation seemed conducive to a further successful advance, unbeknownst to Konev, Trofimenko, and their two corps commanders, Goriachev and Semenov, the German Eighth Army and V Army Corps were quickly and skillfully assembling forces to eradicate this deadly threat to their defenses in northern Romania before it fully matured.

Early on 10 April, the *Grossdeutschland* Panzer Grenadier Division, which fielded a total of roughly 160 tanks, including 40 Panther (Pz V) and 40 Tiger (Pz VI) models, attacked westward along the road from Podu Iloaie to Tirgu Frumos in two columns deployed north and south of the road. Manteuffel described the action:

> The German thrust cut off elements of the Russians from their main forces. The thrust pushed on without stopping to the high ground west of Targul-Frumos and allowed the Germans to get out of the pass at Podu [Podu-Iloaie], which was canalizing their advance. For the Russians, losing Targul-Frumos shut the gateway to the south, since Targul-Frumos dominated the only useable road east of the Sereth [Seret], a river running along difficult ground off to the west.
>
> At about 2200 hours on the 10th, i.e., 48 hours after getting their original order, the Grenadier Regiment had secured Targul-Frumos, the heights to the west, and the high ground north of the town. It could not, however, prevent strong elements of the cut-off Russian attacking force from withdrawing back to their main forces to the north under cover of darkness.[10]

Perceptively, Manteuffel added, "The Russian thrust to the Ploesti oilfields had been halted."[11]

The history of the *Grossdeutschland* Division describes the division's westward assault in even greater detail:

> Early on 10 April, the Grossdeutschland Panzer-Fusiliers set out from Jassy to attack the flank of the enemy force that had broken through to the south between Jassy and Targul-Frumos. Their objective was to destroy the Soviets, even though they had a force the size of an army corps.
>
> Though they were small in number, the momentum of the panzer-fusiliers' attack, which was supported by tanks and assault guns as well as by II Battalion of the Panzer-Artillery Regiment GD, enabled them to take the hills near Danuan [Domian] [one mile east of Podu-Iloaie] in the face of only minor resistance. There they regrouped. III Battal-

ion, Panzer-Grenadier Regiment GD assumed the lead for the subsequent advance along the railroad to the west. Riding on their vehicles, the attackers drove to Podul Iloaei [Podu-Iloaie], where they freed a surrounded group of Rumanian troops. With the latter's help they rolled up the Soviets and brought in a large number of prisoners. The advance continued down the highway to Sarca [Sirca] [five miles west of Podu-Iloaie]. Leutnant [Lieutenant] Kollewe and his 1st Company entered the town, but not a shot was fired. The Bolsheviks had taken refuge in the houses and had to be dragged out. They were completely surprised, for they couldn't believe that there were still German troops with the will to attack. Without pausing I (APC) Battalion, Panzer-Grenadier Regiment GD under Major Krieg took the point and drove to Valea Otlor [Valea Oilor] [ten miles west of Podu-Iloaie], where the first serious resistance was met. Tanks and anti-aircraft guns moved up and that evening the infantry broke into the town. Following a brief close-quarters battle the surviving Soviets fled to the north; the town was in German hands.

The advance toward Targul-Frumos was begun during the night. It was vital that this important city be returned to our hands. In spite of the darkness the attack was a success. The attackers broke into the city following a heavy bombardment which destroyed many Soviet resistance nests. The city was combed for enemy troops, insofar as the darkness allowed. For the most part the attackers established hedgehog positions on the outskirts of the city. Things slowly quieted down when dawn came. Most of the enemy appeared to have retired to the north.

Meanwhile the remaining battalions and the bulk of the Panzer-Fusilier Regiment GD moved up to join the point to set up forward outposts, especially to the north. At approximately 06.00 II Battalion, Panzer-Grenadier Regiment GD attacked the enemy-held village of Balteti [Baltati] [three miles west] from Sarca. Shouting fiercely, the grenadiers stormed the village. Later the battalion joined the attack north through Valea Oilor toward Palieni [Polieni] [three miles northwest of Valea Oilor] by the armoured pioneers and Tigers. Enemy resistance there was weak. A new defence line was manned on the hills about 1,000 metres southeast of Palieni and work began immediately to fortify it.[12]

The *Grossdeutschland* Division launched its concerted counterattack just as Kolesnikov's 206th Rifle, Konev's 3rd Guards Airborne, and Bronsky's 93rd Guards Rifle Divisions were making last-minute preparations to resume their headlong assault toward the south, at a time when only their divisions' rear guards and logistical subunits remained behind to defend the Tirgu Frumos region. As a result, instead of resuming their offensive, the three rifle divisions found their lines of communications with the rear torn asunder and their left flank crushed by *Grossdeutschland* Division's advancing tanks and panzer grenadiers. To their front, several combat groups from the Romanian 1st Guard and 7th Infantry Divisions attacked their forward detachments at the villages of Ganesti, Critesti, and Stornesti, pressing them back to the north.

Caught between the German tanks racing into Tirgu Frumos from the east and the Romanian infantry advancing from the south, the three divisions of Goriachev's 35th Guards Rifle Corps manning these exposed positions south and southeast of Tirgu Frumos had no choice but to fight their way out of the developing trap. Fortunately for Goriachev's forces, since the *Grossdeutschland* Division lacked sufficient motorized infantry to cordon off their withdrawal routes completely, the half-encircled riflemen painstakingly made their way northward between the gaps in the advancing German armor overnight on 10 and 11 April and throughout the following day, finally occupying new defensive positions north and northeast of Tirgu Frumos.

In addition to frustrating the ambitious initial southward thrust by Trofimenko's 27th Army, by day's end on 10 April, the *Grossdeutschland* Division's determined counterstroke also confounded Konev's offensive plans. After a chaotic two-day struggle by Goriachev's rifle divisions to escape encirclement, the fighting in the Tirgu Frumos region quieted down by midday on 12 April. By this time the *Grossdeutschland* Division erected a new defensive line to protect Tirgu Frumos, which extended in a wide arc from the town of Cornesti, five miles northwest of Tirgu Frumos, northeastward south of the village of Liteni to Polieni, six miles northeast of Tirgu Frumos, and then southeast along the Cihudai River to the village of Spinoasa, nine miles east of Tirgu Frumos.

Manteuffel ultimately deployed his *Grossdeutschland* Division into new defensive positions north of Tirgu Frumos, with the Panzer Grenadier Regiment on the division's left wing northwest and north of the town and the Fusilier Regiment on its right wing from northeast of the town eastward to Spinoasa, but he retained his powerful Panzer Regiment in reserve assembly areas close to Tirgu Frumos proper. Meanwhile, throughout the day on 12 April, troops and assault guns from the Panzer Grenadier Regiment cleared isolated parties from the 206th Rifle and 3rd Guards Airborne Divisions from a small pocket west of the town and extended the regiment's defensive positions several miles forward to a new defensive line leading from just north of Cornesti southwestward to Helestieni, seven miles west of Tirgu Frumos, where the *Grossdeutschland*'s defenses tied in with those of the Romanian 1st Guards Division to form a continuous defensive front west of the town. On *Grossdeutschland*'s right flank, a *kampfgruppe* from Edelsheim's 24th Panzer Division continued defending the sector stretching eastward from Spinoasa and north of Podu Iloaie to the village of Letcani, ten miles west of Iasi, where its right flank connected to the defenses of the 7th Romanian Infantry Division, which was defending northwest of Iasi.

After successfully withdrawing the three partially encircled rifle divisions of Goriachev's 35th Guards Rifle Corps from their exposed pocket south of Tirgu Frumos, Trofimenko reorganized his 27th Army's defenses along a line extending from north of Tirgu Frumos eastward to north of Podu Iloaie. By day's end on 12 April, Goriachev deployed Kolesnikov's 206th Rifle, Colonel Konev's 3rd Guards Airborne, and Bronsky's 93rd Guards Rifle Divisions from left to right in defensive positions stretching from the eastern bank of the Seret River near Pascani, 15 miles west of Tirgu Frumos, eastward to the village of Munteni, ten miles northeast of Tirgu Frumos, and then withdrew Khoklov's shattered 202nd Rifle Division into his second echelon. Further to the east on the 35th Guards Rifle Corps' left, Semenov deployed Mikhailov's 78th, Kronik's 180th, and Colonel T. P. Gorobets' 337th Rifle Divisions from his 33rd Rifle Corps in defensive positions extending from the Munteni region eastward along the northern bank of the Cihudai River north of Podu Iloaie to the Zahorna region, nine miles northwest of Iasi.

The Battle of Podu Iloaie (12 April)

Irked by the defeat his forces suffered south of Tirgu Frumos, on 12 April Konev reacted forcefully by ordered Bogdanov, whose 2nd Tank Army had just completed concentrating its two tank corps south of Focuri, ten miles north of Podu Iloaie, to assault the Germans' defenses at Podu Iloaie from the northwest and north. Bogdanov's objective was to eliminate the salient occupied by the 24th Panzer Division, which jutted precariously northward from Podu Iloaie. The only existing Soviet account of this fighting simply notes, "The 40th and 27th Armies conducted prolonged fighting with the counterattacking enemy during the next several days. The 2nd Tank Army, which was committed to combat on 12 April, repelled a counterstroke by an enemy tank group in the Podu Iloaie region in cooperation with the 27th Army."[13] German accounts of this short but intense fight refute this assertion by claiming that Konev's forces actually began the attack. According to these accounts, Konev's attacking force included the 2nd Tank Army's 3rd and 16th Tank Corps and the 93rd Guards and 78th Rifle Divisions from Semenov's 33rd Rifle Corps. In all likelihood, however, the attacking force also included the 180th Rifle Division from Semenov's rifle corps.[14]

Operating jointly, Trofimenko's and Bogdanov's armies launched their first assault against the 24th Panzer Division's defenses north of Podu Iloaie late on 12 April with a force of roughly 70 tanks from the 109th Tank and 15th Motorized Rifle Brigades of Dubovoi's 16th Tank Corps, supported by Bronsky's 93rd Guards and Mikhailov's 78th Rifle Divisions from Goriachev's

35th Guards and Semenov's 33rd Rifle Corps. The attack struck the German defenses at Totoesti, three miles due north of Podu Iloaie, which were manned by four battalions from Edelsheim's 24th Panzer Division. Although the initial Soviet assault succeeded in breaking through the Germans' forward defensive positions, by nightfall a *kampfgruppe* of 15 tanks and 30 assault guns from the 24th Panzer Division, which had redeployed rapidly northward from the village of Damian (midway between Podu Iloaie and Letcani), counterattacked and drove the Soviets back to their jumping-off positions.

Undeterred by this setback, Bogdanov resumed his assaults early on 13 April, this time with about 80 tanks from the 50th and 51st Tank Brigades of Mishulin's 3rd Tank Corps, supported by infantry from the same tank corps' 57th Motorized Rifle Brigade and riflemen from Bronsky's 93rd Guard Rifle Division. This assault struck the Germans' defenses along the northwestern flank of the Totoesti salient. Once again, after the Russians recorded modest initial success, the 24th Panzer Division counterattacked with two *kampfgruppen,* the first equipped with 15 tanks and 30 assault guns and the second with ten tanks and a battalion of assault guns. The combined assaults against the 3rd Tank Corps' flanks quickly brought Bogdanov's assault to a halt and temporarily ended Konev's attempt to resume his offensive in this sector.

JOCKEYING FOR POSITION ALONG THE TIRGU FRUMOS AXIS (13–23 APRIL)

Konev's failed efforts to revitalize his offensive in the Podu Iloaie sector on 12 April ended his attempt to conduct a major offensive into northern Romania with only the 40th and 27th Armies and the 2nd Tank Army. By day's end on 12 April, it was clear to Konev and the *Stavka* alike that the 2nd Ukrainian Front could mount no further major action on its right wing unless and until it could significantly reinforce its shock group. In practical terms, this meant further offensive action would have to be postponed until both Shumilov's 7th Guards Army and Rotmistrov's more powerful 5th Guards Tank Armies were available to spearhead Konev's offensive in the Tirgu Frumos sector. Unfortunately, both armies were still completing the first phase of their regrouping in mid-April and would not be available for action in this sector until month's end at the earliest.

After spending three days reconstructing several bridges across the Prut River, which was swollen to massive proportion by the spring floodwaters, Rotmistrov's 5th Guards Tank Army finally closed into its new assembly areas around Botoshany at day's end on 14 April. However, Shumilov's 7th Guards Army, which had turned its sector on the 2nd Ukrainian Front's extreme left wing over to the 3rd Ukrainian Front's 57th Army between 5 and 7 April, had an even longer distance to traverse during its regrouping. Therefore, its divisions crossed the Prut River on 15 and 16 April across a broad front in the Skuliany and Kuban' regions, 10–20 miles north of Iasi, and concentrated around the town of Copalau, ten miles southeast of Botoshany and 30 miles north of Tirgu Frumos, between 18 and 23 April.

While this regrouping was under way and Konev was refining his plans for the next stage of his offensive, desultory fighting continued along the entire front from Pascani eastward to Podu Iloaie. This fighting broke out as Konev's forward armies struggled to improve their jumping-off positions for the new offensive, and the Germans labored to erect more formidable defenses. The heaviest fighting during this period took place west of Pascani during 13–18 April, north of Tirgu Frumos during 13–16 April, and north of Iasi during13–18 April (Map 7).

After Manteuffel's *Grossdeutschland* Division recaptured Tirgu Frumos on 10 April, the division systematically extended its defensive positions to the north and west over the next two days to better protect its vital strong point at Tirgu Frumos. For example, the division's Panzer Grenadier Regiment launched a sortie to the northeast and northwest from 11 to 13 April, both to expand its defensive perimeter and to test the Soviets' defenses. The *Grossdeutschland* Division's history describes the brief attacks:

> Near Targul-Frumos meanwhile, contact had been established with German and Romanian units attacking from the west. The road from Targul-Frumos east to Jassy was open again. Traffic returned to normal; the supply vehicles rolled.
>
> The advance continued without letup, however, from Targul-Frumos to the north and northeast, toward the advancing enemy. III Battalion of the Panzer-Fusilier Regiment GD reached the ridge southwest of Rusa [Belchesti] [eight miles northeast of Tirgu-Frumos] on the far side of the marshy bottom land [on 11 April]. On its left was I Battalion, which occupied defensive positions on both sides of Polieni [six miles north of Tirgu-Frumos] on 13 April, relieving II Battalion, Panzer-Grenadier Regiment GD, while II Battalion of the Panzer-Artillery Regiment GD was in firing positions on both sides of Facuti [four miles northeast of Tirgu-Frumos].
>
> Meanwhile, northwest of Targul-Frumos, the panzer-grenadiers pushed the main line of resistance forward [on 13 April]. Their forceful assault drove the Bolsheviks out of the towns of Costesti and Pietrisi [Pietresu] [three miles west-northwest of Tirgu-Frumos] and by the evening they had reached the line Point 296 (on the Giurgesu [Giorgesti] highway)-Point 274-Secaresti [one mile further west]. Masses of Soviets

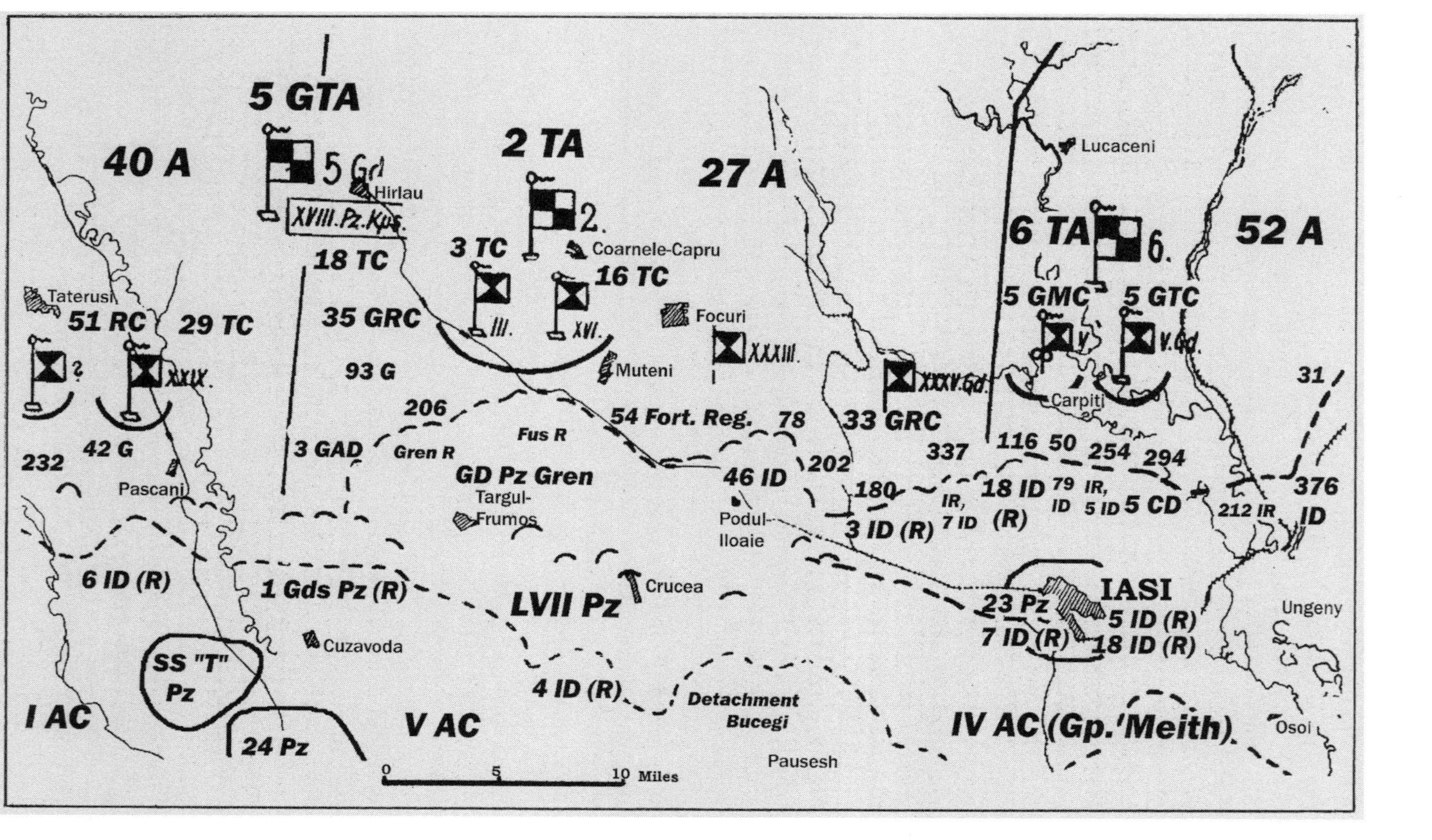

Map 7. The situation in the Tirgu Frumos and Iasi sectors, 20 April 1944

fled, suffering considerable losses to the fire of the heavy weapons in the process.[15]

After advancing about five miles northwestward from the division's outer defensive lines northwest of Tirgu Frumos, the small *kampfgruppe* pierced the defenses of Colonel Konev's 3rd Guards Airborne Division and actually reached the region north of the village of Harmanesti, nine miles northwest of Tirgu Frumos, at midday on 13 April. Although this *kampfgruppe* abandoned its forward positions and withdrew by nightfall, its parent division expanded its defensive perimeter up to three miles northwest of Tirgu-Frumos. Although the Soviets' main defensive belt in this sector was still intact at day's end, this successful German sortie apparently convinced Konev that his defenses in this sector of the 27th Army required further strengthening. Consequently, Konev ordered Trofimenko to reinforce the defenses of Goriachev's 35th Guards Rifle Corps northwest of Tirgu Frumos with Bronsky's 93rd Guards Rifle Division and to reinforce his defenses north of the town with tanks from Bogdanov's 2nd Tank Army.

Before Trofimenko could do so, however, the *Grossdeutschland* Division launched yet another assault, this time on 15 April against his defenses along the Hirlau road, due north of Tirgu Frumos:

> Meanwhile the Soviet resistance stiffened. Patrols revealed the enemy's forward positions; at the highway near Vascani–the north end of Barbatesti [Barbotesti] [six miles northwest of Tirgu-Frumos]–Hill 344–edge of the forest south of Baiceni–hills north of Bals [seven miles north of Tirgu-Frumos]–south end of Ulmi Liteni [six miles north-northeast of Tirgu-Frumos]–south end of Valeni Rusi [Belchesti] [eight miles northeast of Tirgu-Frumos] and along the stream bed [the Cihudai River]. Repeated armoured thrusts, like those north of Bals on 15 April, put the Soviets to flight locally, but resulted in losses. The courageous platoon leader Feldwebel Lux of 11th Company, Panzer-Grenadier Regiment GD was killed that day and an assault gun was lost as the result of a direct hit. On the other side of the coin, an armoured reconnaissance toward Vascani [eight miles northwest of Tirgu-Frumos] by tanks and the armoured personnel carriers of the I (APC) Battalion, Panzer-Grenadier Regiment GD resulted in 16 enemy tanks destroyed.
>
> As a result of these operations it was obvious that the Soviets had moved in considerable reinforcements and would resume their efforts to break through to the south in the near future.[16]

Reacting quickly, Bronsky's guardsmen occupied the sector between Kolesnikov's 206th Rifle and Colonel Konev's 3rd Guards Airborne Divisions, precisely where *Grossdeutschland* had conducted its bold sortie, by day's end on 18 April. While this reinforcement was in progress, Trofimenko ordered Goriachev's guardsmen to conduct local attacks against the *Grossdeutschland* Division's defenses north of Tirgu Frumos on 14 and 15 April and Semenov's 33rd Rifle Corps to do likewise against the 24th Panzer Division's defenses northwest of Podu Iloaie on 15 and 16 April. *Grossdeutschland* Division's history provides some details about the attack north of Tirgu Frumos:

> The obvious point of main effort of the enemy build-up lay along the Vascani-Targul Frumos and Bals-Targul Frumos highways. All hell broke loose in Bals [seven miles north of Tirgu-Frumos] on 16 April when the Bolsheviks succeeded in ejecting the forward outposts of 11th Company, Panzer-Grenadier Regiment GD under the command of Feldwebel Nieswand from the town. An immediate counterattack by assault guns and Tiger tanks, which arrived somewhat later, resulted in the retaking of Bals, but it also confirmed the offensive intentions of the Soviets. The defenders had to expect a Soviet attempt to break through there.
>
> In contrast things were quiet in the enemy positions opposite the panzer-fusiliers, apart from limited patrol activity and occasional artillery bombardments.[17]

While both sides were feeling out one another's intentions from 13 through 18 April, the *Grossdeutschland* Division was the unexpected beneficiary of a spectacular intelligence coup, which confirmed the Soviets' intentions to mount a larger-scale offensive:

> That same day [13 April], from their positions in front of Bals, soldiers of 11th Company, III Battalion, Panzer-Grenadier Regiment GD observed the landing of a small Soviet aircraft that had apparently lost its way. There was a quick burst of machine gun fire and a party of men moved toward the aircraft. While the pilot was being picked up, his passenger tried to flee through the fields. He threw away one piece of equipment after another to help him run faster; but in vain, he was soon caught. He was an astonishing catch: secret papers were found on him. The man was a major, obviously a liaison officer from the Soviet army group [front] to the corps deployed in the area. Examination of his papers revealed important information about the objectives of the Soviet attacks.[18]

As the sporadic fighting continued northwest and north of Tirgu Frumos, further to the east, Konev ordered Koroteev's 52nd Army to probe German Group Mieth's (IV Army Corps's) defenses north of Iasi to provide cover for his major regrouping effort. Koroteev complied by ordering Batitsky, the commander of his 73rd Rifle Corps, to organize an assault with his 254th and 294th Rifle Divisions, supported by a handful of tanks from Kravchenko's 6th Tank Army, against defenses manned by a four-battalion *kampfgruppe* of the 24th Panzer Division, which was defending a sector anchored on the village strong point of Vulturi, six miles due north of Iasi. During the ensuing heavy fighting, which began early on 13 April and lasted for two full days, Koroteev reinforced Batitsky's rifle corps with the 116th Rifle Division from his reserve. However, Group Mieth successfully fended off Koroteev's assaults by reinforcing the defending battalions of Edelsheim's 24th Panzer Division with a fresh *kampfgruppe* dispatched to the region from Major General Kräber's 23rd Panzer Division.

During the same period, a more serious threat to German—or, more properly, Romanian—defenses materialized in the offensive sector of Zhmachenko's 40th Army between Tirgu-Neamt and Pascani, west of the Seret River. Specifically, early on 13 April, two rifle divisions from Avdeenko's 51st Rifle Corps began probing operations against the Romanians' forward defenses on the ridgeline extending from north to south between the Seret River and the Moldava River, ten miles to the west. Two days before, the 51st Rifle Corps' 42nd Guards Rifle Division had captured Pascani from the Romanian 6th Infantry Division and had occupied positions about two miles south of the town. The new and heavier attack on 13 April probably occurred several days later than the 27th Army's assault in the Tirgu Frumos region because of the delays Zhmachenko's army experienced when trying to concentrate his assault force. Since no Soviet accounts of this action exist, the chronology of operations must be based solely on German intelligence and operational reports.

Late on 13 April, the Romanian VI Army Corps' 8th and 6th Infantry Division were defending the sector from Tirgu-Neamt eastward 18 miles to the Seret River south of Pascani. The 8th Infantry Division, whose right flank was anchored on the Moldova River, deployed two of its battalions into forward defensive positions south of the villages of Timisesti and Motca: the first battalion on the eastern bank of the Moldova River, seven miles west of Pascani, and the second one miles to the east along the crest of the ridge running north to south between the two rivers. Further east, the 6th Infantry Division also deployed two battalions forward: the first on the ridge's eastern slope near the village of Brosteni, three miles west of Pascani, and the second astride the road running south from Pascani proper.

Avdeenko's 51st Rifle Corps began its attack at dawn on 13 April with Kozyr's 232nd Rifle Division and most of Bobrov's 42nd Guards Rifle Division, supported by a detachment of ten tanks and tank-mounted infantry probably detached from Lieutenant General A. G. Selivanov's 5th Guards Cavalry Corps, whose main body was resting and refitting in the *front*'s rear area. Avdeenko's assaulting forces struck Romanian security outposts at the village of Critesti, two miles north of Motca, and drove them back to the Romanian 8th Infantry Division's forward defensive positions at Timisesti and Motca, which the Soviets assaulted the next day. Although the Romanian defenders repelled the Russians' attacks on 14 April, Zhmachenko reinforced Avdeenko's rifle corps with Major General A. D. Rumiantsev's 4th Guard Airborne Division on 15 April. The combined Russian force then captured the Romanian strong points at both Motca and Brosteni and advanced southward almost three miles more to the villages of Boureni and Bratesti, where the Romanians employed a full regiment from the newly arrived 20th Mountain Infantry Division to establish a new defensive line astride the ridge between the Seret and Moldava Rivers. Making matters worse for the defending Romanians, another Russian force, probably from Martirosian's 50th Rifle Corps and Selivanov's 5th Guards Cavalry Corps, also began assaulting defenses manned by Romanian Division Group Seret at Tirgu-Neamt, ten miles west of the Moldava River.

With alarm bells sounding loudly, the Romanian VI Army Corps urgently requested assistance from Group Wöhler, and, in response, the German LVII Panzer Corps, which was just beginning to concentrate its forces in the vicinity of the city of Roman, 25 miles to the south, sent a *kampfgruppe* from the SS "*T*" Panzer Division, commanded by SS Lieutenant General Hermann Priess, which the Eighth Army had just regrouped westward from the Kishinev region, to assist the beleaguered Romanians. However, before *Totenkopf's kampfgruppe* could reach the region, on 16 April Zhmachenko halted his army's attacks probably because the 27th Army's offensive further east had already failed. As had been the case with Goriachev's forces struggling south and southeast of Tirgu Frumos, Zhmachenko also feared his forces might be cut off and destroyed by a concerted German counterattack if they were not supported by other successful attacks to the east. Although German intelligence soon identified the arrival of fresh Soviet troops in the Tirgu-Neamt and Pascani regions, which it identified as part of the 5th Guards Tank Army's 29th Tank Corps, the situation in this sector stabilized, with the Romanians clinging to the positions they withdrew to on 15 April.

OPERATIONS ALONG THE DNESTR FRONT (8–25 APRIL)

While the main shock group of Konev's 2nd Ukrainian Front (the 40th and 27th Armies and the 2nd Tank Army) were pounding the Germans' defenses in the Tirgu-Neamt, Tirgu Frumos, and Podu Iloaie sectors and Koroteev's 52nd Army, with minimal support from Kravchenko's 6th Tank Army, was engaging German forces north of Iasi, the armies on Konev's left wing were pressing German forces southward and westward toward and across the Dnestr River north of Orgeev and toward the Dnestr River in the sector extending from the Dubossary region, 23 miles northeast of Kishinev, southward to the Tashlyk region, 26 miles east of Kishinev. Konev assigned the armies on his *front's* left wing, which included Galinin's 4th Guards, Managarov's 53rd, and Zhadov's 5th Guards Armies arrayed from north to south, the vital missions to cross the Dnestr River in the sector from northeast of Orgeev southward to Tashlyk, capture the cities of Orgeev, Dubossary, Grigoriopol', and Tashlyk, and exploit to seize the city of Kishinev. They were to do this in cooperation with the 3rd Ukrainian Front's forces, which were to advance on Konev's left flank once they completed their operation to capture Odessa. In essence, in the *Stavka's* and Konev's view, the seizure of Kishinev, the capital of Romanian Bessarabia, was just as vital to the overall success of their offensive plan as was the capture of Iasi. Nor was the fighting on the left wing of Konev's *front* any less intense than that on his right wing and center.

The 4th Guards Army's Advance to Orgeev

Konev assigned the vital role of piercing German defenses along the Dnestr River, capturing Orgeev, 25 miles north of Kishinev, and leading the march on the Bessarabian capital Kishinev from the north to Lieutenant General I. V. Galanin's 4th Guards Army. By the first week of April, the lead rifle corps of Galanin's guards army had already swept westward across the Dnestr River north of the Rybnitsa region, 30–40 miles north of Orgeev, and was advancing southward toward Orgeev, a town situated on the northern bank of the Reut River, a western tributary of the Dnestr, which flowed into the Dnestr River 15 miles to the southeast.[19] The remainder of Galanin's army was bearing down on the Dnestr's eastern bank north of Dubossary (Map 8).

Forty-five years old in April 1944, Lieutenant General Ivan Vasil'evich Galanin was an experienced combat veteran who had commanded the 4th Guards Army from September 1943 to January 1944 and, after a short stint in command of the 53rd Army, had commanded the 4th Guards Army from mid-February through November 1944. After enlisting in the Red Army during the Civil War, Galanin took part in the suppression of the Kronshtadt mutiny in 1921 and, perhaps due to his proven loyalty to the Bolshevik regime, was sent to the Higher Military Inspectorate School in 1923. A 1931 graduate of the "*Vystrel*'" Course and a 1936 graduate of the Frunze Academy, Galanin served in various staff assignments during the 1930s, culminating in his assignment as deputy chief of staff of the Trans-Baikal Military District from 1936 to 1938. Appointed to division command in August 1938, he fought under Zhukov's command in the Red Army's famous victory over the Japanese Kwantung Army at Khalkhin Gol in August 1939. After war began,

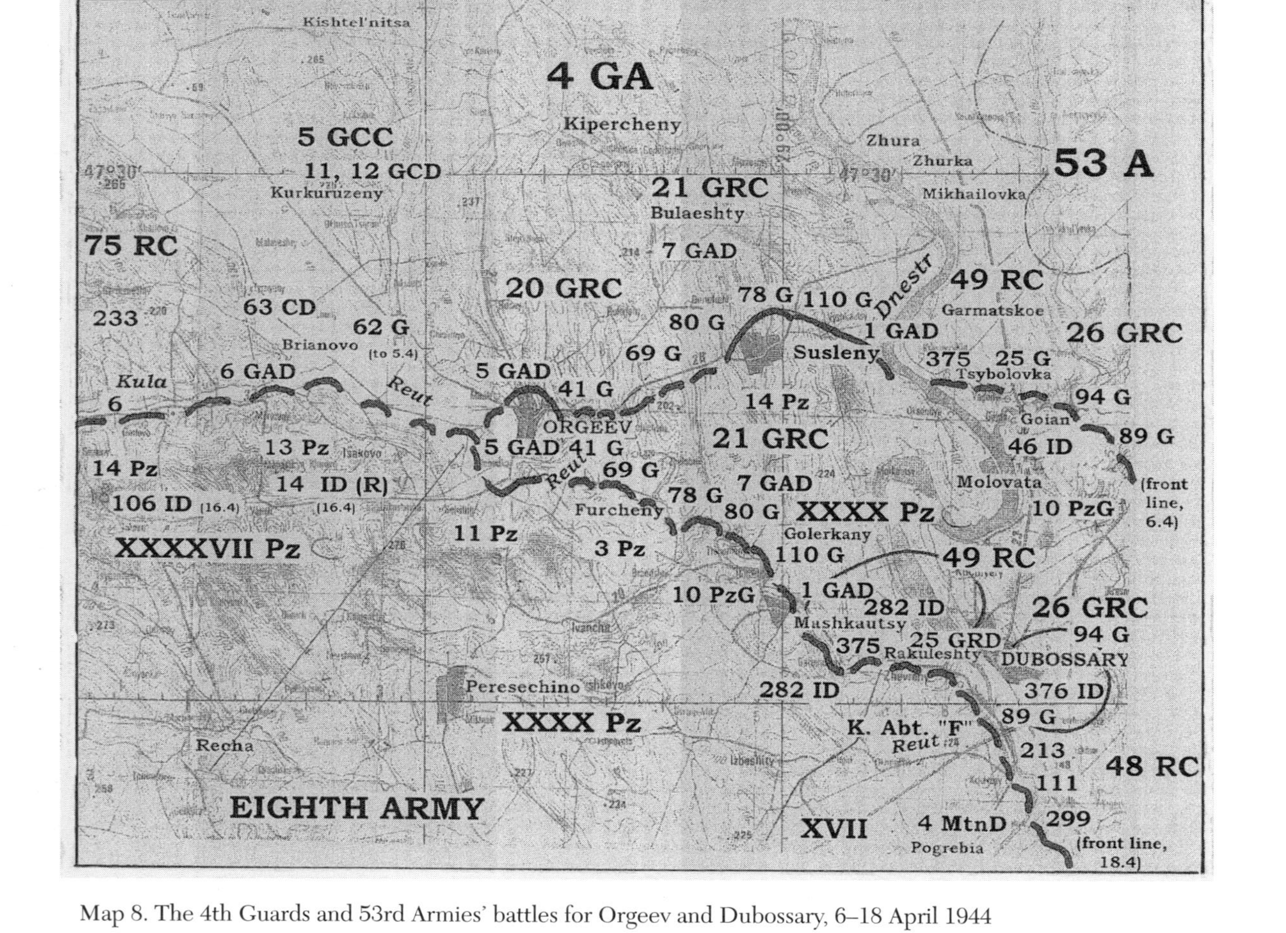

Map 8. The 4th Guards and 53rd Armies' battles for Orgeev and Dubossary, 6–18 April 1944

the NKO assigned Galanin, who had been a rifle corps commander in July 1940, to command the Southern Front's 12th Army during its harrowing retreat across the eastern Ukraine from August through October 1941.

After surviving the Germans' Barbarossa onslaught, Galanin commanded the Volkhov Front's 59th Army during its dramatic victory over German forces at Tikhvin during November 1941 and served as deputy commander of the Western and Voronezh Fronts from late winter through summer 1942. Once again assigned to army command, Galanin led, in succession, the Don Front's 24th Army during the Battle for Stalingrad and the Central Front's 70th Army during the Battle of Kursk defense and the Orel counteroffensive. When the commander of the 4th Guards Army, Marshal of the Soviet Union G. I. Kulik, failed to live up to the *Stavka*'s expectations during the Belgorod-Khar'kov offensive in August 1943, the NKO appointed Galanin to replace Kulik as the guards army's commander. Thereafter, Galanin's 4th Guards Army led the advance of Konev's Steppe (later 2nd Ukrainian) Front to and across the Dnepr River during the fall of 1943, and Galanin commanded both the 4th Guards and 53rd Armies during the same *front*'s offensives on the Right Bank of the Ukraine. During this period Galanin's army spearheaded Konev's *front* during the Korsun'-Shevchenkovskii and Uman'-Botoshany offensives. Later, Galanin would command the 4th Guards Army with distinction during the Iasi-Kishinev and Budapest offensives during August and October 1944, only to relinquish army command in November 1944, possibly because of poor health.[20]

On 1 April Galanin's 4th Guards Army consisted of three rifle corps, the 20th and 21st Guards and the 75th, with a total of 11 rifle divisions, eight of which were either guards rifle or guards airborne divisions. The 20th Guards Rifle Corps, which was commanded by Major General N. I. Biriukov and included the 5th, 6th, and 7th Guards Airborne and the 41st and 62nd Guards Rifle Divisions, was deployed in the army's center and was flanked on the left by Major General P. I. Fomenko's 21st Guards Rifle Corps, with the 69th, 78th, and 80th Guards Rifle Divisions. Finally, Major General A. Z. Akimenko's 75th Rifle Corps, with the 6th, 84th, and 233rd Rifle Divisions, was deployed on the army's right wing and rear.

After crossing the Dnestr River north of Rybnitsa in late March, the main body of Galanin's 4th Guards Army reached the northern approaches to Orgeev and the Reut River on 2 April. In accordance with the mission Konev assigned to his army, Galanin ordered his three rifle corps to begin their advance toward Orgeev and Kishinev the following morning. Attacking at dawn on 3 April, the five guards divisions of Biriukov's 20th Guards Rifle Corps and the three guards divisions of Fomenko's 21st Guards Rifle Corps advanced only two to three miles against stiffening German resistance. Compounding Galanin's slow advance, the three rifle divisions of Akimenko's 75th Rifle

Corps soon became bogged down along the mud-clogged roads well to the rear and were unable to reach their designated jumping-off positions for the offensive.

The 4th Guards Army's official history described the problems it encountered during its advance:

> Overcoming the increasing enemy resistance became more difficult because our forces had inadequate artillery support and ammunition. Of the army's 700 guns no more than 200 were in their firing positions. The remainder lagged behind. They became mired in the sticky mud and were unable to reach the units and support them with their fire. No less difficult was the process of supplying ammunition to the artillery and mortar firing positions. We used every conceivable means of transport, including carrying the shells forward by hand. In spite of these measures, the artillerymen had insufficient quantities of ammunition to conduct their firing missions.[21]

When Galanin's army began its offensive on 3 April, it faced the bulk of the German Eighth Army's XXXXVII and XXXX Panzer Corps, which were deployed abreast from left to right on the army's right (eastern) wing. Major General Baron Hans von Funck's XXXXVII Panzer Corps was deployed along and south of the Kula River, which flowed from west to east into the Reut River west of Orgeev, and farther southeast along the Reut River to just west of Orgeev, with its 370th Infantry and 14th and 13th Panzer Divisions deployed abreast from left to right. On the panzer corps' left wing and in its center, the 370th Infantry Division and Lieutenant General Martin Unrein's 14th Panzer Division manned defenses extending from the village of Mynzalesht', two miles north of Korneshty on the Iasi-Kishinev railroad line 25 miles northeast of Iasi and 40 miles west of Orgeev, eastward to about 15 miles west of Orgeev. On the panzer corps' right wing, Major General Hans Mikosch's 13th Panzer Division defended the 15-mile sector along the Kula and Reut Rivers west of Orgeev. Finally, a *kampfgruppe* of the 13th Panzer was still defending the western portion of the German bridgehead north of Orgeev. The XXXXVII Panzer Corps' left flank tied in with the right flank of the IV Army Corps (Group Mieth's 79th Infantry, *Grossdeutschland,* and 23rd Panzer Divisions) 25 miles northeast of Iasi, and its right flank linked up with the left flank of the XXXX Panzer Corps, which was defending the northern approaches to Orgeev and Kishinev on Army Group Dumitrescu's left flank.

On the XXXXVII Panzer Corps' right (eastern) flank, the XXXX Panzer Corps, under the command of Lieutenant General Otto von Knobelsdoff and reinforced by a *kampfgruppe* from the 13th Panzer Division, defended most of the bridgehead between the Reut and Dnestr Rivers north and northeast of Orgeev, with its left flank anchored on the Reut River just north of Orgeev, its center south of the village of Kirepcheny, ten miles north of Orgeev, and its right on the Dnestr River near the town of Zhura, 15 miles northeast of Orgeev. Knobelsdorff's panzer corps also clung to a sizeable bridgehead east of the Dnestr River, which extended from the river's eastern bank south of Zhura southeastward to Karmanovo, 13 miles northeast of Grigoriopol', to protect the approaches to the river in the Dubossary and Grigoriopol' sectors. Deployed from left to right (northwest to southeast), Colonel Rudolf Lang's 3rd Panzer Division defended the XXXX Panzer Corps' bridgehead north of Orgeev, with its defenses anchored on key strong points at the village of Bulaeshty, ten miles northeast of Orgeev, and Lieutenant General Wend von Wietersheim's 11th Panzer Division, the 46th Infantry Division, Corps Detachment "F," a regiment of the 376th Infantry Division, and the 4th Mountain Division defended the bridgehead on the Dnestr's eastern bank northeast of Dubossary and Grigoriopol'. Knobelsdorff's right flank tied in with the Sixth Army's left flank in the region roughly 20 miles northeast of Grigoriopol'.

So configured, the XXXXVII Panzer Corps faced the rifle corps on the left (eastern) wing of Koroteev's 52nd Army in the Korneshty region northeast of Iasi and against the right (western) wing and center of Galanin's 4th Guards Army north and northwest of Orgeev. Further to the east, the XXXX Panzer Corps opposed the left (eastern) wing of Galanin's 4th Guards Army west of the Dnestr River and Managarov's entire 53rd Army east of the Dnestr River.

Just as Galanin's army was beginning its assault against the XXXXVII Panzer Corps' defensive positions north of Orgeev and along the Kula River to the west, on 3 and 4 April, the Eighth Army shuffled its forces to strengthen its defenses along the approaches to Orgeev, Dubossary, and Grigoriopol'. First, since it faced steadily increasing pressure from the 4th Guards Army north of Orgeev, the XXXXVII Panzer Corps withdrew its *kampfgruppe* from the 13th Panzer Division out of the bridgehead between the Reut and Dnestr Rivers north of Orgeev and regrouped it westward to join the remainder of its patent division, which now became responsible for defending its right wing along the Kula and Reut Rivers west of Orgeev.

Second, to provide better protection along the northern approaches to Orgeev, the XXXX Panzer Corps, which the Eighth Army redesignated as Group Knobelsdorff after the name of its commander, assigned Lang's 3rd Panzer Division responsibility for defending the shrunken bridgehead between the Reut and Dnestr Rivers north of Orgeev, with its defenses anchored on the village strong point of Susleny, eight miles northeast of Orgeev and about 13 miles south of its previous forward defenses near Kipercheny.

In addition, Knobelsdorff withdrew Wietersheim's 11th Panzer Division from its defensive positions east of the Dnestr River and shifted its forces westward into new reserve positions just south of Orgeev, from which it could reinforce the 3rd Panzer Division. This left the corps' 46th Infantry Division, Corps Detachment "F," part of the 376th Infantry Division, and the 4th Mountain Division to defend a smaller bridgehead on the eastern bank of the Dnestr River, which extended from Tsybolevka, nine miles south of Zhura, southeastward to Karmanovo, where it tied in with the defenses on the Sixth Army's left flank. Initially, the XXXX Panzer Corps decided to retain the SS "*T*" Panzer Division in the Kishinev region as a general reserve and, soon after, also withdrew its 376th Infantry Division from the eastern bank of the Dnestr River into reserve assembly areas in the same region. Within days, however, the growing crisis in the Tirgu Frumos region forced the Eighth Army to move the SS "*T*" Division to the Roman region, west of Iasi.

Despite the many daunting problems caused by the spring *rasputitsa,* Galanin's 4th Guards Army resumed its offensive early on 5 April. On his army's right wing, the 6th, 84th, and 233rd Rifle Divisions of Akimenko's 75th Rifle Corps finally reached the Kula River by day's end and tried to force the river in a 13-mile-wide sector between Krasnosheny, 23 miles west of Orgeev, and Brianovo, nine miles west of Orgeev, but they were unable to do so because of the 14th and 13th Panzer Divisions' strong defenses. In the 4th Army's center, the 62nd Guards, 5th and 6th Guards Airborne, and 41st Guards Rifle Divisions of Biriukov's 20th Guards Rifle Corps assaulted the 13th and 3rd Panzer Divisions' defenses west and north of Orgeev but recorded only modest gains in extremely heavy fighting. When Colonel P. I. Afonin's 5th Guards Airborne failed to capture Orgeev from the march, Biriukov reinforced it with Major General K. N. Tsvetkov's 41st Guards Rifle Division and ordered both divisions to regroup and to conduct a coordinated joint assault against Orgeev proper early on 6 April.[22]

Attacking at dawn, the two guards divisions stormed the 13th Panzer Division's defenses at Orgeev and captured the city, and by day's end the 5th Airborne Division managed to seize a small bridgehead across the Reut River in the swampy terrain due south of Orgeev. However, Afonin's assault soon faltered when his airborne troops failed to capture Hill 185, the high ground farther to the south that dominated the bridgehead. During two more days of intense fighting, Biriukov reinforced Afonin's beleaguered airborne division in the bridgehead with Tsvetkov's guardsmen. However, Knobelsdorff quickly countered Biriukov's new attacks by reinforcing the XXXX Panzer Corps' defenses around the swampy bridgehead south of the Reut River with a *kampfgruppe* from the 11th Panzer Division, which was completing its regrouping. Despite these German reinforcements, the two guards divisions managed to capture Hill 185, forming a bridgehead almost five miles wide and over two miles deep across the Reut River south of Orgeev. However, when the rest of Wietersheim's 11th Panzer Division reached the region later on 6 and 7 April, it halted any further advance by Biriukov's 20th Guards Rifle Corps.

Despite the heavy losses Biriukov's corps suffered in the intense fight for Orgeev, the equally heavy fighting in the bridgehead continued unabated on 8 and 9 April as Knobelsdorff's panzer corps counterattacked repeatedly with elements of the 13th Panzer Division in an attempt to crush the Soviets' bridgehead defenses. In a seesaw battle, on 10 and 11 April, Galanin reinforced Biriukov's bridgehead with Major General A. E. Iakovlev's 80th and Major General K. K. Dzhakhua's 69th Guards Rifle Divisions from Fomenko's 21st Guards Rifle Corps, but the Germans responded by reinforcing their defenses with elements of Unrein's 14th Panzer Division, which joined the counterattacks.

Compounding the XXXX Panzer Corps' problems, after repeated assaults by Fomenko's 21st Guards Rifle Corps, the defenses of Lang's 3rd Panzer Division anchored on the strong point of Susleny, in the center of the German bridgehead north of the Reut River nine miles northeast of Orgeev, collapsed under unrelenting pressure by day's end on 12 April (see below). Forced to abandon its bridgehead defenses, Lang's battle-worn panzer-grenadiers withdrew southward across the Reut River, at the same time permitting the forward elements of Fomenko's pursuing guardsmen to capture a bridgehead of their own on the Reut River's southern bank one to two miles east of Orgeev. Within a matter of hours, Fomenko's 21st Guards Rifle Corps was able to combine its bridgehead south of the Reut with the bridgehead controlled by Afonin's and Tsvetkov's guardsmen of Biriukov's 20th Guards Rifle Corps south of Orgeev.

While Biriukov's forces were struggling for possession of Orgeev and the bridgehead to the south, heavy and potentially more decisive fighting was raging to the east, where Lang's 3rd Panzer Division was attempting to defend its bridgehead between the Reut and Dnestr Rivers anchored on the strong point of Susleny. While Biriukov's lead divisions were advancing on and capturing Orgeev from the north, further east the 7th Guards Airborne and the 69th, 78th, and 80th Guards Rifle Divisions of Fomenko's 21st Guards Rifle Corps, supported on their left by the 49th Rifle Corps of Managarov's 53rd Army, had crossed to the Dnestr River's western bank on 1 and 2 April and begun advancing against the 3rd Panzer Division's bridgehead defenses north of Susleny from the northeast and east.

In the vanguard of Fomenko's 21st Rifle Corps, the lead elements of Major General A. G. Motov's 78th Guards Rifle Division reached the eastern bank of the Dnestr River near the villages of Zhura and Mikhailovka, eight miles northeast of Susleny late on 2 April. The following day, the lead elements of Motov's division assaulted across the Dnestr and began a three-day pitched battle with forward elements of the 3rd Panzer Division defending security outposts in the Bulaeshty region, four to five miles north of Susleny. While the remainder of Motov's division joined the assault on Bulaeshty at midday on 2 April, Dzhakhua's 69th and Iakovlev's 80th Guards Rifle Divisions also crossed the Dnestr on the evening of 2–3 April, reinforced Motov's guardsmen, and repeatedly assaulted the 3rd Panzer Division's defenses. After two more days of heavy fighting, during which Fomenko reinforced his three lead divisions with Colonel D. A. Drychkin's 7th Guards Airborne Division, the combined force finally drove Lang's panzer division back to defenses anchored around the strong point at Susleny at midday on 5 April.

As the four rifle divisions of Fomenko's 21st Rifle Corps were struggling against the 3rd Panzer Division's defenses at Bulaeshty and pushing southward toward Susleny, throughout 4 and 5 April, the lead rifle corps on the right wing of Managarov's 53rd Army, Major General G. N. Terent'ev's 49th Rifle Corps, attacked the 3rd Panzer Division's right wing, which was anchored on the Dnestr River four miles east of Susleny. The two divisions in the vanguard of Terent'ev's rifle corps—Colonel Ia. S. Mikheenko's 1st Guards Airborne and Colonel D. F. Sobolev's 110th Guards Rifle Divisions—approached the Dnestr River in the sector extending from the village of Garmatskoe, five miles east of Susleny, southward to the village of Goian, eight miles southeast of Susleny, assaulted across the river against the 3rd Panzer Division's right wing and began a slow advance toward Susleny from the east. After two more days of heavy fighting during which Managarov reinforced Terent'ev's rifle corps with a small armored combat group from the 5th Guards Army's 18th Tank Corps, the combined forces of Fomenko's 21st Guards Rifle Corps and Terent'ev's 49th Rifle Corps captured the 3rd Panzer Division's strong point at Susleny on 7 April. However, although it lost Susleny, the 3rd Panzer Division was able to establish and occupy even stronger defenses just south of the strong point.

The 4th Guards Army's capture of Orgeev and the small bridgehead over the Reut River south of the town and the fall of Susleny to both Galanin's and Managarov's forces did not end the heavy fighting in this key bridgehead north of the Reut. Konev's initial orders to Galanin had required his army to penetrate the German defenses west of the Dnestr River, eliminate the German bridgehead north of the Reut River, force the Reut River, and press its advance toward Kishinev from the north. At the same time, Galanin's forces were to coordinate closely with the forces of Managarov's 53rd and Zhadov's 5th Guards Armies, which were supposed to capture bridgeheads across the Dnestr River in the Dubossary and Grigoriopol' regions, 22–24 miles northeast and east of Kishinev, and then advance toward Kishinev. To fulfill his army's role in Konev's grand design, Galanin ordered Fomenko's 21st and Biriukov's 20th Guards Rifle Corps, deployed abreast from left to right (east to west) just south of Susleny, to assault and crush the 3rd Panzer Division's remaining defenses in the bridgehead north of the Reut River, assault across the river to capture bridgeheads on its southern bank, and then advance southward toward Kishinev.

Complying with Konev's orders, in close cooperation with Terent'ev's 49th Rifle Corps (of Managarov's 53rd Army) on its left flank east of the Dnestr, the divisions of Fomenko's and Biriukov's 21st and 20th Guards Rifle Corps pounded the 3rd Panzer Division's defenses south of Susleny unmercifully with artillery and mortar fire and repeated ground assaults all day on 8 and 9 April. However, the XXXX Panzer Corps quickly reacted by reinforcing the right (eastern) wing of Lang's defenses north of the Reut River with elements of Lieutenant General August Schmidt's 10th Panzer Grenadier Division and the 282nd Infantry Division, which it had withdrawn from the bridgehead on the east bank of the Dnestr River several days before.

After two more days of heavy fighting, on 11 April Iakovlev's 80th Guards Rifle Division of Fomenko's 21st Guards Rifle Corps and Mikheenko's 1st Guards Airborne and Sobolev's 110th Guards Rifle Divisions from Terent'ev's 49th Rifle Corps captured the town of Molovata, which was situated on the Dnestr's western bank nine miles southeast of Susleny, and the eastern portion of the Germans' bridgehead from the defending 282nd Infantry Division. Managarov, the 53rd Army commander, then regrouped the 375th Rifle Division of Terent'ev's rifle corps to the river's western bank and, soon after, also the 25th Guards Rifle Division from Major General P. A. Firsov's 26th Guards Rifle Corps. This, in turn, permitted Fomenko to shift Iakovlev's 80th Guards Rifle Division westward to participate in the advance southward toward the Reut River. In essence, the fall of Molovata rendered the XXXX Panzer Corps' bridgehead defenses north of the Reut River untenable.

By day's end on 12 April, the pressure against the XXXX Panzer Corps' bridgehead defenses was so intense that Knobelsdorff had no choice but to order his force to abandon the northern portion of the beleaguered bridgehead. Overnight on 12–13 April, the 3rd Panzer, 10th Panzer Grenadier, and 282nd Infantry Division's forces withdrew southward, crossed the Reut River, and occupied a new defensive line extending along the river from roughly two miles southeast of Orgeev eastward three miles to the town of Furcheny, and then another seven miles eastward across the Reut River to the western bank of the Dnestr River at the town of Golerkany.

By this time, Motov's 78th and Iakovlev's 80th Guards Rifle Divisions from Fomenko's 21st Guards Rifle Corps had already seized a small bridgehead on the southern bank of the Reut River three to five miles southeast of Orgeev and had linked up their bridgehead with that of Dzhakhua's 69th

Guards Rifle Division (of Biriukov's 20th Guards Rifle Corps) south of Orgeev to form an imposing bridgehead about eight miles wide and one to three miles deep south and southeast of the city. While Fomenko regrouped his remaining divisions westward into the expanded bridgehead on the south of the Reut River, on his left (eastern) flank, Terent'ev's 49th Rifle Corps of Managarov's 53rd Army took control of the sector extending from Furcheny on the Reut River eastward to Golerkany on the Dnestr River.

Despite the significant victories of Galanin's and Managarov's armies at Orgeev, at Susleny, and along the Reut River, the intense fighting had taken a heavy toll on both forces. In fact, their losses were so severe that Galanin's 4th Guards Army was a mere shell of its former self. With the combat strength of his divisions down to roughly 5,000 men each, Galanin was incapable of resuming decisive offensive operations. Although Galanin's forces tried to expand their bridgehead over the Reut River south of Orgeev several times during mid-April, his army had clearly shot its bolt and could accomplish nothing more. Therefore, on 18 April Konev authorized Galanin's army to go over to the defense in the entire sector from Korneshty eastward to the Orgeev region. Galanin complied by erecting defenses with Biriukov's and Fomenko's 20th and 21st Guards Rifle Corps and by withdrawing Akimenko's 75th Rifle Corps into the 2nd Ukrainian Front's reserve.

Konev's decision to allow Galanin's army to go over to the defense along the Reut River essentially ended any hope the *front* commander harbored for conducting an assault against Kishinev from the north. Henceforth, Konev was forced to rely entirely on Zhadov's 5th Guards Army if he expected to participate in any advance on Kishinev from the northeast or east in conjunction with Malinovsky's 3rd Ukrainian Front, which had just captured a series of bridgeheads further south along the Dnestr River. To that end, soon after the fighting along the Reut River died down, in late April Konev transferred the 78th Guards Rifle Division from Galanin's 4th Guards Army to Zhadov's 5th Guards Army to enable the latter to participate in Malinovsky's offensive by attacking in the Tashlyk sector, on the Dnestr River eight miles south of Grigoriopol', on Malinovsky's right flank.

The 53rd Army's Advance to Dubossary

While Galanin's 4th Guards Army was decisively engaged with the forces of Funck's XXXXVII Panzer Corps along the Kula River and with those of Knobelsdorff's XXXX Panzer Corps at Orgeev and Susleny and along the Reut River, Managarov's 53rd Army and Zhadov's 5th Guards Army were bearing down on the Germans' bridgehead defenses east of the Dnepr River, which protected the approaches to the cities of Dubossary and Grigoriopol' (Map 8).

Also an experienced combat veteran, 45-year-old Lieutenant General Ivan Mefod'evich Managarov had commanded the 53rd Army since March 1943, except for the period from December 1943 through February 1944, when he was recovering from wounds he received during a German artillery raid on his command post. Originally a cavalryman by trade, Managarov had joined the Red Guards in 1917, commanded a cavalry detachment, and served as a deputy commander and commander of a cavalry regiment in the southern and Tsaritsyn regions during the Russian Civil War, where his prowess attracted Stalin's attention. Rising in rank quickly after the war ended to become a junior member of Stalin's cavalry clique, Managarov completed the Cavalry School in 1923, served as a cavalry squadron commander in the Leningrad Military District and the Turkestan Front, and was then appointed as the secretary of a cavalry regiment's Commumist Party bureau during the 1920s. After graduating from the Military-Political Academy in 1931, the NKO appointed Managarov, first, as commissar of a new mechanized regiment, later, as commander and commissar of a cavalry regiment, and, finally, in November 1938, as commander of a cavalry division, which he was commanding when war began in June 1941.

After surviving the harrowing first six months of the war in division command, the NKO appointed Managarov to command, in succession, the Far Eastern Front's 26th Rifle Corps in December 1941, the newly formed 16th Cavalry Corps in early January 1942, the 7th Cavalry Corps in March 1942, and, because of his exemplary record in these commands, the 41st Army in December 1942 and the 53rd Army in March 1943. During this period Managarov's army spearheaded the Kalinin Front's offensive against the Germans' Rzhev-Viaz'ma salient during March 1943, the Steppe Front's Belgorod-Khar'kov offensive during August 1943, and the same *front*'s advance to and across the Dnepr River during the fall of 1943. After recovering from wounds received during the fighting for bridgeheads across the Dnepr River during the fall, Managarov's 53rd Army spearheaded the advance by Konev's 2nd Ukrainian Front during the Uman'-Botoshany offensive, which ended with his army poised menacingly on the approaches to Dubossary and the Dnestr River.[23]

On 1 April 1944, Managarov's 53rd Army fielded three rifle corps, the 26th Guards and the 48th, and 49th Rifle Corps, with a total of nine rifle divisions (five of which were either guards or guards airborne divisions), one tank brigade, two tank regiments (one separate and one attached from the *front*'s 8th Mechanized Corps), and two separate antitank rifle battalions. The 26th Guards Rifle Corps, which was commanded by Major General P. A. Firsov and included the 25th, 89th, and 94th Guards Rifle Divisions, was deployed in the army's center, flanked on the left by Major General Z. Z. Rogoznyi's 48th Rifle Corps, with the 111th, 213th, and 299th Rifle Divisions.

Major General G. N. Terent'ev's 49th Rifle Corps, which was deployed on the army's right wing, consisted of the 1st Guards Airborne, 110th Guards Rifle, and 375th Rifle Divisions.

After capturing the city of Kotovsk, 40 miles northeast of Dubossary, on 31 March, Managarov's army advanced steadily southwestward toward Dubossary with its three rifle corps abreast, separated from Zhadov's 5th Guards Army on its left by a boundary line which extended from Elenovka, 20 miles northeast of Dubossary, southwestward to Pogrebia, six miles south of Dubossary. Initially, Managarov's army advanced with the 1st Guards Airborne, 110th Guards, and Major General V. D. Karpukhin's 375th Rifle Divisions of Terent'ev's 49th Rifle Corps on its right wing, adjacent to the eastern bank of the Dnestr River. Further to the east, the 25th, 89th, and 94th Guards Rifle Divisions of Firsov's 26th Guards Rifle Corps advanced in the army's center along an axis aimed at the Dnestr River just north of Dubossary; the 111th, 213th, and 299th Rifle Divisions of Rogoznyi's 48th Rifle Corps, on the army's left wing, advanced directly toward the Dubossary region.

As his army approached the Dnestr River on 4 April, Managarov ordered Terent'ev to regroup Mikheenko's 1st Guards Airborne and Sobolev's 110th Guards Rifle Divisions from his rifle corps to the western bank of the Dnestr River to support the 4th Guards Army's assault on the strong point at Susleny. After Terent'ev's two divisions helped Galanin's 4th Guards Army capture Susleny, Managarov also ordered Firsov to move the 25th Guards Rifle Division from his 26th Guards Rifle Corps across the river to reinforce Terent'ev's forces. Thereafter, the three rifle divisions from Managarov's army on the western bank of the Dnestr River helped Galanin's forces clear the German XXXX Panzer Corps' forces from the northern bank of the Reut River by 12 April.

Once Managarov had concentrated all three divisions of Terent'ev's 49th Rifle Corps and the 25th Guards Rifle Division of Firsov's 26th Guards Rifle Corps west of the Dnestr River, on 13 April, these five divisions assaulted the German 282nd Infantry Division's defenses in the Golerkany sector and, after two days of intense fighting, forced the German infantry to withdraw southward to new defenses along the Reut River west of Dubossary. On 14 April, however, reinforcements from the German 10th Panzer Grenadier and 282nd Infantry Divisions and Corps Detachment "F" finally managed to contain Terent'ev's assault southward along the western bank of the Dnepr River due west of Dubossary. At the same time, the arrival of the fresh German reinforcements also ended any hopes Managarov had of turning the right (eastern) flank of Knobelsdorff's XXXX Panzer Corps and reaching Kishinev by an advance southward along the western bank of the Dnestr. By this time, Managarov's forces west of the Dnestr River were just as exhausted as those in Galanin's 4th Guards Army.

Despite the failure of Galanin's and Managarov's forces to rupture the XXXX Panzer Corps' defenses along the Reut River and push southward toward Kishinev, the remaining two rifle divisions of Firsov's 26th Guards Rifle Corps and the three rifle divisions of Rogoznyi's 48th Rifle Corps maintained constant pressure against the German forces defending the bridgehead on the Dnestr's eastern bank northeast of Dubossary. Ultimately, by 13 April this steady pressure forced Knobelsdorff's XXXX Panzer Corps to withdraw the 46th Infantry Division, Corps Detachment "F," and the 4th Mountain Division, which were defending east of the river, back from their forward defensive line anchored on the village of Karmanovo to a new defensive line five miles to the rear, which stretched from the village of Rogi, on the eastern bank of the Dnestr River four miles north of Dubossary, southeastward to the village of Glinnoe, eight miles northeast of Grigoriopol'.

The decision by Knobelsdorff to withdraw the forces east of the Dnestr River on the XXXX Panzer Corps' right wing back to a denser and more formidable defensive line further to the rear was also hastened by the increased pressure being applied to the panzer corps' right flank by the forces of Zhadov's 5th Guards Army, which were advancing on Grigoriopol' from the northeast. After the 4th Guards and 53rd Armies' attempts to breach the Germans' defenses along the Reut River and advance southward along the Dnestr's western bank aborted, on 18 April Konev ordered Managarov's 53rd Army to go over to the defense, although he did give the army commander permission to conduct local attacks whenever and wherever to improve his army's tactical dispositions. This order essentially ended any role for the 4th Guards and 53rd Armies in future offensive operations to capture Kishinev. From this point forward, the only army in Konev's 2nd Ukrainian Front capable of participating in a general offensive toward Kishinev was Zhadov's 5th Guards Army, which, by the first week in April, had essentially joined the advance by the right (northern) wing of Malinovsky's 3rd Ukrainian Front as it bore down on the Germans' defenses along the Dnestr River from the Grigoriopol' region southward to the Black Sea coast.

The 5th Guards Army's Advance to Grigoriopol' and Tashlyk

Although the 5th Guards Army, operating in early April in conjunction with Major General of Tank Forces F. G. Katkov's severely combat-worn 7th Mechanized Corps, was somewhat weaker than its neighbors, the 53rd and 4th Guards Armies, nevertheless, it was an experienced and battled-hardened force commanded by a general with a proven combat record. Only age 43 in April 1944, Lieutnant General Aleksei Semenovich Zhadov, who would became a Hero of the Soviet Union in 1945, had commanded the 5th Guards Army since it received its guards designation in April 1943 and, before that, had commanded its predecessor 66th Army since October 1942, distinguishing himself at the head of this army during the Don Front's successful counteroffensive at Stalingrad. Like many of his fellow guards army commanders, Zhadov would command the 5th Guards Army with distinction to war's end.

A cavalryman like Managarov, Zhadov had joined the Red Army in 1919 and commanded a cavalry platoon in the famous 1st Cavalry Army's 11th Cavalry Division in the struggle against Baron P. N. Wrangel's White Army in the Crimea during 1920, where he earned Stalin's attention and junior membership in Stalin's cavalry clique. After graduating from the Cavalry Course in 1920, Zhadov fought against the Basmachi insurgents in Central Asia from 1922 through 1924 before being seriously wounded in combat. After recovering from his wounds, Zhadov rose through cavalry ranks during the 1920s, serving as a cavalry platoon commander, commander and political officer of a cavalry squadron, chief of staff of a cavalry regiment, and chief of staff of a cavalry division. In between these assignments, he graduated from a Military-Political Course in 1928 and the Frunze Academy in 1934.

After serving as the deputy inspector of Red Army Cavalry during the final years of the 1930s, the NKO appointed Zhadov to command a mountain cavalry division in 1940 and the newly established 4th Airborne Corps in June 1941, a corps which he was commanding when war began soon after. Zhadov led the airborne corps during the Western Front's futile attempts to defend Belorussia, in the process participating in audacious but failed counterattacks south of Minsk and the subsequent defense of the Dnepr and Sozh Rivers. He then served as chief of staff of the Central and Briansk Fronts' 3rd Army during its unsuccessful defense of Briansk during October but escaped intact from the subsequent Briansk encirclement to plan the army's vital role in the Red Army's winter victories at Elets during the battle for Moscow. As a reward for his outstanding performance during the battle at Elets, the NKO assigned Zhadov command of the Briansk Front's 8th Cavalry Corps during the summer of 1942 and the 66th Army in October 1942. A proven fighter of unquestioned political reliability, Zhadov became one of Stalin's most trusted army commanders.[24]

On 1 April Zhadov's 5th Guards Army fielded two rifle corps, the 32nd and 33rd Guards, with a total of six rifle divisions, five of which were guards divisions, and one separate antitank rifle battalion. The 32nd Guards Rifle Corps, which included the 13th, 95th, and 97th Guards Rifle Divisions and was commanded by Major General A. I. Rodimtsev, who had earned lasting fame commanding the 13th Guards Rifle Division during the Battle for Stalingrad, was deployed on the army's left (western) wing. Lieutenant General N. F. Lebedenko's 33rd Guards Rifle Corps, with the 9th Guards Airborne, 14th Guards Rifle, and 214th Rifle Divisions, was situated on the army's right wing.

Since Konev had ordered Shumilov's 7th Guards Army to begin regrouping from the 2nd Ukrainian Front's left wing to its right wing on 5 and 6 April, by the end of the first week in April, Zhadov's army now occupied a vital position on the 2nd Ukrainian Front's far-left wing. So positioned, the 5th Guards Army's mission was to protect the *front*'s left flank and advance to the Dnestr River in the Grigoriopol' region while maintaining close contact with the 3rd Ukrainian Front's 57th and 46th Armies, which were advancing on the right wing of Malinovsky's *front*. At the time, the remainder of the 3rd Ukrainian Front was in the process of investing and capturing the Black Sea port of Odessa.

The 5th Guards Army's official history summarizes the mission Konev assigned to Zhadov's army in early April, as well as the missions Zhadov assigned to his subordinate corps commanders:

> The commander of the 5th Guards Army received his mission from the front commander at 2300 hours on 1 April when the army was still located 65 kilometers [39 miles] from the [Dnestr] River. [The mission was] to force the Dnestr River and capture the Kateritsa, Budeshty, and Speia regions [a bridgehead five to ten miles deep west of the river] by day's end on 5 April, while pursuing the enemy energetically in the direction of Valetsogulovo and Grigoriopol'.
>
> The 5th Guards Army's commander assigned missions to his corps in accordance with the directive he received. The 32nd Guards Rifle Corps was to force the Dnestr on a broad front by conducting its main attack toward Pugacheny [on the Dnestr's eastern bank five miles south of Grigoriopol'] on the right wing, exploit the attack toward Fintinitsy and Mereny [five miles west of the river], and capture the Chimisheny, Kobuska, Vechi, and Speia line [ten miles west of the river] by day's end on 13 April.
>
> The 33rd Guards Rifle Corps, which was situated in the Krasnyi Moldovanin sector on the right [wing], had the mission of forcing the Dnestr and exploiting the attack toward Chimisheny by delivering its main attack toward Grigoriopol'.
>
> The 7th Mechanized Corps had the mission of crossing its tanks over the Dnestr in the 32nd Guards Rifle Corps' sector and assisting it in capturing a bridgehead by attacking toward Chimisheny. Subsequently, it was to concentrate its tanks on the bank of the Dnestr and be prepared to launch a surprise attack to envelop the city of Kishinev.[25]

At the time Zhadov received Konev's order, the forces on his army's left (northern) wing faced defenses manned by the XXXX Panzer Corps' 4th Mountain Division, and the forces in its center and on its right (southern) wing faced the 320th Infantry Division and Corps Detachment "A," both of which were subordinate to the LII Army Corps, which was defending the German Sixth Army's (Group Dumitrescu's) extreme left (northern) wing. The 5th Guards Army's intelligence organs placed the strength of the opposing German forces at a total of 23 infantry battalions, 22 artillery batteries, 15 tanks, and only 4,100 combat-ready soldiers. However, this estimate fell far short of the over 10,000-man force Zhadov's army ultimately encountered as it advanced toward Grigoriopol'.

Despite possessing an over twofold superiority in manpower and even greater superiority in armor, the 5th Guards Army's subsequent advance toward the Dnestr River developed at a painfully slow pace. Advancing abreast, Zhadov's two guards rifle corps reached positions extending from just east of Karmanovo to Novo-Petrovka, 13–19 miles east of the Dnestr River cities of Grigoriopol' and Tashlyk, by day's end on 4 April. Thereafter, his army made no further forward progress until 10 April, when the German Sixth Army began withdrawing its forces westward after Malinovsky's armies captured Odessa. However, when the German Sixth Army, together with cooperating Romanian forces, began withdrawing back to the Dnestr River in considerable disorder late that day, the 5th Guards Army quickly followed, reaching the river's eastern bank early on 12 April.

Zhadov's forces began river-crossing operations, usually employing only makeshift means, as soon as they reached the Dnestr River's eastern bank. The first formation to do so was Major General A. I. Oleinikov's 95th Guards Rifle Division, which was pursuing in the first echelon of Rodimtsev's 32nd Guards Rifle Corps, which began crossing the Dnestr River at 2200 hours on 12 April after reaching the river's eastern bank near the city of Tashlyk, 27 miles east of Kishinev (Map 9). At the time the only German force available to defend this sector of the Dnestr was the 320th Infantry Division of the Sixth Army's LII Army Corps, which had just completed its harrowing withdrawal back across the river.

Once it reached the river's eastern bank, the 290th Guards Rifle Regiment of Oleinikov's guards rifle division occupied defensive positions in a deep ravine adjacent to the river's bank and launched boats into a water-filled ditch that flowed from the ravine into the main river channel. Protected by the defilade created by the high cliffs on the Dnestr's western bank, the entire regiment managed to cross the river in these boats by 0400 hours on 13 April and established a small bridgehead on its far bank, about three miles south of the village of Pugacheny. Despite answering German artillery, mortar, and machine-gun fire, the first echelon regiments of Oleinikov's division made it into the bridgehead by the following morning. While these forces dug in, during the remainder of the first day in the bridgehead, Zhadov's rear services' organizations moved all of Oleinikov's artillery and mortar batteries, as well as the companies and battalions from his second echelon regiment, into

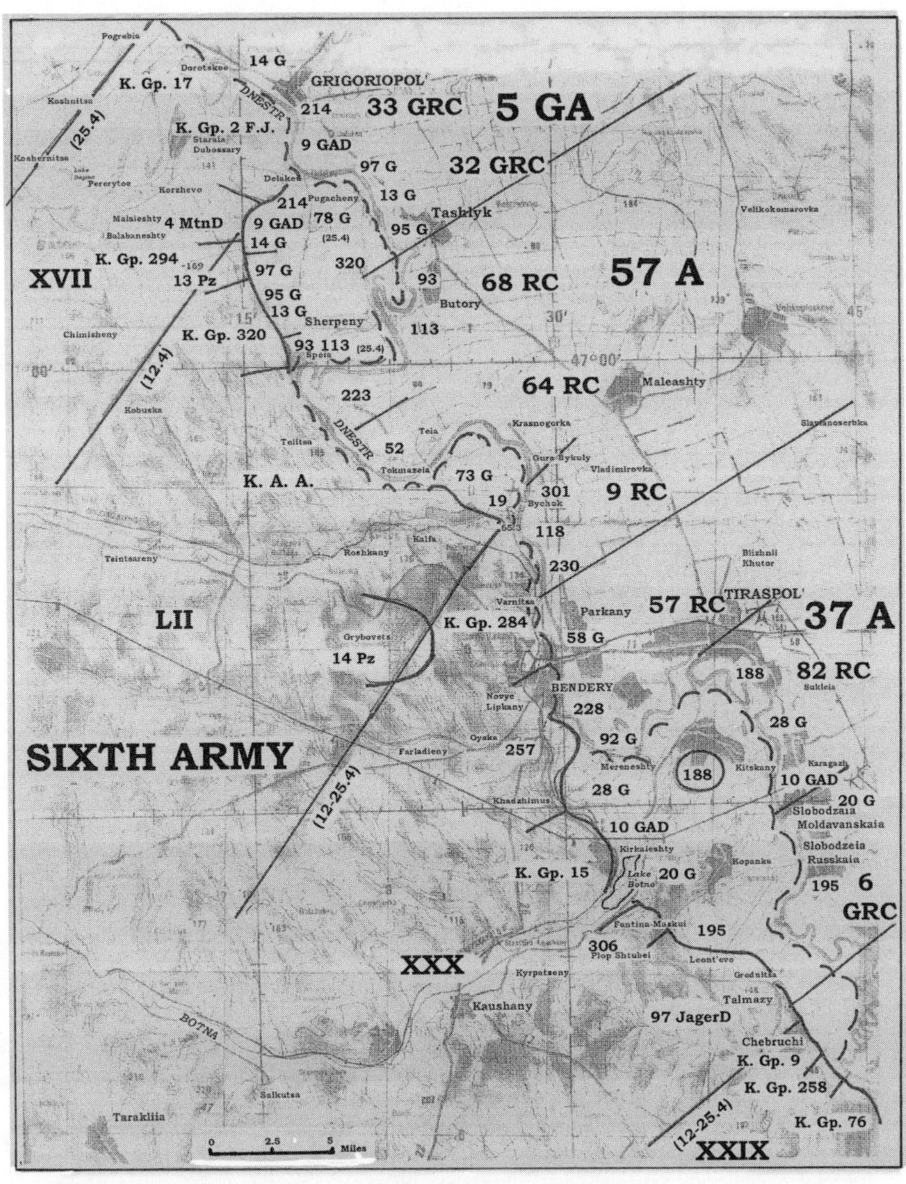

Map 9. The 5th Guards, 57th, and 37th Armies' bridgehead battles, 12–25 April 1944

the bridgehead. After nightfall the next day, his divisional artillery crossed the broad river on a floating bridge emplaced by the 5th Guards Army's supporting engineers.

While Oleinikov's division was securing its bridgehead south of Pugacheny, Major General I. I. Antsiferov's 97th Guards Rifle Division, also from Rodimtsev's 32nd Guards Rifle Corps, and all three divisions of Lebedenko's 33rd Guards Rifle Corps, which were supposed to cross the river further north, closer to Grigoriopol', were unable to carry out their river crossing operations on the night of 12–13 April. Therefore, Rodimtsev ordered Antsiferov to regroup his division southward into the bridgehead established by Oleinikov's 95th Guards Division on 13 April and Major General G. V. Baklanov to move his 13th Guards Rifle Division into the same bridgehead on the following night. As a result, Rodimtsev's entire rifle corps made it safely across the river by 1700 hours on 14 April.

While Rodimtsev was moving the rest of his rifle corps into Oleinikov's bridgehead, on 13 and 14 April, the 97th Guards Rifle Division launched repeated assaults to expand the bridgehead to the north and west and succeeded in capturing the village of Pugacheny on the river's western bank and the low hills nearby. To exploit Rodimtsev's success, late on 14 April, Zhadov ordered Lebedenko to regroup his entire 33rd Guards Rifle Corps southward into the same bridgehead, a task that he completed by day's end on 16 April. While the fresh rifle corps was completing its movement into the bridgehead, Baklanov's 13th Guards Rifle Division captured the town of Speia on the bridgehead's southern flank seven miles southwest of Pugacheny. By this time Zhadov's 5th Guards Armys' had carved out a bridgehead measuring almost seven miles wide and up to five miles deep on the Dnestr's western bank. As yet, however, Zhadov's army did not have a single tank in the bridgehead to fend off German counterattacks, which he knew would inevitably occur.

Beset by real or impending assaults along the Dnestr River from Grigoriopol' in the north southward to Tashlyk, Hollidt's Sixth Army was unable to react quickly or forcefully enough to deal effectively with these threats because its forces were severely disorganized after their difficult withdrawal from the Odessa region. After several days of confusion, on 15 April the Sixth Army finally managed to alert the 294th Infantry Division, which had been in reserve when the Soviet assault on Odessa began and had escaped westward across the river relatively unscathed, and ordered it to move northward as quickly as possible to reinforce the 320th Infantry Division's sagging defenses west of Tashlyk and, if possible, seal off any other developing Soviet bridgeheads of the Dnestr's western bank south of Tashlyk. More important, Knobelsdorff's XXXX Panzer Corps, which by this time had stabilized its defensive front in the sector along the Reut and Dnestr Rivers, transferred the 4th Mountain Division and Mikosch's 13th Panzer Division southward to reinforce the Sixth Army's defenses in the sector between Grigoriopol' and Tashlyk. These forces arrived in the region late on 16 April, too late to eliminate the bridgehead but just in time to contest a major offensive by Zhadov's now concentrated army.

Several days before, on 14 April Konev had ordered Zhadov to concentrate his entire army in the Tashlyk bridgehead, assault and penetrate the Germans' defenses around the periphery of the bridgehead, and exploit westward to capture Kishinev. Accordingly, Zhadov moved the remainder of his army, including some of his armor, into the bridgehead overnight on 14–15 April by using N2P pontoon bridges provided by the 3rd Ukrainian Front's 57th Army on his left (southern) flank. The 5th Guards Army's supporting engineers were also able to erect sufficient bridges over the river by day's end on 15 April to transport six to seven tanks per hour across the river. However, characteristic of the ever-changing spring weather conditions, a brief spell of dry weather caused the water level in the river to fall sharply, thereby preventing the army from moving many tanks and other heavy weaponry to the river's western shore. Zhadov responded by ordering a battalion from his army's engineer-sapper brigade to deploy forward and construct landing berths so that boats could transport the tanks and other heavy equipment across the river. By 16 April, enough heavy weaponry had reached the bridgehead for the 5th Guards Army to resume offensive operations.

While his engineers completed transporting his army's tanks and heavy artillery across the river on the night of 15–16 April, Zhadov regrouped and reinforced his forces within the bridgeheads so they could mount a decisive offensive to break through the Germans' defensive cordon and begin their advance westward toward Kishinev. He concentrated the 13th, 95th, and 97th Guards Rifle Divisions of Rodimtsev's 32nd Guards Rifle Corps deployed from left to right (south to north) in the southern half of the bridgehead on his army's left wing, and the 14th Guards, 9th Guards Airborne, and 214th Rifle Divisions of Lebedenko's 33rd Guards Rifle Corps in a similar combat formation in the northern half of the bridgehead on his army's right wing. A composite tank brigade from Katkov's 7th Mechanized Corps supported Rodimtsev's rifle corps, and the 28th Guards Separate Tank Regiment, which Zhadov "borrowed" from the 57th Army, supported Lebedenko's rifle corps. To protect his vulnerable left flank against possible German counterattacks, Zhadov requested and received the 93rd Rifle Division as a "loan" from the 57th Army, then ordered it to cross the river and occupy defenses around the town of Speia, which anchored the bridgehead's extreme left (southern) flank.

Zhadov's two rifle corps struck the German defenses at dawn on 16 April after the 5th Guards Army's artillery and supporting aircraft from the 17th

Air Army had pounded them for about two hours. After about two hours of intense fighting, the attacking divisions of Zhadov's two guards rifle corps overpowered the 320th Infantry Division's forward security belt and began penetrating into the Germans' first defensive position, by 0930 hours tearing a hole up to one mile wide and almost two miles deep in the center of the German defenses on the bridgehead's western face. During the initial assault, Major General A. M. Sazonov's 9th Guards Airborne and Oleinikov's 95th, Antsiferov's 97th, and Baklanov's 13th Guards Rifle Divisions, supported by the small armor task forces from Katkov's 7th Mechanized Corps and the 28th Guards Tank Brigade, made their most significant gains in the sector two to four miles south of the village of Delakeu, which was located in the river about two miles northwest of Pugacheny, where they penetrated up to one mile into the Germans' second defensive positions.

However, just as the forward assault groups of Rodimtsev's and Lebedenko's attacking divisions completed penetrating the Germans' first defensive position and were approaching the eastern slope of the ridgeline roughly eight miles west of the Dnestr, at 1030 hours the Germans struck back against the two corps' advancing infantry and tanks with an intense artillery preparation of their own, accompanied by massive air strikes against both Rodimtsev's and Lebedenko's forces and the positions of their supporting artillery. After the first wave of German counterattacks halted Zhadov's advancing infantry and tanks in their tracks, at 1500 hours the Germans' launched fresh counterattacks against the center and flanks of his advancing forces before they could dig in. Specifically, two separate *kampfgruppen* formed by the 4th Mountain and 294th Infantry Divisions attacked eastward from the vicinity of Hill 169, about nine miles west of the Dnestr at Tashlyk, striking the center of the bridgehead, while a third *kampfgruppe* from Mikosch's 13th Panzer Division assaulted the left (southern) wing of Zhadov's bridgehead defenses from the high ground west of Speia.

Furious fighting raged throughout the remainder of the day on 16 April, during which Oleinikov's 95th and Baklanov's 13th Guards Rifle Divisions suffered heavy losses and were forced to pull back to avoid outright destruction. By nightfall, the three counterattacking German *kampfgruppen* reached the two guards rifle divisions' rear areas, temporarily encircling their divisional artillery in their firing positions. After withdrawing their lead rifle regiments about one mile under the protection of direct fire from their regimental and divisional artillery, by nightfall Oleinikov's and Baklanov's riflemen finally managed to occupy dug-in defensive positions in and around their artillery firing positions and bring the German onslaught to a halt. When the fighting finally died down late on 17 April, both sides were thoroughly exhausted. Thanks to their concerted counterattacks, the combined *kampfgruppen* of the German XVII and LII Army Corps were able to reestablish a continuous defensive front extending from the Dnestr River at Delakeu, five miles northwest of Tashlyk, southward along the eastern slopes of ridgeline west of the bridgehead to the Speia, eight miles southwest of Tashlyk. Arrayed from left to right (north to south), *kampfgruppen* from the 17th and 294th Infantry, 13th Panzer, and 320th Infantry Divisions manned this new defensive line.

The official history of the 5th Guards Army briefly describes the heavy fighting that took place in the Tashlyk bridgehead on 16 and 17 April and asserts that this fight temporarily ended the struggle by Zhadov's army to expand the Tashlyk bridgehead and break out westward toward Kishinev. However, the same history also admits the army conducted strong local attacks between 18 and 25 April, ostensibly to improve its positions in the bridgehead tactically:

> The army's forces launched two [more] attacks, on 18 and 25 April, but did not achieve success. The army did not possess sufficient forces to advance forward. The artillery, which had lagged behind, was still arriving [forward], the aircraft were shifting to new bases, and the tank units numbered only single [numbers of] tanks. In spite of all of this, the army fulfilled its main mission; it forced the Dnestr, widened the bridgehead, and managed to hold on to it.[26]

However, several histories of divisions subordinate to the 5th Guards Army describe even heavier fighting in the bridgehead before month's end. For example, the history of the 9th Guards Airborne Division asserts:

> While battling to widen the bridgehead, the division and the remainder of the 33rd Guards Rifle Corps advanced five–six miles by 6 May 1944. [However,] the enemy was able to bring reserves forward, create an extremely dense defense, and protect the shortest axis of advance toward Kishinev. Further offensive action along this axis was not feasible.[27]

German archival records convincingly dispute the assertions in the 5th Guards Army's history that the fighting died out in mid-April and prove without a doubt that Zhadov's army did indeed undertake two additional attempts to break out of its bridgehead at Tashlyk before the end of April. These records indicate Zhadov's forces launched two separate heavy assaults from the Tashlyk bridgehead on 18 and 25 April. Furthermore, although the first of these assaults accomplished very little, the second attack occurred after Zhadov's army received sizeable reinforcements from both the 2nd and 3rd Ukrainian Fronts.

After Zhadov's 18 April attacks failed to dent the Germans' defenses, during the ensuing week Konev reinforced Zhadov's army with the 78th Guards

Rifle Division from the 21st Guards Rifle Corps of Galanin's 4th Guards Army, and Malinovsky reinforced his army with the 10th Guards Cavalry Division from Pliev's 4th Guards Cavalry Corps, the 113th Rifle Division from the 68th Rifle Corps of Gagen's 57th Army, and perhaps other forces as well. The official history of the 4th Guards Army's 78th Guards Rifle Division confirms this fact:

> We transferred our sector to the [20th Guards Rifle Corps'] 7th Guards Airborne Division at 1800 hours on 19 April 1944, we reverted to the [21st Guards Rifle] corps' second echelon, and we then concentrated in the region of the village of Bologany [six miles north of Orgeev]. By this time the situation had become quite complicated in the region of the village of Tashlyk in the Dnestr bridgehead, which General A. S. Zhadov's 5th Guards Army had seized. His units in the bridgehead were involved in intense fighting with a significantly superior enemy force.
>
> Our division was alerted at midnight on that date, and, after conducting a night march, it reached the village of Susleny by the morning of 20 April. After crossing the Dnestr, we marched 98 kilometers [59 miles] to the northwest through Gainy [and then southeastward] and concentrated in the region of the village of Tashlyk by 0500 hours on 23 April, where we became subordinate to the 5th Guards Army's 33rd Guards Rifle Corps.
>
> At 1100 hours on 23 April, the division crossed the Dnestr into the bridgehead that had been seized on 13 April and entered combat on the heights southwest of Pugacheny from the march. The enemy, who had concentrated three infantry and two panzer divisions in this area, attacked repeatedly in an attempt to liquidate the bridgehead.
>
> Dense and acrid smoke swirled in the skies, and under its cover, enemy tanks and infantry moved toward the guardsmen's positions. However, together with the units of the 5th Guards Army, the soldiers of the 78th Guards not only held on to the bridgehead but also considerably expanded it in width and depth. This time, we fulfilled the mission.[28]

German records indicate that, while Group Dumitrescu's Sixth Army indeed tried to liquidate the menacing bridgehead as Zhadov claimed, in late April the 5th Guards Army also attempted to resume its offensive from the Tashlyk bridgehead, although the fighting was probably designed to divert the Germans' attention and reserves away from the Iasi sector far to the west. When he deployed his forces to resume his assaults early on 25 April, Zhadov positioned the rifle divisions of Lebedenko's and Rodimtsev's reinforced 33rd and 32nd Guards Rifle Corps from left to right (south to north) in the northern two-thirds of the bridgehead. In addition, prior to the renewed offensive, Gagen, the commander of the 57th Army on Zhadov's left, deployed the 113th Rifle Division of Major General N. N. Mul'tan's 68th Rifle

Corps into the southern third of the bridgehead to reinforce the 93rd Rifle Division of Mul'tan's corps, which was already defending the Speia region. Once concentrated in the bridgehead, Mul'tan's corps was to attack westward on the 5th Guards Army's left flank. Finally, Zhadov planned to exploit his army's penetration operation with Katkov's 7th Mechanized Corps, which by now numbered over 50 tanks, and at least one cavalry division of Pliev's 4th Guards Cavalry Corps.

Attacking just after dawn on 25 April after an intense artillery preparation, the lead elements of Zhadov's reinforced shock group advanced up to two miles across its entire front, once again reaching the base of Hill 169 and the high ground southwest of Delakeu before faltering in the face of heavy German artillery, mortar, and machine-gun fire. By the time the fighting ended late on 26 April, the seven rifle divisions of Zhadov's two rifle corps and the two rifle divisions from Mul'tan's rifle corps had managed to expand the bridgehead's size by roughly one third and forced the Germans to commit the entire 17th Infantry, 4th Mountain, 13th Panzer, and 320th Infantry Divisions (from north to south) to contain his attacking forces.

As noted in this discussion, rather than reaching Kishinev, the 5th Guards Army's offensive on 25 and 26 April was likely a diversionary measure similar to that which Koroteev's 52nd Army conducted north of Iasi on the same day (see Chapter 5). As in the case at Iasi, in this instance Zhadov's assault was a deliberate attempt to distract Army Group South Ukraine's attentions and reserves from the Tirgu Frumos region, where Konev was planning to conduct his next major offensive thrust.

After Zhadov's repeated attempts to crack the German defenses around the Tashlyk bridgehead failed, within the context of the *Stavka*'s overall strategic offensive planning, Stalin, other *Stavka* members, and Konev and Malinovsky debated the future subordination of Zhadov's 5th Guards Army. On the one hand, at least for a time during late April, the *Stavka* seriously considered subordinating Zhadov's army to Malinovsky's 3rd Ukrainian Front so that it could reinforce his six armies when they conducted the second phase of their Iasi-Kishinev offensive, which the *Stavka* intended both Konev's and Malinovsky's two *fronts* to begin in early May. However, on Malinovsky's recommendation and after further reflection, during the first few days of May, the *Stavka* ordered Malinovsky to regroup Chuikov's more powerful 8th Guards Army from his *front's* left (southern) wing northward into the Tashlyk bridgehead to replace Zhadov's 5th Guards Army and spearhead his offensive toward Kishinev. At the same time, the *Stavka* ordered Konev to transfer Zhadov's army northward from the Tashlyk bridgehead to participate in a concerted assault against Iasi from the northeast in mid May.

While the armies in the center and on the left wing of Konev's 2nd Ukrainian Front were pounding German defenses from the Orgeev and Reut River region southward through Grigoriopol' to Tashlyk, Shumilov's 7th Guards Army, which was the only combined-arms army in his *front* that Konev had yet to commit to combat in northern Romania, was beginning a long trek as it regrouped its forces from the Grigoriopol' region on Konev's left wing to his *front*'s right wing north of Tirgu Frumos. Only after Shumilov's powerful guards army reached the region north of Tirgu Frumos and joined his new shock group could Konev hope to unleash a new offensive to envelop Iasi from the west and smash German defenses in northern Romania once and for all.

On 1 April Shumilov's 7th Guards Army consisted of two rifle corps, the 24th and 25th Guards, with a total of five rifle divisions, four of which were either guards or guards airborne divisions, one separate tank brigade, one separate antitank rifle battalion, and two armored train battalions with a total of four armored trains. The 24th Guards Rifle Corps was commanded by Lieutenant General N. A. Vasil'ev and included the 8th Guards Airborne and 72nd and 81st Guards Rifle Divisions, and the 25th Guards Rifle Corps was commanded by Major General G. B. Safiulin and included the 36th Guards and 53rd Rifle Divisions. Once it reached its new assembly areas north of Tirgu Frumos in late April, Konev reinforced Shumilov's army with the 6th Guards Airborne Division.

CONCLUSIONS

Despite several dramatic moments when it appeared as if the armies of Konev's 2nd Ukrainian Front might crumble the Germans' defenses in northern Romania, Konev's first attempt to mount a coordinated offensive against Iasi and Kishinev achieved only limited tactical and operational success but utterly failed strategically. Although the initial thrust by Koroteev's 52nd Army and Kravchenko's 6th Tank Army on the right wing of Konev's *front* reached the Iasi region and threatened to split German defenses apart along the Prut River, the rapid reaction by Group Mieth and the *Grossdeutschland* Panzer Grenadier, and 23rd and 24th Panzer Divisions checked Konev's advance, first at Pyrlitsa east of the Prut River, then at Ungeny, northeast of Iasi, and, later, along the northern approaches to Iasi and, once again, at Pyrlitsa. Likewise, the headlong advance of Zhmachenko's 40th Army west of the Seret River on Konev's extreme right wing captured Pascani but failed to overcome Romanian defenses at Tirgu-Neamt.

Although the dramatic initial advance of Trofimenko's 27th Army in the key Tirgu Frumos sector on the left wing of Konev's *front* captured Tirgu Frumos and the region to the south on 9 and 10 April, once again quick reaction by the *Grossdeutschland* Division prevented Trofimenko from exploiting his gains and sent the divisions in his vanguard reeling back north of the town in considerable disorder. In the same fashion, on the left wing of Konev's *front* north of Kishinev, the combined forces of Galanin's 4th Guards and Managarov's 53rd Armies captured Orgeev and Susleny by 9 April, expelled the Germans from their bridgehead north of the Reut River, and seized a bridgehead of their own on the southern bank of the Reut River. Nevertheless, their forces so exhausted themselves in these battles that they were unable to mount further offensive operations toward Kishinev from the north.

Finally, on the extreme left wing of Konev's *front,* the two rifle corps of Zhadov's 5th Guards Army succeeded in seizing a sizeable and promising bridgehead across the Dnestr River west of Tashlyk by a coup de main on 12 April. However, despite being reinforced by a corps from Gagen's 57th Army, Zhadov proved unable to expand this bridgehead or mount any concerted advance on Kishinev from the east.

As he orchestrated these offensives during the second half of April, Konev consistently believed that if his forces could breech the Germans' partially prepared defenses in multiple sectors across his front, possibly from the march, the German defenses in northern Romania would ultimately collapse. Sadly for Konev, this assumption proved to be incorrect since, for four basic reasons, the German defenses bent but did not break. First and foremost, during his initial offensive, Konev committed his forces into the struggle in piecemeal fashion and in multiple sectors long before all of his *front*'s armies were prepared to participate simultaneously in his offensive operations. Although Konev was justified in assuming he might be able to exploit the weakness of the Axis defenses before they fully jelled, the fighting itself soon proved his *front* could not achieve any dramatic offensive successes unless and until Konev could bring in his powerful 7th Guards and 5th Guards Tank Armies.

Second, Konev's intelligence organs provided him with inadequate and inaccurate information concerning the dispositions and intentions of the defending German and Romanian forces. In addition to overestimating the damage his forces had inflicted on the German panzer forces during their previous offensive operations, his intelligence organs also "lost" many of these divisions and were not able to track them as they moved from one sector to another to check his *front*'s advance. As a result, the relatively fragile rifle divisions in the vanguard of Koroteev's and Trofimenko's 52nd and 27th Armies unexpectedly encountered the *Grossdeutschland* and 24th Panzer Divisions north of Iasi and south of Tirgu Frumos and were no match for the highly skilled German panzer forces, particularly since *Grossdeutschland* Division fielded well over 150 tanks. In similar fashion, although far weaker than their counterparts operating to the west, the 3rd, 11th, 13th, and 14th Panzer Divisions forced the rifle divisions of Galanin's and Managarov's 4th

Guards and 53rd Armies to pay a high price for their limited territorial gains in the Orgeev and Susleny regions.

Third, the 2nd Ukrainian Front's initial offensive failed because the senior leadership of Army Group Wöhler and the German Eighth Army, in particular, Wöhler and his subordinate corps and division commanders, maneuvered and employed their meager operational and tactical resources skillfully enough to fend off each and every Soviet threat effectively and in timely fashion. In particular, the frequent swift maneuvers by Manteuffel's *Grossdeutschland* and Edelsheim's 24th Panzer Divisions staved off potential disaster along the entire front from Iasi to Tirgu Frumos, while the constantly regrouping forces of Wietersheim's 11th, Mikosch's 13th, and Unrein's 14th Panzer Divisions did the same in the Orgeev and Reut River sectors.

Finally, Wöhler's tactical command cadre, such as the regimental commanders in the *Grossdeutschland,* 3rd, 11th, 13th, and 24th Panzer Divisions, as well as the commanders of numerous *kampfgruppen* fielded by the weak divisions on his right wing along the Dnestr River, also proved adept to the rapidly changing combat situation. The actions of these leaders demonstrated that, when well led, superbly trained but badly outnumbered German divisions and regiments still retained the tactical fighting skills that made them so effective, deadly, and famous during the first two years of the war.

As the month of April ended, Stalin, the other members of the *Stavka,* and Konev assessed why the 2nd Ukrainian Front's initial offensive had failed; they concluded that, in order to capture the illusive objectives of Iasi and Kishinev and crush Axis defenses in northern Romania, any future offensive would have to employ all of the forces of Konev's 2nd and Malinovsky's 3rd Ukrainian Fronts. This meant the offensive could not resume until Konev completed regrouping his 7th Guards and 5th Guards Tank Armies to his *front's* left wing in the region west of Iasi and until Malinovsky was able to concentrate the bulk of his *front's* armies in bridgeheads on the western bank of the Dnestr River. Satisfied that both Konev and Malinovsky were about to fulfill these prerequisites, the *Stavka* was convinced the two *fronts* could achieve the strategic success that eluded them in April during their offensive planned for early and mid-May.

Retrospectively in his memoirs, A. M. Vasilevsky, the chief of the Red Army General Staff, who coordinated Konev's and Malinovsky's offensives for the *Stavka,* placed a good face on Konev's progress in April despite the 2nd Ukrainian Front's obvious failures:

> Having defeated the main forces of the German Eighth Army, in so doing destroying more than 60,000 soldiers and officers and taking around 20,000 prisoners, and also seizing a great quantity of weapons and equipment, the forces of I. S. Konev already reached the State border along

> the Prut at the end of March, and then, after forcing it, entered Romanian territory and captured the cities of Botoshany, Radauti, Pascani, and many other towns.[29]

As true as these judgments were, the results Konev's offensive achieved fell far short of both Konev's and the *Stavka*'s expectations. Both resolved to remedy this situation in early May.

Army General I. S. Konev, commander, 2nd Ukrainian Front (commander, 1st Ukrainian Front on 24 May 1944)

Lieutenant General F. F. Zhmachenko, commander, 40th Army

Lieutenant General S. G. Trofimenko, commander, 27th Army

Lieutenant General K. A. Koroteev, commander, 52nd Army

Lieutenant General I. V. Galanin, commander, 4th Guards Army

Lieutenant General I. M. Managarov, commander, 53rd Army

Lieutenant General A. S. Zhadov, commander, 5th Guards Army

Lieutenant General M. S. Shumilov, commander, 7th Guards Army

Colonel General of Tank Forces P. A. Rotmistrov, commander, 5th Guards Tank Army

Lieutenant General of Tank Forces S. I. Bogdanov, commander, 2nd Tank Army

Lieutenant General of Tank Forces A. G. Kravchenko, commander, 6th Tank Army

CHAPTER 4

The 3rd Ukrainian Front's Advance to the Dnestr River and the First Bridgehead Battles (11–25 April 1944)

PRELUDE: THE ODESSA OFFENSIVE (26 MARCH–10 APRIL)

Malinovsky's Plans and Forces

For two important reasons, the *Stavka*'s plan for the Red Army's invasion of Romania during the spring of 1944 initially required the armies of Konev's 2nd Ukrainian Front to conduct its main effort. First, the *Stavka* believed Konev's *front* was sufficiently strong to capture both Iasi and Kishinev without additional support from Malinovsky's 3rd Ukrainian Front. Second, and more important, the *Stavka* had already assigned Malinovsky's forces the equally vital mission of smashing the German Sixth Army and capturing the port city of Odessa on the Black Sea, a mission Malinovsky's forces had begun to carry out on 26 March. Since the *Stavka* anticipated it would take the 3rd Ukrainian Front at least ten days to capture the city, about half of Malinovsky's forces would not be available to join Konev's advance into Romania until after Odessa fell (Map 4).

In the meantime, while the three armies and cavalry-mechanized group deployed on the 3rd Ukrainian Front's left (southern) wing were investing Odessa, the three armies on the *front*'s right wing—specifically Gagen's 57th Army, Sharokhin's 37th Armies, and Glagolev's 46th Army, supported by Major General of Tank Forces A. O. Akhmanov's 23rd Tank Corps—were to join the 5th and 7th Guards Armies on the left wing of Konev's *front* and drive German forces back to and across the Dnestr River. In addition, Sharokhin's and Glagolev's 37th and 46th Armies, which were approaching the road and rail junction at Razdel'naia, 42 miles northwest of Odessa, in the wake of Pliev's exploiting Cavalry-Mechanized Group, were supposed to capture this vital communications center and advance southward to block German forces from retreating westward toward the Dnestr River. This task significantly slowed the forward progress of both Sharokhin's and Glagolev's armies to the Dnestr River.

As of 1 April 1944, Gagen's 57th Army fielded three rifle corps (the 9th, 64th, and 68th), with a total of nine rifle divisions, one of which was a guards division, a separate tank brigade, and a separate antitank rifle battalion. The 9th Rifle Corps, which was commanded by Major General I. P. Roslyi, included the 118th, 230th, and 301st Rifle Divisions; Major General M. B.

Anashkin's 64th Rifle Corps consisted of the 73rd Guards and 19th and 52nd Rifle Divisions; and Major General N. N. Mul'tan's 68th Rifle Corps included the 93rd, 113th, and 223rd Rifle Divisions.

Older than many of his counterparts, 49-year-old Lieutenant General Nikolai Aleksandrovich Gagen had commanded the 57th Army successfully since early May 1943, when the army was reestablished from the remnants of the 3rd Tank Army, which German forces had destroyed south of Khar'kov two months before. A noncommissioned and junior officer in the Tsar's army during World War I, Gagen had joined the Red Army in 1919; commanded at the platoon, company, and battalion levels during the Russian Civil War; and distinguished himself when Red Army forces suppressed White Forces during their uprising in the Petropavlovsk mutiny in 1921. After commanding a battalion and teaching at the Saratov Reserve Command Cadre School during the 1920s, Gagen commanded a rifle regiment and served as an assistant rifle division commander from 1930 through 1935, as the Volga Military District's chief of supply from 1935 through 1938, and as assistant chief of the Infantry School in Kazan' during 1939 and early 1940. Assigned to command the 153rd Rifle Division in the Ural Military District in July 1940, Gagen was commanding this division when war began.

In the wake of the German invasion, Gagen's rifle division was assigned to the 20th Army of the *Stavka*'s reserve in June and to the Western Front's 22nd Army in July, and his division performed credibly enough during the defense of Smolensk to receive the honorific designation of the 3rd Guards Rifle Division in early September. Fortunately for Gagen and his division, the General Staff transferred it northward in early September to reinforce the Leningrad Front's 54th Army; otherwise, it would likely have been encircled and destroyed with the remainder of the 20th Army in the German encirclement at Viaz'ma during October 1941.

Once in the Leningrad region, Gagen led the 3rd Guards Rifle Division that helped defeat the German advance on Tikhvin and led the counteroffensive that drove German forces back to the Volkhov River. For this feat the NKO assigned him command of the newly formed Volkhov Front's s Special Operational Group in late December 1941 and then the newly formed 4th Guards Rifle Corps in January 1942, a post which he occupied nearly continuously until being assigned command of the 57th Army in early May 1943. While in his new command, during the spring of 1942, his 4th Guards Rifle Corps participated in the 54th Army's failed attempt to rescue the 2nd Shock Army, which German forces had encircled in the Liuban' region, and, during August and September 1942, his corps spearheaded an offensive to prevent Manstein's Eleventh Army from attacking Leningrad's defenses and, if possible, to raise the German blockade of the city. Although his rifle corps was virtually destroyed in this offensive and Gagen was wounded in the intense fighting near Siniavino, in late October he resumed command of his reconstituted rifle corps.

After reconstituting Gagen's rifle corps, the *Stavka* assigned it to the newly formed 4th Reserve Army, which then, as the 1st Guards Army, subsequently went into action northwest of Stalingrad in mid-December 1942. Forming part of the shock group of the Southwestern Front's attacking 1st Guards Army, Gagen's rifle corps helped destroy the Italian Eighth Army along the Chir River, thereby helping to prevent the Germans from rescuing their Sixth Army, which was encircled in Stalingrad. During the ensuing winter campaign of 1943, Gagen's 4th Guards Rifle Corps led the dramatic advance by the Southwestern Front's 1st Guards Army deep into the Donbas region and toward Zaporozh'e on the Dnepr River. However, Manstein's famous counteroffensive halted the audacious advance of Gagen's guards rifle corps short of the Dnepr in late February and cut off and largely destroyed the corps in March. Soon after, the *Stavka* reconstituted his guards rifle corps once again and assigned it to the Southwestern Front's 6th Army.

Gagen's proven record for tenaciousness and audacity, particularly on the offense, convinced the *Stavka* to assign him command of the Southwestern Front's 57th Army in early May 1943. Subsequently, he vindicated the *Stavka*'s judgment by effectively leading his army in the defensive battle at Kursk and the Belgorod-Khar'kov counteroffensive during July and August 1943, in the Steppe Front's advance to the Dnepr River during the fall of 1943, and in the 3rd Ukrainian Front's successive offensives in the eastern Ukraine during the winter of 1943 and 1944.[1] A tenacious fighter through and through, Gagen would command the 57th Army until October 1944 and the 26th Army to war's end.

Roughly equivalent in strength to Gagen's 57th Army, on 1 April 1944, Sharokhin's 37th Army fielded three rifle corps, the 6th Guards and the 57th and 82nd Rifle Corps, with a total of nine rifle divisions, six of which were either guards rifle or guards airborne divisions, and a supporting separate armored train battalion. The 6th Guards Rifle Corps, which was commanded by Major General G. P. Kotov, included the 20th Guards and 195th Rifle Divisions; Major General F. A. Ostashenko's 57th Rifle Corps consisted of the 58th and 92nd Guards Rifle and 228th Rifle Divisions; and Major General P. G. Kuznetsov's 82nd Rifle Corps included the 10th Guards Airborne, 28th Guards Rifle, and 188th Rifle Divisions. In addition, Kotov retained the 15th Guards Rifle Division in army reserve and was also supported by a separate armored train battalion.

Although he was just as experienced as his fellow army commanders and had commanded the 37th Army since August 1943, before being assigned to army command, Lieutanant General Mikhail Nikolaevich Sharokhin had spent most of his military career in staff assignments. Sharokhin, 45 years old in April 1944, had begun his military career in 1917 when he was conscripted into the Tsar's army and sent to the northern front. After joining the Red Guards in November 1917, Sharokhin fought German occupation forces in the Pskov region southwest of Petrograd during 1918 and later commanded at the platoon and cavalry squadron levels on the northeastern and Turkestan fronts during the Russian Civil War. Serving as deputy commander and commander of a cavalry machine-gun squadron during the early 1920s, he graduated from a Cavalry Command Course in 1926 and became chief of a regimental school from 1927 to 1931.

After Sharokhin graduated from the Frunze Academy in 1936, somewhat inexplicably the NKO assigned him as chief of staff of a light bomber aviation brigade and, in 1937, as its commander. Thereafter, he occupied a wide variety of key staff positions, including deputy chief and chief of the General Staff's Operations Directorate during 1939 and 1940, deputy chief of the Operation's Directorate after war began, and deputy chief of the General Staff in late 1941 and early 1942. Perhaps because of the favorable impression he made on B. M. Shaposhnikov, the chief of the General Staff, or on A. M. Vasilevsky, his deputy and successor, the *Stavka* assigned Sharokhin to the post of chief of staff of the Kalinin Front's 3rd Shock Army during February 1942, chief of staff of the Northwestern Front in August 1942, chief of staff of the Volkhov Front in October 1942, and commander of the 37th Army in August 1943.

Thereafter, Sharokhin's record paralleled that of Gagen. His 37th Army fought under Konev's Steppe (later 2nd Ukrainian) Front during the advance to and across the Dnepr during the fall of 1943 and under Malinovsky's 3rd Ukrainian Front during its many offensives across the Ukraine during the winter of 1944.[2] A fine staff officer who would command the 37th Army to war's end, becoming a Hero of the Soviet Union in the process, Sharokhin was also known for his steadiness and dogged determination to accomplish his assigned missions.

Advancing in tandem with Sharokhin's 37th Army but slightly to the east was Glagolev's 46th Army. As of 1 April, Glagolev's army fielded three rifle corps—the 31st Guards and 32nd and 34th Rifle Corps—with a total of nine rifle divisions, four of which were guards divisions, and no supporting armor. The 31st Guards Rifle Corps, which was commanded by Major General A. I. Ruchkin, included the 4th, 34th, and 40th Guards Rifle Divisions; Major General D. S. Zherebin's 32nd Rifle Corps consisted of the 60th Guards and 259th and 266th Rifle Divisions; and Major General I. S. Kosobutsky's 34th Rifle Corps included the 236th and 394th Rifle Divisions. In addition, Glagolev retained the 353rd Rifle Division in his army's reserve.

Forty-eight years old in April 1944, Lieutenant General Vasilii Vasil'evich Glagolev had commanded the 46th Army since March 1943 and would continue in army command through war's end. Glagolev had also begun his military career as a private in the Tsar's army during World War I but joined the Red Army in 1918, after which he served in cavalry units in the Urals and north Caucasus regions. After war's end he graduated from the Baku Command Course in 1921 and Command Improvement Courses in 1926 and 1931 and commanded a wide variety of cavalry units up to division level. After his graduation from the Frunze Academy in 1941, the NKO assigned Glagolev to command the 42nd Cavalry Division in the North Caucasus Military District. Glagolev's cavalry division then fought under the 51st Army in the Crimea until November 1941, when the division was partially destroyed and disbanded. The NKO then assigned Glagolev the North Caucasus Military District's 73rd Rifle Division, which he commanded from February through October 1942, under the control of the Southern Front's 24th Army. However, this division was also disbanded in October 1942 after being essentially destroyed along with its parent army during the initial stages of German Operation *Blau*.

After surviving the destruction of two of his divisions, in October 1942 Glagolev received command of the 176th Rifle Division, which was subordinate to the North Caucasus Front's 12th Army, and he commanded that division until November when the NKO assigned him to command the 9th Army's new 10th Guards Rifle Corps. After his new rifle corps earned distinction in the heavy fighting around Groznyi (in Chechnia) deep in the Caucasus region, Glagolev was assigned command of the 9th Army in February 1943 and the 46th Army in March. A determined fighter, Glagolev led the 46th Army in the Battle of Kursk during July and August 1943, the advance to and across the Dnepr River during the fall of 1943, and the Southern (3rd Ukrainian) Front's offensives in the eastern and southern Ukraine during the winter of 1944. As evidence of his sound performance, Glagolev became a Hero of the Soviet Union in the fall of 1943.[3]

In addition to these three armies, the forces on Malinovsky's right wing also included Akhmanov's 23rd Tank Corps, which, although woefully understrength, was organized in a standard configuration of three tank brigades, one motorized rifle brigade, and a variety of supporting self-propelled, tank destroyer, and guards-mortar regiments. Although Akhmanov was experienced as a tank brigade commander, he had taken command of the corps on 12 March, less than three weeks before.

While the three armies on the right wing of Malinovsky's 3rd Ukrainian Front were tasked with continuing to advance toward the Dnestr River while protecting the *front*'s right flank, Malinovsky's offensive plan for the seizure of Odessa required Chuikov's 8th Guards Army and Shlemin's 6th Army to advance in the wake of Pliev's Cavalry-Mechanized Group to envelop Odessa from the northwest and west, while Tsvetaev's 5th Shock Army was to advance directly against Odessa's defenses from the east.

Pliev's Cavalry-Mechanized Group, the armored spearhead leading Malinovsky's advance on Odessa, had already led the 3rd Ukrainian Front's advance across the southern Ukraine. Formed during the midst of the winter campaign to facilitate the conduct of maneuver operations during the trying period of the spring *rasputitsa,* Pliev's force was uniquely configured to overcome supposedly insurmountable weather and terrain conditions. A curious but effective mixture of horse cavalry and tank and mechanized forces, Pliev's Cavalry-Mechanized Group consisted of the combat-tested 4th Guards Cavalry Corps and the 4th Guards Mechanized Corps.

The 4th Guards Cavalry Corps, which was commanded by Pliev himself and was a formidable force in its own right, included the 9th and 10th Guards Cavalry and 30th Cavalry Divisions; three separate tank regiments; separate self-propelled artillery, tank destroyer artillery, guards-mortar, and antiaircraft artillery regiments; and separate tank destroyer artillery and guards-mortar battalions. Rounding out the Cavalry-Mechanized Group, Major General of Tank Forces V. I. Zhdanov's 4th Guards Mechanized Corps was organized with three guards mechanized brigades and one guards tank brigade; separate tank and self-propelled artillery, and tank destroyer artillery regiments; and separate motorcycle, tank destroyer, and guards-mortar battalions. Although Pliev's forces had experienced high attrition rates during its previous operations, it still mustered a force of well over 250 tanks and self-propelled guns to lead its drive on Odessa.

The Cavalry-Mechanized Group's commander, Lieutenant General Issa Aleksandrovich Pliev, was an Ossetian by ethnicity and, at the age of 40 years, was the youngest and arguably the most capable and experienced cavalryman in the Red Army. Too young to participate in either World War I or the Russian Civil War, Pliev had joined the Red Army in 1922, graduated from the Leningrad Cavalry School in 1926, and commanded student detachments at the Cavalry School at Krasnodar in the northern Caucasus region from 1926 to 1930. After serving as chief of operations of the 5th Cavalry Division from 1933 through 1936, Pliev functioned as an advisor to the Mongolian People's Revolutionary Army before returning west to command a regiment in the 6th Cavalry Division during its invasion of eastern Poland in September 1939.

Shortly after the war began in July 1941, the NKO appointed Pliev to command the North Caucasus Military District's 50th Cavalry Division, which was soon assigned to the Western Front to assist in the defense of Smolensk. Pliev subsequently earned new fame by leading his and another cavalry division on a daring but futile raid into the German Army Center's rear area during the August fighting for Smolensk, for which his division received the honorific designation of 3rd Guards. Operating in equally audacious fashion during the Battle for Moscow, Pliev was rewarded by being assigned to command the famous 2nd Guards Cavalry Corps after the death of its commander, General L. M. Dovator, in December 1941 and, thereafter, the 5th Cavalry Corps from April through June 1942, the 3rd Guards Cavalry Corps from July though December 1942, and the 4th Guards Cavalry Corps from November 1943 through April 1944. In between these assignments, he served as deputy commander of the 5th Tank Army from January through early May 1943 and deputy commander of the Steppe Front for Cavalry Forces from May through November 1943.

As a cavalry corps commander, Pliev performed superbly everywhere he served throughout his long career. While his corps had instrumental roles in the Red Army's victories in the Battles of Moscow and Stalingrad, his leadership of an ad hoc cavalry-mechanized group under the 3rd Ukrainian Front's direction during the winter battles in the Ukraine was equally successful, earning for him the designation as a Hero of the Soviet Union for his role in the capture of Odessa in mid-April 1944.[4]

In contrast, Pliev's fellow commander of the 4th Guards Mechanized Corps, General Zhdanov, was far less experienced in corps command. Zhdanov had taken command of his guards mechanized corps on 31 March, the day its former distinguished commander, Major General of Tank Forces T. I. Tanashchishin, who had commanded the corps since July 1942, was killed in battle while his corps was capturing the town of Berezovka. However, Zhdanov was selected for the new post because he had served successfully for several years as a mechanized brigade commander.

By far the most powerful army of Malinovsky's armies participating in the Odessa offensive was Chuikov's veteran 8th Guards Army, which on 1 April 1944 fielded three rifle corps (the 4th, 28th, and 29th Guards), with a total of ten rifle divisions, nine of which were guards divisions, and a separate tank regiment. The 4th Guards Rifle Corps, which was commanded by Lieutenant General V. F. Glazunov, included the 35th, 47th, and 57th Guards Rifle Divisions; Major General S. I. Morozov's 28th Guards Rifle Corps consisted of the 39th, 79th, and 88th Guards Rifle Divisions; and Lieutenant General S. A. Bobruk's 29th Guards Rifle Corps included the 27th, 74th, and 82nd Guards Rifle Divisions. However, for reasons that remain unclear, Lieutenant General Ia. S. Fokanov replaced Bobruk in command on 13 April in the immediate wake of the Odessa offensive. Finally, Chuikov kept the 152nd Rifle Division in his army's reserve.

Arguably the most famous army commander in the Red Army and 44 years old in April 1944, Lieutenant General Vasilii Ivanovich Chuikov had commanded the 8th Guards Army and its predecessor, the 62nd Army, since September 1942 and throughout its dramatic victories during the defense of Stalingrad in the fall of 1942. Chuikov had began his military career as a member of the youth detachment of engineers in the fortress of Kronshtadt during 1917, joined the Red Army in 1918, and participated in the suppression of an uprising by "Left Social Revolutionaries" in Moscow in the same year. During the Russian Civil War, Chuikov served as an assistant company commander on the southern front in 1918 and as a deputy regimental commander and regimental commander on the eastern and western fronts in late 1918 and 1919, in the process earning two awards for bravery.

After graduating from the Frunze Academy in 1925 and the Eastern Faculty of the same academy in 1927, Chuikov served as an advisor to the Chinese government from 1927 through 1929 and as a department chief in the Special Red Banner Far Eastern Army from 1929 through 1932, where he orchestrated Red Army operations in 1929 against Chinese forces in western Manchuria. The NKO appointed Chuikov to head its Command Cadre Improvement Course in 1932 and, after graduating from a course at the Red Army's Academy for Motorization and Mechanization in 1936, to command a new mechanized brigade in December 1936, the 5th Rifle Corps in April 1938, the Belorussian Military District's Bobruisk Army Group of Forces in July 1938, and the same military district's 4th Army in 1939. Chuikov led the 4th Army during the invasion of eastern Poland in September 1939 and, as a reward, the 9th Army during the Soviet-Finnish War from late 1939 to early 1940.

In the Soviet-Finnish War, Chuikov experienced the embarrassment of having his army's 163rd Rifle and 44th Motorized Rifle Divisions destroyed by Finnish forces in the frozen forests near Suomussalmi in central Karelia; as a result, he displayed his ruthlessness in command. Urged on V. I. Mekhlis, a political watchdog Stalin sent to monitor the army commander's response to the catastrophic defeat, Chuikov ordered the execution of the corps and division commanders responsible for these defeats. After Chuikov survived the Finnish debacle, but only barely, the NKO assigned him to virtual exile as military attaché to China from December 1940 through March 1942.

After Chuikov "sat out" the harrowing initial period of the war in Stalin's apparent disfavor, in anticipation of renewed German offensive action during the summer of 1942, the NKO summoned Chuikov back from China in May 1942 and placed him in command of the new 1st Reserve Army. When the German offensive smashed the Red Army's strategic defenses in southern Russia during early July, Chuikov's reserve army formed the 64th Army on 10 July and took up defensive positions along the southwestern approaches to Stalingrad, but it was almost encircled and partially destroyed by the advancing Germans. Surviving this defeat, Chuikov was assigned command of the 62nd Army, which he led during its subsequent determined defenses of Stalingrad city throughout the entire fall. Thoroughly chastened by his previous defeats, Chuikov's tenacious and ruthless defense of Stalingrad's center city and factory district earned fame for him and, in April 1943, the designation of 8th Guards for his victorious but decimated army.

After its strength was fully restored, Chuikov's 8th Guards Army served with distinction as the Southern (later 3rd Ukrainian) Front's main shock force. As such, his army led the *front's* advance during the Izium offensive during July 1943, the Donbas offensive, the capture of Zaporozh'e, the failed Krivoi Rog–Nikopol' offensive during the fall of 1943, and the more successful Krivoi Rog–Nikopol' and Bereznegovatoe-Snigirevka offensives across the southern Ukraine during the winter of 1944. One of Stalin's toughest army commanders, Chuikov could be relied on to carry out every mission assigned to him without hesitation and regardless of cost.[5]

Considerably smaller than Chuikov's army, as of 1 April 1944, Shlemin's 6th Army fielded only two rifle corps (the 34th Guards and the 66th), with a total of six rifle divisions, of which only two were guards divisions, and no additional combat support forces. The 34th Guards Rifle Corps, which was commanded by Major General N. M. Makovchuk, included the 59th and 61st Guards and 243rd Rifle Divisions; Major General D. A. Kupriianov's 66th Rifle Corps consisted of the 203rd, 244th, and 333rd Rifle Divisions. Initially at least, Malinovsky intended to withdraw Shlemin's army into his *front's* reserve once Odessa fell and later commit it to reinforce his other armies along or across the Dnestr as required.

At age forty-five in April, Lieutenant General Ivan Timofeevich Shlemin had commanded the 6th Army since March 1943, one month after German forces destroyed most of the army in the Krasnograd region during Manstein's counteroffensive in the Donbas. A soldier in the Tsar's imperial army during World War I, Shlemin had joined the Red Army in 1918 and commanded an infantry platoon in Estonia and the defense of Petrograd (Leningrad). After war's end, he graduated from the Petrograd Infantry School in 1920, the Frunze Academy in 1925, and the operational faculty of that academy in 1932. In between and after completing these academic courses, Shlemin served on the staff of a rifle regiment and rifle division, on the General Staff, and, after commanding a rifle regiment in 1936 and early 1937, as chief of the General Staff Academy from 1937 through 1940.

The NKO assigned Shlemin as chief of staff of the Baltic Special Military District's 11th Army in 1940, and, after war began in June 1941, he served in that position until appointed as the Northwestern Front's chief of staff in May 1942. During the first year of the war, Shlemin took an instrumental role in planning his army's attack during the Northwestern Front's counterstroke at Staraia Russa in August 1941 and in the Northwestern Front's offensive in the Staraya Russa region during January and February 1942. Transferred to the south as chief of staff of the 1st Guards Army, Shlemin had an equally important role in planning this army's offensives in the Stalingrad region and, as a reward, was assigned to command, in succession, the 5th Tank Army from January through April 1943, the 12th Army in April and May 1943, and the 6th Army in May 1943. Although his 5th Tank Army was without tanks and both it and the 12th Army operated along clearly secondary axes during the Southern Front's operations in early 1943, Shlemin's 6th Army spearheaded the Southwestern Front's offensive in the Donbas during August and September 1943. Thereafter, the 6th Army joined the advance on Zaporozh'e and the Dnepr River during the fall of 1943 and the 3rd Ukrainian Front's drive across the southern Ukraine during the winter of 1944. Although little is known of Shlemin's personality or style of command, he performed competently enough to lead the 46th Army until January 1945, in the process becoming a Hero of the Soviet Union by war's end.[6]

The force Malinovsky ordered to assault the defenses of Odessa from the east was Tsvetaev's 5th Shock Army. Slightly smaller than Chuikov's 8th Guards Army, on 1 April 1944, Tsvetaev's army fielded two rifle corps, the 10th Guards and 37th, with a total of eight rifle divisions, four of them guards, and the 1st Guards Fortified Region. The 10th Guards Rifle Corps, commanded by Major General I. A. Rubaniuk, included the 86th and 109th Guards and 320th Rifle Divisions; Major General S. F. Gorokhov's stronger 37th Rifle Corps consisted of the 49th and 108th Guards and 248th and 416th Rifle Divisions. Tsvetaev retained the 295th Rifle Division in his army's reserve.

Fifty years old in April 1944 and older than most of his counterparts, Colonel General Viacheslav Dmitrievich Tsvetaev had commanded the 5th Shock Army (the former 10th Reserve Army) since December 1942, when it went into action to spearhead the Stalingrad Front's counteroffensive southeast of Stalingrad. Tsvetaev had begun his long military career in 1914 and commanded a company and battalion in the Tsar's army during World War I. After joining the Red Army in 1918, he commanded a company, battalion, regiment, brigade, and, finally, the 54th Rifle Division on the northern and western fronts during the Russian Civil War. After war's end, Tsvetaev graduated from the Higher Academic Course in 1922 and the Frunze Academy's Officer Improvement Course in 1927 and commanded a rifle brigade and rifle division during the suppression of the Basmachi uprising in central Asia.

After teaching at the Frunze Academy from 1931 to 1937, in the wake of Stalin's great purges of the Red Army's officers' corps, the NKO appointed Tsvetaev to command the 57th Rifle Division and, after another short stint as a teacher at the Frunze Academy, as a faculty chief at the same academy in January 1941, where he was serving when war began. During the first 18 months of the war, Tsvetaev commanded an operational group of the Separate 7th Army in Karelia and was deputy commander of the Volkhov Front's 4th Army before being assigned command of the 5th Shock Army in December 1942. Once in army command, Tsvetaev and his 5th Shock Army helped defeat German efforts to rescue their Sixth Army encircled in Stalingrad and then spearheaded the Southern Front's offensives to Rostov and along the Mius River during the winter of 1942–1943.

As the Red Army expanded its offensive operations, Tsvetaev's 5th Shock Army took part in the Southern Front's offensives in the Donbas and Melitopol' regions during the fall of 1943 and the 3rd Ukrainian Front's offensives on the Right Bank of the Ukraine during the winter of 1944. A thoroughly competent commander, Tsvetaev later served as deputy commander of the 1st Belorussian Front from May to September 1944 under its new commander, Konev, and as commander of the 6th and 33rd Armies to war's end, becoming a Hero of the Soviet Union for the role his army played in the storming of Berlin.[7]

In addition to his six armies, cavalry-mechanized group, and separate tank corps, Malinovsky's *front* also included Lieutenant General K. V. Sviridov's 2nd Guards Mechanized Corps, which he had been forced to withdraw into his *front*'s reserve for rest and refitting, and a wide variety of supporting tank regiments, brigades, and self-propelled artillery regiments. An experienced general, Sviridov had commanded his mechanized corps since its creation in October 1942 and would do so continuously until war's end.

Envelopment and Capture of Odessa

On 4 April 1944, Pliev's Cavalry-Mechanized Group and the lead elements of Sharokhin's 37th Army signaled the beginning of the final phase of the Odessa offensive by capturing the town of Razdel'naia, 42 miles northwest of Odessa, thereby splitting Hollidt's German Sixth Army into two distinct parts. With its defenses torn asunder, the western portion of the Sixth Army, consisting of the LII and XXX Army Corps and roughly half of the divisions on the left (western) wing of the XXIX Army Corps, continued defending against the Soviet forces advancing westward and southwestward toward the Dnestr River. The eastern half of the Sixth Army, which included the divisions on the right (eastern) wing of the XXIX Army Corps and the entire XXXXIV and LXXII Army Corps, were soon either fighting in isolation east of Razdel'naia or threatened with encirclement and destruction in the vicinity of Odessa proper (Map 4).

Almost immediately after the Soviets penetrated its defenses, the XXIX Army Corps' 3rd Mountain, 17th, 335th, and 294th Infantry Divisions, which were situated east of Razdel'naia, began moving quickly to the west to escape encirclement. This required the semi-isolated divisions to run a virtual gauntlet through a light cordon of Soviet screening forces facing eastward, which Pliev's Cavalry-Mechanized Group and Chuikov's 8th Guards Army had left behind as the bulk of their main forces lunged southward from the Razdel'naia region to envelop Odessa from the west and southwest.

After Pliev's Cavalry-Mechanized Group captured Razdel'naia, Malinovsky ordered it to race southward as rapidly as possible to sever the withdrawal routes of German forces in the Odessa region. At the same time, he ordered Chuikov's and Shlemin's 8th Guards and 6th Armies to envelop Odessa from the northwest and Tsvetaev's 5th Shock Army to advance directly toward Odessa from the east. By day's end on 7 April, the forward elements of Pliev's forces reached the northern coast of the Dnestr estuary a few miles southeast of the town of Beliaevka, 25 miles west of Odessa. This forced all of the German Sixth Army's forces east of the Dnestr River to run a gauntlet through Pliev's cavalry and mechanized infantry, which had formed a loose cordon of strong points at all major road junctions stretching many miles to his rear.

With Soviet infantry, cavalry, and tanks deployed along their withdrawal routes westward to the Dnestr River, the XXIX Army Corps' 3rd Mountain and 17th, 335th, and 294th Infantry Divisions made their way westward slowly and painfully through the 37th and 46th Armies' blocking forces. After engaging in confused but often intense fighting on 6 and 7 April, the bulk of these divisions made their way safely to new intermediate defensive lines, which the Sixth Army had managed to erect east of the Dnestr and other defenses they created to defend the eastern approaches to the cities of Grigoriopol' and Tiraspol' on the Dnestr.

Further to the south, however, the 302nd, 306th, 9th, and 304th Infantry Divisions, which were subordinate to the Sixth Army's XXXXIV Army Corps, had to fight their way westward through an even heavier cordon of Soviet forces, primarily erected by both Pliev's cavalrymen and the rear guard units of Chuikov's 8th Guards Army. Retreating westward in regimental, battalion, and even smaller groups, these German divisions suffered heavier losses in both men and material as they desperately sought safe haven along the western bank of the Dnestr River. For the distraught Germans, the only saving grace was the fact that Pliev's and Chuikov's forces were focused primarily on their main objective of Odessa rather than the escaping Germans, a reality that permitted a sizeable number of German troops to escape to the west, albeit without much of their heavier weapons and equipment and in considerable disorder.

After engaging in heavy fighting on the northern and eastern approaches to the city, the lead elements of Tsvetaev's 5th Shock Army entered Odessa's northern suburbs on the evening of 9 April. Then, overnight on 9 and 10 April, the forward elements of Chuikov's and Shlemin's 8th Guards and 6th Armies and Pliev's Cavalry-Mechanized Group also approached Odessa's inner defenses from the northwest and west. With the Soviet trap snapping shut around them, the remainder of the defending German LXXII Army Corps began breaking out to the west, permitting the Soviet forces to occupy the city's center at 1000 hours on 10 April after only minor fighting.

The LXXII Army Corps' retreat from Odessa was as difficult and harrowing as the withdrawal of the XXXXIV Army Corps further to the north. A German-based account captured the confusion and horror of the situation:

> The next night [3 April], at the height of the [sleet] storm, Soviet tanks and cavalry broke through to Razdelnaya [Razdel'naia] and turned south, splitting the [Odessa] bridgehead in half. In three more days the Russian force lunged deep behind Odessa to the Dnestr, capturing the city's water intake station near the village of Belyaevka. Sixth Army then began a hasty retreat behind the river amid scenes of wildest confusion. At the railroad bridge and road bridge west of Tiraspol traffic had been jammed up for weeks. The army had built five smaller bridges at various points, and on the muddy approaches to each miles-long columns of trucks, people and cattle stood four and five abreast waiting to cross. Hundreds of trains jammed into Odessa, but only a few could be routed through to the west.
>
> The last Germans crossed the Dnestr on 14 April. The army group reported that the scene behind the river was reminiscent of Stalingrad. The Rumanian railroads had failed completely. The troops had no clothing and no supplies. The wounded were lying in the open at the sidings. The daily ration was 200 grams [seven ounces] of bread.
>
> Probably as much because Malinovsky had gone as far as he wanted to as for any other reason, Sixth Army did manage to get a front on the Dnestr from Dubossary south to the Dnestr Liman [estuary], but not before the Russians, as was their custom, had gained a number of bridgeheads, the largest of them south of Tiraspol at the center of the front.[8]

With Odessa under his *front*'s firm control, Malinovsky's forces could now join those of Konev's *front* in a coordinated advance toward Kishinev and deeper into Romania. However, he could do so only if and when his forces could effectively penetrate the defenses the Germans were still hastily erecting east of and along the Dnestr River.

PURSUIT TO THE DNESTR RIVER AND THE FIRST BRIDGEHEAD BATTLES (11–17 APRIL)

Malinovsky's Initial Plans

Shortly after the 3rd Ukrainian Front reported capturing Odessa, on the night of 10–11 April, the *Stavka* ordered Malinovsky's *front* to mount a concerted offensive to reach the Soviet-Romanian state borders along the Prut and Danube Rivers. In addition to forcing the Dnestr River and occupying Kishinev, this order envisioned Malinovsky's forces occupying all of eastern Bessarabia, while Konev's forces seized western Bessarabia. After receiving their expanded mission, Vasilevsky, the *Stavka*'s representative to the 2nd, 3rd, and 4th Ukrainian Fronts, met with Malinovsky and Lieutenants General A S. Zheltov and F. K. Korzhenevich, the commissar and chief of staff of Malinovsky's *front,* respectively, to prepare an operational plan for conducting the ambitious offensive operation.

In his memoirs, Vasilevsky described the plan he formulated jointly with the *front*'s military council, which subsequently received the *Stavka*'s approval:

> [The 3rd Ukrainian Front] will conduct its main attack with the five armies on its right wing—the 57th, 37th, 6th, 5th Shock, and 46th Armies (a total of 41 divisions reinforced by two artillery divisions—and also all of the front's separate RGK gun and howitzer artillery regiments, tank destroyer, mortar, and engineer brigades, and aviation) in the general direction from Tiraspol' toward Kagul.
>
> We intend to employ Group Pliev to exploit the success of the [front's] main attack toward Komrat [100 miles west of Odessa] and toward the enemy's main withdrawal routes farther to the south and southwest. After forcing the Dnestr at Beliaevka and Akkerman [25 miles west and 30 miles southwest of Odessa, respectively], the 8th Guards Army will conduct a secondary attack along the Black Sea coast toward Tatarbunary [75 miles southwest of Odessa] and reach the Danube River at Vilkova [100 miles southwest of Odessa].
>
> We intend to begin forcing the Dnestr along the entire front on 18–20 April. Meanwhile, the forces of the 57th, 37th, and 46th Armies will widen the bridgeheads on the right bank of the river.[9]

Malinovsky's forces began implementing his plan immediately after receiving the *Stavka*'s approval. Early on 11 April, the 57th, 37th, and 46th, armies, the 8th Guards Army, and the cavalry divisions from Pliev's Cavalry-Mechanized Group, advancing abreast from north to south, began pursuing the disorganized German forces westward toward the Dnestr River, with forward detachments from each of their corps leading the pursuit. However, since they were still busily clearing German stragglers from Odessa's alleys, streets, and buildings, the 5th Shock and 6th Armies were unable to join the pursuit for at least a week. Once they completed securing Odessa, Malinovsky ordered the two armies to advance westward and reinforce his forward armies whenever and wherever required.

The 57th Army's Advance to Butory, Krasnaia Gorka, and Parkany

Supported by small groups of tanks from Akhmanov's 23rd Tank Corps and Lieutenant Colonel V. A. Kulibabenko's 96th Tank Brigade, the three rifle corps of Gagen's 57th Army began their pursuit at dawn on 11 April, advancing 12 miles westward throughout the day against only light resistance from the withdrawing divisions of the Sixth Army's LII and XXX Army Corps.[10] As described by Malinovsky in his order of 8 April, the mission of Gagen's army was "conducting the main attack in your center, force the Dnestr River from the march in the Butor [Butory] Station [three miles south of Tashlyk and 18 miles north of Tiraspol'] and Varnitsa [seven miles west of Tiraspol'] sector and capture a bridgehead on the right bank of the Dnestr River from Telitsa [eight miles southwest of Butory] through Roshkan' [Roshkany] [12 miles southward of Butory and 15 miles northwest of Tiraspol'] and the forest south of Kalfa [11 miles northwest of Tiraspol'] to Varnitsa [seven miles west of Tiraspol']."[11] This required Gagen's army to reach the Dnestr River, force its way across the river, capture a bridgehead roughly 13 miles wide and up to six miles deep on the river's western bank before the Germans could erect strong defenses, and prepare to support the 37th Army's advance toward Kishinev on its left (southern) flank (Map 9).

Gagen's army deployed for the advance to the river with Mul'tan's 68th Rifle Corps advancing through Velikokomarovka toward Butory, three miles south of Tashlyk, on the army's right wing; Anashkin's 64th Rifle Corps through Malaeshty toward Krasnaia Gorka, ten miles south of Tashlyk, in the army's center; and Roslyi's 9th Rifle Corps through Slavianoserbka toward Varnitsa, 15 miles south of Tashlyk and seven miles west of Tiraspol', on the army's left wing. Throughout the advance, the 375th Separate Tank Destroyer Regiment, a company of the 251st Army Motorized Engineer Battalion, and a platoon from the army's military construction detachment supported Mul'tan's corps; a company from the same motorized engineer battalion and a military construction platoon supported Anashkin's corps; and the 595th Tank Destroyer Regiment and engineer and construction support equivalent to the other rifle corps assisted Roslyi's corps. Finally, Akhmanov's 23rd Tank Corps and a smaller tank group from the 68th Tank Brigade were "to concentrate 4 kilometers [2.5 miles] northeast of Malaeshty, prepare to advance in the sector of Anashkin's rifle corps, cross the Dnestr in the Tokmazeia and Bychok sector [midway between Krasnaia Gorka and Varnitsa] and exploit in the general direction of Roshkany and Tsintsareny [7–15 miles west of the Dnestr]."[12]

The 13-mile-wide sector of the Dnestr River Malinovsky assigned to Gagen's army as its objective extended from the town and nearby railroad station of Butory, on the Dnestr's eastern bank three miles south of Tashlyk and roughly the same distance northeast of the town of Sherpeny on the river's western bank, southward to the village of Varnitsa, which was situated on the river's western bank two miles north of Parkany and seven miles west of Tiraspol'. The Dnestr River in Gagen's sector turned sharply westward three miles south of Sherpeny and then flowed westward five miles, southward five miles, and back eastward five miles to Krasnaia Gorka, where it resumed flowing southward toward Bendery, on the river's western bank seven miles west of Tiraspol'. Thus, the river in this sector formed a U-shaped bend, five miles wide and five miles deep, jutting westward to the village of Speia in the north and the village of Tokmazeia in the south. When Gagen's army approached the river's eastern bank, German forces defended the "bottleneck" in this bend east of the river and the river's western bank north and south of the bend.

The terrain on the river's eastern bank was quite low, flat, and free of major obstacles, although it rose gently to a height of roughly 240 feet in the middle of the river bend. In contrast, the terrain on the river's western bank was also relatively low for a distance of almost two miles from the river north and south of the river bend but rose precipitously to heights of up to 450 feet west of the river bend, especially north and south of the village of Telitsa, which was situated less than one mile from the river's western bank. This meant that, while it would be relatively easy for Gagen's forces to seize bridgeheads just north and south of the river bend, it would be far more difficult for his forces to secure the heights in the Telitsa region and those inland from the low ground north and south of the river bend, particularly if the Germans chose to strongly defend this high ground.

Gagen's forces began reaching the eastern bank of the Dnestr River along the front extending from Butory southward to the eastern bank of the river opposite Varnitsa at midday on 12 April. Beginning at about 1200 hours, the forward elements of Major General A. Ia. Kruze's 93rd Rifle Division from Mul'tan's 68th Rifle Corps crossed the Dnestr River near Butory by employing makeshift means and overcame weak forward outposts deployed by the German 320th Infantry Division near the village of Sherpeny on the river's western bank. The remainder of Kruze's rifle division crossed the river over the next several hours, ultimately occupying a small but relatively secure bridgehead on the river's western bank. By day's end, Colonel P. V. Dmitriev's 113th Rifle Division, also from Mul'tan's rifle corps, crossed the river and helped Kruze's riflemen expand and strengthen their bridgehead. At the same time, Mul'tan's third division, Colonel P. M. Tatarchevsky's 223rd Rifle Division, reached the Dnestr River south of Krasnaia Gorka, but was unable to force its way across the river.

While Mul'tan's forces were seizing their bridgehead near Butory, Gagen ordered Anashkin's 64th Rifle Corps, which was advancing westward toward the Dnestr on Mul'tan's left, to move his three rifle divisions forward to the Dnestr north and south of Krasnaia Gorka, penetrate the Germans' defenses in the bend in the river jutting westward between Butory and Krasnaia Gorka, and seize bridgeheads of their own across the river near or north of Krasnaia Gorka. At the time the German XXX Army Corps was defending the eastern base of the bend in the Dnestr River with Division Group 235 of its Corps Detachment "A," which manned defenses on the river's eastern bank from just south of Sherpeny to just north of Krasnaia Gorka, and the western bank of the river from Krasnaia Gorka southward to Bychok with Corps Detachment "A's" Division Group 125.

After Major General S. A. Kozak's 73rd Guards Rifle Division, which was leading the advance by Anashkin's rifle corps toward the Dnestr, cleared German rear guards from the town of Malaeshty, five miles east of the river, late on 11 April, Anashkin ordered Kozak's division, supported by Major General P. E. Lazarev's 19th and Colonel L. M. Miliaev's 52nd Rifle Divisions, which were advancing westward on Kozak's flanks, to continue their advance, liquidate the Germans' bridgehead north of Krasnaia Gorka, and cross the Dnestr south of the village. Moving westward through the darkness, the 73rd Guards Rifle Division's 211th Guards Rifle Regiment captured the northern portion of Krasnaia Gorka at first light on 12 April. The riflemen from Kozak's 214th Guards Rifle Regiment then advanced southward roughly three miles along the river's eastern bank and seized the village of Bychok, while a special reconnaissance group from the division crossed the river north of Krasnaia Gorka on makeshift rafts and captured a small bridgehead on its western bank. However, intense German artillery, mortar, and machine-gun fire prevented both the 211th and 214th Guards Rifle Regiments from reinforcing the reconnaissance group's bridgehead. While the intense fighting raged on the river's western bank west of Krasnaia Gorka, Miliaev's 52nd Rifle Division took advantage of the situation by forcing its way across the river south of the village of Gura-Bykuly, midway between Krasnaia Gorka and Bychok, also on makeshift means. By nightfall on 12 April, Anashkin quickly moved the 211th and 214th Guards Rifle Regiments from Kozak's rifle division into Miliaev's new bridgehead.

Although they had successfully crossed the Dnestr at Gura-Bykuly, Kozak's and Miliaev's rifle divisions could not enlarge their bridgehead because they were pinned down by heavy artillery, mortar, and machine-gun flanking fire from German forces defending their own bridgehead on the river's eastern bank, particularly from artillery dug in on the heights around the villages of Teia, Tokmazeia, and Speia, which dominated the lower ground to the south. To deal with this threat, Anashkin dispatched the 209th Guards Rifle Regiment from Kozak's 73rd Guards Division and the same division's training battalion to reinforce Lazarev's 19th Rifle Division, which was attempting to eliminate the German bridgehead to the north but without much success. Even with these reinforcements, however, Gagen's army was not able to overcome German Division Group 235's firm defenses on the east bank of the Dnestr until 16 April.

Further to south on the left wing of Gagen's 57th Army, the forward detachments of the 118th, 230th, and 301st Rifle Divisions of Major General I. P. Roslyi's 9th Rifle Corps reached the Dnestr's eastern bank between Bychok and Varnitsa, just north of Parkany, late on 11 April. The German XXX Army Corps defended this sector of the river with the remnants of its 384th and 257th Infantry Divisions. As was the case with the 57th Army's other rifle corps, as Roslyi recalled in his memoirs, his corps encountered difficult terrain conditions and lacked adequate support:

> We were able to compensate for the many genuine weaknesses in our preparations to force so formidable a water obstacle only by fast action. The corps reached the Dnestr without its authorized crossing equipment and could not count on reliable artillery and aviation support. The rasputitsa and the lack of roads forced serious alterations in our plans.
>
> Certainly we understood that the mission would not be easy, even though we began preparations for forcing the Dnestr immediately after we overcame the Southern Bug [River], specifically, when our headquarters caught up with Gagen, the army commander, in the Domanevka region. He delineated the boundaries of our corps' attack and assigned us the mission of forcing the Dnestr from the march in the Bychok and Varnitsa sector and capturing a bridgehead on the opposite bank.[13]

After the forward detachments from his three rifle divisions reached the Dnestr River between Bychok and Varnitsa, because of the acute shortage of proper river-crossing equipment, Roslyi's riflemen gathered up local materials, including wood, furniture, and even wooden doors from nearby houses and other buildings and used this material to construct rafts and makeshift boats. The 1050th Rifle Regiment from Colonel V. S. Antonov's 301st Rifle Division began crossing the river shortly after noon, a platoon and company at a time on these fragile rafts and boats. Despite heavy German machine-gun fire, the regiment's 1st Battalion managed to cross the river just south of Bychok, captured the Germans' first trench line, and assaulted Hill 65.3, which was situated less than one mile southwest of Bychok. The regiment's 2nd Battalion and headquarters group also successfully crossed the river an hour later.

Meanwhile, to the south, the 986th and 988th Rifle Regiments of Colonel I. A. Kazakov's 230th Rifle Division also crossed the river near the village of Varnitsa, three to four miles south of Bychok, also a battalion at a time, but in this case employing a locally procured ferryboat that the Germans had abandoned. About two miles to the south, Colonel F. G. Dobrovol'sky's 118th Rifle Division captured the northern portion of the town of Parkany and also managed to secure a small bridgehead on the river's western bank. Despite clearly stiffening German resistance, Antonov's and Kazakov's 301st and 230th Rifle Divisions managed to capture Hill 65.3 and all of Varnitsa by early on 13 April, while Dobrovol'sky's division kept pace in the south. Thereafter, however, a new phase of the battle began as German artillery fire and air strikes struck the corps' forward positions continuously; regrouped German forces, including the 536th, 535th, and 534th Infantry Regiments from the XXX Army Corps' 384th Infantry Division, which were deployed from the Bychok region southward to Varnitsa, and the 257th Infantry Division's 457th Infantry Regiment, which was defending the river's western bank opposite Parkany, began counterattacks aimed at driving Roslyi's troops back into the river.

Although the three rifle corps of Gagen's 57th Army managed to capture multiple small bridgeheads on the western bank of the Dnestr River by day's end on 12 April, they clearly failed to fulfill the mission Malinovsky assigned to them. Instead of capturing one large bridgehead 13 miles wide and six miles deep on the river's western bank, most of the bridgeheads Gagen's forces seized were no more than two miles wide and less than half a mile deep, and all of them were confined to the low ground adjacent to the river's western bank. Since the Germans still controlled the heights around these bridgeheads, they also remained acutely vulnerable to enemy artillery, mortar fire, and machine-gun fire and to destruction by German counterattacks.

While Gagen later credited his army's limited success in crossing the Dnestr to the disorganization of German forces after their hasty withdrawal to the river, he ruefully noted this disorganization did not endure for very long. Consequently, on Malinovsky's orders, Gagen's forces went over to the defense on 14 April, while he prepared his forces to renew their assaults when his *front* commander ordered him to do so. Temporarily, at least, Malinovsky began looking elsewhere to secure an operationally significant foothold on the Dnestr's western bank. By this time the most promising prospects for doing so seemed to be further south, in the offensive sector of Sharokhin's 37th Army.

The 37th Army's Advance to Tiraspol'

After fencing with the withdrawing forces of the German Sixth Army from 7 through 10 April, the forward elements of Sharokhin's 37th Army began approaching the Dnestr River in the Tiraspol' sector late on 11 April.[14] The mission Malinovsky had issued to Sharokhin's army on 8 April was to pursue German forces to the Dnepr River with his three rifle corps advancing abreast, capture the city of Tiraspol', force the river from the march in the sector from one mile north of Parkany (west of Tiraspol') southward to the vicinity of the town of Slobodzeia Russkaia, 13 miles south of Tiraspol', capture a bridgehead roughly 15 miles wide and seven miles deep on the river's western bank southwest of Tiraspol', and prepare to pursue German forces toward Kishinev.

The configuration of the Dnestr River and the surrounding terrain in the sector from Parkany southward through Tiraspol' to Slobodzeia Russkaia seemed to offer Sharokhin's army excellent prospects for successfully fulfilling the mission Malinovsky assigned to it. The bridgehead Sharokhin's forces were to capture resembled a right-angle triangle formed by the Dnestr River, which, after flowing southward past Parkany, turned due eastward just south of Parkany, flowed eastward eight miles to Tiraspol', and then turned 90 degrees southward at Tiraspol' and flowed southward 12 miles past Slobodzeia Russkaia.

As was the case further to the north, this triangular-shaped bridgehead encompassed low-lying terrain, averaging 100–200 feet in elevation, was dotted with small lakes and swamps, and was traversed by several smaller rivers, including the Botna River, which flowed into the Dnestr from the west. Even though a ridge extending from north to south in the bridgehead rose to a height of up to 400 feet, the higher ground west of the bridgehead, which rose sharply to an average height of 450 feet, dominated over the lowlands within the bridgehead itself. In addition, the Germans turned several towns and villages on the approaches to the western heights or on the heights themselves into formidable strong points.

Since the perimeter around this bridgehead was too long for German forces to easily defend and the terrain within it was rather low, flat, and difficult to defend, Malinovsky and Sharokhin believed their forces could capture it with relative ease. Thereafter, they hoped these forces could seize the high ground west of the river's bend before the Germans could react. As was the case further north, however, the problem was that, if the Germans reacted quickly and effectively, they could confine the attacking Russian forces in the lowlands west of the Dnestr.

Sharokhin's army began its advance toward Tiraspol' and the Dnestr River two rifle corps abreast, and his third rifle corps echeloned just behind his advancing army's left wing (Map 9). On his army's right wing, the three rifle divisions of Major General F. A. Ostashenko's 57th Rifle Corps proceeded westward through Blizhnii Khutor (Farm) toward Parkany, seven miles west of Tiraspol', with the mission of capturing Tiraspol' by assaulting the city from the north, seizing Parkany, crossing the Dnestr River, and capturing the town of Bendery and the adjacent narrow strip of high ground on the river's western bank. On his army's left wing to the south, the three rifle divisions of Major General P. G. Kuznetsov's 82nd Rifle Corps advanced through Vladimirovka to Karagazh, six miles south of Tiraspol', with the mission of helping Ostashenko's rifle corps capture Tiraspol', seizing the towns of Karagazh and Slobodzeia Moldavanskaia on the river's eastern bank, and assaulting across the Dnestr River to capture a large bridgehead on the river's western bank, including the German strong points at the town of Kitskany, in the middle of the bridgehead five miles south of Tiraspol', and Kirkaieshty, on higher ground just west of the bridgehead and ten miles southwest of Tiraspol'.

Finally, echeloned to the left rear of Kuznetsov's rifle corps, Major General G. P. Kotov's 6th Guards Rifle Corps was to follow the division on Kuznetsov's left wing, attack from behind Kuznetsov's left wing, capture the towns of Slobodzeia Moldavanskaia and Slobodzeia Russkaia, cross the Dnestr River, and seize the southern portion of the bridgehead on the river's western bank around the German strong point at the village of Kopanka, ten miles south of Tiraspol'.

Ostashenko's 57th Rifle Corps swept westward toward the northern outskirts of Tiraspol' on 10 and 11 April with Major General M. I. Matveev's 92nd Guards, Colonel I. N. Esin's 228th Rifle, and Colonel V. V. Rusakov's 58th Guards Rifle Divisions deployed from left to right (south to north), flanked on the left by Colonel V. Ia. Danilenko's 188th Rifle Division from Kuznetsov's 82nd Rifle Corps. While Matveev's and Esin's rifle divisions cleared German forces from the Tiraspol' overnight on 11–12 April and then raced westward toward the Dnestr River south of Parkany, Rusakov's division advanced to the Dnestr just north of Parkany. However, the 457th Infantry Regiment and other forces of the XXX Army Corps' 257th Infantry Division stoutly defended the river's western bank, containing the main forces of Ostashenko's attacking divisions east of the river. About one mile to the north, however, Rusakov's 58th Guards Rifle Division managed to secure a small bridgehead on the river's western bank near Varnitsa, and, to the south, Esin's 228th Rifle Division did the same near the village of Ternovskaia Plava, just south of Bendery. Both Colonels Rusakov and Danilenko were wounded during this heavy fighting and were replaced by Colonels V. I. Katsurin and S. S. Senin, respectively, who went on to command these divisions throughout the struggle along the Dnestr River.[15]

While Ostashenko's 57th Rifle Corps and the single rifle division from Kuznetsov's 82nd Rifle Corps were clearing German forces from the city of Tiraspol' and the surrounding region, further to the south, the remainder of Kuznetsov's rifle corps and Kotov's 6th Guards Rifle Corps were able to make more spectacular progress. After clearing German forces from Tiraspol' and capturing Karagazh, five miles to the south, by late evening on 11 April, Major General G. I. Churmaev's 28th Guards and Colonel A. N. Petrushin's 10th Guards Airborne Divisions from Kuznetsov's rifle corps forced their way across the Dnestr and captured Kitskany in the swampy flood plain to the west the next day. At the same time, Major General N. M. Dreier's 20th Guards Rifle and Colonel I. N. Kholodov's 195th Rifle Divisions, on the left wing of Kotov's corps, captured the eastern approaches to Slobodzeia Moldavanskaia, eight miles south of Tiraspol', on 10 April. Soon after, Kotov ordered Dreier to complete seizing the town and begin crossing the Dnestr with two of his rifle regiments during the following night.[16]

Kotov's order required Dreier's airborne troopers to occupy jumping-off positions in the village of Novo-Krasnoe, several miles east of Slobodzeia Moldavanskaia, at 2000 hours on 10 April; then to attack through Verbovka toward Slobodzeia Moldavanskaia from behind the right wing of the 195th Rifle Division, destroy the opposing German forces (rear guard element of the XXX Army Corps' 97th Jäger Division), force the Dnestr River from the march, and seize a bridgehead on the river's western bank. Attacking from the march at 2200 hours, the forward battalions of Dreier's two first-echelon rifle regiments drove the Germans' rear guards from the village of Varvarovka and advanced rapidly toward the Dnestr. Meanwhile, a cavalry reconnaissance platoon from the division's reconnaissance company advanced into Slobodzeia Moldavanskaia, where it encountered the German 522nd Security Battalion, which was manning fortified positions. In a coordinated assault alongside the regiments of Kholodov's 195th Rifle Division, the 55th Guards Rifle Regiment of Dreier's division shattered the Germans' defenses, captured the town by 0800 hours on 11 April after a brief but intense fight, and advanced to the eastern bank of the Dnestr.

As the lead elements of his division reached the Dnestr, at 1430 hours Dreier ordered his division's 60th Guards Rifle Regiment to assault across the river and advance to capture the Germans' main strong point at Kopanka, which was situated in the center of the river's broad flood plain. After a running fight, Dreier's 55th and 60th Rifle Regiments captured Kopanka at 1800 hours on 11 April, and, soon after, the rifle regiments of Kholodov's 195th Rifle Division poured across the river and occupied blocking positions facing to the southeast. However, after capturing Kopanka, Dreier's second-echelon rifle regiment, the 57th Guards, which he had previously ordered to assault and capture the hills west of Kopanka and expand the bridgehead to the west, was unable to do so because of intense German fire. By this time the XXX Army Corps' 3rd Mountain and 97th Jäger Divisions, flanked on the left by Division Group 15 (the remnants of the 15th Infantry Division), were manning strong defenses along the western perimeter of the bridgehead.

At day's end on 11 April, Sharokhin ordered Kuznetsov to dispatch Churmaev's and Petrushin's 28th Guards Rifle and 10th Guards Airborne Divisions from his 82nd Rifle Corps into the bridgehead south of Tiraspol' to reinforce the assaults by the divisions of Kotov's 6th Guards Rifle Corps against the German defenses on the heights northwest of Kopanka. While the ensuing combined assault propelled Kotov's forces to the eastern shore of Lake Botna, which was situated on the Botna River about ten miles southwest of Tiraspol' and at the base of the heights defining the western edge of the flatlands west of the Dnestr, another assault by Dreier's entire 20th Guards Division against German defenses around the village of Fantina-Maskui on the lake's southern shore failed to capture the village because Division Group 15 and the newly arrived German 3rd Mountain Division had erected strong defenses on the high ground west of the lake and village.

Dissatisfied with Sharokhin's limited progress, late on 12 April, Malinovsky ordered Sharokhin's army "to penetrate the enemy's defenses north and south of Bendery, reach the Novye Lipkany, Gyska, and Kirkaieshty line [six to seven miles west and southwest of Bendery] and capture the fortress of Bendery by day's end on 14 April."[17] Since not enough time was available for Sharokhin to regroup his forces properly, the army commander simplified his original missions by ordering Ostashenko's 57th Rifle Corps to capture Novye Lipkany, one mile southwest of Bendery, and Varnitsa on the Dnestr's western bank north of Bendery, and Kuznetsov's 82nd Rifle Corps to clear German forces from the Suvorov Heights and the village of Gyska, four miles south of Bendery, which, if captured, would prevent German movement into or out of Bendery along roads to the south and southwest. However, since Sharokhin's artillery preparation against the German defenses, which began at 0700 hours on 13 April, proved utterly ineffective, the assault by Ostashenko's and Kuznetsov's rifle corps ended in total failure.

To help break the stalemate, soon after, Malinovsky decided to reinforce Kuznetsov's rifle corps southeast of Bendery with an M-31 (*Katiusha*) guards-mortar brigade, the 864th Self-propelled Artillery Regiment, and the 301st Guards-Mortar Regiment and also directed Akhmanov's 23rd Tank Corps to reinforce Kuznetsov's forces with additional tanks. However, since these forces arrived too late to provide the necessary support, Kuznetsov's assault, which took place on 16 April, also ended in failure. Heavy fighting also raged for several days throughout the entire expanse of Sharokhin's bridgehead south of Tiraspol' as the four rifle divisions of Kuznetsov's and Kotov's rifle corps struggled to encompass the heights to the west. By day's end on 17 April, Sharokhin's army had managed to expand its bridgehead south of Tiraspol' to a width of roughly nine miles and to a depth of up to nine miles.

Compounding the German Sixth Army's defensive dilemmas, by this time its intelligence organs detected the presence of the forward rifle divisions of the Soviet 46th Army approaching the eastern bank of the Dnestr River in the Glinoe region, 16 miles south of Tiraspol'. German intelligence assessed that the 46th Army's forces would soon attempt to cross the river in this region, seize the southern extension of the triangular-shaped lowlands west of the Dnestr and south of Tiraspol', and assault their strong points at the villages of Talmazy and Chebruchi, which were situated on the heights four to five miles west of the Dnestr River's western bank, 14–16 miles south of Tiraspol', by doing so, expanding the 37th Army's existing bridgehead farther to the south. Fortunately for the Sixth Army, by this time the German XXX Army Corps had managed to establish continuous defenses along the cliffs overlooking the Dnestr River's flood plains from Bendery southward almost 18 miles to the Chebruchi region, manning these defenses with its 257th, 15th, 3rd Mountain, and 97th Jäger Divisions.

Despite the 37th Army's failure to break out into the open country west of the Dnestr River south of Tiraspol', the large bridgeheads it seized by day's end on 17 April were significant and offered clear opportunities for a further successful advance. Driven on by the *Stavka,* Malinovsky began planning for a decisive westward advance, this time exploiting the 37th Army's impressive gains with his reserve 6th Army and 5th Shock Army.

The 46th Army's Advance to Chebruchi and Oloneshty

Malinovsky's 8 April order to Glagolev's 46th Army required its forces to advance toward the Dnestr as rapidly as possible in the sector stretching southward from Chebruchi, 16 miles south of Tiraspol', through Oloneshty, 28 miles southeast of Tiraspol', to Kormazy [Korkmazy], 33 miles southeast of Tiraspol'; force the Dnestr and capture the German strong points on the river's western bank; and prepare to protect the southern flank of Sharokhin's 37th Army as it continued its exploitation westward toward Kishinev. In response to Malinovsky's order, Glagolev ordered his rifle corps to advance abreast in single echelon toward the river (Map 10). On his army's right wing, Major General A. I. Ruchkin's 31st Guards Rifle Corps, with the 40th and 34th Guards Rifle Divisions in the lead and the 4th Guards Rifle Division in second echelon, were to clear German forces from the town of Glinoe on the eastern bank of the Dnestr 16 miles south of Tiraspol', assault across the river at Chebruchi and south of the village, capture the German strong point, and prepare to expand its bridgehead to the west.

On Ruchkin's left (southern) flank, the 236th and 394th Rifle Divisions of Major General I. S. Kosobutsky's smaller 34th Rifle Corps were to advance to the river in the sector east of Raskaetsy, 20 miles south of Tiraspol', capture the towns of Korotnoe and Nezaertailovka, which were adjacent to the river's eastern bank, force the river in this sector, capture the German strong point at Raskaetsy, and prepare to expand their operations toward the west.

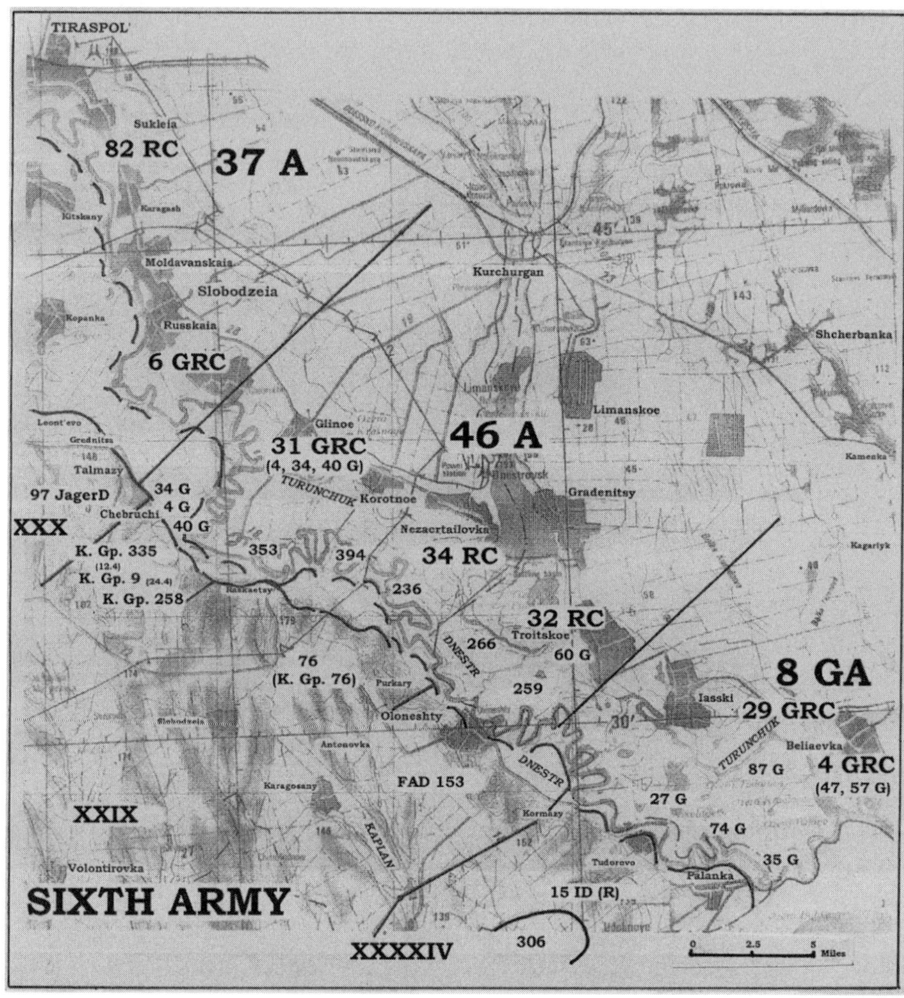

Map 10. The 46th and 8th Guards Armies' bridgehead battles, 12–14 April 1944

Finally, on the 46th Army's left wing, the 60th Guards and 259th and 266th Rifle Divisions of Major General D. S. Zherebin's 32nd Rifle Corps were to approach the river, capture the town of Troitskoe on the river's eastern bank, 28 miles south of Tiraspol', force the river at Oloneshty, capture this German strong point, and prepare to expand its assault in tandem with Chuikov's 8th Guards Army, which was supposed to advance on Glagolev's left (southern) flank.

Although the river sector Malinovsky ordered Glagolev's army to surmount was far straighter than the river in the 57th and 37th Armies' sectors, crossing it still posed several formidable problems for Glagolev's troops. First, in addition to being far wider than it was further north, the river's flood plain in this sector extended up to three miles eastward from the river's eastern bank. Second, wet weather had flooded most of this plain, making it exceedingly difficult to traverse. Compounding Glagolev's problems, except in the Chebruchi region, where low ground extended roughly three miles west of the river to the approaches to Chebruchi on high ground to the west, farther to the south the flood plain on the river's western bank was less than half a mile wide and was dominated by high ground rising to heights of 450–500 feet, which was occupied by enemy forces in ever-increasing strength.

The lead elements of the three rifle corps of Glagolev's army reached the eastern bank of the Dnestr River beginning late on 11 April and immediately began preparing to conduct river-crossing operations the following morning. The first element of Glagolev's army to reach the river was Major General G. F. Panchenko's 40th Guards Rifle Division of Ruchkin's 31st Guards Rifle Corps, which reached the river west of Glinoe, and it was soon joined by Major General F. V. Brailian's 34th Guards Rifle Divisions, which closed up to the river on Panchenko's left flank. Further south, the lead elements of the army's 34th and 32nd Rifle Corps reached the river in several locations southward toward the town of Oloneshty.[18]

Noting that "the remnants of defeated enemy divisions are withdrawing to the western bank of the Dnestr River, where they are putting themselves into order and preparing defenses," Glagolev ordered Panchenko's 40th Guards Rifle Division, together with its supporting 269th Army Pontoon-Bridge Brigade, to:

> Force the Dnestr River in the sector from Chebruchi (incl.) [southward] to Marker 107.5 and reach positions from 500 meters northeast of Hill 145.1 through the western entrance of the forest 2.5 kilometers [1.5 miles] west of Raskaetsy [five miles south of Chebruchi], and subsequently capture Chebruchi and Hill 174.5. Begin the forcing [river crossing] operation at 2100 hours on 13 April 1944. The units of the 6th Rifle Corps [of Sharokhin's 37th Army] will attack on your right flank. The units of the 34th Guards Rifle Division will force the river on your left flank.[19]

Panchenko immediately decided to:

> Make the main attack on the left wing toward the forest west of Raskaetsy and Hill 174.5 with two regiments in first echelon and the third regiment in second echelon.

The 111th Guards Rifle Regiment will force the Dnestr with a forward detachment consisting of assault companies with two field artillery pieces to capture a bridgehead along the line from Chebruchi to Marker 107.5 to protect the crossing of the regiment's main forces.

When the main forces reach the positions of the assault company, the 111th Guards Rifle Regiment will capture the western entrance to the forest west of Raskaetsy and will subsequently reach positions extending from the unnamed heights 130 to Hill 174.5. The artillery infantry support group is the 2nd Battalion, 90th Guards Artillery Regiment. . . .

The 119th Guards Rifle Regiment will force the Dnestr River and, conducting its main attack on its left wing, will capture the southern outskirts of Chebruchi and the road junction two kilometers [1.2 miles] south of Chebruchi and will subsequently reach positions from the western outskirts of Chebruchi to the unnamed heights 130 (6202-A). The artillery support group is the 3rd Battalion, 90th Guards Artillery Regiment. . . .

The 116th Guards Rifle Regiment will force the Dnestr River and reach the region of the western entrance to the forest 2.5 kilometers [1.5 miles] west of Raskaetsy and be prepared to conduct a counterattack toward Chebruchi and Hill 174.5. . . . The artillery of the 90th Guards Artillery Regiment will suppress the enemy's firing system along the forward edge and in the depths, prevent possible enemy counterattacks from Chebruchi, the forest 2.5 kilometers [1.5 miles] west of Raskaetsy, and Raskaetsy, and disrupt the approach of enemy reserves along the roads to Kizyl, Slobodzeia, Chebruchi, and Raskaetsy. Be prepared to fire by 1700 hours 13 April 1944.

The 41st Tank Destroyer Artillery Battalion, my mobile antitank reserve, will be prepared to engage enemy counterattacks with its tanks.[20]

As Glagolev's army prepared to assault across the Dnestr River, the Sixth Army was defending the 15-mile-wide sector along the river's western bank from Chebruchi southward to Oloneshty with the forces on the right (southern) wing of its XXX Army Corps and its entire XXIX Army Corps. On the XXX Army Corps' right wing, the 97th Jäger Division's 207th Regiment defended the four-mile-wide sector from north of Chebruchi northward to Talmazy, while Division Groups 335 and 258 (*Kampfgruppen* 335 and 258), on the XXIX Army Corps' left (northern) wing, defended the six-mile-wide sector from Chebruchi proper southward to Raskaetsy. Further south, the XXIX Army Corps' 76th Infantry Division defended the western bank of the Dnestr in the six-mile-wide sector from just south of Raskaetsy to Purkary, and the forces of the 153rd Field Training Division (FAD 153) and separate security elements defended the five-mile-wide sector from Purkary southward to the Oloneshty region.

Panchenko's 40th Guards Rifle Division began its attack promptly at 2100 hours on the night of 13 April when its forward detachment forced the Dnestr River one-half mile east of Chebruchi and, as ordered, seized a small bridgehead on the river's western bank about 600 yards south of Chebruchi to Marker 107.5 by 0200 hours the next morning. After the remainder of the division crossed into the bridgehead, at 0900 hours the division's 111th Guards Rifle Regiment assaulted Division Group 335's defenses at Chebruchi, capturing the southeastern portion of the town and the hills just to the south. After the XXIX Army Corps reinforced its defenses south of Chebruchi at about midday with additional forces from Division Group 258, both forces launched a series of concerted counterattacks. Panchenko responded by committing his 116th and 119th Guards Rifle Regiments in a coordinated assault on the town's defenses, and later still, his corps commander, Ruchkin, reinforced his division with additional forces from the 34th Guards Rifle Division. However, the Germans met these assaults with fresh counterattacks of their own—Panchenko recorded a total of seven throughout the day—which by nightfall halted his division in its tracks. In the heavy fighting on 13–14 April, during which Panchenko reported 30 soldiers killed and 89 wounded, although his division managed to capture the small bridgehead southeast of Chebruchi, it could not overcome the German defenses even after being reinforced by elements of the 34th Guards Rifle Division.

Nor was the situation any better further to the south, where the 46th Army's 34th Rifle and 32nd Rifle Corps were attempting to cross the river at Raskaetsy southward through Purkary to Oloneshty. For example, Major General N. F. Tsepliaev's 236th and Colonel L. G. Sergeev's 294th Rifle Divisions from Kosubutsky's 34th Rifle Corps managed to capture small but precarious footholds on the narrow strip of flatlands west of the river east of Raskaetsy and Purkary, and Major General A. M. Vlasenko's 259th and Colonel S. M. Fomichenko's 266th Rifle Divisions from Zherebin's 32nd Rifle Corps later seized several meager footholds across the river near Oloneshty. However, the broad flood plains to their rear, which were swollen with water, hindered and sometimes totally prevented the forward movement of heavy weapons, equipment, and necessary supplies, particularly ammunition. In such circumstances, Glagolev had no choice but to call a halt to his offensive.

Compounding Glagolev's obvious problems with the enemy and the terrain was the disturbing fact that Chuikov's 8th Guards Army and Pliev's Cavalry-Mechanized Group, which completed investing Odessa on 10 April, required considerable time to move their forces forward to the Dnestr River on Glagolev's left flank. Thus, while the main forces of Glagolev's 31st Guards and 34th Rifle Corps were struggling for control of bridgeheads across the Dnestr River, the bulk of Zherebin's 32nd Rifle Corps had to defend the army's extended left flank and rear, while Chuikov's forces slowly closed forward to their assigned attack sectors along the southern reaches of the Dnestr River. In fact, the inclement weather and soggy terrain prevented Chuikov's army from even beginning to accomplish his assigned missions.

The 8th Guards Army's and Pliev's Cavalry-Mechanized Group Advance to Palanka and Ovidiopol'

When Malinovsky's offensive to capture Odessa ended successfully on 10 April, the bulk of Chuikov's 8th Guards Army—including his 4th, 28th, and 29th Guards Rifle Corps and most of his supporting artillery—were either in downtown Odessa or on the city's western and northwestern outskirts. At the same time, the forces of Pliev's Cavalry-Mechanized Group were either supporting Chuikov's thrust, advancing southward to capture key points east of the Dnestr River, or preparing to man an extensive cordon west and southwest of the city to prevent elements of the German LXXII Army Corps from escaping. Nevertheless, escape they did in regimental, battalion, and company groups, many of which created serious problems for Pliev's fragile cavalry divisions. Fighting their way along the roads leading from Odessa toward Kagarlyk (25 miles west of Odessa and 15 miles east of the Dnestr River), Beliaevka and Maiaki, on the eastern bank of the Dnestr 25 miles west of Odessa, and further south toward Nikolaevka, Ovidiopol', and Zatoka (on the eastern bank of the Dnestr estuary 20–22 miles southwest of Odessa), these escaping groups struggled to cut their way through Pliev's screening forces from 7 through 10 April.

By the morning of 8 April, the 9th Guards and the 30th and 10th Guards Cavalry Divisions of Pliev's 4th Guards Cavalry Corps had captured the towns of Beliaevka, Il'ichevka, and Maiaki on the eastern bank of the Dnestr River near its mouth and on the northeastern shore of the Dnestr estuary and were occupying blocking positions toward the east. Meanwhile, forces from Zhdanov's 4th Guards Mechanized Corps were manning a defensive screen extending north and south along the road east of Maiaki to block German forces withdrawing from Odessa. Immediately after his forces captured Odessa, Malinovsky ordered Pliev's Cavalry-Mechanized Group and Chuikov's 8th Guards Army to conduct a joint operation to clear German forces from the eastern bank of the Dnestr and occupy positions on the eastern shore of the Dnestr estuary from Il'ichevka southward to the town and railroad station of Karolino Bugaz on the Black Sea coast.

Pliev's cavalry, tanks, and riflemen began carrying out their assigned missions late on 11 April, when the 9th Guards and 30th Cavalry Divisions, later joined by Zhdanov's 4th Guards Mechanized Corps and Colonel N. I. Zav'ialov's 5th Separate Motorized Rifle Brigade, advanced about five miles eastward from Beliaevka and Maiaki on the Dnestr, captured Gross-Leibental (Velikodolinskoe) and Aleksandrovka, and the region to the north and south by 0900 hours. However, during this advance, Pliev's forces encountered large combat groups from the German 304th Infantry Division's 574th and 575th Infantry Regiments and the 335th and 21st Infantry Divisions, supported by the 302nd Panzer Detachment [Abteilung], which were attempting to escape westward from Odessa.

Halting Pliev's forces in their tracks to their front, but hard pressed by Chuikov's forces which were approaching from the east, after a day-long struggle, the 304th Infantry Division's two regiments broke through Pliev's defenses, lunged westward, and crossed the Dnestr River north of Beliaevka, while small groups from the 335th and 21st Infantry Division and their few supporting tanks cut their way westward through Pliev's blocking positions and reached safety on the Dnestr River's western bank near Beliaevka and Maiaki. However, when they found Pliev's defenses too hard a nut to crack, parts of the same two German divisions had no choice but to retreat southwestward toward Ovidiopol' on the eastern bank of the Dnestr estuary.[21]

At dawn on 13 April, Pliev's forces advanced southeastward in pursuit of the fleeing Germans, capturing the villages of Dal'nik, Gribovka, and Rybachi, east and southeast of Ovidiopol', where the Germans had set up intermediate defensive positions. After further heavy fighting, the German forces abandoned most of their heavier equipment, withdrew southward, and ultimately crossed to the west bank of the Dnestr estuary near its mouth at Karolino Bugaz. However, during their retreat they inflicted heavy casualties on Pliev's 10th Guards Cavalry Division, which was trying to block their movement east of Ovidiopol'. So heavy was the fighting that, once his army joined the pursuit westward, Chuikov had to send his 28th Guards Rifle Corps to assist Pliev's forces in clearing the German forces that were fleeing from the region east of the Dnestr estuary. After Pliev's Cavalry-Mechanized Group completed its mission, late on 13 April, Malinovsky ordered it to assemble in the region northwest of Odessa, where, after resting and refitting, the *Stavka* transferred Pliev's 4th Guards Cavalry Corps northward by train to participate in future operations against German Army Group Center in Belorussia.

While Pliev's forces were clearing the retreating Germans from the region west and southwest of Odessa, Chuikov's 8th Guards Army also began operations westward from Odessa toward the southern reaches of the Dnestr River (Map 10). On 11 April, Malinovsky had assigned Chuikov's and Pliev's forces the missions of operating jointly, "to complete liquidating the enemy forces on the left [eastern] bank of the Dnestr estuary and seize a bridgehead on the right [western] bank of the Dnestr estuary along the Kammenyi Most', Turlaki, Britovka, Shabo Tyrg, and Rybachaia Kuren' line [three to five miles west of the Dnestr estuary] by day's end on 14 April."[22] In practical terms, this meant they were to conduct a two-stage operation: in the first stage, the two forces were to clear all German and Romanian forces from the Palanka region at the northern end of the Dnestr estuary and the western coast of the estuary itself to the Black Sea coast; in the second stage, Chuikov's army was to mount an assault across the Dnestr River to support Glagolev's 46th Army on his right.

However, this was no mean task even in the best of conditions, and in April 1944, the prevailing weather conditions were definitely not cooperative. Although by this time Malinovsky's 57th, 37th, and 46th Armies had already reached the Dnestr River along a front from Tiraspol' southward to Oloneshty, Pliev's forces were still scattered to the winds, manning various screening positions east of Beliaevka and Maiaki, and Chuikov's army was just beginning to concentrate west of Odessa. Compounding Chuikov's problems, heavy rains began to fall, swelling the region's streams and rivers and making all movement slow and treacherous at best.

After receiving his new mission, Chuikov decided to move the bulk of his army, Bobruk's and Glazunov's 29th Guards and 4th Guards Rifle Corps, westward toward Beliaevka and Maiaki on the Dnestr River, while Morozov's 28th Guards Rifle Corps would advance southwestward toward Ovidiopol' on the eastern bank of the Dnestr estuary. After assembling and regrouping their forces on 11 and 12 April, Chuikov's guards rifle corps began their westward advance at midday on the 12th, clearing scattered groups of withdrawing German and Romanian forces from their path. Several times during the next several days, the mud-clogged roads and flooded streams and rivers forced Chuikov to ask and receive permission from Malinovsky to delay his march so that his forces could replenish their ammunition and other supplies. In fact, Chuikov later claimed his army had just 0.4 combat loads of ammunition when it began its initial advance, less than one-fifth of the amount his army required to meet its real offensive requirements.

Leading the 29th Guards Rifle Corps' westward, Colonel D. E. Bakanov's 74th Guards Rifle Division recaptured the town of Maiaki at midday on 14 April, while its 240th Guards Rifle Regiment bypassed the town, pressed on toward the west, and crossed the Dnestr River just east of Palanka. For reasons that remain unclear, Lieutenant General Ia. S. Fokanov had replaced the rifle corps' previous commander, General Bobruk, only the day before. Late on 14 April the remainder of Bakanov's division concentrated on the Dnestr's eastern bank opposite Palanka but reported the river's width had reached 10–12 miles and could not be crossed. At the same time, Major General V. S. Glebov's 27th Guards Rifle Division, also from Fokanov's rifle corps, which had just reached Beliaevka on Bakanov's right wing, reported similar conditions along the Dnestr north of Palanka. By this time, the small forces the two divisions managed to dispatch across the Dnestr River faced prepared defenses manned by the Romanian 15th Infantry Division and German 306th Infantry Divisions of the Sixth Army's XXXXIV Army Corps, both of which were still in the process of reorganizing after their harrowing withdrawal from Odessa.

Further to the south, Major General I. Ia. Kulagin's 35th, Colonel V. M. Shugaev's 47th, and Major General A. D. Shemenkov's 57th Guards Rifle Divisions of Glazunov's 4th Guards Rifle Corps, which were marching in long columns along the few roads in the water-logged region east of the Dnestr River, captured the villages of Roksoliany and Franzfeld, reaching Maiaki by day's end on 15 April. It took two more days of arduous marching for the forward elements of these divisions to traverse the eight miles stretching from Maiaki to the eastern bank of the Dnestr southeast of Palanka. Once there, Kulagin's guards division relieved Glebov's 74th Guards Division, while the remainder of Glazunov's corps remained stretched out along the roads to the rear, utterly stymied by the ubiquitous high waters.

East and southeast of the Dnestr estuary, Lieutenant Colonel V. M. Shtrigol's 39th, Major General L. I. Vagin's 79th, and Colonel E. T. Marchenko's 88th Guards Rifle Divisions of Morozov's 28th Guards Rifle Corps first relieved Pliev's beleaguered cavalrymen, a portion of which were still encircled in the town of Ovidiopol' by German forces escaping from Odessa and then cleared the retreating German forces from the eastern bank of the Dnestr estuary and the northern coast of the Black Sea. However, after Morozov's three divisions finally reached the eastern bank of the estuary from Ovidiopol' southward to Karolino Bugaz, they, too, were thwarted in their attempts to cross the estuary because the spring rains had expanded it to a width of up to six miles. Unable to fulfill its mission because of the high waters, Morozov's guards rifle corps turned on its heels and backtracked northward to Palanka, where it rejoined the remainder of Chuikov's army by 30 and 31 April.

Thus, as recorded by Chuikov, the 8th Guards Army's offensive was completely frustrated by the heavy rains, high water, and soggy ground:

> The elements also hindered our plans.
>
> Beginning on 16 April, strong winds began blowing from the south. The water in the Dnestr estuary began to rise. The rising water level at Tsaregradskii Girl' disrupted the crossing by the 79th Guards Rifle Division.
>
> Then the water began to reach the bridgeheads we had seized west of Beliaevka and Maiaki. The Dnestr overflowed its banks in [many] places on 18 April.
>
> On 20 April the water filled up the foxholes the 35th Guards Rifle Division's units had prepared for their offensive. Each day the army's

headquarters received reports from other units that the water was not ceasing its rise. On the night of 25 April, the night before our offensive, the wind strengthened. The water flooded out our artillery positions and ammunition.[23]

In effect, a combination of regrouping difficulties, enemy resistance, and poor terrain and inclement weather conditions caused the offensive by Chuikov's 8th Guards Army to totally abort. Thus, when Malinovsky made his first attempt to assault across the Dnestr River on 13 April, his most powerful army, Chuikov's 8th Guards Army, was not able to participate in any fashion. As a result, Malinovsky's attempt to force the Dnestr from the march failed by day's end on 14 April. Perhaps realizing it would, as early as 12 April, the *Stavka*, its representative Vasilevsky, and Malinovsky were already beginning to formulate plans for a fresh offensive with an even stronger force, this time in close concert with a more powerful offensive by Konev's 2nd Ukrainian Front toward Iasi from the west.

THE SECOND BRIDGEHEAD BATTLES (19–25 APRIL)

Malinovsky's Plans

The *Stavka* began expressing doubts about the feasibility of Malinovsky's initial plans for forcing the Dnestr as early as 12 April. As Vasilevsky recalled:

> [On the night of 12–13 April, the Stavka] called my attention to the inadmissible delay by Malinovsky while liquidating the enemy's forces on the left bank of the Dnestr and the [enemy] grouping the 8th Guards Army was pressing back against the Dnestr Liman' [estuary] at Ovidiopol' and ordered measures be undertaken. R. Ia. Malinovsky promised me he would quickly fulfill the orders I had passed to him from the Supreme High Commander. We agreed to reinforce the 8th Guards Army with a part of the 5th Shock Army's forces and the 9th and 30th Cavalry Divisions, which the front had been employing as infantry during the prolonged battles, to withdraw them from combat immediately, and to give them the next few days to rest.
>
> On the same night, General A. I. Antonov reported to me that the Stavka had received a proposal from the 3rd Ukrainian Front's military council regarding the conduct of a subsequent operation aimed at reaching the Prut and Danube [Rivers], and that the Supreme High Command had immediately requested I report my opinion concerning this [proposal]. I responded I would immediately participate in working out these proposals. The period for beginning the operation, 18–20 April, was

> determined by the time the 6th Army's and 5th Shock Army's forces would be available to be committed into combat along the new axes. Prior to this time, only the forces at hand would conduct the operation. I requested he examine and approve this plan. The plan was approved.[24]

In short, the *Stavka,* Vasilevsky, and Malinovsky agreed that a new and larger-scale offensive across the Dnestr River was necessary and decided to conduct this offensive from the bridgeheads, which Malinovsky's 57th, 37th, and 46th Armies had captured, in conjunction with an assault by the 2nd Ukrainian Front's 5th Guards Army from its bridgehead at Tashlyk, south of Grigoriopol'. Finally, the three generals agreed to begin this expanded offensive during the period from 18 through 20 April.

After working out the *front*'s offensive plan and receiving the *Stavka*'s approval, Malinovsky issued attack orders to his participating armies at 0200 hours on 17 April. While his complete operational order has yet to be released, the order received by Sharokhin's 37th Army read: "Prepare to conduct an offensive operation. . . . In cooperation with the 57th and 6th Armies, [the 37th and 5th Shock Armies] will destroy the enemy grouping between the Dnestr and Prut Rivers in the southern part of Bessarabia. . . . and reach the state [Soviet-Romanian] border."[25]

As had been the case in mid-April, Malinovsky ordered Sharokhin's 37th Army "to capture Bendery, expand your bridgehead on the western bank of the Dnestr by reaching the Gyrbovets and Suvorov Heights [eight miles west of Bendery], and prepare to conduct a subsequent decisive offensive toward Farladieny [six miles southwest of Bendery], Chimishliia [on the Kogil'nik River 38 miles south of Kishinev], and Falchui [on the Prut River 63 miles southwest of Kishinev] by day's end on 19 April." Attacking on the right (northern) flank of Sharokhin's army, Gagen's 57th Army was to assault southwestward through Rezeny, 28 miles west of Bendery and 18 miles south of Kishinev, to Leovo, on the Prut River 48 miles southwest of Kishinev. On Sharokhin's left (southern) flank, Shlemin's 6th Army, which was to occupy offensive positions in the central portion of the 37th Army's bridgehead south of Tiraspol', was to attack southwestward through Kaushany, on the Botna River 14 miles south of Bendery, and Abakliia, just west of the Kogil'nik River and 48 miles south of Kishinev, to Komrat on the Yalpug River 52 miles south of Kishinev. Malinovsky established the boundary between the 37th and 6th Armies along a line extending from Sukleia, east of the Dnestr River southeast of Tiraspol', through Kirkaieshty in the bridgehead to Salkutsa on the Botna River 20 miles south of Bendery, and ordered Sharokhin's 37th Army on the morning of 19 April to turn over the central portion of its bridgehead, specifically, the five-mile-wide sector from Fantina-Mascui on the Botna River southward to Leont'evo, six miles north of Chebruchi, to Shlemin's 6th Army.

Tsvetaev's 5th Shock Army, which Malinovsky designated to join the offensive adjacent to the left (southern) flank of Shlemin's 6th Army, was to cross the Dnestr River in the Slobodzeia Russkaia region the night before the offensive and occupy assault positions in the six-mile-wide sector in the southern portion of the 37th Army's bridgehead from Leont'evo southward to Chebruchi. Tsvetaev's shock army was to penetrate the German defenses at and adjacent to their strong point at Talmazy, midway between Leont'evo and Chebruchi; exploit southwestward through Ukrainka, on the Chaga River 47 miles southeast of Kishinev, to Bessarabka, on the Kogil'nik River 50 miles south of Kishinev; and, in cooperation with Glagolev's 46th Army on its left flank, protect the left (southern) flank of the *front*'s main shock group, the 37th and 57th Armies, during their advance southwestward to the Prut River.

Finally, farther to the south on the extreme left wing of Malinovsky's attacking forces, Glagolev's 46th Army was to assist Tsvetaev's 5th Shock Army in its assault on the German strong point at Chebruchi, and, together with Chuikov's 8th Guards Army, the bulk of whose forces were still on the eastern bank of the Dnestr, was to advance to Berezino and Artsiz, on the Kogil'nik River 60 and 75 miles south of Kishinev, respectively, to protect the shock group's left (southern) flank.

While Malinovsky's overall plan was excessively ambitious, the missions he assigned to his attacking armies were also totally unrealistic. For example, the 37th and 6th Armies' intermediate objectives, the towns of Chimishliia and Abakliia on the Kogil'nik River, were 40–50 miles deep in the Germans' rear area, and the 57th, 37th, and 6th Armies' ultimate objectives, the cities of Leovo and Falchui on the Prut River and Komrat on the Yalpug River, were 65–75 miles distant. Furthermore, on the *front*'s left wing, the 46th and 8th Guards Armies were still facing both strong enemy resistance and deep waters across their fronts. Apparently, the *Stavka* and Malinovsky expected the German and Romanian defensive system to collapse totally once the armies in his shock group penetrated their defenses along the Dnestr north and south of Tiraspol'.

Despite the unrealistic nature of his plan, Malinovsky demonstrated how serious he was by attaching strong artillery and engineer support to his attacking armies. For example, he assigned the 7th and 9th Artillery Penetration Divisions (less one high-powered artillery brigade), two regiments of *Katiusha* multiple rocket launchers, four brigades and one regiment of tank destroyer artillery, six self-propelled artillery regiments, and three multiple engineer-sapper brigades and one assault engineer-sapper brigade to the four armies making his *front*'s main attack. Underscoring his confidence, he also planned to have his attacking armies expend only 0.5 combat loads of ammunition during the penetration phase of the operation, which he assumed would take only one day to complete, when it was customary to consume three to four full combat loads during a normal penetration operation. This meant that his artillery preparation was to be far weaker than usual.

Malinovsky ordered his army commanders to submit their detailed attack plans to his *front's* headquarters for approval by 1200 hours on 18 April, complete the attack preparations by midday on 18 April, and launch their attacks early on 19 April after softening up German defenses with their artillery preparations. Each of the four armies was to begin its advance by assaulting and capturing key German strong points, such as the forts around Bendery and the German fortified strong points in and around Fantina-Mascui, Leont'evo, Talmazy, and Chebruchi before dawn on 19 April, and each was to commit its main forces to combat during the ensuing morning.

The Sixth Army's Defenses

On 18 April, Army Group Dumitrescu defended the western bank of the Dnestr River opposite the 2nd Ukrainian Front's 5th Guards Army and the 3rd Ukrainian Front's six armies with the forces of the German Sixth Army's XVII, LII, XXX, XXIX, XXXXIV, and LXXII Army Corps, which were deployed abreast from the Tashlyk bridgehead south of Dubossary southward past the Soviets' Tiraspol' bridgehead to the western shore of the Dnestr estuary and the Black Sea coast. In addition, Dumitrescu's army group was supported by the III Romanian Army Corps, whose 15th Infantry Division was defending in the XXXXIV Army Corps' sector at Palanka. Army Group Dumitrescu's reserves included the German 9th Infantry Division, which was backing up the XXX and XXIX Army Corps, the German 302nd Infantry Division deployed in the LXXII Army Corps' rear, and the Slovak 1st Infantry Division in general reserve.

On the Sixth Army's extreme left wing, the XVII Army Corps defended the northeastern approaches to Kishinev between the Dubossary region and Grigoriopol with Corps Abteilung "F" and *kampfgruppen* from the 17th Infantry and 2nd Parachute Jäger Divisions. Its forces had just halted the advance of Managarov's 53rd Army along the Dnestr River between Dubossary and Grigoriopol'. On the XVII Army Corps' right, the LII Army Corps defended the sector from Grigoriopol' southward to Bychok with the 4th Mountain Division, the 294th Infantry Division's *kampfgruppe,* and the 320th Infantry Division containing the 2nd Ukrainian Front's 5th Guards Army in its bridgehead west of Tashlyk on its left wing and the three division groups of Corps Detachment "A" defending the sector from Speia to Bychok opposite the 3rd Ukrainian Front's 57th Army on its right wing. In addition, the Sixth Army deployed the German 13th Panzer Division into reserve positions near Cobusca Veche [Staraia Kobuska], in the hills seven miles west of Speia, to help contain the Soviet bridgeheads at both Tashlyk and Bychok.

Further to the south, the Sixth Army's XXX Army Corps defended the 25-mile-wide sector from Bychok southward west of Tiraspol' to just north of Chebruchi with the 384th Infantry Division's *kampfgruppe,* the 257th Infantry Division, the 15th Infantry Division's *kampfgruppe,* and the 97th Jäger Division deployed abreast from left to right (north to south), with the 3rd Mountain Jäger Division's *kampfgruppe* and the 14th Panzer Division in reserve assembly areas west of Bendery prepared to reinforce the corps whenever and wherever necessary. The XXX Army Corps' forces faced the 37th, 6th, and 5th Shock Armies in their small bridgehead in the Varnitsa region northwest of Tiraspol' and in their larger bridgehead from south of Tiraspol' to north of Chebruchi. In addition, by nightfall on 18 April, the Sixth Army was in the process of regrouping the 302nd Infantry Division northward into a new assembly area southwest of Bendery and the 9th Infantry Division into assembly areas west of Chebruchi.

On the XXX Army Corps' right flank, the Sixth Army's XXIX Army Corps defended the 14-mile-wide sector along the Dnestr River from Chebruchi southward to Oloneshty, with its Division Groups 335 and 258 defending the Chebruchi region proper, the 76th Infantry Division defending the Raskaetsy and Purkany regions, and the 153rd Field Training Division defending the Oloneshty region. In addition, the XXIX Army Corps retained portions of the 9th and 302nd Infantry Divisions in close reserve. These forces faced the 46th Army, which had captured only small bridgeheads along its front.

Further to the south on the Sixth Army's right wing, the XXXXIV Army Corps, operating jointly with the Romanian III Army Corps, defended the 25-mile-wide sector from just south of Oloneshty to just north of Cetatea Alba (Akkerman or Belgorod Dnestrovskii) on the western shore of the Dnestr estuary, with the Romanian 15th Infantry Division backed up by the German 306th Infantry Division's *kampfgruppe* defending the Palanka sector opposite the 8th Guards Army and with light security forces deployed along the estuary's western shore. Finally, on the Sixth Army's extreme right wing, the LXXII Army Corps defended the 14-mile-wide sector along the western shore of the Dnestr estuary to the Black Sea, as well as the adjacent Black Sea coast south of the estuary, with the Romanian 24th Infantry Division and a portion of the 302nd Infantry Division defending Cetatea Alba, and the 5th *Luftwaffe* Field Division's *kampfgruppe* and the 304th Infantry Division defending the remainder of the estuary's western shore to the Black Sea coast at Zatoka and Bugaz Station.

Thus, the German Sixth Army and its parent army group defended the most threatened and dangerous sectors of their front—the sectors near Tashlyk and from Tiraspol' southward to Chebruchi, where the Soviets occupied major bridgeheads—with German forces alone and reinforced their defenses in these regions with two panzer and two infantry divisions, which they held in close reserve. Although by this time the Germans were fortunate enough to have been able to erect fairly formidable defenses along the Dnestr River's western bank and adjacent to the Soviets' bridgeheads, Malinovsky's assembling armies still outnumbered them by a factor of more than threefold in infantry, fivefold in armor, and more than tenfold in artillery. However, the presence of the river itself along the entire front, the awkward configuration of the Soviets' bridgeheads, which were situated on low ground surrounded by higher dominating terrain occupied by German forces and artillery, and the inclement spring weather negated much of the Soviets' numerical advantage in infantry and the usefulness of its artillery and armor. In addition, the parlous logistical situation in Malinovsky's *front,* particularly in regard to ammunition and fuel, deprived his forces of the opportunity for employing effectively whatever artillery they could bring to bear against the German defenses.

In fact, the inclement weather and associated logistical and regrouping difficulties ultimately forced Malinovsky to postpone the assault by Sharokhin's 37th Army until 0200 hours on 20 April, two days after Zhadov's 5th Guards Army assaulted the German defenses from his bridgehead west of Tashlyk. In contrast, Gagen's 57th Army, whose right-wing divisions supported Zhadov's assault from his bridgehead west of Tashlyk on 17 and 18 April, had also attacked and eliminated the German bridgehead east of the Dnestr south of Tashlyk on 15 and 16 April and would conduct a general assault to break out of its bridgeheads between Krasnaia Gorka and Varnitsa to envelop Bendery from the north on 19 April. Thereafter, the remainder of Malinovsky's armies attacked in staggered sequence between 20 and 25 April, with the 37th Army and 5th Shock Armies attacking on 20 April and the 6th and 46th Armies joining their offensive on 24 and 25 April, respectively (Map 11). In addition, after their initial attacks failed, the 57th, 37th, 5th Shock Armies, and even Zhadov's 5th Guards Army, tried to resume their attacks on 24 and 25 April. Quite naturally given the piecemeal nature of Malinovsky's offensive, the ensuing fragmented and uncoordinated fighting achieved very little against determined German resistance.

The 57th Army's Assault in the Krasnaia Gorka and Varnitsa Sectors

In accordance with Malinovsky's orders, by 16 April Gagen's 57th Army had already dispatched the 93rd Rifle Division from its 68th Rifle Corps into the bridgehead occupied by Zhadov's 5th Guards Army on the western bank of the Dnestr River near Tashlyk to participate in Zhadov's offensive on 17 and 18 April. When this offensive failed, within days Gagen also sent the 113th Rifle Division from Mul'tan's 68th Rifle Corps across the Dnestr to reinforce the 93rd Rifle Division already in the Speia region and to join Zhadov's

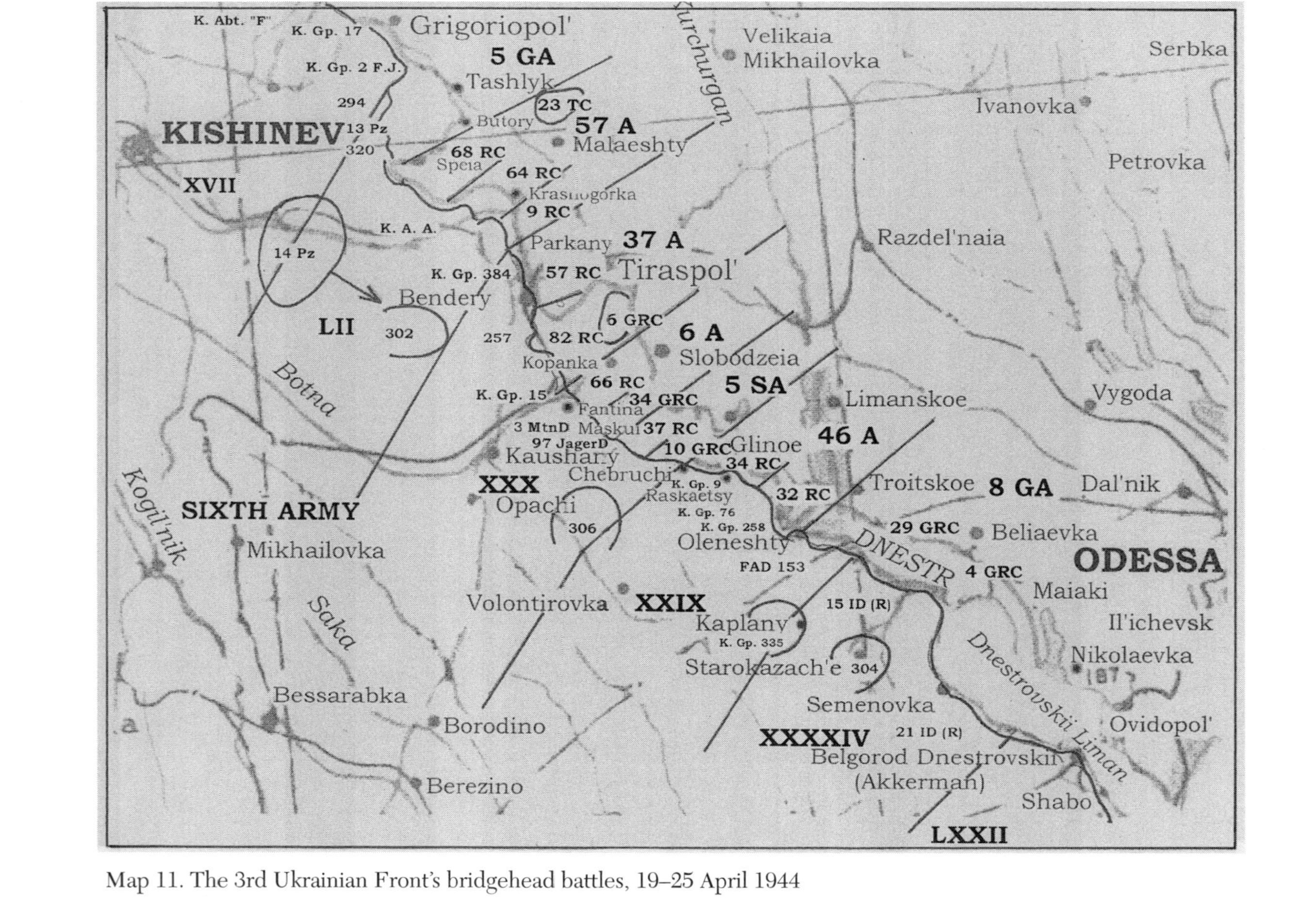

Map 11. The 3rd Ukrainian Front's bridgehead battles, 19–25 April 1944

next offensive effort, which was slated to begin on 25 April. Thus, when Malinovsky began his second major effort to break out of his *front*'s bridgeheads on the western bank of the Dnestr on 19 April, Zhadov's army supported his offensive by attacks of its own from the Tashlyk bridgehead (as discussed in Chapter 3).

During the 5th Guards Army's assaults on 15 and 16 April, the divisions on the right (northern) wing of Gagen's 57th Army supported Zhadov's assault by attacking the defensive positions of the German LII Army Corps' Corps Detachment "A," whose three divisional groups were defending the eastern face of the German bridgehead at the base of the western bend of the Dnestr River south of the Tashlyk bridgehead and north of Krasnaia Gorka. Attacking at dawn on 16 April, Dmitriev's 113th and Tatarchevsky's 223rd Rifle Division from Mul'tan's 68th Rifle Corps, together with Miliaev's 52nd Rifle Division from Anashkin's 64th Rifle Corps, penetrated Corps Detachment "A's" defenses, and, after two days of heavy fighting, captured the villages of Teia and Tokmazeia (three and five miles west of Krasnaia Gorka, respectively), cleared German forces from their bridgehead, and advanced to the eastern bank of the Dnestr, where they occupied defensive positions along the river's bend across the river from Telitsa. The next day, along with the 93rd Division already in the Speia region, Gagen regrouped the 113th Rifle Division northward into the Tashlyk bridgehead to support Zhadov's future attacks.

After clearing the German forces from a westward-jutting bend in the Dnestr River northwest of Krasnaia Gorka, Gagen ordered Anashkin's 64th and Roslyi's 9th Rifle Corps, which were deployed in his 57th Army's center and on its left wing, to attack southwestward from their bridgeheads across the river from Krasnaia Gorka and Varnitsa, penetrate the Germans' defenses, and advance southwestward and southward to envelop the German 384th (K. Gr. 384) and 257th Infantry Divisions defending the Bendery region in conjunction with an attack by the right wing of Sharokhin's 37th Army on Bendery from the southwest.

Attacking at dawn on 19 April, Lazarev's 19th Rifle and Kozak's 73rd Guards Rifle Divisions from Anashkin's 64th Rifle Corps assaulted Corps Detachment "A's" defenses by constricting their bridgehead on the Dnestr's western bank west of Krasnaia Gorka and Bychok, expanded this bridgehead to a depth of about three miles, and, thereafter, struggled for possession of the German strong point on the high ground around the village of Gura Bacutui on the river's western bank opposite Bychok. After several days of heavy fighting, Anashkin's troops captured the German strong point and advanced another mile to the northern shores of an unnamed lake at the base of the river bend, where its advance came to a grinding halt in the face of fresh German defenses anchored on even higher ground south of the lake. By 30

April, additional attacks by Anashkin's two divisions forced Corps Detachment "A" to withdraw its defenses to new positions protecting the approaches to the village of Kalfa, on the Kishinev-Tiraspol' railroad line.

Still further to the south, early on 19 April, Antonov's 301st, Kazakov's 230th, and Dobrovol'sky's 118th Rifle Divisions of Roslyi's 9th Rifle Corps struggled to expand their shallow bridgehead on the Dnestr's western bank from just south of Bychok southward to Varnitsa but were thwarted in their efforts when the Germans reinforced the 384th Infantry Division's *kampfgruppe,* which was defending this sector, with tanks from Unrein's 14th Panzer Division. Although Roslyi's three rifle divisions were able to expand their bridgehead about one-half mile to the west and establish tenuous links with the bridgehead held by Anashkin's 64th Rifle Corps to the north, the lodgment was too small to deploy sufficient armor, and the Germans still held firmly to the heights west of the river, preventing any further advance by Gagen's forces in this sector.

Thus, the multiple attacks by Gagen's 57th Army also failed to record any significant progress by month's end, even though Gagen insisted his forces continue launching new assaults in support of Malinovsky's other armies struggling along the western bank of the Dnestr.

The 37th Army's Offensive against Bendery

After receiving his army's mission from Malinovsky on 17 April, Sharokhin, the 37th Army's commander, ordered the two rifle corps in his army's center and on its right (northern) wing, Ostashenko's 57th and Kuznetsov's 82nd Rifle Corps, to assault the German forts protecting Bendery on the night of 18–19 April. Reinforced by Major General P. M. Chirkov's 15th Guards Rifle Division, which had been in army second echelon during the army's first offensive across the Dnestr River, Ostashenko's army was to conduct its main attack on his 57th Rifle Corps' left wing with Katsurin's 58th Guards and Esin's 228th Rifle Divisions. After breeching the 257th Infantry Division's defenses south of Bendery, the two rifle divisions were to envelop the city from the southwest and secure positions extending from the villages of Novye Lipkany and Ternovskaia Plavnia, one to two miles southwest of Bendery, to render the German defenses in Bendery untenable. Malinovsky's plan sought to encircle the 257th Infantry Division and the 384th Infantry Division's *kampfgruppe* in the Bendery region between Sharokhin's forces advancing from the southwest and the forces of Gagen's 57th Army, enveloping Bendery from the northwest and west.

While Ostashenko's main shock group was assaulting Bendery from the southwest, his third rifle division, Matveev's 92nd Guards Rifle Division, was to tie down German forces defending in the Parkany sector east of Bendery and to advance on the city from the east. Once his corps' three rifle divisions successfully isolated German forces in Bendery, Ostashenko's entire rifle corps was to exploit its success westward and capture the village of Farladieny, five miles southwest of Bendery, which was situated astride the main German communications road leading westward from the Bendery region, to prevent German forces from reinforcing their defenses west of Tiraspol'.

Further south of Bendery, Gagen ordered the three rifle divisions of Kuznetsov's 82nd Rifle Corps—Senin's 188th Rifle, Churmaev's 28th Guards, and Petrushin's 10th Guards Airborne Divisions—which were deployed on the left (southern) flank of Ostashenko's 57th Rifle Corps, to assault and penetrate the German 257th Infantry Division's defenses three to five miles south of Bendery, envelop the city from the south, capture Plavnia, and subsequently advance toward the town of Novyi Grigoreny, about six miles west of Bendery, to cut off German withdrawal routes from Bendery to the west and southwest. Finally, on Kuznetsov's left (southern) flank, Kotov, the commander of the 6th Guards Rifle Corps, was to transfer the sector occupied by Dreier's 20th Guards and Kholodov's 195th Rifle Divisions on the 37th Army's left wing, to the newly arriving forces from Shlemin's 6th Army, which were supposed to reach the region shortly after Sharokhin's army began its attacks. After concentrating his two rifle divisions in new assembly areas around the villages of Mereneshty and Kitskany, five and seven miles south of Bendery, respectively, Kotov's rifle corps was to prepare to support Sharokhin's main attack south of Bendery.

Once the 37th Army had fulfilled its immediate mission by capturing Bendery, Malinovsky's orders required Sharokhin's army to attack northwestward and westward through Farladieny and Chimishliia to envelop Kishinev from the south with a force of five divisions and to conduct a secondary attack with one rifle division westward and southwestward from Khadzhimus, six miles south of Bendery, toward Tarakliia, 25 miles southwest of Bendery, in close cooperation with the forces of Shlemin's 6th Army on his right flank.

Because of severe problems with regrouping his forces and shortages of ammunition, on the very eve of the assault, Sharokhin persuaded Malinovsky to postpone the attack until 0200 hours on 20 April. However, when Sharokhin's forces finally launched their assaults on the morning of 20 April, they accomplished very little. Attacking repeatedly with abandon between 20 and 25 April, the divisions of Ostashenko's and Kuznetsov's rifle corps made no progress whatsoever in the face of a determined German defense, primarily because the XXX Army Corps reinforced its forward defenses during the struggle with the 306th Infantry Division and part of Unrein's 14th Panzer Division. As a result, when the fighting died down late on 25 April, the German defenses north and south of the 37th Army's bridgehead south of Tiraspol' were intact, and Bendery was still in German hands.

The 6th Army's Assault against Fantina-Mascui and Leont'evo

Once Shlemin's 6th Army completed its part in the reduction and capture of Odessa, Malinovsky ordered it, together with Tsvetaev's 5th Shock Army, to spend about a week resting and refitting its forces in assembly areas west of Odessa and then to move westward to the Dnestr River to reinforce his *front*'s advance on Kishinev. On about 14 April, both Shlemin and Tsvetaev received fresh orders from Malinovsky to regroup their armies westward. Shlemin's orders required him to move his two rifle corps, the 66th and 34th Guards, across the Dnestr River and to occupy positions vacated by Kotov's 6th Guards Rifle Corps in the central portion of the 37th Army's bridgehead south of Tiraspol' by day's end on 18 April, the date before Sharokhin's 37th Army was originally supposed to begin its offensive. Once in the bridgehead, Shlemin's rifle corps were to concentrate for their assault in jumping-off positions extending from east of the German strong point at Fantina-Mascui southward five miles to just east of the strong point at Leont'evo. For a variety of reasons, however, Shlemin's forces were not able to cross the Dnestr and fully occupy their jumping-off positions for the attack in timely enough fashion and were forced to delay their offensive until the morning of 25 April. Without explaining exactly why Shlemin's army was unable to satisfy Malinovsky's ambitious offensive timetable, the official history of the army's 203rd Rifle Division, which was commanded by Major General G. S. Zdanovich and was subordinate to Kupriianov's 66th Rifle Corps, describes how its parent rifle corps deployed forward and its immediate mission:

> The 37th Army's 82nd Rifle Corps had captured a bridgehead in the vicinity of Kitskany and Kopanka on the western bank of the Dnestr River by the second half of April, and they intended for us to advance further. To expand the bridgehead, Lieutenant General Shlemin, the commander of the 6th Army, assigned the following missions: the 203rd and 333rd Rifle Divisions will penetrate the enemy's defenses along a front of three kilometers on the night of 24–25 April, capture the northern part of the village of Kyrpatseny [four miles west of Fantina-Mascui], and subsequently reach the dominating [terrain] on Hill 141.1 [two miles beyond].[26]

The German Sixth Army's XXX Army Corps defended the five-mile-wide sector from Kirkaieshty on the Botna River southward through Fantina-Mascui to just north of Leont'evo with its 15th Infantry Division's *kampfgruppe* (K. Gr. 15).

Once the 66th Rifle Corps occupied its jumping-off positions for the offensive, Kupriianov decided to lead his assault with Zdanovich's 203rd and Major General A. M. Golosko's 333rd Rifle Divisions but retained Major

General G. A. Afanas'ev's 244th Rifle Division in his corps' second echelon to exploit the assault once it penetrated the Germans' forward defenses. The assault groups from the two rifle divisions finally occupied their jumping-off positions for the attack by 0400 hours on 24 April.

On the left flank of Kupriianov's 66th Rifle Corps, the three rifle divisions of Major General N. M. Makovchuk's 34th Guards Rifle Corps also began regrouping into the bridgehead beginning late on 18 April but also did not attack until 25 April. The official history of the 59th Guards Rifle Division describes its forward deployment, beginning with its assembly in the Vladimirovka region east of the Dnestr River early on 15 April:

> The division received the following mission on 17 April—to concentrate on the left bank of the Dnestr by first light on 18 April. Part of the division marched along the route from Vladimirovka through Vladimirovka Farm to Hill 58.7. [However], during the march the division received an order to concentrate in new areas. We intended to take over the defensive sector of the 20th Guards Rifle Division's 55th Guards Rifle Regiment and the 195th Rifle Division's 564th and 583rd Rifle Regiments.
>
> The division concentrated in the gardens one kilometer [half a mile] south of Sukleia and west and south of Karagazh [three to five miles southeast of Tiraspol'], by 0400 hours on 18 April. Then, at 1000 hours, the regiments' subunits began crossing to the right [western] bank of the Dnestr and advanced to the village of Kopanka [nine miles south of Tiraspol']. The division began relieving the 20th Guards and 195th Rifle Divisions at 2400 hours. By the morning of 19 April, the 176th and 183rd Guards Rifle Regiments occupied a defensive sector whose forward edge was along a line from Hill 136.6 to Leont'evo. The 179th Guards Rifle Regiment was in second echelon. Over the next five days, the regiments' subunits improved their sector and lines in an engineering sense, conducted observation, and exchanged fire with the enemy. . . .
>
> The division's units occupied their jumping-off positions for the assault along the southwestern slope of Hill 136.6 and, further, toward a forest one kilometer to the southeast on 24 April.[27]

It is likely that Malinovsky delayed the 6th and 5th Shock Armies' offensives for almost a week because the 5th Guards and 57th Armies' assault near Tashlyk on 18 April had failed so quickly and because Shlemin's and Tsvetaev's armies were unable to concentrate all of their forces on time or to accumulate adequate supplies of ammunition with which to support their offensives before 25 April. However, it is less clear why they were unable to support the offensive by Sharokhin's 37th Army on 20 April.

Regardless of the reasons for the delay, Shlemin finally arrayed his two rifle corps in their attack positions across a four-mile-wide front south of

Fantina-Mascui by the evening of 24 April. Once in position, his army deployed for the assault with the three rifle divisions of Kupriianov's 66th Rifle Corps on its right wing and the three rifle divisions of Makovchuk's 34th Guards Rifle Corps on its left wing. Kupriianov placed Zdanovich's 203rd and Golosko's 333rd Rifle Divisions in his first echelon, with the mission of assaulting and penetrating the defenses of the 15th Infantry Division's *kampfgruppe* at and south of Fantina-Mascui, and retained Afanas'ev's 244th Rifle Division in his second echelon to exploit his attack and to capture Fantina-Mascui. On the 6th Army's left wing, Makovchuk deployed Major General G. P. Karamyshev's 59th and Major General L. N. Lozanovich's 61st Guards Rifle Divisions in his rifle corps' first echelon opposite the boundary between the defenses of the 15th Infantry Division's *kampfgruppe* and the 97th Jäger Division at and north of Leont'evo, ordered his two first-echelon divisions to assault and capture the German strong point, and also ordered Colonel M. S. Tkachev's 243rd Rifle Division, which he retained in second echelon because its commander had taken command only two days before, to exploit the attack to the west after Leont'evo fell.

Led by assault battalions formed by the first-echelon rifle regiments of his first-echelon rifle divisions, Shlemin's two corps began their assault at 0200 hours on 25 April after conducting a 15-minute fire raid on the German defenses. Shlemin fired the short artillery raid rather than a proper full preparation because his army was still short of ammunition. During the initial assault, Zdanovich's and Golosko's 203rd and 333rd Rifle Divisions of Kupriianov's rifle corps managed to penetrate the forward defensive positions of the 15th Infantry Division's *kampfgruppe*, advance slightly more than one mile, and capture the German strong point at Fantina-Mascui and the village of Plop-Shtube, about one mile to the southwest. Thereafter, however, intense German artillery, mortar, and machine-gun fire, coupled with incessant effective German air strikes, brought Kupriianov's advance to an abrupt halt. Compounding Kupriianov's problems, the next day, the German 306th Infantry Division reached the forward edge and immediately launched repeated counterattacks, which penetrated the 333rd Rifle Division's right wing in the vicinity of the village of Plop-Shtube, recaptured the village, and turned the 203rd Rifle Division's left flank, forcing Zdanovich's division to abandon its foothold in the Fantina-Mascui strong point as well. Although heavy fighting raged for several more days east of Fantina-Mascui, during which Kupriianov committed his second-echelon division, his 66th Rifle Corps was unable to make any further gains before the fighting died out on 29 April.

Meanwhile, on Kupriianov's left in the sector of Makovchuk's 34th Guards Rifle Corps, Karamyshev's and Lozanovich's 59th and 61st Guards Rifle Divisions began their assault against the 97th Jäger Division's defenses at 0200 hours on 25 April, captured the defenders' forward defensive positions, and advanced roughly one mile westward by day's end but were unable to seize the German strong point at Leont'evo. After failing to achieve any successes in repeated assaults on 26, 27, and 28 April, Shlemin also ordered Makovchuk's rifle corps over to the defense on 29 April.

The 59th Guards Division's history briefly and succinctly summarizes the paltry achievements of Shlemin's abortive offensive:

> The offensive by the units and formations of the 6th Army, which began on 25 April, was not crowned with success. The offensive by the 37th Army's units and formations north and south of the city of Bendery also ended with insignificant gains. The Hitlerite command strove with all of its strength to hold on to its defended positions and brought fresh reserves forward.[28]

The 5th Shock Army's Assault against Talmazy

While Malinovsky's 57th, 37th, and 6th Armies were pounding the German Sixth Army's defenses north and south of Tiraspol' heavily, but in vain, Tsvetaev's 5th Shock and Glagolev's 46th Armies were engaging the Germans' defenses in and around Chebruchi with equally poor results. A fragmentary account from the history of the 5th Shock Army's 108th Guards Rifle Division captures the intensity and frustration of the army's assaults:

> After a three-day rest to refill the division's units with personnel and equipment, on 13 April the division advanced along the march route from Pervomaisk through Milliardivka, Stepanovka, and Varvarovka, to Slobodzeia Moldavanskaia and reached the Dnestr in the Slobodzeia Russkaia region [ten miles south of Tiraspol'] by the morning of 18 April.
>
> The commander of the 37th Rifle Corps assigned our division the mission of forcing the Dnestr on the night of 18–19 April, seizing the flatlands along the river, and subsequently capturing the central part of the town of Talmazy [three miles north of Chebruchi]. The 97th Jäger Division's 204th and 207th Regiments defended the main sector of the defense opposite the division's assault.
>
> The 308th and 311th Rifle Regiments, which were in first echelon, forced the river by handmade means, each with a reinforced battalion in advance. Three artillery battalions and two batteries of antitank artillery supported each regiment. A total of 74 guns and mortars per kilometer [123 per mile] of front, which supported the crossing, reliably suppressed the enemy's defenses in the immediate region of the river's western bank and his artillery batteries situated in the depths.
>
> By the next morning, both regiments had successfully forced the Dnestr and, after destroying the enemy's covering subunits, rapidly over-

came the flood plains and reached the old branch of the river, along which the enemy's main defenses were situated. The 195th [should read 295th] Rifle Division was attacking on the right, and the 49th Rifle Division on the left. The terrain was swampy with a great number of lakes, and, therefore, each formation operated along its own axis without close contact with its neighbor. We attempted to penetrate the defensive lines several times but without any results. The enemy had a high density of firing means [weapons], a trench system, and, first and foremost, favorable terrain conditions. There was a water barrier, the old branch of the river, in front of his forward edge, and it was up to 15 meters [16 yards] wide and two meters [six feet] deep, which was difficult to overcome.

On 4 May our division received the order to go over to the defense.[29]

In accordance with Malinovsky's orders, after crossing the Dnestr River in the Slobodzeia Russkaia region and occupying assault positions in the six-mile-wide sector from Leont'evo southward to Chebruchi, Tsvetaev's army was to attack and capture the German strong point at Talmazy and then exploit southwestward through Ukrainka on the Chaga River and, ultimately, to Bessarabka on the Kogil'nik River deep in the enemy's rear. Throughout its offensive, his army was to cooperate with Glagolev's 46th Army on its left flank and protect the southern flank of the *front*'s 37th and 57th Armies as they advanced southwestward to the Prut River.

To accomplish this mission, Tsvetaev arrayed his two rifle corps in single echelon and kept only a reserve of two rifle divisions to exploit success to the west. Major General S. F. Gorokhov's 37th Rifle Corps was to attack on the army's right (southern) wing, with Colonel S. I. Dunaev's 108th Guards, Major General A. V. Chizhov's 49th, and Colonel A. P. Dorofeev's 295th Rifle Divisions advancing abreast from left to right in the three-mile-wide sector from Talmazy northward to Leont'evo. Gorokhov's three rifle divisions were to penetrate the 97th Jäger Division's defenses between Leont'evo, Grednitsa, and Talmazy; sever the road leading from Leont'evo westward to Kaushany, on the Botna River nine miles west of Leont'evo; and envelop the strong point at Talmazy from the north and northwest.

On Tsvetaev's left wing to the south, Major General I. A. Rubaniuk's 10th Guards Rifle Corps was to conduct its attack in the three-mile-wide sector from Talmazy southward to just north of Chebruchi, with Colonel S. P. Demidov's 86th and Colonel I. V. Baldynov's 109th Guards Rifle Divisions in first echelon and Major General I. I. Svygin's 320th Rifle Division in second echelon, to smash the right wing of the 97th Jäger Division's defenses and envelop Talmazy from the south.

Tsvetaev's two rifle corps began their assault against the German defenses north and south of Talmazy at dawn on 20 April after a short artillery raid but made no progress whatsoever against stiff resistance. Shortly after their assault began, the 97th Jäger Division shifted forces from its left wing, which had been relieved by newly arrived elements of the 306th Infantry Division, to reinforce its defenses around Talmazy, and the XXX Army Corps also released a *kampfgruppe* from the 9th Infantry Division to bolster its defenses south of Talmazy. As a result, Tsvetaev's offensive collapsed in exhaustion after three days of heavy fighting and five more days of desultory fighting.

The 46th Army's Assault on Chebruchi and Raskaetsy

In accordance with his offensive plan, Malinovsky ordered Glagolev's 46th Army to conduct attacks of a clearly secondary nature to assist the advance by the 57th, 37th, and 6th Armies farther to the north. Specifically, Glagolev was to concentrate two of his army's rifle corps—Ruchkin's 31st Guards Rifle Corps and Kosobutsky's 34th Rifle Corps—with a total force of five rifle divisions, in the five-mile-wide sector from Chebruchi southward to Raskaetsy, penetrate the German defenses, capture the twin German strong points, and, together with Chuikov's 8th Guards Army, advance southwestward along the Berezino and Artsiz axis to the Kogil'nik River to protect the left flank of the *front*'s main shock group. Ruchkin's corps was to conduct the army's main attack on Chebruchi with its 4th, 34th, and 40th Guards Rifle Divisions, while Kosobutsky's corps was to attack the German defenses at Raskaetsy with his 236th and 394th Rifle Divisions. Finally, Zherebin's 32nd Rifle Corps, which was deployed on the left flank of Glagolev's army, was to conduct a supporting attack on the German defenses at Purkary, five miles to the south, with a force of two divisions. As before, the German XXIX Army Corps defended the sector from Chebruchi southward to just north of Raskaetsy with the 335th and 258th Infantry Divisions' *kampfgruppen* and the sector from Raskaetsy southward to Purkary with its 76th Infantry Division.

While the assault by Ruchkin's 31st Guards Rifle Corps against the strong point at Chebruchi from the east and south collapsed immediately after it commenced, Kosobutsky's 34th Rifle Corps registered the army's only offensive gains. During three days of heavy fighting, Major General I. I. Fesin's 236th and Major General A. I. Lisitsin's 394th Rifle Divisions, later reinforced by Major General F. S. Kolchuk's 353rd Rifle Division, advanced one to two miles deep in the five-mile-wide sector south of Raskaetsy, threatening to envelop the town from the south. However, the XXIX Army Corps reinforced its defenses at Chebruchi with a *kampfgruppe* from the 9th Infantry Division and brought Kosobutsky's advance in the sector south of Raskaetsy to a halt by shifting most of the 76th Infantry Division's forces to its left wing.

During the same period, Colonel S. M. Fomichenko's 266th Rifle Division, which was deployed on the right wing of Zherebin's 32nd Rifle Corps, registered similar gains against the 76th Infantry Division's defenses just north of Purkary. However, neither assault reached the crest of the heights west of the Dnestr River or the main road running laterally behind the Germans' front lines further to the west. In fact, throughout its entire defensive sector, the XXIX Army Corps' forces halted Glagolev's advancing forces before they reached the high ground west of the Dnestr River. As was the case further north, inadequate artillery support and stout German resistance with devastating artillery, mortar, and machine-gun fire thwarted Glagolev's attempt to end the stalemate in his army's sector along the Dnestr River.

The 8th Guards Army Dilemma

Little needs to be written about the travails of Chuikov's 8th Guards Army, which was supposed to force the Dnestr River on the 3rd Ukrainian Front's left wing during Malinovsky's offensive. Malinovsky's order of 17 April had required Chuikov to concentrate the six rifle divisions of Glazunov's 4th and Fokanov's 29th Guards Rifle Corps east of Oloneshty and Palanka; force the Dnestr River; penetrate the defenses of the 153rd Field Training Division, on the XXIX Army Corps' right wing in the Oloneshty region, and the defenses of the Romanian 15th Infantry Division, on the XXXXIV Army Corps' left wing near Palanka; and advance rapidly to the southwest, ultimately to the mouth of the Danube River.

However, by day's end on 25 April, only two of Chuikov's divisions—specifically, the 4th Guards Corps' 74th Guards Rifle Division and the 29th Guards Corps' 35th Guards Rifle Division—had fully concentrated opposite the Romanian defenses at Palanka. Further to the north, high waters prevented Chuikov from concentrating even a full division opposite Oloneshty. This was the case because the flatlands east of the river for a distance of more than eight miles north of Palanka were still inundated by up to four feet of water, and the Dnestr River was up to four miles wide.

As Chuikov recalled:

> On 25 April we attempted once again to fulfill the front commander's orders and go over to the offensive. But where! The water rose and continued rising everywhere. The islands were already covered. The soldiers filled in the low places with shovels and climbed up on the high ground, while clinging to it as if rooks.
>
> My observation post was situated on the high ground southeast of Palanka. The water reached right up to this high ground.
>
> I communicated by telephone with the *front* commander and told him about the situation. At first, R. Ia. Malinovsky did not believe that the rising water was so great. Certainly, it was difficult to make sure of what was occurring on the banks of the river by telephone. I categorically declared

> that, if the rising water did not stop, in no more than several days we would turn out to be without artillery, and the soldiers would be in rooks' nests on the wood.
>
> I ordered the offensive to cease and the bridgehead to be abandoned. To assist us, a *front* pontoon battalion arrived in Maiaki. With its help, we evacuated the personnel from the bridgehead. This required two days to accomplish. By 27 April we had abandoned the entire bridgehead without a fight.[30]

Acknowledging Chuikov's insurmountable problems, several days later Malinovsky ordered Chuikov to move his entire army northward to drier and more solid ground so that it could take a real role in his *front*'s offensive operations. This order directed Chuikov to regroup his guards army to the Tashlyk region, where Malinovsky believed Chuikov's powerful army could be employed to the greatest effect. However, the distance from Palanka to the Tashlyk region was 36 miles as the crow flies and half again that distance along the few roads between the two regions. Given the poor condition of the roads, it would take at least a week for Chuikov's army to conduct its regrouping and join the *front*'s advance toward its illusive target of Kishinev.

CONCLUSIONS

It is indeed understandable that, in his memoirs, Vasilevsky, the *Stavka*'s representative to Konev's and Malinovsky's *fronts* during their spring offensives, who was personally responsible to Stalin for supervising the operations to penetrate the German defenses along the Dnestr River line, heaped great praise on the accomplishments of Malinovsky's 3rd Ukrainian Front during its April offensives:

> The forces of the 3rd Ukrainian Front inflicted a serious defeat on the German Sixth and Romanian Third Armies. Nine enemy infantry and tank divisions were destroyed in the region between the Dnepr and Southern Bug River alone. Another twenty enemy infantry, tank, and motorized divisions suffered heavy losses and lost their combat capabilities. According to the testimony of prisoners and data from the German archives, the enemy lost 51,000 soldiers and officers killed and wounded here. By 14 April the 3rd Ukrainian Front's forces had liberated the entire left bank of the Dnestr from Tiraspol' to the Black Sea. Forcing the Dnestr from the march, our forces seized bridgeheads on its western bank.[31]

However, by describing Malinovsky's offensive as an unqualified victory, Vasilevsky glosses over many of the *front*'s most notable failures. For example, although Malinovsky's forces captured Odessa and drove German forces from the eastern bank of the Dnestr River, Vasilevsky neglects to mention that the 3rd Ukrainian Front failed to accomplish the most important missions the *Stavka* assigned to it: namely, it failed to seize any operationally or strategically significant bridgeheads across the Dnestr River and did not capture the city of Kishinev. With the exception of the bridgehead that Sharokhin's 37th Army seized south of Tiraspol', virtually all of the other bridgeheads his *front*'s armies captured on the Dnestr's western bank were only tactical in significance since none was large enough for Malinovsky to deploy forces capable of breaking out to the west. Although these bridgeheads were large enough to deploy single or multiple rifle divisions, none was large enough to deploy full armies, including tank and mechanized forces, or requisite supporting artillery necessary to conduct or support offensive operations to break out of these bridgeheads.

Furthermore, all of the bridgeheads Malinovsky's armies captured, including the 37th Army's large bridgehead south of Tiraspol', were confined to the low and often swampy ground on the river's western bank. None of the forces that seized these bridgeheads proved able to capture any high ground on the river's western bank, and, as a result, the dominating high ground adjacent to or around these bridgeheads remained under the control of German or Romanian forces. Therefore, when Malinovsky attempted to resume his offensive operations during the second half of April, his armies on the low ground along the river had to conduct penetration operations against German and Romanian forces dug in on the heights around them. Since these forces were supported by artillery and mortars firing from relatively distant positions along the Dnepr River's eastern bank, the forces conducting the penetration operations conducted their assaults without adequate tank and artillery support, and those few forces which managed to attack successfully quickly advanced beyond the range of their supporting artillery.

Therefore, somewhat reminiscent of the multiple failed offensive operations the Red Army's Voronezh (later 1st Ukrainian) Front conducted across the Dnepr River at Gornostaipol', Liutezh, and Velikii Bukrin in the Kiev region during October 1943, during his twin offensives in April 1944, the configuration of the terrain forced Malinovsky's attacking armies to conduct their penetration operations from low ground along the western edge of the Dnestr River's flood plain against German and Romanian forces occupying formidable defenses on the dominating heights west of the river. Nowhere along the river were Malinovsky's forces able to gain a significant lodgment on those heights.

Of course, there were many extenuating factors that mitigated Malinovsky's April defeats. First, the armies conducting his *front*'s river crossing operations were already seriously weakened and understrength after conducting nearly four months of continuous offensive operations across the southern Ukraine. Most of his armies' rifle divisions were at or less than 60 percent personnel strength (under 5,000 men), and his armies, rifle corps, and supporting tank, mechanized, and cavalry corps and divisions had lost immense quantities of weapons, tanks, and equipment, either in combat or because of attrition during the previous four months of operations. As a result, most of his tank, mechanized, and cavalry-mechanized formations fielded only a fraction of their required tanks and self-propelled guns.

Second, in combination with the terrain, which although flat was laced with rivers and streams, most of which flowed laterally across his forces' axes of advance, the Germans' deliberate decision to destroy the communications infrastructure throughout the Ukraine as they withdrew, combined with the effects of the spring *rasputitsa,* which had prevented similar operations in previous years, made both movement and combat operations difficult for Malinovsky's force to conduct. As a result, by mid-April the lines of communications of Malinovsky's *front* and subordinate armies were woefully overextended, their logistical units and facilities were unable to provide their forces with adequate support, and their logistical umbilicals were tenuous at best.

Third, the difficult terrain and weather conditions during the spring inhibited the forward movement of Malinovsky's surviving artillery, tanks, and other heavy equipment. Consequently, these vital means of fire support trailed far behind the infantry they were to support during his *front*'s advance to the Dnestr River and often was not available to support his forces, either when they assaulted across the river or when they attempted to break out of their restrictive bridgeheads on the river's western bank. Therefore, the lagging artillery and mortars, the restrictive terrain that inhibited their combat employment, and the severe shortages of ammunition combined to deprive Malinovsky's army and corps commanders of their most deadly penetration weapons, their artillery, and their only means to exploit success, their tanks.

Although Malinovsky's forces faced many daunting problems, the difficulties the defending German Sixth Army faced were even more challenging. After conducting a harrowing retreat across hundreds of miles of rain-soaked terrain in the Ukraine and losing immense numbers of men, weapons, equipment, and logistical stocks, to say nothing of territory, the Germans had to regroup their disorganized forces and establish adequate defensive positions and lines along the Dnestr River in an incredibly short period of time. Once ensconced behind these defenses, they had to resist an enemy force many times numerically superior to their own, knowing all the while that further retreat probably meant abandoning the bulk of Romania, if not the Balkan region as a whole, to the Soviets. Ultimately, dread of the horrifying consequences of defeat, combined with excellent small-unit efficiency and cohesion plus a major assist from the terrain and inclement weather, contributed to the Germans' successful defense.

As had been the case numerous times before, although also severely understrength, the Germans' well-trained and surgically effective panzer forces played a significant part in stemming the Red tide along the Dnestr River. Employed as virtual "fire brigades," multiple *kampfgruppen* fielded by the 13th and 14th Panzer Divisions maneuvered rapidly to and fro across the broad battlefield to stiffen the Sixth Army's defenses south of Grigoriopol' and north and south of Tiraspol' and to keep the Soviet forces confined to their low and marshy bridgeheads on the Dnestr's western bank. In similar fashion, although they were weak and often understrength, *kampfgruppen* from the German 9th, 302nd, and 306th Infantry Divisions plugged the gaps in other key sectors of the Sixth Army's front.

When all was said and done, after two weeks of heavy combat, by 25 April the 3rd Ukrainian Front possessed only one operationally significant bridgehead on the Dnestr River's western bank, the bridgehead captured by the 37th and 6th Armies in the Tashlyk region south of Tiraspol'. Even in this region, however, the Soviets' foothold west of the river was tenuous at best. Faced with this reality, Malinovsky concluded that the best, if not only, way his forces could break the stalemate along the Dnestr River was to regroup Chuikov's 8th Guards Army northward from its irrelevent position on his *front*'s left wing and employ it as a fresh shock group to reinvigorate his offensive from the Tashlyk region westward toward Kishinev.

After Malinovsky regrouped Chuikov's army northward, the *front* commander concluded there were only two regions where it could carry out its destructive work effectively enough to reach Kishinev. First, Chuikov's army could join with the 37th and 6th Armies and expand the Tiraspol' bridgehead to the west; second, if Malinovsky could persuade the *Stavka* to assign his *front* control of the bridgehead at Tashlyk, he could deploy Chuikov's army into this bridgehead so that his powerful force could spearhead the *front*'s offensive westward along the shortest route to Kishinev. The only problem with Malinovsky's second solution was that Zhadov's 5th Guards Army occupied the Tashlyk bridgehead and Zhadov's army was subordinate to Konev's 2nd Ukrainian Front.

After pondering these two offensive options, during the last week in April, Malinovsky asked the *Stavka* to transfer the Tashlyk bridgehead to his *front*'s control and permit him to conduct a new offensive spearheaded by Chuikov's army from his new bridgehead. After the *Stavka* approved Malinovsky's request on 28 April, Konev began transferring Zhadov's 5th Guards Army from the Tashlyk region to new assembly areas northeast of Iasi, and Malinovsky regrouped Chuikov's 8th Guards Army into the Tashlyk bridgehead, hoping that, within days, Chuikov's army could mount a triumphal march toward Kishinev. However, whether or not he could do so depended directly on the success that Konev's 2nd Ukrainian Front would achieve as it conducted its climactic offensive against Iasi in early May.

Army General R. Ia. Malinovsky, commander, 3rd Ukrainian Front (commander, 2nd Ukrainian Front on 24 May)

Marshal of the Soviet Union A. M. Vasilevsky, chief of the Red Army General Staff, deputy commissar of defense of the USSR, and *Stavka* representative to the 3rd Ukrainian Front

Marshal of the Soviet Union (then Army General) F. I. Tolbukhin, commander, 3rd Ukrainian Front (on the right), with his chief of staff, General A. S. Zheltov.

Lieutenant General N. A. Gagen, commander, 57th Army

Lieutenant General M. N. Sharokhin, commander, 37th Army

Lieutenant General V. V. Glagolev, commander, 46th Army

Colonel General V. I. Chuikov, commander, 8th Guards Army

Lieutenant General I. T. Shlemin, commander, 6th Army

Colonel General V. D. Tsvetaev, commander,
5th Shock Army

Lieutenant General I. A. Pliev, commander,
Cavalry-Mechanized Group

CHAPTER 5

The 2nd Ukrainian Front's Preparations for the Iasi (Tirgu Frumos) Offensive (24 April–1 May 1944)

KONEV'S STRATEGIC PLAN

After the 2nd Ukrainian Front's first shock group of three armies failed to breech German Army Group Wöhler's defenses west of Iasi in mid-April, Konev took stock of the strategic situation and began formulating a new offensive plan to pierce the German and Romanian defenses in northern Romania, capture Iasi, and expand his offensive southward deeper into the very heart of Romania. This time, however, instead of employing just the 40th and 27th Armies, supported by the 2nd Tank Army, to achieve his offensive aims, Konev decided to reinforce his armies already deployed west of Iasi with his *front's* powerful and relatively fresh 7th Guards and 5th Guards Tank Armies, which had just completed regrouping their forces into the region north of Tirgu Frumos. Thus, the future success of Konev's *front* depended directly on how well these two armies performed in offensive combat.

Konev presented the general concept for his *front's* new offensive into northern Romania to the *Stavka* on 18 April, only a few days after Malinovsky's 3rd Ukrainian Front captured its initial bridgeheads across the Dnestr River east of Kishinev. In brief, Konev's plan required his *front's* main shock group, which would now consist of the 40th and 7th Guards and 27th Armies and the 2nd and 5th Guards Tank Armies, to advance southward from the Tirgu Frumos region toward either Bacau or Vaslui, 52 miles southwest of Iasi and 40 miles south of Iasi, respectively, to envelop German forces defending Iasi from the west, overcome Group Wöhler's Strunga Defense Line south of Tirgu Frumos and Iasi, and advance southward into the very heart of Romania. As he formulated his plan, Konev assumed the forces of Malinovsky's 3rd Ukrainian Front would be able to attack from their bridgehead along the Dnestr to envelop Kishinev from the east.

Specifically, Konev's proposed offensive plan required his shock group, which was to consist of 15 rifle divisions (from Zhmachenko's 40th, Shumilov's 7th Guards, and Trofimenko's 27th Armies) and 470 to 520 tanks and self-propelled guns (from Rotmistrov's 5th Guards and Bogdanov's 2nd Tank Armies), to penetrate German defenses in the 15-mile-wide sector from Pascani eastward to Tirgu Frumos; advance along the left (eastern) bank of the Seret River toward Bacesti, 28 miles southwest of Iasi; and exploit their offensive southward to either the city of Bacau or Vaslui. Konev proposed beginning the offensive on 27–29 April in conjunction with a secondary attack by his forces southward along the Iasi axis and an offensive by Malinovsky's forces along the Dnestr River east of Kishinev.

However, by 22 April it became clear to both Konev and the *Stavka* that Malinovsky's forces were experiencing greater than anticipated difficulties in their attempts to break out westward from their bridgeheads over the Dnestr River, and, unless they were able to do so, Konev's shock group needed to be even stronger than originally planned. Therefore, after consulting closely with Stalin and other members of the *Stavka,* Konev revised his offensive concept to suit the new circumstances and issued new orders to his *front* early on 23 April.

As expressed in his *front's* Operational Directive no. 00324/op, dated 0445 hours 23 April, Konev's new orders required the armies of his *front's* new shock group "to penetrate the enemy's defense in the Sodomeni, Ruginoasa, and Ulmi-Noui sector, east of the Seret River, and conduct their main attack southward along the left bank of the Seret River in the general direction of Sagna and Bacesti," and his two tank armies "to capture Bacau and Vaslui and cut the routes of withdrawal to the west of the enemy's Iasi-Kishinev group of forces" (Map 12; see also Appendix to this volume). To this end, on the right (western) wing of Konev's shock group west of the Seret River, Zhmachenko's 40th Army was to conduct a secondary attack against the Romanian defenses west of Pascani, penetrate those defenses, and advance southward through the town of Tupilati, on the Moldava River 31 miles south of Pascani, and capture the town of Ruginoasa, 19 miles south of Pascani, which was situated astride the vital road running westward from the city of Roman, to isolate the Germans' Iasi group from the west.

East of the Seret River, on the 40th Army's left, Shumilov's 7th Guards Army, supported by the bulk of Konev's artillery, was to penetrate the German defenses west of Tirgu Frumos with a force of six rifle divisions; advance southward through the towns of Sagna, Secueni, Barlicesti, Miclauseni, and Hindresti to capture the city of Roman and the town of Bacesti, 16 miles east of Roman; and then facilitate and support the 5th Guards Tank Army's subsequent advance to the cities of Birlad and Bacau, which were situated 50–60 miles south of the tank army's initial jumping-off positions. On the 7th Guards Army's left, Trofimenko's 27th Army was to penetrate the German defenses east of Tirgu Frumos with a force of four rifle divisions; capture this town and the region to the southeast; advance southward through the villages of Stornesti and Negresti, 10 and 35 miles southeast of Tirgu Frumos, respectively; capture the towns of Dumesti and Boresti [Birzesti], 30 and 45 miles southeast of its initial jumping-off positions and 10–20 miles northwest of Vaslui; and facilitate and support the 2nd Tank Army's subsequent advance,

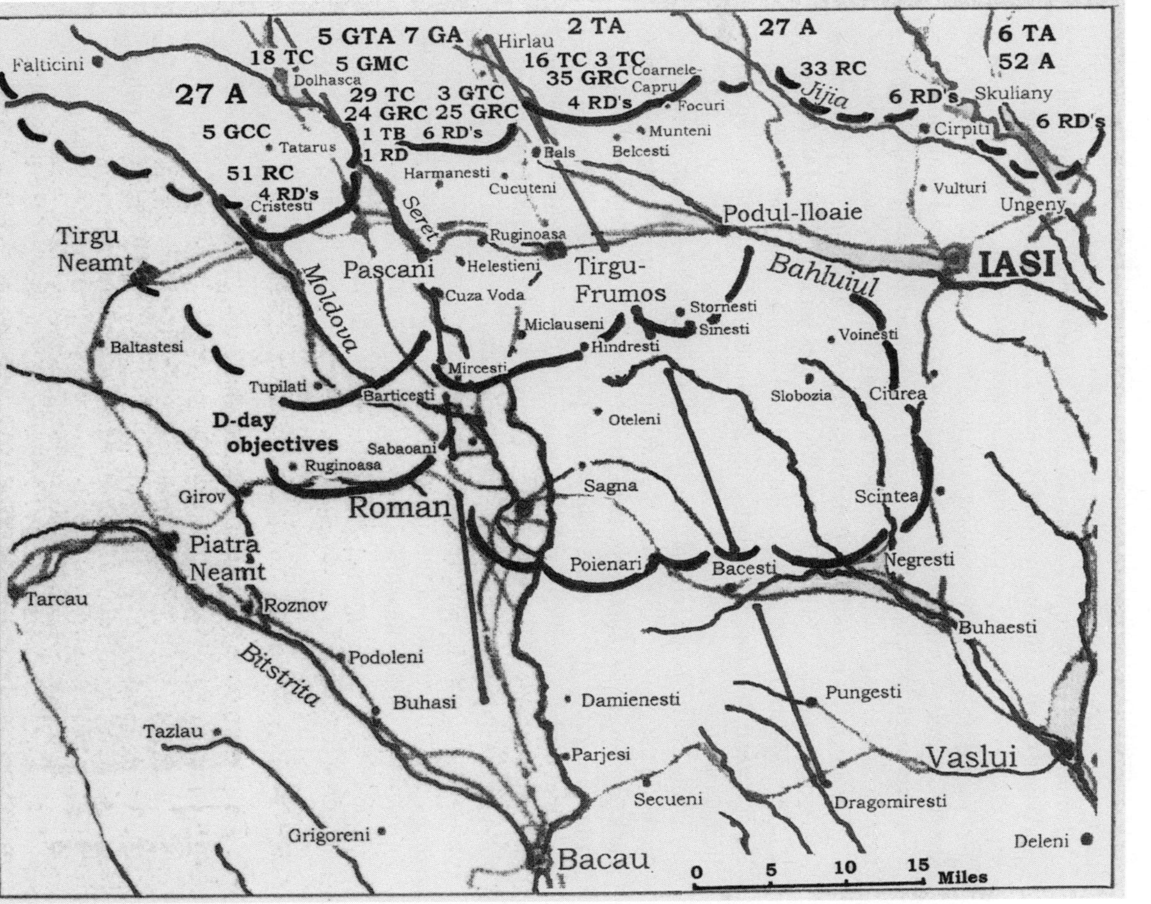

Map 12. The 2nd Ukrainian Front's plan for the Iasi offensive, 24 April 1944

either southward toward Vaslui or northeastward to envelop the German forces defending in the Iasi region from the southwest.

Konev's two tank armies, the 5th Guards and 2nd Tank, which formed the armored spearhead for his main shock group, were to support the shock group's penetration operation and then exploit the penetration southward and southeastward deep into northern Romania. Specifically, the two combat-ready tank corps of Rotmistrov's 5th Guards Tank Army were to support and exploit the 7th Guards Army's penetration west of Tirgu Frumos, swiftly exploit the offensive southward to capture Ruginoasa and Sagna, 11 miles west and seven miles northeast of Roman, respectively, while one tank brigade continued to support the 7th Guards Army's advance southward on along the right (western) bank of the Seret River toward Roman, and capture Roman and the towns of Bacesti and Buhaesti to the east. Subsequently, the main forces of Rotmistrov's two tank corps were to race southward and southeastward to capture the cities of Bacau and Birlad and the towns of Secueni, Dragomiresti, and Racovei in between, a distance of 50–60 miles deep into Romania.

While Rotmistrov's tank army exploited southward deep into Romania on the shock group's right wing, the two armored corps of Bogdanov's 2nd Tank Army were to support the 27th Army's penetration northeast of Tirgu-Frumos; capture the key German strong point by enveloping it from the east; and exploit the offensive southeastward, either to capture the town of Slobodzia, 28 miles southeast of Tirgu Frumos, which controlled the passes through the mountains southwest of Iasi, or to attack eastward to roll up the western flank of the German defenses west of Iasi.

As far as the timing of the offensive was concerned, Konev ordered his forces to submit their final offensive plans to the *front*'s headquarters by day's end on 25 April and be prepared to attack on the morning of 27 April. Once the offensive was under way, Konev expected the armies forming his *front*'s shock group to fulfill their immediate objectives: that is, capture the cities of Tirgu Frumos, Roman, Bacesti, Buhaesti, and Birzesti within 24 hours, and capture their ultimate objectives of Birlad, Bacau, and Iasi within 48 hours.[1]

Konev's new offensive plan, which was far more elaborate and ambitious than his previous one, strengthened his *front*'s proposed shock group and required it to capture both Bacau and Vaslui to cut off the withdrawal routes of the enemy's Iasi-Kishinev grouping to the southwest. Although the plan also required the 2nd Ukrainian Front's forces to be prepared to attack on 27 April, the continued failure of Malinovsky's forces to break out from their bridgeheads on the Dnestr River's western bank and the daunting problems the 2nd Ukrainian Front experienced in regrouping its forces prompted Konev to postpone the "D-day" for his offensive several times, ultimately, until the morning of 2 May.

In the wake of these delays, before his main shock group launched its offensive, Konev also planned to deceive the Germans regarding the location of his main attack by conducting diversionary operations in the Iasi region on 25 and 26 April. The *Stavka* ordered Malinovsky's forces to do the same along the Dnestr River during the same period. To convince the Germans that he intended to make his main attack in the Iasi rather than the Tirgu-Frumos region, Konev ordered Trofimenko, the commander of the 27th Army, to simulate regrouping his army's 35th Guards Rifle Corps from its right wing north of Tirgu Frumos into assembly areas on its left wing northeast of Iasi. Ostensibly, the 35th Guard Rifle Corps would join the army's 33rd Rifle Corps in a concerted attack on the city from the north and northwest. At the same time, Bogdanov was to feign the movement of tanks from his 2nd Tank Army into the same region to support Trofimenko's imaginary offensive. In addition, Konev ordered Kravchenko, the commander of the 6th Tank Army, whose three woefully understrength armored corps were resting and refitting in assembly areas far north of the Iasi region, to simulate the deployment of his entire tank army for an all-out assault on Iasi, together with the 73rd and 78th Rifle Corps of Koroteev's 52nd Army and Trofimenko's 27th Army. In reality, however, Kravchenko was to form a single brigade-size combat group from its 5th Mechanized and 5th Guards Tank Corps to support Trofimenko's simulated diversionary attack against Iasi.

REGROUPING OF FORCES

Konev began regrouping his forces on 23 April. First, he ordered Zhmachenko's 40th Army to concentrate Avdeenko's 51st Rifle Corps in the sector west of Pascani. Second, he ordered Trofimenko's 27th Army to concentrate Goriachev's 35th Guards Rifle Corps in the five-mile-wide sector from the village of Hodora and Tetarului, ten miles north of Tirgu Frumos, and Bogdanov's 2nd Tank Army to regroup its 3rd and 16th Tank Corps into assembly areas to the rear of Goriachev's infantry. At the same time, but with far greater difficulty, he ordered Shumilov's 7th Guards Army to regroup its 24th and 25th Guards Rifle Corps from their assembly areas in the region north of Coarnele-Capru, 20–30 miles north of Tirgu Frumos, into pre-offensive assembly areas about ten miles north of Tirgu Frumos and Rotmistrov's 5th Guards Tank Army to move its 18th and 29th Tank and 3rd Guards Tank Corps from their assembly areas north of the Hirlau region, 20–30 miles northwest of Tirgu Frumos, southward into their pre-offensive assembly area about ten miles northwest of Tirgu Frumos.

The southward movement by the 7th Guards and 5th Guards Tank Armies was particularly painstaking and slow since the road network was exceedingly sparse, and stringent security requirements made it necessary for Shumilov and Rotmistrov to exploit the broken terrain and inclement weather to maintain secrecy during their march south. In addition, the deception plan Konev formulated to mask his attack preparations and offensive intentions, as well as the diversionary attacks associated with his deception plan, also further complicated the regrouping process.

By the time Konev completed regrouping his forces, although his main shock group was far larger than before, the composition of Konev's *front* and its subordinate armies differed very little from its composition on 1 April (see Table 5.1 at chapter's end). Zhmachenko's 40th Army still consisted of three rifle corps—the 50th, 51st, and the 104th—with a total of eight rifle divisions, and Avdeenko and Petrushevsky still commanded the 51st and 104th Rifle Corps. However, Major General P. F. Batitsky had replaced Martirosian as commander of the 50th Rifle Corps on 25 April, and Zhmachenko had shifted several rifle divisions from one rifle corps to another. As a result, Avdeenko's 51st Rifle Corp, which was to conduct the shock group's supporting attack west of Pascani, now consisted of the 42nd Guards and the 133rd and 232nd Rifle Divisions.

The composition of Trofimenko's 27th Army also remained relatively unchanged in late April, consisting of the 35th Guards and 33rd Rifle Corps, which were still commanded by Goriachev and Semenov, with a total of seven rifle divisions. However, Konev assigned Trofimenko's army the 25th and 119th Separate Tank Regiments, which were equipped with KV-model heavy tanks, in place of its two self-propelled artillery regiments to better support the army's assault and shifted several divisions among its two rifle corps. Finally, Bogdanov's 2nd Tank Army retained its previous basic structure, with the 3rd and 16th Tank Corps and the 11th Guards Tank Brigade, and retained the commanders of these forces, Generals Mishulin and Dubovoi and Colonel Erfmeev, respectively. In addition to this nucleus, Bogdanov's tank army also included the 8th and 13th Separate Guards Tank Regiments, which, although present in the tank army during mid-April, did not participate in the April offensive because they were being rested and refitted with new tanks. As a result, the two regiments would go into battle during early May equipped with new Iosef Stalin (IS)–model heavy tanks, which, while formidable, were still untested in combat.

There were two significant additions to Konev's main shock group by the end of April, however: namely, Shumilov's 7th Guards Army and Rotmistrov's famous 5th Guards Tank Army, neither of which had taken part in the *front*'s offensive operations in northern Romania during April. Since it had seen little action since mid-March 1944, Shumilov's 7th Guards Army was relatively fresh and undamaged. Like his counterpart in the 5th Guards Army, the 7th

Guards Army's commander, forty-nine-year-old Lieutenant General Mikhail Stepanovich Shumilov, was one of Stalin's most dependable army commanders. Appointed to command the newly formed 64th Army in August 1942, he had led that army with distinction during the fierce fighting for Stalingrad, and, after his army was awarded with the honorific designation of 7th Guards in March 1943, he led the same army through war's end.

Shumilov had begun his military career during World War I when he served as a noncommissioned officer in the Tsar's army and attended the Chuguev Military School. After he joined the Red Army in 1918, Shumilov commanded a platoon, company, and regiment on the eastern and southern fronts during the Russian Civil War and graduated from the Command and Political Officers Course in 1924 and the "*Vystrel*'" Course in 1929. Rising quickly from regimental to division command during the 1920s and 1930s, Shumilov was appointed to command the 11th Rifle Corps in April 1938 and led that corps in the occupation of eastern Poland during September 1939 and the Soviet-Finnish War during late 1939 and early 1940.

When the Germans began Operation Barbarossa in June 1941, Shumilov's 11th Rifle Corps was defending in the first echelon of the Northwestern Front's 8th Army. After being decimated by the German assault, Shumilov's corps retreated to the Leningrad region before being disbanded in the late summer of 1941. The NKO then assigned Shumilov as deputy commander of the Leningrad Front's 55th Army in late 1941 and early 1942 and the Southwestern Front's 21st Army in the summer of 1942 during the initial stages of German Operation *Blau*. Shumilov's star rose further in August 1942 when he took command of the 64th Army and led it through the Battle of Stalingrad. After the Stalingrad victory, under Shumilov's command, the 7th Guards Army withstood the brunt of the German offensive at Kursk in July 1943, spearheaded the Steppe Front's Belgorod-Khar'kov offensive in August 1943, and led its subsequent offensive to and across the Dnepr River in the fall, during which Shumilov was decorated as a Hero of the Soviet Union. Finally, during the winter of 1944, Shumilov's guards army had a leading role in the 2nd Ukrainian Front's Kirovograd and Korsun'-Shevchenkovskii offensives during January and February and its Uman'-Botoshany offensive during March. Known as a steadfast fighter and reliable Communist Party member, Stalin could count on Shumilov to perform his assigned mission tenaciously, skillfully, and usually without regard for losses.[2]

In late April, Shumilov's guards army still consisted of the 24th and 25th Guards Rifle Corps, commanded respectively by Generals Vasil'ev and Safiulin, but had increased its strength to a total of seven rifle divisions by the addition of the 6th Airborne Division to Safiulin's guards rifle corps and the 6th Rifle Division to his army's reserve. The 7th Guards Army's supporting forces still included the 27th Guards Tank Brigade, a separate antitank rifle battalion, and two separate armored train battalions, although the latter remained well to the rear.

The second and most important addition to Konev's expanded shock group in late April was Rotmistrov's famous 5th Guards Tank Army, which had originally formed as the 5th Tank Army in the early summer of 1942 and, after fighting unsuccessfully around Voronezh in July 1942, won fame by its role in the encirclement of the German Sixth Army at Stalingrad in November 1942. In its new configuration as a guards tank army under Rotmistrov's command, the 5th Guards Tank Army burnished its reputation in July 1943 by fighting the equally famous German II SS Panzer Corps to a standstill on the poppy fields near Prokhorovka and, later, by its signal victory at Korsun'-Shevchenkovskii in January and February 1944.

Although his reputation became a bit tarnished later in the war, as indicated by his rank of colonel general, Pavel Alekseevich Rotmistrov was arguably the Red Army's most famous tank army commander by early 1944, largely by virtue of his army's victory on the field of Prokhorovka during the Battle for Kursk. Only forty-two years old in April 1944, he had joined the Red Army in 1919, fought in the Polish War during 1920, and helped suppress the Kronshtadt mutiny in 1921. After graduating from the Military-Inspectorate's Formation School in 1924, Rotmistrov commanded a platoon and company in the Leningrad Military District's 11th Rifle Division and became an assistant battalion commander in the same division from 1924 through 1930. Upon his graduation from the Frunze Academy in 1931, Rotmistrov was posted to the Far East, where he served as deputy chief of staff of the 36th Rifle Division in the Trans-Baikal Military District, which clashed with Japanese forces in 1932, and deputy chief of operations and then chief of the armored forces of the Special Red Banner Far East Army from 1933 through early 1937. His impressive performance in these posts earned him promotion to colonel and command of a rifle regiment in the same army's 21st Rifle Division from June through October 1937.

After transferring to the Red Army's new tank and mechanized forces, Rotmistrov taught on the tactics faculty of the army's Military Academy for Mechanization and Motorization in 1938; commanded a tank battalion and served as deputy commander of the 35th Light Tank Brigade during the Soviet-Finnish War; and, when the Red Army established mechanized corps in 1940, became first deputy commander of the 5th Tank Division and, in May 1941, chief of staff of the same tank division's parent 3rd Mechanized Corps in the Baltic Special Military District, where he was serving when war broke out in June 1941.

After surviving the destruction of his mechanized corps by German forces during the first three weeks of the war, the NKO assigned Rotmistrov command of the newly formed 8th Tank Brigade in September 1941, which he led with distinction during fighting at Staraia Russa, Kalinin, Klin, and, finally, the Battle for Moscow, where his brigade earned the designation of 3rd Guards. In reward for his brigade's performance at Moscow, the NKO assigned him command of its new 7th Tank Corps in April 1942, and Rotmistrov led this tank corps, then subordinate to the 5th Tank Army, during that army's stunning defeat at Voronezh in July 1942. Once again surviving a major defeat, Rotmistrov's tank corps performed well during the Battle for Stalingrad and, particularly, during the December 1942 counteroffensive south of Stalingrad, when his tank corps fought successfully at Rychkovskii, Verkhne-Chirskii, and Kotel'nikovskii to defeat German efforts to rescue their encircled Sixth Army. Rotmistrov then led his tank corps, by now redesignated the 3rd Guards, during the successful Rostov offensive during January 1943 and the newly formed 5th Guards Tank Army from its formation in February 1943 through April 1944.

Under the control of Konev's Steppe (later 2nd Ukrainian) Front, Rotmistrov commanded the 5th Guards Tank Army successfully and often spectacularly in the Battle of Kursk during August 1943, the Belgorod-Khar'kov offensive during August 1943, the *front*'s advance to the Dnepr River in October 1943, and its bloody and prolonged battles in the Krivoi Rog and Kirovograd regions south of the Dnepr River through year's end. Thereafter, his tank army spearheaded Konev's forces during the Kirovograd and Korsun'-Shevchenkovskii offensives during January and February 1944 and its successful offensive across the central Ukraine during March 1944.

By April 1944 Rotmistrov had earned a stellar reputation for his performance in command:

> Rotmistrov possessed an uncanny ability to quickly assess a situation and devise a creative approach for decisions. Decisions came easily to Rotmistrov, in a word, he was a builder. As an authoritative theorist and practitioner, he took an active part in the reorganizing and structure of the Soviet tank army. This, at times, put him at odds with senior commanders—especially when he believed that he had a better idea. Rotmistrov was conscious of the credentials of his critics and was not impressed by rank or title. He was the supreme pragmatist.
>
> Rotmistrov's fighting style of a hard, direct, and swift blow upset the enemy. Using in full measure the tank unit's agility, he broke up the enemy's main forces, encircled them, and destroyed them in detail. His rapid rise was a combination of his demonstrated erudition and his bold, decisive initiative on the battlefield. In its struggle for survival, the Red Army tolerated such an eccentric nature in its top armored guards theoretician and architect.[3]

Another senior Red Army officer noted:

> Pavel Rotmistrov is also undoubtedly one of our outstanding tank generals. Commanding rich practical experience acquired on the battlefield and a fund of theoretical knowledge, he, too, contributed notably to the postwar development of tank engineering and the training of tank commanders.[4]

The composition of Rotmistrov's 5th Guards Tank Army changed little during the month of April, although the *Stavka* beefed up its armored strength considerably from about 150 tanks and self-propelled guns to about 360 armored vehicles. Throughout the entire month, the tank army's nucleus consisted of Major General of Tank Forces V. I. Polozkov's 18th and Major General of Tank Forces E. I. Fominykh's 29th Tank Corps, both of which were organized in the standard configuration of three tank brigades and one motorized rifle brigade, supported by a variety of self-propelled, tank destroyer, and antiaircraft artillery regiments, mortar and guards-mortar regiments and battalions, motorcycle battalions, and logistical subunits. In addition, the army included Major General of Tank Forces B. M. Skvortsov's 5th Guards Mechanized Corps, which was organized with three mechanized brigades, one tank brigade, and a variety of supporting regiments and battalions. Rotmistrov would retain Skvortsov's mechanized corps in reserve during the May offensive because by this time it lacked most of its heavy weapons and equipment.

While Rotmistrov's tank army lacked a separate tank brigade, it also fielded the 14th and 53rd Guards Separate Tank Regiments, which were equipped with new I. S. Stalin–model heavy tanks, and the 1st Guards Motorcycle Regiment. All of Rotmistrov's corps commanders were experienced and combat-seasoned veterans. Polozkov had commanded the 18th Tank Corps since December 1943, and, although Fominykh had taken command of the 29th Tank Corps from its previous commander, Lieutenant General I. F. Kirichenko, only on 18 April, he too had extensive experience commanding at the brigade level. Finally, Skvortsov, whose mechanized corps would not see action during May, had commanded the 5th Guards Mechanized Corps since February 1943 and would do so until war's end.

Finally, on the eve of his May offensive, Konev temporarily assigned Major General of Tank Forces I. A. Vovchenko's 3rd Guards Tank Corps, which had previously been in his *front*'s reserve to rest and refit, to Rotmistrov's army to replace Skvortsov's weakened 5th Guards Mechanized Corps. Organized as a standard tank corps, the corps' commander, Vovchenko, was also an experienced combat veteran, who had commanded this corps since early March 1943 and a tank brigade before.

In addition to the five armies constituting his shock group, Konev kept several important forces in reserve so that he could reinforce his attacking forces, if necessary. The largest of these forces were the two rifle divisions of Major General E. S. Alekhin's 27th Guards Rifle Corps and Lieutenant General A. G. Selivanov's 5th Guards Cavalry Corps, which, despite the heavy attrition it had endured in previous combat, Konev was prepared to call on to support Zhmachenko's secondary thrust.

Finally, Konev also allocated large amounts of artillery to support his shock group's penetration and exploitation operations. For example, he attached the 16th Artillery Penetration Division to Shumilov's 7th Guards Army to reinforce the 11th Artillery Division, which was already under its control, and he assigned most of the *front*'s 13th Artillery Penetration Division to support his shock group as a whole.

KONEV'S DIVERSIONARY OPERATIONS ALONG THE IASI AXIS (24–26 APRIL)

As required by his *front*'s deception plan, Konev planned to conduct his diversionary attacks against the German IV Army Corps (Group Mieth), which was defending the Iasi region, in three distinct stages, beginning on 24 April (Map 13). First, in the sector of the 27th Army's 33rd Rifle Corps northwest of Iasi, early on 24 April, several reinforced rifle battalions from the lead rifle regiments of Colonel T. P. Gorobets' 337th Rifle Division from Semenov's rifle corps were to conduct a reconnaissance-in-force along the road running southeastward from the village of Harlesti [Zahorna], nine miles northwest of Iasi and at the very center of the defenses manned by the IV Army Corps' Romanian 18th Infantry Division, toward Iasi proper.

Second, regardless of whether this reconnaissance-in-force succeeded, early on 25 April, the 78th, 180th, and 202nd Rifle Divisions of Semenov's 33rd Rifle Corps, supported by the 103rd Tank Brigade from Mishulin's 3rd Tank Corps (from the 2nd Tank Army), were to assault the 18th Infantry Division's defenses in the three-mile-wide sector between the villages of Tautesti and Vinaturi, eight miles northwest and seven miles north of Iasi, respectively, and advance on Iasi from the northwest and north. Third, at dawn on 26 April, the 50th, 373rd, 254th, 116th, and 294th Rifle Divisions from the 73rd and 78th Rifle Corps of Koroteev's 52nd Army, backed up by the 337th Rifle Division from Semenov's 33rd Rifle Corps (from the 27th Army) and spearheaded by two battalion-size tank groups from the 6th Tank Army's 5th Mechanized and 5th Guards Tank Corps, were to assault the enemy's defenses at the town of Vulturi, at the apex of the German defenses six miles due north of Iasi.

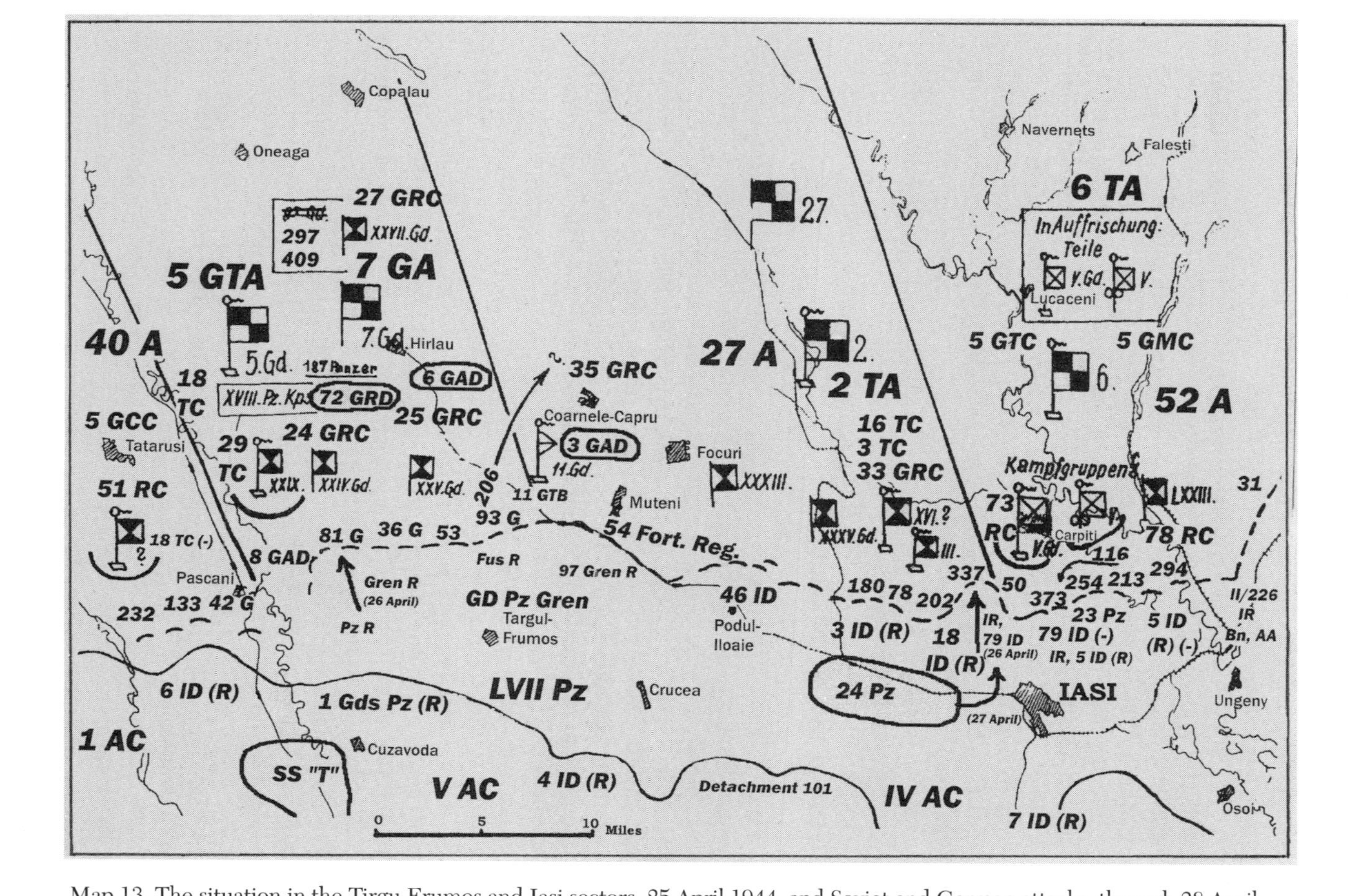

Map 13. The situation in the Tirgu Frumos and Iasi sectors, 25 April 1944, and Soviet and German attacks, through 28 April

The German IV Army Corps, which was defending the northern approaches to Iasi, deployed one regiment each from the German 79th Infantry and Romanian 5th Infantry Divisions and two regiments of the Romanian 5th Cavalry Division to defend the ten-mile-wide sector from Vulturi eastward to the Prut River, and retained the remaining regiments of all three divisions in tactical reserve north of the city. In addition, it also held Kräber's 23rd Panzer Division as its operational reserve south of the city. On the IV Army Corps' left, the Romanian V Army Corps' 18th Infantry Division defended the sector from Tautesti to Vinaturi.

Given the strength of the IV Army Corps and the presence of the 23rd Panzer Division south of Iasi, realistically, Konev harbored little hope that the shock groups conducting his diversionary assaults would fulfill their missions. However, he did believe these forces could pin the 23rd Panzer Division down in the Iasi region and perhaps draw the 24th Panzer Division, then stationed at Podu Iloaie, 15 miles west of Iasi, into the region north of Iasi as well.

After Semenov's 33rd Rifle Corps conducted its reconnaissance-in-force as planned on 24 April, with few gains, the following morning, the 78th, 180th, 202nd, and 337th Rifle Divisions of Semenov's rifle corps, supported by the 103rd Tank Brigade, struck the Romanian defenses between Tautesti and Vinaturi. By day's end, Semenov's attacking riflemen and tanks managed to wedge up to one and one half miles deep into the 18th Infantry Division's defenses along a front of three miles east of Tautesti. Reacting quickly, however, the IV Army Corps was able to restore the Romanian division's shattered defenses, first, by reinforcing it with one regiment from the German 79th Infantry Division late on 25 April, and, second, by counterattacking against the Soviet penetration with the 21st Panzer Grenadier Regiment of Edelsheim's 24th Panzer Division and the German 46th Infantry Division's 97th Grenadier Regiment on 27 April. As a result, after intense fighting, the 33rd Rifle Corps ended its attacks and withdrew its assault force back to its jumping-off positions by day's end on 28 April.

Meanwhile, due north of Iasi, the five rifle divisions of the 52nd Army's 73rd and 78th Rifle Corps and the two small tank groups from the 6th Tank Army assaulted the IV Army Corps' defenses early on 26 April, penetrated the defenses of the Romanian 5th Infantry Division, in the process routing one of the division's regiments, and managed to carve a one-mile-wide and up to two-mile-wide wedge into the defenses of the German 79th Infantry and Romanian 5th Cavalry Divisions. After two days of heavy fighting, however, the 52nd Army's assault also collapsed along the forward slopes of high ground west of the village of Radui Aldei, only five miles north of Iasi, where the 79th Infantry Division's reserve infantry regiment was able to establish effective defenses to block the Soviet advance.

The tide of battle north of Iasi finally turned sharply in the Germans' favor on 28 April when the 23rd Panzer and 79th Infantry Divisions launched a combined counterattack against Koroteev's forces in the Radui Aldei sector, while a small *kampfgruppe* from the 21st Panzer Grenadier Regiment of Edelsheim's 24th Panzer Division's counterattacked northward along the Vulturi road. As a result of these coordinated counterattacks, German forces drove the Soviet troops from their hard-won gains back to their initial jumping-off positions by day's end on 30 April. Although Konev's diversionary assaults north of Iasi failed to seize and hold any ground, they did partially fulfill the goals of Konev's deception plan by tying the German 79th Infantry and 23rd Panzer Divisions down in defensive positions north of Iasi. However, contrary to Konev's hopes, by the time the fighting was over on 30 April, the 24th Panzer Division's *kampfgruppe* was already en route back its parent division's main assembly areas in the Podu Iloaie region to the west.

Although Konev did not realize it at the time, despite the modest results achieved by his diversionary operations, his deception actually succeeded beyond his wildest expectations. For example, as evidenced by its daily intelligence maps, as late as 1 May, Army Group Wöhler's intelligence organs decided the 2nd Ukrainian Front's entire 27th Army and 2nd Tank Army were assembled in concentration areas north and northwest of Iasi, probably in preparation for an assault on Iasi from the north. Only on the morning of 2 May, when the assault by Konev's main shock group against Tirgu Frumos was already under way, did the Germans finally realize that the 2nd Tank Army and half of the 27th Army were bearing down on Tirgu Frumos from the north. The most important question on 2 May was, "Would this German intelligence failure make any difference in the ultimate outcome of the fighting in the Tirgu Frumos region?"

GROUP WÖHLER'S SPOILING ATTACKS (25–28 APRIL)

While his 27th and 52nd Armies were conducting diversionary operations north of Iasi, Konev completed regrouping and concentrating his *front*'s main shock group for the offensive along the Tirgu Frumos axis. This process, in itself, was a complicated task, particularly if it was to be carried out in complete secrecy, as required. First, all of Shumilov's 7th Guards and Rotmistrov's 5th Guards Tank Armies had to regroup southward a distance of 15–20 miles into their designated assault positions between the Seret River and the village of Cucuteni, six miles north of Tirgu Frumos, without being detected. Second, Goriachev's 35th Guards Rifle Corps of Trofimenko's 27th Army had to moved 12 miles eastward from its previous positions northwest of Tirgu Frumos to new concentration areas in the Hodora and Tetarului sector, ten miles northeast of Tirgu Frumos. Finally, Bogdanov had to move his entire 2nd Tank Army, including its 103rd Tank Brigade, which had been fighting near Iasi, into new assembly areas 12–15 miles northeast of Tirgu-Frumos from which it could first support and then exploit the 35th Guards Rifle Corps' attack.

If this regrouping process was not difficult enough in its own right, the Germans complicated matters for Konev by conducting a series of spoiling attacks in the Pascani region and northwest of Tirgu Frumos from 24 through 27 April, at the very time when the divisions of Shumilov's 7th Guards Army were relieving the divisions of Trofimenko's 27th Army (Map 14). In addition to causing considerable damage to Konev's forces locally and disrupting his forces' regrouping, these spoiling attacks also severely disrupted Konev's preparations for the offensive.

Army Group Wöhler's Romanian V Army Corps began planning and organizing these spoiling attacks on 22 and 23 April, immediately after its intelligence organs detected the movement of the Soviet 2nd Tank Army toward the Iasi region but before Konev began conducting his diversionary operations north of Iasi. Although the original intent of these spoiling attacks seemed to be an attempt by the V Army Corps to take advantage of the departure of the 2nd Tank Army from the Tirgu Frumos region, ultimately the V Army Corps' attacks were apparently designed to create enough havoc in the Soviet defenses north of Tirgu Frumos to force them to abandon the attack against Iasi.

Whatever rationale motivated its actions, the V Army Corps ultimately planned to conduct two spoiling attacks, the first near Pascani, west of the Seret River, and the second north of Tirgu Frumos. Accordingly, it ordered Priess's SS "*T*" Panzer Division to regroup northward from its assembly areas around Halaucesti, 14 miles north of Roman, reinforce the Romanian 6th Infantry Division's defenses southwest of Pascani, and assault the Soviet defenses south and southwest of that town. At the same time, Wöhler ordered the Grenadier and Panzer Regiments out of Manteuffel's *Grossdeutschland* Panzer Grenadier Division to attack the Soviet defenses northwest of Tirgu Frumos in tandem with a northward advance by the Romanian 1st Guards Division west of Tirgu Frumos.

The forces of SS "*T*" Panzer Division deployed northward from Halaucesti on 23 April and attacked the Soviet defenses south of Pascani on the morning of 24 April, in close coordination with an assault by the Romanian 6th Infantry Division northward on the SS "*T*'s" left flank. The combined assault struck the 232nd Rifle and 42nd Guards Rifle Divisions of the 40th Army's 51st Rifle Corps. After three days of intense fighting over difficult terrain west of the Seret River, *Totenkopf*'s forces and the supporting Romanians drove the two Soviet rifle divisions back to Pascani and recaptured the

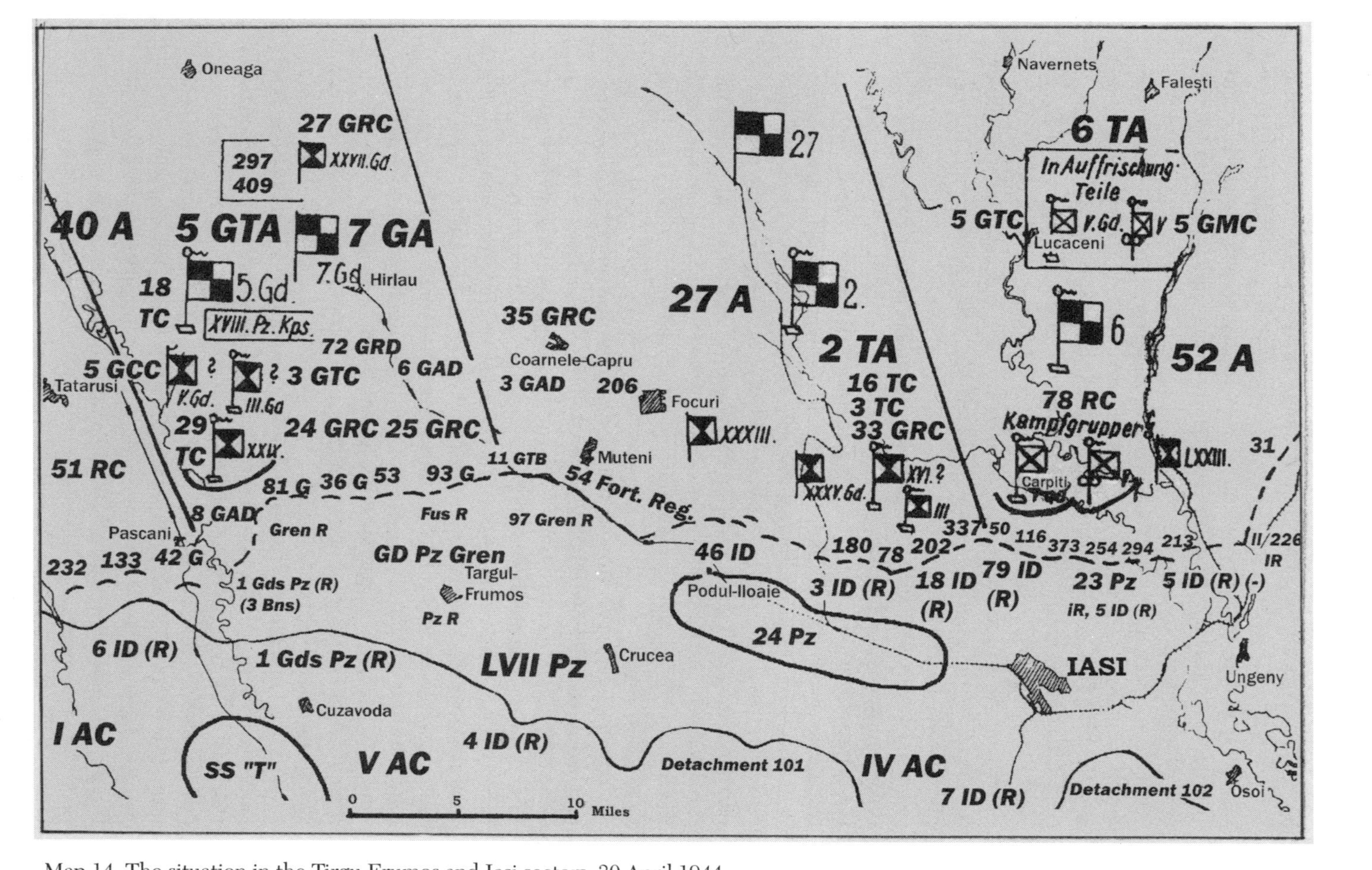

Map 14. The situation in the Tirgu Frumos and Iasi sectors, 30 April 1944

town. However, soon after its forces recaptured Pascani, the V Corps halted its counterattacks, and, by day's end on 28 April, the situation in the Pascani region stabilized. The V Army Corps' decision to halt its counterattacks in the Pascani sector probably resulted from Army Group Wöhler's concerns over the strong Soviet attacks at Iasi. By 28 April, the commitment of part of the 24th Panzer Division in the Iasi region made it essential to call off further operations in the Pascani sector and return SS *"T"* to its previous assembly area so that it could once again serve as the army group's and V Army Corps' general reserve.

Meanwhile, east of the Seret River, the *Grossdeutschland* and Romanian 1st Guards Divisions commenced their assault early on 25 April, with the Grenadier Regiment from the former attacking northwestward from the village of Costesti, four miles northwest of Tirgu Frumos, toward the village of Barbotesti, three miles farther to the northwest, and the latter advancing northward from Radiu, five miles west of Tirgu Frumos, toward Harmanesti, two miles west of Barbotesti. The concentric attacks by the German and Romanian forces through the heavily forested hills northwest of Tirgu Frumos struck the Soviet defenses at the junction of the 7th Guards Army's 24th and 25th Guards Rifle Corps immediately after the two guards rifle corps' lead divisions, the 81st and 36th Guards Divisions, had completed the delicate process of taking over the defensive sectors of the 27th Army's 93rd Guards and 206th Rifle Divisions but before the two guards rifle divisions had a chance to complete their relief, dig in, and thoroughly organize their defenses.

The official histories of the two rifle divisions recorded the subsequent action accurately and vividly. For example, the division history of the 36th Guards Rifle Division, whose commander was Major General M. I. Denisenko and was subordinate to Safiulin's 25th Guards Rifle Corps of Shumilov's 7th Guards Army, reports that the division was struck by a strong German surprise attack soon after it relieved the 27th Army's 206th Rifle Division:

> On the night of 24–25 April, the 36th Guards Rifle Division received the mission of relieving the units of the 27th Army's 35th Guards Rifle Corps and occupying a defense along the Mount Hushenei and Ulmi-Isui line [northwest of Tirgu-Frumos].
>
> The subunits had hardly managed to take over their combat sector when the enemy rained down powerful artillery fire. "Junkers" appeared in the skies. After an intense bombardment and a massive fire raid, units of the 1st Romanian Division, supported by tanks from Motorized Division Grossdeutschland, went over to the attack. The soldiers had still not found their bearings and had not oriented themselves on the terrain. The artillery crews had not yet managed to deploy fully into their firing positions. In addition, the enemy had an obvious superiority in tanks, and his

> aircraft ruled the skies. In spite of all of this, the Upper Dnepr soldiers bravely accepted battle.
>
> The Hitlerites' main attack struck the 106th Rifle Regiment. The enemy tanks succeeded in enveloping its flanks and filtered into its rear area. Fighting in encirclement, the soldiers and their commanders indeed displayed their guards honor and massive heroism. . . .
>
> The subunits of the 104th and 108th Regiments bravely repelled the onslaught of the superior enemy forces. Thirteen enemy tanks with troops carrying automatic weapons riding on them, then succeeded in wedging into the combat formations of the battalions of Senior Lieutenant A. P. Kuz'min and Major K. P. Lapshin at their adjoining flanks. The guardsmen did not falter. . . . Overall, the division destroyed up to 250 Hitlerites and burned or destroyed seven tanks in this fighting.
>
> On the following day—26 April—after bringing up reserves, the Fascist command tried to exploit their attack. However, the regiments parried all of the enemy's attacks and inflicted great losses on him. After exhausting the enemy, the guardsmen themselves advanced forward and threw the Hitlerites back to their jumping-off positions. Digging in on the dominating heights, the guardsmen repelled numerous enemy counterattacks, which inflicted heavy personnel and equipment losses [on the enemy].[5]

The division history of the 81st Guards Rifle Division, whose commander was Major General I. K. Morozov and was subordinate to Vasil'ev's 24th Guards Rifle Corps of Shumilov's guards army, also provides a particularly detailed and accurate description of the heavy fighting it experienced shortly after it relieved the 27th Army's 3rd Guards Airborne Division in the sector south of Harmanesti and northwest of Tirgu Frumos, as well as the overall difficulties Shumilov's army faced:

> On order of the army commander, M. S. Shumilov, on 24 April the division once again joined Hero of the Soviet Union Lieutenant General N. A. Vasil'ev's guards corps.
>
> After an artillery preparation, [on 25 April] the 1st Guards Royal Division of the Royal Romanian 5th Army Corps attacked at the junction of the guards divisions of Generals Bogdanov and Denisenko [the 8th Guards Airborne and 36th Guards Rifle Divisions] with a force of 40 tanks and two full-blooded infantry regiments and drove back the subunits of their flanks. We received the mission from General Vasil'ev to destroy the penetrating enemy and prepare the division to conduct a counterattack in the general direction of Tirgu-Frumos.
>
> Guards Major Andrei Voron's regiment occupied an attack line west of Lake Bulhac and Grigorii Skiruta's regiment to the east of the lake. Timofei Selishchev's regiment was deployed in the division's second ech-

elon on the highway [to the north] southwest of Bolucesti. The artillerymen of Guards Major Konstantin Poliakovsky and Guards Captain Fedor Cherepanov were attached locally by battery [to the forward subunits] and registered on enemy targets.

The gunners and mortar crews of Captain Evgenii Guben and Anatoli Martyniuk swiftly deployed their batteries into the clearings, spread out along the front and in the depth of the shrub growth, and set about adjusting their guns and mortars on enemy targets. The artillery battalion commander, Guards Captain Nikolai Buzuev alerted battery commander Guben to not become preoccupied with the enemy infantry and instead prepare his artillery to repel an enemy tank attack along his axis where they expected it, along the road to Tirgu-Frumos. . . .

The [Romanian's] royal artillery opened heavy fire. Maneuvering to and fro, the assault guns filled up the woods where Guards Captain Iakov Zavadovsky's battalion was concentrating with shell fire. They conducted fire raids with entire artillery battalions against our infantry and artillery batteries occupying their attack lines and firing positions.

After an attack by our artillery and mortars, early in the morning [on 26 April], Voron's and Skiruta's rifle regiments, followed by Selishchev's [regiment], supported by coordinated and precise fire by Poliakovsky's and Cherepanov's artillerymen, disrupted the royal guardsmen's prepared attacks and, after crushing their combat formation, successfully advanced forward, enveloping Dumbravita [nine miles west of Tirgu-Frumos] from the east and west.

After completing their immediate mission of capturing Dumbravita, Major Nikolai Ershov's, Captain Antoli Andreev's, and Senior Lieutenant Pavel Vypasiuk's battalions of Voron's regiment fought for the railroad, the village of Buzhha, and the Cuza Voda Railroad Station.

Captain Nikolai Denisov's, Senior Lieutenant Dmitri Glukhovtsev's, and Captain Kiril Silaev's battalions of Skiruta's regiment repelled enemy counterattacks along the highway and to the east of Cuza Voda Station and Dzhurdzhe. We had to speed up Colonel Skiruta, commit Selishchev's regiment to combat, and bring the reserves closer forward.

Early in the morning, the regiments enveloped Dumbravita from the west and east and, after crushing the enemy, advanced to the south. Without noticing, they left a little something behind for us to work on.

A battalion of the 1st Royal Guards Division's 21st Infantry Regiment did not succeed in withdrawing and continued firing. [After being encouraged to surrender, the battalion was fired on by artillery and broke and ran away in disorder.]

The guardsmen of Colonel Skiruta did not push forward. By that time the regiment had already captured the sector of the railroad south of Dumbravita and was fighting for Radiu [seven miles west of Tirgu-Frumos]. Selishshev's regiment, which had been committed to battle, captured the highway and railroad, advanced to Mount Hushenei, and in cooperation with a regiment from General Denisenko's [36th Guards Rifle] division, repelled an enemy infantry and tank counterattack, while moving back. . . .

The commander of the royal Romanian division reinforced his second-echelon regiment with tanks, counting on not only holding his positions but also throwing us back across the railroad and Mount Hushenei. . . .

The enemy pressure strengthened and then weakened like the stormy waves of a gale, and, while withdrawing from combat under this pressure, Selishchev's regiment drew the royal soldiers after them into the plain between Mount Hushenei and the [village] of Crivesti, where they were surprised by heavy machine guns, guns firing over open sights, mines, and hastily positioned sappers. The artillerymen only awaited the commands of Lieutenant Colonel Saik. And then, when the Romanians entered into this "swamp" between the mountains, all of the prepared firing means of Shamshurov, Ushakov, and Saik came raining down on them.[6]

Finally, the *Grossdeutschland* Division's history provides a detailed account of its spoiling attack from the German perspective:

Subsequently orders came from above for a major offensive action in the division's left sector, with the objective of driving into the woods between Barbatesti (Barbotesti) [seven miles northwest of Tirgu-Frumos] and Vascani [nine miles west-northwest of Tirgu-Frumos], in order to smash enemy preparations which were suspected of going on there. A further objective, especially for the tanks, was Hill 372 and the hill near Dumbravita.

By 25 April all was ready. II and III Battalions, Panzer-Grenadier Regiment GD were to carry the weight of the attack. At about 04.15, after a brief artillery bombardment, the panzer-grenadiers sprang from their foxholes. The Soviets were taken completely by surprise. Their line breached, they fled in panic. The assault guns performed magnificently against the enemy anti-tank guns, especially in the right attack sector under the command of Oberleutnant [Senior Lieutenant] Didens, a specialist in the destruction of anti-tank guns and his battery alone destroyed 31 heavy anti-tank guns and three enemy tanks. He was named in the Wehrmacht communiqué, which declared: "the Soviets attacked north of Jassy with powerful forces. They foundered on the determined resistance of the German and Romanian troops. Local penetrations were sealed off."

> Further to the left the Tigers and Panthers of the Panzer Regiment GD attacked along the highway to Vascani and were able to reach their objective in spite of considerable resistance, especially from tanks and anti-tank guns. This successful operation revealed that they had in fact driven into enemy attack preparations. The Bolsheviks had massed strong infantry and tank forces. . . .
>
> The tanks and assault guns were sent into action on the hills between Vascani and Dumbravita again on 27 April. Believing that in this case, too, a good offense was the best defense, the division command sent them back into the hornet's nest of the enemy assembly area.
>
> The tank battle raged for hours. The attack was an outstanding success; the panzers opened fire from a distance of 80 metres. After a few hits the first tank bearing the red star on its turret went up in flames. The panzer company (the Tiger battalion was under the command of Oberstleutnant Baumungk) reported destroying large numbers of enemy tanks with only minor losses. Once again, however, there was little territorial gain even though the Soviets withdrew.[7]

During this sharp fight, the Romanian 1st Guards Division penetrated the defenses of Morozov's 81st Guards Rifle Division and drove its forces northward to the southern outskirts of the town of Harmanesti, ten miles west-northwest of Tirgu Frumos, and also turned the left flank of Bogdanov's 8th Guards Airborne Division, which was defending on Morozov's right flank, forcing his division to withdraw westward toward the Seret River. Morozov's division was finally able to halt the Romanian advance at Harmanesti and prepared to launch a counterattack of its own with its second-echelon regiment. Meanwhile, to the east, *Grossdeutschland* Division's Grenadier Regiment pushed Denisenko's 36th Guards Rifle Division back to the southern approaches to Barbotesti, seven miles northwest of Tirgu Frumos, where the regiment ended its advance at nightfall.

Meanwhile, while the Romanian 1st Guards Division, which was deployed on the *Grossdeutschland* Division's left, contained the Soviet forces in the vicinity of the town of Dumbravita, along the railroad line from Tirgu Frumos to Pascani, nine miles west-northwest of Tirgu Frumos, early on 25 April, one of the Romanian division's regiments also attacked northward up the valley southwest of Crivesti, five miles north of Dumbravita, but was soon struck by a counterattack from the second-echelon rifle regiment of Morozov's 81st Guards Rifle Division, supported by all of his division's artillery. After a short but bloody encounter, the Romanians broke for the rear, prompting the division commander to ask for assistance from Manteuffel, the commander of the *Grossdeutschland* Division. In response, early the following day, Manteuffel dispatched a small *kampfgruppe* from his division's

Panzer Regiment to help the beleagured Romanians escape from the Soviet trap. After several more hours of fighting, this force stabilized the front west and northwest of Tirgu Frumos and restored a contiguous defense line in this region.[8]

During the three days of fighting northwest of Tirgu Frumos, the attacking German troops also made another notable discovery: the Soviets were employing a new and heavier model tank. This confirmed reports received from German forces fighting in the Chernovtsy sector in far northern Romania about a week before:

> There was a surprise waiting for the tank crews when they inspected the knocked-out Soviet tanks; they were armed with a new 122-mm. gun. The shells came in two parts, with a huge propellant charge. So it was true what German intelligence had reported some weeks earlier: the Soviets were now using a new, much more powerful type of tank, the Josef Stalin, or JS for short. These new tanks subsequently became more prevalent, forcing the development of more powerful defensive weapons, especially anti-tank guns.[9]

As a result of the sorties they conducted northwest of Tirgu Frumos, after the fighting finally ended at day's end on 28 April, the combined German and Romanian forces managed to advance their defense lines forward about six miles northwest and north of Tirgu Frumos. These new defense lines, which incorporated many of Konev's planned jumping-off positions for his offensive, extended from the Seret River at Pascani, eastward three miles to Blagesti, northeastward three miles to just south of Harmanesti, and eastward roughly seven more miles through Vascani and Barbotesti to just north of Cucuteni, six miles north of Tirgu Frumos. By doing so, the V Army Corps seriously disrupted Konev's offensive preparations and combat formation, in the process damaging and severely shaking the determination of at least two of the 7th Guards Army's forward rifle divisions at a time when Shumilov's army was trying to occupy its jumping-off positions for the climactic offensive against Tirgu Frumos and Iasi. It is also quite likely that the German counterattacks forced Konev to delay his general offensive once again, this time to the morning of 2 May.

KONEV'S FINAL OFFENSIVE PREPARATIONS (29 APRIL–1 MAY)

The Main Shock Group's Combat Formation

Undeterred by Army Group Wöhler's spoiling attacks, Konev simply ordered the commanders of his subordinate armies to complete their preparations for the new offensive in accordance with existing plans and his revised "D-day" and to concentrate their forces in attack positions as close as possible to those indicated in his 23 April attack order. His army commanders dutifully complied, moving their forces into their forward jumping-off positions during the two nights of 30 April–1 May and 1–2 May (Map 15).

On 1 May Konev's 2nd Ukrainian Front was still a formidable force, particularly since by this time Konev was able to bring to bear two full combined arms armies (Shumilov's 7th Guards and Trofimenko's 27th) and two tank armies (Rotmistrov's 5th Guards and Bogdanov's 2nd) against Group Wöhler's defenses along the Tirgu Frumos axis. This force was over twice as large as the force he had employed along the same axis during his offensive in mid-April. In addition, a portion of Zhmachenko's 40th Army was poised to support and protect his main shock group's right wing, and a fourth combined-army, Koroteev's 52nd, and part of yet another tank army, Kravchenko's 6th, were prepared to support his shock group's left wing by resuming their assaults on the Germans' defenses north of Iasi. Finally, by the morning of 2 May, Malinovsky's 3rd Ukrainian Front had deployed sufficient forces into its bridgeheads on the western bank of the Dnestr River to pose a credible threat to the German defenses in those sectors as well.

By nightfall of 1 May, the two combined arms armies constituting the nucleus of Konev's main shock group had finally occupied their jumping-off positions for their offensive, each with a full tank army in its rear area poised to exploit their offensive success into the depths (see Table 5.2 at chapter's end).

The Main Shock Group's Dispositions and Missions

When Konev's shock group completed its preparations on 1 May, Shumilov's 7th Guards Army, with Rotmistrov's 5th Guards Tank Army assembled in its rear area, was concentrated on the right wing of the *front*'s shock group, with its two guards rifle corps arrayed from left to right (east to west) in the ten-mile-wide sector from Cucuteni westward to the Seret River (Map 16). Safiulin's 25th Guards Rifle Corps formed for combat on the army's left wing, with Major General A. E. Ovsienko's 53rd Rifle and Denisenko's 36th Guards Rifle Divisions deployed from left to right in first echelon and Major General M. N. Smirnov's 6th Guards Airborne Division in his corps' second echelon.

Opposite Safiulin's jumping-off positions, the Romanian V Army Corps' defenses were manned by forces on the right wing and in the center of *Grossdeutschland* Division's Grenadier Regiment, backed up by *Grossdeutschland*'s Panzer Regiment, which was in lager on the southern outskirts of Tirgu Frumos. Vasil'ev's 24th Guards Rifle Corps formed for combat on the army's right wing, with Morozov's 81st Guards and Bogdanov's 8th Guards Airborne

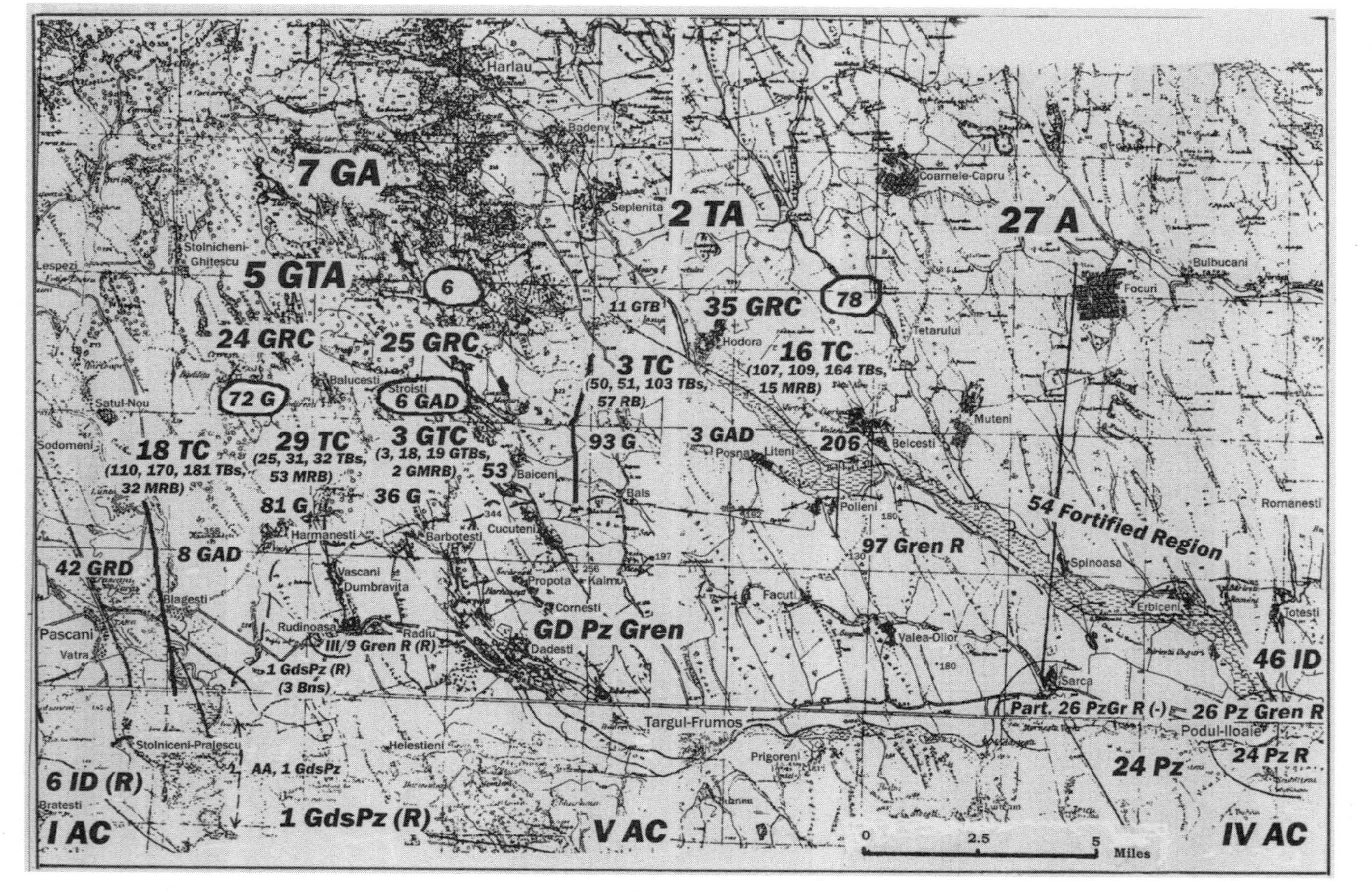

Map 15. The situation in the Tirgu Frumos sector, 0600 hours, 1 May 1944

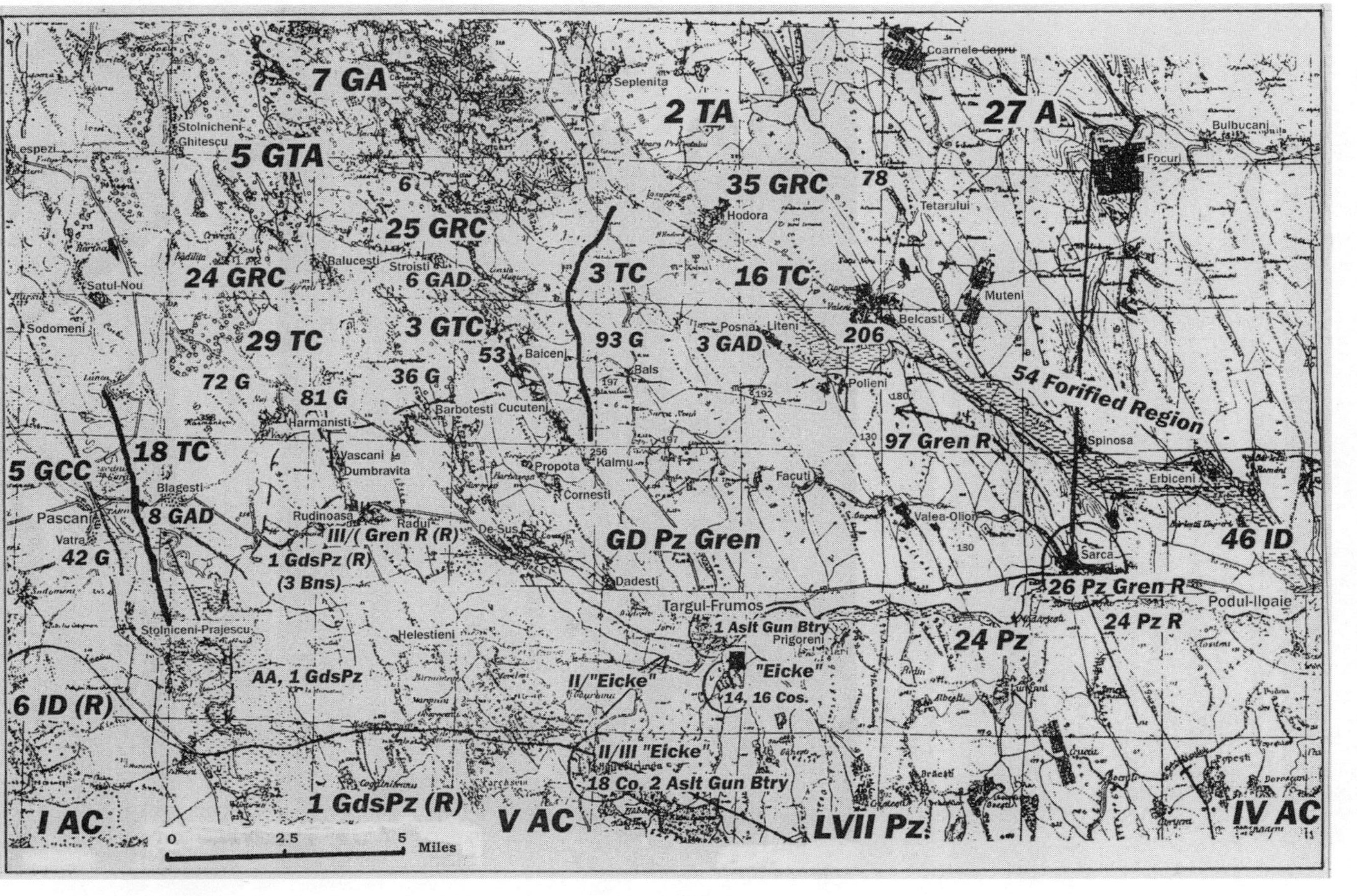

Map 16. The situation in the Tirgu Frumos sector, 0600 hours, 2 May 1944

Divisions deployed from left to right in first echelon and Major General A. I. Losev's 72nd Guards Rifle Division in second echelon. Vasil'ev rifle corps faced defenses manned by the Romanian 1st Guards Panzer Division.

Shumilov's 7th Guards Army retained Colonel I. F. Obushenko's 6th Rifle Division in its rear area as the army's reserve and the 27th Guards Tank Brigade to serve as its antitank reserve. Shumilov intended to employ his reserves whenever and wherever necessary, principally to reinforce his attacks or defeat enemy counterattacks. To support his army's penetration operation, together with his corps and divisions own organic artillery, the 11th Artillery Division and the more powerful 16th Artillery Penetration Division enabled Shumilov to concentrate about 250 guns and mortars along each mile of his offensive front. Finally, while the four regiments of the 5th Antiaircraft Artillery Division protected his entire army against enemy air attacks, the 162nd Separate Guards Antiaircraft Regiment did the same for his army's headquarters.

At a depth of roughly six to 12 miles to the rear of Shumilov's concentrated rifle corps, Rotmistrov deployed his 5th Guards Tank Army for combat with his three tank corps abreast in single echelon. Vovchenko's 3rd Guards Tank Corps deployed in the rear area of the 25th Guards Rifle Corps on Rotmistrov's left wing, Fominykh's 29th Tank Corps concentrated in the center of Rotmistrov's army behind the junction of the 25th and 24th Guards Rifle Corps, and Polozkov's 18th Tank Corps formed on the right wing of Rotmistrov's tank army in the rear of the 24th Guards Rifle Corps but echeloned slightly to the rear of Fominykh's tank corps because of the more restrictive terrain along the eastern bank of the Seret River in its designated attack sector. As of the night of 1 May, Rotmistrov's tank army fielded a total of 271 tanks and 87 self-propelled guns, including roughly 40 IS-2 Stalin heavy tanks in its 14th and 53rd Guards Heavy Tank Regiments, 183 T-34 medium tanks, and 13 IS-122 self-propelled guns, a figure somewhat less than half of its fully authorized armored strength.[10]

The mission of Shumilov's 7th Guards Army was to penetrate the enemy's defenses in the seven-mile-wide sector from the Harmanesti River, three miles northeast of Pascani, eastward to Cucuteni, six miles north of Tirgu Frumos; advance southward in the general direction of Sagna and Secueni, east of Roman; support the commitment of the 5th Guards Tank Army into the penetration; reach positions extending from Barlicesti, five miles west of the Seret River and 12 miles north of Roman, eastward through Miclauseni to Hindresti, at a depth of 13–15 miles into the enemy's defenses, by the end of the first day of the offensive; and capture the city of Roman and positions extending from Duca Station eastward to Bacesti, at a depth of 30–36 miles, by the end of the second day.

On Shumilov's left wing, Safiulin's 25th Guards Rifle Corps was to penetrate the German defenses in the three-mile-wide sector from Cucuteni westward to Barbotesti and advance southward along the Propota, De Sus, and Strunga axis to bypass Tirgu Frumos from the west; on Shumilov's right wing, Vasil'ev's 24th Guards Rifle Corps was to penetrate the Romanian defenses in the three-mile-wide sector from Barbotesti westward to Harmanesti and advance southward along the ridgeline through Dumbravita, Ruginoasa, Helestieni, and Farcaseni to the Cuza Voda region, on the eastern bank of the Seret River ten miles southwest of Tirgu Frumos.

The official history of the 81st Rifle Division, which was attacking in the 24th Guards Rifle Corps' first echelon, describes the mission its corps commander, Vasil'ev, assigned to it orally late on 1 May:

> After an artillery and mortar preparation, in cooperation with the tanks of General Rotmistrov [the 5th Guards Tank Army], penetrate the enemy's defenses along the Cuza Voda Station and Mount Hushenei front on the morning of 2 May. The immediate mission is to capture Cuza Voda, Radiu, and Mount Hushenei. Subsequently, capture Harmanasu [two miles west of Helestieni] and Helestieni and seize a foothold on Mount Krivesti [Hill 358] [two miles south of Helestieni] by day's end.[11]

The mission of Rotmistrov's 5th Guards Tank Army was "to attack together with the [7th Guards Army's] combined-arms formations and, in cooperation with the 2nd Tank Army, capture Tirgu Frumos by an attack in the direction of Dumbravita and the western outskirts of Tirgu Frumos. Subsequently, attack [southward] in the direction of Roman."[12]

Trofimenko's 27th Army, with Bogdanov's 2nd Tank Army assembled in its rear area, was concentrated on the left wing of Konev's shock group, with Goriachev's 35th Guards Rifle Corps concentrated on its right wing northeast of Tirgu Frumos and Semenov's 33rd Rifle Corps on its left wing northwest of Iasi. In between the army's two rifle corps, the army's 54th Fortified Region was deployed in the ten-mile-wide sector extending from the Belcesti and Munteni regions, nine miles northeast of Tirgu Frumos, eastward to the Totoesti region, three miles north of Podu Iloaie. Goriachev's 35th Guards Rifle Corps, reinforced by one rifle division from the 33rd Rifle Corps and followed by the two tank corps of Bogdanov's 2nd Tank Army, was to conduct its attack in the five-mile-wide sector extending from the Hodora Burial Mound, just northeast of Cucuteni, eastward to Belcesti on the shock group's extreme left wing. On Goriachev's left, the 54th Fortified Region was to tie down German forces along its extended front, and, much farther to the east, Semenov's 33rd Rifle Corps was to be prepared to join the offensive by attacking toward Iasi from the northwest if the army's main attack succeeded.

On the 27th Army's right wing and the shock group's left wing, Goriachev's 35th Guards Rifle Corps formed for combat in its sector from Belcesti westward to northeast of Cucuteni with Kolesnikov's 206th Rifle, Colonel I. N. Konev's 3rd Guards Airborne, and Major General N. G. Zolotukhin's 93rd Guards Rifle Divisions arrayed from left to right (east to west) in single echelon backed up by Major General M. N. Mikhailov's 78th Rifle Division from the 33rd Rifle Corps and the 3rd and 16th Tank Corps of Bogdanov's 2nd Tank Army. Forces on the left flank of *Grossdeutschland* Division's Grenadier Regiment manned defenses opposite Goriachev's rifle corps.

On Trofimenko's left wing northwest of Iasi, Semenov's 33rd Rifle Corps formed for combat with his 337th, 202nd, and 180th Rifle Divisions deployed in single-echelon formation along the front extending from Zahorna, ten miles northwest of Iasi, westward to Totoesti, three miles north of Podu Iloaie, but with little or no armor support. Semenov's rifle corps faced two infantry regiments in the center and on the right wing of the German 46th Infantry Division. Finally, deployed in the broad gap between Trofimenko's two rifle corps, the 54th Fortified Region faced the 97th Grenadier Regiment, which was defending on the 46th Infantry Division's left wing. In addition, the German V Army Corps held its 24th Panzer Division in reserve assembly areas around Sarca and Podu Iloaie with orders to respond to any Soviet threats to the Tirgu Frumos, Podu Iloaie, or Iasi regions.

Bogdanov formed his 2nd Tank Army for combat with his two tank corps abreast in assembly areas six to nine miles behind the forces of Goriachev's 35th Guards Rifle Corps. Dubovoi's 16th Tank Corps concentrated on the tank army's left wing to the rear of the rifle corps' 206th Rifle and 3rd Guards Airborne Divisions, and Mishulin's 3rd Tank Corps deployed on the tank army's right wing to the rear of the rifle corps' 93rd Guards Rifle Division.

Since Bogdanov's 2nd Tank Army was also seriously understrength, in fact, even more so than Rotmistrov's, on the eve of the offensive, Konev assigned each of Bogdanov's tank corps a complete heavy tank penetration regiment equipped with new model heavy Iosef Stalin (IS) tanks and heavy self-propelled artillery regiments to support the tank army during its penetration operation. As a result, on 1 May, Mishulin's 3rd Tank Corps fielded a total of 50 tanks and self-propelled guns, including 27 T-34 medium tanks in his tank corps' three organic tank brigades, five IS-85 heavy tanks in the attached 8th Guards Penetration Tank Regiment, and 18 ISU-152 heavy self-propelled guns in the attached 375th Heavy Self-propelled Artillery Regiment. Dubovoi's 16th Tank Corps fielded 55 tanks and self-propelled guns, including 32 T-34 medium and two MK-9 tanks in its three tank brigades, 16 IS-122 heavy tanks in its 6th Guards Tank Penetration Regiment, and five SU-85 self-propelled guns in its 1440th Self-propelled Artillery Regiment. In addition, the tank army's separate 11th Guards Tank Brigade fielded 16 T-34 tanks, increasing the 2nd Tank Army's overall armored strength to a total of 121 tanks and self-propelled guns.[13]

The mission of the main shock group of Trofimenko's 27th Army was to penetrate the German defenses in the three-mile-wide sector from the Hodora Burial Mound eastward to Belcesti with the four rifle divisions of Goriachev's 35th Guards Rifle Corps, and then to advance southward east of Tirgu Frumos to envelop the town from the east. After capturing Tirgu Frumos, his army was to develop the attack to the southeast and capture the villages of Stornesti and Sinesti, 10–11 miles southeast of Tirgu Frumos, respectively, with its main forces, and the mountain pass at Slobodzia, 20 miles southeast of Tirgu Frumos, with forward detachments, by the end of the first day of the operation. Subsequently, Trofimenko's main shock group was to capture the towns of Dumesti, Negresti, and Boresti, which were situated on the railroad line between Roman and Vaslui, 22–42 miles south and southeast of its jumping-off positions, by the end of the second day and support the 2nd Tank Army's advance. Thereafter, Trofimenko's main shock group was to continue its southward advance in tandem with the 2nd Tank Army, while Semenov's 33rd Rifle Corps pressed German forces back toward Iasi, or supported the 2nd Tank Army if it wheeled northward to envelop Iasi from the southwest.

The mission of Bogdanov's 2nd Tank Army was to support the 27th Army's penetration operation, capture Tirgu Frumos by enveloping the town from the east, and prepare to exploit the offensive either toward Vaslui in the south or through Slobodzia toward Iasi to roll up Group Wöhler's left wing and capture Iasi by enveloping the city from the southwest. The official history of the 2nd Tank Army briefly describes its mission:

> The tank army, together with the 35th Guards Rifle Corps, had the mission of penetrating the enemy's defenses in the Cheplenica region and, after developing the offensive toward Tirgu-Frumos, to capture it and be prepared to operate either toward Iasi to destroy the enemy Iasi grouping or toward Slobodzia to seize the passes and reach the valley of the Birladul River.[14]

To fulfill this mission, Bogdanov ordered Dubovoi's 16th Tank Corps to support and exploit the assault by Goriachev's 206th Rifle and 3rd Guards Airborne Divisions, and Mishulin's 3rd Tank Corps to provide similar support for the 35th Guards Rifle Corps' 93rd Guards Rifle Division.

To facilitate the shock group's advance and protect its right (western) flank, Konev ordered Zhmachenko's 40th Army to organize and conduct two secondary supporting attacks in the region north of Tirgu-Neamt and in the Pascani region to tie down German and Romanian reserves. In the first supporting attack, Major General S. P. Timoshkov's 38th Rifle and Major General A. D. Rumiantsev's 4th Guards Airborne Divisions of Petrushevsky's 104th Rifle Corps, supported by elements of Colonel T. F. Umansky's 240th Rifle Division, which had just been transferred to Petrushevsky's corps from Batitsky's 50th Rifle Corps, were to assault defenses manned by the Romanian I Army Corps' *Kampfgruppe* "W" in the sector west of the town of Raucesti, which was situated three miles due north of Tirgu-Neamt. In the second of Zhmachenko's supporting attacks, Kozyr's 232nd, Colonel V. I. Beloded's 133rd, and Bobrov's 42nd Guards Rifle Divisions of Avdeenko's 51st Rifle Corps were to assault the defenses of the Romanian 6th Infantry Division in the sector between the villages of Prajescu and Timisesti, five to nine miles west of Pascani, and then exploit the attack southward along the western bank of the Prut River toward Tupilati on the Moldova River and Ruginoasa astride the road west of Roman.

In addition, once Konev's main shock group accomplished its immediate mission and penetrated the Strunga Defense Line south of Tirgu Frumos, the two rifle corps of Koroteev's 52nd Army deployed north of Iasi, supported by their two small supporting tank groups from Kravchenko's 6th Tank Army, were to attack the German IV Army Corps' defenses north of Iasi from the north and northeast in conjunction with an assault on the city by the 27th Army's 33rd Rifle Corps from the northwest. Finally, shortly after Konev's offensive began, Malinovsky's 3rd Ukrainian Front was to commence penetration operations from its bridgeheads across the Dnestr River, join in the general advance, and capture the city of Kishinev.

ARMY GROUP WÖHLER'S DEFENSE

On 1 May, Army Group Wöhler was responsible for defending Army Group South Ukraine's entire left wing—that is, all of northern Romania from the foothills of the Carpathian Mountains eastward to just west of Orgeev and the Dnestr River. Since the army group consisted of the Romanian Fourth Army and the German Eighth Army, its task organization was complex, with Romanian and German units often subordinate to the same headquarters.

At this time, Group Wöhler defended the sector from north of Tirgu-Neamt eastward across the Seret River, north of Tirgu Frumos and Iasi, and across the Prut River to the region just west of Orgeev and the Dnestr River, with the Romanian I and V Army Corps, a portion of the German LVII Panzer Corps, the German IV Army Corps, the Romanian VI Army Corps, and the German XXXXVII Panzer Corps deployed abreast from west to east (left to right). The Romanian I Army Corps' Division Group Siret defended the city of Tirgu-Neamt and the adjacent region to the north and east, and the same corps' 20th and 6th Infantry Divisions defended the sector from just east of Tirgu-Neamt to the Seret River, with the 8th Infantry Division in reserve. Further to the east, in the sector extending from the Seret River eastward to Sarca, the Romanian V Army Corps defended with its 1st Guards Armored Division deployed forward from the Seret River eastward to just west of Tirgu Frumos and its 4th Infantry Division in reserve well to its rear.

Supplementing the V Army Corps' defense in this most vital of sectors, the German LVII Panzer Corps, whose headquarters was still situated in Roman, defended the sector from west of Tirgu Frumos eastward to Sarca with the *Grossdeutschland* Panzer Grenadier Division and the German 46th Infantry Division's 97th Grenadier Regiment, both of which were theoretically controlled by the Romanian V Army Corps. More important still, the LVII Panzer Corps retained the powerful SS *"T"* Panzer Division in its operational reserve near Halaucesti, northwest of Roman, and the 24th Panzer Division in tactical reserve positions in the Sarca, Podu Iloaie, and Letcani regions, positioned to support either the defense at Tirgu Frumos or north of Iasi.

The German IV Army Corps (Group Mieth), which was responsible for defending the Iasi region where it considered a Soviet offensive most imminent, deployed the German 46th Infantry Division, the Romanian 3rd and 18th Infantry Divisions, the German 79th Infantry Division, and a combined group consisting of the German 23rd Panzer Division and the Romanian 5th Cavalry Division in defensive positions extending from Sarca eastward to the Prut River northeast of Iasi. The defense of Iasi proper was the responsibility of Group Hell, which controlled the 23rd Panzer Division Group and the 79th Infantry Division but was technically subordinate to the IV Army Corps. Finally, the IV Army Corps retained the Romanian 101st and 102nd Mountain Infantry Brigades in reserve, manning defenses in the hills of the Strunga Defense Line south of Iasi.

Group Wöhler defended the sector from the Prut River eastward to the boundary with Army Group Dumitrescu just west of Orgeev with a purely German force. The IV Army Corps' 376th Infantry Division manned defenses from the Prut River to the town of Korneshty, and the XXXXVII Panzer Corps' 370th, 106th, and 14th Infantry Divisions occupied forward defenses from Korneshty to the Orgeev region, with its 3rd Panzer Division in tactical reserve positions west of Kishinev.

The defense of the vital Tirgu Frumos sector, which the Germans believed was also a primary Soviet target, was the joint responsibility of the Romanian V Army Corps and the German LVII Panzer Corps. In the center of this sector, the *Grossdeutschland* Panzer Grenadier Division occupied defenses forming in a wide arc extending from northwest of Tirgu Frumos to northeast of the town, flanked on the left by elements of the Romanian 1st Guards Panzer Division and on the right by the 46th Infantry Division's 97th

Grenadier Regiment. Manteuffel, the commander of the *Grossdeutschland* Division, described the configuration of his defense and the German exploitation of terrain in the region:

> **Defense:**
> From early April the division was deployed on both sides of Targul-Frumos [Tirgu-Frumos]. Remember it had withdrawn over about 500 kilometers [300 miles] in just over three weeks in winter conditions after a three-month battle and had been in action continually for 10 days in the general area. On the left of the Grenadier Division was a Rumanian brigade. The left forward formation of the division was the panzer grenadier regiment, the right formation, the panzer fusilier regiment, and in reserve and depth, the panzer regiment around Targul-Frumos itself. On the right of the division was the 46th Infantry Division, with 24th Panzer Division in depth behind.
>
> From there I could overlook and supervise the employment of the division both orally and visually and had, in addition, a good network of roads and of rapid communications with my commanders. The place had been badly destroyed in the fighting, and, therefore, the enemy probably did not think I would be there. I was therefore seldom disturbed by gunfire while working, eating, or playing bridge.
>
> During these weeks the division clawed itself firmly into the ground in the most literal sense of the words. All the troops vied with one another in preparing a suitable reception for the enemy. To the request from the Führer's headquarters that the division should be used in another place and should therefore be withdrawn, I replied that, in view of the imminent big Russian offensive, the division should be left in its positions since I considered its presence here indispensable until the attack was beaten off in view of its thorough knowledge of the terrain, the number of weapons, its morale and in view of its preparations for defenses against this attack. This request was granted.
>
> **Terrain:**
> North of the east-west line Podul Iloaie–Targul-Frumos–Seret the terrain was passable everywhere and was suitable for armoured combat vehicles. It also offered a broad field of fire. But it was unfavorable in that everywhere north of this line the enemy sat on the commanding hills, although they were 8–10 kilometers [five to six miles] away from our forward positions and could not, as I hoped, make out the details of our defensive system. We therefore advanced our foremost pickets to about 2,500 metres north of Targul Frumos. South of the east-west line there was rising terrain which gave us excellent observation sites and positions

> for anti-aircraft guns and artillery. The natural vegetation throughout the area provided good camouflage for the infantry positions, their heavy weapons, and the assault guns. There was also a Rumanian position in front of a deep, wide wooded area to the south, in which the completely terrified Rumanians now and then did some entrenching. We refused to allow their forces to be integrated with the Germans. The fighting value of the Rumanians was very low and counted for nothing.
>
> Winter gave way to warm, sunny spring weather. The nights were clear and the days saw blue skies with excellent visibility. The subsurface was sandy and generally dry.
>
> Due south of Targul-Frumos there was a hill from which the entire division sector and the probable enemy attack axes could be monitored in the most ideal way through sight and sound. I moved my command post there in the last days of April.[15]

The *Grossdeutschland* Division's history adds a few more details about the division's defenses:

> The defensive measures by the Panzer-Grenadier Division GD were accelerated, but were also concentrated in the areas most likely to be attacked. Reserves were moved up and alert units were formed and positioned behind the main line of resistance. Alternate firing positions for the artillery were scouted, fall-back observation posts were set up, and the radio equipment was checked in the event of a loss of telephone communications; all in preparation for what was coming.
>
> Under the direction of the pioneers, prepared secondary artillery positions were built deep in the defensive zone. Anti-tank barricades were erected on the roads leading to Targul Frumos. Anti-aircraft guns went into firing positions. A breakthrough by the enemy had to be prevented at all costs.[16]

As was the case with most if not all German divisions, Manteuffel and his staff flexibly task-organized the *Grossdeutschland* Division for combat by forming it into several mixed regimental combat groups, or *kampfgruppen*, formed around the nucleus of its three combat regiments (see Table 5.3 at chapter's end).

Grossdeutschland Division's Panzer Grenadier and Fusilier Regiments manned the forward defenses in depth with strong local reserves available to each regimental commander. While the division split up its assault gun battalion and subordinated its lower levels to the operational control of its two regiments, it retained direct control over the division's Panzer Regiment and its Reconnaissance and Engineer Battalions. The division's Panzer Artillery

Regiment, which had abundant ammunition, provided artillery support for the entire division, with priority fire support to its two forward regiments. Of the division's four antiaircraft batteries, three of which were equipped with the famous 88-mm guns, the division employed one of the batteries in dug-in positions north of Targul-Frumos to operate in a ground antitank role and the remaining three batteries for general antiaircraft defense.

After extensive discussions with his staff, Manteuffel decided to employ his Panzer Regiment as the division's principal counterattack force and, depending on the form of the Soviet attack, planned several variants for its combat employment. In each variant, the commanders of the panzer companies reconnoitered their routes forward and the terrain over which they were to operate.

Manteuffel later described the rationale for his defense plan:

> My battle plan was roughly as follows: As I could predict with a probability bordering on certainty that the enemy would attack with strong armoured forces in conjunction with strong artillery aided by god observation possibilities, I decided to repulse the attack through the use of the massed panzer regiment employing a mobile style of warfare. In my comments, I left no doubt whatsoever that the division's regiments would have to defend themselves, for our panzers could not be everywhere. They had to be prepared to stand and fight even if bypassed and outflanked.[17]

Since it was not absolutely clear where the Soviets would make their main effort, a vital feature of Manteuffel's plan was the careful employment of a combination of reconnaissance forces and observation posts to determine the Soviets' intentions in timely fashion and to monitor their actions throughout the course of the ensuing battle. Manteuffel also retained personal command over his Panzer Regiment and supervised its actions beforehand as it rehearsed its role in all of the possible defensive variants. Once complete, Manteuffel's plan called for the rapid transmission of reconnaissance reports throughout the entire division, the establishment of strong forward infantry defensive positions, and a well-coordinated and mutually supporting antitank fire plan. In short, "The infantry and others were dug in 'up to their necks' and were told to stand and fight." Finally, Manteuffel positioned his divisional headquarters in an ideal location, a hilltop position south of Tirgu Frumos on a terrain feature from which Manteuffel claimed, "He could fight the battle with ear and eye."[18]

In the Podu Iloaie region southeast of Tirgu Frumos, Edelsheim's 24th Panzer Division was also working hard to prepare for the expected Soviet onslaught. General Ferdinand von Senger und Etterlin, who was then serving as a junior officer in the panzer division, later described his division's mission and the terrain over which it was required to operate:

> In the beginning of May 1944, the LVII Panzer Corps was on the defense in the Targul-Frumos region in the Moldau [Moldavian] Mountains. It consisted of only weak German formations and Romanian infantry divisions and also controlled the Panzer Grenadier Division Grossdeutschland, which was positioned with its center of gravity north and northwest of Targul-Frumos.
>
> The 24th Panzer Division was in army reserve in the Iasi region behind the right wing of the LVII Panzer Corps.
>
> We were concerned with a sector held by a regiment (in reality, a brigade) [the Fusilier Regiment] of the Panzer Grenadier Division *Grossdeutschland.* Two battalions were dug in along the front line, and the third was in the general area of Facuti, which had been turned into a strong point and contained the regimental battle headquarters. The regiment's task was to hold these positions and, above all, to prevent the loss of the crossing over the chain of lakes at Facuti [four miles northeast of Tirgu-Frumos].
>
> The 24th Panzer Division, the German reserve, had recently been involved in heavy fighting [at Iasi] to the east of the present position, behind the right flank of the LVII Panzer Corps. The [division's] task was to counter any enemy penetration in the right hand sector of the Panzer Grenadier Division *Grossdeutschland.* [To do so], the division was divided into two battle groups [*kampfgruppen*]. . . .
>
> The ground [terrain] did not lend itself to the employment of tanks. There were three fan-shaped deep ravines radiating [northward] out of Sarca [five miles west of Podu-Iloaie] where the 24th Panzer Division was assembled.
>
> a. The southern valley contained the main road to Targul-Frumos.
>
> b. The middle valley running up to and beyond Facuti contained a string of lakes over which there were only a few firm crossing places.
>
> c. The northern valley, along which ran the Cihada stream, was for the most part 2 kilometers [just over one mile] wide and swampy. Between these three valleys were two high ridges, a characteristic of which was their steep northern and relatively gentle southern slopes. Both ridges were only in places intersected by north-south cuttings. There were few woods. The ground was mainly uncultivated and, due to the heavy rains of the previous few days, presented difficult going for even tracked vehicles.[19]

On the evening of 1 May, Edelsheim's 24th Panzer Division had just finished regrouping all of its forces westward from the Iasi region into new assembly areas around Sarca and Podu Iloaie, 8–12 miles due east of Tirgu Frumos. According to the LVII Panzer Corps' defensive plan, it intended to employ Edelsheim's panzer division to defeat any serious Soviet attacks in the region northeast of Tirgu Frumos and north of Sarca, the sector defended by the *Grossdeutschland* Division's Fusilier Regiment. Specifically, the corps' plan required the 24th Panzer Division to regroup into and conduct its counterattacks from the sector extending from Hill 192, about two miles north of the town of Facuti, eastward to the village of Polieni, just over two miles north-northeast of Facuti.

As was the case with the *Grossdeutschland* Division, Edelsheim also flexibly task organized his division into two *kampfgruppen* (see Table 5.4 at chapter's end).

Edelsheim deliberately concentrated all of his division's heavy armored vehicles in the heavier *Kampfgruppe* "W" to serve as his primary shock group and the "soft-skinned elements of the division into *Kampfgruppe* "E" to form another combat element that could maneuver during his counterattacks. Since the original 24th Panzer Division had been destroyed at Stalingrad in early 1943, the new 24th Panzer Division, which was reestablished in early 1944, was far weaker than its illustrious predecessor. As of 1 May, the panzer division's panzer grenadier battalions were at about 60 percent required strength in personnel and 25–30 percent in terms of their required tanks, other vehicles, and other equipment. At the time, the panzer division fielded roughly 24 tanks, 12 assault guns, and eight self-propelled howitzers. This relative paucity of armor forced Edelsheim to task organize his division to employ its tanks and other armored vehicles most effectively and at the most critical time and place during the ensuing battle.

In addition to the *Grossdeutschland* Panzer Grenadier and 24th Panzer Divisions, the LVII Panzer Corps also included the SS "*T*" Panzer Division, which fielded roughly 70 to 100 tanks on 1 May. Although the supporting Romanian forces had little armor, the V Army Corps' 1st Guards Panzer Division, which was defending on *Grossdeutschland* Division's left, fielded up to 80 tanks, but most of these were of lighter Romanian design.

Therefore, given the Soviets' obvious superiority in infantry, armor, and artillery, the defending Germans had to rely on the greater maneuverability and flexibility of their task-organized panzer and infantry *kampfgruppen* to achieve victory, if it was to be achieved at all.

CONCLUSIONS

Although Konev was completely confident that his new reinforced shock group was strong enough to penetrate the German and Romanian defenses in the Tirgu Frumos region, he still realized his forces faced several daunting challenges. First, most of his armies had been fighting almost continuously since early January, and, after five months of nearly unending combat, the replacements the *Stavka* was sending him were not sufficient to compensate for his *front*'s combat losses. As a result, most of his *front*'s divisions numbered between 5,000 and 6,500 men, and some had as few as 4,500 combat soldiers. Furthermore, most of his personnel replacements were men conscripted, often by force, from the local populace during his *front*'s advance across the southern Ukraine and into Bessarabia. In addition, although the Ukrainian *fronts* received priority on receipt of supplies during the entire winter campaign, because of their tenuous supply lines and the wet spring weather, their forces experienced shortages, some quite severe, in all categories of supplies but, particularly, regarding ammunition and fuel.

In addition to these problems in his own forces, both German and Romanian resistance in the Pascani, Tirgu Frumos, and Iasi regions turned out to be far stronger than Konev had anticipated. Although short of operational reserves, the Germans had demonstrated their capability for maneuvering their panzer and panzer grenadier divisions effectively to and fro across the battlefield during mid- and late April, thereby handling crisis after crisis without losing their overall combat effectiveness. To Konev's chagrin, forces such as the *Grossdeutschland* and the 23rd and 24th Panzer Divisions repeatedly rose like phoenixes from the carnage of one battlefield to appear intact and deadly on another battlefield only days later.

In fact, Konev's greatest concerns were about the capabilities of his tank and mechanized forces, which had already conducted months of active combat and, as a result, were now reinforced by additional tanks, along with many newly trained tank crews. Reduced by combat attrition to the real strength of no more than a single full-strength tank corps each, his 2nd and 5th Guards Tank Armies had to operate effectively if they were to propel his attacking forces forward into the Germans' operational depths. Because he was not really sure that they could do so, Konev tried to compensate for their weaknesses by reinforcing them with the new tank penetration regiments armed with Iosef Stalin tanks, the Soviets' answer to the formidable German Tiger tanks, and new heavy self-propelled artillery regiments. However, these units were also relatively fresh, and their weapons were still experimental.

Nor did the 2nd Ukrainian Front's armored specialists display abundant optimism over the prospective success of their *front*'s armored forces. For example, after assessing the terrain in the Tirgu Frumos region and estimating the enemy's armor strength in the region to determine how to employ the *front*'s two tank armies most successfully, on the very eve of the offensive, the 2nd Ukrainian Front's Directorate for Armored and Mechanized Forces concluded:

> The Tirgu-Frumos region consists of open, sharply broken terrain . . . with a great number of ravines, hollows, and hills with steep ascents and descents. These conditions give the enemy the advantage in organizing a firm defense, the selection of firing positions, and dispersing his dispositions not only in the depth but also vertically. . . . In addition, the many small rivers and streams with silted banks and bottoms are major antitank obstacles. . . .
>
> By the beginning of the offensive, the enemy has nine tank divisions and one mechanized division, with an overall total of 275 tanks and assault guns, opposing the 2nd Ukrainian Front. By the beginning of the operation, the main grouping of enemy tank forces, with up to 120 armored vehicles, is located along the Kishinev axis. The enemy has three tank divisions with up to 115 armored vehicles along the Tirgu-Frumos and Iasi axis.
>
> Along the axis of our tank armies' main attack—the Tirgu-Frumos region—the enemy has only one tank division, the SS "Greater Deutschland" with 25 tanks, which is occupying defenses along the Barbotesti, Cucuteni, Hill 192, Polieni, and Erbiceni line.[20]

While this assessment was accurate regarding the terrain, it failed to recognize either the *Grossdeutschland* Division's imposing tank strength of 160 tanks or the near proximity of the 24th Panzer Division to the Tirgu Frumos region. The Soviets would pay dearly for this erroneous assessment.

Nevertheless, according to the 2nd Ukrainian Front's records, the *front* was overwhelmingly superior in armor to the opposing German forces:

> Including the two tank armies (the 2nd and 5th Guards) in the makeup of the front's mobile shock group, we had 380 tanks and 111 self-propelled guns on the main attack axis, for a total of 491 armored vehicles.
>
> At that time, the enemy had a total of 25 armored vehicles along the axis of our forces' main attack. With a penetration front of 20 kilometers [12 miles], the approximate density of tanks and self-propelled guns were: our forces—24.5 [40.8] and the enemy forces—1.2 [2] per kilometer [mile]. The correlation of force [in armor] was 19.6 to 1 [in our favor].[21]

However, on the very eve of Konev's offensive, his intelligence organs reassessed the situation and concluded that, rather than a superiority of more than 16 to 1 (491 to 25) in armor, the actual superiority was better than 4 to 1 (491 to 115), at a time when it was actually about 2 to 1 counting the *Totenkopf* and Romanian 1st Guards Armored Divisions.

Nevertheless, when all is said and done, the forces of Konev's main shock group were clearly numerically superior to the defending Germans and Romanians in every respect when his offensive actually began (see Table 5.5 at chapter's end).

Although German intelligence concluded that a Soviet offensive was imminent, no one in the defending German and Romanian commands knew the exact time the attack would begin:

> In [late] April, the Russians were quiet opposite the division. They fired their artillery occasionally but were obviously saving ammunition. The infantry (as was their custom) made no effort prior to the attack. The prisoners the Germans captured claimed to know nothing of preparations for attack, but it was clear that an attack was imminent. The Germans expected it to be on 30 April or 1 May, and detailed preparations continued in anticipation.
>
> Here is the report of Lieutenant Hans Karl Richter about the victims of the 1st Company of the Panzer Grenadier Regiment Grossdeutschland:
>
>> In the evening of 30 April we took up our positions again. We had put out barbed wire and antitank mines and had prepared positions around Dumrovita for 4 platoons. About 1000 [hours] I met Lieutenant Dieter Bernhagen at the shot-up T-34, which marked our company boundary. The outlook was not at all rosy. I mentioned my thoughts about the unfavorable position of the 1st Company and how poor it would be against the expected Russian tank attack. Dieter agreed with my concerns. We considered it for half an hour; what we should do if the 1st Company and my 3rd Platoon on the right flank of the position should be overrun. In Dumrovita itself, not much could happen, and Lieutenant Bernhagen was a bit more hopeful that against our Tigers the "Ivans" would barely get over the River Kam. We finally agreed that, in the worst possible situation, we would seek to reach Dumbrovita itself and get into a defensive position with the 2nd Company—a hedgehog position.
>
> The Grossdeutschland Division awaited the attack that night, but, as the Eighth Army's War Diary shows, it was not forthcoming despite fire and a probing attack. On the night of the first [of May], a regiment of the 3rd SS Totenkopf Division was moved into the Targul-Frumos concentration area. The remainder was held back as a corps reserve southwest of Targul-Frumos behind the Romanians. The first of May passed quietly, and night came.[22]

Indicative of the Germans' suspicion regarding an impending Soviet attack, overnight on 30 April and 1 May, the German forces conducted interdiction fires with their artillery and mortars at suspected Soviet assembly areas and possible troop concentrations north of their defenses. As described from the *Grossdeutschland* Division's perspective:

> The offensive expected on 1 May 1944 failed to materialize. Air reconnaissance, which watched over the enemy's assembly area all day, reported considerable masses of tanks and a large number of new artillery positions in the anticipated areas of main effort. At the request of the division commander, Generalleutnant von Manteuffel, the famous tank-destroyer Major Rudel and his unit were moved into the area. The Stukas bombed the woods and hollows, bringing death and destruction to the enemy. But at the main line of resistance all remained quiet, almost too quiet for this stage of the game. It was the calm before the storm, a calm which frayed the nerves of the defenders.[23]

On the other side of the front lines, the 27th Army's combat reports recorded the consternation in their ranks caused by these destructive German fires:

> On 1 May 1944, the 27th Army consisted of the 35th Guards Rifle Corps, the 33rd Rifle Corps, the 78th Rifle Division, the 25th and 119th Tank Regiments, the 56th, 57th, and 58th Army Blocking Detachments [probably NKVD], the 54th Fortified Region, and other subunits.
>
> The army's forces occupied their previous defensive positions during 1 May 1944 and conducted reconnaissances-in-force along separate axes with reinforced battalions. During the day, the enemy defended, conducted desultry fire, and tried to conduct reconnaissance, while its aviation bombed the 35th Guards Rifle Corps' combat formations.
>
> Colonel Kolesnikov, the commander of the 206th Rifle Division, perished, and Colonel Nosal', the commander of that division's 722nd Rifle Regiment, was wounded during the bombing by enemy aircraft on 1 May 1944. By the morning of 1 May, the 35th Rifle Corps' 206th Rifle Division occupied positions from the fork of the road and highway south of Lake Hirbu to the isolated farm 1.5 kilometers [one mile] southeast of Lake Hirbu.
>
> Our losses on 1 May were 14 men killed and 34 men wounded.[24]

More ominously from Konev's standpoint, although his *front*'s intelligence organs seriously underestimated the strength of the *Grossdeutschland* Panzer Grenadier Division prior to the offensive, as indicated by a report by the 2nd Ukrainian Front's Armored and Mechanized Directorate, at the last minute, Konev finally realized that the Germans were forewarned of the assault and had moved the SS *"T"* Panzer Division forward to resist their offensive: "The enemy guessed the concept of our operation, hurriedly withdrew the SS Panzer Division 'Death's Head' [*Totenkopf*] from the Piatna axis, and brought it forward into the region north of Tirgu Frumos by the beginning of the operation."[25]

On the eve of the offensive, Konev, his *front*'s intelligence organs, and his subordinate army and corps commanders also did not realize Army Group Wöhler had also alerted the 24th Panzer Division for possible action and was beginning to move this panzer division from its previous assembly areas around Podu Iloaie westward toward Tirgu Frumos. However, they would become aware of this sad reality only a matter of hours after their assaults began.

Table 5.1. The 2nd Ukrainian Front's Order of Battle on 1 May 1944
2nd UKRAINIAN FRONT:
Army General I. S. Konev

40th Army: LTG F. F. Zhmachenko
  50th Rifle Corps: MG P. F. Batitsky
    74th Rifle Division
    163rd Rifle Division
    240th Rifle Division
  51st Rifle Corps: MG P. P. Avdeenko
    42nd Guards Rifle Division
    133rd Rifle Division
    232nd Rifle Division
  104th Rifle Corps: LTG A. V. Petrushevsky
    4th Guards Airborne Division
    38th Rifle Division
  159th Fortified Region
  1898th Self-propelled Artillery Regiment

7th Guards Army: LTG M. S. Shumilov
  24th Guards Rifle Corps: LTG N. A. Vasil'ev
    8th Guards Airborne Division
    72nd Guards Rifle Division
    81st Guards Rifle Division
  25th Guards Rifle Corps: MG G. B. Safiulin
    6th Guards Airborne Division
    36th Guards Rifle Division
    53rd Rifle Division
  6th Rifle Division
  3rd Separate Antitank Rifle Battalion
  27th Guards Tank Brigade
  34th Separate Armored Train Battalion
  38th Separate Armored Train Battalion

5th Guards Tank Army: CGTF P. A. Rotmistrov
  5th Guards Mechanized Corps: MGTF B. M. Skvortsov
    10th Guards Mechanized Brigade
    11th Guards Mechanized Brigade
    12th Guards Mechanized Brigade
    24th Guards Tank Brigade
    104th Guards Self-propelled Artillery Regiment
    1447th Self-propelled Artillery Regiment
    2nd Guards Motorcycle Battalion
    737th Tank Destroyer Artillery Regiment
    285th Mortar Regiment
    409th Guards-Mortar Battalion
  18th Tank Corps: MGTF V. I. Polozkov
    110th Tank Brigade
    170th Tank Brigade
    181st Tank Brigade
    32nd Motorized Rifle Brigade
    1438th Self-propelled Artillery Regiment
    78th Motorcycle Battalion
    1000th Tank Destroyer Artillery Regiment
    736th Tank Destroyer Artillery Battalion
    292nd Mortar Regiment
    106th Guards-Mortar Battalion
    1694th Antiaircraft Artillery Regiment
  29th Tank Corps: MGTF E. I. Fominykh
    25th Tank Brigade
    31st Tank Brigade
    32nd Tank Brigade
    53rd Motorized Rifle Brigade
    1446th Self-propelled Artillery Regiment
    75th Motorcycle Battalion
    108th Tank Destroyer Artillery Regiment
    271st Mortar Regiment
    11th Guards-Mortar Battalion
  14th Guards Separate Tank Regiment
  53rd Guards Separate Tank Regiment
  1st Guards Motorcycle Regiment

27th Army: LTG S. G. Trofimenko
  35th Guards Rifle Corps: LTG S. G. Goriachev
    3rd Guards Airborne Division
    93rd Guards Rifle Division
    206th Rifle Division
  33rd Rifle Corps: MG A. I. Semenov
    78th Rifle Division
    180th Rifle Division
    202nd Rifle Division
    337th Rifle Division
  54th Fortified Region
  25th Separate Tank Regiment
  119th Separate Tank Regiment

2nd Tank Army: LTGTF S. I. Bogdanov
  3rd Tank Corps: LTGTF V. A. Mishulin
    50th Tank Brigade
    51st Tank Brigade
    103rd Tank Brigade
    57th Motorized Rifle Brigade
    1540th Heavy Self-propelled Artillery Regiment
    881st Self-propelled Artillery Regiment
    1818th Self-propelled Artillery Regiment

Table 5.1. *Continued*

74th Motorcycle Battalion
728th Tank Destroyer Regiment
234th Mortar Regiment
126th Guards-Mortar Battalion
121st Antiaircraft Artillery Regiment
16th Tank Corps: MGTF I. V. Dubovoi
107th Tank Brigade
109th Tank Brigade
164th Tank Brigade
15th Motorized Rifle Brigade
6th Guards Separate Tank Regiment
298th Guards Self-propelled Artillery Regiment
1441st Self-propelled Artillery Regiment
51st Motorcycle Battalion
729th Tank Destroyer Regiment
226th Mortar Regiment
89th Guards-Mortar Battalion
1721st Antiaircraft Artillery Regiment
11th Guards Tank Brigade
8th Guards Separate Tank Regiment
13th Guards Separate Tank Regiment
754th Self-propelled Artillery Regiment
1219th Self-propelled Artillery Regiment
87th Motorcycle Battalion

52nd Army: LTG K. A. Koroteev
48th Rifle Corps: MG Z. Z. Rogoznyi
31st Rifle Division
252nd Rifle Division
303rd Rifle Division
73rd Rifle Corps: MG S. S. Martirosian
50th Rifle Division
116th Rifle Division
373rd Rifle Division
78th Rifle Corps: MG G. A. Latyshev
213th Rifle Division
254th Rifle Division
294th Rifle Division
111th Rifle Division
6th Tank Army: LTGTF A. G. Kravchenko
5th Guards Tank Corps: LTGTF V. M. Alekseev
20th Guards Tank Brigade
21st Guards Tank Brigade
22nd Guards Tank Brigade
6th Guards Motorized Rifle Brigade
1416th Self-propelled Artillery Regiment
1458th Self-propelled Artillery Regiment
1462nd Self-propelled Artillery Regiment
80th Motorcycle Battalion
1667th Tank Destroyer Artillery Regiment
454th Mortar Regiment
1696th Antiaircraft Artillery Regiment
5th Mechanized Corps: LTGTF M. V. Volkov
2nd Mechanized Brigade
9th Mechanized Brigade
45th Mechanized Brigade
233rd Tank Brigade
697th Self-propelled Artillery Regiment
745th Self-propelled Artillery Regiment
999th Self-propelled Artillery Regiment
64th Motorcycle Battalion
458th Mortar Regiment
35th Guards-Mortar Battalion
1700th Antiaircraft Artillery Regiment
6th Self-propelled Artillery Brigade
156th Separate Tank Regiment

4th Guards Army: LTG I. V. Galanin
20th Guards Rifle Corps: MG N. I. Biriukov
5th Guards Airborne Division
7th Guards Airborne Division
41st Guards Rifle Division
62nd Guards Rifle Division
21st Guards Rifle Corps: MG P. I. Fomenko
69th Guards Rifle Division
80th Guards Rifle Division
84th Rifle Division

53rd Army: LTG I. M. Managarov
26th Guards Rifle Corps: MG P. A. Firsov
25th Guards Rifle Division
89th Guards Rifle Division
94th Guards Rifle Division
49th Rifle Corps: MG G. N. Terent'ev
1st Guards Airborne Division
110th Guards Rifle Division
375th Rifle Division
63rd Separate Antitank Rifle Battalion
38th Separate Tank Regiment

5th Guards Army: LTG A. S. Zhadov
32nd Guards Rifle Corps: MG A. I. Rodimtsev
13th Guards Rifle Division
95th Guards Rifle Division
97th Guards Rifle Division
33rd Guards Rifle Corps: LTG N. F. Lebedenko
9th Guards Airborne Division

Table 5.1. *Continued*

14th Guards Rifle Division
214th Rifle Division
75th Rifle Corps: MG A. Z. Akimenko
78th Guards Rifle Division
233rd Rifle Division
299th Rifle Division
123rd Separate Antitank Rifle Battalion
1289th Self-propelled Artillery Regiment

5th Air Army: ColGAv S. K. Goriunov
2nd Guards Bomber Aviation Corps: MGAv I. S. Polbin
1st Guards Bomber Aviation Division
8th Guards Bomber Aviation Division
218th Bomber Aviation Division
1st Guards Assault Aviation Corps: LTGAv V. G. Riazanov
8th Guards Assault Aviation Corps
9th Guards Assault Aviation Corps
12th Guards Fighter Aviation Division
2nd Assault Aviation Corps: MGAv (LGAv on 11 May) V. V. Stepichev
7th Guards Assault Aviation Division
231st Assault Aviation Division
4th Fighter Aviation Corps: MG I. D. Podgornyi
294th Fighter Aviation Division
302nd Fighter Aviation Division
7th Fighter Aviation Corps: MGAv A. V. Utin
205th Fighter Aviation Division
304th Fighter Aviation Division
312th Fighter-Bomber Aviation Division
511th Reconnaissance Aviation Regiment
95th Transport Aviation Regiment
85th Medical Aviation Regiment
714th Sep. Signal Aviation Regiment
18th Aviation Regiment, Civil Air Fleet
85th Corrective-Aviation Squadron

Front Reserves
27th Guards Rifle Corps: MG E. S. Alekhin
297th Rifle Division
409th Rifle Division
5th Guards Cavalry Corps: LTG A. G. Selivanov
11th Guards Cavalry Division
12th Guards Cavalry Division
63rd Cavalry Division
1896th Self-propelled Artillery Regiment
150th Guards Tank Destroyer Regiment
5th Guards Separate Tank Destroyer Battalion
9th Guards-Mortar Regiment
72nd Guards-Mortar Battalion
585th Antiaircraft Artillery Regiment
130th Separate Antitank Rifle Battalion
3rd Guards Tank Corps: MGTF I. A. Vovchenko
3rd Guards Tank Brigade
18th Guards Tank Brigade
19th Guards Tank Brigade
2nd Guards Motorized Rifle Brigade
376th Guards Heavy Self-propelled Artillery Regiment
1436th Self-propelled Artillery Regiment
1496th Self-propelled Artillery Regiment
10th Guards Motorcycle Battalion
749th Separate Tank Destroyer Artillery Battalion
266th Mortar Regiment
324th Guards-Mortar Battalion
1701st Antiaircraft Artillery Regiment
7th Mechanized Corps: MGTF F. G. Katkov
16th Mechanized Brigade
63rd Mechanized Brigade
64th Mechanized Brigade
41st Guards Tank Brigade
1440th Self-propelled Artillery Regiment
94th Motorcycle Battalion
109th Tank Destroyer Artillery Regiment
392nd Separate Tank Destroyer Battalion
614th Mortar Regiment
40th Guards-Mortar Battalion
1713th Antiaircraft Artillery Regiment
20th Tank Corps: LTGTF I. G. Lazarov
8th Guards Tank Brigade
80th Tank Brigade
155th Tank Brigade
7th Guards Motorized Rifle Brigade
1895th Self-propelled Artillery Regiment
96th Motorcycle Battalion
1505th Tank Destroyer Artillery Regiment
735th Separate Tank Destroyer Battalion
291st Mortar Regiment
406th Guards-Mortar Battalion
1711th Antiaircraft Artillery Regiment
713th Self-propelled Artillery Regiment
1491st Self-propelled Artillery Regiment
1899th Self-propelled Artillery Regiment
10th Separate Armored Train Battalion
25th Separate Armored Train Battalion
61st Separate Armored Train Battalion

Source: *Boevoi sostav Sovetskoi armii, Chast' 4 (Ianvar'–dekabr' 1944)* [The combat composition of the Soviet Army, Part 4 (January–December 1944)] (Moscow: Voenizdat, 1988), 136–138.

Table 5.2. The 2nd Ukrainian Front's Operational and Combat Formation in the Tirgu Frumos and Iasi Regions Late on 1 May 1944

Force		Sector
1st Echelon	**2nd and 3rd Echelon or Reserve**	
40th Army		West of Radauti, Seret River
50th RC		Radauti, west of Falticeni
74th RD		Radauti, Braesti
163rd RD		Braesti, west of Falticeni
159th FR		West of Falticeni, Brusturi
104th RC		Brusturi, Moldova River
38th RD		Brusturi, Raucesti
4th GAD		Raucesti, Tirgu-Neamt
240th RD (on 2.5)		Tirgu-Neamt, Moldova River
51st RC		Moldova River, Seret River
232nd RD		Moldova River, Boureni
133rd RD		Boureni, Bosteni
42nd GRD	5th GCC (part)	Bosteni, Seret River
7th Guards Army		Seret River, east of Cucuteni
24th GRC		Seret River, east of Harmanesti
8th GAbnD	18th TC, 5th GTA (one TB)	Seret River, west of Harmanesti
81st GRD	29th TC, 5th GTA, 72nd GRD	West and east of Harmanesti
25th GRC		East of Harmanesti, east of Cucuteni
36th GRD	3rd GTC, 5th GTA	East of Harmanesti, Barbotesi
53rd RD	6th GAbnD	Barbotesti, east of Cucuteni
27th Army		East of Cucuteni, Vulturi
35th GRC		East of Cucuteni, Belcesti
93rd GRD	3rd TC, 2nd TA	East of Cucuteni, east of Bals
3rd GAbnD	16th TC, 2nd TA	East of Bals, Liteni
202nd RD	78th RD	Liteni, Belcesti
54th FR		Belcesti, Avantul
33rd RC		Avantul, Vulturi
180th RD		Avantul, west of Zahorna
202nd RD		West and east of Zahorna
337th RD		East of Zahorna, Vulturi
52nd Army		Vulturi, north of Korneshty
73rd RC		Vulturi, Redui
50th RD		Vulturi
116th RD	5th GTC, 6th TA (combat group)	East of Vulturi
373rd RD		West of Radui
78th RC		Redui, Prut River
254th RD		East of Radui
294th RD	5th MC, 6th TA (combat group)	North of Hill 222
213th RD		West of Prut River
48th RC	111th RD	Prut River, north of Korneshty
31st RD		Prut River, Livodka
252nd RD		Livodka, Pyrlitsa
303rd RD		Pyrlitsa, Korneshty
	27th GRC (297th, 409th RDs)	*front* rear area

Table 5.3. Task Organization of the *Grossdeutschland* Panzer Grenadier Division on 1 May 1944

The **divisional staff** with a mixture of hard and soft skinned vehicles
The **Panzer Regiment** comprising:
1. One battalion of MK IV tanks with four companies and a total of 40 tanks
2. Two battalions of MK V [Tiger] tanks, each battalion with four companies and 40 tanks, for a total of 80 tanks
3. One battalion of MK VI [King Tiger] tanks with four companies and a total of 40 tanks
4. For a grand total of 160 tanks

Two infantry regiments [Grenadier and Fusilier], each with three battalions with four companies of 100 men each and heavy weapons companies:
1. The **Panzer Grenadier Regiment** with one battalion in halftracks and one in lorries
2. The **Panzer Fusilier Regiment** with one battalion in halftracks and two in scout cars

A **Reconnaissance Battalion** at two-thirds strength
An **Antiaircraft Battalion** with three batteries of 88-mm guns and one battery of 37-mm guns
An **Armored Artillery Regiment** with four battalions, each battalion with three batteries, one tracked and three lorry-drawn
An **Assault Gun Battalion** with about 40 guns
An **Engineer [Pioneer] Battalion**

Summary: *Grossdeutschland* Division had 160 tanks, 24 infantry companies with a total bayonet [combat] strength of 2,400 men, 12 artillery batteries, 40 assault guns, and a comprehensive air defense, part of which could be employed in an antitank role.

Table 5.4. Task Organization of the 24th Panzer Division on 1 May 1944

***Kampfgruppe* "E"** (Commander, Lieutenant Colonel von Einem)
1. Two motorized panzer grenadier battalions [*abteilungen*]
2. One motorized panzer artillery battalion

***Kampfgruppe* "W"** (Commander, Colonel von Waldenburg)
1. *Kampfgruppe* headquarters (26th Panzer Grenadier Regiment headquarters)
   a. Headquarters squadron (11./26) with:
      i. Reconnaissance section [*zug*]
      ii. Panzer hunter [anti-tank] section
      iii. Security section
   b. Infantry gun squadron (9./26) with:
      i. Three 150-mm infantry guns on Panzer 38 tanks
   c. Antiaircraft squadron (10./26) with:
      i. Nine 20-mm self-propelled antiaircraft guns
2. Panzer battalion [*abteilung*] (Hq III./24)
   a. Two panzer squadrons (10. and 12./24), each with:
      i. Six–eight MK IV (75-mm L-48 canon) tanks
   b. One panzer squadron (9./24) with:
      i. Nine assault guns III (75-mm L-48 canon)3. Medium panzer grenadier battalion (Hq I./26)
   a. Two panzer grenadier squadrons (1. and 2./26) with:
      i. 18 medium SPW [armored personnel carriers]
   b. One heavy squadrons 4./26) with:
      i. Panzer hunter [antitank] section with three 75-mm guns
      ii. Canon section with three 75-mm canons (L-24) on SPW
      iii. Infantry gun section with two 75-mm guns
      iv. Engineer [Pioneer] section on SPW
4. Light panzer grenadier battalion (Hq PzAA. 24)
   a. One panzer grenadier squadron with
      i. 22 light infantry panzer vehicles
   b. One panzer grenadier squadron in trucks
   c. One heavy squadron with:
      i. Panzer hunter [antitank] section with three 75-mm. guns
      ii. Canon section with four 75-mm. canons (L-24) on SPW
      iii. Grenade launcher section with three 81-mm. grenade launchers on SPW
      iv. Engineer [Pioneer] section on SPW
5. Panzer artillery battalion [*abteilung*] (Hq I./89)
   a. One battery of heavy 150-mm field howitzers on "Hummel" (IV) self-propelled mounts
   b. One battery of 150-mm assault howitzers on Panzer IV "Brummbar"

Source: F. M. von Senger und Etterlin, *Der Gegenschlag* (Neckargemund: Scharnhorst Buchkameradschaft, 1959), 113–114.

Table 5.5. Correlation of Opposing Forces along the Tirgu Frumos and Iasi Axes on 1 May 1944

SOVIET	GERMAN
2nd Ukrainian Front	
Tirgu Frumos Sector	
40th Army (51st Rifle Corps)	6th Infantry Division (R)
5th Guards Cavalry Corps	
7th Guards Army	1st Guards Panzer Division (R)
5th Guards Tank Army	
18th Tank Corps	Panzer Grenadier Division *Grossdeutschland*
29th Tank Corps	
3rd Guards Tank Corps	SS Panzer Division *"Totenkopf"*
27th Army (35th Rifle Corps	
	24th Panzer Division
	46th Infantry Division
Shock Group Strength	
14 rifle divisions	Two infantry divisions
One fortified region	One panzer grenadier division
Five tank corps	
One cavalry corps	Two panzer divisions
Two tank brigades	
Six separate tank regiments	
491 tanks and SP guns	250 tanks and assault guns (est.)
2,250 guns and mortars	
Iasi Sector	
27th Army (33rd Rifle Corps)	3rd Infantry Division (R)
52nd Army (73rd, 78th Rifle Corps)	18th Infantry Division (R)
Two combat groups, 6th Tank Army	79th Infantry Division
	23rd Panzer Division
	5th Cavalry Division (-)(R)
Nine rifle divisions	Three infantry divisions
Two tank brigades	One panzer division
	One cavalry division
Overall *Front* Strength:	
377,500 men	160,000 men
600 tanks and SP guns	350 tanks and assault guns (est.)
8,300 guns and mortars	
515 aircraft	600 aircraft
Depth of Advance	
6–10 kilometers	
Casualties	
Personnel unknown	Unknown
250 tanks and SP guns	

CHAPTER 6

The 2nd Ukrainian Front's Iasi (Tirgu Frumos) Offensive (2–8 May 1944)

THE BATTLE ON 2 MAY

At precisely 0515 hours Moscow time on 2 May 1944, sudden loud explosions and bright muzzle flashes from over 1,000 guns and mortars rudely shattered the pre-dawn silence and semidarkness of the warm spring morning, startling German and Romanian troops defending foxholes, trenches, and bunkers north of Tirgu Frumos and announcing that the long-awaited Soviet offensive had at last begun (Map 17). Exactly 30 minutes later, another 800 guns and mortars rent the quiet dawn northwest of the town, and the rumble of distant artillery fire also resounded far to the east and west. Experienced or inexperienced alike, the defending German and Romanian troops instinctively went to ground to wait out the torrent of fire, whose end they knew would inevitably be followed by an assault by massed Soviet infantrymen and tanks.

From the perspective of the *Grossdeutschland*'s expectant but surprised panzer grenadiers and fusiliers:

> At precisely 04.20 on the morning of 2 May, there began a firestorm the likes of which had seldom been seen before. The hail of fire lasted more than 60 minutes. The waves of tanks, including the latest types, moved forward toward the German lines through the morning mist and the clouds of smoke produced by the artillery fire which moved slowly to the rear.[1]

As expected, less than an hour later, the distinctive flashes of massed rocket launchers and the eerie screaming sounds of rockets hurling toward their positions signaled the defenders that the ground assault was imminent. In fact, they could already hear heavy machine-gun and rifle fire, accompanied by muffled explosions and the sharp crack of tank and self-propelled gunfire through the cacophony of violent noise that enveloped them. Minutes later, they could see long ranks of infantry and the dark and menacing hulls of tanks emerging from the smoke and dust, the advancing troops shouting loudly the guttural chant "Urrah" as they pushed though the gloom toward their positions. The offensive had indeed begun.

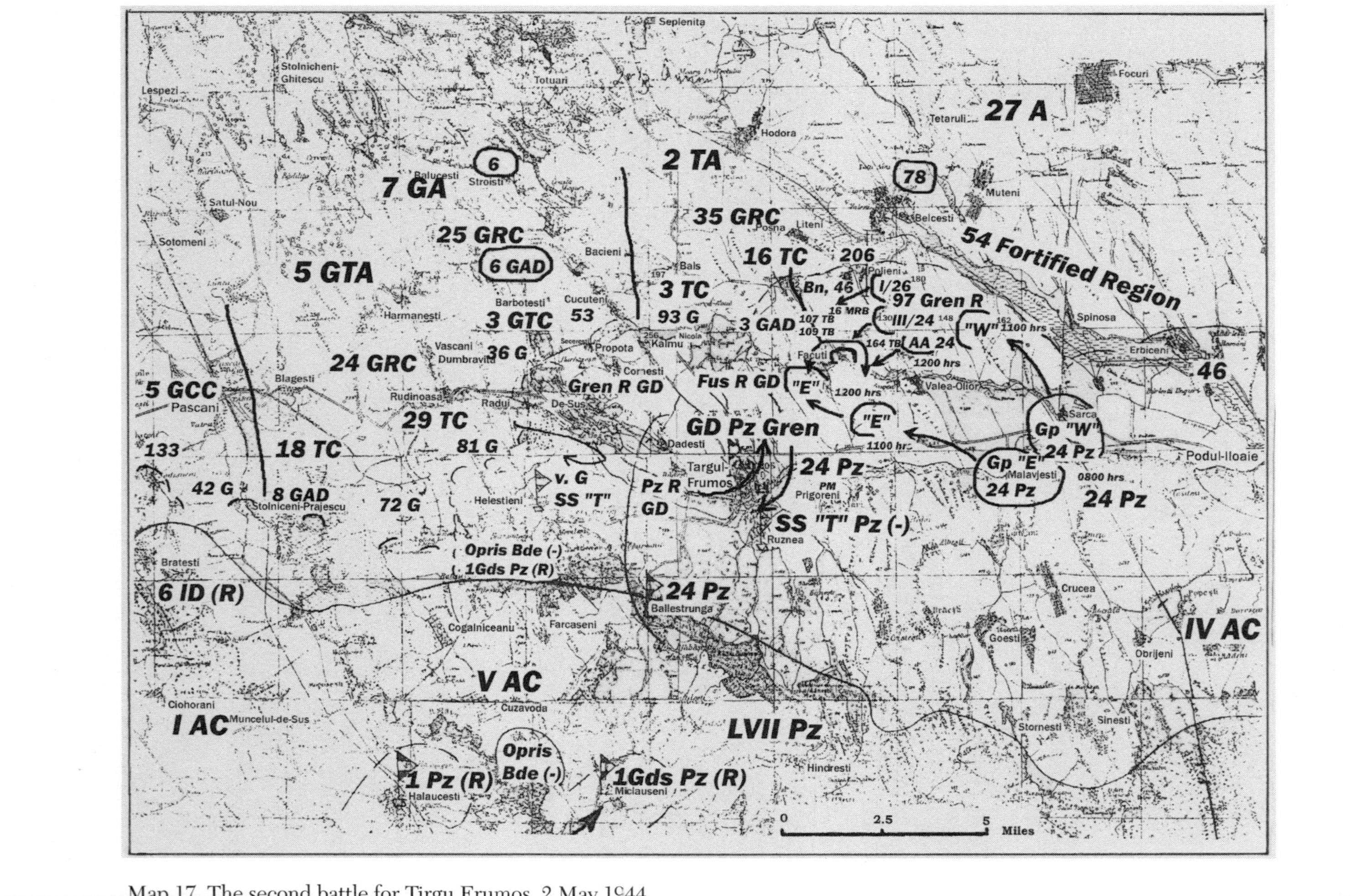

Map 17. The second battle for Tirgu Frumos, 2 May 1944

Preceded by an intense artillery and mortar bombardment against the Germans' forward defenses north of Tirgu Frumos and concentrated air strikes by aircraft from the 5th Air Army against German artillery positions and force concentrations to the rear, the assault battalions of the first-echelon rifle divisions leading the attack of the two combined-arms armies in Konev's main shock group commenced their operations promptly at 0615 hours on the morning of 2 May 1944. As Konev's main shock group struck the German defenses north of the Tirgu Frumos region, farther to the east, the two rifle corps from Koroteev's 52nd Army, once again operating closely with a small number of tanks from Kravchenko's 6th Tank Army, launched secondary supporting attacks against the German IV Army Corps' defenses north of Iasi.

The 2nd Ukrainian Front's daily combat journal describes the intense fighting that took place on the first day of Konev's offensive:

> 2 May 1944. The front's forces launched an offensive along the Tirgu-Frumos axis at 0615 hours on 2 May after a 60-minute artillery preparation. As a result of fierce fighting with [enemy] infantry, tanks, and aircraft, they succeeded in penetrating the enemy's strongly fortified defense to a depth of from 4 to 10 kilometers [2.5 to six miles] along the 20-kilometer [12-mile] front from Blagesti to Hodora. The fighting was marked by great doggedness and bitterness on both sides and characterized by a great number of enemy counterattacks. . . .
>
> More than 50 enemy tanks and assault guns were destroyed or burned, and 250 prisoners were captured as a result of the fighting.
>
> In cooperation with the 5th Guards Tank Army, the 7th Guards Army advanced from four to ten kilometers [2.5 to six miles]. . . .
>
> The 52nd Army attacked toward Iasi after a 30-minute artillery preparation but was unable to advance. The 6th Tank Army fought within the 52nd Army's combat formation.[2]

Manteuffel later recorded his impressions of the Soviet's initial assault against his *Grossdeutschland* Division's defenses:

> On 2 May 1944, the day began at about 04.00 hours with a lively artillery fire, which was mainly concentrated on the forward positions and did not extend to the rear. Our camouflage must have been very good, for our losses in men and material was very low; it was thus essentially harassing fire, which, as was often the case with the Russians, they stubbornly kept up. Looking back, I believe that it was intended to soften up our infantry and heavy weapons positions before they committed their tanks.
>
> The attack by the Russian armour began about an hour after the artillery opened fire and about thirty minutes later tank fire began falling on

> Targul Frumos. I watched the tanks roll toward the city from my command post.[3]

In the main shock group's attack sector, the first-echelon rifle divisions of the 7th Guards Army's 24th and 25th Guards Rifle Corps and the 27th Army's 35th Guards Rifle Corps began their assault with specially tailored assault groups consisting of riflemen and sappers supported by 75-mm regimental guns and, occasionally, by individual tanks and self-propelled guns. Advancing in the wake of small groups of sappers, defended by sub-machine gunners, who cut lanes through the German minefields and barbed wire entanglements detected by the reconnaissance parties hours before, the assault groups quickly attacked and overcame the Germans' security outposts in their forward security belt.

As the bursting shells of Konev's artillery preparation crept slowly but relentlessly forward through the depth of the German and Romanian forward defenses, the assault groups followed, each advancing along a specific preplanned route, with the intent to engage and destroy specific enemy strong points, which reconnaissance organs had identified before the offensive began. While the assault groups were carrying out their deadly work, the main forces of the four attacking rifle corps' eight first-echelon rifle divisions also began their advance, each of them supported by their own tank regiments, followed, in turn, by the lead tank brigades of the 5th Guards and 2nd Tank Armies' tank corps and, finally, the tank brigades of the four tank corps' main forces.

The 7th Guards and 5th Guards Tank Armies' Assault

Almost immediately after beginning their assault, the lead assault groups and rifle regiments of Shumilov's 7th Guards Army encountered fierce and determined resistance across their entire front from the swampy region adjacent to the eastern bank of the Seret River eastward to the heavily forested hills near Cucuteni. The official history of Denisenko's 36th Guards Rifle Division, which was advancing in the first echelon of Safiulin's 25th Guards Rifle Corps, on the left wing of Shumilov's guards army, describes the intensity of the fighting:

> In the beginning of May, the 36th Guards Rifle Division, together with other units of the 7th Guards Army, tried to drive the enemy from their occupied positions and capture the Tirgu-Frumos fortified region. While advancing forward in cooperation with the tank crews of the 3rd Guards Tank Corps, the regiments seized the strongly fortified centers of resistance at Dumbravita, Georgesti, and Cucuteni. Less than ten kilometers

[six miles] remained to Tirgu-Frumos. However, we did not succeed in overcoming that distance. The enemy halted the advance of our attacking regiments with powerful fire and numerous counterattacks.

Both sides suffered losses. Just during the period of 2–5 May, the enemy lost 350 soldiers and officers, three tanks, 16 machine guns, three mortars, and three guns. The division lost 74 men killed and 181 wounded. Major G. P. Ioffe, the commander of the 106th Rifle Regiment, and Senior Lieutenant I. A. Gelikh, the assistant chief of staff for reconnaissance of the 104th Rifle Regiment, died heroes' deaths on the field of battle. A veteran of the division, he [the latter] had traveled along the trying roads of war from Stalingrad to the foothills of the Carpathian Mountains and, during that time, had risen from a corporal in reconnaissance to an experienced staff officer.

The courageous attempts by the division's soldiers to crush the enemy's resistance did not produce success. The units of the Romanian 1st Division and the SS Motorized Division "*Grossdeutschland,*" which opposed them and were dug in to pillboxes and bunkers, resisted fiercely. The penetration of so powerful a defense as there was in the Tirgu-Frumos fortified region required greater forces and, even more important, more careful preparation. However, we had devoted little time to this, as well as to our system of fires. The ammunition was clearly inadequate. These circumstances could not have failed to reflect negatively on the results of the offensive. After achieving no positive results at all, the *front* commander ordered us to make the transition to a firm defense.[4]

In the same fashion but in even greater detail, the official history of Morozov's 81st Guards Rifle Divisions, which was advancing in the first echelon of Vasil'ev's 24th Guards Rifle Corps on the right wing of both Shumilov's 7th Guards Army and Denisenko's 36th Guards Rifle Division, confirms the ferocity of the fighting north of Tirgu Frumos:

The early morning quiet on the 2nd of May in the hilly and forested terrain, which was intersected by narrow strips of settlements, was shattered by volleys of hundreds of guns and mortars of Soviet artillery. The artillery preparation lasted for 45 minutes and concluded with powerful volleys of "Katiushas" and a headlong attack by tanks and infantry.

Actually, just as could be expected from railroad workers, the resistance offered by the Romanian infantry was weak. As soon as the Soviet tanks appeared in front of their trenches, with infantry advancing steadily behind them, few of the [Romanian] soldiers remained. We penetrated the defense after crushing the resistance of the Romanian 1st Guards Division's resistance.

Retreating southward, the enemy clung to every house and hillock, trying with all of his might to halt us as far as possible forward from the fortified region that stretched from west to east cutting across the region between the Seret and Prut Rivers. The Royal forces offered particularly strong resistance in the sector from the village of Helestieni to Mount Hushenei [Hill 358] [seven to eight miles west of Tirgu-Frumos] along the line [extending] from the railroad station at Cuza Voda to the village of Radui. Here, the enemy committed his corps' reserves and counterattacked fiercely against our regiments, particularly along the Mount Hushenei axis, where the guardsmen of Lieutenant Colonel Selishchev had attacked successfully [several days before]. The division's units were forced to halt and go over to the defense. [At this time] Skiruta's regiment was north of Harmanesti, Major Voron's regiment was north of Helestieni, and Selishchev's regiment was north of Mount Krivesti.

Lieutenant Colonel Selishchev climbed up onto Mount Hushenei and reported, "Here I am, comrade division commander, like a sailor tied loop to loop with the battalion of Major Irzhevsky. I am preparing my sons for a rush closer to the fortified region."

After an agonizing six days of attempts to penetrate the Tirgu-Frumos fortified region, the armies of General Shumilov and Marshal Rotmistrov did not succeed. Here they then went over to the defense.[5]

The perspective was quite different on the German side of the firing line opposite the left wing of Vasil'ev's 24th Guards Rifle Corps. Lieutenant Hans-Karl Richter's 3rd Platoon of Lieutenant Bernhagen's 1st Company in the 1st Battalion of *Grossdeutschland*'s Panzer Grenadier Regiment, which was defending a strong point just west of Dumbravita [nine miles west of Tirgu Frumos] on the division's extreme left wing and at its boundary with the Romanian 1st Guards Panzer Division, recalled the terrifying Soviet artillery bombardment and infantry and tank assault:

At 04.20 hours [Berlin time] the world seemed to disintegrate. The front was ablaze. The flash of bursting shells was all that was visible as far as the eye could see. We cowered in our holes. Everyone knew that the big moment had come; the one we had already been awaiting for twenty-four hours. I kneeled by the field telephone; but what should I say? The command knew what was coming anyway.

Feldwebel Boehne lay above at the entrance to the cellar and watched. "The swine," was all that he said. Then we saw it ourselves. The enemy were now using white phosphorus. The broad hollow between Dumbrovita [Dumbravita] and the hill upon which the 1st Company was dug in resembled a sea of fire. That had to be the focal point of the Russian at-

> tack. I cranked the field telephone in vain. The line had been severed. While I was doing this, the ground began to tremble. A direct hit had almost leveled the house above our cellar. We looked at our watches and waited, but the firing continued unabated. When it finally appeared to leap over us an hour later, the air was filled with the roar of hundreds of motors and the rattling of tanks.
>
> Then machine gun fire sprang up. We were outside in a flash. An unreal scene like we had never seen before met our eyes. In the broad valley about 80 to 100 tanks were racing toward the hollow, toward my 3rd Platoon. Star shells, mauve-coloured flares and thousands of tracers flitted in all directions.[6]

The imposing force bearing down on Lieutenant Richter's forlorn platoon was the massed riflemen of Morozov's 81st Guards Rifle Division. The rattling tanks were infantry support tanks assigned to Colonel N. M. Brizhinev's 27th Guards Tank Brigade, which was supporting Denisenko's and Morozov's riflemen, and the lead tank brigades of Fominykh's 29th Tank Corps.

Konev's forces had begun their destructive work right on schedule. First seven and then eight reinforced rifle divisions advancing in the first echelon of the 25th and 24th Guards Rifle Corps of Shumilov's 7th Guards Army and the 35th Guards Rifle Corps of Trofimenko's 27th Army struck the German and Romanian defenses simultaneously, just as the violent artillery preparation roared to an end. The artillery preparation—which had engulfed an 18-mile-wide and six-mile-deep swath of ground extending from the Seret River at Pascani eastward to Polieni—with its destructive fires, smashed buildings, trees, pillboxes, and trench lines alike, killing, wounding, burying, or simply deafening the awed and frightened defenders. Under the protective fire of tanks and heavy self-propelled guns and a dense curtain of artillery and mortar fire, the combined infantry and tank assault tore though the Germans' forward defenses, isolating strong points and forcing the shaken defenders to readjust their shaken defenses to greet the torrent descending on them.

On the extreme right wing of Shumilov's 7th Guards Army, just east of the Seret River, Bogdanov's 8th Guards Airborne Division from Vasil'ev's 24th Guards Rifle Corps, supported by a composite tank brigade from Polozkov's 18th Tank Corps from the 5th Guards Tank Army, struck defenses manned by the reconnaissance battalion and three infantry battalions of the Romanian 1st Guards Panzer Division. Within a matter of several hours, Bogdanov's airborne troopers and their accompanying tanks smashed through the Romanian defenses with relative ease, by noon capturing Hill 256, two miles southeast of Blagesti, and cutting the Pascani and Tirgu Frumos road. Continuing their headlong advance, during the afternoon Bogdanov's forces drove the Romanian troops southward in small groups and in considerable disorder across the main east-west railroad line near Helestieni Station to the eastern outskirts of the town of Stolniceni-Prajescu, which was located on the western bank of the Seret River four miles south of Pascani. However, because it lacked bridging equipment, and, in any case, the town was not in its sector of advance, the forces of Bogdanov's division did not try to cross the river. In addition, since his tank support was relatively weak, and the forces on his left, Morozov's 81st Guards Rifle Division, were lagging far behind, Bogdanov called off his pursuit at nightfall and ordered his forces to go over to the defense in the marshlands east of the Seret River.

Simultaneous with Bogdanov's assault but on his left flank, riflemen and supporting tanks from Morozov's 81st Guards Rifle Division assaulted the forward defensive positions and strong points manned by the Romanian 1st Guards Panzer Division and the panzer-grenadier battalion defending on the extreme left wing of the *Grossdeutschland* Division's Panzer Grenadier Regiment, which included Lieutenant Richter's platoon. After shattering the Romanian defenses southwest of Harmanesti and bypassing and isolating many of the German strong points, including the one defended by Richter, Morozov's forces advanced southward up to three miles, capturing the strong points at Vascani and Dumbravita, eight to nine miles northwest of Tirgu Frumos at 1100 hours and the village strong point of Ruginoasa and a nearby sector of the main railroad line from Tirgu Frumos to Pascani, one mile to the south at 1400 hours. Continuing their assault, Morozov's lead rifle regiment forces reached the northern approaches to the strong point village of Helestieni, three miles south of the railroad and six miles west of Tirgu Frumos, by day's end. During this advance Major Selishchev's regiment of Morozov's division enveloped Helestieni from the west and captured the crest of Mount Hushenei (Hill 358), about one mile southwest of the strong point. However, although Selishchev's riflemen had seized the high ground dominating the western approaches to Helestieni, they were unable to advance any further because a *kampfgruppe* dispatched northward by the SS "*T*" Panzer Division blocked them.

Immediately after the riflemen and infantry support tanks from Vasil'ev's 24th Guards Rifle Corps penetrated the Romanian and German forward defenses, the lead tank brigades of Fominykh's 29th Tank Corps charged into and through these defenses and pushed on relentlessly toward the western outskirts of Tirgu Frumos without regard to their flanks and rear.

As Bogdanov's and Morozov's rifle divisions advanced southward, dramatically expanding the width and depth of their parent rifle corps' penetration, their offensive front expanded, and their forward ranks thinned. Inevitably, a yawning gap began forming between the two advancing divisions. Therefore, shortly after the two divisions severed the Tirgu Frumos and Pascani road and railroad line at midday, Vasil'ev ordered Losev's 72nd Guards Rifle Division to advance into combat from his rifle corps' second echelon and plug the gap between Bogdanov's and Morozov's rifle divisions. Deploying southward quickly, Losev's riflemen crossed the road and railroad line and occupied forward positions between Bogdanov's and Morozov's forces, permitting Morozov to regroup his regiments to the east for a concentrated assault on the German strong point at Helestieni.

During the first day of the offensive, Vasil'ev's three rifle divisions savaged the Romanian and German defenses at and west of Harmanesti, advanced up to seven miles in over 12 hours of heavy and often confused fighting, cut and crossed the main road and railroad from Tirgu Frumos to Pascani, and forced the German LVII Panzer Corps to commit a *kampfgruppe* (*Kampfgruppe* "G") from its SS "*T*" Panzer Division to bolster the Romanian's sagging defenses near Helestieni and reinforce the defenses on the *Grossdeutschland* Division's threatened right wing.

However, although Vasil'ev's forces successfully penetrated the Romanians' and Germans' first defensive belt, many if not most of the vital strong points in the German forward defenses managed to hold out against the Soviet onslaught, often simply by hunkering down into all-round hedgehog defenses. While this tactic seriously disrupted the orderly advance and resupply of Vasil'ev's advancing riflemen by forcing them to leave men behind to contain the pesky strong points, it also adversely affected the progress of Fominykh's exploiting armor, which by this time was reaching the western outskirts of Tirgu Frumos.

The Eighth Army's situation report dated 0830 hours 2 May cryptically but accurately described the situation as it developed early in the day:

> After heavy artillery preparations, which included up to 150 barrels, Stalin organs, and rocket launchers, at least 5, and supported by very heavy close air support, the enemy attacked the reinforced Pz GD [Panzer Grenadier Division Grossdeutschland] across the whole front. The attack was led by at least six shock divisions with over 300 tanks.[7]

As the report explained, the Soviets were making their main effort from the northwest through the *Grossdeutschland* Division's Panzer Grenadier Regiment and "the luckless Lieutenant Richter, on whose left flank the Romanians faltered and failed."[8] From his vantage point in the German forward defenses, which were soon in the Soviets' rear area, Lieutenant Richter described how his platoon coped with the looming disaster once the Soviet infantry had bypassed his strong point:

> Why wasn't the artillery firing? The Rumanians were responsible for our sector. I sent a runner to the rear, but he returned with bad news. When

the preparatory fire started, the Rumanian artillery commanders and the observation posts had left their positions, like the infantry, and had probably fallen back toward the much-talked about bunker line [Strunga Line]. Now all we had left was the rocket launchers and the three assault guns.

But there was no time for reflection. The first tanks had already reached the outskirts of Dumbrovita. They didn't get very far. The assault guns had been watching, and, within a few seconds, seven heavy tanks were in flames. Fahnenjunker-Feldwebel [Officer Cadet Sergeant Major] Gerber, who was in command of the 1st Platoon on the left wing, suddenly came running across the open ground, and he and his platoon occupied the west side of our pre-planned hedgehog. Meanwhile, on the right wing our soldiers were fighting an almost hopeless battle.

The first wave of Russian tanks had already passed over them. Another hundred followed in the second wave, and they had infantry with them. Tremendous masses of infantry. It was time. When the first salvo of rockets landed in the midst of the Russians, I fired the signal flare. That meant pull back. Two squads of the 3rd Platoon were able to comply with the order and were taken in by us at the outskirts of the village. But the others stayed put; they probably saw no way out. They shot the infantry off the tanks, but then the T-34s were upon them. All at once the entire hill in 1st Company's sector seemed to be swarming with tanks. From a distance of 100 metres one could watch hand grenade duels and see soldiers jump to their feet and be cut down. Unable to help, we had to sit and watch.

We had posted four MG-42s [machine guns] on the rooftops and these fired without interruption. Then something happened that no one who was there will ever forget. A shout went through the ranks of the soldiers of the 2nd Company. Ammunition gone, exhausted, some without weapons, our comrades stood up in their foxholes and raised their hands. Then we saw them fall. I don't know what happened, only at that instant no one was thinking about cover. The men stood and fired rifles and machine-guns freehand. Our rocket launchers [*Nebelwerfers*] must have realized that something awful was happening over on the hill. Rockets howled over us without letup and tore huge gaps in the seemingly endless mass of brown figures. Still we stayed. Heavy rifle fire and a flurry of grenades were the first indication that the Russians had reached the first houses in Dumbrovita.

We fought our way back slowly, frequently fighting hand to hand. We stopped and set up a hedgehog position just in front of the rocket launchers. A Leutnant, probably the battery commander, had been very badly shaken up by the grisly murders on the hill. He lay on a roof with tears in his eyes, directing his battery's fire as it destroyed what looked like entire enemy units.

Suddenly there were Russian tanks thirty metres in front of the firing positions, but the assault guns were standing guard. A few shots and three heavy tanks were burning. The crews didn't get far. Two tanks had broken through, however, and these split up the two platoons on the left wing. Two rifle squads and the company headquarters squad defended the battery's firing position until the last rocket had been fired. Then, at the last second, the brave Leutnant commanding the battery was hit. Badly wounded, we took him along in the prime mover. The assault guns had pulled back to the rail line. The Russians had already crossed it. Finally, after a hand-to-hand struggle lasting 30 minutes, we were able to fight our way through at an underpass. Sadly, our medic, Unteroffizier Hoffmann, was blown apart by a tank shell.

We reestablished contact with our people at about noon, the last squad of the battalion to do so. The day was not yet over, however. With four armoured personnel carriers, I assumed responsibility for securing the left flank, which was open for many kilometers.[9]

Meanwhile, combat was also raging on the right flank of Richter's platoon, where the remainder of his 1st Battalion and the Panzer Grenadier Regiment's 2nd Battalion were defending the four-mile-wide sector extending from just east of Dumbravita northeastward through Barbotesti. Once again Richter describes the action, which took place opposite the left wing of Morozov's 81st Guards Rifle Division and the right wing of Denisenko's 36th Guards Rifle Division:

From their positions, the men of III [II] Battalion, Panzer-Grenadier Regiment GD saw what happened to their comrades [the 1st Battalion near Dumbravita]—and knew that for them there was only one chance. Somewhat further back, at the edge of a hollow, there was a 75mm Pak [antitank gun]. Crouched behind the anti-tank gun's armour shield, Unteroffizier Emde (4th Heavy Company, I Battalion) sat spellbound at the sight mount and stared through the telescope sight at the approaching enemy tanks. Behind him, by one of the two rails, was his loader, the next armour-piercing round already in his hands. The gun tractor, which was off to one side, was hit by a shell, and burst into flames. Then . . . a heavy blow, a flash of fire; the gun jumped back. In the area of the target a flash—smoke—fire. A tank blew apart. The loader rammed another shell into the breech; the anti-tank gun barked again, another enemy tank went up in flames. In less than twenty minutes, Emde destroyed seven enemy tanks, just he and his loader. Then his gun was hit, and it was over. The firing stopped. The surviving enemy tanks noticed this and raced toward the lone anti-tank gun in order to run over it and grind it into the dirt

> beneath their tracks. Unteroffizier Emde and his loader were just able to reach safety. Later his commanding officer, Oberst Lorenz, awarded Emde the Iron Cross, First Class.
>
> Due northwest [northeast] raged the Battle of Giurgesti (Georgesti]. II Battalion's 5th Company had been ejected from its positions, and its handful of men had fallen back to a section of trench several hundred metres in front of the village. Then a group of German soldiers emerged from the wood to the right: Leutnant Thurau of I Battalion had managed to fight his way through and went into position farther left near the highway. He had to hold, even though eight more enemy tanks had already arrived. Fire! Fire!! Armoured-piercing shells brought them to a halt. On the road fork off to the left on the hill, near Point 298, they could see 26 enemy tanks and more than 300 men. Where was the regiment's pioneer platoon? Was it over there? Then Stukas came and dived on the mass of tanks. Smoke, dust, fire. For the moment there was quiet. To the right, the Russians had broken into II Battalion's trenches. Oberleutnant Wechmann, together with several runners and a few stragglers he had picked up, stormed the trench and took it back, shooting wildly in all directions. The Soviets fled. The German right wing was again back in the main line of resistance.[10]

The torrent of Soviet armor that flowed into and around the defenses of Lieutenant Richter's 1st Battalion and the 2nd Battalion to the east belonged to Fominykh's 29th Tank Corps from Rotmistrov's 5th Guards Tank Army, whose lead tank brigade, together with Brizhinev's 27th Guards Tank Brigade, was supporting the advance of Vasil'ev's riflemen. Replicating practices he had employed to penetrate the enemy's defenses in his previous offensives, most notably in his tank army's spectacular victory at Korsun'-Shevchenkovskii during January 1944, Rotmistrov had ordered Fominykh to support the infantry to his front during the penetration with his lead tank brigade, commit his full tank corps into the penetration as soon as it developed, and advance toward his initial objective, the western outskirts of Tirgu-Frumos, as rapidly as possible and without regard for his flanks and rear. Fominykh followed Rotmistrov's orders to the letter. In columns of brigades led by forward detachments, his tanks lunged forward, bypassing German strong points and deploying into assault formation only when absolutely necessary to accomplish their mission.

The after-action report prepared by the Armored and Mechanized Directorate of Konev's *front* describes the initial assaults by the 5th Guards Tank Army:

> Overcoming strong enemy fire resistance and repelling frequent counterattacks by enemy infantry and tanks, by the end of the day on 2 May,

> the 5th Guards Tank Army drove the enemy back to Hill 358 [the 29th Tank Corps one mile west of Helestieni], Hill 326 and Hill 225 [the 29th Tank Corps up to two miles southeast of Ruginoasa], De-Sus [the 29th Tank Corps three miles northwest of Tirgu-Frumos], and Cornesti [the 3rd Guards Tank Corps five miles north of Tirgu-Frumos] line by delivering attacks in the direction of Dumbravita and the western outskirts of Tirgu-Frumos.[11]

Fominykh's armor, followed by the riflemen from Morozov's 81st Guards Rifle Division, passed through and around the German forward defenses east of Dumbravita, captured Ruginoasa, and rushed forward southeastward along the road and railroad line running through the broad valley approaching Tirgu Frumos from the northwest. After capturing or bypassing the villages of Radui and De-Sus, the lead tanks reached the village of Dadesti, just two miles northwest of Tirgu Frumos, and formed into attack formation to assault directly into the center of the town. With most of his infantry now fighting in the Soviet rear area, Manteuffel, who was observing the Soviet advance from his command post on high ground south of the town, had no choice but to rely on his precious 88-mm antiaircraft guns and panzer reserves to halt the Soviet tank attack:

> Our infantry in the forward positions had allowed them to roll past, partly in order to leave the prize to the antiaircraft battery of 88's dug in at [Hill 372], the northern entrance to Targul-Frumos. The majority of the attacking tanks, about 25 in number, were hit and set afire, and the rest, about ten, stumbled into our Panzer Regiment's concentration area and were destroyed there. I very soon had the impression that the main attack would come from the area northwest of Targul-Frumos toward Targul Frumos and therefore ordered the Panzer Regiment to position itself behind a rise west of Targul-Frumos, behind the left wing of the [Ruginoasa] sector, which was held by the Panzer-Grenadier Regiment. Dug in on the rise, very well camouflaged, was a battery of assault guns. Approximately two companies of Russian tanks, about 30 vehicles, attacked the rise just as I was driving up to it.
>
> The infantry deployed in front of the rise had allowed the tanks, which were moving at high speed, to roll past. The battery let the tanks approach to about 30 metres and then knocked out every one of them. Most of the enemy tanks exploded into tiny pieces. I later showed some of them to the experts to prove to them the outstanding effectiveness of our armour-piercing ammunition. We suffered no losses.[12]

Although the battery of German 88-mm. guns managed to destroy many of the tanks in the forward detachments of Fominykh's assaulting force west of Tirgu Frumos and disrupted the coherence of his advancing tank formations, the remaining tank brigades of his 29th Tank Corps were still pouring into the valley west of the town, posing a continued deadly threat to the coherence of Manteuffel's defenses. However, as described by Manteuffel, a hastily organized but effective counterattack by *Grossdeutschland* Division's Panzer Regiment late in the morning ended this threat once and for all:

> Another Soviet company drove in Indian file, that is to say one behind the other, past Ruginoasa, where the Rumanians had disintegrated as expected. It was spotted in time by a company of our tanks and completely destroyed. My initial favorable impression was confirmed at about 08.00. There now came wave after wave of tanks, which we blasted and put to flight by from well-sited, prepared firing positions. As I was speaking to the commander of the Panzer Regiment [Oberst Willy Langkeit] in his command vehicle (by radio), very large-caliber tank shells began whizzing past our vehicles. They had been fired from great range. We soon ascertained that they were being fired by heavy tanks in stationary positions from a distance of some 3,000 meters.
>
> At first we both thought that several of our own Tiger tanks had become disoriented, because we had never before experienced such heavy caliber fire from the Russians. A company of Tigers [the 9th Company of Oberleutnant Dr. Fritz Stadler, from Vienna, Austria] was summoned, and these opened fire on the enemy tanks. One could clearly see the shells were striking the [enemy] tanks, but all bounced off! The commander of the Tiger Battalion, Oberstleutnant Baumungk, who was present, ordered his tanks [10–12 in number] to attack the enemy tanks. The Tigers approached to within approximately 2,000 to 1,800 meters of the enemy tanks and opened fire on them. Four of the enemy tanks were soon burning; three, as far as I could see, immediately left the position at high speed. I then ordered a nearby company of Mark IV tanks to swing around Ruginoasa from the east to pursue and knock out these "escapees." Our swift and maneuverable "small" tanks had the good fortune to come up under cover to within approximately 1,000 meters and engage them from the rear.
>
> As we later found out, they were the new "Stalin" tanks: big gun, heavy armor, low silhouette, but also slow and not maneuverable enough. In my opinion, the crews were also not sufficiently familiar with the new vehicle.[13]

The heavy Iosef Stalin tanks referred to by Manteuffel in his description of the fighting southeast of Ruginoasa belonged to the 14th Guards Separate Heavy Tank Regiment, whose 13 IS-122 heavy tanks had been attached to

Fominykh's 29th Tank Corps during the assault. Although Soviet records do not indicate how many of these tanks the Germans destroyed during this fighting, the ability of *Grossdeutschland*'s Panzer Regiment to break up and ultimately repel Fominykh's assault indicates that the new tanks did not operate very effectively.

Manteuffel later summed up the morning's action in his panzer grenadier regiment's sector:

> By about 11.00 [hours], the Panzer Regiment had destroyed about 250 tanks in the area of the Panzer-Grenadier Regiment's positions. I saw hesitation in the enemy attack. The Russians still had plenty of tanks but they merely fired at us from extreme range without attacking. We at first had no interest in attacking so deep into the enemy's positions with our tanks to finish them off—we hoped to take them on the next day or at another place.[14]

Thus, the initial crisis the defending Germans faced west of Tirgu-Frumos ended by mid-morning on 2 May as a considerable success. The skillful counterattack by *Grossdeutschland* Division's Panzer Regiment drove the riflemen of Morozov's 81st Guards Rifle Division and the exploiting tanks of Fominykh's 29th Tank Corps back up the valley west of Tirgu Frumos, recaptured De Sus, and reached the eastern outskirts of Radui, thereby securing the western approaches to Tirgu Frumos, at least temporarily. However, no sooner had Manteuffel resolved this crisis than a second crisis erupted on the Panzer Grenadier Regiment's right wing and along the Fusilier Regiment's entire front.

Because he committed his Panzer Regiment to the full-scale counterattack northwest of Tirgu Frumos, Manteuffel lacked forces with which he could plug any gaps that developed elsewhere along his division's front. By mid-morning just such a gap had formed as the result of a strong Soviet tank and infantry assault further east at the junction of the *Grossdeutschland* Division's Grenadier and Fusilier Regiments. Consequently, at about 0900 hours, *Grossdeutschland*'s headquarters received an alarming report from its Fusilier Regiment that 34 Russian tanks had broken through their front lines between Barbotesti and Cucuteni, six miles north-northwest of Tirgu Frumos, and had penetrated southward to a depth of roughly three miles into the streets of the village of Cornesti, where the regiment's headquarters was situated. During the heavy and often hand-to-hand fighting in the town, in which the regimental commander personally participated, the defending Fusiliers had reportedly "shot up 24 tanks."[15]

The Soviet force that created this threat were the two first-echelon rifle divisions of Safiulin's 25th Guards Rifle Corps and supporting armor from

Vovchenko's 3rd Guards Tank Corps of Rotmistrov's 5th Guards Tank Army, which were attacking on the left wing of Shumilov's 7th Guards Army at the very center of Konev's main shock group. While Vasil'ev's 24th Guards Rifle Corps and Fominykh's 29th Tank Corps were wrecking havoc on the Romanian and German defenses west and northwest of Tirgu Frumos, at dawn on 2 May, the assault groups and first-echelon rifle regiments of Safiulin's 25th Guards Rifle Corps, supported by the lead tank brigades of Vovchenko's 3rd Guards Tank Corps, launched an assault against the right wing of *Grossdeutschland* Division's Panzer Grenadier Regiment and the left wing of the division's Fusilier Regiment. Safiulin conducted his assault in the three-mile-wide sector from the German strong point at Barbotesti eastward to the Cucuteni region with Denisenko's 36th Guards and Ovsienko's 53rd Rifle Divisions.

The sector extending from Barbotesti eastward through Securesti to Cucuteni opposite Safiulin's assembled host was defended by the 3rd Battalion of *Grossdeutschland*'s Panzer Grenadier Regiment. A participant in the battle described the scene:

> Where was the neighboring unit on the right? Where was the nearest machine gun nest of III Battalion, Panzer-Grenadier Regiment GD? They should have contact on the left with Oberstleutnant Wechmann of II Battalion, which was supposed to be in front of Secaresti. Where were they then? Hill 344 had been lost; it was in Russian hands. But the men of the 11th Company were still holding out in the gardens at the north end of Cucuteni and were in contact with the Haputmann commanding the company; there, at least, they were together.
>
> Then, suddenly, [they saw] two T-34s on the street. Hollow charges up! Frisch ran forward and set off the tanks, but then two assault guns approached and opened fire. Frisch, now having reached the enemy tanks, armed the charge. Boom! Hurray, its burning.! There were loud shouts, arms were thrown in the air from joy. Then, from the side, machine-gun fire. Sustained fire. Time to keep their heads down.[16]

Just as was the case to the west, Safiulin's assault collapsed the German defenses between these strong points, and Vovchenko's tanks quickly exploited the penetration, creating the crisis described by Manteuffel. During the heavy fighting, which lasted throughout the entire day, the Soviet infantry and supporting tanks captured the strong points at Barbotesti and Cucuteni and penetrated southward through the village of Propota into the town of Cornesti, prompting the Fusilier Regiment to issue its urgent call for help to Manteuffel.

Even though the Soviets succeeded in penetrating the Fusilier Regiment's defenses at several points and managed to advance up to three miles to the south, after quickly regrouping its panzers to the northeast, *Grossdeutschland's* Panzer Regiment and the beleagured Fusiliers were at last able to separate the Soviet tanks from their supporting infantry and contain and finally repel the assault. Once again, Manteuffel describes this, his second major crisis on the first day of the battle:

> I had promised my friend Oberst Niemack, the commander of the Panzer-Fusilier Regiment, that I would come to his aid with the Panzer Regiment at 12.00 [Berlin time]. The situation there had meanwhile become extremely critical and full of danger. There was a renewed heavy attack by strong Russian armoured forces after 11.00. I therefore ordered the panzers to break off the battle in the sector west of Targul Frumos and assemble in the Targul Frumos area.
>
> The commander of the Panzer Regiment, who was in Targul Frumos, took the initiative and made all the necessary preparations to supply the regiment with fuel and ammunition as quickly as possible. A mixed battalion of Panzer Vs and VIs under the command of the Tigers was left behind the Panzer-Grenadier Regiment's sector. I myself drove forward to the Panzer-Fusilier Regiment with a company of Panzer IVs. I assessed the situation and the terrain and sent the following panzer regiment to the attack while it was still on the move.[17]

Manteuffel's Panzer Regiment reached the beleagured Fusiliers at 1155 hours and immediately destroyed 30 Russian tanks. At the same time, further to the east, the 24th Panzer Division also reached the region and began a counterattack of its own.

The counterattack by the *Grossdeutschland* Division's Panzer Regiment halted the advance by Safiulin's riflemen and Vovchenko's tanks in the streets of Cornesti, destroyed many of Vovchenko's tanks, recaptured the strong point at Probota, and drove the Soviet infantry and tanks back about two miles to the forward edge of the Germans' former second defensive belt, thereby limiting Safiulin's advance to a total depth of only about two miles. The fighting in this sector was so fierce and the German resistance so strong that it forced Vovchenko to commit virtually all three of his tank brigades to support Safiulin's hard-pressed riflemen. By day's end, a frustrated Rotmistrov ordered Vovchenko to cease his futile assaults and instead regroup his tank corps westward to support a renewed advance by the 29th Tank Corps the next day. Manteuffel reported:

> By nightfall the intervention of the Panzer Regiment had completely restored the situation in this sector of the division. . . . During the latter part of the night, or before it became first light, a half-battalion each of Panzer

> Vs and VIs was positioned in both sectors so that they could place fire in front of our infantry when it became first light.[18]

The regrouping of the *Grossdeutschland* Division's Panzer Regiment from its previous positions west and northwest of Tirgu Frumos eastward late in the morning, to conduct its counterattack against Soviet forces in the Cornesti sector, afforded Vasil'ev's 25th Guards Rifle Corps and Fominykh's 29th Tank Corps yet another opportunity to resume their tank and infantry assaults against the Germans' newly restored defenses west and northwest of the town, which they did immediately with fresh resolve. However, as they did so, beginning at 1200 hours, a regiment from the SS "*T*" Panzer Division (Group v. "G") launched a counterattack of its own northward from the strong point at Helestieni toward Ruginoasa, in conjunction with an attack westward through Radui toward Ruginoasa with the "swift and maneuverable" Mark IV tanks in position that Manteuffel had left behind west of Tirgu Frumos.

Richter vividly describes his rescue by the twin German panzer forces, whose combined assault apparently caught the Soviets by surprise:

> The I Battalion was scattered. There were small groups of men everywhere. With great difficulty Major Schwarzrock had managed to fight his way out of his command post, around which three T-34s were circling. Tired and depressed, we sat in the armoured personnel carriers and waited for what was to come. The enemy hadn't penetrated far, but the soldiers could no longer stand the strain. . . . The pickets on the hill must have fallen asleep, for suddenly there were four T-34s right in front of our half-tracks. However, this time luck was on our side. As if summoned by a magic hand, the tanks and assault guns of the SS Division "Totenkopf" suddenly appeared from the south; before any of the T-34s could take aim they had all been hit. Then there began a terrible tank battle, practically in no-mans land. Oberst Rudel's Ju 87s swooped down repeatedly, showing the panzers the way. The 4 APCs of 2nd Company went with them, and they found plenty of work to do. The Russian infantry appeared to be following their tanks in thousands; now, all the fury of the soldiers who had seen their comrades fall to the murderer's hands was unleashed.
>
> The attempt by the Russians to break through was frustrated.[19]

Under the cover of these panzer counterattacks, the infantrymen from the smashed left wing of the *Grossdeutschland* Division's Panzer Grenadier Regiment, including Richter's platoon, withdrew from their strong points near Dumbravita and Ruginoasa and established new defensive positions on the eastern outskirts of Radui, less than two miles southeast of Ruginoasa, protected by Manteuffel's and SS "*T*'s" panzers.

Despite the limited successes the riflemen of Vasil'ev's 24th Guards Rifle Corps and the tanks of Fominykh's 29th Tank Corps achieved west of Tirgu Frumos, the failure of Safiulin's 25th Guards and Vovchenko's 3rd Guards Tank Corps' combined infantry and tank assaults on the *Grossdeutschland* Division's defenses north of Tirgu Frumos seemed to ensure the viability of the LVII Panzer Corps' defenses in the entire region. However, to the German panzer corps' discomfiture, if not consternation, this was not yet the case.

This was so because the strong Soviet infantry and tank assaults against the defenses of the *Grossdeutschland* Division's Fusilier Regiment northeast of Tirgu Frumos and east of Cucuteni were making noticeable and alarming progress and threatening to collapse the entire left wing of the panzer corps' defenses. Fortunately for Lieutenant General Friedrich Kirchner's LVII Panzer Corps, however, the failure of the Soviet assaults against its center and its left wing meant that vital panzer reserves were now available to counter the new Soviet threat. In addition, because of the panzer corps' excellent foresight, by now Edelsheim's relatively fresh 24th Panzer Division was prepared to march to the sounds of the Soviet guns.

The 27th Army's and 2nd Tank Army's Assaults

While the LVII Panzer Corps was maneuvering its operational and tactical panzer reserves to support the *Grossdeutschland* Panzer Grenadier Division's positional defense north and west of Tirgu Frumos, the Soviet attacks to the east forced the panzer corps to conduct a more mobile defense to contend with this equally deadly threat to its defenses. In this instance, Edelsheim's 24th Panzer Division had the most vital role in the defense.

Konev initiated his assault northeast of Tirgu Frumos with the combined forces of the 35th Guards Rifle Corps from Trofimenko's 27th Army and the 3rd and 16th Tank Corps of Bogdanov's 2nd Tank Army. The 27th Army's daily combat journal entry for 2 May accurately describes the first day of Trofimenko's offensive:

> In accordance with the battle plan, which the army commander approved on 24 April 1944, and the combat order, which he issued on 1 May 1944, the army's forces commenced combat operations with the mission of penetrating the enemy's defenses and, after destroying his units, reach the Buda, Stornesti, Obrijeni, and Podu-Iloaie line and seize the mountain passes on the Slobodzia and Sinesti road with forward detachments by the end of the first day of battle. The army commander decided to conduct the attack with three rifle divisions (the 3rd Guards Airborne, 93rd Guards Rifle, and 206th Rifle) [abreast from right to left] [of the 35th Guards Rifle Corps] and retain one [of the rifle corps'] division (the 78th

Rifle) in second echelon. The penetration of the defense was conducted along a 5.5-kilometer [3.3-mile] front in the sector from Cucuteni [eastward] to the fork in the road and the path one kilometer [0.6 miles] southwest of Lake Hirbu. The penetration was carried out in close cooperation with the 2nd Tank Army. . . .

The 33rd Rifle Corps [on the army's left wing northwest of Iasi] received an enciphered order from the army commander on 1 May 1944 to begin the attack at 0615 hours on 2 May 1944 after an artillery preparation.

The enemy [is] the panzer division "*Grossdeutschland,*" which is defending in front of the army's right wing with two motorized regiments in the forward area. The defensive works along the forward edge consist of pillboxes and trenches and a considerable number of tanks dug into the earth. Up to 20 tanks and concentrated infantry and the presence of pillboxes and dugouts and a three- to four-meter-wide [9–12-foot-wide] antitank ditch have been noted in the Tirgu-Frumos region. . . .

In fulfillment of its assigned missions, the army's forces launched their attack at 0615 hours on 2 May 1944 after a 30-minute artillery preparation. Overcoming stubborn enemy resistance, the units of the 35th Guards Rifle Corps and 54th Fortified Region (on the army's right wing), in coordination with units of the 2nd Tank Army, wedged into the enemy's defenses and advanced four to six kilometers [2.4–3.6 miles] along the Tirgu-Frumos axis by 1100 hours and fought primarily in their existing positions in other sectors. Beginning at first light, our aviation conducted bombing and strafing strikes against enemy strong points and artillery positions in the army sector, primarily in the Tirgu-Frumos region, with groups of 6–12 aircraft.

Enemy infantry and tanks (up to 70 tanks) counterattacked against the 35th Rifle Corps' and the 54th Fortified Region's attacking units at 1100 hours and pressed them back somewhat. Beginning at 1100 hours, groups of enemy aircraft repeatedly bombed the attacking units, conducting more than 250 aircraft sorties. The 35th Guards Rifle Corps lost 156 men killed and 275 wounded, and the 54th Fortified Region lost four killed and 14 wounded during the day.

The 33rd Rifle Corps attempted to attack toward the south but achieved no success after encountering stubborn resistance and was fighting in its previous positions at day's end. It managed to capture 15 Romanian soldiers during the morning but suffered 24 killed and 113 wounded.[20]

The after-action report prepared by the Armored and Mechanized Directorate of Konev's *front* provides additional details about the operations of Bogdanov's 2nd Tank Army during Trofimenko's initial assault:

> Attacking [southward] toward Tirgu-Frumos along the Hirlau-Tirgu-Frumos road, separate groups of tanks from the 2nd Tank Army's 107th Tank Brigade [16th Tank Corps] penetrated [the enemy's defenses], reached the road two kilometers [1.2 miles] east of Tirgu-Frumos, and captured [the village] of Facuti [four miles northeast of Tirgu-Frumos] (the 16th Tank Corps' 109th Tank Brigade) by 1110 hours on 2 May 1944.
>
> By this time, the 2nd Tank Army's left flank turned out to be open, and the threat of an attack on the army from the east materialized. In accordance with a decision made by the commander of the 16th Tank Corps, the 164th Tank Brigade and the 1st Motorized Rifle Brigade were wheeled toward the east to protect the [left] flank of the 16th Tank Corps and the 2nd Tank Army as a whole.
>
> By committing up to 40 tanks into combat from the direction of the northeastern outskirts of Tirgu-Frumos and from the direction of the town of Bosna (south of Polieni) [two miles northeast of Facuti], the enemy pushed the 16th Tank Corps' units back, but they fought stubbornly and occupied defenses along the southern slope of Hill 192 [two miles north of Facuti].
>
> The units of the 3rd Tank Corps fought with mixed success in the vicinity of Hills 256 and 197 [four miles north of Tirgu-Frumos] and the northern outskirts of Cucuteni throughout the entire day.[21]

As was the case on his shock group's right wing to the west, the massed infantry and tanks concentrated on the left wing of Konev's shock group struck the German defenses in the six-mile-wide sector from Cucuteni eastward to Liteni, six miles north and northeast of Tirgu Frumos, at 0615 hours Moscow time on 2 May after firing a powerful 30-minute artillery preparation. In this sector, Konev's assaulting forces consisted of three rifle divisions from Goriachev's 35th Guards Rifle Corps of Trofimenko's 27th Army, supported by the army's 8th and 13th Heavy Tank Regiments, and all of Mishulin's 3rd and Dubovoi's 16th Tank Corps of Bogdanov's 2nd Tank Army.

Goriachev conducted his assault with Kolesnikov's 206th Rifle, Colonel Konev's 3rd Guards Airborne, and Zolotukhin's 93rd Guards Rifle Divisions arrayed from left to right [east to west] in the sector from Polieni westward to Cucuteni against defensive positions manned by the 3rd Battalion of the *Grossdeutschland* Division's Grenadier Regiment, the same division's Fusilier Regiment, and the battalions of the left wing of the 46th Infantry Division's 97th Grenadier Regiment. As was the case in the 7th Guards Army's sector, Goriachev led his attack with specially tailored assault groups followed by the main forces from his divisions' first-echelon rifle regiments. Bogdanov's two tank corps, whose forward brigades were to support Goriachev's initial assault, were to commit their remaining tank and motorized rifle brigades to the fight immediately after Goriachev's riflemen and infantry support tanks penetrated the Germans' forward defenses. Deployed along an extended front to the east, the machine-gun and artillery battalions of the 27th Army's 54th Fortified Region were to support Goriachev's assault by protecting his left flank and capturing German strong points on the southern bank of Lake Hirbu, just east of Belcesti, and the Cihudai River, which flowed southeastward from Munteni to Podu Iloaie.

As of the morning of 2 May, the LVII Panzer Corps' defense plan called for its forward deployed forces to hold and contain any Soviet assaults until it was able to mount counterattacks to eliminate any Soviet penetrations. This plan meant that *Grossdeutschland* Division's 3rd Battalion, Grenadier Regiment, its Fusilier Regiment, and the 46th Infantry Division's 97th Grenadier Regiment would be "left to their own devices" to defend the region northeast of Tirgu Frumos and north of Facuti until the panzer corps' principal counterattack force, the two *kampfgruppen* of Edelsheim's 24th Panzer Division, were able to deploy for action. According to Manteuffel's account of the 24th Panzer Division's operations:

> As a prerequisite for the counterattack, the order was given to hold the defensive position at Facuti at all costs, and the screening forces were ordered to establish and firmly hold smaller defensive positions on both sides of the break-in, a rapid switch from delaying to defensive tactics typical of what the Germans called elastic fighting.
>
> 24th Panzer launched its two kampfgruppen in different directions and with different missions but with one and the same aim: to destroy the enemy, a simultaneous combination of two tactics. Kampfgruppe "E" was ordered to stop the enemy, which had outflanked Facuti, and Kampfgruppe "W" was to attack the enemy in the flank and rear as long as he was still moving forward in the attack.
>
> The counterattack was to take the enemy by surprise in the flank and from the rear and destroy him. Subsequently, the division was to concentrate the two Kampfgruppen "E" and "W" and regain the commanding positions north of Facuti within only a few hours.[22]

The initial assault by Goriachev's 35th Guards Rifle Corps shattered the German forward defenses, creating an immediate crisis in the headquarters of the *Grossdeutschland* Division's Fusilier Regiment. Advancing southward astride the Hirlau-Tirgu Frumos road, the assault groups and follow-on riflemen from Zolotukhin's 93rd Guards Rifle Division, supported by small groups of tanks from the lead tank brigades of Mishulin's 3rd Tank Corps, broke through at the boundary between the Grenadier Regiment's

3rd Battalion and the Fusilier Regiment's 3rd Battalion just south of the town of Bals, six miles north of Tirgu Frumos; captured the German strong point on nearby Hill 197, just west of Bals; and advanced almost three more miles to the northern outskirts of the village of Kalmu and Hill 256, where the Grenadiers and Fusiliers finally halted the Soviets' advance, but just barely.

A German participant describes the assault's effects:

> What was happening near Bals, on the [Grenadier Regiment's] left? That's where III Panzer-Fusilier Battalion was supposed to be. Damned heavy firing there. Were they still there? It didn't look that way. The MG 42s were still firing, but the enemy tanks were already behind them. Now they were rolling toward Nicolne [Nicola] [three miles south of Bals], where the artillery was. There was a flash, the guns of 1st Battery were firing over open sights. Boom! The first enemy tank blew up, then another and yet another. The battery had been able to hit five enemy tanks, and while this was happening 2nd and 3rd Batteries were able to pull out and disappear toward the rear.
>
> On the "Kalmu," Hill 256, there was an observation post. Weren't they going to leave? Couldn't they tear themselves away from the panorama of battle, from the wide-ranging view to the north? Those were brave boys. Finally, the enemy infantry were stopped. Oberleutnant Kendel of III Battalion, Panzer-Fusilier Regiment GD defended the road bitterly and single-mindedly, but was unable to hold Nicolne. He and his men had to fall back to new positions father south of the town.[23]

Advancing in tandem further to the east, the riflemen of Colonel Konev's 3rd Guards Airborne and Kolesnikov's 206th Rifle Divisions, supported by tanks from the forward detachments of Dubovoi's 16th Tank Corps, shattered the Fusilier Regiment's defenses from Hill 192 eastward to just west of the village of Polieni, captured the hilltop strong point, and drove the beleagured Fusiliers back toward Facuti. Encouraged by his tanks' spectacular early forward progress, which propelled Goriachev's advancing infantry forward almost three miles, at roughly 1000 hours, Bogdanov ordered Dubovoi to begin committing his 16th Tank Corps into what Bogdanov thought was a wide open gap in the German defenses. Advancing in brigade columns, with his 109th and 107th Tank Brigades in the lead and his 164th Tank and 1st Motorized Rifle Brigades following some distance behind, the tank fist of Dubovoi's tank corps thrust rapidly southward toward Facuti. The 6th Guards Heavy Tank Regiment, which was equipped with 16 Iosef Stalin (IS) 122-mm heavy tanks, rumbled menacingly southward amid Dubovoi's advancing tank columns.

Within a half an hour, Dubovoi's tanks reached the northern outskirt of Facuti and began penetrating into the town, which was stoutly defended by small units subordinate to the Fusilier Regiment's headquarters. A German war correspondent, Heiner Mayer, who was situated at the command post of Oberst Niemack, the commander of the Fusilier Regiment, describes the fighting in and around Facuti:

> Situated close to the wall of the house behind a cottage [in Facuti], the narrow opening led into the makeshift bunker. Below, the regiment's adjutant spoke without interruption to the battalion command posts. The Oberst [Colonel] sat in front of the entrance on a half-charred beam. If he bent down, the earpiece of the second receiver just reached his ear. Now and then he listened in. He said little. Beside him, on the bunker's earthen roof, a brown leather briefcase; inside were the most secret, important files and orders. Across the case lay a submachine-gun.
>
> To the left a treeless path led down to a brook spanned by a narrow bridge. It was the only one across the very swampy stream bed. There behind the wall of a collapsed dam was an anti-tank gun, the sole available heavy weapon. Three-hundred metres father down the brook sat a T-34, pouring smoke. It had been knocked out by the anti-tank gun several moments earlier. The village was burning from end to end.
>
> The young operations office came hurrying up and reported that 32 enemy tanks had now been counted in the village. From the bunker the adjutant called, "Herr Oberst, all communications have been lost, even to division!"
>
> A formation of enemy bombers swept over the village. A growing hail of bombs fell among the foxholes on the slope. On the far side of the valley, behind the front, Soviet infantry went into position. Continuous bursts of machine-gun fire forced everyone to take cover. From the most forward holes someone shouted, "Is the Oberst still there?"
>
> The liaison officer from a nearby artillery battalion arrived with the news that there was one chance to retreat, upstream. If the Herr Oberst wanted to establish a second line of defence there . . .
>
> The Oberst cut him off and said forcefully, "I hear retreat, there'll be none of that here! Are your guns still in their old positions?" The artilleryman replied that they were. "Then fire as long as you have ammunition! By the way, ask my operations officer what I think of attempts to fall back!" The Oberst bent down in the bunker entrance: "Just so that everyone is clear on this: there will be no such attempt here! Let each of my officers know again, by radio or runner: the village will be held no matter what!"

A Feldwebel came and reported that he had destroyed a T-34 with a panzer-faust [panzer fist antitank weapon] a few houses away. His left hand was bleeding. The Oberst thanked him warmly and ordered him to have his wound bandaged and then come into his bunker.

Our infantry came back from the front. The rigours of five hours of close-quarters fighting could be seen in their faces. The Oberst knew them; he also knew what they'd been through that morning. Several of them were wounded. "The tanks have broken in," one of them reported, "thirty-three tanks are tearing up our positions. Now they are entering the village. Herr Oberst it is simply impossible . . ."

Herr Oberst sprang to his feet. "Impossible? . . . Do we know that? Oh, my fusiliers. Here we have hand grenades, mines, hollow charges, haven't we gone through situations like this before? Let them come. We are here and are tougher than thirty-three tanks."

An Oberleutnant was brought in. Before they got him, he had knocked out the first of the thirty-three tanks among the houses. "Bring me an Iron Cross, First Class!" called the Oberst. The adjutant took off his own and passed it up from the bunker. Above in the street a tank shell smashed the medical officer's house to rubble. Houses were burning all around. They could hear the rattle of heavy tracks. Heavy artillery shells fell in the town. Rifle bullets hissed. Ricochets buzzed and howled before landing in the mud somewhere. "Now let's get them!" shouted the Oberst, and he picked up his submachine-gun. The spell was broken. . . .

Eight of the Soviet giants, some of the latest type, were destroyed in close combat, man against tank. The battle went on for hours. The rest of the tanks withdrew. The will of one man had overcome them; he was tougher than armour plate, tougher than the column of tanks.

And then, ringing out from the right, from the east, tank cannon; their hard crack was music to the ears of the men in Facuti. They had come at literally the last moment. The enemy tanks swung their guns around to the right to met the new threat. Here and there one of them went up in flames, some withdrew to the north.[24]

Above the din of battle resounding through the streets of the half-destroyed town of Facuti, the cracking tank fire announced to the beleagured Fusiliers that succor was near at hand; the panzers of Edelsheim's 24th Panzer Division were rushing to their rescue, not a moment too soon.

Shocked by the intensity and ferocity of the Soviets' initial onslaught, at 0900 hours Colonel Niemack, the commander of the Fusilier Regiment, had requested immediate assistance from his parent division and the LVII Panzer Corps. While the panzer corps ordered Edelsheim's 24th Panzer Division to initiate its counterattack plans, Manteuffel responded by dispatching the bulk of his Panzer Regiment to the rescue. With Manteuffel himself in the lead, the *Grossdeutschland* Division's Panzer Regiment counterattacked northward along the Hirlau road, bringing the Soviet attack in this sector to an abrupt halt shortly after noon. After making several vain attempts to dislodge the German tanks during the afternoon, Zolotukhin's 93rd Guards Rifle Division and Mishulin's 3rd Tank Corps halted their attacks to rest and regroup and, if possible, resume their assaults the next morning.

Further to the east, however, a far more complex and potentially more significant battle was developing as Edelsheim's panzer division responded to Niemack's call for help. In accordance with its defense plan and even before it realized the full scope of the damage done by the Soviet tank attack, the LVII Panzer Corps swung into action immediately after learning the Soviets were beginning their initial assaults northeast of Tirgu Frumos by ordering Edelsheim's 24th Panzer Division to implement its counterattack plan. This order, which the panzer corps issued at about 0730 hours, arrived just in time to avert a major disaster. Von Senger recalled the situation in the 24th Panzer Division's headquarters early that fateful morning and the rationale behind the 24th Panzer's future actions:

> On 2 May 1944 at first light, the enemy attacked along the whole front of Targul-Frumos under a heavy artillery barrage and broke through the Panzer Division "GD" on two thrust lines: strong panzer force in the Bals region heading south along the main road from Harlau [Hirlau] to Targul-Frumos and panzers and infantry from PT [Hill] 192 to Facuti. With the beginning of the attack, the 24th Panzer Division was placed under the command of the LVII Panzer Corps and received the order to destroy the enemy who had broken through toward Facuti and restore the original positions.
>
> The division faced a difficult decision; should their main effort be made north or south of the chain of lakes [the Fadariesal Lakes, which stretched from Facuti eastward to Sarca]? If made to the north, there was a danger that the enemy would break through at Facuti and threaten Targul-Frumos. If made to the south, it was doubtful whether the division would have the strength to retake the high ground at PT 192 [two miles north of Facuti]. Following known Soviet tactical principles, it could be expected that they would build up strong antitank defenses in support of their break-in, which, once established, could only be breached by a costly and large-scale counterattack. Additionally, to mount a counter-stroke against Facuti and the narrow crossing place would hinder mobile operations. The division then decided to risk the temporary loss of Facuti and to place its main thrust against the flank of the enemy breakthrough

> and hinder the establishment of an antitank front around PT 192. Simultaneously, however, it was necessary to prevent the enemy penetration developing toward Targul-Frumos. The first task was given to Kampfgruppe "W," and the latter task to Kampfgruppe "E."[25]

The 24th Panzer Division's commander, Edelsheim, issued an order to his subordinate *kampfgruppen* orally at 0800 hours on 2 May, in a format von Senger described as "of interest for its brevity and simplicity":

> a. Enemy broke into the positions of the Panzer Fusilier Regiment "GD" in the area PT 192 [two miles north of Facuti]. Advancing with strong tank forces and infantry toward Facuti. Apparent intention to seize the crossing there.
>
> b. Own forces fighting defensively throughout whole area. Situation unclear.
>
> c. Division will destroy enemy north or south of the chain of lakes and restore the old front line around PT 192 as soon as possible.
>
> d. K. Gp. "E." Follow the road toward Targul-Frumos, turn north on road leading to Facuti, and then advance to the [Fadariesal] lakes. Further orders to follow.
>
> e. K. Gp. "W." Move from Sarca to north of the lakes in the general direction of Pt 148 and 192. Tasks to destroy enemy who have broken through and restore the old front of PT 192. Contact to be made with own troops in the area between Polieni and Facuti.
>
> f. Divisional Command Post one kilometer [0.6 miles] southwest of Valea-Oilor.[26]

Since heavy fighting was already raging along the northern approaches to Facuti and northward to Polieni, where a single infantry battalion of the 46th Infantry Division was clinging desperately to the eastern shoulder of the Soviet penetration, the situation was indeed urgent and required immediate action. Therefore, without regrouping his forces into their ideal march formation, Colonel von Waldenburg, the commander of *Kampfgruppe* "W," ordered his group to leave the village of Sarca, six miles southeast of Facuti, immediately, move rapidly northward, and reassemble at Hill 148, three miles northeast of Facuti, to await further orders. Waldenburg's *kampfgruppe* assembled on the designated hill at about 1100 hours, just as the Soviet infantry and tank attacks against the German defenses at Facuti were intensifying. In the meantime, Lieutenant Colonel Haus-Egon von Einem's *Kampfgruppe* "E" moved westward from its lager at Malevjesti, two and one half miles southwest of Sarca, reached the jumping-off positions for its counterattack southwest of Valea-Oilor and three miles south of Facuti, also at 1100 hours, and prepared to advance northward toward Facuti on the division commander's orders.

Shortly after 1100 hours, Waldenburg's *Kampfgruppe* "W" received another order from division headquarters, which read: "Enemy infantry have crossed the lakes west of Facuti and are advancing south. Facuti is still in own hands. K. Gp. 'E' attacking from the south. K. Gp. 'W' to carry out its task as soon as possible."[27] Waldenburg responded quickly by ordering:

> a. The panzer troop move over PT 130 [Hill 130, 1.5 miles northeast of Facuti] toward Facuti as quickly as possible to report on the situation;
>
> b. An antitank screen be formed to protect the assembly area. It was to remain on the reserve [southern] slope facing north so as to achieve surprise;
>
> c. The light antiaircraft squadron to deploy along the forward edge of the assembly area so that it could fulfill the secondary task of engaging enemy infantry at long range; and
>
> d. The artillery to be prepared to protect not only Facuti but also PT 192 [Hill 192, two miles north of Facuti] in order to impede the establishment of an antitank front.[28]

Once it deployed to Hill 130 [1.5 miles northeast of Facuti], the commander of the panzer troop of *Kampfgruppe* "W" reported:

> 30–40 enemy tanks of unknown type [in reality, IS models] attacking Facuti. Heavy fighting underway in the village. Movement southwest of the village, probably enemy infantry. A lot of movement and battle noises around PT 192 [Hill 192, two miles north of Facuti]. No sign of own troops between Polieni and Facuti.[29]

The Soviet forces assaulting the defenses of the battalions on the Fusilier Regiment's right wing, which were bottled up in Facuti at that time, included Colonel Konev's 3rd Guards Airborne Division of Goriachev's 35th Guards Rifle Corps and the 6th Guards Heavy Tank Regiment and portions of Colonel P. D. Babkovsky's 109th Tank Brigade from Dubovoi's 16th Tank Corps. Another part of this force, including Colonel T. P. Abramov's 107th Tank Brigade from Dubovoi's tank corps and two regiments from Zolotukhin's 93rd Guards Rifle Division, were already in the process of maneuvering around Facuti from the west; after doing so, they reached the junction of the Facuti and Tirgu Frumos road, only 2.5 miles east of Tirgu Frumos, at 1110 hours. By this time Colonel M. V. Kopylov's 164th Tank Brigade and supporting 16th Motorized Rifle Brigade, which were following in the path of Dubovoi's two forward tank brigades, were approaching Facuti from the north, while providing some armor support to the riflemen of Kolesnikov's 206th Rifle Division, which were attacking the German strong point at the village of Polieni, two miles north of Facuti, which was defended by a single battalion from the 46th Infantry Division's 97th Infantry Regiment.

Based on this new report, Waldenburg, the commander of *Kampfgruppe* "W," assessed:

> The enemy armor is occupied with the capture of Facuti in order to seize a crossing site over the [Fadariesal] lakes. He appears to be unaware of the kampfgruppe's presence because of the difficult terrain and seems to have discounted the threat to his flanks. The infantry belonging to the enemy's "deep penetration group" [mobile group] have already crossed the lakes, and the second wave of this group is still trying to clear PT 192 [Hill 192 two miles north of Facuti] of our own infantry. By attacking northward the kampfgruppe could probably recapture PT 192 without too much difficulty. There would be the danger, however, that the greatly superior enemy around Facuti would turn back and take Kampfgruppe "W" in the flank. In addition, from the heavy crack of gunfire, it appeared as though the enemy tanks were equipped with a new, large caliber and long-range gun, and, therefore, their destruction by the lighter-gunned German tanks could only be achieved by exploiting surprise to the full. On the other hand, everything possible had to be done to prevent the Russians from establishing an antitank front around PT 192, which if done, would make the task of restoring the former front line extremely costly if it were even possible.[30]

Given these considerations, Waldenburg decided to destroy the Soviet forces at Facuti by a surprise assault employing all of his tanks supported by all of his mechanized infantry, while his remaining forces prevented the enemy from moving additional forces and weapons onto Hill 192. While it was clear his secondary forces could not recapture the hill, they could certainly provide necessary security for the *kampfgruppe*'s main forces as they attacked toward Facuti. Waldenburg's orders read:

> a. The *kampfgruppe* will destroy the enemy attacking Facuti;
> b. The panzer group [battalion] will move at once toward the southwest to achieve surprise. It is to cross the ridge in a determined rush along a broad front;
> c. The mechanized infantry [medium panzer grenadier battalion] are to support our panzers until those of the enemy are destroyed. They will then attack the enemy infantry and relieve our own forces at Facuti; and
> d. The remainder of the *kampfgruppe* is to move to the high ground

> west of Polieni, from where it is to secure the right flank of the *kampfgruppe,* establish contact with the "in-position" infantry, prevent any further enemy advance, and impede by fire the enemy's ability to bring heavy weapons forward to PT 192 [Hill 192]. This group will be supported by all of the artillery.[31]

After receiving their orders, all of the subordinate elements of Waldenburg's *kampfgruppe* regrouped into their jumping-off positions and were prepared to begin their counterattack by 1200 hours on 2 May. Once positioned for the counterattack, the *kampfgruppe*'s panzer battalion [*abteilung*], which was equipped with about 16 MK IV tanks and nine assault guns, was located in defilade positions on the eastern slope of Hill 130, 1.5 miles northeast of Facuti; the 1st Battalion, 26th Panzer Grenadier Regiment, was situated near Hill 180 on the panzer battalion's right wing, one half mile north of Hill 130; and the Panzer Reconnaissance Battalion [Panzer AA] from the 24th Panzer Grenadier Regiment was located on Hill 90, on the panzer battalion's left wing, one half mile south of Hill 130. Finally, the *kampfgruppe*'s headquarters served as its emergency reserve, and its panzer artillery battalion was prepared to deliver necessary artillery support. Configured in this fashion, *Kampfgruppe* "W" was deployed facing west on a front of about two miles.

The separate elements of Waldenburg's *kampfgruppe* began their assault southwestward toward Facuti and westward toward Hill 192 shortly after 1200 hours, in close coordination with a simultaneous assault launched by Einem's *Kampfgruppe* "E" northward toward Facuti from the region southwest of Valea-Oilor. Sweeping rapidly westward over the crest of Hill 130 and into the valley beyond, the 24 panzers and assault guns of *Kampfgruppe* "W's" panzer battalion swept aside the light screen of riflemen providing flank security for the forces of Goriachev's and Dubovoi's 35th Guards Rifle and 16th Tank Corps fighting around and south of Facuti and struck the Soviet forces besieging Facuti on their left flank and rear.

The surprise German assault prompted the 35th Guard Rifle Corps to report: "At 1100 hours [1200 hours local time], enemy infantry and tanks (up to 70) counterattacked against the 35th Guards Rifle Corps' and the 54th Fortified Region's attacking units and pressed them back somewhat."[32] Almost simultaneously, through its own command channels, the 16th Tank Corps reported: "Committing up to 40 tanks into combat from the direction of the northeastern outskirts of Tirgu Frumos and from the direction of the town of Bosna (south of Polieni), the enemy pushed back the 16th Tank Corps' units, which conducted stubborn fighting around the southern slope of Hill 192."[33]

In addition, sheepishly and well after the fact, the 2nd Ukrainian Front's Armored Directorate reported:

> By this time [1200 hours], the 2nd Tank Army's left flank turned out to be open and the threat of an attack from the east arose. By virtue of a decision by the commander of the 16th Tank Corps, the 164th Tank Brigade and the 15th Motorized Rifle Brigade were turned to the east to protest the [left] flanks of the 16th Tank Corps and the 2nd Tank Army as a whole.[34]

In reality, however, Dubovoi did not begin ordering the forces of his 16th Tank Corps to redeploy to counter the German assault until well after the Germans had begun their counterattack, and, by the time he did, both of his second-echelon mobile brigades had already marched straight into the 24th Panzer Division's trap.

While clearly conflicting, the reports prepared by the 35th Guards Rifle and 16th Tank Corps were also "sugar coated," in the sense that they woefully overestimated German strength, probably because both forces counted German armored personnel carriers and self-propelled artillery pieces as tanks and also because their intent was to deliberately obscure the embarrassing consequences of the German counterattacks.

In reality, however, the coordinated panzer and panzer grenadier assault by the 24th Panzer Division's two *kampfgruppen* caught the Soviet forces fighting in and around Facuti by surprise and produced general disorder and confusion in their ranks. The panzer group of Waldenburg's *Kampfgruppe* "W" struck the rear of the riflemen of Colonel Konev's 3rd Guards Airborne Division and the *tankists* of Babkovsky's 109th Tank Brigade, who were besieging the German garrison in Facuti, throwing them into disorder and prompting Konev and Babkovsky to issue frantic calls for assistance. In response to these appeals, Dubovoi ordered Kopylov's 164th Tank Brigade, which was then in the 16th Tank Corps' reserve, to regroup its tanks southeastward to protect the corps' left flank and the 15th Motorized Rifle Brigade, which was attacking the German forces at Polieni, two and one half miles north of Facuti, to erect a protective screen on the tank corps' left flank.

However, while Kopylov was in the midst of moving his tank brigade rapidly southeastward toward Hill 130, it ran directly into, first, *Kampfgruppe* "W's" artillery and antitank screen and, soon after, the *kampfgruppe's* panzer grenadier and panzer battalions, which had already routed Babkovsky's 109th Tank Brigade west of Facuti. Almost simultaneously, Dubovoi's virtually unarmored 15th Motorized Rifle Brigade also ran a fiery gauntlet southward through *Kampfgruppe* "W's" deployed subgroups, only to suffer the same fate as its sister tank brigades. Caught in their flanks and rear by withering and deadly tank, artillery, and machine-gun fire, in short order, Babkovsky's 109th and Kopylov's 164th Tank Brigades and the 16th Motorized Rifle

Brigade, accompanied by the riflemen from Colonel Konev's 3rd Guards Airborne Division, were left with no choice but to begin a harrowing withdrawal northward from Facuti toward Hill 192 through the same devastating fires.

Once again, war correspondent Mayer describes the situation in the Fusilier Regiment's sector after the 24th Panzer Division's successful counterattack:

> Tanks, armored cars and APCs of the 24th Panzer Division appeared; they rolled past the village of Facuti and set out in pursuit of the surviving enemy tanks. The panzer-fusiliers followed slowly on foot. Soon II Battalion, Panzer-Fusilier Regiment was back in its old foxholes; on the left III Battalion stayed due south of Nicolne [Nicola]and dug in to stay. The town in front of them was full of the enemy.
>
> And behind near Targul Frumos? Thirteen enemy tanks, including several Stalins, got through, while the others lay disabled on the field, were shot to pieces or blew apart. The Tigers, Panthers and Panzer IVs had finished them. The 88mm flak troops at the outskirts of the city enjoyed a great day. They kept up a hectic rate of fire. The main force of enemy tanks succumbed to hits from 88mm shells. Scarcely one of them returned to its departure position.[35]

While this intense fight was raging around and northeast of Facuti, south of the town, Einem's *Kampfgruppe* "E," supported on its left flank by reinforcing tanks and infantry from the *Grossdeutschland* Division's Panzer Regiment, engaged the tanks of Abramov's 107th Tank Brigade and its supporting infantry in the valley west of Valea-Oilor. Although the opposing forces were relatively evenly matched, the news of what was occurring to its rear seemed to unnerve the commander of the tank brigade task force, prompting him also to order his forces to withdraw to the north, in this case along a circuitous route west of Facuti.

Thus, the two *kampfgruppen* of Edelsheim's 24th Panzer Division essentially routed the exploiting tanks and infantry of Dubovoi's 16th Tank Corps and Colonel Konev's 3rd Guards Airborne Division in a matter of hours, forcing them to conduct a fighting withdrawal toward the north and the northwest. By nightfall on 2 May, the defeated Soviet forces withdrew to new defense positions extending from Hill 184, midway between the Hirlau-Tirgu Frumos road and Facuti, northeastward to Hill 192, two miles north of Facuti, and then further eastward to the northern outskirts of Polieni. Although the forces of Trofimenko's 27th and Bogdanov's 2nd Tank Armies still clung stubbornly to a salient about two and one half miles deep into the German defenses northwest of Facuti, the 24th Panzer Division's quick reaction and skillful counterattack deprived them of both Facuti and the critical high ground on and around Hill 192.

Within only hours after the 24th Panzer Division succeeded in restoring much of LVII Panzer Corps' original defensive positions north of Facuti, the panzer corps ordered Edelsheim's panzer division to turn its hard-won gains over to the *Grossdeutschland* Division's Fusilier Regiment and concentrate in the Tirgu Frumos region by nightfall. Refusing to rest on its laurels, the panzer corps was already preparing to greet the new Soviet onslaught, which it knew would materialize the next morning.

Dotting the "Is" and crossing the "Ts" on the day's frenetic action, the situation report the Eighth Army issued at 1815 hours on 2 May modestly summarized the LVII Panzer Corp's accomplishments on the first day of Konev's new offensive:

> The main attack was beaten off with 300–350 tanks destroyed. Enemy reinforcements are coming in from the north. The battle is expected to continue on 3 May. Grossdeutschland reports indicate that they have lost 400 wounded, 6 tanks destroyed, and 8 damaged. Our own air support has been continuous and has included Stuka, CAP [air cover for ground troops], and tank busting aircraft.[36]

Mayer, the war correspondent, later added his epitaph to the first day of battle:

> In the course of these bitter defensive battles, by the evening of 2 May 1944, the units of the Panzer-Grenadier Division GD alone destroyed 96 enemy tanks, some of them super-heavy types. The Panzer Regiment GD commanded by Oak Leaves wearer Oberst Langkeit was responsible for the greater part of this success. It destroyed a total of 56 enemy tanks. The 41st kill of the day brought the total number of enemy tanks destroyed by the regiment since it first saw action in March 1943 to one thousand tanks.
>
> Thus ended the first day of the great defensive battle in front of Targul Frumos. Even if ground had been lost, the positions as such were still firmly in our hands. Losses, especially men killed and the large number of missing, had been painful.[37]

Supporting Attacks

While the four armies of Konev's main shock group were conducting his main attack along the Tirgu Frumos axis, his other armies launched five separate supporting or diversionary attacks along his main shock group's right and left flanks. These actions included supporting attacks conducted by the forces of Zhmachenko's 40th Army north of Tirgu-Neamt and west of Pascani, a supporting attack by Semenov's 33rd Rifle Corps of Trofimenko's 27th Army northwest of Iasi, and diversionary attacks by Koroteev's 52nd Army and Kravchenko's 6th Tank Army north and northeast of Iasi.

Of these five attacks, the only one that achieved any success whatsoever was the assault conducted by Petrushevsky' 104th Rifle Corps in the sector of Zhmachenko's 40th Army north of Tirgu-Neamt. Attacking at dawn on 2 May, in part to divert German attention from Konev's main attack at Tirgu Frumos, Timoshkov's 38th Rifle and Rumiantsev's 4th Guards Airborne Divisions penetrated Divisional Group Siret's defenses west of the town of Raucesti, three miles north of Tirgu-Neamt, and advanced up to four miles deep to the eastern approaches to the village of Nemtisor on the Neamful River, five miles northwest of Tirgu-Neamt. In addition to threatening the Romanian defenders at Tirgu-Neamt with envelopment from the west, the attack by Petrushevsky's two divisions also threatened to disrupt communications between Army Group Wöhler's LXXVIII Army Corps, which was defending further northwest in the foothills of the Carpathians, and the Romanian I Army Corps, which was defending Tirgu-Neamt and Pascani. However, by 7 May a small force dispatched by German LXXVIII Army Corps counterattacked and restored the front northwest of Tirgu-Neamt.

Further to the east, Zhmachenko's 40th Army conducted another supporting attack early on 2 May to assist the advance of Konev's shock group and protect its right flank. In this attack, Kozyr's 232nd, Beloded's 133rd, and Bobrov's 42nd Guards Rifle Divisions from Avdeenko's 51st Rifle Corps, supported by small groups of tanks from Selivanov's 5th Guards Cavalry Corps, assaulted the defenses of the Romanian 20th and 6th Infantry Divisions in the sector from Prajescu to Timisesti west of Pascani. However, this assault faltered immediately after it began without registering any appreciable gains. The 2nd Ukrainian Front reported Avdeenko's 51st Rifle Corps lost 89 men killed and 379 wounded in the process.[38]

Although it was included in the plan Konev prepared for his main shock group, in reality the attack conducted by Semenov's 33rd Rifle Corps of Trofimenko's 27th Army in the region northwest of Iasi clearly fell into the category of a supporting attack. In this instance, early on 2 May, Major General G. S. Merkulov's 180th, Colonel I. M. Khoklov's 202nd, and Colonel T. P. Gorobets's 337th Rifle Divisions of Semenov's rifle corps assaulted the defenses of the Romanian 3rd and 18th Infantry Divisions northwest of Iasi. However, as the 27th Army reported: "The 33rd Rifle Corps attempted to attack to the south but had no success after encountering heavy resistance and was fighting along its previous lines at day's end. While it succeeded in taking 15 Romanian soldiers captive in the morning, the corps lost 24 men killed and 113 wounded."[39]

In Konev's fifth and final supporting attack, the six rifle divisions subordinate to Martirosian's 73rd and Latyshev's 78th Rifle Corps of Koroteev's

52nd Army, supported by two small combat groups from Kravchenko's 6th Tank Army, assaulted the German 79th Infantry and 23rd Panzer Divisions' defenses north of Iasi early on 2 May but achieved virtually nothing. As the 2nd Ukrainian Front cryptically reported: "After a 30-minute artillery preparation, the 52nd Army conducted an offensive toward Iasi but was not able to advance. The 6th Tank Army fought in the combat formation of the 52nd Army."[40]

Thus, none of Konev's five supporting or diversionary attacks achieved their intended goals. Only one of them, the attack by Petrushevsky's rifle corps of the 40th Army, succeeded in penetrating the enemy's defenses, and none forced Army Group Wöhler or any of his subordinate commands to transfer any forces away from the Tirgu Frumos sector. All five, however, contributed to the particularly inauspicious beginning of what the *Stavka* and Konev intended to be a dramatic advance into northern Romania.

Although the Red Army's casualty figures remain relatively opaque, fragmentary reports prepared by the 2nd Ukrainian Front indicate that Shumilov's 7th Guards Army lost 123 soldiers killed and another 573 wounded on 2 May, and the 27th Army lost 184 soldiers killed and 402 wounded during the same period. This report accords with the 27th Army's casualty reports, which claimed Goriachev's 35th Guards Rifle Corps and 54th Fortified Region lost a total of 160 soldiers killed and 289 wounded on 2 May.[41]

However, Konev's tank losses during the first day of his offensive are far more difficult to determine than his personnel losses. German documents, which indicate the Soviets lost up to 350 tanks destroyed on the first day of combat, seem woefully overinflated, since the documented strength of Konev's 5th Guards and 2nd Tank Armies on 1 May was a total of 491 tanks and self-propelled guns. Although the Soviet archives have produced no documents detailing the tank losses of Rotmistrov's 5th Guards Tank Army, the intense nature of the combat it participated in makes it reasonable to assume its three tank corps lost up to half of its 358 tanks and self-propelled guns, for a total of roughly 180 armored vehicles.

As far as Bogdanov's 2nd Tank Army is concerned, its 16th Tank Corps reported it fielded a total of 55 tanks on the morning of 2 May and lost 33 tanks from 2 to 8 May, about half of which were destroyed on 2 May. Likewise, the same tank army's 3rd Tank Corps reported that it lost 33 of its 50 tanks in the fighting from 1 through 8 May, probably half of which were destroyed on the first day of the battle. This would place the 2nd Tank Army's armored losses on 2 May at no more than 40 tanks and raise the tank losses of the *front* shock group on 2 May to a total of about 220 tanks. While this is far less than the Germans' tally, given the relatively weak initial armored strength of Konev's shock group, these losses were heavy enough to seriously damage any hopes Konev harbored about successfully resuming his offensive on 3 May.

However, Konev was a fighter. Consequently, with the *Stavka*'s encouragement, he ordered his shock group to regroup, reinforce its forward forces, and resume its offensive with even greater intensity the following morning.

THE BATTLE ON 3 MAY

Konev's Revised Offensive Plan

Overnight on 2–3 May, Konev refined his offensive plan and his shock group's offensive formation based on the previous day's action and ordered the four armies in his main shock group to concentrate their forces for a fresh assault the next day in far narrower sectors than the day before. Meanwhile, the forces in his shock group replenished their ammunition, regrouped into new jumping-off positions, prepared to resume their attacks the next morning, and, during the few moments when it was possible, also tried to rest.

On his main shock group's right wing northwest of Tirgu Frumos, Konev's revised offensive plan required Shumilov's 7th Guards Army to regroup all of the forces in the second echelons of Vasil'ev's and Safiulin's 24th and 25th Guards Rifle Corps forward into first-echelon assault positions. In addition, Shumilov's army was to shift the axis of its main attack to the narrow sector where the 5th Guards Tank Army's 29th Tank Corps had conducted its dramatic but failed exploitation the previous day: specifically, the front extending northeast and south of Radui, which was situated about two miles east of Ruginoasa on the road and railroad from Pascani to Tirgu Frumos and about six miles northwest of Konev's immediate objective.

Shumilov complied by ordering Safiulin's 25th Guards Rifle Corps to relieve Denisenko's 36th Guards Rifle Division, which was fighting in the sector west of Propota, five miles north of Tirgu Frumos, with Smirnov's 6th Guards Airborne Division, which had spent the first day of battle in his corps' second echelon. Once relieved, Denisenko's guards division was to shift its forces to the right and concentrate in the region just north of Radui, on the railroad six miles northwest of Tirgu Frumos. Shumilov then ordered Vasil'ev's 25th Guards Rifle Corps to regroup Losev's 72nd Guards Rifle Division to the left and concentrated both his 72nd and Morozov's 81st Guards Rifle Divisions in a relatively narrow two-and-one-half-mile-wide sector between Hill 358, just southwest of Helestieni, and the right flank of Denisenko's division at Radui.

At the same time, Konev ordered Rotmistrov's 5th Guards Tank Army to withdraw Vovchenko's 3rd Guards Tank Corps from its former sector between Barbotesti and Cucuteni on his shock group's left wing and regroup it, together with all of its serviceable armored vehicles, to the Ruginoasa and Radui regions, where it was to reinforce the remnants of Fominykh's

29th Tank Corps. Finally, Rotmistrov withdrew the single tank brigade of Polozkov's 18th Tank Corps, which was supporting Bogdanov's 8th Guards Airborne Division in the marshland east of the Seret River, and sent its remaining tanks to reinforce Vovchenko's and Fominykh's 29th and 3rd Guards Tank Corps. With all of Rotmistrov's serviceable armored vehicles concentrated in a single iron fist northwest of Tirgu Frumos, Konev then ordered Rotmistrov to withdraw the rest of his tank army to assembly areas north of Blagesti in his shock group's rear area.

This regrouping enabled Konev to concentrate four of Shumilov's rifle divisions, two of Rotmistrov's tank corps with about 180 armored vehicles, and much of Shumilov's and his *front*'s artillery in the seven-mile-wide sector extending from Hill 358 northeastward through Radui to just west of Propota. Once concentrated in their assault positions, deployed from left to right, Smirnov's 6th Guards Airborne and Denisenko's 36th Guards Rifle Divisions (from Safiulin's 25th Guards Rifle Corps) and Morozov's 81st and Losev's 72nd Guards Rifle Divisions (from Vasil'ev's 24th Guards Rifle Corps) were to penetrate the German defenses northwest of Tirgu Frumos and support the commitment of Fominykh's 29th and Vovchenko's 3rd Guards Tank Corps (from Rotmistrov's 5th Guards Tank Army) into the penetration. Once through the penetration, the two tank corps were to advance along the road from Ruginoasa through Radui, De Sus, and Dadesti and the adjacent broad valley and enter Tirgu Frumos from the west.

On his shock group's left flank to the east, Konev's new plan required Trofimenko's 27th Army to reinforce Goriachev's 35th Guards Rifle Corps with Mikhailov's 78th Rifle Division from his army's second echelon and use Mikhailov's fresh division to replace Kolesnikov's 206th Rifle Division in the Polieni sector. After it was relieved, Kolesnikov was to regroup his division to the right [west] and occupy assault positions due north of Hill 192, just over one mile west of Polieni and two miles north of Facuti. As a result of this regrouping, Goriachev concentrated Zolotukhin's 93rd Guards, Colonel Konev's 3rd Guards Airborne, and Kolesnikov's 206th Rifle Divisions in the four-mile-wide sector extending from Hill 256, just west of the Hirlau-Tirgu Frumos road, eastward to Hill 192. At the same time, Konev ordered Bogdanov's 2nd Tank Army to regroup Dubovoi's 16th Tank Corps into the narrow one-mile-wide sector between the village of Nicola and Hill 197, east of the Hirlau-Tirgu Frumos road and on the left flank of Mishulin's 3rd Tank Corps, which was to concentrate in a one-mile-wide sector west of the road.

This regrouping enabled Konev to concentrate three of Goriachev's rifle divisions, two of Bogdanov's tank corps with about 70 armored vehicles, and much of Trofimenko's artillery in the four-mile-wide sector extending from Hill 256 through Nicola to Hill 192. Once concentrated in their new assault positions, deployed from left to right, Kolesnikov's 206th Rifle Division, Colonel Konev's 3rd Guards Airborne Division, and Zolotukhin's 93rd Guards Rifle Division (from Goriachev's 35th Guards Rifle Corps) were to penetrate the German defenses north of Tirgu Frumos and support the commitment of Dubovoi's 16th and Mishulin's 3rd Tank Corps (from Bogdanov's 2nd Tank Army) into the penetration. Once through the penetration, the two tank corps were to exploit southward along the Hirlau road and enter Tirgu-Frumos from the north.

Ever optimistic, Konev assumed the combined forces of Rotmistrov's and Bogdanov's four tank armies and the seven rifle divisions of Shumilov's two rifle corps and Trofimenko's single reinforced rifle corps, which, including infantry support armor, still fielded more than 300 tanks and self-propelled guns, was a more than adequate force with which to defeat the Germans, which his intelligence organs informed him consisted of two German panzer divisions with about 100 tanks. Even if his forces were no longer able to envelop Iasi from the west, he reasoned, they could at least capture the illusive prize of Tirgu Frumos.

On the German side, based on its previous experiences, Kirchner's LVII Panzer Corps, as well as Manteuffel and Edelsheim, understood quite well that, with the determined Konev in command, the Soviet offensive was far from over. Therefore, overnight on 2–3 May the panzer corps and its two subordinate panzer division commanders also regrouped their forces to meet the expected renewed Soviet assault. The previous afternoon, the LVII Panzer Corps had already ordered Edelsheim to withdraw his 24th Panzer Division's two *kampfgruppen* from the vicinity of Hill 192 and concentrate them in the region just west of Tirgu Frumos. Doing so quickly and efficiently, later in the evening, Edelsheim concentrated his 24 tanks and assault guns in assembly areas between the western edge of Tirgu Frumos and the village of Dadesti, two miles to the northwest, and dispatched the 2nd Battalion of his 24th Panzer Grenadier Regiment to the village of Kalmu, on the Hirlau road three miles due north of Tirgu Frumos, where it reinforced the *Grossdeutschland* Division at the junction of its Panzer Grenadier and Fusilier Regiments' defenses.

At the same time, Manteuffel sent the *Grossdeutschland* Division's engineer [pioneer] battalion, which had been in division reserve near Tirgu Frumos, northward to reinforce his Panzer Grenadier Regiment's defenses between Cornesti and Kalmu, four miles north of Tirgu Frumos, and regrouped his Panzer Regiment from its former assembly area northeast of Tirgu Frumos to new assembly areas between Dadesti and De Sus, four to five miles northwest of Tirgu Frumos to back up his Panzer Grenadier Regiment's defenses astride the road and valley east of Radui. Finally, the LVII Panzer Corps ordered the SS "*T*" Panzer Division to concentrate its *Kampf-*

gruppe "E" (the 6th SS Panzer Grenadier Regiment "Theodor Eicke"), with its main forces in the Helestieni region, six miles west of Tirgu Frumos.

By the time it completed its regrouping, the LVII Panzer Corps had assembled the bulk of the combat power of Manteuffel's, Edelsheim's, and Priess's *Grossdeutschland,* 24th, and *Totenkopf* divisions precisely opposite the sectors where Konev intended to deliver his main attack. The results were predictable.

The daily entry in the 2nd Ukrainian Front's combat journal succinctly describes the actions of Konev's main shock group when it resumed offensive operations early on 3 May and provides context regarding what was transpiring on the remainder of the front in northern Romania:

> The front's forces continued their offensive along the Tirgu-Frumos and Iasi axes, and the 8th and 5th Guards Armies conducted local operations along the Kishinev axis to improve their tactical positions. The 40th Army lost 89 men killed and 379 men wounded, the 7th Guards Army lost 123 men killed and 573 wounded, and the 27th Army lost 184 men killed and 402 wounded on 2 May 1944. . . .
>
> By day's end on 3 May, together with the 7th Guards Army, the 5th Guards Tank Army was deployed with the 18th Tank Corps two kilometers [1.2 miles] north of Blagesti, and the 3rd Guards and 29th Tank Corps two kilometers [1.2 miles] south of Ruginoasa. The 2nd Tank Army was fighting on the approaches to Tirgu-Frumos with units of its 16th Tank Corps. By day's end the tank army was fighting 2.5 kilometers [1.5 miles] southeast of the Papa-Mort Burial Mound. The 6th Tank Army's situation is unchanged.
>
> The 5th Air Army conducted 1,319 combat sorties, 615 of these strafing and bombing enemy personnel and equipment in the Tirgu-Frumos, Cucuteni, Costineci, Movileni, Baskany, and other regions on 2 and 3 May. Thirty-eight enemy aircraft were shot down in 24 air battles, and ten enemy aircraft were burned and 12 enemy aircraft damaged at the Roman airfield. Enemy aviation flew more than 2,000 aircraft sorties over the two days.
>
> The roads are in trafficable condition.[42]

Indulging in a bit of understatement, the *Grossdeutschland* Division's history provides a German perspective of combat on the second day of the battle:

> In spite of their bloody losses of the previous day, the Soviets continued their attacks on 3 May 1944. Numerous tanks rolled into the positions of

the grenadiers and fusiliers, some of them new; they formed points of main effort here and there but soon disappeared to the rear. But waiting for them in ambush positions, deep in the division's combat zone, were the Tiger, Panthers and assault guns. The anti-aircraft gun concentrated on them, anti-tank gunners aimed at the steel giants' most vulnerable spots. It was tank slaughter again, an unparalleled massacre.

There was plenty of activity in the air the entire day by both sides. From the other side came close-support aircraft, the feared IL-2s, spewing death and destruction from their wing-mounted cannon and machine-guns. The Ratas spiraled above them and now and then dived down to attack some target they had spotted on the ground. The most commonly seen German aircraft were the Stukas, which dived howling on their targets and released their bombs just before pulling up. Their bombing accuracy was great. There were also the German tank-hunters, who took on individual enemy tanks with their cannon and destroyed them from the air.[43]

Konev's Assault

Only hours after they completed their complex regrouping on the right wing of Konev's shock group, the combined forces of Shumilov's 7th Guards and Rotmistrov's 5th Guards Tank Armies struck the German defenses west of Tirgu Frumos at 0600 hours on 3 May, but as the 2nd Ukrainian Front reported, "with completely no success" (Map 18). The fighting was particularly fierce in the Radui sector, along the Tirgu Frumos-Pascani road six miles northwest of Tirgu Frumos, where Denisenko's 36th and Morozov's 81st Guards Rifle Divisions, supported by the bulk of Fominykh's and Vovchenko's tanks, unmercifully pounded the defenses of the *Grossdeutschland* Division's Grenadier Regiment. However, effective German machine-gun, mortar, artillery, and antitank fire along the immediate front, combined with long-range antitank fire from Manteuffel's 88-mm antiaircraft guns and both long-range tank fire and local counterattacks by his Panzer Regiment, repelled each and every Soviet assault. Attacking repeatedly but with increasing futility, Shumilov's rifle divisions were decimated, and about half of Rotmistrov's remaining 180 tanks and self-propelled guns fell victim to the Germans' deadly fire. The attack by the right wing of Konev's shock group collapsed in complete exhaustion by nightfall without registering any significant forward progress.

The after-action report prepared by Konev's Armor and Mechanized Directorate partially explained why Shumilov's and Rotmistrov's assault failed:

> After encountering the enemy's second defensive belt, which was outfitted with pillboxes, dugouts, and minefields, the 5th Guards Tank Army

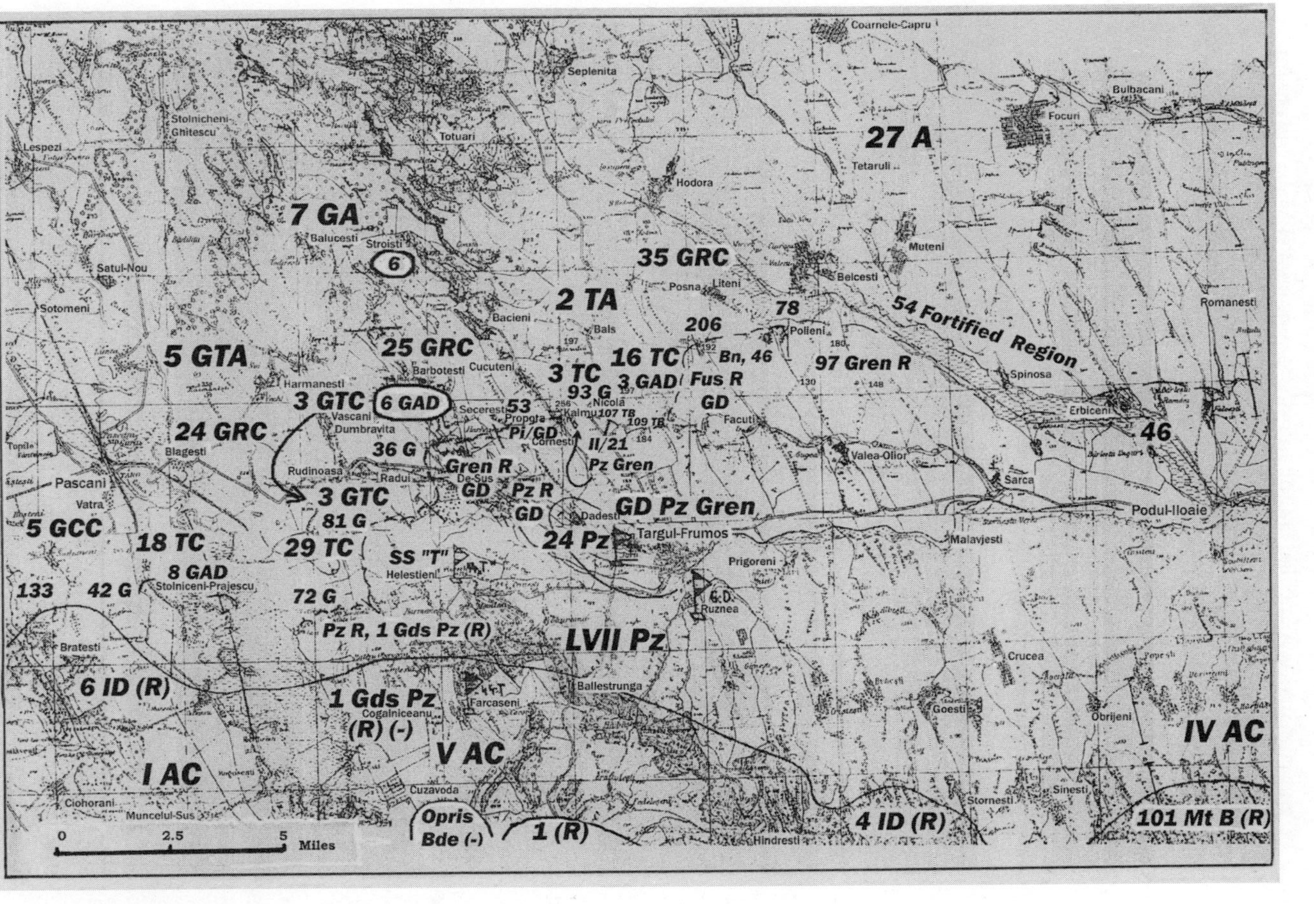

Map 18. The second battle for Tirgu Frumos, 3 May 1944

> and 7th Guards Army had completely no success on 3–4 May. The enemy stopped our formations' offensive by counterattacks with tanks and infantry and by operating from ambushes.[44]

Meanwhile, on the left wing of Konev's main shock group, despite recording some local tactical successes, the three rifle divisions of Goriachev's 35th Guards Rifle Corps and the 16th and 3rd Tank Corps of Bogdanov's 2nd Tank Army also failed to accomplish their assigned missions. As described in the daily entries in the 27th Army's combat journal:

> The army's forces continued combat operations on the night of 2–3 May 1944 with detachments, brought their artillery forward, and prepared to continue the offensive. After methodically suppressing the enemy's firing points with artillery and mortar fire, at 0600 hours the army's forces attacked southward. Overcoming stubborn enemy resistance and repelling his counterattacks, the formations on the right wing advanced forward a short distance. However, the forces in the center and on the left wing had no success, failed to advance, and were fighting along their previous lines at day's end. The enemy counterattacked repeatedly in the Facuti, Ulmi, and Veci sectors with a force of up to a battalion of infantry and 5 to 12 tanks, and enemy aviation in groups of up to 30 aircraft bombed the 35th [Guards] Rifle Corps' units. More than 200 aircraft sorties were counted during the day.
>
> The 3rd Guards Airborne Division seized four prisoners, confirming the operations of the SS Panzer Division "Deaths Head" in that region. The 35th [Guards] Rifle Corps lost 156 killed and 275 wounded, and the [54th] Fortified Region lost two killed and four wounded during the day. The 33rd Rifle Corps lost 15 killed and 73 wounded, and the corps seized five Romanian soldiers as prisoners.[45]

The after-action report prepared by Konev's Armor and Mechanized Directorate provides additional details concerning the operations conducted by the two tank corps of Bogdanov's 2nd Tank Army:

> On 3 May 1944, the units of the 107th Tank Brigade of the 2nd Tank Army's 16th Tank Corps penetrated to the northern outskirts of Tirgu-Frumos for the second time, but, since they were not supported by the combined-arms formations, they were forced to withdraw to the southeastern slope of Hill 256 after an unequal struggle with enemy tanks, artillery, and infantry. After repelling enemy counterattacks, by day's end on 3 May, the formations of the 2nd Tank Army went over to the defense in positions from the southern outskirts of Cucuteni through Hill 184 (incl.),

> the unnamed lake northeast of Hill 184, and the southeastern slope of Hill 102 to the northern outskirts of Ulmi-Veni, with their tanks distributed throughout the infantry's combat formation.[46]

Although the assault by the three rifle divisions of Goriachev's 35th Guards Rifle Corps and the massed armor of Mishulin's 16th and Dubovoi's 3rd Tank Corps fared somewhat better than Shumilov's and Rotmistrov's assaults to the west, it ultimately proved just as frustrating to the Soviet commanders. After attacking at 0600 hours, Zolotukhin's 93rd Guards and Colonel Konev's 3rd Guards Airborne Divisions from Goriachev's guards corps once again managed to penetrate the Germans' forward defenses at the junction of *Grossdeutschland* Division's Panzer Grenadier and Fusilier Regiments near Kalmu, on the road from Hirlau to Tirgu Frumos, four miles north of Tirgu Frumos. By 0800 hours, the assaulting riflemen and tankists pushed just over one mile southward, driving the German defenders from Hill 256, which was situated just southwest of Kalmu, and from the western slope of Hill 184, which was located slightly to the south and east of the Hirlau road.

Exploiting the gap in the German defenses, Abramov's 107th and Babkovsky's 109th Tank Brigades from Dubovoi's 16th Tank Corps rushed forward about two miles, reaching the northern outskirts of the village of Dadesti and Hill 189, just two miles north of Tirgu Frumos. However, while the *Grossdeutschland* Division's forces firmly held the flanks of the Soviet penetration, the 2nd Battalion of the 24th Panzer Division's 21st Panzer Grenadier Regiment, supported by about 12 tanks from the 24th Panzer Division's panzer regiment, repelled the assault and forced the attacking Soviet force to withdraw to their original jumping-off positions.

In addition to seeing his main attack fail once again, none of the supporting attacks by Konev's other armies achieved any success on 3 May. For example, on the shock group's right flank west of the Seret River, the three divisions of Avdeenko's 51st Rifle Corps from Zhmachenko's 40th Army resumed their assaults near Pascani but achieved no more success than they had the day before. In addition, while attacking the Germans' prepared defenses, Konev's forces suffered even heavier casualties than they had the day before. For example, the 7th Guards Army lost 135 soldiers killed and 575 wounded, the 27th Army lost 173 soldiers killed and 352 wounded, and along its secondary axis, the 40th Army lost 56 soldiers killed and 225 men wounded during the futile fighting on 3 May.

Once again, the careful defensive preparations by the LVII Panzer Corps and its subordinate divisions proved effective and thwarted all of Konev's attempts to renew his offensive. Although both the *Stavka* and Konev realized that defeat was at hand, they would still have "one more go" at the German defenses the next day.

THE BATTLE ON 4 MAY

When Konev's shock group resumed its attacks on the morning of 4 May, it did so in basically the same combat formation as the day before but with roughly two-thirds of the 300 tanks and self-propelled guns it fielded the day before (Map 19). Deprived of much of the shock group's armor punch, the results of the attack were again predictable. Once again, the 2nd Ukrainian Front's daily combat journal tersely described the utter futility of the assault:

> While repelling enemy counterattacks, the front's forces conducted stubborn combat on 4 May 1944. There were more than 15 counterattacks in the sectors of the 7th Guards Army and the 27th Army's 35th Guards Rifle Corps in which 130–140 tanks and assault guns and up to five infantry regiments took part.
>
> The 40th Army lost 56 men killed and 225 men wounded, the 7th Guards Army lost 135 killed and 575 wounded, and the 27th Army lost 173 killed and 352 wounded on 3 May. . . .
>
> The weather was cloudy with 10/10th [100%] overcast and with continuous rain during the second half of the day. The air temperature was 8–17 degrees of warmth [8–17 Centigrade], and the country roads deteriorated and became difficult for vehicular transport.[47]

The daily entry in the 27th Army's combat journal for 4 May describes the fighting in Trofimenko's and Bogdanov's sectors, as well as the emerging stalemate across the remainder of Konev's front:

> On the night of 3–4 May, the [27th] Army's forces remained in the positions they previously occupied and conducted reconnaissances-in-force with detachments and destructive fires against identified enemy targets along separate axes. After an artillery preparation, the formations on the left wing and the formations on the right wing resumed the offensive along their previous axes at 0645 and 0800 hours [respectively] but, after encountering heavy fire resistance and repelling attacks by infantry and tanks, were unable to achieve success in advancing forward. The enemy conducted repeated counterattacks in the Cornesti, Facuti, Ulmi, and Veci sectors and in other sectors with forces in up to infantry battalion strength, supported by groups of from four to 14 tanks, defended stubbornly, and conducted reconnaissances-in-force against our dispositions. Enemy aviation bombed our formations with groups of up to 40 aircraft, and the enemy conducted aviation reconnaissance, flying a total of 158 identified sorties.

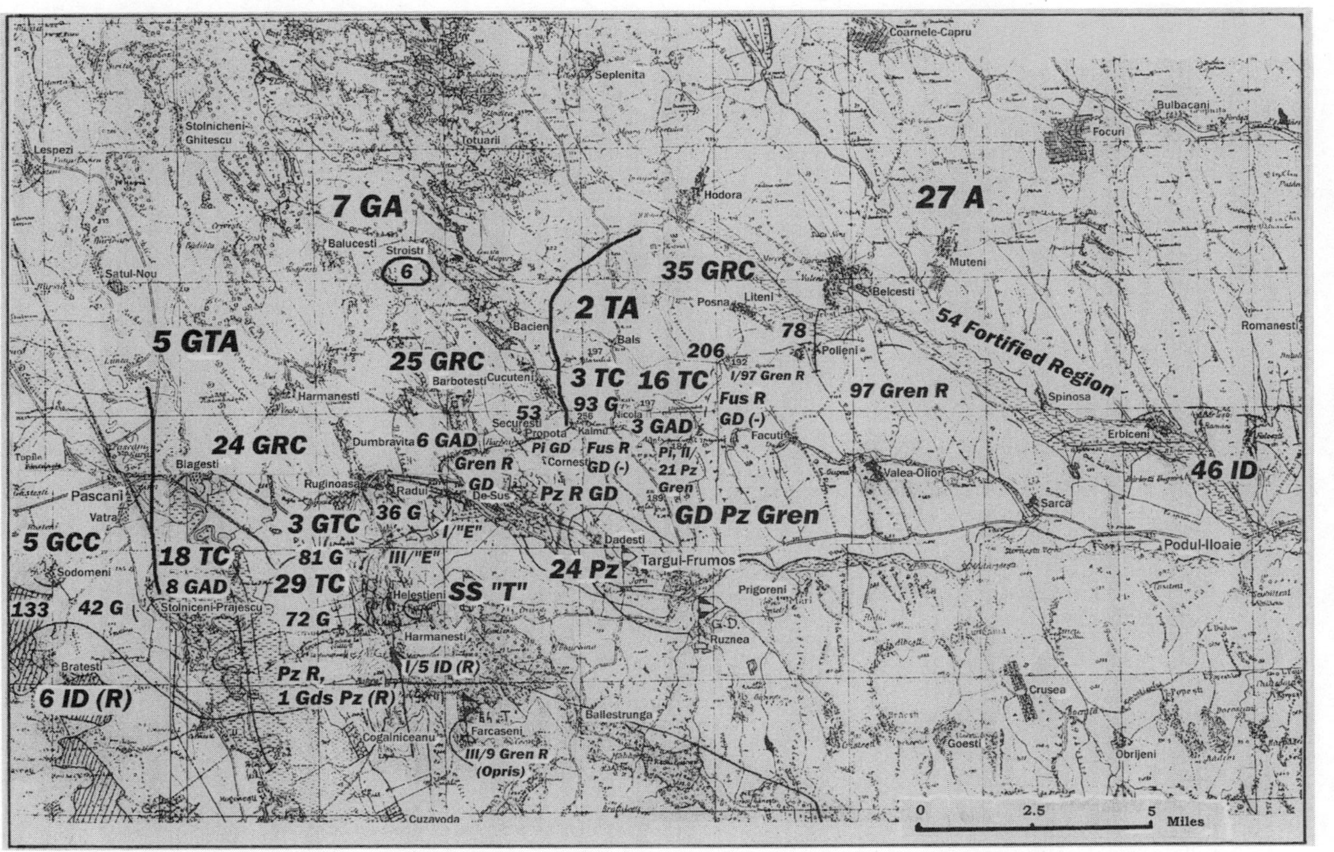

Map 19. The second battle for Tirgu Frumos, 4 May 1944

At 0600 hours on this day, the 35th Guards Rifle Corps began an artillery preparation lasting two hours, after which it began an attack along the Tirgu-Frumos axis at 0800 hours. Its 3rd Guards Airborne Division captured six soldiers from the SS Panzer Division "Grossdeutschland." The 35th Guards Rifle Corps lost 55 killed and 237 wounded, and the 33rd Rifle Corps lost 64 killed and 202 wounded during the day.

The neighbor on the right, the 7th Guards Army, continued to fight in its existing positions, and, on the left, the 52nd Army was under pressure at Bursukeri and Bulturul.[48]

Grossdeutschland Division's history underscores the futility of Konev's efforts on 4 May:

> On 4 May there existed the impression that the Soviet attack had lost some of its force. Concentrating their infantry and tank forces, the enemy now tried to break through only at selected points. They showered these objectives with artillery, mortar and rocket fire in an effort to destroy totally any and all resistance. And then they set off again, with masses of tanks and infantry, and sought to steamroller everything in their path.[49]

Admittedly, from Konev's perspective, the fighting that took place in the Tirgu Frumos region on 4 May was largely ceremonial in that it was simply designed to demonstrate his resolve to the defending Germans and disrupt any attempt by them to mount counterstrokes, as was their custom after completing a successful defense. Therefore, while Shumilov's and Rotmistrov's riflemen and tanks lightly probed the German defenses west and northwest of Tirgu Frumos, Trofimenko's riflemen and Bogdanov's seriously depleted armored forces tried to recapture the village of Kalmu and the dominating heights to the south and southeast.

As evidenced by the *Grossdeutschland*'s history, the increasing desperation of the attacking Soviets, which became more apparent by the hour, summoned up an equal degree of dogged determination on the part of the exhausted defenders:

> Summoning the last of their strength, the infantry, who had been in heavy combat for two days, pulled themselves together to defend once again. One particular focal point for the defenders was the already famous "Kalmu"—Point [Hill] 256. As the dominating hill position it exerted a special attraction on both opponents. It was now a no-man's land; armoured assault pioneers of the GD stormed it several times, but each time they were thrown out of their positions. Each time, though, they regrouped and stormed this "Whore Hill," as it had become known, with

flamethrowers and other assault weapons. On this day they finally succeeded in taking it for good.

Counterattacks by the battalions, some of which were down to 60 to 70 men, resulted in an improvement in their positions. The enemy were driven back. It was squad-size groups of men that repeatedly pulled themselves together and counterattacked. One such effort was organized by Hauptmann Mayer of II Panzer-Grenadier Battalion. He led his battalion headquarters staff and a squad from 8th Company in an assault which carried them back into Giugesti. Mayer was wounded in the attack, while Oberfeldwebel Vies was fatally hit.[50]

Unlike the previous day, however, none of the Soviets' "local" assaults on 4 May achieved any success. By day's end, a resigned Konev gave up all hopes of resuming his offensive and ordered Rotmistrov to withdraw his tank army from combat the next day and reassemble its shattered remnants in the region north of Balucesti. However, he ordered Rotmistrov to leave the bulk of his surviving tanks with Shumilov's riflemen to provide defensive support and establish tank ambush points in the close Soviet rear area.

THE BATTLES DURING 5–7 MAY

Just as Konev suspected, immediately after repelling his feeble attacks on 4 May, the LVII Panzer Corps indeed began preparing concerted counterattacks of its own to improve its defensive positions north of Tirgu Frumos and, if possible, forestall another Soviet offensive. To this end, the panzer corps ordered Manteuffel to regroup his *Grossdeutschland* Division's Panzer Regiment northward to the Cornesti region, four miles north of Tirgu Frumos; to shift his division's Fusilier Regiment to new attack positions west of the Hirlau-Tirgu Frumos road; and to conduct a combined counterattack with its Fusilier and Panzer Regiments against the Soviets' defensive positions along the axis through Cucuteni, five miles north of Tirgu Frumos northward toward the village of Baiceni, eight miles north of Tirgu Frumos (Map 20).

Before doing so, however, Manteuffel took stock of his division's losses and reorganized his battle-worn division:

> 5 May was far quieter than the previous days; the Soviets were spent. Their strength was exhausted and all of their bloody sacrifices gained them nothing.
>
> II Battalion, Panzer-Grenadier Regiment was tactically disbanded on account of its considerably weakened combat strength. Battalion headquarters and the Reinehr Company were assigned to I (APC) Battalion

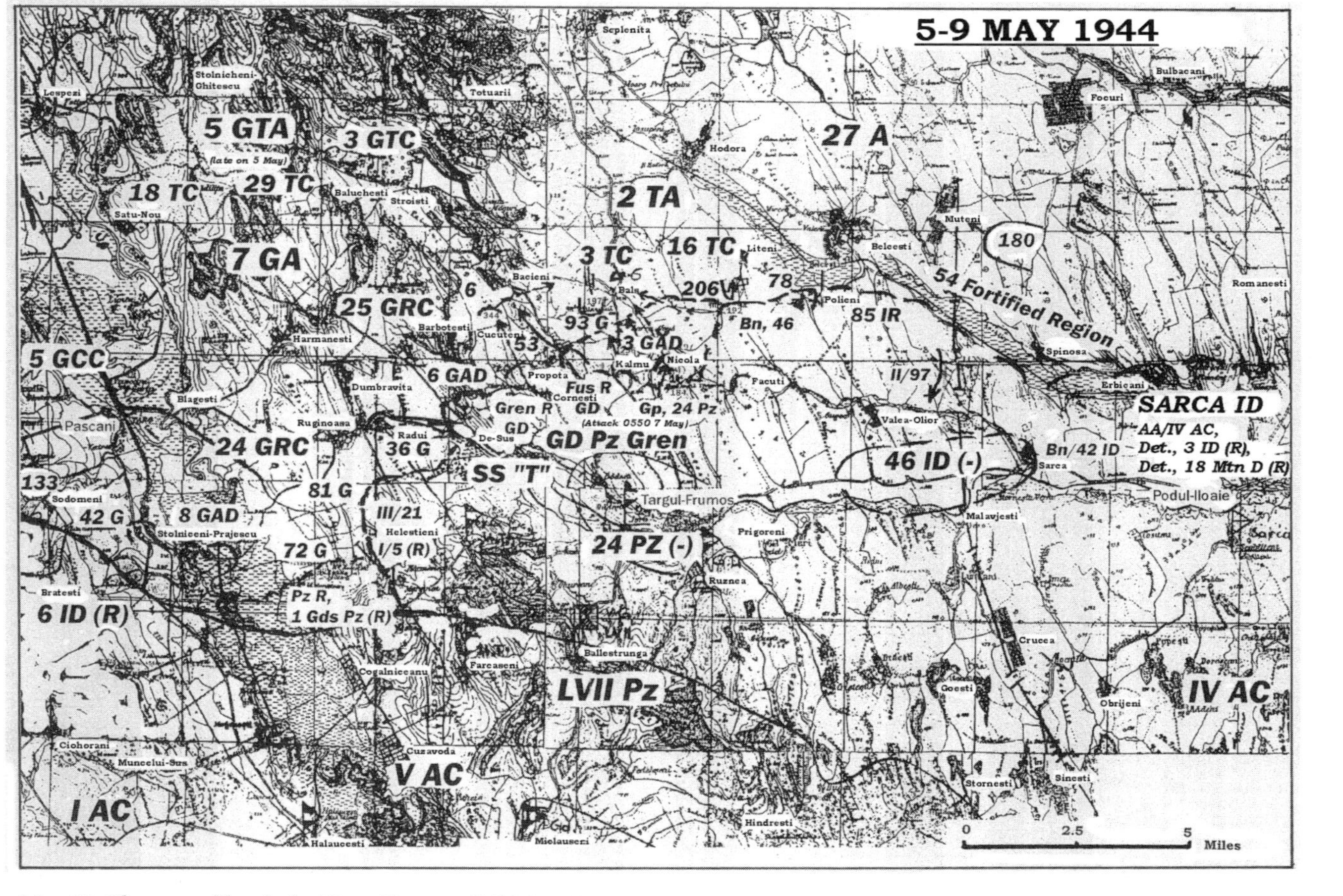

Map 20. The second battle for Tirgu Frumos, 5–7 May 1944

and the Morscheck Company to III Battalion. This measure was made necessary by the shortage of officers and, especially, NCOs.[51]

Simultaneously, the LVII Panzer Corps also ordered Edelsheim to regroup his entire 24th Panzer Division northward to new attack positions near Kalmu and Hill 184, four to five miles north of Tirgu Frumos, and then to counterattack northward along the Hirlau-Tirgu Frumos road against the Soviets' defensive position on Hill 197 and around the village of Bals. Simultaneously, Lieutenant General Kurt Röpke, the commander of the German 46th Infantry Division, was to regroup his entire division westward and concentrate it in the sector between Hills 184 and 192 and then attack to eliminate the Soviet salient northwest of Facuti. As its forces were regrouping, the LVII Panzer Corps ordered the counterattack to begin at dawn on 7 May. In the meantime, only desultory and inconsequential local fighting went on throughout the region.

As recorded in the 2nd Ukrainian Front's combat journal for 5 and 6 May:

On 5 May 1944, the front's forces continued offensive operations along the Tirgu-Frumos axis and conducted combat of local significance in separate sectors. Fifty prisoners were captured. . . . The 7th Guards Army lost 90 men killed and 623 men wounded; the 27th Army, 119 killed and 443 wounded; and the 52nd Army, 74 killed and 332 wounded on 4 May.

The 5th Guards Tank Army's 18th Tank Corps is in the Conchesti [Contesti] and Valia Siaca [Valea Seaca] regions [five to seven miles northwest of Pascani], with tank ambushes in the Hastasti [Hornita] region [seven miles northwest of Pascani]. After leaving tank ambushes in the groves north of Hill 326 [near Harmanesti], the 29th Tank Corps is in the Balucesti [Balcescu] region [25 miles north of Tirgu-Frumos]. The 3rd Guards Tank Corps is in the Balucesti [Balcescu] and Stroisti [Stroesti] regions and the forests to the north [28–34 miles north of Tirgu-Frumos], after it left a portion of its tanks to operate with the 7th Guards Army's infantry.

The 2nd Tank Army is fighting along the southeastern slopes of Hill 256 and the Popa-Mort Burial Mound [near Kalmu].

The 6th Tank Army's 5th Guards Cavalry Corps' and 27th Guards Rifle Corps' positions have not changed.

The 5th Air Army conducted 302 aircraft sorties, and enemy aviation conducted up to 800.

On 6 May 1944, the *front's* forces strengthened their occupied positions and conducted combat operations with small detachments in separate sectors.

Engineer-wise, the enemy has strongly fortified his positions and regrouped his forces, while fortifying the Tirgu-Frumos and Iasi regions.[52]

The 27th Army's daily combat journal entries for 5 and 6 May 1944 confirm the relative inactivity along Konev's front:

> On 5 May 1944, while fulfilling its previously assigned missions, the forces on the army's right wing began an attack at 0840 hours after an artillery preparation but failed to achieve success and advance forward because of strong resistance. . . .
>
> The 93rd Guards Rifle Division seized one prisoner from the SS Panzer Division "Grossdeutschland." The 35th Guards Rifle Corps lost 35 killed and 125 wounded, the 33rd Rifle Corps lost 12 killed and 52 wounded, and the 54th Fortified Region lost two killed and five wounded.
>
> Neighbors: The 7th Guards Army on the right and the 52nd Army on the left were fighting along previous lines.
>
> On 6 May 1944, the army regrouped and did not undertake offensive operations.[53]

The after-action report prepared by Konev's Armor and Mechanized Directorate confirms this inactivity and also describes the departure of Rotmistrov's tank army from the combat area:

> After turning its combat sector over the combined-arms formations, the 2nd Tank Army has withdrawn from combat with its 49 remaining tanks and self-propelled guns by 0600 hours 6 May 1944.
>
> The 5th Guards Tank Army has withdrawn from combat by day's end on 5 May 1944, and its main forces have concentrated in the region of Satu-Nou, Bascani, and the forest north of Balucesti [Balcescu] to restore its strength and put itself in order with 148 tanks and 67 self-propelled guns, for a total of 215 armored vehicles.[54]

All of these combat reports prepared on 5 and 6 May simply "put a good face" on Konev's operations by implying the 2nd Ukrainian Front was still on the offense, when it clearly was not. In fact, after withdrawing Rotmistrov's 5th Guards Tank Army into reserve assembly areas on 5 May, Konev began withdrawing Bogdanov's 2nd Tank Army the next day. All of these measures simply played into the Germans' hands.

THE LVII PANZER CORPS' COUNTERSTROKE (7 MAY)

Once the LVII Panzer Corps' counterattack force regrouped into its designated counterattack positions, it struck Konev's defenses north and northeast of Tirgu Frumos precisely at 0550 hours on 7 May (Map 21). The combined assault by the *Grossdeutschland* Division's Fusilier Regiment and the 24th Panzer and 46th Infantry Divisions collapsed the defenses of Shumilov's 7th Guards and Trofimenko's 27th Armies in several sectors west and east of the Hirlau–Tirgu Frumos road and forced Konev to call on the 16th Tank Corps of Bogdanov's 2nd Tank Army to contain the Germans' assault.

The 27th Army's daily combat journal entries for 7 May describe the Germans' assault:

> On 7 May 1944, after a massive fire raid, the enemy launched an attack in a strength of up to 60 tanks and assault guns and no fewer than three infantry regiments supported by constant air strikes by groups of 30–60 aircraft against the 35th Guards Rifle Corps' sector at 0550 hours. We identified more than 500 combat sorties during the day. The army conducted stubborn defensive fighting on its right wing all day long. As a result of the powerful enemy attacks, the 35th Guards Rifle Corps was pushed back slightly in separate sectors during the first half of the day, but halted the enemy's advance by day's end.
>
> The 35th Guards Rifle Corps lost 86 killed and 291 wounded.
>
> Neighbors: On the right, the 7th Guards Army fought with enemy infantry and tanks in the Cucuteni region, and on the left the 52nd Army's situation was unchanged.
>
> On 7 May 1944, the army received an extract from the commander of the 2nd Ukrainian Front's order No. 00348/op, dated 7 May 1944, concerning a transition to the defense, which read, "The *front's* forces will make the transition to a rigid defense, and the defense will be deeply echeloned and antitank in nature."
>
> The Army lost 14 men killed and 37 men wounded during the day on 7 May.[55]

The after-action report by the *front*'s Armor and Mechanized Directorate adds further details to the 27th Army's description of the German counterattacks:

> 7 May 1944—After bringing the 24th Panzer Division forward to the region north of Tirgu-Frumos, the enemy launched a counteroffensive from the Propota region [eastward] toward Barbotesti, Hill 344, Cucuteni, and Hill 256 and from the region northeast of Tirgu-Frumos toward Hills 184 and 192 at first light on 7 May 1944.
>
> On the right wing, we repelled all of the enemy attacks in the Barbotesti, Cucuteni, and Hill 344 regions with tanks in ambush positions, together with combined-arms formations. On the left wing, after failing to halt the enemy attack, the 206th Rifle Division began to withdraw toward

> Hill 192. However, the 16th Tank Corps, which was transferred to that region by a forced march, restored the situation together with the 206th Rifle Division. . . .
>
> Thus, beginning on 8 May both sides made the transition to a firm defense.[56]

The *Grossdeutschland* Division's history summarizes the action in the Kalmu sector:

> Finally, on 7 May, the panzer-fusiliers counterattacked on the left wing of the division's sector with the assault guns and Panthers [tanks] and supported by the armoured assault pioneers. Their objective was to take once and for all Hill 254, called "Kalmu," which was higher than any of the neighboring hills. Possession of the hill meant a good view to the north into enemy territory and, with it security, for from there any massing of tanks or enemy approach could be spotted in good time. Of course, the Soviets were aware of this, and they transformed the hill into a fire-spewing fortress immediately after its capture.
>
> The initial attempt failed, however a second attack made at first light with the support of 20mm flak on self-propelled carriages was more successful. The attackers entered Nicolne [Nicola] and tracer fire from the light flak drove the Russians from the town. Attacking from the left flank, panzer-fusiliers of the Regimental Headquarters Company under Oberleutnant Emminghaus, supported by pioneers, stormed the "Kalmu" Hill and took it in bitter hand-to-hand fighting. Artillery and rocket batteries pounded Point 365 to soften it up for attack. This proved successful and a short time later the positions were handed over to units of the 24th Panzer Division, which simultaneously took over this sector. The elements of the Armoured Reconnaissance Battalion GD deployed near Point 256 had to withstand significant Soviet counterattacks, which resulted in the hill changing hands several times. The fighting raged on until 10 May. Statements by prisoners revealed that the regiments of the 3rd Guards Airborne Division had been completely wiped out in the fighting there.[57]

During the attack by Manteuffel's division, which, in reality, took the form of a large-scale raid, several mixed panzer and panzer fusilier *kampfgruppen* from the division first smashed their way through the defenses of Ovsienko's 53rd Rifle Division, which was defending the sector south of Cucuteni and Baiceni on the left wing of Safiulin's 25th Guards Rifle Corps, drove Ovsienko's riflemen back, and captured both Cucuteni and Baiceni. This bold thrust forced Shumilov to commit Obushenko's 6th Rifle Division, his 7th Guards

Army's only reserve, to restore the situation. However, Obushenko's division deployed forward too late to catch and damage Manteuffel's fleet-footed *kampfgruppen*.

Immediately after capturing the twin Soviet strong points at Cucuteni and Baiceni and wrecking havoc on Safiulin's forward defenses, *Grossdeutschland's kampfgruppen* wheeled eastward, crossed the Hirlau–Tirgu Frumos road, and struck and collapsed the right flank of Zolotukhin's 93rd Guards Rifle Division, throwing both it and Goriachev's 35th Guards Rifle Corps into considerable disorder. Before Goriachev could reinforce the defenses on his right wing, the two German *kampfgruppen* abandoned their gains and returned to their jumping-off positions near Propota. In reality, therefore, *Grossdeutschland* Division's "raid" was simply a diversion designed to ease the task of the Germans' 24th Panzer and 46th Infantry Divisions' forces, which were conducting a far more important counterattack further to the east. It succeeded in doing so in spades.

Assisted by *Grossdeutschland*'s northward dash on its left flank, Edelsheim's 24th Panzer Division began its assault against the forward defenses of Goriachev's 35th Guards Rifle Corps' north of Kalmu and Hill 184 early on 7 May and smashed his two defending rifle divisions with relative ease. Already under attack from the west, before the riflemen of Zolotukhin's 93rd Guards and Colonel Konev's 3rd Guards Airborne Divisions realized what was happening to them, the panzer division's *kampfgruppen* captured Hill 256 and the nearby village of Nicola and reached the southern approaches to Hill 197 and Bals. Further to the east, other elements of the 24th Panzer Division and Major General Kurt Röpke's 46th Infantry Division swept through the defenses of Kolesnikov's 206th Rifle Division on and west of Hill 192, wheeled northward, captured Hill 192, and recaptured the salient defended by the Soviet forces southwest of the key hill.

By day's end on 7 May, the LVII Panzer Corps' combined counterattack force had eliminated the pesky Soviet salient northwest of Facuti and established a new defense line extending from just north of Propota eastward through Kalmu to Hill 192 and Polieni. Adding insult to injury, by doing so they erased most of the gains Konev's forces had made since beginning their offensive early on 2 May.

In an order he dispatched to Trofimenko, the 27th Army's commander, late on 7 May, an angry Konev blamed Goriachev, the hapless commander of the army's 35th Guards Rifle Corps, for the embarrassing failure. Claiming that "the forces of the 35th Guards Rifle Corps did not display steadfastness" during combat on 7 May and that they had "surrendered the important commanding heights on Hill 256 to the enemy," Konev demanded that Trofimenko "reprimand the commander of the 35th Guards Rifle Corps, Lieutenant General Goriachev, and his artillery commander" and "investigate all of the circumstances surrounding the surrender of Hill 256 and immediately bring the guilty to trial before the judgment of a military tribunal." Asserting that there was "no reason whatsoever to justify the surrender of Hill 256," Konev ordered Trofimenko to "fight for the hill to the last bullet, right up to hand-to-hand fighting, restore the situation on Hill 256 and firmly hold on to Hill 256 and personally organize the battle for the hill." In addition, Konev ordered Trofimenko "to restore order in your forces, especially in the artillery," and to do so by clearing "the 'hangers-on' [riffraff] out the divisions' rear areas," and by replacing "the units that have suffered losses with units from the second echelons and army reserves."[58]

Despite Konev's anger and caustic words, Trofimenko's forces were unable to recapture Hill 256, and Goriachev retained his corps command. Finally acknowledging the reality that Konev's offensive had failed, as early as 6 May, a resigned *Stavka* ordered Konev to halt his offensive and erect a firm defense along the Tirgu Frumos and Iasi axes (see Appendix). However, while requiring Konev "to go over to a firm defense along the entire sector of the front," the *Stavka*'s order authorized him "to conduct local offensives with limited aims in separate sectors of the front to create more favorable jumping-off positions for subsequent offensives."[59]

Indicative of its desire to continue offensive operations in northern Romania, the *Stavka* also indicated that this lull would be only temporary by adding, "the *front*'s forces will prepare to regroup and immediately start creating reserves of ammunition and fuel. Prepare to regroup no later than 25 May."[60] A subsequent directive, which the *Stavka* issued on 23 May, ultimately postponed the date Konev's forces were to be prepared to launch a new offensive for an additional seven days, presumably from 25 May to 2 June.[61] Clearly, therefore, the *Stavka* intended that Konev not end his offensive efforts after his failure at Tirgu Frumos.

In response to the *Stavka*'s directive of 6 May, the next day Konev issued similar orders to his subordinate armies. In its daily report, the 27th Army recorded: "On 7 May the army received an excerpt from the commander of the 2nd Ukrainian Front's order No. 00348/op dated 7 May 1944 concerning a transition to the defense, [which read,] 'The *front*'s forces will go over to a firm defense, and the defense will be deeply echeloned and antitank [in nature].'"[62]

CONCLUSIONS

Wöhler and his superior and subordinate commanders were understandably proud of the LVII Panzer Corps' combat performance during its defense of the Tirgu Frumos region. A retrospective analysis of the battles, prepared many years later under Manteuffel's supervision, explains why the panzer corps' defense was such a matter of pride:

> We believe this [the Targul-Frumos defense] to be a classic example of mobile defense. It contains all of the elements: it shows what is meant by hitting the enemy in his weak spot, at the right time and at the right place—therefore, the significance of timing and direction—and it demonstrates the tremendous value of surprise. This example underlines the need for independent action by commanders at all levels on the battlefield within the framework of the mission, which must dispense with detail but which sets clear aims. Finally, it shows how successful even depleted units can be against a numerically far superior enemy, if their morale is high, if they are led with resource and skill, and react and act quickly and with dash and determination.
>
> There is another lesson to be learned from this example and that is that one cannot rely only on pre-arranged counterattacks but must be able, as at Facuti, to "play it off the cuff." In such cases, the counterattack must be in the form of a quick counterblow, employing speed, surprise, deception and concentration of force to bring the necessary strength to bear at the decisive spot.[63]

Manteuffel also shared his thoughts as to why his *Grossdeutschland* Panzer Grenadier Division achieved such remarkable success before and during the battles in early May by distilling basic principles illustrated by the conduct of his division's defense:

1. The accurate assessment of the situation in general;
2. The detailed defensive preparations, carried out diligently and reliably, which assured the closest cooperation of all arms within the division, and in which each weapon was able to exploit its technical and tactical characteristics to the full;
3. The marksmanship and skill of the anti-tank weapons and the artillery;
4. The preparedness and steadfastness, as well as the bravery, of the artillery, the infantry, assault gun, and the flak [antiaircraft] artillery as well as the aggressive spirit of the tank crews;
5. The exemplary fighting spirit of all officers, NCOs and men, who knew that each could depend on the other; and
6. The accurate assessment of the battle situation in the various phases of the battle and of the terrain by the division command.[64]

Not to be outdone, von Senger also drew equally favorable conclusions regarding the role Edelsheim's 24th Panzer Division had in the signal victory:

> There are a number of lessons to bring out:
>
> a. The brevity of the orders and the absence of any detailed preconceived plans, which would have cramped initiative and been unlikely to have matched the actual situation.
>
> b. The clear concept of an "operation" when mounting a counterstroke, the destruction of the enemy through a combination of concentration, mobility and surprise, and the recapture of ground followed as a consequence of the enemy's destruction. Such an operation calls for the courage to take risks, to accept gaps and then turn the inevitability of penetration to one's own advantage. . . .
>
> There are a number of other points to be noted from this battle:
>
> a. The flexibility and decisiveness of the German commanders, which enabled them to exploit the mobility of relatively small forces to surprise and destroy greatly superior enemy ones. In a word, to exercise generalship.
>
> b. The need to establish early contact with the "in-position" troops and the immediate search for information by pushing forward tank troops to observe.
>
> c. The adoption of a reverse slope position when covering the assembly area from any advance south of PT 192.
>
> d. The clear knowledge of Soviet tactics, which enabled countermeasures to be taken, as exemplified by the holding action of the *fernkampfgruppe* [far *kampfgruppe*] and preventing the establishment of an antitank front around PT 192.
>
> As the battle of Facuti demonstrates, a counterstroke calls for a sense of urgency, coupled with a determination to seize the initiative by bold and resolute action.[65]

From the Red Army's perspective, the *Stavka*, Konev's 2nd Ukrainian Front, and his subordinate armies also well understood why the May offensive failed, albeit after the fact. For example, in a document entitled, "Short Conclusions on the Conduct of Operations from 2 through 8 May 1944," the 27th Army's staff assessed the fighting at that time, citing many cogent reasons for the army's and the *front*'s failure:

> The operations were not successful. The reasons for the failures [were as follows]:
>
> 1. The enemy organized a firm and deeply-echeloned defense. . . . ;
>
> 2. Cooperation between types of forces was not sufficiently well organized, and an increase in artillery, air, and tank strikes into the depth of the enemy's defenses was not planned to a sufficient extent. Normally, at the very moment of the artillery and aviation preparation, almost all of our ammunition ran out, and our aviation had used up its planned aircraft

sorties, and, when the infantry rose up on the attack and, particularly, when they penetrated to the enemy's forward edge, the artillery fire quieted down, the aircraft discontinued their strikes, and, in a majority of instances, the tanks lagged behind. The infantry, which was deprived of any support whatsoever and was subjected to enemy air and tank attacks, quite naturally, had no success in advancing.

It is essential to plan for the cooperation of types of forces during the offensive so that the artillery, aircraft, and support and accompanying tanks protect the actions of the infantry with their fires throughout the entire depth of the battle.

3. There was very little antitank artillery within the infantry's combat formations, and when the enemy conducted tank counterattacks, in a majority of cases, they could not repel them, and, in the best case, the infantry was forced to go to ground and fight the tanks with their own organic weapons or simply withdraw.

4. The tank armies did not support the infantry attacks with the massed fire of tanks but, instead, committed them into combat five to ten tanks at a time, which the enemy then quickly knocked out, and the tank units suffered unjustified losses without offering almost any assistance to the infantry.

5. There were instances when, as a result of poor cooperation with the ground forces, and, probably also due to a lack of knowledge about the situation, our aircraft bombed our forces' own combat formations, not only along the forward edge, but also up to five kilometers [three miles] into the depths.

6. The infantrymen themselves, which, in the majority of instances, were poorly trained and not fully equipped and properly outfitted, absorbed the full weight of the battle on themselves and did not display decisive offensive actions. . . . Combat experience indicates that, if we do not have satisfactorily armed, prepared, and steadfast infantry, then, despite the artillery and air support, their effectiveness will be insignificant. It follows that we should pay greater attention to training the infantry.

7. The issues of command and control and communications requires further improvement, and it is imperative that commanders at all levels direct the battle from their observation posts and see the field of battle, especially on the axes of main attacks. . . .

8. The enemy's defense system and his system of fires were not detected to a sufficient degree before the battle began, and, as a result, the artillery fire during the artillery preparation had little effect.[66]

Similarly, the 2nd Ukrainian Front's Armor and Mechanized Directorate issued its own assessment of the missions assigned to the *front*'s tank forces before the offensive and their performance during its course:

Before beginning our conclusions regarding the actions of the front's tank and mechanized forces during the Targul-Frumos operation, we must note:

1. The 5th Guards Tank Army and the 2nd Tank Army, which had the mission of attacking toward Tirgu-Frumos and, subsequently, toward Iasi and Roman, did not fulfill their missions;

2. By the beginning of the Tirgu-Frumos operation, the *front*'s tank and mechanized forces were not prepared for offensive operations in terrain of such a hilly or mountainous nature and, especially, for penetrating a fortified belt in these conditions;

3. Surprise was completely absent at the beginning of the operation because the enemy had comparatively detailed knowledge about the grouping and intentions of our forces through our soldiers and commanders who fell captive to the enemy. . . . [Consequently,] he brought one more tank division forward, SS Tank Division "Deaths Head" and reinforced his defenses with antitank weapons;

4. The experiences of combat in mountains indicates that the employment of tank armies simultaneously either to penetrate a defense or to exploit success is inexpedient since the latter, by suffering significant losses in the forward edge, will not be able to strengthen the attack into the depth of the enemy's defense.

After the enemy defense has been penetrated to a depth of two to three kilometers [1.2–1.8 miles], it is necessary to commit a second penetration echelon into the battle, which, after penetrating the enemy's defense to a depth of six to eight kilometers [3.6–4.8 miles], will finally create conditions conducive to committing the tank army into the penetration. . . .

Colonel General of Tank Forces Kurkin, commander of the 2nd Ukrainian Front's Tank and Mechanized Forces

Colonel Zadorozhnyi, chief of staff of the 2nd Ukrainian Front's Tank and Mechanized Forces[67]

Only a few Soviet archival documents are available to assess the tank losses of Konev's tank armies during the fighting in the May offensive. The first of these is a report by the 2nd Tank Army, which described the tank army's precise armor strength on 1 May 1944 and losses the army's forces suffered from 1 through 8 May 1944. This report, which was signed by Major General A. I. Radzievsky, Bogdanov's chief of staff, and was prepared on 8 May, stated that the tank army fielded a total of 121 tanks and self-propelled guns on 1 May, allocated as follows:

3rd Tank Corps	27 T-34s
8th Guards Heavy Tank Regiment	5 IS-85s

375th Heavy Self-Propelled Artillery Regiment	18 ISU-152s
TOTAL	50
16th Tank Corps	32 T-34s and 2 MK-9s
6th Guards Heavy Tank Regiment	16 IS-122s
1140th Self-Propelled Artillery Regiment	5 SU-85s
TOTAL	55
11th Guards Tank Brigade	16 T-34s

Radzievsky reported the following non-recoverable (permanent) losses from 1 through 8 May:

3rd Tank Corps	21 tanks
16th Tank Corps	23 tanks
6th Guards Heavy Tank Regiment	10 tanks
11th Guards Tank Brigade	9 tanks
375th Heavy Self-propelled Artillery Regiment	11 self-propelled guns
TOTAL	74[68]

The second of these documents, which is an extract from an after-action report prepared by Lieutenant General Mishulin, the commander of the 2nd Tank Army's 3rd Tank Corps, entitled, "A Report about the Combat Operations of the 3rd Tank Corps during the Period from 2 through 5 May 1944," summarizes the tank corps' role in the battle, as well as the tank losses it incurred:

> From 0500 hours 2 May 1944 to 0610 hours 2 May 1944, the artillery of the 35th Guards Rifle Corps and 3rd Tank Corps and other artillery units conducted an artillery preparation against the forward edge and tactical depth of the enemy's defenses. The artillery preparation that was conducted was not effective since the enemy, who was informed about the readiness of our units for the offensive, withdrew his personnel and equipment from the forward edge by 0500 hours 2 May 1944 and moved them back to the forward edge after the end of the artillery preparation.
>
> At 0615 hours on 2 May 1944, the formations and units of the 3rd Tank Corps launched an offensive in the general direction of Tirgu-Frumos from their jumping-off regions.
>
> During the combat from 2 through 5 May 1944, the corps' units caused the following enemy losses: 26 tanks destroyed, including ten T-6 tanks, and 14 tanks damaged, including nine T-6. Twenty-five guns were destroyed. . . . six prisoners, ten light machine guns, and six heavy machine guns were seized.
>
> The corps' losses during combat from 2 through 5 May 1944 amounted to:

T-34 tanks	6 damaged and 10 burned
ISU-152s	4 damaged and 11 burned
KV tanks	2 damaged
Personnel	80 men killed and 321 men wounded.[69]

This documentary evidence, as well as the course of the battle, makes it quite clear that Army Group Wöhler and the LVII Panzer Corps were forewarned about Konev's impending offensive, in part because of their fortuitous capture of the Soviet liaison officer. In addition, faulty operational and tactical security within Konev's forces, including careless radio discipline, also seems to have contributed to the Germans' intelligence successes. In contrast, however, the Red Army's previous operational record and Konev's pattern of aggressive behavior made it clear to the Germans that an offensive by Konev's *front* was inevitable. The only remaining doubts concerned precisely when and where the offensive would occur.

Based on the performance of Konev's forces during the May offensive, it is also quite clear that, after months of continuous combat and its associated inevitable combat attrition, his forces were not capable of organizing and conducting an effective strategic penetration and exploitation operation. In addition to the inadequate time available to plan the offensive, his forces were too poorly trained and equipped to mount so ambitious an offensive, and his *front*'s logistical and communications systems were poorly developed, relatively inefficient, and starved of equipment, ammunition, fuel, and other vital supplies necessary to sustain an offensive on such a large scale.

Nonetheless, and with considerable justification, Konev assumed that the defending German and Romanian forces were in a similar state or even in a worse condition. When it turned out that they were not, this reality—combined with crisper German command and control and the greater operational and tactical flexibility and skill displayed by the Germans' panzer and infantry divisions, regiments, and battalions—ultimately spelled doom for Konev's offensive. From the *Stavka*'s perspectives, the failure of Konev's *front* at Tirgu Frumos also spelled doom for the future operations by Malinovsky's 3rd Ukrainian Front along the Dnestr River.

2nd Ukrainian Front troops cross the Soviet-Romanian border

Soviet tankers enter Botoshany

Adolf Hitler (second from right) discusses operations with Ion Antonescu and Field Marshal Wilhelm Keitel (on Hitler's right)

Army General I. S. Konev, commander, 2nd Ukrainian Front (on the right), planning the offensive

Lieutenant General A. G. Kravchenko, commander, 6th Tank Army (on the left)

Lieutenant General F. F. Zhmachenko, commander, 40th Army, planning his offensive

Army General I. S. Konev, commander, 2nd Ukrainian Front (on the left), with General S. K. Goriunov, commander, 5th Air Army, observing operations from the *front*'s forward observation post

Army General I. S. Konev, commander, 2nd Ukrainian Front (on the right), with Colonel General of Tank Forces P. A. Rotmistrov, commander, 5th Guards Tank Army, observing preparations for the offensive

2nd Ukrainian Front's tanks in assembly areas for the offensive

Soviet infantry assault

Soviet antitank riflemen engaging German tanks

Soviet artillery on the march

Soviet T-34-85 medium tank

Soviet IS-2 (Iusef Stalin-2) heavy tank

CHAPTER 7

The 3rd Ukrainian Front's Plans and the German Sixth Army's Counterstrokes along the Dnestr River (2–30 May 1944)

MALINOVSKY'S PLANNING AND REGROUPING (2–8 MAY)

Initial Planning (2–6 May)

Reflecting Stalin's continued resolve to expand the Red Army's April incursion into Bessarabia into a full-fledged invasion of northern Romania and, if possible, an even deeper advance into the Balkans, during late April the *Stavka* ordered Malinovsky's 3rd Ukrainian Front to mount yet another offensive toward Kishinev from his bridgeheads across the Dnestr River. This time, Malinovsky's forces were to begin their offensive as early as possible during the first week of May so as to coincide with and exploit the results of the offensive by Konev's 2nd Ukrainian Front against Iasi. In late April, the *Stavka* directed Malinovsky to regroup his forces into their new assault positions as rapidly as possible, break out from their bridgeheads on the western bank of the Dnestr River, and attack westward and southwestward to capture Kishinev and the Komrat region by month's end in close coordination with the offensive by Konev's 2nd Ukrainian Front against Tirgu Frumos, Iasi, and Vaslui.

Almost a week before, Malinovsky had anticipated Stalin's wishes by requesting that the *Stavka* transfer all of the 2nd Ukrainian Front's operational sector east of the Dnestr River to his 3rd Ukrainian Front's control. This encompassed the front occupied by Zhadov's 5th Guards Army, which was deployed on Konev's extreme left wing in the sector extending from Dubossary southward to Grigoriopol' and the bridgehead west of Tashlyk. Once this sector and the vital Tashlyk bridgehead were under his control, Malinovsky was convinced his forces would be able to overcome most if not all of the adverse circumstances that had thwarted his previous attempts to break out westward from the Dnestr. If and when the *Stavka* approved his request, Malinovsky intended to concentrate his *front*'s freshest and most powerful army, Chuikov's 8th Guards, in the Tashlyk bridgehead and employ it together with Tsvetaev's 5th Shock Army, which he planned to regroup from the Tiraspol' bridgehead northward into the sector between Dubossary and Grigoriopol', to spearhead his new offensive toward Kishinev.

Even before the *Stavka* approved his request, on 28 April Malinovsky ordered Chuikov to regroup his army, which had been conducting futile operations in the flooded regions along the eastern bank of the lower Dnestr River, northward into assembly areas east of Grigoriopol' so it could move into the Tashlyk bridgehead when he received the *Stavka*'s approval. Chuikov later recalled the circumstances of his regrouping:

> We did not have time to rest. We had already received a new order from the front commander on 28 April—to transfer the army's base of operations to the Kotovsk region [42 miles northeast of Grigoriopol']. The order required us to conduct the force regrouping at night and conceal it from the enemy. This regrouping reinforced the 3rd Ukrainian Front's right wing at the junction with the 2nd Ukrainian Front.
>
> The forces began moving from the Maiaki region toward the Grigoriopol' and Pugacheny regions on the night of 1 May.
>
> After completing a 120-kilometer [72-mile] march, the 8th Guards Army's forces halted in their new concentration region on 3 May. The army received the mission to relieve the units of General A. S. Zhadov's 5th Guards Army in the Pugacheny and Sherpeny regions in the bridgehead on the right bank of the Dnestr River by the morning of 7 May, to firmly defend it [the bridgehead], and to concentrate our forces and weapons for an offensive. By the time the relief began, the army had [assembled] six of its eight divisions with small quantities of ammunition.[1]

At roughly the same time, Malinovsky ordered Tsvetaev to begin regrouping his 5th Shock Army from its sector in the southern portion of the bridgehead south of Tiraspol' northward into the sector between Dubossary and Grigoriopol' on the *front*'s extreme right wing and to conduct an attack in the sector just north of Grigoriopol' in support of the offensive by Chuikov's guards army westward from the Tashlyk bridgehead. Although Chuikov and Tsvetaev were supposed to regroup their armies in stages that were closely coordinated by time so that they could launch a concerted offensive, it took longer for Tsvetaev to do so since his forces required more time to disengage and withdraw from its positions in the bridgehead south of Tiraspol'.

As Chuikov's 8th Guards Army was closing into its new assembly areas late on 3 May, at midnight the *Stavka* issued a new directive to Konev and Malinovsky, transferring the sector of Konev's *front* east of the Dnestr River to the control of Malinovsky's *front* and containing new instructions to both *fronts* regarding their respective roles in a new offensive to capture Iasi and Kishinev. Addressed also to Vasilevsky, who was still coordinating both *fronts*' operations, the directive directed Konev "to transfer the sector of the front now occupied by [his] 5th Guards Army to the 3rd Ukrainian Front effective 2400 hours on 6 May," and, after its relief, "to employ the [army] to reinforce [his] *front*'s right wing" in the Iasi region. Once his forces had completed their regrouping, Konev was to arrange for the forces on his *front*'s new left wing, between Orgeev and Dubossary west of the Dnestr River, "to cooperate with the 3rd Ukrainian Front in the capture of Kishinev by enveloping the latter from the north."[2]

As far as Malinovsky was concerned, the directive ordered him "to complete the relief of the 5th Guards Army by the time indicated" and "to regroup his *front*'s main forces to the Grigoriopol' [Tashlyk] and Bendery sectors and conduct an offensive no later than 15–17 May by mounting a main attack on his *front*'s right wing in the general direction of Birlad and Focsani [75–120 miles southwest of Kishinev and 90–130 miles southwest of his jumping-off positions]." Finally, after establishing a new boundary line between the two *fronts,* which extended from Perekrestovo Station southwestward through Elenovka, Krasnyi Moldovanin, Floreshty, Petricani, Kotomori, and Solesti to Bacau, effective 2400 hours on 6 May, the *Stavka* demanded that the two *front* commanders conduct their regrouping "secretly from the enemy."[3]

Immediately after receiving the *Stavka*'s 3 May directive, Konev ordered Zhadov's 5th Guards Army to prepare for its relief by Tsvetaev's 5th Shock and Chuikov's 8th Guards Armies and immediately begin to regroup its forces to new assembly areas in the region northeast of Iasi. Zhadov later described the process:

> Finally, during the first few days of May, we received an order to withdraw the army from the bridgehead into the front commander's reserve and to concentrate it in the Botoshany region on Romanian territory. After completing an almost 300-kilometer [180-mile] march, the formations reached the designated region in the middle of May.
>
> The bridgehead on the Dnestr was given to one of the 3rd Ukrainian Front's armies. As we later realized, he [Malinovsky or Chuikov] did not succeed in concealing such a large-scale regrouping from the enemy. Several days after our withdrawal from the bridgehead, the German-Fascist forces undertook a powerful attack against the forces that had replaced us. Its results turned out to be depressing for us; our forces then retreated from the bridgehead.[4]

The *Stavka*'s intent when it issued its new directive was quite clear. At the time it was preparing it late on 3 May, the main shock group of Konev's 2nd Ukrainian Front was already encountering stronger than expected resistance along the Tirgu Frumos axis, prompting the *Stavka* to conclude that Konev's offensive might falter unless it could bring strong pressure to bear against the German defenses in other sectors of the front. Therefore, while the fighting raged in the Tirgu Frumos region, the *Stavka* once again changed the location and timing of its offensive into northern Romania. First, it ordered Malinovsky to regroup the bulk of his *front*'s forces—specifically, Chuikov's and Tsvetaev's 8th Guards and 5th Shock Armies—into new concentration areas north of Grigoriopol' and into the Tashlyk bridgehead and then to launch an offensive in these sectors sometime between 15 and 17 May. At the same time, it directed Konev to support Malinovsky's offensive with an attack by Managarov's 53rd Army in the sector just west of Dubossary and the Dnestr River on his *front*'s left wing.

Second, by instructing Konev to regroup Zhadov's 5th Guards Army to the region northeast of Iasi, the *Stavka* hoped to form a new shock group in the center of Konev's front, which would be capable of capturing the Iasi region in close coordination with Malinovsky's advance on Kishinev. Konev's new shock group was to consist of Koroteev's 52nd Army and Kravchenko's 6th Tank Armies, which were already operating in the region; Zhadov's 5th Guards Army, which was regrouping into the region; and Trofimenko's 27th Army and Bogdanov's 2nd Tank Army, which the *Stavka* planned to regroup eastward from the Tirgu Frumos region to the Iasi region beginning on about 7 May, if their offensive at Tirgu Frumos faltered. Once assembled, this shock group was to begin its assault shortly after Malinovsky's forces broke through the German defenses along the Dnestr River. Tentatively, at least, the *Stavka* ordered Konev to be prepared to launch his new attack against Iasi on 25 May, one week after the 53rd Army on his left wing joined Malinovsky's assault on Kishinev.

The *Stavka*'s new plan did little to alter its ultimate objectives. While the objectives of Konev's original shock group had been the cities of Bacau and Birlad, 48–60 miles south of its jumping-off positions north of Tirgu Frumos, the objectives it assigned to Malinovsky's new shock group were Birlad and Focsani, 90–130 miles southwest of its starting positions. In both cases, the *Stavka*'s objectives included the capture of both Iasi and Kishinev.

Rounding out this flurry of orders, in accordance with the *Stavka*'s new intentions, on 6 May Konev issued fresh attack orders to Managarov's 53rd Army, which was deployed on his *front*'s new left wing, requiring it to cooperate with Malinovsky's larger shock group on the 3rd Ukrainian Front's right wing during the advance on Kishinev. Konev's order instructed Managarov "to prepare and deliver your main attack with a force of four rifle divisions on the left wing in the general direction of Zagaikany and Gratgieshty [8–16 miles south of the Reut River] to envelop Kishinev from the north and, at the same time, capture Kishinev while cooperating with the forces of the 3rd Ukrainian Front." After concentrating "no fewer than 100 [167] tubes per kilometer [mile] of front in the main attack sector," Managarov was "to submit a plan for conducting the operation on 10 May by special courier" and await Konev's further orders regarding the precise timing of his attack.[5]

In short, after reshuffling his rifle divisions, a shock group formed by Managarov's 53rd Army supported by tanks from Lieutenant General of Tank

Forces I. G. Lazarov's 20th Tank Corps was to assault the German defenses in the seven-mile-wide sector from the Dnestr River at Dubossary westward to Mascauti. This sector, which was opposite the junction of the German XXXXIV Army and XXXX Panzer Corps' defenses, was defended by the 282nd Infantry Division from the former and Corps Detachment "F" from the latter, which manned defenses to contain Soviet forces in several small bridgeheads on the Reut River's southern bank just west of its junction with the Dnestr River.

After penetrating the German defenses, Managarov's shock group was to advance along the Zagaikany and Gratgieshty axis and capture Kishinev by enveloping it from the north. Managarov assigned the task of conducting the actual assault to the three guards rifle divisions of Firsov's 26th Guards Rifle Corps and reinforced Firsov's guards corps with one additional guards rifle division from Terent'ev's 49th Rifle Corps, whose remaining two rifle divisions were to defend the remainder of the 53rd Army's front westward to south of Orgeev. In turn, Firsov arrayed his 98th, 110th, 94th, and 25th Guards Rifle Divisions in single-echelon attack formation in his assigned attack sector between the Dnestr River and Mascauti.

Two days before, on 4 May, Malinovsky had already dispatched an order to Chuikov's 8th Guards Army, which was in the process of relieving Zhadov's 5th Guards Army in the Tashlyk bridgehead: "To the commander of the 8th Guards Army. Conduct your main attack with your left wing in the general direction of Chimisheny and Kostiuzshany [8 and 20 miles west of the Tashlyk bridgehead, respectively] to envelop Kishinev from the south. I will personally indicate the time of the attack."[6]

While Chuikov moved his guards army into the Tashlyk bridgehead and carried out its complex relief of Zhadov's forces, Malinovsky undertook every effort to accelerate the regrouping of Tsvetaev's 5th Shock Army from its positions in the bridgehead south of Tiraspol' northward to its new assault positions north of Grigoriopol' and, at the same time, reshuffled his *front*'s forces to reinforce Tsvetaev's army once it reached its new assembly areas. However, despite Malinovsky's best efforts, the regrouping process proceeded at a snail's pace.

First, Malinovsky disbanded Shlemin's 6th Army, which was situated in the center sector of the bridgehead south of Tiraspol', and assigned its forces to the armies on its flanks. Specifically, he subordinated Kupriianov's 66th Rifle Corps (with new rifle divisions and its sector), which was on the right wing of Shlemin's army, to Sharokhin's 37th Army in the northern half of the Tiraspol' bridgehead and Makovchuk's 34th Guards Rifle Corps, which was on the left wing of Shlemin's disbanded army, together with the 203rd, 243rd, and 248th Rifle Divisions, to Tsvetaev's 5th Shock Army in the southern half of the bridgehead. Second, he transferred Gorokhov's 37th Rifle Corps from

Tsvetaev's 5th Shock Army to Glagolev's 46th Army, on Tsvetaev's left. Finally, he assigned Zherebin's 32nd Rifle Corps from Glagolev's army to Tsvetaev's army and ordered Tsvetaev to regroup his army, which now consisted of the 34th Guards, 10th Guards, and 32nd Rifle Corps, to the region north of Grigoriopol', one rifle corps at a time.

The first of Tsvetaev's corps to reach the Grigoriopol' region was Makovchuk's 34th Guards Rifle Corps, whose 203rd, 243rd, and 248th Rifle Divisions began reaching their new concentration areas on about 8 May and were in position by 10 May. However, since it was still in close contact with German forces and space within the bridgehead prevented large-scale movements, Rubaniuk's 10th Guards Rifle Corps had to remain in its sector of the Tiraspol' bridgehead north of Chebruchi and was not able to begin turning its defenses over to the 46th Army and begin moving northward until after 8 May. Soon after, Zherebin's 32nd Rifle Corps, which manned the 46th Army's sector south of Chebruchi, also began redeploying its divisions northward.

Malinovsky's orders to the 5th Shock Army required Tsvetaev to begin his attack in the sector north of Grigoriopol', even if he was unable to concentrate his army completely before the required assault date. Specifically, he ordered Tsvetaev to begin his assault with Makovchuk's 34th Guards Rifle Corps, together with Akhmanov's 23rd Tank Corps, in conjunction with Chuikov's mid-May attack. After concentrating in the region opposite the German bridgehead on the Dnestr River's eastern bank just south of Dubossary, Makovchuk's guards rifle corps was to attack in close coordination with Managarov's 53rd Army on its right and Chuikov's 8th Guards Army on its left; penetrate defenses manned by a *kampfgruppe* of the German 17th Infantry Division on the eastern bank of the Dnestr River; capture the German strong points at Koshnitsa and Pererytoe, five to seven miles deep; and liquidate the German bridgehead on the Dnestr's eastern bank north of the 8th Guards Army's bridgehead at Tashlyk. Pursuant to Malinovsky's order, late on 9 May, Makovchuk deployed his rifle corps in a two-echelon attack formation opposite the German bridgehead with Zdanovich's 203rd and Tkachev's 243rd Rifle Divisions deployed abreast from left to right (south to north) in first echelon and Colonel N. Z. Galai's 248th Rifle Division in second echelon.

Once it was fully reorganized and regrouped, at the end of the first week in May, Malinovsky's 3rd Ukrainian Front was a far more formidable offensive force than it had been during April, when the defending German and Romanian forces had thwarted its two previous attempts to breach their defenses along the Dnestr (see Table 7.1 at chapter's end). Although his *front* fielded five rather than six full armies, a total of 50 rather than 51 divisions, and two rather than three tank and mechanized corps, Malinovsky had increased the strength of these forces after their April battles. More important still, the tank force earmarked to take part in Malinovsky's May offensive, Akhmanov's 23rd Tank Corps, which had played little or no part in the earlier fighting, was now completely refitted and prepared to have a major role in the offensive. Most important of all, by mid-May Malinovsky was finally prepared to bring Chuikov's 8th Guards Army, supported by Tsvetaev's 5th Shock Army, to bear along the shortest and most direct axis of advance toward Kishinev. Therefore, if Malinovsky could regroup his forces in time, both he and the *Stavka* had every reason to be more optimistic about his *front*'s prospects for success.

The Altered Plan (8 May)

On the heels of this flurry of new offensive planning, the severe defeat Konev's shock group suffered along the Tirgu Frumos axis threw all the subsequent planning by the *Stavka,* Konev, and Malinovsky into doubt if not utter chaos. In short, the defeat German Army Group Wöhler inflicted on Konev's shock group at Tirgu Frumos from 2 through 5 May cast serious doubt on the feasibility of the offensive by Malinovsky's *front* and the left wing of Konev's *front* against the German Sixth Army's defenses at Kishinev, at least in the immediate future.

Therefore, only hours after Konev issued his final attack order to Managarov's 53rd Army poised along the Reut River, at 1515 hours on 6 May, the *Stavka* dispatched yet another directive to his and Malinovsky's *fronts.* Echoing the one it sent to Konev, the *Stavka*'s directive required Malinovsky's *front* "to go over to a firm defense along its entire sector," with "a deeply echeloned defense," while paying "special attention to defense along the Tiraspol' axis and the boundary with the 2nd Ukrainian Front," and "reliably dig in on the bridgeheads on the right bank of the Dnestr River." However, as was the case with Konev's *front,* Malinovsky's forces were "to immediately begin creating reserves of ammunition and fuel," and be "prepared to attack no later than 25 May."[7] However, because of regrouping problems in both Malinovsky's and Konev's *fronts* and unexpected German actions along the Dnestr River, on 23 May the *Stavka* issued yet another directive, this time instructing Malinovsky to postpone his new offensive for seven days until 30 May, presumably so that it would coincide with Konev's new offensive north of Iasi, which the *Stavka* also delayed from 24 to 30 May (discussed in Chapter 8).

Although the *Stavka*'s actions throughout the entire month of May indicate its clear intent to mount some sort of major offensive along the Iasi and Kishinev axes, no Soviet sources adequately explain the rationale for it. Although Chuikov attempts to do so in his memoirs, he provides conflicting insights on this complex decision-making process:

The front commander assembled all of his army commanders at a meeting in the village of Malaeshty on 6 May, at which he oriented us on the combat situation. R. Ia. Malinovsky claimed German forces on the right bank of the Ukraine were beaten, their remnants had retreated behind the Dnestr, and this created the prerequisites for an advance on Kishinev, the liberation of Bessarabia, and an attack toward Bucharest and Ploesti. We were assigned the mission of concentrating our forces.

Together with our formations' headquarters, we left to think about what needed to be done to conduct such a large-scale offensive.

As early as the morning of 8 May, however, we received an order from the *front* commander which postponed subsequent operations along the Dnestr until August. The *front*'s forces were required to go over to a firm and deeply echeloned defense with no fewer than three prepared lines to a total depth of 30–40 kilometers [18–24 miles].

This order itself signified some changes in our operational concepts in the south.

A *Stavka* order signed by I. V. Stalin and A. I. Antonov followed on 6 May. It clarified the reason for the changes in the offensive, which the *front* commander had previously provided to us. Time was necessary to put our forces in order, bring our rear services forward, restore our communications, and begin preparations for the summer offensive.

The *Stavka* ordered the 3rd Ukrainian Front to prepare defensive positions along its entire front as far [south] as the Black Sea.

It is true that this directive did not completely end the matter of a possible new offensive. We were ordered to prepare for an offensive on about 25 May.

Jumping forward, I can say that the offensive was once again postponed by a 26 May directive from Stalin, this time for an indeterminate period.

Inasmuch as the previous order and concept the *front* commander issued to us on 6 May mandated preparations for an offensive, in this regard the primary means of reinforcement, such as the 9th Artillery Penetration Division and other artillery regiments, although with small quantities of ammunition, were sent into the bridgehead where we had to prepare positions for the offensive. Certainly, such a grouping of forces did not at all correspond to the subsequent mission—a transition to the defense and the construction of powerful defensive positions.

The bridgehead had only one pontoon bridge across the Dnestr in the vicinity of the village of Butory. If the units of the 8th Guards Army entered the bridgehead on the nights of 5, 6, and 7 May and the units of the 5th Guards Army left from the bridgehead on the nights of 8 and 9

> May, then there was only a single crossing to serve the two armies in turn. However much it hoped to do so, the 8th Guards Army was not able to carry out any sort of regrouping until 9 May. It would have been desirable to withdraw the artillery's main force from the bridgehead to the eastern bank of the Dnestr, from where it would have been significantly better able to support the units defending in the bridgehead by its fire. We had to do that at Stalingrad, where we held the artillery on the eastern bank of the Volga and defended on the western bank. But we were not able to do that: one single crossing was not capable of supporting such a regrouping.
>
> If time and the presence of crossings over the Dnestr had permitted us to withdraw the RVGK [the Reserve of the Supreme High Command or the *Stavka*'s Reserve}, army, and corps artillery to the eastern bank, then, after leaving it in various regions—one grouping at Krasnaia Gorka and another in the forests east of Speia—and without overloading the single crossing, we could have fired on the entire forward edge of the bridgehead with flanking fires, we would have protected the resupply of shells, and we would not have created the great congestion of forces in the same bridgehead.[8]

Within the context of Chuikov's description of the dilemma Malinovsky's *front* faced during early May, the *Stavka*'s apparently contradictory directives point to several conclusions. First, the *Stavka*'s decision to postpone the offensive, first until 25 May, and, later, until early June, was a direct result of the defeat Konev's forces suffered in the Tirgu Frumos region. Second, despite its 6 May halt order, by referring to a "possible" offensive, Chuikov acknowledges the qualification the *Stavka* added to its directive, in which it declared its intent to pursue further offensive action in late May or early June. Third, albeit with a bit of self-justification on his part, he also describes the precarious position his army found itself in while it was conducting its relief of the 5th Guards Army. Fourth, without saying so directly, he underscores the intelligence success the Germans achieved, which allowed them to identify his army's vulnerabilities and organize so devastating a counterstroke. Finally, but only tangentially, Chuikov also describes the situation that gave rise to the offensive Konev's 2nd Ukrainian Front attempted to conduct in the Iasi region before month's end.

Regardless of the missions the *Stavka*'s directives assigned to its two Ukrainian *fronts* in May and the ensuing dispute concerning Stalin's ultimate intentions, the German Sixth Army's subsequent operations along the Dnestr River during the second week of May rendered all of these missions and directives utterly irrelevant.

GERMAN SIXTH ARMY'S COUNTERSTROKES ALONG THE DNESTR RIVER (8–30 MAY)

The 8th Guards Army's Defense of the Tashlyk Bridgehead (8–15 May)

Almost immediately after the *Stavka* postponed its offensive operations along the Dnestr River in early May, the German Sixth Army leaped to take advantage of this unforeseen opportunity. After detecting the difficulties Malinovsky's 3rd Ukrainian Front was experiencing as it attempted to relieve Zhadov's 5th Guards Army with Chuikov' 8th Guards Army in the Tashlyk bridgehead, General of Artillery Maximilian de Angelis, who had replaced Hollidt as the Sixth Army's commander in late April, accomplished something in May 1944 that no other *Wehrmacht* force had been able to accomplish since late 1942: it managed to penetrate a major Red Army bridgehead defense and destroyed or drove away most of the bridgehead's defenders (Map 21). Furthermore, the Sixth Army added insult to the 3rd Ukrainian Front's injury by doing so not once but twice against two Soviet bridgeheads in two separate locations.

In his memoirs, Chuikov correctly provided both rationale and context for the Sixth Army's counterstroke:

> This bridgehead (we will henceforth call it Pugacheny) was like a thorn in the flesh for the enemy. In a straight line, it was around 30 kilometers [18 miles] from it to Kishinev, the capital of Moldavia, and the seizure of Kishinev opened the gates for an offensive on Bucharest, Ploesti, and the Balkans. The Hitlerite command knew this well.
>
> An attack directly against Romania and a withdrawal of this Ally from the war threatened Fascist Germany with many complications, including the loss of the Balkans. Therefore, the Hitlerite command could not fail to undertake an offensive along the Dnestr, if only with the aim of liquidating the bridgeheads we had seized on its right bank and, by digging in along its entire right bank, therefore, establish a barrier to the offensive by Soviet forces into the Balkans.
>
> We should have expected the Hitlerites to activate operations, and this also accounts for the *Stavka* of the Supreme High Command's anxiety when it constructed defensive positions along the left bank of the Dnestr.[9]

In addition, Chuikov's description of the bridgehead's physical characteristics, and the nature of the Red Army's defense within it, underscored its acute vulnerability:

> The bridgehead, which was occupied by units of the 5th Guards Army, stretched across the front of 12 kilometers [7.2 miles] with a depth of from

> five to eight kilometers [three to five miles]. It was completely exposed to artillery fire. The predominant heights over the bridgehead were in the enemy's hands. Forest masses and small woods were along the Dnestr to the right [north] of the bridgehead. The enemy was able to conceal the reinforcement of his forces in these [woods] and deployed batteries of heavy artillery in them.
>
> This in itself gave rise to the decision to widen the bridgehead up to the Balabaneshty, Chimisheny, and Speia line to rest our flanks firmly on the Dnestr and protect the crossings from enemy artillery fire. However, we could not fulfill this mission immediately after reaching the Dnestr: three divisions of nine lagged behind. Ammunition had not been brought forward, and there were insufficient means of reinforcement. The forces of the 5th Guards Army and, later, the 8th Guards Army had neither anti-tank nor anti-personnel mines.[10]

Apparently understanding the problems Chuikov's and Zhadov's armies were having with the relief effort, during the first week of May, the Sixth Army reorganized its forces and deployed a fresh shock group of unprecedented size opposite the Soviets' front lines north and south of Dubossary and around Malinovsky's bridgehead west of Tashlyk. First, the Sixth Army formed Group Knobelsdorff, named after the commander of the XXXX Panzer Corps, which combined all German forces defending the 35-mile-wide sector along the Reut and Dnestr River front from the Orgeev region southward to Speia under a single headquarters. Once formed, Knobelsdorff's group included the XXXXIV Army Corps, which was defending the Dnestr River front north of Dubossary; the XXXX Panzer Corps, which had been defending the Orgeev sector; and the LII Army Corps, which had been defending the sector from Dubossary to Grigoriopol'. Its mission was to forestall any Soviet offensive emanating from the Dubossary region or the Tashlyk bridgehead and, more important, to attack and eliminate the Red Army's Tashlyk bridgehead once and for all.

After his special operational group formed, Knobelsdorff ordered the XXXXIV Army Corps to take over the defense of the sector extending from the Reut River west of Orgeev southeastward along the Reut and Dnestr Rivers to just south of Dubossary, with its 11th Panzer, 10th Panzer Grenadier, and 282nd Infantry Divisions, the three division groups subordinate to Corps Detachment "F," and Group Schmidt (ARKO 128)(Artillery Command 128-ARKO 128) deployed from left to right, to defend against an expected assault by the Soviet 53rd and 5th Guards Armies. Farther to the south, in close cooperation with the forces of the former LII Army Corps, which were containing the Soviets' forces in the Tashlyk bridgehead, the XXXX Panzer Corps, under Knobelsdorff's personal control, was to penetrate and destroy

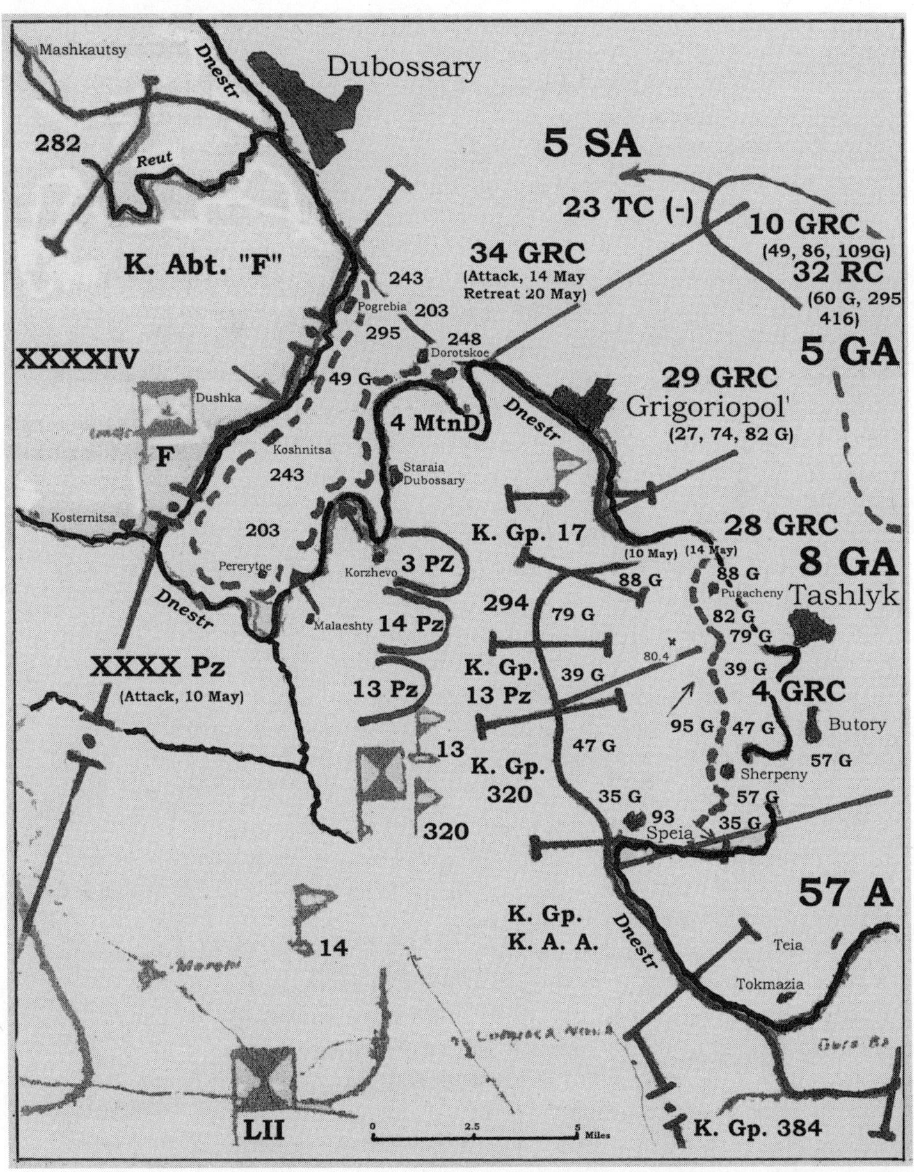

Map 21. The 8th Guards and 5th Shock Armies' bridgehead battles, 10–20 May 1944

the Soviet forces (8th and 5th Guards Armies) in the Tashlyk bridgehead and restore the Sixth Army's defenses along the river.

Specifically, in the XXXX Panzer Corps' sector, *kampfgruppen* made up of the remnants of Lieutenant General Otto Hermann Brücher's 17th, Major General Werner von Eichstadt's 294th, and Lieutenant General Georg Postel's 320th Infantry Divisions and the three divisional groups subordinate to Corps Detachment "A," which were deployed in forward defensive positions extending from the village of Koshernitsa, situated at the tip of the Dnestr River's western bend 12 miles west of Grigoriopol', southward to the bend in the river near Speia, seven miles southwest of Tashlyk, were to protect the forward deployment and concentration of Knobelsdorff's panzer forces. The commander of Knobelsdorff's infantry group was General of Infantry Erich Buschenhagen, the Commander of the Sixth Army's LII Army Corps.[11]

Deploying into assembly areas behind this infantry screen, the XXXX Panzer Corps' panzer fist consisted of the 13th Panzer Division, now commanded by Colonel Friedrich von Hake, which was already in the forward line, Lang's 3rd and Unrein's 14th Panzer Divisions, the 13th Regiment of Lieutenant General Julius von Braun's 4th Mountain Division, and elements of Major General Robert Bader's 97th Jäger Division. This fist was to deliver a concentrated concentric assault across the 8th Guards Army's defensive front, hopefully while it was relieving the 5th Guards Army. Since all three panzer divisions had been in near continuous combat for months and were seriously understrength, they went into combat organized as regimental-size *kampfgruppen.* Finally, Knobelsdorff's assault forces also included the 259th and 286th Assault Gun Brigades, which were attached to them by the Sixth Army, and the 2nd Parachute Infantry Division, which remained in reserve positions prepared to reinforce the assault. The new group contained essentially all of the Sixth Army's armor, which, at this point, probably amounted to roughly 115 tanks and assault guns.

Knobelsdorff organized the forces of his XXXX Panzer Corps for their assault by concentrating its three panzer divisions in the forests east of Balabaneshty, 12 miles west of Tashlyk, with the *kampfgruppe* of Lang's 3rd Panzer Division on his group's left wing, the *kampfgruppen* of Unrein's 14th Panzer Division in its center, and Braun's 13th Panzer Division *kampfgruppe* on its right wing. Attacking abreast in a roughly five-mile-wide sector, the three panzer divisions were to penetrate the Soviet defenses northwest and west of Height Marker 80.4, dominating high ground two miles southwest of Pugacheny, which the Germans called *Stahlhelmhohe,* or "Steel Helmet Hill," and capture the vital Soviet strong point. Thereafter, and supported by the adjacent infantry, the XXXX Panzer Corps' tank fist was to advance to the Dnestr south of Pugacheny to eliminate the Soviet bridgehead.[12] To achieve surprise, which he considered necessary if his forces were to be successful,

Knobelsdorff ordered his troops to begin their assault several hours before dawn on 10 May after a short but intense artillery bombardment against the Soviets' defensive positions.

On the night of 9–10 May, the rifle divisions subordinate to Glazunov's 4th and Morozov's 28th Guards Rifle Corps from Chuikov's 8th Guards Army were still in the process of relieving the rifle divisions of Zhadov's 5th Guards Army, which manned the bridgehead's defenses. To the north and on the river's eastern bank, the three rifle divisions of Foklanov's 29th Guards Rifle Corps were taking over the defenses of the 5th Guards Army from the village of Dorotskoe, four miles northwest of Grigoriopol', southward to the village of Delakeu, three miles south of Grigoriopol'. However, Chuikov estimated it would take several more days for Foklanov's guards rifle corps to complete its relief of Zhadov's forces in the Grigoriopol' region. Finally, to the north adjacent to Chuikov's right flank, the three rifle divisions of Makovchuk's 34th Guards Rifle Corps, which were in the vanguard of Tsvetaev's regrouping 5th Shock Army, were just beginning to relieve the 5th Guards Army's forces in the eight-mile-wide sector from Dubossary southward to Dorotskoe, opposite the Germans' bridgehead on the river's eastern bank.

Within the Tashlyk bridgehead itself, Morozov's 28th Guards Rifle Corps was in the process of taking over the northern half of the bridgehead, with its 39th, 79th, and 88th Guards Rifle Divisions arrayed in single echelon from left to right (south to north) manning defensive positions extending from the high ground west of Marker 80.4 northward to the Dnestr River near Delakeu. Shtrigol's 39th Guards Rifle Division, which was deployed on the rifle corps' left wing, manned defenses extending from the road junction southeast of Hill 172.4 northward to just northwest of Marker 80.4, flanked on the right by Vagin's 79th Guards Rifle Division, which defended northward to just northwest of Marker 80.4. On Vagin's right flank, Marchenko's 88th Guards Rifle Division manned defenses on the corps' right wing from the Dnestr opposite Delakeu southwestward along the bridgehead's northern flank.[13]

In the southern half of the bridgehead on the 28th Guards Rifle Corps left flank, the three rifle divisions of Glazunov's 4th Guards Rifle Corps were still in the process of relieving the 5th Guards and 57th Army's forces, which were defending this sector. Shugaev's 47th Guards Rifle Division had already relieved the 5th Guards Army's 95th Guards Rifle Division in the sector extending from southeast of Hill 172.4 southward to the low hill designated by Marker 164.5, but Kulagin's 35th Guards Rifle Division was in the process of taking over the defenses of the 57th Army's 93rd Rifle Division in the sector between Marker 164.5 and Speia. For example, the 100th Guards Rifle Regiment of Kulagin's division had occupied its sector on the division's right wing, but the 102nd Guards Regiment was still in the process of relieving the

93rd Rifle Division's forces in the corps' center and on its left wing.[14] Nor had Shemenkov's 57th Guards Rifle Division completed its movement across the Dnestr and into the bridgehead.

Meanwhile, north of Dorotskoe adjacent to Chuikov's right flank, the three rifle divisions of Makovchuk's 34th Guards Rifle Division from Tsvetaev's 5th Shock Army, backed up by the lead elements of Akhmanov's 23rd Tank Corps, were beginning to concentrate their forces in anticipation of a future assault against the German bridgehead on the Dnestr River's eastern bank north of Grigoriopol'.

After conducting a reconnaissance-in-force at 0200 hours, at 0330 hours Knobelsdorff unleashed his panzer fist in a general assault against the 8th Guards Army's bridgehead defenses. Putting a good face on his defense, Chuikov recalled his surprise over the assault and the harrowing first several hours of action:

> By 8 May the enemy had concentrated four infantry and three panzer divisions, with a total strength of about 250 tanks against the Pugacheny bridgehead, which was defended by four rifle divisions of the 8th Guards Army.
>
> By that time, our divisions occupying the bridgehead had not yet received personnel or weapons replacements. There were a total of ten tanks in the army's dispositions in the bridgehead, and half of these were captured tanks.
>
> Undoubtedly, the enemy attentively monitored the movements of all of our forces in the bridgehead. He held the dominating heights in the region and reconnaissance aircraft often appeared.
>
> The Hitlerites began an artillery preparation against the forward edge and in the depth of our defense at 0250 hours on 10 May.
>
> After 40 minutes of intense artillery fire, the infantry and tanks advanced, supported by aircraft. This furious enemy assault caught us by surprise.
>
> However, we repelled the initial attacks. A night attack, which also counted on surprise, failed. The Hitlerites were forced back after suffering significant losses in personnel and weapons.
>
> When first light arrived, after resuming the artillery and aviation preparation and after committing 40–50 tanks and self-propelled guns into the fighting, supported from the skies by 40 bombers, the enemy pushed the units on the 28th Guards Rifle Corps's right flank back to the northwestern part of Pugacheny and then into the center of that village. It was clear that the enemy was striving to reach our crossings by attacking through Pugacheny and along the bank of the Dnestr, by doing so cutting off the units of both corps.[15]

Although Chuikov's account inflates the strength of the attacking German forces and understates the strength of his own force and puts a positive face on their resistance, his description of the attack is essentially correct. After several hours of heavy fighting, by 1000 hours the *kampfgruppen* from Lang's 3rd and Unrein's 14th Panzer Divisions penetrated the forward defenses of Morozov's 28th Guards Rifle Corps west of Marker 80.4, forcing Shtrigol's 39th and Vagin's 79th Guards Rifle Divisions to abandon their first defensive positions. Shtrigol's guards division, which was defending with its 120th, 117th, and 112th Guards Rifle Regiments abreast from left to right (south to north) and with only the 1st Battalion of the 112th Regiment in reserve, bore the brunt of the German assault. The official history of the 39th Guards Rifle Division describes the action:

> The enemy began an artillery preparation at 0250 hours on 10 May and attacked across the entire front with large forces at 0300 hours, focusing their main attack against the 39th Guards Rifle Division. The [division's] regiments repelled five fierce attacks between 0300 and 0700 hours as the fighting evolved into a hand-to-hand struggle. We were able to throw the enemy back only in the 120th Guards Rifle Regiment's sector. The 117th and 112th Guards Rifle Regiments, which were defending on the right wing and in the center, were forced to withdraw to the second trench line.
>
> The enemy intensified his offensive on the morning of the following day. He was able to press back the left flank of the 47th [Guards] Rifle Division. The enemy began to envelop the battalions of the 120th Guards Rifle Regiment. Up to 15 tanks and up to a battalion of infantry raced into the penetration that was forming. After suffering heavy losses in personnel, especially among the officers but also in the artillery, which, for the most part, was destroyed and suppressed by enemy aircraft, tanks, and artillery, the guardsmen began to withdraw under the pressure of superior forces and dug in 500 meters west of Hill 80.4. The enemy occupied Pugacheny. During the day the enemy attacked six times with significant forces supported by tanks.[16]

Continuing their advance, the lead elements of the two *kampfgruppen* from Lang's 3rd and Unrein's 14th Panzer Divisions reached the region roughly two miles south of Pugacheny at 1300 hours. As the lead tanks in Lang's spearhead approached the Dnestr River, Morozov, the commander of the 28th Guards Rifle Corps, who was situated in the southern part of the village of Pugacheny, personally gathered up reserves to defend the village and ordered his antiaircraft guns to conduct direct fire on the advancing German tanks. The heavy antitank fire finally brought the German assault to a standstill. During this fight, Vasiliy Zaitsev, who had earned fame as a sniper at Stalingrad and was now a captain in command of one of Chuikov's antiaircraft artillery batteries, was wounded in both legs.[17] However, both Chuikov and Morozov credit Zaitsev with blunting the German panzer assault before it reached the river and, in essence, saving two-thirds of Chuikov's guards army from destruction.

While the heavy fighting raged for possession of Pugacheny, a force of about 60 tanks from the *kampfgruppe* from Unrein's 14th Panzer Division launched a heavy assault against the defensive positions of Shtrigol's 39th Guards Rifle Division, which was deployed in the center of Morozov's 28th Guards Rifle Corps; penetrated Shtrigol's defenses; and raced eastward to cut the Pugacheny-Sherpeny road. This assault threatened to cut the 8th Guards Army's bridgehead defenses in half and capture the Soviets' only crossing site over the Dnestr River. Making matters worse, all of Chuikov's forward corps and divisions began sending desperate calls for more ammunition.

Meanwhile, along the bridgehead's southern flank, the *kampfgruppen* from Hake's 13th Panzer, Postel's 320th Infantry, and Bader's 97th Jäger Divisions pressed the three guards divisions of Glazunov's 4th Guards Rifle Corps to the rear, but more slowly than in the northern and central sectors. The history of Kulagin's 35th Guards Rifle Division of Glazunov's 4th Guards Rifle Corps accurately describes the action:

> The enemy opened heavy artillery and mortar fire against the forward edge of our defense at 0230 hours on 10 May. Large forces of enemy infantry supported by tanks and assault guns struck the forward edge 40 minutes later. On the division's left wing, the Hitlerites had already managed to occupy the trenches of the 93rd Rifle Division's 51st Regiment, which our 102nd Regiment was supposed to take over, during the artillery preparation. In difficult circumstances, the 102nd Regiment was forced to occupy defenses in an antitank ditch west of [the village of] Gospodskii Dvor. The enemy focused his main attack on the 39th Guards Rifle Division's defensive sector. The Hitlerites also conducted main attacks in the sector of the 47th Guards Rifle Division, as well as in the sector of the 100th Regiment's defenses.
>
> For good reason, the enemy command presumed that the ravine where the 100th Regiment's right flank was anchored was the weakest place in the defense. Therefore, he sent a large force of infantry and tanks through that ravine with the mission of reaching Hill 80.4 and, by doing so, providing himself with space for subsequent operations.
>
> After taking over the defensive sector of the 284th Regiment's artillerymen, the chief of the 100th Regiment's artillery, Senior Lieutenant V. I. Varennikov, ordered all of his regiment's artillery and a considerable number of the mortar subunits concentrated on the slopes of the hill

adjacent to the ravine. Considering the antitank ditch, he deployed the artillery there based on the assumption that the enemy would try to penetrate into the rear through the ravine. . . . [The ensuing ambush broke up an attack by 32 enemy tanks, supposedly destroying 16 tanks and two armored personnel carriers.]

At the time a difficult situation arose in the defensive sector of the 47th Guards Rifle Division's 140th Regiment. The chief of artillery of the 100th Regiment, V. I. Varennikov, ordered one battery to change its firing positions immediately and support its neighbor on the right with fire. [This enemy attack too was repelled]. . . .

The situation was also difficult in the 28th Guards Rifle Corps' sector, where the Hitlerites pressed our units back and occupied the village of Pugacheny and Hill 80.4. As a result, the right flank of the 35th Guards Rifle Division was wide open.[18]

As he recalls in his memoirs, by nightfall Chuikov understood just what the Germans were trying to achieve:

During the night of 10 May, I had already decided to concentrate all of the 29th Guards Rifle Corp's artillery, which was located in the Grigoriopol' region on the eastern bank of the Dnestr River, in the Pugacheny and Delakeu sectors and to the south in front of the 28th Guards Rifle Corps. I sent Lieutenant General M. P. Dukhanov, the army's deputy commander, to the headquarters of Lieutenant General Ia. S. Fokanov's 29th Guards Rifle Corps to arrange this maneuver. The artillery assigned to this corps opened fire on the enemy's flanks and rear, albeit after a delay, but its effect on the enemy was soon apparent. A fire strike by a brigade of multiple-rocket launchers [Katiushas] and direct fire by 203-mm guns was delivered against the enemy's tanks and infantry, which were penetrating along the Delakeu-Sherpeny road. Several tanks were destroyed or burned, and the infantry was either destroyed or withdrew as a result of this strike.

More than 4,000 enemy soldiers and officers were killed, more than 60 tanks were destroyed or burned, and 15 enemy aircraft were shot down in air battles or by antiaircraft during the day of fighting on 10 May.[19]

Although Chuikov undoubtedly once again inflated the Germans' losses, German accounts do mention the intense artillery and the *Katiusha* [*Werfer*] fire that pounded their positions beginning at 2300 hours on 10 May and seriously hindered their subsequent advance.[20]

At this moment, Malinovsky was resting at the 3rd Ukrainian Front's headquarters in the town of Razdel'naia, 21 miles east of Tiraspol'. Awakened by the heavy cannonading, he soon ordered all of the *front*'s aircraft to join the struggle for the bridgehead. Chuikov observed the initial massed air strikes the next morning from his army's headquarters on the eastern bank of the Dnestr between Butory and Tashlyk, where Colonel General V. A. Sudets, the commander of the *front*'s 17th Air Army, and General M. I. Nedelin, the commander of the *front*'s artillery, had joined him to observe the devastating fires.

Although this intense artillery fire forced the Germans to suspend active operations over night on 10–11 May, nevertheless, Knobelsdorff's forces resumed their offensive the following morning after several local Soviet counterattacks to regain the initiative had failed. Once again, Chuikov describes the German assault:

> At 0630 hours a large enemy infantry force supported by more than 150 tanks and armored personnel carriers and bomber aircraft attacked from the grove northwest of Speia toward Sherpeny [on the Dnestr three miles east of Speia], where two divisions of the 4th Guards Rifle Corps were defending. Exceptionally fierce fighting raged. The enemy increased the pressure despite suffering huge losses. The position of our infantry became more and more difficult. In spite of the resistance by the Soviet forces, the enemy's tanks succeeded in penetrating into the village of Sherpeny by 1100 hours on 11 May. The units of the 35th and 47th Guards Divisions were threatened with being cut off from the army's main forces and from the crossing sites in the vicinity of the village of Butory. The defensive front of these divisions stretched along the road from Sherpeny to Speia, inclusively.
>
> The enemy strove with all of his strength to reach our main army crossing during the second half of the day. Units from the 57th Guards Division, which were committed to the fighting, halted the enemy attack.[21]

Echoing Chuikov's account, the history of Shtrigol's 39th Guards Rifle Division of Morozov's 28th Guards Rifle Corps put a slightly more positive face on the fight:

> The Fascists resumed the offensive on 11 May with a force of about 1,000 infantry supported by 60 tanks. After a strong artillery preparation, they tried to throw the division's units back into the Dnestr and liquidate the bridgehead. Suffering huge losses, the enemy launched five assaults during the day, but all of them were repelled.[22]

In contrast, the history of Kulagin's 35th Guard's Rifle Division of Glazunov's 4th Guards Rifle Corp provides a more detailed account of the fighting on 11 May and the disastrous consequences for the bridgehead defenses:

The Fascist command once again threw his infantry battalions supported by tanks and assault guns into the attack at 0500 hours on 11 May. Enemy aircraft bombed the forward edge continuously. The enemy conducted his main attack with forces from the 17th, 320th, 72nd, and 355th Infantry Divisions in cooperation with the 13th Panzer Division from the vicinity of Hill 80.4 toward Hill 47.5. After penetrating of the 47th Guards Rifle Division's rear subunits, 12 assault guns and 20 armored transporters with infantry penetrated into the 35th Guards Rifle Division's rear and reached the southwestern outskirts of the village of Sherpeny and the eastern side of the village of Speia. Developing their obvious success, the Hitlerites threw a regiment of infantry supported by 30 tanks and 30 assault guns forward into this penetration and continued to push back the 142nd Regiment, the neighbor on our right.

After occupying their previous positions, the 35th Guards Rifle Division's units began to take measures to liquidate the penetration by reinforcing their right wing with antitank guns. All the while, actively operating enemy aircraft bombed our combat formation and the crossing sites over the Dnestr. We recorded 2,000 aircraft sorties during the day. As a result, the division's units received no ammunition at all throughout the day. The fierce two-day struggle consumed all of our units' ammunition reserves. By midday the artillery had no more shells and was not able to support the rifle subunits. As a result, the 118th Artillery Regiment lost four 76-mm guns, two 122-mm howitzers, 11 mortars, and four 45-mm guns. Displaying courage and bravery, the artillerymen fought against the enemy's tanks to their very last rounds. Colonel A. I. Loginov, the commander of the 118th Artillery Regiment, personally corrected the fire and perished bravely on the field of battle. While carrying out their orders, the artillerymen serving the remaining five 76-mm guns withdrew to the Dnestr crossing without a single shell.

Meanwhile, after repelling attacks by superior forces against their front and while holding off an attack by tanks and assault guns against their rear, the 100th Regiment began to retreat in the direction of the village of Speia, under the protection of a battery of guns commanded by V. I. Varennikov, the chief of the regiment's artillery. After occupying a defense in the forest southeast of Speia, they repelled an attack by enemy infantry and tanks and held firmly to their defensive positions. The 101st Regiment was fighting with infantry and tanks, which had penetrated on the right wing and were threatening to reach the division's rear. By employing guns captured in battle, the regiment began withdrawing toward the forest and the defense lines occupied by the 100th Regiment. The 102nd Regiment was fighting with superior enemy forces, which were attacking against both its front and its flanks. Because of the absence of

> ammunition, the regiment was forced to withdraw toward the division's main forces in the village of Speia, where it held on to its defenses until it received an order to evacuate to the eastern bank of the Dnestr. After fulfilling the corps commander's order, the division's units crossed to the left bank of the Dnestr during the evening of 11 May and concentrated in the vicinity of the village of Butory on the morning of 12 May.[23]

In fact, Knobelsdorff had indeed altered the direction of his main attack on 11 May by wheeling the bulk of his three panzer divisions southward to drive the Soviet troops from Sherpeny and seize the Soviet's sole crossing sites over the Dnestr at Butory. Only the intervention of fresh Soviet troops prevented his attacking panzers and assault guns and their supporting infantry from reaching their critical final objectives. Notwithstanding Knobelsdorff's failure to crush Chuikov's forces entirely, Chuikov's defenses in the Tashlyk bridgehead were indeed in a shambles.

During the carnage on 11 May, Malinovsky joined Chuikov in the Butory region to assess the situation and ordered the army commander to make every effort to resupply his forces in the bridgehead with ammunition. However, Chuikov was not able to do so until nightfall, and, when he did, he had to do so from the *front*'s ammunition bases since his army's ammunition bases were already depleted.

Knobelsdorff's forces resumed active offensive operations once again at 0300 hours on 12 May, this time by launching several separate assaults in succession at three different locations. However, Chuikov described the assaults as far less fierce than before, adding, "We felt the enemy was tiring."[24] The 39th Guards Rifle Division's account of the fighting from 12 to 14 May confirms Chuikov's judgment:

> The following day [12 May] was less tense. The enemy attacked three times during the day with a force of 700–800 infantry supported by 30 tanks and assault guns.
>
> All of the means of antitank defense and the artillery and mortars in the division's regiments were put out of action as a result of the fierce fighting.
>
> After an artillery preparation, in which multibarrel mortars [*werfers*] took part, an enemy force of up to a battalion of infantry supported by 12 tanks and assault guns attacked once again at 2000 hours on 13 May. We repelled this attack with rifle fire from the subunits and with the help of *Katiusha* guards-mortars.
>
> An enemy force of up to a battalion of infantry accompanied by 17 tanks and supported by bomber aircraft attacked the division's units twice more from 1700 up to 1900 hours but suffered heavy losses and withdrew.

> The 120th Guards Rifle Regiment turned its sector over to the 82nd Guards Rifle Division's 246th Rifle Regiment [from Fokanov's 29th Guards Rifle Corps] on the morning of 14 May and concentrated two kilometers [one mile] southwest of the village of Pugacheny. After turning their sectors over to the regiments of the 82nd Guards Rifle Division, the 112th and 117th Guards Rifle Regiments concentrated in the forest one kilometer [one half mile] east of Vainovo. The division received orders to attack.
>
> After a 20-minute artillery preparation, the division attacked at 0400 hours on 15 May but failed to achieve any success.
>
> After an hour's artillery preparation and two volleys of multiple-rocket launchers, the battalions of the 120th and 117th Guards Rifle Regiments, supported by assault aircraft, once again attacked the enemy at 1900 hours. Overcoming strong resistance, the battalions advanced forward slowly over night and captured the southeastern slopes of an unnamed hill early on the morning of 16 May.
>
> After an artillery preparation, an enemy force of up to a battalion of infantry supported by 12 tanks and assault guns attacked the subunits of the 120th and 117th Guards Rifle Regiments at midday on 16 May. The guardsmen forced the enemy to withdraw to their jumping-off positions by a counterattack.
>
> Once again the enemy counterattacked against the 117th and 120th Regiments five times between 13 and 19 May with a force of up to two battalions supported by nine tanks under the protection of heavy artillery fire. The units repelled six enemy attacks during this period.
>
> In response to an order by the 28th Guards Rifle Corps' commander, the division turned its defensive sector over to the 88th Guards Rifle Division at 2000 hours on 18 May and reached its new concentration area at "Vinogradar'" Collective Farm.[25]

As this account confirms, at this critical juncture, Fokanov's 29th Guards Rifle Corps had finally completed relieving the 5th Guards Army's rifle divisions in the sector north and south of Grigoriopol' and soon began sending its divisions into the Tashlyk bridgehead to support Morozov's beleagured 28th Guards Rifle Corps, which was clinging precariously to its bridgehead defenses from Pugacheny southward five miles to Sherpeny. During the same period, Makovchuk's 34th Guards Rifle Corps from Tsvetaev's 5th Shock Army also finally made its presence known by attacking the German bridgehead on the river's eastern bank north of Grigoriopol'. More important still, although he had suffered significant losses, Chuikov was able to complete regrouping his surviving artillery force from within the bridgehead back to the river's eastern bank and bring it to bear in the bridgehead struggle. Characteristic of Chuikov, although the German assault had decimated two of his rifle corps, he persistently ordered the remnants of these corps to continue to attack to take back whatever portion of the shrinking bridgehead they could.

In three days of heavy fighting, Knobelsdorff's forces were able to eliminate much of the 8th Guards Army's bridgehead, ultimately compressing it into a restrictive area along the river roughly seven miles wide but only one half to two miles deep. Exhausted by the battle, both Malinovsky and Chuikov ultimately gave up the fight:

> The front commander ordered our army to cease its struggle to widen the bridgehead on 15 May and to go over to a stubborn defense of its existing positions. Despite this [order], after a fire raid, the 226th Guards Rifle Regiment attacked the enemy in the village of Sherpeny at 1600 hours on 16 May and captured it after repelling numerous enemy counterattacks.
>
> After committing the last reserves he could assemble and concentrate after his retreat behind the Dnestr, the enemy repeatedly attacked our units from 16 through 22 May, but all of his attacks were repelled with heavy losses.[26]

What Chuikov failed to report in his partially face-saving account was that, while his army was locked in the fierce struggle for the Tashlyk bridgehead, Malinovsky mounted another attempt to rescue the 8th Guards Army from its precarious situation. He did so on 13 May by ordering Tsvetaev's 5th Shock Army, which was in the midst of completing its major reorganization and regrouping from its former bridgehead south of Tiraspol' into the Grigoriopol' sector on Chuikov's right flank, to assault the German defenses north of Grigoriopol' to relieve the pressure on Chuikov's forces.

The 5th Shock Army's Counterstroke North of Grigoriopol' (14–20 May)

The second major battle along the Dnestr River during the first half of May developed in conjunction with and as a direct result of Group Knobelsdorff's counterstroke against Chuikov's 8th Guards Army. During the period when Knobelsdorff was organizing and launching his assaults against Chuikov's defenses around the Tashlyk bridgehead, the three rifle corps of Tsvetaev's 5th Shock Army were in the process of regrouping from their former bridgehead south of Tiraspol' northward to the Grigoriopol' region (Map 21). Although the three rifle divisions of Makovchuk's 34th Guards Rifle Corps were already in their new assembly areas north of Grigoriopol' on or shortly after 10 May, his 10th Guards and 32nd Rifle Corps and their reshuffled rifle divisions were either en route to their designated sectors or about to move into their new assembly areas.

In the meantime, as he prepared to fulfill the offensive mission Malinovsky had assigned to him several days before, Tsvetaev ordered Makovchuk's 34th Guards Rifle Corps, which was deployed adjacent to Chuikov's left flank opposite the German bridgehead north of Grigoriopol', to accelerate the concentration of his forces. Once in position, Makovchuk's three divisions were to assault and collapse the Germans' bridgehead defenses and advance westward to Koshnitsa and Pererytoe to relieve the pressure the Germans were applying against the right wing of Chuikov's forces in the Tashlyk bridgehead. This assault was especially important, since, if successful, it would eliminate the heavy artillery and mortar fire the Germans were delivering against Chuikov's forces from the higher ground north of the river. Finally, while Makovchuk's rifle divisions were making their assault, Tsvetaev ordered his two other rifle corps, Rubaniuk's 10th Guards and Gorokhov's 32nd Rifle, to reinforce Makovchuk's assault as soon as they completed their regrouping into the region.

The division history of the 34th Guards Rifle Corps' 203rd Rifle Division, which was written by the division's commander, Colonel G. S. Zdanovich, provides the most accurate and detailed account of the 5th Shock Army's fight north of Grigoriopol':

> The assault on the [Germans'] bridgehead was supposed to begin on 14 May. The 243rd and 203rd Rifle Divisions were to participate in the attack, supported on the left by the 248th Rifle Division. They were to be supported by two artillery and two mortar regiments and also by a tank brigade [probably from the 23rd Tank Corps]. . . .
>
> Our artillery struck at 0300 hours on the morning of 14 May, as soon as first light began. After a 30-minute artillery preparation against the enemy's forward edge, the soldiers of the 592nd and 610th Rifle Regiments, which were cooperating with the tank brigade, advanced forward with a powerful "Ura!"
>
> The strong and unexpected attack caused disorder in the enemy's ranks. They offered almost no resistance.
>
> Dzhafer's battalion penetrated into Dorotskoe [five miles west of Grigoriopol']. Majors Kolesnikov's and Gursky's regiments had already captured the village of Pererytoe [ten miles southwest of Grigoriopol'] and the nearby woods at about 0900 hours in the morning. The mission assigned by Colonel General Tsvetaev had been fulfilled; we had essentially succeeded in driving the Germans from the ill-fated Dnestr "bottle."[27]

The early dawn assault by Makovchuk's 34th Guards Rifle Corps smashed the defenses of the 17th Infantry Division's *kampfgruppe* and, within a matter of a few hours, forced the surprised German forces to abandon their defensive positions between the villages of Pogrebia and Dorotskoe (across the base of the river bend), withdraw from their entire bridgehead, and fall back to new defenses along the western bank of the Dnestr River north and south of Koshernitsa, 12 miles west of Grigoriopol'. As a result, by nightfall on 14 May, arrayed from south to north, the two rifle divisions in the first echelon of Makovchuk's 34th Guards Rifle Corps—Zdanovich's 203rd and Tkachev's 243rd—occupied the long westward-jutting salient formed by the river, flanked on the south, west, and north by defending German forces. To assist Makovchuk in his defense, Tsvetaev, the 5th Shock Army's commander, also committed the forward elements of Rubaniuk's 10th Guards Rifle Corps into the fighting on Makovchuk's right wing as soon as Rubaniuk's forces reached the combat area. The first of Rubaniuk's reinforcing rifle divisions, Colonel V. F. Margelov's 49th Guards, soon occupied defenses facing north near the village of Koshnitsa, nine miles west of Grigoriopol'. Indicative of the intense fighting, within 24 hours Margelov was wounded by German artillery fire and replaced by Colonel S. V. Salychev.

The relatively exposed positions the Soviets occupied in the river salient north of Grigoriopol' and in the other relatively isolated or poorly positioned bridgeheads they held elsewhere along the Dnestr provided the Germans with ideal targets for reduction or outright elimination. In addition, German intelligence organs apparently kept close track of the extensive regrouping Malinovsky was conducting all along the Dnestr River and were quickly able to identify and engage Soviet forces when they were most vulnerable as they regrouped into and out of these exposed positions. As a result, to Malinovsky's consternation, beginning on 13 May and continuing until month's end, although understrength, concentrated German *kampfgruppen* were able to crush several of these exposed Soviet positions and literally destroy the forces defending them.

The first instance when this took place occurred in the sector of Makovchuk's 34th Guards Rifle Corps of Tsvetaev's 5th Shock Army, whose 203rd, 243rd, and 248th Rifle Divisions had driven the German 17th Infantry Division's *kampfgruppe* from its narrow bridgehead defenses east of the Dnestr River on 14 May. Zdanovich, the commander of the 203rd Rifle Division, provides a particularly detailed, graphic, candid, and accurate account of his division's tragic ordeal by fire in its exposed river salient northwest of Grigoriopol':

> Soon we received an order to force the Dnestr, beginning on the morning of 15 May. I sent the new mission assigned by the commander and the division headquarters down to my regiments immediately.
>
> I transferred my observation post [OP] to the high ground at the very neck of the "bottle" [the eastern end of the river salient]. Although this

eased the regiment's command and control and improved its observation, the enemy could observe the same spot from the higher right bank of the Dnestr and even fire on us with machine guns.

Massive enemy artillery and air raids continued all day. The Germans were trying to prevent our forces from maneuvering and assist in the conduct of their own defensive work. At the same time, they transported all of their available reserves in Staraia Dubossary [on the southern side of the river salient's narrow eastern neck three miles south of Dorotskoe] to our bank and threw them into a counterattack during the evening. Major Gursky repelled it with an automatic weapons company and then withdrew Captain Dzhafer's 2nd Battalion from the peninsula north of Korzhevo [on the river's southern bank six miles south of Dorotskoe], where he occupied new defenses. At that time, a beloved soldier, Viktor Vladimirovich Sendek, the 610th Regiment's deputy commander for political affairs, was killed during an artillery raid. The 619th Regiment also repelled an enemy counterattack and simultaneously tried to push them off the peninsula [salient], but without any results.

The division's regiments were stretched along the [Dnestr's] bank in a single line over a distance of just over eight miles. The army commander knew about this, but he also knew that the Hitlerites had brought two panzer divisions and a motorized regiment up to the "bottle." However, we did not receive an order to defend.

The Germans began active operations overnight on 15 May, that is, on the eve after we were supposed to cross the Dnestr. They transferred the 14th Panzer Division and the 116th Motorized Regiment across the river from the march and, after conducting a heavy fire raid, advanced into the attack from four directions. They committed up to two battalions with tanks from the peninsula north of Korzhevo [2.5 miles southeast of Staraia Dubossary on the river's southern bank] toward Hill 15.1, up to two battalions against the village of Pererytoe [on the river's northern bank ten miles west of Grigoriopol'], and up to two companies toward the woods at Lake Dogma [one mile northwest of Pererytoe]; around 150 soldiers also advanced toward Koshnitsa [eight miles west of Grigoriopol'] from the gardens two kilometers [1.2 miles] west of Koshnitsa [on the northern bank of the river salient].

Fierce combat raged, which, by virtue of the number of losses among the senior officer cadre, was the heaviest the division had ever experienced. Our units, which were preparing to cross the Dnestr, were not able to pay requisite attention to defense and, therefore, had not dug blindages, trenches, or dugouts. In addition, when German bombers appeared in the transparent May skies following the artillery raid, the situation became critical.

The telephone operators had barely established communications with the 619th Regiment, all of whose actions I could clearly see since the regiment was located literally only a kilometer [0.6 miles] from my OP. Seeing that the Fascists were conducting fire against its positions, I tried to communicate with Lieutenant Colonel Iaremchuk. But instead of the regimental commander, his deputy chief of staff took the phone and said:

> Mefodiy Platonovich Iaremchuk has been seriously wounded, and his assistants, Majors Aleksandr Mikhailovich Bachkin and Vasiliy Aleksandrovich Antonov, have also been wounded by bomb fragments. The Party organizer and the agitator of the regiment, Captains Arsentiy Petrovich Obernikhin and Nikolai Vasil'evich Fediakin, the battalion commander, Captain Aleksei Alekseevich Bronsky, and all of the company commanders are also out of action.

Through my stereoscope I could see the enemy attacking the regiment's positions from the fairly high ground that rose above the bank at the village of Staraia Dubossary. I asked, "What is the strength of the forces attacking you?" "I cannot know," I heard in the receiver, "Perhaps a regiment."

By this time, the 619th Regiment's right wing faltered and began to withdraw toward the division's OP. "All staff officers into the ranks!" I commanded, "Stop the retreating soldiers and throw the enemy back."

The battle was seething only a half kilometer [0.3 miles] from my observation post. The staff officers encountered the soldiers of the 619th Regiment in the brush along the bank of the river. Seeing their officers in the ranks with them, the soldiers quickly regained their confidence and became controlled and combat ready. The attack was repelled.

However, reports that the Germans were bringing up reserves were already reaching the division's OP.

The 3rd Battalion of the 619th Regiment, which was commanded by my former adjutant, Captain V. M. Timchenko, was located in the rear area. I ordered, "Immediately summon Timchenko's battalion." At that very moment, one of the shells exploded not very far from me. It hurled me aside and scorched my side. "You are wounded Comrade General!" cried my radio operator as he rushed to help me.

I stopped him with a quick gesture and ordered him to radio a message that the 619th [Regiment] was to repel the attack at all cost. There were several enemy attacks; however, the regiment managed to repel all of them.

The artillery again struck our positions at 1600 hours, and about 20 German bombers also appeared in the skies. Once again—it was another enemy attack.

Now it became clear that the Germans were about to attack the division's OP. We had to stop them at all cost. "All officers, security troops, and signalmen into the ranks," I ordered. Then and there, the soldiers took to the ground along the slope of a small hill about 100 meters [328 feet] from the OP.

We beat off the first attack, but the enemy resumed active operations an hour later.

However, there are 60 minutes in an hour. And we were accustomed to value each and every minute during the war, particularly in critical situations. This was how it was this time. During the hour between the Hitlerites' first and second attacks, we managed to create what resembled a coherent defense at the OP—we entrenched, assembled a number of soldiers, and occupied a more proper position.

Colonel Bespal'ko said, "Permit me to lie down with the soldiers, and you, Comrade General, must go off to the medical battalion. Your entire blouse is covered with blood."

I responded, "If required, we will all join the ranks. In the event of a new attack against the OP, only our guest, Colonel Savitsky, the chief of staff of the 34th Guards Rifle Corps, will be left. Therefore, there is nowhere to hurry to Ignatiy Fedorovich."

It was the middle of May. A blizzard of falling petals from cherry and apple trees rained down onto the gardens. And when the wind blew carrying the sour powdery smoke, one could clearly sense the smell of lilacs.

My head was splitting with pain, my temple was hammering from the loss of blood, and I was tormented by a terrible thirst.

"We could vacation in these places, fish, and get sunburned,"—the strange but utterly absurd idea ran through my mind at this time. And the enemy was only 100 meters away.

I distinctly heard the guttural commands of the German officers exhorting their troops into the attack. Already dark stains were pushing through the light green foliage of the shrubbery, and, gradually increasing in number, they blended together into a dense moving rank—the Fascists were closing in.

"The training company is approaching to help us," reported Savitsky; "Only we must hold out." "We are holding," I answered as I drew my pistol. And all of the others there followed my example—both Colonel Bespal'ko and Colonel Artem'ev, the chief of the 34th Guards Rifle Corps' political section, and Major Sadovnikov, the division procurator, who had just arrived.

I turned to the few soldiers who were located at the OP and shouted, "Soldiers, we will stand to the death!"

This division had advanced more than 1,700 kilometers [1,056 miles] from the Don [River] to the Dnestr [River] and had fought in 120 offensive battles. However, here once again I had to recall the old motto from a time when defense was difficult, "Stand to the Death!"

The enemy's ranks snaked in front of us in the growing darkness. Stooping low and clinging to the pliable brush, the Hitlerites advanced toward us in short rushes. They were advancing forward without greatcoats. And for some reason, the image of how colorless the tin buttons on their dress uniforms were gleaming in the sun is still etched in my memory.

Some kind of birds suddenly burst into the skies. This, in particular, disrupted the quiet of that moment.

It is difficult to say to how many meters away the Fascists approached. Only when they pushed forward, throwing themselves into their final dash with a savage roar as if it defended them from bullets and dissipated fear, did the concerted volleys by our soldiers ring out. One could hear shots chattering in staccato fashion and the explosion of grenades. No, the Soviet soldiers did not repel the attack in silence. They also shouted all sorts of things, while raising themselves menacingly from their small foxholes, ready to throw themselves into furious hand-to-hand combat.

Colonel Savitsky, who remained at the OP, managed to report to the army's headquarters that the division headquarters' entire cadre was repelling the enemy's attack under the leadership of their commander. They [the army headquarters] informed him that they were sending another ten tanks to assist him. But Savitsky did not hear these words; he had already been mortally wounded.

Then I distinctly recall how someone in the ranks shouted, "Comrade General. Help is arriving! We will stand our ground!!!"

The training company suddenly appeared next to us. And not far away, shots rang out somewhere in the rear area, and the metallic clank and rumble of our tanks gradually swelled. Timchenko's battalion was also approaching.

The motto, "Stand your ground," rushed through my mind. And once again, for some reason, the idea of resting and fishing in these places also ran through my mind. I raised my head with difficulty. Although I saw pretty little circles dancing fleetingly before my eyes, nevertheless, I also saw how the enemy's rank were faltering and how they began rolling back.

"Bespal'ko is dead," "Bespal'ko is dead," "Bespal'ko is dead."

What is it? A dream? Is it gibberish?

I had to give way to a medic. For some reason, he had bandages in his hand that smelled of carbolic acid.

I checked my pulse and listened to the beating of my heart. "Killed." "Who was killed?" I asked. "Colonel Bespal'ko," he answered.

All sorts of things happen in war. Losses as upsetting as this one hardly ever take place on a daily basis. At the same time, it was impossible to become used to them, and each left a special ache in your heart. And how can you become resigned when a man who was your brother dies, a man with whom you shared extraordinary trust, with whom you shared blood and bread, and with whom you have marched together for so long through the fiery roads of war?

I lost consciousness . . .

After an operation and prolonged squabbling with doctors, I was not evacuated to the rear but instead remained in the division's medical battalion. I rested in bed in a small peasant house in the Moldavian village of Gortop. . . .

My chief of staff, Aleksandr Vasilevich Semenov, commanded the division in my absence, and combat raged in the bridgehead in the bend of the Dnestr.

On order of the army commander, the OP of Major General Nikolai Matveevich Makovchuk, the commander of our 34th Guards Rifle Corps, was transferred to this area.

The corps' units, which were being pressed from all sides by the advancing enemy, were defending with exceptional bravery but were also suffering heavy losses. Colonel Semenov, who had replaced me, had already been killed by day's end on 15 May, and Lieutenant Colonel Degtiarev, the artillery commander, had received a severe contusion.

On the night of 16 May, the Germans landed no fewer than two battalions of infantry ashore at the northern outskirts of the village of Koshnitsa, which was occupied by units of the 49th Guards Rifle Division. The enemy managed to cut the road to the village of Dorotskoe at the very [eastern] exit from the bend. This made the resupply of our forces with ammunition and other supplies quite difficult. It also became almost impossible to evacuate the wounded from the bridgehead.

The 203rd Rifle Division fought all day without a commander. Only at 1000 hours in the morning and under heavy artillery fire was the newly assigned division commander, Lieutenant Colonel Vasiliy Ivanovich Shorin, able to reach the 592nd Rifle Regiment's OP. However, within two hours he was killed during a bombing strike. Then, by order of the corps commander, Major Anton Mikhailovich Kolesnikov, the commander of the 592nd Rifle Regiment, was placed in command of the division's forces that were still situated in the bridgehead.

The enemy constructed a bridge at the northern outskirts of Koshnitsa on the night of 17 May. After crossing armored transporters and self-propelled guns, he began a decisive attack, supported by 16 gun, seven mortar, and two 6-barrel [*werfer*] batteries along with continuous bombing by aircraft during the morning, and he dissected the neck of the peninsula, encircling the 243rd and 203rd Rifle Divisions by 1200 hours.

The situation was perilous for the encircled units. Their ammunition and supplies were inadequate, and the number of wounded steadily increased. The inhabitants of Pererytoe did all they could for the soldiers; they fed them, bandaged them, and looked after those who were wounded.

The army headquarters tried to bring ammunition and supplies forward on armored transporters and tanks repeatedly, but this did not succeed.

After taking command of the encircled units, by using captured guns and ammunition, somehow Major Kolesnikov managed to create a firm defense under continuous enemy fire.

After satisfying themselves that they could not overcome the Soviet soldiers, the enemy began dropping leaflets on our positions that read, "The division is encircled. General Zdanovich is dead. Surrender! This leaflet will serve as a pass."

"Thank you for providing the toilet paper," the soldiers answered in utter contempt.

The Hitlerites captured Koshnitsa on 19 May. This forced the corps commander, General Makovchuk, to move to Kolesnikov's OP.

The fire raids conducted by the Fascists' artillery became even fiercer. It thinned out our infantry and put many guns out of action.

Many times, the crew of the 4th Battery, which was commanded by Sergeant Moskalenko, used their rifles and grenades to repel the enemy's attempts to seize the guns. The fragments from the exploding shells slaughtered all of the horses and wounded many of the soldiers.

Sergeant Moskalenko was killed during a new bombing strike, and someone from the ranks of the artillerymen then took command. By this time, the battery had only four shells per tube, each soldier had five to six rounds of ammunition, and there was one grenade for every two soldiers.

But the men did not falter. They stood to the death.

There was only one escape—to penetrate!

Therefore, after receiving permission from the army's military council, Major General Makovchuk ordered the forces to regroup on the night of 20 May and penetrate the enemy's defenses by launching a strong attack in the region at the neck of the bend.

A decisive battle was at hand. We had to assemble all of the personnel and weapons located on the peninsula into a single fist, bring forward the carts transporting the wounded and material, distribute the forces prior to the onset of darkness, and do so inconspicuously. The soldiers in the battalion of the 592nd Regiment led by the Komsomol' organizer, Lieutenant D. A. Chumachenko, were assigned the responsible combat mission of protecting the rear.

Before darkness fell, our artillery rained heavy fire down upon the concentration of enemy tanks east of Koshnitsa, and the *Katiushas* fired several volleys against the infantry, who were concealing themselves in the woods west of the village. The attack stunned the enemy and caused heavy casualties.

The encircled units completed their regrouping during this period. All of the wounded who could move took their places in the ranks. Those who could not move were laid on carts and the gun carriages.

Upon receipt of a prearranged signal, tightly encircling the carts, the field kitchens, and the guns harnessed to the horses, all of the soldiers of the 203rd and 243rd Divisions who were capable of carrying weapons advanced forward into the penetration with a powerful "Ura!"

The Hitlerites opened disorganized fire and then began fleeing in panic from the avalanche rushing toward them.

Our tanks were advancing in front of us. They crushed and crumbled the enemy's ambushes. One armored vehicle, which was not able to maneuver, slid down a steep precipice into the Dnestr River. Together with its crew, two famous officers in our division, Heroes of the Soviet Union and Captains I. T. Shikunov and G. I. Korneev, also perished. [This tank was extricated from the water in 1969 and installed as a monument to the fallen heroes at the former location of the division's OP.] Overwhelmed by surprise and the impetuosity of the penetration, many Hitlerites took cover in their foxholes and did not offer any sort of resistance.

The corps' main forces escaped from encirclement by 0100 hours on the night of 20 May. Almost all of the wounded, guns, and equipment were saved.

Major Kolesnikov was wounded during the penetration but did not leave the field of battle until he was satisfied that all of the soldiers of the 203rd were safely out. All, that is, except those who remained to cover the withdrawal. The 12 soldiers under the command of Komsomol' organizer Chumachenko did not manage to withdraw quickly enough behind the penetrating [escaping] units and remained in the bridgehead.

However, Soviet men do not lose heart, even in the most trying of situations. Three days later, the soldiers from Chumachenko's group returned to us. They hid in groves of trees during the day, and they advanced forward during the night. Using their bayonets, they soundlessly overcame the enemy's ambushes. Their path was not easy, but doggedness and will, as well as soldierly bravery, prevailed, and they returned to us.

Although 35 years have passed, I will never erase from my memory the division's intense struggle on the bridgehead in the bend of the Dnestr, which became the last for so many soldiers and officers.[28]

Placing this battle in proper context, while Knobelsdorff's panzer fist was attacking and compressing the bridgehead that Chuikov's 8th Guards Army was defending at Tashlyk, on 14 May the three divisions of Makovchuk's 34th Guards Rifle Corps from Tsvetaev's 5th Shock Army drove the *kampfgruppe* from the German 17th Infantry Division from its bridgehead defenses northwest of Grigoriopol' adjacent to Chuikov's right flank. Since this attack deprived Knobelsdorff of his valuable artillery and mortar firing positions north of the Tashlyk bridgehead, he ordered his forces to counterattack and drive the Soviet forces from their newly secured positions north of the Dnestr on his group's left flank.

To that end, Knobelsdorff ordered a *kampfgruppe* formed by Eichstadt's 294th Infantry Division to cross the Dnestr River near Staraia Dubossary and a *kampfgruppe* from Corps Detachment "F" to do the same from the north side of the river toward Koshnitsa. Once both forces were across the river, he planned to reinforce them with another *kampfgruppe* from Unrein's 14th Panzer Division and mount a concerted assault across the narrow waist of the river's salient to trap the Soviet forces in the region and restore the original German defense line between Pogrebia and Dorotskoe.

The ensuing battle developed just as Zdanovich described. After Knobelsdorff's successful initial assaults gained footholds on the southern and northern flanks of Makovchuk's defenses in the river salient, Tsvetaev reinforced Makovchuk's beleagured rifle corps on 17 and 18 May by sending Margelov's newly arrived 49th Guards Rifle Division from Rubaniuk's 10th Guards Rifle Corps to protect Makovchuk's right flank in the Koshnitsa region and Dorofeev's 295th Rifle Division from Zherebin's 32nd Rifle Corps, which was also just reaching the combat area, to reinforce Makovchuk's left wing near Dorotskoe. Despite these reinforcements, however, Makovchuk's defensive positions, which were subjected to intense and constant German fire from three sides, were essentially untenable. Therefore, the advancing Germans cut off the 34th Guards Rifle Corps' routes of withdrawal late on 19 May, forcing the remnants of Makovchuk's rifle corps to run a gauntlet of fire back to relative safety on the night of 19–20 May.

This short but exceedingly violent episode was over by 20 May. Despite the obvious bravery and valor of Makovchuk's forces, the appalling losses his rifle corps suffered during this battle seemed to epitomize the Red Army's frustrating experiences along the Dnestr River.

The 320th Rifle Division's Battle (13–14 May)

The third instance when a German force was able to perform the unique feat of penetrating and destroying a Red Army bridgehead and the forces defending it took place on 13 May. German forces defending in and around their strong points at Chebruchi and Raskaetsy struck back at Russian forces who were defending a nearby bridgehead the 5th Shock Army had seized in mid-April (Map 11 on p. 148). This defeat also marked the end of Malinovsky's many futile attempts to advance on Kishinev during May 1944.[29]

The target of this German assault was Major General I. I. Svygin's 320th Rifle Division, which had helped seize the bridgehead on the Dnestr's western bank east of Chebruchi on 18 April when it was subordinate to Makovchuk's 10th Guards Rifle Corps from Tsvetaev's 5th Shock Army. However, when Malinovsky reorganized and regrouped his *front*'s forces beginning on 6 May, he ordered Tsvetaev to transfer Svygin's rifle division together with its bridgehead sector from Makovchuk's rifle corps to Glagolev's 46th Army, which took over Tsvetaev's sector when the latter regrouped his forces northward to Grigoriopol'. In turn, Glagolev assigned Svygin's rifle division to Gorokhov's 37th Rifle Corps, which Malinovsky had just subordinated to his army, and tasked Gorokhov's corps with defending the Dnestr bridgeheads east and south of Chebruchi, on the 46th Army's right wing.

As a result, by the evening of 12 May, Svygin's 320th Rifle Division was defending a bridgehead 0.6–1.2 miles deep along a 1.8-mile-wide front in the low-lying marshlands along the Dnestr's western bank, flanked on its right by the 37th Rifle Corps' 108th Guards Rifle Division and on the left by the river itself and the remainder of the 46th Army. However, Svygin's defenses were particularly vulnerable because the defending Germans controlled all of the high ground to the west and southwest from which they could deliver fire against any point within the bridgehead with any and all types of weapons. The Germans also subjected the only crossing site linking the forces on the left and right banks of the river to a steady rain of artillery and machine-gun fire, which severely impeded a resupply of forces in the bridgehead with arms and ammunition. Compounding the 320th Rifle Division's difficulties, the Dnestr River and its adjacent marshes separated Svygin's bridgehead from those to the north and south.

The responsibility for organizing the German attack in this sector rested with Lieutenant General August Wittmann's 3rd Mountain Division of the Sixth Army's XXX Army Corps, which was defending the Talmazy and Chebruchi sector of the Soviets' bridgehead at Tiraspol', and *kampfgruppen* organized by the remnants of the XXIX Army Corps' 9th, 258th, and 76th Infantry Divisions, which were defending the sector from Chebruchi southward past Raskaetsy. The German attack plan called for *kampfgruppen* from all four forces to launch converging assaults against the Soviets' bridgehead defenses, to collapse those defenses, and to trap and destroy the Soviet forces against the western bank of the Dnestr.

After a powerful 50-minute artillery preparation, which began at 0330 hours on 13 May, the combined German force struck Svygin's defenses at

0420 hours with an infantry assault (in reality, a reconnaissance-in-force), supported by a few tanks and assault guns. Although Svygin's riflemen managed to repulse the initial German assault with heavy answering fires and forced the attackers to fall back to their jumping-off positions, the Germans began a fresh artillery preparation at 0600 hours and resumed their assaults at 0700 hours with a force the defenders estimated as two full infantry regiments supported by numerous assault guns. These assaults emanated from three directions, Chebruchi, Raskaetsy, and the sector directly opposite the boundary between Svygin's 478th and 481st Rifle Regiments, which were defending in his rifle division's first echelon.[30]

The Germans' effective artillery fire disrupted the communications between Svygin's two forward rifle regiments, which, due to the pressure from the attacking German infantry, had no choice but to give ground grudgingly. At the same time, the assault by the 3rd Mountain Division's *kampfgruppe*, which struck due east toward the river through the rifle regiment of Svygin's right wing, reached the river's bank, cut the bridgehead into two distinct parts, and separated Svygin's rifle division from the 108th Guards Rifle Division on its right, preventing the latter from reinforcing the former. With the Germans' assaults also making progress in the center, by 0800 hours the bridgehead shrank further in size, forcing the defenders' backs literally to the riverbank. Unable to maneuver, Svygin's riflemen became even more vulnerable to the steadily increasing volume of German fire. German aircraft then appeared over the battlefield, inflicting further casualties on the defenders.

At 0930 hours, the attacking German *kampfgruppen* intensified their fires and succeeded in destroying Svygin's crossing site over the Dnestr River, while German infantry encircled the increasingly desperate defenders. Faced with a hopeless situation, the riflemen displayed "unmatched bravery, as the heroes literally fought to their last bullet." Although the fighting lasted for two more hours, the die was already cast. By day's end, the Germans completely destroyed Svygin's 478th and 481st Rifle Regiments, although elements of his third regiment managed to escape across the river by swimming. According to Soviet archival documents, "Major General I. I. Shvygin, the division commander, together with other members of the division's command group, died valiantly on the field of battle while inspiring his soldiers."[31] Shvygin had commanded the 320th Rifle Division since 7 July 1943 and led it during all of the 3rd Ukrainian Front's major offensives through the Donbas region and southern Ukraine.

The short, violent, but decisive German assault against the 320th Rifle Division ended the Sixth Army's May counterstrokes along the Dnestr River. Through tremendous exertions and at considerable risk, somehow de Angelis's Sixth Army had managed to overcome the crippling effects of its March and early April defeats in the Ukraine and at Odessa to withstand Malinovsky's repeated attempts to force the Dnestr River and capture Kishinev. Furthermore, in addition to meeting these daunting challenges, it was able to capitalize on Malinovsky's mistakes by inflicting two grievous and almost unprecedented defeats on Malinovsky's forces. At least in part, this feat alone delayed another Red Army offensive in the region for another three months.

CONCLUSIONS

The counterstrokes de Angelis's Sixth Army conducted against Malinovsky's 3rd Ukrainian Front along the Dnestr River proved effective, timely, and ultimately decisive with regard to the *Stavka*'s intent to resume major offensive operations deep into Romania during May 1944. Strategically, while Konev's defeat in the Tirgu Frumos region during early May actually encouraged the *Stavka* to try to mount an even larger-scale offensive later in the month with both Konev's and Malinovsky's *fronts,* the setbacks that Malinovsky's forces experienced at Tashlyk and west of Grigoriopol' during mid-May ended once and for all any hopes the *Stavka* entertained for resuming offensive operations with its two Ukrainian *fronts* deeper into Romania and the Balkans later during the spring.

Operationally, Group Knobelsdorff's well-planned, exquisitely coordinated, and effective counterstroke severely damaged Malinovsky's two strongest armies—Chuikov's 8th Guards and Tsvetaev's 5th Shock—and shattered the confidence of Malinovsky and the 3rd Ukrainian Front's command cadre. Catching the Soviets by surprise, the assaults inflicted heavy casualties on Chuikov's 8th Guards Army and probably caused considerable casualties in the withdrawing divisions of Zhadov's 5th Guards Army as well. More important still, the German assault recaptured well over half of the Soviets' Tashlyk bridgehead, depriving them of their most important launching pad for any future offensives toward Kishinev.

Although the Soviets have yet to account for the casualties their forces suffered during these operations, the 14th Panzer Division alone recorded capturing 3,050 Red Army soldiers, seven tanks and assault guns, 447 artillery pieces, 193 grenade launchers, 380 machine guns, 106 flamethrowers, and 102 antitank rifles.[32] Given the normal ratio of captured to dead and wounded and the fact that the 14th Panzer Division constituted less than one-sixth of Knobelsdorff's attacking force, it is likely that Chuikov suffered as many as 30,000 casualties, or roughly one-fourth of his army's personnel. After suffering such heavy casualties and equally heavy losses of weapons and other equipment, it would be weeks if not months before the 8th Guards Army would be fit to spearhead another offensive operation.

By ordering Tsvetaev's 5th Shock Army to intervene on Chuikov's behalf by attacking the German bridgehead north of Grigoriopol' on 14 May, Malinovsky provided the German Sixth Army with yet another opportunity to score another operational coup de main. Counterattacking into a virtually untenable cul-de-sac with one-third of his army, Tsvetaev's army fell victim to another German counterstroke, which decimated three rifle divisions from his army's 34th Guards Rifle Corps and severely damaged two more divisions from his other two rifle corps. Although his army's casualties are also unknown, it is likely the 5th Shock Army lost as many as 20,000 men dead, wounded, missing, or captured. As a result, Tsvetaev's army too was no longer capable of conducting further offensive operations until it was thoroughly rested and refitted.

Finally, the XXX and XXIX Army Corps' assaults on the hapless 320th Rifle Division in the bridgehead at Chebruchi destroyed this division, inflicted another 5,000 casualties on the defending Soviets, and severely truncated Malinovsky's bridgehead south of Tiraspol', all the while further undermining the confidence of his *front*'s command cadre and soldiers.

Tactically, the Sixth Army's counterstrokes were notable in several important respects. First, German intelligence organs were able to detect Malinovsky's intent and actions in timely enough fashion for the army to undertake effective countermeasures. In addition to divining Malinovsky's attack plans, the Sixth Army kept track well enough of his force regroupings to be able to launch their assaults at the most critical moment, when the Soviet forces were regrouping and, hence, were most vulnerable.

Second, as was the case with Army Group Wöhler's defense at Tirgu Frumos, the Sixth Army was able to reorganize its seriously depleted, understrength, and bone-tired panzer and infantry divisions into numerous small but flexible and effective *kampfgruppen*, maneuver these *kampfgruppen* effectively, and concentrate and employ them with deadly effect. Third, and perhaps most important, despite the serious defeats the German Sixth Army suffered in the southern Ukraine, at Odessa, and during its withdrawal to the Dnestr River, and despite the Soviets' consistently clear numerical superiority in infantry, tanks, and artillery throughout the entire battle along the Dnestr River, the morale of de Angelis's troops remained high and, however understrength his corps and divisions became, the regiments, battalions, and companies within them remained highly cohesive forces.

Most important of all from Army Group South Ukraine's perspective, the timing and the effectiveness of the German Sixth Army's counterstrokes could not have been more ideal. Just as Wöhler's defeat of Konev's forces at Tirgu Frumos during early May convinced the *Stavka* to postpone further offensive operations into Romania until late May, de Angelis's victory over Malinovsky's forces during mid-May forced Stalin and the *Stavka* to postpone any further offensive action in the region until August 1944.

Table 7.1. The 3rd Ukrainian Front's Order of Battle on 1 May 1944
3rd UKRAINIAN FRONT:
Army General R. Ia. Malinovsky

57th Army: Lieutenant General N. A. Gagen
- 9th Rifle Corps: MG I. P. Roslyi
  - 118th Rifle Division
  - 230th Rifle Division
  - 301st Rifle Division
- 64th Rifle Corps: MG M. B. Anashkin (MG I. K. Kravtsov on 9 May)
  - 73rd Guards Rifle Division
  - 19th Rifle Division
  - 52nd Rifle Division
- 68th Rifle Corps: MG N. N. Mul'tan
  - 93rd Rifle Division
  - 113th Rifle Division
  - 223rd Rifle Division
- 93rd Separate Antitank Rifle Battalion
- 96th Tank Brigade

37th Army: Lieutenant General M. N. Sharokhin
- 6th Guards Rifle Corps: MG G. P. Kotov
  - 20th Guards Rifle Division
  - 195th Rifle Division
- 57th Rifle Corps: MG F. A. Ostashenko
  - 10th Guards Airborne Division
  - 15th Guards Rifle Division
  - 58th Guards Rifle Division
  - 228th Rifle Division
- 82nd Rifle Corps: MG P. G. Kuznetsov
  - 28th Guards Rifle Division
  - 92nd Guards Rifle Division
  - 188th Rifle Division
- 864th Self-propelled Artillery Regiment

46th Army: Lieutenant General V. V. Glagolev
- 31st Guards Rifle Corps: MG A. I. Ruchkin (MG S. S. Bobruk on 28 May)
  - 4th Guards Rifle Division
  - 34th Guards Rifle Division
  - 40th Guards Rifle Division
- 32nd Rifle Corps: MG D. S. Zherebin
  - 60th Guards Rifle Division
  - 259th Rifle Division
- 34th Rifle Corps: MG I. S. Kosobutsky
  - 236th Rifle Division
  - 266th Rifle Division
  - 353rd Rifle Division
  - 394th Rifle Division

8th Guards Army: Colonel General V.I. Chuikov
- 4th Guards Rifle Corps: LTG V. F. Glazunov
  - 35th Guards Rifle Division
  - 47th Guards Rifle Division
  - 57th Guards Rifle Division
- 28th Guards Rifle Corps: MG S. I. Morozov
  - 39th Guards Rifle Division
  - 79th Guards Rifle Division
  - 88th Guards Rifle Division
- 29th Guards Rifle Corps: LTG Ia. S. Fokanov
  - 27th Guards Rifle Division
  - 74th Guards Rifle Division
  - 82nd Guards Rifle Division
- 1st Guards Fortified Region
- 5th Guards Separate Tank Regiment

6th Army: Lieutenant General I. T. Shlemin
- 34th Guards Rifle Corps: MG N. M. Makovchuk
  - 59th Guards Rifle Division
  - 61st Guards Rifle Division
  - 243rd Rifle Division
- 66th Rifle Corps: MG D. A. Kupriianov
  - 203rd Rifle Division
  - 244th Rifle Division
  - 333rd Rifle Division

5th Shock Army: Colonel General V. D. Tsvetaev
- 10th Guards Rifle Corps: MG I. A. Rubaniuk
  - 86th Guards Rifle Division
  - 109th Guards Rifle Division
  - 320th Rifle Division
- 37th Rifle Corps: MG S. F. Gorokhov (MG F. S. Kolchuk on 28 May)
  - 49th Guards Rifle Division
  - 108th Guards Rifle Division
  - 248th Rifle Division
- 295th Rifle Division
- 416th Rifle Division

Cavalry-Mechanized Group: Lieutenant General I. A. Pliev
- 4th Guards Mechanized Corps: MGTF V. I. Zhdanov
  - 13th Guards Mechanized Brigade

Table 7.1. *Continued*

14th Guards Mechanized Brigade
15th Guards Mechanized Brigade
36th Guards Tank Brigade
292nd Guards Self-propelled Artillery Regiment
62nd Motorcycle Battalion
1512th Tank Destroyer Regiment
748th Separate Tank Destroyer Artillery Battalion
129th Guards-Mortar Battalion
4th Guards Cavalry Corps: LTG I. A. Pliev
9th Guards Cavalry Division
10th Guards Cavalry Division
30th Cavalry Division
128th Separate Tank Regiment
134th Separate Tank Regiment
151st Separate Tank Regiment
1815th Self-propelled Artillery Regiment
152nd Guards Tank Destroyer Regiment
4th Guards Separate Tank Destroyer Battalion
68th Guards-Mortar Battalion
12th Guards-Mortar Regiment
255th Antiaircraft Artillery Regiment

17th Air Army: ColGAv V. A. Sudets
1st Mixed Aviation Corps: MGAv V. I. Shevchenko
5th Guards Assault Aviation Division
288th Fighter Aviation Division
9th Mixed Aviation Corps: LTGAv O. V. Tolstikov
305th Assault Aviation Division
306th Assault Aviation Division
295th Fighter Aviation Division
244th Bomber Aviation Division
262nd Fighter-Bomber Aviation Division
371st Fighter-Bomber Aviation Regiment
39th Reconnaissance Aviation Regiment
96th Corrective-Reconnaissance Aviation Regiment
282nd Sep. Signal Aviation Regiment
3rd Medical Aviation Regiment
14th Aviation Regiment, Civil Air Fleet

Front Reserves:
10th Separate Automatic Weapons Battalion
2nd Guards Mechanized Corps: LTG K. V. Sviridov
4th Guards Mechanized Brigade
5th Guards Mechanized Brigade
6th Guards Mechanized Brigade
37th Guards Tank Brigade
23rd Guards Tank Regiment
24th Guards Tank Regiment
25th Guards Tank Regiment
99th Motorcycle Battalion
1509th Tank Destroyer Regiment
744th Separate Tank Destroyer Artillery Battalion
408th Guards-Mortar Battalion
23rd Tank Corps: MGTF A. O. Akhmanov
3rd Tank Brigade
39th Tank Brigade
135th Tank Brigade
56th Motorized Rifle Brigade
1443rd Self-propelled Artillery Regiment
82nd Motorcycle Battalion
1501st Tank Destroyer Artillery Regiment
457th Mortar Regiment
442nd Guards-Mortar Battalion
1697th Antiaircraft Artillery Regiment
5th Guards Motorized Rifle Brigade
28th Guards Separate Tank Regiment
52nd Separate Tank Regiment
398th Guards Heavy Self-propelled Artillery Regiment
1200th Self-propelled Artillery Regiment
1201st Self-propelled Artillery Regiment
1202nd Self-propelled Artillery Regiment
1891st Self-propelled Artillery Regiment
3rd Guards Motorcycle Regiment
53rd Motorcycle Regiment
67th Motorcycle Battalion
22nd Separate Armored Train Battalion
26th Separate Armored Train Battalion
28th Separate Armored Train Battalion

Source: *Boevoi sostav Sovetskoi armii, Chast' 4 (Ianvar'-dekabr' 1944)* [The combat composition of the Soviet Army, Part 4 (January–December 1944)] (Moscow: Voenizdat, 1988), 139–140.

3rd Ukrainian Front troops on the Soviet-Romanian border

Soviet troops advancing during the spring *rasputitsa* (period of rains)

3rd Ukrainian Front's tanks on the attack

3rd Ukrainian Front's forces crossing the Dnestr River

Colonel General I. V. Chuikov, commander, 8th Guards Army, issuing orders in the field

Hero of the Soviet Union Captain Vasilii Grigor'evich Zaitsev, famed sniper at Stalingrad and commander of an antiaircraft battery in the 8th Guards Army

Major General A. I. Rodimtsev, commander, 32nd Guards Rifle Corps, 5th Guards Army (on the right) with Major General A. I. Oleinikov, commander, 95th Guards Rifle Division, at the division's observation post along the Dnestr River

Lieutenant General V. D. Tsvetaev, commander, 5th Shock Army (second from the left), planning the offensive

Army General F. I. Tolbukhin, commander, 3rd Ukrainian Front (on the right), with Lieutenant General S. S. Biriuzov, his chief of staff (center), and Georgii Dimitrov, head of the Bulgarian Communist Party (on the left)

CHAPTER 8

Denouement (30 May–6 June 1944)

SOVIET PLANNING TO 26 MAY

The *Stavka*'s Plans

In the wake of Army Group Wöhler's defeat of Konev's 2nd Ukrainian Front at Tirgu Frumos and in the midst of the German Sixth Army's counterstrokes against Malinovsky's 3rd Ukrainian Front along the Dnestr River, Stalin and his *Stavka* abruptly reshuffled the command cadre in their Ukrainian *fronts*. On 15 May they ordered Malinovsky to replace Konev as the commander of the 2nd Ukrainian Front, effective 24 May, and Army General F. I. Tolbukhin, the commander of the 4th Ukrainian Front, whose forces had just completed liberating the Crimea, to replace Malinovsky as the commander of the 3rd Ukrainian Front, effective 22 May (see Appendix). In addition, the *Stavka* order relieved Lieutenant General S. S. Biriuzov from his duties as chief of staff of the 4th Ukrainian Front, appointed him as the 3rd Ukrainian Front's chief of staff, effective 20 May, and reassigned Lieutenant General F. K. Korzhenevich, the 3rd Ukrainian Front's previous chief of staff, as chief of staff of the new 4th Ukrainian Front.[1]

In its directive, the *Stavka* asserted it made these changes so that Marshal of the Soviet Union G. K. Zhukov, who had been serving as commander of the 1st Ukrainian Front throughout April and May, would be available "to direct the operations of several *fronts* in the future," presumably meaning the summer campaign. In addition, however, the *Stavka* wanted to assign Konev, whom it correctly believed was one of its most capable and effective *front* commanders, to command its 1st Ukrainian Front, whose forces faced the German defenses in eastern Poland. At the time, the *Stavka* and General Staff were beginning to plan their summer offensive, which was to begin in late June and early July with major offensives, first, into central Belorussia and, about two weeks later, into eastern Poland. Supposedly, Stalin wanted his best *front* commanders, K. K. Rokossovsky and I. S. Konev, to command the 1st Belorussian and 1st Ukrainian Fronts, his largest, most powerful, and most capable *fronts* spearheading his critical summer offensive.

Consequently, in addition to receiving command of Konev's 2nd Ukrainian Front, Malinovsky also inherited the plans Konev had already formulated and begun implementing for yet another offensive toward Iasi and, with these plans, another opportunity for Malinovsky to redeem his bruised pride after the setbacks he experienced along the Dnestr River.

However, whatever hopes Malinovsky harbored about achieving an offensive victory turned out to be short-lived. The day before he took command of his new *front* and only three days after the intense fighting died out along the Dnestr River, on 23 May the *Stavka* issued a new directive postponing the date the 2nd and 3rd Ukrainian Fronts were to be prepared to conduct a new offensive for seven days, that is, from 25 May to 1 June 1944. Worse still from Malinovsky's perspective, three days later the *Stavka* sent him another directive, this time postponing both his and Tolbukhin's offensives indefinitely.

Signed by Stalin and dated 0235 hours on 26 May, the *Stavka*'s new directive ordered Malinovsky's *front*, "to postpone the period of readiness for the attack until receipt of special orders from the *Stavka*. The *fronts'* forces will reliably defend their occupied positions with strong second echelons and reserves."[2] Confirming its decision to halt offensive operations in northern Romania, the next day the *Stavka* ordered Rotmistrov to regroup his 5th Guards Tank Army northward to eastern Belorussia, where the *Stavka* planned to employ it to spearhead its new summer offensive in that region.

In effect, this directive, plus the departure of Rotmistrov's 5th Guards Tank Army for Belorussia, placed all offensive operations by the 2nd and 3rd Ukrainian Fronts on hold until further notice. However, the extensive regrouping of forces that Konev had begun as early as 6 May in order to prepare his *front*'s forces for their new offensive in the Iasi region attracted the attention of German Eighth Army's intelligence organs, prompting both it and its parent Army Group Wöhler to prepare plans and forces to meet and defeat the anticipated Soviet threat.

After receiving the *Stavka*'s approval on 6 May to begin preparations for a new offensive in the Iasi region later in the month, Konev ordered Zhadov's 5th Guards Army to turn its bridgehead at Tashlyk over to Malinovsky's 3rd Ukrainian Front and regroup its forces into new assembly areas northeast of Iasi. Initially at least, the 5th Guards Army was supposed to be ready to conduct offensive operations by 25 May. Thereafter, however, the German Sixth Army's counterstrokes along the Dnestr River delayed the departure of Zhadov's army from the Tashlyk region since many of its rifle divisions had to exit the bridgehead under German fire. Ultimately, Zhadov's guards army did not begin concentrating in the region northeast of Iasi until 15 May and did not complete its concentration into its new assembly areas until the first week in June. Inevitably, along with other factors, this delay forced the *Stavka* to postpone the start date of the new offensive, first until 1 June, and later indefinitely.

Konev's Plans

While Zhadov's army was slowly en route to its new assembly areas, immediately after his defeat at Tirgu Frumos, Konev ordered Bogdanov and Trofimenko to regroup their 2nd Tank and 27th Armies eastward from the Tirgu Frumos region and concentrate them in new assembly areas north and northwest of Iasi (Map 22). Once in their new locations, the two armies were to attack the German defenses north of Iasi in cooperation with Koroteev's 52nd Army and a portion of Kravchenko's 6th Tank Army, either on 25 May or shortly after that date. In outline form, Konev's offensive plan called for the formation of a new shock group consisting of Trofimenko's 27th, Koroteev's 52nd, and Zhadov's 5th Guards Armies, supported by all of the armor available to Bogdanov's and Kravchenko's 2nd and 6th Tank Armies. Once formed, this shock group was to assault the German defenses along a 20-mile-wide front that extended from north of Podu Iloaie eastward north of Iasi to the Prut River.

On the left wing of Konev's new shock group, the 48th and 73rd Rifle Corps of Koroteev's 52nd Army, supported by armored combat groups from Kravchenko's 6th Tank Army, were to assault and penetrate the German defenses in the nine-mile-wide sector that extended from the village of Vulturi, six miles north of Iasi, eastward to the Prut River northeast of Iasi. Once it became available for action, Zhadov's 5th Guards Army was to reinforce and exploit the 52nd and 6th Tank Armies' assault, capture Iasi, and exploit southward to seize the sector of the Strunga Defense Line 10–15 miles due south of Iasi.

On the shock group's right wing, the 33rd Rifle and 35th Guards Rifle Corps of Trofimenko's 27th Army, for the first time operating together as a concentrated force, supported by the 3rd and 16th Tank Corps of Bogdanov's 2nd Tank Army, were to attack and penetrate the German defenses in the 11-mile-wide sector extending from Avantul, six miles northeast of Podu Iloaie, eastward to Vulturi; capture Podu Iloaie and envelop German forces in Iasi from the west; and exploit southward to seize the sector of the Strunga Defense Line 8–13 miles south and southeast of Podu Iloaie.

In addition, Konev ordered Major General E. S. Alekhin's 27th Guards Rifle Corps, which had been in his *front*'s reserve in the Botoshany region far to the rear, to regroup to the Iasi region and support the 52nd and 27th Armies' assaults. The 27th Guards Rifle Corps' combat journal duly recorded:

> During the first half of May 1944, the 27th Guards Rifle Corps was situated in the 2nd Ukrainian Front commander's reserve and was occupied with combat preparations and training. Beginning at 2000 hours on 14 May 1944, it was assigned to the 27th Army in accordance with an enciphered telegram from the 2nd Ukrainian Front commander.[3]

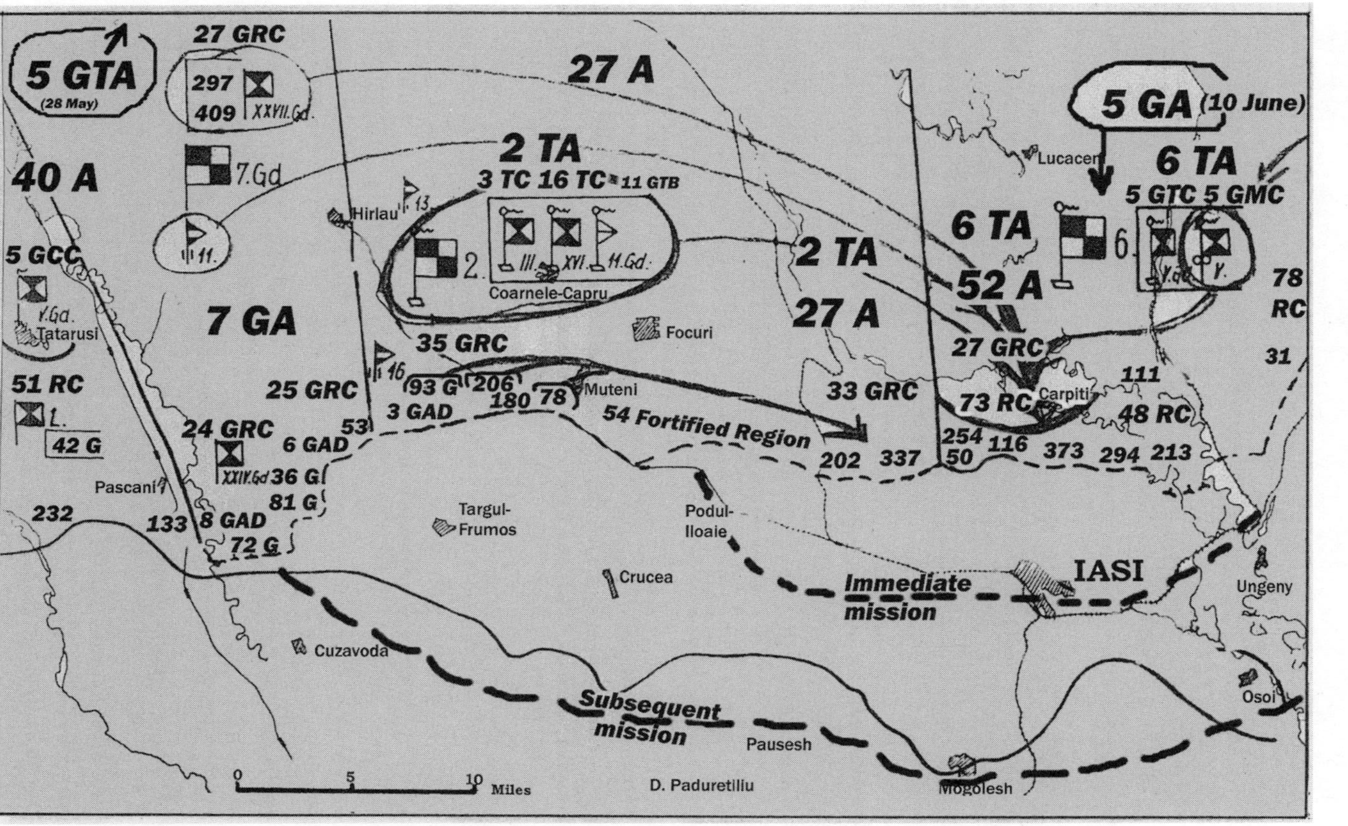

Map 22. The situation in the Tirgu Frumos and Iasi sectors and the 2nd Ukrainian Front's Plan and Regrouping, 24 May

Finally, although no records have been released to clarify the matter, at least prior to 27 May when it departed for eastern Belorussia, the *Stavka* may also have planned to support Konev's offensive with elements of Rotmistrov's 5th Guards Tank Army.

Konev's new offensive plan assigned the five armies constituting his shock group the immediate mission of seizing the Podu Iloaie and Iasi line and the city of Iasi and the subsequent mission of clearing all Axis forces from the region stretching from the Tirgu Frumos region eastward to the Prut River south of Iasi and seizing a significant portion of the Axis' Strunga Defense Line further to the south. From the standpoint of the correlation of opposing forces in the Iasi region, once Konev reinforced his shock group in the Iasi region with his 5th Guards Army and 27th Guards Rifle Corps, the *Stavka* believed Konev's *front* was certainly strong enough to achieve these objectives, which were far more limited in nature than the objectives it had assigned to his forces in its previous offensives. In fact, despite the impending departure of the 5th Guards Tank Army, the seven armies, 18 rifle corps, and 56 rifle or airborne divisions Konev's *front* had at its disposal on 1 June were virtually identical to the *front*'s composition on 1 May (see Table 8.1 at chapter's end). Furthermore, Konev would be conducting his offensive against Iasi in late May with a shock group of five armies, whereas he had conducted his offensive at Tirgu Frumos in early May with a force of four armies.

Although the *Stavka* postponed the 2nd Ukrainian Front's offensive against Iasi indefinitely within days after Malinovsky took command, for the most part, his new *front* had already carried out the massive force regroupings called for by Konev's previous offensive plan. Unfortunately for Malinovsky, as had been the case along the Dnestr in mid-May, the German Eighth Army's intelligence organs had already detected his *front*'s extensive regrouping and, unaware of the *Stavka*'s change of heart, assumed it was associated with Soviet preparations for a fresh offensive. Armed with this knowledge, and aware of the Sixth Army's recent success along the Dnestr River, Wöhler's Eighth Army had no choice but to react to its intelligence and prepare to disrupt the anticipated Soviet offensive.

ARMY GROUP WÖHLER'S IASI COUNTERSTROKE (30 MAY–5 JUNE 1944)

Army Group Wöhler's Offensive Plan

As described by one of the few histories detailing Army Group South's and Army Group South Ukraine's wartime operations:

> The Eighth Army's commander [General Wöhler] worked out a plan, which included an offensive operation with limited objectives north of Jassy.

> The attack by the Eighth Army's units began completely unexpectedly on 30 May after a short fire preparation. Thus, the Wehrmacht's only major offensive operation on the Eastern Front during 1944 began. During the beginning of the battle, the Luftwaffe also managed to assemble strong air formations and attacked during the early morning hours and achieved air superiority for several hours.[4]

Although this account overlooks the victories de Angelis's Sixth Army achieved along the Dnestr River only a week before, it certainly underscores the unique nature of Wöhler's offensive north of Iasi.

As of 24 May, Army Group Wöhler's German Eighth Army was defending the Iasi region with Group Mieth, a composite group headquarters consisting of the Romanian IV and German IV Army Corps, whose defensive sector extended roughly 40 miles from the vicinity of the village of Spinoasa, six miles northwest of Podu Iloaie, eastward across the Prut River, nine miles northeast of Iasi, to the Korneshty region, on the Iasi-Kishinev railroad line 16 miles east of the Prut River (Map 23). On Group Mieth's left wing, the Romanian 18th Mountain Division manned defenses in the 13-mile-wide sector from Spinoasa eastward to Tautesti, eight miles northwest of Iasi, and, in Group Mieth's center, the Romanian 3rd and 11th Infantry Divisions, respectively, defended the four- and nine-mile-wide sectors between Tautesti and Vulturi and Vulturi to the Prut River. On Group Mieth's right wing east of the Prut River, the German 376th Infantry Division manned defenses in the 16-mile-wide sector from the river northeast to Korneshty. Finally, Group Mieth retained the German 79th Infantry and Romanian 5th Cavalry Divisions in tactical reserve in the Iasi region, and the 23rd Panzer Division, which had been assigned to Group Mieth but was now in the Eighth Army's reserve, was still situated in the Iasi region.

At the same time, the Eighth Army's LVII Panzer Corps, whose headquarters was still in the city of Roman, defended the approaches to Tirgu Frumos with its *Grossdeutschland* Panzer Grenadier and 46th Infantry Divisions, which were defending north and northeast of the town, and the SS *"T"* Panzer Division, which was defending the sector from Tirgu-Frumos westward to the Seret River. The LVII Panzer Corps retained the 24th Panzer Division in its reserve in assembly areas around and south of Tirgu-Frumos, and the Romanian V Army Corps defended the sector from south of Focuri eastward to north of Sarca on the LVII Panzer Corps' right wing with its 1st Infantry Division.

So configured, the Army Group Wöhler's Eighth Army defended the Tirgu Frumos and Iasi regions with German forces deployed forward in the most threatened sectors, with its Romanian divisions manning less important

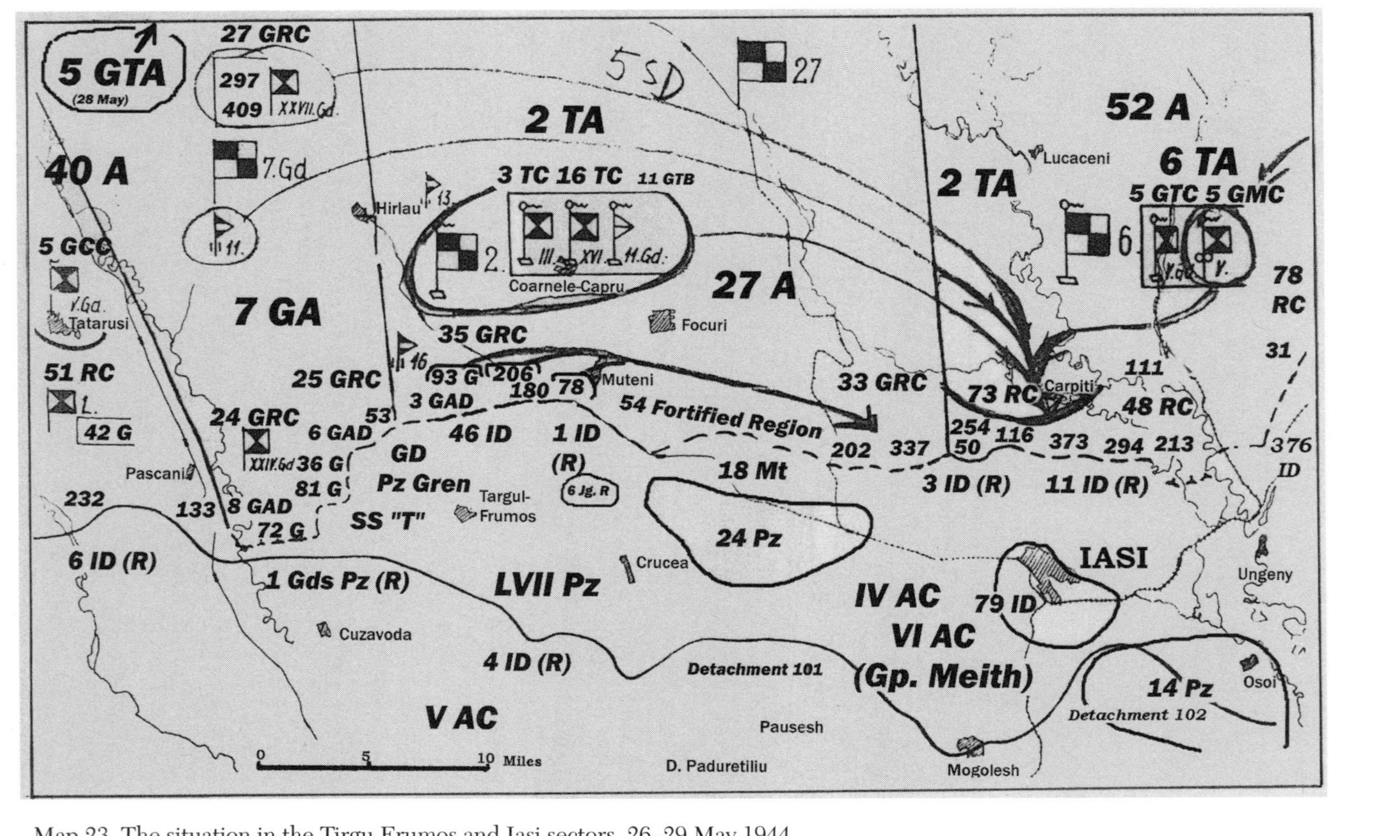

Map 23. The situation in the Tirgu Frumos and Iasi sectors, 26–29 May 1944

sectors, and with two panzer divisions, the 23rd and 24th, in tactical or operational reserve in the vicinity of Iasi and Tirgu Frumos.

As early as 24 May, the Eighth Army's intelligence organs began detecting signs that the Soviets were regrouping their forces from the Tirgu Frumos region eastward and from the region east of the Dnestr River westward into the region north of Iasi.[5] After four days of collection and collating intelligence data, the full scope and presumed intent of this regrouping became quite apparent. By day's end on 28 May, for example, the Eighth Army's Ic (intelligence officer) assessed that the Soviets either had already transferred or were in the process of transferring the 2nd Tank Army, the 27th Army's 35th Guards Rifle Corps, and five additional rifle divisions, including those belonging to the 27th Guards Rifle Corps, from the region north of Tirgu Frumos eastward to new assembly areas north of Iasi. During the same period, it also began detecting the transfer of the entire Soviet 5th Guards Army and, presumably, portions of the 4th Guards and 53rd Armies as well, from the Dnestr River front to the region northeast of Iasi. In terms of its scale, these intelligence organs assessed this regrouping involved at least 11 rifle divisions, two tank corps, and one tank brigade.

From its vantage point north of Tirgu Frumos, Manteuffel's *Grossdeutschland* Panzer Grenadier Division also confirmed the Soviets' attack preparations, described in part in the Eighth Army's pending counteraction:

> By the end of May Romania was ripe for further trouble. Aerial reconnaissance believed it had detected a shifting of enemy forces from the area northwest of Targul Frumos into the area northwest of Jassy, which suggested that they had new offensive intentions. The Soviets were searching for a German weak spot. This shifting of forces by the enemy resulted in the division command dispatching armoured patrols provided by the Armoured Reconnaissance Battalion GD into the area northwest of Jassy to determine the enemy's intentions. The patrols discovered a massing of enemy forces in the area north of Letcani [ten miles west of Iasi], very close to the Jassy–Targul Frumos highway. Something was brewing opposite the positions of the 46th Infantry Division. For a ridge was the only thing separating these positions from the highway, which was so vital to the German supply organization.
>
> The direct threat posed to Jassy, the dangerous proximity of enemy positions to the highway and the apparent attack preparations in the gorges and ravines to the north forced the German command to take countermeasures. The Panzer-Grenadier Division GD received orders to immediately withdraw from its present combat zone and attack north from the area due south of Podul-Ilaoie, Danian and Letcani.[6]

While the Germans' assessment of the scale and destination of this regrouping was essentially correct, they could not have realized that the *Stavka* had already altered and finally abandoned their plans for an offensive.

Prudently assuming that a major Soviet offensive was imminent, the Eighth Army reflected on what the Sixth Army had been able to achieve during its counterstrokes along the Dnestr River in mid-May and decided to attempt to replicate the Sixth Army's prodigious feats. Therefore, Wöhler decided to form a large panzer shock group, concentrate it in the Iasi region, and employ it to attack and destroy the Soviet troop concentration north of Iasi. At the time, Soviet forces had crossed the Jijia River, which flowed from the Focuri region, ten miles north of Podu Iloaie, eastward 15 miles past the town of Carpiti (Cirpiti), on the northern bank of the Jijia ten miles north of Iasi, and then southeastward parallel to and roughly three miles west of the Prut River before joining the Prut River about 20 miles southeast of Iasi. Thus, Soviet forces had occupied a virtual bridgehead extending from east to west roughly halfway (four miles) between the Jijia River and Podu Iloaie and Iasi. Thus, although Wöhler's counterstroke was essentially preemptive in nature, since it sought to drive Soviet forces from their bridgehead and back north across the Jijia River, the planned counterstroke also incorporated important concrete territorial objectives.

Specifically, while the Eighth Army's panzer shock group was to destroy the Soviet forces concentrated north of Iasi before they could launch their offensive against the city, the counterstroke also sought to destroy the Soviet bridgehead north of Iasi by recapturing the entire region between the Jijia River and Iasi proper from the village of Polingeni, on the southern bank of the Jijia River ten miles north of Podu Iloaie, in the west to the Cirpiti region, ten miles north of Iasi, in the east. To accomplish this task, the Eighth Army's forces would have to penetrate the Soviet defenses and advance northward a distance of only four to five miles. If successful, in addition to forestalling a probable Soviet offensive, the counterstroke would also drive the Soviet forces back roughly ten miles from Iasi proper and from the key road and railroad lines that extended from Iasi westward to Podu Iloaie, eliminate the Soviets' bridgehead north of Iasi, and provide more suitable terrain to defend Iasi in the future.

Pursuant to this plan, to form its requisite shock group the Eighth Army regrouped its forces in distinct stages between 26 and 29 May. First, Army Group Wöhler released Kräber's 23rd Panzer Division to Group Mieth's control and also reinforced Group Mieth with Edelsheim's 24th Panzer Division from the LVII Panzer Corps and Unrein's 14th Panzer Division, which the German Army High Command (OKH) had just transferred from the Sixth to the Eighth Army. In addition, Wöhler alerted Manteuffel's *Grossdeutschland* Panzer Grenadier Division to be prepared to turn its defensive sector at

Tirgu Frumos over to the 46th Infantry and SS *"T"* Panzer Divisions on 31 May and move eastward to the Podu Iloaie sector to join the counterstroke by attacking northward on the shock group's left wing. Ultimately, the 14th Panzer Division reached the Iasi region late on 26 May, and the 24th Panzer Division closed into assembly areas north of Iasi late on 29 May. The *Grossdeutschland* Division followed, concentrating in the Podu Iloaie region between 31 May and 1 June and occupying attack positions north of Letcani, midway between Podu Iloaie and Iasi, late on 1 June.

The Eighth Army planned to conduct its counterstroke in two distinct operational phases, which it assigned twin codenames: Operations "Sonja" and "Katja." During Operation Sonja, which was to begin at dawn on 30 May, *kampfgruppen* formed by Edelsheim's 24th and Kraber's 23rd Panzer Divisions, which were deployed from left to right (west to east) abreast in the four-mile-wide sector between the village of Redui Aldei, five miles north of Iasi, and the western bank of the Jijia River, six miles northeast of Iasi, were to assault the Soviet defenses from jumping-off positions along the ridges that ran from north to south east of Redui Aldei. Supported by Lieutenant General Friedrich-August Weinknecht's 79th Infantry Division, which was operating on the panzer shock group's left flank, after their *kampfgruppen* penetrated the Soviets' forward defenses, the two panzer divisions were to advance northwestward, then capture Hills 168, 165, 198, and 166 and seize the village of Stanca, nine miles north of Iasi, and the adjacent high ground along the southern bank of the Jijia River opposite the town of Cirpiti.

On the left flank of the attacking panzer fist, Weinknecht's 79th Infantry Division was to advance northward from its positions east of Vulturi, six miles north of Iasi, capture Hills 93, 162, and 167, and protect the panzer shock group's left flank; the Romanian 11th Infantry Division, through which the panzer fist was to attack, was to support the panzer shock group throughout its advance and protect its right flank. Group Mieth, which controlled both phases of the counterstroke, held Unrein's 14th Panzer Division in reserve, with the missions of either supporting or exploiting the advance and relieving Edelsheim's 24th Panzer Division once it secured its final objectives, which it was supposed to accomplish by day's end on 31 May.

After being relieved by the 14th Panzer Division, on 1 June the 24th Panzer Division was to regroup rapidly to the region south of Tautesti, eight miles northwest of Iasi, and, together with the *Grossdeutschland* Division, initiate Operation Katja, early on 2 June. During Operation Katja, several *kampfgruppen* formed by Manteuffel's *Grossdeutschland* Panzer Grenadier and Edelsheim's 24th Panzer Divisions were to attack northward from jumping-off positions west and east of Tautesti; penetrate the Soviet defenses in the six-mile-wide sector from Avantul, six miles northeast of Podu Iloaie, eastward to Tautesti; capture the villages of Horlesti, Zahorna, Epureni, and Tipilesti; and then attack northward and eastward to outflank the remaining Soviet forces south of the Jijia River and seize Popricani, three miles southwest of Cirpiti, and the high ground along the river's southern bank from Epureni, ten miles northeast of Podu Iloaie, eastward to Cirpiti. During this second phase of the counterstroke, which was to last roughly two to three days, the Romanian 18th Infantry Division was to protect the panzer shock group's left flank, and the Romanian 3rd Infantry Division was to cover its right flank. Hoping to replicate his recent exploits along the Dnestr, Wöhler then designated General von Knobelsdorff to command the panzer group conducting Operation Katja.

In essence, Wöhler's counterstroke was designed to bring almost all of the Eighth Army's limited panzer forces to bear against the Soviet defenses north of Iasi. As had been the case with the Sixth Army's counterstroke along the Dnestr River, Group Mieth banked on catching the Soviets unaware while they were still in the midst of regrouping for their offensive.

The panzer shock group designated to spearhead Operation Sonja assembled in its jumping-off positions late on 29 May. As it had at Tirgu Frumos, Edelsheim's 24th Panzer Division fielded two *kampfgruppen* designated "W" and "E" after their commanders, Colonel von Waldenburg and Lieutenant Colonel von Einem (see Table 8.2 at chapter's end).

As had been the case at Tirgu Frumos, Einem's *Kampfgruppe* "E" consisted of the division's soft-skinned armored personnel carriers protected by about 20 assault guns, while Waldenburg's *Kampfgruppe* "W" included all of the division's available armor, which amounted to about 30 tanks, for a total armored strength of about 50 tanks, assault guns, and self-propelled artillery pieces in the panzer division. Kraber's 23rd Panzer Division, which was weaker still, fielded one *kampfgruppe* with about 20 armored vehicles, and Unrein's 14th Panzer Division fielded several *kampfgruppen* organized around its 103rd and 108th Panzer Grenadier Regiments and 36th Panzer Regiment, with a total strength of roughly ten tanks, 15 assault guns, and five self-propelled guns ("*Wespen*" ["Wasps"]).

Although the armor strength of the panzer divisions conducting Operation Sonja was far less than had been authorized by their tables of organization, Group Mieth believed that the shock group's approximately 100 tanks, assault guns, and mobile artillery pieces, combined with the always effective armored personnel carriers of the accompanying panzer grenadiers, were more than a match for the estimated three to four understrength Soviet rifle divisions defending along their front, in particular, since these Soviet forces were supported by no more than 30–40 tanks and self-propelled guns. Furthermore, during Operation Katja, the second phase of the counterstroke, when the counterattacking German forces would likely encounter elements of the Soviet 2nd Tank Army, the heavier armored force of the *Grossdeutschland* Panzer Grenadier Division, with about 100 tanks and assault guns, would take part in the attack.

The 2nd Ukrainian Front's Dispositions on 29 May

By the evening of 29 May, the forces of Malinovsky's 2nd Ukrainian Front in the region north of Iasi were occupying a classic defense-in-depth. This defense consisted of a main defensive belt, four to six miles deep, whose forward edge extended from east to west from the western bank of the Jijia River westward north of the villages of Redui Aldei, Vulturi, and Tautesti, and whose rear boundary rested on the Jijia River. The main defensive belt consisted of three defensive positions, each extending to a depth of from one to two and one half miles, which included a complex network of interconnected company strong points and battalion defensive regions anchored on the high ground and in the villages situated in between the forward edge and the Jijia River. Between these defensive positions were numerous cut-off and intermediate positions. The forward positions in the second defensive belt, which was also about six miles deep, were situated on the high ground along and north of the Jijia River and between the Jijia and Prut Rivers.

Malinovsky assigned Koroteev's 52nd and Trofimenko's 27th Armies joint responsibility for defending a roughly 30-mile-wide swath of his *front*'s main defensive belt extending from the Korneshty region east of the Prut River westward across the Prut and Jijia Rivers and the high ground north of Iasi to Avantul, six miles northeast of Podu Iloaie. By late on 29 May, Koroteev's 52nd Army was deployed to defend the roughly 25-mile-wide sector extending from the Korneshty region east of the Prut River westward across the Prut and Jijia Rivers to the village of Horlesti, two miles northwest of Tautesti and ten miles northwest of Iasi, with all three of his rifle corps deployed abreast in a single echelon.

On Koroteev's left (eastern) wing, Latyshev's 78th Rifle Corps defended the broad sector east of the Prut River with its 303rd, 252nd, and 31st Rifle Divisions deployed abreast from left to right. Further to the west in Koroteev's center, Major General I. E. Buslaev's 213th and Colonel L. G. Sergeev's 294th Rifle Divisions from Rogoznyi's 48th Rifle Corps defended the five-mile-wide sector from the western bank of the Prut River across the Jijia River to just west of Redui Aldei, with Major General Iu. I. Sokolov's 111th Rifle Division in assembly areas in the corps' second echelon north of the Jijia River. Finally, on the army's right (western) wing, Colonel K. I. Sazonov's 373rd, Major General V. A. Smirnov's 116th, and Colonel N. A. Ruban's 50th Rifle Divisions from

Martirosian's 73rd Rifle Corps defended the eight-mile-wide sector from just west of Redui Aldei westward to Horlesti, backed up by Colonel M. K. Puteiko's 254th Rifle Division, which constituted the army's second echelon.

In turn, Trofimenko deployed his army for the defense with Gorobets's 337th and Khokhlov's 202nd Rifle Divisions of Semenov's 33rd Rifle Corps defending from left to right (east to west) in the five-mile-wide sector from Horlesti westward to Avantul. At the time Semenov's third rifle division, Major General V. I. Kalinin's 206th, which had taken part in the fighting at Tirgu Frumos and whose new commander had replaced Colonel Kolesnikov on 15 May, was still en route to the Iasi region to rejoin its parent corps.

According to Malinovsky's defense plan, Kravchenko's 6th Tank Army and Bogdanov's 2nd Tank Army were responsible for providing armored support to Koroteev's and Trofimenko's combined-arms armies, respectively. At the time, the two mobile corps of Kravchenko's 6th Tank Army were still resting and refitting deep in the rear, in assembly areas 20–30 miles north and northeast of Iasi, with Volkov's 5th Guards Tank Corps in the far rear and Alekseev's 5th Mechanized Corps somewhat closer to the front. While trying to refurbish his tank army, at Malinovsky's direction Kravchenko concentrated all of his tank army's remaining armor, roughly 50 tanks, in Lieutenant Colonel A. A. Chernushevich's 233rd Tank Brigade from Volkov's 5th Mechanized Corps and ordered Chernushevich's tank brigade to support Koroteev's rifle forces whenever and wherever required.

By this time, Bogdanov's 2nd Tank Army had already regrouped Erfmeev's 11th Guards Tank Brigade, which had been in his tank army's reserve, and the forward elements of Dubovoi's 16th Tank Corps into forward assembly areas near the village of Epureni, which was centrally located just south of the Jijia River and about four miles behind the forward defenses of Semenov's 33rd Rifle Corps. However, the bulk of Dubovoi's tank corps was still located in assembly areas near Ceplenita, 13 miles north of Tirgu-Frumos, while most of Bogdanov's second tank corps, Mishulin's 3rd, was in a lager around the town of Focuri, ten miles north of Podu Iloaie, preparing to move southeastward into the region northwest of Iasi. After the heavy fighting during the first half of May, Bogdanov's tank army fielded about 60 tanks, including about ten heavy IS model tanks of various calibers.

Finally, as of 29 May, Zhadov's 5th Guards Army was still regrouping into assembly areas 35–40 miles northeast of Iasi, and, although they had already been assigned to Trofimenko's 27th Army, the two rifle divisions from Alekhin's 27th Guards Rifle Corps were still en route from the north to join Trofimenko's army.

Based on the configuration of Malinovsky's defenses north of Iasi, when they began Operation Sonja, the German 23rd, 24th, and 14th Panzer Divisions and the German 79th and Romanian 11th Infantry Divisions would initially face the 52nd Army's 213th, 294th, and 373rd Rifle Divisions, all of which were understrength and backed up by little or no armor. However, once its panzer shock group penetrated the Soviets' forward defenses, Group Mieth's attacking force was also likely to encounter at least two more rifle divisions, probably the 254th and 111th, and as many as 50 Soviet tanks and self-propelled guns from the 6th Tank Army. Given these force ratios, which were clearly favorable to the attacking Germans, there was every reason for Group Mieth to count on reaching its ultimate objective, the Jijia River at Cirpiti.

In addition, when they began Operation Katja, Knobelsdorff's panzer group made up of the *Grossdeutschland* Panzer Grenadier and 24th Panzer Divisions, backed up by the Romanian 3rd and 18th Infantry Divisions, would initially face the Soviet 50th, 337th, and 202nd Rifle Divisions, perhaps backed up by the 206th Rifle Division and by whatever tank forces Bogdanov's 2nd Tank Army would be able to deploy into the region prior to their assault. While this was a reason to be optimistic about the attack's prospects for success, the Eighth Army realized that it had to secure its objectives before larger tank forces from the 2nd Tank Army intervened.

Therefore, on the eve of its offensive, the assumptions Group Mieth made while planning its counterstroke were essentially correct. The 2nd Ukrainian Front had not yet completed regrouping its forces into the Iasi region, and, as a result, its defenses north of Iasi were indeed vulnerable. However, just how vulnerable these defenses were depended on several key factors, including the tactical effectiveness of the assaulting German forces, the resiliency of the Soviets' forward defenses, and the proximity of regrouping Soviet reserves, especially Bogdanov's 2nd Tank Army, to the points where the Germans were making their main effort.

Operation "Sonja" (30–31 May)

Few Soviet sources make any mention of the 2nd Ukrainian Front's operations north of Iasi during late May and early June 1944. One notable exception, however, is a brief description of the defensive battle found in the 6th Tank Army's official history. While revealing a few details about the involvement of Kravchenko's forces in the fighting, this account provides precious little context and studiously avoids mentioning the 27th Army's and 2nd Tank Army's roles in the battle:

> The German-Fascist command understood that the 2nd Ukrainian Front's seizure of a bridgehead on the right bank of the Prut River threatened them with a new offensive by Soviet forces along that important [Iasi] axis. After retreating from the Right Bank of the Ukraine and from the

western part of Moldavia during March 1944, the German-Fascist command strove to hold on to favorable positions along the line of the Prut River, with the intent of once again attacking into the Ukraine.

However, in order to undertake their offensive, it was necessary for the enemy to drive Soviet forces back from the positions they occupied on Romanian territory and return to the extremely favorable positions from which it seemed possible not only to control the great hilly plateau on Moldavian territory along the left bank of the Prut right up to the city of Bel'tsy but also to deploy enough suitable shock groups. Therefore, after resting and refitting his forces, which had successfully withdrawn back across the Prut in March and April, and bringing fresh forces forward from other axes, the Hitlerite command decided to undertake a counterstroke north of Iasi on 30 May 1944.

After a strong aviation and artillery preparation against the positions of the rifle divisions of the 2nd Ukrainian Front's 52nd Army north of Iasi, the enemy attacked early on the morning of 30 May with a large number of tanks and infantry. The situation in the bridgehead became quite dangerous several hours after the Hitlerites began their offensive. Therefore, in response to an order from the 2nd Ukrainian Front's military council, the 6th Tank Army's formations were immediately moved forward into the 52nd Army's area of operations so that both forces could jointly repel the enemy's offensive.

The 5th Dnestr Mechanized Corps was the first to enter battle in the bridgehead. Operating in cooperation with the 52nd Army's 73rd Rifle Corps, its brigades (the 233rd Tank, and the 9th, 45th, and 2nd Mechanized) inflicted a severe defeat on the enemy and restored the situation in the bridgehead. The enemy lost up to 200 tanks and self-propelled guns, 74 guns, 39 armored transporters and armored vehicles, 35 trucks, 192 machine guns, and 8,000 soldiers and officers in this fighting.

This fighting, which lasted for nine days, was rather intense for the soldiers of the 6th Tank and 52nd Army. Although the poorly trained forces still did not always operate skillfully, their courage and steadfastness was exemplary. During the course of these operations, they learned the art of delivering appreciable blows on the enemy. . . .

The enemy suffered a serious defeat in the nine days of fierce fighting in the bridgehead. 315 tanks and self-propelled guns, 29 armored transporters and armored vehicles, and 62 guns were burned or destroyed, and up to 10,000 soldiers and officers were destroyed.[7]

The Battle on 30 May. Group Mieth's panzer fist sprang into action at 0400 hours on 30 May, on the heels of an intense artillery preparation fired jointly by German and Romanian artillery. Led by engineers [pioneers] with mine-clearing equipment, the *kampfgruppen* from Edelsheim's 24th and Kraber's 23rd Panzer Divisions burst northward on both sides of the so-called Enache Wald [Enache Forest], which was situated astride the hills flanking the village of Redui Aldei on the east and west.[8] Running the gauntlet of heavy flanking fire from Soviet artillery positioned on Hill 125, just over one mile west of the Enache Wald, and from the Cotmani Wald to the southeast, the panzers penetrated the Soviet defenses at the junction of Sergeev's 294th and Sazonov's 373rd Rifle Divisions and lunged forward east of Hill 165 toward Hill 198 and the village of Stanca, which lay some five miles beyond (Map 24).

Advancing in the vanguard of Waldenburg's *Kampfgruppe* "W," the 24th Panzer Division's Reconnaissance Battalion (PzAA 24) and the 1st Battalion of the panzer division's 26th Panzer Grenadier Regiment reached the approaches to Hill 198, about two and one half miles deep into the Soviets' defenses, at 0900 hours but were immediately subjected to heavy flanking fire from Soviet artillery emplaced on Hills 191, 198, and 197. After being reinforced by its tanks, *Kampfgruppe* "W" overcame the resistance offered by the second-echelon rifle regiment of Sazonov's rifle division on Hill 198, wheeled to the northwest, and reached the approaches to the fortified village of Stanca and Hill 166, which was located just to the south, at 1400 hours. There, its forward movement was halted by a cluster of Soviet antitank guns, and antitank riflemen dug in on the southern outskirts of Stanca and the forward slope of Hill 166, reinforced by withdrawing elements of Sazonov's rifle division.

Advancing on *Kampfgruppe* "W's" left and supported by infantrymen from Weinknecht's 79th Infantry Division, initially at least, Einem's *Kampfgruppe* "E" kept pace with Waldenburg's advancing panzers. Einem's assaulting *kampfgruppe* penetrated the Soviets' first defensive position in the center of Sazonov's 373rd Rifle Division and captured Hill 165, about one and one half miles deep into the Soviet defenses. However, the attack by the accompanying infantry from the 79th Infantry Division faltered in the face of strong Soviet resistance, and Einem's *kampfgruppe* was forced to continue on by itself, to protect the left flank of *Kampfgruppe* "W," which, by this time, was attempting to envelop Stanca and nearby Hill 166 from the south with its panzers.

Meanwhile, across the ridges farther to the east, the *kampfgruppen* from Kräber's 23rd Panzer Division brushed aside the defending Soviet infantry on the right wing of Sergeev's 294th Rifle Division, captured Hill 198 south of the Jijia River and halfway to Cirpiti, and forced Sergeev's riflemen to withdraw eastward into the swampy flatlands west of the Jijia River. Once Kräber's panzer-grenadiers reached the bluffs on the western bank of the river, dug-in Soviet infantry and heavy artillery fire from the river's eastern bank halted their advance.

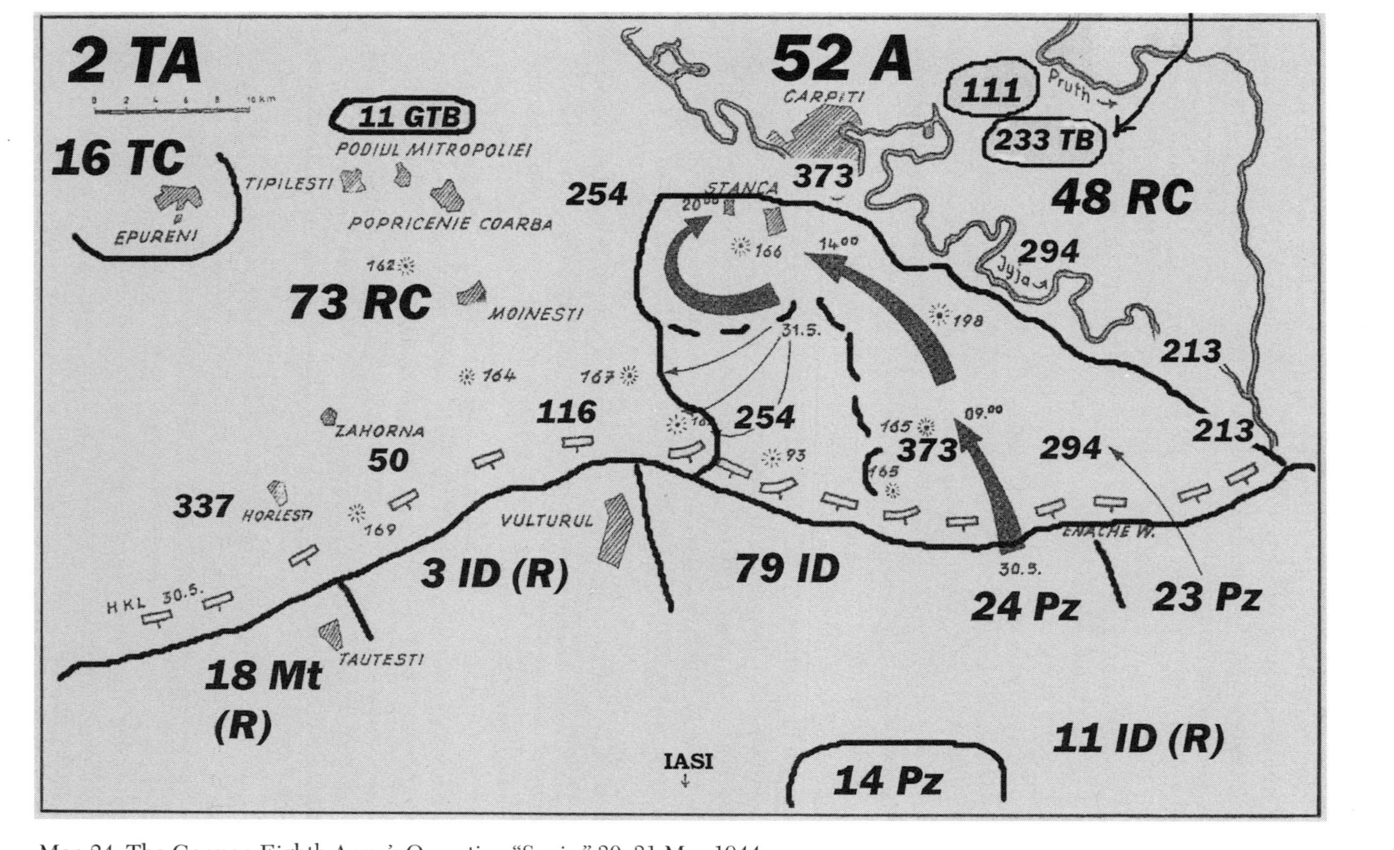

Map 24. The German Eighth Army's Operation "Sonja," 30–31 May 1944

After heavy fighting, particularly in the Sarca region and along the left flank of their penetration, by 2000 hours on 30 May, the 24th Panzer Division's two *kampfgruppen* had captured the village of Stanca and, together with the 23rd Panzer Division, had carved a narrow four-mile-wide corridor extending from its jumping-off positions in the Enache Wald northwestward to Stanca. However, Edelsheim's corridor was a tenuous one at best, since dug-in Soviet forces, still clinging stubbornly to strong defensive positions in several small bridgeheads on the western bank of the Jijia River, threatened their right wing, and other Soviet forces were holding firm to their defenses around the southern approaches to the town of Cirpiti. Other Soviet forces, in particular those of Puteiko's 254th Rifle Division, were delaying the 79th Infantry Division's advance and were still clinging to numerous strong points on the 24th Panzer Division's left wing and flank.

The powerful assault early on 30 May by Group Mieth's concentrated panzer fist caught the defending riflemen of Rogoznyi's 48th Rifle Corps quite by surprise. Before they could react, Edelsheim's and Kräber's panzers overran the forward defenses of Sergeev's 294th and Sazonov's 373rd Rifle Divisions with relative ease and turned the right (western) flank of Buslaev's 213th Rifle Division, forcing it to withdraw eastward into the Jijia River valley. After fighting a stubborn but fragmented rearguards action, Sazonov's forces recoiled westward onto the high ground at and west of Hill 165 and northward toward Hill 166 and Sarca, while Puteiko's and Buslaev's 294th and 213th Rifle Divisions withdrew into new defenses along the western bank of the Jijia River. Once there, Koroteev demanded that they hold out on the river's western bank and ordered Rogoznyi to dispatch Sokolov's 111th Rifle Division from his 48th Rifle Corps' second echelon to shore up his defenses along the river.

Soon after, Koroteev also alerted Puteiko's 254th Rifle Division, which was in his army's reserve, and ordered it to reinforce the shattered defenses of Sazonov's 373rd Rifle Division along the western flank of the German penetration and also stoutly defend the Stanca region. At the same time, he ordered Martirosian's 73rd Rifle Corps to regroup part of Smirnov's 116th Rifle Division, which was on his rifle corps' left wing, to shore up the western shoulder of the German penetration. Finally, at Koroteev's request, late in the day, Malinovsky ordered Kravchenko's 6th Tank Army to release whatever tank forces he could muster to assist Koroteev in repelling the German assault.

Group Mieth's panzer shock group fulfilled most of its assigned missions by day's end on 30 May (Map 25). An entry in the German Armed Forces High Command's (OKW) daily log for 31 May evidenced satisfaction with the Eighth Army's progress on 30 May:

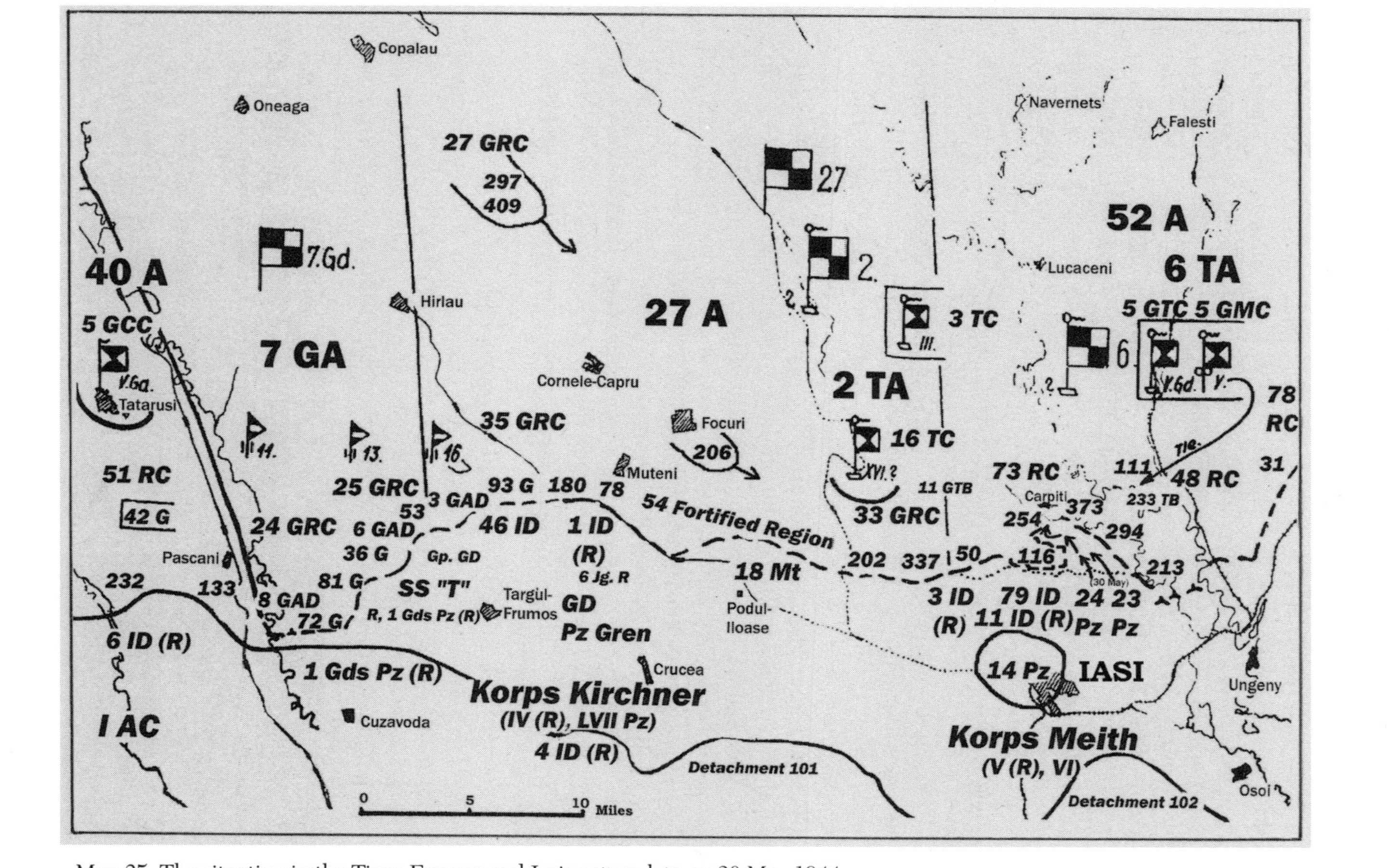

Map 25. The situation in the Tirgu Frumos and Iasi sectors, late on 30 May 1944

> In the East, infantry and panzer formation, supported by German and Rumanian tactical and fighter bomber formations, broke through strongly fortified and deeply echeloned defensive positions north of Jassy and threw the Soviets back to the river in fierce combat. The territory won was held against strong Bolshevik counterattacks. Fighters and fighter-bombers destroyed 69 enemy aircraft over this area.[9]

Having captured the village of Sarca, Group Mieth's forces were now poised to advance on Cirpiti, only two miles to the northeast. But first, it had to eliminate the pesky Soviet salient formed on its left flank. This became its primary task the next day.

The Battle on 31 May. Heavy fighting continued raging north of Iasi on 31 May, as Edelsheim's 24th Panzer and Weinknecht's 79th Infantry Divisions, now reinforced by the *kampfgruppen* from Unrein's 14th Panzer Division, fought to reduce the pesky Soviet salient on their left flank. A history of Army Group South noted the increased Soviet resistance:

> The Soviet formations recovered from their initial surprise and strengthened their resistance. However, the German attack continued once again on the second day of the battle. On this day alone, the Soviets lost 37 tanks, including their newest models, to the 8.8.cm antiaircraft guns and the assault guns. Fighters and fighter-bombers shot down 87 enemy aircraft.[10]

During the day, Waldenburg's *Kampfgruppe* "W" from the 24th Panzer Division consolidated its positions north of Stanca but could make no further forward progress northward toward the Jijia River against the forces of Puteiko's 254th Rifle Division, which were dug in west of Stanca, and Sazonov's 373rd Rifle Division, whose forces defended Cirpiti on the river's northern bank. To the south, infantry from Weinknecht's 79th Infantry Division and Einem's *Kampfgruppe* "E" slowly and painfully cleared Soviet forces from the salient they occupied on the shock group's left flank, captured Hill 93, and broadened the base of their penetration to just under five miles. On the penetration's right (eastern) flank, Kräber's 23rd Panzer Division, now supported by infantry from the Romanian 11th Infantry Division, consolidated its defenses on the bluffs overlooking the Jijia River but was unable to eliminate the Soviet bridgeheads on the river's western bank (Map 24).

By the time the day's heavy fighting ended, Mieth's shock group had accomplished most of its assigned mission by driving a V-shaped wedge into the Soviet defenses south of Cirpiti, with the point of the "V" anchored on the village of Stanca. Although it confuses the two phases of the Eighth Army's counterstroke, the history of Army Group South describes how Operation Sonja ended:

> On the third day of the battle, the Russian command threw new formations into the battle, which were transported from sectors of the front not involved in the attack. Therefore, the Eighth Army attack ground to a halt on 2 June. The same combat groups had to withdraw from the superior enemy. However, the army regained its composure during the evening and continued the attack on the next day.[11]

With its initial task accomplished, on the evening of 31 May, the two *kampfgruppen* of Edelsheim's 24th Panzer Division turned their positions over to the 79th Infantry and 14th Panzer Divisions and began regrouping to new assembly areas south of Tautesti, seven miles northwest of Iasi, to prepare to join the *Grossdeutschland* Panzer Grenadier Division in Operation Katja, the second phase of the Eighth Army's counterstroke.[12]

After the 24th Panzer Division regrouped westward, by midnight on 31 May, infantry from the 79th Infantry Division was dug in at the apex of Group Mieth's advance just south of Cirpiti, flanked on the left by the 14th Panzer and Romanian 3rd Infantry Divisions, whose forward positions stretched southwestward past the northern outskirts of Vulturi, and on the right by the 23rd Panzer and Romanian 11th Infantry Divisions, which were containing Soviet forces in their bridgeheads on the western edge of the Jijia River valley.

By this time Koroteev's 52nd Army had managed to stabilize its defenses and was already seeking ways to push the Germans back. In the 52nd Army's center southeast of Cirpiti, Buslaev's 213th and Sergeev's 294th Rifle Divisions from Rogoznyi's 48th Rifle Corps, which was responsible for defending the eastern flank of the German penetration along the western bank of the Jijia River northwestward to Cirpiti, were clinging tenaciously to their narrow bridgeheads along the Jijia River's western bank. On the 52nd Army's right (western) wing (in the sector of Martirosian's 73rd Rifle Corps on the western flank of the German penetration), Sazonov's 373rd Rifle Division, which had now reassembled its remnants, was dug in at and south of Cirpiti proper, and riflemen and artillerymen from Puteiko's 254th and Smirnov's 116th Rifle Divisions, supported by a small number of tanks sent forward by Kravchenko's 6th Tank Army, were defending the five-mile-wide front extending from the Jijia River at Cirpiti southward to Vulturi.

Urged on by the *Stavka,* which was unhappy with the Germans' success in light of what had occurred only weeks before along the Dnestr River, overnight on 31 May, Malinovsky ordered Koroteev to mount strong counterattacks as soon as possible to expel German forces from the approaches to Cirpiti, and ordered Kravchenko's 6th Tank Army to support Koroteev's counterattacks. In response, Koroteev ordered Rogoznyi's 48th Rifle Corps to move Sokolov's 111th Rifle Division from his second echelon north of the Jijia River into forward assembly areas along the river's northern bank from which it could launch a counterattack across the river to expand the 294th Rifle Division's shallow bridgehead southeast of Cirpiti. At the same time, he directed Martirosian's 73rd Rifle Corps to attack the German salient south of Cirpiti from the west. However, since Kravchenko's 6th Tank Army was not able to assemble its tank group fast enough to support Koroteev's counterattacks, Koroteev requested and received Malinovsky's permission to delay the counterattacks until the morning of 2 June.

While messages were flashing to and fro between Malinovsky's and Koroteev's headquarters, Malinovsky also ordered Kravchenko to alert Volkov's 5th Mechanized Corps to deploy Chernushevich's 233rd Tank Brigade to support Rogoznyi's counterattack against the eastern flank of the German penetration and Volkov's 2nd, 9th, and 45th Mechanized Brigades to support Martirosian's assaults on the penetration's western face. However, after Koroteev's and Kravchenko's forces spent all day on 1 June regrouping for their dawn counterattack on 2 June, the second phase of the German Eighth Army's counterstroke, Operation Katja, suddenly rendered all of Malinovsky's counterattack plans largely irrelevant.

Operation "Katja" (2–6 June)

The only existing Soviet account of the intense fighting that took place during Operation Katja is contained in the 2nd Tank Army's official history, which, like the 6th Tank Army's history quoted above, provides enticing details regarding the 2nd Tank Army's fight, but no context whatsoever:

> During May the German-Fascist command created a large force grouping, which numbered up to four panzer and three infantry divisions (the "Greater Germany," 14th, 23rd, and 24th Panzer Divisions; the German 79th Infantry Division; and the Romanian 3rd and 11th Infantry Divisions). It was clear that, while pursuing definite military-political and military-economic aims, the German command was preparing to strike a strong blow aimed at the destruction of our forces north of Iasi and reaching the Prut River, the state boundary of Romania.
>
> The forces of our 27th Army were defending in this sector of the front. The 2nd Tank Army was withdrawn into the front's reserve during the second half of May and was concentrated with its 3rd Tank Corps in the Focuri region and its 16th Tank Corps in the Cheplenitsa [Ceplenita] region [14–16 miles north of Tirgu-Frumos].

On the morning of 1 June, the headquarters of the 35th Rifle Corps, with which we had direct communications, reported to the tank army headquarters that the enemy had begun an offensive.

The *front* headquarters forewarned the tank army commander so that the army would be prepared, together with the 27th Army's formations, to repel the German attack and prevent them from penetrating north of Iasi and reaching the Jijia River.

The enemy did not succeed in penetrating the 35th Rifle Corps' defenses on 1 June. Beginning on the morning of 2 June, the enemy committed their panzer divisions into combat, and, as a result, he succeeded in wedging up to a depth of eight kilometers [five miles] into our defenses during the second half of the day, although at a cost of heavy losses.

Fulfilling the *front* commander's orders, the 2nd Tank Army moved forward to the Hill 164–Epureni line [15–18 miles northwest of Iasi] with the mission of preventing the enemy from developing his offensive north of that line. Subsequently, it had the mission of restoring the situation in the 27th Army's sector.

The 3rd Tank Corps attacked the enemy from the march during the second half of the day and captured the region around Movileni Station (east of Hill 164) [four miles west of Epureni] and the heights west of the station. The 16th Tank Corps' forward detachment reached the region north of Epureni by day's end on 2 June and attacked the enemy on the morning of 3 June, throwing him back south from Epureni.

The enemy resumed his fierce attacks on the morning of 4 June. The pressure was intense. He pushed the units on the 16th Tank Corps' left flank [the 15th Motorized Rifle Brigade] back in several sectors, by doing so threatening to capture Epureni. . . . [This attack was halted by a counterattack organized by Major General P. M. Latyshev, the member of the tank army's military council (commissar).]

The enemy attacked once again at midday on 4 June with a force of up to a battalion of infantry reinforced by tanks. Eleven enemy tanks [including several Tiger models] penetrated into the brigade's dispositions . . . [but were repelled by the brigade's artillery battery firing over open sites]. . . .

The tank army repulsed all of the Fascists' attempts to penetrate our defenses on 4 and 5 June. After failing to achieve success, the Germans halted their offensive and, beginning on 6 June, went over to the defense along the entire front.

When summarizing this fighting and characterizing enemy command's attempts to conduct active combat operations between the Prut and Seret Rivers, the army commander, General S. I. Bogdanov, stated that these

> were the desperate efforts of the enemy to compel us to relinquish our offensive along this axis.[13]

After regrouping westward from the Cirpiti region to new assembly areas south of Tautesti overnight on 31 May, on 1 June Edelsheim's 24th Panzer Division, which was still organized in two *kampfgruppen,* concentrated in new jumping-off positions in the valley south of the village of Horlesti, roughly ten miles northwest of Iasi. By this time, Colonel von Bulow had replaced Waldenburg in command of the division's panzer *kampfgruppe.* On the same day, Manteuffel regrouped his *Grossdeutschland* Panzer Grenadier Division from the Tirgu Frumos region to new assembly areas between Podu Iloaie and Letcani, nine miles west of Iasi. The *Grossdeutschland* Division's history describes its redeployment:

> On 31 May elements of the SS-Division Totenkopf began relieving the division's left wing, while elements of the 24th Panzer Division relieved its right wing.
>
> The panzer-fusiliers were the first to leave their positions. They had the shortest route into the assembly area and moved to the extreme eastern end of this in the area [west of Tautesti] north of Letcani. The batteries of the Panzer-Artillery Regiment GD went into position on both sides of the town and in the hollows behind the hills. They were strengthened by the addition of static artillery, including heavy rocket launchers, whose role was to support the attack.
>
> The panzer-grenadiers took up positions farther west, but north of the highway. With them was III (Tiger) Battalion, Panzer Regiment GD under Oberstleutnant Baumungk.[14]

The two German divisions forming the panzer shock designated to conduct Operation Katja occupied jumping-off positions for their assault overnight on 1–2 June in the six-mile-wide sector extending from the valley north of Hill 177, two and one half miles south of the village of Avantul, eastward to the road from Epureni to Radui-Tatar, about one mile northeast of Tautesti.

While this new panzer group was assembling, General von Knobelsdorff, who had wrought havoc on Chuikov's 8th Guards Army only two weeks before, took command of the group to lead it during its counterstroke. When fully assembled in their jumping-off positions in the two-mile-wide sector west and east of Tautesti, *kampfgruppen* Bulow and Einem from Edelsheim's 24th Panzer Division fielded a total of about 40 tanks and assault guns, and Manteuffel's *Grossdeutschland* Division concentrated a slightly stronger force in the remaining four-mile-wide sector westward to south of Avantul. However, records indicate that, out of a total armor strength of about 100 tanks and assault guns, the *Grossdeutschland* Division fielded only 19 serviceable Tigers and 12 Panzer IVs in its 3rd Battalion on 1 June but a slightly larger force on 2 June.[15]

Knobelsdorff's plan for Operation Katja required the 24th Panzer Division's two *kampfgruppen* to attack due north from the Tautesti region; penetrate the Soviet defenses and capture the Soviet strong points at Horlesti and Zahorna, ten miles northwest of Iasi; wheel northeastward to turn the right (western) flank of the Soviet forces defending north of Vulturi; and then exploit northward to seize the villages of Tipilesti and Popricani on the heights overlooking the southern bank of the Jijia River. Advancing on the 24th Panzer's right, after it left one infantry division to protect the panzer division's right flank once the penetration was complete, the Romanian 3rd Infantry Division was to employ its two other regiments to follow and support the panzer division's advance and clean up pockets of bypassed Soviet troops.

Deployed along a far broader front to the west, arrayed from west to east, two *kampfgruppen* formed from the *Grossdeutschland* Division's Grenadier and Fusilier regiments, the former with the division's Tiger tank battalion attached, were to advance northward in tandem; penetrate the Soviets' defenses and capture the Soviet strong points at Avantul, Movileni Station, and Epureni; and then exploit northward to seize the high ground overlooking the southern bank of the Jijia River between Polingeni and Epureni.

According to the *Grossdeutschland* Division's history:

> The initial objectives had been revealed: for the panzer-fusiliers, who would be attacking on the right, Hill 278.3, about 2,000 metres south of Isvoare Epurennu [Epureni]; for the panzer-grenadiers the hills either side of Orsoaeia (Ursoaei) [Movileni Station]. A common objective was the line of hills due south of the Prut [actually the Jijia] Valley, as it was important to gain a vantage point overlooking the valley.[16]

During the assault the Romanian 18th Mountain Infantry Division was to advance on and support *Grossdeutschland*'s left flank, and the Romanian 5th Infantry Division, which was originally in reserve assembly areas south of Letcani, was to take over responsibility for the sector west and east of Totoesti to permit the 18th Mountain Infantry Division to support *Grossdeutschland*'s advance to the north.

The Soviet defenses opposite Knobelsdorff's panzer fists were fairly weak on the night of 1 June. Although Trofimenko's 27th Army was responsible for the defense of this sector, his defending force consisted of the three already weakened rifle divisions of Semenov's 33rd Rifle Corps and the left wing of his 54th Fortified Region. Although Malinovsky had ordered Trofimenko to concentrate his entire army in the region northwest of Iasi by early June, by the end of May, the three rifle divisions of Gorokhov's 35th Guards Rifle Corps were still manning the 27th Army's defenses north and northeast of Tirgu Frumos. This meant that Trofimenko's army was defending the sector from Tautesti westward to Avantul with Gorobets's 337th and Khokhlov's 202nd Rifle Divisions from Semenov's 33rd Rifle Corps, backed up by Kalinin's 206th Rifle Division, which had just reached the region and was in Semenov's second echelon, and the broad sector west of Avantul with several artillery–machine-gun battalions subordinate to the 54th Fortified Region.

At the time, a portion of Erfmeev's 11th Guards Tank Brigade from Bogdanov's 2nd Tank Army had just moved into its new reserve assembly areas north of Tipilesti, east of Epureni and just south of the Jijia River, but they had a small force of only about ten tanks. In addition, advanced parties and forward detachments from the 2nd Tank Army's 3rd and 16th Tank Corps had reached their new assembly areas near Popricani and Epureni, respectively, but their main forces were still in the process of moving toward their designated assembly areas. After the heavy losses they had suffered during the fighting at Tirgu Frumos three weeks before, Bogdanov's two corps numbered only about 50 tanks, although some of them were heavy IS models.

Therefore, when they commenced their initial assault during Operation Katja, Knobelsdorff's two panzer and panzer grenadier divisions and two Romanian infantry divisions faced three weak Soviet rifle divisions, one of which (Kalinin's 202nd) had been severely damaged in fighting two weeks before, and a handful of Soviet tanks. Only after the main forces of Bogdanov's two tank corps and the remainder of Trofimenko's 27th Army—specifically, Goriachev's and Alekhin's 35th and 27th Guards Rifle Corps—reached the region would the balance of forces tip decisively in the Soviets' favor. Since it would take between two and five days for these reinforcements to reach the region, Knobelsdorff's shock group was embarking on a "race with the clock" if it hoped to fulfill its assigned missions before significant Soviet reinforcements arrived.

The Battle on 2 June. The multiple panzer *kampfgruppen* of Manteuffel's *Grossdeutschland* Panzer Grenadier and Edelsheim's 24th Panzer Divisions began their assault just before dawn on 2 June (Map 26). Advancing quickly and dramatically, they pushed northward up the gentle valleys and along the sparsely wooded ridgelines into and through the Soviets' forward defenses. Far more powerful than Group Mieth's previous panzer fist, the four *kampfgruppen* struck the Soviets' forward defensive positions between Hill 177, two and one half miles south of Avantul, and east of Tautesti, tearing numerous gaping holes in the forward defenses of Semenov's three defending rifle divisions.

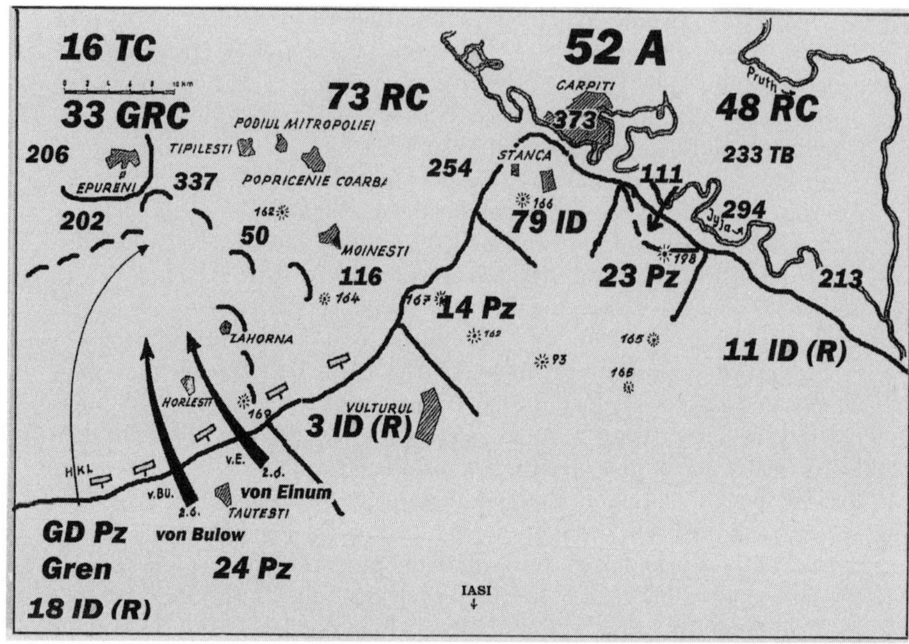

Map 26. The German Eighth Army's Operation "Katja," 2 June 1944

Attacking from jumping-off positions just east of Tautesti, the panzer grenadiers of the 24th Panzer Division's *Kampfgruppe* Einem, supported by the 1st Battalion of the 228th Assault Gun Battalion, struck the Soviets' defenses precisely at the boundary between Semenov's 33rd Rifle Corps of Trofimenko's 27th Army and Martirosian's 73rd Rifle Corps of Koroteev's 52nd Army. The assault collapsed the defenses of Gorobets's 337th Rifle Division, which was defending on Semenov's left wing, bypassed the strong point at Horlesti from the east, and headed straight for the town of Zahorna, which was defended by Gorobets's second-echelon rifle regiment. While Gorobets's rifle division attempted to refuse its flank to the east, Ruban's 50th Rifle Division, which was defending on the right wing of Martirosian's 73rd Rifle Corps, attempted to erect a new defensive line facing west along the Epureni-Radui road and dispatched its second-echelon rifle regiment to reinforce Gorobets's defenses at Zahorna.

At the same time, attacking northward from jumping-off positions west of Tautesti, the 24th Panzer Division's panzer force, *Kampfgruppe* von Bulow, collapsed the center of Gorobets's defenses, forced the rifle regiment defending on the 337th Rifle Division's right wing to withdraw rapidly to the north, and captured the Soviet strong point at Horlesti from the march. Alerted to the German assault, Kalinin's 206th Rifle Division, which was in the second echelon of Semenov's rifle corps, hastily manned its assigned defenses at and forward of Epureni.

Unleashing its heavier armored force further to the west, the two *kampfgruppen* subordinate to Manteuffel's *Grossdeutschland* Panzer Grenadier Division struck the entire front of Khokhlov's 202nd Rifle Division on the right wing of Semenov's 33rd Rifle Corps, the left wing of the 27th Army's 54th Fortified Region, and the right wing of Gorobets's 337th Rifle Division. As described in the *Grossdeutschland* Division's history:

> The infantry, tanks, and assault guns attacked at first light on 2 June. The advance was supported by heavy fire from howitzers and rocket launchers and the first enemy-occupied villages were taken. The resistance stiffened; they had reached the Soviet main line of resistance. The battle zone that the attackers had to traverse consisted of deeply-excavated positions, camouflaged minefields of unknown size and numerous anti-tank and mortar positions.[17]

This multipronged assault tore numerous holes through the Soviets' defensive front, both on the *Grossdeutschland* Division's left wing, where the *kampfgruppe* formed from its Grenadier Regiment was advancing northward along and east of the railroad line through Avantul to Movileni Station, and on the division's right wing, where the Fusilier Regiment's *kampfgruppe* was moving northward through the valley north of Letcani along the Bogonos and Zahorna road. However, the assault was not without difficulty:

> Farther right in the attack lane of the panzer-grenadiers, the Panthers of I Battalion, 26th Panzer Regiment under Hauptmann Graf Rothkirch were so held up by the swampy ground that they had to go around, which cost time. Oberleutnant Hasler and his men stormed ahead, jumped into the trenches and rolled them up. Hand-to-hand fighting broke out. Heavy fire from Stalin Organs [Katiusha multiple-rocket launchers] frequently forced the men to take cover, but each time the panzer-grenadiers advanced between salvos.
>
> The Tigers and Panthers exchanged fire with the enemy at extreme range, destroying anti-tank guns and setting enemy tanks on fire at ranges in excess of 2,000 metres.
>
> However the enemy very quickly recognized the intentions of the Germans.
>
> The Soviets committed whole swarms of close-support aircraft, which made things difficult for the attackers. The anti-aircraft gunners, as well

> as those of the Army Flak Battalion GD and the regiments' flak companies, did the best they could. With only three working guns, the flak company of the Panzer-Fusilier Regiment GD brought down a number of enemy aircraft in a few hours; the heavy batteries of the Army Flak battalion GD alone claimed more than five enemy aircraft shot down that day.
>
> These losses were not enough to deter the pilots of the enemy close-support aircraft, however. They repeatedly swept over the battlefield, dropped their fragmentation bombs and then returned to strafe the attackers. The latter were forced to take cover and the momentum began to go out of the German attack. Mine-clearing troops from the Armoured Assault Pioneer Battalion GD accompanied the advancing infantry spearheads. The mines, invisible to the eye and immune to almost all types of mine detector, were everywhere. Oberleutnant Kruger ran into an enemy counterattack but was able to fend it off and put the enemy to flight.[18]

Despite these problems, the coordinated assault by *Grossdeutschland*'s Grenadier Regiment forced the riflemen of Khokhlov's 202nd Rifle Division to retreat northward in considerable disorder, although, with assistance from the 54th Fortified Region, Khokhlov's right-wing rifle regiment somehow managed to cling stubbornly to the strong point at Avantul and adjacent high ground to the northwest. However, the Fusilier Regiment's *kampfgruppe* on *Grossdeutschland* Division's right wing utterly demolished the forces on the right wing of Gorobets's 337th Rifle Division, forcing them to retreat northward from Horlesti toward safety at the strong point at Zahorna.

After a full day of heavy fighting, the 24th Panzer Division's *Kampfgruppe* "E" captured Zahorna at 1930 hours, and, thereafter, both of the division's *kampfgruppen* attacked the forward defenses of Kalinin's 206th Rifle Division, which was defending along the forward slopes of the high ground south of Epureni and Tipilesti. By this time, a few tanks from Erfmeev's 11th Guards Tank Brigade were able to reinforce Kalinin's defenses. According to prearranged plans, the 24th Panzer Division then began wheeling its *kampfgruppen* toward the northeast so that is could mount an assault toward the Soviets' strong point defenses at Popricani, Hill 162, and Moinesti the next morning. By doing so, Edelsheim hoped to be able to roll up the Soviet 52nd Army's right flank and continue its advance to the Jijia River west of Cirpiti.

Meanwhile, on the left (western) wing of Knobelsdorff's shock group, the *kampfgruppen* of Manteuffel's *Grossdeutschland* Division assaulted the Soviets' defensive positions along the road leading from Avantul northeastward to Epureni during the afternoon and early evening but encountered stronger resistance as they reached the southern approaches to Epureni. Avoiding specifics, the *Grossdeutschland*'s history recorded the advance to the southern outskirts of the town:

> In spite of everything the advance continued. The bare, grass-covered hills were taken one after another. Far to the rear the anti-aircraft guns provided sustained covering fire, while the panzers shot up every anti-tank gun they could see as well as enemy tanks on the back side of the hills. This supporting fire played havoc with the enemy and reduced their firepower. This was the moment when the panzer-fusiliers and panzer-grenadiers chose to force the next hill, to climb and occupy it. When they reached the top they placed sustained fire on the enemy.[19]

On Manteuffel's left wing, the remnants of Khokhlov's 202nd Rifle Division and the artillery machine-gun battalions on the 54th Fortified Region's left wing managed to hold firm on the high ground northwest of Avantul but lost control of the village itself, while, in Manteuffel's center, Kalinin's 206th Rifle Division, supported by other remnants of Khokhlov's 202nd Rifle Division and tanks from Erfmeev's 11th Guards Tank Brigade, clung tenaciously to their defenses south of Epureni. At nightfall, Manteuffel began turning the western half of his division's sector—that is, the sector west of Epureni—over to the Romanian 18th Mountain Division and prepared to move part of his forces northeastward toward Tipilesti to support the 24th Panzer Division's advance, while the remainder of his division fought on to capture the Soviet strong points at Orsoaei [Movileni Station] and Epureni.

By day's end on 2 June, the *kampfgruppen* making up Group Knobelsdorff's new panzer fist managed to advance northward to a depth of from two and one half to five miles along a front of almost six miles and reached positions only one to three miles south of the Jijia River. As Army Group South's history recorded, "[The army] continued its attacks on the next day. Another 23 enemy tanks were destroyed and regained the excellent high ground northwest of Jassy."[20] Making matters more challenging for the defending Soviets, the panzer spearheads of Knobelsdorff's shock group were coiled and ready to strike both northward toward Epureni and northeastward toward Cirpiti, thereby threatening to collapse the entire Soviet defensive belt south of the Jijia River.

In addition to severely damaging the Soviet defenses west of Vulturi, Group Knobelsdorff's assault on 2 June also disrupted the counterattacks Malinovsky planned to conduct early on the same day to restore his defenses south of Cirpiti. In fact, Koroteev's 52nd Army actually began its counterattacks at dawn on 2 June, almost simultaneously with the Germans' assault to the west. In the sector east and southeast of Cirpiti, for example, Sokolov's 111th Rifle Division from Rogoznyi's 48th Rifle Corps, supported by about 30 tanks from Chernushevich's 233rd Tank Brigade of Volkov's 5th Mechanized Corps and elements of Sergeev's 294th Rifle Division, crossed the Jijia River and assaulted the 23rd Panzer Division's defenses on Hill 198, roughly four miles southeast of Cirpiti. Although Rogoznyi's strong assault ultimately failed, it did widen and deepen the 52nd Army's bridgehead on the river's western bank and propelled Soviet riflemen onto the eastern slopes of the key hill.

Meanwhile, Puteiko's 254th and Smirnov's 116th Rifle Divisions, both from Martirosian's 73rd Rifle Corps of Koroteev's 52nd Army, together with the 2nd, 9th, and 45th Mechanized Brigades from Volkov's 5th Mechanized Corps, also counterattacked at dawn on 2 June, this time near the village of Stanca, two miles southwest of Cirpiti, against the western flank of the German penetration into the sector defended by Group Mieth's 79th Infantry and 14th Panzer Divisions. However, immediately after Martirosian's reinforced rifle corps began its assault, news arrived about the powerful German panzer attack to the west. Since this assault collapsed the 73rd Rifle Corps' right wing and threatened its rear area, Martirosian called off his counterattack and ordered Smirnov's 116th Rifle Division and part of Volkov's mechanized group to erect new defenses in the sector from Hill 164 and the village of Moinesti on his corps' left wing and rear.

At this point, at about mid-morning on 2 June, Malinovsky and his subordinate army commanders, Trofimenko, Koroteev, and Bogdanov, worked frantically to bolster their defenses and stave off further disaster. First, Malinovsky ordered Bogdanov to regroup his 2nd Tank Army's 3rd and 16th Tank Corps into new concentration areas extending from Hill 164, just west of Movileni Station, eastward to Epureni to back up the sagging defenses of Semenov's shattered 33rd Rifle Corps and block any further German advance northward to the Jijia River. Second, he ordered Shumilov's 7th Guards Army to take over the defensive sector of the 27th Army's 35th Guards Rifle Corps north of Tirgu Frumos to permit Trofimenko to regroup the three rifle divisions of Goriachev's guards rifle corps southeastward to the Epureni sector on his army's left flank. Third, Malinovsky ordered Trofimenko to accelerate the regrouping of Alekhin's 27th Guards Rifle Corps so that it, too, could bolster the 27th Army's defenses northwest of Iasi.

After receiving its alert orders, Mishulin's 3rd Tank Corps moved hastily to the vicinity of Movileni Station, 15 miles northwest of Iasi, arriving just in time to fend off an attack on the station by the forward elements of *Grossdeutschland* Division. At nightfall, Mishulin's armor, together with riflemen from the remnants of Khokhlov's 202nd and Kalinin's 206th Rifle Divisions and artillerymen and machine gunners from the 54th Fortified Region, were able to establish stable defenses just south of Movileni Station and the high ground to the west. By this time, the *Grossdeutschland* Division had turned this portion of its sector over to the Romanian 18th Mountain Infantry Division.

To the east where the situation for the Soviets was most critical and dangerous, the forward detachment of Dubovoi's 16th Tank Corps finally reached the Epureni region, 13 miles northwest of Iasi, after dark on 2 June, where it reinforced the beleagured riflemen of Kalinin's 206th and Khokhlov's 202nd Rifle Division, whose defenses on the southern outskirts of Epureni were still being supported by the few remaining tanks of Erfmeev's 11th Guards Tank Brigade. However, the forward detachment was of only limited assistance since it fielded only a handful of tanks. The remainder of Dubovoi's 3rd Tank Corps spent the night frantically marching southeastward toward the battlefield. Making matters worse for Trofimenko, it would take far longer for the foot-bound troops of his 35th and 27th Guards Rifle Corps to arrive in the region and reinforce his army's defenses. In the interim, Trofimenko had no choice but to hold until the necessary reinforcements arrived.

The Battle during 3–6 June. The *kampfgruppen* of Knobelsdorff's panzer shock group resumed their heavy assaults against the Russians' shrinking defensive perimeter south of the Jijia River once again early on 3 June after a short artillery preparation (Map 27). As before, although brief, the description of the fighting in Army Group South's history remained positive:

> This success [on 2 June] was expanded on the next day as they succeeded in storming the last Russian position on the high ground. The Russians lost another 25 combat vehicles [tanks] and 33 aircraft. While fighting with the Russian combat vehicles, Major Rudel from the "Immermann" Fighter-Bomber Squadron distinguished himself by destroying several "T-34s" and assault guns making deep attacks.[21]

This time the *kampfgruppen* of Manteuffel's *Grossdeutschland* Panzer Grenadier Division concentrated their forces in assaults both northward toward Orsoaei [Movileni Station] and Epureni and northeastward toward the Soviets' strong points at Tipilesti, Popricani, and Hill 162, which were situated on or near the southern bank of the Jijia River about three miles northeast of Zahorna. As a result:

> On 3 June the fighting raged on. The heavy weapons opened fire at first light, helping the attack groups as they strived to reach their objectives. The town of Orsoaei fell after heavy fighting. Unteroffizier Kuhnanz of 6th Company, Panzer-Grenadier Regiment GD was killed and Major Sussmann, the commander of II (Self-propelled) Battalion, Panzer-Artillery Regiment GD, died a tragic death. Early that morning he set out with his adjutant, Leutnant Schurmann, his driver and the commander of the motorcycle squad, Unteroffizier M. Grosspointner, in a VW Schwimmwagen to scout the area. They drove into a previously unknown minefield. A powerful explosion hurled the vehicle into the air and cast its occupants onto the ground in a wide circle. The major landed on

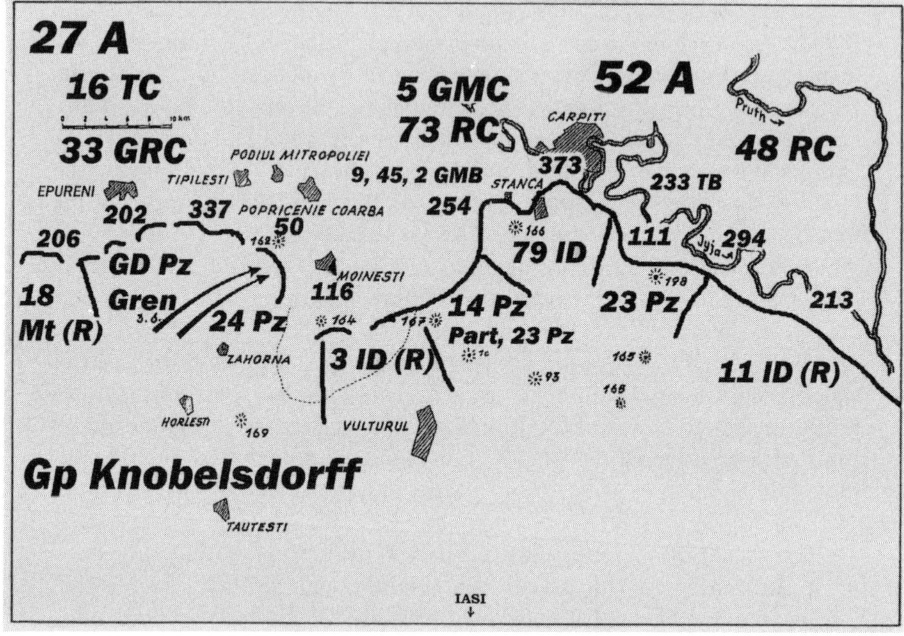

Map 27. The German Eighth Army's Operation "Katja," 3 June 1944

> another anti-personnel mine, which blew him to pieces. The others were seriously injured; Unteroffizier Grosspointner, the driver of the vehicle, lost a leg below the knee and suffered other serious injuries.
>
> By evening the infantry, especially the panzer-fusiliers, were able to capture the high ground on either side of Point 181, north of Zahorna [one mile south of Epureni]. The attack objectives were taken in heavy, close-quarters fighting and a large number of prisoners were brought in. There too the captured positions were immediately improved for defensive purposes.[22]

At the same time, the two *kampfgruppen* of Edelsheim's 24th Panzer Division assaulted eastward toward Moinesti and Hill 164 in an attempt to roll up the right wing of the Soviet forces defending north of Vulturi. As Edelsheim's attacks developed, the Romanian 3rd Infantry Division, supported by Unrein's 14th Panzer Division on its right, also assaulted the Soviet strong points north of Vulturi and south of Hill 164 in support of the 24th Panzer Division's advance.

The fighting on 3 June was far more intense than the day before because the Soviets were able to strengthen their resistance with newly arrived reinforcements. For example, after the main forces of Dubovoi's 16th Tank Corps reached the Epureni region early in the day, Dubovoi ordered a tank brigade group and his 15th Motorized Rifle Brigade to blunt *Grossdeutschland* Division's assault south of Epureni by counterattacking with a force of about 20 tanks, including several IS-model heavy tanks. Although the counterattack failed to penetrate *Grossdeutschland* Division's defenses, it did succeed in halting its assault just south of the town.

Meanwhile, east and southeast of Epureni, the remnants of Gorobets's 337th Rifle Division from Semenov's 33rd Rifle Corps, together with Ruban's 50th and Smirnov's 116th Rifle Divisions from Martirosian's 73rd Rifle Corps of the 52nd Army, which were by now reinforced by the mechanized group from Volkov's 5th Mechanized Corps and large antitank reserves from the 52nd Army, mounted strong resistance from positions extending from Hill 162, just south of Popricani, southward through the village of Moinesti to Hill 164. In complex, intense, and often futile fighting, the *Grossdeutschland* Division's *kampfgruppen* failed to dislodge the riflemen and antitank gunners of Ruban's 50th Rifle Division from their defenses on Hill 162, and the 24th Panzer Division's assaults faltered in front of the defenses of Smirnov's 116th Rifle Division at Moinesti and on Hill 164.

After further concentrating its forces, the *Grossdeutschland* Division finally assaulted and captured Hill 162 on 4 June but could advance no further because of the Russians' strong defenses and because it was distracted by the heavy fighting raging on south and southeast of Epureni (Map 28). As described in the *Grossdeutschland*'s history:

> After shifting elements of the Panzer-Grenadier Regiment GD to the right of the panzer-fusiliers, at approximately 14.00 on 4 June the men of reinforced II Battalion, Panzer-Grenadier Regiment, together with the remaining handful of Tigers, attacked from the area north of Vanatori [Vinatori] along the Jassy-Papricani Coarb [Popricani] road toward the enemy-occupied town of Moinesti. By evening they had entered the village in the face of determined Soviet resistance. There were only four Tigers left, all commanded by officers, whose privilege it was to take command of the nearest serviceable tank when their own was put out of action. A nearby natural obstacle, the wood about 1,000 metres southwest of Papricani Coarba , was defended by the Soviets particularly stubbornly and simply could not be taken.
>
> As soon as the attacking groups reached their objectives, Romanian troops were moved up and these occupied the newly-won positions.

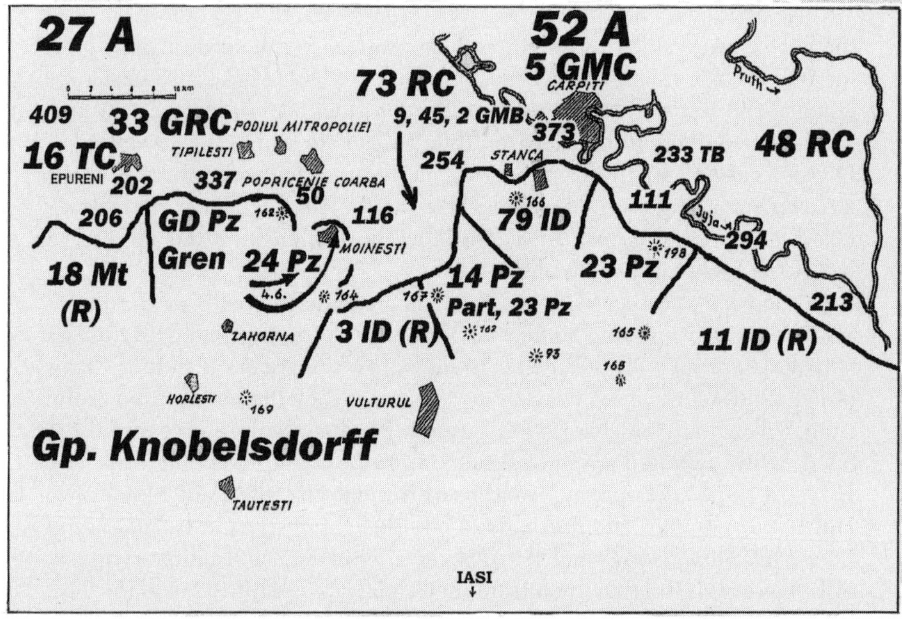

Map 28. The German Eighth Army's Operation "Katja," 4 June 1944

> However, the higher-ups were not very convinced of the Romanians' will to resist, and so German counterattack groups were held behind each of the Romanian positions and these were forced to intervene on more than one occasion.[23]

By this time, all of Dubovoi's tank corps was participating in the defense of Epureni, probably also reinforced by the forward elements of Mishulin's 3rd Tank Corps. Further south, Edelsheim's *kampfgruppen* of the 24th Panzer Division finally captured Hill 164 and the Soviet strong point at Moinesti with help from *Grossdeutschland*'s Grenadier Regiment and infantrymen from the Romanian 3rd Infantry Division. However, strong Soviet resistance also halted this attack by day's end.[24]

Nor did the heavy fighting diminish the following day. Advancing abreast from west to east, early on 5 June, the concentrated *kampfgruppen* of the *Grossdeutschland* and 24th Panzer Divisions once again assaulted the Soviets' entire defensive front from just north of Hill 162 eastward to just north of Hill 167, two miles north of Vulturi (Map 29). This time, they were joined by a *kampfgruppe* from Unrein's 14th Panzer Division, which, after being

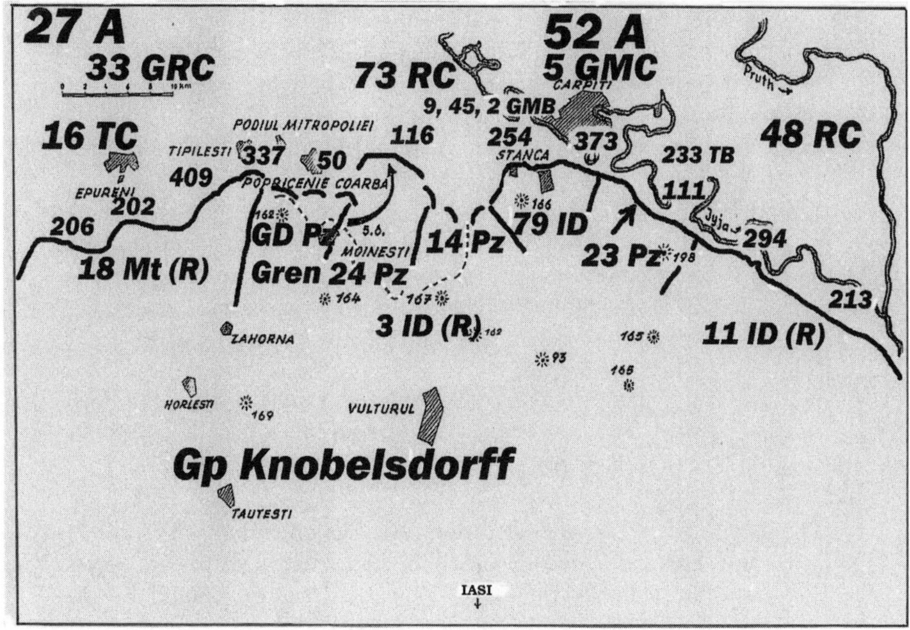

Map 29. The German Eighth Army's Operation "Katja," 5 June 1944

reinforced by most of Kräber's 23rd Panzer Division's tanks, fielded a force of six tanks and 25 assault guns and conducted its attack from jumping-off positions southwest of the village of Stanca. Although it provides no details about its renewed assault, the *Grossdeutschland* Division's history describes a particularly disconcerting Soviet counterattack that threatened to rout a defending Romanian force and, tangentially, outlines the ill effects of the recent fighting on its own combatworthiness:

> This is exactly what happened west of Zahorna on 5 June, when the enemy, with considerable support from bombers and close-support aircraft, charged the Romanian positions on a 2–3 kilometre [one to two-mile] front and soon put the defenders to flight. Elements of the Armoured Reconnaissance Battalion GD were able to restore the situation by evening, returning the Romanians to their foxholes. Unfortunately this did not make for a rosy outlook for the future, especially when the GD was no longer on the scene.
>
> The losses of the past days once again forced the panzer-fusiliers to amalgamate units. The remnants of III Battalion were combined with

> those of II Battalion, while actual command of the regiment was temporarily in the hands of Major Krieg, filling in for Oberst Niemack who had been ordered to Fuhrer Headquarters to receive the Swords. Niemack was the 69th recipient of this high decoration, which was awarded him for his courageous actions in front of Targul Frumos on 2 May 1944.[25]

Although Knobelsdorff's general assault reached the southern approaches to the village strong points of Tipilesti and Popricani on the southern bank of the Jijia River, it faltered once again because Trofimenko committed the lead rifle division of Alekhin's 27th Guards Rifle Corps, Major General E. P. Grechanyi's 409th Rifle Division, and probably the remainder of Mishulin's 3rd Tank Corps, into the fighting.

Fighting raged along the entire front on 5 and 6 June as Knobelsdorff's forces tried to break the Soviets' defenses once and for all and reach the Jijia River (Map 30). However, as recorded by Army Group South's history:

> The Eighth Army suspended further offensive operations on 6 June because they had completely occupied the high ground northwest of Jassy, and, therefore, achieved their attack objectives. In this manner, the army considerably improved its defensive position.
>
> The army conducted mopping-up operations the next day and then the front quieted down.[26]

Grossdeutschland's history confirms this lull, adding, "On 6 June the fighting died down somewhat; the men were able to better install themselves in the former Soviet trenches, which were now used in reverse to their intended direction."[27]

Notwithstanding its accomplishments and the assertions of Army Group South's history, by this time Knobelsdorff's panzer shock group had lost much of its combat punch and its forward momentum—in reality, before it accomplished all of the objectives the Eighth Army had assigned to it. Although Group Mieth's and, later, Group Knobelsdorff's panzer shock groups eliminated most of Koroteev's bridgehead south of the Jijia River east of Cirpiti, they failed to dislodge the 52nd Army's forces from their smaller bridgeheads on the river's southern bank. In addition, when the battle ended, Trofimenko's 27th Army still controlled Epureni and a sizeable bridgehead on the southern bank of the Jijia River from Epureni eastward to the river's southern bank opposite Cirpiti.

After Knobelsdorff's counterstroke ended, Group Mieth had to withdraw the 14th Panzer Division out of line north of Vulturi on 7 June and employ it to reinforce the 23rd Panzer Division's sector along the Jijia River in order to repel new attacks by the 52nd Army's 48th Rifle Corps. At the same time,

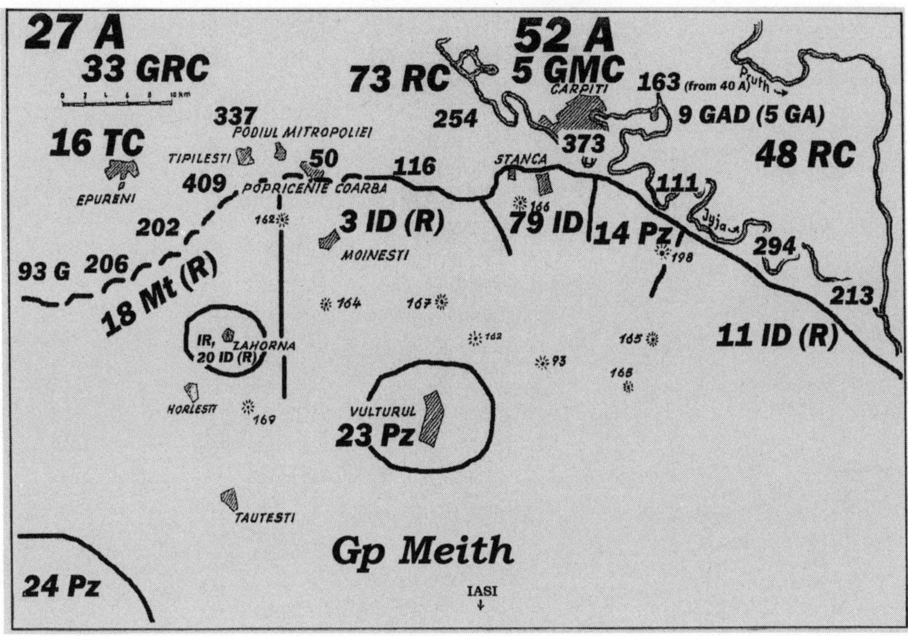

Map 30. The situation in the Iasi sector, 7–8 June 1944

Group Mieth withdrew Edelsheim's severely worn down 24th Panzer Division from combat and dispatched it southward into assembly areas for rest and refitting.

However, urged on by Malinovsky, Trofimenko's forces continued to mount local attacks against Group Mieth's defenses northwest of Iasi, this time with reinforcements from Goriachev's 35th Guards Rifle Corps and tanks from Bogdanov's 2nd Tank Army. *Grossdeutschland*'s history describes the strongest of these attacks, which Trofimenko's riflemen and Bogdanov's tanks conducted in the sector south of Epureni on 7 June:

> However, the quiet was deceptive, for on 7 June the enemy counterattacked north of Zahorna with considerable air support. Hill 181 [two kilometers south of Epureni] was lost and the Soviets managed to drive into Zahorna itself.
>
> An immediate counterstroke, carried out by the Assault Gun Brigade GD under Oberleutnant Diddens and a battle group from the Armoured Reconnaissance Battalion GD led by Rittmeister Schroedter, returned Zahorna to German hands. However, the attackers were pinned down

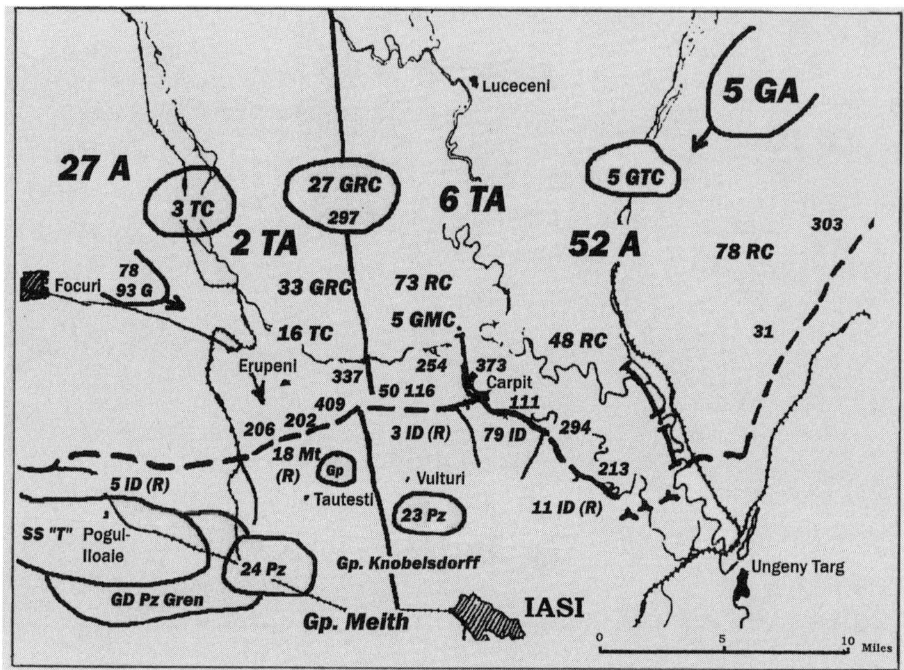

Map 31. The situation in the Tirgu Frumos and Iasi sectors, 8 June 1944

by heavy defensive fire about 1,000 metres south of Point 81. Both battle group commanders, Oberleutnant Diddens and Rittmeister Schroedter, were put out of action with serious wounds. The German attack was called off and a new defensive line was occupied at the limit of the advance.

There now followed a pause in the fighting, apart from some local skirmishing, which allowed the German troops to more or less improve their positions.[28]

Trofimenko spearheaded this particularly fierce assault against the *Grossdeutschland* Division's defenses south of Epureni with Zolotukhin's and Grechanyi's 93rd Guards and 409th Rifle Divisions, which had just reached this sector, supported by the remnants of Khokhlov's and Kalinin's 202nd and 206th Rifle Divisions and a few tanks from Dubovoi's 16th Tank Corps (Map 31). In addition to further damaging the defending German forces, the ferocity of the attack convinced Mieth that his forward defenses northwest of Iasi were still overly vulnerable. Therefore, although the fighting north of Iasi died out on 8 June, signaling the end of Operation Katja, only days after silence descended over the battlefield, Mieth withdrew the forces on his left wing to more defensible terrain, one to two miles south of Epureni. However, in grim determination, he held firmly to his forward defenses south of Tipilesti, Popricani, and Cirpiti and southward along the Jijia River.

CONCLUSIONS

The decision by Army Group Wöhler and the German Eighth Army to conduct the major counterstroke in the Iasi region was based on two principal assumptions, one of which was correct and the other only a perception. Although entirely justified, their perceived assumption was that the Soviet 2nd Ukrainian Front was regrouping its forces during late May so that it could conduct yet another major offensive in the Iasi region during early June. Although this assumption ultimately proved to be incorrect, the Eighth Army's detection of Malinovsky's attack preparations left it with no choice but to attempt to preempt the impending offensive.

The Eighth Army's assumption that it would be able to replicate the success the Sixth Army achieved in its counterstroke along the Dnestr River by conducting a counterstroke of its own north of Iasi, if given the opportunity to do so, proved to be at least partially correct. In fact, Wöhler and the Eighth Army's command were fascinated by the apparent ease with which de Angelis's Sixth Army had destroyed or severely damaged the Soviets' most threatening bridgeheads across the Dnestr River in its counterstrokes during early and mid-May. However, even if their fascination with de Angelis's signal victories was not enough to justify launching a major counterstroke in the Iasi region, then their fears of an impending Soviet offensive certainly provided adequate justification for conducting the counterstroke.

Of course, Wöhler could not have known that the *Stavka* first delayed Malinovsky's offensive on 23 May and, later, postponed it indefinitely on 26 May. Nor would this knowledge have made any difference in Wöhler's operational planning. Preoccupied with the Sixth Army's impressive counterstrokes, Wöhler believed he could and should replicate the Sixth Army's performance, both to improve his army's own defenses and to improve the sagging morale of his Romanian Allies. In contrast, the *Stavka*'s decision to call a halt to its attempts to invade northern Romania ultimately did have a significant effect on the success of Wöhler's counterstroke. After deciding to go over to the defense, both the *Stavka* and Malinovsky either cancelled or slowed the regrouping of their forces into the Iasi region. In concrete terms, this meant that many of the Soviet forces, which the Germans assessed were either in or near the Iasi region in late May, were actually not there. This certainly increased the Eighth Army's prospects for achieving success.

Finally, regardless of what Wöhler's counterstroke actually achieved, it had no effect whatsoever on the Soviets' future offensive planning. This was the case, because, beginning on 26 May, the *Stavka* and the 2nd Ukrainian Front had abandoned any intention of resuming offensive operations in the region until August 1944. In short, by late May the *Stavka* was devoting its full attentions to organizing its forthcoming offensives against German forces in eastern Belorussia and southeastern Poland.

As far as the Eighth Army's counterstroke itself was concerned, during a week of intense fighting, first, Group Mieth's forces, and, later, Knobelsdorff's panzer shock group drove the Soviet forces back between two and five miles, thereby providing the German Eighth Army with greater defensive depth north of Iasi. However, because of the timely intervention of Bogdanov's 2nd Tank Army, Trofimenko's rapid redeployment of his 27th Army's forces, and the vigorous reaction of Koroteev's 52nd Army, the counterstroke failed to achieve its ultimate aims. Specifically, Eighth Army's two shock groups failed to expel the Soviets' defending forces from the entire region south of the Jijia River line from Movileni Station to the Prut River and left Soviet forces in possession of bridgeheads, albeit small ones, on the Jijia River's southern bank.

Although the actual casualties both sides suffered during Wöhler's counterstroke remain obscure, the intense fighting certainly exacted a heavy toll in terms of both men and equipment on the Soviets and Germans alike. For example, the 24th Panzer Division alone reported capturing 453 Red Army prisoners and destroying 28 tanks, 47 artillery pieces, 52 antitank guns, and 34 aircraft during Operation Katja, for a total of 1,000 prisoners, 134 tanks (primarily from the 16th Tank Corps), 102 field guns, and 118 antitank guns since 1 April 1944. During the same period, however, the division lost 92 officers and 1,825 of its own men, most of them panzer grenadiers.[29] In addition, during the fighting from 2 through 7 June, the *Grossdeutschland* Division claims to have destroyed 70 Russian tanks, 45 artillery pieces, and 36 antitank guns, while its antiaircraft gunners claimed to have shot down 19 enemy aircraft, and its engineers asserted they cleared more than 10,300 mines. While the division neglects to mention its number of dead, it acknowledges its medical company treated more than 2,000 wounded.[30]

The German High Command celebrated the end of the fighting north of Iasi on 9 June 1944, with an optimistic communiqué announcing:

> In the battles in the Jassy area German-Romanian troops under the command of Romanian Cavalry General Racovit, General der Panzertruppe Knobelsdorff and General der Infantrie Mieth, with outstanding support from strong German-Romanian bomber and close-support squadrons, drove the Bolsheviks from in-depth, fiercely-defended positions in heavy

fighting and in doing so were able to improve their own positions significantly.[31]

After the vicious fighting in early June, relative quiet descended over the entire front in northern and eastern Romania from the Tirgu-Neamt region in the west, eastward through the Iasi and Orgeev regions, and southward along the bloody banks of the Dnestr River. Konev's and Malinovsky's attempts to seize Iasi and Kishinev and, with these, a significant foothold in northern Romania, first, by a twin coup de main during mid-April, and, later, by a concerted offensive during early May, ended in abject failure in late May. In recognition of this sad reality, at the *Stavka*'s request, a resigned Malinovsky submitted his new defense plans to Moscow on 11 June (see Appendix).

As he did so, Malinovsky also included his assessment of Wöhler's June counterstroke:

> Having conducted an unsuccessful offensive along the Iasi axis and having lost equipment equivalent to four panzer divisions, while suffering great losses in personnel as a result of the ten-day battle, and having failed to achieve success, the enemy has gone over to the defense.[32]

Table 8.1. The 2nd Ukrainian Front's Order of Battle on 1 June 1944
2nd UKRAINIAN FRONT:
Army General R. Ia. Malinovsky

40th Army: LTG F. F. Zhmachenko
50th Rifle Corps: MG S. P. Merkulov
74th Rifle Division
163rd Rifle Division
240th Rifle Division
51st Rifle Corps: MG I. M. Liubovtsev
42nd Guards Rifle Division
133rd Rifle Division
232nd Rifle Division
104th Rifle Corps: LTG A. V. Petrushevsky
4th Guards Airborne Division
38th Rifle Division
159th Fortified Region

7th Guards Army: LTG M. S. Shumilov
24th Guards Rifle Corps: MG P. P. Avdeenko
72nd Guards Rifle Division
81st Guards Rifle Division
25th Guards Rifle Corps: MG G. B. Safiulin
6th Guards Airborne Division
36th Guards Rifle Division
53rd Rifle Division
6th Rifle Division
8th Guards Airborne Division
3rd Separate Antitank Rifle Battalion
27th Guards Tank Brigade
34th Separate Armored Train Battalion
38th Separate Armored Train Battalion

27th Army: LTG S. G. Trofimenko
27th Guards Rifle Corps: MG E. S. Alekhin
297th Rifle Division
409th Rifle Division
33rd Rifle Corps: MG A. I. Semenov
202nd Rifle Division
206th Rifle Division
337th Rifle Division
35th Guards Rifle Corps: LTG S. G. Goriachev
3rd Guards Airborne Division
93rd Guards Rifle Division
78th Rifle Division
180th Rifle Division
54th Fortified Region
25th Separate Tank Regiment

2nd Tank Army: LTGTF S. I. Bogdanov
3rd Tank Corps: LTGTF V. A. Mishulin
50th Tank Brigade
51st Tank Brigade
103rd Tank Brigade
57th Motorized Rifle Brigade
375th Guards Heavy Self-propelled Artillery Regiment
74th Motorcycle Battalion
728th Tank Destroyer Regiment
234th Mortar Regiment
126th Guards-Mortar Battalion
121st Antiaircraft Artillery Regiment
16th Tank Corps: MGTF I. V. Dubovoi
107th Tank Brigade
109th Tank Brigade
164th Tank Brigade
15th Motorized Rifle Brigade
6th Guards Separate Tank Regiment
1441st Self-propelled Artillery Regiment
51st Motorcycle Battalion
729th Tank Destroyer Regiment
226th Mortar Regiment
89th Guards-Mortar Battalion
1721st Antiaircraft Artillery Regiment
11th Guards Tank Brigade
754th Self-propelled Artillery Regiment
1219th Self-propelled Artillery Regiment
87th Motorcycle Battalion

52nd Army: LTG K. A. Koroteev
48th Rifle Corps: MG Z. Z. Rogoznyi
111th Rifle Division
213th Rifle Division
294th Rifle Division
73rd Rifle Corps: MG S. S. Martirosian
50th Rifle Division
116th Rifle Division
373rd Rifle Division
78th Rifle Corps: MG G. A. Latyshev
31st Rifle Division
252nd Rifle Division
303rd Rifle Division
254th Rifle Division

5th Air Army: ColGAv S. K. Goriunov
2nd Guards Bomber Aviation Corps: MGAv I. S. Polbin
1st Guards Bomber Aviation Division
8th Guards Bomber Aviation Division
218th Bomber Aviation Division
1st Guards Assault Aviation Corps: LTGAv V. G. Riazanov
8th Guards Assault Aviation Corps
9th Guards Assault Aviation Corps

Table 8.1. *Continued*

12th Guards Fighter Aviation Division
2nd Assault Aviation Corps: LGAv V. V. Stepichev
7th Guards Assault Aviation Division
231st Assault Aviation Division
4th Fighter Aviation Corps: MG I. D. Podgornyi
294th Fighter Aviation Division
302nd Fighter Aviation Division
7th Fighter Aviation Corps: MGAv A. V. Utin
9th Guards Fighter Aviation Division
205th Fighter Aviation Division
304th Fighter Aviation Division
312th Fighter-Bomber Aviation Division
511th Reconnaissance Aviation Regiment
207th Corrective Reconnaissance Aviation Regiment
95th Transport Aviation Regiment
714th Sep. Signal Aviation Regiment
18th Aviation Regiment, Civil Air Fleet

6th Tank Army: LGTF A. G. Kravchenko
5th Mechanized Corps: LTGTF M. V. Volkov
2nd Mechanized Brigade
9th Mechanized Brigade
45th Mechanized Brigade
233rd Tank Brigade
697th Self-propelled Artillery Regiment
745th Self-propelled Artillery Regiment
64th Motorcycle Battalion
458th Mortar Regiment
35th Guards-Mortar Battalion
1700th Antiaircraft Artillery Regiment
5th Guards Tank Corps: LTGTF V. M. Alekseev
20th Guards Tank Brigade
21st Guards Tank Brigade
22nd Guards Tank Brigade
6th Guards Motorized Rifle Brigade
1458th Self-propelled Artillery Regiment
1462nd Self-propelled Artillery Regiment
80th Motorcycle Battalion
1667th Tank Destroyer Artillery Regiment
454th Mortar Regiment
127th Guards-Mortar Battalion
1696th Antiaircraft Artillery Regiment
156th Separate Tank Regiment
6th Self-propelled Artillery Brigade
1494th Self-propelled Artillery Regiment

4th Guards Army: LTG I. V. Galanin
20th Guards Rifle Corps: MG N. I. Biriukov
5th Guards Airborne Division
7th Guards Airborne Division
41st Guards Rifle Division
62nd Guards Rifle Division
21st Guards Rifle Corps: MG P. I. Fomenko
69th Guards Rifle Division
80th Guards Rifle Division
84th Rifle Division

53rd Army: LTG I. M. Managarov
26th Guards Rifle Corps: MG P. A. Firsov
25th Guards Rifle Division
94th Guards Rifle Division
49th Rifle Corps: MG M. P. Seriugin
1st Guards Airborne Division
375th Rifle Division
89th Guards Rifle Division
110th Guards Rifle Division
63rd Separate Antitank Rifle Battalion
38th Separate Tank Regiment

5th Guards Army: LTG A. S. Zhadov
32nd Guards Rifle Corps: MG A. I. Rodimtsev
13th Guards Rifle Division
95th Guards Rifle Division
97th Guards Rifle Division
33rd Guards Rifle Corps: LTG N. F. Lebedenko
9th Guards Airborne Division
14th Guards Rifle Division
78th Guards Rifle Division
214th Rifle Division
123rd Separate Antitank Rifle Battalion

Front Reserves
75th Rifle Corps: MG A. Z. Akimenko
233rd Rifle Division
299th Rifle Division
5th Guards Cavalry Corps: MG S. I. Gorshkov
11th Guards Cavalry Division
12th Guards Cavalry Division
63rd Cavalry Division
1896th Self-propelled Artillery Regiment
150th Guards Tank Destroyer Regiment
5th Guards Separate Tank Destroyer Battalion
9th Guards-Mortar Regiment

Table 8.1. *Continued*

72nd Guards-Mortar Battalion	40th Guards-Mortar Battalion
585th Antiaircraft Artillery Regiment	1713th Antiaircraft Artillery Regiment
1st Infantry Division (Rum)	18th Tank Corps: MGTF V. I. Polozkov
7th Mechanized Corps: MGTF F. G. Katkov	110th Tank Brigade
16th Mechanized Brigade	170th Tank Brigade
63rd Mechanized Brigade	181st Tank Brigade
64th Mechanized Brigade	32nd Motorized Rifle Brigade
41st Guards Tank Brigade	1438th Self-propelled Artillery Regiment
1289th Self-propelled Artillery Regiment	78th Motorcycle Battalion
1440th Self-propelled Artillery Regiment	1000th Tank Destroyer Artillery Regiment
94th Motorcycle Battalion	736th Tank Destroyer Artillery Battalion
109th Tank Destroyer Artillery Regiment	292nd Mortar Regiment
392nd Separate Tank Destroyer Battalion	106th Guards-Mortar Battalion
614th Mortar Regiment	1694th Antiaircraft Artillery Regiment
	10th Separate Armored Train Battalion
	25th Separate Armored Train Battalion
	61st Separate Armored Train Battalion

Source: *Boevoi sostav Sovetskoi armii, Chast' 4 (Ianvar'-dekabr' 1944)* [The combat composition of the Soviet Army, Part 4 (January–December 1944)] (Moscow: Voenizdat, 1988), 167–170.

Table 8.2. Task Organization of the 24th Panzer Division on 30 May 1944

***Kampfgruppe* "E"** (Commander, Lieutenant Colonel von Einem)
1. Two motorized panzer grenadier battalions [*abteilungen*] (the 2nd Battalion, 21st Panzer Grenadier Regiment [II./21] and the 2nd Battalion, 26th Panzer Grenadier Regiment [II./26])
2. 2nd Company, 40th Panzer Pioneer (Engineer) Battalion
3. Part of the 323rd Assault Gun Brigade

***Kampfgruppe* "W"** (Commander, Colonel von Waldenburg)
1. *Kampfgruppe* headquarters (26th Panzer Grenadier Regiment headquarters)
2. Panzer battalion [*abteilung*] (3rd Battalion, 24th Panzer Regiment [III./24])
3. Medium panzer grenadier battalion (1st Battalion, 26th Panzer Grenadier Regiment [I./26] and the 24th Panzer Reconnaissance Battalion [PzAA. 24])
4. Panzer artillery battalion [*abteilung*] (1st Battalion, 89th Artillery Regiment [I./89], with one battery of heavy 150-mm field howitzers on "*Hummel*" ["Bumble-bee"] (IV) self-propelled mounts and one battery of 150-mm assault howitzers on Panzer IV "*Brummbar*" ["Growler"])
5. 3rd Battalion, 40th Panzer Pioneer Battalion

Division Reserve
1. Division Escort Squadron and the remainder of the 40th Panzer Pioneer Battalion

Source: F. M. von Senger und Etterlin, *Die 24. Panzer-Division vormals 1. Kavallerie-Division 1939–1945* (Neckargemund: Kurt Vowinckel Verlag, 1962), 242–243.

CHAPTER 9

Conclusions

THE "DISCOVERY"

During the almost 60 years since the end of World War II, Soviet and Russian military historians and theorists have carefully erased from the historical record any mention of the 2nd and 3rd Ukrainian Fronts' first Iasi-Kishinev offensive, during which the Red Army's two *fronts* attempted to invade Romania in April and May 1944. As is the case with so many other military operations the Red Army conducted during the war, they have done this deliberately, in the process relegating this offensive to a lengthy list of "forgotten battles" of the Soviet-German War. Only recently have Russian historians begun recognizing that this offensive ever took place and partially resurrected it from the "forgotten" category. For example, the four-volume official history of the Soviet Union's "Great Patriotic War," prepared by the Russian Federation's Ministry of Defense in 1998 and 1999, for the first time includes a brief but incomplete description of the offensive, which ends by concluding:

> Thus, during the Tyrgu-Frumos [Tirgu-Frumos] operation, the 2nd Ukrainian Front's forces tried unsuccessfully to complete a deep penetration of the enemy's defense and reach the territory between the Prut and Seret Rivers. By order of the Stavka, they themselves went over to the defense along existing lines on 6 May. . . .
>
> The several attempts by the [3rd Ukrainian Front's] participating armies to conduct attacks from their [Dnestr] bridgeheads and seize new bridgeheads led to nothing. By order of the Stavka, the 3rd Ukrainian Front went over to the defenses on 6 May.[1]

From the standpoint of establishing a complete and accurate record of the Soviet-German War, very few histories of the war written by German historians or other Western historians relying primarily on German sources even mention this Red Army offensive. Following the Soviet and Russian example, these historians relegate this offensive to the "dustbin" of history by ignoring it and focusing instead on the heavy fighting that took place in the Ukraine from January through April 1944. The few exceptions to this rule are General von Senger und Etterlin's perceptive book, *Der Gegenschlag,* and the lecture of General Manteuffel, which, although tactical in focus, correctly concludes that the Germans' successful defenses along the Tirgu Frumos axis actually halted "the Russians' thrust toward the Ploesti oilfields."

Today, however, more careful examination of the archival records of German forces, which were defending northern Romania during April and May 1944, as well as recently released Soviet archival materials, not only support von Senger's and Manteuffel's contentions but also prove irrefutably that Stalin, his *Stavka,* and the Red Army's 2nd and 3rd Ukrainian Fronts indeed intended to capture the cities of Iasi and Kishinev during the spring of 1944 and, if possible, extend their offensive operations and Soviet political influence into the depths of Romania, if not the Balkan region as a whole. Thus, the "discovery" of this forgotten offensive fundamentally alters longstanding perceptions of the military strategy Stalin and his *Stavka* pursued during 1944, if not the entire final two years of the war, by revealing what should be properly termed Stalin's "Balkans strategy."

STRATEGIC IMPLICATIONS

Every officially sanctioned Soviet and, more recently, Russian history of the Soviet-German War published since war's end categorically asserts that, immediately after the Red Army completed its successful winter campaign in the Ukraine during mid-April 1944, Stalin ordered his *Stavka* and General Staff to begin preparations to conduct a series of successive strategic offensives through Belorussia and Poland during the summer of 1944, which, from a military and political perspective, were designed to hasten the destruction of the *Wehrmacht* and Hitler's Third Reich in the shortest possible time by exploiting the most direct route into the heart of Germany. Only after completing these more important offensives, these sources argue, did Stalin finally unleash the Red Army on an invasion of Romania and the Balkan region. According to this strategic paradigm, when the Red Army actually implemented the *Stavka*'s plan, it began its offensive into Belorussia in late June, its offensive into southern Poland in mid-July, and its offensive into Romania in late August.

Furthermore, these same histories argue that, just as the Balkan region was a secondary strategic objective for Stalin during the Red Army's summer–fall campaign of 1944, it remained of secondary importance when the Red Army conducted its offensives during the winter campaign of 1945. Therefore, just as the Red Army invaded Romania in late August 1944, but only after its offensives in Belorussia and eastern Poland succeeded, likewise, during its winter campaign of 1945, the Red Army captured Budapest and western Hungary and invaded Austria in February and March 1945, but only after its offensive through Poland to the Oder River succeeded.

However, the "discovery" of the Red Army's attempt to invade Romania in mid-April and May 1944 casts serious doubts on this prevailing strategic paradigm. In short, the precise timing, immense scale, complex nature, and obvious objectives of the Red Army's offensive into Romania during April and May 1944 now clearly indicate that Stalin and his *Stavka* were paying considerable attention to strategic imperatives other than those described in this prevailing strategic paradigm. Simply stated, vital military, economic, and political factors prompted Stalin to order his Red Army to mount a major offensive of immense potential strategic significance into Romania between mid-April and late May 1944.

From the perspective of strictly military considerations, Soviet and Russian military historians have argued that Stalin had no choice but to begin his summer campaign of 1944 with an assault against the *Wehrmacht*'s defenses in Belorussia. This was so, they argue, because the failure of the Red Army's 1st Baltic, Western, and Belorussian Fronts to reduce the German defenses in eastern Belorussia during the winter of 1944, coupled with the Leningrad and 2nd Baltic Fronts' advance to the Pskov and Ostrov regions on the eastern border of the Baltic region and the 2nd Belorussian Front's advance to the Kovel' region during the same period, formed the so-called Belorussian balcony, which protruded dangerously eastward toward Moscow and had to be eliminated before the Red Army could begin a coherent advance toward Berlin. Similarly, they argue, the successful advance by the 1st Ukrainian Front to the border with eastern Poland during April dictated that the *Stavka* follow up its summer offensive into Belorussia with an immediate offensive into Poland. Then and only then, they assert, was it militarily feasible for the *Stavka* to mount an offensive into northern Romania.

Therefore, based on purely military considerations, this paradigm provides no rationale for Konev's and Malinovsky's 2nd and 3rd Ukrainian Fronts to advance beyond the Seret, Prut, and Dnestr Rivers in northern Romania during the spring of 1944. While it would be entirely reasonable for them to conduct local operations to seize favorable terrain conducive to the conduct of future offensive operations, any attempt by them to advance deeper into Romania or the Balkans region was likely to jeopardize the *Stavka*'s more vital offensives through Belorussia and Poland toward Berlin.

However, for a variety of reasons, these arguments regarding military imperatives are incorrect. First, time and time again prior to 1944, the *Stavka* had already demonstrated its willingness to employ the Red Army to conduct simultaneous and even successive strategic offensives along multiple axes. Although the Red Army's capabilities for doing so successfully proved quite limited during 1941, 1942, and the first half of 1943, it did so with far greater success during the second half of 1943 and the first half of 1944. Therefore, based on its past practices and the Red Army's previous accomplishments, the *Stavka* could certainly do so once again during the spring and summer of 1944.

Second, as it conducted its strategic planning in April 1944, there was no reason for the *Stavka* to rule out conducting an immediate offensive into Romania for the sake of mounting successful offensives into Belorussia and Poland in mid-summer. This was true because, in the first instance, the German's defenses in Belorussia were already essentially untenable and, in the second instance, because there was ample time available to reinforce Red Army forces facing eastern Poland without abandoning an offensive into Romania. At the time, powerful Red Army forces threatened German Army Group Center, which was defending Belorussia, from three sides. Although the Germans still grimly clung to their fortress bastions at Vitebsk, Orsha, Mogilev, and Bobruisk, the Red Army's Baltic *fronts* outflanked them from the north, and its 1st and 2nd Belorussian Fronts outflanked them from the south.[2] Thus, by mid-April the Germans' Belorussian salient had already become largely untenable and was vulnerable to destruction during the summer after the Red Army reinforced its *fronts* operating in the region only modestly.

Furthermore, the Red Army's 1st Ukrainian Front, which had reached extreme western Ukraine by mid-April 1944 and was supposed to invade southeastern Poland in mid-July, shortly after the Belorussian *fronts* began their offensive to the north, would have been able to begin its invasion on schedule even if the *Stavka* conducted its invasion of Romania during April and May. As previous experience indicated, in this case the 2nd and 3rd Ukrainian Fronts, which were supposed to provide reinforcements to the 1st Ukrainian Front prior to its offensive, would have sufficient time to do so if they completed their offensive into Romania by late May or early June.

Last but not least, from the military perspective, a successful invasion by the 2nd and 3rd Ukrainian Fronts into Romania during April and May 1944 would deprive Hitler's Axis of its vital defense lines in northern Romania, thereby facilitating a subsequent advance by the Red Army into the entire Balkan region whenever the *Stavka* desired. Therefore, from a purely military standpoint, the offensive into Romania was both feasible and desirable.

In addition to these purely military considerations, there were also strategically vital economic and political motives for Stalin and his *Stavka* to mount an invasion of Romania during April and May 1944. Economically, for example, as von Senger pointed out, if successful, a full-fledged Red Army invasion of Romania could deprive the Axis of its vital oilfields in Romania, thereby seriously degrading Germany's ability to continue the war. More important still from a political standpoint, a successful invasion of Romania would likely topple the pro-German Romanian government and drive Romania from the war, and perhaps even force Bulgaria to abandon its looser ties with Hitler's Germany. In fact, the loss of a significant portion of Romania to the Red Army would shake if not shatter the Axis' defenses throughout the entire Balkans, inject a sizeable Red Army presence in the region, and end all hopes by Stalin's "Big Three" counterparts, Roosevelt and Churchill, that they could halt the spread of Soviet influence into the Balkan region.

In short, since Stalin's Western Allies were already planning Operation Overlord to land their forces on the coast of France, the Red Army's entry into Romania would end, once and for all, Stalin's anxiety over his Allies establishing a "second front" in the Balkans. Ever the realist, Stalin judged that the potential political gains associated with the Red Army's advance into Romania during April and May 1944 more than outweighed any associated military risks. Nor was it coincidental that, after his spring 1944 venture failed and the Red Army's summer offensives to the north succeeded, Stalin unleashed the Red Army' forces on a new invasion deeper into Romania and the Balkans during August 1944.

Furthermore, although it will be the subject of a future book, it is now quite clear that Stalin continued to pursue a similar "Balkan strategy" during the winter of 1945 after his Allies assured him at the Yalta Conference in early February that Berlin would be his for the taking. As a result, within hours after receiving these assurances, Stalin abruptly halted the Red Army's advance on Berlin along the Oder River, only 30 miles from Berlin, and instead shifted its main axis of advance—first, into western Hungary and, later, into the depths of Austria—for essentially the same political reasons that had motivated him to invade Romania during April, May, and August 1944. Just as Stalin had altered his strategy for a drive on Berlin by attempting to invade Romania in April and May 1944 only to resume his advance along the Berlin axis in June, a year later the Red Army began its final drive on Berlin on 16 April 1945, the day after Vienna fell. Therefore, the Red Army's failed offensive into Romania during April and May 1944 is remarkably consistent with Stalin's strategic behavior during 1945.

LESSON LEARNED

Regardless of Stalin's motives for authorizing the offensive into Romania, for a variety of reasons, the Red Army's first Iasi-Kishinev offensive ended as a spectacular failure. After failing to overcome Axis defenses from the march during mid-April, Konev's 2nd Ukrainian Front was equally unsuccessful in its better-prepared offensive against Axis forces defending in the Tirgu-Frumos and Iasi regions in May. During the same period, although Malinovsky's

3rd Ukrainian Front was able to seize some bridgeheads across the Dnestr River in early April, its twin efforts to expand those bridgeheads later in the month achieved little more. Complicating the *Stavka*'s strategic plans, while Konev and Malinovsky were organizing a third effort to capture Iasi and Kishinev during mid-May, for the first time since late 1942, counterattacking German forces actually managed to inflict serious defeats on major Red Army forces defending bridgeheads across a major river.

Since Soviet and Russian military theorists and historians have concealed this offensive from public view, precious few critiques of the combat performance of the two *fronts* that conducted the first Iasi-Kishinev offensive exist. In addition to fragmentary critiques scattered throughout the multiple classified war experience volumes compiled by the Red Army General Staff, other critiques appear in the semiofficial histories of the armies and divisions that took part in the offensive and the memoirs of those who led these forces. In general, these critiques attribute the offensive's failure, first and foremost, to the relative weakness of both attacking *fronts,* and, secondarily, to the failure of Konev and Malinovsky to coordinate their operations effectively. This applies in particular to the period in mid-April, when Konev attempted to capture Iasi before he concentrated his forces enough to do so successfully and, during late April, when, as many observers concluded, the *Stavka* should have transferred the sector of Konev's *front* east of the Dnestr River to Malinovsky's *front* so that both commanders could have brought the bulk of their forces to bear precisely where they would have the greatest impact, specifically, along the Iasi and Kishinev axes. When the two *front* commanders finally attempted to do so in early May (by regrouping their 5th and 8th Guards and 5th Shock Armies), say these observers, it was already too late to have any beneficial effect.

Most of these critiques also highlight the relative weakness of Konev's and Malinovsky's *fronts* when they began their offensives during mid-April and ascribe their subsequent failure to this weakness. For example, they point out that the 2nd and 3rd Ukrainian Fronts had been on the offensive almost constantly since late December 1943 and, during this period, had lost over half of their initial complement of soldiers as casualties. Furthermore, the replacements the two *fronts* received, many of which the Red Army conscripted while on the march, were poorly trained and equipped, and there was no time available to train them while the two *fronts* were continuing their hasty advance into northern Romania. Hence, although their forces were numerically superior to the Germans when the two *fronts* attacked during April and May, their soldiers were not skilled enough to contend with the *Wehrmacht*'s better-trained veterans.

For example, a report prepared by the 2nd Ukrainian Front's Operations Directorate on 17 May 1944 typified numerous other critiques regarding many shortcomings in the *front*'s combat performance during April and May:

> During the course of our forces' successful offensive operations, the enemy employed one of several characteristic tactical techniques to resist our offensive during the penetration of his defensive belts and, in particular, while we were fighting in the depths [of his defense]. The enemy began extensively employing separate groups of tanks and self-propelled guns, which often operated very carefully from ambush or ran to and fro across the battlefield, opening fire on our combat formations from a distance of two kilometers [1.2 miles] or greater.
>
> In these instances, our forces were inadequately prepared to fight with these mobile groups of enemy tanks, their advance tempo slowed, and, in some cases, our infantry and tanks simply halted their attacks.
>
> After discovering that the enemy's tanks (self-propelled artillery) were outside of the range of their direct fire, our accompanying artillery became silent and, since they were incapable of towing the guns forward by hand, our tanks and self-propelled guns conducted the fight with the enemy's tanks and self-propelled guns alone.
>
> As a rule, given our overall unsatisfactory observation [target acquisition], we had no special observers to watch for tanks, and we did not establish special signals in the event the enemy's tanks appeared. Therefore, frequently the artillery did not see the tanks at all or discovered them too late.
>
> Our infantrymen and artillerymen, who are poorly trained in target identification, did not employ sufficiently effective means for identifying the tanks, and, as a result, when the tanks appeared, our artillery opened fire too late and conducted their fire in disorganized fashion and frequently without any observation.[3]

While these and other comments by Soviet and Russian critics are indeed correct, they tend to ignore the fact that the defending German forces had also been fighting for as prolonged a period as their Red Army counterparts and had suffered many serious and costly defeats and heavy losses in men and equipment. Furthermore, when Konev's and Malinovsky's forces invaded Romania, in many sectors they faced green and poorly motivated and equipped Romanian troops. Despite this fact, fighting with a determination born of desperation, the Axis forces were able to hold firmly to most of their defenses in April and early May and, thereafter, mount successful counterstrokes of their own during early May and early June.

Difficult spring weather conditions and the adverse effect of the heavy rains and flooding on the terrain also certainly exacerbated the already significant logistical problems the two *fronts* were experiencing as they operated at the end of their overextended lines of communications characterized by a rickety patchwork logistical network that was just being constructed. First, the two Ukrainian *fronts* were conducting offensive operations in a region whose hilly, broken, and often lightly wooded terrain differed substantially from the rolling grass-covered flatlands of the Ukraine to which their troops were long accustomed.

Second, for the first time in the war, the two *fronts* were attempting to conduct offensive operations after warmer weather melted the icy surface they had exploited to conduct mobile military operations in previous winters. Predictably, the *rasputitsa* proved as formidable an obstacle to the two *fronts'* advancing forces as the Germans' resistance and, in some cases, even more formidable.

Third, compounding the problems cited above, pursuant to orders, as they conducted their fighting withdrawal, the Germans systematically destroyed everything of value both for destruction's sake and to create obstacles to the Red Army's forward movement. They blew up railroads, beds, tracks, and culverts alike; they cratered roads and demolished dams; and they destroyed every building or installation regardless of military value. In short, they left a vast wasteland for the Red Army to traverse in their wake.

As a result, whether attacking or defending, in addition to experiencing customary shortages of food, which made soldierly foraging an essential art, and the normal effects of prolonged combat attrition, virtually every formation and unit within the 2nd and 3rd Ukrainian Fronts suffered significant losses in weaponry and heavy equipment and experienced severe ammunition and fuel shortages. For example, archival documents indicate that, prior to its offensive along the Tirgu Frumos axis on 2 May, the 2nd Ukrainian Front's 2nd Tank Army was supplied with between two and five combat loads of ammunition and two to two and one-half refills of gasoline and diesel fuel, which was not excessively low to conduct such an operation.[4] However, it would be disingenuous to offer these realities as excuses for Konev's and Malinovsky' offensive failures, since, as was always the case, the two *front* commanders, as well as their subordinate officers and soldiers alike, frequently relied on sheer ingenuity or "native wit" to resolve their logistical dilemmas.

THE HUMAN COST

As is the case with many military battles and operations that took place during the Soviet-German War, the losses in personnel and equipment suffered by both sides during the first Iasi-Kishinev offensive and the German counterstrokes remain quite opaque. For example, the Russians have not included any of these operations in their official list of Red Army wartime operations and have omitted them from their recently released but as yet incomplete calculation of personnel losses incurred in specific military operations. In addition, although they have released figures on the number of casualties each Red Army operating *front* suffered during the war, they have failed to break these losses down by year, quarter, or month.

Alternatively, for one reason or another, they have included casualty totals in a variety of other older works, perhaps to demonstrate the sacrifices the Soviet Union made in order to liberate their future Socialist allies in eastern and central Europe—in this case, Romania. For example, a 1974 book concerning the Red Army's role in the liberation of Romania claims that Konev's 2nd Ukrainian Front suffered a total of 78,648 casualties during the period from 27 March to 20 August 1944, including 16,170 killed in action and 62,478 wounded casualties out of the *front*'s total strength of roughly 550,000 men.[5] This period extends from the latter stages of the Uman'-Botoshany offensive up to the beginning of the Iasi-Kishinev offensive of August 1944.

In addition, the same source indicates the 52nd and 27th Armies and the 2nd and 6th Tank Armies suffered another 14,871 casualties, including 2,800 dead and 11,600 wounded during the German counterstrokes from 30 May through 5 June and, in addition, 96 tanks and self-propelled guns and 132 aircraft destroyed and another 18 tanks and self-propelled guns damaged.[6] Thus, according to this source, the 2nd Ukrainian Front lost a total of 93,519 soldiers, roughly 17 percent of its total force, during the fighting in April and May. This figure, in turn, represents roughly 29 percent of the total losses of 266,973 soldiers, including 66,059 dead and 200,914 wounded that it suffered during the entire winter campaign up to 17 April.[7]

Regarding the 3rd Ukrainian Front's losses, the recent four-volume history of the war states that Malinovsky's *front* lost a total of 32,633 men from 20 April through 10 May 1944, including 6,882 killed in action, captured, and missing, and 25,751 wounded, out of an initial strength of approximately 280,000 soldiers.[8] However, this figure does not include the heavy losses the *front* suffered during the deadly counterstrokes the Germans conducted after 10 May, which probably added another 30,000 men to the total casualty toll, bringing it to roughly 60,000 men. Therefore, according to these calculations, the 3rd Ukrainian Front lost roughly 21 percent of its force during the fighting in April and May, which, in turn, represents roughly 22 percent of the total casualties of 269,235 soldiers, including 54,997 killed, captured, or missing, and 214,238 wounded, it suffered during the entire winter campaign up to 17 April.[9]

Therefore, the two Ukrainian *fronts* probably suffered a total of about 150,000 casualties during their offensive into Romania out of approximately

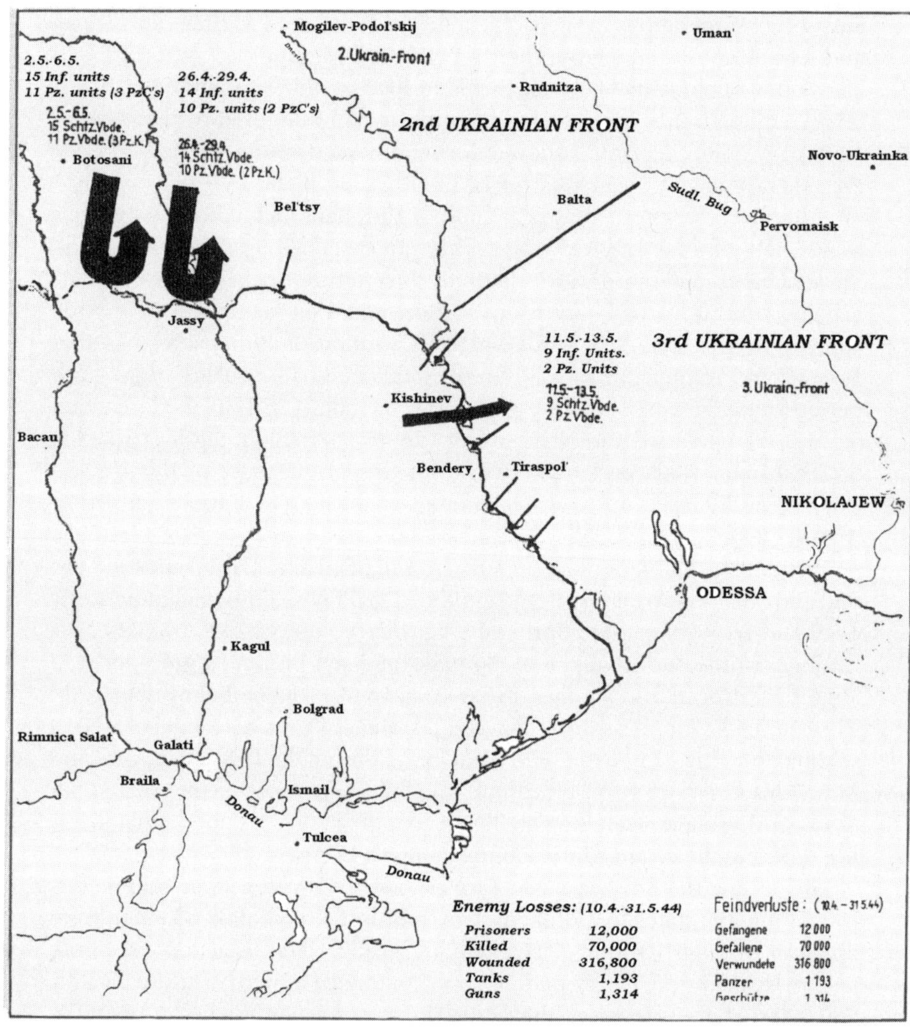

Map 32. German summary of Red Army operations and losses along the southwestern axis, 10 April–31 May 1944

830,000 soldiers assigned to the two *fronts,* for an overall casualty rate of roughly 18 percent. While these figures are rather low when compared with the losses suffered by other Red Army *fronts* in strategic offensive operations, they do indicate that heavy fighting took place in what until recently was presumed to be a quiet sector of the front (Map 32).

As far as Axis losses were concerned, casualty figures are even harder to determine. In the first instance, Soviet and Russian estimates of German losses are wildly inaccurate since these sources routinely inflate German and Axis losses as greatly as they understate their own. For example, the 1974 study states that the 2nd Ukrainian Front killed, wounded, or captured 200,000 Axis troops from 27 March through 20 April 1944, including 27,170 men during the period from 30 May through 5 June.[10] At the same time, it claims that the Axis lost 500 tanks and 366 aircraft during the fighting from 30 May through 5 June, which is actually about five times greater than the Germans' overall initial armor and aircraft strength in this sector.

While no overall loss total is available for German and Romanian forces, overall losses can be estimated from the loss totals that the histories of specific German divisions admit. For example, the 24th Panzer Division, which was in combat nearly continuously in the most active sectors during the entire period from early April to early June, lost a total of 1,917 officers and men from early April through early June, including 446 killed and missing and 1,471 wounded, out of a total of about 12,000 men.[11] This casualty rate of about 15 percent should apply to other equally active divisions, although many were far more understrength. Applied loosely to the overall combat strength of Army Groups Wöhler and Dumitrescu, which amounted to roughly 300,000 men, Axis losses amounted to roughly 45,000 men.

Thus, Stalin's decision to order the 2nd and 3rd Ukrainian Fronts to invade Romania in April and May 1944 represented a deliberate gamble on his part to exploit apparent Axis weakness. By securing possible military victory in Romania, Stalin hoped to paralyze the Germans economically by seizing the Romanian oilfields and to "steal the march" on his Western allies politically by propelling the Red Army and, by extension, Soviet power and influence, into the Balkans. If successful, the offensive ultimately promised to create conditions favorable for the extension of Soviet power into Hungary and the Danube basin. At the same time, whether successful or unsuccessful, the invasion required no significant alterations to Stalin's basic strategy for the defeat of Nazi Germany.

Ironically, even though Stalin's Romanian gambit of April and May 1944 failed, during late August 1944, Stalin was able to implement the same "Balkan strategy," this time with spectacular success to war's end.

APPENDIX

Soviet Documents

1. To the Commander of the 2nd Ukrainian Front Concerning a Plan for the Capture of Iasi and Kishinev, dated 1945 hours 5 April 1944.

For a report to Comrade Ivanov [Stalin], communicate your views on the forcing [river crossing] operations with the aim of capturing Iassy and Kishinev and your evaluation of the enemy along these axes.

Antonov[1]

2. *Stavka* VGK Directive no. 220072, dated 2210 hours 5 April 1944, to the Commander of the 2nd Ukrainian Front Concerning the Acceleration of your Reaching the Siret [Seret] and Bahluiul Rivers.

In connection with the unimpeded advance of the 40th and 27th Armies' reconnaissance detachments between the Prut River and the Siret River, the Stavka VGK orders:

1. Advance the front's right wing to the line of the Siret and Bahluiul Rivers and capture the Dorohoi, Botoshany, and Iasi regions.
2. Immediately report all orders issued.

Stavka VGK
I. Stalin
A. Antonov[2]

3. Report no. 00281/op, dated 2400 hours 5 April 1944, by the Commander of the 2nd Ukrainian Front to the Supreme High Commander on a Plan for Developing an Offensive toward the South.

I am reporting:

1. Separate German units and Romanian units are defending along the Seret River on the front's right wing

The enemy is offering stout resistance along the Kishinev axis. The enemy has reinforced the Kishinev axis at the expense of units withdrawing from the 3rd Ukrainian Front's front.

The enemy has already transferred the 62nd, 46th, 79th, and 370th Infantry Divisions and the 3rd and 24th Panzer Divisions to reinforce the Kishinev axis.

In addition, the enemy has also reinforced the Kishinev axis with units transferred from the left bank of the Dnestr.

According to information from prisoners, the enemy is striving to organize a dense defense along the Kishinev axis.

2. To envelop the Germans' main southern grouping, I believe it is necessary to conduct an offensive with the *front*'s right wing, consisting of the 40th and 37th Armies reinforced by the 3rd Guards Tank Corps and, subsequently, Shumilov's [7th Guards] Army.

I will assign the 40th and 27th Armies the mission to reach the Radauty [Radauti], Falticeni, Tirgu-Neamt, Piatra, and Bacau line. When it reaches that line, the 40th Army will go over to the defense to protect the *front*'s right flank.

I will conduct my main attack along the Bolotino, Tirgu-Frumos, Roman, and Bacau axis.

I will employ the 27th Army, reinforced by the 3rd Guards Tank Corps, along the main attack axis now. Subsequently, I will commit Shumilov's army and Rotmistrov's tank army, which will consist of two tank corps (after filling it out with 120 tanks from among those arriving), along this axis.

The operation will begin on 8 April 1944 with the 40th and 27th Armies' offensive. The immediate mission of these armies is to reach the Seret River. Subsequently, the operation will be strengthened as the units of the 3rd Guards Tank Corps and the armies of Shumilov and Rotmistrov arrive.

The missions of the armies on the *front*'s left wing—the 4th Guards, 53rd, and 5th Guards and the 2nd and 6th Tank—will be to continue the offensive to capture the Kishinev region and reach the Prut River.

I request you approve [this proposal] and designate the *front*'s subsequent missions.

Based on the situation and terrain conditions, I presume the *front* will subsequently conduct an attack toward Focsani.

I. Konev I. Susaikov M. Zakharov[3]

4. *Stavka* VGK Directive no. 220073, dated 2245 hours 6 April 1944, to the Commander of the 2nd Ukrainian Front on the Development of an Offensive toward the South.

The Stavka VGK approves the Report No. 00281/op that you submitted on 6 April 1944 and points out:

1. The reinforcement of Trofimenko's 27th Army with only the 3rd Guards Tank Corps for operations to the south along the Siret [Seret] River will be insufficient. Immediately transfer one tank army, either Bogdanov's or Kravchenko's, to the western bank of the Prut River.

2. With regard to the axis toward Kishinev, two tank armies, Rotmistrov's, Kravchenko's, or Bogdanov's, will be entirely sufficient. In addition, you must bear in mind that the 3rd Ukrainian Front's right wing will reach the region south of Kishinev, which will ease your capture of Kishinev.

3. Regroup Shumilov's 7th Guards Army to the region west of Rybnitsa.

4. Immediately commit the corps on the right wing of Zhmachenko's 40th Army, which are situated in the Khotin region and to the south, and employ them to reinforce the 40th Army's units attacking toward the Siret River.

5. The commander of the 2nd Ukrainian Front is responsible for protecting the boundary with the 1st Ukrainian Front and to do so will keep one rifle division in the region of the town of Seret.

6. Report fulfillment.

The *Stavka* VGK
I. Stalin
A. Antonov[4]

5. Operational Directive no. 00324/op of the 2nd Ukrainian Front, dated 0445 hours 23 April 1944.

Top Secret, Special Importance Map 1:100,000

1. The enemy is defending along the Roman axis.

2. The mission of the *front's* shock group of armies is to penetrate the enemy's defense in the Sodomeni, Ruginoasa, and Ulmi-Noui sector and conduct its main attack along the left bank of the Seret River in the general direction of Sagna and Bacesti.

The tank armies will capture Bacau and Vaslui and cut the routes of withdrawal to the west of the enemy's Iasi-Kishinev group of forces.

I order:

3. The commander of the 40th Army to penetrate the enemy's defense in the Prajescu and Timisesti sector and develop the attack in the general direction of Tupilati and Ruginoasa. . . .

4. The commander of the 7th Guards Army, after creating a grouping consisting of six rifle divisions and all of his main mass of artillery to achieve a density of 150 [250] tubes per one kilometer [mile] of front, to penetrate the enemy's defenses in the Harmanesti River and Cucuteni sector.

Conduct your main attack in the general direction of Sagna and Secueni.

One division with one tank brigade of the 5th Guards Tank Army will attack along the right bank of the Seret River with the missions of rolling up the enemy's defense along the Seret River.

Keep one division in second echelon behind your left wing.

Capture the Barlicesti, Miclauseni, and Hindresti line by the end of the first day of the offensive.

Capture the city of Roman and the Duca Station and Bacesti line by the end of the second day of the offensive.

The boundary line on the right is as before, and on the left up to Coarnele-Capru as before and beyond to Hodora, Height Marker 256, Halmu, Tirgu-Frumos, Slobozia, and Bacesti, with all points except Hodora inclusive for the 7th Guards Army.

The army will cooperate with and support the commitment of the 5th Guards Tank Army into the penetration.

5. The commander of the 27th Army will penetrate the enemy's defense in the Tetarului and Hodora Burial Mound sector with a force of four divisions.

Conduct your main attack on your right wing in the direction of Tirgu-Frumos and beyond to Stornesti and Negresti.

Capture Tirgu-Frumos and the Stornesti and Sinesti regions and the mountain passes to Slobodzia with forward detachments by the end of the first day.

Capture the Dumesti and Boresti line by the end of the second day.

The army will cooperate with and support the commitment of the 2nd Tank Army into the penetration.

Fulfill the mission toward Iasi on your left wing.

The boundary line on the left is as before.

6. The commander of the 5th Guards Tank Army will exploit the 7th Guards Army's penetration in the Ruginoasa and Probota sector on the first day of the operation and swiftly develop the offensive in the direction of Ruginoasa and Sagna.

One brigade will attack along the right bank of the Seret River toward Roman in cooperation with the 7th Guards Army.

Capture the city and road junction at Roman and Bacesti and reach the Roman, Bacesti, and Buhaesti line by the end of the first day, with your main grouping in the Bacesti region.

Allocate one tank brigade with automatic weapons assault troops for the surprise and swift seizure of the passes.

Subsequently exploit the offensive to Birlad. Part of your force will capture the city of Bacau and reach the Secueni, Dragomiresti, and Racovei line by the end of the second day.

7. The commander of the 2nd Tank Army, in cooperation with the 27th Army, will penetrate the enemy's defenses in the Tetarului and Hodora Burial Mound sector and capture Tirgu-Frumos by enveloping it from the east. Subsequently, be prepared to develop the offensive toward Slobodzia or Iasi to roll up the enemy's defense opposite the 27th Army's center and left wing.

8. Be prepared to begin the offensive on 27 April 1944. The date and hour of the offensive will be in accordance with a special order.

9. Submit detailed plans on 25 April 1944.

10. Confirm receipt.

Konev
Zakharov
Susaikov[5]

6. *Stavka* VGK Directive no. 220093, dated 2400 hours 3 May 1944, to the Commander of the 2nd and 3rd Ukrainian Fronts and the Representative of the *Stavka* [A. M. Vasilevsky] Regarding the Transfer of the 5th Guards Army and the Missions of Liberating Kishinev.

The Stavka VGK orders:

1. Transfer the sector of the front now occupied by the 2nd Ukrainian Front's 5th Guards Army to the 3rd Ukrainian Fronts effective 2400 hours on 6 May; the latter will complete the relief of the 5th Guards Army by the time indicated.

2. Establish the following boundary line between the 2nd and 3rd Ukrainian Front effective 2400 hours on 6 May: Perekrestovo Station, Elenovka, Krasnyi

Moldovanin, Floreshty, Petricani, Kotomori, Solesti, and Bacau (all points except Elenovka and Bacau are inclusive for the 3rd Ukrainian Front).

3. The commander of the 3rd Ukrainian Front will regroup his *front*'s main forces to the Grigoriopol' and Bendery sector and launch an offensive no later than 15–17 May by conducting your main attack on the right wing in the general direction of Birlad and Focsani.

4. After its relief, the commander of the 2nd Ukrainian Front will employ the 5th Guards Army to reinforce the *front*'s right wing. The left wing will cooperate with the 3rd Ukrainian Front in the capture of Kishinev by enveloping the latter from the north.

5. Carry out all force movements secretly from the enemy.

6. Report all orders issued.

The *Stavka* VGK
I. Stalin
A. Antonov[9]

7. *Stavka* VGK Directive no. 220094, dated 1515 hours 6 May 1944, to the Commander of the 2nd Ukrainian Front Concerning a Transition to the Defense.

The Stavka VGK orders:

1. Upon receipt of this directive, the 2nd Ukrainian Front will go over to a firm defense along the entire sector of its front. You are permitted to conduct local offensives with limited aims in separate sectors of the front to create more favorable jumping-off positions for subsequent offensives.

2. When organizing your defense, pay special attention to the Roman and Iassy [Iasi] axes.

3. Employ a deeply echeloned defense. Prepare no fewer than three defensive lines in the *front*'s sector, with an overall defensive depth of 30–40 kilometers [18–24 miles].

4. The *front*'s forces will prepare to regroup and immediately start stockpiling reserves of ammunition and fuel. Prepare to regroup no later than 25 May [in accordance with *Stavka* Directive no. 220106 dated 23 May, the date of preparedness for an offensive was postponed for seven days].

5. Report on all orders given.

The *Stavka* VGK
I. Stalin
A. Antonov[7]

8. *Stavka* Directive no. 220095, dated 1515 hours 6 May 1944, to the Commander of the 3rd Ukrainian Front Concerning a Transition to the Defense.

Copy to the Stavka Representative

The Stavka VGK orders:

1. Upon receipt of this directive, the 3rd Ukrainian Front will go over to a firm defense along the entire sector of its front with its main grouping in accordance with *Stavka* Directive no. 220093 dated 3 May.

2. Employ a deeply echeloned defense. Prepare no fewer than three defensive lines with an overall defensive depth of 30–40 kilometers [18–24 miles] in your *front*'s sector.

3. Pay special attention to defense along the Tiraspol' axis and the boundary with the 2nd Ukrainian Front. Reliably dig in on the bridgeheads on the right bank of the Dnestr River.

4. The *front*'s forces will prepare to move [attack]. Immediately begin creating reserves of ammunition and fuel. Prepare to move [attack] no later than 25 May.

5. Report on all orders given.

The *Stavka* VGK
I. Stalin
A. Antonov[11]

9. 2nd Ukrainian Front Directive no. 00337/op, dated 1700 hours 6 May 1944, to the Commander of the 53rd Army Concerning the Conduct of an Offensive toward Kishinev.

1. The enemy in front of the 53rd Army is continuing to occupy his previous positions.

I order:

2. The commander of the 53rd Army to prepare an offensive. Deliver your main attack with a force of four rifle divisions on your left wing in the general direction of Zagaikany and Gratgieshty to envelop Kishinev from the north and, at the same time, capture Kishinev while cooperating with the 3rd Ukrainian Front's forces.

Provide for an artillery density of no fewer than 100 [167] tubes per kilometer [mile] of front in your main attack sector.

3. Submit a plan for conducting the operation on 10 May by special courier.

4. I will subsequently indicate the time the offensive is to begin.

5. Confirm receipt.

Konev[10]

10. 2nd Ukrainian Front Order no. 00348/op, dated 1900 hours 7 May 1944, to the Commander of the 27th Army.

Copy to the Commander, 7th Guards Army

During the combat on 7 May, the forces of the 35th Guards Rifle Corps did not display steadfastness and surrendered the important commanding heights on Hill 256 to the enemy.

I order:

1. You will reprimand the commander of the 35th Guards Rifle Corps, Lieutenant General Goriachev, and his artillery commander.

2. Investigate all of the circumstances surrounding the surrender of Hill 265 and immediately bring the guilty to trial before the judgment of a military tribunal. No reason whatsoever can justify the surrender of Hill 256. You must fight for the hill to the last bullet, right up to hand-to-hand fighting.

3. Restore the situation on Hill 256 and firmly hold on to Hill 256. You will personally organize the battle for the hill.

4. Restore order in your forces, especially in the artillery. . . . Fill out your companies. Clear the "hangers-on" [riffraff] out the divisions' rear areas. Replace the units that have suffered losses with units from the second echelons and army reserves. . . .

Konev[6]

11. From the Documents of the 2nd Tank Army for 1944, dated 8 May 1944.

To: The chief of staff, 2nd Ukrainian Front
The chief of the 2nd Ukrainian Front's Armored and Mechanized Forces
The chief of the 2nd Ukrainian Front's Operations Department

I am reporting about the 2nd Tank Army's composition on 1 May 1944.

1. 3rd Tank Corps	T-34s	27
8th Guards Heavy Tank Regiment	IS-85s	5
375th Heavy Self-propelled Artillery Regiment	ISU-152s	18
TOTAL		50
2. 16th Tank Corps	T-34s	32
	MK-9s	2
6th Guards Heavy Tank Regiment	IS-122s	16
1140th Self-Propelled Artillery Regiment	SU-85s	5
TOTAL		55
3. 11th Guards Tank Brigade	T-34s	16

The losses from 1 through 8 May are:

1. 3rd Tank Corps, irrecoverable [permanent] losses—21 tanks

2. 16th Tank Corps, irrecoverable losses—23 tanks; 6th Guards Heavy Tank Regiment, irrecoverable losses—10 tanks

3. 11th Guards Tank Brigade, irrecoverable losses—9 tanks

4. 375th Heavy Self-propelled Artillery Regiment, irrecoverable losses—11 self-propelled guns

Total irrecoverable losses are 74 tanks and self-propelled guns.

Major General Radzievsky,
Chief of Staff, 2nd Tank Army[8]

12. The 2nd Ukrainian Front's Combat Report for April 1944. Account of the 2nd Ukrainian Front's Combat Activities for the Month of April 1944. Report no. 20892 dated 10 May 1944 to the Operations Directorate of the Red Army General Staff.

Top Secret.

Copy No. 1.

The 2nd Ukrainian Front's combat activities for the month of April encompassed:

A) Pursuit of the enemy after the successfully conducted Uman' operation, during which the *front*'s right wing and center managed to prevent the enemy from occupying a defense along the Prut and Seret Rivers, reach the foothills of the eastern Carpathians [Mountains] and the Pashkani [Pascani] and Iassy [Iasi] line, and, on the *front*'s left wing, reach the Dnestr River, force the river, and establish bridgeheads for operations for the capture of the city of Kishinev.

B) Preparations and the commencement of operations: 1) along the Roman axis; 2) along the Iasi axis; and 3) along the Kishinev axis.

The Grouping and Nature of the Enemy's Operations

As a result of the Uman' operation, which the forces of the 2nd Ukrainian Front conducted successfully, the enemy conducted a fighting withdrawal toward the west and southwest during the first half of the month of April. The enemy's situation was complicated by the fact that our attack toward Iasi, together with the 3rd Ukrainian Front's attack on Kishinev, created a threat to the enemy's flanks and rear. According to information received from the Intelligence Directorate, in this situation the plan of action of the enemy's Army Group South consisted of regrouping part of its forces to the north and moving fresh forces up from the depths in order to prevent a penetration by our forces into the Sixth Army's rear.

The armies were assigned the [following] missions:

1) The Eighth Army was to hold on to positions between Balta and Pervomaisk to forestall a threat to the flank of the withdrawing Sixth Army and then occupy final position along the Orgeev and Skuliany line between the Prut and Dnestr Rivers.

2) Moving up from the depth, the Romanian Fourth Army was to hold the Prut River line between Chernovtsy and Iasi. If the Russians were to cross the Prut River, then the Romanian Fourth Army was to occupy a defense of the crossings through the Carpathians to Tyrgu-Niamt [Tirgu-Neamt]. . . .

Based on these missions and correctly assessing our possible actions, at first the enemy directed his forces to the Kishinev axis, where he had withdrawn his main forces operating before the *front,* having reinforced this axis with four infantry divisions transferred from the 3rd Ukrainian Front and having created a density of one infantry division every two to four kilometers along the Kishinev axis.

Simultaneously, the enemy reinforced the Roman and Iasi axes with Romanian units moving up from the depths, having created a density of one infantry division every five to eight kilometers along these axes. By the middle of April, the enemy managed to occupy a previously prepared defensive belt outfitted with pillboxes and bunkers, which proceeded along terrain favorable for defense along the Moldava River, Pascani, Iasi, Korneshty, mouth of the Reut River, and Dnestr River line. During the month of April, the enemy managed to reinforce his grouping in front of the 2nd Ukrainian Front with 15 divisions, including one tank and two cavalry divisions, and, if 23 divisions, including six tank divisions, were deployed in front of the 2nd Ukrainian Front on 1 April 1944, then 37 divisions, including seven tank divisions, were deployed in front of [the *front*] on 1 May 1944.

The General Factors Influencing the Conduct of Offensive Operations

Operations in the conditions of the spring *rasputitsa* and the absence of roads developed to a depth of 350–400 kilometers by the middle of April, but, at the same time:

1) The reinforcing artillery, in particular the artillery divisions, became overextended and lagged behind the infantry's combat formations. Because of the rasputitsa, up to 75 percent of the reinforcing artillery fell behind along the roads during the first half of the month of April.

2) The separation of the forces from the railroads reached up to 300 kilometers, which complicated the supply of ammunition and fuel.

3) The regrouping of forces became difficult; for example, the regrouping of the 5th Guards Tank Army from the *front*'s left wing to the Roman axis (200 kilometers) required up to 10 days.

4) The extensive flooding made it impossible to arrange for normal conditions for crossing the Dnestr, Prut, Zhizhia, Seret, and Suchava Rivers.

Due to the reasons set forth above, the *front's* forces did not manage to penetrate the enemy's defenses along the Pascani and Iasi line from the march. By exploiting the severely broken terrain and previously prepared defensive positions, the enemy managed to occupy a defense with new Romanian divisions transferred from [in front of] the 3rd Ukrainian Front.

The Combat Operations of the *Front's* Right Wing

These may be divided into two periods, the first from 1 through 18 April with the right wing consisting of the 40th, 27th, and 52nd Armies, and the second after 18 April, consisting of the 40th, 7th Guards, 27th, and 52nd Armies and the 5th Guards, 2nd, and 6th Tank Armies. During the first period, the missions of the front's right wing were to deny the enemy the opportunity to dig in along the Prut and Seret Rivers, reach the foothills of the Carpathians, capture Iasi, and cooperate in the destruction of the enemy's Kishinev grouping.

The armies were assigned the [following] missions:

The 40th Army (with eight rifle divisions) was to capture bridgeheads on the Seret River along the Dorneshti [Dornesti] and Pascani front.

The 27th Army (with seven rifle divisions) was to conduct its main attack in the general direction of Bolotino and Podu-Iloaie and capture Iasi by day's end on 7 April.

The 52nd Army (with 10 rifle divisions) was to capture Iasi with three rifle divisions in cooperation with the 27th Army and, on its left flank, secure the Lunka-Byrnovei [Lunga-Birnova], Komarno [Comarna], Nisporiany [Nisporeny], and Pitushka line with its main forces by day's end on 8 April 1944.

Simultaneously, the *komfront* [*front* commander] was to move [the following] forward to the Roman and Iasi axes:

A) The 5th Guards Tank Army, with the mission to concentrate in the Khyrlau [Hirlau] region by the morning of 10 April 1944 and, without waiting for its full concentration, to attack in the general direction of Tyrgu-Frumos on the morning of 11 April 1944 and capture Roman on 11 April 1944.

B) The 2nd Tank Army with the mission to pass through the 27th Army's combat formation during the course of 9 April and attack in the general direction of Hirlau, Tyrgu-Frumos, and, subsequently, toward Iasi.

With the exception of the 40th Army on the right flank, the forces on the right wing did not fulfill these missions. The reasons were:

1. Because of the poor roads and crossings on the march, the 5th Guards and 2nd Tank Armies were delayed and entered combat [as follows]: the 5th Guards Tank Army on 15 April 1944 instead of on 11 April and the 2nd Tank Army on 12 April instead of on 9 April; and the strengthening of the attack occurred too late and with excessive intervals of time.

2. Having brought the 23rd, 24th, and "GD" [*Grossdeutschland*] Tank [Panzer] Divisions forward and while operating in a system of prepared positions, the enemy himself went over to a counteroffensive and threw the 27th Army's units back from Tyrgu-Frumos on 11 April. A correlation [of forces] of 3:1 in infantry, 1:6 in tanks, and 2:1 in artillery was created, which did not herald success for our subsequent offensive.

On 12 April 1944, the *front* commander made the decision to regroup his forces and conduct his main attack west of Iasi. During the second period, the *front*'s right wing was assigned the mission to penetrate the enemy's defenses in the Sodomen' [Sodomeni], Ruzhinos [Ruginoasa], and Ulmii Noui [Ulmi-Noui] sector and conduct its main attack along the left bank of the Seret River in the general direction of Sagna and Bechesti [Bacesti]; capture Bakeu [Bacau] and Vaslui with the tank armies; and cut off the routes of withdrawal to the west of the enemy's Iasi and Kishinev group of forces.

A) The 40th Army—was to attack in the general direction of Tupilats [Tupilati] and Ruginoasa with a force of four rifle divisions.

B) The 7th Guards Army—was to conduct the main attack in the general direction of Sagna and Secueni with a force of six rifle divisions and capture the city of Roman by the end of the second day of the offensive. The army was to cooperate with and protect the 5th Guards Tank Army's commitment into the penetration.

C) The 27th Army—was to attack in the direction of Tirgu-Frumos and, subsequently, toward Storneshti [Stornesti] and Negreshti [Negresti] with a force of four rifle divisions and capture the Dumeshtii [Dumesti] and Boreshtii [Boresti] line by the end of the second day.

D) The 5th Guards Tank Army—was to exploit the 7th Guards Army's penetration and attack in the direction of Ruginoasa and Sagna on the first day of the operation and reach the Roman, Beshesti [Bacesti], and Vul'pesheshi [Vulpecesti] region.

E) The 2nd Tank Army—was to penetrate the enemy's defenses in cooperation with the 27th Army and capture Tirgu-Frumos by envelopment from the east.

The forces set about fulfilling their assigned missions on 26 April 1944 but were unable to penetrate the enemy's heavily fortified belt to its entire depth.

The offensive which was continued in the ensuing days was also unsuccessful. The reasons were because the enemy consolidated his combat formations and because the existing correlation of forces along the main attack axis of 3:1 in infantry, 3:1 in artillery, and 2:1 in tanks turned out to be inadequate for penetrating the fortified belt by the method of hasty preparations. At this point, the enemy himself prepared for an offensive on 26 April 1944 but was forestalled by an artillery preparation begun by our forces.

The Combat Operations of the *Front's* Left Wing (4th Guards, 53rd, 5th and 7th Guards, and 5th Guards Tank Armies)

The forces were fulfilling the mission of continuing to pursue the withdrawing enemy, cut him off from Dnestr River crossings, force it [the river] from the march, and capture the city of Kishinev. During the period of 6–10 April 1944, the most prolonged fighting took place for Dubossary, Pavlovka, and Grosulovo. The enemy went over to the defense along that line with the mission to protect the withdrawal of his forces to the right bank of the Dnestr River. The enemy's main grouping was operating in front of the [front's] left wing, and the withdrawal of his units was planned. Therefore, the subsequent struggle for the Dnestr was augured to be protracted and prolonged.

Considering the existing situation, the front commander transferred the front's main forces from its left wing to its right wing and transferred part of the forces on the left wing—the 5th Guards Tank Army beginning on 4 April and the 7th Guards Army beginning on 7 April 1944—to the Roman axis. On the left wing, the units of the 53rd and 5th Guards Armies reached the Dnestr River along the Dubossary and Tashlyk front on 12 April 1944 and began forcing the Dnestr River and struggling for bridgeheads.

In order to create a shock group on the left wing, on 17 April the *front* commander ordered the 4th Guards Army to go over to the defense along the Kondrateshty and Pakharnichen' front and reinforce the 5th Guards Army's units. After the regrouping was carried out, on 25 April the units of the 53rd and 5th Guards Armies began an offensive with the mission of capturing the city of Kishinev. The 53rd Army conducted its main attack in the direction of Zagaikana [Zagaikany]; and the 5th Guards Army, reinforced by the 7th Mechanized Corps, conducted its main attack toward Chimisheni [Chimisheny] to envelop Kishinev from the south.

As a result of the intense fighting, the armies were not able to penetrate the entire depth of the enemy's defensive belt and recorded negligible advances.

The most important reasons for this lack of success were that our attacking forces encountered previously prepared defensive lines along which the enemy managed to plant his withdrawn forces and consolidate his combat formations. Our superiority in infantry, tanks, and artillery was quite small. The correlation of forces along the 5th Guards Army's front (the main attack axis) was 2:1 in infantry, 2.5:1 in artillery, and 7:4 in tanks. The enemy's air forces maintained air supremacy. Our aviation could not be fully employed because of the poor state of the airfields and insufficient quantities of fuel.

The Operations of the Armored Formations

The tank armies operated greatly understrength in tanks (on average, the 5th Guards Tank army consisted of 54 tanks and self-propelled guns, the 6th Tank Army of 23, and the 7th Mechanized Corps of 13). This determined their insignificant penetrating power. It [the penetrating power] grew to a significant degree only by the beginning of the Roman operation when the 3rd Guards Tank Corps arrived from the Stavka's reserves and a number of tanks were received as reinforcements, particularly in the 5th Guards Tank Army. The tank formations operated only in cooperation with the infantry. The 5th Guards Tank Army, which was designated to operate as an echelon to develop success along the Roman axis, also operated within the combat formations of the infantry because of the lack of success in penetrating the enemy's defensive belt. The tank formations were employed correctly along axes.

The shortcomings in the tank and mechanized forces were:

A) Reconnaissance was conducted poorly and often limited to a formal "interrogation" [questioning] of the combined-arms commander.

B) There was haste in committing the tanks into combat, unit by unit, without the protection of its artillery and infantry, which resulted in the tanks suffering unnecessary losses.

C) Cooperation with the infantry and artillery was lost in the enemy's tactical depths.

D) In practice, not enough attention was paid to surprise—the main prerequisite for a successful operation—and *maskirovka* [deception].

E) The poorly organized evacuation of tanks increased the number of irreplaceable losses.

F) Command and control was organized unskillfully, and the headquarters lost contact with their combat formations and were not able to influence the course of the fighting.

Concerning the employment of the artillery, during the period of pursuit up to mid-April, the forces operated only with their own artillery, and almost all of the reinforcing artillery lagged behind the infantry because of the poor roads. Because of the lagging artillery, the infantry attacks to capture the enemy's intermediate defensive positions ended up taking two to three days. Only after mid-April did it become possible to bring the artillery forward in timely fashion. The distribution of the artillery according to the axes corresponded to the concept of the conducted operation. Because the *front*'s forces approached right up to the fortified belt, which was equipped in many sectors with pillboxes and bunkers prepared well in advance, it is imperative to reinforce the *front* with high-power artillery.

Conclusions: The *front*'s forces fulfilled the mission of destroying the enemy's Uman' grouping brilliantly and completed that destruction in two months of uninterrupted fighting, while projecting combat operations on its right wing onto Romanian territory. . . . During this fighting, the forces displayed great physical endurance and skill in circumstances of the *rasputitsa* and river obstacles to conduct offensive operations successfully. The existing correlation of forces (2.3:1 in infantry, 2.6:1 in tanks, and 2.7:1 in artillery) and the enemy's occupation of previously prepared defensive lines demands:

A) Reexamination of the *front's* operational plans; and

B) Time necessary for the forces to put themselves in order and accumulate material and ammunition. To do so, it is necessary to go over to a rigid defense, which the forces are accomplishing on the basis of a *Stavka* directive.

Possible enemy actions: Large-scale offensive operations during the month of May are not likely; however, this does not exclude the possibility of the enemy conducting local operations with the mission of throwing our forces back across the Prut River by means of attacks conducted from the Tirgu-Frumos and Podu-Iloaie line.

Note: The material we have on this axis does not reflect the problems of command and control of the forces; therefore, this issue is not addressed in this present report.

Colonel Postnikov, the chief of the 2nd Ukrainian Direction [Axis] of the Operations Directorate of the Red Army General Staff, 10 May 1944[15]

13. *Stavka* VGK Directive no. 220097, dated 15 May 1944, Concerning the Changes in Command of the 2nd, 3rd, and 4th Ukrainian Fronts.

1. To provide Marshal Zhukov with the opportunity to direct the operations of several *fronts* in the future, relieve him from temporary command of the 1st Ukrainian Front.

2. Appoint Marshal Konev as commander of the 1st Ukrainian Front after freeing him from his duties as commander of the 2nd Ukrainian Front.

3. Appoint Army General Malinovsky as commander of the 2nd Ukrainian Front after freeing him from his duties as commander of the 3rd Ukrainian Front.

4. Appoint Army General Tolbukhin as commander of the 3rd Ukrainian Front after freeing him from his duties as commander of the 4th Ukrainian Front.

5. Free Lieutenant General Biriuzov from his duties as chief of staff of the 4th Ukrainian Front and appoint him as chief of staff of the 3rd Ukrainian Front. Comrade Biriuzov will arrive at his new place of duty and will begin performing his responsibilities as chief of staff of the 3rd Ukrainian Front no later than 20 May of this year.

6. Free Lieutenant General Korzhenevich from his duties as chief of staff of the 3rd Ukrainian Front and appoint him a chief of staff of the 4th Ukrainian Front.

7. Comrade Tolbukhin will take command of the 3rd Ukrainian Front no later than 22 May of this year.

8. Comrade Malinovsky will take command of the 2nd Ukrainian Front no later than 24 May of this year.

9. Comrade Konev will take command of the 1st Ukrainian Front no later than 27 May of this year.

The *Stavka* VGK
I. Stalin
A. Antonov[12]

14. *Stavka* VGK Directive no. 220107, dated 0235 hours 26 May 1944, to the Commanders of the 2nd and 3rd Ukrainian Front Concerning the Change in the Period of Readiness for an Offensive.

The Stavka VGK orders:

1. Postpone the period of readiness for the move [attack] until receipt of special orders from the Stavka. The fronts' forces will reliably defend their occupied positions in accordance with Stavka Directive no. 220094 dated 6 May (no. 220095 dated 6 May for the 3rd Ukrainian Front) with strong second echelons and reserves.

2. Organize combat training for the forces to prepare them for subsequent offensive actions. The combat training will involve all forces and headquarters, to which end you will establish the order of withdrawal of forces into second echelon. During this training, pay special attention to the less trained divisions and headquarters.

3. Submit defensive plans in accordance with the ongoing changes in force composition and one-month combat training plans to the General Staff by 1 June.

The *Stavka* VGK
I. Stalin
A. Antonov[13]

15. Report no. 00413/op by the Commander of the 2nd Ukrainian Front to the Supreme High Commander Regarding a Plan for Defensive Operations along the Roman and Iasi Axes, dated 11 June 1944.

I am submitting a plan for the 2nd Ukrainian Front's defensive operation for your approval.

1. The enemy grouping facing the 2nd Ukrainian Front.

After an unsuccessful offensive along the Iasi axis, having lost the equipment of four panzer divisions while suffering great losses in personnel as a result of the ten-day battle, and having failing to achieve success, the enemy has gone over to the defense.

By combat means and all types of reconnaissance, the enemy's grouping opposite the 2nd Ukrainian Front has been established [as follows]:

a) The Carpathian axis.

In the Krasnoputna and Seret River sector, 165 kilometers [103 miles]—one German division and five Romanian [divisions] and up to four separate regiments.

In the second line—two divisions, one Romanian motorized division, one German brigade, and up to four separate regiments.

The average density per one kilometer [one mile] of front is up to 0.5 [0.8] battalions and 2.5 [4.2] guns. The greatest density is in the Oglinsi and Pascani sector, where the density is up to 1.5 [2.5] battalions per one kilometer [one mile] of front.

Total along this axis—eight divisions, one motorized division, one brigade, and up to eight separate regiments.

b) The Roman axis.

In the Seret River and Tirgu-Frumos sector, 30 kilometers [18 miles]—up to two Romanian infantry divisions.

In the second line—up to two Romanian infantry divisions and up to three tank divisions.

The average density per one kilometer [one mile] of front is up to 0.6 [one] battalion and up to ten [17] guns.

c) The Iasi axis.

In the Tirgu-Frumos and Prut River sector, 65 kilometers [39 miles]—two German divisions, five Romanian divisions, and four German tank divisions.

In the second line—two infantry divisions, two Romanian cavalry divisions, and one German motorized division.

The average density per one kilometer [one mile] of front is one [1.7] battalion and up to ten [17] guns.

d) The Kishinev axis.

In the Prut River and Dnestr River sector, 135 kilometers [81 miles]—six German infantry divisions, one Romanian infantry division, and one German motorized division.

In the second line—two German infantry and two tank divisions.

The average density per one kilometer [one mile] of front is up to 0.5 [0.8] battalions and up to seven [12] guns.

Thus, the enemy has nine German infantry divisions, four tank divisions, and one motorized division and 13 Romanian divisions in the first line, and an overall total of 22 infantry divisions, four tank divisions, and one motorized division.

In the second line—German forces of up to three infantry divisions and up to four tank divisions and Romanian forces of six infantry divisions, one tank division, one motorized division, and two cavalry divisions.

Overall, the enemy has up to 33 infantry divisions, including separate regiments, nine tank and three motorized divisions, one artillery division, and one antiaircraft artillery division in the first and second lines opposite our front.

For the past two days, 8–9 June, the enemy has been conducting some sort of regrouping along the Iasi axis, which has not yet been revealed to the *front*. Prisoners from Romanian units have been captured in some sectors where there were German forces.

The Romanian prisoners are indicating that there is discontent among the soldiers due to their heavy losses.

We have noticed work on preparing defensive belts along the forward edge and in the depths.

Rumors are circulating among the soldiers that, in the immediate future, the Germans must leave after being relieved by Romanian forces.

Supposedly, separate subunits of German forces remain to serve as blocking detachment since the German command does not particularly believe in the doggedness of the Romanian soldiers.

Rumors have surfaced that some sort of German divisions must leave for France.

Actually, it is possible that the German command will complete the transfer of a portion of its forces from Romania to France.

Agent and aviation reconnaissance measures have established the possible loading of German forces in railroad cars.

2. The plan for the defensive operation.

Considering the presence of up to nine enemy tank divisions, we cannot exclude the possibility that the enemy can still repeat his attempts to conduct active military operations in the region west of the Prut River or along the Bel'tsy axis.

Considering this possibility and based on the importance of these axes, I intend to group the 2nd Ukrainian Front's forces in the defense and deploy the reserves as follows:

a) The Carpathian axis.

The defensive front is 165 kilometers [103 miles]. I will deploy the 40th Army, which consists of eight divisions and two fortified regions, along this broad front, with five of these divisions, two fortified regions, and one rifle regiment in the defense.

One rifle division, two fortified regions, and one rifle regiment will be deployed along the 110-kilometer [66-mile] front immediately blocking the exits from the Carpathians.

The greatest density [of forces] will be along the 55-kilometer [33-mile] front on the left wing, where I will deploy four rifle divisions.

There will be two rifle divisions and two rifle regiments in the army's second echelon.

The [right] boundary line will be the existing boundary line with the 1st Ukrainian Front. The boundary on the left is from Staryi Badrazh through Grunesti, Sulitsa, Lespezi, and along the Seret River to Pascani (all points except Staryi Badrazh and Pascani are inclusive for the 40th Army).

The 40th Army commander will be responsible for the junction [boundary] with the 7th Guards Army.

b) The Roman axis.

The width of the front is 30 kilometers [18 miles]. I will deploy the 7th Guards Army, which consists of seven divisions and one tank brigade, in the defense, five of these divisions in the first line and two divisions in reserve behind the army's left wing.

I will create the greatest density [of forces] on the left wing of the defense.

The left boundary line is from Zagaikany through Braneshty, Plugari, and Hodora to Tirgu-Frumos (all points except Hodora inclusive for the 7th Guards Army).

The commander of the 7th Guards Army is responsible for the junction [boundary] with the 5th Guards Army.

c) The Iasi axis.

The width of the front is 65 kilometers [39 miles]. I will deploy three armies in the defense.

The 5th Guards Army, which consists of six rifle divisions, with four of these in the first line and two divisions in the army's reserve, along a front of 20 kilometers [12 miles].

The left boundary line is from Recha through Glodiany, Bederei, Iakobenii, and Gropnitsa to Byrleshi (all points except Glodniany and Bederei are inclusive for the 5th Guards Army).

The 5th Guards Army commander is responsible for the junction [boundary] with the 27th Army.

The 27th Army, which consists of nine rifle divisions, with six divisions in the first line and three rifle divisions in the army's reserves, along a front of 20 kilometers [12 miles].

The left boundary line is from Strymba through Pynzariany, Albinets, Goreshty, and Rednu-Miropoliei to Rediului Teter (all points except Rednu-Miropoliei inclusive for the 27th Army).

The commander of the 27th Army is responsible for the junction [boundary] with the 52nd Army.

The 52nd Army, which consists of seven rifle divisions, with six divisions in the first line and one division in the army's reserve, along a front of 25 kilometers.

The left boundary is from Floreshty through Glin'zhen', Novaia Chelakovka, and Kirilen' to Bogdaneshty (all points inclusive for the 52nd Army).

The commander of the 4th Guards Army is responsible for the junction [boundary] with the 52nd Army.

d) The Kishinev axis.

The width of the front is 135 kilometers [81 miles]. I will deploy two armies in the defense.

The 4th Guards Army, which consists of nine divisions, with seven divisions in the first line and two divisions in the army's reserve, along a front of 80 kilometers [48 miles].

The left boundary line is from Slobodzeia through Syrkova, Kishtel'nitsa, and Branicheni to Bykovets (all points inclusive for the 4th Guards Army).

The commander of the 53rd Army is responsible for the junction [boundary] with the 4th Guards Army.

The 53rd Army, which consists of eight divisions, with six in the first line and two divisions in the army's reserve behind the right wing, along a front of 55 kilometers [33 miles].

The desirable boundary line is from Anan'ev through Dubovo, Dubossary, Fauresht', Petrikani, and Kotu-Mori to Soleshti (all points except Dubovo inclusive for the 2nd Ukrainian Front).

The commander of the 3rd Ukrainian Front is responsible for the junction [boundary] with the 2nd Ukrainian Front.

e) The *front* reserve will include:

The 5th Guards Cavalry Corps—in the region north and south of Suchav behind the 40th Army's center and right wing.

The 18th Tank Corps—in the Kornele-Kaprei region behind the 5th Guards Army.

The 34th Guards Rifle Corps, which consists of three rifle divisions—in the Reumeni, Shodana, and Andreshenii region.

I will deploy the 6th Tank Army—behind the 52nd Army, with one corps in the bridgehead and the other corps in the Skulian region.

I will deploy the 23rd Tank Corps in the region of the Taksabianskii crossings along the left bank of the Prut River. The corps can be employed to reinforce either the Iasi or Roman axes, and also for counterattacks toward Petreshti and Korneshty, as well as along the Bel'tsy and Orgeev axes.

I will deploy the 57th Rifle Corps, which consists of four rifle divisions, in the Staraia Sarata, Kishkareni, and Synzhereia regions along the Bel'tsy axis.

I will deploy the 7th Mechanized Corps in the forested region north of Rasponeni along the Orgeev axis.

Therefore, two-thirds of the *front,* namely, 40 rifle divisions and two fortified regions, will be in the first defensive line. Fifteen rifle divisions will be in the armies' reserves. Seven rifle divisions, one cavalry corps, one tank army, and two tank and one mechanized corps will be in the *front*'s reserve.

I have a total of 550 tanks and self-propelled guns in our tank units as of 10 June 1944.

Such a grouping of the *front*'s forces will ensure an echeloned defense in depth and, in the event it becomes necessary, will provide an opportunity to create a grouping for an offensive operation along the Iasi or Roman axes.

3. Defensive lines.

The *front* will generally complete the construction of three defensive lines by 15 June 1944.

In addition, work on rear defensive lines along the Prut River and along the Dnestr River will be completed by this time.

4. I request:

a) You approve the submitted plan for the *front*'s defensive operation:

b) You establish [the following] boundary line with the 3rd Ukrainian Front—from Ana'ev through Dubovo, Dubossary, Floreshty, Petricani, and Kotu-Mori to Solesti (all points except Dubovo are inclusive for the 2nd Ukrainian Front).

c) You protect the operational junction [boundary] with the 1st Ukrainian Front in the Chernovtsy region with no less than a rifle corps.

d) You accelerate the *front's* receipt of the tanks we have yet to receive out of the 500 earmarked for us, that is, 370 tanks, and, additionally, you issue the *front* 150 foreign model tanks for the 6th Tank Army.

e) And in exchange for the departed 2nd Tank Army, you provide the *front* a tank corps by stationing it on Romanian territory.

Attachments:

Commander of the 2nd Ukrainian Front,
Army General Malinovsky
Member of the 2nd Ukrainian Front's Military Council,
Lieutenant General of Tank Forces Susaikov
Chief of Staff of the 2nd Ukrainian Front,
Colonel General Zakharov[14]

16. The 2nd Ukrainian Front's Combat Report for May 1944. Account of the 2nd Ukrainian Front's Combat Activities for the Month of May 1944. Report no. 25494 dated 15 June 1944 to the Operations Directorate of the Red Army General Staff.

Top Secret.

Copy No. 1.

The 2nd Ukrainian Front's combat activities for the month of April were directed at the creation of a rigid defense and the combat training of the forces.

The Grouping and Nature of the Enemy's Operations

Having strengthened his grouping in front of the 2nd Ukrainian Front to 15 divisions and while operating along a previously prepared defensive belt along the Moldava River, Pascani, Iasi, Korneshty, mouth of the Reut River, and Dnestr River line, the enemy was able to repel an offensive by our front's forces along the Tirgu-Frumos, Iasi, and Kishinev axes during the first few days of May. During May he reinforced his grouping with another two infantry divisions (the 11th Infantry Division and the 8th Mountain Infantry Division), and, as a result, a total of 37 divisions, including 25 infantry, seven tank, one motorized, one airborne, and three cavalry divisions, were deployed in front of our front by the beginning of June. Simultaneously, the enemy filled out his units with personnel and weapons, in particular, with tanks.

At the end of the month of May, [the enemy] undertook local operations to liquidate our bridgehead north of Iasi and, at the same time, to protect the lateral road from Kishinev through Iasi to Tirgu-Frumos. To do so, he concentrated a large tank group (the 23rd, 14th, and 24th Tank Divisions) and an infantry group (the Romanian 3rd and 11th Infantry Divisions and the German 79th Infantry Division) north of Iasi. He went over to the attack in the general direction of Kyrpitsi [Cirpiti] with these forces at first light on 30 May after an hour-long artillery preparation and massed air strikes (a total of up to 1,800 air sorties were conducted during the day).

As a result of three days of fierce fighting, the enemy succeeded in wedging from one to four kilometers deep into our defenses along a front of nine kilometers. Having failed to achieve the success he desired north of Iasi, in order to broaden his offensive front, simultaneously with the offensive north of Iasi, on 2 June 1944, the enemy attacked from the railroad and Tautoshti [Tautesti] line toward Epurenii [Epureni] with the "Velikaia Germaniia" [*Grossdeutschland*] Tank Division, 18th Mountain Infantry Division (Romanian), and 5th Infantry Division (Romanian).

As a result of seven days of continuous intense battles (from 30 May through 5 June) the enemy wedged into our defenses along a 19-kilometer front and to a depth of from one to four kilometers. In these battles the *front*'s forces inflicted a serious defeat on four tank and four infantry divisions (the 14th, 23rd, 24th, and SS *Grossdeutschland* Divisions; the Romanian 3rd and 11th Infantry Divisions; the Romanian 18th Mountain Infantry Division; and the German 79th Infantry Division). According to incomplete information, the enemy lost more than 17,000 men killed and wounded, and 315 tanks and self-propelled guns, 29 armored vehicles and armored transporters, and 4,521 aircraft were destroyed or burned.

The enemy halted his offensive on 6 June 1944. At the same time, the enemy himself, if only by a negligible advance, forced the units on the 52nd Army's right flank to dig into very unfavorable positions. The Zhizhia and Prut Rivers, with swampy floodlands, were immediately to the rear of the forward edge of the units on the 52nd Army's right flank, and this deprived them of the possibility of a deep constructed defense.

The Grouping and Nature of the Operations by the 2nd Ukrainian Front's Forces

> Operating from the march, the 2nd Ukrainian Front's forces were not able to overcome the resistance of an enemy who successfully occupied previously prepared defensive belts outfitted with pillboxes and bunkers. In order to organize a penetration of a fortified belt, it was necessary to have time both for carrying out an appropriate regrouping and for bringing the lagging rear services forward and accumulating ammunition. The 2nd Ukrainian Front's forces carried out their transition to the defense on the basis of a Stavka operational directive dated 6 May 1944 and front directive no. 00348/op dated 8 May 1944. . . .
>
> I consider it necessary: . . .

B) To conduct a local operation by part of the 27th and 52nd Armies' forces with the mission to capture the Iassy bridgehead and the city of Iassy without which the bridgehead defense on the right flank of the 52nd Army will always be a most vulnerable spot.

Overall Conclusions

> 1. On the whole, the 2nd Ukrainian Front's defenses are constructed correctly. The armies' and *front's* reserves are sufficiently powerful to conduct an attack and destroy the penetrating enemy.

Thoughts Concerning the Operations of the 2nd Ukrainian Front's Forces during the Month of June 1944

> The enemy's measures directed toward the creation of groupings along the Tirgu-Frumos and Iasi axes and northwest of Kishinev, as well as the possibilities for reinforcing his forces operating in front of the 2nd Ukrainian Front at the expense of forced operating in front of the 3rd Ukrainian Front, will allow him to propose possible active operations along the axes indicated above with the aim of liquidating our forces in the Romanian salient. Therefore, the missions of our forces during the month of June must be a rigid defense. But, while occupying a rigid defense, it is necessary to continue preparing our forces for offensive operations, since the front can accomplish active missions if it is reinforced with two rifle corps and one tank corps.
>
> Colonel Postnikov, the chief of the 2nd Ukrainian Direction [Axis] of the Operations Directorate of the Red Army General Staff, 13 June 1944[16]

Notes

1. Introduction

1. M. M. Kozlov, ed., *Velikaia Otechestvennaia voina 1941–1945: Entsiklopediia* [The Great Patriotic War 1941–1945: An encyclopedia] (Moscow: "Sovetskaia entsiklopediia," 1985), 746. Hereafter cited as *VOV* with appropriate page(s). Throughout, unless otherwise noted, translations from the Russian and German are mine.

2. Ibid., 506.

3. M. M. Minasian, ed., *Istoriia Velikoi Otechestvennoi voiny Sovetskogo Soiuza 1941–1945 v shesti tomakh, tom chetvertyi* [A history of the Great Patriotic War of the Soviet Union in six volumes, vol. 4] (Moscow: Voenizdat, 1962), 82 and 87.

4. D. F. Ustinov, ed., *Istoriia Vtoroi Mirovoi voiny 1939–1945 v dvenadtsati tomakh, tom bos'moi* [A history of the Second World War in eleven volumes, vol. 8] (Moscow: Voenizdat, 1977), 93 and 96.

5. I. S. Konev, *Zapiski komanduuishchego frontom 1943–1945* [Notes of a *front* commander 1943–1945] (Moscow: Voenizdat, 1981), 199.

6. A. V. Antosiak, *V boiakh za svobodu Rumynii* [In the battles for the liberation of Romania] (Moscow: Voenizdat, 1974), 65–66.

7. V. I. Chuikov, *Gvardeistsy Stalingrada idut ne zapad* [The Stalingrad guardsmen march to the west] (Moscow: Sovetskaia Rossiia, 1972), 238.

8. V. A. Zolotarev, ed., *Velikaia Otechestvennaia Voina 1941–1945: Voenno-istoricheskie ocherki v chetyrekh knigakh, Kniga 3* [The Great Patriotic War 1941–1945: A military-historical survey in four books, book 3] (Moscow: "Nauka," 1999), 45, 46–48.

9. Ibid., 48.

2. Prelude

1. A. M. Vasilevsky, *Delo vsei zhizni* [Life's work] (Moscow: Izdatel'stvo politicheskoi literatury, 1983), 360–361.

2. Unfortunately, Konev's memoirs, I. S. Konev, *Zapiski komanduiushchego frontom 1943–1945* [Notes of a *front* commander 1943–1945] (Moscow: Voenizdat, 1981), cover only the period after January 1943. See also P. M. Portugal'sky, *Marshal I. S. Konev* (Moscow: Voenizdat, 1985). Both of these works and most other biographies of Konev studiously ignore Konev's role in Operation Mars and provide scant information on his activities and performance as a commander during 1941 and 1942.

3. Thereafter, while leading the 1st Ukrainian Front to victory at war's end, Konev grew in reputation and stature to become one of the Red Army's finest and most accomplished *front* commanders and a clear counterweight to Zhukov.

4. For these positive and negative comments on Konev's personality, see Oleg Rzheshevsky, "Konev," in Harold Shukman, ed., *Stalin's Generals* (London: Weidenfeld and Nicolson, 1993), 91–107. Rzheshevsky is the first to surface and discuss Konev's problems during the purges.

5. Petro G. Grigorenko, *Memoirs*, translated by Thomas P. Whitney (New York: W. W. Norton, 1982), 112–113.

6. F. I. Vysotsky, M. E. Makukhin, F. M. Sarychev, and M. K. Shaposhnikov, *Gvardeiskaia tankovaia* [Guards tank] (Moscow: Voenizdat, 1963), 102.

7. V. S. Golubovich, *Marshal Malinovsky* (Moscow: Voenizdat, 1984); and John Erickson, "Rodion Iakovlevich Malinovsky," in Shukman, *Stalin's Generals,* 117–124.

8. Richard Woff, "Rokossovsky," in Shukman, *Stalin's Generals,* 187.

9. Earl F. Ziemke, *Stalingrad to Berlin: The German Defeat in the East* (Washington, DC: Office of the Chief of Military History, United States Army, 1968), 290–291.

10. A. N. Grylev, *Dnepr, Karpaty, Krym: Osvobozhdenie Pravoberezhnoi Ukrainy i Krym v 1944 godu* [The Dnepr, the Carpathian, and the Crimea: The liberation of the Right Bank of the Ukraine and the Crimea in 1944] (Moscow: "Nauka," 1970), 175. According to this source, the Fourth Romanian Army, which had been deployed from Romania from 26 to 31 March, initially consisted of the German LXXVIII Army Corps and the Romanian 4th Mountain, 5th Cavalry, and 6th, 7th, and 8th Infantry Divisions. Other forces joined the Romanian Fourth Army in April, including the V Army Corps headquarters on 3 April; the 1st Guards Infantry Division on 5 April; the 1st Panzer, 2nd Reserve Mountain Infantry, the 4th Infantry, and the 18th Mountain Infantry Divisions on 9 April; the 20th Infantry Division on 11 April; the 1st Cavalry Division on 15 April; the I Army Corps headquarters and the 1st Infantry Division on 16 April; and the 103rd Mountain Infantry Brigade on 21 April. In addition, the Romanian VI and VII Army Corps headquarters; the 3rd, 11th, and 13th Infantry Divisions; and the 101st and 102nd Mountain Infantry Brigades arrived between 2 and 28 April and were assigned to the German Eighth Army.

11. For further details on the Romanian Army's participation in these operations, see Mark Axworthy, Cornel Scafes, and Cristian Craciunoiu, *Third Axis Fourth Ally: Romanian Armed Forces in the European War, 1941–1944* (London: Arms and Armour, 1995), 145–155.

12. Ibid.

13. V. A. Zolotarev, ed., "General'nyi shtab v gody Velikoi Otechestvennoi voiny: Dokumenty i materialy 1944–1945 gg." [The General Staff in the Great Patriotic War: Documents and materials 1944–1945], in *Russkii arkhiv: Velikaia Otechestvennaia, T. 23 (12–4)* [The Russian archives: The Great Patriotic [War], vol. 23 (12–4)] (Moscow: "TERRA," 2001), 136.

14. V. A. Zolotarev, ed., "Stavka VGK: Dokumenty i materially, 1944–1945" [The *Stavka* VGK: Documents and materials, 1944–1945], in *Russkii arkhiv: Velikaia Otechestvennaia, T. 16 (5–4)* [The Russian archives: The Great Patriotic [War], vol. 16 (5–4)] (Moscow: "TERRA," 1999), 71. Hereafter cited as Zolotarev, "Stavka VGK, 1944," with appropriate page(s).

15. Grylev, *Dnepr, Karpaty, Krym,* 175.

16. Zolotarev, "Stavka VGK, 1944," 281–282.

17. Ibid., 72.

18. Ibid.

19. *Sbornik voenno-istoricheskikh materialov Velikoi Otechestvennoi voiny, vypusk 15* [A collection of military-historical materials of the Great Patriotic War, issue 15] (Moscow: Voenizdat, 1955), 92–93. Classified secret.

20. Vasilevsky, *Delo vsei zhizni,* 363–364.

3. The 2nd Ukrainian Front's April Offensive (8–23 April 1944)

1. V. A. Zolotarev, ed., *Velikaia Otechestvennaia Voina 1941–1945: Voenno-istoricheskie ocherki v chetyrekh knigakh, Kniga 3* [The Great Patriotic War 1941–1945: A military-historical survey in four books, book 3} (Moscow: "Nauka," 1999), 47.

2. N. V. Ogarkov, ed., *Sovetskaia voennaia entsiklopediia, Tom 3* [Soviet military encyclopedia, vol. 3] (Moscow: Voenizdat, 1977). Hereafter cited as Ogarkov, *SVE* with appropriate volume and page(s). After war's end, Zhmachenko went on to serve as deputy commander of the Central Group of Forces in Austria, deputy commander of the Belorussian and Carpathian Military Districts, and chief of DOSAAF in the Ukraine.

3. Ibid., vol. 8 (1980), 125.

4. Ibid., vol. 1 (1976), 509. During July and August 1944, Bogdanov's 2nd Tank Army spearheaded the 1st Belorussian Front's controversial offensive from the Kovel' region westward to the gates of Warsaw, but they failed to capture the Polish capital city when it encountered strong German counterstrokes. During 1945, Bogdanov's army fought alongside Katukov's 1st Guards Tank Army in the 1st Belorussian Front's advance from the Vistula River to the Oder River and its climactic April assault on Berlin.

5. Richard N. Armstrong, *Red Army Tank Commanders: The Armored Guards* (Atglen, PA: Shiffer Military/Aviation History, 1994), 155.

6. Ogarkov, *SVE,* vol. 4 (1977), 371.

7. Armstrong, *Red Army Tank Commanders,* 450.

8. For details regarding the Eighth Army's daily intelligence assessment during this battle and the army's precise dispositions, see "Anlagen z. KTB–Ic/AO Feindlagekarten, Jan–Jun 1944," *AOK 8, 58298/30* file, in National Archives microfilm series T-312, Roll 70, and "Anlagen z. KTB–Ia Tägliche Lagekarten, Jan–Jun 1944," *AOK 8, 58298/24* file, in National Archives microfilm series T-312, Roll 68.

9. Hasso von Manteuffel, "The Battle of Targul-Frumos," transcript of a lecture delivered to the U.S. Army War College, Ft. Leavenworth, KS, 1948, 3.

10. Ibid.

11. Ibid.

12. Helmuth Spaeter, *The History of the Panzerkorps Grossdeutschland,* vol. 2, translated by David Johnson (Winnipeg, Canada: J. J. Fedorowicz, 1995), 312–313.

13. V. A. Zolotarev, ed., *Velikaia Otechestvennaia Voina 1941–1945: Voenno-istoricheskie ocherki v chetyrekh knigakh, Kniga 3* [The Great Patriotic War 1941–1945: A military-historical survey in four books, book 3] (Moscow: "Nauka," 1999), 47.

14. For details on this fighting, see F. M. von Senger und Etterlin, *Der Gegenschlag* (Neckargemund: Scharnhorst Buchkameradschaft, 1959), 60–62.

15. Spaeter, *History of the Panzerkorps Grossdeutschland,* 313.

16. Ibid., 313–314.

17. Ibid.

18. Ibid., 313.

19. For details on the 4th Guards Army's offensive, see *Ot Volzhskikh stepei do Avstriiskikh Al'p* [From the Volga steppes to the Austrian Alps] (Moscow: Voenizdat, 1971), 97–100.

20. Ogarkov, *SVE,* vol. 2 (1976), 464. Galanin entered the reserves in 1946 and died in 1958.

21. T. F. Vorontsev, ed., *Ot Volzhskikh stepei do Avstriiskikh Al'p,* 98.

22. For details on the 41st Guards Rifle Division's fighting to seize the Orgeev bridgehead, see A. A. Iaroshenko, *V boi shla 41-ia gvardeiskaia: Boevoi put' 41-i gvardeiskoi strelkovoi Korsun'sko-Dunaiskoi ordena Suvorova divizii* [The 41st Guards went into battle: The combat path of the 41st Guards Korsun'-Shevchenkovskii, Order of Suvorov Rifle Division] (Moscow: Voenizdat, 1982), 104–107.

23. Ogarkov, *SVE,* vol. 5 (1978), 113.

24. Ogarkov, *SVE,* vol. 3 (1978), 318.

25. I. A. Samchuk, P. G. Skachko, Iu. N. Babikov, and I. L. Gnedoi, *Ot Volgu do El'by i Pragu: Kratkii ocherk o Boevoi puti 5-i gvardeiskoi armii* [From the Volga to the Elbe and Prague: A short survey of the combat path of the 5th Guards Army] (Moscow: Voenizdat, 1978), 171.

26. Ibid., 179.

27. For further details on this fighting, see I. A. Samchuk and P. G. Skachko, *Atakuiut desantniki: Boevoi put's 9-i gvardeiskoi Krasnoznamennoi ordena Suvorova i Kutuzova Poltavskoi vozdushno-desantnyoi diviziii* [The airborne troops are attacking: The combat path of the 9th Guards Red Banner, orders of Suvorov and Kutuzov, Poltava Airborne Division] (Moscow: Voenizdat, 1975), 97–102.

28. B. I. Mutovin, *Cherez vse ispytaniia* [Through an entire education] (Moscow: Voenizdat, 1986), 161–162.

29. A. M. Vasilevsky, *Delo vsei zhizni* [Life's work] (Moscow: Izdatel'stvo politicheskoi literatury, 1983), 366.

4. The 3rd Ukrainian Front's Advance to the Dnestr River and the Bridgehead Battles (11–25 April 1944)

1. N. V. Ogarkov, ed., *Sovetskaia voennaia entsiklopediia v vos'mykh tomakh, Tom 2* [Soviet military encyclopedia in eight volumes, vol. 2] (Moscow: Voenizdat, 1976), 453–454. Hereafter cited as Ogarkov, *SVE,* with appropriate volume and page(s). After war's end, Gagen commanded a rifle corps from 1945 through January 1947 and served as deputy commander of the Coastal and Far Eastern Military Districts from February 1947 until his retirement due to poor health in 1959.

2. Ogarkov, *SVE,* vol. 8 (1980), 492. After commanding an army during 1945 and 1946, Sharokhin became chief of a General Staff directorate in April 1946, deputy chief of the General Staff's Military-Scientific Directorate in December 1951, chief of the Ministry of Defense's higher military-educational institutions in April 1953, and a consultant to the Ministry of Defense's Inspector-General from May 1957 to his retirement in 1960.

3. Ogarkov, *SVE,* vol. 2, 570. After Glagolev commanded the 31st Army in the 2nd Belorussian Front's Belorussian offensive during the summer of 1944, in December 1944 the NKO assigned him to command the powerful 9th Guards Army, which spearheaded the 3rd Ukrainian Front's successful Vienna and Prague offensives during March and April 1945. After war's end, among other assignments, Glagolev served as commander of the Soviet Army's Airborne Forces.

4. Ogarkov, *SVE,* vol. 6 (1978), 356–357. Pliev would also command a cavalry-mechanized group in the Belorussian offensive during June and July 1944, the 1st Guards Cavalry-Mechanized Group in the 2nd Ukrainian Front's Budapest and Vienna offensives during late 1944 and 1945, and the Trans-Baikal Front's Soviet-Mongolian Cavalry-Mechanized Group in its dramatic dash from Mongolia to Peking, China, in the Red Army's Manchurian offensive during August 1945. Pliev received his second award as Hero of the Soviet Union in September 1945 for his superb performance in the Manchurian offensive. After war's end, Pliev also commanded the Soviet Army's Strategic Rocket Forces in Cuba during the Cuban Missile crisis of 1962.

5. Ogarkov, *SVE,* vol. 8, 486–487. Chuikov commanded the 8th Guards Army to war's end, in the process leading it in the advance by Zhukov's 1st Belorussian Front across Poland and during the storming of Berlin. After the war ended, as evidence that he had clearly become one of Stalin's favorites commanders, Chuikov served as a deputy and the first deputy Supreme Commander of the Soviet Army from 1945 to 1949, as commander of the Group of Soviet Forces in Germany (GSFG) from 1949 through 1953, and as chairman of the Soviet Control Commission in Germany in 1953. After Stalin's death, Chuikov commanded the Kiev Military District from 1953 through April 1960, and, thereafter, rose to become commander of Soviet Army's Ground Forces and deputy Minister of Defense, the chief of the USSR's Civil Defense in 1964, and the army's Inspector-General in 1972.

6. Ibid., 522. After war's end, Shlemin served as chief of staff of the Soviet Southern Group of Forces (SFG) in Hungary from 1945 to 1948 and the Central Group of Forces (CFG) in Czechoslovakia from 1949 to 1954, as deputy chief of staff and chief of the Operations Directorate the Soviet Ground Force's Main Staff in 1948 and 1949, and as a teacher and deputy chief of the General Staff Academy from 1954 to his retirement in 1962.

7. Ibid., 404. After war's end, Tsvetaev served as deputy commander and later commander of the Soviet Southern Group of Forces in Hungary from 1945 through 1947 and chief of the Frunze Academy from 1948 until his retirement.

8. Earl F. Ziemke, *Stalingrad to Berlin: The German Defeat in the East* (Washington, DC: Office of the Chief of Military History, United States Army, 1968), 289–290.

9. A. M. Vasilevsky, *Delo vsei zhizni* [Life's work] (Moscow: Izdatel'stvo politicheskoi literatury, 1983), 365.

10. For German force dispositions throughout the battles along the Dnestr River, see "Ia, KTB, Akte F, Tasche 16, Lagekarten, Mar–May 1944," *AOK 6, 50624/3* file, in National Archives microfilm series T-312, Roll 1468.

11. For details about the 57th Army's planning to cross the Dnestr River and the army's subsequent bridgehead battle, see "57-ia armiia: Dokumenty po forsirovaniiu p. Dnestr s khoda voiskami 57-i armii v aprele 1944 g." [The 57th Army: Documents on the forcing of the Dnestr River from the march by the 57th Army in April 1944],

in *Sbornik Boevykh dokumentov Velikoi Otechestvennoi voiny, vypusk 30* [A collection of combat documents of the Great Patriotic War, issue 30] (Moscow: Voenizdat, 1957), 79–109. These documents, compiled by the General Staff's Military-Scientific Directorate, include the 57th Army's and 68th Rifle Corps' 10 and 11 April operational orders and planning schedules for the river-crossing operation, the army's war experience report, and the 68th Rifle Corps' after-action report, all classified secret. Hereafter cited as *SBDVOV* with appropriate article and issue.

12. Ibid., 87–88.

13. I. P. Roslyi, *Poslednii priva', v Berline* [The last stopping place, in Berlin] (Moscow: Voenizdat, 1983), 206.

14. For details about the 37th Army's planning to cross the Dnestr River and the army's subsequent bridgehead battle, see "1944 god. 3-i Ukrainskii Front, 37-ia armiia: Dokumenty po forsirovaniiu p. Dnestr s khoda voiskami 37-i armii v aprele 1944 g." [1944. 3rd Ukrainian Front, the 37th Army: Documents on the forcing of the Dnestr River from the march by the 37th Army in April 1944], in *SBDVOV*, issue 30, 71–78. These documents, compiled by the General Staff's Military-Scientific Directorate, include the 37th Army's operational order dated 8 April and the army's war experience report, both classified secret. For the 37th Army's complete order to cross the Dnestr River, see "1944 god. 3-i Ukrainainskii Front" [1944. 3rd Ukrainian Front], in *SBDVOV*, issue 2 (1947), 100–102.

15. Both Rusakov and Danilenko returned to command of their divisions, the former on 10 June and the latter on 3 May.

16. For details on the 20th Guards and 195th Rifle Divisions' roles in this battle, see F. P. Bologov, *V shtabe gvardeiskoi divizii* [In the headquarters of a guards division] (Moscow: Voenizdat, 1987), 152–160; and V. S. Vylitok and S. F. Leskin, *Novomoskovskaia krasnoznamennaia: Boevoi put' 195-i Novomoskovsk Krasnoznamennoi strelkovoi divizii* [The combat path of the 195th Novomoskovsk Red Banner Rifle Division] (Moscow: Voenizdat, 1979), 170–174.

17. A. K. Blazhei, *V armeiskom shtabe* [In an army headquarters] (Moscow: Voenizdat, 1967), 117.

18. For additional details, see "Nastuplenie voisk 46-i armii v aprele 1944 g. s forsirovaniem p. Dnestr" [The offensive of the 46th Army in April 1944 with the forcing of the Dnestr River], in *SBDVOV*, issue 24 (1955), 56–64, which contains the 46th Army's operational order dated 10 April, the 40th Guards Rifle Division's operational order dated 13 April, and the same division's report dated 14 April.

19. Ibid., 59.

20. Ibid., 59–60.

21. For further details on the operations of Pliev's Cavalry-Mechanized Group from 1 to 13 April, see N. I. Zav'ialov, *Versty muzhestva* [Sacred versts] (Kiev: Politicheskoi literatury Ukrainy, 1981), 280–285; I. A. Pliev, *Dorogami voiny* [Along the roads of war] (Moscow: "Khiga," 1985), 90–94; and A. Ia. Soshnikov, ed., *Sovetskaia kavaleriia* [Soviet cavalry] (Moscow: Voenizdat, 1984), 266–267.

22. V. I. Chuikov, *Gvardeitsy Stalingrada idut na zapad* [The Stalingrad guardsmen march to the west] (Moscow: Sovetskaia Rossiia, 1972), 234.

23. Ibid., 235–236.

24. Vasilevsky, *Delo vsei zhizni*, 365–366.

25. Blazhei, *V armeiskom shtabe,* 119.

26. G. S. Zdanovich, *Idem v nastuplenie* [We are on the attack] (Moscow: Voenizdat, 1980), 161–162.

27. A. M. Chmelev, *Proshla s boiami* [Advancing under fire] (Kishinev: Karta Moldaveniaske, 1983), 68–69.

28. Ibid., 71.

29. V. P. Savil'ev and N. P. Popov, *Gvardeiskaia Nikolaevskaia: Boevoi put' 108-i gvardeiskoi strelkovoi Nikolaevskoi Krasnoznamennoi, ordena Suvorovoa divizii* [The guards Nikolaev: The combat path of the 108th Guards Nikolaev, Red Banner, and Order of Suvorov Rifle Division] (Moscow: Voenizdat, 1978), 63–64.

30. Chuikov, *Gvardeitsy Stalingrada idut na zapad,* 236.

31. Vasilevsky, *Delo vsei zhizni,* 367.

5. The 2nd Ukrainian Front's Preparations for the Iasi (Tirgu Frumos) Offensive (24 April–1 May 1944)

1. "Boevye prikazy i operativnye direktiy 2 Ukrainskogo fronta za 1944 g." [Combat orders and operational directives of the 2nd Ukrainian Front for 1944], *TsAMO* (*Tsentral'nyi arkhiv Ministerstva Oborony* [Central Archives of the Ministry of Defense (of the Russian Federation)]), f. 381, op. 8378, ed. khr. 308, l. l. 1–6.

2. N. V. Ogarkov, ed., *Sovetskaia voennaia entsiklopediia, Tom 8* [Soviet military encyclopedia, vol. 8] (Moscow: Voenizdat, 1980), 545–546. Hereafter cited as Ogarkov, *SVE,* with appropriate volume and page(s).

3. Richard N. Armstrong, *Red Army Tank Commanders: The Armored Guards* (Atglen, PA: Shiffer Military/Aviation History, 1994), 376–377. See also Ogarkov, *SVE,* vol. 7 (1979), 150–151.

4. S. M. Shtemenko, *The General Staff at War 1941–1945: Book 1* (Moscow: Progress, 1981), 479. Rotmistrov's career as a tank army commander soured somewhat in August 1944, when, after successfully spearheading the Red Army's offensive in Belorussia during late June and July, the *Stavka* relieved him from his command, probably because of the heavy losses his army suffered during the offensive, particularly during the struggle for possession of the city of Vilnius. Thereafter, Rotmistrov served as deputy chief of the Red Army's Armored and Mechanized Forces to war's end, as chief of tank and mechanized forces in the Group of Soviet Forces in Germany (GSFG) from 1945 to 1948, as chief of the faculty at the Voroshilov General Staff Academy from 1948 through 1958, as head of the Armored Forces Academy from 1958 through 1964, and as assistant Minister of Defense of the USSR from 1964 through 1968. After his "demotion upward" in 1944, but also belatedly, Rotmistrov became a marshal of armored forces in 1962 and a Hero of the Soviet Union in 1965.

5. K. V. Amirov, *Ot Volgi do Al'p: Boevoi put' 36-i gvardeiskoi strelkovoi verkhnedneprovskoi krasnoznamennoi ordena Suvorova in Kutuzova II stepeni divizii* [From the Volga to the Alps: The combat path of the 36th Guards Upper Dnepr, Red Banner, and Order of Suvorov and Kutuzov II degree rifle division] (Moscow: Voenizdat, 1987), 125–127.

6. I. K. Morozov, *Ot Stalingrada do Pragi: Zapiski komandira divizii* [From Stal-

ingrad to Berlin: The notes of a division commander] (Volgograd: Nizhne-Volzhkoe knizhnoe izdatel'stvo, 1976), 177–179.

7. Helmuth Spaeter, *The History of the Panzerkorps Grossdeutschland,* vol. 2, translated by David Johnson (Winnipeg, Canada: J. J. Fedorowicz, 1995), 315–317. See the daily dispositions of German forces in "Anlagenband z. KTB–Ia Tägliche Lagenkarten, Jan–Jun 1944," *AOK 8, 58298/24* file, and "Anlagenband z. KTB–Ia Tägliche Lagenkarten, Apr–Jul 1944," *AOK 8, 58298/28* file, in National Archives microfilm series T-312, Rolls 68 and 69. Daily German intelligence assessments are in "Anlagen z. KTB–Ic/AO Feindlagenkarten, Jan–Jun 1944," *AOK 8, 58298/30* file, in National Archives microfilm series T-312, Roll 70.

8. For a detailed account by a participant in the rescue operation conducted to the Ruginoasa and Dumbravita region by *Grossdeutschland* Division's Panzer Regiment, see Hans-Joachim Jung, *The History of the Panzerregiment "Grossdeutschland,"* translated by David Johnson (Winnipeg, Canada: J. J. Fedorowicz, 2000), 179–183. Mateufel's *Kampfgruppe* reportedly consisted of 23 Panzer IV's, 3 Tiger, and 6 Panther tanks.

9. Spaeter, *History of the Panzerkorps Grossdeutschland,* 317.

10. "Doklad o boevykh deistviiakh bronetankovykh i mekhanjzirovanykh voisk 2 Ukrainiskogo fronta v Tyrgul-Frumosskoi operatsii, 2–8.5.1944" [A report concerning the combat operations of the 2nd Ukrainian Front's armored and mechanized forces in the Tirgu Frumos operation, 2–8 May 1944], in "Zhurnal boevykh deistvii 2 Ukrainskogo fronta za aprel'-mai 1944 g." [The journal of combat operations of the 2nd Ukrainian Front for April–May 1944], *TsAMO,* f. 240, op. 2779, ed. khr. 1155, l. 290.

11. Morozov, *Ot Stalingrada do Pragi,* 180.

12. Ibid., 291.

13. "Dokumenty 2 Tankovoi armii za 1944g." [Documents of the 2nd Tank Army for 1944], *TsAMO,* f. 308, op. 4148, l. 159.

14. F. I. Vysotsky, M. E. Makukhin, F. M. Sarychev, and M. K. Shaposhnikov, *Gvardeiskaia tankovaia* [Guards tank] (Moscow: Voenizdat, 1963), 103.

15. General Hasso von Manteuffel, "The Battle of Targul-Frumos," transcript of a lecture delivered to the U.S. Army War College, Fort Leavenworth, KS, 1948), 5–7. Author's copy.

16. Spaeter, *History of the Panzerkorps Grossdeutschland,* 317.

17. Quoted in ibid., 322; for a different translation, see Manteuffel, "Battle of Targul-Frumos," 8.

18. Manteuffel, "Battle of Targul-Frumos," 9.

19. F. M. von Senger und Etterlin, briefing presented to the U.S. Army War College, undated, 1. Author's copy. More details can be found in F. M. von Senger und Etterlin, *Der Gegenschlag* (Neckargemund: Scharnhorst Buchkameradschaft, 1959), 110–131.

20. "Doklad o boevykh deistviiakh bronetankovykh i mekhanjzirovanykh viosk," ll. 289–290.

21. Ibid., 291.

22. Manteuffel, "Battle of Targul-Frumos," 10.

23. Spaeter, *History of the Panzerkorps Grossdeutschland,* 317.

24. "Zhurnal boevykh deistvii 27 armii za mai 1944 g." [The journal of combat operations of the 27th Army for May 1944], *TsAMO,* f. 381, op. 8378, ed. khr. 439, l. 2.

25. "Doklad o boevykh deistviiakh bronetankovykh i mekhanjzirovanykh viosk,", 292.

6. The 2nd Ukrainian Front's Iasi (Tirgu Frumos) Offensive (2–8 May 1944)

1. Helmuth Spaeter, *The History of the Panzerkorps Grossdeutschland,* vol. 2, translated by David Johnson (Winnipeg, Canada: J. J. Fedorowicz, 1995), 317.

2. "Zhurnal boevykh deistvii 2 Ukrainskogo fronta za aprel'-mai 1944 g." [The combat journal of the 2nd Ukrainian Front for April–May 1944], *TsAMO* (*Tsentral'nyi arkhiv Ministerstva Oborony* [Central Archives of the Ministry of Defense (of the Russian Federation)]), f. 240, op. 2779, ed. khr. 1155, ll. 217–220.

3. Quoted in Spaeter, *History of the Panzerkorps Grossdeutschland,* 328–329. For a different translation, see General Hasso von Manteuffel, "The Battle of Targul-Frumos," transcript of a lecture delivered to the U.S. Army War College, Ft. Leavenworth, KS, 1948. See the daily dispositions of German forces in "Anlagenband z. KTB–Ia Tägliche Lagenkarten, Jan–Jun 1944," *AOK 8, 58298/24* file, and "Anlagenband z. KTB–Ia Tägliche Lagenkarten, Apr–Jul 1944," *AOK 8, 58298/28* file, in National Archives microfilm series T-312, Rolls 68 and 69. Daily German intelligence assessments are in "Anlagen z. KTB–Ic/AO Feindlagenkarten, *AOK 8, 58298/30* file, in National Archives microfilm series T-312, Roll 70.

4. K. V. Amirov, *Ot Volgi do Al'p: Boevoi put' 36-i gvardeiskoi strelkovoi verkhnedneprovskoi krasnoznamennoi ordena Suvorova in Kutuzova II stepeni divizii* [From the Volga to the Alps: The combat path of the 36th Guards Upper Dnepr, Red Banner and Order of Suvorov and Kutuzov II degree rifle division] (Moscow: Voenizdat, 1987), 127–128.

5. I. K. Morozov, *Ot Stalingrada do Pragi: Zapiski komandira divizii* [From Stalingrad to Berlin: The notes of a division commander] (Volgograd: Nizhne-Volzhkoe knizhnoe izdatel'strvo, 1976), 181–182.

6. Quoted in Spaeter, *History of the Panzerkorps Grossdeutschland,* 329. For a different translation, see Manteuffel, "Battle of Targul-Frumos," 11.

7. Manteuffel, "Battle of Targul-Frumos," 12.

8. Ibid.

9. Quoted in Spaeter, *History of the Panzerkorps Grossdeutschland,* 328–329.

10. Ibid., 331–332.

11. "Doklad o boevykh deistviiakh bronetankovykh i mekhanjzirovanykh voisk 2 Ukrainiskogo fronta v Tyrgul-Frumosskoi operatsii, 2–8.5.1944" [A report concerning the combat operations of the 2nd Ukrainian Front's armored and mechanized forces in the Tirgu Frumos operation, 2–8 May 1944], in "Zhurnal boevykh deistvii 2 Ukrainskogo fronta za aprel'-mai 1944 g." [The journal of combat operations of the 2nd Ukrainian Front for April–May 1944], *TsAMO,* f. 240, op. 2779, ed. khr. 1155, l. 292.

12. Quoted in Spaeter, *History of the Panzerkorps Grossdeutschland,* 323–324, and Manteuffel, "Battle of Targul-Frumos," 13. As in other passages, the translations in these two versions of the same account vary somewhat.

13. Quoted in Spaeter, *History of the Panzerkorps Grossdeutschland,* 324, and Manteuffel, "Battle of Targul-Frumos," 13.

14. Quoted in Spaeter, *History of the Panzerkorps Grossdeutschland,* 325.

15. Spaeter (ibid.) claims that 32 tanks broke into Cornesti, while Manteuffel ("Battle of Targul-Frumos," 14) places the number at 34.

16. Spaeter, *History of the Panzerkorps Grossdeutschland,* 332.

17. Quoted in ibid., 325, and Manteuffel, "Battle of Targul-Frumos," 14.

18. Quoted in Spaeter, *History of the Panzerkorps Grossdeutschland,* 325.

19. Quoted in ibid., 329–330. The SS Panzer Division *Totenkopf* had begun the day with its *Kampfgruppe* "Eicke," which consisted of one assault gun battery and its 13th and 14th Companies, in lager just south of Tirgu Frumos and the 2nd and 3rd Battalions of *Kampfgruppe* "Eicke" and the 18th Company and two assault gun batteries in the village of Strunga, southwest of Tirgu Frumos. During the day, Group "Eicke" regrouped to new positions in the southern outskirts of Tirgu Frumos and *Kampfgruppe* "G," which included the division's panzer regiment, moved to the Helestieni region to assist *Grossdeutschland* Division's Grenadier Regiment and rescue the Romanian 1st Guards Panzer Division.

20. "Zhurnal boevykh deistvii 27 armii za mai 1944 g." [The journal of combat operations of the 27th Army for May 1944], *TsAMO,* f. 381, op. 8378, ed. khr. 439, ll. 4–6.

21. "Doklad o boevykh deistviiakh bronetankovykh i mekhanjzirovanykh voisk," l. 292.

22. Manteuffel, "Battle of Targul-Frumos," 17.

23. Spaeter, *History of the Panzerkorps Grossdeutschland,* 332.

24. Quoted in ibid., 333–334.

25. F. M. von Senger und Etterlin, briefing presented to the U.S. Army War College, undated, 2. More details can be found in F. M. von Senger und Etterlin, *Der Gegenschlag* (Neckargemund: Scharnhorst Buchkameradschaft, 1959), 117.

26. Von Senger und Etterlin, *Der Gegenschlag,* 120.

27. F. M. von Senger Un Etterlin, briefing presented to the U.S. Army War College, undated, 3.

28. Ibid.

29. Ibid.

30. Ibid., 4.

31. Ibid., 4–5.

32. "Zhurnal boevykh deistvii 27 armii za mai 1944 g.," *TsAMO*, f. 381, op. 8378, ed. khr. 439, l. 6.

33. "Doklad o boevykh deistviiakh bronetankovykh i mekhanizirovannykh voisk," l. 292.

34. Ibid.

35. Quoted in Spaeter, *History of the Panzerkorps Grossdeutschland,* 334.

36. Manteuffel, "Battle of Targul-Frumos," 15.

37. Quoted in Spaeter, *History of the Panzerkorps Grossdeutschland,* 334.

38. "Zhurnal boevykh deistvii 2 Ukrainskogo fronta za aprel'-mai 1944 g.," l. 220.

39. "Zhurnal boevykh deistvii 27 armii za mai 1944 g.," l. 5.

40. "Zhurnal boevykh deistvii 2 Ukrainskogo fronta za aprel'-mai 1944 g.," l. 217.

41. "Zhurnal boevykh deistvii 27 armii za mai 1944 g.," l. 5.

42. "Zhurnal boevykh deistvii 2 Ukrainskogo fronta za aprel'-mai 1944g.," ll. 220–221.

43. Spaeter, *History of the Panzerkorps Grossdeutschland,* 334–335.

44. "Doklad o boevykh deistviiakh bronetankovykh i mekhanjzirovanykh voisk," l. 293.

45. "Zhurnal boevykh deistvii 27 armii za mai 1944 g.," l. 7.

46. "Doklad o boevykh deistviiakh bronetankovykh i mekhanjzirovanykh voisk," l. 293.

47. "Zhurnal boevykh deistvii 2 Ukrainskogo fronta za aprel'-mai 1944g.," ll. 223–225.

48. "Zhurnal boevykh deistvii 27 armii za mai 1944 g.," ll. 7–8.

49. Spaeter, *History of the Panzerkorps Grossdeutschland,* 335.

50. Ibid.

51. Ibid.

52. "Zhurnal boevykh deistvii 2 Ukrainskogo fronta za aprel'-mai 1944g.," ll. 225–227.

53. "Zhurnal boevykh deistvii 27 armii za mai 1944 g.," ll. 9–10.

54. "Doklad o boevykh deistviiakh bronetankovykh i mekhanjzirovanykh voisk," l. 294.

55. "Zhurnal boevykh deistvii 27 armii za mai 1944 g.," ll. 11–12.

56. "Doklad o boevykh deistviiakh bronetankovykh i mekhanjzirovanykh voisk," ll. 293–294.

57. Spaeter, *History of the Panzerkorps Grossdeutschland,* 335–336.

58. "Zhurnal boevykh deistvii 2 Ukrainskogo fronta za aprel'-mai 1944g.," ll. 220–221.

59. V. A. Zolotarev, ed., "Stavka VGK: Dokumenty i materially, 1944–1945" [The *Stavka* VGK: Documents and materials, 1944–1945] in *Russkii arkhiv: Velikaia Otechestvennaia, T. 16 (5–4)* [The Russian archives: The Great Patriotic (War), vol. 16 (5–4)] (Moscow: "TERRA," 1999), 84. Hereafter cited as Zolotarev, "Stavka VGK, 1944," with appropriate page(s).

60. Ibid.

61. *Stavka* Directive No. 220106 dated 23 May, referenced in Zolotarev, "Stavka VGK, 1944," 85.

62. "Zhurnal boevykh deistvii 27 armii za mai 1944 g.," ll. 12.

63. Manteuffel, "Battle of Targul-Frumos," 17–18.

64. Quoted in Spaeter, *History of the Panzerkorps Grossdeutschland,* 326; also Manteuffel, "Battle of Targul-Frumos," 18.

65. Von Senger und Etterlin, briefing presented to the U.S. Army War College, 5–6.

66. "Kratkie vyvody po provedeniiu operatsii so 2 po 8.5.44g." [Short conclusions on the conduct of operations from 2 through 8 May 1944], in "Zhurnal boevykh deistvii 27 armii za mai 1944 g.," ll. 14–15.

67. "Doklad o boevykh deistviiakh bronetankovykh i mekhanjzirovanykh voisk," ll. 296–297.

68. "Dokumenty 2 Tankovoi armii za 1944g." [Documents of the 2nd Tank Army for 1944], *TsAMO,* f. 308, op. 4148, d. 206, ll. 159–160.

69. "Iz otcheta o boevykh deistviiakh 3 TK v period co 2 po 5 maia 1944g." [A report about the combat operations of the 3rd Tank Corps during the period from 2 through 5 May 1944], *TsAMO,* f. 307, op. 4148, ed. khr. 222, ll. 629–637.

7. The 3rd Ukainian Front's Plans and the German Sixth Army's Counterstrokes along the Dnestr River (2–30 May 1944)

1. V. I. Chuikov, *V boiakh za Ukrainy (Gvardeitsy Stalingrada v boiakh protiv fashistskikh zakhvatchikov za osvobozhdenie Sovetskoi Ukrainy)* [In the battles for the Ukraine (The guardsmen of Stalingrad in battles against the Fascist invaders for the liberation of the Soviet Ukraine)] (Kiev: Politicheskoi literatury Ukrainy, 1972), 178–179.

2. V. A. Zolotarev, ed., "Stavka VGK: Dokumenty i materially, 1944–1945" [The *Stavka* VGK: Documents and materials, 1944–1945] in *Russkii arkhiv: Velikaia Otechestvennaia, T. 16 (5–4)* [The Russian archives: The Great Patriotic (War), vol. 16 (5–4)] (Moscow: "TERRA," 1999), 82. Hereafter cited as Zolotarev, "Stavka VGK, 1944," with appropriate page(s).

3. Ibid.

4. A. S. Zhadov, *Chetyre goda voiny* [Four years of war] (Moscow: Voenizdat, 1978), 173–174.

5. "Zhurnal boevykḥ deistvii 2 Ukrainskogo fronta za aprel'-mai 1944g." [The combat journal of the 2nd Ukrainian Front for April-May 1944], *TsAMO* (*Tsentral'nyi arkhiv Ministerstva Oborony* [Central Archives of the Ministry of Defense (of the Russian Federation)]), f. 240, op. 2779, ed. khr. 1155, ll. 228.

6. Chuikov, *V boiakh za Ukrainy,* 179.

7. Zolotarev, "Stavka VGK, 1944," 85.

8. Chuikov, *V boiakh za Ukrainy,* 179–181.

9. Ibid., 181.

10. Ibid.

11. Rolf Grams, *Die 14. Panzer-Division 1940–1945* (Bad Nauheim: Verlag Hans-Henning Podzun, 1957), 210. For German Sixth Army's daily dispositions throughout this period, see "Ia, KTB, Akte F, Tasche 16, Lagekarten, Mar–May 1944," *AOK 6, 50624/3* file, in National Archives microfilm series T-312, Roll 1468.

12. For details on the German deployment and conduct of the operation, see Grams, *Die 14. Panzer-Division,* 210–211.

13. A. V. Morozov, *39-ia Barvenkovskaia: Boevoi put' 39-i gvardeiskoi strel'kovoi Barvenkovskoi ordena Lenina, dvazhdy Krasnoznamennoi, ordena Suvorova II stepeni i Bogdan Khmel'nitskogo II stepeni divizii* [The 39th Barvenkovo: The combat path of the 39th Guards Barvenkovo order of Lenin, twice Red Banner, order of Suvorov 2nd degree and Bogdan Khmel'nitsky 2nd degree Rifle Division] (Moscow: Voenizdat, 1981), 58–59. For another perspective on the fighting in the bridgehead, see V. A. Beliavsky, *Strely skrestilis' na Shpree* [Rifle fire crisscrosses along the Spree] (Moscow: Voenizdat, 1972), 155–165. Actually, the 39th Guards Rifle Division relieved the 5th Guards Army's 9th Guards Airborne Division literally on the eve of the German assault, and the 9th Guards Airborne Division had to exit the bridgehead on 13 May under heavy German artillery fire and air strikes. The 79th Guards Rifle division began relieving the 5th Guards Army's 13th Guards Rifle Division on 5–6 May, hence, it was able to clear out of the bridgehead before the German assault began.

14. N. N. Afanas'ev, *Ot Volgi do Shpree: Boevoi put' 35-i gvardeiskoi strel'kovoi Lozovskoi Krasnoznamennoi ordena Suvorova i Bogdan Khmel'nitskogo divizii* [From the Volga to the Spree: The combat path of the 35th Guards Lozovaia, Red Banner,

and Order of Suvorov and Bogdan Khmel'nitsky Rifle Divisions] (Moscow: Voenizdat, 1982), 173–174.

15. Chuikov, *V boiakh za Ukrainy,* 181–182.

16. Morozov, *39-ia Barvenkovskaia,* 60–61.

17. Chuikov, *V boiakh za Ukrainy,* 182.

18. Afanas'ev, *Ot Volgi do Shpree,* 175–176.

19. Chuikov, *V boiakh za Ukrainy,* 183.

20. Grams, *Die 14. Panzer-Division,* 212.

21. Chuikov, *V boiakh za Ukrainy,* 184. Chuikov claims the Germans lost 5,000 dead and wounded and up to 50 tanks destroyed or burned on 11 May.

22. Morozov, *39-ia Barvenkovskaia,* 61.

23. Afanas'ev, *Ot Volgi do Shpree,* 177–178.

24. Chuikov, *V boiakh za Ukrainy,* 185.

25. Morozov, *39-ia Barvenkovskaia,* 62–63.

26. Chuikov, *V boiakh za Ukrainy,* 185.

27. G. S. Zdanovich, *Idem v nastuplenie* [We are on the attack] (Moscow: Voenizdat, 1980), 166.

28. Ibid., 167–169.

29. For more details based on Soviet archival records, see A. A. Maslov, *Fallen Soviet Generals* (London: Frank Cass, 1998), 141–142.

30. Ibid., citing archival document f. 1633, op. 1, d. 2, ll. 27–28.

31. Ibid.

32. Grams, *Die 14. Panzer-Division,* 215.

8. Denouement (30 May–6 June 1944)

1. V. A. Zolotarev, ed., "Stavka VGK: Dokumenty i materially, 1944–1945" [The *Stavka* VGK: Documents and materials, 1944–1945] in *Russkii arkhiv: Velikaia Otechestvennaia, T. 16 (5–4)* [The Russian archives: The Great Patriotic (War), vol. 16 (5–4)] (Moscow: "TERRA," 1999), 86. Hereafter cited as Zolotarev, "Stavka VGK, 1944," with appropriate page(s).

2. Ibid., 92.

3. "Zhurnal boevykh deistvii 27gv sk za mai 1944 g." [The 27th Guards Rifle Corps' journal of combat operations for May 1944], *TsAMO* (*Tsentral'nyi arkhiv Ministerstva Oborony* [Central Archives of the Ministry of Defense (of the Russian Federation)]), f. 381, op. 8378, ed. khr. 304, l. 198.

4. Werner Haupt, *The Battles of Army Group South,* translated by Joseph Welch (unpublished manuscript), 243.Originally published as *Die Schlachten der Heeresgruppe Sud: Aus der Sicht der Divisionen* (unknown: Podzun-Pallas-Verlag, 1985).

5. For example, see the daily intelligence maps in "Anlagen z. KTB-Ic/AO Feindlagekarten, Jan–Jun 1944," *AOK 8, 58298/30* file, in National Archives microfilm series T-312, Roll 70. The daily situation in Army Group Wöhler and the German Eighth Army is found in "Anlagenband z. KTB–Ia Tägliche Lagekarten, Jan–Jun 1944," *AOK 8, 58298/24* file, in National Archives microfilm series T-312, Roll 68; and "Anlagenband z. KTB–Ia Tägliche Lagekarten, Apr–Jul 1944," *AOK 8, 58298/28* file, in National Archives microfilm series T-312, Roll 69.

6. Helmuth Spaeter, *The History of the Panzerkorps Grossdeutschland,* vol. 2, translated by David Johnson (Winnipeg, Canada: J. J. Fedorowicz, 1995), 338.

7. G. T. Zavision and P. A. Korniushin, *I na Tikhom okeane: Voenno-istoricheskii ocherk o boevom puti 6-i gvardeiskoi tankovoi armii* [To the Pacific Ocean: A military-historical account of the combat path of the 6th Guards Tank Army] (Moscow: Voenizdat, 1967), 54–55, 58.

8. For details about the 24th Panzer Division's advance, see F. M. von Senger und Etterlin, *Die 24. Panzer-Division vormals 1. Kavallerie-Division 1939–1945* (Neckargemund: Kurt Vowinckel Verlag, 1962), 244–246.

9. Haupt, *Battles of Army Group South,* 243.

10. Ibid.

11. Ibid.

12. For the 14th Panzer Division's role in the counterstroke, see Rolf Grams, *Die 14. Panzer-Division 1940–1945* (Bad Nauheim: Verlag Hans-Henning Podzun, 1957), 220–221.

13. F. I. Vysotsky, M. E. Makukhin, F. M. Sarychev, and M. K. Shaposhnikov, *Gvardeiskaia tankovaia* [Guards tank] (Moscow: Voenizdat, 1963), 105–108.

14. Spaeter, *History of the Panzerkorps Grossdeutschland,* 338.

15. Hans-Joachim Jung, *The History of the Panzerregiment "Grossdeutschland,"* translated by David Johnson (Winnipeg, Canada: J. J. Fedorowicz, 2000), 211.

16. Spaeter, *History of the Panzerkorps Grossdeutschland,* 338.

17. Ibid.

18. Ibid., 339.

19. Ibid.

20. *Battles of Army Group South,* 243.

21. Spaeter, *History of the Panzerkorps Grossdeutschland,* 339.

22. Ibid., 339–340.

23. Ibid., 340.

24. German intelligence records, which are normally exceedingly accurate, at least tactically, show the 73rd Rifle Corps as being reinforced by the 58th Rifle Division on 3 June at a time when Soviet order of battle documents indicate the 58th Rifle Division was then subordinate to the 22nd Rifle Corps of the 1st Ukrainian Front's 3rd Guards Army. German records show the 58th Rifle Division remained with the 52nd Army at least until month's end. Regardless of whichever document is correct, at least one rifle division reinforced the 73rd Rifle Corps on 3 June, perhaps one from the 27th Guards Rifle Corps. See *Boevoi sostav Sovetskoi armii, Chast' 4 (Ianvar'-dekabr' 1944)* [The combat composition of the Soviet Army, Part 4 (January–December 1944)] (Moscow: Voenizdat, 1988), 167–170.

25. Spaeter, *History of the Panzerkorps Grossdeutschland,* 340–341.

26. *Battles of Army Group South,* 243.

27. Spaeter, *History of the Panzerkorps Grossdeutschland,* 341.

28. Ibid.

29. Von Senger und Etterlin, *Die 24. Panzer-Division,* 249.

30. Spaeter, *History of the Panzerkorps Grossdeutschland,* 341.

31. Ibid.

32. Zolotarev, "Stavka VGK, 1944," 284–286.

9. Conclusions

1. V. A. Zolotarev, ed., *Velikaia Otechestvennaia Voina 1941–1945: Voenno-istoricheskie ocherki v chetyrekh knigakh, Kniga 3* [The Great Patriotic War 1941–1945: A military-historical survey in four books, book 3] (Moscow: "Nauka," 1999), 48. Hereafter cited as Zolotarev, *VOV.*

2. At least in part, the perilous German situation in Belorussia was due to successful offensive operations conducted by Rokossovsky's 1st Belorussian Front, which Soviet historians have also largely covered up. See David M. Glantz, *Forgotten Battles of the Soviet-German War (1941–1945),* vol. 6: *The Winter Campaign (24 December 1943–April 1944) (Part Three: The Western Axis)* (Carlisle, PA: Self-published, 2004).

3. "1944 god, 2-i Ukrainskii front: Ukazaniia po bor'be s tankami i samokhodnymi orudiiami protivnika pri boe v glubine oborony" [1944, 2nd Ukrainian Front: Instructions on the struggle with tanks and self-propelled artillery during combat in the depth of defenses], *Sbornik boevykh dokumentov Velikoi Otechestvennoi voiny, vypusk 6* [Collection of combat documents of the Great Patriotic War, issue 6] (Moscow Voenizdat, 1948), 18. Hereafter cited as *SBDVOV* with appropriate issue and page(s). For other General Staff critiques of this offensive, as well as orders of specific tactical themes, see "1944 god, 2-i Ukrainskii Front: Ukazaniia po organiizatsii protivitankovoi oborony (mai 1944 g.)" [1944, 2nd Ukrainian Front: An order of the organization of antitank defenses (May 1944)], *SBDVOV,* issue 4 (1948), 128–135; "Boevye deistviia shturmovykh otriady i grupp: 1944 2-i Ukrainskii front" [The combat actions of assault detachments and groups: 1944 2nd Ukrainian Front], *SBDVOV,* issue 3 (1947), 89–91; "1944 2-i Ukrainskii front: Ukazaniia o deistviiakh tankovykh i mekhanizirovannykh voisk v gorno-lesistoi mestnosti" [1944 2nd Ukrainian Front: An order concerning the operations of tank and mechanized forces in mountainous and forested terrain], *SBDVOV,* issue 6, 135–137: "Prikaz voiskami 2-i Tankovoi armii no. 0230 6 maia 1944 g." [2nd Tank Army order no. 0230 on 6 May 1944], *SDBVOV,* issue 15 1952), 44–44; and "1944 god, 57-ia armiia, 3-i Ukrainskii front, Prikaz voiskami 57-i armii no. 00143 21 maia 1944 g." [1944, 57th Army, 3rd Ukrainian Front, 57th Army order n0.00143 of 21 May 1944], *SBDVOV,* issue 9 (1949), 32–35.

4. "Prikaz voiskami 2-i tankovoi armii No. 0217, 30 aprelia 1944 g." [2nd Tank Army's order No. 0217, 30 April 1944], in *SBDVOV,* issue 15 (1952), 21–23.

5. A. V. Antosiak, *V boiakh za slobodu Rumynii* [In battles for the liberation of Romania] (Moscow: Voenizdat, 1974), 67.

6. Ibid., 66. According to G. F. Krivosheev, ed., *Rossiia i SSSR v voinakh XX veka: Poteri vooruzhennykh sil* [Russia and the USSR in 20th-century wars: Losses of the Armed Forces] (Moscow: "Olma-Press," 2001), the 2nd Ukrainian Front numbered 594,700 men on 24 December 1943 and lost a total of 266,973 men, including 66,059 killed, missing, and captured during its operations in the Ukraine through 17 April 1944. Returnee wounded and new conscripts probably amounted to roughly half of its losses, bringing its total strength in mid-April to just under 600,000 soldiers.

7. Krivosheev, *Rossiia i SSSR v voinakh,* 292.

8. Zolotarev, *VOV,* 48.

9. Krivosheev, *Rossiia i SSSR v voinakh,* 292.

10. Antosiak, *V boiakh za slobodu Rumynii,* 66–67.

11. F. M. von Senger und Etterlin, *Die 24. Panzer-Division vromals 1. Kavallerie-Division 1939–1945* (Neckargemund: Kurt Vowinkel Verlag, 1962), 249.

Appendix

1. V. A. Zolotarev, ed., "General'nyi shtab v gody Velikoi Otechestvennoi voiny: Dokumenty i materialy 1944–1945 gg." [The General Staff in the Great Patriotic War: Documents and materials 1944–1945], in *Russkii arkhiv: Velikaia Otechestvennaia, T. 23 (12–4)* [The Russian archives: The Great Patriotic (War), vol. 23 (12–4)] (Moscow: "TERRA," 2001), 136.

2. V. A. Zolotarev, ed., "Stavka VGK: Dokumenty i materially, 1944–1945" [The *Stavka* VGK: Documents and materials, 1944–1945], in *Russkii arkhiv: Velikaia Otechestvennaia, T. 16 (5–4)* [The Russian archives: The Great Patriotic (War), vol. 16 (5–4)] (Moscow: "TERRA," 1999), 71. Hereafter cited as Zolotarev, "Stavka VGK, 1944," with appropriate page(s).

3. Ibid., 281–282.

4. Ibid., 72.

5. "Boevye prikazy i operativnye direktiy 2 Ukrainskogo fronta za 1944 g." [Combat orders and operational directives of the 2nd Ukrainian Front for 1944], *TsAMO* (*Tsentral'nyi arkhiv Ministerstva Oborony* [Central Archives of the Ministry of Defense (of the Russian Federation)]), f. 381, op. 8378, ed. khr. 308, ll. 1–6.

6. Zolotarev, "Stavka VGK, 1944," 82.

7. Ibid., 84.

8. Ibid., 85.

9. "Zhurnal boevykh deistvii 2 Ukrainskogo fronta za aprel'-mai 1944 g.," *TsAMO*, f. 240, op. 2779, ed. khr. 992, 1. 228.

10. Ibid., ll. 220–221.

11. "Dokumenty 2 Tankovoi armii za 1944 g." [Documents of the 2nd Tank Army for 1944], *TsAMO*, f. 308, op. 4148, d. 206, ll. 159–160.

12. "Zhurnal boevykh deistvii 2 Ukrainskogo fronta za aprel'-mai 1944 g.," *TsAMO*, f. 240, op. 2779, ed. khr. 992, ll. 3–11.

13. Zolotarev, "Stavka VGK, 1944," 86.

14. Ibid., 92.

15. Ibid., 284–286.

16. "Zhurnal boevykh deistvii 2 Ukrainskogo fronta za aprel'-mai 1944 g.," *TsAMO*, f. 240, op. 2779, ed. khr. 992, ll. 27–30.

Selected Bibliography

Abbreviations

TsAMO *Tsentral'nyi arkhiv Ministerstva Oborony* [Central Archives of the Ministry of Defense (of the Russian Federation)]

Archival Documents

"Anlagenband z. KTB–Ia Tägliche Lagekarten, Apr–Jul 1944," *AOK 8, 58298/28* file. National Archives microfilm series T-312, Roll 69.

"Anlagenband z. KTB–Ia Tägliche Lagekarten, Jan–Jun 1944," *AOK 8, 58298/24* file. National Archives microfilm series T-312, Roll 68.

"Anlagen z. KTB–Ic/AO Feindlagekarten, Jan–Jun 1944," *AOK 8, 58298/30* file. National Archives microfilm series T-312, Roll 70.

Boevoi sostav Sovetskoi armii, Chast' 4 (Ianvar'-dekabr' 1944) [The combat composition of the Soviet Army, Part 4 (January–December 1944)] (Moscow: Voenizdat, 1988), 167–170.

"Boevye prikazy i operativnye direktiy 2 Ukrainskogo fronta za 1944 g." [Combat orders and operational directives of the 2nd Ukrainian Front for 1944], *TsAMO,* f. 381, op. 8378, ed. khr. 308.

"Doklad o boevykh deistviiakh bronetankovykh i mekhanjzirovanykh voisk 2 Ukrainiskogo fronta v Tyrgul-Frumosskoi operatsii, 2–8.5.1944" [A report concerning the combat operations of the 2nd Ukrainian Front's armored and mechanized forces in the Tirgu Frumos operation, 2–8 May 1944], in "Zhurnal boevykh deistvii 2 Ukrainskogo fronta za aprel'-mai 1944 g." [The journal of combat operations of the 2nd Ukrainian Front for April–May 1944], *TsAMO,* f. 240, op. 2779, ed. khr. 1155, ll. 289–292.

"Dokumenty 2 Tankovoi armii za 1944g." [Documents of the 2nd Tank Army for 1944], *TsAMO,* f. 308, op. 4148, d. 206.

"Ia, KTB, Akte F, Tasche 16, Lagekarten, Mar–May 1944," *AOK 6, 50624/3* file. National Archives microfilm series T-312, Roll 1468.

"Iz otcheta o boevykh deistviiakh 3 TK v period co 2 po 5 maia 1944g." [A report about the combat operations of the 3rd Tank Corps during the period from 2 through 5 May 1944], *TsAMO,* f. 307, op. 4148, ed. khr. 222, ll. 629–637.

Komandovanie korpusnogo i divizionnogo zvena Sovetskikh vooruzhennykh sil perioda Velikoi Otechestvennoi voiny 1941–1945 gg. [Commanders at the corps and division level of the Soviet Armed Forces during the period of the Great Patriotic War 1941–1945]. Moscow: Frunze Academy, 1964.

Sbornik voenno-istoricheskikh materialov Velikoi Otechestvennoi voiny, vypusk 15 [A collection of military-historical materials of the Great Patriotic War, issue 15]. Moscow: Voenizdat 1955. Classified secret.

"Zhurnal boevykh deistvii 2 Ukrainskogo fronta za aprel'-mai 1944 g." [The journal of combat operations of the 2nd Ukrainian Front for April–May 1944], *TsAMO,* f. 240, op. 2779, ed. khr. 992, 1155.

"Zhurnal boevykh deistvii 27 armii za mai 1944 g." [The journal of combat operations of the 27th Army for May 1944], *TsAMO,* f. 381, op. 8378, ed. khr. 439.

"Zhurnal boevykh deistvii 27gv sk za mai 1944 g." [The 27th Guards Rifle Corps' journal of combat operations for May 1944], *TsAMO,* f. 381, op. 8378, ed. khr. 304.

Zolotarev, V. A., ed. "General'nyi shtab v gody Velikoi Otechestvennoi voiny: Dokumenty i materialy 1944–1945 gg." [The General Staff in the Great Patriotic War: Documents and materials 1944–1945]. In *Russkii arkhiv: Velikaia Otechestvennaia, T. 23 (12-4)* [The Russian archives: The Great Patriotic (War), vol. 23 (12-4)]. Moscow: "TERRA," 2001.

Zolotarev, V. A., ed. "Stavka VGK: Dokumenty i materially, 1944–1945" [The *Stavka* VGK: Documents and materials, 1944–1945]. In *Russkii arkhiv: Velikaia Otechestvennaia, T. 16 (5-4)* [The Russian archives: The Great Patriotic (War), vol. 16 (5-4)]. Moscow: "TERRA," 1999.

Secondary Sources

Afanas'ev, N. N. *Ot Volgi do Shpree: Boevoi put' 35-i gvardeiskoi strel'kovoi Lozovskoi Krasnoznamennoi ordena Suvorova i Bogdan Khmel'nitskogo divizii* [From the Volga to the Spree: The combat path of the 35th Guards Lozovaia, Red Banner, and Order of Suvorov and Bogdan Khmel'nitsky Rifle Division]. Moscow: Voenizdat, 1982.

Amirov, K. V. *Ot Volgi do Al'p: Boevoi put' 36-i gvardeiskoi strelkovoi verkhnedneprovskoi krasnoznamennoi ordena Suvorova in Kutuzova II stepeni divizii* [From the Volga to the Alps: The combat path of the 36th Guards Upper Dnepr, Red Banner, and Order of Suvorov and Kutuzov II degree rifle division]. Moscow: Voenizdat, 1987.

Antosiak, A. V. *V boiakh za svobodu Rumynii* [In the battles for the liberation of Romania]. Moscow: Voenizdat, 1974.

Armstrong, Richard N. *Red Army Tank Commanders: The Armored Guards.* Atglen, PA: Shiffer Military/Aviation History, 1994.

Axworthy, Mark, Cornel Scafes, and Cristian Craciunoiu. *Third Axis Fourth Ally: Romanian Armed Forces in the European War, 1941–1944.* London: Arms and Armour, 1995.

Beliavsky, V. A. *Strely skrestilis' na Shpree* [Rifle fire crisscrosses along the Spree]. Moscow: Voenizdat, 1972.

Blazhei, A. K. *V armeiskom shtabe* [In an army headquarters]. Moscow: Voenizdat, 1967.

Bologov, F. P. *V shtabe gvardeiskoi divizii* [In the headquarters of a guards division]. Moscow: Voenizdat, 1987.

Chmelev, A. M. *Proshla s boiami.* [Advancing under fire]. Kishinev: Karta Moldaveniaske, 1983.

Chuikov, V. I. *Gvardeistsy Stalingrada idut ne* zapad [The Stalingrad guardsmen march to the west]. Moscow: Sovetskaia Rossiia, 1972.

Chuikov, V. I. *V boiakh za Ukrainy (Gvardeitsy Stalingrada v boiakh protiv fashistskikh zakhvatchikov za osvobozhdenie Sovetskoi Ukrainy)* [In the battles for the Ukraine (The guardsmen of Stalingrad in battles against the Fascist invaders for the liberation of the Soviet Ukraine)]. Kiev: Politicheskoi literatury Ukrainy, 1972.

Glantz, David M. *Forgotten Battles of the Soviet-German War (1941–1945),* vol. 6: *The Winter Campaign (24 December 1943–April 1944) (Part Three: The Western Axis).* Carlisle, PA: Self-published, 2004.

Golubovich, V. S. *Marshal Malinovsky.* Moscow: Voenizdat, 1984.

Grams, Rolf. *Die 14. Panzer-Division 1940–1945.* Bad Nauheim: Verlag Hans-Henning Podzun, 1957.

Grigorenko, Petro G. *Memoirs.* Translated by Thomas P. Whitney. New York: W. W. Norton, 1982.

Grylev, A. N. *Dnepr, Karpaty, Krym: Osvobozhdenie Pravoberezhnoi Ukrainy i Krym v 1944 godu* [The Dnepr, the Carpathian, and the Crimea: The liberation of the Right Bank of the Ukraine and the Crimea in 1944]. Moscow: "Nauka," 1970.

Haupt, Werner. *The Battles of Army Group South.* Translated by Joseph Welch. Unpublished manuscript. Originally published as *Die Schlachten der Heeresgruppe Sud: Aus der Sicht der Divisionen* (Unknown: Podzun-Pallas-Verlag, 1985).

Iaroshenko, A. A. *V boi shla 41-ia gvardeiskaia: Boevoi put' 41-i gvardeiskoi strelkovoi Korsun'sko-Dunaiskoi ordena Suvorova divizii* [The 41st Guards went into battle: The combat path of the 41st Guards Korsun'-Shevchenkovskii, Order of Suvorov Rifle Division]. Moscow: Voenizdat, 1982.

Jung, Hans-Joachim. *The History of Panzerregiment "Grossdeutschland."* Translated by David Johnston. Winnipeg, Manitoba, Canada: J. J. Fedorowicz, 2000.

Konev, I. S. *Zapiski komanduuishchego frontom 1943–1945* [Notes of a *front* commander 1943–1945]. Moscow: Voenizdat, 1981.

Kozlov, M. M., ed. *Velikaia Otechestvennaia voina 1941–1945: Entsiklopediia* [The Great Patriotic War 1941–1945: An encyclopedia]. Moscow: "Sovetskaia entsiklopediia," 1985.

Krivosheev, G. F., ed. *Rossiia i SSSR v voinakh XX veka: Poteri vooruzhennykh sil* [Russia and the USSR in 20th-century wars: Losses of the Armed Forces]. Moscow: "Olma-Press," 2001.

Manteuffel, Hasso von. "The Battle of Targul-Frumos." Transcript of a lecture delivered to the U.S. Army War College, Ft. Leavenworth, KS, 1948. Author's copy.

Maslov, A. A. *Fallen Soviet Generals.* London: Frank Cass, 1998.

Minasian, M. M., ed. *Istoriia Velikoi Otechestvennoi voiny Sovetskogo Soiuza 1941–1945 v shesti tomakh, tom chetvertyi* [A history of the Great Patriotic War of the Soviet Union in six volumes, vol. 4]. Moscow: Voenizdat, 1962.

Morozov, A. V. *39-ia Barvenkovskaia: Boevoi put' 39-i gvardeiskoi strel'kovoi Barvenkovskoi ordena Lenina, dvazhdy Krasnoznamennoi, ordena Suvorova II stepeni i Bogdan Khmel'nitskogo II stepeni divizii* [The 39th Barvenkovo: The combat path of the 39th Guards Barvenkovo order of Lenin, twice Red Banner, order of Suvorov 2nd degree and Bogdan Khmel'nitsky 2nd degree Rifle Division]. Moscow: Voenizdat, 1981.

Morozov, I. K. *Ot Stalingrada do Pragi: Zapiski komandira divizii* [From Stalingrad to Berlin: The notes of a division commander]. Volgograd: Nizhne-Volzhkoe knizhnoe izdatel'strvo, 1976.

Mutovin, B. I. *Cherez vse ispytaniia* [Through an entire education]. Moscow: Voenizdat, 1986.

Ogarkov, N. V., ed. *Sovetskaia voennaia entsiklopediia v vos'mykh tomakh* [Soviet military encyclopedia in eight volumes]. Moscow: Voenizdat, 1976–1980.

Pliev, I. A. *Dorogami voiny* [Along the roads of war]. Moscow: "Khiga," 1985.

Portugal'sky, P. M. *Marshal I. S. Konev.* Moscow: Voenizdat, 1985.

Roslyi, I. P. *Poslednii priva'- v Berline* [The last stopping place, in Berlin]. Moscow: Voenizdat, 1983.

Samchuk, I. A., and P. G. Skachko. *Atakuiut desantniki: Boevoi put's 9-i gvardeiskoi Krasnoznamennoi ordena Suvorova i Kutuzova Poltavskoi vozdushno-desantnyoi diviziii* [The airborne troops are attacking: The combat path of the 9th Guards Red Banner, orders of Suvorov and Kutuzov, Poltava Airborne Division]. Moscow: Voenizdat, 1975.

Samchuk, I. A., P. G. Skachko, Iu. N. Babikov, and I. L. Gnedoi. *Ot Volgu do El'by i Pragu: Kratkii ocherk o Boevoi puti 5-i gvardeiskoi armii* [From the Volga to the Elbe and Prague: A short survey of the combat path of the 5th Guards Army]. Moscow: Voenizdat, 1978.

Savil'ev, V. P., and N. P. Popov. *Gvardeiskaia Nikolaevskaia: Boevoi put' 108-i gvardeiskoi strelkovoi Nikolaevskoi Krasnoznamennoi, ordena Suvorovoa divizii* [The guards Nikolaev: The combat path of the 108th Guards Nikolaev, Red Banner, and Order of Suvorov Rifle Division]. Moscow: Voenizdat, 1978.

Shtemenko, S. M. *The General Staff at War 1941–1945: Book 1.* Moscow: Progress, 1981.

Shukman, Harold, ed. *Stalin's Generals.* London: Weidenfeld and Nicolson, 1993.

Soshnokov, A. Ia., ed., *Sovetskaia kavaleriia* [Soviet cavalry]. Moscow: Voenizdat, 1984.

Spaeter, Helmuth. *The History of the Panzerkorps Grossdeutschland,* vol. 2. Translated by David Johnston. Winnipeg, Manitoba, Canada: J. J. Fedorowicz, 1995.

Ustinov, D. F., ed. *Istoriia Vtoroi Mirovoi voiny 1939–1945 v dvenadtsati tomakh, tom bos'moi* [A history of the Second World War in eleven volumes, volume eight]. Moscow: Voenizdat, 1977.

Vasilevsky, A. M. *Delo vsei zhizni* [Life's work]. Moscow: Izdatel'stvo politicheskoi literatury, 1983.

von Senger und Etterlin, F. M. *Der Gegenschlag.* Neckargemund: Scharnhorst Buchkameradschaft, 1959.

Vorontsev, T. F., ed., *Ot Volzhskikh stepei do Avstriiskikh Al'p* [From the Volga steppes to the Austrian Alps]. Moscow: Voenizdat, 1971.

Vylitok V. S., and S. F. Leskin. *Novomoskovskaia krasnoznamennaia: Boevoi put' 195-i Novomoskovsk Krasnoznamennoi strelkovoi divizii* [The combat path of the 195th

Novomoskovsk Red Banner Rifle Division]. Moscow: Voenizdat, 1979.

Vysotsky, F. I., M. E. Makukhin, F. M. Sarychev, and M. K. Shaposhnikov. *Gvardeiskaia tankovaia* [Guards tank]. Moscow: Voenizdat, 1963.

Zav'ialov, N. I. *Versty muzhestva* [Sacred versts]. Kiev: Politicheskoi literatury Ukrainy, 1981.

Zavision, G. T., and P. A. Korniushin, *I na Tikhom okeane: Voenno-istoricheskii ocherk o boevom puti 6-i gvardeiskoi tankovoi armii* [To the Pacific Ocean: A military-historical account of the combat path of the 6th Guards Tank Army]. Moscow: Voenizdat, 1967.

Zdanovich, G. S. *Idem v nastuplenie* [We are on the attack]. Moscow: Voenizdat, 1980.

Zhadov, A. S. *Chetyre goda voiny* [Four years of war]. Moscow: Voenizdat, 1978.

Ziemke, Earl F. *Stalingrad to Berlin: The German Defeat in the East.* Washington, DC: Office of the Chief of Military History, United States Army, 1968.

Zolotarev, V. A., ed. *Velikaia Otechestvennaia Voina 1941–1945: Voenno-istoricheskie ocherki v chetyrekh knigakh, Kniga 3* [The Great Patriotic War 1941–1945: A military-historical survey in four books, book 3]. Moscow: "Nauka," 1999.

Index

A Personal Guide to the People, Places, and Things of Legendary Camelot and the World Beyond, as Revealed by the Tales Themselves, Discussed and Related by the Authoress with Warm Concern. Herein Are the Greatest and the Humblest in the Realm, Interpreted in Hundreds of Entries Arranged Alphabetically for Convenient Reference and Secure Pleasure.

by

Phyllis Ann Karr

PENDRAGON™ FICTION

PENDRAGON™ FICTION

The Arthurian Companion

The Legendary World of Camelot and the Round Table

by
Phyllis Ann Karr

A CHAOSIUM BOOK
1997

A shorter version of this book appeared previously under the title of *The King Arthur Companion*

Special thanks are extended to the following individuals and institutions for permission to quote from or to otherwise employ materials owned by them: Carnegie Institution of Washington (D.C.), for *The Vulgate Version of the Arthurian Romances* (8 vols.), ed. by H. Oskar Sommer, 1909-1916; to Charles Scribner's Sons, for *The Realms of Arthur*, by Helen Hill Miller, 1969; University of Chicago Press, for *The Complete Works of the Gawain Poet*, by John Gardner, 1965; the Council of the Early English Text Society, for *Arthurian Localities*, by J. S. Stuart Glennie, 1869; Mr. Frank Graham, for *A Topographical and Historical Description of Cornwall*, by John Norden, 1728, reprinted 1966; Harper & Row, Publishers, Inc., for *Reader's Handbook of Famous Names* (2 vols.), by E. Cobham Brewer, 1899, reprinted 1966; Lyle Stuart, Inc., for *Le Morte d'Arthur*, in an edition by A. W. Pollard (1920, 1961).

Cover art by Ed Org. Interior map Eric Vogt. Cover layout by Eric Vogt. Editors Janice Sellers, Sam Shirley, Eric Vogt. Proofreading by Janice Sellers. Interior layout Eric Vogt. Editor-in-Chief Lynn Willis.

First Edition 1 3 5 7 9 8 6 4 2

Chaosium Publication 6200. Published in April 1997.

ISBN 1-56882-096-8

Printed in Canada on 100% recycled acid-free paper (includes at least 20% post-consumer waste).

or less probable example of a female knight. Had I begun reading Spenser's *Faerie Queen* in time, I could have increased the list by two undoubted lady knights—Britomart, who plays a major role in the action, and Palladine, who is only mentioned in Book III, Canto VII, but who may have been meant for the "hero" of one of Spenser's unwritten books.

In references to Malory, I have followed the book and chapter divisions called Caxton's. The Roman numeral refers to the book, the Arabic to the chapter. This, of course, can only be helpful to readers who have access to an edition of Malory that is likewise divided according to Caxton; still, some help is better than no help, and the size of the number will at least tell readers about how far into Malory's narrative the incident cited my be found.

Where the words King and Queen stand alone and are capitalized, they refer to Arthur and Guenever. I have tried to keep the spelling of names more or less standardized but, in some cases like those of Morgan/Morgana and Guenever/Guenevere, I gave up the attempt and spelled as a medieval author might have in the days before dictionaries. The name of Tristram's love is spelled Isoud in my copy of Malory, so it somehow crept into this volume under that spelling, though I think Isolde is much more graceful. The word "court", as in a monarch's court, should be understood as referring to Arthur's court unless otherwise specified or otherwise obviously attached to another ruler.

Compiling this book has been an educational experience for me (and for my mother, who proofread these pages and bore with my oral expoundings); I hope it may add a bit to other readers' appreciation of Arthurian literature.

Rice Lake, Wisconsin
August 3, 1979/August, 1982

About the Entries

A dagger (†) beside or within a boldface entry indicates that the entry is not found in Malory.

I have tried to keep the entries in alphabetical order. Where spelling is so unstandardized and variants so rife, however, any alphabetical order is tricky. For most of the characters named in Malory, I have tried to use the spelling, or one of the alternate spellings, from Pollard's edition, that being the version I had most readily to hand while assembling this work. In some half-dozen cases I have preferred a variant from Sommer's version of the Vulgate or even from Tennyson, as sounding to me less confusing, more mellifluous, or possibly better known; in such cases, and elsewhere as they seemed needed, I have tried to provide sufficient cross-references.

Titles such as King, Queen, and so on are disregarded in alphabetization, and appellations like "Lady of the Lake" and "Queen of the Out Isles" will usually be found under the first distinctive word. Examples: Lady of the *L*ake, Queen of the *O*ut Isles, King *A*grippe's Daughter, Damsel des *M*ares, Giant of the *M*ount of Araby. The italicized letter indicates the word under which the entry will be found. The "first distinctive word" can sometimes be an adjective—I wanted to get all of Chrétien's "Haughty Knights of ..." together—and occasionally for some reason that seemed good enough I may have disregarded my own rule. I tried to give enough cross-references; when in doubt, try checking under any word you can think of. I have listed all the female Elaines together, regardless of how I found the name spelled (Eleine, Helayne, etc.), but I have not attempted to standardize the masculine version of this popular name. The title "Sir" has been omitted from before the names of most knights, unless used to show that a hermit is a retired knight.

In a very few cases, a "see under" note means that an item is entered under a different set of alphabetizing rules than those to which I generally adhered: for instance, **La Beale Isoud**—see under **ISOUD**. (One might with reason have expected to find La Beale Isoud among the B's.)

Numerous characters, especially damsels and ladies, are left nameless in the romances. This does not necessarily mean that they are minor figures, only that certain literary conventions have changed between medieval days and our own. For instance, in *Erec & Enide*, when the titular couple are married about a third of the way through (ca. line 2025), Chrétien de Troyes calls her Enide for the first time in the text, explaining that she cannot be counted a married woman unless she is called by her true name, the name with which she was christened. Before that, it seems, the other characters had less clue to her christened name than the readers had. Chrétien does not apply this rule, or whatever other rules he may use for withholding the names of certain knights, kings, etc., consistently throughout his works—for instance, he gives us Fenice's name at once; nevertheless, the passage may help throw light on the problem of characters left nameless. Where such characters were identified, or where I could identify them simply (by the name of a castle, a relative, etc.), I did so as, for instance, the Damsel of La Beale Regard and King Agrippe's Daughter. I did not particularly like to identify a woman only by the name of a male relative, but it seemed the most convenient course, and readers are left free to to give these ladies names to their own taste. Where I could not readily use such a simple tag, I chose a name arbitrarily. This seemed handier than giving a lump sub-section of "unnamed Damsels", and the names can always be changed to taste. Such names are enclosed in double quotation marks: **"ORNAGRINE."** In a few cases, like that of the king 'Premier Conquis', the quotation marks were bestowed by Sommer, not by me. These names I enclose in single quotation marks, rather than double ones.

In most cases, a cross-reference like **Mungo**†—see **KENTIGERN** means that this is one character with two different names, while a reference like **Bellagere of Magouns**—see under **ANGLIDES** means that the first-named character has no separate note, but that information about him or her may be found under the second-named character.

This volume is selective rather than exhaustive. For instance, of at least six Ywaines, I include only two. I discuss minor characters rather more generously if they were females, kings and dukes, villains, giants, retainers or relatives of major figures, and so on than if they simply were knights, even Round Table knights, of whom there is no shortage.

A few words concerning Chrétien's characters: If they already appeared in the first edition—except for some characters from *Yvain*, this usually means that they reappeared in post-Chrétien works—as a general rule I left them alphabetized under the Malorian or Vulgate spelling of the name, with cross-references where they seemed necessary. In a very few cases, such as Bademagu/Bagdemagus and Calogrenant/Colgrevance, Chrétien's treatment seemed sufficiently different from that of his successors to warrant a separate and additional entry under the Chrétien spelling. Of course, it is less accurate to speak of "Chrétien's" and "Malory's" spellings than of the spellings of the authors' translators and editors; for Chrétien's characters, I have usually followed D.D.R. Owen's spellings and translations with some cross-references from Ruth Harwood Cline's versions, but occasionally I have preferred Cline's, and I left Lunette's listing with the two "t's" Julian Harris employed, rather than changing it to Owen's single-"t" version.

Information indicated as coming from Vulgate VII is to be accepted with extreme caution, due to peculiar research conditions affecting that volume only.

The notes do not pretend to perfect objectivity.

Lists of Families and Retainers

Occasionally you will find appended to a character's entry a list of known family members and retainers for that character. I was prompted to attempt such lists by the prominence of blood feuds. While seemingly not "court cases" except in the event of treachery, such feuds appear to be recognized unofficially. Malory, for instance, has Gawaine and his brothers indulging in several of them with no reprisals from their royal uncle. If someone slays one of your kinsmen, even in battle or tournament, the code apparently permits you to hunt him down and slay him in turn, preferably in honest battle. This may make the difficult tangle of interlinking family relations rather interesting. Such lists are doubtless incomplete, and are starting points at best. They do not include enemies, they do not reflect animosities within the family, and so on. The allegiances of retainers frequently shift.

Despite the importance of family, medieval folk seem to have had fewer exact words than we do for pinpointing relations. "Cousin" covers almost anything outside of father, mother, brother, sister, son, and daughter. "Cousin" sometimes seems interchangeable with "nephew." In Malory VI, 1, for instance, Lionel, Lancelot's cousin, is called his nephew (though this may be the result of a different tradition). When in doubt, "kinsman" or "kinswoman" covers the relationship. For convenience in all of this book, I have tried to use our familiar modern terms where available.

Castles and Cities

When discussing places, I felt it appropriate to try to locate in the real world as many of the places of the days of Arthur as I could. The efforts have been made in good faith; many of the arguments I used have been included as notes in relevant entries. Such efforts are among the most arcane of literary exercises. The reader may or may not find my logic compelling, but he or she should not understand the result to be an archaeological guide to actual Arthurian artifacts and ruins.

The distinction between a castle and a city is slight. Malory tells us that Camelot, Astolat, and Dover had castles, and we can assume that most of the rest of the cities listed likewise had their castles. Conversely, a number of references in Malory make it apparent that almost every castle had a town or village around or near it.

Almost every knight seems to have his castle, or to be capable of acquiring one. The lord of any given castle can change. Therefore I have not always given the names of the castellans.

I have tried to include every castle to which Malory gives a proper name, even in passing. I also included some of the castles to which he gives no names, but which seem interesting. I did not try to include every nameless castle held by a nameless or insignificant knight or lady.

Almost all identifications are tentative, except that sometimes I found a castle clearly stated as being in a particular territory. More often, I made an educated guess as to the approximate area of the country by attempting to trace the knights' adventures. Some castles I could not locate even generally.

Court Cities

Many modern treatments, especially movies, may give the impression that Arthur held his court only at Camelot and stayed there permanently. This is inaccurate. Like English monarchs of historical times, Arthur made his progresses, keeping his court on the move. Far from amassing material possessions promiscuously, these kings and nobles had to keep their property, at least what they meant to take around for daily use, portable and ready to be constantly packed, transported, unpacked, and repacked by the servants. I wonder if all this moving about might have influenced the development of royal generosity and gift-giving, so lauded by Chrétien de Troyes.

By making his progresses, the King was able to hold court and dispense justice all around his kingdom, not simply among those who were able to travel to one particular capital. Also, by moving around, the court would not so totally deplete the food of a given area (although nobles who hosted the courts of such monarchs as Elizabeth I might take years to recover from one courtly visitation).

When Arthur moved his court, did he take along the Round Table? We can assume this table was moved at least twice. Uther Pendragon gave it to King Leodegrance, and Leodegrance gave it back to Uther's son, Arthur, as a wedding present, along with Guenevere. So it was not absolutely immobile. In those days tables were generally boards laid across trestles at meal times, rather than our solid, full-joined pieces of furniture; the Round Table, likewise, may have been a large circular board or several boards which, when laid together across locally available trestles, formed the circle. Thus, there may have been no problem in moving the Round Table from court city to court city.

Arthur, in Malory X, 68, while attending the tournament at Lonazep castle, sends Kay to check which knights of the Round Table are present at the tournament by reading the names on their sieges, or chairs.

(Apparently these names appear only when the knights are near enough to come and take their seats.) By Malory's own identification, Joyous Garde and therefore the neighboring Lonazep are much too far from Camelot for such a quick and comparatively casual errand between the two places. From this it seems that both the Round Table and its chairs must have been moved around from court to court.

The cities designated court cities are those at which Malory definitely tells us Arthur held his court at least once. I suspect that Arthur also held court at almost any good-sized city in his kingdom. For instance, he apparently had some site near Lonazep castle to set up court; it would be surprising if he did not sometimes hold court at Canterbury.

The length of Arthur's courts might perhaps be gauged by a comment (Vulgate V, 335) that an important court at Camelot, on Whitsunday, when Arthur was planning a large-scale war on King Claudas of France, lasted a whole week, after which the barons went home.

Malory records these court cities: Caerlon, Camelot, Cardiff, Carlisle, Kynke Kenadonne, London, York.

Religious Centers

It can be very hard to distinguish a "religious center" from a "magical place" or a "castle."

It is also sometimes hard for me to be sure about whether a given religious center is wholly Christian. I cannot remember finding any Pagan holy places explicitly mentioned by Malory; however, many of the "Christian" or assumedly Christian holy sites were originally Pagan, and it well may be that elements of Paganism were still carrying through in Arthur's time, blending more quietly and peaceably with the Christian than we might have expected.

In a realistic Romano-British setting of the actual fourth or fifth centuries, I doubt cathedrals would be much in evidence. In Malory, however, I feel confident they are available. I cannot recall that Malory ever uses the word "cathedral", but he uses bishops, archbishops, and "great churches." Malory certainly knew St. Paul's cathedral, though he cannily avoids committing himself as to whether or not Arthur knew it [I, 5]. The greatest church of Camelot, St. Stephen's, probably was another cathedral.

Hermits were everywhere. They "held great household, and refreshed people that were in distress" [Malory XVIII, 13]. A favorite form of retirement for a knight appears to have been turning hermit. I suspect that many former knights merely converted their manors into their hermitages. Women, too, became hermits, or "recluses." A lady may have become a recluse even while her husband was still living elsewhere, as wives sometimes entered or were put into convents during the lifetimes of their royal or noble spouses, who were thus enabled to remarry.

Early usage has "convent" meaning a house of either male or female religious. An abbey would be under the rule of an abbot or abbess, a priory under that of a prior or prioress. In an abbey, the abbot or abbess would have a prior or prioress under him or her; therefore, a priory would be a smaller establishment. Sometimes Malory refers to the house of a hermit as a priory, presumably with the hermit as prior or prioress. For ready identification, I would suggest using "monastery" for a convent of men and that good old word "nunnery" for one of women.

An "almery" in Malorian usage is probably either an ambry—a cupboard or storage place in a church or elsewhere—or an almonry—a place where alms were distributed to the poor or where lived the almoner who distributed them for a bishop or prince. (The almoner, I suppose, may not have been a religious official himself, especially if he was a prince's official.)

It seems superfluous to make the next distinction if one knows it already, but many people (including myself in casual speech) use the terms "monk" and "friar" interchangeably. A monk lives in a monastery and stays put; I have even read somewhere that making too many trips abroad can be considered hazardous to his spiritual program. A friar travels around by vocation; itinerant preaching and well-doing is the nature of his calling. Friars were an invention of the later Middle Ages and should not have been around in Arthur's time. I cannot recall that even Malory, who can be quite anachronistic and who lived after the advent of friars, put them into his book anywhere.

Although Vulgate III tells us that regular religious orders were not yet established in Great Britain in Arthur's time, numerous houses would seem to take such names or descriptive phrases as "White Abbey" and "Black Abbey" from the habits of their congregations—habits frequently associated with specific orders. Malory probably did not trouble himself with the question of whether or not regular orders were established in Arthur's day; moreover, all the religious of a house may well have adopted the same color habit, even before such habits became associated with specific, regular orders.

At one time, I would have guessed that the occasional isolated church or chapel Arthurian characters find in the wilderness was largely a literary invention. It seems that I would have been mistaken. In her study *Mary Magdalen: Myth and Metaphor*, Susan Haskins, quoting from a 1906 county history of Norfolk, mentions a thirteenth-century hermit named Joan, one of a number of recluses, who lived in the graveyard of Mary Magdalene of Wiggenhall, a church built in a wilderness far removed on all sides from human habitation. [NY, etc.: Harcourt Brace, ©1993, p. 181]

In this volume I have listed or cross-referenced named institutions;

institutions that are given a fairly definite location, even if that location is no more than proximity to such-and-such a castle; a few institutions that, although unnamed, play a fairly important role in the action; and some of the more prominent cathedral cities. I have not attempted to include all individual hermitages, even where their location is specified; some of these may be filled in by finding the hermits and recluses by name. Nor have I tried to list the many holy wells and ancient arrangements of standing stones to be found about Arthurian country, although I have given a few examples of these.

I have included a few sites more properly historical than directly related to Malorian and Vulgate romance.

Magical Places

I find in Malory no clear cases of transfer into an entire "other world" of faery, such as are encountered, for instance, in old Celtic myth and in such tales as that of True Thomas the Rhymer. The nearest thing to a world of faery in Malory seems to be "The Lake", which is more fully described in the Vulgate, and which seems to be an illusion masking a city in our own plane rather than a portal into another realm. In the Arthurian romances I have perused, there seems to be but one world for mortals to adventure in, and the faeries and necromancers either coexist in the mortal world, or conceivably come into it from time to time through ways not open to mere lay mortals. If there is any "secondary world", it is the religious and mystical plane of the Grail adventures, where nothing seems to happen that does not have an allegorical meaning.

Even an otherwise superficially mundane adventure at an apparently mortal castle can have spiritual and allegorical significance in the Adventures of the Grail. I have included cross-references to castles described in the Grail Quest only if such castles seem to have some magical significance or potential significance independently of their Grail context. For example, I include a reference to the "Castle of the Leprous Lady", but not to the Castle of Maidens.

I have included references to castles definitely mentioned as being the stronghold of some necromancer for some period of time. I have not, however, attempted to reference castles if the only hint of occupation by a magic-worker was a name or unspecific reference. Nor have I listed every site at which something magical or mystical occurred, unless the event seemed bound up with or to alter supernaturally the nation of the place itself.

About the Text

In general, internal references will be of two kinds. If the reference was only to the last preceding sentence, then the citation will be inside the period concluding that sentence. If the reference is to the last two or more sentences, then the citation will be found outside the last pertinent period.

About the Heradlry

Included with the descripions of the most important knights and kings are coats of arms which have been attributed to them by medieval enthusiasts. The majority of these arms are taken from a medieval manuscript compiled toward the end of the 15th century and commonly known as the *D'Armagnac Armoral*, and more formally called *La Forme quon tenoit des torynoys*. This was apparantly compiled as a guide for the pageants called Round Tables, wherein noblemen dressed in Arthurian arms and engaged in tournaments, each roleplaying their favorite knights. The manuscript was well known and copied with little change several times.

Some of the more important personages have been omitted from that old list. The compiler, who was French, either did not know of or chose to ignore many popular British figures. For the sake of visually noting these important figures in the text, Greg Stafford has attributed arms to them for the sake of completeness.

The Arthurian Companion

Chief Incidents in Le Morte D'Arthur

BOOK I.	Birth and crowning of Arthur; rebellion of petty British kings; acquisition of Excalibur; birth of Mordred.
BOOK II.	The book of Balin and Balan.
BOOK III.	Marriage of Arthur and the adventures of Tor, Gawaine, and Pellinore following the marriage feast.
BOOK IV.	Nimue imprisons Merlin; Morgan's attempt to put Accolon on the throne; adventures of Ywaine, Gawaine, and Marhaus following Ywaine's temporary banishment from court.
BOOK V.	Arthur wars with Rome and is crowned Emperor in Rome.
BOOK VI.	Adventures of Lancelot with Morgan, Turquine, Kay, and others.
BOOK VII.	The tale of Gareth Beaumains.
BOOK VIII.	The first book of Tristram of Lyonesse.
BOOK IX.	The tale of La Cote Male Taile. Further adventures of Tristram and others.
BOOK X.	Further adventures of Tristram and Isoud, including not a little about Palomides.
BOOK XI.	Lancelot engenders Galahad on Elaine of Carbonek. Her intriguing later drives him mad. Other knights search for him.
BOOK XII.	Lancelot is found living with Elaine of Carbonek and is persuaded to return to court, bringing his son most of the way with him. Further adventures of Tristram, including the baptism of Palomides.
BOOKS XIII –XVII.	The Adventures of the Holy Grail.
BOOK XVIII.	The incident of the poisoned apples; the Winchester tournament and Lancelot's affair with Elain of Astolat.
BOOK XIX.	Meliagrant's kidnaping of Guenevere; the healing of Sir Urre of Hungary.
BOOK XX.	Lancelot and the Queen surprised together. The split in the Round Table; Gawaine and Arthur war against Lancelot.
BOOK XXI.	Mordred attempts to seize the crown; the last battle; the final days of Lancelot and Guenevere in religious retirement.

ABBLASOURE

All Malory tells us of Abblasoure can be found in XIII, 14:

> And at the last it happened [Galahad] to depart from a place or a castle the which was named Abblasoure; and he had heard no mass, the which he was wont ever to hear or ever he departed out of any castle or place, and kept that for a custom.

Could it be that Galahad heard no mass here because the inhabitants, if any, were Pagan? We are not told Galahad's emotions during his visit. He seems to have gotten along peaceably; this may have been early ecumenism, or he may have found the place deserted, even ruinous.

After leaving Abblasoure, he prayed at a desolate old chapel on a mountain, where a heavenly voice directed him to go to the Castle of Maidens and destroy the wicked customs there.

Rhayader Gwy, in Radnor, Wales, is handy both to mountains and to the Castle of Maidens if Llanidloes is accepted as the latter.

ABERCURNIG†

Glennie states that Abercorn, on the Firth of Forth, "where was anciently a famous monastery", was the Abercurnig of Gildas. By Glennie's map, Abercorn seems about five miles east of Linlithgow on the south bank of the firth.

ACCOLON OF GAUL

A lover of Morgan le Fay's and a knight of Arthur's court, Accolon conspired with Morgan to kill kings Arthur and Uriens and make themselves king and queen of England. When the actual fight came about through Morgan's plots, Accolon did not realize who his opponent was until after Arthur had given him his death wound. Upon recognizing Arthur, the dying Accolon confessed all and begged forgiveness. Arthur forgave him, but sent his dead body to Morgan as "a present." [Malory IV, 6-12]

ACORIONDE OF ATHENS†

One of Alexander's twelve companions, who accompanied him from Greece to Britain, where Arthur knighted them all at the outset of Count Angrs' rebellion. Surviving this rebellion, Acorionde eventually returned with Alexander to Greece; when they landed at Athens, Acorionde was the man who took Alis', crowned emperor by mistake, word that Alexander had arrived ready to fight for his throne. [Chrétien de Troyes, **Cligés**, ll. 102-385; 1093-ca. 2210; 2457-2525]

ADRAGAIN†

A former knight, he became a black friar in Gaul. After kings Ban and Bors were defeated by King Claudas, Adragain visited Britain, where he reproached Arthur for not coming to the aid of Ban and Bors as he had promised earlier, when they had crossed the Channel to help him against the rebel kings. King Uriens honored Adragain for the sake of his brother Mador (de la Porte?). On his way to Britain, Adragain visited Elaine of Benwick and Evaine in the Royal Minster, telling Elaine that her son Lancelot was safe, happy among friends. Adragain was in a position to know, being an uncle of Seraide, a damsel of the French Lady of the Lake. [Vulgate III]

Adventurous, Castle—see **CARBONEK**

ADVENTUROUS SHIELD

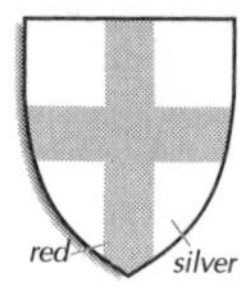

Josephe, son of Joseph of Arimathea, converted King Evelake, giving him the baptismal name Mordrains, and helped him win a war against King Tolleme. The war was won partly with the help of this shield, which had a sweet aroma and of which it was said that it would render its bearer victorious and be the cause of many miracles. At the time of Mordrains' war against Tolleme, the shield bore the figure of Christ on the Cross, and touching this image healed at least one man's battle wound. Thereafter the image disappeared, leaving the shield white as snow. When Josephe lay on his death bed, he marked the shield anew with a cross drawn with the crimson of his nosebleed. He left the shield, so marked, as a token for Mordrains, who was to leave it in his turn in the same abbey where lay Nascien the Hermit, there to await Galahad. [Vulgate I and VI]

Only Galahad could take the Adventurous Shield. Anyone else who tried to bear it away would be killed or maimed within three days. A White Knight, apparently an angel waiting to avenge the shield, struck down and wounded King Bagdemagus two miles from the hermitage when he tried taking it. [Malory XIII, 9-11]

ADVENTUROUS SHIELD, ABBEY OF THE (White Abbey)

Sommer seems to call this simply White Abbey, apparently as its proper name, one confusingly generic [Vulgate III, 21].

At this abbey Galahad found his Adventurous Shield. Here the holy Nasciens was either buried or to be buried. This is also, seemingly, the same abbey where there was a tomb from which issued such a noise that those who heard it either almost lost their wits or did lose their strength. The monks thought it was a fiend. Galahad, exorcising it, found on opening the tomb that the body was "a false Christian man." The soul returned, protesting, apparently to Hell, leaving a foul stink, and the monks reburied the body to get it out of the hallowed churchyard. This incident resembles that at the "Abbey of the Burning Tomb", and it is not unlikely that both tales sprang from the same original story, but in the state of the legends today, I would hesitate to recombine them.

The only clue I could find in Malory as to this abbey's whereabouts is that it was about four days from Vagon. That covers quite a territory. Putting Vagon at or near Basingstoke and going strictly by the "minster" or "church" in the name yields possible locations at Kidderminster in Worcestershire, Leominster in Herefordshire, or Church Stratton in Shropshire.

AGLOVALE

King Pellinore's "first son begotten in wedlock" [Malory X, 23]. Malory mentions him only about half a dozen times, once as one of the knights killed by Lancelot and his men during the rescue of Guenevere from the stake. One could have expected Aglovale to be a more important figure than this indicates. He was, of course, a member of the Round Table, and is named in Malory XIX,11.

AGRAVADAIN DES VAUS DES GALOIRE† ([A]Gravadain du Chastel Fort?)

Castellan of the castle Des Mares. Merlin caused King Ban to sleep with Agravadain's daughter, the Damsel des Mares, while on a visit. This coupling resulted in Sir Ector de Maris. After Agravadain's death, his son became castellan of Des Mares.

Agravain, Tertre†—see DRUAS' HILL

AGRAVAINE (Agravain the Arrogant; Agravain the Proud)

The second and probably the most unpleasant son of King Lot and Queen Margawse of Orkney. The romances seem agreed that, although a good knight of arms, he was not a likable character. Vulgate IV characterizes him as envious and evil-disposed, without love or pity; he was very handsome, but his beauty was the best part of him. (Sounds to me as if he may have been spoiled in childhood, perhaps because of his beauty.) At the same time, he was a member of the Round Table, and got around quite a bit on adventures.

There seems some dispute as to whether Agravaine or Mordred was the more culpable in the conspiracy against Lancelot and Guenevere. In Malory, Mordred seems to emerge as the chief force, especially since—in Malory—Agravaine is killed during Lancelot's escape from the Queen's chamber. In the Vulgate, where Lancelot's escape is not so bloody, Agravaine, not Mordred, seems the chief villain until he is killed when Lancelot rescues the Queen from the stake. Agravaine is motivated chiefly, however, by a desire to hurt Lancelot, while Mordred is motivated by a desire for the throne.

Chrétien shows Agravain the Arrogant holding his brother Gawaine back from responding too hastily to Guigambresil's accusation of treachery. Here, despite his soubriquet, Agravain seems to appear to rather good advantage, even offering to fight on his brother's behalf. Later in the same romance, Gawaine lists Agravain as the second oldest son of King Lot and his lawful wife. [**Perceval**, ll. 4766-4796; ca. 8138] The contrast between Agravain's surname of "Arrogant" or "Proud" and the seemingly sympathetic nature of his cameo appearance in this romance suggest to me that Chrétien had found his usual characterization already established in Arthurian lore. Perhaps, also, he would have come back into the action had Chrétien finished the story.

"AGRAVAINE'S HOUSE"†

The Duke of Cambeninc conquered this manor, which was in Bresquehan Forest, and gave it to Sir Agravaine. Later, a damsel carrying a sword led Gawaine to the house. Here numerous knights fought him. They demanded a helmet of his blood for a ransom. Refusing to give it under constraint, Gawaine gave it gladly on learning it was needed to heal a wounded Knight. The wounded knight turned out to be his brother Agravaine, although so thin and pale that Gawaine did not recognize him at first.

Some time previously, two damsels had come when Agravaine was asleep, anointed his right leg and left arm with a strange ointment, and then ridden off well pleased with their revenge. Agravaine's squire had witnessed this, and Agravaine suspected the damsels were sweethearts of knights he had wounded. He could not be healed except by the blood of the two best knights in the world. Gawaine's blood, when rubbed on the wounded leg, healed it. Gawaine later found Lancelot at Duke Galeholt's Isle Perdue and sent back a helmet of Lancelot's blood, which healed Agravaine's arm.

One time Gawaine met the daughter of the man from whom the Duke of Cambeninc had conquered this house. She and another damsel were in the company of Agravaine and Mordred. One of the damsels was apparently Agravaine's sweetheart; the other had a younger sister enamored of Gawaine. [Vulgate III]

Agrestizia—see under AMIDE

AGRIPPE, KING†

A minor monarch of—my guess—somewhere in Wales. [Vulgate IV]

AGRIPPE'S DAUGHTER

King Vadalon was besieging King Agrippe. (If my personal translation is correct, Vadalon claimed Agrippe had killed Vadalon's brother, the King of Norgales.) Food ran short and all the wells except one supplying the besiegers were dried up. King Agrippe's daughter poured strong poison into this last well, killing 5000 besiegers and forcing the others to return to their own country. Vadalon had the princess tracked and seized. Thinking death too lenient, he had two iron bands fixed so tightly round her body that they cut skin in several places. She defied Vadalon, telling him she would find a deliverer, but would let no one remove the bands unless he also swore to avenge her. Vadalon, she said, would recognize her avenger because he would carry the shield of Vadalon's brother, whom Agrippe was said to have killed. The princess, who could travel only in easy stages, was on her way with a few companions to Arthur's court to find a champion when Sir Bors found her resting in her pavilion. Swearing to bear the shield in question for a year and a day and to punish Vadalon, Bors gently broke her bands with his bare hands. [Vulgate IV]

AGUISEL, KING OF SCOTLAND†

Chrétien lists him among Arthur's vassal kings, summoned to court for Erec's Pentecost wedding. Aguisel came riding a Cappadocian horse and bringing his two sons, Cadret and Coi. [**Erec & Enide**, ll. 1963-2024]

AGWISANCE (Anguish), KING OF IRELAND

Agwisance was one of the rebel kings at the beginning of Arthur's reign, but later apparently became a companion of the Round Table, being listed in Malory XIX, 11. I believe Agwisance to be identical with King Anguish of Ireland, the father of La Beale Isoud. Anguish used to exact

tribute from King Mark. When Mark finally refused tribute, Anguish chose his wife's brother, Sir Marhaus, as champion. Mark's champion was Tristram, who killed Marhaus and freed Cornwall from Anguish's truage, but got a poisoned wound from Marhaus' sword and finally had to come to Anguish's court in disguise to be healed. Anguish became Tristram's friend, and, when Tristram's disguise was uncovered and the Irish queen tried to kill him, Anguish himself excused his brother-in-law's death and sent Tristram away with kind words. Later, when Bleoberis and Blamore de Ganis summoned Anguish to Arthur's court on a charge of treacherously murdering their cousin, Tristram came along by chance in time to fight as Anguish's champion and win his acquittal. This expedited Tristram's errand of seeking La Beale Isoud to be Mark's bride; Anguish only regretted that Tristram did not ask her for himself instead. [Malory VIII]

I also much suspect that King Anguish of Ireland is to be identified with King Anguish of Scotland.

KING AGWISANCE'S FAMILY
Daughter: La Beale Isoud
Son? Nephew?: Lanceor
Father-in-law: King Marhalt
Brother-in-law: Marhaus
Cousin: Lady of the Launds

ALAIN, KING OF ESCAVALON†

The father of Floree, Gawaine's love, and possibly the father also of Sir Galeshin. In addition, we know the name of one of Alain's nephews, Arguais. [Vulgate IV]

ALENTIVE†

A town apparently in or near Surluse [Vulgate IV].

ALEXANDER†

Father of Cligés and actual hero of the first third of the romance bearing his son's name, Sir Alexander seems to have spent much more time than Cligés did as one of Arthur's knights.

The older son of the emperor of Greece and Constantinople (who was also named Alexander) and his empress, Tantalis, Alexander was already grown by the time his brother Alis was born. Young Alexander might have ruled Greece, but he insisted on receiving his knighthood from the great King Arthur and no one else. For this reason he journeyed to Britain with a dozen companions: Cornix, Licorides, Nabunal of Mycene, Acorionde of Athens, Ferolin of Salonica, Calcedor from Africa, Parmenides, Francagel, Torin, Pinabel, Nerius, and Neriolis. Arthur welcomed them into his court at once. Alexander became Gawaine's close friend and coincidentally fell in love with Gawaine's sister Soredamors. When Count Angrs of Windsor rebelled against Arthur, who was summering in Brittany that year, Alexander and his companions chose the moment to request knighthood, which Arthur granted them; they used the water of the English Channel for their ritual bath. Alexander proceeded to put down the rebellion and capture Angrs, for which Arthur rewarded him with the kingdom of Wales to hold until he should inherit Greece, while Guenevere wisely sped his hesitant courtship so that he and Soredamors could wed without further delay. Cligés was born about fourteen months later. Meanwhile, the old emperor of Greece died commanding a search for his firstborn son; the ship sank on its way to Britain, and the single survivor, favoring Alis, made his way home with the mendacious report that it had sunk on its way back, drowning Alexander with everyone else. Alis was crowned emperor. Learning this, Alexander returned to Greece with his wife and young son, prepared to go to war for his rights. A compromise was effected whereby Alis kept the title, on condition of never marrying, while Alexander did the actual ruling. Perhaps in the tradition that was later to include Tirant lo Blanc and Don Quixote himself, Alexander died of sickness. Cligés was just about old enough to attend his father's sickbed and receive the parental charge to prove his prowess in Britain. Soredamors soon followed her husband. [Chrétien de Troyes, **Cligés**, ll. 45-2639]

I suppose it possible that Chrétien's knight transmogrified over the centuries into Malory's Alisander le Orphelin, though their life histories keep them separate characters.

ALEXANDER'S SHIRT†

Guenevere gave this garment to Alexander when her husband dubbed him knight. It was of white silk, sewn entirely with gold or silver thread, except that Soredamors, who helped sew it, had worked some golden hairs from her own head in beside the metallic threads to see if she could ever find a man able to tell the difference. The metallic gold threads eventually tarnished as Sir Alexander wore the shirt, while the hair became lovelier. At length Guenevere, making a conversation piece of the shirt while Alexander was wearing it one evening in company with her, Soredamors, and his own companions, divined the love between him and her handmaiden, whom she prodded to reveal her part in making the shirt. When Alexander learned this, the garment became infinitely more valuable to him than before, and he treated it as a wonderful relic. While having no other special properties, it helped lead to the lovers' brief but happy marriage. [Chrétien de Troyes, **Cligés**, ll. 1147-1196, 1380-1418, 1553-1647]

ALICE LA BEALE PILGRIM

Alice was called "La Beale Pilgrim" after her father, Duke Ansirus the Pilgrim, "of the kin of Sir Lancelot." When Alice heard of the way in which Sir Alisander le Orphelin was defending the remains of the castle La Beale Regard against all comers, she went to Arthur's court and announced that whatever knight could defeat Alisander would gain her hand and land. She then set up her pavilion beside the ruins of La Beale Regard. Seeing Alisander defeat Sagramore le Desirous, Alice

> leapt out of her pavilion, and took Sir Alisander by the bridle, and ... said: Fair knight, I require thee of thy knighthood show me thy visage.

He did, and she immediately fell in love with him. At his request, she unwimpled and showed him her face, which had a similar effect on him. They wed, and when his year of defending the ruins was up, they "went into their country of Benoye, and lived there in great joy" until King Mark contrived to murder Alisander [Malory X, 38-39]. Presumably

Alice charged their son, Sir Bellengerus le Beuse, to avenge his father's death, as Alisander's mother had charged Alisander to avenge the murder of his father, Prince Boudwin.

ALIER, COUNT†

He was warring against the lady of Noroison when the latter and two of her damsels found Ywaine, who defeated their enemy for them. Little is said of the whys of this war: Alier would appear to have been the aggressor, and he managed to burn some of the lady's buildings before Ywaine conquered him; but he was allowed to surrender and swear to repay and rebuild her losses as far as possible. [Chrétien de Troyes, **Yvain**, ll. ca. 2940; 3131-3340]

ALIPHANSIN†

A leader of the Sesnes. He was involved in the attack on Vandaliors, the castle of the rebel kings. [Vulgate II]

ALIS†

Younger brother of Arthur's Greek knight Alexander, Alis was crowned emperor of Greece and Constantinople when their father died and the ship sent to Britain sank on the way, leaving a single survivor who, preferring the younger brother, brought back a false account of the elder's death. At first reluctant to believe Alexander was still alive when Acorionde came from their ship to tell him so, Alis decided on the advice of his counselors to avoid another Polyneices and Eteocles situation (see Greek legend—e.g., Edith Hamilton's **Mythology**) by cobbling up a compromise which gave the true power to Alexander while Alis retained the name of emperor in return for a promise never to marry and thus ensure the eventual passage of the crown to Alexander's son Cligés. This promise Alis, who seems never to have shown much strength of personality, finally broke after Alexander's death, when his nobles pestered him to marry. They had already picked out the emperor of Germany's daughter Fenice for his bride. Cligés helped his uncle keep Fenice from her former fiancé the Duke of Saxony, but the princess, having fallen in love with Cligés, enlisted her nurse Thessala to cheat Alis by means of a potion that made him dream about having relations with her and mistake his dreams for fact, while the marriage remained unconsummated. When Cligés returned to Constantinople after spending about a year in Britain, Alis made over to him everything except the crown and the empress. Cligés reciprocated by helping himself to the only-too-eager empress, stealing her away (the scheme being her own) to live secretly with her in a marvelous tower built to order by Cligés' serf John, while Alis and the rest of the empire supposed her dead of disease. Discovered by one Bertrand, Cligés and Fenice escaped to Britain, where he enlisted his great-uncle Arthur to war against his other uncle Alis; but before it could happen Alis died of grief-induced madness. [Chrétien de Troyes, **Cligés**, ll. 45-80, ca. 2390 ff.]

While functioning more or less as antagonist, Alis seems more weak and misled than malicious, and at least as much sinned against as sinning. But **Cligés** is a romance that drips with moral amibguities, and I for one much suspect that they were as apparent to the late twelfth-century mind as to the late twentieth.

ALISANDER LE ORPHELIN

After King Mark murdered his brother Prince Boudwin, Boudwin's wife Anglides escaped from Cornwall with her infant son Alisander. She reached Magouns Castle, where she raised Alisander. On the day he was made knight, she gave him his father's bloody doublet and shirt, charging him to avenge Boudwin's death. Sir Alisander bore his father's shirt "with him always till his death day, in tokening to think of his father's death." (Unlike La Cote Male Taile, however, Alisander seems not to have actually worn it.) Riding to London by Tristram's advice, to seek Lancelot, Alisander took a wrong turn and ended up at a tournament of King Carados', where he did so well that Morgan heard of him and determined to meet him. After the tournament, Alisander fought and killed Sir Malgrin for the sake of a damsel whom Malgrin was persecuting. Morgan arrived in time to watch at least part of this battle and then spirited Alisander, who "had sixteen great wounds, and in especial one of them was like to be his death", away in a horse litter. She searched his wounds, first aggravating them further and then healing them, apparently to increase his gratitude. Next, putting him to sleep for three days, she took him to the castle La Beale Regard, where she tried to make him her lover. He maintained, "I had liefer cut away my hangers than I would do her such pleasure."

The damsel who was rightful owner of La Beale Regard helped Alisander by summoning her uncle to burn down the castle, thus driving Morgan away. Having escaped before the holocaust by a privy postern, Alisander and the Damsel of La Beale Regard returned to the site. Alisander had promised Morgan not to leave the castle for a year and a day, so he now announced he would defend what once had been his chamber against all comers for that period of time. Alice La Beale Pilgrim heard of this, came, and fell in love with him, marrying him and giving him a son, Sir Bellengerus le Beuse. After his year at the ruins, Alisander returned with her to Benoye. He never managed to avenge his father, being murdered in his turn by Mark first. Nor did Alisander ever reach Arthur's court:

> And it happed so that Alisander had never grace nor fortune to come to King Arthur's court. For an he had come to Sir Lancelot, all knights said that they knew him, he was one of the strongest knights that was in Arthur's days, and great dole was made for him. [Malory X, 32-40]

While I think it most likely that Malory's Alisander and Chrétien's Greek knight Alexander both coincidentally derive their names from the quasilegendary historical figure of Alexander the Great, Alisander might conceivably derive from the father of Cligés, the state of orphanhood having gotten transferred in the intervening centuries. Of course, Alisander and Alexander's biographies are so different as to keep them entirely separate characters.

ALMESBURY

After Arthur's death, Guenevere retired to the nunnery at Almesbury, where she became a "nun in white clothes and black", and, as befitted her former rank in the world, Abbess [Malory XXI, 7]. Almesbury is "little more than thirty mile" from Glastonbury [Malory XXI, 11]. It surely must be Amesbury, Wiltshire.

ALPHIN†

This castle is thirty English miles from Camelot [Vulgate VI].

"ALTERIA", HER HUSBAND, and CHILDREN†

Having happened upon Lunete imprisoned in the chapel at the spring of Broceliande Forest, and promised to defend her next day in trial by combat, Ywaine journeyed on in search of shelter for the night and found a strong new fortress with the land laid bare outside its walls. The people of this castle did their best to honor their noble guest, but kept breaking into tears until he insisted they tell him their trouble. His host turned out to be Gawaine's brother-in-law, having married the great knight's full sister. They were being persecuted by a giant named Harpin of the Mountain, who had captured their six sons, killed two, and was threatening to murder the other four the very next day, unless the parents turned over their daughter for him to give to his vilest servants as a sex toy. Gawaine would surely have come to his relatives' aid, but was absent in Gore and knew nothing of their situation. Ywaine promised to fight Harpin if he came to be finished off in time for the knight to get on to his previous pressing appointment. Fortunately, Harpin arrived with the captive sons just as Ywaine was distressfully feeling he could wait no longer. (All in all, it was a very busy day for Ywaine and his lion.) On leaving the rescued family safe, he requested Gawaine's niece and surviving nephews to take the dead Harpin's dwarf to Arthur's court and greet their uncle in the name of the "Knight with the Lion." This they did, arriving two days after Guenevere's return from Gore. [**Yvain**, ll. 3770-4312; 4737-4758]

Counting Soredamors and Clarissant, this gives Gawaine at least three sisters in Chrétien's work. Being unable to find any name for the one in **Yvain**, and a little unwilling to list her simply as "Gawaine's Other Sister", I coined the name "Alteria" from the Latin for "other."

AMABLE†

Malory seems to know nothing of her, unless she can be identified with a nameless damsel who meets Lancelot on the road and guides him to both Sir Turquine and Sir Peris de Forest Savage to stop their evil practices by exterminating them. Before parting with him, this damsel remarks it is a shame he has no lady but Guenevere, whereon he gives her an exposition on the joys and virtues of celibate bachelorhood [Malory VI, 7-10]. It is also possible she appears elsewhere in Malory, but anonymously.

Indeed, she apparently has a name in only one of the manuscripts that Sommer collated. Even nameless, however, she plays a major role throughout the Vulgate **Lancelot**. One day, when he had just met Amable and her brother beside a fountain, Lancelot drank from the fountain and fell deathly sick—the water had been poisoned by venomous serpents in it. Amable used a combination of medicines and sweating therapy to cure him. In the process, she fell sick herself for love of him. On his recovery, he explained to her that he could not return her love because he already had a highborn lady. Amable found a way out, a way which modern society might find risible, but which accorded very well with the traditions of chivalric romance. "All I ask is that you always and everwhere stand my friend", she told Lancelot. "As for myself, I will vow never to love any other man and always to remain a virgin. Thus you may love your other lady as a woman and me as a maiden, without wronging either of us." Lancelot agreed, and Amable thus became the lady he loved best after Guenevere. Even the Queen, learning the situation, accepted Amable without the jealousy she displayed toward the Elaines.

No stay-at-home, Amable frequently appears throughout the rest of the Vulgate **Lancelot**, enjoying various rescues at the hands of Lancelot and others, entertaining her rescuers at her castle, and so on. Amable may have been a friend or cousin of King Brandegoris' daughter, for Lancelot once found Amable in a pavilion, and they were visited there by Brandegoris' daughter, with her son by Bors. [Vulgate V]

AMANS (Aniause), KING

Amans seems to have been a contender for the kingship of Carmelide (Cameliard), which he fought to reconquer while Arthur, King Ryons, and Sesnes were busy with each other. King Bors killed Amans in battle. [Vulgate II]

AMANS' (Aniause's) DAUGHTERS

Vulgate VI makes them the king's daughters, and Amans in the Vulgate is probably Aniause in Malory, but Malory makes the relationship less clear [Malory XVI, 7-9,13]. I recap the Vulgate version, which is more coherent.

Amans entrusted all his land and men to the elder of his daughters, but she proved a bad ruler. So Amans expelled her and put the younger daughter in charge. As soon as Amans died, the elder daughter went to war against the younger and succeeded in gaining most of the property. When Sir Bors, on the Grail Quest, came to the younger sister's last remaining castle, he found the lady, although young and beautiful, poorly dressed. She prepared an elaborate meal for him; he ate only bread and water. She gave him the best chamber and a fine bed; he slept on the floor, but rumpled the bed to appear as if he had slept in it, out of regard for her feelings. In her castle, he had symbolic dreams which indicated the choices he should make the following day in Grail tests. He listened to the debate of the two sisters, declared that the younger seemed to be in the right, championed her cause against the older sister's champion, Priadan (Pridam) le Noir, and won.

In the context of the spiritual allegory of the Grail Quest, King Amans symbolized Christ, the elder sister the Old Covenant, and the younger sister Holy Church, dressed in mourning for the sins of evil-doers. Amans and his daughters seem also to have had their own flesh-and-blood existence, independently of the allegory.

AMANS' LAND

Amans, who appears in the Vulgate and is probably to be identified with Malory's King Aniause, took advantage of the war between Arthur, Ryons, and the Sesnes to attack Carmelide (Cameliard). Thus, Amans' land would most likely have bordered Cameliard. Sir Bors later helped Amans' daughter hold her land. Since the area south of Cameliard is Bertilak de Hautdesert's territory, and Bertilak seems to be more or less allied with the powerful Morgan le Fay, I would put King Amans' land north of Cameliard, between about the Mersey River in the south to about the mouth of the Ribble River (at Preston) in the north. Knowing no other name for this territory, I can only call it by that of its king.

AMANT

A knight of King Mark's. Mark killed Bersules, another of his knights, in a rage for praising Tristram. Amant, witnessing this, threatened to appeach Mark of treason before Arthur. Since Mark could not just then defeat Amant and the two squires (Amant and Bersules'), Mark said, "An thou appeach me of treason I shall thereof defend me afore King Arthur; but I require thee that thou tell not my name." Sir Amant agreed and allowed Mark to depart for the nonce, while he and the squires buried Bersules. When the trial by combat came, "by misadventure Mark smote Amant through the body. And yet was Amant in the righteous quarrel." Mark got away from there in a hurry.

> Then were there maidens that La Beale Isoud had sent to Sir Tristram, that knew Sir Amant well. Then by the license of King Arthur they went to him and spake with him; for while the truncheon of the spear stuck in his body he spake: Ah, fair damosels, said Amant, recommend me unto La Beale Isoud, and tell her that I am slain for the love of her and of Sir Tristram ... and all was because Sir Bersules and I would not consent by treason to slay the noble knight, Sir Tristram .... [And] when Sir Tristram knew all the matter he made great dole and sorrow out of measure, and wept for sorrow for the loss of the noble knights, Sir Bersules and Sir Amant. [Malory X, 7,14-15]

AMAUGUIN†

In lines 311-341 of **Erec & Enide**, Chrétien de Troyes names King Amauguin among Arthur's allies and advisors. Almost certainly, he is identical with the Amauguin found among Arthur's knights in the list beginning in line 1691 of the same work.

AMIDE (Agrestizia, Dindrane)

She was Sir Percivale's sister and Sir Galahad's lady, the latter relationship being platonic. I found the name Amide in one place only, a footnote of Sommer's in Vulgate IV, p. 343. Another reference suggests that she was yet one more Elaine. Both Wolfram von Eschenbach (fl. 1200) in his German **Parsifal** and the thirteenth-century French romance **Perlesvaus** gave the name Dindrane or Dindraine to Percivale's sister, while the fourteenth-century Italian romance **Tavola Ritonda** called her Agrestizia, all of which I learned from Ronan Coghlan's **Encyclopaedia of Arthurian Legends** (1991). The same source reveals that at some point French romance assigned the name Amite (with a "t") to Galahad's mother. Usually, Percivale's sister seems to be left nameless, as in Malory; but if any nameless damsel needs a name, it is she, as the above-mentioned romancers presumably noticed. Sources we regard as more authoritative clearly make Galahad's mother Elaine of Carbonek, but French romance apparently insisted on linking a lady with the name Amite, which is almost identical to Amide, to a Grail knight in some way; and I prefer "Amide" to "Dindraine" for its softer sound and suggestion of the Latin word for "love."

Amide came and found Sir Galahad at the hermitage of Sir Ulfin:

> Galahad, said she, I will that ye arm you, and mount upon your horse and follow me, for I shall show you within these three days the highest adventure that ever any knight saw.

After stopping for a short rest at a castle near Collibe, she led him on to the seaside, where they found a ship with Sirs Bors and Percivale waiting. All being aboard, "the wind arose, and drove them through the sea in a marvellous pace." Eventually their ship encountered King Solomon's Ship (q.v.). Amide was able to tell the knights part, if not all, of the history of King David's Sword and to assure Galahad, who was somewhat reluctant to attempt drawing the sword, that he was the one knight to whom the warnings did not apply. When Galahad needed a new belt to gird on the sword, Amide produced one:

> Lo, Lords, said she, here is a girdle that ought to be set about the sword. And wit ye well the greatest part of this girdle was made of my hair, which I loved well while that I was a woman of the world. But as soon as I wist that this adventure was ordained me I clipped off my hair, and made this girdle in the name of God. Ye be well found, said Sir Bors, for certes ye have put us out of great pain, wherein we should have entered ne had your tidings been.

Girding Galahad with the sword, she exclaimed,

> Now reck I not though I die, for now I hold me one of the blessed maidens of the world, which hath made the worthiest knight of the world. Damosel, said Galahad, ye have done so much that I shall be your knight all the days of my life.

Amide and the knights returned to land. She was with them when they destroyed the evil brothers of Carteloise Castle and when they saw the white hart with four lions and the marvels of the chapel in the forest. At the castle of the Leprous Lady, though her companions could have defended her, Amide willingly submitted to the custom and gave her blood to heal the Leprous Lady.

> So one came forth and let her blood, and she bled so much that the dish was full. Then she lift up her hand and blessed her; and then she said to the lady: Madam, I am come to the death for to make you whole, for God's love pray for me.

Before dying, she directed her knights to put her body into a boat and promised they would find her again at Sarras, where they must bury her. Ironically, the night after Amide's blood healed the Leprous Lady, the castle was destroyed by tempest and lightning, and all within killed, in Heaven's vengeance for the death of Amide and the maidens who had died giving their blood before her.

Lancelot found and boarded the ship bearing Amide.

> And as soon as he was within the ship there [Lancelot} felt the most sweetness that ever he felt, and he was fulfilled with all thing that he thought on or desired. Then he said: Fair sweet Father, Jesu Christ, I wot not in what joy I am, for this joy passeth all earthly joys that ever I was in. ... So with this gentlewoman Sir Launcelot was a month and more. If ye would ask how he lived, He that fed the people of Israel with manna in the desert, so was he fed.

Next Galahad found the ship and joined his father. They spent half a year together in the ship, sometimes landing for awhile to find "many strange adventures and perilous." After Galahad left the ship, it brought Lancelot to Carbonek, where he half-achieved the Grail. True to Amide's prediction, when Galahad and his companions Bors and Percivale arrived at Sarras, they found the ship with her body already there, and had time to bury her richly before King Estorause clapped them into prison. [Malory XVII, 1-14, 21]

The warning connected with the girdle of King David's Sword was that if ever the maid who replaced the original hempen girdle should break her virginity she would "die the most villainous death that ever died any woman." It is possible that Amide's death at the castle of the Leprous Lady hints at some irregularity in her life; but the facts that the castle was destroyed by the wrath of God, and that Amide's body, saint-like, apparently stayed fresh and sweet, and even seems to have filled the ship with an atmosphere of spiritual joy, belies the idea. Besides, Amide's death seems preferable to that of other ladies in the tales.

AMITE†

Apparently, French romance gave this name to Galahad's mother. See under Amide.

AMUSTANS†

Once Arthur's chaplain and later a hermit, Amustans knew Guenevere in her childhood and was instrumental, by scolding Arthur and helping get deathbed confessions from Genievre and Bertholai, in reconciling Arthur with Guenevere after Genievre's last attempt to supplant her half-sister. [Vulgate IV]

AMYR (Anir)†

In his introduction to Chrétien's **Yvain**, Julian Harris recaps old, pre-Chrétien rumors of Arthur's son Amyr, or Anir, and his marvelous tomb. Amyr is apparently unknown to later romancers, at least under that name; one of the old legends Harris mentions has it that he was killed by Arthur himself, reminding us of the Vulgate's Lohot. See Borre, Loholt.

ANDRED

Sir Tristram's cousin and nemesis, Andred seems to have filled more or less the role at Mark's court that Mordred filled at Arthur's as a general rotter, spying on and ambushing Tristram [Malory VIII, 32-34] and spreading, through his paramour, false news of Tristram's death in order to get the land of Tristram [Malory IX, 20]. In Book XIX, 11, Malory mentions that "all that were with King Mark that were consenting to the death of Sir Tristram were slain, as Sir Andred and many other" (apparently by Sir Bellangere le Beuse). Edward Arlington Robinson, in his generally excellent **Tristram**, makes Andred a half-wit and transfers Tristram's murder from Mark to Andred. Malory's Andred, however, must have had some competence as a fighter, for, when the Saxons attacked under Elias, Andred led one of Mark's three divisions in the battles of defense [Malory X, 28].

ANEURIN†

Glennie lists Aneurin, along with Merlin, Llywarch Hen, and Taliessin, as one of the four great bards of the Arthurian age.

ANGIS†

When Lancelot left court because of Guenevere's anger over the Elaine of Astolat incident, Angis was his squire and only companion [Vulgate VI]. Malory does not mention Lancelot's return to court between the tournament of Winchester and his last interview with Elaine [Malory XVIII]. The Vulgate says it was a very brief return; its very brevity convinced Arthur that Morgan's accusation of Lancelot and Guenevere's guilt was false.

ANGLIDES

When King Mark killed her husband, Prince Boudwin, Anglides escaped to Magouns Castle in Sussex with her young son, Alisander le Orphelin. The Constable of Magouns, Sir Bellangere, who was married to Anglides' cousin, told Anglides that the castle was hers by inheritance. Anglides raised Alisander there. When he was knighted, she gave him his father's bloody doublet and shirt, told him how Mark had stabbed Boudwin before her eyes, and charged her son to avenge the deed. [Malory X, 32-34]

ANGRS, COUNT OF WINDSOR†

On the unanimous advice of all his lords in council, Arthur chose Angrs of Windsor, as the most trustworthy man in Britain, to serve as his regent while he paid Brittany a royal visit. Angrs was a brave, excellent knight and would have been a fine choice, had he not also been a criminal traitor. In October, messengers from London and Canterbury crossed the Channel to bring Arthur word that Angrs was planning rebellion. Comparing the Count of Windsor to Charlemagne's Ganelon—whom medieval Europe considered history's worst traitor after Judas Iscariot—Arthur hastened back to Britain, his army swelled with Bretons. Angrs, meanwhile, despoiled London to win over and enrich men of his own, then fled back to Windsor, which he had spent the summer fortifying. At first the defenders, feeling secure, came out without their armor to sport and exercise on their own side of the Thames, in full view of Arthur's camp. This stirred up Sir Alexander and his Greek companions to make a sally across the ford, capturing four rebels, whom he gave to Guenevere. She would have followed the code of chivalry, which forbade slaying a defeated opponent who surrendered; but Arthur, following the code of feudal justice which required death to traitors, demanded them from her and had them drawn by four horses around Windsor. Enraged at seeing men he had loved put to such a death, Angrs and his people planned a night attack of their own. The moonlight betrayed them, so the slaughter was great on both sides. Finally Angrs with seven surviving companions retreated to their stronghold. Alexander, following, marshalled thirty knights (six of them Greeks) and came up with the ruse of trading their armor and shields with those of fallen rebels. Thus disguised, they easily gained admission to the castle, where the only men wearing armor were those just returned from the battlefield, who were already disarming. Though surprised and outnumbered as to armed warriors, the rebels still killed half of Alexander's men while losing only three of their own. Angrs himself slew Alexander's comrade Calcedor and might have proved Alexander's own match, had not being in the wrong worked to the count's disadvantage. With his last four armed men, Angrs made it into the keep and expected help from the townspeople; but another of Alexander's companions, Nabunal, advised the infiltrators to bar the outer gates in time to keep the Windsor people out, and Alexander stunned Angrs into defeat with one great blow from a heavy pole that he found ready to hand, thus ending the rebellion. Exhibiting Angrs to his subjects of Windsor, Alexander promised them mercy if they would surrender to the king, which they did. Angrs and his few surviving battle companions begged their captors to behead them at once, but this mercy would apparently have violated Alexander's knightly honor. Chrétien tells us only that Arthur wasted not a moment in bringing Angrs to justice, presumably drawing him with four horses. I must further assume that this sentence extended to the armed men captured with him. Since no mass slaughter is mentioned, this time Arthur apparently acted according to Alexander's hopes and treated Angrs' other people with mercy. [Chrétien de Troyes, **Cligés**, ll. 422-440, 1047-ca. 2205, & Owen's notes]

It has been suggested that Chrétien patterned Count Angrs' rebellion on that of Mordred as described by Wace. If we do not dismiss Chrétien's account as an apocryphal reworking of the Mordred story, Angrs must have committed his villainy fairly early in Arthur's reign, for Alexander's son Cligés, not yet conceived at the time of Angrs' death, was later to make his own knightly mark at Arthur's court. I have recapped this episode, which seems noticeably more serious in nature than much of Chrétien's writing, at some length in part because it seems to me to underscore how very far removed Chrétien's seminal treatments of the Matter of Britain seem from our modern vision of Good versus Evil in virtually pure, if not cosmic, forms. While Arthur is clearly in the right, his savagery in demanding strict "justice" contrasts tellingly with the mercy that Guenevere and Alexander would have preferred; in having his first rebel captives dragged to death in full sight of their comrades, moreover, Arthur shows questionable strategy, since the spectacle infuriates Angrs while graphically demonstrating to the rest of his men what they can expect should they surrender, thus ensuring that they will fight to the bitterest end. Many of Angrs' knights, moreover, must have erred rather in adhering to their immediate loyalty than in breaking a more removed allegiance—a tangle of conflicting loyalties that could hardly have been lost on a medieval reader!—and for this some of them are shamefully tortured to death. Angrs himself is shown not as a monster of evil, but as a brave knight retaining some admirable qualities even in the midst of his villainy. Alexander succeeds in defeating him by means of a ruse that could strike an impartial judge as sneaky, underhanded, not playing fair, and hardly worthy of "the good guys"—yet for all his youth, idealism, mercy, and virtue, the heroic Alexander apparently sees nothing in the trick that might sit uncomfortably with his knightly honor. **Cligés** may have been largely ignored by later Arthurian writers because so much of it is only periphally an Arthurian romance. This seems unfortunate. Where is the novelist to explore the story of Angrs and his ill-fated rebellion for our own age?

Anguingueron—see **ENGYGERON**

Anguish, King—see **AGWISANCE, KING**

Aniause, King—see **AMANS, KING**

Aniause's Daughters—see **AMANS' DAUGHTERS**

Anir—see **AMYR**

ANNA†

According to Geoffrey of Monmouth, Arthur's full sister and the wife either of King Lot or of King Budic of Brittany. In a note to l. 8135 of Chrétien's **Perceval**, D.D.R. Owen indicates Anna as presumably Ygerne's (Igraine's) daughter and the second of the queens of the Rock of Canguin. (Cline, however, in a note to l. 8135 of her translation, follows Hilka in mentioning Morcads, which is much closer to Morgawse/Margawse, as the name of Arthur's sister and Lot's wife.)

See also Anu.

ANNOWRE

A sorceress who loved Arthur and enticed him to her tower in the Forest Perilous. When she could not get him to make love to her, she plotted his death.

> Then every day she would make him ride into that forest [where his own knights were looking for him], to the intent to have King Arthur slain. For when this Lady Annowre saw that she might not have him at her will, then she laboured by false means to have destroyed King Arthur.

Nimue learned of the situation and came into the same forest, seeking Lancelot or Tristram to help the King. She found Tristram and brought him to the tower in time to see two strange knights defeating Arthur and unlacing his helm. "And the Lady Annowre gat King Arthur's sword in her hand to have stricken off his head." Tristram rushed up shouting, "Traitress, traitress, leave that", and killed the two knights. Meanwhile, Nimue shouted to Arthur not to let Annowre escape, so the King chased Annowre and smote off her head, which Nimue hung up by the hair to her saddlebow. [Malory IX, 16]

ANSIRUS THE PILGRIM, DUKE

He was called "the Pilgrim" because of his passion for going on pilgrimage, "for every third year he would be at Jerusalem." He passed his nickname on to his daughter, Alice la Beale Pilgrim. Ansirus was of Lancelot's kin, apparently in the British branch of the family. His daughter and her knight, Alisander le Orphelin, settled in "their country of Benoye", which presumably was Ansirus' dukedom.

Antor—see ECTOR

ANU†

A goddess whom Lewis Spence quotes one R. Briffault, in a work titled **The Mothers** (London, 1927), as calling Arthur's sister [**Magic Arts**, p. 146].

See also Anna.

ARAGON, SON OF THE KING OF†

He came to Britain to win renown and honor, and fought in the Noauz tournament. His coat of arms featured an eagle and a dragon side by side. [Chrétien de Troyes, **Lancelot**, ll. 5783-5823]

Arans, Aranz—see AROUZ, COUNT

ARBRAY

Sir Sadok, flying from Mark's ambush at Tintagil, passed Lyonesse (Liones) Castle and continued to Arbray, where he found Sir Dinas, the Seneschal of Cornwall. They gathered the people and stocked the towns and castles of Cornwall. Arbray Castle, therefore, appears to have been within the land of Lyonesse. [Malory X, 50]

ARCAUS†

Son of the King of Saxony and the leader of Mordred's first division, apparently the Saxon division, in the last battle [Vulgate VI].

ARGIUS

This knight "of the blood of King Mark" led a third of Mark's army in battle against Elias and the invading Sessoins. Dinas the Seneschal and Andred were Mark's other two commanders. [Malory X, 28]

ARGUSTUS

While on the Grail Quest, Lancelot "rode into a forest, and held no highway. And ... he saw a fair plain, and beside that a fair castle." A tournament was in progress between the castle knights, in black, and other knights, in white. Lancelot entered on the side of the castle and was defeated and shamed. In sorrow he rode on through a deep valley, past a mountain, and to a chapel where a recluse lived. She explained to him that the tournament had a spiritual meaning. Although the combatants "were earthly knights", the

> tournament was a token to see who should have most knights, either Eliazar, the son of King Pelles, or Argustus, the son of King Harlon. But Eliazar was all clothed in white, and Argustus ... in black, the which were [over]come.

The knights in black symbolized sinners, those in white virgins and good men. [Malory XV, 5-6]

Finding nothing more about King Harlon and his son Argustus, I hypothesize that their country was in northern Logres or southern Scotland, so that Harlon's son and Pellam's could conveniently arrange their tournament. The last specific site Lancelot appears to have visited was the place I have called "Chapel of the Demon" (q.v.). At least two, perhaps three, days of travel seem to have passed between the time Lancelot left the chapel and the time he came to the tournament; it was hardly, however, uninterrupted travel. The similarity of the names suggests that possibly Harlon's son Argustus was also Aguarus, the nephew of the dead man whom Lancelot found in the chapel.

ARIES

A cowherd, reputed father of Sir Tor, and actual father of twelve sons besides. At the time of Arthur's marriage, Aries reluctantly yielded to Tor's desire and brought him to Arthur's court at London to request knighthood for the boy. After comparing Tor with his twelve supposed younger brothers and finding him unlike any of them, Arthur dubbed the boy. Merlin then explained that King

Pellinore had begotten Tor on the housewife Vayshoure when he took her maidenhead. Being assured both by Merlin and by the woman that Tor had been begotten before ever she was wedded, Aries remarked, "[I]t is the less grief unto me." [Malory III, 3]

ARMOURER, THE†

Among Arthur's knights in the list Chrétien de Troyes begins in line 1691 of **Erec & Enide**. Chrétien gives him no other name, but tells us that he preferred war to peace.

ARNOLD LE BREUSE

He and his brother, Sir Gherard le Breuse, were a murderous pair who "guarded" a passage of the water of Mortaise as an excuse to kill passing knights. Gareth slew them both on his way with Lynette to Castle Dangerous. This was Gareth's first conquest, not counting Sir Kay. [Malory VII, 6]

AROUZ (Arans, Aranz), COUNT†

Count of Flanders, he was killed when he came out to resist Arthur's army on its way to fight King Claudas in the war on behalf of Guenevere's cousin Elyzabel [Vulgate V].

ARRANT, KING OF DENMARK

This king of Denmark, who was a brother of one of the kings of Ireland, was killed in battle beside the Humber along with his four allies, the kings of Ireland, Vale, Soleise, and the Isle of Longtains, when they tried to invade Arthur's realm [Malory IV, 2]. I got the name Arrant from Vulgate VII.

ARROY

Sirs Marhaus, Gawaine, and Uwaine "came into a great forest, that was named the country and forest of Arroy, and the country of strange adventures", and here they chose for their guides three damsels whom they met at a fountain [Malory IV, 18]. Aside from the intervention of the Damosel of the Lake in Gawaine's adventure, there is not much of the supernatural in the succeeding episodes, as Malory records them.

Gawaine ended up in the middle of the Pelleas and Etnard affair, which may have been near the magical Lake, since Nimue loved Pelleas. Marhaus came to the Duke of the South Marches, while Uwaine rode westward and arrived in Wales. After meeting each other again in Arroy at the close of these adventures, the trio took twelve days to reach Camelot, which may argue quite a distance, or bad roads, or a leisurely trip.

Considering all things, I incline to identify Arroy as Warwickshire, reasonably convenient to Wales, the South Marches, and to Malory's Camelot.

ARS, KING†

According to Chrétien de Troyes, the father of Sir Tor. While the similarity of name seems to make it probably that he should be identified with Aries, Chrétien names Tor's father as a king while Malory makes him a cowherd and only putatively the hero's parent; thus, I feel the symbol † is appropriate after the name of King Ars. [**Erec & Enide**, ca. l. 1527]

ARTHUR

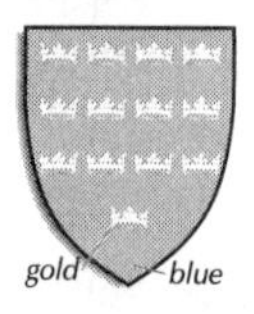

Arthur was no chessboard king. The point is made frequently in the romances that he was a good knight in his own right, capable of fighting in the field or tournament, of slaying terrific giants, and so on. His men loved him because he would jeopardize his life like any of them, even riding incognito to seek adventure. Once he jousted down Lamorak, who, according to Malory, was the third best knight of the world [Malory IX, 14]. Another time, to demonstrate his strength, Arthur seized Gawaine at a tournament, lifted him out of the saddle, and carried him along, armor and all, on his horse's neck [Vulgate V]. (Gawaine already had won the tournament, and Arthur had forewarned him to go along with whatever he did.) And although on at least one occasion Arthur had a clerk read a letter from Elaine of Astolat aloud to the court, Arthur was literate, like many of his knights and ladies, but unlike King Claudas. [Malory XVIII, 20; cf. Vulgate VI, 238]

Tennyson's Arthur can do no wrong. The Arthur of T. H. White is an idealistic and faithful man who has to be enchanted into going to bed with Morgawse, as well as a gentle, forgiving husband who is trapped into sentencing Guenevere to the stake and rejoices at her rescue. It is this version of Arthur that seems to have colored almost all modern treatments.

The Arthur of the Vulgate, Malory, and other medieval works, however, is a lusty and jealous man who does not need to be enchanted before hopping into bed with at least two other lovely ladies and probably more besides Morgawse; who appears to have fathered at least one bastard son and possibly more besides Mordred (see Amyr, Borre, and Loholt); who would have sentenced Guenevere to death or to horrible maiming before her exile, if Lancelot had not saved her in trial by combat during the affair of Genievre; and who goes into a jealous rage and cries for the blood of both Guenevere and Lancelot when their guilt is made clear to him.

He is also something of a practical joker. When Sir Baudwin of Britain made a vow never to be jealous of his wife, Arthur arranged for Baudwin to be out hunting one night. Then Arthur brought a young knight of his own to the chamber of Baudwin's wife, commanded

Arthur and the Orkney Kin

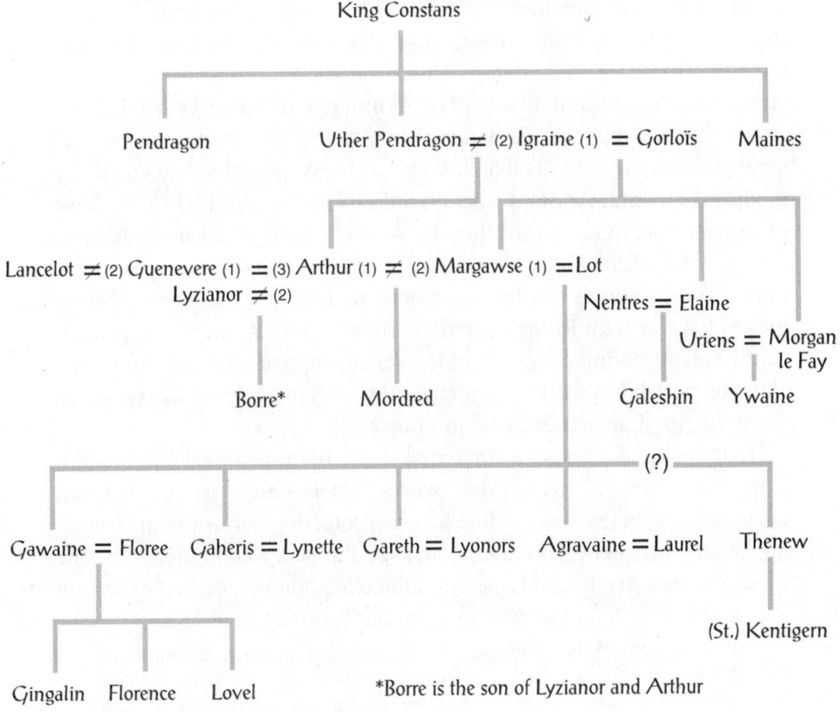

- *Gawaine's amours and wives are not well known and may vary from version to version.*
- *Thenew may have been Lot's daughter by Margawse, by an earlier wife, or by an amour. Thenew claimed an immaculate conception for her own son, Kentigern.*
- *King Lot is descended from Peter, one of the companions of Josephe, son of Joseph of Arimathea. King Uriens is descended from Josephe's brother Galaad.*

= *Indicates a known marriage.*

≠ *Indicates a union either known to be illicit or a union not proven to be a marriage.*

admittance, and forced the young man into bed with the lady—though he did put a sword between them, threaten the knight with death if he touched the lady, and sat playing chess with one of her damsels at the bed's foot for the rest of the night. In the morning, Arthur showed Baudwin his wife apparently caught with a lover in her bed, thus testing Baudwin's vow of non-jealousy. Wonder of wonders, Baudwin passed, remaining truly non-jealous, whereupon Arthur explained the situation and praised the lady. [**The Avowynge of King Arthur**]

Also among Arthur's faults according to the medieval versions, and surely more serious faults than lust and jealousy, are pride and greed. By medieval thought, Arthur's final downfall was brought less by the love of Lancelot and Guenevere than by Arthur's own greed in wishing to conquer the world. Early versions give Mordred his chance at usurpation while Arthur is on the Continent to fight the Romans. Malory moves the war with Rome to fairly early in Arthur's career and gives it a triumphant ending, but the older version appears to survive in the Vulgate, which has the Romans attacking Arthur while he and Gawaine are besieging Lancelot's castle in France.

High among Arthur's genuine virtues, by both medieval and modern standards, was loyalty to his word. After Lancelot had rescued Guenevere from the stake, while he was protecting her in Joyous Garde, the Bishop of Rochester came to arrange the peace commanded by the Pope between Arthur and Lancelot. Lancelot naturally wanted to be sure it was safe to deliver Guenevere up to her husband.

> And then [the Bishop] shewed Sir Launcelot all his writing, both from the Pope and from King Arthur. This is sure enough, said Sir Launcelot, for full well I dare trust my lord's own writing and his seal, for he was never shamed of his promise. [Malory XX, 14]

Chrétien de Troyes has been called the adoptive father of Arthurian literature. In his romances, which antedate and clearly contain many seeds of the Vulgate and Malorian versions, Arthur usually seems less a flawed human being than a quasi-otherworldly ideal. He does appear to show feet of clay in **Cligés** (the same romance which calls him, ca. l. 310, "the best king" this world ever saw or will see), when he insists upon death by torture for Count Angrs and his rebels, but this case is wrapped up with various medieval codes; and I find **Cligés** a work even more remarkable than most of Chrétien's for gray areas between good and bad. Arthur also seems strangely weak at his first appearance in the last and possibly strangest of the series, **Perceval**, when he allows himself to fall into frozen despair over the Red Knight of Quinqueroi's insult to himself and Guenevere, while his court continues to laugh and joke about him [ll. 900-973]. On the whole, however, he seems the personification of worldly (as opposed to otherworldly) kingliness. He can summon men from England, Flanders, Normandy, France, and Brittany as far as the Spanish peaks over the Pyrenees for his projected war on behalf of his great-nephew Cligés; yet Britain seems filled with little otherworldly kingdoms and castles that know not his sway, from Brandigant to Gore to the Rock of Canguin. Both Arthur's magnificence and some (exaggerated!) glimpse into medieval society may be gleaned from the remark that the king felt upset at having only a mere 500 nobles of his household with him at Robais. [**Erec & Enide**, ll. 6411-6443] Chrétien lost no chance of emphasizing Arthur's generosity—a pearl among virtues, especially in medieval eyes; one guesses that the generosity of the rich must have been a key element in medieval economy. Possibly less to Arthur's credit, Chrétien also shows him early on declaring that a king's word, once spoken—even if less than judiciously—should never be retracted. [**Erec & Enide**, ll. 27-68] In **Yvain** [ll. 6350-6446], we find Arthur cast in the role of the wise judge of folklore, shrewd as the Old Testament's Solomon or Daniel as he tricks the elder daughter of the Lord of Noire Espine into confessing her greed and mercilessness.

Chrétien's Arthur swears by the souls of his father Uther Pendragon, his mother, and his son—implying either that they are all three of them dead or that he so believes. [**Yvain**, ll. 649-690] Unfortunately, I cannot find that Chrétien gives us a name for Arthur's son; but in **Perceval** [ca. ll. 8730-8745] we learn that his mother is, indeed, Igraine and that she is ruling the Rock of Canguin, along with her daughter, Arthur's sister, and the niece, Clarissant, whom Arthur surely does not know he has—though whether the castle of Canguin lies in this world or the Otherworld appears a very moot question. In this episode, Igraine calls Arthur a young man, a mere hundred years old, which looks like a piece of literary humor that serves the additional purpose of heightening the Good King mystique.

Don Quixote, who apparently knows nothing about Arthur's being carried to Avalon, mentions a tradition that instead of dying he was magically turned into a crow, from which form he will eventually return to rule again. The good Don also remarks that in Castilian Arthur is usually called Arts or Artus (with or without accent mark depending on the English translation). [Cervantes, **Don Quixote**, Part I, Chapter 13] "Artus" is the name I found in the Vulgate. In **The Magic Arts in Celtic Britain** [chapter XII, pp. 145-163, esp. pp. 146, 147, 151-2, 160], Lewis Spence adds to Quixote's words an account of a nineteenth-century Cornishman admonishing a hunter to stop shooting at ravens, because King Arthur was still alive as one. Spence even provides reasons for this belief: quoting various sources, he records possible derivations of the name "Arthur", not only from *aruthr*—a variant of Welsh *uthr*, meaning "cruel" and suggestive of an early splitting of a single character into father and son—but alternatively from Welsh *arrdhu*, meaning "very black", suggestive of a connection with the raven god Bran. (Spence argues that Arthur was once the hero-god of a religious cult, an interesting theory which I record here without personally believing on the evidence I have so far seen.)

It would appear that Don Quixote got his information about the Matter of Britain not from his own or his author's errant fancy, but from existing tradition. One book available to us and known to have been in Quixote's library—the Catalan romance **Tirant Lo Blanc**, first published in 1490—seems to offer a further tiny glimpse into this Iberian Arthurian tradition: Queen Morgan le Fay arrives, in a black-shrouded ship, at the Greek emperor's port of Pera. She is clad in black velvet and attended by 130 lovely maidens, chief among whom are Hope, Honor, Chastity (named to celebrate courtly love), and Beauty; they are searching for Morgan's brother Arthur. The Greek emperor happens to be holding, lodged in a fair silver cage, a strange lord whose name he cannot learn, but who has a wondrous sword called Excalibur, as well as an aged knight attendant called Breunis Saunce Pit. Morgan recognizes the unnamed prisoner as her brother, whereupon Arthur looks into Excalibur, which seems to have somewhat the same properties as a crystal ball or other oracle of wisdom, and gives to all the company's questions answers replete with the courtly philosophy of the time. At the end, he is of course released and restored to his sister, and after a splendid celebration, during which Arthur and Morgan honor the emperor's daughter and Tirant by dancing with them, the Arthurian party exchanges their ship's black cloth for brocade and departs. This whole episode is almost surely to be understood as an elaborately staged masque; nevertheless, it is interesting to find Breunis (surely our old friend Breuse Sans Pitie) as well as Morgan cast in an unimpeachable light, and I cannot recall ever before finding this particular quality recorded of Excalibur. [Joannot Martorell & Mart Joan de Galba, **Tirant Lo Blanc**, tr. by David H. Rosenthal; NY: Schocken Books, ©1984, chapters clxxxix-ccii (pp. 333-339)] In **The Arthurian Tradition** [Rockport, Mass., etc., ©1989], p. 23, John Matthews refers to a version of the epic in which Merlin departs into an "esplumoir", sometimes interpreted as a moulting cage for hawks; I find this interesting in view of Arthur's silver cage and oracular resources in **Tirant**.

Lewis Spence further cites evidence pointing to Arthur himself having at one time been the Maimed King of the Grail legend [**Magic**

Arts, chapters XII & XIII, pp. 145-173] and he mentions three more close relatives of Arthur: a sister, Anu; a brother, Madawg ap Uther; and a nephew, Eliwlod [pp. 146, 159].

KING ARTHUR'S FAMILY AND RETAINERS
Grandfather (paternal): King Constans of England
Father: Uther Pendragon
Mother: Igraine
Uncles (paternal): Maines, Pandragon (both killed before Arthur's conception)
Uncle (maternal?): Duke Elise
Foster Father: Ector (not de Maris)
Foster Brother: Kay
Wife: Guenevere
Paramours: Margawse, Lyzianor, Countess of Orofoise's Sister
Sons: Borre (by Lyzianor), Mordred (by Margawse); cf. Amyr, Loholt
Full Sister?: cf. Anna
Half-sisters (by Igraine): Margawse, Elaine of Tintagil, Morgan le Fay
Brothers-in-law: King Lot (m. Margawse), King Nentres (m. Elaine), King Uriens (m. Morgan)
Nephews (by Lot and Margawse): Gawaine (favorite), Agravaine, Gaheris, Gareth Beaumains
Other Nephews: Ywaine (by Uriens and Morgan), Galeshin (by Nentres and Elaine)
Nieces: Soredamors, "Alteria", Clarissant
Mentor: Merlin
Cousin: Hoel of Brittany (also an ally)
Allies (sampling): Kings Ban and Bors, Carbarecotins, Archbishop of Canterbury
Lieges (sampling): Damsel of the Marches, Lady of Nohaut
Would-be-paramours: Annowre, Camille

No effort has been made to include all of Arthur's allies and liege subjects on this list.

ARTHUR'S CUP†

Weighing fifteen marks, it was fashioned of gold; the workmanship was worth more than the gold, and the inset jewels worth more than either. Arthur promised this cup to any man, even a foot-soldier, who took the rebel Count Angrs' castle; if the man were a knight, he would get any other possible reward he asked along with the cup. On capturing Angrs, Sir Alexander accepted only the cup and promptly talked Gawaine into accepting it from him for friendship and courtesy. [Chrétien de Troyes, **Cligés**, ll. 1515-1552, 2201-2248]

ARTHUR'S IVORY THRONES†

Sir Bruiant of the Isles gave these to Arthur and Guenevere. The two thrones, made of gold and ivory with no wood at all, were absolutely identical. Each had the form of a leopard finely carved on one side and that of a crocodile on the other. Arthur sat in one and had Erec sit in the other at the latter's coronation as king of Outre-Gales, which suggests that Arthur may from time to time, as a signal honor, have sat other people in the throne that would otherwise have been the Queen's. It also sounds as if these thrones, despite their weight, must have been among the items carried about with the court from city to city. [Chrétien de Troyes, **Erec & Enide**, ll. 6713-6735]

ASELAPHES†

In the time of Joseph of Arimathea, the devil Aselaphes killed the Pagan King Tholomer to keep him from being converted by Josephe [Vulgate I].

ASTLABOR, KING

The father of Sirs Palomides, Safere, and Segwarides [Malory X, 82-83]. Since they are Saracens, Astlabor's kingdom would be somewhere in Moorish lands.

ASTOLAT

Malory identifies this as Guildford, which is in present-day Surrey, south of London [XVIII, 8].

"ASTRIGIS"†

This treacherous lady tried to trick Gawaine, through her lies, into killing her husband. Gawaine fought the husband; when the husband told his side, Gawaine did not know whom to believe. He tried to take them both to find someone who could tell him which was in the right. On the way, the woman gave him the slip. Her husband remarked,

> You knights of the Round Table are compelled by your oath to help any woman without knowing whether she deserves it or not. Would it not be more reasonable and honorable to inquire before you act if you are espousing a good cause?

The lord of the castle La Tour Quarrée, where they repaired, agreed with the husband. [Vulgate V, appendix]

Both the wife and the husband are unnamed in the account. I have given her a minor place name.

AUBAGU†

A horse of King Arthur's [Chrétien de Troyes, **Erec & Enide**, ll. 4110-4142; Chrétien mentions only the name, nor does D.D.R. Owen supply any enlightening note.].

"Automne"—see under **"PRINTEMPS, ÉTÉ, & AUTOMNE"**

Avalon—see **AVILION**

Avarlon—see **PINEL**

AVENABLE (Grisandoles)†

Avenable, the daughter of Duke Mathem, disguised herself as a squire, took the name Grisandoles, and went to the court of the Emperor of Rome. Here she worked her way up to seneschal, presumably being knighted on the way.

One night the Emperor dreamed of a sow with a gold circle on her head and of twelve "loueaus." (I could not find an exact definition of "loueau", but the context explains it as well as need be.)

At that time Merlin was in the forest of Romenie. He took the semblance of a stag, ran through the palace, and told the Emperor that only "the wild man" could explain the dream. Merlin also played this same wild man. The Emperor promised his daughter to whomever found either the stag or the wild man. Eventually Grisandoles, instructed by the stag, found the wild man. The wild man laughed thrice on the way back: when he looked at Grisandoles, when he saw many poor people before an abbey, and when he saw a squire strike his master three times during Mass at a chapel. Brought before the Emperor, the wild man explained that he was a Christian and that he had laughed the first time because a good and beautiful woman had found both stag and wild man where many men had failed, the second time because the beggars at the abbey had a rich treasure buried under their feet, and the third time because a great treasure was hidden at the place where the squire struck his master. The Emperor's dream, which Merlin, as the wild man, related before expounding, to prove his knowledge, meant that the Empress' twelve handmaidens were twelve young men in disguise. The Empress and her twelve lovers were burned at the stake. Merlin advised the Emperor to marry Avenable and not act contrary to her will when they were married. Merlin also assured the Emperor that his daughter was really his and would not resemble the late Empress, her mother. Letters appearing over the door then revealed that the stag and the wild man were both Merlin. The Emperor sent for Avenable's parents and brother Patrices, married Avenable, married his daughter to Patrices, and lived long and happily with his new wife. [Vulgate II]

This seems to be a tale of Merlin's youth, and the Emperor in question may have been a predecessor of the Lucius whom Arthur conquered and killed. Even if the Emperor is identified with Lucius, a romancer might be justified in having the widowed Avenable-Grisandoles come back to Britain with other Continental knights, like Sir Priamus.

AVILION (Isle of Avalon)

This is the place of Arthur's passing. He either died or was taken alive into a magical retreat. I conceive that Avilion must have been a sort of sanctuary: hallowed, neutral ground.

Avilion includes Glastonbury and the territory between the Mendip and the Quantock Hills, Somerset. Malory in his last book seems to confirm this traditional identification. Helen Hill Miller, in **The Realms of Arthur**, points out that:

> It is no figurative island. Until recent centuries, the territory between the Mendip and the Quantock Hills, extending far inland from Bristol Channel, was a marsh across which only those who knew secret hidden causeways could travel. ... As late as the 19th century the sea broke in ... and spread a brackish flood over miles of flat pasture.

Here, at Glastonbury, Joseph of Arimathea planted his miraculous Flowering Thorn. Later, a number of former knights gathered as hermits around Arthur's grave near Glastonbury.

Avilion may have been simply a geographical territory, difficult of access because of the marshlands. Certainly the place seems to have had normal residents leading normal lives. It must also have been the residence of the mysterious "great lady Lile of Avelion", who appears, from Malory's references to her, to have been a powerful sorceress [II, 1,4]. I suspect, however, that Lady Lile of Avelion may be an unconscious personification of the island, or "l'i[s]le" of Avilion itself. Arthur may be in a mystical or magical sleep in Avilion, but Malory himself seems more of the opinion that the great king died like any other man.

Nevertheless, Avilion comes across to me as a mystical center of repose, quite possibly Christian grafted onto Pagan with elements of the old creed remaining, and beneficent if a shade melancholy—a "peaceable kingdom" of healing, sanctuary, and permanent, inviolate truce. Or, perhaps, it might have been a gateway to the underworld of the dead.

AXILLES†

He was Sir Bors' squire. Bors eventually knighted him and invested him with the castle of Le Terte Deuee [Vulgate V].

Baale†—see **KALET**

BADEMAGU, KING OF GORE†

While the Bademagu who appears in Chrétien's **Lancelot** clearly became the Bagdemagus of later romance, I see enough scarcely reconciliable differences to give them separate entries. For one thing, I find no suggestion that Chrétien's Bademagu would ever become a vassal or Arthur or any other earthly king, let alone one of Arthur's company of Round Table champions. Bademagu is too self-contained and, quite possibly if not probably, too unearthly.

From whatever source Chrétien drew the material for his version of the Knight in the Cart story, Bademagu's realm shows its otherworldly roots—whether Celtic faeryland or thinly Christianized afterlife—more clearly than the kingdom of Bagdemagus was later to do. Despite his country's custom of holding all foreigners who stray into it prisoner, Bademagu shows himself at every step an exemplary man and monarch, devoted to honor and loyalty, consistently if often unsuccessfully aiming for peace and justice in all things—in contrast to his son Meleagant (Meliagrant), who always strives for the opposite of everything for which his father stands. When Meliagrant brings them back captive from Arthur's court, Bademagu keeps Guenevere safe from ravishment and Kay alive, despite his son's designs upon the lady and attempts to do in the wounded knight by getting the doctors to use baneful treatments. Bademagu also provides a good surgeon for Lancelot when the latter arrives wounded, having left horse, arms, and some of his armor behind in order to cross the Sword Bridge; the new horse and arms the hero needs to fight Meliagrant are provided by Bademagu.

Much as Meliagrant exasperates Bademagu, the father continues to love his son, successfully pleading with Guenevere to ensure that Lancelot spare Meliagrant's life, for his parent's sake, during their first combat, and managing to stop their second in time to prevent bloodshed. At last, boasting of what he will do at Arthur's court, Meliagrant appears to succeed in breaking the bond between himself and his father; but this scene comes in the finishing pages, allegedly added by one Godefroi de Leigni with Chrétien's approval, and one may wonder if the break would truly have been final. As Chrétien's translator D.D.R. Owen points out, the arguments of the "Old and Young Knights of the Meadow" in the same romance foreshadow those of the king of Gore and his son. Bademagu and Meliagrant may also remind us of David and Absalom in the Old Testament. Ultimately, Bademagu and Meliagrant put me in mind of God and Satan—in the Book of Job, for instance—a notion not wholly out of place if the romance of Gore is indeed a secularization of the Harrowing of Hell and similar romances of the afterlife, an impression I find hard to avoid.

While Lancelot, like other knights, is often acclaimed, within his own story and in certain situations, as "the best knight in the world", I will venture to guess that it is Bademagu's pronouncement to this effect, ca. l. 3235, on seeing Lancelot cross the Sword Bridge, that marks the beginning of Lancelot's ascendancy over Gawaine in later works by other authors. It was also for the later romancers to solidify and demythologize Bademagu into Bagdemagus, giving him and his land a human history and rationale; but, since Chrétien himself clearly did quite a bit of demythologizing, how can we logically complain?

[Chrétien de Troyes, **Lancelot**; Bademagu first named ca. l. 650, appears in person ca. l. 3155, figures prominently thereafter.]

BADEMAGU'S DAUGHTER

While Lancelot was engaged with the challenger I have very tentatively identified with the Haughty Knight of the Heath, King Bademagu's daughter rode up and asked Lancelot, as a favor, to give her his opponent's head, and she would reward him. Eventually he complied, to her great joy, and she left repeating her promise. I am in some quandary whether or not to identify her with the "Damsel of the Crossroads" (q.v.), but the maiden who asks for the proud knight's head apparently makes no reference to any favor Lancelot may already owe her.

Later, while Bademagu was holding court in Bath on his birthday, Meliagrant arrived boasting of his appointment to fight Lancelot or, in Lancelot's continued absence, the great Gawaine himself at Arthur's court within a year and a day. Meliagrant's pride caused a rift with his father; the maiden who was Bademagu's daughter and Meliagrant's sister overheard their quarrel, guessed that the missing Lancelot was being secretly held prisoner somewhere, mounted a fine mule, and went in search of him. After a month of hard searching, she found him in the tower Meliagrant had built to hold him. Someone had left a pickaxe lying about, so she passed it up to Lancelot, who, even weakened as he was by bad provisions, used it to break out. Reminding him of the favor he had done her by striking off the proud knight's head, she took him to a favorite retreat of hers and nursed him back to health, then provided him with a wonderful horse before they parted with courtly pledges of an affection that was almost certainly platonic. Since she had overheard him (before he knew of her presence) name Meliagrant as his imprisoner, it probably did not bother her that she was healing Lancelot so that he could fight and quite possibly kill her brother. [Chrétien de Troyes, **Lancelot**, ll. 2793-ca. 2950; 6246-6728]

See also Bagdemagus' Daughters.

BADEMAGU'S SURGEON†

A good and trustworthy Christian, he knew more about how to heal wounds than did all the doctors of Montpellier (which was renowned as a center of medical studies). When Lancelot arrived in Gore, he should have had three weeks or a month to recover from the wounds sustained on his way, especially from crossing the Sword Bridge, but he absolutely insisted on waiting no longer than overnight. Bademagu's surgeon proved his skill by getting Lancelot battle worthy in that one night. [Chrétien de Troyes, **Lancelot**, ll. 3492-3526]

BAGDEMAGUS (Baudemagus), KING OF GORE

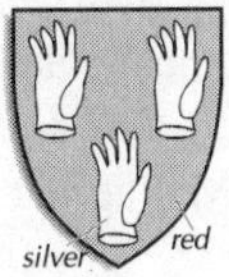

Although Bagdemagus seems pretty well forgotten in our day, he was one of the more important companions of the Round Table.

King Uriens of Gore gave his country to his nephew Bagdemagus (see Gore). At the time Arthur interred the second group of rebel kings with all honors, Merlin revealed to him that Bagdemagus was Arthur's cousin as well as Uriens' kinsman (Malory II, 11; the name is here spelled Basdemegus, but there is no reason to doubt the identity). Bagdemagus later left Arthur's court in anger because Sir Tor had been chosen instead of himself to fill a vacant seat at the Round Table. Riding into the forest, Bagdemagus and his squire came to a cross where Bagdemagus stopped to say his prayers. The squire noticed a prediction written on the cross, saying that Bagdemagus would not return to court until he had won a knight of the Round Table, fighting body to body.

> So, sir, said the squire, here I find writing of you, therefore I rede you return again to the court. That shall I never, said Bagdemagus, till men speak of me great worship, and that I be worthy to be a knight of the Round Table. And so he rode forth, and there by the way he found a branch of an holy herb that was the sign of the Sangreal, and no knight found such tokens but he were a good liver.

Bagdemagus also found the rock under which Merlin was imprisoned and spoke with Merlin, but could not lift the rock.

> And so Bagdemagus departed and did many adventures, and proved after a full good knight, and came again to the court and was made knight of the Round Table. [Malory IV, 5]

Strangely enough, after the incident of the holy herb (that was a sign of the Sangreal), Bagdemagus did not achieve the Holy Grail. Indeed, when he started out on the Quest, he attempted to take the Adventurous Shield reserved for Galahad, and as punishment was stricken down by an apparently angelic knight in white armor outside the abbey [Malory XIII, 9]. Malory XVII, 17, and Vulgate VI agree that sometime on the Grail Quest Bagdemagus was killed by Gawaine; neither account, however, describes the actual death scene, and Malory brings Bagdemagus back as one of Lancelot's advisors in XX, 19. This last reference is likely an error. When Bagdemagus was killed on the Grail Quest, Arthur mourned his loss more than that of any other three together of those killed [Vulgate VI].

Once, at a tournament, Bagdemagus requested a knight named Sauseise to strike down his son Meliagrant, "for I would he were well beaten of thy hands, that he might depart out of this field." Sauseise would have succeeded "had there not come rescues." (Malory X, 41: Meliagrant seems to have survived the tournament in good shape, despite the failure of his father's tender ruse to get him out of danger.) Later, Lancelot was very nervous about how to tell Bagdemagus he had killed Meliagrant to defend the Queen; Bagdemagus, being a fair and just man, forgave him [Vulgate IV]. Besides his son Meliagrant, Bagdemagus had at least one and possibly two daughters.

In her delightful modern romance **The King's Damosel**, Vera Chapman uses Bagdemagus as the name of her villain. He is so dissimilar to the Bagdemagus of Malory and the Vulgate, however, that I must assume them mere coincidental namesakes.

KING BAGDEMAGUS' FAMILY AND RETAINERS
Son: Meliagrant
One or more Daughters
Uncle: King Uriens
Aunt: Morgan le Fay
Squire: Melias de Lile

BAGDEMAGUS' DAUGHTER(S)

An unnamed daughter of King Bagdemagus helped deliver Lancelot from Castle Chariot, where he was being held by Morgan and other queens. The damsel's condition for helping Lancelot escape was that he help her father in a tournament against the King of Norgales. [Malory IV, 4]

Vulgate IV mentions a stepsister of Sir Meliagrant. She hated him because he had calumniated her, causing her father to cut her off, so that she retained only a poor inheritance from her mother. This damsel was benefactress to the wife of a serf named Roliax, whom Meliagrant made Lancelot's jailor. Thus the stepsister was able to help Lancelot escape. This damsel may be identical with Malory's daughter of King Bagdemagus, or she may be a separate character; she may even be a daughter of Bagdemagus's wife, perhaps by a former marriage, and not of Bagdemagus himself. In her story we can definitely recognize that of Bademagu's daughter in Chrétien's **Lancelot**, mixed in with certain elements Chrétien used with other ladies in **Yvain**.

Lancelot later learned, as he rode through the wood of Sapine, that Meliagrant's stepsister was to be burned at Florega the next day for the death of Meliagrant. Lancelot saved her in the nick of time and threw her accuser into the fire instead. [Vulgate IV]

See also Bademagu's Daughter.

Baillon†—see **TANEBORC**

BALAN

Born in Northumberland, Sir Balan was a good and unfortunate knight. Although never apparently, in Malory's version, a knight of the Round Table, he helped his brother Balin le Savage capture King Ryons for Arthur and win Arthur's war against Lot, Ryons, Nero, and the other kings of the second rebellion. He and his brother Balin, who is the more famous of the two, finally killed each other in a tragic battle, neither knowing the other's identity until too late. [Malory, II]

(Tennyson's idyll, "Balin and Balan", though an excellent tale in its own right, could hardly be called a retelling of Malory's book of Balin.)

BALANTON (Barenton?)†

See under Broceliande, Esclados, Laudine, and Ywaine.

D.D.R. Owen identifies Barenton as the marvelous spring of Chrétien's **Yvain** [note to l. 189], and it seems to me unlikely that two different marvelous springs in the same forest would have such similar names; but I do not venture to answer whether it was called either Barenton or Balanton in Chrétien's day—the only name I find in Owen's translation of **Yvain** that might cover the spring and castle thereto pertaining is Landuc—nor do I answer the question whether the Broceliande of Chrétien's romance is in Britain or Brittany. Chrétien's Arthur visits his Breton lands in **Erec** and **Cligés**; on the other hand, Ywaine starts from Carlisle in Wales with hopes of reaching Broceliande in two days' time and, while he may not succeed in this schedule, subsequent events in the romance (part of which runs concurrently with Lancelot's adventures in Gore) suggest no crossing of waters to and from Brittany.

By Chrétien's description, the cold spring bubbled or "boiled" up beneath a very fine pine tree. A pure gold basin hung from the pine, and the slab beside the spring was of emerald, bored out like a cask, with four bright rubies underneath it. On the other side of the spring was a small but pretty chapel. [**Yvain**, esp. ll. 410-448]

In **The Golden Bough**, Sir James Frazer observed that Breton peasants resorted in times of drought to a fountain or stream called Barenton. It would hardly have been as expensively decorated as the one Chrétien describes.

BALD SQUIRE, THE†

As the first day of the tournament between Meliant of Liz and Tibaut of Tintagel was winding down, a very tall, bald-headed squire came out to collect booty from the battlefield. One of the ladies mockingly called him a fool for trying to plunder broken equipment from the thick of things, advising him instead to appropriate the fresh horses and gear of the strange knight who had sat the day out watching peaceably from beneath a tree in the meadow.

This knight was Gawaine, who had arrived by chance and abstained from hazarding himself in the tourney because he had more important personal business elsewhere. Replying to the squire's rather rude words in kind, Gawaine soon sent him packing without revealing his (Gawaine's) identity or what his business was.

[Chrétien de Troyes, **Perceval**, esp. ll. 5114-5164]

Baldwin—see **BAUDWIN**

BALIN LE SAVAGE (The Knight with the Two Swords)

Born in Northumberland, Balin somehow slew a cousin of Arthur's, for which Arthur imprisoned him for half a year. Balin was out of prison, but impoverished and still remaining at Arthur's court, when a damsel to whom I have arbitrarily assigned the name "Malvis" came to Camelot girded with the sword referred to as Balin's Sword (q.v.). When Balin, alone of the knights at court, had drawn the sword, the first English Lady of the Lake (not Nimue, but the one I have styled "Nineve") came to Arthur to demand either Balin's head or that of "Malvis" in return for Excalibur. The Lady of the Lake claimed that Balin had slain her brother. As Arthur tried to put her off, Balin saw her, heard she was asking for his head, and loppedoff hers instead, explaining that she had caused his mother to be burnt. Arthur, annoyed, dismissed Balin from court. Sir Lanceor of Ireland rode out after Balin, challenged him, and died of Balin's spear when they jousted; Lanceor's lady Colombe, finding him dead, slew herself before Balin could stop her. Balin's brother Balan found him here, and shortly thereafter King Mark happened by. When Mark asked their names, Balan told him, "Sir ... ye may see he beareth two swords, thereby ye may call him the Knight with the Two Swords."

Balin and Balan next got back Arthur's favor by capturing his enemy King Ryons in ambush and then joining the battle before Castle Terrabil on Arthur's side. Lamorak de Galis was to claim, years later, that Balin had been the one who had killed King Lot in that battle.

> Oh, where is Balin and Balan and Pellinore? said King Arthur [after the battle]. As for Pellinore, said Merlin, he will meet with you soon; and as

> for Balin he will not be long from you; but the other brother will depart, ye shall see him no more. By my faith, said Arthur, they are two marvellous knights, and namely Balin passeth of prowess of any knight that ever I found, for much beholden am I unto him; would God he would abide with me.

(Lancelot had not yet come to Britain, and Gawaine was still young and scarcely tried.)

Balin did return to Arthur, but only very briefly. Seeing Sir Herlews le Berbeus and his lady ride by his pavilion toward the castle of Meliot, Arthur sent Balin after them, and on the way back Herlews was slain by Sir Garlon, who rode invisible. Balin thereupon rode with Sir Herlews' lady in pursuit of Garlon, whom they traced by his other murders and depredations. They stopped one night at the castle of the Leprous Lady. Eventually tracking Garlon to King Pellam's castle, Balin succeeded in exterminating the villainous knight. He and the lady lingered, however, to collect some of Garlon's blood in order to heal a youth Garlon had left wounded. This gave Garlon's brother Pellam time to call for his weapon and go after Balin. Balin's sword breaking at the first stroke, he fled from Pellam until he found Longinus' Spear and dealt Pellam the Dolorous Stroke. The castle collapsed about them, killing Sir Herlews' lady. In three days Merlin released Balin from the wreckage.

After one or two other adventures, Balin came to the castle I have described under Meliot. Here, to fulfill the customs of the place, Balin fought his brother Balan; Balan (having conquered the previous defender of the island) wore that knight's red armor, while Balin borrowed a shield offered to him for the occasion by one of the castle's knights. Thus neither recognized the other until after both were mortally wounded. Merlin later refurbished Balin's sword for Galahad. (The sword that Pellam had broken may have been the one Balin had, even before he drew that of "Malvis"; he wore only one of his two swords into the hall where he found and slew Garlon.) [Malory II; X. 24]

Although apparently never a companion of the Round Table, and seemingly doomed to do unfortunate deeds, Balin seems to have been a very sincere and well meaning knight as well as a capable and valorous one.

Balin's Lady—see **HERLEWS' LADY**

BALIN'S SWORD

An (apparently) wicked damsel wore this sword to Arthur's court, claiming that only a passing good knight of his hands and deeds, one who was without villainy and of gentle blood on both sides, could pull it out and free her of the encumbrance. This is a classic type of test for knightly virtue; in this case it seems to have been a trap to get

Balin to draw the sword and with it slay the damsel's brother, who had killed her sweetheart. Yet, when Balin drew it, she requested it back, saying that if he kept it, it would be the destruction of him and the man he loved most in the world. This prediction came true when Balin and Balan, not knowing each other, gave each other their death wounds in battle.

Merlin put a new pommel on Balin's sword and put it in a block of floating red marble. He also left the scabbard at the castle where Balin was buried, for Galahad to find. [Malory II, 19; see also Meliot.]

When Galahad arrived in Camelot some years later, he was already wearing the empty scabbard, having apparently picked it up on his way. The sword had just come floating down to Camelot in its block of marble, for the court to marvel at it and read in golden letters on its jewel-decked pommel: "Never shall man take me hence, but only he by whose side I ought to hang, and he shall be the best knight of the world." Lancelot had refused to make the attempt, remarking that whoever tried and failed would receive a grievous wound of that sword. At Arthur's urging, Gawaine reluctantly made the attempt, for which, sure enough, the sword later wounded him. Percivale also made the attempt, but, being almost as pure as Galahad, suffered no retribution from this sword. (However, he did wound himself in the thigh with his own sword in self-penance for having almost been seduced by the fiend.) Galahad, of course, drew the sword. [Malory XIII, 2-5]

Merlin had also predicted that with Balin's Sword Lancelot would slay the man whom he loved best, which was Gawaine. Either there is a confusion here between Lancelot and his son—for it is Galahad who deals Gawaine a grievous, not a mortal, wound with Balin's Sword [Malory XVII, 1]—or else Galahad sent the sword back by Sir Bors to his father Lancelot, who later used it in the fatal combat with Gawaine.

BAN, KING OF BENWICK

The French kings Ban and his brother Bors, who were wedded to the sisters Elaine and Evaine, were two of Arthur's major allies in his wars against the rebel kings at the beginning of his reign. It was largely through their assistance that Arthur won the battle of Bedegraine against the first rebel alliance. Ban and Bors returned to their own kingdoms, however (Ban fathering Ector de Maris along the way), before the second alliance of rebel kings reared its head. Arthur failed to pay back the favor and come to France in time to help Ban and Bors against King Claudas. Escaping with his queen, Elaine, and their small son Lancelot, Ban looked back, saw his castle in flames, and died, probably of heart seizure. Elaine, hurrying to her husband, left young Lancelot unattended for a few moments, and Viviane, the French Damsel of the Lake, appropriated him. [Vulgate II, III]

KING BAN'S FAMILY AND RETAINER
Brothers: King Bors, Gwenbaus
Wife: Queen Elaine of Benwick
Paramour: Damsel des Mares
Sons: Lancelot (by Elaine), Ector de Maris (by Damsel des Mares)
Sister-in-law: Queen Evaine
Nephews: Sir Bors de Ganis, Lionel
Retainer: Phariance

BAN, KING OF GOMERET (Gormoret)†

Chrétien records him among Arthur's vassal kings, summoned to court for Erec's wedding. Ban's company of 200 was composed entirely of beardless youths, all very merry, and each one bringing some sort of hawk or falcon. [**Erec & Enide**, ll. 1963-2024] Tentatively, I would avoid identifying him with King Ban of Benwick.

Chrétien mentions King Ban of Gomeret a second time in his last romance, as the monarch who knighted the second of Percivale's two older brothers. [**Perceval**, ll. 465-469]

BAN'S CROWN†

When Gwenbaus decided to stay behind in Britain with his princess in the Forest Perilous (or Forest Perdue), his brother King Ban of Benwick left his crown with them. Gwenbaus enchanted the forest grove. The crown may not have been magical in itself, but it gained a magical association; the enchantment was not broken until Lancelot came, sat in the chair, and wore the crown. [Vulgate V]

BANDES, KING

His daughter was loved by a Saracen knight, Sir Corsabrin, who would not suffer her to marry anyone else, and who spread the story that she was out of her mind. The princess enlisted the aid of Sir Palomides, who fought and killed Corsabrin during Duke Galeholt's tournament in Surluse. "And therewithal came a stink out of [Corsabrin's] body when the soul departed, that there might nobody abide the savour." [Malory X, 46-47]

Barant le Apres—see **HUNDRED KNIGHTS, KING OF THE**

Barenton—see under **BALANTON**

BATH

Chrétien names this as one of King Bademagu's court cities, which affects the geographical placement of the land of Gore [**Lancelot**, ll. 6246-6287].

Baudemagus—see **BAGDEMAGUS**

BAUDWIN, BISHOP†

The bishop who sits on the dais beside Sir Ywaine in **Sir Gawaine and the Green Knight** also plays a major, if rather unclerical, role in **Sir Gawaine and the Carl of Carlisle**. Very likely this notable churchman of Arthur's in pre-Malory romances is to be identified with Sir Baudwin of Britain.

BAUDWIN OF BRITAIN

One of the most important of the less-remembered knights, Baudwin seems to have been a major figure in various pre-Malory romances. In **The Avowynge of King Arthur** we learn that he made three interesting vows prompted by early experiences campaigning in Spain: never to deny anyone meat and drink, never to fear death, and never to be jealous of his wife or any other woman. It is possible that Sir Baudwin should be identified with Bishop Baudwin.

The little Malory gives about him is telling. On Arthur's accession, he made Sir Baudwin constable of the kingdom at the same time he made Kay seneschal. When Arthur left for his war against the Emperor of Rome, he made Baudwin joint governor of England in his absence, along with the Sir Constantine who later succeeded to the throne of Britain. Later, apparently after the death of his wife, Baudwin became a holy hermit and a "full noble surgeon and a good leech", forsaking his lands to settle in "wilful poverty" with at least two servants somewhere in the neighborhood of Camelot and Astolat. His hermitage was "under a wood, and a great cliff on the other side, and a fair water running under it" some two or three miles from Camelot. Here, after the tournament at Winchester, Baudwin healed the gravely wounded Lancelot, whom he recognized by a scar on the latter's neck. [Malory I, 7; V, 3; XVIII, 12-13]

BEALE ADVENTURE, ABBEY OF

Arthur founded this abbey fairly early in his reign, on or near the Humber River, at the site of his victory over the five invading kings of Denmark, Ireland, Soleise, the Vale, and the Isle of Longtains [Malory IV, 4]. Judging from the text, it would be a place where the river is crossable on horseback in calm weather [cf. Malory IV, 3]. Perhaps Selby or Cawood?

Beale Isoud—see **ISOUD**

BEALE REGARD

Morgan le Fay was holding this castle, but it was not the one Arthur had given her. She usurped it from an unnamed but lively damsel, the niece of the Earl of Pase. When Morgan imprisoned Sir Alisander le

Orphelin here, the Damsel of La Beale Regard helped him escape by writing to her uncle the earl, asking him to come and destroy La Beale Regard with wildfire. Alisander afterward defended the site against all comers and thus met his love, Alice la Beale Pilgrim.

Alisander had started out, on Tristram's advice, for London. Presumably he left from Magouns Castle (Arundel), but "by fortune he went by the seaside, and went wrong." At a tournament made by King Carados, he caught the eye of Morgan, who, after a side-battle of Alisander's against one Sir Malgrin, got Alisander into La Beale Regard. [Malory X, 36-38]

Since it is difficult to see how Alisander could miss London and end up in Scotland, I suspect that here Sir Cador of Cornwall is meant as the giver of this tournament, and not King Carados of Scotland.

In southwest Southampton is a town called Beaulieu. "Beautiful place", "beautiful view", La Beale Regard?

BEALE REGARD, DAMSEL OF LA

This unnamed damsel, rightful heir to the castle La Beale Regard, was cousin to both Morgan le Fay and the Earl of Pase. Morgan appropriated La Beale Regard and brought Alisander le Orphelin there with intent to seduce him. To foil Morgan, the damsel sent a request to the Earl of Pase, who hated Morgan, to come and destroy the castle with wildfire, which he did, while the damsel helped Alisander to escape by a privy postern, where she had his horse and harness ready for him. Since Alisander had promised Morgan to stay there a year, he waited in the garden while the castle was destroyed and then returned to defend his former bedroom against all comers. Alice la Beale Pilgrim came to the place and fell in love with him. The damsel of La Beale Regard, who might be considered as having a prior claim on Alisander, appears to have taken this in good humor and even, possibly, to have helped the romance along; at least, she did not hinder it.

One day Alisander went into a fit of being besotted on his lady, a sort of occupational hazard of being both knight and lover. While Alisander was in this helpless state, Mordred came along and started to mock him by leading his horse away. When the damsel of La Beale Regard saw this,

> anon she let arm her, and set a shield upon her shoulder, and therewith she mounted upon his horse, and gat a naked sword in her hand, and she thrust unto Alisander with all her might, and she gave him such a buffet that he thought the fire flew out of his eyen.

This brought him out of his trance and enabled him to rout Mordred. One pictures him saying, "Thanks—I needed that."

> But then Sir Alisander and Alice had good game at the damosel, how sadly she hit him upon the helm. [Malory X, 37-39]

The damsel of La Beale Regard's knowledge and skill in arming herself and using a sword to such good advantage suggest her as a possible female warrior.

BEALE-VALET

This castle seems to be mentioned only once by Malory, as a place where Sirs Palomides and Dinadan spent a night [X, 25]. I would guess it to be somewhere in the southwest. If "Valet" is "valley", the castle might well be in a mountainous region. Exmoor Forest is very up and down, and Beale-Valet might be or be near to Ilfracombe, Barnstaple, or South Matton.

Beaumains—see GARETH

BEAUREPAIRE (Belrepeire)†

The castle and lands of Blancheflor (q.v.). (D.D.R. Owen uses "Beaurepaire" in his translation, Ruth Cline "Belrepeire.") One might guess that Chrétien intended to bring Percivale back eventually to help Blancheflor rule this place. [Chrétien de Troyes, **Perceval**, ll. 1699-2975; first named ca. l. 2385]

A footnote of Cline's quotes Hilka as noting that Belrepeire is the name of the castle of Morcads, Gawaine's mother in the "Enfances Gauvain", which Ronan Coghlan's **Encyclopaedia of Arthurian Legends** tells me is a French poem of the thirteenth century (thus post-dating Chrétien's work).

BEAUVIVANTE (Maledisant, Bienpensant)

The history of Sir La Cote Male Taile and his damsel as recorded in Malory IX parallels, or perhaps parodies, the history of Gareth and Lynette in his Book VII. La Cote Male Taile's damsel is first called Maledisant ("Evil-speaking") for her raillery against her champion. Later, when she reveals to Lancelot that she had rebuked La Cote Male Taile not for hate but for love, fearing him too young and tender to risk his life questing, Lancelot names her Bienpensant ("Well-thinking"). Finally, after her marriage with La Cote Male Taile, she is called Beauvivante ("Well-living"). With so many unnamed damsels in the tales, it seems hardly fair that a single maiden should be given three distinctive, personality-tailored names. Her story suggests, however, that anyone with some knowledge of French can coin similar names for otherwise nameless characters. See also Maledisant's Shield.

BEDEGRAINE

Malory identifies this as Sherwood Forest. So, at least, I interpret "the castle of Bedegraine, that was one of the castles that stand in the forest of Sherwood" [I, 17], coupled with the description in that and surrounding chapters of the battle fought in Bedegraine Forest between Arthur, with his allies Ban and Bors, and the eleven rebel kings. In a valley in the "forest of Bedegraine", before the battle, Merlin secretly lodged Ban and Bors' host of 10,000 men on horseback, though this may argue more for Merlin's magic than Bedegraine's extent.

BEDEGRAINE CASTLE

Apparently the major one of the castles that stood in Bedegraine (Sherwood) Forest [Malory I, 12, 17]. Inspired by the prominence of the Sheriff of Nottingham in the legends of Robin Hood, I am tempted to identify Bedegraine Castle with the city of Nottingham.

BEDIVERE (Bedevere, Bedwyr)

One of Arthur's first knights, and the last one left alive with him after the battle with Mordred on Salisbury Plain, Bedivere was the knight who had to throw Excalibur back to the Lady of the Lake.

Malory mentions Bedivere first as one of Arthur's two companions (the other was Kay) in the adventure of the giant of Saint Michael's Mount on the way to the Continental campaign against the Emperor Lucius. Soon after the slaying of the giant, Bedivere, Gawaine, Lionel, and Bors were selected to carry Arthur's warlike message to Lucius. We do not, apparently, meet Bedivere again in Malory's account until he shows up at the tournament of Winchester and at the attempt to heal Sir Urre, which last marks him, if such evidence is needed, as a member of the Round Table. Bedivere, his brother Lucan the Butler, and a pair of bishops served as Arthur's messengers to Mordred to try to arrange a treaty. After the last battle, Bedivere obeyed, with famous reluctance, Arthur's command about Excalibur and then saw Arthur borne away in the boat with Morgan and her companions. Bedivere later found Arthur's grave at the hermitage of the former Archbishop of Canterbury. Bedivere became a hermit with the bishop. [Malory V, 5-6; XVIII, 11; XIX, 11; XXI, 3; XXI, 5-6]

This seems to be all Malory tells us of Bedivere. Nevertheless, I class him among the major knights. Along with Kay, he seems to have been one of the earliest companions of Arthur to have remained in the romances through the centuries, although by the time Malory got hold of the material other knights had crowded him from prominence. Sutcliff, in **Sword at Sunset**, makes Bedivere (under the earlier version of his name) the Queen's lover, Lancelot having come too late into the body of Arthurian literature to fit Sutcliff's pseudo historical retelling. In **The Hollow Hills**, Stewart seems to follow Sutcliff's lead in assigning the Queen's-lover role to Bedwyr. White identifies Bedivere with Pedivere in **The Once and Future King**, but in this instance I think he distorts Malory. Chapman includes Bedivere in his character as hermit in the cast of **King Arthur's Daughter**.

BEDOIIER THE MARSHAL†

Among Arthur's knights in the list Chrétien de Troyes begins in line 1691 of **Erec & Enide**. Chrétien tells us that Bedoiier (spelled with two "i's", at least in D.D.R. Owen's translation) was expert at chess and backgammon.

Bedwyr—see **BEDIVERE**

Bele Garde, Bele Prise—see **DOLOROUS TOWER**

Belec, Lady of†—see under **BELOE**

Belias—see **DEUX SYCAMORES, FONTAINE DES**

BELINANS, KING OF SORGALES (Sugales?)†

This chap got a mention in Vulgate VII.

Bellangere of Magouns—see under **ANGLIDES**

BELLENGERUS LE BEUSE (Bellangere le Beuse)

> And by Alice he [Sir Alisander le Orphelin] gat ... Bellengerus le Beuse. And by good fortune he came to the court of King Arthur, and proved a passing good knight; and he revenged his father's death [apparently by killing King Mark]. [Malory X, 40]

Bellengerus became a knight of the Round Table, being listed in Malory XIX, 11. He accompanied Lancelot into exile and was made Earl of the Launds [XX, 18]. Very likely he was named for Sir Belangere, the constable of Magouns Castle, who had taken in Bellengerus' grandmother, Anglides, when she fled from King Mark.

BELLEUS

A "passing good man of arms, and a mighty lord of lands of many out isles", Belleus was one of the victims of what was probably Sir Lancelot's worst habit: making free with other people's pavilions. One night Lancelot found a pavilion of red sendal, went in, and went to bed. After a while Sir Belleus came, it being his own pavilion, got into bed, and began to hug Lancelot, innocently and naturally believing the person who already lay in bed to be his leman. Up jumps Lancelot and, before anyone stops to ask questions, Belleus is wounded nigh unto death, to the horror of his lady, who arrives on the scene while Lancelot is staunching the wound he has given Belleus. Belleus shows himself to be of an understanding nature:

> Peace, my lady and my love, said Belleus, for this knight is a good man, and a knight adventurous, and there he told her all the cause how he was wounded; And when that I yielded me unto him, he left me goodly and hath staunched my blood.

The lady, who is left unnamed, demands to know Lancelot's name. On learning it she requires Lancelot to see to it, for the harm he has done her lord and herself, that Belleus be made a knight of the Round Table. This Lancelot does. [Malory VI, 5,8] Malory seems not to mention Belleus again. Presumably, if he survived until the time of the rift between Arthur and Lancelot, he clove to Lancelot's party.

BELLIANCE LE ORGULUS

Sir Lamorak saved Sir Frol of the Out Isles from four knights who were fighting Frol all at once. Shortly thereafter Lamorak and Frol had a tiff and separated. Three or four days later Lamorak came along again and saw Frol give Gawaine a fall when Gawaine tried to take Frol's lady. Lamorak jousted with Frol to avenge Gawaine, and by mischance smote Frol fatally.

Frol's brother, Sir Belliance le Orgulus, came to avenge Frol. Learning Lamorak's identity, Belliance said,

> Ah, thou art the man in the world that I most hate, for I slew my sons for thy sake, where I saved thy life, and now thou hast slain my brother Sir Frol.

Lamorak tried to beg Belliance's pardon, but Belliance insisted on fighting. Lamorak fought him down but refused to kill him, thereby winning his friendship so that they swore never again to fight each other [Malory VIII, 40-41].

Belliance is probably the "Sir Bellangere le Orgulous, that the good knight Sir Lamorak won in plain battle", who is listed as a knight of the Round Table [Malory XIX, 11]. He should not be confused with Bellengerus le Beuse, who is also sometimes called "Bellangere", as in XIX,11.

Belliance was among those killed during Lancelot's rescue of Guenevere from the stake [Malory XX, 8].

Bellicent—see MARGAWSE

BELLINOR†

When Lancelot and his followers left Arthur, Sir Bors' seat at the Round Table was given to Bellinor. Sir Bellinor was a king's son, but I know not of which king. [Vulgate VI]

Beloc, Lady of†—see under BELOE

BELOE† (Belec, Beloc)

When Arthur returned from France on news of Mordred's rebellion, the party bearing Gawaine's body stopped at Beloe Castle. The lady of Beloe grieved for Gawaine as the only man she had ever loved. Upon this, the lord of Beloe, who had never liked Gawaine, killed his wife.

For this murder, he was killed in turn by Arthur's knights, who then carried the lady's body with Gawaine's. [Vulgate VI, 358-359]

Mordred had attacked Arthur at Dover, trying to prevent his landing. Beloe must be between Dover and, probably, London or Camelot.

Belrepeire—see BEAUREPAIRE

BENIGNE (Blenined, Blevine)†

She was the Damsel of Glocedon Castle and a cousin of the Damsel of Hongrefort. At Galdon Castle, Sir Bors saved Benigne from being drowned by knights who had already slain her lover. Shortly thereafter, she joined her cousin of Hongrefort, who was searching for Sir Bors. [Vulgate IV]

BENOYE (Benoic, Benwick)

The more famous Benoye, or Benwick, was in France. There seems to have been another Benoye, in Britain—the dukedom of Duke Ansirus the Pilgrim. Ansirus' daughter, Alice La Beale Pilgrim, married Sir Alisander le Orphelin and they retired "into their country of Benoye, and lived there in great joy." [Malory X, 38-39]

Glennie identifies Albany, the area of Scotland roughly between the Firth of Tay to the east and Loch Fyne to the west, possibly with the Firth of Forth as part of its southern boundary, as Benoic. Alice heard of Alisander and journeyed down to see him when he was defending the site of the castle La Beale Regard, which I consider likely to have been somewhere near the southern coast of England. Since Alice's father had the custom of being in Jerusalem every third year, a simple jaunt all the way across Logres might have seemed little enough to her, so Albany remains a strong contender for Benoye.

On the other hand, Benoye might have neighbored La Beale Regard, being perhaps somewhere in Dorsetshire or Wiltshire.

Or Benoye might have been the country not of Alice's father, but of Alisander's father, Prince Boudwin. Boudwin was the brother of Mark of Cornwall; Mark murdered Boudwin, and Boudwin's wife had charged Alisander to avenge his father. "But, as the book saith, King Mark would never stint till he had slain [Alisander] by treason."

It seems likely that Prince Boudwin's principal holdings would have been in or near Cornwall. Had Alisander returned to his father's lands in this part of the country, would he not have attacked Mark first? Also, Malory tells us that Alisander never came to Arthur's court; it seems that he should have managed that trip, had he remained in southern or south-central Logres or in Cornwall, within reach of such major court cities as Camelot, Caerleon, and London. Mark, however, might have contrived to get an assassin up into Scotland. All in all, I prefer Glennie's identification of Albany as the British Benoye.

BENWICK (Benoye, Benoyc)

The kingdom of Lancelot's father, King Ban. In XX, 18, Malory says:

> And so [Lancelot and his party] shipped at Cardiff, and sailed unto Benwick: some men call it Bayonne, and some men call it Beaune, where the wine of Beaune is.

John W. Donaldson identifies Benwick with Burgundy (Burgoyne, Bourgogne). The French Benwick is probably not to be identified with the territory of Benwick to which Alisander le Orphelin and his wife Alice retired.

BERCILAK (Bertilak) DE HAUTDESERT and WIFE†

Sir Bercilak was the Green Knight of **Sir Gawaine and the Green Knight**. It is uncertain whether Bercilak himself was magical; I am of the opinion that he was an ordinary mortal—albeit a prime specimen—who cooperated with Morgan, and that the transformation and all other magic involved was her work. Here is the way Gardner translated lines from the poem describing Bercilak in his human appearance:

> An immense man, indeed, mature in years;
> A beard broad and bright, and beaver-hued;
> His stance was proud and staunch, on stalwart shanks;
> His face flashed like fire; his speech was free;
> Surely a man well-suited ...
> To lead as lord in a land of gallant men.

BERLUSE

The lieutenant of the castle of Sir Tor le Fise Aries. King Mark had killed Berluse's father before Berluse's eyes, and would have killed the son had he not escaped into the woods. Nevertheless, when Mark turned up at Sir Tor's castle, Berluse, motivated by love of Tor and of Lamorak, who was also a guest there, gave Mark truce and hospitality for the duration of his stay. Berluse warned Mark, however, to beware if ever they met outside the castle. [Malory X, 9]

From the similarity of the names, I suspect some connection between Berluse and the Sir Bersules whose story is given along with Amant's.

Berrant le Apres—see **HUNDRED KNIGHTS, KING OF THE**

Bersules—see under **AMANT**

Bertain—see **BERTE**

BERTE (Bertain)†

Father of Tibaut's vavasour Garin [Chrétien de Troyes, **Perceval**, ca. l. 5230].

BERTELOT

Bertelot was the brother of Breuse Sans Pitie. Sir Bliant, defending Lancelot from the brothers while Lancelot was mad, struck off Bertelot's hand [Malory XII, 2]. It is possible, but unlikely, that Bertelot could be identified with Sir Bertholai of the Vulgate.

BERTHOLAI†

Despite his advanced age, Bertholai was called the "best knight of Carmelide." Apparently this meant the best in arms, because he was not an endearing character. He was banished for the malevolent murder of another of King Leodegrance's knights. Finding Genievre, who was also living in exile after the attempt by Cleodalis' relatives to substitute her for Guenevere, Bertholai instigated a second attempt to substitute her for her more famous look-alike. They captured Arthur by luring him into the woods on a boar hunt and separating him from his companions. Then, with drugs and flattery, Genievre won his love and convinced him that she was Guenevere, the true-born. Arthur had Genievre acknowledged Queen and renounced Guenevere. Genievre wanted her rival's death, but eventually Guenevere was merely(?) condemned to lose the skin of her head (scalp?), cheeks, and palms, and be exiled forever.

This split the court. Lancelot renounced allegiance to Arthur, insisting on defending Guenevere against three knights. (This caused a curious rivalry between Lancelot and Kay, who also wanted to serve as Guenevere's champion.) Gawaine lent Excalibur to Lancelot for the battle. Thus Lancelot saved Guenevere's skin, and Arthur gave her into Duke Galeholt's keeping. Galeholt set her up comfortably with Lancelot in Surluse. At Gawaine's urging, Arthur tried to win back Lancelot, but failed.

In his infatuation with Genievre, Arthur let his duties slip. When the Pope learned what had happened, he ordered Arthur to take back Guenevere and, when Arthur refused, interdicted Britain for twenty-one months. In the tenth month of interdiction, Genievre and Bertholai had paralytic strokes, losing the use of their limbs and all their senses except sight and hearing. They began to decay while still alive. The hermit Amustans upbraided Arthur and helped get deathbed confessions from Genievre and Bertholai, who confessed to save their souls. Gawaine took the news to Surluse, and finally Guenevere and Lancelot were persuaded to return to Arthur. By the time Guenevere arrived, after spending more than two and a half years in Surluse, Bertholai and Genievre were dead. [Vulgate IV]

It is possible (though unlikely) that Bertholai could be identified with Malory's Sir Bertelot, the brother of Breuse Sans Pitie.

Bertilak de Hautdesert†—see **BERCILAK DE HAUTDESERT**

BERTRAND†

A noble, chivalrous, and spirited young knight from Thrace who had the bad luck one day near Constantinople to chase his sparrowhawk over a garden wall and find the supposedly dead and buried Empress Fenice sleeping naked with her lover Cligés. Thus discovered, Cligés sliced one of Bertrand's legs off below the knee. Bertrand escaped anyway to take his report to Emperor Alis. What happened to Bertrand after that Chrétien does not say, but his case illustrates the moral ambiguities of this romance: Bertrand, though functioning as betrayer, is far less blameworthy in the matter than the betrayed hero and heroine, and the loss of his leg seems most unjust. I for one cannot suppose this reading is due to modern perception alone. [Chrétien de Troyes, **Cligés**, ll. 6425-6533]

BIENFAIT MONASTERY†

It was near the forest of Bresquehan, and had the Duke of Cambeninc for its patron [Vulgate III].

Bienpensant—see **BEAUVIVANTE**

BILIS, KING OF ANTIPODES†

Chrétien lists him among Arthur's vassal kings, summoned to court for Erec's wedding. Bilis was the lord of the dwarfs and the smallest of them all, yet he was full brother to Brien, a giant. To show off his splendor, Bilis brought two vassal kings of his own, Grigoras and Glecidalan, also dwarfs. All three were noble gentlemen, well liked and served at Arthur's court as befitted their rank. [**Erec & Enide**, ll. 1963-2024]

BLACK CHAPEL

According to the Vulgate, this is the name of the chapel to which the last of Arthur's knights carried the wounded king after the last battle. It is located somewhere between Salisbury and the sea. Malory's account might lead one to believe that the last knight took Excalibur to the lake from this chapel, and afterward carried Arthur from here directly to the boat of Morgan and the other queens. The Vulgate, however, specifies that after passing the night at the Black Chapel, Arthur and his last warrior set out in the morning, reaching the sea at noon, and Arthur sent his knight from the seaside to throw Excalibur into the lake on the other side of the hill. Also according to the Vulgate, the last knight later found

Arthur's grave at the Black Chapel. This seems to vary from Malory, who apparently makes the chapel near Salisbury distinct from that where Arthur lies buried. [Vulgate VI; Malory XXI, 4-7]

BLACK CROSS, THE†

When Josephe and his followers arrived in Britain, Kamaalot (Camelot) was the richest city of the Pagans. The then king, Agrestes, pretended to convert; after Josephe left the city, Agrestes martyred twelve of Josephe's relatives. A cross Josephe had erected was stained black with their blood. Agrestes went mad and committed suicide, after which his people called Josephe back. The Black Cross was still standing in the forest of Camelot in Arthur's time. [Vulgate I]

BLACK CROSS, ABBEY OF THE

Kay carried Ywaine here to be healed after a treacherous attack by King Mark. Thus it would seem to be in Cornwall, probably in the northern part of the modern county, within easy reach of Tintagil.

BLAISE (Bleise)

Blaise was Merlin's master. After teaching him, Blaise retired to the forest of Northumberland to write down his pupil's deeds. Although so greatly eclipsed by his former pupil, Blaise must have had some skill in his time. Merlin frequently visited him in Northumberland. [Malory I, 17; other sources]

BLAMORE DE GANIS

Blamore was brother to Sir Bleoberis de Ganis, cousin to Lancelot, and a knight of the Round Table. Of the two brothers, Blamore was accounted the better man of arms.

Blamore and Bleoberis once arraigned King Anguish of Ireland for the death of a cousin of theirs. Blamore was the one who fought the actual trial by combat against Anguish's champion, Sir Tristram. Defeated, Blamore tried to insist on death rather than surrender. Bleoberis seconded his brother's request, but Tristram and the judges refused to allow it.

> And then, by all their advices ... the two brethren were accorded with King Anguish, and kissed and made friends for ever. And then Sir Blamore and Sir Tristram kissed together, and there they made their oaths that they would never none of them two brethren fight with Sir Tristram, and Sir Tristram made the same oath. And for the gentle battle all the blood of Sir Launcelot loved Sir Tristram for ever.

Malory mentions Blamore several more times—fighting at the tournament of the Castle of Maidens, joining a quest to find Tristram, taking a fall from Sir Palomides at Duke Galeholt's tournament in Surluse. Blamore and Bleoberis were two of the guests at Guenevere's small dinner party when Sir Patrise was poisoned. Later, they followed Lancelot into exile, and Blamore was made Duke of Limosin in Guienne. After the passing of Arthur, Blamore and Bleoberis eventually joined Lancelot, the former Archbishop of Canterbury, and others in their hermitage at Arthur's tomb. After Lancelot's death, Blamore and Bleoberis, along with Bors and Ector, went into the Holy Land to die warring against the Turks. [Malory VIII, 21-23; IX, 31, 36; X, 44; XVIII, 3; XX, 18; XXI, 10, 13]

BLANCHE ESPINE, CASTEL DE LA†

Its lord, Maten, was Arthur's enemy. Lancelot, Bors, Gareth, and Bagdemagus, passing by this fine castle, found a hundred ruffians ill-using Mordred. The four knights rescued their companion. On learning from him that Maten had attacked him simply for belonging to the Round Table, they fired the town, killed Maten, and burned the castle. [Vulgate V]

At this time, Mordred seems to have been an earnest and promising young knight. At least, his villainy had not yet surfaced. Still, it is of course possible that he maligned Maten.

Blanche Espine appears to be on the way from Camelot to the land of the giant Mauduit. Where Mauduit's land was I am not sure, but in non-Arthurian traditions, Cornwall is called a land of giants, and certain Arthurian stories bear this out, although not precluding the possibility that giants inhabited other areas as well.

Warbelow Barrow might be identified with La Blanche Espine.

> Between Camelford and Launceston [Cornwall], on Wilsey Downs, is Warbelow Barrow, an ancient fortification of considerable size, in the centre of which is a large mound, popularly called King Arthur's Grave. [Glennie, p. 12]

BLANCHE LANDE, DAMOISELLE DE LA†

Sir Gaheris' sweetheart, according to Vulgate V. I do not know where the "White Land" (Blanche Lande) was. See also under "Clarisin."

BLANCHEFLOR†

The lady of Beaurepaire was Gornemant of Gohort's niece and Percivale's love.

When Percivale, newly knighted, leaves Gornemant and comes to Beaurepaire, he finds the town and castle in terrible plight—impoverished, spent, and starving. Nevertheless, they offer him what hospitality they can. Blancheflor, her eyes either smiling or sparkling with laughter, depending on the translation, greets the newcomer with an offer of all she has on hand: a freshly shot deer, along with a gift of five loaves or rolls and some boiled or reheated wine from another uncle of hers, a prior. (D.D.R. Owen explains in a note that inferior wine was improved by reheating it.) That night, having given her guest a fine bed, she comes in and weeps beside it until he wakes and tenderly asks what troubles her. She reveals that Clamadeu of the Isles is bent on having her and has his seneschal Engygeron besieging her. He has killed most of her original 310 knights, captured 48, and left her with only 50 to defend her starving stronghold. Tomorrow the castle must be surrendered, but she has the knife ready to kill herself before letting Clamadeu have her person. "That's all", she finishes. "Now I'll let you get back to sleep." (Sounds pretty calculated to me.) He naturally comforts her, taking her into bed with him for the rest of the night to do so—whether or not they remain innocent seems largely to depend upon the reader's own interpretation—and afterward defeats first Engygeron and then Clamadeu for her, sending them to Arthur. The timely if chance arrival of a ship laden with food also helps Beaurepaire.

Anxious about his mother, Percivale leaves Blancheflor, promising to return. One may guess that he would have, had Chrétien completed his story; at any rate, Blancheflor is apparently the sweetheart memory of whose complexion later sends him into a long and rapt contemplation of three drops of blood on the snow. [Chrétien de Troyes, **Perceval**, ll. 1774-2937; 4162-4210ff.; her name is given ca. l. 2417, and Cline quotes Loomis as noting that it was a common name in Old French literature.]

BLANCHEFLOR'S UNCLE THE PRIOR†

Blancheflor calls him a very religious and saintly man, who has sent her the bread and wine which is all, with a deer newly shot by one of her servants, that she has to offer Percivale for supper.

Blancheflor is also Gornemant's niece, so the prior might be Gornemant's brother. If so, the frequency with which younger sons entered religion would suggest that Gornemant was the elder. I also see some possibility that, although Blancheflor praises her uncle Gornemant for being a very worthy, rich man, her contrast of the fine cheer he must lately have given Percivale with the poor fare that is all she has to give—most of it thanks to the charity of another and presumably less well-off uncle—might be construed as a veiled complaint against Gornemant. Against this interpretation we should weigh the fact that both Engygeron and Clamadeu fear to be sent prisoner to Gornemant because, in their war against Blancheflor, Engygeron has killed a(nother?) brother of Gornemant's. [Chrétien de Troyes, **Perceval**, ca. ll. 1910-1915; see also Engygeron; Clamadeu of the Isles]

BLANK, CASTLE

Sirs Bliant and Selivant, brothers, kept Sir Lancelot here for a time at their castle, nursing him during a fit of madness [Malory XII, 1-2]. Do not confuse Castle Blank with the castle of Bliant. In earlier versions they might have been the same, but in Malory they are different. Castle Blank might or might not have been near Listeneise.

"Blank" in Malorian names almost certainly means "white" (from the French *blanc*). For Castle Blank I tentatively suggest either Whitehaven on the coast of Cumberland or Barnard Castle in Durham, near the border of North Riding on the river Tees.

"BLAVINE"†

An unnamed female recluse who lived near enough the (commonest?) haunts of Breuse Sans Pitie to warn travelers against him. Unless Breuse's home territory was near the priory of the Queen of the Waste Lands, this likely was a different reclusive lady. [Vulgate III]

BLEEDING LANCE, THE

D.D.R. Owen points out in a note to line 3190 (& ff.) of Chrétien's **Perceval** that the bleeding lance described in this passage is not yet "recognisably" the spear of Longinus. As Chrétien describes it, it is pure white, with drops of blood forming, one at a time in succession, on its white tip to run along the shaft and onto the hand of the squire who bears it at the head of the Grail procession. Later, the young king of Escavalon sends Gawaine in search of the bleeding lance, identifying it as the weapon prophesied to demolish the realm of Logres. Curiously, the Escavalon people make no mention of the Grail, apparently regarding the lance strictly in its own right; and, whatever the object of the Grail quest—to see a vision, to bring the artifact back for safekeeping, or (as it appears in Chrétien's romance) simply to ask the right questions—the object of Gawaine's quest is definitely stated to be bringing the bleeding lance back to the king of Escavalon … who will, however, accept a year's honest but unfruitful searching as fulfillment of Gawaine's vow, in lieu of the lance itself. [**Perceval**, ca. ll. 3190-3202; 6162-6200]

See also Longinus' Spear.

Bleise—see **BLAISE**

Blenined—see **BENIGNE**

BLEOBERIS DE GANIS

red black silver

Godson of King Bors, brother to Sir Blamore de Ganis, and cousin to Lancelot; as Bleoberis explains the relationship, he and Blamore "be sister's children unto my lord Sir Lancelot du Lake."

Malory first mentions Bleoberis as standardbearer for his godfather in the battle of Bedegraine during the first rebellion of British kings against Arthur. Like his brother, Bleoberis became a knight of the Round Table.

One time, before King Mark's marriage with La Beale Isoud, Bleoberis rode into Mark's court, demanded a gift, and, on being granted it for the sake of his renown and his place as a knight of the Round Table, he helped himself to Sir Segwarides' wife as the fairest lady at court and rode off with her. Segwarides came to rescue his wife, and Bleoberis defeated him. Next Tristram, who was at the time her lover, came on the same errand and defeated Bleoberis. The lady, however, was miffed at Tristram for letting her husband attempt her rescue first and refused to return with Tristram, insisting instead that Bleoberis take her to the abbey where Segwarides lay wounded. Bleoberis complied. Another time, Lancelot and Bleoberis came upon Lamorak and Meliagrant in the midst of a battle over which queen was lovelier, Morgawse or Guenevere. Seeing Lancelot about to enter the fray on Meliagrant's side in defense of Guenevere's beauty, Bleoberis quelled the quarrel with some very sensible words:

> My lord Sir Launcelot, I wist you never so misadvised as ye are now … for I warn you I have a lady, and methinketh that she is the fairest lady of the world. Were this a great reason that ye should be wroth with me for such language?

Presumably the lady that Bleoberis mentions here is distinct from Segwarides' wife, but we never learn more about her.

Bleoberis and his brother arraigned King Anguish of Ireland, as described under Blamore. Bleoberis was castellan of Ganis Castle, probably in Cornwall and probably named after the kingdom of his godfather. Active in tournaments and in jousting adventures in the books of Tristram, and one of Guenevere's guests at the intimate dinner party when Sir Patrise was poisoned, Bleoberis later followed Lancelot into exile and was make Duke of Poitiers. Later still, he became one of the hermits at the grave of Arthur. At last, after Lancelot's death, Bleoberis joined his brother Blamore and their cousins Ector and Bors as crusaders in the Holy Land, thus becoming one of the last of Arthur's former knights of the Round Table to perish. [Malory II, 15; VIII, 15-18, 21-23; IX, 13-14, 37; XXI, 10, 13]

Blevine—see **BENIGNE**

BLIANT, CASTLE OF

Do not confuse with Sir Bliant's Castle Blank. The castle of Bliant was one of Pellam's castles, standing on an "island beclosed in iron, with a fair water deep and wide." Pellam gave the castle and island to Lancelot, who had just recovered from a long bout of madness, including a period of nursing at Castle Blank, and who thought he could never go back to Arthur's court. As Le Chavaler Mal Fet, Lancelot held Bliant against all jousters, naming it Joyous Isle and living here with Pellam's daughter Elaine. [Malory XII, 5-7]

Pick out a nice lake in the Lake District and put the Castle of Bliant on it. Alternatively, we could bend Malory a little here. Since it looks confusing to have Sir Bliant of Castle Blank and the castle of Bliant so closely connected in this account of Lancelot's madness, the names of the castles might be switched, giving Sirs Bliant and Selivant the castle of Bliant, and Pellam getting Castle Blank. Castle Blank might then be Whitehaven, and the Joyous Isle the shallow peninsula or headland surrounding it.

BLIOBLEHERIS†(?)

Among Arthur's knights in the list Chrétien de Troyes begins in line 1691 of **Erec & Enide**. Lacking any other evidence than similarity of name, I hesitate to identify Bliobleheris with Malory's Bleoberis de Ganis.

Bohart (le Cure Hardy)—see **BORRE**

Bohort—see **BORS**

BOILING WELL, FOREST OF THE

Sir Lancelot's grandfather, King Lancelot, had a great and honorable love for his cousin's beautiful, saintly wife. The cousin, a duke, misconstrued the relationship. As King Lancelot was on his way home through the perilous forest, he stopped to drink at a fountain. Here his cousin, the duke, ambushed him and cut off his head, which fell into the fountain. The fountain started to boil and scalded the duke's hands when he tried to remove the head. The duke and his men buried the king near the fountain. As they were entering their castle, a stone fell from the roof and killed them.

King Lancelot's widow erected a tomb. The tomb bled every day in several places, at the hour of the murder. Two lions fought fiercely over a stag near the tomb. They wounded each other grievously, but the drops of blood from the tomb healed them. Henceforth, they guarded the tomb, taking turns to hunt their food. A hermitage, also, was either near this site already or was built nearby in the years between King Lancelot and his more famous grandson.

When Sir Lancelot came to the well, having been directed by his grandfather in a dream, he killed the lions, retrieved his grandfather's head, opened the tomb, and, with the help of the hermit, reburied the body, with the head, at the front of the altar, where King Lancelot's wife was buried. Because Sir Lancelot was not pure, however, the water continued to boil. Only when Galahad arrived did the water cease boiling; the fountain was thereafter called Galahad's Fountain. [Vulgate I and V]

Malory omits the above history, but describes Galahad's coming to the place. Galahad departed from the "Abbey of King Mordrains"

> and so came into a perilous forest where he found the well the which boileth with great waves. ... And as soon as Galahad set his hand thereto it ceased, so that it brent no more, and the heat departed. For that it brent it was a sign of lechery, the which was that time much used. But that heat might not abide his pure virginity. And this was taken in the country for a miracle. And so ever after was it called Galahad's well. [Malory XVII, 18]

Because Malory's work seems largely a summarization, that Malory recounts Galahad's visit to the boiling well immediately after his visit to Mordrains' abbey does not necessarily mean they are in the same region. The Vulgate tells us that Lancelot lost his way while returning from this forest to Le Tertre Deuee and saw the white stag conducted by four lions. This appears to place the "Forest of the Boiling Well", the castle of Le Tertre Deuee, the abbey of la Petite Aumosne, and possibly King Vagor's Isle Estrange in the general vicinity of Carteloise Forest in southern Scotland.

BOIS EN VAL†

The illusory, magical lake in Benwick, Gaul, at the foot of a hill near Trebes Castle. Here the Damsel of the Lake took the young son of King Ban and Queen Elaine and disappeared with him into her lake, where she raised him. Of course, it only looked like a lake to the uninitiated; it was really a rich city.

Bois en Val means "Wood in a Valley."

BOOK CONTAINING THE HISTORY OF THE GRAIL, A†

Christ Himself wrote this book [Vulgate I].

BOOK OF THE FOUR EVANGELISTS (The Gospels), THE

Oaths were sworn upon this [cf. Malory III, 15]. Possibly any book may be used for swearing oaths upon.

> [Lancelot] made bring forth a book [and said] Here we are ten knights that will swear upon a book never to rest one night where we rest another this twelvemonth until that we find Sir Tristram. [Malory IX, 36]

BORRE (Bohart le Cure Hardy, Lohot, Loholz, Amyr?)

Arthur's son by his pre-Guenevere leman, Lyzianor, Sir Borre became "a good knight" and a companion of the Round Table [Malory I, 17]. Borre is probably identical with "Sir Bohart le Cure Hardy that was King Arthur's son", listed by Malory in XIX, 11. (Another knight with the surname "le Cure [Coeur] Hardy"—"the strong heart"—was Sir Ozanna, who seems to have been no relation to Borre.)

That Borre should be identified with Lohot, or Loholz, who appears in the Vulgate and is mentioned at least once by Chrétien de Troyes, is reasonably evident from the similarity of the mother's name in each instance. See Loholt; also see Amyr.

BORS (Bohort) DE GANIS

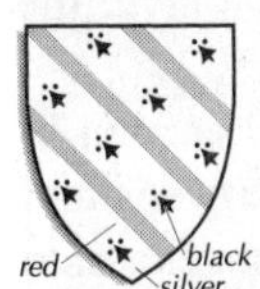

One of the major knights of the Round Table, Bors was the younger brother of Sir Lionel and a favorite cousin of Lancelot.

According to the Vulgate, after the death of King Bors, his sons Lionel and Bors the younger were taken by the father's conqueror, King Claudas. Seraide rescued the two children from Claudas and brought them to her mistress Viviane, the French Damsel of the Lake, to join their cousin Lancelot under Viviane's care.

Malory's first mention of Bors appears to be when Arthur sends him, with Lionel, Gawaine, and Bedivere, to carry a message of war to the Emperor Lucius. The four get the continental campaign against Rome off to a flying start. In battle with the Romans, Bors is named to Arthur's personal guard.

Sir Bors begat a child, Helin le Blank, on the daughter of King Brandegoris. Aside from this one lapse, Bors was celibate.

After Duke Galeholt's death, Seraide brought Galeholt's sword to Sir Bors, according to Vulgate IV.

Bors's prominence in Malory really begins in the Grail adventures. While on this quest, Bors championed the younger daughter of King Amans (Aniause). At the time, he was practicing ultra-austerity, eating only bread and water and sleeping on the floor. Vulgate VI tells us that when the lady gave him the best room in her castle and a splendid bed, he rumpled the bed to make it appear he had slept in it. Possibly he remembered that his hostess had seemed hurt when he ate only bread and water instead of the fine dinner she had prepared. In her castle, he had two dreams or visions, pointing out the choices he should make the next day after winning the battle of his hostess and leaving her. The choices were whether to save his own brother Lionel from a captor who was beating him with thorns or to save a virgin from deflowerment (Bors saved the virgin) and, afterward, whether to sleep with a temptress or allow her to jump from her tower and make her gentlewomen jump with her (he let them jump—they all turned out to be demons who disappeared on the way down).

Lionel later met Bors and attacked him in a towering rage for having been abandoned; Bors refused to defend himself against his brother until after an old holy man and a fellow companion of the Round Table had both been slaughtered trying to stop Lionel—then, when Bors at last took up weapon, a column of fire from Heaven intervened to stop the fight. None of Bors' decisions on this quest were made without much soul-searching, and he had also to undergo at least his share of false counsel by tempters in the guise of holy folk. Eventually joining Galahad, Percival, and Amide, Bors became the third of the three Round Table Knights to achieve fully the Holy Grail, and the only one of the three to return alive to Arthur's court.

Curiously, after the Grail Quest, we find Bors advising Lancelot in the latter's affair with Guenevere, and even acting as go-between and peacemaker for the pair of adulterers. Accompanying Lancelot into exile, he was made king of all of Claudas' lands. Bors appears to have acted as Lancelot's executive officer during the fighting with Arthur, and later when Lancelot returned after the deaths of Arthur and Mordred to put down the remnants of Mordred's rebellion. Bors was the first, according to Malory, to find and join Lancelot as another hermit in the retreat of the former Archbishop of Canterbury. After Lancelot's death, Bors returned to settle affairs in his own country, and from thence he went, with Ector, Blamore, and Bleoberis, to die on crusade in the Holy Land.

By the time of the Winchester tournament and the affair of Elaine of Astolat, Bors could be recognized by a distinctive scar on his forehead. [Malory V 6; XI, 4; XII, 9; XVI, 7-17; XVII-XXI; for the scar see XVIII, 15]

SIR BORS' FAMILY AND RETAINER
Father: King Bors
Mother: Queen Evaine
Brother: Lionel
Uncle: King Ban of Benwick
Aunt: Queen Elaine of Benwick
Cousins: Lancelot, Ector de Maris
Mentors: Lionses, Phariance, Viviane, Seraide
Paramour (one-night): King Brandegoris' Daughter
Son: Helin le Blank
Squire: Axilles
Would-be-lover?: Damsel of Hongrefort

BORS (Bohort), KING OF GAUL (Gannes)

With his brother, King Ban of Benwick, King Bors was one of Arthur's major allies during Arthur's wars of accession. Ban and Bors were instrumental in helping Arthur win the battle of Bedegraine against the first rebel alliance, but perished when Arthur failed to return the favor and aid them against their enemy, King Claudas.

King Bors married Evaine, the sister of his brother's wife Helayne (Elaine of Benwick). The sons of Bors and Evaine were Lionel and Sir Bors de Ganis. [Vulgate II-IV; Malory I, 10-15]

King Bors' Family and Retainers
Brothers: King Ban, Gwenbaus
Wife: Queen Evaine (Elaine of Benwick's sister)
Sons: Lionel, Sir Bors de Ganis
Sister-in-law: Queen Elaine of Benwick
Godson: Bleoberis de Ganis
Nephews: Lancelot, Ector de Maris
Retainers: Lionses?, Phariance

BOUDWIN, PRINCE

The good Prince Boudwin, well beloved by all the people of Cornwall, was King Mark's brother. Once, when the Saracens landed in Cornwall shortly after the Sessoins had gone, Boudwin "raised the country privily and hastily", put wildfire in three of his own ships, caused them to be driven among the ships of the Saracens, and so burned their entire navy. Then Boudwin and his men set on the Saracens and slew them all, to the number of forty thousand. Mark went wild with jealousy and murdered Boudwin. Boudwin's wife, Anglides, escaped with their young son, Alisander le Orphelin, to Magouns Castle. [Malory X, 32]

BOUDWIN'S DOUBLET AND SHIRT

Boudwin was murdered by his brother, King Mark. Boudwin's widow Anglides kept the bloody garments to give her son Alisander when he grew up and was of an age to think about avenging his father. [Malory X, 32-35]

This is similar to Sir La Cote Male Taile's wearing the coat in which his father was murdered until he could avenge that deed [Malory IX, 1].

BRAGWAINE

She was the chief gentlewoman of La Beale Isoud and accompanied her to Cornwall from Ireland. The Irish queen, Isoud's mother, entrusted Bragwaine and Gouvernail with a love potion to give Isoud on the day of her marriage with Mark to ensure their wedded love. I believe that in some versions Bragwaine's carelessness is blamed for Tristram's accidentally drinking the love potion with Isoud on shipboard, but Malory is careful not to fix blame on anyone for the mischance. Chrétien de Troyes, who apparently knew some version of the story, alludes to Bragwaine, here called Brangien, being substituted for her mistress Iseut on the latter's wedding night. [**Erec & Enide**, l. 2075]

Bragwaine seems to have been an herbwoman in her own right, as well as Isoud's well loved favorite. Once two other handwomen of Isoud's conspired to kill Bragwaine out of envy—she was sent into the forest near Mark's court to gather herbs and there waylaid and bound to a tree for three days until Sir Palomides fortunately came by and rescued her.

When La Beale Isoud heard of Tristram's marriage to Isoud la Blanche Mains, she sent Bragwaine to Brittany with letters to Tristram. Bragwaine returned to Cornwall with Tristram, Gouvernail, and Kehydius. On a later occasion, also carrying letters from La Beale Isoud to Tristram, Bragwaine found him on his way to the tournament at the Castle of Maidens. At his invitation she went with him, and was given a place near Guenevere during the tourney. Not long thereafter, Lancelot met Bragwaine fleeing as fast as her palfrey could go from Breuse Sans Pitie. Lancelot, of course, rescued her. [Malory VIII, 24, 29; IX, 10, 27, 32, 36]

Bragwaine appears to have been an interesting, capable, and discreet dame, as well as an adventurous one, or, at least, one who attracted adventure.

BRANDAN, SAINT†

A sixth-century saint who sailed west from Ireland into the Atlantic in search of the "Islands of Paradise."

Brandeban—see **BRANDELIS**

BRANDEGORIS (Brandegore, Brangoire), KING OF STRANGGORE

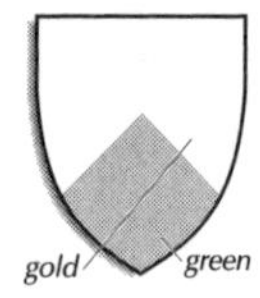

One of the rebel kings at the beginning of Arthur's reign, he pledged to bring 5,000 mounted men to the battle of Bedegraine. In that battle Brandegoris, King Idres, and King Agwisance unhorsed Sirs Griflet and Lucas. [Malory I, 12-15]

Surviving the battle, Brandegoris seems not to have joined the second coalition of rebel kings, for he is almost certainly to be identified with King Brandegore, on whose daughter Sir Bors begat a son, Helin le Blank. Bors revisited Brandegoris when Helin was fifteen years old and, with Brandegoris' consent, brought the boy to Arthur's court. King Brandegoris himself, however, seems never to have officially joined Arthur's court. [Malory XII, 9]

Brandegoris also fathered a son, Evadeam [Vulgate II].

BRANDEGORIS' DAUGHTER

She was to be the prize of a tournament at the Castel de la Marche, held for the purpose of getting her a good husband. Sir Bors won the tournament, but, having sworn to remain chaste all his life, cried off by pleading that he was not ready to take a wife until his current quest, to avenge King Agrippe's daughter, was done. Brandegoris's daughter fancied Bors. With the connivance of her old nurse, who gave Bors a ring to make him love the princess, the damsel spent that night with Bors, and Sir Helin le Blank was the result. The spell was broken in the morning when the ring fell off.

The twelve best knights of this tournament, after Bors, gave the princess "gifts" of varying silliness or bloodthirstiness. One, for instance, promised to cut off the heads of all the knights he conquered and send them to the princess.

The details given above come from Vulgate IV, but the princess is mentioned three or four times by Malory, once as the daughter of King Brandegore [XII, 9] and always as the mother of Helin le Blank.

BRANDELIS (Brandeban, Brandeharz, Brandelz)†

He was the Duke of Taningues [Vulgate IV].

BRANDES, COUNT OF GLOUCESTER†

Chrétien lists him among the counts and other lords, vassals of Arthur, summoned to court for Erec's wedding. Along with his retinue, Brandes brought 100 spare horses. [**Erec & Enide**, ll. 1934-1962] Tentatively, I resist identifying him with any of the several characters of similar name found in the Vulgate and Malory.

BRANDIGANT†

The castle of King Evrain, situated on an island four leagues across, in a river about thirty Welsh leagues from Guivret the Little's castle of Penevric. Brandigant was so strong and self-sufficient that Guivret assured Erec it needed fear no siege or attack whatever. The river alone would have proved a barrier equal to any assault, but Evrain fortified his castle because he thought it more attractive that way. Happily, Evrain was a friendly and hospitable monarch, and seemingly much regretted that his nephew Mabonagrain guarded one of his gardens, to the deadly peril of visiting knights. [Chrétien de Troyes, **Erec & Enide**, ll. 5367-6155] See "Garden of the Joy."

The similarity of Brandigant and Evrain to Gore and Bademagu in Chrétien's later romance **Lancelot** is hard to miss.

BRANDILES

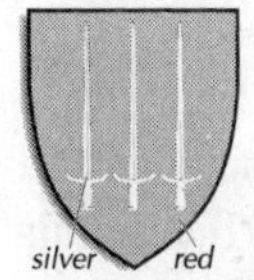

Malory mentions this knight of the Round Table perhaps half a dozen times. He was one of the knights invited to Guenevere's small, select dinner party [XVIII,3], one of the party who were a-Maying with Guenevere when Meliagrant ambushed them [XIX, 1], and one of those killed during Lancelot's rescue of the Queen from the stake [XX, 8]. Sir Brandiles' sister was Gawaine's lady and the mother of Gawaine's sons Florence and Lovel [XIX, 11].

In the Vulgate, Floree, daughter of King Alain of Escavalon, is named as the mother of Gawaine's oldest son Guinglain. Assuming Guinglain to be Malory's Gingalin, Floree might be identified with Sir Brandiles' sister, making Brandiles the son of King Alain. See Floree.

In the metrical romance **The Wedding of Sir Gawaine and Dame Ragnell**, Ragnell is made the mother of Guinglain. (It would seem from the names, however, that Floree must have been the mother of at least one of Gawaine's sons, Sir Florence.) In another, fragmentary romance collected by Hall, one Sir Brandles appears as the son of Sir Gilbert and brother of Sirs Gyamoure and Terry. This Brandles fights Gawaine for deflowering his chance-met sister (who clearly enjoyed it), proves Gawaine's equal, and parts from him at nightfall with the mutual promise to finish the fight another time; Brandles then beats his sister and abandons her. Sir Brandelys is one of Arthur's knights in **Sir Gawain and the Carl of Carlisle**. See Louis B. Hall, **The Knightly Tales of Sir Gawain.**

BRANDILES' SISTER

Either one of Gawaine's wives or one of his favorite paramours, since according to Malory she bore Gawaine two sons, Sirs Florence and Lovel [Malory XIX, 11]. Probably she should be identified with Floree; see also Brandiles.

BRANDUS DES ILLES†

The lord of Dolorous Garde before Lancelot conquered it. Brandus fled before Lancelot, tried to attack Arthur, and shortly thereafter, disguised as a vavasour, invited Gawaine, Ywaine, and their companions to La Dolorous Chartre, where they met some of their companions alive whose names they had read on false graves at Dolorous Garde. What Brandus had not told Gawaine and Ywaine was that he intended to imprison them, too, in Dolorous Chartre. Lancelot rescued them. [Vulgate III]

Brandus may perhaps be identified with Malory's Sir Brian of the Isles.

Brangien—see BRAGWAINE

Brangoire—see BRANDEGORIS

BRASIAS, SIR

A hermit living near Windsor, he hosted Lancelot when the latter left Arthur's court in London after a quarrel with Guenevere. (It was this quarrel that led to the dinner at which Sir Patrise was poisoned, for Guenevere gave the dinner "to show outward that she had as great joy in all other knights of the Round Table as she had in Sir Lancelot.") [Malory XVIII, 2-5, 21].

Brasias probably is to be identified with Sir Brastias.

BRASTIAS

Brastias originally was a knight of Duke Gorloïs. Merlin disguised Sir Ulfius as Sir Brastias on the night Uther begat Arthur. Later, on his accession to the throne, Arthur made Brastias "warden to wait upon the north from Trent forwards, for it was that time the most party the king's enemies." Brastias served Arthur well in the first wave of rebellion. With Ulfius, Brastias traveled across the Channel to summon Kings Ban and Bors to Arthur's aid. On the way, the two of them had to joust down eight of King Claudas' knights who tried to stop them. Brastias fought in the battle of Bedegraine, but afterward seems to drop out of Malory's account, with no mention that he remained with Arthur long enough to serve at the Round Table. [Malory I, 2, 7, 10-14] Brastias must already have been at least approaching middle age by the time of Arthur's coronation, and he may have retired early into a hermitage. He probably is to be identified with the hermit Brasias of Malory's Book XVIII.

BRAVAÏN†

Bravaïn is among Arthur's knights in the list Chrétien de Troyes begins in line 1691 of **Erec & Enide**.

BREON THE SON OF CANODAN†

Among Arthur's knights in the list Chrétien de Troyes begins in line 1691 of **Erec & Enide**.

BRESQUEHAN†

This forest is near the River Saverne (Severn?). A little river running through the Bresquehan formed the boundary between Norgales and Cambenic. [Vulgate II; III, p. 310]

Breunis Saunce Pit—see **BREUSE SANS PITIE**

BREUNOR

He was the wicked lord of Castle Pluere and, according to Malory, Duke Galeholt's father. Do not confuse this Sir Breunor with Sir Breunor le Noir, who is La Cote Male Taile.

Breunor le Noir—see **COTE MALE TAILE, LA**

BREUSE SANS PITIE (Breunis Saunce Pit, Bruns Saunce Pit, Bruns Saunce Pité)

The "most mischievoust knight living" in Arthur's day, Sir Breuse, while not without skill and prowess at arms, regularly practiced every dirty trick available to force or guile. He even enlisted the aid of other knights by claiming that he was an innocent victim and the knight chasing him was Breuse Sans Pitie (the unreliability of shields as identify-

ing devices enabled him to get away with this one for a while). Among his favorite tricks was riding over an unhorsed knight; on one occasion, for instance, Breuse outjousted Gawaine and then rode over him twenty times in an effort to kill him.

Although he had at least one castle somewhere, Breuse seems likely to turn up almost anywhere; attack, kidnap, murder, and rape anyone, child or adult, for the sheer deviltry of it; and then disappear again, often pursued but never brought finally to justice. Unlike almost all other villains in Malory, Breuse seems never to be captured, utterly defeated, and either slain or converted to Arthur's side and the company of the Round Table. (Of course, Breuse was not afraid to turn tail and run when occasion demanded—but see the Brown Knight Without Pity.)

In one passage, Malory gives Breuse a brother, Bertelot, but Bertelot is not nearly so prominent. Another time, King Mark writes to Morgan le Fay and the Queen of Norgales begging them to rouse up Breuse Sans Pitie, among others, in a general manhunt for Alisander le Orphelin. [Malory IX, 26; X, 1, 35, 53; XII, 2; etc.]

In Vulgate VII I found what seemed to be a hint that Breuse was allied with the Saxons, but of this I am even less sure than of most data I took from the text of that volume.

The fifteenth-century Catalan romance **Tirant Lo Blanc** shows Breuse, or Breunis, in an unexpectedly good light, as the single aged, and obviously loyal, attendant of King Arthur. (See Arthur.)

BREUSE SANS PITIE'S CASTLE

Searching for Lancelot, Tristram "rode by a forest, and then was he ware of a fair tower by a marsh on that one side, and on that other side a fair meadow." Before the tower Breuse Sans Pitie and eight of his knights were attacking Palomides, all at once. When Tristram came to the rescue, he drove Breuse and his men into the tower, which suggests this was Breuse's own stronghold. [Malory X, 1-2] The last place Tristram is known to have been before this was the Castle of the Hard Rock, but he might have come any distance from there to this tower.

Surely the infamous Breuse Sans Pitie had one or two castles tucked away about the island. I suspect that at least one of them would have been in or on the edge of the Saxon lands, for there is evidence that Breuse was allied with the Saxons on at least one occasion.

Brewnor le Noir—see **COTE MALE TAILE, LA**

Briades†—see under **DEUX SYCAMORES, FONTAINE DES**

BRIAN OF THE ISLES

Lord of the castle of Pendragon, Sir Brian was "a noble man and a great enemy unto King Arthur." He collected knights and ladies as his prisoners, among them La Cote Male Taile. Lancelot delivered the prisoners, fighting Brian until the latter yielded rather than be killed. Learning who it was that had defeated him, "Sir Brian [was] full glad, and so was his lady, and all his knights, that such a man should win them." Lancelot departed with La Cote Male Taile and his damsel on other adventures. Possibly Sir Brian made a show of changing his ways and was left for a time in charge of his castle. However,

> as Sir Lancelot came by the Castle of Pendragon [on his return to Arthur's court] there he put Sir Brian de les Isles from his lands, for cause he would never be withhold with King Arthur; and all that Castle of Pendragon and all the lands thereof he gave to Sir La Cote Male Taile [Malory IX, 6, 9].

This may be the same Sir Brian of the Isles whom Malory introduces, much earlier, as sworn brother to Nimue's cousin Sir Meliot de Logres, and who appears again at the tournament at Dame Lyonors' Castle Dangerous, fighting against Arthur's side [Malory III, 13; VII, 28]. There are, however, many minor knights named Brian or Briant in Malory. I suspect that Brian of the Isles may be identified with the Vulgate's Sir Brandus des Illes, the former lord of La Dolorous Garde and Dolorous Chartre.

BRIEN†

Brien was a giant, half a foot taller than any (other?) knight in Arthur's kingdom, yet full brother of King Bilis, who was the smallest of all the dwarfs and a vassal of Arthur's. Chrétien mentions Brien in **Erec & Enide**, lines 1963-2024; I cannot tell whether he is named as one of the kings summoned to Erec's wedding or merely as Bilis' brother, nor am I sure whether or not he should be identified with Chrétien's Briien of the double "i."

BRIESTOC†

Apparently this was in the vicinity of the Dolorous Tower, for the Lady of Briestoc lost all her knights while attempting to rescue Gawaine from Carados [Vulgate IV]. It is possible that Briestoc could be counted as a subkingdom, but one can more easily imagine Carados destroying the force of a single castle than that of an entire subkingdom.

If Turquine's Hill is accepted as Cadbury, and Carados' Dolorous Tower put somewhere in the middle of modern Devonshire, the Briestoc might be identified with Botreaux. On the other hand, if Botreaux were Briestoc, the lady would have had troublesome neighbors at Tintagil—

first the giants and later King Mark—too close for her to be that concerned about Carados farther away. Almost due south of Tintagil, about eight miles from the tip of the southern coast of Cornwall, is Brodock, or Brotheck. Norden lists it only as a parish, but the name is at least as close as "Botreaux" to "Briestoc."

BRIESTOC, LADY OF†

Apparently a sovereign lady, she lost all her knights while attempting to rescue Gawaine from Carados of the Dolorous Tower [Vulgate IV].

BRIIEN [with two "i's"]†

Among Arthur's knights in the list Chrétien de Troyes begins in line 1691 of **Erec & Enide**.

Brinos de Plessie—see BROMEL LA PLECHE

BRISEN (Brisane)

Dame Brisen, "one of the greatest enchantresses that was at that time in the world living", came to King Pellam and offered to arrange matters so that his daughter Elaine could lie with Lancelot. Pellam setting them up in his nearby Castle of Case for the trick, Brisen had a message brought to Lancelot by a man in the likeness of one he knew well, who brought him a ring that looked like one of Guenevere's and told him that his lady awaited him in Case Castle. When he arrived, Brisen gave Lancelot a cup of wine, which may have been drugged, before sending him upstairs to Elaine, who was already abed. Some time later, Brisen accompanied Elaine as handmaiden to Arthur's court for the festivities celebrating the victory over Claudas of France. Again Brisen helped her mistress enjoy Lancelot's love, this time, apparently, through simple intrigue. Elaine's chamber was next to the Queen's, Lancelot and Guenevere planned to sleep together, and Brisen simply beat Guenevere's messenger to Lancelot and guided him to Elaine's room instead. Lancelot went mad after that night's wor, and turned up, a few years later, at Carbonek, where eventually Dame Brisen recognized him and tactfully cast him into an enchanted sleep for an hour until he could be carried before the Sangreal, which healed him. [Malory XI, 2, 7-8; XII, 4]

BRITAIN

Having married Laudine, Ywaine requests her permission to leave her castle and lands in order to "return to Britain" and make the round of tournaments [Chrétien de Troyes, **Yvain**, ll. 2503-ca.2540]. If it is not reading too much into a twentieth-century translation of a twelfth-century romance, this sounds as if "Britain" was understood as including only those territories actually governed by Arthur and his pledged vassals—of whom Dame Laudine was not one, cordial though their relations had become by the time Ywaine asked his year's leave of absence.

BRITTANY (Little Britain)

Also called Armorica in the old days, I assume it was in about the same place but with more territory than the modern province. Brittany, not Great Britain, may well have been the birthplace of Arthurian romance as we know it. France and Brittany almost surely contain such important sites as Broceliande Forest and the lake in which Lancelot was raised. Sometimes, indeed, the reader of old romances hardly can be sure whether the author had British or Breton places in mind. My putting one Benoye or Benwick in Britain and another in France, and a magical Lake with its Damsel on both sides of the Channel, ultimately may be the result of a fusion or confusion of British and French sites in the original romances.

The works of Chrétien de Troyes indicate Brittany as among Arthur's lands, describing two of his visits there, at both of which his Breton subjects rejoice. One occurs when Arthur for some reason, perhaps topical to Chrétien's own time, chooses Nantes in Brittany for the site of Erec's coronation as king of Outre-Gales. [**Erec & Enide**, ll. 6533 ff., & Owen's note to l. 6549] During Alexander's time with Arthur, which we may suppose to take place before Erec's adventures, when Arthur wishes to pay Brittany a visit, he consults his lords as to whom he should leave in charge of Britain. (They unwisely choose Count Angrs.) Both the care Arthur uses to select a regent and the time he plans to stay suggest that Brittany was not part of his regular yearly round: he spends the entire summer and might have been about to spend the winter as well, had it not been for his regent's rebellion. Arthur musters men from all of Brittany to swell his army before returning to deal with Angrs. [**Cligés,** ll. 422-440; ca. 570; 1047-ca. 1093]

In **Yvain**, however, Chrétien certainly appears to move Broceliande Forest into England.

BROCELIANDE, BULLHERD OF†

On their way from the vavasour of Broceliande to the storm-making spring, knights met a gigantic and hideous churl herding wild bulls in a clearing. The giant was seventeen feet tall, dark-skinned and black-bearded, with a bald forehead more than two spans wide. Hair grew in tufts on the rest of his head; his ears were mossy and elephantine, his brows heavy, his face flat, his chin running into his chest, his eyes owl-like, his nose catlike, his mouth wolf-like, his teeth boar-like, his mustache tangled, his spine humped and twisted, and his clothing the recently flayed hides of two bulls.

Despite his fierce appearance and great club, he seemed ready to answer questions, if not politely, at least fully and peaceably. He showed himself quite ready to explain how he handled his animals by teaching them to fear his superior strength, and to provide directions to the spring, which he described to the best of his uneducated ability: he called the bubbling of the spring "boiling" although the water was colder than marble; characterized the pine simply as a tree that kept its leaves all year; called the gold basin iron; and did not recognize the material (emerald) from which the slab was made. D.D.R. Owen surmises that this giant was originally a denizen of the Celtic otherworld; his description of the spring seems to provide a study in how lack of sophistication can magnify the merely marvelous into the totally inexplicable. [Chrétien de Troyes, **Yvain**, ll. 269-409 & Owen's notes]

BROCELIANDE, FOREST OF†

This is in the Morbihan, next to Cornuailles in Brittany [Glennie, 13]. Here is found the consecrated fountain of Balanton, and here Merlin "drees his weird."

The fountain of Balanton appears to be where Merlin met his lady Viviane, and around which he made to spring up an enchanted Garden of Joy to please her.

BROCELIANDE, VAVASOUR OF, and HIS DAUGHTER†

Either on the edge or in a large clearing of Broceliande Forest lay a heath with a moated wooden fortress, kept by a courteous vavasour who summoned his people by striking thrice on a gong of pure copper. He had a tall, slender, and beautiful daughter of courtesy equal to his own. Together, they gave Calogrenant, Ywaine, and any other passing knights hospitality, asking them to return if possible and recount their adventures. Nor did the father and daughter show any less courtesy and good cheer to Calogrenant when he returned on foot to describe his defeat by the guardian of the marvelous spring, which lay near enough to make the round trip within one day. Indeed, they congratulated him on being the first they knew of to escape death or capture in that place. Had the story been written in our century, it seems doubtful that they would have faded from it with no later mention. [Chrétien de Troyes, **Yvain**, ll. 175-269; 548-580; 777- ca. 800]

BROKEN SWORD WHEREWITH JOSEPH WAS STRICKEN THROUGH THE THIGH

At Mategrant's castle, in Broceliande, the seneschal broke this sword while wounding Joseph of Arimathea in the thigh with it. Joseph miraculously extracted the broken piece of metal from his wound and predicted that the sword would never be joined until the one handled it who would achieve the Grail. The broken sword was held in great honor at Mategrant's castle, at least for a while. [Vulgate I] Later, Sir Eliazer brought it from Mategrant's castle to Carbonek [Vulgate IV].

Malory omits this early history of the sword, but tells how Eliazer, Pellam's son, brought it forth for Galahad and his companions to attempt mending it. After Bors and Percivale tried unsuccessfully, Galahad soldered the broken pieces by simply setting them together with his hands. [Malory XVII, 19]

Kissing this sword would keep whomever kissed it safe from being mortally wounded for the day [Vulgate IV].

BROMEL LA PLECHE (Brinos de Plessie, Brunout, Bruiol de Plessie)

After Galahad's birth, Sir Bromel, "a great lord" who had long loved Elaine of Carbonek, came to ask her to marry him. At last, trying to be rid of him, she told him she loved Lancelot. Bromel threatened to slay Lancelot. When Elaine exhorted him to do the great knight no treason, he vowed, "this twelvemonth I shall keep the pont [bridge] of Corbin for Sir Lancelot's sake, that he shall neither come nor go unto you, but I shall meet with him." Sir Bors happened to come first, however, defeated Bromel, and charged him to go the following Whitsunday to Lancelot and yield to him as knight miscreant. [Malory XI, 3-4] According to the Vulgate, in which his name is Brunout or variants thereof, Elaine tells him she will love him instead of Lancelot if he proves himself better. When Brunout arrives in Camelot on Whitsunday, he comes in time to join Arthur's troops in the war against King Claudas. [Vulgate V]

BROWN KNIGHT WITHOUT PITY

The Brown Knight had a castle somewhere in the vicinity of the Duke de la Rowse, and his hobby was slaying other knights and imprisoning their ladies. He had collected thirty ladies when Gareth came by and slew him. [Malory VII, 32] If he had not been slain, I would have identified him with Breuse Sans Pitie.

BRUIANT OF THE ISLES†

This knight gave two magnificent gold and ivory thrones to Arthur and Guenevere as a gift [Chrétien de Troyes, **Erec & Enide**, ll. 6713-6735]. Because the giving of such a gift hardly seems compatible with either villainy or enmity to Arthur, I hesitate to identify Chrétien's Bruiant with Malory's Brian of the Isles, especially considering how often the surname "of the Isles" appears in the romances. The thrones, indeed, strike me as enough to identify Bruiant as among Arthur's allies. See Arthur's Ivory Thrones.

Bruiol de Plessie—see **BROMEL LA PLECHE**

BRUMANT L'ORGUILLEUS†

He was a nephew of King Claudas. One Eastertime, the knights of Claudas' court were discussing who was the best knight of the world. Everyone said it was Lancelot except Brumant, who said it was not Lancelot because Lancelot had never dared sit in the Siege Perilous. Although Claudas tried to dissuade him, Brumant swore to sit in the Siege Perilous on Whitsunday. By the time Brumant arrived at Camelot, he was weeping. (Perhaps he had sobered up and realized what kind of vow he had sworn.) He gave Lancelot a letter, telling him to read it in the event of Brumant's death. Then, saying, "I shall die for doing what you never ventured to do", Brumant sat in the Siege Perilous. A fire fell on him, from whence no one knew. It gave him just time to say, "By pride one gets but shame. I die by God's vengeance", before it consumed him to ashes. An evil smell filled the hall, but passed quickly. All the knights moved away from the holocaust except Lancelot, who, refusing to move from his own chair beside the Siege Perilous, remained unharmed. The letter Brumant had given Lancelot told the whole story of the rash vow. When Brumant's three brothers got the news from England, they took comfort in the thought that Brumant's was an honorable death. [Vulgate V]

BRUN OF PICIEZ†

Brun and his brother Grus the Wrathful are among Arthur's knights in the list Chrétien de Troyes begins in line 1691 of **Erec & Enide**.

Brunout—see **BROMEL LA PLECHE**

Bruns Saunce Pit(é)—see **BREUSE SANS PITIE**

BURNING TOMB, ABBEY OF THE

This white abbey is in the land of Gore. Here both Lancelot and later Galahad found the tomb of King Bagdemagus, slain by Sir Gawaine during the Grail Adventures. [Malory XVII, 17, 18]

Malory, however, not only never describes the actual killing—which is not unusual; Malory has many characters, including Tristram, killed "offstage"—but also resurrects Bagdemagus during Arthur's war with Lancelot, in XX, 19. Sommer failed to find Gawaine's alleged slaying of Bagdemagus actually described in the Vulgate manuscripts, either.

More important than Bagdemagus' tomb, in this same abbey is a burning tomb wherein a soul in torment has been waiting 354 years for Galahad to release him from the punishment he had incurred for sinning against Joseph of Arimathea—apparently some sort of private purgatory. [Malory XVII, 18] See also Abbey of the Adventurous Shield.

BYANNE†

The daughter of King Clamadon, Byanne may or may not have been responsible for the magic in her tale. She first appeared at Arthur's court with her lover Evadeam, son of King Brangoire (Brandegoris), Evadeam being in the form of an ugly dwarf. Byanne insisted, despite Kay's chaffing, that Arthur dub her dwarf knight. She herself fixed his left spur, while the King fixed his right. They did not give their names, but Merlin said the dwarf was highly born. After leaving court, Evadeam defeated at least one knight, Tradelmant, the grandson of the King of Norgales, and sent him back to Arthur's court. Later, while searching for Merlin, Ywaine and his companions met Byanne, who begged them to succor her dwarf. When they arrived, however, Evadeam had defeated five attacking knights all by himself.

Later, while Gawaine was riding around the woods in a reverie, he passed Byanne without saluting her. As a punishment, she told him he would for a time resemble the next person he met. That person was Evadeam, still in dwarf form. Wandering in the shape of the dwarf, Gawaine came near the place of Merlin's imprisonment. Merlin sent greetings to the King and Queen, and said that no one would ever hear his voice again. Later still, Gawaine met a damsel (I presume Byanne again) beset by two knights and succored her. She had set it up to test him, enchanting the knights so that they could not be hurt. After swearing to help every damsel and never to forget to bow to any woman, Gawaine regained his true form. [Vulgate II]

I consider Byanne to be among the possible potential female knights on the grounds that she served her knighted dwarf in the capacity of a squire. She may also, of course, be considered an enchantress.

CADOALANT†

Chrétien names this king as a very valiant and wise ally of Arthur's. He was present at Erec's coronation, going with three others to escort Enide to the hall. [**Erec & Enide**, ll. 311-341; 6810-6855]

CADOC OF TABRIOL AND HIS LADY†

On Erec's third day of adventuring with his wife to prove his prowess, they met Sir Cadoc's lady weeping because two giants had just captured her lover. Erec gave pursuit and found Cadoc, naked, bound, and perched on a nag, his captors beating him with scourges until the blood ran. Erec challenged, battled, and killed both giants, armed though they were with great, iron-shod clubs. Then he gave the grateful Cadoc back to his lady, requesting them to take the story to King Arthur, which they did. If the usual pattern holds, Cadoc and his lady would then have joined Arthur's court. [Chrétien de Troyes, **Erec & Enide**, ll. 4306-4577]

CADOR OF CORNWALL

The father of that Sir Constantine who was king after Arthur, Cador appears in Malory V as a knight of the Round Table, one of Arthur's counselors, and a trusty officer in the war against Emperor Lucius. The name may be a variant of "Carados"—in Malory XIX,11, Constantine is called "Sir Carados' son of Cornwall." Do not confuse Cador of Cornwall with Carados of Scotland or with Carados of the Dolorous Tower.

CADORCANIOIS, COUNT†

Among Arthur's knights in the list Chrétien de Troyes begins in line 1691 of **Erec & Enide**.

CADRET†

A much-feared knight, son of King Aguisel of Scotland and brother of Coi. Cadret and Coi accompanied their father to Arthur's court for Erec's wedding. [**Erec & Enide**, ll. 1963-2024]

CAERLEON (Carlion)

Located on the Usk River above the Severn estuary in Monmouthshire, Wales, this city is sometimes called Caerleon-upon-Usk. By Vulgate III, this was Arthur's favorite city in which to hold court. After Camelot, it is still possibly Arthur's most famous court city. In some romances, indeed, it eclipses Camelot. As a fortress, Malory tells us that it "has a strong tower" [I, 8].

In his **Lancelot**, ll. 31-34, Chrétien de Troyes mentions that King Arthur has just left Caerleon to hold court at Camelot, making it sound as though the two are in geographical proximity. Again, he makes it the city in which the Haughty Knight of the Heath and his damsel find Arthur holding a small and intimate little court of only 3,000 famous knights [**Perceval**, ll. 4004ff.].

Cai—see **KAY**

Caitis, Tertre as†—see **DRUAS' HILL**

CALCEDOR FROM AFRICA†

One of Alexander's twelve companions who accompanied him from Greece to Britain, where Arthur knighted them all at the outset of Count Angrs' rebellion, Calcedor was killed by Angrs himself during the climactic fighting. Calcedor's tincture was apparently gold. [Chrétien de Troyes, **Cligés**, ll. 102-385; 1093-1932]

Caliburn—see **EXCALIBUR**

CALLES, DUKE†

Duke Calles wanted to settle half his land on his daughter upon her marriage. When his three sons opposed the idea, he disinherited them in favor of the daughter. They surprised her husband in a wood and murdered him, then seized many of the Duke's castles. Gareth, Gaheris, and Agravaine arrived at the castle in which the Duke's sons were besieging their own father, and entered on the side of Calles. The first day they fought Gareth killed one of the sons. Lancelot and Lionel arrived in company with "Ornagrine." These two knights, hearing a false account of the war, entered on the side of the rebellious sons and killed the Duke. [Vulgate V]

CALOGRENANT† (Galogrinans, Colgrevance?)

This good-looking and seemingly good-natured knight of Arthur's appears in the opening of Chrétien's **Yvain**, where he tells a group of notable auditors, including Ywaine, Dodinel, Sagramore, Kay, Gawaine, and, eventually, Guenevere, the story of his adventures seven years earlier in Broceliande Forest. These adventures duplicate those his cousin Ywaine later seeks and completes, except that Calogrenant was defeated by the champion of the marvelous spring—so that in retelling the story his aim is to inform and entertain, rather than boast. If Loomis (as cited by D.D.R. Owen) is correct is seeing Calogrenant as a doubling of Kay (*Cai–lo–grenant*, "Kay the grumbler"), then Calogrenant looks like the "good" alter ego, possessing virtues that are the reverse of Kay's notorious faults. According to this fascinating theory, the words that Kay and Calogrenant exchange would provide a study in argument with one's self more interesting, probably, to our modern tastes than are the various long soliloquies of some of Chrétien's other characters, and foreshadowing such modern works as Poe's **William Wilson** and Stevenson's **Dr. Jekyll and Mr. Hyde**.

Returning to more solid ground, I hazard the guess that Calogrenant must be Ywaine's first cousin on King Uriens' side, since he seems to be identified as Ywaine's cousin but not as Gawaine's [**Yvain**, ll. 42-ca. 582, and Owen's notes].

My earlier edition identified Calogrenant with Malory's Sir Colgrevance of Gore. My confidence in that identification is no longer unqualified.

CAMBENET

This territory, as far as Malory is concerned, sems to rate mention only in the title of Duke Eustace of Cambenet [I, 14; "Duke Cambines" appears in X, 49].

According to the Vulgate, Cambenic is a rich and prosperous city, and the name of its duke is Escan [Vulgate II]. Cambenic seems to be on or near the Severn River, for when King Lot and his sons helped Duke Escan, they drove the Sesnes into the Severn. A little river running through Bresquehan Forest formed the boundary between Norgales and Cambenic [Vulgate III]. This suggests that Cambenic was the southern half of Shropshire, possibly also including Herefordshire or the northern part thereof.

I assume that Escan is to be identified with Eustace and Cambenic with Cambenet. To save both names, Cambenet might be applied to the whole territory of the dukedom and Cambenic to its principal castle-city.

Cambenet, Duke of—see EUSTACE

Cambenic—see under CAMBENET

Cambines, Duke—see under EUSTACE

CAMELIARD (Carmelide)

The Vulgate identifies the kingdom of Arthur's father-in-law, Leodegrance, as the territory between Bedingran (Sherwood Forest) and King Ryons' country (Norgales). Thus, Cameliard would include the eastern half of Cheshire joined to Derbyshire or the western half of Derbyshire, arching above Staffordshire so as not to cut into the territory of Bertilak de Hautdesert and the Green Chapel.

CAMELOT

According to D.D.R. Owen, when Chrétien de Troyes begins his romance **Lancelot** with Arthur's court at Camelot on Ascension Day, it is the earliest known mention of this city. Chrétien remarks that Arthur had just left Caerleon, another of his famous court cities, which suggests that the two lie in geographical proximity. The way in which Chrétien simply drops the name in, without elaboration, seeming to make nothing special of it, suggests to me either that he had some specific place in mind and may not have gotten its name quite right, or that "Camelot" was in fact already established in whatever sources—now lost—he may have used. Neither of these possibilities precludes the other.

The debate as to where Camelot really was may never be decided. Malory, however, twice clearly identifies it as Winchester [II, 19 and XVIII, 8]. The major church of Camelot is Saint Stephen's, where Arthur and Guenevere were married.

Though today the word "Camelot" has become virtually synonomous with "King Arthur", I cannot perceive that in the medieval material it is more than just another one of Arthur's many court cities. It looks to me as if the puzzle over its actual identity has enhanced its mystique far beyond its medieval importance.

CAMILLE†

An enchantress of Saxon descent, she held the castle of La Roche and helped her people against Arthur. At the same time she loved Arthur—which did not prevent her having a lover, Gadrasolain, in the castle.

After a battle with the Saxons, Arthur accepted an invitation to visit Camille in La Roche. He had a good time with her, but afterward he and Gaheris were captured with the help of Hargodabran and forty knights. A damsel of Camille's went to Lancelot, Duke Galeholt, Gawaine, and Ector, telling them that Camille meant to convey Arthur to Ireland. These four knights came into La Roche to save Arthur. The damsel's tale had been a ruse which enabled Camille to capture them also. She released Lancelot, however, who was demented with grief at being captured. Lancelot, wearing Arthur's arms and using Arthur's sword Sequence, grievously wounded Hargodabran in battle and then penetrated into La Roche, where he killed Gadrasolain and many others, and freed Arthur with his companions. Threatening to kill Camille unless she surrendered the castle, Arthur left Gawaine, whom she feared more than any other knight, in charge of La Roche. Kay found a former sweetheart of Gadrasolain's. This damsel, whom Camille had kept imprisoned for three years, warned Kay that if Camille escaped with her books and boxes all was lost. Kay burned the books and boxes. Camille, to Arthur's grief, threw herself from the rocks and perished.

It was after this episode that Lancelot, Galeholt, and Ector became members of Arthur's court (and of the Round Table at once?). [Vulgate III]

CAMPACORENTIN†

In this forest an unnamed knight, chasing an assailant, came upon two damsels bathing. One of them shot him in the thigh with an arrow which appears to have been magic, for only the best knight in the world could draw it out. The wounded knight went to Arthur's court looking for help; since Lancelot was absent, no one could help him. Returning to his own castle, he met Lancelot; since Lancelot was traveling incognito, the wounded knight refused to believe he was good enough to make the attempt. Later, learning that the incognito knight had been Lancelot, the wounded knight set off in his litter to find him again. Eventually he found him at La Fontaine des Deux Sycamors and was delivered of the arrow. Some manuscripts call the forest of the bathing damsels "la forest perilleuse." The wounded knight's own castle was apparently not far from King Vagor's Isle Estrange, which may put it and hence the forest of Campacorentin somewhere in southern Scotland. [Vulgate IV]

Canains—see KANAHINS

Canguin, Ferryman of—see FERRYMAN ...

CANGUIN (Chanpguin, Sanguin), ROCK OF†

The castle of Queen Ygerne (Igraine), near the Galloway border. D.D.R. Owen prefers the Chanpguin spelling; Roach and Cline use "Canguin", which seems to me far easier on the modern eye and tongue—although the "Sanguin" variation is tempting, for its double sound of blood and hope. Igraine's "retirement home", if so I may call it, smacks more than a little of otherworldly connections, perhaps even forming a branch of the more or less Christianized Afterlife; even Owen, while apparently preferring the theory that the Gawaine adventures were originally intended to form a separate romance, points out the parallel between Igraine's Canguin and the Fisher King's Grail Castle. [Chrétien de Troyes, **Perceval**, ll. 7233 on, & Owen's notes to 7233 & 8817]

See Igraine, Igraine's Clerk, the Ferryman of Canguin, and the Wondrous Bed.

CANODAN†

Parent of Arthur's knight Breon [Chrétien de Troyes, **Erec & Enide**, ll. 1691-1750].

CANTERBURY

Although I do not find that Malory states Arthur held court here, it may well have been a court city. Mordred had himself crowned king and apparently held his parliament here, and also retreated here after the battle of Dover. Mordred's alliance with the Saxons works in with an identification of Kent as Saxon (Sessoin) territory. The name may also be applicable to the "Saxon shore" of Britain.

Chrétien de Troyes gives Canterbury a brief mention in **Cligés**, when messengers from London and Canterbury reach Arthur in Brittany with news of Count Angrs' rebellion. [ca. l. 1057]

As the seat of the Archbishop, this city is a major Christian religious center. I do not know whether folk were going on pilgrimage to Canterbury in the days of Arthur, before the martyrdom of Thomas à Becket.

CANTERBURY, ARCHBISHOP (or Bishop) OF

This churchman blessed the seats of the Round Table at the ordination of Arthur's first knights of the Table. Years later he resisted Mordred's attempt to usurp the throne, for which he was forced into religious retirement at Glastonbury. A political power as bishop, he seems also to have been a holy man, as evidenced by his life as a hermit. After burying the body of Arthur when the queens brought it to him, he became the nucleus of a group that finally included Bedivere, Bors, Lancelot, and others who embraced the religious life at Arthur's grave. When Lancelot died, the former Archbishop saw a vision of angels heaving up Lancelot's soul into Heaven. [Malory III, 2; XXI, 1, 6-12] Chrétien de Troyes mentions that the Archbishop of Canterbury officiated at Erec and Enide's Pentecost wedding. [**Erec & Enide**, ca. l. 2032] This archbishop might perhaps be identified with Dubric (q.v.).

CARADOS, KING OF SCOTLAND

This Carados seems to be the one who joined the first wave of rebellion against Arthur, pledging 5,000 mounted men to the effort and fighting in the battle of Bedegraine. Carados of Scotland must have been reconciled with Arthur and avoided the second rebellion, for he later appears as a knight of the Round Table during the attempt to heal Sir Urre. Chances are he also was the Carados involved in the trial of Anguish of Ireland: "King Arthur assigned King Carados and the King of Scots to be there that day as judges" when Sirs Bleoberis and Blamore arraigned King Anguish for murder. [Malory I, 12-16; VIII, 20-23; XIX, 11]

CARADOS OF THE DOLOROUS TOWER

This Carados, who was "made like a giant" and whom Lancelot later called "a full noble knight and a passing strong man", enjoyed capturing and imprisoning other knights. Sir Lancelot arrived on the scene

when Carados was carrying Gawaine away on his saddle-bow. Lancelot killed Carados and freed Gawaine and the other prisoners. Carados' brother, Sir Turquine, died in the attempt to avenge Carados' death on Lancelot.

Carados and Turquine illustrate the problem of Malory's chronology. Lancelot fights and kills Turquine in Book VI, 7-9. Turquine reappears, along with Carados, at the tournament at Castle Dangerous in VII, 26-29, where they do not appear to be villainous. The rescue of Gawaine and the slaying of Carados, for which Turquine seeks revenge, is not described until VIII, 28. Nor is the problem alleviated by the presence of at least one other Carados in Malory's account. Shall we blame it all on Caxton? Although in VIII, 28, Malory calls Carados of the Dolorous Tower "the mighty king", I am reasonably sure this Carados is not to be confused with King Carados of Scotland.

CARAHS†

Among Arthur's knights in the list Chrétien de Troyes begins in line 1691 of **Erec & Enide**.

CARBARECOTINS (Carbarentins, Kabbaranturs), KING OF CORNOAILLE†

I believe that his territory was the French Cornoaille in Brittany, not the Cornwall in Great Britain. Carbarecotins was an ally of Arthur, whom he joined in the war against Claudas to free Elyzabel. [Vulgate V]

CARBONEK (Corbenic, Corbin)

Carbonek was a magical place, the castle where the maimed Fisher King guarded the Holy Grail until Galahad's coming. It also seems, however, to be a place where more or less normal day-to-day life was possible for the residents, and once Sir Bors de Ganis visited Carbonek without even realizing it was a place of supernatural marvels. On a later visit, having experienced some of the marvels, Bors remarked to King Pellam, "[T]his castle may be named the Castle Adventurous, for here be many strange adventures." [Malory XI, 4]

From portions of the Vulgate, I have the impression that the 'Castle Adventurous' was only part of Carbonek where the visions and power of the Grail were most immediate. "Adventurous", of course, seems one of those words which could be applied to any place a person felt it appropriate.

In a wide valley before one reached the main castle was another fine castle, where a damsel waited in a scalding bath five years until the best knight in the world came to rescue her. Near her tower a serpent, or dragon, lurked in a tomb. On the tomb was written in gold letters, "Here shall come a leopard of king's blood, and he shall slay this serpent, and this leopard shall engender a lion in this foreign country, the which lion shall pass all other knights." Lancelot lifted the tomb and the dragon issued out, spitting fire, to give him a long, hard fight before he slew it. The "leopard" of the inscription was, of course, Lancelot; the "lion" Galahad. [Malory XI, 1; Vulgate IV]

During the Grail adventures, Lancelot arrived at Carbonek in the vessel with the body of Amide, after seven months or more of random adventuring on the sea. Finding the back gate to Carbonek guarded by two lions, he drew his sword; but a dwarf (or, according to the Vulgate, a flaming hand) struck him, knocking the weapon from his grasp. The lions threatened, but did not molest him as he passed between them. [Malory XVII, 14; Vulgate VI]

Carbonek would be somewhere in Listeneise, which I have identified with the Lake District. Keswick seems to me a nice choice. It is inland, but not by that many miles; and it seems to be on a lake. Considering the mystic, miraculous nature of the Grail Adventures, a miraculous temporary canal from the sea to accomodate Lancelot's midnight arrival by boat does not seem farfetched. To avoid the necessity of such a tide, however, Whitehaven or Ravenglass might be identified with Carbonek, perhaps moving Bliant Castle (or Joyous Isle) to one of the lakes.

See also Grail Castle.

CARDIGAN† (Cardican?)

According to Chrétien de Troyes, the stronghold of Cardigan was one of Arthur's places to hold court [**Erec & Enide**, l. 27ff.].

Malory mentions Cardican in passing, as a castle where Sirs Percivale and Aglovale lodged for a brief time while searching for Lancelot [XI, 12]. From the name alone, I assume Malory's Cardican Castle to be Cardigan city, at the southwest tip of Cardiganshire, Wales; and would identify it with Chrétien's Cardigan.

CARDIFF

Arthur held court in this city in Glamorganshire, Wales.

Cardoile, Carduel—see CARLISLE

Carlion—see CAERLEON

CARLISLE (Cardoile, Carduel in Wales)

One of Arthur's court cities. Malory uses both names. For the identification of Cardoile (Caer Lliwelydd, or Cardueil) with Carlisle, see, e.g., Glennie, cxliv; D.D.R. Owen, note to l. 7 of **Yvain**; and Cline, note to v. 336 of **Perceval**.

Chrétien de Troyes seems to make more of this city than of Camelot and maybe even Caerleon. It is in Carlisle that he begins the romance of **Yvain**; in Carlisle that he shows Percivale first finding Arthur's court; and, in **Erec & Enide**, Erec tells Guivret the Little that he hopes to find Arthur's court either at Carlisle or Robais (which suggests that they might lie in some proximity to each other). [**Yvain**, l. 7ff.; **Perceval**, ca. ll. 335-339, 840-1304; **Erec & Enide**, ll. 5260-5293]

CARLISLE, SUFFRAGAN OF

A suffragan is a bishop serving as assistant to the bishop of a diocese. It was the Suffragan of Carlisle who finally baptized Sir Palomides at Tristram's behest. [Malory XII, 14]

Carmelide—see CAMELIARD

CARNANT†

In this town or city of Outre-Gales, Erec's father King Lac had a superbly endowed castle for his residence. [Chrétien de Troyes, **Erec & Enide**, ll. 2293-2328]

CAROHAISE†

Located in Cameliard, this was apparently Leodegrance's capital, or at least one of his most important cities [Vulgate II].

CARSENEFIDE†

Enide's mother. Chrétien does not tell us Dame Carsenefide's name until almost the end of the romance, several hundred lines after Arthur, meeting her, remarks that it is easy to see how Enide came by her beauty. [**Erec & Enide**, esp. ll. 6594-6627 & 6888-6917]

CART

Useful as carts must have been for transporting things, in Arthur's day the cart served the same purpose as the pillory did for Chrétien's own contemporaries: traitors, murderers, the losers of judicial combats, thieves, highway robbers—all these were forced to ride in the cart, and thereafter lost all legal rights and were never again heard, honored, or welcomed in any court. This, adds Chrétien, was what had given rise to what appears to have been a twelfth-century superstition about seeing a cart in one's path, similar to the one we know about a black cat crossing in front of one. Small wonder that Lancelot hesitated a little to ride in a cart, even for the sake of rescuing Guenevere from Meliagrant! [**Lancelot**, ll. 323-398]

CART, DWARF OF THE

Lancelot had ridden two horses to death pursuing Meliagrant, Guenevere, and Kay, when he caught up with a cart and asked the dwarf driving it if he had seen the Queen. The dwarf, a surly and vulgar fellow, only bade him get into the cart if he wanted to find out what had happened to her. Riding in a cart was a horrific disgrace but, having just ridden two horses to death and thus being afoot with no other way to travel, Lancelot climbed in. Gawaine soon caught up, and the dwarf gave him the same advice; Gawaine, still having his horse, chose to ride alongside. The dwarf silently allowed this—indeed, the dwarf seems not to have spoken again, even when they passed people who questioned them about what the knight had done. After depositing both knights without explanation at the castle of the "Lady of the Deadly Bed", the dwarf drove off and disappeared from the story. [Chrétien de Troyes, **Lancelot**, ll. 322-462]

Could it be that Lancelot's following the dwarf's injunction and Gawaine's refusal to do the same has any bearing on the fact that Lancelot was able to cross the Sword Bridge into Gore while Gawaine, at this stage in Arthurian romance the greatest of the knights, could not manage the Water Bridge and finally had to be rescued?

CARTELOISE CASTLE

Here Galahad and his companions killed the three incestuous and wicked sons of Earl Hernox, who had raped and murdered their own sister and imprisoned their father. After his rescue, Hernox died in Galahad's arms. [Malory XVII, 7-9]

Carteloise Castle is in the Marches of Scotland. It would be on the west coast, near the border between Scotland and England. Here, where Glennie would be most helpful, he is silent. Port Carlisle might be a fair choice for Carteloise, but it is hard to see how Hernox's sons could have pursued their evil course with such impunity so near one of Arthur's court cities, unless the King had not been there on his progresses for some time. I would place Carteloise somewhere on the Solway Firth. It should probably be not too close to King Pellam's territory of Listeneise; yet we do seem to be in Grail territory, for, after leaving Carteloise Castle, Galahad and his companions entered a waste forest where they encountered very holy visions. Perhaps Carteloise could be identified with Workington, Maryport, or Allonby; or, on the Scotland side of the Solway, Kirkendbright or Southerness.

CARTELOISE FOREST

After leaving Carteloise Castle, Galahad and his companions entered a "waste forest." Assuming that this forest would be near the castle, I have called it Carteloise. Here Galahad's party saw the mystical white hart, representing Christ, walking within a guard of four lions, representing the four evangelists. Others had seen the hart and lions before, but Galahad and his companions appear to have been the first and only folk to follow the animals to a

> valley, and thereby was an hermitage where a good man dwelled, and the hart and the lions entered also. So when they saw all this they turned to the chapel, and saw the good man in a religious weed and in the armour of Our Lord, for he would sing mass of the Holy Ghost: and so they entered in and heard mass. And at the secrets of the mass they three saw the hart become a man, the which marvelled them, and set him upon the altar in a rich siege; and saw the four lions were changed, the one to the form of a man, the other to the form of a lion, and the third to an eagle, and the fourth was changed unto an ox. Then took they their siege where the hart sat, and went out through a glass window, and there was nothing perished nor broken; and they heard a voice say: In such a manner entered the Son of God in the womb of a maid Mary, whose virginity ne was perished ne hurt. And when they heard these words they fell down to the earth and were astonied; and therewith was a great clearness.

When they came to themselves, the holy man expounded the vision, also remarking that he supposed the white hart would be seen no more. [Malory XVII, 9] Although Malory says "they three saw" it, actually there were four, not counting the hermit: Galahad, Percival, Bors, and Percival's sister Amide.

CASE, CASTLE OF

Another castle of Pellam's, five miles from Carbonek. Here Dame Brisen caused Lancelot to lie with her.

CASTOR

Lancelot was at Carbonek in one of his mad fits, subdued but unknown, at the time King Pellam's nephew Castor was grooming for knighthood.

> [S]o [Castor] desired of [Pellam] to be made knight, and so ... the king made him knight at the feast of Candlemas. And when Sir Castor was made knight, that same day he gave many gowns. And then Sir Castor sent for the fool—that was Sir Lancelot. And when he was come afore Sir Castor, he gave Sir Lancelot a robe of scarlet and all that longed unto him.

Now well groomed, Lancelot fell asleep in the garden, where Elaine and Brisen found and recognized him at last and cured his madness by exposing him to the Holy Grail. Under the name of Le Chevaler Mal Fet, Lancelot planned to live with Elaine in Pellam's Joyous Isle.

> Sir, said Sir Castor ... ever meseemeth your name should be Sir Lancelot du Lake, for or now I have seen you. Sir, said Lancelot, ye are not as a gentle knight: I put case my name were Sir Lancelot, and that it list me not to discover my name, what should it grieve you here to keep my counsel, and ye be not hurt thereby? but wit thou well an ever it lie in my power I shall grieve you, and that I promise you truly. Then Sir Castor kneeled down and besought Sir Lancelot of mercy: For I

> shall never utter what ye be, while that ye be in these parts. Then Sir Lancelot pardoned him. [Malory XII, 4, 6]

CAVERON OF ROBENDIC†

Among Arthur's knights in the list Chrétien de Troyes begins in line 1691 of **Erec & Enide**.

Cei—see KAY

CELIBE† (Seloude, Tibise)

This is the forest through which Galahad follows Percivale's sister to Goothe Castle [Vulgate VI].

CHALEINS, DUKE OF CLARANCE

Chaleins appears at Duke Galeholt's tournament in Surluse, where he did "great deeds of arms, and of so late as he came in the third day there was no man did so well except King Bagdemagus and Sir Palomides." To this tourney he brings along a knight called Elis la Noire. Chaleins appears again at a tournament given by Arthur on Candlemas Day following the death of Elaine of Astolat; to this tourney he brings a hundred knights. [Malory X, 44, 48; XVIII, 22] Apparently Chaleins became a companion of the Round Table, being listed in Malory XIX, 11.

I suggest he be identified with the Vulgate's Galeshin.

CHAMPAYNE, Guienne, etc.

After Lancelot breaks with Arthur and goes back across the Channel with his kinsmen and supporters, here is how he parcels out his lands:

> [Lancelot] crowned Sir Lionel, King of France; and Sir Bors [he] crowned him king of all King Claudas' lands; and Sir Ector de Maris ... King of Benwick, and king of all Guienne, that was Sir Launcelot's own land.

He also makes others of his supporters Dukes of Limosin in Guienne, Poictiers, Querne, Sentonge, Provence, Landok, Anjou, and Normandy; and Earls of Perigot, Roerge, Bearn, Comange, Arminak, Estrake, Pardiak, Foise, Masauke, Tursauk, the Launds, Agente, and Surlat. [Malory XX, 18]

Lionses, whom Malory calls "lord of the country of Payarne", and who fights on the side of Arthur, Ban, and Bors, is probably identical with Leonce, the wisest and most loyal man in Gannes according to the Vulgate [Malory I, 10; Vulgate III]. This makes Payarne another French territory.

CHANART†

King Claudas made his nephew Chanart co-commander-in-chief (with Claudin) of his army for the war with Arthur over Elyzabel. A good knight, Chanart succeeded in unhorsing Gawaine—though

Gawaine later unhorsed him during the same battle. After Claudas' departure, Chanart helped welcome Arthur into Gannes. [VulgateV]

CHANGING COLORS, FOUNTAIN OF†

This fountain was located near La Tour Quarée on the Salerne River. I have not been able to locate the Salerne. Once Josephe preached here. The water of the fountain frequently changed color. Josephe explained that the color changes were produced by the approach of sinful and unclean persons; I am unsure whether Josephe himself caused the fountain to take on this attribute, or whether it had already existed and Josephe only explained it.

Josephe caused an inscription to be left here on a stone: "The adventure of the fountain will be achieved by the great lion with the marvellous neckband." The neckband signified obedience; the lion was probably Galahad. I do not know what the "adventure" was, unless this is another version of the Boiling Well.

A wounded knight who heard Josephe preach mistook his comparison of the Trinity to a healing fountain for a reference to the actual fountain at hand. He wanted to drink of it, but every messenger was afraid to bring him a cup of the waters that changed color. The knight appealed to Josephe, who gave him a short lesson in theology. The knight promised to believe in God if He would heal him. Josephe filled a cup at the fountain; the knight drank the water and was healed. [Vulgate V]

Chanpguin—see **CANGUIN, ROCK OF**

Charcoal Burner—see **PERCIVALE'S CHARCOAL BURNER**

CHARIOT (Charroie), CASTLE

According to the Vulgate, this castle was in the marches of Carmelide (Cameliard) and Bedigran, across the teritory of King Ryons. King Amans fought to reconquer it while Arthur, Ryons, and the Sesnes were busy with each other. [Vulgate II, VIII]

For a time, at least, Morgan le Fay and her cohorts appear to have used this castle as their base of operations. After Amans' attempt to conquer it, Morgan le Fay and her cohorts found Lancelot asleep and kidnaped him, bringing him to Castle Chariot (called Charroie in the Vulgate). According to Malory's account, which differs in important details from that of the Vulgate, Morgan's companions on this occasion were three—the queens of Norgales, Eastland, and the Out Isles—and Lancelot was released by King Bagdemagus' daughter, who asked him to help her father at a tournament between him and the King of Norgales on the "Tuesday next coming." [Malory VI, 3-4]

CHESTER

Chrétien identifies this as among Arthur's court cities. [**Yvain**, ca. l. 2677]

CLAELLUS†

The seneschal of King Pellam of Listenois, according to Vulgate VII (which, however, also seems to give Minadoras as Pellam's seneschal).

CLAMADEU OF THE ISLES†

Desiring Blancheflor of Beaurepaire, Clamadeu of the Isles sent his seneschal Engygeron to besiege her. When Clamadeu himself approached after almost a year, confident in the expectation of imminent victory, he learned that Blancheflor's strange new champion (Percivale) had defeated Engygeron on the very day when Beaurepaire should have surrendered. On the advice of his mentor, who called him "young man", Clamadeu undertook the attack himself, but was foiled first by a chance ship that arrived full of provisions and was willing to sell them to Blancheflor's people, and then by Percivale, who defeated him in personal combat. Like his seneschal, Clamadeu begged not to be sent prisoner either to Beaurepaire or to Gornemant's castle, in both which places his life wouldn't have been worth much; so Percivale sent him to King Arthur instead. After a visit home to release the prisoners Engygeron had captured in the fighting at Beaurepaire, Clamadeu arrived at Arthur's court, where he was welcomed and made a member for the rest of his life. [Chrétien de Troyes, **Perceval**, ll. 1999-2909]

The similarity of names might suggest an identification of Clamadeu with the Vulgate's King Clamadon. For myself, I would hesitate to make that identification.

CLAMADEU'S MENTOR†

This graying knight of Clamadeu's advised him that an attack would conquer Beaurepaire, since Clamadeu's forces were strong and well fed, while Blancheflor's people were weak with hunger and long siege. Clamadeu's mentor may have been a sound military strategist, but Percivale and a chance-arriving ship with a full cargo of food defeated his planning.

D.D.R. Owen translates this character as Clamadeu's major-domo, but while the OED gives "major-domo" as the title of the highest royal official under the Merovingians, its earliest example of the word in English usage is dated 1589; moreover, a comparison of "major-domo" with "seneschal" in the same dictionary shows an overlap of office and functions, and Clamadeu already had a seneschal in Engygeron. Possibly the "major-domo" served as acting seneschal while Engygeron was besieging Beaurepaire for his master—but then, who watched things at home while the "major-domo" accompanied Clamadeu to the siege site? Ruth Cline simply renders this character as an aging knight who had trained Clamadeu and become his counselor. [Chrétien de Troyes, **Perceval**, ll. 2393ff.]

CLAMADON, KING†

The father of Byanne.

CLARANCE

Duke Chaleins of Clarance gets a little more mention in Malory than Duke Eustace of Cambenet, generally turning up at tournaments. The most logical territory for Chaleins would be the territory of the historical Dukes of Clarence, whose seat was County Clare, Munster, Ireland, from the thirteenth century.

Clarance, Duke of—see **CHALEINS;** see also **GALESHIN**

CLARENCE†

This city is mentioned in Vulgate II. I assume it to be identical with the holding of the Duke of Clarance in Ireland. Clarence apparently is near another city or castle, Vambieres.

CLARIANCE (Clarence, Clarion), KING OF NORTHUMBERLAND

One of the kings in the first wave of rebellion against Arthur, Clariance pledged 3,000 men of arms to the cause and fought in the battle of Bedegraine. Apparently he became a companion of the Round Table, for he is listed among those at the attempted healing of Sir Urre. Probably he is to be identified with the "King of Northumberland" who appears, for instance, at Arthur's Candlemas tournament after Elaine of Astolat's death, to which he brings a hundred good knights and where he gives Hoel of Brittany a fall, and with the King of Northumberland who is father to Sir Epinegris.

Vulgate VII tells of a king or ally of the Sesnes named Clarions. He is probably distinct from Clariance of Northumberland.

CLARIONS†

This Saxon king was involved in the attack on Vandaliors, a castle of the rebel kings early in Arthur's reign. It was from Clarions that Gawaine won his warhorse Gringolet.

"CLARISIN"†

After rescuing the unnamed damsel I have called "Clarisin", Sir Gaheris tried to get her to go to bed with him. She argued him down, pointing out that he already had a sweetheart, the Damoiselle de la Blanche Lande, in that country; that "women are easily conquered, and therefore the wrong is all the greater to deceive them, and will bring you more shame than honour"; and that she already loved another knight and wished to remain true. At last Gaheris admitted she was right and stopped trying to seduce her. [Vulgate V]

I have borrowed the name for this woman from Malory V, 12. Arthur is besieging a stubborn city in Tuscany.

> Then came out a duchess, and Clarisin the countess, with many ladies and damosels, and kneeling before King Arthur, required him for the love of God to receive the city, and not take it by assault, for then should many guiltless be slain.

Arthur promised the ladies safety, "but the duke shall abide my judgment." Thus the town was surrendered without further bloodshed, but Arthur sent the duke of the Tuscan city to Dover as a life prisoner.

CLARISSANT†

The granddaughter of Queen Igraine (Ygerne), Clarissant is tall, beautiful, wise, gracious, and seems in every way a paragon. This may befit her status in more ways than one: her mother (presumably that woman whom later romancers were to name Margawse) was pregnant with Clarissant when she followed Igraine to the Rock of Canguin. But as far as the outer world—even Igraine's famous son Arthur—knows, Igraine has been dead for sixty years when Gawaine finds her! and Gawaine has believed his mother (who is also Clarissant's mother) dead for twenty years. By this and other indications, we may suspect at least the possibility that the Rock of Canguin belongs to the Otherworld, even a Christianized Otherworld. Could Clarissant conceivably have been born in Heaven without passing through earthly life and death? She might certainly strike one as healthily angelic. Small wonder if Guiromelant loves her—although from a distance, from the other side of an all but impassable river; Clarissant testifies that they have never actually met, but only passed messages, and her acceptance of him as her lover apparently remains tentative.

Chrétien left things in a pleasant tangle at Canguin: Gawaine knows the situation, for Guiromelant has told him; but Gawaine has not yet revealed his own identity to his grandmother, mother, and sister. He has revealed it to Guiromelant, who hates him, and they have arranged to fight as soon as Arthur's court can be summoned to see them. Meanwhile, Igraine and her people are hoping to make a match between Clarissant and Gawaine, whom they want to keep permanently as their lord; not yet knowing he is Clarissant's brother, they see only how well the pair suit each other. I must confess that what Chrétien would have made of Gawaine's adventure at Canguin intrigues me far more than how he might have finished Percivale's Grail adventure. [**Perceval** ll. 7527 on; Clarissant is named ca. l. 8268]

From Ronan Coghlan's **Encyclopaedia of Arthurian Legends** [c1991], I learn that the French prose **Perlesvaus** and, apparently, other continuators had Clarissant wed Guiromelant and give birth to a daughter, Guigenor. I am far from sure that that is the way I would have continued it.

CLAUDAS, KING OF GAUL

Malory mentions this important villain about a dozen times, always as an offstage menace or defeated enemy. The most significant thing Malory tells us of his character comes from Merlin's counsel to Arthur during the first wave of rebellion after the accession:

> And on these two kings [Ban and Bors] warreth a mighty man of men, the King Claudas, and striveth with them for a castle, and great war is betwixt them. But this Claudas is so mighty of goods whereof he getteth good knights, that he putteth these two kings most part to the worse .... [Malory I, 10]

The Vulgate gives much fuller information, calling him "brave but treacherous" and saying that his "character was a strange mixture of good and bad qualities." His original territory was "la terre deserte" in Gaul, so called because Uther Pendragon and Hoel had devastated it, sparing only Bourges. This alone would be enough to explain Claudas' antipathy to Uther's son Arthur, as well as his attempts to gain other lands. I also suspect that Claudas may have been trying to do in France what Arthur did in Britain: consolidate the petty kingdoms into one. Possibly the difference was that after conquering the petty kings, Arthur was willing to incorporate those who were still alive into his own government, leaving them as rulers of their old territories with him as their liege lord, and even making them companions of the Round Table. Claudas appears to have aimed simply at annihilating the opposition.

Claudas succeeded in defeating and bringing about the deaths of Ban and Bors after they had returned from helping Arthur. Claudas loved the wife of Phariance and for her sake made Pharien seneschal of Gannes after driving out King Bors. [Malory brings Phariance to Britain with Ban and Bors to help Arthur in I, 10.] Claudas also took in King Bors' sons Lionel and Bors the younger, but surely regretted it when they killed Claudas' own son Dorin (who had already become quite dislikable by his death at age 15). Seraide rescued Lionel and Bors from Claudas.

Besides sending spies from time to time to Arthur's court (the spies were quite likely to decide to stay in Logres), Claudas himself went at least once, in disguise, to spy out Arthur's land. He was very impressed by Arthur's good qualities.

Eventually Arthur and Guenevere declared all-out war on Claudas in the affair of Guenevere's cousin Elyzabel. Despite the facts that Claudas accepted excellent advice, enlisted Rome as an ally, allowed those of his people who so wished to leave the country before the war started, and gave great largess to win the hearts of those who stayed, despite his excellent comanders-in-chief Claudin (his son or stepson) and Chanart, he was at last utterly routed. In one battle near Gannes, he refused, with tears in his eyes, to leave his people in their danger on the battlefield. He might have ended the war by freeing Elyzabel after the first battle, but he refused—perhaps because it was Lionel, who had long ago killed Dorin, who asked for her release. Claudas did arrange an exchange of prisoners taken in battle; Claudas gave each of his prisoners a meal and a good horse, while Gawaine on the other side was giving the freed prisoners a rich garment apiece and lavish entertainment. Finally, forced to decamp, Claudas told his barons they should now do whatever seemed to them best, but he himself had no hope of personally making peace with Arthur and with Lancelot, whose father's lands he had taken so long before. Claudas then slipped out of Gannes to take refuge in Rome. [Vulgate III-V]

Claudas could not read, needing his clerks to read to him [Vulgate V].

Malory mentions Claudas' final defeat: "King Arthur had been in France, and had made war upon the mighty King Claudas, and had won much of his lands" [Malory XI, 6].

KING CLAUDAS' FAMILY AND RETAINERS
Son: Dorin
Son or stepson: Claudin
Lover: Phariance's wife
Nephews: Brumant l'Orguilleus, Chanart
Kinsman (otherwise unspecified): Bertolle
Seneschal: Phariance
Knight of Gaul: Esclamor

CLAUDIN (Claudine)

According to Malory XVII, 21, he was King Claudas' son; according to Vulgate V, he was the king's stepson. Claudas made Claudin co-commander-in-chief (with Chanart) of his army for the war with Arthur. Gawaine admired Claudin's prowess in battle; Bors and Gawaine agreed that, after Lancelot and Gawaine himself, Claudin was the best knight. With Chanart and another good Gaulish knight, Esclamor (probably distinct from King Esclamor), Claudin welcomed Arthur into Gannes after Claudas escaped. [Vulgate V]

Claudin was one of three Gaulish knights who arrived at Carbonek to meet Galahad, Percivale, Bors, three Irish knights, and three Danish knights at the climax of the Grail Quest. Together, these twelve knights represented the twelve apostles at the Last Supper. At Carbonek they witnessed the mysteries of the Grail as performed by Joseph of Arimathea (or perhaps by his son Josephe). From the Vulgate we learn that all but one of the knights were to die on the Quest. After leaving Carbonek, the twelve knights went on their separate ways, apparently in small groups, as the Apostles were sent forth in all directions. Since Sir Bors was the survivor, Claudin presumably died before reaching home.

Claudin would seem to be the French equivalent to Galahad, or at least to Percivale.

CLEODALIS†

He was King Leodegrance's seneschal, and the supposed father of Genievre [Vulgate II].

CLIGÉS†

This hero is not born until about line 2380 of the romance bearing his name. D.D.R. Owen tells us in a note to his translation that a still-extant 13th-century text, **Marques De Rome**, may preserve another version—also with hero named Cligés—of whatever main source Chrétien de Troyes followed.

The name "Cligés" can sound much like "cliches." I do not know whether this pun would have occurred in Chrétien's lifetime, but I suspect that it might have pleased him. At the age of fifteen, his golden-haired Cligés, orphaned son of Alexander and Soredamors, is not only more handsome and charming than Narcissus, but already highly accomplished in arms. He twice defeats the Duke of Saxony's nephew in joust (the second time killing him); on the spur of the moment, and with a slight leg wound, he leads the combined armies of Greece and Germany against the attacking Saxons; he singlehandedly rescues his uncle Alis' bride Fenice from twelve abducting Saxons; he then asks Emperor Alis to knight him and proceeds to fight the seasoned Duke of Saxony into submission in single combat … all this while acting with irreproachable loyalty to his uncle although himself secretly in love with Fenice. After all this, Cligés begs Alis to let him go to Britain in order to put his prowess to the test! True, his dying father Alexander had charged Cligés to prove himself in Britain someday; also, we may suspect the youth of wishing to escape his tricky love triangle for a while. Nevertheless ….

He takes four different chargers—white, sorrel, tawny, and black—with him to Britain. Arriving at Wallingford and learning that Arthur is about to hold a tournament near Oxford, he sends his squires to London to buy him three extra suits of armor—black, crimson, and green. (Money is definitely not a problem for this lad.) Wearing the black armor and riding the black horse, Morel, Cligés starts the first day of the tournament by defeating Sir Sagramore in the opening joust, afterward carrying off all the honors in the melee, until it is considered an honor even to dare go against him and be taken prisoner. Getting back to his lodging, he hides the black armor and has the green displayed, so that when his prisoners come to present themselves, they cannot find him. Next day, wearing the green armor and riding his tawny horse, he defeats Lancelot in the opening joust and proceeds to fight so well that he is called far better than the unknown black knight of the day before. This time he hides the green armor at the day's end and displays the crimson, in which he rides his sorrel horse on the third day, defeating Percivale and repeating his general success. By now people are tumbling to the fact that this is the same unknown knight in different armor, and Gawaine—still at this stage in the romances Arthur's greatest knight—modestly decides to try his hand on the fourth and last day. When Cligés shows up this time, he matches the great champion so well that Arthur declares it a draw and ends the tournament a little early. Cligés reveals his identity: through his mother, he is Gawaine's nephew and thus Arthur's great-nephew. All are delighted, and the young knight stays with Arthur's court until the following summer, traveling throughout Britain, France, and Normandy performing knightly deeds—it seems like crowding quite a bit into a year or less—while Arthur makes more of him than of any other nephew.

On returning to Greece, Cligés enjoys a secret liaison with Fenice, in a hideaway built to order for them by his loyal serf John. Being discovered, the lovers escape back to Britain, where Arthur prepares to go to war to help win Cligés the emperorship of Greece and Constantinople, which should rightfully have been his anyway. Alis conveniently dies before the war can start, so Cligés peacefully becomes emperor and marries Fenice.

Aside from those two relatively short sojourns, Cligés appears to have spent no other time in Britain, which makes his story only peripherally Arthurian. [Chrétien de Troyes, **Cligés**, ca. l. 2380 to end]

Clochides†—see under **DEUEE, LA TERTRE**

CLUB OF IRON

After killing the Giant of Saint Michael's Mount, Brittany, Arthur kept the giant's iron club as a trophy [Malory V, 5].

COAT (Kirtle) OF THE GIANT OF SAINT MICHAEL'S MOUNT, BRITTANY

This was decked with gems and embroidered with the beards of fifteen kings whom the giant had vanquished. Arthur kept it, along with the giant's iron club, as a souvenir after killing him. [Malory V, 5]

COATS OF ARMS—see Appendix

COGUILLANT OF MAUTIREC†

He fought in the Noauz tournament. His shield featured pheasants beak to beak. [Chrétien de Troyes, **Lancelot**, ll. 5783-5823]

COI†

A much-feared knight, he accompanied his father King Aguisel of Scotland and brother Cadret to Arthur's court for Erec's wedding. [Chrétien de Troyes, **Erec & Enide**, ll. 1963-2024]

Cole†—see **KALET**

COLGREVANCE OF GORE (Calogrenant, Galogrinans?)

Malory mentions "Sir Colgrevaunce de Gorre" as early as the battle of Bedegraine against the rebel kings, where he fights on Arthur's side [I, 17]. In IX, 24, Malory notes that Bors, Lancelot, and others "had made promise to lodge with Sir Colgrevance" for a night.

This knight of the Round Table had at least two deaths, both of them spectacular. During the Grail Quest, Colgrevance happened to find Sir Lionel ready to slay his own brother Bors, who had earlier left him a suffering captive in order to go rescue a virgin. Colgrevance loved Bors and tried to stop Lionel. They fought long, but Lionel got the upper hand. Colgrevance cried out to Bors for help; Bors, however, was busy doing the Right Thing by refusing to raise a hand against his brother. So Lionel, who had already cut down a hermit for coming between him and Bors, slew Colgrevance. Colgrevance died with a prayer on his lips, and then, at last, with tears, Bors dressed to defend himself. [Malory XVI, 14-16]

You can't keep a good man down, though. Colgrevance shows up again among the knights who try to heal Sir Urre, in Malory XIX, 11. Colgrevance of Gore was among the knights who went with Mordred and Agravaine to surprise Lancelot and Guenevere together. Lancelot was unarmed, and Colgrevance was the first to go into the Queen's chamber.

> [Lancelot] unbarred the door, and with his left hand he held it open a little, so that but one man could come in at once; and so there came striding a good knight, a much man and large, and his name was Colgrevance of Gore.

Lancelot deflected his blow, killed him, and took his arms and armor. Colgrevance thus became the evening's first casualty. [Malory XX, 2-4] He might have been better off staying dead the first time; it was a more pious death and in a worthier cause.

It is, of course, possible that the Colgrevance slain by Lionel was different from the Colgrevance of Gore slain by Lancelot—in which case there were two companions of the Round Table by that name.

My confidence is no longer automatic, as it was at the time of the first edition, that Colgrevance and Calogrenant are one and the same character.

COLLIBE

During the Grail Adventures, Sir Percivale's sister brings Galahad from a hermitage apparently in the vicinity of Carbonek Castle to a ship in which they find Sirs Bors and Percivale. Galahad and the damsel pass by a sea called Collibe on the way. [Malory XVII, 1-2]

COLOMBE

When Sir Lanceor rode out after Sir Balin, Lanceor's lady Colombe came after him.

> And when she espied that Lanceor was slain, she made sorrow out of measure, and said, O Balin, two bodies thou hast slain and one heart, and two hearts in one body,and two souls thou hast lost. And therewith she took the sword from her love that lay dead, and fell in a swoon. And when she arose she made great dole out of measure, the which sorrow grieved Balin passingly sore, and he went unto her for to have taken the sword out of her hand, but she held it so fast he might not take it out of her hand unless he should have hurt her, and suddenly she set the pommel to the ground, and rove herself through the body. [Malory II, 6]

COLUMBA, SAINT† (Columkill)

A sixth-century Irish saint of the family of the kings of Ulster. With twelve followers, he left Ireland and evangelized Scotland, founding 300 religious houses there. The first, that on the island of Iona, was founded in 563 A.D. According to Glennie, Columba was supposed to possess prophetic power. Phyllis McGinley, who calls him "Ireland's most typical saint", gives a physical description from old chronicles: tall, fair-skinned, dark-haired, gray-eyed, and with a melodious, far-sounding voice. She also retells the tale of why he left Ireland—in self-banishment for the horror of having started a war over his right to copy a book. [**Saint-Watching**, Viking, 1969]

"CONJURATION, CHAPEL OF THE"

After leaving the hermit who had expounded his visions at the Chapel of the Stony Cross, Sir Lancelot, apparently after less than an afternoon's travel, came to a chapel where an old man was laid out dead in a shirt of fine white cloth. The old religious man of the place feared that the dead man was damned because, after being a man of religion for more than a hundred years, he had put off the habit of his order. The living old man, who was probably a priest, put about his own neck a stole (a priestly garment, still required in the twentieth century before a priest may administer the sacraments) and, taking up a book, conjured up a fiend to tell him how the dead man had died and where his soul had gone. The priest and Lancelot learned from the fiend that the dead man had left his hermitage by permission, to help his nephew Aguarus win a war against the Earl of Vale. The earl had then sent two of his nephews to the hermitage for revenge. They had to burn Augurus' uncle all night in a fire before they could manage to kill him; even then, though he died, his body was left whole. The same fiend, coming in the morning, had found the naked body in the fire, removed it, and laid it out in the white shirt. The dead man's soul was in Heaven. [Malory XV, 1-2]

Conlotebre, Conlouzebre†—see **TALEBRE**

CONSTANS, KING OF ENGLAND†

He was Arthur's grandfather. Constans' three sons were Maines, Pendragon, and Uther (later Uther Pendragon). Constans died a natural death. [Vulgate II] Malory seems not to mention Constans, unless he is to be identified with "Constantine the son of Heleine", whose holding the empire is cited as precedent for Arthur's refusal to pay truage to Rome [Malory V, 1].

CONSTANTINE

Almost all that Malory tells us of Sir Constantine is that he was the son of Cador (sometimes called Carados) of Cornwall, that Arthur left him and Sir Baudwin of Britain as joint governors of the realm during his continental war with Emperor Lucius of Rome, that he was a knight of the Round Table, that he became King after Arthur, and that he tried unsuccessfully to keep Sirs Bors, Ector de Maris, Blamore, Bleoberis, and other former companions of the Table with him in England after Lancelot's death [Malory V, 3; XIX, 11; XXI, 13]. Still, even allowing for the fact that the flower of Arthur's knighthood was either slaughtered or moved to Gaul and/or hermitages during and after the wars with Lancelot and Mordred, it does seem that the man who eventually succeeded Arthur must have been a person of some importance. Arthur would have done better to have reappointed Constantine governor, instead of Mordred, when he went to fight Lancelot in France. I suspect that Constantine may have tried to keep up the Round Table.

Corbenic, Corbin—see **CARBONEK**

COREUSEUSE†

King Ban's sword [Vulgate II]. Perhaps it passed down to Lancelot?

CORNEUS, DUKE

The father of Sir Lucan the Butler [Malory I, 10].

CORNIX†

Cornix was one of Alexander's twelve companions who came with him from Greece to Britain, where Arthur knighted them all. Chrétien de Troyes singles Cornix out as being very dear to Alexander—perhaps his favorite? Nevertheless, he was not among those with Alexander's party when it penetrated Windsor to end Count Angrs' rebellion. Cornix survived that rebellion, but Chrétien tells us nothing more about him. [**Cligés**, ll. 102-385; 1093-ca. 2210]

CORNOUAILLE

Distinct from the Cornwall of Great Britain, the French Cornouaille is an area on the southwest coast of Brittany.

CORNWALL

"Old Cornwall" included Devon. Arthurian Cornwall would have consisted of present-day Devon and Cornwall, and the sunken land of Lyonesse (Liones) to the west, of which the Scilly Islands are the touted remains. Subkingdoms include Lyonesse, the South Marches, and Tintagil.

Chrétien tells us that Arthur regularly reinforced his army with men drawn from Cornwall.

CORSABRIN

A paynim and "a passing felonious knight" [Malory X, 47]. See under King Bandes.

COTE MALE TAILE, LA (Sir Breunor, Brewnor, or Bruin le Noire)

The tale of Sir Breunor in Malory IX parallels or—I think—parodies the tale of Sir Gareth in VII. Again we have the young man arriving at court and being given a nickname by Sir Kay in mockery. Breunor is called La Cote Male Taile ("the evil-shapen coat") because he wears his father's coat with the marks of his father's death wounds, being determined to avenge his father's murder.

Breunor gets off to a more visibly promising start than Gareth. At his request, Arthur knights him the day after his arrival, and almost immediately afterwards when a lion breaks loose from its tower and comes hurtling at the Queen and her knights, only Breunor stands his ground to slay the beast. That same day the damsel first called Maledisant and finally Beauvivante comes into court looking for a knight to achieve the quest of a "great black shield, with a white hand in the midst holding a sword", which she carries with her. Breunor takes the quest and, like Lynette, Maledisant promptly and continuously mocks him. Unlike Lynette, however, Maledisant later confesses that she has been prompted all along by love for Breunor, wanting to get him off the dangerous quest because he seems too young and likely to be killed on it. Also, in Malory's version of Gareth and Lynette, Gareth finally weds not Lynette but her sister; the romancer corrects this in the later tale and matches Breunor with Maledisant-Beauvivante.

I confess I lose the train of Breunor's quest with Maledisant and cannot quite figure out what it was all about; Breunor, however, unlike Gareth, is sometimes realistically allowed to be defeated on his first quest. Eventually Lancelot makes him lord of the castle of Pendragon in place of Sir Brian de les Isles. A little after this, La Cote is made a knight of the Round Table. He does finally succeed in avenging his father, though Malory does not give the details. The last we seem to hear of La Cote Male Taile, aside from his appearance at the attempt to heal Sir Urre, is as one of the guests at Guenevere's small dinner party when Sir Patrise is poisoned. La Cote Male Taile was brother to Sir Dinadan. [Malory IX, 1-9; XVIII, 3; XIX, 11]

COTOATRE†

The lake below Cotoatre was the home of the smith Trebuchet. D.D.R. Owen remarks that Cotoatre has been identified with the Firth of Forth, called in medieval times "Scottewatre"—an identification Cline clearly accepts, for she does not even use the name "Cotoatre", simply calling Trebuchet's home area the Firth of Forth. [Chrétien de Troyes, **Perceval**, ll. 3675ff. & Owen's note to 3675]

CRADELMAS, KING

One of the rebels at the beginning of Arthur's reign, Cradelmas pledged 5,000 mounted men to the cause and fought in the battle of Bedegraine [Malory I, 12, 15]. Possibly he should be identified with Tradelmans.

"CROSSROADS, DAMSEL OF THE"†

Gawaine and Lancelot met her at a crossroads after leaving the "Castle of the Deadly Bed" in their pursuit of Guenevere and her abductor. In return for their promises—Gawaine's to be ever at her service, Lancelot's to do anything she might desire and completely subject himself to her will—the damsel told them the name of Guenevere's abductor—Meliagrant, son of King Bademagu of Gore—and his destination: "the kingdom from which no stranger returns." She also pointed out the ways to the Water Bridge and the Sword Bridge, adding descriptive particulars and cautions. Strangely, unless she is to be identified with King Bademagu's daughter, she seems to disappear from the romance. [Chrétien de Troyes, **Lancelot**, ll. 612-713]

CROWN OF GOLD

After being made knight by Galahad, Sir Melias rode into an old forest, where he found a lodge of boughs. Inside this lodge, on a chair, was a subtly wrought crown of gold. Melias took the crown and almost at once was accosted by another knight, who fought him for taking what was not his, won back the crown, and left Melias wounded until Galahad came and found him again. [Malory XIII, 13-14] This happens during the Grail adventures. The crown symbolizes worldly pride and covetousness, and may be an illusory temptation rather than an actual physical object.

CUBELE† (Noble, Tubelle)

A castle in a valley, seemingly some two days' ride from the castle of King Amans' daughter, which is near Cameliard. Sir Bors, arriving here, learnèd of an impending tournament between the Earl of Plains and the Lady of Hervin's nephew. Malory mentions this castle in XVI, 14; he, however, does not give it a name, and Vulgate VI does—indeed, various manuscripts of the Vulgate give it various names.

CUCKOLD'S HORN†

No man who was a cuckold could drink from this horn without spilling the beverage. See under Magic Mantle.

CULROSS†

The monastery where Saint Kentigern, whom I have reason to believe may have been a nephew of Sir Gawaine, was placed under the discipline of Saint Servanus [Glennie, 51].

Culross is on the north bank of the Firth of Forth, five to ten miles west of Charlestown.

DAGONET, SIR

The King's fool, or court jester, Arthur "loved him passing well, and made him knight with his own hands." Sir Griflet called him "the best fellow and the merriest in the world." Kay sent him after La Cote Male Taile on the latter's first quest; although La Cote bested him, the clash lent Maledisant ammunition for further raillery: "Fie for shame! now art thou shamed in Arthur's court, when they send a fool to have ado with thee, and especially at thy first jousts." Dagonet appears adventuring about the countryside in the long rambling books of Tristram. Once, riding alone with two squires, Dagonet meets Tristram in a fit of madness. The madman ducks Dagonet and the squires in a nearby well, to the merriment of nearby shepherds who have been feeding Tristram. Dagonet and the squires, thinking the shepherds put Tristram up to it, begin to beat them, whereupon Tristram kills one of the squires. Escaping to King Mark, Dagonet warns him against going near "the well in the forest, for there is a fool naked, and that fool and I fool met together, and he had almost slain me." Later, joining a party of some half-dozen knights of the Round Table, Dagonet takes the suggestion of the wounded Mordred, dons Mordred's armor, and rides after Mark with such a fierce show that he makes Mark ride for dear life. Palomides happens along in time to rescue Mark. [Malory IX, 3, 19; X, 12-13]

Tennyson makes exquisite use of Dagonet in the idyll **The Last Tournament**.

Also see the Fool.

DAMAS

Sir Damas, a villainous knight, was unjustly keeping a manor from his good younger brother Sir Ontzlake, and imprisoning all good knights so that they would not champion Ontzlake. Morgan used the situation to get Arthur and her lover Accolon into a fight as the brothers' champions. Arthur, ironically enough, was championing the wicked brother, Damas, while Accolon, who was actually meant to kill Arthur, was officially representing the good brother, Ontzlake. After Arthur, through Nimue's help, had won, he commanded that Ontzlake should hold the manor from Damas for the yearly fee of a palfrey, "for that will become [Sir Damas] better to ride on than upon a courser"—Damas had no business riding into battle on a warhorse, like an honorable knight. [Malory IV, 6-12]

A knight named Damas was killed during Lancelot's rescue of Guenevere from the stake. It might have been a different Damas, or it might be that Ontzlake's brother reformed and joined Arthur's court. Malory also mentions at least one and possibly two knights named Darras—an old knight with five sons who gives Tristram lodging after the tournament at the Castle of Maidens, and a knight of the Round Table who appears at the attempt to heal Sir Urre—and the names Damas and Darras may have been easy to confuse. [Malory IX, 34-37; XIX, 11; XX, 8]

DAMAS' CASTLE

Sir Ontzlake's manor, near the castle of his brother Damas, was two days' journey from Camelot. From the magical aspects of the adventure, it could be anywhere within that radius. [Malory IV, especially 12]

DAMES, CHASTEL AS and CHASTEL AS PUCELES†

The "Castle of Ladies" and "Castle of Virgins" were located on opposite banks of a river, probably in or near the forest of Carduel (Carlisle). Here, during a tournament between the two castles, Sirs Ector de Maris and Lionel once helped the knights of the Puceles, who were inferior in number, while Lancelot, to balance the influence of his kinsmen, entered on the side of the Dames. Lancelot, however, did not get into the fray until a damsel came by and dropped a hint that he should fight by asking him if she could have his shield, since he obviously had no use for it. [Vulgate IV]

"Chastel as Puceles" is, of course, the equivalent of "Castle of Maidens", which may have been a popular name.

DANEBLAISE†

Another of King Leodegrance's castle-cities in Cameliard [Vulgate II].

DANGEROUS, CASTLE

The castle of Dame Lyonors (or Lionesse) is also called the Castle Perilous. Malory tells of another Castle Perilous, however, one almost certainly different from that of Lyonors.

When Sir Ironside besieged Castle Dangerous, Lynette came to Arthur's court at Caerleon to find a champion for her sister. Lyonors' castle may perhaps be found by attempting to retrace Lynette's return with Gareth Beaumains. After leaving Caerleon, Gareth fights and kills two wicked brothers at a "great river and but one passage." The Severn makes a horseshoe curve at Newnham, below Gloucester, and continues to make little bends between Newnham and Gloucester. Malory's "great river and but one passage" might be somewhere here.

Continuing on, Gareth fights and kills the Black Knight of the Black Laund, that same day, in a valley. Still, apparently, the same day, he defeats the Green Knight (not to be confused with the title character of **Sir Gawaine and the Green Knight**), who lodges him and Lynette for a night and next morning escorts them partway through a forest. This day Gareth defeats the Red Knight by a white tower at the Pass Perilous. I would guess this to be a mountain rather than a river pass, and put it in the Cotswolds, perhaps at Stroud. The Red Knight also lodges them overnight.

The following day Gareth defeats Sir Persant of Inde near a "city rich and fair", which is "seven mile" from Castle Dangerous. Castle Dangerous is later described, in a cry made throughout Britain, Ireland, and Brittany, as "beside the Isle of Avilion." Sir Persant's city might be Tetbury or Chippenham, and Castle Dangerous seven miles beyond that, toward Avilion. [Cf. Malory VII, 2-12, 26]

Dareca†—see **MONENNA**

DAVID OF TINTAGIL†

Chrétien lists him among the counts and other vassals whom Arthur summoned to court for Erec's wedding. David of Tintagil never suffered sorrow or grief. [**Erec & Enide**, ll. 1934-1962] The geography looks wrong for an identification of this David with the saint.

DAVID (Dewi), SAINT†

Born c. 496 to Prince Xantus of Cereticu (Cardiganshire) and a nun named Malearia, Saint David was an uncle of Arthur. After entering religious life on the Isle of Wight, the ascetic David moved to Menevia, Pembrokeshire, where he founded twelve convents. In 577 the archbishop of Caerleon resigned his see to David, who moved the seat of the diocese to Menevia, which became the metropolis of Wales under the name St. David's. According to Drayton, he lived in the valley of Ewias between the Hatterill Hills, Monmouthshire. The waters of Bath were said to owe their qualities to the blessing of David. He reportedly died in 642, aged 146.

(King) DAVID'S SWORD AND SCABBARD

Balin's sword was Galahad's first sword. Galahad's second sword was King David's Sword, which he found on Solomon's Ship (q.v.).

de, del, des ( )—see the word following **"de"**, etc.

"DEADLY BED"†

See "Lady of the Deadly Bed." It probably isn't what you think.

"DEADLY BED, CASTLE OF THE"†

It was situated near a high, dark rock that dropped steeply away. On the other side were meadows and a town. This must have been near the marches leading to King Bademagu's land of Gore. [Chrétien de Troyes, **Lancelot**, ll. 422-611]

"DEADLY BED, LADY OF THE"†

The "Dwarf of the Cart" brought Lancelot and Gawaine to a castle or keep apparently held by this lady near the marches of Gore. Though Lancelot had arrived riding in a cart and Gawaine on horseback, the chatelaine treated them with equal hospitality. At bedtime, she assigned each of them a long, wide, handsome bed, adding that a third bed, which waited raised half an ell above the other two, was not to be slept in by anybody who did not merit it. Gawaine accepted this with his usual quiet courtesy, while Lancelot demanded to know why the third bed was forbidden. Now she scorned him for having ridden in a cart, telling him it was not for any knight so shamed to ask or know the reason. All the more determined, Lancelot climbed into the forbidden bed, which had a fine mattress covered with sable furs, white sheets, and a yellow velvet coverlet starred with gold. At midnight a lance with blazing pennon shot down like lightning from the rafters and almost skewered the occupant as it set the bed afire. Only grazed, Lancelot sat up, put out the fire, threw the lance into the middle of the hall, then lay back down and slept as soundly as before.

In the morning, they saw Meliagrant's party pass the castle. Now the lady, who may meanwhile have enjoyed a flirtation with Gawaine, made it up to Lancelot for her ridicule about the cart by giving him a horse and a lance so that he could continue with Gawaine in their pursuit of Meliagrant. [Chrétien de Troyes, **Lancelot**, ll. 422-611]

DELECTABLE ISLE

Sir Palomides avenges the death of King Hermance of the Red City and the Delectable Isle in Malory's tenth book. Spurn Head peninsula, at the mouth of the Humber River, between Lincolnshire and East Riding, Yorkshire, satisfies Malory's description. (If Glastonbury can be considered an island, so should a peninsula.)

"DESOLATE, CHAPEL"

In this desolate chapel, located on a mountain in the vicinity of Ablasoure, Galahad heard a heavenly voice directing him to go to the Castle of Maidens and destroy the wicked customs there [Malory XIII, 14].

DEUEE, LE TERTRE†

Sir Clochides loved King Esclamor's daughter, but Esclamor did not love Clochides. So the princess had Clochides take her to a strong castle he built on a hill. Clochides had only one approach to Le Tertre Deuee, and he defended it for twenty years against all comers, imprisoning defeated companions of the Round Table and killing all others. Finally Sir Bors de Ganis defeated and mortally wounded Clochides, but, before dying, Clochides made him promise to keep up the customs. Bors did so. In three months he killed more than sixty knights, and by the time his cousin Lancelot arrived, fourteen members of the Round Table were imprisoned here. Lancelot recognized Bors by his sword, which had once been Duke Galeholt's. Then the knights were freed, the customs dropped, everybody reconciled and happy, and I do not know what became of Clochides' princess. Bors knighted his squire Axilles and invested him with the castle. [Vulgate V]

Le Tertre Deuee was in the vicinity of the "Forest of the Boiling Well" and the abbey La Petite Aumosne; possibly also in the vicinity of King Vagor's Isle Estrange. Further on, the Vulgate tells us it was in "the perilous forest", perhaps either Carteloise Forest or an adjacent forest to the east. "The perilous forest" is an appellation belonging to more forests than just one or two.

DEUX SYCAMORES, FONTAINE DES†

This brook and the nearby castle would seem to have been somewhere in southern Scotland or northern Logres, possibly not far from Carteloise Forest. The brook, or fountain, was defended by two brothers, Sirs Belias and Briadas, sons of Sir Broades, who also had at least one daughter. These two brothers, who wore black armor, were defending the place to demonstrate that they were good enough for the Round Table. Their story had an unhappy ending. Hearing that one of them had unhorsed Gawaine, Lancelot came to encounter them, and ended by killing both them and their father. [Vulgate V]

Cadzow is one possible place in which Fontaine des Deux Sycamores may be located.

> Overhanging the brawling Avon [Scotland], and on the skirt of the noble chase which, with its wild cattle and ancient oaks, is all that now remains of that Caledonian Forest, once haunted by Merlin, and which stretched from sea to sea, stands Cadzow Castle [Glennie, p. 84].

DEVIL'S ROAD†

A road said to be haunted by devils, where Lancelot heard strange voices but saw nothing [Vulgate IV]. It was somewhere not far from the castle of Gais on the Thames.

DIN DREI†

> Immediately to the south of Melrose ... rise those three summits of the Eildons, the *Tremontium* of the Romans, which Mr. Nash identifies with the Din Drei of Aneurin. ... These three summits ... with their various weirdly appurtenants—the Windmill of Killielaw, the Lucken Hare, and Eildon Tree—mark the domes of those vast subterranean Halls, in which all the Arthurian chivalry await, in an enchanted sleep, the bugle-blast of the Adventurer who will call them at length to a new life. [Glennie, p. 60]

If the bend in the Tweed River at Melrose, Roxburgh County, southern Scotland, were considered as three sides of a rectangle, with Silkirk and St. Boswells at roughly the two lower points, Din Drei would not be far from the middle of the imaginary base line. Din Drei is in Rhymer's Glen.

Arthur and all his knights asleep in Scotland seems to be a different tradition from that preserved in Malory and the Vulgate, but perhaps both Din Drei and Avilion lead to the same otherworldly plain, where distances work differently. Even before Arthur's passing, Din Drei and Rhymer's Glen might have been an entrance into a world of Faery. (See also Ercildoune.)

DINADAN

A good knight with a sense of humor and, what seems even rarer among the companions of the Round Table, a sense of practicality, Dinadan was never willing to rush into a fight for the sake of wounds and glory. He wanted to know first that he had some chance of success and that he was going in on the right side.

Dinadan had more than a little satirical talent. Malory characterizes his lampoon against Mark of Cornwall as "the worst lay that ever harper sang", probably in the sense of hardest hitting. Dinadan was equally able, however, to laugh at himself. One of Malory's best episodes for Dinadan-watching is Duke Galeholt's tournament in Surluse, to which Dinadan first came in disguise and did great deeds of arms. He was unmasked by the fifth day, if not earlier—Galeholt sent Lancelot to unhorse him, apparently with a bit of clowning on both sides. On the evening of the sixth day, seeing Galeholt in a dark mood at being served fish, which he hated, Dinadan got "a fish with a great head" and served it up elaborately to Galeholt with the quip, "Well may I liken you to a wolf, for he will never eat fish, but flesh." This snapped Galeholt out of his bad humor. Dinadan then asked Lancelot, "What devil do ye in this country, for here may no mean knights win no worship for thee." Lancelot, entering into the spirit, replied by praying to be delivered from Dinadan's great spear: "God forbid that ever we meet but if it be at a dish of meat." Next day Lancelot entered the lists with a maiden's gown over his armor, unhorsed Dinadan before the latter recovered from his surprise, and then, with a group of co-pranksters, carried Dinadan into the forest and clothed him in the damsel's dress. A good time was had by all, and the Queen was vastly amused.

(In his excellent edition of Malory, John W. Donaldson interprets the tournament of Surluse as an attempt by Duke Galeholt and a co-conspirator to get Lancelot killed, and finds evidence in Dinadan's actions, especially the serving of the fish, that the shrewd, joking knight saw through the plot and meant to warn or protect Lancelot. This is an ingenious interpretation, but I have not yet been able to locate in the full edition of Malory the lines describing Galeholt's murderous intent, nor is it consistent with what we know from the Vulgate of the great friendship between Galeholt and Lancelot. It seems to me more likely that Dinadan's part in the Surluse tournament reflects pure high spirits.)

Dinadan, one knight who claimed to have no lady love, was the brother of La Cote Male Taile. Dinadan was "gentle, wise, and courteous", "a good knight on horseback", "a scoffer and a japer, and the merriest knight among fellowship that was that time living. And he … loved every good knight, and every good knight loved him again." Tristram in particular loved him above all other knights except Lancelot. Alas, Mordred and Agravaine took a dislike to him, apparently because of something he said to them about the matter of Lamorak's death, and, although he had once rescued them from Breuse Sans Pitie, "cowardly and feloniously" they killed him during the Grail Quest, though Malory does not give fuller details. [Malory VII, 2; X, 10, 20, 25, 27, 40-49, 55]

DINAS

Originally King Mark's seneschal of Cornwall, Dinas renounced his allegiance to Mark in anger at Mark's treatment of Tristram, gave up all the lands that he held of Mark, and became Tristram's trusty friend and ally, helping Sir Sadok and others garrison Lyonesse on Tristram's behalf. Eventually, probably after Tristram's death, Dinas came to Arthur's court, where he became a knight of the Round Table. He followed Lancelot into exile and was made Duke of Anjou. From what we are told of Dinas, he seems an honorable and capable man.

He did not, however, have the most enviable love life, if the following is a fair example:

> … hunting she slipped down by a towel, and took with her two brachets, and so she yede to the knight that she loved, and he her again. And when Sir Dinas came home and missed his paramour and his brachets, then was he the more wrother for his brachets than for the lady.

He caught up with them, smote down his rival, and then the lady asked to come back to Dinas.

> Nay, said Sir Dinas, I shall never trust them that once betrayed me, and therefore, as ye have begun, so end, for I will never meddle with you. And so Sir Dinas departed, and took his brachets with him, and so rode to his castle. [Malory IX, 40; X, 50; etc.]

DINASDARON IN WALES†

Another of Arthur's court cities. It was here that first Engygeron and after him Clamadeu came, sent by Percivale, to present themselves prisoner. [Chrétien de Troyes, **Perceval**, ca. ll. 2753-2754]

Dindraine, Dindrane—see AMIDE

DO†

Parent of Sir Girflet (Griflet) according to Chrétien de Troyes [**Erec & Enide**, ll. 1691-1751]. This is according to D.D.R. Owen's translation, but I suspect that "Do" was either a variant of or a scribe's error for "Dieu." Else the post-Chrétien writers confused a human character's name with that of the Deity. See Griflet le Fise de Dieu.

DODINAS (Dodynel, Dodinel) LE SAVAGE

Son of Belinans, the brother of King Tradelmans of Norgales [Vulgate II], Dodinas was a knight of the Round Table and one of those who seem to be much in evidence, but upon whose personality I can get little if any grip. Chrétien de Troyes gives him, as Dodinel the Wild, the place of ninth best on the list of Arthur's knights that begins in line 1691 of **Erec & Enide**; but Harris remarks, in his introduction to **Yvain**, that Chrétien "included among the ten … some who were of no importance whatever", being more interested in catchy names. Chrétien also included Dodinel (though without the soubriquet "Wild") with Sagramore, Kay, Gawaine, Ywaine, and eventually Guenevere as they sit listening to Sir Calogrenant at the beginning of **Yvain**. Dodinas is again listed among Arthur's knights in **Sir Gawaine and the Green Knight**. He may have been prominent in certain pre-Malory romances, and the prominence echoed wanly through into Malory, but the major adventures did not. Dodinas may well have been a friend of Sagramore's, for they ride together three times in the books of Tristram; on the third occasion, Gawaine and Ywaine are also with them. Dodinas may have been one of the Queen's most immediate circle, for he was in her party when they went a-Maying and Meliagrant ambushed them. [Malory VIII, 16; X, 4, 66; etc]

DOLOREUSE CHARTRE†

A small but strong castle near Dolorous (Joyous) Garde. The lord of Doloreuse Chartre was the villainous Sir Brandus des Illes, who was also lord of Dolorous Garde until Lancelot conquered it and made it Joyous Garde. [Vulgate III]

Dolorous Garde—see JOYOUS GARDE

Dolorous Mount†—see under **KAHEDIN**

DOLOROUS TOWER

The castle of Sir Carados, who collected knights he had defeated and kept them in his dungeons until Lancelot defeated and killed him [Malory VIII, 28]. After Lancelot killed Carados, this castle was renamed La Bele Garde or La Bele Prise, and apparantly Sir Melians li Gai and his bride became its lord and lady [Vulgate IV].

I do not think this Sir Carados is to be identified with King Carados of Scotland, nor the Dolorous Tower with Dolorous Garde. Sir Carados and Sir Turquine were brothers, so their holdings reasonably might have been close together. I have some scanty evidence that Turquine's Hill may have been in the southwest, in the region of the South Marches. Carados might have been a spiritual ancestor of the outlaw Doones of Exmoor, with his tower somewhere in the middle of modern Devonshire. A possible identification for the Dolorous Tower is Trematon Castle,

> {A} place wherin the former Earles and other chiefe gouernors of *Cornwall* made their abodes ... howsoeuer ... it falleth daylie to ruyne and decaye: The inner buyldinges are fallen downe, only some ragged walls remayne; and in the base courte some Lodginges doe stande, and the Prison. [Norden]

Trematon is near Saltash, where the Tamar flows into the sea on the south coast, near the present-day border between Cornwall and Devon.

DOORS OF IVORY AND EBONY†

Passing the man with the silver leg, the Ferryman of Canguin led Gawaine into Queen Igraine's castle through a pair of doors, one of ivory and the other of ebony. Both were finely carved and sculpted, trimmed with gold and precious magic stones, and hung with gold hinges. The bolt, likewise, was gold. The paving beneath these doors was multicolored in black, white, reds, blues, and violets, brightly polished. Apparently, these doors opened directly into the chamber of the Wondrous (and dangerous) Bed. [Chrétien de Troyes, **Perceval**, ca. ll. 7676-7696]

Does this remind anyone besides me of those two gates of classical mythology, one of ivory through which false dreams passed, the other of horn for true dreams, below which lived Sleep and Death? [See, e.g., Edith Hamilton, **Mythology**, ch. 1, section on "The Underworld"; in index, see "Sleep" or "Death."]

DORIN†

Son of King Claudas. See under Claudas.

DORNAR (Dornard, Durnore)

A son of King Pellinore, apparently his third in wedlock, and a knight of the Round Table, Dornar is greatly eclipsed by his brothers Lamorak, Percivale, and even Aglovale and the bastard half-brother Tor. Dornar appears at Duke Galeholt's tournament in Surluse and at the attempt to heal Sir Urre. He seems to have met his death before or during Lancelot's sojourn with Elaine of Carbonek in the Joyous Isle, for while Aglovale and Percivale are searching for Lancelot they visit their mother, who mourns the death of her husband Pellinore and two of her four sons. [Malory X, 23, 48; XI, 10; XIX, 1]

'DOUTRE LES MARCHES', KING†

He was an ally of Duke Galeholt [Vulgate III].

DOVER

An important port city, especially for travel between Britain and the Continent. Dover has a good battlefield, Barham Down, nearby. It also boasts Dover Castle. Arthur used it for keeping at least one lifetime political prisoner, the duke of a Tuscan town. [Malory V, 12]

Chrétien recognized Dover's importance: the messengers who brought Arthur, then in Brittany, news of Count Angrs' treachery came through Dover. [Cligés, ll. 1047-1066]

DRAGON BANNER†

Merlin gave Arthur this banner for his battle against the rebel kings. It was sometimes carried in battle by Sir Kay, sometimes by Merlin himself. On at least one occasion when Merlin was bearing it, the dragon on the banner spat fire and flame; this, however, may have been a specific magical act of Merlin's rather than a property of the banner itself. [Vulgate II]

DROS D'AVS (Droes d'Aves)†

Approaching Tintagel, Gawaine sees a party of knights crossing the heath, followed by a squire bringing a Spanish horse. Questioning the squire, Gawaine learns that he serves Droes d'Aves (with or without the accent marks, depending on the translation), who is going to take part in a tournament between Meliant of Liz and Tibaut of Tintagel. Gawaine knows Dros well. So, I suspect, did Chrétien's target audience, from some contemporary literature apparently lost or terribly obscure to us today. A connection with Druas of Druas' Hill is probably not impossible, though it would seem to require a shift over the years from heroic to sinister figure.

DRUAS†

Brother to Sir Sornehan.

DRUAS' HILL† (Le Tertre as Caitis)

Sir Druas defended this hill against all knights who tried to pass over it, killing or wounding them. If Druas was defeated, his dwarf would offer the victor a horn. Blowing this horn would bring Druas' brother, Sornehan.

Sir Agravaine mounted the hill, encountered and killed Druas near a fountain, but—though forewarned—blew the horn when the dwarf offered it. Sornehan was sick at home, but, on hearing the horn, he rose and went out, despite the pleading of his young son not to go. Sornehan defeated Agravaine and would have slain him, but a damsel happened to come by and she asked Sornehan to do her a favor. When he granted it unheard, she asked for Agravaine's life, pointing out that thus Sornehan would save his own life, Agravaine being the brother of the great Gawaine. Sornehan imprisoned Agravaine in the tower on the hill and enclosed the hill with a wall having only one gate, where was a warning that Sornehan would fight whomever mounted the hill. Later Sornehan defeated and imprisoned Gaheris when he tried to cross the hill. Sornehan's niece, whom Gaheris had once saved, succored him and Agravaine secretly.

Gareth finally defeated Sornehan, rescued his brothers, and sent Sornehan as prisoner to the Lady of Roestoc. The hill, hitherto called *letertre as caitis,* was henceforth called *li tertres Agravaine.* [Vulgate V]

Gareth's sending Sornehan to the Lady of Roestoc suggests a northern site.

DUBRIC, SAINT (Dubricus)†

The Archbishop of Caerleon who crowned Arthur King. According to Geoffrey of Monmouth, Dubric was primate of Britain and so eminent in piety that he could cure any sick person by his prayers. He abdicated later to become a hermit.

Malory seems to know nothing of him, unless Saint Dubric is to be identified with the Archbishop of Canterbury. To Tennyson, however, Dubric is the "high saint" who not only crowned Arthur but officiated at his marriage, and who is as eminent in the spiritual realm as Merlin in the magical.

DUNDEVENEL† (Dundonald)

A church founded by Saint Monenna after Arthur's victories over the Pagans [Glennie, p. 82].

On the west coast of Scotland, on the Firth of Clyde, a few miles north of Ayr, is a small island. A little north of the island is a small, pointed peninsula. A little north of this peninsula is the mouth of the River Irvine. If an isosceles triangle were drawn using the coast from the peninsula to the river's mouth as one side and the Irvine as another side, Dundevenel would be roughly in the middle of the base line between the peninsula and the river's curve, slightly closer to the river.

Dundonald—see **DUNDEVENEL**

DUNPELEDUR† (Dunpender Law)

> On Dunpeledur … as likewise on the three fortified rocks Edinburgh, Stirling, and Dumbarton, at Dundonald, in Ayrshire, and Chilnacase, in Galloway, S. Monenna … founded a church, and nunnery. These foundations appear to synchronise with the re-establishment of the Christian Church in these districts by Arthur. [Glennie, p. 54]

Glennie goes on to suggest that the 'Castle of Maidens' at Edinburgh takes its name from one of Monenna's nunneries, and that Thenew, daughter of King Lothus and mother of Saint Kentigern, was a nun at Dunpeledur.

Dunpeledur is in East Lothian, a few miles south of the River Tyne, apparently a little east of modern Haddington.

Dunpender Law—see **DUNPELEDUR**

Durnore—see **DORNAR**

Eastland—see SORESTAN

EASTLAND (Sorestan?), QUEEN OF

In Malory VI, 3-4, the Queen of Eastland, Morgan, and the Queens of Norgales and the Out Isles kidnap Lancelot and take him to Castle Chariot, wishing him to choose one of them for his paramour. The Vulgate version of this episode has only three kidnapers: Morgan, the Queen of Sorestan, and Sebile the enchantress [Vulgate V]. From this and other evidence, I suspect Eastland to be identical with Sorestan; thus the Queen of Eastland is to be identified with the Queen of Sorestan. Incidentally, the reputations of the Queens of Eastland, Norgales, and the Out Isles as dames of magic seem to rest—as far as Malory is concerned—on their association with Morgan and on Lancelot's assertion that they are all four "false enchantresses."

ECTOR (Antor)

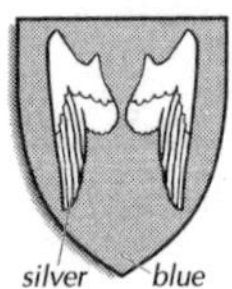

Merlin selected this "lord of fair livelihood in many parts in England and Wales", whom he called "a passing true man and a faithful" to Uther, to be Arthur's foster father. Accepting the task at Uther's behest, for which Uther granted him great rewards ahead of time, Ector followed Merlin's directions and gave Arthur to his wife for suckling, entrusting his own son, Kay, to a wetnurse. Some years later, when Kay tried to claim credit for drawing the Sword from the Stone, Ector saw through the claim and made his son "swear upon a book how he came to that sword."

Modern romancers have presented us with the tale that Arthur was always aware he was not Ector's true son and that he grew up believing himself a bastard and destined to a humbler lot in life than Kay. According to Malory, however, Arthur was completely surprised and dismayed when the incident of the Sword in the Stone prompted Sir Ector to reveal as much of the truth as he knew. (Apparently Ector himself did not know the full story of Arthur's birth and parentage.)

> Alas, said Arthur, my own dear father and brother, why kneel ye to me? ...
>
> Then Arthur made great dole when he understood that Sir Ector was not his father. Sir, said Ector unto Arthur, will ye be my good and gracious lord when ye are king? Else were I to blame, said Arthur, for ye are the man in the world that I am most beholden to, and my good lady and mother your wife, that as well as her own hath fostered me and kept. ... God forbid I should fail you.

Ector asked of Arthur only that Kay be made seneschal of all Arthur's lands, which the young King eagerly promised. I see no reason to believe from all this that Arthur occupied a lesser position in Ector's household during his formative years than did Kay, except for a slight age difference, or to assume that Arthur did not fully expect to be made knight in his turn. Ector was clearly an ideal foster father.

This Sir Ector must not be confused with Sir Ector de Maris, Lancelot's brother. Vulgate II names Arthur's foster father Antor. Tennyson gives him the name Anton (**The Coming of Arthur**).

ECTOR DE MARIS (Hector des Mares)

This major knight of the Round Table was Lancelot's English-born half-brother. Through Merlin's unsolicited contrivance, King Ban of Benwick fathered Ector on the Damsel des Mares [Vulgate].

Malory seems first to mention Ector de Maris in Book VI. Lancelot left court with his cousin Lionel to seek adventure. Lancelot was napping under a tree when Lionel saw Sir Turquine ride by, pursued him without waking Lancelot, and was captured by Turquine, while Morgan and her cohorts chanced along from another direction and kidnaped the slumbering Lancelot. Ector, meanwhile, learning how Lancelot had left court, "was wroth with himself" and went out to find and join him. Coming to Turquine's stronghold and being informed of the danger by a local forester, Ector challenged Turquine and was defeated in his turn, stripped, beaten with thorns, and imprisoned along with Lionel and others until Lancelot could come to rescue them. A little later Ector, Sagramore, Gawaine, and Ywaine saw Lancelot riding in Kay's arms, thought it was indeed Kay, and tried—unsuccessfully, of course—to joust him down. When Mark sent Tristram to Ireland for La Beale Isoud, a storm drove him ashore "fast by Camelot." Ector de Maris and another knight of Arthur's, Morganore, welcomed Tristram with a joust.

> Alas, said Sir Ector [on being defeated], now I am ashamed that ever any Cornish knight should overcome me. And then for despite Sir Ector put off his armour from him, and went on foot, and would not ride.

When Tristram later dropped out of sight after the Castle of Maidens tournament, however, Ector was one of nine knights who joined Lancelot in a vow to search for him.

Despite the defeats mentioned above, Ector was a good man of arms, showing up well at tourneys. At least once during Duke Galeholt's Surluse tournament, Ector got the better of the formidable Palomides.

Chancing to meet during a search for Lancelot, Ector and Percivale took time out for a friendly little fight that ended with both wounded nigh unto death and lying helpless on the ground. At Percivale's prayer, the Sangreal came and healed them. Traveling on together, Ector and Percivale found Lancelot living with Elaine of Carbonek at Joyous Isle and persuaded him to return to Arthur's court.

While on the Grail Quest, Ector met and rode for a while with Gawaine. One night each had a vision. In Ector's vision, he saw Lancelot humbled and himself turned away from a rich man's wedding feast. Later, when Ector came knocking at Carbonek (his brother Lancelot being already within), King Pellam denied him admittance, saying that he was "one of them which hath served the fiend, and hast left the service of Our Lord." This may reflect the high standards of the Grail rather than Ector's depravity, for Ector seems no worse than most "worldly" knights and a good deal better-living than many.

Naturally rallying at once to Lancelot's side when the break came with Arthur, Ector helped rescue Guenevere from the stake. He afterward accompanied Lancelot into exile and was crowned King of Benwick. Later, he was one of the last to refind Lancelot at the hermitage of the former Archbishop of Canterbury. Ector did not arrive until Lancelot was dead.

> [A]nd then Sir Ector threw his shield, sword, and helm from him. And when he beheld Sir Launcelot's visage, he fell down in a swoon. And when he waked it were hard for any tongue to tell the doleful complaints that he made for his brother. Ah Launcelot, he said, thou were head of all Christian knights, and now I dare say ... that thou were never matched of earthly knight's hand.

After returning to settle affairs in Benwick, Ector went with Bors, Blamore, and Bleoberis to die fighting the Turks in the Holy Land. [Malory VI, 1-2, 7-9,13; VIII, 19; IX, 36; X, 79; XI, 13-14; XII, 7-10; XVI, 1-2; XVII, 16; XX, 5-8, 18, etc.]

Ector's first love was Perse. Later he took a niece of the Lady of Roestoc's dwarf and cousin of the Lady of Roestoc. She died, and he was eventually reunited with Perse. [Vulgate V, appendix]

Do not confuse Ector de Maris with the older Ector who was Arthur's foster father.

EDWARD OF ORKNEY

Brother to Sir Sadok, cousin to Gawaine, and a knight of the Round Table. [Malory X, 68; XIX, 11]

EDWARD OF THE RED CASTLE

He and his brother, Hue of the Red Castle, extorted a barony from the Lady of the Rock. Sir Marhaus, winning it back for her, killed Edward in combat. [Malory IV, 26-27]

EDYOPE†

This castle was in the "Waste Forest"—in Wales or in the Waste Lands of Listeneise [Vulgate VII].

ELAINE OF ASTOLAT (Elaine le Blank)

For his own excellent artistic purposes, T. H. White combines Elaine of Astolat and Elaine of Carbonek into one character and identifies them both with the damsel in the scalding bath (**The Once and Future King**, Book III, especially chapters 11 and 40). In Malory, Elaine of Astolat is definitely distinct from her namesake of Carbonek. Elaine of Carbonek may have been the damsel in the scalding bath (though I am far from convinced of it), but there is no way to combine the two Elaines.

The younger Elaine, Tennyson's "lily maid of Astolat" (**Lancelot and Elaine**), was the daughter of Sir Bernard of Astolat and the sister of Sirs Lavaine and Tirre. Lancelot, traveling secretly to the tournament at Winchester, lodged with Sir Bernard and borrowed the shield of the recently wounded Sir Tirre, leaving his own shield with Elaine for safe-keeping. He also did for her what he had never done for any other woman, including Guenevere: with a view to heightening his incognito, he accepted Elaine's token to wear in the lists. Elaine fell deeply in love with him. When she learned he was wounded and lodged with Sir Baudwin the hermit, she insisted on going herself to nurse him. She asked to be his paramour if he would not marry her, and even Sir Bors counseled him to love Elaine if he could, but Lancelot remained true to Guenevere. After Lancelot left her, Elaine died for love of him. According to her dying instructions, her body was put in a barge and steered down to Westminster, where King, Queen, Lancelot, and the rest of the court grieved to see the body and read the explanatory letter in its hand, which requested Lancelot to give the Mass-penny for her soul. [Malory XVIII, 9-20]

ELAINE OF CARBONEK

Do not confuse her with Elaine of Astolat.

Vulgate II calls Elaine of Carbonek, King Pellam's daughter, the wisest woman who ever lived. "The best of the world" seems to be a figure of speech with the old romancers, however, and I am not sure the statement is meant to be taken as literal fact.

When Lancelot first came to Carbonek, rescued the damsel in the scalding bath, and killed a troublesome dragon, Elaine fell in love with him. At that time, she seems to have been acting as the "damosel passing fair and young" who bore the Holy Grail at dinnertime in the castle. With the help of Dame Brisen and the connivance of King Pellam, Elaine managed to sleep one night with Lancelot by tricking him into thinking she was Guenevere. Thus was Galahad begotten, who was by his holy life to expiate the fornication of his father and mother and to heal his grandfather Pellam and Pellam's kingdom of the effects of the Dolorous Stroke. When Lancelot woke up in the morning and saw how he had been tricked, he came near smiting Elaine down with his sword.

> Then ... Elaine skipped out of her bed all naked, and kneeled down afore Sir Launcelot, and said: Fair courteous knight ... I require you have mercy upon me, and as thou art renowned the most noble knight of the world, slay me not, for I have in my womb him by thee that shall be the most noblest knight of the world. ... Well, said Sir Launcelot, I will forgive you this deed; and therewith he took her up in his arms, and kissed her, for she was as fair a lady, and thereto lusty and young, and as wise, as any was that time living.

He threatened, however, to slay Dame Brisen if ever he saw her, but nothing ever came of the threat.

After Galahad's birth, Elaine and Brisen came to Arthur's court to help celebrate Arthur's victory over Claudas. Again they tricked Lancelot into Elaine's bed by pretending she was Guenevere. This time Guenevere herself, whose room was next door and who had been expecting Lancelot in her own bed, heard them. She came into Elaine's room, found them together, and jealously accused Lancelot, setting off a fit of his madness. After wandering a long time insane and unknown, he came again to Carbonek, where he was eventually recognized and cured by exposure to the Grail. Pellam now set him up with Elaine in the Joyous Isle. Lancelot agreed to this arrangement because he thought he could never again return to Arthur's court after his disgrace. As Le Chavaler Mal Fet, he lived with Elaine in the Castle of Bliant and kept the Joyous Isle against all comers for perhaps two years. Then, to Elaine's grief, Ector de Maris and Percivale came to the Joyous Isle and persuaded Lancelot to return to court. By this time Galahad, who had been growing up at his grandfather's castle Carbonek on the mainland, was fifteen years old; Elaine promised that he could come to Arthur's court to be made knight that same feast of Pentecost.

When Lancelot came once again to Carbonek during the Grail Quest, he learned to his sorrow that Elaine had died in the interim. [Malory XI, 1-3, 7-9; XII, 1-9; XVII, 16]

It is possible, as T. H. White has it, that Elaine of Carbonek was herself the damsel Lancelot rescued from the scalding bath (**The Once and Future King**). I doubt this. According to the Vulgate, the damsel in the bath was being punished for sin, and as Grail-bearer Elaine must have been free of fleshly sin before her night with Lancelot. (After that night, of course, they had to find a new damsel to carry the Grail. Amide may have fulfilled this office for a time.)

ELAINE OF TINTAGIL, QUEEN OF GARLOTH

The second daughter of Gorloïs and Igraine, she was married to King Nentres of Garloth at about the same time her mother was married to Uther Pendragon and her sister Morgawse to King Lot (Malory I, 2). Elaine became the mother of Galescin. She is greatly eclipsed by her sisters Morgan and Morgawse. Chapman identifies her with "Vivian called Nimue" and makes her the youngest of Igraine's "witchy" daughters (**The Green Knight**, Part 1). This is ingenious and symmetrical, but I found nothing in Malory or the Vulgate to substantiate it, or even to suggest that the other two sisters shared Morgan's talent for necromancy.

ELAINE, QUEEN OF BENWICK

Wife of King Ban and mother of Sir Lancelot. After the death of her husband and the appropriation of her young son by Viviane, Queen Elaine founded a religious house, the Royal Minster, on the scene of her losses in Benwick and lived there for many years as a saintly woman. This we find in the Vulgate. Malory only records that Merlin, visiting her, assured her she would live long enough to witness her son's fame and glory. [Malory IV, 1]

She visited her nephews Bors and Lionel when they were in Gaul during Arthur's war against King Claudas. From her nephews she got news of her son. Later, when the war was won, she visited Lancelot himself in Gannes, afterward returing to her minster. [Vulgate V]

Her sister was Evaine, who married Ban's brother Bors.

ELAINE'S SLEEVE

In the tournament at Winchester, Lancelot wore the token of Elaine of Astolat, a scarlet sleeve embroidered with pearls. Lancelot did this to insure his incognito status, since he was well known never to have worn anybody's token before. Elaine might have broken her heart for love of him even had he refused to accept her token; of course, it caused Guenevere much pain, anger, and jealousy when she learned of it. [Malory XVIII, 9-15]

ELEINE

The beautiful, golden-haired daughter of King Pellinore and the Lady of the Rule, Eleine killed herself with the sword of her lover Sir Miles after he was treacherously slain by Loraine le Savage. The tragedy was compounded in that Pellinore himself passed by before Miles' actual death, and Eleine appealed to him, but he was in eager pursuit of another quest—the rescue of Nimue—and did not stop to help them. Only after finding them both dead on his return, all of Eleine eaten by lions except for the head, did Pellinore learn that she was his own daughter. [Malory III, 12-15]

Elian—see HELIN LE BLANK

ELIAS

A captain of the Sessoins and "a good man of arms", Elias commanded an invading Saxon host against King Mark. Elias led his men nobly in battle before Tintagil. After many of them were killed and the rest became loath to do battle again, he offered to settle the invasion in single combat. Mark's champion was Tristram. Elias put up a good fight. Tristram remarked at the end, "Sir Elias, I am right sorry for thee, for thou art a passing good knight as ever I met withal, except Sir Lancelot." With Elias dead, Mark took prisoners and sent the rest of the Sessoins back to their own country. [Malory X, 28-30]

ELIAZAR

He was a holy knight, the son of King Pellam, living at Carbonek. Eliazar brought back from Mategant's castle to Carbonek the broken sword with which Joseph had been wounded. [Vulgate IV; see also Swords] Eliazar fought a tournament with symbolic overtones; see under Argustus.

Curiously, Eliazar is not among the twelve knights who represented the twelve apostles at the Mass celebrated by Joseph in Carbonek during the climax of the Grail adventures. Indeed, Pellam, Eliazar, and "a maid which was [Pellam's] niece" must specifically be sent out of the room before the Mysteries can begin. [Malory XVII, 19)

ELIEZER†

Gawaine's squire. He is a fairly important character in Vulgate VII.

In Vulgate VI, p. 329, Gawaine's squire balks at taking Gawaine's challenge to Lancelot in the war of vengeance for the deaths of Gareth and Gaheris. The squire tells him that, "A wrong cause often makes a good knight blunder, while a right one transforms an indifferent knight into a hero." Either this is a case of squire rebellion, a suggestion that squires are not the subservient ciphers they sometimes seem to be considered, or an indication that Gawaine's squire, like Tristram's Gouvernail, may be a special case. The specific squire in Vulgate VI is left unnamed, but for the sake of convenience I would identify him with Eliezer.

Like Gouvernail, Eliezer seems to be a "career squire", one with little or no intention of becoming a knight.

"ELINOR"†

Chrétien de Troyes leaves the damsel nameless who thrice served as Guenevere's messenger to Lancelot during the Noauz tournament. I chose the name "Elinor" for her because, like Jane Austen's Elinor of **Sense And Sensibility**, she was prudent and sensible, both of which qualities she must have needed to seek out one particular knight and give him private messages in the middle of a tournament. It is tempting to wonder if the "Shrewd Damsel at the Window" might have accompanied Guenevere from Gore to turn up a second time at Noauz. [**Lancelot**, ll. 5641-5937.]

ELIOT

Dinadan taught his satirical lay against King Mark to a minstrel and harper named Eliot, who in turn taught it to many other harpers. After singing it to Tristram, Eliot asked if he dared sing it before Mark. Tristram said yes, promising to be his warrant—although Tristram himself does not seem to have attended dinner in Mark's hall on the occasion. When Mark spoke angrily at the song's end, Eliot excused himself by explaining that Dinadan had made him sing it and a minstrel had to obey the lord whose arms he bore. Told by Mark to leave quickly, Eliot escaped to Tristram, who wrote to Lancelot and Dinadan and "let conduct the harper out of the country" (probably the country of Cornwall). [Malory X, 27, 31]

ELISE, DUKE

This "worshipful duke", seemingly named Elise, is apparently mentioned only once by Malory, at Duke Galeholt's tournament in Surluse. The duke is mentioned, however, as "uncle unto King Arthur." He had a son, also, it seems, named Sir Elise. [Malory X, 46]

ELIWLOD†

According to Lewis Spence, Eliwlod was the son of Arthur's brother Madawg ap Uther and thus Arthur's nephew. He appears in a poem known as "The Dialogue of Arthur and Eliwlod." In the poem, Eliwlod seems to appear as an eagle to Arthur, perhaps while the latter lies wounded in Avalon, and urges him to accept Christianity. This poem was translated by one Herbert, and Lewis Spence lists among his sources two titles by A. Herbert: **Brittania after the Romans**, 2 v., London, 1836-1841; and **An Essay on the Neo-Druidic Heresy**, London, 1838. Beyond this much, I cannot find that Spence throws any further light on the subject, even as to the approximate date of the poem. [**Magic Arts**, p. 159]

ELIZABETH, QUEEN OF LYONESSE

The sister of King Mark was "a full meek lady, and well she loved her lord", King Meliodas of Cornwall. While she was pregnant with Tristram, Meliodas was waylaid on a hunt and imprisoned by an enchantress who loved him.

> When Elizabeth ... missed her lord, and she was nigh out of her wit, and also as great with child as she was, she took a gentlewoman with her, and ran into the forest to seek her lord.

Here she gave birth to her son.

> But she had taken such cold for the default of help that deep draughts of death took her .... Now let me see my little child, for whom I have had all this sorrow. And when she saw him she said thus: Ah, my little son, thou hast murdered thy mother, and therefore I suppose, thou that art a murderer so young, thou art full likely to be a manly man in thine age.

With this wry humor, and charging her gentlewoman to ask the king to name his son Tristram, "that is as much to say as a sorrowful birth", she gave up the ghost and died. [Malory VIII, 1]

ELYZABEL†

Guenevere's cousin and, seemingly, her most intimate confidante, Elyzabel was a brave and resourceful woman as well as a discreet one. On one occasion, when Lancelot, Bors, and Lionel were all from court and Guenevere had no one else to confide in about Lancelot, she took to her bed with no attendant but Elyzabel. Once the Queen sleepwalked in a nightmare. Elyzabel, awaking, sprinkled her with holy water and said, "Go quickly to bed—the King is coming", thus bringing her to her senses.

In her efforts to find the missing Lancelot, Guenevere once sent Elyzabel to the Royal Minster in Gaul to bring back the French Damsel of the Lake, Viviane. King Claudas, who was at that time popular and residing in Gannes, welcomed and feasted Elyzabel at first, but then suspected she was a spy for Lancelot and his cousins. He had her, her squire, and her dwarf seized and searched. The dwarf threw Guenevere's box containing the message to Viviane into the river, but Claudas' seneschal saw him do it. Claudas imprisoned them all and sent two squires to Britain as spies. The spies were so impressed by Arthur's court that one of them stayed on, entering Guenevere's service. When, a year later, Guenevere asked him where he came from, he told her all. Thus she learned that her cousin was a prisoner. She wrote an indignant letter to Claudas, sealed it with her seal, and sent it by the squire. Claudas forced the squire to return it with an insulting answer. This led to the war in which Arthur defeated Claudas for once and all and freed Elyzabel. [Vulgate V]

ENGLAND (Logres, Logris)

The "country of Logris … that is for to say the country of England" [Malory XII, 5], excluding Scotland, Wales, and Cornwall. Sub-kingdoms include Arroy, Avilion, Cameliard, the Delectable Isle, King Amans' Land, Leicester, Listeneise, Malahaut, Nohaut, Northumberland, and Roestoc.

ENGYGERON (Anguingueron)†

The seneschal of Clamadeu of the Isles spent the better part of a year besieging Beaurepaire in order to win it and its lady Blancheflor for his lord. He had almost reduced it to abject surrender when Percivale arrived and defeated him in single combat. Conscientiously remembering Gornemant's instructions to grant mercy whenever defeated opponents begged for it, Percivale would have sent Engygeron prisoner to Blancheflor; Engygeron pointed out that she would certainly have him killed, not only for besieging her and her people, but for having had a hand in her father's death. (I find no further details about that incident.) All right, said Percivale, then present yourself prisoner at this castle, describing Gornemant's. Engygeron recognized it from the description and explained that they hated him there, too, for having killed one of Gornemant's brothers in the Beaurepaire fighting. Thereupon Percivale ordered him to turn himself in at Arthur's court in Dinasdaron, which final charge Engygeron accepted. The day after his arrival at Arthur's court, he found his lord Clamadeu following him, having suffered almost exactly the same fate at Percivale's hands. Since Clamadeu settled down as a member of Arthur's court for the rest of his life, it might not be preposterous of us to guess that Engygeron did the same.

"Engygeron" is D.D.R. Owen's transcription of the name. "Anguingueron" is Ruth Harwood Cline's.

ENIDE (Enid)†

Wife of Sir Erec (Geraint), whom see. Chrétien de Troyes describes her as so beautiful that Nature herself, who created her, could never again reproduce her (but this is more or less what Chrétien says of most of his heroines). At any rate, Enide was so lovely that Arthur easily solved his dilemma of killing the White Stag (q.v.) and having to choose the loveliest maid among the five hundred highborn damsels at court, simply by following Guenevere's suggestion and naming golden-haired Enide as soon as she appeared with Erec, since not even the most zealous lover of any other maid could dispute this choice! The poverty of Enide's immediate family sprang from her parents' pride. Her mother, Carsenefide, was sister to the Count of Lalut and by her father Liconal's account Enide had any number of would-be suitors, but he refused them all his parental permission until Erec arrived, to whom he betrothed her at once, to her own silent satisfaction. Enide had at least two female cousins, one of them being Mabonagrain's lady.

Her vavasour father being so impoverished he had only a single manservant, Enide could tend horses like an expert stablehand, a talent which must have come in handy when her husband later took her as his only attendant on a series of madcap adventures inspired by her fearing aloud that her bridal doting upon him was enervating his knightly prowess and reputation. Among his methods to punish her fear was forbidding her to speak a word to him without first being addressed. Poor, patient Griselda, that famous medieval model of wifely virtue, would have obeyed her lord to the strictest letter; but Enide proved herself no patient Griselda by disobeying Erec on several occasions, though not without severe mental anguish, whenever she saw robbers or other dangers bearing down on him to his apparent (though feigned) ignorance. Even while berating her for disobeying his injunction not to speak, he secretly recognized and rejoiced in the love her disobedience displayed. Such was Enide's affection that it survived even the test to which her husband put it, which must make her one of the most remarkable examples of loyalty in all Arthurian romance. [Chrétien de Troyes, **Erec & Enide**; also "Gereint Son of Erbin" in the Welsh **Mabinogion**, and Tennyson's **Idyll of the King** "Geraint and Enid."]

ENIDE'S COUSIN†

When Enide was about to leave Lalut with her affianced husband Erec, another niece of the count's, a maid of talent, prudence, and intelligence, wanted to give her a fine dress as a going-away present. Erec, however, preferred bringing his betrothed to court in her ragged old white dress in order to have Guenevere give her fine apparel. So, instead, the cousin gave her finest dappled palfrey to her cousin. This was almost certainly the same horse that later served Enide so well during her enforced adventures following Erec. [Chrétien de Troyes, **Erec & Enide**, ll. 1353-1406 and 2583ff.]

ENIDE'S DAPPLED PALFREY†

Presented to the heroine by her cousin, who called it swift as a bird, gentle as a boat (presumably on quiet waters), and calm enough for a child to ride, this splendid northern mount was almost certainly the one Enide later rode on the madcap adventures Erec initiated to prove that his knightly prowess still continued after marriage. There may have been a touch of Faery in this horse's origin. Unhappily, somewhere during the adventures this excellent palfrey was lost—I suspect during the episode with Count Oringle of Limors. [Chrétien de Troyes, **Erec & Enide**, ll. 1353-1406, 2583ff., 5173-5180]

ENIDE'S SADDLE†

Given to her, along with a remarkable sorrel palfrey, by Guivret the Little and his sisters, this saddle had ivory bows, decorated with gold, on which the complete story of Aeneas and Dido was carved. The craftsman had spent seven years making it. [Chrétien de Troyes, **Erec & Enide**, ll. 5337-5366]

ENIDE'S SORREL PALFREY†

This mount, presented to Enide by Guivret the Little and his sisters to replace the notable dappled palfrey she had lost while following Erec's adventures, had a tricolored head with one cheek white, the other black, and a line greener than a vine separating the white and black sides. (One thinks of the "horse of a different color.") D.D.R. Owen remarks that both this palfrey and Enide's earlier one may have been supernatural in origin. [Chrétien de Troyes, **Erec & Enide**, ll. 5316-5336 & note to l. 5316]

EPINEGRIS (Epinogrus)

> Well, said Sir Tristram, I know that knight well with the covered shield of azure, he is the king's son of Northumberland, his name is Epinegris; and he is as great a lover as I know, and he loveth the king's daughter of Wales, a full fair lady.

Epinegris seems to make his first appearance in Malory at the Castle Dangerous tournament in the book of Gareth Beaumains. Later, Tristram and Dinadan encounter him while they are in the midst of a discussion about whether or not knights in love make the better fighters. With the words quoted above, among others, Tristram eggs Dinadan on to make the test, Dinadan having boasted about his lack of a lady. After asking, "Sir … is that the rule of you errant knights for to make a knight to joust, will he or nill?", Epinegris, the lover, unhorses Dinadan. He appears a little after this in unsuccessful pursuit of Breuse Sans Pitie.

Later still, Palomides finds Epinegris wounded. They tell each other their woes. Palomides complains of his love for La Beale Isoud. Epinegris says his case is much worse, for in the tournament of Lonazep he had won his lady (here, the daughter of an earl) by killing her father and one of his two knights. The next day, as they reposed by a well, Sir Helior le Preuse came, challenged, and fought Epinegris, defeating him and winning away the lady. Palomides brings Epinegris safe to a hermitage, then finds Helior, wins back the lady, defends her against yet another challenger (who turns out to be Palomides' brother Safere), and returns her to Epinegris.

Epinegris is mentioned again at the tournament of Winchester and as one of the knights of the Round Table who attempt to heal Sir Urre. [Malory VII, 26; X, 55, 65, 82-84; XVIII, 10; XIX, 11]

ERBIN†

Father of Geraint according to the Welsh **Mabinogion**.

ERCILDOUNE, CASTLE OF (Rhymer's Tower)†

Here, in the thirteenth century, lived Thomas the Rhymer, who, according to the ballad of "True Thomas", visited the Queen of Faery in her own land and who, according to Glennie, became a guide to those adventurers trying to find the sleeping Arthur. Perhaps already in Arthur's day this was a gateway into the otherworld of Faery.

Glennie puts Rhymer's Tower at present-day Earlston, north of Melrose, Roxburgh County, Scotland, with Rhymer's Glen slanting down below Melrose and including Din Drei.

EREC†—see also **GERAINT**

Chrétien de Troyes gave us our earliest known written version of this knight's story, although Chrétien alludes to earlier sources, and a large body of scholarly opinion would consider the **Mabinogion** story "Gereint Son of Erbin" evidence that Chrétien was telling the truth about this, rather than using a literary device to introduce his own new characters. The son of King Lac, Erec resembled Absalom for good looks, King Solomon for speech, a lion for pride, and Alexander (presumably the Great) for giving and spending—a virtue, in the world Chrétien describes. Already before the age of twenty-five Erec was a renowned knight of the Round Table: Chrétien names him as second, after Gawaine and before Lancelot, in the roll call of Arthur's knights. (Since this placement comes during Erec's own story, however, it may be colored by flattery.) [**Erec & Enide**, ca. l. 1691]

After finding Enide in Lalut and marrying her in Arthur's court at Pentecost, Eric was acclaimed victor in the tournament between Evroic and Tenebroc, then retired with his bride to his father's kingdom of Outre-Gales, where he settled into marital bliss until one morning he overheard Enide lament that he might be losing his reputation. Chrétien's Erec, unlike the **Mabinogion**'s and Tennyson's Gereint, does not suspect his wife of infidelity, nor do her words invite such misinterpretation; from the beginning, he understands her lament on the fateful morning as exactly what it is: a fear for his chivalric honor. This may make his subsequent actions—taking her along as his only companion on an extended round of often foolhardy adventures, forbidding her to speak to him without permission and scolding her whenever she disobeys in order to warn him of impending peril, and so forth—even less explicable to our modern sensibilities. He appears to do it all for the sole purpose of proving to her his unsullied knighthood and manliness. (Had I been Enide, I'm not at all sure how long I would have continued to love Erec!) Tennyson has probably made the story far more accessible to the modern reader, yet Chrétien's version retains a rambling, tongue-in-cheek charm peculiarly its own.

In Erec's favor, when he conceives his plan for adventuring alone with only his wife for human company (clearly an unusual move, especially for a king's son, in an age when "aloneness" in the modern sense was rare), he may wish to test himself at least as much as her. Chrétien's Erec bids Enide wear her best gown, as if to show her off, whereas his counterpart Geraint makes her wear her worst, as if to shame her; in refusing his father's pleas to take along thirty or forty knights, a supply of money, etc., Erec begs him to take care of Enide, should she return widowed, and freely give her half the kingdom. [**Erec & Enide**, ll. 2540-2741, & Owen's notes]

Fine a warrior as he undoubtedly was, Erec got some boost from Lady Luck. The robber knights he encountered his first day out, in one band of three and a later band of five, had sufficient chivalry to come at him and be demolished one at a time (though Enide had feared otherwise). The second day, Count Galoain had a change of heart as soon as he was gravely wounded by our hero and ordered his men to cease their pursuit. Erec next encountered Guivret the Little, who battled him only for the exercise and became his friend. He ended that day by coming to where Arthur and his court happened to be hunting; bent on pursuing his own way incognito, Erec jousted Kay down for trying to force hospitality upon them (considerately using the butt end of his lance, since the seneschal foolishly if typically tried to tilt although not wearing armor), but Gawaine cleverly tricked our hero into spending the night in the king's pavilions. Arthur fortunately had some ointment made by his sister Morgan (in her beneficial aspect) with which they could treat Erec's wounds. Insisting on leaving again after a single night, on his third day Erec rescued Sir Cadoc of Tabriol by killing two giants who had cruelly kidnaped him. Lucky as Erec's persistence proved for Cadoc and his lady, it cost Erec and Enide something—returning to her, he fell down as if dead. She would have killed herself in despair, but their luck held when Count Oringle of Limors and his company heard her cries and arrived in time to save her. Oringle would have forcibly married the supposed widow, but that evening, after some hours of rest, Erec woke, saw the situation, rescued her, and kindly forgave her the fault that everybody else has so much difficulty seeing in the first place.

Escaping Count Oringle's people, Erec and Enide had the further good fortune again to meet Guivret the Little, who, having heard the news of his neighbor's doings, was on the way with 1,000 men to the rescue. This fortune Erec did his best to spoil by jousting with Guivret before they recognized eath other—Chrétien himself remarks on Erec's foolishness in galloping to the encounter without identifying himself. On learning who they were, however, Guivret took them to his nearby castle of Penevric, where his two sisters skillfully nursed the model of chivalric reputation back to health. Healed, he rounded off his grand adventure by defeating Mabonagrain to achieve the adventure called the Joy of the Court. (See "Garden of the Joy".) He then found Arthur at Robais and, on the king's request, agreed to stay at court three or four whole years, providing Arthur ask Guivret the Little to stay also. They stayed until the death of old King Lac, Erec's father. Erec showed his grief as befit a king, with alms, prayers, and generous gifts until, having distributed all his immediate wealth, he received his father's land back from Arthur in a Yuletide coronation at Nantes in Brittany. [Chrétien, **Erec & Enide**]

Erec has been identified with Sir Harry le Fise Lake, a very minor figure in Malory.

EREC'S ROBE†

Worn by Erec on his coronation as king of Outre-Gales, this extraordinarily rich robe depicted the four Liberal Arts—Geometry, Arithmetic, Music, and Astronomy—in feminine personifications, perhaps connected with the four fairies who had made the robe of watered fabric. It was lined with the multicolored skins of spice-eating and probably fabulous Indian beasts called barbioletes. It had four stones in the tassels: two chrysolites on one side and two amethysts on the other. [Chrétien de Troyes, **Erec & Enide**, ll. 6736-6809]

EREC'S SCEPTER†

Made entirely of a single emerald, it was as thick as a man's fist and carved with the likenesses of every known kind of wild beast and man, fish and bird. Arthur put it into Erec's hand at the latter's coronation, whether as gift or loan I cannot say; but Chrétien's Arthur is incredibly generous. [Chrétien de Troyes, **Erec & Enide**, ll. 6856-6887]

Erminide—see HERMIND

ESCADES†

According to the Vulgate, the guardian knight of the *pont despee* or Sword Bridge into Gore. Escades was succeeded in this role by Meliagrant. See Gore.

ESCALON LI TENEBREUX†

This castle had once been called Escalon li Envoisies. The lord of Escalon had relations with his paramour in the chapel of his castle on Ash Wednesday, where they were found at it by a holy man. From that day, castle and church were enveloped in darkness. Only the churchyard remained light, also giving off a sweet fragrance because of the many holy folk buried there.

Only the knight who succeeded in the adventure of this castle could defeat Sir Carados of the Dolorous Tower. But any knight who entered the cold, dark, malodorous chapel was driven back by a rain of blows from invisible hands.

Fourteen years went by, reapers on the surrounding farms supplying the castle dwellers with food, before Lancelot arrived to make it through the chapel and open the far door, thus bringing back light and freeing the castle from the spell. Henceforth the place was called Escalon li Aaisies. The sight of a certain tomb in the churchyard healed Lancelot's wounds.

From the neighborhood of Escalon li Tenebreux, the only way to the Dolorous Tower, where Lancelot finally defeated Sir Carados and freed Gawaine and other prisoners, went past the chapel of Morgan and through the Val Sans Retour. [Vulgate IV]

Escan, Duke—see **EUSTACE**

Escarans—see **ESTORAUSE, KING OF SARRAS**

ESCAVALON†

According to Sommer, this subkingdom is called Kaerlyon, Scatanon, Catonois, or Ycastanon in various manuscripts of the Vulgate. Based on this statement, and on the Roman name for Caerleon being Isca, in my first edition I suggested identifying Escavalon, as a city, with Caerleon and, as a country, with Monmouthshire. At that time, I had not yet read much of Chrétien's work.

Escavalon and its royal family feature rather prominently in Chrétien's last romance. Gawaine leaves Arthur's court at Caerleon and reaches Tintagil, where Tibaut offers to give him an escort and provisions for the very poor country he must pass through on his further way to Escavalon. All this makes my earlier identifications unviable. Of course, the geography of the British Isles might not have been Chrétien's strongest point (although his placement of Bath in Gore is certainly clear and unambiguous); neither was my earlier surmise based on too much in the way of hard evidence, if one hypothesizes that "Kaerlyon", where it occurs for "Escavalon", was a scribal error or idiosyncracy.

Of Escavalon, Chrétien tells us that its fortress was very strong and overlooked an arm of the sea, its town was so prosperous that one might have thought it enjoyed a continuous fair, and its population was good-looking (i.e., healthy and well-fed?). The very poor country that Tibaut warned Gawaine about encountering between Tintagel and Escavalon seems to have been forgotten. [**Perceval**, ca. ll. 5318-5325; 5703-6216]

At least some of the people of Escavalon seem fairly well versed on the bleeding lance. [*Ibid.*, ca. ll. 6162-6190] Could this suggest some affinity between Escavalon and the Grail castle?

ESCAVALON, KING OF†

Near the outset of Chrétien's Grail romance, Percivale's mother tells him that his oldest brother served and was knighted by the king of Escavalon. Apparently this king died in circumstances that allowed Guigambresil to accuse Gawaine of his murder, challenging Arthur's knight to trial by combat before the young and elegant king of Escavalon, the old king's son, "handsomer than Absalom." When Gawaine arrives at Escavalon, he seems not to realize that he has reached his destination. He meets the young king, who is out hunting, but neither recognizes the other, and the king greets him hospitably, sending him on to the castle with a messenger to bid his sister entertain this new guest well. She does, until a vavasour comes in who happens to know Gawaine. The vavasour rouses the entire town, which hates Gawaine for its old king's murder, and when Guigambresil arrives, he finds Gawaine and the king's sister defending themselves against a mob. Guigambresil locates the king, who, finally learning his guest's identity, rules that the royal promise of hospitality remains sacred but, on the advice of another(?) vavasour, postpones the trial by combat for one year on condition that Gawaine use that year to search for the bleeding lance. [Chrétien de Troyes, **Perceval**, ca. ll. 464; 4792; 5703-6216]

ESCAVALON, MAYOR and MAGISTRATES (Aldermen) OF†

Chrétien describes these worthies as so sleek and paunchy they could certainly not have been taking any purgatives. Their immediate mobilization and willingness not only to summon the townsfolk but to lead the mob attack on Gawaine as soon as a vavasour calls his presence to their attention strikes me as less stereotypical than their appearance. [Chrétien, **Perceval**, ll. 5905ff.]

ESCAVALON, SISTER OF THE KING OF†

This lively damsel obeyed her brother's command to welcome their unknown guest with great spirit if not quite to the letter—her brother's instructions were "do as much for him as you would for me", but she soon entered into a flirtation with Gawaine that must have been anything but sisterly. On learning who he was—allegedly her father's murderer—she fell into a long swoon but, upon recovering, immediately set about arming him and otherwise preparing their joint defense against the mob she shrewdly guessed would come. When it came, she helped fight it off by hurling their huge chessmen—ten times larger than ordinary ones—down upon the rabble, meanwhile shouting that in making the man welcome she had simply obeyed her kingly brother. Anyone who might still imagine the maids of medieval romance to be pallid and timid creatures chiefly useful at waiting to be rescued ought to consider this one's fighting spirit, fired by a rage that continued to burn within her after her brother had come home and dispelled the mob; she trembled and whitened on his entrance, but I suspect that Chrétien, like us, could recognize that as a natural physical reaction after stress. [**Perceval**, ca. ll. 5730-6135]

ESCAVALON, VAVASOUR(S) OF THE KING OF†

Two of them appear to play a part in the Escavalon episode of Chrétien's **Perceval**. The first discovers the king's sister enjoying an obviously hot flirtation with Gawaine and, though Gawaine is universally hated in Escavalon for allegedly murdering its previous ruler, this vavasour is the first to recognize him and raise the alarm, summoning the mayor and magistrates to lead the mob. I do not think he is the same wise vavasour, a native of that town and advisor to the country round, whom the young king finds in the square after dismissing the mob, and who advises him to postpone Gawaine's trial by combat with Guigambresil for a year and meanwhile send Gawaine in quest of the bleeding lance. [Chrétien, **Perceval**, ca. ll 5835ff., 6088ff.]

ESCLADOS THE RED†

This was the knight whom Sir Ywaine found guarding the marvelous spring in Broceliande Forest. Presumably Esclados was also Dame Laudine's first husband, and the same man Ywaine's cousin Sir Calogrenant had met seven years earlier in the same place—though the whole situation might seem to smack somewhat of ritual blood battles for the lordship, and Laudine's sensechal later reveals that the custom has been kept for sixty years. (Dare I wonder if Esclados really was Laudine's *first* spouse?)

Esclados shows himself a generous conqueror in leaving Calogrenant free and taking only his horse—by chivalric rule, the conqueror could take the conquered man prisoner, along with his arms and armor, as well as his steed. In the mortal battle with Ywaine, both combatants, while striking at each other from the saddle, take care not to hit the horses—this in contrast to Lancelot and Meliagrant who, about this same time in another romance, kill each other's horses in similar combat. Dame Laudine sounds wonderfully sincere in her grief for Esclados after his death at Ywaine's hands. It looks as if we have here no villain, but a brave and conscientious champion whose death, even at the hands of the hero, constitutes a tragedy.

At the same time, I remain puzzled as to his value in "protecting" his people from the horrific storms produced by the spring, when it is only after such a storm that he appears, to chastize whatever adventurer has already caused the damage. [Chrétien de Troyes, **Yvain**, ll. 478-547; 811ff.; named l. 1970; 60 years' custom ca. l. 2105]

ESCLAMOR, KING†

A subking probably contemporary at least with Arthur's early days, if not with his later ones. Esclamor's territory seems to have been in the neighborhood of the "Forest of the Boiling Well." See Le Tertre Deuee.

Escorant—see **ESTORAUSE**

ESLIT†

Among Arthur's knights in the list Chrétien de Troyes begins in line 1691 of **Erec & Enide**.

ESTORAUSE (Escorant, Escarans, etc.), KING OF SARRAS

He "was a tyrant, and was come of the line of paynims, and took them [Galahad and his companions] and put them in prison in a deep hole." On his deathbed, however, he sent for them and begged forgiveness. By divine guidance, Galahad was chosen king of Sarras after Estorause's death, thus bringing the Grail Quest to its conclusion. [Malory XVII, 22]

ESTRANGOR

Malory gives Brandegoris as King of Stranggore [I, 12, 13; XII, 9], while the Vulgate gives Karados as the King of Estrangor [Vulgate II]. Therefore, I cannot bring myself to identify Estrangor with Stranggore. Carados seems a fairly common name, and the Vulgate's King Karados may be Malory's King Carados of Scotland. Remembering Malory's "many kings in the north", I incline to this view and suggest the peninsula on the north shore of Solway Firth, between Luce Bay and Wigtown Bay, or even the whole area of land between Solway Firth and the Firth of Clyde.

Alternatively, Karados might be identified with Malory's Cador of Cornwall, the father of Constantine, who became king after Arthur.

Estre-Gales—see **OUTRE-GALES**

Estroite March†—see **LESTROITE MARCHE**

Estroite Marche, Damsel of—see under **LESTROITE MARCHE**

"Été"—see under **"PRINTEMPS, ÉTÉ, and AUTOMNE"**

"ETHERIA"†

The damsel bearing the Grail has pre-eminence in the mystic procession of the Grail Castle; but I think that the damsel immediately following her, who bears a silver platter or carving dish, should be remembered too. [Chrétien de Troyes, **Perceval**, ca. l. 3228]

For this platter bearer, I borrowed the name "Etheria" from a Galician noblewoman whose account of her own fourth century A.D. pilgrimage to Palestine is cited by Susan Haskins in **Mary Magdalen, Myth And Metaphor** (NY: Harcourt Brace [1993], p. 105).

ETTARD (Ettarre)

See under Peleas, and remember that Ettard had not asked Pelleas to love her and pester her with his unsolicited devotion.

EUGENE, BISHOP†

According to Vulgate IV, he was the man who crowned Guenevere and officiated at her marriage. See also Archbishop of Canterbury and Dubric.

EUSTACE, DUKE OF CAMBENET (Duke Escan of Cambenic)

He pledged 5,000 mounted men to the first rebellion of sub-kings against Arthur and fought in the battle of Bedegraine. That is all I can find of him in Malory unless he is to be identified with the "Duke Cambines" who appears at Duke Galeholt's tournament in Surluse. [Malory I, 12-17; X, 49] According to Vulgate II, this duke's name was Escan, and Cambenic was a rich and prosperous city.

EVADEAM†

The son of King Brangoire (Brandegoris), Evadeam was 22 years old when he appeared, in the form of an ugly dwarf, with his lady Byanne at Arthur's court. See Byanne.

EVAINE†

Sister of Queen Elaine of Benwick, Queen Evaine was the wife of King Bors and the mother of Lionel and Bors de Ganis. After the death of her husband and the seizure of her young sons, she joined her sister at the Royal Minster, but died there much sooner than did Elaine. [Vulgate III-IV]

Evelake—see MORDRAINS

EVRAIN, KING†

Ruler of the castle of Brandigant and uncle of Sir Mabonagrain, Evrain appears to be a friendly, kind-hearted, and hospitable monarch. At the same time, I can find no indication that he was among Arthur's vassals, or needed to be, seeing that the strength and self-sufficiency of his island fortress (possibly an outpost of the Otherworld) would reportedly have defied anybody's siege. [Chrétien de Troyes, **Erec & Enide**, ll. 5367ff.]

EVROIC

The name Chrétien de Troyes uses for York (q.v.) [**Erec & Enide**, l. 2131, & D.D.R. Owen's note to same.].

Ewaine—see YWAINE

EXCALIBUR (Caliburn) and SCABBARD

Arthur's great sword. Unfortunately, Malory gives two accounts of its origin: as the sword Arthur drew out of the stone and anvil to prove his right to be King, and as the sword Arthur rowed across the Lake to receive from the mysterious arm—which apparently belonged to a damsel of the Lady of the Lake. Unless postulating that between these two events Excalibur was lost (a loss of such magnitude that Malory should have mentioned it), I see no way to reconcile the versions and still keep both swords Excalibur. (John Boorman's film **Excalibur**, however, reconciles the versions deftly.)

In Chrétien's final romance, we find Gawaine belting on Escalibor, which can cut iron as easily as wood. Gawaine has come to Escavalon to defend himself against Guigambresil's charge of treason; earlier, Chrétien emphasized that Gawaine takes only his own property along on this trip. Gawaine's possession of his uncle Arthur's sword baffles D.D.R. Owen, but Ruth Cline notes that the Vulgate includes an alternative tradition, in which Arthur gives Excalibur to Gawaine, who then consistently uses it throughout. [**Perceval**, ca. ll. 4803-4804; 5901-5904 & Owen's note to 5902 & Cline's to 5904] I found Gawaine consistently using Excalibur throughout the rest of the Vulgate.

Malory says nothing of this alternative tradition, but gives Gawaine a sword named Galatine. Might we consider Galatine the sword Arthur drew from the stone and then gave to his favorite nephew when he himself received Excalibur from the Lady of the Lake?

Also according to the Vulgate, Arthur seems to have had a second sword, named Sequence. This might be identified with the sword from the stone. The reason Arthur chose to keep the first sword and give Gawaine the one he had received from the Lady of the Lake might have been to prevent another such incident as Morgan's attempt to kill Arthur by means of a counterfeit Excalibur.

Merlin warned Arthur during the war with the rebel kings that the sword from the stone was not to be drawn until Arthur's moment of greatest need. When Arthur drew it, at the time the battle was going against him, the sword "was so bright in his enemies' eyes, that it gave a light like thirty torches", enabling him to win the battle [Malory I, 9].

After this it seems to have settled down and been merely a tremendously good weapon, not a preternaturally luminous one. Regarding the appropriateness, however, of Gawaine's being given a sword that on at least one occasion shone as brightly as thirty torches—if the sword from the stone is considered as the one Arthur gave him—it is a fairly common theory that Gawaine descends from a solar deity.

In the Vulgate, where Gawaine continues to use Excalibur in the war against Lancelot, Arthur apparently takes it back after Gawaine's death. Here, as in Malory, it is Excalibur that Arthur commands his last knight to throw into the water after the final battle. In the Vulgate account, Arthur regrets that Lancelot cannot have the sword, for Lancelot alone is now worthy of it. [Vulgate VI]

The scabbard of Excalibur, "heavy of gold and precious stones", was, in Merlin's opinion, worth ten of the sword, because as long as a fighter had the scabbard upon him, he would lose no blood, no matter how severely wounded [Malory I, 25; IV, 14]. The importance of the scabbard is an argument for making Excalibur the sword given by the Lady of the Lake, since it is more difficult to account for a scabbard belonging specifically to a sword that appeared sheathed in stone and anvil. Morgan stole this scabbard and threw it into a convenient body of water fairly early in Arthur's career [Malory IV, 14].

In the fifteenth-century Catalan romance **Tirant Lo Blanc**, Excalibur seems to possess a kind of oracular magic: gazing into his great sword enables Arthur to give every questioner an answer replete with the wisdom of medieval courtly philosophy. This, however, occurs in a passage that surely describes an elaborate and presumably rehearsed masque. (See Arthur for further description and bibliographical citation.)

FALERNE, LA †

A castle in Norgales belonging to the Duke of Cambenic, but under the immediate control of another castellan or lord [Vulgate III].

'False Guenevere, The'†—see GENIEVRE

FARAMON, KING OF FRANCE and DAUGHTER

Malory mentions this monarch only in VIII, 5, where the daughter of King Faramon of France, being in love with Tristram, sends him letters and "a little brachet that was passing fair." Receiving no regard from the knight, the princess dies for love of him. (Tristram keeps the brachet.)

Faramon may have been a kind of high king of France in Uther Pendragon's time, for in Vulgate V, when Frolle of Alemaigne tries to seize Gaul, Arthur maintains that his own claim is stronger than Frolle's, since his father Uther was suzerain of Faramon in King Ban's day.

Faux Amants, Val des †—see VAL SANS RETOUR

FELELOLIE

The sister of Sir Urre of Hungary, Felelolie accompanied her mother and brother throughout Europe searching for the best knight of the world, who alone could heal Urre's wounds. When they had found Lancelot in Logres and Urre was healed, "Sir Lavaine cast his love unto Dame Felelolie … and then they were wedded together with great joy." [Malory XIX, 10, 13]

FENICE†

She was the golden-haired and, of course, incredibly beautiful daughter of the Emperor of Germany, who first betrothed her to the Duke of Saxony but then broke this arrangement in order to marry her to Emperor Alis of Greece and Constantinople. Fenice, however, fell in mutual love at first sight with young Cligés, the Greek emperor's nephew. She went ahead with the arranged marriage but, not wishing to become known as another Iseut, let her nurse Thessala brew Alis a drink which made him dream so realistically every night about marital relations that he supposed his marriage consummated, while his bride lay still virginal at his side. At last Fenice had Thessala prepare her a death-counterfeiting drink so that Cligés could spirit her out of her tomb and live with her in secrecy, in a hideaway built by Cligés' serf John. The trick cost Fenice great physical pain (see Three Physicians of Salerno) but finally succeeded. When discovered, the lovers fled and would have enlisted Arthur, who was a great-uncle of Cligés, to help him win the throne of Greece and Constantinople; but Alis considerately died in time to let Cligés and Fenice come back peacefully to reign as emperor and empress. Cligés always trusted his wife, but Chrétien adds that no later emperor of Greece and Constantinople, remembering Fenice, ever trusted his.

In spite of the rule he himself cites for withholding Enide's name until after her marriage, Chrétien tells us Fenice's as soon as she appears, adding that she was as matchless in beauty as her namesake the phoenix bird. [Chrétien de Troyes, **Cligés**, ll. 2653 to end & D.D.R. Owen's notes to same]

FERGUS, EARL

A Cornish knight, Fergus "was but a young man, and late come into his lands" when Sir Marhaus came along to kill his troublesome neighbor, the giant Taulurd. When next we meet Fergus in Malory, he is one of Tristram's knights and acts as messenger for Tristram. Later we learn that he has become a fellow of the Round Table. With Tristram, Dinas, and others, Fergus grieves for Prince Boudwin and refuses to raise hand against Sir Sadok for helping Boudwin's wife Anglides escape with her son. His last appearance seems to be at the attempt to heal Sir Urre. [Malory IV, 25; IX, 18; X, 26, 32, 35; XIX,11]

The Vulgate has at least one Fergus, but I am not sure he can be identified with Malory's character.

FEROLIN OF SALONICA†

One of Alexander's twelve companions who accompanied him from Greece to Britain, where Arthur knighted them all at the outset of Count Angrs' rebellion. Ferolin seems to have been among those who followed Alexander into Windsor to capture Angrs. Ferolin survived that episode, but Chrétien tells us nothing more of him. [**Cligés**, ll. 102-385; 1093-ca. 2210]

FERRYMAN OF CANGUIN†

The man in charge of ferrying passengers across the water to the country of the Rock of Canguin (he has oarsmen under him to do the actual work) claims as his due either the charger of every knight downed at the landing-place, or the knight himself—presumably for ransom. Having thus obtained Greoreas' nephew, defeated by Gawaine, the ferryman takes them both across, the one as prisoner and the other as guest, along with Gawaine's steed Gringolet, to his own fine and comfortable house near the river, where he feeds and lodges both men—guest and prisoner—with equally rich fare and good cheer.

Canguin may possibly belong to the Otherworld, but its ferryman seems no grim Charon of classical myth. He might more nearly resemble a kind of Virgil to Gawaine's Dante: a friendly guide and, within certain bounds, even mentor. He shows a cheerful, courteous, and sympathetic personality, perhaps not lacking in a streak of mischief: when Gawaine asks who is the lord of this land, his ferryman host replies that he has never known—this might be a riddle, for the ferryman is a dependent of the castle and seems to know everything else about it; but, as we later learn, its lord is to be the man who can survive sitting on the Wondrous Bed, and that man has not yet come and is therefore still unknown when Gawaine (who of course turns out to be the very man) asks his question. [Chrétien de Troyes, **Perceval**, ll. 7371-8978]

FISHER KING, THE (The Rich Fisher, Rich Fisherman, The Maimed King; see also **PELLAM, ARTHUR)**

Alias the Maimed King, he was the guardian, or any one of a line of guardians, of the Holy Grail.

Since Chrétien de Troyes gave us what appears to be the earliest known extant account of the Grail episode, it may be a good idea to review what he tells us of the Fisher King, alias the Rich Fisherman. In Chrétien's version, this monarch turns out to be Percivale's cousin on the mother's side, a king who had been wounded in battle by a javelin through both thighs. (Percivale's father had also been maimed with a thigh wound—weapon unspecified—and the javelin was the one weapon Percivale had learned in boyhood to use, for hunting.) The maimed monarch of the Grail Castle is called the "Fisher" because his only recreation is fishing, with hook and line, from a little boat, his wound having rendered all other sports impossible for him. He shows himself courteous and hospitable, seeming wise and reasonably cheerful. His father, another king, brother to Percivale's mother, is the man who sits in a room off the main hall of the castle and is served with consecrated hosts from the Grail. I cannot find in Chrétien's work any indication that the Fisher King's country is a waste land, except in the sense of "uninhabited"—the Fisher King's castle or manor would seem to be the only habitation for many leagues about and it, apparently, is often invisible to travelers. The Fisher King, however, can spread a fine meal; the description of "waste land" in Chrétien's romance would seem more appropriate for Blancheflor's land around the castle of Beaurepaire after her war with Clamadeu. Asking the right questions would have restored the Fisher King to wholeness, enabling him to rule his land, and would also have spared Percivale himself many hardships; but if it would have healed the land, I am missing something vital in Chrétien's version. [**Perceval**, ll. 3011-3421; 3194; 4638-4683; 6394-6431]

Malory and others identify the Fisher King as Pellam. Lewis Spence [**Magic Arts**, pp. 152, 155, 172, etc.] cites evidence that at one time the

Maimed or Fisher King was Arthur himself, an idea used to superb dramatic advantage by John Boorman in **Excalibur**, the only movie and one of the very few modern fictional treatments of any kind that I have yet seen which does the Grail Quest well.

Spence makes much of the connection between the title "Fisher King" and the ancient Celtic salmon of knowledge [**Magic Arts**, pp. 171, 172]. Without denying this application, I feel bound to add a reminder that the fish is an even more ancient symbol of Christianity than is the cross. (The recurrence of symbols surely delights students of comparative religion.)

FISHER KING'S CANDLESTICKS†

Following the lance bearer and preceding the Grail maiden came two handsome young men, each carrying at least ten candles in a branched candlestick of gold inlaid with black enamel [Chrétien de Troyes, **Perceval**, ca. ll. 3212-3218]. Candles were costly, and the radiance cast by twenty of them at once must have seemed extremely brilliant nocturnal illumination before the advent of electric, gas-, or limelight.

FISHER KING'S CARVING-DISH†

In Chrétien's seminal version, a second maiden follows the Grail maiden. This second maiden, whom I call "Etheria", carries a silver carving-dish (Owen's translation) or platter (Cline's). Chrétien gives no further details concerning this carving-dish. Its purpose seems obscure if, as Chrétien later explains, the Fisher King's father receives as his entire meal a single Mass wafer from the Grail. [**Perceval**, ca. ll. 3227-3228; 6415-6429] The platter may serve as a paten, either to cover the Grail or, perhaps, to convey the wafer from Grail to recipient. Or, the Grail being seen as the cup, might the platter echo the dish of the paschal lamb at the Last Supper?

FISHER KING'S FATHER†

According to Chrétien de Troyes, the Fisher King's father, also a king, was brother to Percivale's mother and to her other brother the hermit. (In this version, it all seems to be pretty much a family affair.) In addition, the Fisher King's kingly father is the person served from the Grail, which is processionally borne to him in the little room where he has lived for twelve years at the time of his nephew's first visit. The only food served him is Mass wafers, apparently one per meal. This is all he lives upon. The diet was far from unknown among saints beloved in the Middle Ages; indeed, growing up Catholic in the 1950s, I myself encountered it told of some saints of our own times. [**Perceval**, ca. ll. 6413-6432]

FISHER KING'S NIECE†

This lovely blonde damsel sent her uncle the Fisher King a gift, the sword forged by Trebuchet, with the message that she would be well pleased if he passed it along to a worthy recipient. He passed it along to Percivale.

I strongly suspect, but cannot absolutely prove, that she is the same cousin whom Percivale meets next morning on his way away from the Fisher King's dwelling. She sits mourning her lover, who lies in her lap newly slain by the Haughty Knight of the Heath, and whose body she refuses to leave until she has buried it. Recognizing Trebuchet's sword, she tells its present bearer much about it and about the Rich Fisher. This cousin was reared as a young child with Percivale in his mother's nursery. Now she asks his name: he has not known it (at least consciously) before this moment, but in answering her question he instinctively calls himself Percivale—commentators understand this as a crucial point in his development. His cousin then chides him for failing to ask the questions that would have healed their uncle and spared people a lot of grief. [Chrétien de Troyes, **Perceval**, ca. ll. 3144-3153; 3430-3690]

FISHER KING'S OARSMAN†

Our only identifiable glimpse of this man comes when Percivale sees him rowing the boat from which his master is fishing with hook and line. The boat's maximum capacity is given as about four men, but the oarsman is the Fisher King's sole companion. He leaves all the talking to his master. While I think it likely that the same attendant rows the Rich Fisher every time he goes out fishing, we cannot be absolutely sure of this. [Chrétien de Troyes, **Perceval**, ca. ll. 2998-3034; 3500-3506]

FISHER KING'S TABLE†

Like other tables of the age, it was in pieces, reassembled before each meal. The top was a single broad length of ivory. The trestles were ebony, proof against rot or fire. When set up, the table was spread with a cloth spread whiter than any the Pope himself ever ate off.

Since the Fisher King (who is not, in Chrétien's version, the one served by the Grail) and his guest Percivale dined on peppered venison, good wine, fruits, spices, and electuaries set before them on this table, I venture to guess that Chrétien describes it and the formality of assembling it merely as an example of the Fisher King's wealth and courtliness, rather than as a thing imbued with mystical properties of its own. [**Perceval**, ca. ll. 3254-3336]

FLANDERS

Arthur and his host sailed from Sandwich to war against Lucius, landing at Barflete in Flanders [Malory V, 4].

FLECHE, CASTLE DE LA†

A well situated and splendidly appointed castle a day's ride or less from Windesant [Vulgate IV].

FLOEMUS†

Apparently King Lot's seneschal [Vulgate VII].

FLOREE

According to the Vulgate, she was the daughter of King Alain of Escavalon and the mother of Gawaine's oldest son, Guinglain. Vulgate VII seems to describe the encounter: after Gawaine rescued her, Floree came to his bed somewhat in the manner of Sir Bercilak's lady in **Sir Gawaine and the Green Knight**. Since Floree meant it, it went farther, and Guinglain apparently resulted from this adventure. I do not know for sure whether Gawaine married Floree or not, but according to **The Wedding of Sir Gawaine and Dame Ragnell** he was married several times.

Malory does not name Floree, but in XIX, 11, he calls Sir Brandiles' sister the mother of Gawaine's sons Florence and Lovel. Although Malory does not name Brandiles' sister as the mother of Gawaine's son Gingalin, who surely is identical with the Vulgate's Guinglain, the name of the second son, Florence, is so similar to the name Floree that it strongly suggests a mother-son connection. Floree, then, might be identified with Sir Brandiles' sister, but see under Brandiles and Ragnell.

FLOREGA†

Lancelot was six miles from Florega, in the wood of Sapine, when he learned that Meliagrant's stepsister was to be burned at Florega the next day. That night, on his way to Florega, Lancelot stopped at a house of religion where he found Duke Galeholt's tomb. [Vulgate V] From this I surmise that Sapine Wood was in or near Duke Galeholt's favorite kingdom of Surluse. The judgment of Meliagrant's sister at Florega suggests a location exactly between Surluse and Gore.

FLORENCE

The elder, apparently, of Gawaine's two(?) sons by Sir Brandiles' sister, Florence became a knight of the Round Table. With his brother Lovel, he joined the party that helped Mordred and Agravaine try to trap Lancelot with the Queen. All but Mordred were killed by the escaping Lancelot. [Malory XIX, 11; XX, 2-4]

Malory also mentions a Sir Florence in Arthur's Continental campaign against the Emperor of Rome.

> Then ... the king called Sir Florence, a knight, and said to him they lacked victual. And not far from hence be great forests and woods, wherein be many of mine enemies with much bestial: I will that thou ... tgo thither in foraying, and take with thee Sir Gawaine my nephew [and others].

The foragers run afoul of a force of Spanish knights, defeat them, and win plenty of rich spoils. [Malory V, 9-11] Although Malory's internal chronology is confusing, he puts the war against Emperor Lucius much too early in the work to make me feel comfortable identifying this Florence with Gawaine's second son; moreover, it seems unlikely that Arthur would put Gawaine's son, rather than Gawaine himself, in charge of an expedition which included Gawaine.

FONTAINE AUX FEES, LA†

La Fontaine aux Fees was located beneath a sycamore in the forest of Camelot. Here forest dwellers claimed to have seen fairy ladies. [Vulgate IV]

Fontaine des Deux Sycamores—see **DEUX SYCAMORES, FONTAINE DES**

FOOL, THE†—see also **DAGONET**

In Chrétien's **Perceval**, the Fool or court jester and the maiden struck by Kay usually appear together. The Fool it was who used to say of the maid that she would not laugh until she saw the man who would be the supreme knight. This seems a prophecy in Chrétien's work (Ruth Cline cites evidence that it might once have been a geis, or magical injunction), and Chrétien's Fool proceeds to prove his prophetic powers by predicting that, for striking the maid and kicking the Fool himself into the fire, Sir Kay will in the fullness of time receive a broken arm from the avenging Percivale. This warning the jester gleefully repeats every time Percivale sends someone to court with the message that, if he lives, he will avenge the maiden Kay struck, until it must come as rather a relief to the seneschal when it finally happens. (As we later glean from the Ugly Squire's words to Gawaine, ca. ll. 7038-7040, Kay's broken arm is an appropriate penalty because it injures the same members—hand and arm—used in committing the offense; I presume that the kick given to the Fool must have been seen as trifling compared with the blow dealt the maid, or Kay should have suffered a broken leg as well as a broken arm.) [**Perceval**, ca. ll. 1050-1066; 1239-1274; 2864-2881; & here & there to 4316; ca. 4575]

For the maid, see "Verrine." I feel far from confident, however, that the Fool of Chrétien's Grail romance should be automatically identified with Malory's Dagonet.

FORD, KNIGHT AND DAMSEL OF THE†

There seem to have been a great many waterways in and near the marches of Gore. On his way to the Sword Bridge, but long before he reached it, Lancelot came to a river ford guarded by a knight. This knight shouted three warnings to Lancelot not to cross, but Lancelot was deeply engaged just then in the knightly duty of contemplating his lady, and his horse was thirsty. As soon as Lancelot's mount was in the water drinking, the guardian of the ford rode in and knocked the oblivious champion from his saddle. At last awake to his immediate situation, Lancelot demanded to know the reason for this attack, swearing he had never heard the other man. Not that it would have made any ultimate difference, of course, but the knight of the ford put up a better than average fight before Lancelot, blaming himself for weakness, got his opponent on the run. At length the guardian's damsel intervened, helping her knight obtain first mercy and then freedom (by the rules, Lancelot could have taken him prisoner). The damsel even risked rape by promising to do Lancelot whatever favor he desired, but he released her from this pledge and carried away the good wishes of both. The whole episode seems irresistibly burlesque. [Chrétien de Troyes, **Lancelot**, ll. 714-940]

FOREIGN LAND, THE (La Terre Foraine)

This name applies to a region on the border of Gore. It seems also to apply to Listeneise, since Pelles is identified as king of "the foreign country." [Malory XI, 2] I suspect the name is a descriptive tag rather than a proper name. Maante is the capital [Vulgate I].

Forth, Firth of—see **COTOATRE**

Foul Ladye, The†—see **RAGNELL**

FOUNTAIN OF THE SILVER PIPE

When Sir Accolon of Gaul awoke after going to sleep on an enchanted ship,

> he found himself by a deep well-side, within half a foot, in great peril of death. And there came out of that fountain a pipe of silver, and out of that ... ran water all on high in a stone of marble.

From this fountain a dwarf of Morgan's brought Accolon to Sir Ontzlake's manor by a priory, where Morgan prepared the knight for fighting Arthur. [Malory IV, 8] This fountain, which was apparently near Sir Damas' castle and Ontzlake's manor, seems to have been a "fountain" as we moderns think of fountains, rather than a plain brook or spring in the woodland or elsewhere, which is probably the more common meaning of the word "fountain" in the language of Malory's time.

Turquine's Hill had a fountain suspiciously similar to the one described above [Vulgate V]. This leads me to believe that the two sites were probably the same, at Cadbury.

FOUR STONES, CASTLE OF

Sir Balan mentions this [Malory II, 6]. Perhaps it was somewhere mountainous, or near a dolmen or cromlech, and hence got its name. According to Vulgate IV, Meliagaunt's body, after Lancelot killed him, was taken to the Castle of Four Stones. From this it would appear that Four Stones was either Meliagaunt's own castle, or the castle of a friend.

FRANCAGEL†

One of the twelve companions who accompanied Alexander from Greece to Britain, where Arthur knighted them all at the outset of Count Angrs' rebellion, he seems to have been with Alexander's party when it penetrated Windsor to capture Angrs. Francagel survived the rebellion,but Chrétien de Troyes tells us nothing more about him. [**Cligés**, ll. 102-385; 1093-ca. 2210]

FRANCE (Gaul)

This must have included more or less the area of present-day France, with a few sub-kingdoms unsubjugated or imperfectly subjugated, like Benwick. Malory leaves me confused as to whether France was one small subkingdom of Gaul, or vice versa, or whether they were in fact completely interchangeable names. I opt for interchangeability.

The interesting King Claudas may have been trying to bring France under one crown. Malory mentions another French monarch, King Faramon of France, in the story of Tristram; according to Vulgate V, Faramon appears to have been a sort of high king of France during Uther Pendragon's time.

Frol of the Out Isles—see under **BELLIANCE LE ORGULUS**

FROLLE, KING(?) OF ALEMAIGNE†

Frolle, who was a head taller than most men, tried to take advantage of Arthur's war with Claudas to invade Gaul himself. Arthur, arriving in Gaul, said that his own claim was older than Frolle's, since Uther Pendragon had been suzerain of Faramon, King of Gaul, in King Ban's day. Arthur substantiated his claim by killing Frolle in single combat. [Vulgate V]

Further Wales—see **OUTRE-GALES**

GAHERES†

A nephew of the King of Norgales, Gaheres received Gareth's seat at the Round Table after Gareth was killed duriing Lancelot's rescue of Guenevere from the stake [Vulgate VI]. Do not confuse Gaheres with Gareth's brother Gaheris, who was killed with Gareth during the rescue of Guenevere.

GAHERIS (Gaheriet, Guerrehes)

The third son of Lot and Morgawse.

As Gaheriet, he appears among Arthur's knights in the list Chrétien de Troyes begins in line 1691 of **Erec & Enide**. Presumably this is the same Gaheriet whom Chrétien has Gawaine name as King Lot's third son in about line 8141 of **Perceval**. (Cline uses the spellings Gaheris and Gareth for Lot's third and fourth sons in this passage; D.D.R. Owen uses the versions Gaheriet and Guerrehet; "Guerrehet" seems not nearly so close to "Gareth" as to "Guerrehes", the name I found in the Vulgate for Gaheris. At this point, I can offer no clear explanation for these spellings.)

Vulgate IV remarks that Lot's third son was a good knight, and that his right arm was longer than his left.

He first came to court in youth with his mother and brothers Gawaine, Agravaine, and Gareth (who must have been very young indeed) when Morgawse visited Arthur between the two early waves of rebellion. Morgawse and her sons returned to Arthur's court after the second rebellion, at the burial of Lot; Morgawse clearly returned home afterward with Gareth, but the three older boys apparently stayed. Before his own dubbing, Gaheris served as squire to his oldest brother Gawaine, toward whom he acted, at the same time, as a sort of advisor and second conscience. During the celebration of Arthur's marriage, when Gawaine said he would kill Pellinore in revenge for King Lot's death, Gaheris held him back, "for at this time I am but a squire, and when I am made knight I will be avenged on him", and besides, if they killed Pellinore now they would trouble the feast. Pellinore's eventual death is not described in detail, but his widow later complains that Gawaine and Gaheris "slew him not manly but by treason." When Gawaine was sent on the quest of the White Hart, Gaheris, still his squire, accompanied him. On this adventure Gawaine defeated Sir Ablamar and was about to ignore his plea for mercy when Ablamar's lady came between them and took Gawaine's stroke. As she fell headless, Gaheris rebuked his older brother:

> Alas, said Gaheris, that is foully and shamefully done, that shame shall never from you; also ye should give mercy unto them that ask mercy, for a knight without mercy is without worship.

Retiring into Ablamar's castle for the night, Gaheris shrewdly warned Gawaine not to unarm: "Ye may think ye have many enemies here." Almost at once four knights angrily attacked Gawaine, and Gaheris fought very capably at his brother's side.

Like all his brothers, Gaheris became a knight of the Round Table. While Gareth was out on his first series of knightly adventures, Morgawse visited Arthur's court at Pentecost. Gawaine, Agravaine, and Gaheris, not having seen her for fifteen years, "saluted her upon their knees, and asked her blessing." Later, however, Gaheris slew his mother in anger at her taking Pellinore's son Lamorak for a lover. The two had an assignation at Gawaine's castle near Camelot, where Morgawse was staying on another visit, at her sons' invitation. Gaheris watched and waited as Lamorak went to the queen's bedroom.

> So when the knight, Sir Gaheris, saw his time, he came to their bedside all armed, with his sword naked, and suddenly gat his mother by the hair and struck off her head.

> When Sir Lamorak saw the blood dash upon him all hot, the which he loved passing well ... [he] leapt out of the bed in his shirt as a knight dismayed, saying thus: ... Alas, why have ye slain your mother that bare you? with more right ye should have slain me .... The offence hast thou done, said Gaheris, notwithstanding a man is born to offer his service; but yet shouldst thou beware with whom thou meddlest, for thou hast put me and my brethren to a shame, and thy father slew our father; and thou to lie by our mother is too much shame for us to suffer. And as for thy father, King Pellinore, my brother Sir Gawaine and I slew him. Ye did him the more wrong, said Sir Lamorak, for my father slew not your father, it was Balin le Savage: and as yet my father's death is not revenged. Leave those words, said Sir Gaheris, for an thou speak feloniously I will slay thee. But because thou art naked I am ashamed to slay thee. But wit thou well, in what place I may get thee I shall slay thee; and now my mother is quit of thee; and withdraw thee and take thine armour, that thou were gone.

(T. H. White, who makes Gaheris something of a nonentity, transfers the matricide to Agravaine [**The Once and Future King III**, 26].)

After Duke Galeholt's tournament in Surluse, Gaheris joined with his brothers (except Gareth) to ambush and kill Lamorak. As with other killings, Malory has his characters allude to the incident rather than describe it himself: finding that Gaheris and Agravaine have just killed a knight for saying that Lancelot was better than Gawaine, Tristram rebukes the two brothers both for this and for Lamorak's death, of which he has just learned from Palomides. Tristram jousts them down and says he is leaving it at that only for the sake of their relationship to Arthur. Remounting, they chase him in anger, and he unhorses them again.

Among other adventures, Gaheris fought the Cornish knight Matto le Breune and took away his lady, whose loss drove Matto out of his mind. Malory weds Gaheris to Lynette. Vulgate V gives him the Damoiselle de la Blanche Lande as a sweetheart. The accounts are not mutually exclusive. Gaheris, like other knights, demonstrates considerable taste for sampling various damsels. See also "Clarisin."

On at least one occasion Gaheris visited King Mark, bringing him and Isoud news of the Castle of Maidens tournament. Mark and Gaheris seem to have enjoyed each other's company well enough. Gaheris was among the guests at Guenevere's intimate dinner party when Sir Patrise was poisoned; Agravaine, Gaheris, and Mordred may have been present, however, largely because Gawaine and Gareth were invited. Gaheris took no part with Agravaine and Mordred when they tried to trap Guenevere with Lancelot. After Guenevere's trial, Arthur asked Gawaine to help lead the Queen to the stake. Gawaine refused.

> Then said the king to Sir Gawaine: Suffer your brothers Sir Gaheris and Sir Gareth to be there. My lord, said Sir Gawaine, wit you well they will be loath … but they are young and full unable to say you nay. Then spake Sir Gaheris, and the good knight Sir Gareth, unto Sir Arthur: Sir, ye may well command us to be there, but wit you well it shall be sore against our will; but an we be there by your strait commandment ye shall plainly hold us there excused: we will be there in peaceable wise, and bear none harness of war upon us.

According to the Vulgate, however, they were armed and fought back when Lancelot and his men attacked the guard to save the Queen. It is also hard to believe that Gawaine's statement of Gaheris' youth is to be taken literally. The result was the same in any case: Gaheris and Gareth were both killed. [Malory I, 19; II, 11; III, 4-8; VII, 25, 35; IX, 19 38; X, 24, 54-56; XVIII, 3; XIX, 11; XX, 2, 8; etc.]

To Gaheris' further discredit, the Vulgate records how he widowed Lancelot's cousin "Iblis." Vulgate V, however, also depicts him showing a concern for common folk which other knights might also have shown, but examples of which are rarely recorded. While involved in settling a quarrel among the knightly class, Gaheris accidentally frightened a poor man. The poor man fled, leaving his donkey alone in the woods. Returning, he found it devoured by wolves. As the donkey had been essential to his livelihood, he would now be forced to beg. Gaheris, having inadvertently caused the trouble, requested his host—whose life he had just saved, and who thus owed him a favor—to give the poor man a horse. The host obliged, and the peasant's livelihood was saved.

In Sommer's edition of the Vulgate, the name Gaheries is given to the brother we know as Gareth, Malory's Gaheris being called Guerrehes in the Vulgate.

Gaheris de Kareheu†—see under **PINEL LE SAVAGE**

GAIDON DE GALVOIE†

I have found him only in Sommer's appendix to Vulgate V. He married the Lady of Galvoie.

GAIHOM (Gohorru)†

The Vulgate says this is the capital of the kingdom of Gore. In my first edition, I proposed identifying Gaihom with the city of Pembroke in present-day Wales, but this suggestion was based on the placement of Gore in Wales, which Chrétien's **Lancelot** seems to preclude. See Gore.

GAIS†

A castle set on the Thames; Sir Trahans, the castellan, and his sons Melians and Drians were all surnamed "li Gais", after the castle [Vulgate IV]. Melians apparently became castellan of the Dolorous Tower.

Galadon—see **GALDON CASTLE**

GALAFORT†

The first British castle which Joseph of Arimathea and his followers entered. At Josephe's advice, Duke Ganor, who then held the castle, erected there the Tower of Marvels, where no knight of Arthur's would fail to find a jouster as good as himself. The duke also began a church of the Holy Virgin at Galafort. [Vulgate I]

If Joseph came directly here from the Continent, Galafort would probably be somewhere in the southeast. If he went to Sarras first, and if my identification of Sarras as the Isle of Man is accepted, Galafort would probably be somewhere on the northwest coast.

Galagars—see under **GRIFLET**

GALAHAD

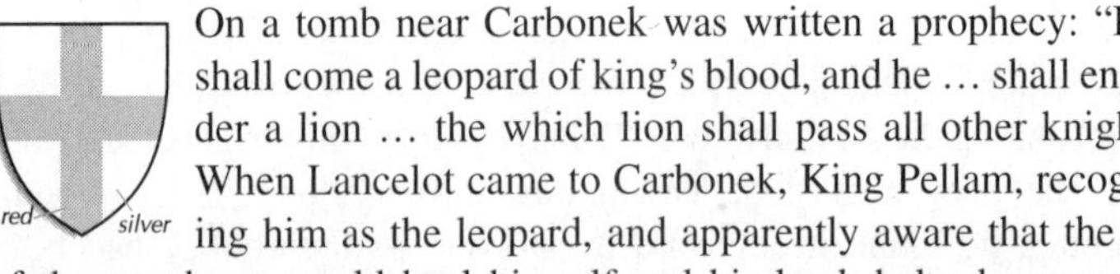

On a tomb near Carbonek was written a prophecy: "Here shall come a leopard of king's blood, and he … shall engender a lion … the which lion shall pass all other knights." When Lancelot came to Carbonek, King Pellam, recognizing him as the leopard, and apparently aware that the lion of the prophecy would heal himself and his land, helped arrange for Lancelot to beget Galahad on Elaine. Lancelot's own baptized name had been Galahad before it was changed by Viviane, and this is no doubt where Elaine got the name for her son. Sir Bors visited Carbonek while Galahad was a babe in arms, and remarked on his likeness to Lancelot.

> Truly, said Elaine, wit ye well this child he gat on me. Then Sir Bors wept for joy, and he prayed to God it might prove as good a knight as his father was.

There is some confusion as to Galahad's upbringing. According to the Vulgate, Galahad lived at Carbonek with his grandfather during the time Lancelot lived with Elaine at Joyous Isle and, when Lancelot departed, Galahad, wanting to remain near his father, traveled to the convent where Pellam's sister was abbess and lived there until he was about eighteen. When Lancelot leaves Joyous Isle, Malory has Elaine tell him that "at this same feast of Pentecost shall … Galahad be made knight, for he is fully now fifteen winter old." A few chapters later, however, when an unnamed gentlewoman brings Lancelot to the convent to visit his son, the nuns present Galahad as "this child the which we have nourished." It appears to me that Malory cut out three years Galahad spent at the convent, but failed to make his account fully consistent in so doing.

Lancelot's visit to the convent came on the eve of Pentecost. At this time Lancelot dubbed Galahad knight, but Galahad did not return at once to Arthur's court with his father. Next day the sword which had once been Sir Balin's floated down the river to Camelot. After Gawaine and Percivale, at the King's behest, had attempted without success to draw the sword, "a good old man, and an ancient" (Nascien?) brought Galahad to court "on foot, in red arms, without sword or shield, save a scabbard hanging by his side." The old man led Galahad to the Siege Perilous, which was now found to bear his name, and sat him in it. After dinner, Arthur took Galahad to the river, where the young knight drew the sword from its floating marble. Now a gentlewoman rode to them to tell Lancelot he was no longer the greatest knight in the world and to predict the Grail Quest. Disturbed by the thought that he would never see all his knights together again after the Quest, and wanting to prove Galahad, Arthur held one last tournament before the Quest. At this tourney Galahad "defouled many good knights of the Table save twain, that was Sir Launcelot and Sir Percivale." When Guenevere looked at Galahad's face after the tourney, she said:

> Soothly I dare well say that Sir Launcelot begat him, for never two men resembled more in likeness, therefore it tis no marvel though he be of great prowess … he is of all parties come of the best knights of the world and of the highest lineage; for Sir Launcelot is come but of the eighth degree from our Lord Jesu Christ, and Sir Galahad is of the ninth degree from our Lord Jesu Christ.

That evening the Holy Grail, veiled in white samite, appeared in Arthur's hall to feed the knights at supper, and Gawaine was first to vow to quest for a clear look at the vessel. Later the Queen questioned

Galahad about his father and place of birth. He told her readily of his country, but would neither affirm nor deny his relationship to Lancelot. When Guenevere assured him he need not be ashamed of his father, whom he so much resembled,

> then Sir Galahad was a little ashamed and said: Madam, sith ye know in certain, wherefore do ye ask it me? for he that is my father shall be known openly and all betimes.

Embarking on the Quest, Galahad rode four days, apparently alone, without adventure before coming to the "Abbey of the Adventurous Shield", where he met Ywaine and Bagdemagus. Galahad agreed to let Bagdemagus try to take the Adventurous Shield first. The White Knight who waited outside struck down Bagdemagus. Then, when Galahad came with the shield, the knight saluted him courteously and told him the shield's history. Bagdemagus' former squire Melias de Lile, who had begged to accompany Galahad, now begged to be made knight, and Galahad obliged. The two returned briefly to the abbey and Galahad cleared the churchyard of an unquiet soul, who cried, when Galahad blessed it, "Galahad, I see there environ about thee so many angels that my power may not dere [harm] thee." Melias and Galahad left again and parted at a crossroads, but Melias soon got into trouble and Galahad had to rescue him. Leaving the wounded Melias with an old monk, Galahad went on to Abblasoure and thence to "Chapel Desolate", where a voice directed him to destroy the wicked customs at the Castle of Maidens. Galahad went at once and drove out the seven wicked brothers, who swore to avenge themselves by killing all of Arthur's knights they could overcome—which was none, since the first three they met were Gawaine, Gareth, and Ywaine, who soon exterminated them all seven. For this deed Gawaine later was rebuked by a hermit who said, "Sir Galahad himself alone beat them all seven the day to-fore, but his living is such he shall slay no man lightly."

Meanwhile, meeting Lancelot and Percivale by chance, Galahad unhorsed both, but then fled, "adread to be known", when a nearby recluse began praising him. Galahad's next recorded adventure came as he passed a rather bloody tournament and entered on the side that was being literally slaughtered. Gawaine and Ector de Maris got into the melee, and Galahad wounded Gawaine with the stroke which had been predicted as punishment for an unworthy attempt to draw Balin's sword.

From here Galahad rode to Ulfin's hermitage, where Percivale's sister came to lead him to a ship in which Bors and Percivale, tested and purified by their own adventures, were waiting. Sailing in this vessel, the four came to King Solomon's Ship, where Galahad drew King David's Sword from its scabbard and was girded with it by Amide.

Returning to their own ship, the party came ashore at Carteloise Castle, where they slew the murderous and incestuous brothers who had thrown their own father, Earl Hernox, in prison and raped and murdered their sister. Hernox counted himself blessed to die in Galahad's arms, counseling the young knight to go to the Maimed King as soon as possible. Leaving Carteloise, Galahad and his companions followed the mystical white hart and four lions through the forest to a chapel where they experienced a Eucharistic vision during Mass.

Next the knights came to the "Castle of the Leprous Lady", defending Amide till she agreed to give blood willingly, which caused her death. After putting her body into a ship and setting it adrift, the three knights separated for a time. Lancelot found the ship with Amide's body and embarked in it. After about a month, Galahad joined him; they journeyed together in the ship for half a year, serving God and sometimes going ashore for strange adventures on beast-infested islands. Finally a "knight armed all in white" appeared on shore, leading a white horse, and summoned Galahad to his own further adventures. Lancelot had already been at Carbonek and gone away again by the time Galahad arrived there, so that father and son never saw each other again. Galahad went first to the "Abbey of King Mordrains", where he healed and saw released from mortal coil that long-lived sufferer.

Next Galahad entered the Forest of the Boiling Well, where he stopped the water from boiling, and came to the burning tomb of Simeon, an ancestor of his, who was enduring a kind of purgatory for a sin against Joseph of Arimathea. After releasing Simeon's soul, Galahad met Bors and Percivale again, and they came at last to Carbonek, where Galahad mended the broken sword wherewith Joseph had been stricken through the thigh. The three British knights met nine other knights of various countries and all experienced the climactic Mysteries of the Grail, celebrated by Joseph of Arimathea. Instructed by Joseph, Galahad healed the Maimed King by anointing him with blood from Longinus' Spear. Then Galahad, Bors, and Percivale embarked in a ship with the Sangreal (which miraculously preceded them aboard). They were carried to Sarras, where they found and buried Amide's body. The Pagan king of Sarras, Estorause, threw them into prison for a time, but freed them when on his deathbed, begging for and receiving their forgiveness. A voice now directed the city council to make Galahad their king. He reigned there for one year, at the end of which Joseph of Arimathea came again to accompany his soul, borne up by a great company of angels along with the Grail and the Spear, into Heaven. (According to the Vulgate, Galahad had been given the grace to die at an hour of his own choosing.)

I have recapped Galahad's whole earthly career according to Malory partly to show the sequence of the various miracles which only Galahad could accomplish and partly because, of all the knights whose reputations have suffered with the changing times, Galahad's has perhaps suffered the most. Gawaine's reputation probably comes in second, but his was on the decline much earlier, and our century seems able to understand more easily the frivolous ladykiller Gawaine has become than it can understand Galahad's high ideals and purity.

Therefore, in modern versions, Galahad tends to become a prissy, a hypocrite, a fool, somebody else's half-witted pawn, or all of these together. Tennyson's Sir Galahad—"My good blade carves the casques of men ...."—has hardly helped matters, of course, nor has John Erskine's **Galahad**, though the latter gives a more sympathetic picture than might have been expected. Fraser's Harry Flashman even believes that Galahad was lustier in bed than his father Lancelot ever was [**Flashman in the Great Game**, chapter 4].

Malory's Galahad, however, far from going around quipping about the purity of his heart, gave Bagdemagus first chance at the Adventurous Shield. Later, aboard King Solomon's Ship, he allowed Bors and Percivale the first attempts to draw King David's Sword and said, on their failure, "I would draw this sword out of the sheath, but the offending is so great that I shall not set my hand thereto", and had to be reassured by Amide. If this was not humility, it was at least courtesy toward his companions. Galahad's reluctance to slay any man lightly also contrasts favorably with the almost casual killings so many of the other knights, including his own father Lancelot, committed in battles or comedies of errors. On the one occasion when the battle rage that regularly seized Lancelot descended on Galahad and his companions, at Carteloise Castle, it was Bors, not Galahad, who rationalized the slaughter.

> Then when they beheld the great multitude of people that they had slain, they held themself great sinners. Certes, said Bors, I ween an God had loved them that we should not have had power to have slain them thus. But they have done so much against Our Lord that He would not suffer them to reign no longer. Say ye not so, said Galahad, for if they misdid against God, the vengeance is not ours, but to Him which hath power thereof.

Galahad does not seem to have been reassured that he and his friends had served as Heaven's tools until a local priest seconded Bors' opinion. Galahad's wishing to accompany his father from Carbonek and their sojourn together in the ship also points to a better father-son relationship than is sometimes supposed. Nor do I find any evidence to support Harry Flashman's belief about Galahad's sex life, any reason to suppose that his regard for Amide, though deep, was not platonic, nor any reason to imagine that Galahad's purity made less a man of him. It may also be remarked, in this age of cult leaders, that Galahad seems not to have abused his power as king of Sarras, nor to have clung to it. Indeed, remembering the legend that he had been granted to name the time of his own death, one may speculate that perhaps he chose to leave such power before it could corrupt him. [Malory XI, 1, 3; XII, 1-17; XVII, 1-14; Vulgate, chiefly vol. VI]

Galahad, Duke—see GALEHOLT

Galahad's Fountain—see FOREST OF THE BOILING WELL

Galahalt—see GALEHOLT

GALAPAS

A giant who fought with the Romans against Arthur.

> [Galapas] was a man of an huge quantity and height, [Arthur] shorted him and smote off both his legs by the knees, saying, Now art thou better of a size to deal with than thou were, and after smote off his head. [Malory V, 8]

GALATINE

Sir Gawaine's sword [Malory V, 6]. See the note for Excalibur.

GALDON CASTLE† (Galadon)

On the Galide River, probably in the part of the country in or around Stranggore [Vulgate].

GALEGANTIN OF WALES†

Among Arthur's knights in the list Chrétien de Troyes begins in line 1691 of **Erec & Enide**.

Galehodin—see GALIHODIN

GALEHOLT, DUKE OF THE LONG ISLES AND OF SURLUSE (Galahalt the Haut Prince; Galahad; Galehot; etc.)

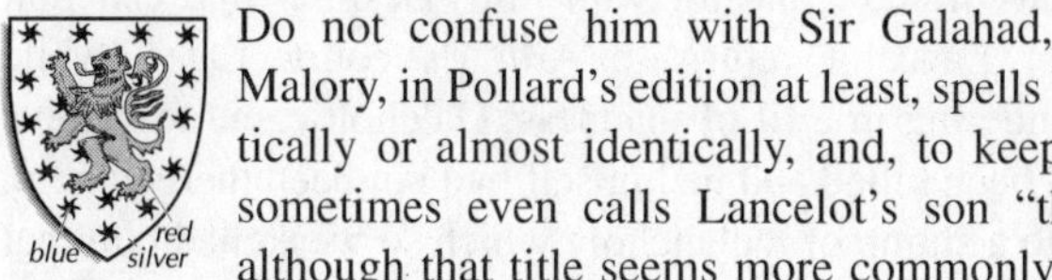

Do not confuse him with Sir Galahad, Lancelot's son. Malory, in Pollard's edition at least, spells their names identically or almost identically, and, to keep matters simple, sometimes even calls Lancelot's son "the high prince", although that title seems more commonly to belong to the older Galahalt. To try to avoid confusion, I have followed a spelling Sommer uses in the Vulgate and also tried to use Galeholt's title of Duke consistently rather than sporadically.

Malory makes Duke Galeholt the son of the evil Sir Breunor of Castle Pluere, but perhaps we can take this with a grain of salt. At least, Galeholt does not condone Breunor's evil customs, nor start a feud to avenge his death. Vulgate IV calls Galeholt "the son of the beautiful giantess."

In the Vulgate, Duke Galeholt is prominent for a longer time than Sir Galahad. Although called "Duke", he had conquered thirty kingdoms, of which Surluse was his favorite. Malory's mentioning the Long Isles specifically, along with Surluse, suggests that Galeholt considered them his second best kingdom. Some of the kingdoms, of course, were probably little more than city-castles, and the majority of them may not have been too far-flung; still, Duke Galeholt was one of the strongest as well as one of the most lovable of Arthur's early foes. Arthur's own knight Galegantin (Galegantis), the only member of Arthur's court who had yet seen him, described him as "a young bachelor, most gentle, kind-hearted, and generous." [Vulgate III, 202]

Galeholt attempted to win Arthur's allegiance. Instead, Lancelot won Galeholt's allegiance for Arthur. Galeholt then became Lancelot's close friend and confidant in the latter's affair with Guenevere. The Lady of Malohaut, who had been in love with Lancelot, became Guenevere's confidante and Galeholt's paramour. During the affair of "the false Guenevere" (Genievre), Galeholt gave Lancelot and Guenevere shelter in Surluse. Is it possible that Lancelot's son was named as much in honor of Lancelot's friend as because Lancelot's own baptismal name had been Galahad?

Duke Galeholt was one of the wisest of princes. In order to make himself a still worthier knight, he went to mix with Arthur's court, first deputizing King Bagdemagus of Gore to administer his territories and turn them over to Galeholt's nephew Galihodin in the event of Galeholt's death. The only hard evidence I can produce that Galeholt became a companion of the Round Table is that Malory lists him, perhaps posthumously, among the would-be healers of Sir Urre; but it would be surprising if the illustrious Haut Prince had been kept out of that company.

Galeholt's clerks, especially Helyes of Thoulouse, determined by study that he had only a few more years to live, but could prolong his life by keeping his friend Lancelot with him. Despite this, Galeholt unprotestingly let Lancelot return to Arthur's court. Later, while Lancelot was wandering in a fit of madness, Galeholt came to believe that Lancelot had been killed and he himself had not been there to help. Galeholt went into a slump of melancholy which so weakened him that a wound breaking open and a strange illness attacking him simultaneously killed him. Lancelot found his body buried in a religious house and carried it to Joyous Garde for reburial.

Galeholt hated to eat fish. [Vulgate III-IV; Malory VIII, 24-27; X, 48; XIX, 11; etc.]

At one point [X, 50], Malory has King Mark learning that Galeholt and Bagdemagus have arranged the Surluse tournament with intent to slay or shame Lancelot for jealousy. This is very difficult to reconcile with the Vulgate's insistence on the friendship between Galeholt and Lancelot and with Malory's own depiction of Bagdemagus' character. Possibly Mark misunderstood the situation, or possibly Malory just needed an occasion for Mark to exercise his malice, and trumped up a peculiarly flimsy and inconsistent one.

See also Ossa Cylellaur.

DUKE GALEHOLT'S FAMILY AND RETAINERS
Father: Breunor of Castle Pleure
Mother: "a beautiful giantess"
Nephew: Galihodin
Lover: Lady of Malohaut
Ward: King Gloier's Daughter
Clerk: Helyes of Thoulouse
Knights and nobles of Surluse: Ossaise, Earl Ulbawes
Protege: King Marsil
Allies: King 'Doutre les Marches', King 'Premier Conquis', King of the Hundred Knights
Special friend: Lancelot

GALES THE BALD†

Among Arthur's knights in the list Chrétien de Troyes begins in line 1691 of **Erec & Enide**. The Everyman's edition of 1987 definitely gives his name as "the Bald" and, while unfortunately I lack the French original or any other English translation for immediate comparison, I have no reason to suspect a misprint for "Bold."

GALESHIN†

A knight of the Round Table. Sommer in a footnote makes him the son of King Nentres of Garlot (and thus the son of Elaine of Tintagil and a nephew of Arthur), but points out that the Vulgate in other places makes him the son of King Alain of Escavalon (and thus the brother of Floree) or the son of the King of Norgales and thus the brother of Dodinal le Savage. [Vulgate IV, p.90] Further on, Sommer explains that Galeshin and Dodinal are cousins, not brothers [Vulgate IV, p. 229]. Also in the Vulgate, Galeshin is identified as the Duke of Clarence, a title he was given by Arthur; "Galeshin" certainly could be a variant of the name Malory uses for the Duke of Clarence, "Chaleins." Take your choice. Galeshin would seem to be a most flexible character.

GALIHODIN (Galehodin)

Nephew of Duke Galeholt and lord of Peningue Castle. Galihodin may have become ruler of Norgales after Ryons.

Once Sir Aglovale killed a relative of Galihodin in battle. The dead man's brother (not Galihodin) later found Aglovale and attacked him. Aglovale, being unarmed at the moment, fled. A large party of knights pursued him past the house of a wealthy burgher who lived on a hill. Gawaine and some of his companions were staying with this burgher. They piled out and rescued Aglovale, killing sixty knights. The burgher was horrified: "You have ruined me! Gilehodin will kill me and mine. You will go away and I shall have to bear the consequences." Gawaine, confident that Galihodin would pardon them even if they had killed half his men, because three of them were of high lineage, promised to make the burgher's peace with his lord. Sure enough, Galehodin was so impressed by manly explanation that he not only pardoned Gawaine's party and scolded his own people, but invested the burgher with the castle of Peningue and promised to dub him knight on Whitsunday. [Vulgate V]

Malory has Galihodin a "nigh cousin" to Galeholt and "a king within the country of Surluse." Galihodin helps Lancelot play a practical joke on Dinadan at the tournament in Surluse. Later Galihodin shows up with twenty knights and tries to win La Beale Isoud by jousting, but Palomides, with Tristram's permission, jousts him and his knights down. Galihodin became a knight of the Round Table; he was among the guests at Guenevere's small dinner party and among the knights who tried to heal Sir Urre. Following Lancelot into exile, Galihodin was made Duke of Sentonge. He later joined Lancelot and others in the hermitage of the former Archbishop of Canterbury, but returned to his own country after Lancelot's death. [Malory X, 49, 56, 65-66; XVIII, 3; XIX, 11, XX, 18; XXI, 10, 13]

GALLERON OF GALWAY

This knight of the Round Table became Sir Palomides' godfather. Palomides had just struck Galleron down in single combat when Tristram came along, entered conversation with the Saracen knight, and asked why he was still postponing his baptism. Palomides replied that he had still one battle to do in the name of Christ before being baptized, in fulfillment of a vow he had made years before. Tristram borrowed the armor of the wounded Galleron and gave Palomides his battle. This formality over, Palomides was baptized by the Suffragan of Carlisle, with Tristram and Galleron as godfathers.

Malory also mentions Galleron, very briefly, as one of the attempted healers of Sir Urre and as one of the knights who was killed trying to help Mordred and Agravaine trap Lancelot with the Queen. [Malory XII, 12-14; XIX, 11; XX, 2]

Galloway—see also **GALWAY**

GALLOWAY, KING OF†

An uncle of Erec's, this bountiful and generous monarch was at Nantes for his nephew's coronation; in Chrétien's earliest romance, we find him going with King Cadoalant, Guivret the Little, and Yder the son of Nut to escort Enide and Guenevere to the great hall. Presumably, if not among Arthur's vassals, the King of Galloway was among his friends and allies. [Chrétien de Troyes, **Erec & Enide**, ll. 6810-6855]

In Chrétien's last romance, however, Galloway seems to have become a land of some mystery and peril—D.D.R. Owen cites evidence that the actual country suffered bad repute, and that four mss. include a couplet identifying it as an evil land with perverse people. The rest of Chrétien's text may not bear this out: as I interpret the peril, it comes from a few renegade individuals; the general populace seems passively sympathetic, and if the King of Galloway was to reappear in Gawaine's adventures, it must have been in the part that Chrétien never managed to add. [**Perceval**, ca. ll. 6520-7370 & Owen's note to 6602]

GALOAIN, COUNT†

Possibly one of the most interesting villains of medieval romance, Count Galoain makes his appearance in Chrétien's **Erec & Enide**, lines 3121-3662.

Galoain's land bordered that of Guivret the Little and, on the other side, seems to have lain about a day's ride from King Lac's Outre-Gales: Erec and Enide reached it about noon on their second day, but on the first day out from his father's kingdom Erec had had to fight off a total of eight robber knights, which must have taken some time.

One of Galoain's squires, who was carrying lunch to the men mowing in the fields, stopped and gave it to Erec and Enide instead, completing his hospitality by finding them good lodging with one of Galoain's townsmen. Galoain learned of this when he saw the fine horse (captured from one of yesterday's robber knights) that Erec gave the squire in an exchange of generosity. The count visited the couple and promptly fell in love with Enide. First, noticing something of the way in which Erec was currently treating her, Galoain proposed that she simply stay with him instead. When she heatedly refused, he threatened to kill Erec. Understanding, now, that she needed trickery to save her husband, she lied to the count, pretending to agree but begging him not to kill Erec at once, lest people blame her for it—let him, instead, send knights in the morning to seize her forcibly: Erec could then be slain in battle defending her. She proceeded to let Erec have a good night's sleep in ignorance before waking him early and warning him why they must leave without further delay, rather to the surprise of their host, who knew nothing of the treachery his lord planned. Barely were they on their way when a hundred of the count's knights crowded into the townhouse (this must have been quite a scene!) to find them gone. At once Galoain set off with his men, breathing fire and promising signal favor to anyone who brought him Erec's head. When they caught up, Erec began by laying Galoain's seneschal low, then encountered the count himself. This was a hard, if rapid, battle, Galoain proving himself the best opponent Erec had met so far; but our hero managed to run a yard or so of lance through his stomach and knock him from his steed. Recovering consciousness, the badly wounded Galoain saw how wickedly he had been behaving, forbade his men to continue the chase, and praised Enide for her prudent deception. Chrétien adds that Galoain's wound did not prove fatal and that he lived a long time after that. One hopes that he lived the rest of his life well. The lunch his squire had been taking to the field workers included rich cheese, fine white cakes, and good wine; this suggests that Galoain had already been treating his people well. (One further hopes that he or his squire soon sent a replacement repast to those field workers.) Despite a certain incredulity when listening to his squire describe Erec and Enide, Galoain seems to have shown quite an acceptable level of courtesy until falling in love with Enide; indeed, his worst fault up to that point appears to have been vanity about his own good looks.

Chrétien remarks that his shield was painted yellow, but does not further describe it.

Galogrinans—see **CALOGRENANT, COLGREVANCE**

GALVOIE, LADY OF†

The Lady of Galvoie, the chatelaine, sent a damsel to Arthur's court to request either Lancelot or Gawaine to fight for her. Since both were absent, she settled for Bors.

The Lady's father had rescued Sir Kahenin from captivity. Kahenin had built a castle on an island and given both castle and island to his rescuer. After the deaths of Kahenin and the Lady's father, Kahenin's son Mariales seized the castles. When the Lady arraigned him before King Pellam, Mariales argued that his father had built the castle. Bors came to Pellam's court at Carbonek, defeated—but did not kill—Mariales, and made him restore the castle to the Lady. (It was on this quest that Bors spent two nights at Carbonek without learning of the Adventurous Palace where the Grail was kept.)

The Lady of Galvoie married Gaidon, a knight who was her inferior by birth, but a man of great worth and prowess. He fought for her against Mariales, who was still making trouble. Together with Sir

Bors, they were eventually able to patch up peace and friendship with Mariales. [Vulgate V]

I am not sure whether Galvoie is the castle Kahenin built on an island or another castle nearby, but in any case the castle(s) would be in the territory of King Pellam, Listeneise.

GALWAY (Galloway)

As I recall, Malory only mentions Galway as part of a personal name—as, for instance, Sir Galleron of Galway (who, however, is listed among twelve knights, "and all they were of Scotland", either of Gawaine's kin or well-wishers to his family) [Malory XX, 2]. There was strong connection between Ireland and Scotland in the early days.

The last Arthurian adventures Chrétien de Troyes wrote take place in the marches of Galloway. Just over the Galloway border lies the city, which may be the Guiromelant's Orqueneseles, to which the Haughty Maid of Logres sends knights for her palfrey. Also near the border—I remain unsure on which side—we find Ygerne's Rock of Canguin. A note of D.D.R. Owen's remarks that in Chrétien's time Galloway had a regrettable reputation, and that four mss. include a couplet describing it as an evil land with perverse people. I cannot see that the perversity of its population in general is borne out by Gawaine's adventures, nor that the unpleasant individuals whom he encounters near Galloway are any worse than villains elsewhere. [**Perceval**, ll. 6519-9188, & Owen's note to 6602]

GANDELU†

Tenth best of Arthur's knights, according to the list Chrétien de Troyes begins in line 1691 of **Erec & Enide**.

GANIEDA (Ganicenda, Gwendydd)†

According to the Red Book of Hergest, she was the twin sister of Merlin. Glennie, from whom I gleaned this tantalizing scrap, does not make it clear whether she, also, was a necromancer. I only wish I could tell you more!

In **Namer of Beasts, Maker of Souls**, an exquisite 1995 Arthurian novelette based on a kabbalistic interpretation, Jessica Amanda Salmonson refers to Merlin's twin sister Ganicenda as Divine Wisdom, with her head in heaven and her feet in Sheol.

GANIS, ABBEY OF

This abbey was near the castle of Ganis.

GANIS, CASTLE OF

Malory names Sir Bleoberis de Ganis as its lord [IX, 37]. The abbey of Ganis is nearby. Bleoberis was the godson of King Bors of Gaul (Gannes), the father of Bors de Ganis. I am not sure whether the

"Ganis" of Sir Bors' name refers to this castle, which is apparently in Britain, or to his native land across the Channel.

Carew, in his **Survey of Cornwall**, notes that Cornish residents believe that the local place name Bodrugan is a degeneration of Bors de Ganis. Bodrugan is in about the south center of modern Cornwall, in the division called Powder Hundred, on the east side of Dodman Point.

Ganora—see GUENEVERE

Garantan†—see "UNCOURTEOUS LADY, CASTLE OF THE"

GARAUNT

A knight of Cameliard, mentioned once in passing by Malory. His only apparent claim to interest is that he was a cousin of Guenevere. [Malory X, 36] The similarity of names makes it conceivable that he could be identified with Sir Geraint, the name Tennyson uses for Erec.

GARETH OF ORKNEY (Beaumains, Guerrehet)

The youngest true-born son of Lot and Morgawse, Gareth was one of the best knights of his arms of the world and probably remains today the best loved of the Orkney brothers, as well as one of the best loved members of Arthur's Round Table. His story is quite familiar. The last of the brothers (except, presumably, Mordred) to come to court, he appeared anonymously and asked Arthur for three gifts. The first was to be fed for a twelvemonth, at the end of which time he would ask the other two. Kay took charge of feeding him, nicknamed him Beaumains ("Fair-hands") in mockery, and put him in the kitchen. Both Lancelot and Gawaine befriended him, the latter not recognizing him as brother, and even Kay seems to have taken pride in Beaumains' strength in the sports of casting bars or stones. At the end of the year, Lynette came to court requesting a champion for her sister Lyonors against Sir Ironside, alias "The Red Knight of the Red Launds", who was besieging their castle. Beaumains made his remaining requests: that he be given Lynette's adventure, and that Lancelot be sent after them to dub him knight on command.

To Lynette's chagrin, Arthur granted both gifts. Kay rode after them to give the kitchen boy his first test, and Beaumains promptly jousted him down; Lancelot came shortly thereafter and gave Beaumains a fall, but when they fought with swords, Gareth fought so well that Lancelot "dreaded himself to be shamed" and called a truce and knighted the young man. Despite Lynette's continued mockery, Gareth completed the adventure, conquering and either converting or slaying numerous knights on the way—Gherard and Arnold le Breusse, the four brothers Percard, Pertelope, Perimones, and Persant, and finally Ironside himself. (Tennyson, who changes and simplifies the tale somewhat in one of his best idylls, **Gareth and Lynette**, ends it with Gareth's victory at Lyonors' castle and marries Gareth to the livelier sister, Lynette.)

Malory continues the story quite a bit further: Gareth begs to see the lady he has just saved from Ironside, but Lyonors tells him he must first labor for a year to win greater fame and her love. Already in love with him, however, she enlists her brother Sir Gringamore to bring him to her with a mock kidnaping of Gareth's dwarf. Biding together in the castle after this practical joke, Gareth and Lyonors decide to consummate their love in advance of the wedding ceremony, but Lynette uses a bit of magical art to keep her sister an honest woman. Meanwhile, Pertelope, Perimones, Persant, and Ironside arrive at Arthur's court to describe their young conqueror's exploits. Queen Morgawse also comes to visit her brother Arthur, and her older sons learn of their relationship with Beaumains.

At Gareth's advice, Lyonors holds a great tournament at her castle on the feast of Assumption. Lyonors gives her lover a ring which enables him to fight in the tournament incognito (see Lyonors' Ring), but he is recognized when his dwarf cunningly gets possession of the ring. Then Gareth slips away from the tournament and obtains lodging at the castle of the Duke de la Rowse by promising the Duchess to yield to the absent Duke whenever he meets him. Continuing, he kills a knight named Bendelaine in battle and defends himself successfully against twenty of Bendelaine's men who attack him seeking revenge. He then defeats and slays the Brown Knight without Pity, rescuing thirty ladies from his castle. He next meets the Duke de la Rowse and offers to yield to him as per his promise, but the Duke insists on having a fight instead, is defeated, and swears fealty to Gareth and Arthur. At last Gareth and Gawaine meet, neither knowing the other, and battle for two hours before Lynette arrives to stop the fight by shouting to Gawaine that his opponent is his brother. Lynette heals their wounds with her craft, and so Gareth is finally restored to Arthur's court and wed to Dame Lyonors. [Malory, Book VII]

Vulgate IV tells us that Gareth had a splendid physique and a fine head, was a favorite with ladies and liked their company, was generous and charitable, and was Gawaine's favorite brother. Vulgate V tells us that on one occasion Arthur offered Gareth the crown of Orkney, but Gareth declined until the Grail should be achieved.

Malory, who does not seem to like Gawaine, is always careful whenever the other Orkney brothers do evil (as when they bring about the deaths of their mother Morgawse and her lover Sir Lamorak) to make it clear that Gareth had no part in the villainy. According to Malory,

Gawaine's vengefulness caused a rift between him and the unvengeful Gareth, so that the younger brother preferred Lancelot's company. [Malory VII, 34; X, 58; etc.]

Against his will, Gareth obeyed Arthur's command to join the group of knights taking Guenevere to the stake. According to Malory, Gareth and his brother Gaheris went unarmed and were cut down by mischance in the confusion, Lancelot not recognizing them. (The Vulgate has Gareth and Gaheris wearing arms during this scene and giving a good account of themselves before their deaths.) It was for Gareth's death that Gawaine turned against Lancelot and pressed the war, to the ultimate destruction of Arthur's Round Table. [Malory, XX, 8; Vulgate VI]

In Chrétien's **Perceval**, ca. l. 8141, Gawaine names Gareth as the fourth son of King Lot; at least, Ruth Cline renders the name as Gareth—D.D.R. Owen gives it as Guerrehet. See under Gaheris.

GARETH'S DWARF

When Gareth first came to Arthur's court, he was accompanied by two men mounted on horseback like himself and a dwarf on foot, who held all three horses while the men escorted Gareth into the hall. Once Gareth was established at court, the two men and the dwarf seem to have left, all without saying a word. Presumably they were servants or retainers from home and returned to Orkney. At the end of Gareth's year in the kitchen, when he obtained Lynette's adventure, the dwarf, apparently the same one, showed up again with his young master's horse and armor. After conquering Kay, Gareth mounted the dwarf on Kay's horse. Little is said of the dwarf's opinions or services during the journey to Castle Dangerous; after Gareth had conquered the last knight on the way, the dwarf was sent on ahead to the castle, where he sang his master's praises to Lyonors, describing all his victories and telling the lady that her champion was the king of Orkney's son, nicknamed Beaumains by Sir Kay and dubbed knight by Sir Lancelot—he declined, however, to give Gareth's real name. Lyonors had the dwarf carry ample provisions to a hermitage in her territory and then guide Beaumains and her sister to the hermitage from Sir Persant's city to spend the night, all which instructions the dwarf capably fulfilled. Returning alone to Castle Dangerous, the dwarf met Sir Ironside and boldly defied him on Gareth's behalf, again praising his master and telling Ironside, "... it is marvel that ye make such shameful war upon noble knights."

Later, when Ironside was conquered and Lyonors had sent Gareth away, supposedly to prove his worth for a year, she made the dwarf the nub of a lover's prank. Her brother Sir Gringamore, acting on her instructions, came stalking up from behind and kidnaped the dwarf while Gareth slept. Awakened by the dwarf's cries, Gareth promptly got up and rode in pursuit. Meanwhile, Gringamore got the dwarf to his own castle, where Lyonors and Lynette were waiting to question the dwarf as to Beaumains' birth and lineage, playfully threatening him with lifelong imprisonment unless he told all. Probably recognizing the farcical nature of the affair, he replied that he "feared not greatly" to reveal his master's name and family (in effect, this entailed only adding Gareth's true name to what he had already told Lyonors) and met her threat with another in kind, mentioning all the damage Gareth would do in the country if he were angered. Gareth arrived, still thinking the matter was in earnest, and no doubt really would have done great slaughter in order to save his dwarf, whom he had had considerable trouble in tracking, had any slaughter proven necessary.

In the tournament at Castle Dangerous, Gareth fought wearing Dame Lyonors' ring, which concealed his identity by continually changing the color of his armor. When he rode off the field to "amend his helm" and take a drink of water, however, the dwarf took charge of the ring, ostensibly to prevent Gareth's losing it while he drank. Whether Gareth's returning to the field without the ring was due to his own eager haste and forgetfulness or to the dwarf's cunning is unclear, but certainly the dwarf was well pleased to keep the ring, for he wished his master to be recognized. After the tournament, the dwarf followed Gareth into the woods, returned briefly to the castle to deliver Lyonors her ring and her lover's au revoir, and then rejoined Gareth. Presumably, although the dwarf now fades from attention, he continued to accompany and serve his master. [Malory, Book VII]

Malory gives much more information about Gareth's dwarf than about any other, but Gareth's may perhaps be considered an example of dwarf-knight relationships and of the duties of dwarfs to knights, which seem to resemble closely the duties of squires, except that squires would be expected to fight at need.

GARETH'S(?) SWORD

Sir Gringamore, brother of Dames Lyonors and Lynette, gave this, "a noble sword that sometime Sir Gringamore's father won upon an heathen tyrant", to Sir Gareth; or, perhaps, merely lent it for the tournament at Castle Dangerous [Malory VII, 27].

GARIN and FAMILY†

Garin was a vavasour of Tibaut of Tintagil.

En route to Escavalon, Gawaine coincidentally came to Tintagil as the tournament between Meliant and the reluctant Tibaut was about to begin. Gawaine was carrying a pair of shields and hung them both on the tree beneath which he parked. I surmise that they were standard-issue "Arthur's court" shields rather than two bearing his own device because, seeing them, Garin guessed that two of Arthur's knights had arrived and would help the town—Tibaut's side. On this assumption, he advised his lord to let the tourney proceed. Though Gawaine's daylong inaction must have disappointed Garin, he nevertheless welcomed Arthur's knight into Tintagil at the day's end, offering him hospitality for the night, which Gawaine accepted. Garin naturally asked why his guest had refrained from fighting, and pronounced the explanation—that the stranger was on his way to defend himself in trial by combat against a charge of treason and feared being delayed by tournament injury—good and honorable. Leaving his guest with his wife and two daughters, Garin and his son Herman set out to confer with their lord Tibaut, as was apparently their regular daily usage, but met him on the way. Tibaut's elder daughter had told him that the stranger was a merchant passing himself off as a knight to avoid paying tolls, an imposture which seems to have been a hanging offense. Garin explained the true state of things and they returned to his house, where they found Tibaut's younger daughter, the Maid with Little Sleeves, who was a friend of Garin's daughters, begging Gawaine for her sake to fight only one day in the tournament. The outcome of his assent was quite happy for Garin's family, since Gawaine had the second, third, and fourth horses he won next day sent as gifts to Garin's wife and two daughters. On finally asking his guest's name, and learning whom he had hosted, Garin tried to get Gawaine to spend a second night beneath his roof and be more completely honored, but the champion refused (perhaps fearing further delay). [Chrétien de Troyes, **Perceval**, ca. ll. 4922-5655]

GARLON

Although brother to Pellam, the guardian of the Grail, Garlon was a real rotter. He must have had some knowledge of magic, or else a working arrangement with a magician, because he went around invisible, slaying knights at will. When he showed up visible at his brother's banquet in Listeneise, he is described as having a "black face", which here probably means dour. Balin killed him, very sensibly, considering that any man as dangerous and treacherous as Garlon should be put out of action definitely and permanently. The act, however, angered Pellam, who chased Balin through the castle (probably Carbonek) until Balin found Longinus' Spear and struck Pellam with it in self-defense. Thus Garlon became the immediate occasion of the Dolorous Stroke. [Malory II, 12-15]

GARLOTH (Garlot)

King Nentres of Garloth married Elaine, the sister of Morgan le Fay and Margawse, and half-sister of Arthur. With few clues as to the location of this kingdom, I suggest East Lothian.

GARRAS, KING OF CORK†

Among the vassal kings Arthur summoned to court for Erec's wedding, Garras brought 500 richly clad knights. [Chrétien de Troyes, **Erec & Enide**, ll. 1963-2024]

GARRAVAIN OF ESTRANGOT†

Among Arthur's knights in the list Chrétien de Troyes begins in line 1691 of **Erec & Enide**.

GAUDIN OF THE MOUNTAIN†

He was captured by Gawaine in the tourney between Evroic and Tenebroc a month after Erec's wedding. [Chrétien de Troyes, **Erec & Enide**, ll. 2215-2234]

GAWAINE

Oldest son of King Lot and Queen Morgawse, chief of the Orkney clan (which included his brothers Agravaine, Gaheris, Gareth, and Mordred), Arthur's favorite nephew, and one of the most famous knights of the Round Table.

These are some highlights of his career according to Malory: he first came to court with his mother and three full brothers between the two early rebellions of the petty British kings against Arthur. He seems to have returned about the time of Arthur's marriage and the establishment of the Round Table, when he asked and received Arthur's promise to make him knight—they had now learned of their uncle-nephew relationship. At Arthur's wedding feast, Gawaine was sent, by Merlin's advice, on the quest of the white hart. On this quest, he accidentally slew a lady who rushed between him and her lord, whom he had just defeated in battle and was about to behead; for this his brother Gaheris, then acting as his squire, rebuked him severely, and Guenevere ordained that Gawaine should "for ever while he lived … be with all ladies, and … fight for their quarrels."

When the five kings of Denmark, Ireland, the Vale, Soleise, and Longtains invaded Britain, Gawaine, Griflet, and Arthur followed Kay's example to strike them down and save the battle. After this campaign, Gawaine was elevated to the Round Table on King Pellinore's advice. Nevertheless, Gawaine later slew Pellinore in revenge for Lot's death (though Malory only alludes to the incident without describing the scene). When Arthur banished Gawaine's favorite cousin, Ywaine, on suspicion of conspiracy with his mother, Morgan le Fay, Gawaine chose to accompany Ywaine. They met Sir Marhaus and later the three knights met the damsels "Printemps, Été, & Automne" in the forest of Arroy. Leaving his companions to make the first choice of damsels, Gawaine ended with the youngest (who, however, left him and went with another knight). It was on this adventure that Gawaine became involved in the affair of Pelleas and Ettard, playing Pelleas false by sleeping with Ettard, for which cause "Pelleas loved never after Sir Gawaine."

These adventures lasted about a year, by the end of which time Arthur was sending out messengers to recall his nephews. In Arthur's continental campaign against the Roman emperor Lucius, Gawaine and Bors de Ganis carried Arthur's message to Lucius, to leave the land or else do battle. When Lucius defied Arthur's message, hot words passed on either side, culminating when Gawaine beheaded Lucius' cousin Sir Gainus in a rage, which forced Gawaine and Bors to take rather a bloody and hasty leave. Malory seems to insinuate that Gawaine was accessory to Gaheris' murder of their mother, though "Sir Gawaine was wroth that Gaheris had slain his mother and let Sir Lamorak escape." Certainly Gawaine was with his brothers Agravaine, Gaheris, and Mordred when they later ambushed and killed Morgawse's lover, Lamorak, for which Gawaine seems to have lost Tristram's goodwill. Despite Gawaine's vengefulness, however, Lancelot, who had once rescued him from Carados of the Dolorous Tower, remained his friend until the end.

At the time of Galahad's arrival in Camelot, Gawaine reluctantly, and at Arthur's command, was the first to attempt to draw Balin's Sword from the floating marble; shortly afterward, it was Gawaine who first proposed the Quest of the Holy Grail, in the midst of the fervor which followed the Grail's miraculous visit to court. Gawaine rather quickly tired of the Quest, however, and had very bad fortune on it besides; in addition to being seriously wounded himself by Galahad, in divine retribution for having attempted to draw Balin's Sword, he slew both King Bagdemagus and Yvonet li Avoutres—the latter and apparently the former also by mischance in friendly joust.

> Sir Gawaine had a custom that he used daily at dinner and at supper, that he loved well all manner of fruit, and in especial apples and pears. And therefore whosomever dined or feasted Sir Gawaine would commonly purvey for good fruit for him.

Sir Pinel le Savage, a cousin of Lamorak's, once tried to use this taste to avenge Lamorak, by poisoning the fruit at a small dinner party of the Queen's.

Gawaine had "three sons, Sir Gingalin, Sir Florence, and Sir Lovel, these two were begotten upon Sir Brandiles' sister."

Gawaine was not party to Agravaine and Mordred's plotting against Lancelot and the Queen; indeed, Gawaine even warned his brothers and sons against what they were doing. When Lancelot killed Agravaine and all three of Gawaine's sons in escaping from Guenevere's chamber, Gawaine was ready to forgive all their deaths, and pleaded earnestly with Arthur to allow Lancelot to defend Guenevere and prove their innocence in trial by combat. Not until Lancelot slew the unarmed Gareth and Gaheris in rescuing Guenevere from the stake did Gawaine feel bound to take vengeance, in pursuit of which vengeance he stirred Arthur to besiege Lancelot first in Joyous Garde and later, after the Pope had enjoined peace in Britain, in Lancelot's lands in France. Gawaine would continually challenge Lancelot to single combat; Lancelot would defeat but refuse to kill Gawaine, who would challenge him again as soon as his wounds were healed.

Learning of Mordred's usurpation, Arthur returned to England, to meet Mordred's resistance at Dover; in this battle, the wounds Gawaine had received from Lancelot broke open fatally. Between making his last confession and dying, Gawaine wrote a letter to Lancelot, asking his prayers and forgiveness and begging him to hurry back to England to Arthur's assistance. His death took place at noon, the tenth of May, and

> then the king let inter him in a chapel within Dover Castle; and there yet all men may see the skull of him.

His ghost appeared to Arthur in a dream the night of Trinity Sunday, accompanied by the ladies whose battles he had fought in life. In the dream Gawaine warned Arthur to avoid battle with Mordred until after Lancelot had arrived. [Malory I, 19; II, 10, 13; III, 2, 6-8; IV, 4, 16-23, 28; V, 6; VIII, 28; X, 55; XIII, 3,7; XVI, 1-2; XVII, 17; XVIII, 3; XIX, 11; XX, 2; XXI, 3; etc.]

These are not all of Gawaine's adventures even according to Malory, and a recapitulation according to earlier sources would be far more favorable to the famous knight. Malory did not seem to like him, making him a rather unpleasant personality and not even all that impressive a fighter, when compared with other great champions, being defeated by Lancelot, Tristram, Bors de Ganis, Percivale, Pelleas, Marhaus, Galahad, Carados of the Dolorous Tower, and Breuse Sans Pitie. [Malory IV, 18; VIII, 1; VIII, 28; IX, 26] Presumably Lamorak, Gareth, and others could also have defeated him, had he finished a fair fight with them. (Once, indeed, he did fight Gareth unknowingly, but left off at once when Lynette revealed Gareth's identity. VII, 33)

Modern treatments are based largely on Malory. By the time we reach Tennyson, Gawaine's courtesy had degenerated into smooth talk and his chivalry into casual love affairs. William Morris turned him from one of

Guenevere's most ardent defenders into one of her chief accusers. Edward Arlington Robinson retained the superficiality of Tennyson's character. John Erskine seems simply to have accepted this version of Gawaine as a matter of course. Hal Foster, while making him a major and generally likable character in **Prince Valiant**, tends to emphasize his lightness and lady-killing qualities. T. H. White, while generally not unsympathetic, turned him into a rather brusque personality and even gave the adventure of the Green Knight to Gareth instead. [**The Once and Future King**, Book IV, ch. 9] It remained for **Monty Python and the Holy Grail** to sink Gawaine to his lowest point yet: in a line that goes by so fast you're likely to miss it, Gawaine is named as one of the knights slain by the vicious white rabbit! Vera Chapman created a second Gawaine, nephew and namesake of the more famous, rather than attempt to rehabilitate Malory's character. One of the few exceptions to the modern picture of Gawaine is Sutcliff's, in **Sword at Sunset**, and her Gwalchmai seems to owe as little to the pre-Malory Gawaine as to the post-Malory one.

Once, however, before his place was usurped by Lancelot, Gawaine was considered the greatest of all the knights, the epitome both of prowess and courtesy, the touchstone against whom all others must prove themselves. This is the Gawaine we find in Chrétien de Troyes.

Chrétien's first romance, **Erec & Enide**, names Gawaine as one of his uncle Arthur's most prudent counselors [ll. 27-69; 275-310], and gives him as first of all Arthur's good knights in the roll call beginning at line 1691.

In Chrétien's next romance, **Cligés**, Gawaine is much impressed by the titular knight's performance during the first three days of the Oxford tournament, and decides to open the last day's combat himself. He modestly says that he fully expects to have no better luck than Sagramore, Lancelot, and Percivale in tilting against the still-unknown champion, but thinks he may fare better in the sword play: at this stage of the legend, nobody has every beaten Gawaine at swordfighting. When the combat comes, Gawaine and Cligés knock each other from their horses, then fight with swords until Arthur calls a halt while the outcome still remains undecided. Gawaine is delighted to learn that he is the young champion's uncle, his sister Soredamors having married Cligés' father Alexander.

In Chrétien's **Lancelot**, Gawaine accompanies his good friend Lancelot part of the way on their journey to King Bademagu's Gore. When Lancelot rides in the cart for the sake of getting to the queen, Gawaine declines the dishonor and follows along on his horse; later, when Lancelot insists on sleeping in the forbidden "Deadly Bed",

Gawaine quietly accepts the lesser bed his hostess offers him. My own reading of these episodes is that Gawaine shows greater prudence in the first and greater modesty in the second. Other interpretations are certainly possible, and it might be argued that Lancelot's success in crossing the Sword Bridge and Gawaine's failure in crossing the Water Bridge can be traced to Lancelot's riding in the cart and Gawaine's refusal to do so; also it would have shown greater courtesy and generosity on Gawaine's part, when offered him the choice by his friend, to take the Sword Bridge and leave the comparatively less hazardous Water Bridge to Lancelot. On the other hand, Gawaine has not, like Lancelot, ridden two horses (one of them borrowed) to death and left himself without a mount and therefore in need of the ignominous cart ride; while, as to the one's success and the other's failure to cross the bridges into Gore—if Gore is indeed a branch of the eschatological Otherworld, I might venture the very tentative theory that Lancelot's desire for Guenevere renders him, in some spiritual sense, already dead. This might make the next world more accessible to him than to the still vital and generally virtuous Gawaine, who, while already displaying amorous tendencies, seems to restrict them to more available ladies—for instance, the lively Lunette of **Yvain**, which can be called a companion piece to **Lancelot**. In **Yvain**, Chrétien tells us of yet another sister of Gawaine's, whom I call for convenience "Alteria."

Chrétien's last and unfinished romance, **Perceval**, gives us our fullest view of the author's approach to this hero: at about line 4750, the emphasis twists over from Percivale to Gawaine and, except in one short episode, stays there until Chrétien laid down his pen. Here we see several instances of Gawaine's modesty, or prudence, with his name: he never refuses to give it when asked outright, but rarely if ever volunteers it, and sometimes requests those he meets not to ask his identity for a certain period of time. [ca. ll. 5610-5620; 8117-8145; 8350-8359; 8720-8835] He has superior medical and herbal knowledge [ll. 6908-6958]. We get a flashback glimpse of him acting as judge or magistrate—perhaps filling in for his royal uncle?—meting out strict justice to uphold Arthur's laws, yet incapable of understanding why one so chastized should harbor a grudge against the judge [ll. 7108-7131]. We find him carrying Excalibur [l. 5902]. We learn that the poor love him for his generosity [ll. 9204 ff.], and we watch him put his own concerns at risk in order to please a child, the Maid with Little Sleeves, whom he treats as courteously as if she were fully grown. At the same time, we see his flirtatiousness in full swing with the young king of Escavalon's sister, and we find hanging over his head at least one and possibly two charges of murder. The likeliest explanation I see is that all such charges refer to men slain in honest battle (Gawaine stands ready to defend himself in trial by combat), and a similar charge is raised against his cousin Ywaine over the death of Esclados the Red. In **Perceval**, Gawaine finds himself again in what may well be an outpost of the Otherworld—the Rock of Canguin, where he meets his grandmother Ygerne, his mother (here unnamed), and the sister, Clarissant, he never knew he had. Before learning who they are, he answers the old queen's questions concerning King Lot's four sons (without revealing that he is himself the oldest of them, Gawaine gives the same list we have from later sources), King Uriens' two Yvains, and King Arthur's health.

As early as Chrétien's pages we also meet Gawaine's great charger Gringolet, whom later romancers retained long after they appear to have forgotten Gawaine's sisters. As I recall, in **Gawaine at the Grail Castle** Jessie Weston suggests that in now-lost versions of the story, Gawaine may have achieved the Grail. The Gawaine of **Sir Gawaine and the Green Knight** is certainly an idealistic young knight very nearly as worthy, pure, and polite as mortal can be—though I must add, in fairness, that critical opinion is divided as to whether the sexual mores of the Gawaine in this poem reflect the general character of the Gawaine of other early romances, are a conscious deviation from the tradition on the part of an individual author, or even have anything to do with his behaviour toward Sir Bercilak's wife, whom he refuses, by this theory, through refusal to betray his host's hospitality. For an excellent study of Gawaine's pre-Malory character, at least in the English romances, see **The Knightly Tales of Sir Gawaine**, with introductions and translations by Louis B. Hall.

Even as late as the Vulgate, Gawaine is definitely second only to his close friend Lancelot as the greatest knight of the world (excluding spiritual knights like Galahad). In this version Gawaine comes across as much steadier and more dependable than Lancelot, much less prone than Lancelot to fits of madness, to berserk lust in battle, to going off on incognito adventures for the hell of it without telling the court in advance, or to settling down uninvited in somebody else's pavilion and killing the owner on his return. The Vulgate tells us that Arthur made Gawaine constable of his household and gave him the sword Excalibur for use throughout his life. For a time, as Arthur's next of kin and favorite nephew, Gawaine was named to be his successor. Gawaine was well formed, of medium height, loved the poor, was loyal to his uncle, never spoke evil of anyone, and was a favorite with the ladies. Many of his companions, however, would have surpassed him in endurance if his strength had not doubled at noon. [Vulgate IV] In the Vulgate, when Gawaine appears in Arthur's dream, he comes not with ladies and damsels exclusively, but with a great number of poor people whom he succored in life. [Vol.VI, p. 360]

The romancers seem agreed on the fact of Gawaine's strength always doubling or, at least, being renewed at noon.

> Then had Sir Gawaine such a grace and gift that an holy man had given to him, that every day in the year, from underne [9:00 a.m.] till high noon, his might increased those three hours as much as thrice his strength ... And for his sake King Arthur made an ordinance, that all manner of battles for any quarrels that should be done afore King Arthur should begin at underne. [Malory XX, 21]

Modern scholars seem satisfied that this is because Gawaine was originally a solar god. The Vulgate gives a more Christian explanation, alluded to by Malory: the hermit who baptized Gawaine and for whom the child was named prayed for a special grace as a gift to the infant, and was granted that Gawaine's strength and vigor would always be fully restored at noon. For this reason many knights would not fight him until afternoon, when his strength returned to normal. [cf. Vulgate VI, p. 340-341] Sometimes the reason for Gawaine's noon strength is described as being kept a secret; the fact, however, must have become obvious early in Gawaine's career. Nor was Gawaine the only knight to enjoy such an advantage; Ironside's strength also increased daily until noon, while Marhaus' appears to have increased in the evening.

Also among the numerous ladies whose names are coupled with that of Gawaine are Floree, who may be identical with Sir Brandiles' sister, and Dame Ragnell, his favorite wife and the mother of his son Guinglain (surely identical with Gingalin) according to **The Wedding of Sir Gawaine and Dame Ragnell**, which mentions that Gawaine was often married (and presumably, often widowed)—-which is one way to reconcile the various tales of his loves and romances. (See the list "Love—Marital & Otherwise")

I have heard his name pronounced both Gah-WANE (rhymes with Elaine) and GAH-w'n. The first seems by far the most popular today, but I prefer the second; I have no scholarly opinion to back me up, but GAH-w'n seems the preferred pronunciation in the dictionaries I have checked, it seems to match the pronunciation of the modern derivative name Gavin, and emphasizing the first syllable seems a better safeguard against aural confusion with such names as Bragwaine and Ywaine.

Sir Gawaine's Family and Retainers
Father: King Lot
Mother: Margawse
Brothers: Agravaine, Gaheris, Gareth
Half-brother: Mordred
Sisters: Soredamors, "Alteria", Clarissin, Thenew?
Wives and paramours & flirtations: Floree, Sir Brandiles' sister

(Floree and Sir Brandiles' sister are probably the same), Ragnell, Helain de Taningues' sister, Hellawes, Helaes, Lore de Branlant, the King of Norgales' daughter, the Lady of Roestoc?, the Lady of Beloe, Lunette, "Lady of the Deadly Bed"?, King of Escavalon's sister
Special case: The Maid with Little Sleeves
Sons: Gingalin, Florence, Lovel
Uncle: Arthur
Aunts: Elaine of Tintagil, Morgan le Fay
Baptizer (godfather): Hermit Gawaine
Father-in-law?: King Alain of Escavalon
Brother-in-law?: Brandiles
Brothers-in-law: Gringamore (by the marriages of Gaheris and Gareth); Alexander of Greece (by the marriage of Soredamors); unnamed husband of "Alteria"
Sisters-in-law: Laurel (m. Agravaine), Lynette (m. Gaheris), Lyonors (m. Gareth)
Nephews: Melehan, Cligés, "Alteria's" six sons, Saint Kentigern?, Ider?
Niece: "Alteria's" daughter
Cousins: Ywaine (by Morgan), Galeshin (by Elaine), Edward of Orkney, Sadok
Squire: Eliezer
Ally: Lady of Briestoc
Charger: Gringolet

GAWAINE THE HERMIT†

The more famous Sir Gawaine was baptized by and named for this saintly hermit. When begged to give the infant a gift, the hermit Gawaine prayed to Heaven, obtaining the grace that Sir Gawaine, however exhausted before noon, would always grow fresh and vigorous again at midday. [Vulgate VI, p. 340-341]

GAWAINE'S CHESSBOARD SHIELD and IVORY PIECES†

Trapped by a mob in a tower room without his own arms and armor (of which he had been relieved when arriving as a guest), Gawaine accepted such arms as the king of Escavalon's sister could provide him on short notice. When she could not find him a shield, Gawaine seized a chessboard, spilling its chessmen to the floor, and assured his hostess that it would serve him as well as he could wish. The ivory pieces were ten times larger than most chessmen, and shortly did service as missiles for the lady to hurl down upon the mob; the board must have been proportionate in size. Thus, heaving it up and tilting its chessmen off sounds like an example of Gawaine's strength. It also sounds, to me, like a bit of tall-tale humor. [Chrétien de Troyes, **Perceval**, ca. ll. 5880-6006, esp. 5890-5897]

GAWAINE'S GIRDLE†

The wife of Sir Bertilak de Hautdesert pressed Gawaine to accept her sash of green silk, richly embroidered in gold, as a love token, assuring him that it would save its wearer from all injury. Since he had to offer his neck to the Green Knight's axe next day, the promise of a sash that might save him from injury proved too tempting to resist.

Whether the girdle actually had this saving property is in doubt, since while Gawaine wore it the Green Knight did draw blood. Gawaine determined to wear the sash ever afterward, obliquely across his chest, as a reminder of his failing. The rest of Arthur's court thought he had done rather well and determined to wear similar sashes to honor him. This was the origin of the Order of the Garter. [**Sir Gawaine and the Green Knight**]

GAWAINE'S HERB†

It was not Gawaine's discovery, of course; it was simply a plant he knew for its remarkable healing properties. I am not aware that herbal lore was included in the usual knightly education, though it probably should have been: fortuitously finding this herb near the Galloway border, Gawaine used it on the wounded Greoreas. Gawaine explained that it was potent enough to heal a sick tree (providing the tree had not entirely dried). Considering how well and quickly it restored Greoreas, this might not have been an exaggeration. [Chrétien de Troyes, **Perceval**, ca. ll. 6909-7074]

GAWAINE'S SHIELD†

According to **Sir Gawaine and the Green Knight**, Gawaine had an image of the Virgin Mary painted on the inside of his shield to inspire him in battle. Possibly he had taken the idea from his royal uncle's shield, Pridwen.

GAZEWILTE†

The lord of this castle, Sir Persides, imprisoned his wife here for five years, until Ector de Maris defeated him and rescued her. I found no clue to the location of this castle.

GENIEVRE†

King Leodegrance was a busy man. On the same night he engendered Guenevere on his wife, he engendered a second daughter on the wife of Cleodalis, his seneschal. The two children were born on the same day, looked exactly alike (despite having different mothers), and, just to keep things simple, Leodegrance gave them both the same name. (Sommer distinguishes the bastard daughter as "the false Guenevere", but this seems to me unfair—it was not her fault she was born with Guenevere's looks, and she had just as much right as the true-born daughter to the name she was given. Therefore, I have used an alternate spelling for the name Guenevere—the spelling Sommer gives both Gueneveres in Vulgate II—for this second one.)

Genievre was raised as the supposed daughter of Cleodalis, which must have been either a good trick or a courteous pretense, considering her looks and name. Rich relatives of Cleodalis, hating Leodegrance, tried to substitute Genievre for Guenevere on Arthur's wedding night, but the attempt to kidnap Guenevere was foiled by Ulfius and Brastias. At Leodegrance's order, Cleodalis took Genievre away from Carohaise; he also disowned her. On the same night as the attempted abduction, Bertholai, one of Leodegrance's knights, murdered another knight out of hatred, and was disinherited and banished for the deed. Some time afterward, Bertholai came to the place where Genievre was living. [Vulgate II] See Bertholai for the rest of the story.

See also Guenevere.

GERAINT (Gereint)†—see also **EREC**

Malory does not mention Geraint, unless he is to be identified with Sir Garaunt. Possibly this companion of the Round Table is best known today from Tennyson's Idylls **The Marriage of Geraint** and **Geraint and Enid**. According to Tennyson, Geraint was a "tributary prince of Devon" and knight of the Round Table who met and married Enid, only child of Earl Yniol, in a romantic adventure that involved Geraint's defeating Yniol's enemy and nephew Edyrn son of Nudd ("The Sparrow-Hawk") and restoring Yniol to his earldom. (Edyrn reformed and became a knight of the Round Table himself.) Geraint proudly presented his wife as a handmaid to Guenevere; later, growing nervous at the rumors of Guenevere's guilt with Lancelot, the prince used the proximity of his own land in Devon to "a territory, /Wherein were bandit earls and caitiff knights" as a pretext to leave court and take Enid home to his own castle, away from courtly corruption. Here Geraint became so enmeshed in loving domesticity as to forget all calls of knightly honor, duty, and glory. Enid, more mindful than her husband of his rusting reputation, and fearing the cause to be herself, murmured in soliloquy one morning: "I fear that I am no true wife." He was just waking up, heard this sentence, misconstrued it, and took her out for a long test of faithfulness. They rode alone, without even a squire, and he commanded her to ride some distance before him and never dare speak to him. They kept coming to groups of thieving knights and other robbers. Enid would see them and hear their plans, disobey her husband's orders about silence in order to warn him, and he would scold her, slay his attackers, appropriate their gear and horses (which he made Enid drive on ahead of her), and thus make more than enough to pay their expenses on the road. After numerous adventures of increasing peril, including a couple of other men who tried to make Enid marry them, Geraint was at last convinced of her worth and they were reconciled.

Tennyson probably took his story from "Gereint Son of Erbin" in the Welsh **Mabinogion**. As we have this work, it was written down a century or so after the death of Chrétien de Troyes; one scholarly opinion holds that the Welsh version derives directly from Chrétien's **Erec & Enide**, while another and apparently stronger opinion considers both versions derived from some common source.

GERMANY, EMPEROR OF†

In Chrétien's **Cligés**, this potentate betrothed his daughter Fenice to the Duke of Saxony, but jumped at the chance to break this engagement and give her to Emperor Alis of Greece and Constantinople instead. This caused plenty of fighting, which might have been seen as further political shrewdness in an age when knights often enough hacked away at one another for far less reason. [**Cligés**, ll. 2640-4213]

Gherard le Breuse—see under ARNOLD LE BREUSE

Gifflet—see GRIFLET

GILDAS†

An actual person, an historian and probably a monk, who flourished ca. 560 A.D. Brewer gives his dates as 493-570 and calls his work "utterly worthless as history, extremely dull, meagre, and obscure." I am sure that I encountered Gildas some years ago as a rather unpleasant character in a competent but undistinguished modern Arthurian novel which I had borrowed and returned, and the author of which I have forgotten. Poor Gildas almost has to be better than the above sentences suggest!

GINGALIN (Guinglain)

Sir Gawaine's son, apparently the oldest. According to **The Wedding of Sir Gawaine and Dame Ragnell**, Ragnell was Gingalin's mother.

In Malory IX, 18, we find Gingalin jousting with Tristram at Tintagil, apparently for the sport of it, and being defeated, his horse killed under him. King Mark witnesses the fight. Mark does not learn Tristram's identity, for Tristram rides off into the woods; Mark does send a squire out to Gingalin, and, on learning who the defeated knight is, welcomes him and gives him a horse. It sounds as if Gingalin was on rather close terms with Mark, but Mark may, for once, have simply been showing the hospitality of the times.

Gingalin became a knight of the Round Table, being listed, with his brothers Florence and Lovel, among those who attempted to heal Sir Urre. Gingalin, Florence, and Lovel were among the knights who tried to trap Lancelot with the Queen and were slain when he escaped; in this episode, however, Arthur later tells Gawaine, "Remember ye he slew two sons of yours, Sir Florence and Sir Lovel", without adding Gingalin, so it is conceivable there may have been two Gingalins. [Malory XIX, 11; XX, 2-4, 7]

GIRDLES FOR KING DAVID'S SWORD

See under Solomon's Ship.

Girflet—see **GRIFLET**

Glade, Proud Knight of the—see **HAUGHTY KNIGHT ...**

GLASTONBURY

Here the Archbishop of Canterbury became a hermit after defying Mordred. Here Bedivere, Lancelot, and other knights joined the former Archbishop as hermits at Arthur's grave. All this is at the end of Malory's book, but there must have been enough at Glastonbury already to attract the Archbishop. According to a tradition not found in Malory, Joseph of Arimathea planted a flowering thorn tree here, which bloomed in winter until it was uprooted by Oliver Cromwell. You can still see trees in Glastonbury reputed to be descendants of the original flowering thorn.

All indications point to Glastonbury's having been a Pagan holy place before Christianization. Glastonbury Tor, for instance, is a high, conical hill with an ancient pathway to the top. As part of a ritual, the tor was to be ascended in tiers, the celebrants walking around each tier alternately clockwise or counter-clockwise before climbing to the next.

GLECIDALAN, KING†

A dwarf monarch who held his land from King Bilis, whom he accompanied to Arthur's court for Erec's wedding [Chrétien de Troyes, **Erec & Enide**, ll. 1963-2024].

GLOEVANT† (Glocuen, Gloovent)

A forest, probably in or near Stranggore [Vulgate IV].

GLOIER, KING, DAUGHTER OF

Gloier was king of Soreloise (Surluse). When Duke Galeholt conquered the country, he cared for his dead enemy's orphaned daughter. [Vulgate III]

GLOUCHEDON†

Gawaine declared he would not have parted with his fresh-won horse Gringolet for this castle [Vulgate II, 343]. From the name, Glouchedon might be Gloucester (Roman name Glevum) or Colchester.

Probably identical with Glouchedon is the castle of Glochedon, the chatelaine of which was a cousin of the Damsel of Hongrefort Castle.

Hongrefort was in or near the forest of Landoine. Glocedon Castle seems to have been near Galdon Castle, and probably both would have been within easy reach of Hongrefort.

Gloovent†—see GLOEVANT

GLOVES

Gloves may be given as pledges and as challenges to trial by combat.

> Hold, said Sir Maliagrance, here is my glove that [Guenevere] is traitress unto my lord, King Arthur, and that this night one of the wounded knights lay with her. And I receive your glove, said Sir Lancelot. And so they were sealed with their signets, and delivered unto the ten [wounded] knights. [Malory XIX, 7]

GODEGRAIN, COUNT†

Chrétien lists him among the vassal lords whom Arthur summoned to court for Erec's wedding. Godegrain brought 100 knights. [**Erec & Enide**, ll. 1934-1962]

Gohorru†—see GAIHOM

GOHORT†

After leaving Arthur's court in Carlisle, Percivale came to a river wider than a crossbow could shoot across, dark, swift-flowing, and turbulent, though contained within its bed. (I.e., the riverbed was deep?) Following the riverbank, he came to a rocky cliff. Eventually, on that rock, overlooking a slope that ran down toward the ocean, a magnificent castle came into view. Facing the wide bay where sea and river fought, the castle had a turret on each of its four corners, a round outerwork, and a stone bridge fortified with more towers and ending in a drawbridge. This was the castle of Gornemant of Gohort, who instructed Percivale in knighthood and formally buckled on his right spur. [Chrétien de Troyes, **Perceval**, ll. 1305-1698]

In telling Blancheflor about his last overnight stop before reaching her, Percivale says he does not know the castle's name, but the name of his host was Gornemant of Gohort. Considering how extraordinarily naive Percivale still is at this point, I rather think that Gohort is indeed the name of Gornemant's castle with its surrounding territory, and that Percivale's failure to understand this is part of the joke. Blancheflor's failure to point it out can easily be ascribed to courtesy. [Ibid., ca. ll. 1883-1909]

The description of Gornemant's castle resembles later descriptions, in the same romance, of both the Grail Castle and the Rock of Canguin.

See Gornemant.

Golden Ring, Youth with the—see YOUTH ...

GONDEFLE†

A leader of the Sesnes, involved in the attack on Vandaliors Castle early in Arthur's reign. [Vulgate II]

GOOTHE

The recluse Queen of the Waste Lands told Percivale, who was on the Quest of the Holy Grail, to go to Goothe Castle, where Galahad had a cousin-germain. If he could not find Galahad there, he was to ride on straight to Carbonek. Since she told him he could rest at Goothe "this night", it should have been near her priory. [Malory XIV, 2]

It is possible that Goothe was the castle to which Percivale's sister brought Galahad [Malory XVII, 2]. This would put Goothe in or near Grail territory, not far from Carbonek, and near the sea. The lady of the castle to which Percivale's sister brought Galahad was Percivale's sister's mistress; possibly she was Galahad's cousin-germain.

GORE (Gorre)

From the Vulgate we learn that this important though apparently small kingdom, the strongest of its size in Great Britain, borders on Sugales and is surrounded by water, the Tembre being its boundary toward Legres. By the dictionary, a gore can be a triangular piece of land, a promontory, or a wedge-shaped portion of a field.

We are almost certainly safe in assuming Sugales to be South Wales. In southwest Wales is a peninsula, the one including the city of Pembroke, which has a city named Tenby near where it connects with the mainland. I would make this peninsula the kingdom of Gore, or Gore could be the whole southwestern tip, comprising more or less the present-day county of Pembroke, with the city of Pembroke as Gaihom.

The above were my thoughts in 1982. Chrétien de Troyes, however, clearly names Bath as one of King Bademagu's court cities. This would place his land of Gore in the Bristol area, south of the Cotswolds, on the southern shore of the Bristol Channel, which would be the "arm of the sea" mentioned in the **Lancelot**.

Chrétien actually calls Gore "the kingdom from which no stranger returns." Its bridges—the Water Bridge and the Sword Bridge—resemble the bridges to the Christian afterlife as described in such medieval eschatological romances as the widespread accounts of Saint Patrick's Purgatory. Chrétien's translator D.D.R. Owen cites an explanation of the name "Gorre" as a corruption of Old French *voirre* ("glass"), suggesting an identification of Gore with Glastonbury—which is also commonly recognized as Avalon, where Arthur was taken after his last battle.

How so many strangers managed to stray into a land accessible only by the Water Bridge and the Sword Bridge—the first has as much water over as under it, and no man before Lancelot ever crossed the latter and lived—remains unexplained, although we do find many prisoners living in the marches of Gore, on the Logres side of the perilous bridges. (Do the marches of Gore equate with Purgatory?) It also remains a mystery to me how the natives of Gore can exercise their right to come and go freely: by which bridge, for instance, does Meliagrant cross fully armed, on horseback, and later bring Guenevere and Kay, the latter on a litter, back to his father's castle on the far side of the bridges? Lancelot's success made Gore open for anyone, including the former prisoners, to come and go freely—again, how and by what (new?) bridges?

All in all, Lancelot's rescue of Guenevere and the other prisoners looks very much like a secularized pastiche of Christ's Harrowing of Hell. This in no way precludes the strong likelihood that it also derives from Pagan views of the Otherworld. This could help explain the strange atmosphere pervading Chrétien's recounting of the episode, which may be a late version of a Pagan myth, but at the same time provides our first known account with Lancelot as hero and thus may well have been the springboard for later Arthurian retellings.

The Vulgate gives a further rationalized and secularized history of Gore. Uther Pendragon warred against King Uriens of Gore, captured him, and threatened to hang him. Uriens' nephew Baudemagus (or Bagdemagus) surrendered the land in order to save Uriens' life. Uriens later reconquered Gore and gave it to Bagdemagus as a reward for his loyalty. After Bagdemagus' coronation, Uriens retired into a hermitage. (Possibly this explains his wife Morgan's independent castles and various lovers. Malory, however, has Uriens becoming a knight of the Round Table.) Bagdemagus, in order to repeople his war-wasted kingdom, established the custom of two bridges, the "pont desouz ewe" (bridge under water) of one beam, and the "pont despee" (sword bridge) of a single plank of steel. Each bridge had a knight guardian; everyone—knights, ladies, and others—who crossed either bridge was made to swear to stay in Gore until a strong champion arrived who could deliver them. Escades, the guardian of the pont despee, was succeeded by Bagdemagus' son Meliagrant, a pround and evil-disposed knight who though himself as good as Lancelot. Almost needless to say, Lancelot was the champion who eventually delivered the prisoners.

Elsewhere in the Vulgate, it appears that these prisoners were not confined in the territory on the Gore side of the bridge, but also resided in a largish area called the Terre Foraine (Foreign Land) before the bridges were reached (in Chrétien's account, we find "foreign" prisoners living on both sides of the bridges). Except that they could not move away until freed by their champion, and that they wore a distinctive type of dress, the prisoners seemed to live comfortably and under no restraint save their parole. The Terre Foraine of Gore would be its marches, or borders.

Some further appreciation of what it might have been to live as a "foreign" prisoner in Gore may, perhaps, be gleaned from the pages of John Demos' study of Eunice Williams, or Marguerite A'ongote Gannenstenhawi, who was taken captive from New England to French Canada in 1704. [**The Unredeemed Captive**, NY: Knopf, 1995] I found it of particular interest that old Iroquois beliefs, possibly still lingering even among Eunice's Catholicized Indian community, included reaching the grand and lovely lodge of the afterlife by crossing bridges too shaky and narrow to accommodate flesh bodies; these bridges were even guarded by fierce dogs which caused many disembodied souls to fall into the deep and precipice-bounded waters of the rivers beneath. [Ibid, pp. 240-241] How students of comparative mythology and religion must delight in such unexpected parallels!

I cannot imagine Chrétien's King Bademagu ever becoming a knight or even a subordinate ally king of Arthur's. Too much of the otherworld deity seems still to cling about Bademagu. The Vulgate's Bagdemagus, however, despite the seemingly unfriendly custom of holding strangers prisoner, was later to become a companion of the Round Table and one of Arthur's staunchest and most likable allies, which role we still find him playing in Malory.

DUKE GORLOÏS

Duke of Tintagil, Igraine's husband, and the father of Morgawse, Elaine, and Morgan, Gorloïs long warred against Uther Pendragon. Eventually Uther summoned Gorloïs to make peace, but Uther's motive seems to have been to see Igraine, whom he charged the duke to bring along. When Uther tried to seduce her, she told her husband at once and they returned home to Cornwall, where Gorloïs prepared his strong castles Tintagil and Terrabil, putting Igraine in charge of the first and himself in the second. On the same night that Uther, given Gorloïs' appearance by means of Merlin's magic, begot Arthur on Igraine, the real Gorloïs was killed in a sally at Terrabil. [Malory I, 1-2]

My edition of Malory does not give Igraine's husband the name Gorloïs (or any other name), but Tennyson uses it, and Brewer credits to Malory a quotation in which it appears.

GORNEMANT OF GOHORT†

Fourth best of Arthur's knights, according to the list Chrétien de Troyes begins in line 1691 of **Erec & Enide**, Gornemant of Gohort was to reappear in the same author's final romance as Percivale's tutor and mentor.

After his brief first visit to Arthur's court and his David-like defeat of the Red Knight of Quinqueror, Percivale comes to Gornemant's castle. Welcoming him, Gornemant sees his potential, gives him a day's good training in the techniques of knightly combat, and begs him, over supper, to stay for a month or a year. Percivale, anxious to return home and check on the health of his mother, refuses. Accordingly, next morning Gornemant gives him new clothes (to wear under the Red Knight's armor) and the accolade of knighthood, along with parting instructions about how to behave. These include an injunction to stop saying "My mother taught me" this or that, and henceforth to give all the credit for his education to the vavasour who fitted on his spur and made him a knight. This directive may reflect the anti-feminine sentiment of the age, or it may be a simple effort to make the youth appear less of an ignorant bumpkin. More important to the storyline, Gornemant also stresses the importance of not talking too much. Again, he may simply hope to keep his protégé from showing off too much ignorance; this advice is to do the lad a grave disservice by preventing him from asking the crucial questions at the Grail Castle, which he might have asked had he preferred the spirit of his mother's earlier advice never to have a companion, on road or in any lodging, for long without asking his name.

Gornemant was one of Blancheflor's uncles and had given her some assistance in her defensive war against Clamadeu and Engygeron, for he had lost a brother at Engygeron's hands in that conflict.

The description of Gornemant's castle and its location near a river bears a striking resemblance to the descriptions of both the Grail Castle and the Rock of Canguin and their locales, both found later in the same romance. This, along with the verbal resemblance of the names "Gohort", "Gorre", and "Gohurru", make me wonder if in Gornemant's little realm we may glimpse yet another pocket of the Otherworld, and if the day Percivale passes there really equates to a single twenty-four-hour interval in the everyday world. [**Perceval**, ca. ll. 1305-1698; 3202ff.; 3246; 3293; see also under Blancheflor]

GORNEVAIN†

Among Arthur's knights in the list Chrétien de Troyes begins in line 1691 of **Erec & Enide**.

GOUVERNAIL

Tristram's tutor and squire.

> And then [King Mediodas, Tristram's father] let ordain a gentleman that was well learned and taught, his name was Gouvernail; and then he sent young Tristram with Gouvernail into France to learn the language, and nurture, and deeds of arms.

Gouvernail apparently chose a permanent career as squire in preference to becoming a knight himself. After seven years of teaching Tristram in France, he returned as Tristram's servant. When Tristram commanded Gouvernail to leave him alone on the island where he would fight Sir Marhaus to the uttermost, "either departed from other sore weeping." Gouvernail is usually found at Tristram's side, serving him faithfully and well and advising him prudently. On at least one occasion, Gouvernail was instrumental in saving his master's life, when he, with Sirs Lambegus and Sentraille, pulled Tristram up from the sea cliffs of Cornwall; when, immediately after this, Tristram escaped into the woods with La Beale Isoud, Gouvernail was the only man he kept with him.

It is tempting to pair Gouvernail with Isoud's favorite handmaiden, Bragwaine. The only grounds for such a match that I find in Malory, however, are that Gouvernail is entrusted, along with Bragwaine, with the love potion intended for Isoud and Mark, and when Tristram and Isoud find it by mischance, Tristram jokingly remarks that Bragwaine and Gouvernail have kept what he supposes is merely good wine for themselves. Also, when Tristram, Sir Kehydius, Bragwaine, and Gouvernail are blown ashore near Castle Perilous, North Wales, Tristram takes Kehydius adventuring in the forest, saying, apparently to Bragwaine, "Here shall ye abide me these ten days, and Gouvernail, my squire, with you."

I have not discovered what happened to Gouvernail after Tristram's death.

[Malory VIII, 3, 6, 16, 21, 24, 31, 35; IX, 10; X, 4]

GOVERNAL OF ROBERDIC†

He fought in the Noauz tournament. His red shield bore a golden band across it. [Chrétien de Troyes, **Lancelot**, ll. 5783-5823] It is tempting to imagine that Tristram's faithful squire finally had a knightly career of his own, but the only grounds I see for this theory are the similarity of names and the fact that Chrétien was acquainted with some version of the Tristram tale.

GRAIL CASTLE† (see also **CARBONEK**)

Chrétien de Troyes does not give the Grail Castle a name. He describes it as a square tower of dark gray stone, flanked by two smaller towers, with hall, arcade, and drawbridge; all located in a valley between a river in a deep, rocky bed and a wood. The building is at first invisible to Percivale, even after the Fisher King in his boat has described it; its finally coming into Percivale's view could have either a mystical explanation, or a natural one involving angles and perspective. When he meets his cousin (the Fisher King's niece) next day, however, she remarks that there is no lodging within forty leagues along the way he has come. Hearing that he has lodged comfortably, she knows it could only have been at her uncle's house. She does not identify it as an Otherworldly outpost, but her general reaction seems to suggest as much.

The description of this castle and its locale somewhat resembles those of both Gornemant's Gohort and Ygerne's Rock of Canguin in the same romance. [**Perceval**, ca. ll. 2876-3592]

GRAIL, HOLY (Sangreal)

There are entirely plausible pre-Christian meanings of this mystical dish or cauldron of plenty, but I do not examine them here. The **New Catholic Encyclopedia** [©1967] verifies its general modern identification with the cup or chalice used by Jesus at the Last Supper, but adds that it might alternatively have been identified with the dish of the paschal lamb. The same source points out that two classes of Grail romances developed, mainly between the years 1180 and 1240: the Quest type and the Early History type. The Early History romances explained it as above (i.e., the dish from which Christ and his apostles ate the lamb, or else the chalice from which He drank), adding that Joseph of Arimathea used it to collect His blood as He hung on the cross. Joseph of Arimathea later brought the Grail to Britain, where it was put into the keeping of the Fisher Kings, or Rich Fishers, at Carbonek Castle. King Pellam was the last Fisher King to guard it here; when Galahad and his companions achieved the Adventures of the Grail, the sacred vessel moved to Sarras and thence to Heaven.

Chrétien de Troyes' **Perceval** is generally acknowledged as the earliest known Grail romance; he himself speaks of having drawn it from a book given him by Count Philip of Flanders, but this book seems to be as lost and mysterious as the Grail itself ever was. As for the Welsh **Peredur**, its date relative to that of Chrétien's account seems to be controversial: while the **Mabinogion** stories are commonly considered to antedate Chrétien's time, it seems that they were actually committed to writing more than a century after Chrétien's death. In any case, as Ronan Coghlan observes [**Encyclopaedia of Arthurian Legends**, ©1991, "Perceval" entry], in **Peredur** the salver holds the bloody head of Peredur's cousin, whom he must avenge; I would consider this twist as setting Peredur, whatever its antiquity and origin, pretty well apart from the Grail romances properly speaking.

Chrétien's being the earliest known account, it might be as well to list the order of the Grail procession as he describes it:

1. The lance bearer
2. Two lads each carrying a ten-candle candlestick

3. The Grail maiden

4. The maiden (I call her "Etheria") bearing the silver platter

Chrétien names neither the Grail Castle nor the Grail maiden. Nor does he give the Fisher King a personal name, though he identifies him as an uncle of Percivale's. (In fact, I suspect that the family relationships in Chrétien's poem would be very difficult to reconcile with the line of Rich Fishers as per later romances.) Nor does he tell us the Grail's previous history; what little he says of the lance's seems exceedingly sketchy. It was only in later versions that Chrétien's silver plate was to become the paten covering the chalice, and the bleeding lance, the spear with which the Roman centurion Longinus had pierced Christ's side. Ruth Harwood Cline notes that Chrétien never even calls it "the Holy Grail"—the closest he comes is once having Percivale's hermit uncle call it a holy thing. [**Perceval**, l. 6426 & Cline's note to same] Otherwise, to Chrétien, it is always simply "the Grail." D.D.R. Owen even remarks that the glow accompanying it could conceivably emanate from the maiden rather than the vessel. [Note to l. 3190] This did not prevent the "San Greal" (Holy Dish") vs. "Sang Real" ("Royal Blood") debate from developing over its apparently post-Chrétien appellation, Sangreal. W. W. Skeat, in his **Concise Etymological Dictionary**, which Spence quotes without giving its date, rejects the "Sang Real" division as a deliberate falsification. [Spence, **Magic Arts**, p. 163] Which did not stop the authors of that hilarious piece of pseudo scholarship that made a little stir in the 1980s, **Holy Grail, Holy Blood**, from latching onto "Sang Real" and claiming that it refers to the actual living bloodline descended from Jesus Christ and still today living in France! In my own opinion, the medieval authors may well have seen both possibilities and delighted in so appropriate a wordplay. "Royal Blood" could, of course, simply transfer the emphasis from the dish itself to its contents.

The Cistercian chronicler Helinandus (d. ca. 1230) explained the word "Grail" as deriving from Latin *gradale*, a wide and rather deep dish in which costly foods were served gradatim ("successively": one morsel after another); it was popularly called "Graalz" because it was pleasing (*grata*). **The New Catholic Encyclopedia** rejects the derivation from *gradatim* or *grata* as fanciful, but considers a derivation from *cratalis, crater* (a mixing bowl) plausible.

I find two common types of Grail Quest stories: the mystical and the material. The material search, in which the Grail is a lost or otherwise out-of-reach physical artifact sought with the intention of bringing it back, presumably for safekeeping in the king's treasury or some religious museum, seems to be the more popular type today. For myself, I infinitely prefer the mystical interpretation, in which the search for the

Grail more or less approximates the American Indian vision quest. Having delivered this opinion, I must add that Chrétien's narrative, the one that probably kicked it all off, seems to involve yet a third type of search, one in which the object is simply to ask the right questions. Indeed, Chrétien's version might conceivably be viewed as an antidote to the Garden of Eden story: Eve and Adam sin in eating the fruit of the Tree of the Knowledge of Good and Evil—i.e., they yield to their curiosity. Percivale sins in not asking the right questions through fear of seeming rude—i.e., he stifles his curiosity. What, exactly, might Chrétien have been hinting? I must also confess that, when it comes to sending Gawaine after the bleeding lance, Chrétien does indeed seem to set his hero on a more or less material search with the object of bringing the thing back.

The Vulgate cycle incorporates both types of Grail romance, the Quest and the History. It is clearer, perhaps, in the Vulgate than in Malory that to the medieval reader seeking the Grail meant not so much "seeing" or "finding" it (it had, after all, been seen, and it was known to reside most of the time at Carbonek) as to behold it clear and unveiled—i.e., to receive mystic or religious enlightenment. Arriving at Carbonek Castle was fairly easy. One time Sir Bors visited there without suspecting he was near a place of great and perilous adventure. But finding Carbonek was no guarantee that the Grail would feed or heal you, or even that you would be let into the castle. Ector de Maris, arriving as his brother Lancelot sat with the castle folk to be fed by the Sangreal, was turned away as unworthy [Malory XVII, 16]; Lionel, coming just as Galahad and eleven other knights were sitting down to the climactic mysteries, was similarly turned away at the door. To sleep at Carbonek, in the part which Sir Bors named the "Castle Adventurous", could be extremely harrowing, if not downright dangerous—one might see all sorts of visions, including battling beasts; might be grievously wounded by mystical weapons and healed again, after a while, by the Grail; and so on.

Notice that of the twelve knights who achieve the Grail Quest in Malory, only three—Galahad, Percivale, and Bors—are British. The rest represent various other European countries. Were it not for the popularity of the material treasure-hunt type of Grail Quest story in our own time, I would not even bother to point out that, though in Malory all these twelve knights "achieve" the Grail, they obviously cannot all take it home!

The Grail fed the worthy, giving each the food he liked best (shades here, very likely, of its Pagan origins). It healed wounds. It was not confined to Carbonek, but appeared of itself from time to time and place to place to heal knights [cf. Malory XI, 14 and XIII, 17-20], and once it passed through Arthur's hall at Camelot when the knights were sitting at dinner and fed them itself, thus touching off the great general Grail Quest.

To embark on the Grail Quest, you must confess your sins; you must not take along your lady; and it would not be a bad idea to restrict yourself to a diet of bread and water, maybe wear a hair shirt, and garb yourself in some symbolic outer garment (Sir Bors wore a scarlet coat while on the Quest). You need not be a virgin—Bors achieved the Grail, although he had once trespassed on his virginity—but you must remain celibate while on the Quest. Take heed: if you enter this Quest unworthily, you will return worse than when you set out; this may explain why Lancelot, relapsing into his old sinful affair with Guenevere, grew careless about keeping it secret, why the Round Table seems generally to have gone to pot after the Quest, and why even Bors (after his return to court) did some rather surprising things for a saintly man to do.

Although women are absolutely forbidden to accompany their knights on the Quest, the fact that a maiden damsel was the Grail Bearer at Carbonek and that Percivale's saintly sister, Amide, played a major role in the Adventures suggest to me that a damsel may undertake the Quest alone, under the same moral conditions as a knight. It is interesting, indeed, that, although Nascien absolutely forbade any knight who went on the Grail Adventures to travel with a woman, the only three knights who achieved the Grail were, in fact, those who traveled at least part of the time with a damsel, Amide. (Vera Chapman, in her excellent modern Arthurian romance **The King's Damosel**, has Lynette achieving the Grail.)

According to Malory, after Galahad's death the Grail was taken up into Heaven and never seen again on earth. Other traditions, however, place it still in England. Some years ago I saw it, or at least a relic believed to be it, on a television documentary; it was a bowl-like wooden cup, olivewood I think, no longer quite whole. I have also found a carving of it on a Cornish church pew, which showed it more the shape of a soup mug than of a goblet, as we usually think of it.

There seems to be an opinion drifing around that the Grail was the mystical uniting force behind Arthur's Round Table. I disagree. Far from powering the Round Table, the Grail seems to have helped destroy it. When all the companions left at once on the Quest, they were of course all unavailable at the same time for a long period. Many of them were killed on the Quest. Those who did come back were all, presumably, worse than when they had left, with the possible exception of Bors (and I have my doubts of him; he seems to have acted as go-between in the affair of Lancelot and Guenevere). Galahad and Percivale, the court's most spiritual knights, had died in the odor of sanctity. It must have taken some time before Arthur could even be sure which knights were definitely not returning, so that he could fill up their seats with new members and restore the Table to its full strength.

My own favorite Grail story—if indeed it is the Grail story I take it to be, even though it lies outside Arthurian literature—is that of Saint Robert, q.v. I also find it interesting to speculate on Mary Magdalen's possible connection with the development of the Grail legends: she was an extremely popular saint in the Middle Ages; her most common symbol was an alabastron or vase, apparently the vessel in which she was supposed to have carried spices to anoint Jesus; a pre-Chrétien hymn to her speaks of her having made a cauldron [of iniquity?] into a shallow cup, transforming a vessel of shame [surely meaning herself] into one of glory; she was supposed to have lived in the wilderness for many years, nourished only by heavenly food (reminiscent of the Grail diet); and the presence of Joseph of Arimathea as one of her companions in certain accounts of their coming to Europe looks much like a direct tie between her legendary history and that of the Grail.

Two fairly recent films merit mention here. John Boorman's **Excalibur**, at least its full theatrical-release version, impressed me as showing a marvelous, mystical Grail Quest worthy in every way of the best medieval tales. (The powerful second half of the movie seems unhappily to be chopped away to almost nothing on network TV.) In a completely different vein, **Indiana Jones and The Last Crusade**, which one might have expected to be sheer material scavenger-hunt stuff, turned out to have a refreshing little whiff of the mystical.

GRAIL MAIDEN

Chrétien, who seems to have first described her, does not tell us who she is. According to D.D.R. Owen, he describes the scene in such a way as to allow the possibility that the radiance issues from the damsel rather than from the object she carries. [Chrétien de Troyes, **Perceval**, ca. ll. 3219-3227 & Owen's note to 3190]

The following data drawn from Susan Haskins' study of Mary Magdalen may or may not have any bearing on this whole question: the alabastron or vase was from medieval times Mary Magdalen's most common attribute; it could symbolize the "Eternal Feminine", containing both death and life; a hymn to the Magdalen by Odo of Cluny (d. 942) refers to her making a cauldron out of a shallow cup and to the transformation of a vessel of shame into one of glory; Mary Magdalen was one of the most popular female saints of the Middle Ages, quite possibly the most popular after the Virgin Mary; her legendary biography had Mary Magdalen arriving in French territory, with companions who sometimes included Joseph of Arimathea, in a rudderless vessel; and, while in that period it was a virtual article of faith to identify her both with the sister of Martha and Lazarus and with the reformed prostitute who wiped Christ's feet, she was nevertheless commonly listed with the virgin saints. She also was supposed to have spent the last thirty years of her life as a naked hermit, clad only with her own long red-gold hair, in a desert place removed from food and water—angels rapt her into Heaven for her meals. [Haskins, **Mary Magdalen: Myth And Metaphor**, NY, etc., c1993, esp. pp. 217, 222-3]

See also Elaine of Carbonek.

GRAIN†

Among Arthur's knights in the list Chrétien de Troyes begins in line 1691 of **Erec & Enide**.

GRAISLEMIER OF FINE POSTERNE†

Chrétien lists him among the vassal lords whom Arthur summoned to court for Erec's wedding. Graislemier brought twenty companions with him. He was the brother of Guingomar, lord of the Isle of Avalon, who also came. [**Erec & Enide**, ll. 1934-1962]

Granidel—see GUINDOEL

Gravadain du Chastel Fort†—see under AGRAVAINE DES VAUS DE GALOIRE

GREEN CHAPEL†

Gawaine, arriving at the Green Chapel and findng it an ancient, hollow barrow or cave, overgrown with clumps of grass, in a steep, craggy valley, considered the possibility that a fiend used it for his devilish devotions—an understandable enough impression, since Gawaine had come here in midwinter to undergo his stroke in the beheading game with the Green Knight.

Helen Hill Miller puts the Green Chapel below Leek Moor, in northern Staffordshire, where the Black Brook and the Dane River converge. Glennie provides an alternative location, placing the Green Chapel on the southern bank of Solway Firth, at about the tip of the small peninsula north of Abbey Holme. I much prefer Miller's identification.

Green Knight†—see BERCILAK DE HAUTDESERT

GREOREAS and HIS LADY†

Sir Greoreas raped a maiden, for which crime against Arthur's law Gawaine, acting as judge, sentenced him to eat with the dogs for a month, hands tied behind his back.

Some time later, probably measurable in years, Greoreas was gravely wounded near the Galloway border. As I read the evidence, he must have tried the adventure of bringing the Haughty Maid of Logres her piebald palfrey and thus won his wounds from the Haughty Knight of the Rock on the Narrow Way. At this time Greoreas was traveling with a lady of his own. I can find nothing to indicate whether or not she was the one he had earlier forced, but surely her presence would not have prevented him from assisting any other damsel who asked his help. In any case, his conqueror apparently appropriated his charger, leaving the pair with only the lady's palfrey (either a northern horse or a black one, depending on the ms. and the translator). Yet the conqueror left the wounded knight's lance and shield: it was the incongruity of seeing them hanging from a tree above a riding horse rather than a warhorse that first attracted Gawaine to the place. Too weak to recognize his one-time judge, Greoreas weakly warned him against crossing into Galloway, but begged him, if by any chance he should return alive from such an adventure, to check their condition and provide for the lady if he found her knight dead.

Gawaine returned indeed, bringing not only the Haughty Maid of Logres but a powerful healing herb with which he bound up Greoreas' wounds, assisted by Greoreas' lady and using her fine white wimple for bandages. Immediately Greoreas felt strengthened enough to beg Gawaine to bring him the nag yonder ugly squire was riding, so that he could get to a nearby priest in time to receive the last sacraments. By the time Gawaine brought the nag, Greoreas was sufficiently recovered not only to recognize his former judge, but to steal his horse Gringolet while Gawaine was helping the lady onto her northern (or black) palfrey. This treachery astonished Gawaine, who had never recognized Greoreas; with Greoreas, old anger outweighed present gratitude, and he waited only long enough to reveal his identity and explain his revenge before riding after his already-disappearing lady.

Both his knowing about the nearby priest, and his later sending his nephew, on Gringolet, to find Gawaine and bring back his head, suggest that Greoreas was living in the vicinity.

[Chrétien de Troyes, **Perceval**, ca. ll. 6519-7360]

GREOREAS' NEPHEW†

Having stolen Gawaine's horse Gringolet, Greoreas mounted his nephew on the great steed and sent him to find Gawaine and bring him back his head. The nephew found Gawaine, mounted on the Ugly Squire's Sorry Nag, on the river bank facing the Rock of Canguin. Gawaine waited for him and, although so much worse mounted, easily defeated him—the encounter reminds me of the slapstick in animated cartoons. Presently Gawaine gave his enemy's nephew to the Ferryman of Canguin, in lieu of his newly recovered Gringolet, to pay for passage over the river. By rules of combat, the defeated man was his conqueror's prisoner. In any case, Greoreas' nephew would not appear to have lost by the transfer, for the brief battle had left him badly wounded; since the Ferryman treated him and Gawaine with equal courtesy, like two guests rather than guest and prisoner, we can probably assume that the nephew's wounds were well cared for. (There remains the possibility, of course, that the nephew was henceforth stuck permanently in the country of Canguin.) [Chrétien de Troyes, **Perceval**, ca. ll. 7284-7488]

GRIFLET LE FISE DE DIEU (Girflet, Giflet, or Gifflet Son of Do)

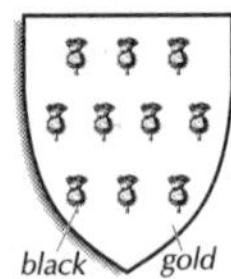

At the beginning of Arthur's reign,

> on All Hallowmass at the great feast, sat in the hall the three kings [Arthur, Ban, and Bors], and Sir Kay seneschal served in the hall, and Sir Lucas the butler ... and Sir Griflet, that was the son of Cardol, these three knights had the rule of all the service that served the kings. [Malory I, 10]

Shortly after this feast, Sir Griflet proved a good man in the battle of Bedegraine [Malory I, 14-17].

A few chapters farther on, however, we find Griflet still a squire.

> Then on a day there came in the court a squire on horseback, leading a knight before him wounded to the death, and told ... how there was a knight in the forest had reared up a pavilion by a well, and hath slain my master, a good knight, his name was Miles; wherefore I beseech you that my master may be buried, and that some knight may revenge my master's death. ... Then came Griflet that was but a squire, and he was but young, of the age of the king Arthur, so he besought the king for all his service that he had done him to give the order of knighthood. Thou art full young and tender of age, said Arthur, for to take so high an order on thee. ... Sir, said Merlin, it were great pity to lose Griflet, for he will be a passing good man when he is of age, abiding with you the term of his life. And if he adventure his body with yonder knight at the fountain, it is in great peril if ever he come again.

Nevertheless, Arthur dubs Griflet, who goes out to joust with the knight at the fountain. The knight at the fountain is King Pellinore, who leaves Griflet badly wounded; Arthur then has a go at Pellinore, and Merlin finally stops the fighting by casting Pellinore into sleep. (See Magical Acts in the Appendix.) [Malory I, 21-24]

During the battle with the five invading kings on the bank of the Humber, when things looked bad for Arthur's side, Griflet joined Arthur, Kay, and Gawaine in trying to get Guenevere to safety; the invading kings catching up with them, Griflet did his part and slew one of the enemy monarchs. It was after this battle that Griflet—along with King Uriens, Sir Hervise de Revel, a couple of older knights called the King of the Lake and Sir Galagars (whom Malory mentions only this once), Gawaine, Kay, and Tor was made a companion of the Round Table. [Malory IV, 4-5]

Griflet's epithet "le Fise de Dieu" ("the son of God") seems to suggest religious leanings. It is therefore surprising that we do not hear more of him during the Grail Adventures.

According to Malory, Griflet was one of those slain by Lancelot's party during Lancelot's rescue of Guenevere from the stake [Malory XX, 8]. In the Vulgate, however, Griflet, not Bedivere, is the last knight left alive with Arthur and the one who must throw Excalibur into the lake [Vulgate VI]. I cannot make up my mind whether Griflet is one of the more minor of the "major" knights or one of the more major of the "minor" ones.

Surely he is to be identified with Chrétien's Girflet, making him one of the earliest knights of Arthurian romance. In the list beginning at line 1691 of **Erec & Enide**, Chrétien identifies Girflet as the son of Do, q.v. In **Perceval**, Chrétien gives Giflet two further cameo appearances: about line 2882 Giflet simply rises to obey Arthur's commands when Clamadeu comes to court; about lines 4721-23, in the sudden questing-fever roused by the Loathly Damsel, Giflet the son of Do vows to go and find the Castle Orgulous that she has just described.

GRIGORAS, KING†

A dwarf monarch who held his land from King Bilis, in whose retinue he came to Arthur's court for Erec's wedding [Chrétien de Troyes, **Erec & Enide**, ll. 1963-2024].

Grim Baron of Castle Hewin†—see under GROMER SOMER JOURE

GRINGAMORE

The brother of Dames Lyonors and Lynette, Sir Gringamore lived in the Isle of Avilion and is described as carrying all black arms, though this could have been for anonymity. Do not confuse him with Gringolet, Sir Gawaine's horse, nor with Sir Percard "The Black Knight" of Gareth's earlier adventure.

After Gareth had defeated Sir Ironside, Dame Lyonors sent Gringamore to kidnap Gareth's dwarf, so that they could learn who and what the champion "Beaumains" was who had freed Castle Dangerous from Ironside's siege. When brought to Gringamore's castle, the dwarf used the occasion to boast of his master; on Gareth's arrival, Gringamore and his sisters welcomed them both as guests. Without revealing herself as the lady of Castle Dangerous, Lyonors attracted Gareth's love with passionate flirtation. Observing the looks that passed between them, Gringamore called her aside into a chamber to tell her how much he approved the match, and then went to Gareth to assure him of the lady's love. [Malory VII, 19-20]

GRINGOLET (Gringalet)†

Chrétien de Troyes knew Gringolet, first mentioning him in **Erec & Enide**; D.D.R. Owen, in a note to line 3955 of that romance, remarks that the traditional name of Gawaine's horse is possibly derived either from Welsh *ceincaled* ("handsome-hardy") or *guin-calet* ("white-hardy"). I feel called upon to observe that, while my dictionary of Medieval French is presently out of reach, my New Cassell's French-English, English-French [©1962] gives "gringalet" as a noun meaning "weak, puny man." Owen says nothing of this modern French word, which strikes me as odd; if the term existed in its approximate present-day meaning in Chrétien's milieu, there must have been affectionate humor in giving such a name to such a mighty charger.

With all his sterling qualities, Gringolet was not, it seems, a one-rider horse: on at least one occasion, Sir Kay coolly borrowed him on assumed permission, took a little gallop, and kept his seat until he attempted a joust with Erec [Chrétien, **Erec & Enide**, ll. 3959-4073].

The most memorable role I have so far found Gringolet playing comes in Chrétien's **Perceval**. Sending his squires and other horses home before undertaking the quest of the bleeding lance, Gawaine keeps Gringolet alone. At one point, near the Galloway border, he loses the steed to Greoreas, but subsequently recovers him from Greoreas' nephew. Next day, challenged by the Haughty Maid of Logres to jump his horse across the Perilous Ford, Gawaine achieves the crossing twice—but only thanks to Gringolet's strength and dexterity. The first time, the charger misses the farther bank and lands in the water, but swims until his four feet touch bottom, when he heaves himself and his rider to dry ground in one impressive leap up the extremely steep side. This little accident may cause Gawaine to feel that he has not fully met the Haughty Maid's challenge (even though the Guiromelant assures him that no other knight has ever attempted that crossing and lived), for he insists on returning the same way. Perhaps Gringolet learned from his first attempt, because the second time he jumps from bank to bank perfectly. [**Perceval**, ca. ll. 6206-6208; 7070-7359; 8475-8917]

GRIP, EARL

He warred on King Howel in Brittany, and was killed by Tristram [Malory VIII, 36].

Grisandoles†—see AVENABLE

GROMER SOMER JOURE

While hunting alone in Inglewood, Scotland, Arthur once fell into the power of Sir Gromer Somer Joure, who threatened to take vengeance because, Gromer claimed, Arthur had wrongfully given some of his lands to Gawaine. Gromer finally agreed to let Arthur go for a year, on Arthur's parole to return at the end of that time prepared to meet his death if he could not answer the question, "What is it women most desire?" Arthur got the answer from Dame Ragnell, who turned out to be Gromer's sister; as soon as Gromer heard it, he cursed Ragnell as the only one who could have taught it to the King.

The Wedding of Sir Gawaine and Dame Ragnell, the source of the above information, leaves the impression that Arthur and Gromer parted enemies, the King vowing never to fall into Gromer's power again. Malory, however, mentions "Gromore Somir Joure" as one of the knights who accompanied Mordred and Agravaine in their attempt to trap Lancelot with the Queen, and who were killed during Lancelot's escape. All these knights "were of Scotland, outher of Sir Gawaine's kin, either well-willers to his brethren." [Malory XX, 2-5] This suggests that somewhere along the line Gromer became reconciled with Arthur and Gawaine and joined Arthur's court, possibly as a companion of the Round Table.

Glennie refers to the basic story, calling Gromer only "The Grim Baron of Castle Hewin" and Ragnell only "The Foul Ladye", and pinpointing Arthur's meeting with the Grim Baron at Tarn Wadling in Inglewood.

GRONOSIS†

Kay the Seneschal's son, according to Chrétien de Troyes, who calls Gronosis "well versed in evil", yet lists him among Arthur's knights [**Erec & Enide**, ll. 1691-1750].

GRUMMORE GRUMMURSUM

A "good knight of Scotland" who became a companion of the Round Table, being listed among the would-be-healers of Sire Urre [Malory VII, 26; XIX, 11]. This is about all Malory tells us of him, and in the second reference his name is given as "Sir Gromere Grummer's son." I do not think he should be identified with Gromer Somer Joure. Grummore Grummursum is a minor knight—but with a name like that, I simply could not resist the temptation to include him here.

GRUS THE WRATHFUL†

Grus and his brother Brun of Piciez are among Arthur's knights in the list Chrétien de Troyes begins in line 1691 of **Erec & Enide**.

GUARD, KNIGHTS OF THE (Knights of the Watch)†

When Gawaine comes to the Rock of Canguin, Queen Ygerne commences her questions about Arthur's household by asking her guest if he is one of the knights of the guard (Owen's translation) or watch (Cline's translation), who have done many valiant deeds. She does not mean the Round Table, for she proceeds to ask about that separately after Gawaine has answered that he is not a knight of the guard; he does admit to belonging to the Round Table, calling himself "neither the best nor the worst" of that company. [Chrétien de Troyes, **Perceval**, ca. ll. 8111-8130]

Unless the Knights of the Guard are to be equated with the Queen's Knights, I do not recall yet meeting them as a specific body anywhere else in Arthurian lore. Arthur's court must certainly have had its share of other knights, whether waiting and hoping to join the Round Table or content with lifelong service in less exalted but still essential places.

GUENEVERE (Ganora, Genievre, Guenever, Guenhumara, Vanora, Wander, etc.)

Arthur first saw Guenevere when he went, with his allies Kings Ban and Bors, to rescue her father King Leodegrance of Cameliard from King Ryons. When Arthur's barons insisted he take a wife, he told Merlin:

> I love Guenever the king's daughter Leodegrance of the land of Cameliard, the which holdeth in his house the Table Round that ye told he had of my father Uther. And this damosel is the most valiant and fairest lady that I know living.

He insisted on marrying her, despite Merlin's warning that she would have Lancelot for a lover. Leodegrance sent Arthur the Round Table, along with a hundred knights, as a wedding gift.

When Arthur prepared to go and meet the five invading kings of Denmark, Ireland, the Vale, Soleise, and the Isle of Longtains, he took Guenevere along on the campaign, saying that she would cause him "to be the more hardy" and promising to keep her safe. While they were camped beside the Humber, the invading kings attacked by night. Arthur, Kay, Gawaine, and Griflet tried to get the Queen over the Humber River to safety, but

> the water was so rough that they were afraid to pass over. Now may ye choose, said King Arthur, whether ye will abide and take the adventure on this side, for an ye be taken they will slay you. It were me liefer, said the queen, to die in the water than to fall in your enemies' hands and there be slain.

At Kay's urging and example, the four men slew the five invading kings who were bearing down on them, for which Guenevere praised Kay greatly and promised to bear his fame among the ladies.

Malory records that Guenevere "made great sorrow … and swooned" at the departure of her husband and his men for their continental war with the Emperor Lucius, and that she came to meet him at Sandwich on his return.

As Arthur had his Knights of the Round Table, Guenevere had her own company, the Queen's Knights, who carried white shields; at first, the Queen's Knights were apparently made up of youthful aspirants to the Table, but eventually there seems to have been considerable overlapping in the membership of the two companies. Malory is unclear on when and how Guenevere and Lancelot became more to each other than she was to all of her knights, but by the time Lancelot slew Turquine and Peris de Forest Savage, gossip was already hot enough that the damsel who guided the great knight to Peris could mention it to his face, while by the time Tristram and La Beale Isoud gave in to their passion, the relationship was sufficiently established and known that Isoud could send Palomides to Arthur's court charging him

> there recommend me unto Queen Guenever, and tell her that I send her word that there be within this land but four lovers, that is, Sir Launcelot du Lake and Queen Guenever, and Sir Tristram de Liones and Queen Isoud.

Perhaps Guenevere shows to her worst advantage in this long, stormy love affair. Lancelot called forth her jealousy in a way that Arthur seems never to have done (although, ironically, Arthur probably deserved her jealousy more, Lancelot being drawn into side affairs and appearances of affairs through trickery and misfortune). She accepted Lancelot's explanation of the engendering of Galahad and forgave him, but later, when Elaine of Carbonek tricked Lancelot into her bed at Arthur's court itself, within earshot of Guenevere's own room, the Queen's rather understandable fury drove Lancelot mad. While he wandered out of his wits she spared no expense to find him, financing the knights who went out searching, so that when Percivale and Ector de Maris finally found him at Joyous Isle, Percivale could say that "I was sent by the queen for to seek you." The affair seems to have become even more tempestuous after the Grail Quest. Lancelot quickly forgot the vow he had made during the holy adventures to break it off with Guenevere—Malory's wording seems to put the responsibility for the resumption of the affair more on Lancelot than on the Queen—but he also became more careless about secrecy. When he realized the scandal they were causing and began championing as many ladies and damsels as possible to throw the gossips off the scent, Guenevere waxed angry and jealous again, speaking to him so hotly that he followed his cousin Bors' advice and left court again, hiding with the hermit Sir Brasias at Windsor until the Queen should repent her words and want him back.

It was at this time that Guenevere held a "privy dinner" for twenty-four other knights of the Round Table, to show that she took joy in all of them—at which dinner Sir Patrise of Ireland died of a poisoned apple meant for Gawaine.

Guenevere was accused of the crime, reproached by Arthur himself for being unable to keep Lancelot at hand when she needed him, and driven to beg Sir Bors to champion her in Lancelot's place; Lancelot, meanwhile, secretly informed of the situation by Bors, laid low and let Guenevere stew, not showing up until the very last minute. Shortly after this incident, Lancelot tried to stay in London with the Queen while the rest of the court went to Winchester for a great tournament. This time Guenevere told Lancelot to leave her and attend the tournament, lest their enemies use the occasion for further scandal. "Madam", said Sir Lancelot, "I allow your wit, it is of late come since ye were wise." Somewhat illogically, after accepting Guenevere's reasoning, he went to Winchester in disguise, and his wearing of the favor of Elaine of Astolat in the lists led to another jealous rift, which was not quite healed until Elaine's death bore testimony to Lancelot's avoidance of sexual entanglement with her. In justice, Guenevere seems genuinely to have pitied the dead Elaine. She also prudently insisted that from now on Lancelot wear her favor in tournament, to avoid such injury as he sustained at Winchester when his kinsmen, not knowing him, ganged up on him.

Guenevere shows to better advantage in the adventure of Sir Meliagrant, which Malory (or his first editor, Caxton) places after the last-mentioned incidents, but which probably occurred earlier. When Meliagrant and his men ambushed Guenevere and her party while they were out a-Maying, she kept her head; seeing her ten unarmored knights outnumbered, defeated, and wounded, she surrendered rather than let them be slain, even calling on the four who were still on their feet to leave off fighting, since it was hopeless. She managed, however, to slip her ring to a child of her chamber and send him back to Lancelot. When Lancelot arrived and cowed Meliagrant, Guenevere seems to have promoted the cause of peace and truce, though she prudently insisted that, as long as they remained in Meliagrant's castle, her wounded knights should be put in her own chamber so that she could be sure they received the best treatment. Lancelot came to her at the garden window that night, injured his hands in pulling out the window bars to get in, and so left blood in her bed, giving Meliagrant the chance to accuse her of lying with the injured knights. Again Lancelot had to fight her trial by combat to save her from burning, and this time she "wagged her head … as though she would say: Slay [Meliagrant]", which may have been more prudence than bloodthirstiness and was certainly understandable, all things considered.

When cornered at last together in the Castle of Carlisle by Mordred, Agravaine, and their dozen knights, Lancelot offered, after slaying thirteen of the attackers and driving Mordred away wounded, to take Guenevere with him at once to safety. She, however, refused to go, probably hoping that the good of the court might yet be salvaged, telling him only that if he saw they would burn her, then he might rescue her as he thought best. Most modern versions depict Arthur as being forced with a heavy heart to bow to the righteousness of the law in sentencing Guenevere, but a close reading of Malory and the Vulgate version gives the impression of what might be called a kangaroo court, save that the King himself was presiding, with Arthur seeming to rejoice in the law (though it is just possible his rage was less for Guenevere's inconstancy than for the deaths of his thirteen knights) and hotly refusing Gawaine's plea to allow Lancelot to fight a trial by combat yet again and prove their innocence—which would, of course, have averted the final catastrophe. Indeed, Arthur apparently forbade any trial by combat at all and, far from hoping that Lancelot would come to the rescue, as in T. H. White's version, seems to have tried to burn her at once, before Lancelot got his chance. Guenevere probably never knew that even Lancelot had seemed to falter a little in his resolve to save her: talking the matter over with his kinsmen, he said

> and this night because my lady the queen sent for me ... I suppose it was made by treason, howbeit I dare largely excuse her person, notwithstanding I was there by a forecast near slain.

Despite Arthur's attempt to burn her, she returned to him and showed herself a loyal wife and prudent queen while he was overseas besieging Lancelot. She was not taken in by Mordred's forged letters purporting that Arthur was dead, but she pretended to agree to marry Mordred, thus getting him to let her go to London, supposedly to buy what she wanted for the wedding, actually to barricade herself well in the Tower of London with men and provisions. When Mordred laid siege to the Tower she answered him "that she had liefer slay herself than to be married with him." Learning at last of Arthur's actual death (or "passing"), Guenevere "stole away" with five of her ladies to Almesbury, where she became a "nun in white clothes and black", and lived in great penance, "fasting, prayers, and alms-deeds", "and never creature could make her merry", which last must have been especially severe, as Malory elsewhere shows her possessed of a keen sense of humor and fun. She became Abbess. She had one more meeting with Lancelot; he sought her out, with thoughts of taking her back with him to his kingdom in

France. Counseling him to keep his realm in peace, take a wife, and pray for his old lover, she refused to leave her sanctuary and penance. "And therefore, lady", said Lancelot, remembering his broken resolutions of the Grail Adventures, "sithen ye have taken you to perfection, I must needs take me to perfection, of right." He did not see her again until, learning of her death in a vision, he and eight companions went on foot from Glastonbury to Almesbury to bring back her body for burial. [Malory I, 18; III, 1, 5; IV, 2-3; V, 3, 12; VI, 10; VIII, 31; X, 49; XI, 6-9; XVIII 1-21; XIX, 1-9; XX, 3-17; XXI, 1, 7-11, etc.]

Malory does not show, except perhaps between the lines, as in the number of cases of conquered knights being sent to her and in her presiding at Duke Galeholt's tournament in Surluse when Arthur himself was unable to attend [X, 40-49], how good a queen Guenevere was, that part of her character being overshadowed by her affair with Lancelot. The Vulgate, which calls her, after Elaine of Carbonek, the wisest woman who ever lived [vol. II], throws more light on this and other points. That she was an excellent day-to-day administratress is evidenced by how greatly the affairs of the kingdom slipped while Arthur banished her for two and a half years to live in infatuation with her look-alike, Genievre, giving knights, court, and common people much cause to yearn for their wise and generous true Queen. Guenevere was understandably reluctant to return to Arthur after Genievre's death, for, as she said, he had in effect dissolved her marriage by condemning her to death in this case, and she was well content in Surluse with a man who would make her a much better husband. Except for Elaine of Carbonek (whom she made some attempt to accept—cf. Malory XI, 7) and Elaine of Astolat, whom she did not meet alive and grieved for dead, she seems to have befriended all women, even accepting Amable as Lancelot's platonic lady love. She seems to have inspired more than common devotion in Gawaine, who lent Lancelot Excalibur when he fought to save her from Arthur's sentence in the Genievre episode, and in Kay, who openly envied Lancelot his position as her champion.

In Malory Book VI, chapter 10, an unnamed damsel remarks to Lancelot: "It is noised that ye love Queen Guenevere, and that she hath ordained by enchantment that ye shall love none other but her." This is the only hint I remember reading that Guenevere may have dabbled in magic; I think this evidence either comes under the heading of gossip and metaphor, or that it reflects some confusion with Lancelot's mentor Viviane, the French Damsel of the Lake, who according to the Vulgate largely engineered the affair (with a bit of intriguing assistance from Duke Galeholt and the Lady of Malohaut).

A Middle English romance, **The Adventures at Tarn Wadling**, currently available in Louis Hall's **Knightly Tales of Sir Gawaine**, describes an interesting meeting of Guenevere with her mother's ghost. The ghost describes her penitential suffering, the sins—especially pride—that led to it and the virtues that would have helped her avoid it, asks Masses for her salvation, and warns against Arthur's greed as the cause of his future downfall. The description of the ghost's appearance would stir professional jealousy in the heart of any monster-movie makeup artist; nevertheless, Guenevere has Gawaine at her side and, after her initial fright, questions the spirit bravely and compassionately, afterward ordering a million Masses for her.

Guenevere had gray eyes (cf. **Sir Gawaine and the Green Knight**) and more than one commentator has remarked that the root of her name means "white", suggesting a pale complexion and very fair blond hair. According to the Vulgate, she was also the best chess player of Arthur's court.

Chrétien de Troyes, while emphasizing Arthur's generosity as a shining and royal virtue, did not neglect to show Arthur's queen as possessed with a goodly share of the same virtue, along with graciousness and wisdom. Consider, for example, the rich garments she gives Enide for the asking [**Erec & Enide**, ll. 1585-1654] and the wise counsel she offers Alexander and Soredamors after divining their unvoiced lovesickness for each other [**Cligés**, ll. 2249-2360]. In **Perceval**, ca. ll. 8174-8200, Gawaine devotes his golden tongue to about twenty-six lines in eloquent praise of Guenevere. (He does not yet know that the venerable queen inquiring about Arthur's wife is Arthur's mother.)

QUEEN QUENEVERE'S FAMILY AND RELATIONS
Father: King Leodegrance
Husband: King Arthur
Half-sister: Genievre
Lover: Lancelot
Would-be-lover: Meliagrance
Cousins: Elyzabel, Garaunt, Guiomar, Guy, Labor

'Guenevere, the False'—see GENIEVRE

GUENEVERE'S COMB†

When Guenevere was captured by Meliagrant, on the way into Gore she either lost her comb or left it behind as a marker. I would incline toward the latter interpretation, since the comb lay clearly visible on a stone slab near a spring in the middle of a meadow. The comb was of gilded ivory, very fine, and still had some of the queen's hairs in it. "Portia" (q.v.) at first tried unobtrusively to keep Lancelot from spotting it. When he did, and she told him whose it was (I remain uncertain how "Portia" herself knew this), he ecstatically cherished the hairs but let his guide keep the comb. It could be thinking more like a modern than a medieval mind to wonder why it apparently never occurred to this devout lover that the object of his undying adoration might appreciate getting such a fine and valuable personal item back from his hand. [Chrétien de Troyes, **Lancelot**, ll. 1356-ca. 1510]

GUENEVERE'S SHIELD†

This shield showed an armed knight and a beautiful lady embracing, but separated by a cleft down the middle, the cleft being wide enough for a person to place one hand through it without touching either side. The French Damsel of the Lake sent the shield to Guenevere, to help her in the greatest pain and cause her the greatest joy. The cleft in the shield was to close when the knight had gained the lady's complete love and was a member of Arthur's court. At this time, although he had been dubbed by Arthur and had already pledged his love in person to Guenevere, Lancelot was still adventuring around the country.

During the siege of La Roche, the crack was closed. While Arthur was Camille's prisoner in that castle, the French Damsel of the Lake came to counsel Guenevere to love Lancelot with all her heart. After the fighting, Lancelot finally became a member of Arthur's court. [Vulgate III]

GUENEVERE'S SLEEVE

Guenevere gave Lancelot a sleeve of gold to wear on his helmet at tournaments so that his kinsmen would know him. Lancelot apparently wore it from then on. What else could he do, after not only wearing Elaine of Astolat's sleeve at the tournament of Winchester, but being grievously wounded by his cousin Sir Bors, who did not know him, in that same tourney? All of this had caused Guenevere to insist he now take her token [Malory XVIII, 21].

Guenhumara—see GUENEVERE

GUERGESIN, DUKE OF HIGH WOOD†

Chrétien de Troyes lists him among the vassal lords whom Arthur summoned to court for Erec's wedding. Guergesin came very richly equipped. [**Erec & Enide**, ca. l. 1962]

Guerrehes—see GAHERIS

Guerrehet—see GARETH

Guidel—see GUINDOEL

GUIGAMBRESIL (Guinganbresil)†

High steward or advisor to the kings of Escavalon, he enters Arthur's court during the questing fever inspired by the Loathly Damsel at the time of Percivale's second visit to court and rather puts a damper on things by charging Gawaine with treason in the death of the old king of Escavalon. Gawaine willingly pledges himself to meet his challenger within forty days at Escavalon in trial by combat before his alleged victim's father, the young king. When next we see Guigambresil, he is returning to Escavalon, to find Gawaine and the young king's sister defending themselves against a mob. Guigambresil has known nothing until this moment of Gawaine's arrival, so it seems possible that Gawaine actually beat him back to Escavalon. In any case, taking stock of the situation, Guigambresil hurries to find the young king and advise him that, since he has unwittingly made Gawaine his guest, he is obligated to see that no harm comes to him. We should surely understand Guigambresil as meaning "no harm before our combat"; nevertheless, his conduct looks wholly honorable. Whatever the story behind his accusation, I find it difficult to interpret Guigambresil as villainous.

Guigambresil's shield was gold with an azure band covering an exactly measured third of it.

[Chrétien de Troyes, **Perceval**, ll. 4747-4797; ca. 6030-6202]

GUIGENOR†

According to one or more of Chrétien's continuators, the daughter of Guiromelant and Clarissant, q.v.

GUINABLE, COUNT†

Apparently a member of Arthur's court, he overheard Guenevere's *sotto voce* plaint when she left with Kay to take up Meliagrant's challenge at the beginning of the "Knight of the Cart" adventure [Chrétien de Troyes, **Lancelot**, ll. 198-221].

GUINAS†

Sir Guinas, seeking to measure Gawaine's strength, erected twelve pavilions near his castle and filled them with knights to dispute passage to all passing knights. When Gaheris and Sagramore had each unhorsed one of Guinas' knights, Guinas' dwarf told them they were free to proceed, and gave Sagramore a new lance to replace the one he had broken. Here we see that not all knights who guard passages need be bloodthirsty scoundrels, nor all such disputed passages mortally perilous traps. Some of the guardians may be sportsmen, and the disputed passages safe (barring accidents) places to pick up glory.

Gareth eventually conquered Guinas and made him promise to surrender to Gawaine. [Vulgate V]

I found no clue to the location of Guinas' castle. Guinas' sportsmanship suggests a locale in more settled areas, possibly in territory in or near that held by the chivalrous Duke Galeholt.

GUINCEL†

Chrétien tells us that he was captured by Gawaine in the tourney between Evroic and Tenebroc about a month after Erec's wedding [**Erec & Enide**, ll. 2215-2234].

GUINDOEL† (Gindiel, Granidel, Guidel, Raginel)

This castle seems not to have been far from Listeneise, for when Gawaine and Ector separated at the fork in the road beyond the "Chapel of the Conjuration", Gawaine took the right fork and ended at Carbonek, while Ector took the left fork, despite numerous warnings of shame waiting along that road, and ended at Guindoel.

Sir Marigart had once loved Lady Oruale, the rightful chatelaine of Guindoel. When she refused to wed him, and her cousin killed Marigart's brother for insulting her before her people, Marigart invaded the castle by night, killed the cousin, and raped the lady. Declining, now, to marry her, he imprisoned her in a cave guarded by two lions, while he settled down to vanquishing knights (stripping them and having them dragged through the streets) and dishonoring maidens of the village. Marigart may have set up the warnings along the road himself. Four years, forty maidens, and an unknown number of knights later, Ector arrived to kill Marigart, restore Oruale, and offer to be her knight always and everywhere. [Vulgate IV]

Guinebas—see **GWENBAUS**

GUINEMANS†

Apparently either a leader of the Sesnes or one of their allies in the attack on Vandaliors Castle, early in Arthur's reign [Vulgate II].

Guinganbresil—see **GUIGAMBRESIL**

Guinglain—see **GINGALIN**

GUINGOMAR, LORD OF THE ISLE OF AVALON†

Chrétien lists him among the vassal lords whom Arthur summoned to court for Erec's wedding. Guingomar was Morgan le Fay's lover. His brother was Graislemier. [**Erec & Enide**, ll. 1934-1962]

I would guess that Chrétien's Guingomar became the Vulgate's Guiomar.

GUIOMAR†

A cousin of Guenevere, he was one of Morgan's earliest lovers. Guenevere's anger over Morgan's affair with Guiomar led to the rift between the two women, Guenevere banishing Guiomar from court and

Morgan leaving to learn witchcraft from Merlin. I found Guiomar's name in Vulgate VII, the story in Vulgate IV.

Compare Guingomar.

GUIROMELANT(, THE)†

Ruth Cline consistently uses "the" with his name; D.D.R. Owen does not.

I cannot yet visualize the geographical element involved: sometimes the Rock of Canguin and Guiromelant's country seem to face each other across a river, and sometimes an additional tongue of land seems to lie between them. Gawaine has the Ferryman row him over from the Canguin side to meet the Haughty Maid of Logres and her companion, the Haughty Knight of the Rock on the Narrow Way. After defeating the knight, Gawaine accepts the damsel's challenge to leap his horse across the Perilous Ford. On the far side of this ford, he meets Guiromelant, who is out hunting with a sparrow hawk on his wrist and two bird dogs in the field. Guiromelant reveals himself as lord of the city they can see, which he boasts of holding from no other overlord except God alone—it is called Orqueneseles and I tentatively identify it with the city where the Haughty Maid the previous day sent Gawaine for her palfrey. Guiromelant proceeds to tell Gawaine all about the Haughty Maid, whom he once loved: since she did not love him, he slew the sweetheart she did love and appropriated her. Strangely—to Guiromelant's mind—even this failed to win her affection, and she ungratefully took her first opportunity to escape with yet another knight, thus earning Guiromelant's contempt. Now he has turned his undying devotion to a worthier object: the young lady of Canguin. At first questioning Gawaine about Canguin, and becoming sarcastic almost to the point of rudeness when Gawaine confesses how little he knows about it, Guiromelant proceeds to enlighten him as to the identities of Queen Ygerne, her daughter, and granddaughter (whom he knows to be Gawaine's sister, though I remain unsure whether he knows her name). Much though he loves her, he hates her brother enough to rip his heart out in her sight, because Gawaine's father Lot killed Guiromelant's father and Gawaine himself killed one of Guiromelant's first cousins. By the way, Guiromelant goes on to the stranger, will you kindly do me the favor of delivering this emerald finger ring to my lady along with the message that I love and trust her so much I feel confident she would rather that her brother Gawaine die a painful death than that I should scratch my toe. At last Guiromelant asks Gawaine's name, learns it, and observes that Gawaine has been overfoolish or overbold in revealing it: "If only I were armed for combat, I'd cut your head off right now … . As it is, we'll have to hold our fight in a week, for greater glory: I'll have my army on hand, and you'll have time to summon Arthur and his court, since they're just two days away at Orkney right now." Gawaine accepts all this, even though he would prefer to make more peaceable amends; Chrétien never got beyond the arrival of Gawaine's messenger at Arthur's court. [**Perceval**, ca. ll. 8370 to end]

From Ronan Coghlan's **Encyclopaedia of Arthurian Legends** (©1991) I learn that at least one continuator had Guiromelant succeed in marrying Igraine's granddaughter Clarissant and begetting a daughter, Guigenor, on her. I sincerely hope that wasn't the outcome Chrétien had in mind. Guiromelant strikes me as one of the least likable characters in his author's entire output, comparing unfavorably even with Count Galoain. I cannot think him nearly good enough for Clarissant, who explains (ca. ll. 9015-9042) that Guiromelant has seen her only from a distance, never having crossed to her side of the river; that she is his only to the extent of a few messages sent back and forth; and that he was astonishingly foolish to say she would prefer her brother's death to her admirer's scratching his toe.

GUIROMELANT'S RING†

Before knowing who Gawaine was, Guiromelant gave him this ring, which was of gold set with a large emerald, to give Clarissant in token of his (Guiromelant's) love. Even after learning that Guiromelant was in fact his enemy, and setting a date to fight with him, Gawaine carried out this commission; nor did Guiromelant ever seem to question that he would do so. [Chrétien de Troyes, **Perceval**, ca. ll. 8807-8810; 9009-9014]

GUIVRET THE LITTLE†

He was a dwarf king of entirely noble heart. So, at least, Chrétien's translator D.D.R. Owen assures us, suggesting possible descent from Huon's Auberon. Guivret's liegemen were all Irish, and he boasted that none of his neighboring lords went against his wishes.

When Erec and Enide escaped from Count Galoain's land, they crossed a mown and hedged meadow, then passed over a drawbridge spanning a wide moat. Guivret looked down from his tower, saw them, and, calling for his arms and armor, rode after them for no other purpose than to measure his strength against that of the unknown knight. If we go by the romances, this must have been a perfectly legitimate way of getting one's knightly exercise. Apparently it did not demand any initial declaration of intent, no doubt to guarantee that the attacked stranger fought back without stinting himself. Erec and Guivret dealt each other mighty blows from nine a.m. until after three p.m., no mean feat considering that in the initial joust, while knocking each other off their horses, each had driven the tip of his lance as far as the other's intestines! At last the dwarf king's sword broke and he reluctantly yielded, exchanging names with the conquering stranger. Delighted to learn that his opponent was King Lac's son, Guivret proposed repairing together to the manor house of a doctor of his, a mere seven or eight leagues distant; Erec, not to be outdone in manly endurance, insisted on continuing his own journey. So the two tore their shirt tails to bind up each other's wounds (without benefit of plaster), swore friendship, and parted, Guivret promising to come to Erec's assistance whenever needed. This promise he fulfilled within thirty-six hours: hearing that his neighbor Count Oringle of Limors had found a seemingly dead knight and wanted to wed his beautiful widow, the dwarf king—although only suspecting the young couple's identity—set off at once with a thousand men to the rescue. He encountered Erec and Enide that night as they were already escaping and took them to his castle of Penevric, where his two sisters nursed Erec back to health. Guivret then escorted Erec and Enide to Castle Brandigant and afterward to the court city of Robais, where they found King Arthur. On being told of their approach, Arthur remarked that he knew of no better lords anywhere than those two, which shows that Arthur had already known Guivret, at least by reputation. It seems curious that Chrétien does not mention Guivret the Little much earlier in the romance, along with the other good dwarf kings, Bilil, Grigoras, and Glecidalan. Perhaps, unlike them, Guivret had not been Arthur's vassal. In any case, at Erec's insistence, Arthur invited Guivret, along with Erec, to remain at court, which both did—Erec until his father's death called him back to rule Outre-Gales, Guivret possibly longer (he was still around, at any rate, for Erec's coronation). Guivret's coat of arms appears to have included gold lions. [Chrétien de Troyes, **Erec & Enide**, ll. 3663-3929 & Owen's note to 3678; 4937-5366; 6411-6532; 6810-6855]

GUY

A knight of Cameliard, mentioned once by Malory, in passing, along with Sir Garaunt [X, 36]. Guy and Garaunt's claim to fame is that they were cousins of Guenevere.

GWENBAUS (Guinebas)

The brother of Kings Ban and Bors, Gwenbaus accompanied them to England when they came as Arthur's allies during the early war against the rebel kings. Malory characterizes Gwenbaus simply as "a wise clerk." From the Vulgate we learn that he was a clerk of necromancy and did a bit of hobnobbing with Merlin. Gwenbaus met, loved, and remained with a king's daughter in the Forest Perilous in England until his and her deaths (apparently natural). See Forest Perilous.

Gwendydd†—see **GANIEDA**

HANDSOME COWARD†

Since Chrétien de Troyes lists this knight of the intriguing appellation as the fifth best of Arthur's knights [**Erec & Enide**, ll. 1691-1750], one guesses that his cowardice was the same sort displayed by the Cowardly Lion of L. Frank Baum's Oz books (who is quite a different personality from the otherwise delightful comic character played by Bert Lahr!). Chrétien might also have been hinting at something by putting the Handsome Coward in immediate juxtaposition with the Ugly Brave. I regret my inability to give the French original of these appellations, which could vary in different English translations.

HARD ROCK (Roche Dure), CASTLE OF THE

Tristram "won the tournament of the Castle of Maidens that standeth by the Hard Rock" [Malory X, 7]. From this it appears that the Castle of the Hard Rock either was near to or identical with a Castle of Maidens. Roche Dure or Hard Rock may have been an earlier or an alternative name for it.

HARGODABRANS†

A leader of the Sesnes, involved in the attack on Vandaliors, Hargodabrans was 15 feet tall. He worked with the sorceress Camille against Arthur at La Roche; grievously wounded and taken prisoner by Lancelot, he stabbed himself when carried to the tents. [Vulgate II, III]

Harlon, King—see under ARGUSTUS

HARPE, CASTEL DE LA†

This may have been a castle of King Bagdemagus, since Lancelot and Meliagrant's stepsister joined her father here [Vulgate V].

Vulgate VII has the Damoisele a la Harpe, a sister or cousin of Helaes de la Forest Perilleuse. This suggests a location in or near the Forest Perilous. Helaes de la Forest Perilleuse may well be Malory's Hellawes, the sorceress of Castle Nigramous.

HARPE, DAMOISELE À LA†

She took Oriolz the Dane to heal him. She was either a sister or a cousin of Helaes de la Forest Perilleuse. [Vulgate VII] The name suggests she may have been castellaine of the Castel de la Harpe.

HARPIN OF THE MOUNTAIN and HIS DWARF†

Excepting Meliagrant, Harpin of the Mountain may be Chrétien's most unmitigated portrait of evil. One doubts that anything at all could be found to say in defense of this archetypal ogre's character. True, one might call him punctual to his appointments—probably a rare virtue in that age—but then, as far as he knew, he came to the one appointment described for the sole purpose of enjoying himself by tormenting victims. (See under "Alteria.")

Harpin did not deign to wear armor, substituting a bearskin. Probably this confidence in his own strength was also what prompted him to carry a massive pointed stake in lieu of other weapon. Had he had proper armor and bladed or other metal weaponry, the task of Ywaine and his lion in destroying him might have left them with less energy for fighting Lunette's accusers a few hours later.

Harpin died with a large slab sliced off his face, a hunk clawed or bitten from his hip, one arm hacked off at the shoulder, and a sword thrust through the liver. Anyone inclined to pity him might bear in mind not only how he had threatened to treat "Alteria's" daughter—by giving her to his vilest servants for their sex toy—but how he had actually treated her six brothers, killing two before their father's eyes and bringing the surviving four, clad only in filthy shirts, hands and feet bound tightly, mounted on skinny and limping nags tied tail to tail, and flogged bloody by a dwarf who resembled a toad and wielded a four-knotted scourge, to witness their sister's surrender or else be murdered themselves. Harpin's only motive for all this appears to have been frustrated lust for the young lady.

The dwarf survived to be taken by his erstwhile victims to Arthur's court. What happened to him after that, Chrétien does not tell us.

[**Yvain**, ca. ll. 3852-4312]

HARRY LE FISE LAKE

A companion of the Round Table, "[a] good knight and an hardy." His biggest moment in Malory comes during a scuffle with Breuse Sans Pitie in Book I, chapter 53. He is also listed in XIX, 11. In XX, 5, he appears as one of the knights who sided with Lancelot after Mordred surprised the great knight with Guenevere. "Le Fise Lake" suggests a close relationship with Lancelot du Lake; Harry has been identified, however, with Chrétien's title hero Erec, the son of King Lac.

HAUGHTY KNIGHT OF THE HEATH (Proud Knight of the Moor, Glade, etc.) and HIS DAMSEL†

This Haughty Knight rode an Irish steed, from which he was unhorsed by Erec in the tournament between Evroic and Tenebroc a month after Erec's wedding [**Erec & Enide**, ll. 2171-2214].

Both the adjective and the place noun of his name vary with the translation. Perhaps I make a wild jump in identifying him with a knight who appears at a house where Lancelot is lodging for the night in the marches of Gore. This man, looking more arrogant than a bull, rides up with one leg thrown jauntily over his charger's neck, asks for the fool who intends to cross the Sword Bridge, berates Lancelot for having ridden in a cart, and offers to ferry him across the water for the toll of his head, "if I feel like taking it." Lancelot rejects the offer, but humors the proud knight with an immediate battle on the nearest convenient field. In this fight, both horses are soon killed. The first time Lancelot defeats his opponent, he offers him mercy on condition that he himself get into a cart. While the loser begs for mercy on any other terms, King Bademagu's daughter rides up and asks Lancelot, as a favor, to give her the head of the defeated knight, whom she calls the most perfidious traitor who ever lived. Torn between the great knightly virtues of Pity—which bids him extend mercy to vanquished foes—and Generosity—which bids him do the damsel the favor she asks—Lancelot lets his opponent rehelm, rearm, and fight again. This time, Lancelot even puts himself under the handicap of fighting without moving from his original stance, but defeats him easily and lops off his head, presenting it to the delighted maiden. [Chrétien, **Lancelot**, ll. 2580-ca. 2950] My only reasons for identifying the unnamed knight killed by Lancelot with the one so briefly mentioned as being unhorsed by Erec is that Lancelot's challenger, whether or not as bad as the damsel claims, is certainly haughty, that the field whereon they fight happens to be a heath, that the knight of **Eric & Enide** was apparently not one of Arthur's, and that any new tag I might devise for Lancelot's opponent would probably include the element "Haughty" or "Proud" anyway.

The principal difficulty with the above identification is that a Haughty Knight of the Heath, alternatively called the Proud Knight of the Moor or of the Glade, reappears alive in Chrétien's last romance as the sweetheart of the damsel whom Percivale, on his very first adventure after leaving home, finds sleeping in a tent pitched in a woodland glade. Interpreting his mother's parting instructions rather liberally, Percivale roughly helps himself to the damsel's emerald ring, one of three waiting meat pasties and a silver cupful of wine, and an unwilling kiss from the maiden's lips. Returning to the tent after the intruder's departure, the Haughty Knight takes news of the ring, pasty, and wine in stride, but flies into fury when his damsel confesses the forced kiss. Clearly among those who believe "when a woman says no, she means yes", the Haughty Knight assumes that, if she is willing to admit a kiss, she must in fact have gone all the way with the stranger. Punishing both her and, by some twist of logic, her unoffending horse, he makes her follow him with neither change of raiment for herself nor oats, veterinary care, nor new shoes for her mount, until he can find and decapitate the rude stranger.

Nor does he content himself with wreaking vengeance on the particular unknown who committed the original offense: he slays any knight who stops to talk, however innocently, with his maltreated damsel along the way. Some time later, immediately after leaving the Fisher King's castle, Percivale (now knighted and a little better acquainted with chivalric niceties) finds his cousin, the Fisher King's Niece, mourning her headless lover, who has just become the Haughty Knight's latest victim. Percivale rides in pursuit, finds first the damsel and her horse, in very sorry state, and then the Haughty Knight himself, who appears in such a way as to suggest he has been using his poor sweetheart as bait. He retells the story to Percivale, who reveals his own identity as the youth of the tale. Some mss. describe Trebuchet's Sword as breaking in the ensuing battle, but a deal of scholarly opinion considers this passage of about twenty lines as a later interpolation. Whether with Trebuchet's Sword or that of the Red Knight of Quinqueroi, Percivale defeats the Haughty Knight but grants his plea for mercy, charging him to take his lady somewhere she can rest and be healed, and then to go to Arthur's court, tell the whole story, and give Kay the usual message that Percivale intends to come back and avenge the maiden whom the seneschal struck. These directives the Haughty Knight carries out, with the observation that he really loves his sweetheart. It may have been considered sufficient amends in that era. When she is well enough, they find Arthur's court at Caerleon, where the knight presents his damsel to the queen and relays his message. If the usual pattern holds, they presumably join the court. [**Perceval**, ca. ll. 635-834; 3430-3466; 3691-4085; named ca. 3817]

HAUGHTY KNIGHT OF THE ROCK ON THE NARROW WAY (Proud Knight of the Passage with the Narrow Way)†

The knight with whom the Haughty Maid of Logres escaped from Guiromelant. It appears to me that, when she sends passing knights to fetch her little palfrey, the Haughty Knight of the Rock (etc.) is the champion on whom she relies to come and put them to death or disgrace in single combat. The day after she leaves Gawaine at the riverbank facing Canguin, she returns with her Haughty Knight of the Rock. Sure enough, Gawaine has himself ferried across the river to meet them. He soon defeats the Haughty Knight and sends him over to Canguin; the damsel's turn does not come until later in the day.

This Haughty Knight bore a quartered shield. By Guiromelant's testimony, he guarded the Galloway border and was a formidable opponent—even though, Guiromelant adds, he never dared come near him (Guiromelant) again.

[Chrétien de Troyes, **Perceval**, ca. ll. 8309-8582]

HAUGHTY MAID (Damsel, Woman) OF LOGRES (Nogres)†

Chrétien scholars Cline and Frappier call her Chrétien's "vamp." She takes her name from the land where she was born, and from which she was taken as a child. Whether this land was Logres or Nogres apparently depends on the ms.; Cline prefers Nogres, but D.D.R. Owen claims to follow the majority opinion in preferring Logres.

Gawaine first meets her as he approaches the Galloway border, soon after leaving the wounded Greoreas. The Haughty Maid sits beneath a tree admiring her face in a looking glass. The beauty of her face and body are worth admiring; nevertheless, the mirror could well symbolize vanity to the medieval mind (as to the modern: I suspect that this image of the beauty admiring herself strikes us much in the same way it struck Chrétien's original readership). Her every word dripping scorn, she challenges Gawaine to cross to the city (of Orqueneseles?) and bring back her little piebald palfrey, threatening that if he does, she will ride with him to watch the shame and disaster he will suffer. When he successfully brings her mount, she refuses to let him help her into the saddle: she will not endure his touch. She follows him back to Greoreas and his lady and apparently sits quietly watching Greoreas steal Gringolet, whereupon she mocks Gawaine's necessity of mounting the Ugly Squire's "Sorry Nag", saying she only wishes it were a mare, so that his shame would be even worse. She accompanies him to the riverbank facing Canguin, where she leads her palfrey into a waiting barge, warns Gawaien that the knight approaching on Gringolet is Greoreas' nephew come to kill him, and quietly slips away while Gawaine is engaged winning back his own steed. Next day the Haughty Maid reappears, bringing the Haughty Knight of the Rock on the Narrow Way. Upon Gawaine issuing forth, defeating her champion, and sending him wounded back to Canguin, she informs Gawaine that it was a case of the weaker man winning and challenges him to prove his worth by leaping his horse across the Perilous Ford, telling him that the man he just defeated has been doing this every day (a short passage of questioned authenticity adds that his purpose was to bring her flowers picked on the other side). After achieving this feat, thanks to Gringolet, Gawaine learns from Guiromelant that he is in fact the first to cross this ford.

Up until now, the Haughty Maid has made herself universally hated by her behavior. From Guiromelant, we learn some of the reason behind her actions: this worthy boasts of having slain her original sweetheart in order to take her himself. Of course, he scorns her now, for showing the inexplicable taste to escape from him with the Haughty Knight of the Rock (etc.) at her first opportunity. When Gawaine crosses the Perilous Ford a second time and returns to her, she shows him quite a different side of herself, explaining that she has been behaving as she has because, in her grief for her slain love, she has hoped to anger some knight into ending her own life. Now she begs Gawaine to give her a death that will serve for an example to prevent all maidens henceforth from insulting other knights. He naturally refuses, instead taking her back to Canguin, where she is welcomed for his sake. [**Perceval**, ca. ll. 6671-7370; 8289-9002; & Cline's & Owen's notes]

For the symbolism of the mirror, which may mark the Haughty Maid on her first appearance as a *vanitas* or personification of vanity, see, e.g., Susan Haskins, **Mary Magdalen: Myth and Metaphor** (©1993), esp. p. 168. The mirror also, however, came to serve as a symbol of truth (e.g., ibid., p. 258), which is presumably its significance in works with the title Mirror for … or Mirror of …, and in the owl and looking-glass associated with Tyll Eulenspiegel. Whether it might have had this "truth" symbolism as early as Chrétien's generation, I cannot as yet say.

HAUTDESERT†

I have assumed that Sir Bercilak, or Bertilak, de Hautdesert, alias the Green Knight of the famous metrical romance, took his surname from the name of his castle. According to **Sir Gawaine and the Green Knight**, the castle is less than two miles from the Green Chapel. Helen Hill Miller puts the Green Chapel at a certain deep ravine below Leek Moor, northern Staffordshire.

HEBES LE RENOUMES

A squire of Tristram's, sent to Tristram first by King Faramon's daughter, with a love letter and a gift brachet. After Faramon's daughter had died of love, Hebes returned to the great knight. He remained in Britain when Mark sent Tristram to Ireland to be cured of the wound from Marhaus' spear. Hebes accompanied Gawaine, however, to Ireland for the tournament for the Lady of the Launds, hoping "to be made knight", and there recognized Tristram, promised not to reveal his true identity, and asked to receive his knighthood from Tristram's hands. Tristram obliged, after which Hebes "did right well that day" at the tournament and afterward held with Tristram. When the Irish queen, Isoud's mother, discovered Tristram was the man who had killed her brother Marhaus, it was Sir Hebes who bodily prevented her from slaying Tristram in his bath.

After Tristram's death, Hebes remained in Arthur's court as a companion of the Round Table, being listed among those who tried to heal Sir Urre. He accompanied the exiled Lancelot into France, where Lancelot made him Earl of Comange. [Malory VIII, 5, 9-11; XIX, 11; XX, 18]

Hector des Mares—see under **ECTOR DE MARIS**

HELAES DE LA FOREST PERILLEUSE (Helaes the Beautiful)

Helaes was an orphan, the Countess of Limos, the sister of one Clapor le Riche and the niece of one Meleager le Rous, a sister or cousin of the Damoisele à la Harpe, and also unmarried and a determined lover of Sir Gawaine. Enlisting the aid of Oriolz the Dane, she won a place in Gawaine's bed. [Vulgate VII]

It is likely that Helaes should be identified with Malory's sorceress Hellawes of the Castle Nigramous.

HELAIN DE TANINGUES†

This squire was castellan of a castle in the neighborhood of Taningues. Gawaine visited him anonymously. Helain confided to the knight, "My people have often blamed me for delaying my entry into the order of chivalry", but, after a dream twelve years before, his mother had made him promise not to request anyone but Sir Gawaine to dub him. Gawaine revealed himself and dubbed Helain the next day, also promising Helain's beautiful sister to be her true knight. [Vulgate III]

HELAIN DE TANINGUES' SISTER†

After dubbing her brother, Gawaine promised this unnamed damsel to be her true knight, giving her a girdle and a locket which the Lady of Roestoc had given him [Vulgate III].

Helaine (as a woman's name)—see **ELAINE**

Helaine the Peerless†—see under **PERSIDES**

HELIADES†

A very late king in our period, Heliades was given Scotland by Mordred during the latter's rebellion [Vulgate VI]. If he fought with Mordred in the last battle, he was, of course, killed there.

HELIAP†

As nearly as I can make out the text of Vulgate VII, Heliap was Sir Sagramor's lady love.

HELIN LE BLANK (Hellaine, Helain, Elian)

Like Percivale and Galahad, Helin, the son of Sir Bors and King Brandegoris' daughter, appears to have been knighted at the age of 15, and at about the same time as Galahad. He became a knight of the Round Table and "proved a good knight and an adventurous." [Malory XII, 9; XIX,

11] He was eventually to become emperor of Constantinople [Vulgate IV]. "Le Blank" signifies "the white" and is also an appellation of Elaine of Astolat; I find the resemblance in the names of two such different characters very interesting.

HELLAWES

The lady of Castle Nigramous and the Chapel Perilous, she tried to kill Lancelot with a kiss, so that she could keep his dead body always to cherish and serve. Failing in her attempt, she died of love for him. She had a similar passion, though not so deadly, for Gawaine. [Malory VI, 15]

Very likely Malory's Hellawes should be identified with the Vulgate's Helaes de la Forest Perilleuse.

HELYAN OF IRELAND†

When Arthur refilled the seats of the Round Table after Lancelot and his followers had left, Lancelot's seat was given to Sir Helyan. This alone suggests that Helyan was an excellent knight, at least "of his hands." He was a king's son, but of which Irish king I do not know. [Vulgate VI] Presumably he perished with Arthur in the last battle.

HELYES OF THOULOUSE†

Duke Galeholt's chief clerk, Helyes had nine other clerks under him, including Petroines and a clerk of Cologne. Galeholt said of Helyes that he surpassed all other clerks as gold all other metals. Helyes had enough knowledge and power to call up at least one wonder, and might have performed miracles had he chosen to study along those lines. See also Helyes' Book and Magical Act 33 on page 534.

HELYES' BOOK†

This little book could have enabled Helyes of Thoulouse to perform miracles, had he cared to study it. On at least one occasion, he used it to conjure up an apparently demonic apparition to help elucidate a prophecy concerning Duke Galeholt's term of life. None of Galeholt's other clerks had success when they tried to consult this book; perhaps they were not learned enough. [Vulgate IV]

HEMISON

Sir Hemison was a lover of Morgan le Fay, living with her at one of her castles. One time Morgan gave a Cornish knight lodging, but next morning informed him that he was her prisoner until he told her who he was. She gave him, however, the place of honor at her side, which aroused Hemison's jealousy until he almost attacked the stranger, but "left it for shame." When the stranger privately told Morgan his identity, she regretted her promise to let him go so easily, but made him promise to carry a shield of her design at the next tournament (see Morgan's Shield). As the Cornish knight departed, the jealous Hemison prepared to follow him, and Morgan's strenuous objections only resulted in a quarrel and sent Hemison away the more "wood wroth."

> Fair friend, said Morgan, ride not after that knight, for ye shall not win no worship of him. Fie on him, coward, said Sir Hemison, for I wist never good knight come out of Cornwall but if it were Sir Tristram de Liones. What an that be he? said she. Nay, Nay, said he, he is with La Beale Isoud, and this is but a daffish knight. ... For your sake, said Sir Hemison, I shall slay him.

Well, Hemison was wrong. It was Tristram. After the fight, Hemison begged his varlet to bring him back to Morgan's castle,

> for deep draughts of death draw to my heart that I may not live, for I would fain speak with her or I died: for else my soul will be in great peril an I die.

His varlet got him to the castle, "and there Sir Hemison fell down dead. When Morgan le Fay saw him dead she made great sorrow out of reason" and buried him with honor. [Malory IX, 41-43]

Herlews le Berbeus—see under **BALIN LE SAVAGE**

HERLEWS' LADY

When Herlews was mortally wounded by the invisible Garlon, he told Balin le Savage to take his horse and follow his lady in "the quest that I was in as she will lead you, and revenge my death when you may." She seems to have been a capable, loyal, and hardy damsel, surviving the ordeal—which killed at least three score other maidens—of giving a dish of her blood to the Leprous Lady, and carrying with her the truncheon with which Garlon had slain Herlews until Balin called for it to stick into Garlon's body and complete the revenge. She was killed when Balin dealt King Pellam the Dolorous Stroke and the castle fell down upon them. [Malory II, 12-16] One would have said she deserved a better fate; one would have said that Balin deserved a better fate, too. See also under Balin le Savage.

HERMAN†

Garin's son. All Chrétien tells us about him is that he rode with his father to confer with their lord Tibaut of Tintagel. This suggests a good relationship between father and son, as well as steadiness and reliability on the young man's part. [**Perceval**, ca. l. 5257]

HERMANCE, KING OF THE DELECTABLE ISLE AND THE RED CITY

Tristram and Palomides found the body of King Hermance in a rich vessel covered with red silk, which grounded on the bank of the Humber River. In the dead king's hand was a letter telling how he had been traitorously slain by two poorly born brethren whom he had brought up, and pleading for some knight to avenge him. Palomides took the quest, journeyed to the Red City, met Sir Ebel, a faithful old retainer who had written the letter for his dead king, and Sir Hermind, the king's brother. Palomides fought and slew the wicked brothers, Sirs Helius and Helake, and freed Hermance's kingdom. [Malory X, 59-64] King Hermance may well have been alive and ruling, but keeping to himself, during the first part of Arthur's reign.

HERMIND (Erminide)

The brother of King Hermance of the Red City, Hermind fought Sir Palomides for the right of avenging Hermance's death, but yielded to Palomides as the better warrior. Hermind may have become king after his brother, though there is no evidence for this; Palomides apparently left Hermance's territory in the hands of the people. [Malory X, 62-64] Hermind did become a knight of the Round Table, being listed among those who tried to heal Sir Urre. He was one of the men killed during Lancelot's rescue of the Queen from the stake. [Malory XIX, 11; XX, 8]

HERNOX, EARL

The lord of Carteloise Castle, Earl Hernox was good but unfortunate. His three sons raped and murdered their sister and imprisoned their father. After Galahad and his companions Bors and Percivale had killed the sons in righteous battle, Hernox died, counting himself blessed, at least, that he died in Galahad's arms. [Malory XVII, 7-9]

HERTANT†

A Saxon warrior, involved in the attack on Vandaliors Castle early in Arthur's reign, Hertant was the nephew of the Saxon king or leader Minadus [Vulgate II].

HERVISE (Hervi) DE REVEL

An excellent knight who, Vulgate III tells us, was already of a "great age" at the beginning of Arthur's reign. Malory mentions him twice, the first time as doing "marvellous deeds with King Arthur" in the battle against the rebel kings at Terrabil, the second time as being chosen, on Pellinore's advice, to fill one of the empty seats at the Round Table after the battle with the five invading kings (of Denmark, etc.) at the Humber [II, 10; IV, 4]. Hervise de Revel may be a character with a rich history of his own, who was either incorporated into the Arthurian cycle or whose original importance was crowded into the background by more recently added characters.

Robert Browning's poem **Hervé Riel** is about a Breton sailor and hero of the late seventeenth century.

HEWIN, CASTLE†

Glennie calls this the stronghold of the Grim Baron. It is in Cumberland, perhaps eight miles south of Carlisle, in an area called Inglewood Forest.

The Grim Baron demanded that Arthur bring him the answer to the riddle "What is it that women most desire?" within a year and a day. Arthur got the answer from the Foul Ladye, who demanded—and married—Gawaine as her reward. Although rather famous (Chaucer has a version of it, for instance), this story is found neither in Malory nor in the Vulgate.

HIGH MOUNTAIN, COUNT(?) OF THE†

Chrétien lists him among the vassal lords whom Arthur summoned to court for Erec's wedding. He brought a very fine company along with him. [**Erec & Enide**, ll. 1934-1962]

HODDAM† (Hoddelm)

The episcopal seat of Saint Kentigern. Hoddam is a few miles north of the mouth of the River Annan, on the north bank of Solway Firth.

Hoel—see **HOWELL**

Holy Grail—see **GRAIL, HOLY**

HOLY HERB

> And ... there by the way [King Bagdemagus] found a branch of an holy herb that was the sign of the Sangreal, and no knight found such tokens but he were a good liver [Malory IV, 5].

Strangely, Bagdemagus is unlisted among knights who later achieve the Adventures of the Grail. Gawaine supposedly kills him sometime during the Quest, although the details are fuzzy.

Holy Island of Saint Cuthbert†—see **MEDGAUD**

HONGREFORT†

This castle was in or near the forest of Landoine. Its lord left the castle to his two daughters, but their uncle, Galindes, besieged them because the Damsel of Hongrefort refused to marry his seneschal. Sir Bors, brought to the area by the younger sister, defeated four of Galindes' knights, killing two and sending the other two to the Damsel of Hongrefort. One of these two prisoners was the seneschal himself. Very reluctantly he gave his word to deliver himself to the Damsel and kept it, even though he passed through Galindes' camp on his way to the castle. His fears were fully justified, for the chatelaine, in her haste and rage, had her proposed bridegroom and his companion bound hand and foot and shot from a mangonel into Galindes' camp. Galindes swore to treat any captured enemies in similar fashion. Bors learned of this the next time he went out to fight Galindes' knights on behalf of the Damsel. He finished the fight, defeating fifteen or sixteen men in succession and finally conquering Galindes himself. Bors had to finish this fight with his shield, because at a crucial point Seraide came and tested him by asking for his sword, which he courteously gave her. In displeasure at the chatelaine's treatment of the prisoners, Bors then rode off with Seraide.

The Damsel of Hongrefort, who had been much taken with Bors, left the castle in charge of her sister and rode off with four knights, seven squires, and three other damsels, wearing their garments inside-out and riding horses without manes or tails, to do penance and find Bors. She met Bors again in Gloevant Wood, but did not know him because he was carrying the shield King Agrippe's daughter had given him. She and her cousin, the Damsel of Glocedon, finally found and recognized him in Roevant Wood, where she obtained his pardon. [Vulgate IV]

HONOLAN, COUNT OF†

Naming him among Arthur's knights in the list beginning line 1691 of **Erec & Enide**, Chrétien de Troyes adds that the Count of Honolan had a fine head of fair hair, never had regard for truth, and received the horn of an ill-fated king (Arthur himself?) who appears to be unidentified in this passage save by the definite article.

HONTZLAKE

In Malory Book III, chapters 5 and 12, Sir Hontzlake of Wentland comes into Arthur's court and forcibly abducts Nimue, who has not yet become an enchantress and who has ridden into court to claim a stolen brachet. King Pellinore pursues them, kills Hontzlake, and rescues Nimue.

In Malory Book IV, chapters 7 and 8, the name Ontzlake appears, this time attached to the good brother of the evil Sir Damas. Here Sir Ontzlake keeps a fair manor through "prowess of his hands … and dwelleth [therein] worshipfully, and is well beloved of all people." See also Damas.

HORN, KNIGHT WITH THE†

Among Arthur's knights in the list Chrétien de Troyes begins in line 1691 of **Erec & Enide**. His appellation may vary with the English translation; might he be identified with Huon of the Horn, Oberon's friend and hero of his own *chanson de geste*?

HORN OF ELEPHANT'S BONE

In the best tradition, this great horn hung near Castle Dangerous, ready for knights-errant to blow when they came to fight Sir Ironside [Malory VII, 15].

HORN OF IVORY

This horn bound with gold was used to summon knights to the Castle of Maidens, the one of evil customs. Possibly the horn had some magical or mystical quality, since it could be heard for two miles around. [Malory XIII, 15]

HOWELL (Hoel) OF BRITTANY (Little Britain)

Sometimes called King, sometimes called Duke, Hoel was Arthur's cousin and ally. Lady Hoel, his wife, was killed by the Giant of Saint Michael's Mount, Brittany, who in turn was slain by Arthur, Kay, and Bedivere.

Hoel was the father both of the second wife of King Meliodas of Cornwall and of Isolt le Blanche Mains. Tristram's stepmother became his sister-in-law! Hoel's son was Sir Kehydius, who became enamoured of La Beale Isolt. [Malory V, 5; VIII, 2; etc.]

HOEL'S FAMILY
Cousin: Arthur
Son: Kehydius
Daughters: King Meliodas' second wife (Tristram's stepmother), Isoud la Blanche Mains
Sons-in-law: King Meliodas, Tristram

HUE OF THE RED CASTLE

Hue and his brother, Sir Edward of the Red Castle, extorted a barony from the Lady of the Rock. Sir Marhaus defeated them, killed Edward, and sent Hue to Arthur's court. [Malory IV, 26-27] Malory seems to say nothing more about Hue, but if he followed the usual pattern he probably reformed and became a companion of the Round Table.

HUNDRED KNIGHTS, KING OF (with) THE (Barant, Berrant le Apres)

One of the rebel kings at the beginning of Arthur's reign, he was a "passing good man and young." Malory gives his name once as Berrant le Apres and once as Barant le Apres (the alternate spellings may be the result of editor's work), but he is far more commonly known as "The King of [or, with] the Hundred Knights." He pledged 4,000 mounted men of arms to the rebellion. Two nights before the battle of Bedegraine, this monarch

> met a wonder dream ... that there blew a great wind, and blew down their castles and their towns, and after that came a water and bare it all away. All that heard of the sweven [dream] said it was a token of great battle.

He acquitted himself well in the battle and did not join Lot's later rebellion, going over to Arthur's side instead and becoming a member of the Round Table. [Malory I, 8-17; X, 60; XIX, 11]

Vulgate II gives his country, or perhaps his city, as Malahaut, suggesting the Lady of Malohaut may have been his vice-regent or vassal. He had a son named Marant and a daughter named Landoine, and was an ally of Duke Galeholt, one of the two allies Galeholt loved and trusted most. [Vulgate III] He seems to be one of the more important minor characters.

Pondering on his title and on the fact that he must have had many more than a hundred knights at his command, I wonder if this monarch might not have kept a table something like Arthur's, perhaps even round, which seated a hundred. Since Arthur had got the Round Table from King Leodegrance, who had got it from Uther Pendragon, the King of the Hundred Knights would have had Uther's or Leodegrance's example for such a table.

HUNTRESS OF WINDSOR

This unnamed lady lived in Windsor Forest, hunted daily with women only, and one day accidentally shot Lancelot in the buttock with an arrow as he lay beside a well near Brasias' hermitage [Malory XVIII, 21].

Curiously, in the Vulgate it is a male hunter who shoots Lancelot by mistake.

HUON†

I do not recall meeting Huon de Bordeaux, alias Huon of the Horn, in Arthurian literature—unless he can be identified with the Knight of the Horn whom Chrétien de Troyes lists among Arthur's good knights [**Erec & Enide**, ll. 1691-1750].

"IBLIS"†

One night Gaheris came to four pavilions. He helped himself to food in the first and in the fourth lay down in bed with a sleeping lady, not noticing that her husband was also asleep in the same bed. In the middle of the night the husband awoke, found Gaheris, and dragged the lady out of bed by her hair. Gaheris woke, saw him mistreating the lady, and cleft him to the shoulders with no further questions, to the lady's additional grief. In the morning, Gaheris insisted she go with him, even extracting a promise from her that she would never love any other knight after him. Her four brothers tried to rescue her and Gaheris defeated them, leaving one seriously wounded in the charge of a physician who promised to heal him in eight weeks. Gaheris and the lady spent the night in a convent of white nuns. Here she craftily took the veil, thus escaping from Gaheris without breaking her word. She afterward did much for the convent, and led a saintly life. [Vulgate V]

I borrowed the name "Iblis" for this lady from that of Lanzelet's wife according to the German **Lanzelet** of Ulrich von Zatzikhoven (about which work I know nothing further). It seemed a not unfitting name in that the lady of the Vulgate is a cousin-german of Lancelot, Bors, and Lionel. After the initial appearance of this volume and of my novel **Idylls of the Queen**, a learned friend informed me that Iblis is the name of a demon or devil in Islamic lore. Since this does not alter the Ulrich von Zatzikhoven evidence before me, I have decided at this time to leave the name as is in my own work.

IDER

Malory mentions this knight at the beginning of the war against the Emperor Lucius, calling him Ywaine's son. A few chapters earlier, Ywaine himself appears quite young. This indicates either that Malory did not arrange his material in strict chronology or that Ider was the son of some other Ywaine, not Ywain son of Uriens and Morgan. Malory seems not to mention Ider again, unless he is identical with "Sir Idrus the good knight", who seems likewise to be mentioned but once. Ider and Idrus were on Arthur's side, but I find no firm evidence that he or they were members of the Round Table. [Malory V, 2, 6; cf IV, 19]

KING IDRES OF CORNWALL

One of the rebel kings at the beginning of Arthur's reign. When the Saracens attacked Wandesborow Castle, forcing the rebel kings to suspend their war against Arthur, King Idres with four thousand men of arms was put into the city of Nauntes in Britain "to watch both the water and the land." [Malory 1, 12, 14, 15, 18]

Igerne—see **IGRAINE**

IGNAURES†

This knight was a popular lover, and fought in the Noauz tournament. His shield was half green and half azure, with a leopard on the green side. D.D.R. Owen tells us that Ignaures and his amorous activities formed the subject of an anonymous lay. [Chrétien de Troyes, **Lancelot**, ll. 5783-5823 & note to l. 5808] Looking at the letters in his name and tentatively sounding them out, I cannot help but wonder if some of Ignaures' exploits could have gone into Gawaine's later reputation.

IGRAINE (Igerne, Ygerne, Ygraine, etc.), DUCHESS OF TINTAGIL and later QUEEN OF ENGLAND

Arthur's mother, she "was called a fair lady, and a passing wise." The first part of her story is basic: how she repulsed Uther Pendragon's advances, telling her husband Duke Gorloïs, "I suppose that we were sent for that I should be dishonoured; wherefore, husband, I counsel you, that we depart from hence suddenly, that we may ride all night unto our own castle."; how on the night of her husband's death at Castle Terrabill Merlin introduced Uther into her bed at Tintagil disguised as the Duke, how that night Arthur was engendered, and how afterward Uther married Igraine, urged thereto by Sir Ulfius and others as well as by his own desire. Uther did not tell her who had lain with her on the night of her husband's death, however, until half a year after the marriage, when at last, as she waxed larger,

> he asked her, by the faith she owed to him, whose was the child within her body, then [was] she sore abashed to give answer. Dismay you not said the king, but tell me the truth, and I shall love you the better by the faith of my body.

After making her tell her story, he told her his. "Then the queen made great joy when she knew who was the father of her child." Malory does not record Igraine's sentiments when Uther took away her son to give him over to Merlin, nor is it clear from this account why Merlin demanded secrecy in the matter, when one might have expected that Uther's barons had wished him to marry precisely in order to produce an heir—although later interpretations have made the spiriting away of the child seem a political necessity.

Igraine's children by Duke Gorloïs were Morgawse, Elaine, and Morgan le Fay; the first two daughters were married to King Lot and King Nentres respectively, and the last put into a nunnery at the time of Igraine's marriage to Uther.

What seems often overlooked is that Igraine was still around during at least the first part of Arthur's reign. After Uther's death she would presumably have been Queen Dowager, and later she would have been recognized as Queen Mother, though Merlin appears to have arranged a sort of practical joke in bringing about this recognition. Arthur had Merlin send for Igraine so that he could talk to her himself and learn the truth of his birth.

> In all haste, the queen was sent for, and she came and brought with her Morgan le Fay her daughter, that was as fair a lady as any might be, and the king welcomed Igraine in the best manner.

But Sir Ulfius came in and appeached Igraine of treason,

> For an she would have uttered it in the life of King Uther Pendragon of the birth of you ... ye had never had the mortal wars that ye have had; for the most part of your barons ... knew never whose son ye were ... and she that bare you of her body should have made it known openly in excusing of her worship and yours, and in like wise to all the realm, wherefore I prove her false to God and to you and to all your realm, and who will say the contrary I will prove it on his body.

> Then spake Igraine and said, I am a woman and I may not fight, but rather than I should be dishonoured, there would some good man take my quarrel. More, she said, Merlin knoweth well, and ye Sir Ulfius, how King Uther came to me in the Castle of Tintagil in the likeness of my lord, that was dead three hours to-fore, and ... after the thirteenth day King Uther wedded me, and by his commandment when the child was born it was delivered unto Merlin and nourished by him, and so I saw the child never after nor wit not what is his name, for I knew him never yet. And there, Ulfius said to the queen, Merlin is more to blame than ye. Well I wot, said the queen, I bare a child ... but I wot not where he is become. Then Merlin took the king by the hand, saying, This is your mother. And therewith Sir Ector bare witness how he nourished him by Uther's commandment. And therewith King Arthur took his mother, Queen Igraine, in his arms and kissed her, and either wept upon other. And then the king let make a feast that lasted eight days.

Nothing more was said about trial by combat or treason; Ulfius' accusation seems to have been staged to make the revelation more dramatic. [Malory I, 1-33, 21]

What happened to Igraine after that? Centuries before Malory, Chrétien de Troyes had provided an answer I find pleasant to recap. After the burial of Uther Pendragon, Arthur's mother Ygerne (Igraine) came with all her stock of treasure to the Rock of Canguin (somewhere near the Galloway border), where she had a fine and beautiful castle built. Igraine's daughter—unnamed by Chrétien, but Lot's widow and Gawaine's mother, which would make her Margawse according to later chroniclers—joined Igraine at Canguin, and there gave birth to Igraine's granddaughter, Clarissant. Orphaned young ladies and widowed old ladies unjustly deprived of their lands joined the two queens and young princess in Canguin. They also had five hundred squires in the palace: a hundred old and white-haired, a hundred graying middle-agers, a hundred younger ones who shaved weekly, a hundred whose beards had just begun to grow, and a hundred still too young for facial hair; all, it seems, were good archers in addition to their other martial training, but they awaited a lord to knight them. This lord must needs be sufficiently perfect to survive the ordeal of the Wondrous Bed: no knight tainted with cowardice, flattery, avarice, or any other sin could survive an hour inside the palace. Eventually, Igraine's illustrious grandson Gawaine arrived, unrecognized and unrecognizing, to survive the Wondrous Bed and be greeted as Canguin's long-awaited lord; but Chrétien did not live to complete the tale. By the time of Gawaine's arrival, the outside world had considered Igraine dead for at least sixty years, her daughter for more than twenty. This and other details suggest the possibility that the Rock of Canguin forms part of the eschatological Otherworld.

[**Perceval**, ll. ca. 7230 to end; Ygerne & her daughter identified ll. 8730-8760]

IGRAINE'S CLERK†

A wise man, learned in astronomy, he embellished the Rock of Canguin with the Wondrous Bed and other marvels [Chrétien de Troyes, **Perceval**, ca. ll. 7545-7551]. Readers absolutely determined to find Merlin in Chrétien's pages might conceivably identify him with this clerk. I think it would be a stretch, but certainly Merlin owed Igraine something for what he had put her through.

IGRAINE'S SQUIRE†

Queen Igraine, of course, has half a thousand squires in her palace at the Rock of Canguin. Gawaine singles out one who strikes him as seeming especially brave and intelligent, reveals his identity to this lad, and sends him to Arthur's court at Orkney with news of Gawaine's present whereabouts and his arrangement to fight Guiromelant in a week. This message the squire is to deliver privately to both Arthur and Guenevere. The lad assures Gawaine he has access to a fine hunter (the suitable kind of horse for a messenger), as well as everything else he needs. We watch him reach Arthur's court, but Chrétien laid down his pen before describing how he carried out his mission. [**Perceval**, ca. ll. 9077-end] I suspect that he should be identified with a squire noticed earlier in the same romance, among the crowd of castle maidens who follow Clarissant in to hail Gawaine for achieving the adventure of the Wondrous Bed. This youth is the only male among the ladies, and wears a cloak or mantle of scarlet wool lined with ermine and black sable; there seems little reason for such a detailed description of a character not slated to reappear and play a more important role. [Ibid., ca. ll. 7911-7917]

IRELAND

Ireland has special importance in the saga of Tristram, and Malory speaks of it, along with Brittany and the Out Isles, as one of the major divisions of Britain. King Anguish of Ireland, La Beale Isoud, and Sir Marhaus are among the Irish characters of the romances. King Anguish long extracted tribute from King Mark of Cornwall.

IRELAND, SON OF THE KING OF†

A bold and valiant knight, he rode a spirited horse swifter than a stag and fought on the Pomelegloi side in the tournament of Noauz. As the first day of that tournament ended, he considered himself to have won the honors; the point was not, however, universally conceded. On the second day, he was unhorsed with some damage by Lancelot, whose weapon pinned his shield and arm to his side. [Chrétien de Troyes, **Lancelot**, ll. 5642-5985]

IRONSIDE (The Red Knight of the Red Launds)

This is the knight who was besieging Lyonors in Castle Dangerous when Lynette came to Arthur's court for a champion and was given Gareth Beaumains. After defeating Ironside, Gareth sent him to Arthur. Ironside had hanged nearly forty armed knights by the neck from trees, perhaps the most shameful death that could be inflicted on a knight, but this was forgiven because he had done it to fulfill a promise to a lady, his former love. Her brother had been slain, either by Lancelot or by Gawaine as she thought, and she had made Ironside swear "to labour daily in arms unto [sic] I met with one of them; and all that I might overcome I should put them unto a villainous death." The lady who exacted this promise seems never mentioned again, but Ironside became a knight of the Round Table. Malory mentions him at least twice more, as one of the guests at Guenevere's small dinner party and as one of ten knights to ride a-Maying with the Queen when Meliagrant ambushed her. He also appears among the would-be healers of Sir Urre.

While he besieged Castle Dangerous, Ironside's shield, arms, and harness were all blood red. This may create some confusion, but Ironside does not seem to have been related to the brothers Percard, Pertolepe, Perimones, and Persant, whom Gareth defeated on his way to Castle Perilous, even though Perimones also wore all red arms and armor.

Ironside's strength, like Gawaine's, increased daily until noon, until he had the strength of seven men [Malory VII, 2-18, 35; XVIII, 3; XIX, 1, 11].

In **Sir Gawaine and the Carl of Carlisle**, Ironside is called the father of Sir Raynbrown, "the knight with the green shield", by the fair damsel of Blanche Land. He was armed both in the winter and the hot summer, in constant combat with giants, and his horse was named Sorrel-Hand.

Iseult—see **ISOUD**

ISLE ESTRANGE† (Estrangor, Lo Leu Estrange)

This is the kingdom and/or castle of King Vagor. The castle was strong, with but one narrow entrance. The name suggests an island or perhaps a valley. The place is probably small, and may be near the "Forest of the Boiling Well." I believe it is probably close to Carteloise Forest in southern Scotland.

ISLE OF MAIDENS

See under King of the Isle of Maidens (below), and also under the Captive Damsels of Pesme Avanture. I can find no further hints in Chrétien's romance **Yvain** as to the whereabouts and culture of this island kingdom itself.

ISLE OF MAIDENS, KING OF THE†

This young monarch was only eighteen when he went out seeking adventures and came to Pesme Avanture. His experience there does not exactly cover him with glory—he looks like a feckless coward who cares more for his own skin than for his people's welfare—but at least the charge of malice is never laid against him. See the various personages listed under Pesme Avanture.

ISLE PERDUE†

A retreat of Duke Galeholt's, this castle was thickly surrounded by woods and located on an island [Vulgate III]. Probably it was in or near Galeholt's favorite country, Surluse.

Do not confuse this Isle Perdue with those described with the entry for the castle of Meliot.

ISLES, THE

Pellinore has not forgotten his kingdom in Malory, as he has in the musical **Camelot**. He is King Pellinore of the Isles. Since two of his sons are Percivale and Lamerake of Wales (or, de Galis), his Isles could be in or near Wales. Anglesey and Holyhead Islands off the coast of northern Wales would answer this description.

Study of the works of Chrétien de Troyes gives an alternative interpretation. In notes to line 419 of **Perceval**, both D.D.R. Owen and Ruth Cline identify the Isles of the Sea (Owen's translation), a.k.a. the islands of the sea (Cline's), as the Hebrides, Cline citing the authority of Hilka. In the passage including line 419, Percivale's mother tells him that his father's name (which Chrétien does not reveal) was known throughout the Isles of the Sea; again, in and around line 4093, Gawaine remarks that he has never known or heard of any knight from all the islands of the sea whose feats could rank with Percivale's. Apparently the same islands are meant in both passages. The context of these references, coupled with the surprising number of characters Chrétien includes, especially in **Perceval**, surnamed "of the Isles", causes me to wonder whether the islands in question could conceivably be the British Isles themselves.

ISOUD, LA BEALE (Iseult, Isolt, Ysolde, etc.)

The daughter of King Anguish of Ireland and the niece, on her mother's side, of Sir Marhaus, La Beale Isoud was already "a noble surgeon" when Tristram came to Ireland, disguised under the name Tramtrist, to seek a cure for the wound Marhaus had given him with a venomed spear. Isoud healed Tristram, who fell in love with her during the process and taught her to play the harp, "and she began to have a great fantasy unto him." About this time Palomides also visited Ireland and began to court Isoud. She sponsored Tristram in a tournament against Palomides—curiously, the winner of the tournament was to receive the Lady of the Launds in marriage, but Tristram clearly declined the prize, contenting himself, as the winner, with forbidding Palomides to wear armor for a year. Chased from Ireland by the anger of Isoud's mother, who finally realized he was Marhaus' killer, Tristram had a rivalry with King Mark for the love of Sir Segwarides' wife, but this affair ended by the time Mark sent his nephew back to Ireland to fetch Isoud to be the king's wife. (Mark had heard of her beauty and goodness from Tristram himself, but Mark's true purpose in sending for her was to get Tristram slain on the mission.)

On his way, Tristram had the fortune to represent King Anguish in a trial by combat, which made Tristram welcome again at the Irish monarch's court despite the death of Marhaus. Isoud's mother gave the princess' favorite handwoman, Bragwaine, a love potion meant for Isoud and Mark to drink on their marriage night, but on the ship Tristram and Isoud happened to find it and drink it under the impression it was innocent wine, thus cementing a love which had already been burgeoning. On the way back to Cornwall they halted at Castle Pluere where, in defense of Isoud and himself, Tristram killed Sir Breunor and his lady and ended their evil customs; Breunor's son Duke Galeholt came to avenge his father, with the King of the Hundred Knights for his ally, but after a fight both became Tristram's friends.

Isoud married King Mark as arranged, but if by that time she had not already consummated her love for Tristram, she must have wasted little time in proceeding to do so. Some little while later, Tristram met Sir Lamorak when the latter was weary with jousting down thirty knights.

Lamorak, feeling slighted because Tristram refused to give him a good fight under such unequal circumstances, waylaid a knight who was taking Morgan le Fay's magical drinking horn, designed to test the loyalty of wives, to Arthur's court, and made him take it to Mark's court instead. See Morgan's Drinking Horn.

Thus Mark learned that Isoud, along with 96 out of 100 other court dames, was an unfaithful wife, and would have burned them all had not his barons sensibly opposed the mass execution and saved their ladies. Tristram's cousin Andred, however, played the spy until he caught Tristram with Isoud. Tristram was taken bound to "a chapel that stood on the sea rocks" and there condemned to death, but he broke his bonds, fought off his captors, and at last jumped down and fell upon the crags.

Isoud, meanwhile, was sent to a "lazar-cote", or house of lepers. Gouvernail, Sir Lambegus, and Sir Sentraille de Lushon pulled Tristram from the rocks, he rescued Isoud, and they spent a loving interlude in a fair manor in the forest until Mark learned where they were, came one day when Tristram was out, and fetched Isoud home again. She sent her lover a message, by way of a cousin of Bragwaine's, that he should seek help in healing his latest wound—an arrow wound in the shoulder, given him by a man whose brother he had killed—from Isoud la Blanche Mains, Howell's daughter. Traveling to Brittany, Tristram not only gave Howell some welcome help in Howell's war against Earl Grip, but also fell in love with and married his new surgeon; conscience-smitten on the marriage night, however, he refrained from taking her maidenhead, and she was too innocent and untaught in the ways of love to recognize the omission.

Lancelot, learning of Tristram's marriage, denounced him as untrue to his first lady, while La Beale Isoud sent a letter of complaint to Guenevere, who returned her a letter of comfort. La Beale Isoud then sent Bragwaine to Brittany with letters in which she begged Tristram to return, bringing his wife, "and they should be kept as well as she herself." Tristram at once headed back for Cornwall, bringing his brother-in-law Sir Kehydius, along with Bragwaine and Gouvernail, but leaving La Blanche Mains in Brittany. After various valorous adventures, the party arrived at Mark's court, where the affair gained a new dimension when Kehydius fell in love with La Beale Isoud and began writing her poems and letters. Though not returning his love, she pitied him and tried to comfort him in another letter, which Tristram found and misinterpreted. In the rage of accusations that followed, Isoud was driven into a swoon, while Kehydius jumped from an upper window to escape Tristram's sword and landed, much to Mark's astonishment, in the middle of Mark's game of chess. Fearing repercussions, Tristram fled to the forest, where he brooded until he went mad, so that even Palomides, who had all this while been his rival for the love of La Beale Isoud, pitied him.

With an eye to Tristram's lands, Andred fomented a rumor that Tristram was dead. This drove La Beale Isoud almost mad, so that she propped a sword up breast-high in a plum tree in her garden and tried to run against it. The attempt was stopped by Mark, who "bare her away with him into a tower; and there he made her to be kept, and watched her surely, and after that she lay long sick, nigh at the point of death." Mark now found but did not recognize Tristram, who was naked and wild but had recently slain the giant Tauleas. Admiring this deed, Mark had the naked madman carried to his castle, where eventually La Beale Isoud and Bragwaine recognized him by means of their pet brachet, the gift of King Faramon's daughter to Tristram. Isoud's love restored Tristram to his wits. Unfortunately, Mark and Andred recognized Tristram the same way, and Mark would have sentenced him to death but, on the insistence of his barons, banished him from Cornwall for ten years instead.

Isoud sent Bragwaine after Tristram with letters. After a long search, Bragwaine found Tristram and attended the tournament at the Castle of Maidens with him, expecting to return from there with his answering letters to his lady. Tristram, Palomides, and Dinadan left the tournament early and privately, however, Tristram with a wound from a joust with Lancelot. This left Lancelot, nine other knights, and Bragwaine to search for Tristram, while Isoud learned how well her lover had done at the tournament from Gaheris and others of Arthur's knights who visited Cornwall and who got into a free-for-all of battle and treachery with Mark and Andred. Meanwhile Tristram, Palomides, and Dinadan fell into the hands of one Sir Darras, who threw them into his prison because Tristram had killed three of his sons in the tournament. Eventually Bragwaine headed back for Cornwall, and Sir Darras repented when Tristram fell deathly sick and released his captives. Tristram and Palomides began appointing days to do battle with each other, one or the other of them consistently missing the appointment due to wounds or imprisonment.

After various adventures, Lancelot brought Tristram to Arthur's court, where he was welcomed into the company of the Round Table. Both Mark and La Beale Isoud had their spies to report on Tristram's fame, he for hate and she for love and pride in her paramour. Finally Mark took Sirs Amant and Bersules and went disguised into Logres with intent to slay Tristram. Amant and Bersules revolted and ended up dead, while Mark only got into plenty of trouble, but finally Arthur made truce between Mark and Tristram and they returned to Cornwall together. Arthur, Lancelot, and Guenevere kept up a correspondence with Tristram and Isoud, Lancelot warning them to beware of Mark; the damsel who carried the letters was also in Mark's confidence and shared them with him, causing him to return letters of such a nature as to call down a satiric lay of Dinadan's upon his head.

Tristram saved Mark from a Saxon invasion led by Elias. For thanks, when Mark learned of a plot afoot to slay Lancelot at the Surluse tournament, the Cornish king planned to send Tristram in disguise, hoping he would be mistaken for Lancelot. Tristram was badly hurt and Mark, pretending great love, spirited him away secretly to prison. Isoud appealed to Sir Sadok to learn where Tristram was; the upshot of this move was that Sadok, joined by Mark's former seneschal Sir Dinas, raised the country of Lyonesee for war with Mark, while Percivale came and made Mark free Tristram and promise his safety. Mark forged letters to make it appear that the Pope was ordering him to go on crusade, and thus, arguing "this is a fairer war than thus to arise the people against your king", tricked Dinas and Sadok into disbanding their rebellion. Mark then threw Tristram back into prison.

Now Tristram sent La Beale Isoud a letter requesting her to ready a ship for their escape. She reacted promptly and capably, preparing the ship and enlisting Dinas and Sadok to put Mark himself into prison until she and Tristram were safely in England. Lancelot gave them a home in Joyous Garde. Here "they made great joy daily together with all manner of mirths that they could devise, and every day Sir Tristram would go ride a-hunting", but even here Isoud prudently insisted he ride armed, in case of "perilous knights" or further efforts on Mark's part. Malory records other episodes, such as how Tristram and Isoud left Joyous Garde for a time to attend the tournament at Lonazep. The pair remained in Joyous Garde and Isoud continued in at least occasional correspondence with Guenevere, during the period when Guenevere's jealousy of Elaine of Carbonek drove Lancelot to madness.

Lancelot being found, Tristram proposed they go to court to help celebrate. Isoud's answer seems to be a model of lady's love for knight. She would not go herself, "for through me ye be marked of many good knights, and that caused you to have much more labour for my sake than needeth you", but she insisted he go, to prevent the accusation that she was keeping him in idle dalliance to the rusting of his honor. (Compare with the tale of Enid.) She also sent four knights with him, but within a half mile he sent them back. On this journey he met Palomides and they finally had their battle, ending in their reconciliation and Palomides' baptism. The feast they attended at Camelot saw the beginning of the Grail Quest, but Tristram returned to Joyous Garde and Isoud rather than seek the holy vessel.

Here Malory, or his early editor, simply drops the tale of Tristram and Isoud, remarking, "Here endeth the second book of Sir Tristram that was drawn out of French into English. But here is no rehersal of the third book." Much later, Malory remarks that Mark finally slew Tristram as he sat harping before Isoud, but does not go into further particulars, not even to tell us where it happened. Presumably Isoud did not long survive Tristram.

La Beale Isoud was not without a sense of humor; once she invited Dinadan into Joyous Garde and chid him gently for his stand against love. At his quipping refusal to fight against three knights for her, despite her beauty, "Isoud laughed, and had good game at him", not neglecting hospitality, however. Bleoberis and Ector de Maris once described Isoud to Guenevere in the following terms:

> [S]he is peerless of all ladies; for to speak of her beauty, bounte, and mirth, and of her goodness, we saw never her match as far as we have ridden and gone. O mercy Jesu, said Queen Guenever, so saith all the people that have seen her and spoken with her. God would that I had part of her conditions ....

It is worth remarking that these two women, who would seem to have had every cause for jealousy of each other except a man, never displayed such jealousy, but remained friends and admirers of one another. [Malory VIII-XII; XIX, 11]

I have recapped Malory's version of Isoud's story at length because the books of Tristram are notoriously the most rambling portion of **Le Morte d'Arthur**, capable of bogging down the most interested reader, and the thread of narrative often becomes difficult to follow. I have found no other early version so conscientiously dovetailing Tristram's story with Arthur's.

LA BEALE ISOUD'S FAMILY AND RELATIONS
Father: King Anguish (Agwisance) of Ireland
Husband: King Mark
Lover: Tristram
Uncle (maternal): Marhaus
Gentlewoman: Bragwaine
Mentor: Brother Ogrins

ISOUD LA BLANCHE MAINS (Iseult, Isolt, Yseult, etc., of the White Hands)

She was the daughter—apparently the younger daughter—of Howell of Brittany, presumably by that wife who was so brutally slain by the Giant of Saint Michael's Mount, which would have cast a tragic shadow on her childhood and on that of her brother Kehydius.

As La Beale Isoud had cured Tristram of the wound of Marhaus' envenomed spear, so Isoud of the White Hands met him when

Bragwaine and Gouvernail had him conveyed to Brittany expressly so that she, also a good surgeon, could heal him of the wound of a poisonous arrow. Tristram became infatuated with his newest nurse and married her as much, it appears, because her name was the same as that of his real love as for any other reason. It was a virginal marriage.

> And so when they were abed both Sir Tristram remembered him of his old lady La Beale Isoud. And then he took such a thought suddenly that he was all dismayed, and other cheer made he none but with clipping [hugging] and kissing; as for other fleshly lusts Sir Tristram never thought nor had ado with her ... the lady weened there had been no pleasure but kissing and clipping.

La Blanche Mains sailed with Tristram on at least one occasion, when their barget was blown ashore on the coast of Wales, where La Beale Isoud learned of Tristram's marriage and invited both him and his wife to Cornwall. Tristram left La Blanche Mains behind. Apparently he never saw her again. In Cornwall, he spoke of his denying his wife her conjugal rights as a praiseworthy deed:

> But as for thee, Sir Kehydius ... I wedded thy sister Isoud la Blanche Mains for the goodness she did unto me. And yet, as I am true knight, she is a clean maiden for me ....

Malory is silent on the later life of Isoud La Blanche Mains of Brittany. Robinson gives a sympathetic picture of her in his **Tristram**. [Malory VIII, 35-38; IX 10, 17]

JAGENT

Malory mentions "a great tournament … beside Camelot, at the Castle of Jagent" [X, 8].

JOHN†

A serf of Cligés and a notably skilled craftsman, John built to his master's order a marvelous tower in which to secrete Fenice after her feigned death. John did this on his master's promise to set him, his wife, and their children free forevermore; later, apparently while still waiting for Cligés to keep his promise, the serf showed the courage of a knight and the arguing power of a lawyer when facing Emperor Alis, who threatened him with death and torture if he did not reveal where Cligés and Fenice had fled after being discovered. Following Alis' death, the trustworthy John was in the party that came from Greece to Britain to hail Cligés as the new emperor of Greece and Constantinople. Presumably Cligés rewarded his former serf richly.

Either Chrétien de Troyes intentionally painted John as a most remarkable serf, or else John's case might make us re-examine the supposedly servile role and potential of "underlings" in Arthurian romance. [**Cligés**, ll. 5370ff.]

JOSEPH OF ARIMATHEA and JOSEPHE

Joseph of Arimathea was the disciple of Jesus. Josephe was Joseph's son, first bishop of Britain, miraculously consecrated by Christ Himself. According to a tradition which I encountered orally and not in connection with the Arthurian cycle, Joseph first visited Britain with Jesus during the latter's hidden years before His public preaching; they came ashore in Cornwall. After Christ's resurrection, Joseph and Josephe converted Nascien and Mordrains and their families and returned to Britain, bringing Christianity, the Holy Grail, the flowering thorn which Joseph planted at Glastonbury, and a number of followers, as described in detail in Volume I, **Lestoire del Saint Graal**, of the Vulgate.

Unlike Nascien and Mordrains, Joseph and Josephe did not miraculously survive into Arthur's times. Either Joseph or Josephe did, however, return to Carbonek Castle to celebrate the climactic mysteries of the Grail at a Mass attended by Galahad and his companions. Galahad himself is called a direct descendant of Joseph; since both Pellam and Lancelot were descended from Joseph's convert Nascien, the relation would seem either to be spiritual, like that of a godparent and godchild, or to have come through intermarriage between Nascien's male and Joseph's female descendants. Josephe's cousin (Joseph's nephew?) Lucans first was appointed guardian of the ark containing the Grail, before Josephe reassigned the keepership of the holy vessel to Nascien's descendant Alain (or Helias) le Gros. Joseph's younger son Galaad, born after the arrival in Britain, becomes the direct ancestor of King Uriens.

Malory, or his editors, seem to know nothing of Josephe, ascribing some of his deeds (such as marking the Adventurous Shield) to Joseph [Malory II, 16; IX, 2; XIII, 3, 11; XVII, 18-20, 22].

"JOY, GARDEN OF THE" (Joy of the Court)†

One of Enide's cousins, falling in love with King Evrain's nephew Mabonagrain, returned with him to Evrain's castle Brandigant, where she made him swear to stay with her in the garden where he was knighted and never to leave until some other knight could here defeat him in honest combat. Mabonagrain conscientiously defeated and decapitated every oncomer, placing their heads on sharpened stakes all around the garden. I suppose this final touch must have been to prove his good faith, to discourage champions from intruding upon his love retreat, or both. Aside from the macabre note lent it by all these staked heads, the garden sounds admirably suited for a hideaway: magically enclosed by nothing but air, it was filled with every kind of fruit, herb, and bird known to humanity, all growing, bearing, or singing the whole year round.

Presumably none of the defeated knights had been told how the adventure called the Joy of the Court came to be, for Erec had to defeat (though not to behead) Mabonagrain in order to learn why they had fought. Nor was any knight compelled to undertake it: on the contrary, the whole castle-town tried to discourage them. Nor—most surprising of all?—did anyone seem to blame either Mabonagrain's lady or Mabonagrain himself for causing all the earlier knights' deaths.

Chrétien explains that the adventure was called the Joy of the Court in anticipation of the joy the court would experience if and when it were finally won (i.e., with Mabonagrain's defeat). D.D.R. Owen points out that very likely there was also a play on the French words for "court" and "horn", seeing that, after defeating Mabonagrain, Erec was obliged to round his victory off by blowing a horn that hung in the garden. The whole episode seems otherworldly in origin. It may also make a twentieth-century American think of the archetypal Fastest Gun in the West and all his eager challengers. [Chrétien de Troyes, **Erec & Enide**, ll. 5367-6410 & Owen's notes] (See also Mabonagrain, Mabonagrain's Lady, Evrain, and Brandigant.)

JOYOUS (Dolorous) GARDE, LA

This stronghold was La Dolorous Garde when Lancelot captured it, became La Joyous Garde while he held it, and turned once more into La

Dolorous Garde after his banishment from England.

Vulgate III gives a more complete account than does Malory of Lancelot's actual capture of the castle. The graveyard was full of graves or purported graves of knights who had died or reputedly died fighting the castle's champions. Among the tombstones was a large slab of metal, bedecked with gems, on which was written: "Only he who conquers La Doloreuse Garde will be able to lift this slab, and he will find his name beneath it." When Lancelot lifted the slab, he read: "Here will repose Lancelot of the Lake, the son of King Ban." Thus Lancelot, who had been appropriated in infancy by the French Lady of the Lake, learned his parentage for the first time.

La Dolorous Garde also had a chapel with a door leading to a cave. As Lancelot entered the cave, the earth quaked and a dreadful noise filled the air. Two copper knights holding huge swords struck at him as he entered the next chamber. Here he found a deep and evil-smelling well from which ghastly noise rose, and beyond it an ugly monster guarding the way with an axe. Lancelot had to break his shield upon the monster, strangle it, and push it into the well. At last a damsel of copper became visible, holding the keys of the enchantments, one large and one small. With the large key Lancelot opened a copper pillar. Terrible noises issued from thirty copper tubes. With the small key Lancelot opened a small coffer, out of which rose a whirlwind. Then at last the enchantments were broken. The obstacles vanished, as did the tombs in the churchyard and the helmets on the wall of knights previously vanquished; Dolorous Garde became Joyous Garde.

Malory tells us that Joyous Garde had at least three gates [XX, 12], that Tristram and La Beale Isoud spent some time here as Lancelot's guests [X, 52], and that the procession bearing Lancelot's body from Glastonbury reached Joyous Garde within fifteen days [XXI, 12]. He further records, "Some men say it was Alnwick, and some men say it was Bamborough." [XXI, 12]

Glennie identifies Bamborough with Castle Orgulous and prefers Aberwick, or Berwick on Tweed, for Joyous Garde. I like his placement of Castle Orgulous, but when Malory is more or less definite, as in the case of Joyous Garde, that outweighs Glennie. Therefore I put Joyous Garde at Alnwick, saving Benwick for another site, perhaps the city of Windesan.

Joyous Isle—see **BLIANT, CASTLE OF**

Kabbaranturs—see **CARBARECOTINS, KING OF CORNOAILLE**

Kadin—see **KANAHINS**

KAHEDIN†

In the questing fever which the Loathly Damsel set off at Arthur's court, a knight called Kahedin promised to go straight, without stopping for a rest, to Mount Dolorous and climb it [Chrétien de Troyes, **Perceval**, ca. ll. 4724-4726].

The situation seems to mark him as one of Arthur's knights; the way his name is dropped in without prelude or follow-up seems to mark him as a knight fairly well known to Chrétien's target audience. An identification with Malory's Sir Kehydius might be possible, but the evidence before me is too scanty to make it more than a guess.

KAINUS LE STRANGE (Kay de Stranges, Kay the Stranger)

A knight of the Round Table. Malory mentions him appearing at the tournament of Lonazep (where he was jousted down by Palomides), as being among the would-be healers of Sir Urre, and as being among those killed during Lancelot's rescue of Guenevere from the stake [X, 79; XIX, 11; XX, 8]. He should not be confused with Arthur's foster-brother Kay.

KALEPH†

A castle in Norgales [Vulgate I].

KALET† (Baale, Cole, Karelet)

The castle of Lancelot's friend Count Dagins. Here Lancelot and his party passed the night after rescuing the Queen from the stake. [Vulgate VI, 283]

In Malory, Lancelot and the Queen were surprised together at Carlisle [XX, 22]. Presumably it was there, also, that the Queen was to be burnt, since she had a very hasty trial. The Vulgate version differs widely in important details, but my notes do not include evidence that the locale is changed. Thus, Kalet (not mentioned by Malory) would be within two day's ride of Carlisle in the direction of Joyous Garde, allowing perhaps the maximum time for escaping before stopping to rest. This precludes identification of Kalet with Kaleph, since Kaleph is in Norgales—surely too far, and in the wrong direction.

KANAHINS (Canains, Kadin)†

When Lancelot was preparing to depart from Britain in exile, he sent the squire Kanahins to Camelot with his shield so that it could be hung in St. Stephen's cathedral [Vulgate VI].

KARADIGAN†

Apparently the castle of Lyzianor, who bore Arthur a son. The exact words are, "*chastel de Karadigan que Lysianors la bele demoisele tenoit en sa bailie ou li rois Artus engendra Lohot.*" [Vulgate VII, 206]

KARADOS, KING OF ESTRANGOR†

Although apparently one of the rebels against Arthur, Karados had been a companion of the Round Table (during the time of Uther Pendragon?). He did not occupy his seat during the rebellion. [Vulgate II]

I am not sure whether or not he should be identified with either King Carados of Scotland, Sir Carados of the Dolorous Tower, or Cador of Cornwall, father of Constantine who became King after Arthur.

KARADUS THE SHORT-ARMED†

Among Arthur's knights in the list Chrétien de Troyes begins in line 1691 of **Erec & Enide**. Chrétien tells us that Karadus had a very cheerful disposition. He might be identified with Karados, but I do not like to press that possibility to the point of combining their entries.

Karelet—see **KALET**

KAY (Cai, Cei, Kai, Kex)

Arthur's foster-brother, Seneschal of England, knight of the Round Table, and my own personal favorite of all the male characters in the Arthurian cycle.

Whereas Gawaine's character underwent a degradation from the time of Chrétien to that of Malory, Kay's remained remarkably constant—perhaps because his surly, jaundiced attitude and freakish attempts at glory-grabbing provided so perfect a foil for the chivalric ideal. In some ways, one might opine that Kay serves the same dramatic function in Arthur's court that Loki serves, up to a point, in Asgard, the chief differences being that Kay's sharp-tongued sallies and occasional trickery (in Chrétien's **Lancelot** he puts on quite an elaborate act in order to be the first knight to try rescuing Guenevere from Meliagrant; there is his famous attempt to claim credit for drawing the sword from the stone) almost invariably win him either contemptuous retorts, or embarrassment and even bodily injury—and that Kay never goes bad, but remains loyal in his unpolished way, to Arthur to the end. (Ronan Coghlan's **Encyclopaedia of Arthurian Legends** mentions that in the **Perlesvaus** Kay joins a rebellion against Arthur, but this is surely an exceptional treatment and, from Coghlan's description, I gather that it reflects simply another reworking of the Sword in the Stone incident.)

Might Kay also have served somewhat the same function for medieval folk that Hallmark's Maxine character has served us late

20th-century Americans since her appearance in the 1980s: a sort of escape valve, a personage who openly lets out with all the grouchy and surly statements so many of us spend so much of our energy repressing?

Moreover, my studies leave me with the strong impression that seneschals often served as scapegoats for their liege lords: any adverse sentiment that the public feared to voice, perhaps even to think, against a ruler, they directed against the ruler's seneschal instead. Heaven forfend, of course, that we imagine the populace could ever have felt any grievance against so wonderful a king as Arthur! Nevertheless, if sensechals in general came to have a certain reputation, it might have rubbed off on even Arthur's officer. Whatever the reason, throughout most of the medieval romances I have examined, Kay can be depended upon to speak rudely, boast a lot, bully young hopefuls like Gareth, Percival, and La Cote Male Taile, and be unhorsed in usually every joust.

D.D.R. Owen surmises that Chrétien took Kay's personality from some lost source. All that seems certain, however, is that Chrétien gave us our earliest extant portrait of this cranky version of a hero who in presumably more ancient lore could breathe nine days and nights under water, or make himself as tall as the tallest tree. [**Erec & Enide**, Owen's note to l. 3959; & Lewis Spence, **Magic Arts**, p. 146] His stature was heroic in Geoffrey of Monmouth, Wace, and the old Welsh myths which spell his name Cai or Cei. Both his heroic and his churlish aspects appear in Malory.

On Merlin's instruction, Kay's father Sir Ector gave the infant Arthur to his wife for nourishing and put Kay out to a wetnurse; this indicates an age difference of no more than a few years in the boys. There is no evidence in Malory that either Kay or Arthur realized they were not born siblings; there are, however, indications of real brotherly affection between the two.

To help find the man who would prove himself King by pulling the marvelous sword from the stone and anvil, Merlin and the Archbishop of Canterbury called a great tournament in London on New Year's Day. Sir Ector brought Kay, who had been knighted on All Hallowmass two months before, and Arthur, who appears to have been serving as Kay's squire. On the way to the tournament, Kay discovered he had left his sword at the house where they were lodging and sent Arthur back to get it. When Arthur arrived,

> the lady and all were out to see the jousting. Then was Arthur wroth, and said to himself, I will ride to the churchyard, and take the sword with me that sticketh in the stone, for my brother Sir Kay shall not be without a sword this day. ... And as soon as Sir Kay saw the sword, he wist well it was the sword of the stone and so he rode to his father Sir Ector, and said: Sir, lo here is the sword of the stone, wherefore I must be king of this land.

Sir Ector saw through Kay's claim and insisted on taking both young men back to the churchyard (which had providentially been abandoned by the men who were supposed to have been guarding it) and repeating the experiment. Curiously, the closest thing to a rebuke Kay seems to have received was that Ector made him "swear upon a book how he came to that sword", after which he requested as his only favor from his foster-son, who was having some trauma accepting the situation, that Arthur make Kay his seneschal. Promising "that never man shall have that office but he, while he and I live", Arthur carried this out at his coronation.

The first serious threat of rebellion was made at Pentecost, and, on Merlin's advice, Arthur sent for Kings Ban and Bors as allies. At the feast celebrating their arrival, on All Hallowmass, Kay served in the hall, assisted by Sirs Lucan and Griflet—which seems to be noted as an honor for all parties. At the tournament following this feast Kay "did that day marvellous deeds of arms, that there was none did so well as he that day", but was finally unhorsed by one Sir Placidas, at which Griflet and other knights in Kay's party angrily avenged his fall. The kings awarded the prize of this tournament to Kay, Griflet, and Lucan. Kay proved his worth in practical warfare during the bloody battle of Bedegraine against the rebel kings, and again in the battle against Nero and King Lot before Castle Terrabil.

Kay's greatest moment of glory came during the invasion of the five kings of Denmark, Ireland, the Vale, Soleise, and the Isle of Longtains. While Arthur, his wife, and his army were camped by the Humber River, the enemy army surprised them with a night attack. Trying to get the Queen to safety, Arthur, Kay, Gawaine, and Griflet were trapped on the edge of the rough water.

> And as they stood so talking, Sir Kay saw the five kings coming on horseback by themselves alone, with their spears in their hands. ... Lo, said Sir Kay, yonder be the five kings; let us go to them and match them. That were folly, said Sir Gawaine, for we are but three [maybe Gawaine is not counting the King] and they be five. That is truth, said Sir Griflet. No force, said Sir Kay, I will undertake for two of them, and then may ye three undertake for the other three. And therewithal, Sir Kay let his horse run as fast as he might, and struck one of them through the shield and the body a fathom, that the king fell to the earth stark dead.

Inspired by this example, Gawaine, Arthur, and Griflet each struck down another of the five invaders.

> Anon Sir Kay ran unto the fifth king, and smote him so hard on the helm that the stroke clave the helm and the head to the earth. That was well stricken, said King Arthur, and worshipfully hast thou holden thy promise, therefore I shall honour thee while that I live ... [and] always Queen Guenever praised Sir Kay for his deeds, and said, What lady that ye love, and she love you not again she were greatly to blame; and

> among ladies, said the Queen, I shall bear your noble fame, for ye spake a great word, and fulfilled it worshipfully.

It was after this battle that Kay became a companion of the Round Table, on the advice of Pellinore, who pointed out,

> for many times he hath done full worshipfully, and now at your last battle he did full honourably for to undertake to slay two kings. By my head, said Arthur, he is best worth to be a knight of the Round Table of any that ye have rehearsed ....

When, on his way to fight Emperor Lucius on the Continent, Arthur stopped to exterminate the giant of Saint Michael's Mount, Brittany, Kay and Bedivere were the two companions he chose to take on the secret expedition. Having slain the giant, Arthur assigned Kay the task of cutting off the head and bearing it to Howell. In the battle with Lucius, Kay was among Arthur's personal bodyguard.

From about this point Malory's Kay slides downhill. He turns up among the knights rescued from Sir Turquine, and when Lancelot departs suddenly after vanquishing Turquine, Kay takes an oath with Lionel and Ector de Maris to find him again. Kay's next action on being released from prison may be typically stewardly: he sees to supper.

> [T]here came a forester with four horses laden with fat venison. Anon, Sir Kay said, Here is good meat for us for one meal, for we had not many a day no good repast.

In an often-retold incident, Kay, having become separated from Ector and Lionel, is set on by three knights at once beneath the window which happens to be of Lancelot's badchamber. Lancelot descends by a sheet, rescues Kay, and in the morning, before Kay is awake, leaves with Kay's horse and armor, whether accidentally or on purpose. Lancelot thus gets the chance to strike down several knights who mistake him for "the proud Kay; [who] weeneth no knight so good as he, and the contrary is ofttime proved." Lancelot's reputation, on the other hand, is already such that Kay, disguised perforce as Lancelot, makes it back to court without being challenged.

Kay's treatment of Gareth, whom he nicknamed Beaumains, is one of the most widely known and typical tales of the seneschal, though it is usually glossed over that, despite his bullying, Kay seems to have taken a certain pride in Beaumains. When Gareth displayed his strength in courtyard sports, "[t]hen would Sir Kay say, How liketh you my boy of the kitchen?" Kay's mockery of La Cote Male Taile and of Percivale is in similar vein, though neither of them came under his authority as Beaumains did, and for most of Percivale's story we must go outside Malory, to tales stemming from Chrétien's **Perceval**.

During the rambling adventures of Malory's books of Tristram, in which Kay occasionally appears, Tristram, meeting him by chance, pretty well sums up his reputation:

> [N]ow wit ye well that ye are named the shamefullest knight of your tongue that now is living; howbeit ye are called a good knight, but ye are called unfortunate, and passing overthwart of your tongue.

In fairness to Tristram, this is said in response to Kay's repetition of the old saw about no good knights ever coming out of Cornwall. On the other hand, some chapters later, when Kay finds Ywaine treacherously and gravely wounded by Mark, the seneschal makes sure of getting Ywaine safely to the Abbey of the Black Cross for healing.

Kay plays no part in the Grail Adventures except to remind Arthur, shortly before Galahad's arrival on Pentecost, of the King's old custom of never sitting down to dinner on the feast day until they have seen some adventure. Malory mentions him as one of the guests at Guenevere's small dinner (where Sir Patrise was poisoned), as the chief of three knights whom Arthur sends to bring in the barge bearing the body of Elaine of Astolat, as one of the small party of unarmed knights who ride a-Maying with Guenevere and are ambushed and kidnaped by Meliagrant, and as one of those who attempt to heal Sir Urre. This is the last we hear of Sir Kay in Malory's pages; perhaps he becomes confused with Sir Kainus le Strange, who is killed by Lancelot and his party during their rescue of Guenevere from the stake. [Malory I, 3, 5-17; II, 10; IV, 3-4; V, 5, 8; VI, 9, 11-12, 18; VII, 1-4; IX, 1-3, 15, 38; X, 6, 79; XI, 12; XIII, 2; XVIII, 3, 20; XIX, 1-9, 11]

The Vulgate fills in further details. Kay got his sharp tongue from his nurse, apparently the one who took charge of him when his own mother took over Arthur's nursing. On more than one occasion he bore Arthur's standard into battle. He was deeply devoted to Guevevere, although in a more platonic way (in practice if not in desire) than Lancelot. Rivalry arose between the two, as in the affairs of "the false Guenevere" Genievre and of Meliagrant, as to which should defend her in trial by combat. (Lancelot always won the honor.) Kay is said to have murdered Arthur's bastard son Borre in order to get credit for killing a giant Borre had exterminated; the Vulgate "Merlin" adds that this was the only treacherous deed Kay ever committed.

In the Vulgate version, Kay plays a more prominent part in the Meliagrant affair, beginning when he comes into court armed and announces he is leaving because his services are not appreciated. Arthur and Guenevere beg him to stay, which he does on condition he be allowed to defend the Queen against Meliagrant, who has offered to free the exiles in Gore's Terre Foraine in return for the chance to attempt Guenevere's capture (this differs from Malory's version, in which Meliagrant ambushes Guenevere's party a-Maying). Meliagrant defeats Kay and later accuses Kay in particular of sleeping with the Queen (in Malory, it is a general accusation against the ten wounded knights).

Kay met his death during Arthur and Gawaine's siege of Lancelot's city in France—the Emperor of Rome took advantage of Arthur's presence on the continent to invade Burgundy and advance on the British. In the resulting battle, Gawaine killed the Emperor's nephew; the Emperor, seeking revenge, mortally wounded Kay, whereon Arthur slew the Emperor.

According to Wace, Kay was given the title of Duke of Anjou. In **Sir Gawain and the Carl of Carlisle**, the Carl presents Kay with a blood-red horse swifter than any other the knight has ever seen. I do not remember ever finding a lady for Kay in the old romances; perhaps his courtly devotion to Guenevere precluded a more mundane relationship with another woman.

Despite Kay's reputation as braggart, when he comes back to court in Lancelot's armor, he frankly gives Lancelot all the credit for the conquests made by the knight in Kay's armor [Malory VI, 18]. In the Vulgate version of the episode, vol. V, near the end of the **Livre de Lancelot del Lac**, on top of incident after incident of frequently senseless and avoidable bloodshed committed by such "good" knights as Lancelot and Bors, Kay's statement that he has not overcome any knight since leaving court strikes me as not only honest, but downright commendable.

Perhaps the contrast between Kay's early prowess at arms and the frequent defeats of his middle and later years is explained by the performance of his duties as seneschal occupying too much of his time to allow him to keep in fighting trim. It is not hard, by reading between the lines, to see that he must have been conscientious and competent in his official capacity. As for his reputation as braggart and churl, I suspect that, just as later kings needed scapegoats for popular dislike of various mistakes and policies, so did Arthur. The seneschal, largely responsible for the practical, day-to-day functioning of the court, would have been a logical candidate for the role of scapegoat. If Arthur's bastard son Borre, or Lohot, is to be identified with Arthur's son Anir, or Amyr, of shadowy early legends, it is interesting that, while Borre's death is charged to Kay, Anir's is charged to Arthur himself.

I also theorize that Kay's mockery of and jousts with young hopefuls like Beaumains and Percivale may have been part of a program to weed out country lads who came to court with no qualifications for knighthood beyond their own aspirations; there may well have been a great many of these, especially after the easy knighting of Sir Tor, but only the tales of those who really were of noble birth and valorous worth have been preserved for us.

A popular device of old romancers was to contrast Kay's churlish behavior with Gawaine's courtesy, always, of course, to Gawaine's advantage. **The Knightly Tales of Sir Gawain**, with introductions and translations by Louis B. Hall, in addition to being a gold mine about Gawaine, has also a rich vein of information about Kay. It interests me that, whereas Gawaine's reputation seems still to be slipping, various modern treatments have been rehabilitating Kay. Of course, in order to do it, most of the ones I have seen discard Kay's medieval personality as thoroughly as most of the occasional modern versions that feature a heroic Gawaine (Hal Foster's being a notable exception) do so by discarding Gawaine's medieval personality.

Kay de Stranges—see **KAINUS LE STRANGE**

KAY OF ESTRAUS†

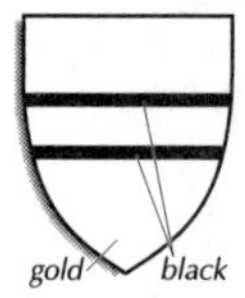

He is among Arthur's knights in the list Chrétien de Troyes begins in line 1691 of **Erec & Enide**. Chrétien mentions him again as fighting in the Noauz tournament, with a shield made in Toulouse but not otherwise described [**Lancelot**, ll. 5824-5842]. He should not be confused with Kay the seneschal; I think, however, that he might be identified with Kainus le Strange.

Kay the Stranger—see **KAINUS LE STRANGE**

KEHYDIUS

Howell's son and the brother of Isoud la Blanche Mains. Kehydius was with Tristram and La Blanche Mains when they blew ashore near the Isle of Servage and Tristram slew Sir Nabon le Noire. Kehydius later accompanied Tristram, Gouvernail, and Bragwaine back to Cornwall; this time they were blown ashore near Castle Perilous, North Wales, where Tristram took Kehydius into the forest with him for a few days of adventure, leaving Gouvernail with Bragwaine at the boat. Kehydius begged for and obtained first chance to joust with the first knight they encountered. He promptly got a fall and a severe wound—the knight was Lamorak, who proceeded to give Tristram himself a fall, though Tristram redeemed his honor with sword, and they ended by agreeing never to fight each other again.

When Tristram and his party finally got to Mark's court, Kehydius fell in love with La Beale Isoud and wrote love letters to her. She felt sorry for him and wrote a letter in return. Malory does not say what, exactly, was in her letter; but when Tristram found both sides of the correspondence, he misconstrued the situation, charged Isoud with falseness, and rounded on Kehydius with drawn sword. While Isoud swooned, Kehydius jumped out the window and landed in the middle of Mark's chess game, much to Mark's astonishment. Kehydius, thinking quickly, covered up by saying he had fallen asleep at the window and so tumbled out. This incident reads like domestic comedy; the outcome of the whole affair, however, was tragic for Kehydius, who at last died of his love, as her other unrequited lover, Palomides, remarks to Tristram later at Joyous Garde: "[W]ell I wot it shall befall me as for her love as befell to the noble knight Sir Kehydius, that died for the love of La Beale Isoud." [Malory VIII, 36-38; IX, 10-11, 17; X, 86]

See also Kahedin.

KENTIGERN, SAINT (Saint Mungo)†

The royal virgin Thenew, daughter of the Scots King Lothus, had the misfortune to give birth to Kentigern in 518, Glennie reports. Her story of an immaculate conception notwithstanding, she was placed in a boat and cast adrift from Aberlady Bay. Kentigern was put into Culross monastery under the discipline of Saint Servanus. If King Lothus was the Arthurian King Lot, then his daughter would have been Gawaine's sister, and Kentigern would have been Gawaine's nephew!

KERRIN, KING OF RÏEL†

Chrétien lists him among the vassal monarchs whom Arthur summoned to court for Erec's wedding. An aged king, Kerrin brought no young men with him: his company was composed of 300 old men, the youngest being seven score years of age. Arthur held them all in great affection. [**Erec & Enide**, ll. 1963-2024]

Kex†—standard version of **KAY** used in the Vulgate

King of the Hundred Knights—see **HUNDRED KNIGHTS, KING OF THE**

Kink Kenadon—see **KYNKE KENADONNE**

Kirtle of the Giant of Saint Michael's Mount, Brittany—see **COAT OF THE ...**

Knight with the Two Swords—see **BALIN LE SAVAGE**

KYNKE KENADONNE (Kink Kenadon)

Malory tells us it is a city and castle "upon the sands that marched nigh Wales", and that "there is a plentiful country" around it [VII, 1 and VII, 34]. Malory seems to mention this city only in the story of Gareth and Lynette. Not being a Welsh scholar, I can only suggest it be identified with Carnarvon city in present-day Carnarvon County. This sounds like a good old name, and Arthur seems to prefer cities beginning with "C", or at least the hard-"C" sound, for his major courts.

John W. Donaldson tentatively identifies Kynke Kenadon with Kyneton, Radnorshire. Radnor, however, is a landlocked county, and Malory clearly puts this town by the seaside. Several of Donaldson's place identifications strike me as even more questionable than some of my own.

LABIGODS THE COURTLY†

Among Arthur's knights in the list Chrétien de Troyes begins in line 1691 of **Erec & Enide**.

LABOR†

This trusty and valiant knight was Guenevere's cousin and helped her escape when the barons who had taken Mordred's part were trying to force her to marry Mordred [Vulgate V].

LAC†

King of Outre-Gales (Estre-Gales or Further Wales) and father of Erec, according to Chrétien de Troyes [**Erec & Enide**, esp. l. 1874].

Ladinas, Duke—see under **ROWSE, DUKE AND DUCHESS DE LA**

Lady Leech of Cornwall—see **LEECH**

Lake, King of the—see under **GRIFLET**

LAKE, LADY (Damsel) OF THE

There are two distinct Ladies of the Lake in Malory. There seem to be three in all, taking the Vulgate into account: one who raised Lancelot in France, one who gave Arthur his sword, and Nimue. Likely all started as one character but, in the present state of the legends, I see nothing for it but to split them.

The French Lady seems to be basically good. So does Nimue; although she imprisons Merlin, she thereafter acts beneficently to Arthur and his court. However, the one who gave Arthur his sword, even in that instance cooperating with Merlin, appears to have been evil. [Malory I, 25; II, 1-4]

Tennyson makes the Lady of the Lake a good, mysterious, almost angelic benefactress of Arthur, but Viviane a villainess who seduces and imprisons Merlin as part of her design to bring back Paganism.

For convenience I distinguish them as follows: Viviane (the French Damsel of the Lake, who raised Lancelot), "Nineve" (Malory's first English Lady of the Lake, who gave Arthur his sword), and Nimue (the second English Lady of the Lake, who gained the position after "Nineve's" death and who became benefactress to Arthur's court). Though "Nineve" is never actually named, "Nineve" is a variant of both the names Nimue and Viviane, and it is a handy one for my purpose.

Both Nimue and Viviane are credited with imprisoning Merlin; whereas Viviane must be in France to raise Lancelot, Malory definitely puts Nimue in Britain. Take your choice as to which one actually did away with the great necromancer. Viviane definitely, and Nimue apparently, had other damsels of the lake under them. The Vulgate says the

Damsels of the Lake owed their knowledge of magic to Merlin; Malory corroborates this as far as Nimue is concerned, but not as far as "Nineve" is portrayed.

LAKE, THE

Here dwelt the Lady (or Damosel) of the Lake, who gave Arthur his sword Excalibur. As Merlin once told Arthur, "within that lake is a rock, and therein is as fair a place as any on earth, and richly beseen." Malory puts the Lake definitely in Britain, apparently somewhere near Carleon. [Malory I, 25] The Vulgate just as clearly puts the Lake in Benoyc, France, and it is where the Damosel of the Lake raised Sir Lancelot from infancy. Hence, there must have been at least two magical Lakes, with one chief Lady of the Lake at a time in each.

Since the Lakes were magical and illusory (although the illusion was apparently quite tangible, even permitting the uninitiated to boat on the water's surface), there is no need to search for real lakes with which to identify them.

LALUT†

Located about seven leagues or less from Cardigan, by Erec's estimation, this county (ruled by a count) kept the custom of annually awarding a fine sparrow-hawk to the loveliest lady present or, in other words, the lady lucky enough to have a knight able to defeat any and all challengers. If a knight could win it for his lady three years in a row, he would win it for good. Chrétien describes this place as a fortress and a town; by the way in which it could fill up to bursting yearly with the people of the country roundabout and never, seemingly, have come to Arthur's attention before Erec visited it, I suspect an otherworldly origin. Whether or not this town was once of Faery, it was where Erec first met the ethereally lovely Enide and her parents. [Chrétien de Troyes, **Erec & Enide**, ll. 342-1478]

LALUT, COUNT OF†

He was the brother of Enide's mother and thus Enide's uncle. Chrétien de Troyes gives the story no obvious otherworldly overtones at all, but, if my guess is right, there may be a touch of faery origin in this whole family and its home. See Lalut. [**Erec & Enide**, ll. 342-1429]

LAMBEGUS

One of Tristram's knights, he boldly pursued Sir Palomides once when Palomides had succeeded by ruse in getting La Beale Isoud for a short while. Palomides defeated Lambegus easily. On a later occasion, however, Lambegus was useful enough, helping Gouvernail and Sir Sentraille de Lushon rescue Tristram from the rocks by pulling him up with towels.

After Tristram's death Lambegus remained in Arthur's court as a knight of the Round Table. He was among those killed during Lancelot's rescue of Guenevere from the stake. [Malory VIII, 30, 35; XIX, 11; XX, 8]

LAMBETH

Malory mentions Lambeth in XIX, 4: "Then Sir Launcelot … took the water at Westminster Bridge, and made his horse to swim over Thames unto Lambeth." I do not know whether in this context Lambeth is a castle, a religious center, or simply a place name for undeveloped real estate.

LAMBOR†

A castle about midway between Camelot and the Humber. Arthur stopped here with his men for a night on his way from Camelot to Joyous Garde and reached the Humber on the second day, which is a very fast pace, even on horseback. [Vulgate VI]

LAMORAK DE GALIS (Lamerake of Wales)

He was King Pellinore's son, apparently the second born in wedlock. His brothers were Aglovale, Dornar, Percivale, and Tor; his known sisters, Eleine and Amide. A companion of the Round Table, Lamorak was "the most noblest knight [but] one that ever was in Arthur's days as for a worldly knight."

> [S]o all the world saith, that betwixt three knights is departed clearly knighthood, that is Launcelot du Lake, Sir Tristram de Liones, and Sir Lamorak de Galis: these bear now the renown.

So Sir Persant of Inde tells Gareth Beaumains, adding that if Gareth conquers Ironside he "shall be called the fourth of the world." At the Michaelmas jousts marking Gareth's marriage, Lamorak overthrew thirty knights, to Tristram's forty and Lancelot's fifty. At the end of these jousts, both Lamorak and Tristram "departed suddenly, and would not be known, for the which King Arthur and all the court were sore displeased." It may have been before this tournament, though it is described later in the **Morte D'Arthur**, that Lamorak, traveling with one Sir Driant, gave another thirty knights their falls within sight of King Mark's pavilion. Mark sent Tristram to match Lamorak, sorely against Tristram's will, for, as the Cornish knight pointed out, he himself was fresh, while Lamorak would be spent with his thirty conquests. Nevertheless, Tristram obeyed Mark far enough to give Lamorak a fall (Lamorak's horse also being tired and going down before Tristram's spear). He then refused to fight Lamorak with the sword, "for I have [already] done to thee over much unto my dishonour and to thy worship." Lamorak did not appreciate Tristram's courtesy. While still in a pique over Tristram's refusal to fight, he met the messenger bearing

Morgan's magic drinking horn to Arthur's court and made him bear it to Mark's court instead, which almost resulted in the execution of La Beale Isoud and more than ninety other ladies. This angered Tristram.

While Tristram was in Brittany, Lamorak was shipwrecked near the Isle of Servage and nursed back to health (apparently having caught a chill in the water) by fishermen. Here Tristram and Isoud la Blanche Mains, also shipwrecked, met him, and the two knights buried their differences to plot how to exterminate the evil Sir Nabon le Noir, whom Lamorak especially hated for having shamefully drawn a cousin of his, Sir Nanowne le Petite, limb from limb. Nabon holding a tournament about this time, both Tristram and Lamorak attended; Lamorak, having borrowed horse and armor from Nabon himself, gave him such a good fight that, when he "was so sore bruised and short breathed, that he traced and traversed somewhat aback", Nabon spared him: to Tristram fell the honor of killing Nabon. On his way back to Arthur's court, Lamorak encountered Sir Frol of the Out Isles and Sir Belliance le Orgulus, had a friendly encounter with Lancelot, and a not-so-friendly one with Gawaine.

Lamorak next encountered Tristram when the latter's party was blown ashore near Castle Perilous, North Wales. Here Tristram remembered his annoyance at the drinking-horn incident and Lamorak remembered the friendship they had pledged each other in the Isle of Servage; they fought a long time, Tristram at first promising it would be to the death, but ended by yielding to each other and swearing eternal friendship in honor of one another's prowess. Not long thereafter, Lamorak got into a battle with Meliagrant over which queen was the more beautiful, Morgawse or Guenevere. See under Bleoberis de Ganis for the incident.

Lamorak's love for Morgawse was his undoing, for Lamorak was the son of the man who had killed King Lot in battle, and Lot's sons felt it an insult that the son of their father's killer should become their mother's lover and potential husband. They therefore first killed Morgawse, as described under Gaheris, while she was in bed with her lover. Gaheris refusing to fight Lamorak at that time, Lamorak left the place, but "for the shame and dolour he would not ride to King Arthur's court, but rode another way." He surfaced again at Duke Galeholt's tournament in Surluse, where he did great deeds of battle and complained to Arthur of the wrongs done him by Lot's sons. Arthur expressed his grief at his sister's death, wished that she had been married to Lamorak instead, and promised to protect Lamorak from Lot's sons and arrange a truce if Lamorak would stay with him. Lamorak, however, refused to remain with Arthur and Lancelot and departed alone. Palomides later describes, first to Ector de Maris, Bleoberis, and Percivale, and later to Tristram, Gareth, and Dinadan, what happened then:

> [Of] his age he was the best that ever I found; for an he might have lived till he had been an hardier man there liveth no knight now such .... And at his departing [from the Surluse tournament] there met him Sir Gawaine and his brethren, and with great pain they slew him feloniously ... would I had been there, and yet had I never the degree at no jousts nor tournament thereas he was, but he put me to the worse, or on foot or on horseback; and that day that he was slain he did the most deeds of arms that ever I saw knight do in all my life days. And when him was given the degree by my lord Arthur, Sir Gawaine and his three brethren, Agravaine, Gaheris, and Sir Mordred, set upon Sir Lamorak in a privy place, and there they slew his horse. And so they fought with him on foot more than three hours, both before him and behind him; and Sir Mordred gave him his death wound behind him at his back, and all to-hew him for one of his squires told me that saw it.

[Malory I, 24; VII, 13, 35; VIII, 33-41; IX, 10-14; X, 17-24, 40-49, 54, 58, etc.]

LANCE BEARER, THE†

Carrying the lance that drips blood down upon his hand (see Longinus' Spear), this squire leads the Grail procession as Percivale sees it in Chrétien's version. [**Perceval**, ca. ll. 3191-3201]

LANCELOT OF THE LAKE (Launcelot du Lake, du Lac)

Lancelot, probably the most famous of all Arthur's Knights of the Round Table, was the most illustrious of an illustrious family which included King Ban his father, King Bors his uncle, Sirs Lionel and Bors de Ganis his cousins, and Sir Ector de Maris his bastard British-born half-brother.

Lancelot, then called by his christened name of Galahad, was an infant when his parents, Ban and Elaine of Benwick, fled their city with a few retainers. When King Ban looked back and saw his castle burning, he suffered a seizure of some kind, possibly a heart attack. Queen Elaine, hurrying to him, left her son alone for a few moments. It was then that Viviane, the French Damsel of the Lake, took him, brought him to her rich city in the illusory magical Lake at Bois en val, and raised him, renaming him Lancelot. The widowed Elaine remained nearby, building the Royal Minster on the hill where Ban had died. Lancelot's cousins Lionel and Bors, with their mentors, were eventually welcomed into Viviane's Lake with Lancelot to finish their knightly education.

When Lancelot reached 18 years of age and was itching to become a knight, Viviane gave him a last lecture on the history and duties of that state of life; provided him with a sword of proven worth, a snow-white horse, and the rest of his outfit, all in white and silver; and brought him, accompanied by Lionel, Bors, Seraide, and others, to Arthur's court, where the King dubbed him on Saint John's Day. He may have become a member of the Queen's Knights at this time; before officially settling

Lancelot's Kin

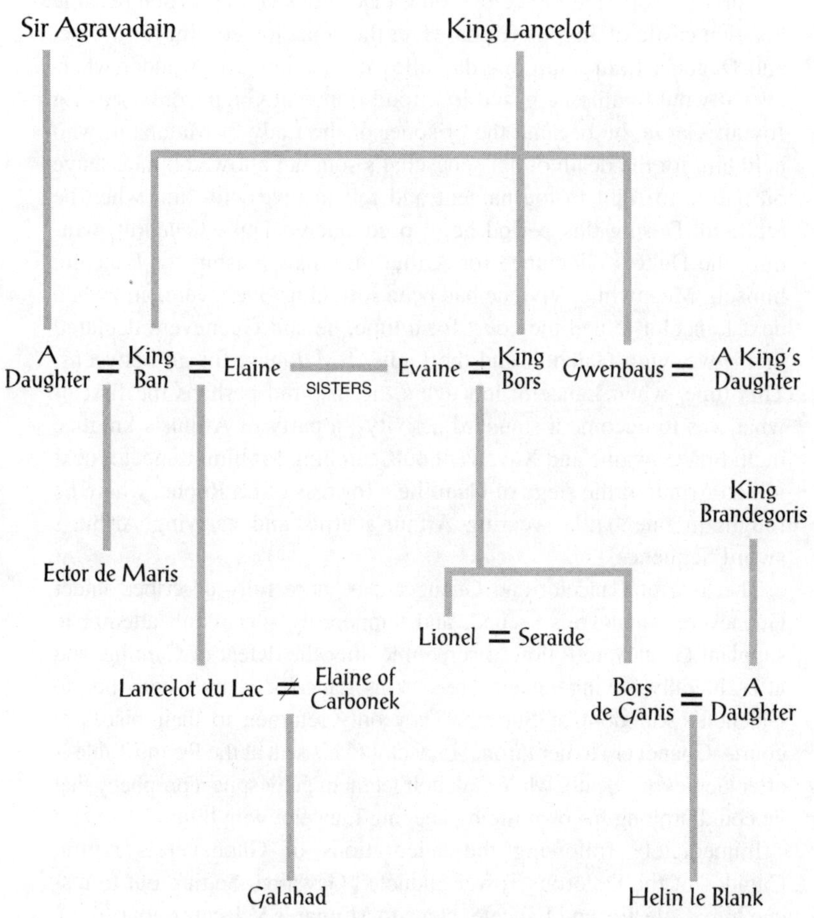

= *Indicates a known marriage.*

≠ *Indicates a union either known to be illicit or a union not proven to be a marriage.*

down at Arthur's court, however, he spent some time wandering in knight errantry, beginning when he left to succor the Lady of Nohaut—his first rivalry with Kay seems to have been over which of them would serve as her champion.

During this period Lancelot won La Dolorous Garde, which became his own castle of Joyous Garde. Here the court joined him for a time, and Dagonet found him one day allowing his horse to wander wherever it would while he gazed in a fond trance at Guenevere. Leaving Joyous Garde, he became the prisoner of the Lady of Malohaut, who held him for the death of her seneschal's son, but allowed him to leave on parole to fight in tournament and fell in love with him when he returned. During this period he also conquered Duke Galeholt, winning the Duke's allegiance for Arthur and his frienship for Lancelot himself. Meanwhile, Viviane had been softening Guenevere, and when next Lancelot joined the court for a time, he and Guenevere declared their love, with Galeholt and the Lady of Malohaut for go-betweens. This time, when Lancelot left again, he inspired perhaps the first of what was to become a standard activity—a party of Arthur's knights, including Gawaine and Kay, went out searching for him. Lancelot next joined Arthur at the siege of Camiille's fortress of La Roche, where he fought in one battle wearing Arthur's arms and carrying Arthur's sword Sequence.

The love of Lancelot and Guenevere is more fully described under Guenevere. Genievre's second, and temporarily successful, attempt to supplant Guenevere followed sometime after the defeat of Camille, and after literally saving Guenevere's skin, Lancelot retired with her to Galeholt's kingdom of Surluse. They only returned to their places at court—Guenevere to her throne, Lancelot to his seat at the Round Table—after Genievre's death, while Galeholt let them go despite a prophecy that he could prolong his own life by keeping Lancelot with him.

Immediately following the celebrations of Guenevere's return, Carados of the Dolorous Tower abducted Gawaine. Setting out to rescue him, Galeshin and Lancelot came to Morgan's Val sans retour (q.v.). As a true lover, Lancelot was able to free Morgan's prisoners here, but she succeeded in kidnaping him in return. She let him go long enough to kill Carados and free Gawaine, but then, by a ruse, sent Lancelot's ring (a gift from Guenevere) back to court with a pretended message from the knight that he would never return. This drove Lancelot mad until the Damsel of the Lake found him wandering in Cornwall and cured him. Meanwhile, however, Duke Galeholt had gotten a false report of Lancelot's death, which caused his own. Before Lancelot's return to court, Meliagrant succeeded in abducting Guenevere, also taking Kay prisoner; Lancelot pursued them to Gore, freeing not only Guenevere and Kay but also the occupants of Gore's "Terre Foraine." Lancelot made up his differences with the Queen in her bed and eventually killed Meliagrant in trial by combat before Arthur.

Some time later, traveling on other adventures, Lancelot found Duke Galeholt's grave and almost killed himself in grief, but was prevented by Seraide, at whose direction he had his friend's body taken to Joyous Garde for reburial. Lancelot was gone so long on his adventures that Gawaine and other knights went out searching for him again, while Guenevere, distraught, sent Elyzabel to France to summon Viviane. After her departure, a damsel whom Lancelot had succored arrived at court with the news that he was still alive, which was so welcome that Arthur gave the messenger her choice of castles (she chose Leverzep).

Lancelot, meanwhile, met his virgin love, Amable. Lancelot was found at last by his cousin Lionel, only to be separated again when Lionel went off to pursue and be captured by Sir Terican (Turquine) while Lancelot was napping. Lancelot was captured while asleep by Morgan and her cohorts, but escaped through the help of Duke Rochedon's daughter, succored Meliagrant's sister (see King Bagdemagus' Daughter), and visited Carbonek, where he engendered Galahad on Pellam's daughter Elaine. After this he visited the Forest Perilous (q.v.), repaid Duke Rochedon's daughter by saving her from an unwanted marriage and forcing Morgan's friend the Queen of Sorestan to restore her inheritance, and finally rejoined the court at a tournament in Camelot, which Amable also attended and where Guenevere accepted her platonic relationship with Lancelot. After the tournament, Lancelot, Bors, Gareth, and Bagdemagus went out looking for Lionel and Ector de Maris and saved Mordred from Maten's men at the Castel de la Blanche Espine (q.v.); Lancelot eventually killed Terican and freed Lionel and the other prisoners.

After a few other adventures, Lancelot fell again into Morgan's hands, who tricked him into her castle, drugged him with wine and a powder blown into his nose, and held him for two winters and a summer; during this time, Lancelot painted his own history, including his love for Guenevere, on his bedroom walls. Inspired by a spring rose that reminded him of the Queen, he finally broke the iron bars of his window and escaped. He then rescued Lionel again, this time from a trumped-up charge of treason in King Vagor's country, fought Bors at Le Tertre Deuee (q.v.), visited the site of his grandfather's death in the Forest of the Boiling Well, killed Merlan le Dyable, and rescued Mordred at the castle of the Fontaine des Deux Sycamores. Mordred at this time was still a promising young knight, who won Lancelot's praise as they traveled together and who saw with him the mystic stag and four lions in the forest moonlight. Lancelot witnessed the revelation in the woods near Peningues that marked the turning point in Mordred's life and parted company with him after the tournament of Peningues. Lancelot had been included in the priest's prophetic greeting of them as "the two most unfortunate knights who ever lived", and he was much shaken when Mordred slew the prophet before the latter had time to predict his—Lancelot's—fate. It was after the Peningues tournament that Lancelot rescued Kay from attacking knights and then left in the morning with Kay's horse and armor.

Lancelot returned to court in time to witness the attempt of Sir Brumant l'Orguilleus to sit in the Siege Perilous. By now it had been learned the Dame Elyzabel was being held prisoner by King Claudas, and Arthur and Guenevere went to war, finally defeating Claudas and driving him into exile. After Claudas' defeat, Queen Elaine of Benwick came to visit her son and other male relatives at Gannes.

After Arthur's return from the Continent, Elaine of Carbonek visited the victory celebration, tricked Lancelot into her bed again, and so aroused Guenevere's jealousy that Lancelot went mad again. He wandered for up to two years and finally ended at Carbonek, where he was recognized, restored to sanity by exposure to the Grail, and given Joyous Isle to live in with Elaine. Under the self-imposed impression that he could never again return to Arthur's court, he called himself "Le Chevaler Mal Fet" and guarded the island against all challengers. Eventually Ector de Maris and Percivale found him here and persuaded him to return.

During the Grail Adventures, Lancelot suffered unaccustomed defeats and humiliation at arms, as well as experiencing a few visions and semivisions of his own. After meeting and adventuring for a time with his son Galahad in the vessel with Amide's body, he arrived at Carbonek. Here, having resolved to amend his life of his adulterous love for Guenevere, he had a Grail vision of his own—not the full experience of Galahad and his companions, but one which put Lancelot into a swoon for nearly a month, from which he awakened filled with the ineffable marvels he had seen.

Returning from the Grail Quest, however, Lancelot soon relapsed into his old love, but became more careless about secrecy. Then followed more stormy episodes between the lovers, including the incidents of the poisoning of Sir Patrice of Ireland and the passion and death of Elaine of Astolat. Eventually trapped alone with Guenevere by Agravaine and Mordred, Lancelot fought his way free, leaving the Queen behind with reluctance and returning to rescue her from the stake with great slaughter of Arthur's men, including Lancelot's old favorite Gareth. Arthur and Gawaine, who had always until now been counted one of Lancelot's dearest friends, first besieged Lancelot, his kinsmen and supporters, and Guenevere in Joyous Garde. At the Pope's intervention, Lancelot restored Guenevere to Arthur, who took her back and pardoned her, but exiled her lover. Lancelot returned to his lands in France, where he parcelled out the territories and titles among his kinsmen and followers. Arthur and Gawaine pursued Lancelot across the Channel and besieged him in Gannes. Lancelot met Gawaine in single combat, but with the utmost reluctance; as always, when Lancelot won, he refused to kill Gawaine. At news of Mordred's rebellion, Arthur and his men returned to Britain without making up their differences with Lancelot. Gawaine, dying at Dover, wrote a plea to Lancelot to return and aid Arthur, but, thanks to the famous premature battle at Salisbury, Lancelot and his men arrived too late; Mordred and virtually all the men of both armies were dead, and Arthur had passed. Lancelot was able, however, to mop up the last of the rebellion, which was being kept alive by Mordred's two sons. Both of these lads exterminated, Lancelot found the chapel where Arthur's grave was marked and joined the former Archbishop of Canterbury and others, including many of his kinsmen, as a hermit. Here the great knight died, in Tennyson's words, "a holy man." His body was taken to Joyous Garde and buried beside that of Duke Galeholt.

I have recapped Lancelot's career, with many, many omissions, as given in the Vulgate, Volumes III-VI. After a few forecasts [II, 8 19; III, 1], Malory brings him onstage in V, 2, in time for Arthur's campaign against Emperor Lucius. Malory gives the episode of Lancelot's abduction by Morgan and her cohorts, his escape and slaying of Sir Turquine, and the incident of returning to court in Kay's armor in Book VI; the begetting of Galahad and Lancelot's madness and subsequent sojourn with Elaine of Carbonek in Joyous Isle in Books XI and XII; Lancelot's Grail adventures in Books XIII, XV, and XVII; the poisoning of Sir Patrise and the Elaine of Astolat affair in Book XVIII; Meliagrant's kidnaping of Guenevere in Book XIX; and the last, tragic adventures in Books XX and XXI, including Lancelot's last interview with Guenevere in her convent [XXI, 9] and his bringing her body to Glastonbury, having learned of her death in a vision [XXI, 10-11]. Most of these episodes, especially the Meliagrant affair, are given somewhat differently in Malory, but the outlines are recognizable. Malory also describes Lancelot's mentorship of La Cote Male Taile [IX], his friendship with Tristram [IX, X], and his miraculous healing of Sir Urre of Hungary [XIX, 10-12] following the Meliagrant affair.

According to Malory, the only "worldly" knight who could conceivably have beaten Lancelot in single combat (except during the Grail Adventures or perhaps in Lancelot's first few years of knighthood) was Tristram; their big battle, however, ended in a draw, each surrendering to the other on learning one another's identity [Malory X, 5]. Coupled with this strength, skill, and prowess was an unfortunate tendency to blood-lust in battle; the film **Monty Python and the Holy Grail**, while hardly a reliable general picture of Arthur's court and reign, seems to me to have caught this facet of Lancelot's character to near perfection. One of his unluckiest habits was that of going to sleep in somebody else's pavilion without the owner's knowledge, which usually led to bloodshed and not infrequently to somebody's death. (See Belleus and "Iblis"—"Iblis" was widowed by Gaheris, but my impression is that Lancelot was the knight most frequently involved in this sort of incident.) Another of his habits was that of taking off secretly on unannounced adventures:

> And when Sir Lancelot was thus missed they marvelled where he was become; and then the queen and many of them deemed that he was departed as he was wont to do, suddenly. [Malory XIX, 7]

This, coupled with his absences on fits of madness, must have kept him very much away from court. Nevertheless, he attained great political influence; his "will was law throughout the kingdom of Logres." [Vulgate V]

Eventually jealousy of Lancelot grew among the other knights of the Round Table, caused in part by Arthur's praise [Vulgate V].

When Morgan and her cohorts kidnaped Lancelot, Morgan did not recognize him because he had short hair, his hair and nails having fallen out during the sickness from which Amable cured him, and his hair not having fully grown back [Vulgate V]. At some point in his career, he acquired a wound on his cheek; it was by this scar that the hermit Baudwin recognized him after the Winchester tournament at which he carried Elaine of Astolat's token [Malory XVIII, 13]. Lancelot had an inconvenient habit of talking in his sleep of his love for Guenevere [Malory XI, 8].

His relationship with his son Galahad sems to have been very good, friendly and loving on both sides. With Morgan he seems to have had a curious relationship—she varied between hating him and trying to seduce him.

SIR LANCELOT'S FAMILY AND RETAINERS
Father: King Ban of Benwick
Mother: Queen Elaine of Benwick
Mentor-guardian (self-appointed): Viviane
Half-brother: Ector de Maris

Cousins: Lionel, Bors de Ganis, "Iblis", Oruale de Guindoel
Lover: Guenevere
Virgin lady: Amable
Paramour: Elaine of Carbonek
Would-be-paramours: Elaine of Astolat, Hellawes, Lady of Malohaut
Son (by Elaine of Carbonek): Galahad
Grandfather of son: King Pellam
Squires: Angis, Kanahins
Protégés: Lavaine, Nerovens de Lile, Urre of Hungary
Especial friend: Duke Galeholt
Dearest foe?: Morgan le Fay
Insistent guide: "Ornagrine"

When and how did Lancelot make his way into the Arthurian cycle? According to D.D.R. Owen, the appearance of Lancelot's name in the list of Arthur's champions beginning line 1691 of **Erec & Enide**, considered Chrétien de Troyes' earliest surviving Arthurian romance (thought to have been composed ca. 1170), is the first known mention of this famous knight. For myself, I find it difficult, on internal evidence alone, to believe that Lancelot actually sprang into being at this point in Chrétien's creative process. Chrétien names him as third best of Arthur's knights—a high position for a newly introduced character with no other role to play in the romance in question. (The well established champion Gawaine comes first in this list, and Erec himself second, as befits a titular hero; the place of "third best" ought surely to have gone to another knight already widely known, if not in Arthurian tales, then in other stories of chivalry.) Again, in Chrétien's second romance, we find Lancelot prominent among Arthur's knights; but his one dramatic function here is to open the second day of the Oxford tournament by jousting with and being defeated by the youthful titular hero. [**Cligés**, ll. 4759-4823] One might argue that Chrétien already had it in mind when he wrote **Erec & Enide** to make Lancelot the hero of another romance; yet when this Lancelot romance finally materialized, in **The Knight of the Cart**, Chrétien himself credited a patroness with proposing the subject matter, which scholarly opinion considers to have been personally distasteful to him, and which apparently engaged his interest so insufficiently that he left it for another clerk to finish.

The evidence I have so far seen in favor of the theory that Lancelot's direct original can be found in ancient Welsh myth seems to boil down to wishful thinking fastened around the "L", "n", and "s"(?) sounds in the name Llwch Lleminawc/Llenlleawc, which does not convince me. At the same time, I feel that Chrétien must have used a character already popular by 1170. It would be nice to know more about the actual date of Ulrich von Zatzikhoven's **Lanzelet**, and what traditions or sources he may have used.

In any event, Chrétien's **Lancelot** (alias **The Knight of the Cart**) would seem to be the earliest known extant treatment of this particular story featuring Lancelot as its hero. While longer and more detailed, Chrétien's account is essentially close enough to those of the Vulgate and of Malory to make it plausible that they ultimately took it from him. Allusions in Chrétien's **Yvain** identify part of its hero's adventures as running simultaneously with events in **Lancelot**, which might be of interest to anyone trying to pin down where, exactly, the Meliagrant affair figures in Arthurian chronology. (I have given my most complete summary of this episode under the entry for Meliagrant.)

LANCELOT'S "FOREIGN" HOSTS†

When on his way through the marches of Gore to the Sword Bridge, the evening after leaving the "Church of the Tombs" and parting from "Portia", Lancelot met a vavasour returning from hunting in the woods, his game lashed to his large gray hunting horse. The vavasour took Lancelot home as a guest to his family, which included a wife, two unmarried daughters, and five sons—two of them already knighted. They had been born in Logres, but somehow strayed into Gore, where they had been living captive for a long time. Two of the sons, one knighted and the other not, accompanied Lancelot next day, guiding him through the Stony Passage, briefly joining an uprising raised by more prisoners from Logres at the rumor that the champion foretold to free them had finally arrived, and then lodging for the night with another well-to-do knight. At some point in their journey, Lancelot knighted the younger of his guides. After an apparently uneventful day of travel, they found hospitality at the household of a knight and lady with an unspecified number of sons and daughters—"foreign" prisoners or not, these people were as gracious as Lancelot's earlier hosts. This stopping-place was where the man I have very tentatively identified with the Haughty Knight of the Heath challenged and fought Lancelot to the death, and this third knightly host supplied Lancelot with a horse to replace the one slain in that combat. The original two young men continued with Lancelot the next day until reaching the Sword Bridge that evening. They witnessed his crossing; I assume that, after seeing him reach the other side in safety (his injuries they could not see), they returned to their own home, spreading the news. [Chrétien de Troyes, **Lancelot**, ll. 2023-3150]

LANCELOT'S RING†

The fairy who raised Lancelot—Chrétien does not further identify her—gave him a ring whose stone had the power to free him from any spell or magical illusion. Once, for instance, finding himself and his companions trapped in a strong castle in the marches of Gore, and suspecting enchantment, he held the ring up before his eyes, gazed at the stone, and called on God and his lady the fairy, trusting her to hear and rescue him: by the fact that nothing happened, he knew that the castle was real and solid, that they had to fight their way out by natural means. Later in the same adventure, he used his ring again to prove that the two lions or leopards apparently set to guard the farther end of the Sword Bridge were, unlike the bridge itself and the castle described above, mere illusory enchantments. [Chrétien de Troyes, **Lancelot**, ll. 2330-2373; 3124-3149]

Vulgate III identifies the fairy as the (French) Lady of the Lake, and tells us that the ring was a last gift she gave Lancelot before leaving him at Arthur's court to be knighted.

"LANCELOT'S TOWER"†

Chrétien describes an island in the middle of the large, broad arm of the sea that lay beside Gore. Upon this island Meliagrant had a tower built for the special purpose of imprisoning Lancelot: the stone for this tower had to be ferried over the water, and its construction took almost fifty-seven days. Later on, however, in the part added by Godefroi de Leigni, the tower seems to be not on an island, but standing lonely on the shore beside the arm of the sea. [**Lancelot**, ll. 6128-6166; 6420-ca. 6460; see also Meliagrant; King Bademagu's Daughter]

LANCEOR

Son of one of the kings of Ireland (Malory does not specify which), Lanceor was "an orgulous [haughty] knight" of Arthur's court, but not, apparently, of the Round Table, early in Arthur's reign. Jealous of Balin's success in drawing the sword worn by "Malvis", Lanceor pursued Balin, jousted with him, and was killed. Lanceor is mainly memorable for being one of the comparatively few knights with a lady who is named—Colombe—and because their tomb (erected over them, curiously enough, by King Mark) became a kind of landmark when Merlin accurately predicted that Lancelot and Tristram would someday fight each other there [Malory XI, 4-8].

LANCES, CHAPEL OF THE†

An old, dilapidated church in a wasteland. On a marble tomb in the churchyard were the words: "Do not enter. Unless you are the wretched knight who has lost the chance of finding the Holy Grail through his luxury, you cannot achieve the adventure of the churchyard." Inside was a burning tomb with twelve other tombs, each with a lance, surrounding it. When any knight entered, the lances advanced and beat him to unconsciousness. He would wake to find himself outside again. On the door of the chapel was written: "Only the son of the Dolorous Queen can enter this churchyard without shame." By the Dolorous Queen was meant Elaine of Benwick; the adventure, of course, was for Lancelot.

Going on from this church, one reached a fork in the road. A warning on a stone read: "Do not take the road on the left, for it will bring you to shame." This road led to Guindoel Castle. The road on the right led to Carbonek. This puts the chapel between Scotland and Listeneise. [Vulgate IV]

LANDOINE (Landoigne)†

Daughter of the King of the Hundred Knights [Vulgate V].

LANDOINE† (Landone)

A forest, probably on the way to Gore [Vulgate IV].

Lands of the Two Marches—see **LISTENEISE**

LANDUC†

I would incline to interpret this as Chrétien's name for the castle and lands, including the marvelous spring, in the forest of Broceliande, where Ywaine finds and weds Dame Laudine. It appears, however, to have been uncommon in Chrétien's society to identify a person as "of somewhere" while the person was still living there. I remain unpersuaded that this rule would necessarily apply to Dame Laudine in the single line and general literary context where Chrétien names her. Nevertheless, it is possible that "Landuc" was her father Laudunet's duchy, and lay elsewhere, and that she held the Broceliande castle, spring, and appertaining lands as her late husband's widow rather than as her parent's child. In any case, whether or not they comprised Landuc, the lands Laudine held as widow of Esclados the Red extended two to four leagues in every direction and included more than one castle; the property was sufficiently extensive to entertain Arthur's court for a week. [**Yvain**, esp. l. 2151 & Owen's note; ll. 2466-2483] As so often with various locales in such Arthurian romance as Chrétien's, one suspects a whiff of the otherworld about Landuc.

LAUDINE OF LANDUC†

The wife of Ywaine, q.v. Chrétien gives us her name only in line 2151 of **Yvain**; but, according to D.D.R. Owen's note to that verse, most of the manuscripts have not "Laudine of Landuc", but "la dame de Landuc." Was Landuc her father Duke Laudunet's domain, or was it the castle and territory of her husband Esclados ... or were they, perhaps, one and the same property, inherited from her father and shared with her successive husbands? Owen, citing Loomis, suggests that "Laudine" might derive from a form of "Lothian" and point to early Scottish origins. Ruth Harwood Cline states that Chrétien giving his name as "of Troyes" implies that he was not at that time living in Troyes [introd. to **Perceval**, p.ix], but Susan Haskins quotes a mystery play of 1486 in which Mary Magdalen is chatelaine of the castle of Magdalen, thus explaining her name [**Mary Magdalen: Myth and Metaphor**, NY, ©1993, p.166-167]. It would appear that Landuc might or might not be the name of the castle in which Ywaine finds Laudine residing.

How seriously are we expected to interpret Laudine's angry statements of undying hatred for Ywaine at various stages of the romance? The proper actress could so deliver these speeches as to give Laudine's subsequent capitulations perfect psychological plausibility.

LAUDINE'S DAMSEL†

Not Lunette, but a second capable maiden of Dame Laudine's, this damsel arrives alone, mounted on a black palfrey with white feet, to find Ywaine at Chester, where Arthur is holding a mid-August court and tournament. Having taken off her mantle—this may have some significance in courtly protocol—she marches into the tent and up to Arthur, greets him and all his other knights, singles Ywaine out for a tirade of about sixty lines reminding him that he had promised to return to his wife by Saint John's Day, informs him that he has broken Laudine's heart by failing to keep his word, and demands Laudine's ring back. When he sits stricken dumb, she pulls the ring off his finger and takes her leave, commending the king and everyone else except the guilty party to God.

In her tirade, she lays an all but formal accusation of treachery against that person who brought about Ywaine's marriage to Laudine. It sounds as if she means Lunette and may have some connection with Laudine's seneschal, who later makes the accusation formal.

[Chrétien de Troyes, **Yvain**, ll. 2672-2801]

LAUDINE'S RING†

When worn by a true lover, its stone had the power to protect him from wounds and loss of blood, making his flesh harder than iron. Laudine gave it to her new-wedded lord Ywaine when he left for his year on the tournament round. After he stayed away about six weeks overtime, she sent a damsel who reclaimed it on her behalf, with the message "Don't come home." [Chrétien de Troyes, **Yvain**, ll. 2579-2615; ca. 2770-2775]

LAUDINE'S SENESCHAL and HIS BROTHERS†

Described as neither stammerer nor laggard, although either unwilling or for some reason himself ineligible to take on the role of guardian of the marvelous spring, this knight urges Laudine's council to advise her to take Ywaine as her new husband after the death of Esclados.

Arthur is coming, and the seneschal emphasizes Arthur's supposed intention of warring against them and laying waste their land. The thought that a single good man as their lady's husband and the spring's protector can avert this catastrophe shows the perceived value of strong leadership; the context also shows that the seneschal feels himself unqualified to provide this same leadership. His moral defects appear later: when Ywaine overstays the year's leave of absence Laudine granted him, the seneschal charges Lunette with treason for having promoted the marriage. Feeling cocky in her innocence, Lunette offers to have her case defended in trial by combat by one against three. Instead of declining this offer, which would have been the courtly course and one she expected him to take, he enlists his two brothers to help him await her single champion. Then, when Ywaine shows up (incognito) with his lion, the seneschal insists on the beast's staying out of the three-against-one combat. The seneschal's foresight is foiled, however; disobeying Ywaine's orders, the lion eventually jumps into the fray and wounds the seneschal mortally, facilitating Ywaine's victory. Laudine's seneschal and his brothers end burnt on the pyre originally intended for Lunette.

I suspect a connection between this seneschal and Laudine's unnamed damsel (see above), but can find no allusion in the text to any such liaison. Instead, Lunette herself states envy of her own position to have been the seneschal's motive. It also occurs to me that the seneschal's original speech to Laudine's council plays in so beautifully with Lunette's own matchmaking as to suggest that when the marriage seems to go badly sour, the seneschal may turn against Lunette in order to forestall being accused himself.

[Chrétien de Troyes, **Yvain**, ll. 2070-2106; 3648-97; 4385-ca.4570]

LAUDUNET, DUKE†

Father of Dame Laudine. Chrétien de Troyes tells us that a lay was sung of Duke Laudunet; it apparently has not survived. [**Yvain**, l. 2151 & Owen's note]

Launcelot du Lac, du Lake—see LANCELOT OF THE LAKE

LAUNDS, LADY OF THE

Her "nigh cousin", King Anguish of Ireland, held a tournament to find her a husband.

> And what man won her, three days after he should wed her and have all her lands. This cry was made in England, Wales, Scotland, and also in France and Brittany.

Both Palomides and Tristram fought in this tournament; Palomides at first was winning, but Tristram (rather surprisingly urged thereto by La Beale Isoud) bested the Saracen and made him swear not to bear arms for a year. Everybody seems to have forgotten completely that the original purpose of the tournament was to find the Lady of the Launds a mate. [Malory VIII, 9-10]

LAUREL

The niece of Lyonors and Lynette, Dame Laurel was "a fair lady" who was wedded to Agravaine at the same time Lyonores was married to Gareth and Lynette to Gaheris [Malory VII, 35].

LAVAINE

Sirs Tirre and Lavaine were the sons of Sir Bernard of Astolat and the brothers of Elaine, the Lily Maid. They had recently been knighted when Lancelot stopped at Astolat on his way to the Winchester tournament. The main importance of the older brother, Tirre, seems to be that he had been wounded the same day he was made knight and was still lying abed with his wounds, so that his shield was available for Lancelot to borrow. Lavaine, the younger son, went with Lancelot to the tournament, made a good showing, and helped the gravely wounded Lancelot away to the hermit Baudwin. Returning to Winchester—apparently sent by Lancelot to seek Bors or some other kinsman—Lavaine first encountered his sister Elaine and later located Bors, bringing them both to the wounded Lancelot. Lavaine remained at court after Elaine's death, "and ever in all places Sir Lavaine gat great worship so that he was renowned among many knights of the Table Round". In Arthur's Christmas tournament, Lavaine encountered Arthur himself in the lists and they smote each other down. Made a companion of the Round Table at the same time as Sir Urre of Hungary, Lavaine married Urre's sister Felelolie. Remaining in Lancelot's faction during the break with Arthur, Lavaine accompanied Lancelot into exile and was made Earl of Arminak. [Malory XVIII, 9-23; XIX, 13; XX, 5, 18]

LEECH OF CORNWALL, A LADY

> Then the king [Mark] let send after all manner of leeches and surgeons, both unto men and women, and there was none that would behote [Tristram] the life. Then came there a lady that was a right wise lady, and she said plainly unto King Mark, and to Sir Tristram ... that he should never be whole but if Sir Tristram went in the same country that the venom [of Marhaus' spearhead] came from. [Malory VIII, 8]

I assume from the context that she was a leech or surgeon; she may, of course, have been an herb-woman or even one who simply knew how to speak out with authority. Mark and Tristram took her advice seriously and followed it, to Tristram's healing.

LEICESTER†

Mentioned in Vulgate II, this subkingdom presumably corresponds to modern Leicestershire.

KING LEODEGRANCE (Leodegance, Leodegran) OF CAMELIARD (Carmelide)

The father of Guenevere and Genievre, Leodegrance held in his house the Round Table, which he received from Uther Pendragon. He was not involved in the rebellion of the kings at Arthur's accession, possibly because he already had his hands full with King Ryons. Leodegrance appealed for Arthur's help against Ryons; Arthur came, bringing with him his allies Ban and Bors, and succored Cameliard. At this time Arthur first saw Guenevere. When Arthur later requested her hand in marriage, Leodegrance was honored and delighted. Casting about in his mind for a gift that would please his new son-in-law, Leodegrance reasoned that "he hath lands enow, him needeth none; but I shall send him a gift shall please him much more, for I shall give him the Table Round", together with a hundred knights [Malory I, 18; III, 1; Vulgate].

KING LEODEGRANCE'S FAMILY AND RETAINERS
Daughter: Guenevere
Daughter (by wife of seneschal): Genievre
Son-in-law: Arthur
Seneschal: Cleodalis
Knights: Bertholai, Garaunt, Guy (Guenevere's cousins (q.v.))

Leonce—see LIONSES

LEPROUS LADY, CASTLE OF THE

This castle may have been on the other side of the waste forest near Carteloise Castle. The Leprous Lady could only be cured by a dish of warm blood from the right arm of a clean virgin who was a king's daughter, and not just any virginal king's daughter at that—they had to find the right one. Accordingly, every maiden damsel who passed by was forced to donate enough of her blood to fill a silver dish. Near the castle was a graveyard full of tombs of damsels who had died by this custom. Twelve of those interred were kings' daughters; all who donated were apparently related in some way to kings. It looks as if the people of the castle interpreted the position of king's daughter rather loosely. Did they also so interpret virginity?

The custom was not always fatal. When Sir Balin and the lady of the slain Sir Herlews le Berbeus arrived at this castle, she survived being bled very nicely, leaving again after a night's rest and "right good cheer."

Sir Percivale's sister Amide finally cured the Leprous Lady, giving her blood of her own free will. Amide died of it, and almost immediately thereafter the vengeance of God destroyed the castle and all its people. [Malory II, 13 and XVII, 9-11]

The "Castle of the Leprous Lady" should not be far from Carteloise Castle and forest. It must also be near a river or harbor, since Galahad and his companions put Amide's body into a barge and let it drift to Sarras to meet them there. If Carteloise is put on the north shore of Solway Firth, the Leprous Lady's castle might be located at, say, Annan.

LESTROITE MARCHE†

The lord of Lestroite Marche held it against the King of Norgales, the Duke of Cambeninc, and the King of the Hundred Knights with the latter's seneschal Marganor, putting the castle somewhere in the marches between Norgales and Cambenet; indeed, its name means "the narrow march."

The lord of Lestroite Marche had one child, a daughter, who for some reason could not hold the castle after him. To help defend the castle and try to find his daughter a good husband at the same time, this lord established the custom that any knight who accepted his hospitality must spend half a day defending the castle. Ector de Maris, at that time a Queen's Knight, vanquished Marganor and restored peace to the area, although he cried off from marrying the damsel by pleading that he already had a lady. [Vulgate III]

LESTROITE MARCHE, DAMSEL OF†

For some reason, although other damsels and ladies acted as apparently independent chatelaines, this damsel could not hold her father's castle in her own right after his death. The lord of Lestroite Marche therefore tried to find her a good husband by insisting that each of his knightly guests spend half a day defending the castle. The damsel fell in love with Ector de Maris, who defeated Sir Marganor during his half-day's service; Ector hedged by telling her he already had a lady. Then the damsel gave him a ring with a stone that had the power to make the man who received it love with ever-increasing force the woman who gave it. [Vulgate V]

LETRON OF PREPELESANT†

Among Arthur's knights in the list Chrétien de Troyes begins line 1691 of **Erec & Enide**, Letron is noted for his polished manners.

Leu Estrange—see **ISLE ESTRANGE**

LEVERZEP† (Leverserp, Leverzerp, Loverseph, etc.)

This sounds like a variant of the name Lonazep, but Malory places Lonazep Castle near Joyous Garde, while Vulgate III and VII tell us that Leverzep belonged to the Duke of Cambeninc and place Leverzep on the way from Bedingran to Orofoise. Leverzep and Lonazep must be two different castles.

Near Leverzep is the Round Mountain, site of a hermitage.

LEVERZEP, DAMSEL OF†

She was rescued by Lancelot on one of his long adventures away from court. He sent her back to let the court know he was still alive, and Arthur was so delighted with the news that he rewarded her with the castle of her choice. She chose Leverzep, where she had been born. [Vulgate V]

LIANOUR, DUKE

Duke of the Castle of Maidens, Lianour and his eldest son were slain be seven evil brothers who then raped the Duke's elder daughter, appropriated his property and treasure, and set about oppressing the common folk and taking all passing knights and damsels prisoner. After seven years of this, the seven brothers were routed by Galahad and his companions. Lianour's elder daughter had died, so the castle was restored to her younger sister. [Malory XIII, 15]

LICONAL†

Enide's father, though Chrétien does not tell us his name until almost the end of the story, several hundred lines after Arthur, being introduced at last to both the lady's parents when they come to court for their son-in-law's coronation, has commented on Liconal's handsome appearance [**Erec & Enide**, esp. ll. 6594-6627 & 6888-6917].

LICORIDES†

One of the twelve who accompanied Alexander from Greece to Britain, where Arthur knighted them all at the outset of Count Angrs' rebellion. Chrétien remarks on the boldness of Licorides. He seems to have been among those who followed Alexander into Windsor to capture Angrs. Licorides survived the rebellion, but Chrétien tells us nothing more of him. [**Cligés**, ll. 102-385; 1093-ca. 2210]

LILE OF AVELION

Called "the great lady Lile of Avelion", this enigmatic person may have been an enchantress. Avelion is almost certainly Avilion or Avalon, suggesting religion, mysticism, magic, and benevolence; yet Lady Lile helped the damsel "Malvis", whom Merlin characterized as wicked. Perhaps in this case Lile, although good, mistakenly helped the wrong side—the Round Table heroes were often enough guilty of helping the wrong side, through siding with the first party who appealed to them, or unquestioningly taking the part of any woman against any man. [Malory II, 1-4]

Lile would not have been a Lady of the Lake, for Lancelot's Lady of the Lake, Viviane, was in France. The first English Lady of the Lake came to demand the heads of Balin and the very damsel whom Lile had helped, and the second English Lady of the Lake was Nimue.

I have treated Lile in the above notes as a person because in Malory she does seem definitely a person, not a personification, even though she remains an offstage figure. My opinion, however, is that this mysterious dame came into being when some scribe or translator mistook the French for "the island of Avalon" (*l'ile d'Avilion)* for a personal name.

LIMORS†

The castle of Count Oringle [Chrétien de Troyes, **Erec & Enide**, ll. 4713-4962].

Limors, Count of—see **ORINGLE**

Lindisfarne†—see **MEDGAUD**

Linet—see **LYNETTE**

LINTHCAMUS† (Lintheamus)

Here Saint Cadoc built a monastery. Since Glennie gives Linthcamus among his Arthurian locales, Cadoc either must have preceded or have been contemporary with Arthur.

Linthcamus is at present-day Cambuslang, near the River Clyde, in the northern part of Lanark County, Scotland.

LIONEL

silver red black

The first son of King Bors, the older brother of Sir Bors de Ganis, and the cousin of Lancelot, Lionel owed his name to a birthmark shaped like a lion. At the death of King Bors, one of his former retainers, Sir Pharien, appropriated Lionel and Bors, aged 21 and 9 months, and took over their training. The growing boys occupied what must have been a rather uneasy place in the court of King Claudas, and finally gave Claudas' son Dorin his death wound during a fray at dinner. Seraide, who had been sent by Viviane, rescued Lionel and Bors by giving them the shape of greyhounds for a while. They, along with their tutors Pharien, Lambegues, and Leonce, were welcomed into Viviane's Lake, where they finished their education at the side of their cousin Lancelot, and where Lionel took Seraide to be his lady. Lionel and Bors accompanied Lancelot to England, where they were to become knights of the Round Table. [Vulgate III]

As early as V, 6, Malory has Arthur sending Lionel, with Bors, Gawaine, and Bedivere, on an embassy to Lucius during the war with Rome. Soon after their return from the Continent, Lionel accepted Lancelot's invitation to seek adventures, they two alone. While Lancelot was asleep, Lionel saw three knights fleeing from a single adversary. Lionel got up without waking his cousin and took off after them. The single knight was Turquine, who defeated them all, took them prisoner, threw them into his dungeon, stripped them naked, and beat them with thorns. Meanwhile, Lancelot was captured by Morgan and her companions, so that Lionel had a longish wait before his cousin arrived to rescue him.

At least once during the middle years of Arthur's reign Lionel joined a search, headed by Lancelot, for Tristram. Lionel, Bors, and Ector de Maris were the first to leave court, sent and supplied by Guenevere, to find Lancelot when he disappeared in a fit of madness caused by Guenevere's jealousy of Elaine of Carbonek; Lionel spent at least two years on this search. It is possible, though no specific names are mentioned, that Lionel was among those kinsmen of Lancelot's who once sought Tristram's death out of envy because his fame was overshadowing Lancelot's—a murderous effort which Lancelot himself stopped when it came to his attention.

As T. H. White noticed in the **Once and Future King**, Lionel was unlucky about getting beaten with thorns. On the Grail Quest,

> [Sir Bors] met at the departing of the two ways two knights that led Lionel, his brother all naked, bounden upon a strong hackney, and his hands bounden to-fore his breast. And every each of them held in his hands thorns wherewith they went beating him so sore that the blood trailed down more than in an hundred places of his body ... but he said never a word; as he which was great of heart he suffered all that ever they did to him, as though he had felt none anguish.

Bors was about to rescue him when he saw a knight about to rape a virgin on the other side of the road. So, with a prayer to Jesu to keep Lionel, Bors went to help the maiden instead. This, rather understandably, irked Lionel; no matter how nobly he bore suffering, he was also capable of bearing a strong grudge. When next the brothers met, Lionel threatened to kill Bors for his unbrotherly action. Bors made no defense, but a good old hermit ran out to put himself between the brothers. Lionel hewed the old holy man down. Then Sir Colgrevance, a fellow companion of the Round Table, came along and tried to save Bors. Lionel killed Colgravance, too. It took a fiery cloud from Heaven to stop Lionel. On the Heavenly voice instructing Bors to go and join Percivale, Bors, relieved to find that Lionel had not been struck dead by God's vengeance, prepared to go.

> Then he said to his brother: Fair sweet brother, forgive me for God's love all that I have trespassed unto you. Then he answered: God forgive it thee and I do gladly.

Lionel, of course, sided with Lancelot when the break with Arthur came. Accompanying Lancelot into exile, Lionel was crowned King of France. After all, though, he died in England—he was slain apparently during the last of Mordred's rebellion, when he took fifteen other lords from Dover to London to seek Lancelot, who may already have found Arthur's grave (see Melehan). [Malory V, 6; VI, 1-9; IX, 36; X, 88; XI, 10; XII, 9; XVI, 9-17; XX, 5, 18; XXI, 10]

Liones—see **LYONESSE, LYONORS**

Liones Castle—see **LYONESSE CASTLE**

Lionesse—see **LYONORS**

Lionors, Lisanor—see **LYZIANOR**

LISTENEISE (Lands of the Two Marches, Listinoise)

Malory gives Pellam as King of Listeneise and Pelles as King of the Waste Lands. After much consideration I believe Pelles and Pellam to be one and the same. Therefore I feel justified in identifying Listeneise with "The Waste Lands", "The Lands of the Two Marches", and "The Foreign Country" of the Grail Adventures. It is the country of the Grail, which the maimed Fisher King keeps at Carbonek (or Corbenic) Castle; "three countries" were laid waste by the Dolorous Stroke. Listeneise seems also, however, sometimes to play the role of a more normal country, with Pellam carrying out the usual political functions of a king.

For various reasons, I place Listeneise in the present-day Lake District, which is in Cumberland and Westmoreland Counties, due east of the Isle of Man, and includes the Cumbrian Mountains, Windermere, Derwentwater, and Skiddaw Peak. One of my reasons is that Rosemary Sutcliff points out that the Lake land remains unmentioned in the Domesday book, which ends abruptly at the Cumberland fells. (**The Shield Ring**, author's note) Remaining unincorporated and Norse-Saxon in Norman England, the Lake District may have acquired an aura of mystery which carried over into Malorian legend. Also, the Isle of Man makes a very handy Sarras.

LITTLE PIEBALD PALFREY†

The Haughty Maid of Logres' horse, at least according to her own statement. This well trained little mount waited in a garden of a city (Orquesneles?) just over the Galloway border, while the Haughty Maid sent knights to fetch it out to her, and a tall knight sat in the garden warning them of dire consequences to themselves if they did. Apparently the Haughty Knight of the ... Narrow Way waited somewhere outside to vanquish each knight who took the bait, though in Gawaine's case other adventures happened to intervene. The docile palfrey itself was presumably innocent of guile in all this, though at the same time it knew the routine quite well. Its head was black on one side and white on the other, somewhat reminiscent of Enide's sorrel palfrey. [Chrétien de Troyes, **Perceval**, ca. ll. 6711-6837]

LITTLE SLEEVES, MAID WITH (Maiden with the Small Sleeves)†

For her story, see under Garin, Meliant of Liz, Tibaut of Tintagil, and Tibaut's Elder Daughter. D.D.R. Owen calls Tibaut's younger daughter the Maiden with the Small Sleeves; I find Cline's Maid with Little Sleeves more mellifluous, even outside the verse translation. Whichever adjective is chosen, this little maid's sleeves were so tight that they looked painted on. While this may have been a fashionable affectation, I cannot help but wonder if it might not mean that the damsel was having problems outgrowing her clothes: she strikes me as one of Chrétien's youngest creations, if not *the* youngest. While possibly hovering on womanhood, she could equally well be seen as under ten. I doubt that she was completely guiltless in the obvious sibling rivalry with her older sister, but Garin's daughters loved the little maid well, which argues in favor of her amiability. It could have been her extreme youth that finally won Gawaine to break his own resolve and fight as her champion. After winning the second day's tourney for her, he made her the same promise he made to so many a more mature fair one, vowing to be ever ready to drop any other business and hurry to her call for assistance. She replied by seizing his foot and kissing it—an unusual gesture, which she explained by saying she wanted to make sure he would always remember her face wherever he went. I like to think that had Chrétien finished the story, we would have seen much more of the Maid with Little Sleeves. [Chrétien, **Perceval**, ca. ll. 4982-5651]

LLYWARCH HEN (Llywarch the Aged)†

Glennie lists him as one of the four great bards of the Arthurian age; see under Taliessin.

LOATHLY DAMSEL (Ugly Maid)†

The third day after Percivale returned to Arthur's court, avenged the maiden whom Kay had struck (see "Verrine"), and been welcomed, a damsel of extreme ugliness rode a tawny mule into the rejoicings at Caerleon. Her black hair was in two braids, her neck and hands were blacker than iron, her eyes like tiny holes, her nose like that of a cat or monkey, her lips like a donkey's, her teeth yellow as egg yolks, her chin bearded like a billy-goat's, her chest (!) had a hump, her back a lump, her spine was crooked, and her hips twisted. She carried a whip in her right hand. Addressing herself first to Percivale, she excoriated him for failing to ask the crucial questions about the Grail when he visited the Fisher King. Turning then to the king and other knights, she informed them that she intended that evening to reach Castle Orgulous (the Proud Castle), where 566 eminent knights, each with his noble and beautiful lady, waited to give a joust or combat to anyone who came seeking it. She added that anyone who wanted to win the whole world's esteem would be well advised to rescue a damsel under siege on the hill below Montesclaire: whoever raised this siege and saved the damsel would be able to gird on safely the Sword with the Strange Baldric. She then departed, leaving the knights in a flurry of questing fever. Gawaine began by swearing to go to Montesclaire, while Giflet declared in favor of Castle Orgulous, Kahedin chose Mount Dolorous, and Percivale vowed to repair his earlier omission. Gawaine, at least, was to be foiled—quickly on the heels of the Loathly Damsel came Guigambresil to give him even more pressing business. [Chrétien de Troyes, **Perceval**, ca. ll. 4609-4749]

In a footnote to this passage, Cline cites evidence connecting the ugly maid with the lovely grailbearer: Chrétien supplied no link, but two continuations (**Peredur** and **Perlesvaus**) identified them as contrasting manifestations of the same individual; and Loomis suggests a connection with the Sovranty of Ireland. She also reminds me of Dame Ragnell. The color of the Loathly Damsel's mule seems to have symbolized ill omen and deceit.

LOATHLY DAMSEL'S TAWNY MULE†

In medieval times, its color could symbolize ill omen or deceit. The Loathly Damsel tells Arthur's court that she cannot linger because by nightfall she must be far away at Castle Orgulous; this may suggest that her mount can travel faster than one might expect. If the Loathly Damsel is indeed herself one of those marvelous ladies we find in the Arthurian landscape, who can wear either an ugly or a beautiful aspect, then her mule might be similarly marvelous. [Chrétien de Troyes, **Perceval**, ca. ll. 4603-4690, & Cline's note to 4610]

LOGRES (Logris)

According to Lewis Spence, Logres was the eastern part of ancient Britain [**Magic Arts**, p. 167]. Other sources, Chrétien de Troyes for one, seem to apply the name generally to Arthur's kingdom (e.g., Chrétien's **Lancelot**, l. 1313, & D.D.R. Owen's note to same).

In **Perceval**, lines 6169-6170, Chrétien explains the name as signifying "the land of ogres", which it allegedly was in pre-Arthurian times.

Logres, Haughty Maid of—see HAUGHTY MAID OF LOGRES

LOHOLT (Loholz, Lohot)†

King Arthur's son and a very meritorious youth, according to Chrétien de Troyes, who puts him among Arthur's knights in the list beginning in line 1691 of **Erec & Enide**. The Vulgate gives the name of Lohot's mother as Lisanor, which seems to mark her as identical with Lyzianor, whom Malory calls the mother of Arthur's son Borre, opening the possibility that Loholt and Borre are the same man, despite the dissimilarity of their names. According to the Vulgate, Lohot killed the giant Logrin, but was killed in turn by Kay, who wished credit for the giant's death. See also Amyr, Borre.

LONAZEP

This castle, close to Joyous Garde, was the site of a famous tournament [Malory X, 52].

LONDON

This must have been a good place to buy armor: Cligés sent his squires here from Wallingford to buy three full suits of it—one black, one crimson, and one green—for him to wear in the Oxford tournament. They accomplished this within a fortnight. [Chrétien de Troyes, **Cligés**, ll. 4600ff.]

LONDON CATHEDRAL

> So in the greatest church of London, whether were Paul's or not the French book maketh no mention, all the estates were long or day in the church for to pray [for the choice of a king]. [Malory I, 5]

"Paul's" would of course be old St. Paul's cathedral.

LONG ISLES, THE

Duke Galeholt conquered thirty kingdoms, of which Surluse and the Long Isles seem the most notable. This suggests that the Long Isles may have been close to Surluse. Some evidence, however, points to a Welsh location for Surluse; Holyhead and Anglesey (which are more roundish than long) have already been assigned to King Pellinore on stronger evidence. Islay, Jura, Kintyre, and Arran, in Scotland, certainly answer the description of "long islands", and the fact that they are far distant from Wales may be secondary to a conqueror of Galeholt's caliber.

LONGINUS' (Longius') SPEAR (The Spear of Vengeance?)

Balin found this spear in a chamber of King Pellam's castle: "a marvellous spear strangely wrought" standing on a table of clean gold with four silver legs, in a chamber "marvellously well dight and richly, and a bed arrayed with cloth of gold." Since Pellam was pursuing him for killing Garlon, Balin snatched up the spear to defend himself and dealt Pellam the Dolorous Stroke, at which "three counties" were wasted and most of the castle caved in. Although Balin had not known it, this was the spear with which the centurion Longinus smote Our Lord on the cross. [Malory II, 15-16]

It would seem to be as well the same Spear of Vengeance which other knights beheld in the Grail Castle, Carbonek. Sometimes they saw it bleeding; sometimes it came and wounded them when they slept in the Castle Adventurous [cf. Malory XI, 4-5]. Galahad healed the Maimed King by anointing him with blood from the spear [Malory XVII, 21].

In XVII, 5, Malory tells us that Pelles was smitten through both thighs with the spear because he dared try to draw David's Sword when he found Solomon's Ship. I suppose that the spear did not come at once of itself, but that some time elapsed before Balin unwittingly administered the punishment of the Dolorous Stroke as described above.

After Galahad's death, the spear was taken to Heaven along with the Grail [Malory XVII, 22].

See also the bleeding lance.

"LOQUACIOUS HERALD OF NOAUZ"†

Whether this herald-at-arms was native to Noauz or not, I cannot say; he was there for the tournament between the lady of Noauz and she of Pomelegloi. Seeing a new red shield outside the door of a miserable lodging and not recognizing the device (it would be a large part of the herald's profession to keep up with coats of arms), he went in through the open door, found Lancelot, and recognized him right away. The herald's immediate reaction was to cross himself: Lancelot had gone missing in Gore and was almost certainly feared dead. Charged by the great knight in no uncertain terms to keep his identity secret, the herald promised never to do anything that might annoy him, and promptly went out shouting through the streets, "Now the one has come who will take their measure!" without telling anyone whom he meant. His call must have been a popular saying, for Chrétien records this episode as its origin.

The poor herald was sorely embarrassed the first day: suspecting Lancelot's identity, perhaps from his style of fighting, Guenevere tested it by sending him a message, by the damsel I nickname "Elinor", to "do his worst"; he obeyed her. The second day she repeated her injunction but, satisfied of his identity, soon reversed herself and sent the welcome message to do his very best. Thus enjoined, Lancelot lost no further time in justifying the herald's expectations and restoring his boisterous enthusiasm. [Chrétien de Troyes, **Lancelot**, ll. 5546-5985]

LORAINE LE SAVAGE

"A false knight and a coward", he came up from behind and slew Sir Miles of the Launds with a spear [Malory III, 15]. I cannot find that he was ever overtaken and made to answer for the deed; presumably that task would have fallen to King Pellinore, who had learned that Miles was the lover of Pellinore's daughter Eleine. Loraine's modus operandi suggests that of Garlon or of Breuse Sans Pitie.

LORE DE BRANLANT†

She was a cousin of a knight named Sir Drians li Gaiz of Gais Castle. Branlant seems to have been the name of Lore's own castle; her seneschal was called Bruns de Branlant. Lore was among the many ladies who loved Gawaine. [Vulgate VII]

LORE, LADY†

King Arthur sits with his court about him in Orkney, and they all break down with grief for Gawaine, who is missing and for whom they fear the worst. Up in a gallery, Lady Lore witnesses their grief. It is unclear to me whether or not she also witnesses the arrival of Gawaine's messenger (Igraine's squire from the Rock of Canguin), who is just in process of arriving with news of Gawaine's whereabouts and arrangement to fight Guiromelant. In any event, Lady Lore leaves the gallery and comes down to the Queen, showing distress and shock. The Queen asks her what the trouble is … and there Chrétien laid down his pen forever. It is Lore's first appearance in this romance, though the abruptness of her introduction suggests to me that she may have been already known in other Arthurian contexts of the era. [**Perceval**, ll. ca. 9229 to end]

I would more incline to identify her with Lore of Carduel than with Lore de Branlant.

LORE OF CARDUEL (Lore de Kardoil, Lore la Fille Doon, Lorete)†

Carduel is surely Cardoile, or Carlisle. Dame Lore of Carduel served as the King's cupbearer. At a lovers' rendezvous between the two couples Lancelot and Guenevere, and Duke Galeholt and the Lady of Malohaut, Lore of Carduel and Duke Galeholt's seneschal were also present. [Vulgate III]

In Vulgate VII Lore is a sister or—more likely—a cousin of Guenevere, and either the sister or the lover of Sir Giflez (Griflet?). In some extremely tricky (at least to me) passages, Lore and the Queen appear to help Giflez cross a lake. Four knights seem to have captured Gareth; Kay, after killing one of them, gives his destrier to Lorete (Lore), who then proceeds with the Queen to rescue, mount, and arm Gareth. Once he is armed, the women apparently stand back and watch; however, there is at least a hint that Lorete might do a bit of fighting.

L'Orguellouse Emprise†—see **ORGUELLOUSE EMPRISE**

KING LOT (Loth) OF LOTHIAN AND ORKNEY

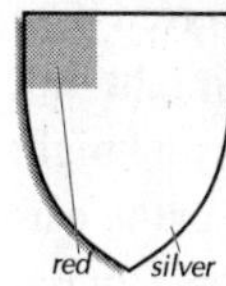

Lot married Morgawse, daughter of Igraine and Gorloïs, at the same time Uther Pendragon married Igraine. The father of Gawaine, Agravaine, Gaheris, and Gareth, Lot was one of the rebel kings at the beginning of Arthur's reign. He showed himself a good strategist during the battle of Bedegraine:

> Then all the eleven [rebel] kings drew them together, and then said King Lot, Lords, ye must other ways than ye do ... ye may see what people we have lost, and what good men we lose, because we wait always on these foot-men, and ever in saving of one of the foot-men we lose ten horsemen for him; therefore this is mine advice, let us put our foot-men from us, for it is near night, for the noble Arthur will not tarry on the foot-men, for they may save themselves, the wood is near hand. And when we horsemen be together, look every each of you kings ... that none break upon pain of death. And who that seeth any man dress him to flee, lightly that he be slain, for it is better that we slay a coward, than through a coward all we to be slain.

Acting upon Lot's advice, the kings at least saved themselves, though not the battle.

After Bedegraine, Lot's wife Morgawse came to Arthur's court, "in manner of a message, but she was sent thither to espy the court." Although we know from the Vulgate account that Morgawse did not share Lot's enmity against Arthur, from Malory's account it appears that at this point Lot was sounding Arthur out, leaving himself free to opt for either peace or further rebellion according to Arthur's strength and disposition. Unfortunately, Arthur begat Mordred on Morgawse and later, learning that a boy born on May Day would destroy him, had Mordred, along with all the other lords' sons born about that time, put on a ship and sent out to sea to die. Whether Lot knew that Arthur had cuckolded him, or whether he believed Mordred—apparently killed with the other babies—to have been his own son, his enmity against Arthur was now cemented, and he joined Ryence and Nero as ringleaders of the second rebellion of twelve kings. This time the crucial battle was fought before Terrabil Castle. During the first part of the battle, Merlin cunningly "came to King Lot ... and held him with a tale of prophecy, till Nero and his people were destroyed." Learning too late of their destruction, Lot cried,

> Alas ... I am ashamed, for by my default there is many a worshipful man slain. ... Now what is best to do? ... whether is me better to treat

> with King Arthur or to fight, for the greater part of our people are slain and destroyed? Sir, said a knight, set on Arthur for they are weary and forfoughten and we be fresh. As for me said King Lot, I would every knight do his part as I would do mine.

So he went into battle and was killed by King Pellinore (though there must have been some confusion, for Pellinore's son Lamorak later claimed it had been Balin who dealt the fatal stroke).

There is an almost Grecian fate about Lot's death. Merlin had known that either Arthur or Lot must die at Terrabil that day, and preferred it be Lot, yet even Merlin regretted the necessity. "Alas he might not endure", says Malory, "the which was great pity, that so worthy a knight as [Lot] was should be overmatched." All the rebel kings died in the battle, and Arthur buried them all with full honors in St. Stephen's Church in Camelot. "But of all these twelve kings King Arthur let make the tomb of King Lot passing richly, and made his tomb by his own ...." [Malory I, 2, 18-19, 27; II, 10-11; X, 24]

Chrétien de Troyes places King Lot among Arthur's living knights in the list beginning line 1691 of **Erec & Enide**, and identifies him as Gawaine's father in **Yvain** [ca. l. 6267] and **Perceval** [l. 8135].

Lot may also have been the father of Thenew, and thus the grandfather of Saint Kentigern.

LOTHIAN

The modern place name of Lothian (West, Mid, and East) in Scotland is just south of the Antonine Wall. King Lot, or Loth, of Lothian and Orkney apparently was king of all northern Scotland from the Orkneys to at least some of the area south of the Antonine Wall. Lot may have been High King of Scotland, with sub-kings under him, before Arthur's advent.

LOUIS†

At the "Church of the Tombs", Lancelot found the tomb where Louis would lie. It waited with, possibly between, the tombs ready-inscribed for Gawaine and Ywaine. This suggests that Sir Louis must have been a knight of no small renown. [Chrétien de Troyes, **Lancelot**, ca. l. 1880]

LOVE POTION

The Queen of Ireland entrusted this, in a little flasket of gold, to Dame Bragwaine and Gouvernail when Tristram came to take the Queen's daughter, La Beale Isoud, to Mark. Bragwaine and Gouvernail were to see that Mark and Isoud drank it on their wedding day; but Tristram and Isoud found it one day on the ship and, thinking it was simply good wine that Gouvernail and Bragwaine had been keeping for themselves, drank it and loved. [Malory VIII, 24]

LOVE RING†

The Damsel of Lestroite Marche gave this ring to Sir Ector de Maris. It had a stone with the power to make the one who received it love with ever-increasing force the one who gave it. [Vulgate III]

The old nurse of King Brandegoris' daughter had a similar ring, though it is not specified that its power lay in the stone. She gave this ring to Sir Bors de Ganis to compel him to love the princess. [Vulgate IV]

LOVEL

One of Gawaine's three sons, apparently the youngest, "begotten upon Sir Brandiles' sister." Lovel became a companion of the Round Table. Joining his uncles Agravaine and Mordred in their attempt to trap Lancelot with the Queen, Lovel was killed by the escaping Lancelot. [Malory XIX, 11; XX, 2-4]

Loverseph, Loverzeph†—see LEVERZEP

LUCAN THE BUTLER (Lucanere de Buttelere, Lucas)

Son of Duke Corneus and possibly brother of Bedivere, Sir Lucan appears to have been a good knight and sensible, and gentle in the best sense of the word. One of Arthur's earliest knights, he may have been appointed butler at the same time Kay was named seneschal; at least, he appears in that post, serving with Kay and Griflet, at the feast given by Arthur in honor of his newly arrived allies Kings Ban and Bors. Lucan fought valiantly in the battle of Bedegraine; we can probably assume that he also fought at Terrabil and on Humber bank. Through most of Malory's work Lucan remains in the background, presumably carrying out his duties as butler. He does appear half a dozen times in the books of Tristram and those immediately following the Grail Adventures, chiefly jousting at tournaments. At least once during the books of Tristram Lucan shows up riding by and for adventure; he has now attained Round Table status. Outjousted and injured by Tristram, he is brought safely to the abbey of Ganis by Ywaine.

Lucan remained with Arthur when the split came between the King and Lancelot. When Arthur was encamped before Benwick, it was Lucan who met Lancelot's messengers, a damsel and her dwarf.

> And when she came to the pavilion of King Arthur, there she alighted; and there met her a gentle knight, Sir Lucan the Butler, and said: Fair damosel, come ye from Sir Launcelot du Lake? Yea sir, she said, therefore I come hither to speak with my lord the king. Alas, said Sir Lucan, my lord Arthur would love Launcelot, but Sir Gawaine will not suffer him. ... I pray to God, damosel, ye may speed well, for all we that be about the king would Sir Launcelot did best of any knight living.

As one of the last two knights left alive with Arthur after the last battle at Salisbury, Lucan tried to prevent the King from attacking Mordred.

> Now give me my spear, said Arthur unto Sir Lucan, for yonder I have espied the traitor that all this woe hath wrought. Sir, let him be, said Sir Lucan, for he is unhappy; and if ye pass this unhappy day ye shall be right well revenged upon him. Good lord, remember ye of your night's dream, and what the spirit of Sir Gawaine told you this night, yet God of his great goodness hath preserved you hitherto. Therefore, for God's sake, my lord, leave off by this, for blessed be God ye have won the field, for here we be three alive, and with Sir Mordred is none alive; and if ye leave off now this wicked day of destiny is past.

Arthur insisted on attacking Mordred, killing him but getting his own death wound in the process. Lucan and Bedivere got Arthur to a little chapel. Hearing people cry in the battlefield, the King sent Lucan to see what was going on. Lucan found robbers and pillagers stealing from the corpses.

> When Sir Lucan understood this work, he came to the king as soon as he might, and told him all what he had heard and seen. Therefore by my rede, said Sir Lucan, it is best that we bring you to some town.

When Lucan tried to help Bedivere lift Arthur, a wound opened and part of Lucan's bowels burst out, and so he died. [Malory I, 10-14; IX, 37; X, 74; XVIII, 11, 23; XIX, 11; XX, 19; XXI, 4-5]

In Malory, Bedivere, the other survivor of the last battle, is called Lucan's brother. I am not sure whether this means blood relationship, or brother in the sense that both were of the Round Table. In Vulgate VI, where Griflet and not Bedivere is the last knight left alive with Arthur, Lucan is nevertheless the next-to-the-last, and dies when Arthur embraces him.

Sir Lucan entered Arthurian literature early: Chrétien de Troyes casually mentions him as Lucan the cup-bearer [**Erec & Enide**, ca. l. 1528].

LUCIUS, EMPEROR OF ROME

"Emperor Lucius, which was called at that time, Dictator or Procuror of the Public Weal of Rome", sent twelve ancient, venerable ambassadors to Arthur's court to command from him the traditional obeisance and truage paid by the kings of Britain to Rome, and threatening dire war against Arthur if he refused to pay. Arthur refused to pay, citing the examples of "Belinus and Brenius, kings of Britain, [who] have had the empire in their hands many days, and also Constantine the son of Heleine." Arthur then crossed the Channel to meet Lucius on the Continent, perhaps reasoning that thus he could keep the destruction of warfare out of Britain. Lucius summoned Rome's allies to his aid, gathered his army and his personal bodyguard of "fifty giants which had been engendered of fiends", and set out to meet Arthur in France. Arthur sent Gawaine, Bors, Lionel, and Bedivere in embassy to command Lucius to return to Rome. Haughty words passed on both sides, Lucius showing himself as proud as Arthur, and finally Gawaine fell into a rage and slew Lucius' cousin Sir Gainus in the Emperor's presence. The ensuing skirmish turned into a battle, with much bloodshed and taking of Roman prisoners. Lucius arranged an ambush to rescue the Roman prisoners as they were being sent to Paris. The attempt was foiled by Lancelot and Cador. A senator who escaped from the fray reached Lucius with this counsel:

> Sir emperor, I advise thee for to withdraw thee; what dost thou here? ... for this day one of Arthur's knights was worth in the battle an hundred of ours. Fie on thee, said Lucius, thou speakest cowardly; for thy words grieve me more than all the loss that I had this day.

Lucius proceeded to the crucial battle with Arthur and met death from Arthur's own sword, following which Arthur marched on Rome, took it, and was crowned Emperor of Rome by the Pope himself. [Malory V]

It seems that Arthur was not able to maintain himself as both King of Britain and Emperor of Rome, for the Romans attacked him again when he was besieging Lancelot in France toward the end of his reign [Vulgate VI]. We may perhaps surmise that there was originally but one campaign against Rome (in some medieval versions, Mordred makes his bid for the throne while Arthur is absent on the Roman campaign rather than while Arthur is in France for the specific purpose of fighting Lancelot). It also makes sense, however, to accept a successful British war against Rome, as described by Malory, during the early or middle years of Arthur's reign, followed by a revolt of Rome against Arthur in the last, troubled years of his reign, as described in Vulgate VI.

I am not sure whether it was Lucius or his predecessor who married Avenable.

Lucius' Bodyguard—see under **LUCIUS**

LUNETTE (Lunete)†

When Ywaine has chased Laudine's mortally wounded husband Escades into the castle, has gotten himself trapped in a little hall between two gates, and runs the risk of death if he is discovered, Laudine's chief handmaid and advisor Lunette remembers that once her lady sent her on an errand to Arthur's court, and Ywaine alone, of all the knights there, deigned to speak to her. (The unfailingly courteous Gawaine must have been away from court during her visit.) Perhaps, she supposes, she did not comport herself with as much prudence and courtliness as she should have. Now she repays Ywaine's courtesy on that occasion by befriending him, bringing him food, and giving him a magic ring of invisibility. As the opportunity ripens, she further repays him by successfully matchmaking for him and Dame Laudine.

Upon Arthur bringing his court to Laudine's castle, Lunette and Gawaine strike up a lively flirtation and friendship, with him (predictably) swearing to be her knight. Chrétien likens Gawaine to the sun and Lunette to the moon—largely on account of her name, which he only now tells us. Virtually alone among Chrétien's golden-haired heroes, heroines, and anybody described as handsome or beautiful, Lunette is definitely a brunette. [ca. l. 2415]

Gawaine would assuredly have defended her against Laudine's seneschal's formal charge of treason; unhappily, he is away just then in Gore, so that the trial by combat falls to Ywaine, who fortunately turns up in the nick of time.

Along with good sense, wit, and a certain store of mischief, Lunette has a strong streak of generosity: when it looks as if she is about to be burned, the other ladies of Laudine's court mourn, "Now who will advise our lady to give us fine clothes? Nobody else ever makes requests for other people any more."

All in all, even though Laudine is the hero's romantic interest, Lunette steals the spotlight to such an extent that one might be tempted to call her the true heroine of Chrétien's **Yvain**.

A "Lunete" appears in Vulgate VII as a cousin-germain of Niniane (Nimue and/or Viviane). I assume that, like her cousin of the Lake, Lunette is here a magician (cf. the magic ring Chrétien's Lunette gives Ywaine), but she may be simply a damsel.

It has been suggested that Lunette became Malory's Dame Linet, the Damsel Savage. While such a metamorphosis is conceivable, I find their tales, positions, and personalities too different to maintain the identification today.

LUNETTE'S RING†

When so worn that the stone was enclosed in the hand, this ring conferred invisibility upon the wearer. [Chrétien de Troyes, **Yvain**, ll. 1026-1281]

LYNETTE (Linet, The Damosel Savage)

When Sir Ironside laid siege to Lynette's sister Lyonors in Castle Dangerous, Lynette came to Arthur's court to find a champion. At first reluctant for some reason to tell her sister's name, she seemed about to reveal it in order to gain a worthy knight when Beaumains, hot from his year in the kitchen and not yet knighted, asked for the adventure. Since this was serious business—Gawaine himself had just called the Red Knight "one of the perilloust knights of the world"—we may understand Lynette's annoyance at being given an unproved kitchen page for her sister's champion, especially when Lancelot and Gawaine, the two knights Ironside most sought to fight, were both at court. She industriously rebuked Gareth all the way from Arthur's court to the city of Sir Persant of Inde. It is possible that, like Beauvivante, she hoped to discourage her youthful knight from risking his life, but during his battle with Perimones, it was Perimones whom she cheered on. The triumphant Gareth threatened to kill Pertelope, Perimones, and Persant, each in turn, unless "his lady" told him to spare them; she always did, though couching the instruction in scornful terms the first few times. By the time they came to Persant's city, though, she had relented, begged Gareth's pardon, and warned him sincerely against taking on Persant and later Ironside. In Ironside's case, she also craftily couseled Gareth to wait until after noon, when Ironside's strength would be on the decline, before issuing his challenge. (He scorned the suggestion, of course.) At one point in the battle with Ironside, when Gareth was temporarily on the bottom, Lynette cheered on her former kitchen knave, reminding him that Lyonors was looking on and thus stirring him to victory. Like the Isouds and other ladies, Lynette had surgical skill, tending the wounds of both Gareth and Ironside after the fight.

Not long thereafter, when Gareth and Lyonors "were accorded to abate their lusts secretly", Lynette used her craft and a magic salve to keep them honest before marriage. Although this is Malory's only instance of Lynette in the apparent role of sorceress, and although she could simply have gotten hold of Sir Priamus' restorative balm or some similar unguent, the evidence suggests some sorcerous, rather than merely surgical, knowledge on her part. For instance, when the leeches examined the wounds Lynette's knight inflicted on Gareth, they "said that there was no man … should heal him throughout of his wound but if they healed him that caused that stroke by enchantment." Then Lynette "laid an ointment and a salve to him as it pleased to her, that he was never so fresh nor so lusty."

Lynette's brother was Sir Gringamore; her niece was Dame Laurel. When Lyonors was wedded to Gareth, the quick-tongued, crafty, and lively though somewhat puritanical Lynette was wedded to Gaheris. [Malory VII]

Perhaps she is best remembered today for Tennyson's graceful version in **Gareth and Lynette**, one of the most enjoyable of his idylls. Tennyson has Gareth fall in love with and marry Lynette rather than Lyonors, which perhaps seems more satisfying to the modern mind. Because the Tennysonian names seem to me more musical than the

Malorian, and because Malory names the other sister Lionesse, which sounds confusingly like the country of Lyonesse, I have used Tennyson's names instead of Malory's in this work.

The King's Damosel, a charming modern romance by Vera Chapman, which catches the medieval spirit with a good admixture of modern taste, uses Lynette for its heroine. Chapman (who does take considerable liberties with Malory) has Lynette leaving Gaheris almost at once to become a carrier of messages for Arthur. In Chapman's version, Lynette, although not a virgin, achieves the Grail. She reappears in Chapman's other romances, **The Green Knight** and **King Arthur's Daughter**, which show her surviving the downfall of Arthur's kingdom to help plant the seeds of Arthur's spirit in future generations.

LYONESSE (Liones)

My edition of Malory spells the land Liones throughout, employing the same spelling as for Dame Liones, Gareth's love. To avoid confusion, I have gone to the more common modern variant spelling Lyonesse for the land, a now-sunken peninsula of which only the Scilly Islands remain.

LYONESSE (Liones) CASTLE

Sir Sadok passed this castle on his way to Arbray Castle, while escaping from Mark's ambushment at Tintagil [Malory X, 50]. I would guess Lyonesse Castle to be on the border between the land of Lyonesse and the rest of the Cornish peninsula, and Arbray to be a castle in the heart of Lyonesse.

At the northwest point of Land's End, modern Cornwall, are "the ruynes of an auntiente castle .. vpon a loftie craggie rocke, where yet appeare the ruined walls and forlorne trenches" [Norden]. The site is right for Lyonesse Castle.

LYONORS (Liones, Lionesse)

Sister of Lynette, chatelaine of Castle Dangerous (also called Castle Perilous), lady and wife of Sir Gareth, Dame Lyonors also had a brother, Sir Gringamore, and a niece, Dame Laurel. I have preferred Tennyson's version of her name.

Though rather outshadowed by her sister, Lyonors does show considerable character of her own. Hers must have been a wealthy castle, for she was able to host a tournament there for Arthur's knights and others. She also seems to have been a competent chatelaine, to judge by her foresight when Gareth's dwarf brought her word that his master and her sister were nearing the castle. She sent the dwarf to a hermitage appertaining to Castle Dangerous, taking the hermit

> wine in two flagons of silver, they are of two gallons, and also two cast of bread with fat venison baked, and dainty fowls; and a cup of gold. ... And go thou unto my sister and greet her well, and commend me unto that gentle knight, and pray him to eat and to drink and make him strong ....

She was coy, for even after Gareth defeated Ironside for her, she declared she would not love her champion until he was "called one of the number of the worthy knights. And therefore go labour in worship this twelvemonth, and then thou shalt hear new tidings." In this she may only have acted according to the postures of her milieu. Apparently endowed, however, with a sense of humor, she enlisted her brother's aid for an elaborate practical joke involving the kidnaping of Gareth's dwarf and encompassing Lyonors' own flirtation, under an assumed identity, with Gareth (who had not until then seen the lady of Castle Dangerous close up). No prude, she was ready enough to go to bed with Gareth now, before marriage, though Lynette prevented it. On the whole, we may hope that Lyonors and her husband enjoyed a happy wedded life. [Malory VII]

LYONORS' RING

Sir Gareth wished to fight in a tournament without being known.

> Then Dame [Lyonors] said unto Sir Gareth: Sir, I will lend you a ring, but I would pray you as you love me heartily let me have it again when the tournament is done, for that ring increaseth my beauty much more than it is of himself. And the virtue of my ring is that, that is green it will turn to red, and that is red it will turn in likeness to green, and that is blue it will turn in likeness to white, and that is white it will turn in likeness to blue, and so it will do of all manner of colours. Also who that beareth my ring shall lose no blood, and for great love I will give you this ring.

Gareth wore the ring and his armor appeared now of one color and now of another, which confused combatants and onlookers, although they seemed to realize it was the same knight in all these different colors. "What manner a knight is yonder knight that seemeth in so many divers colors?" asked Tristram. When Gareth rode out for a moment to amend his helm and take a drink, his dwarf contrived to get the ring, wishing, for greater glory, that Gareth be known. Then "King Arthur had marvel what knight he was, for the king saw by his hair that it was the same knight." [Malory VII, 27-29]

LYZIANOR (Lionors, Lisanor)

The daughter of Earl Sanam, Dame Lyzianor "came thither [to Arthur] for to do homage, as other lords did after the great battle" of Bedegraine. She pleased Arthur so well that he begat on her Sir Borre, "that was after a good knight, and of the Round Table" [Malory I, 17].

This was, of course, before Arthur met Guenevere. Lyzianor seems to have been chatelaine of Karadigan Castle. [Vulgate VII, p. 206]

In Vulgate II, Sommer uses Lisanor for her name, and her son by Arthur is called Lohot. To try to avoid confusion with Lyonors of Castle Dangerous, I have here preferred the variant name for Arthur's early paramour as given in Vulgate VII.

Barbara Ferry Johnson's competent novel **Lionors** is based on this character. Johnson's portrayal is along totally different lines from those I have etched in, making Lionors Arthur's secret, lifelong lover and also, for some reason, transforming her son into a daughter called Elise (not to be confused with the heroine of Chapman's book, **King Arthur's Daughter**).

MAAGLANT†

A leader of the Sesnes, involved in the attack on Vandaliors Castle early in Arthur's reign [Vulgate II].

MAANTE†

Capital of Listeneise [Vulgate I].

MABONAGRAIN†

Nephew of King Evrain, Mabonagrain while still a squire served a year as hired warrior to the Count of Lalut. I *think.* Pronouns and antecedents are such that I see some possibility of the count who hired Mabonagrain being, not he of Lalut (who was Enide's mother's brother), but an older brother of Enide's father. While serving this year, Mabonagrain and one of Enide's cousins fell in love with each other and made a pact, she requiring him to vow he would grant her an as-yet-unstated favor whenever she should ask it. She returned to Brandigant Castle with him, where King Evrain eventually knighted him in the "Garden of the Joy." She then explained to Mabonagrain that she wished him to fulfil his vow by staying with her in that same garden until a knight came and vanquished him in armed combat. His strict adherence to her wish produced the adventure called the Joy of the Court, wherein many knights perished until Erec arrived and defeated Mabonagrain. (See "Joy, Garden of the")

I can find nothing in the original wording, as translated by D.R.R. Owen, to require the death of every unsuccessful challenger, and certainly Mabonagrain himself retained his life when defeated by Erec. Possibly he beheaded all his earlier challengers to prove his good faith, or to discourage future challengers, or to ensure that he would not have to fight any particular knight more than once. In any event, he disclaimed any blame for their deaths on the grounds that he had to keep his knightly word in order not to prove a false and disloyal perjurer, an excuse eveyone understood so well that they blamed neither him nor his lady for all those deaths. On the contrary, both he and she were delightedly drawn into the general rejoicings over his defeat, which celebrations lasted three days before Erec insisted on leaving. Sounding overjoyed at his own defeat, especially when he learned that his conqueror was King Lac's son, Mabonagrain presumably settled down into a fine, socially conscious knight.

He was a foot taller than any other knight known (presumably excluding those of giant blood), and Chrétien remarks on his height as a blemish to his otherwise handsome appearance. He wore crimson armor, at least while defending the garden. [Chrétien de Troyes, **Erec & Enide**, ll. 5367-6410]

As I learned through personal correspondence with Jessica Amanda Salmonson, Mabonagrain would appear to be a descendant or avatar of Mabon, a Welsh god of death, which casts light on both his role in Erec's adventure and the paradisal garden with its fence of impaled heads.

MABONAGRAIN'S LADY†

Fairer than Helen of Troy, this damsel was the daughter of Enide's father's brother, and thus another cousin of Enide's. Finding her in the "Garden of the Joy" at Brandigant Castle, Enide felt unsure whether she recognized her or not, and finally had to ask. Both had been little more than children when the cousin left with Mabonagrain.

One is tempted to hypothesize that this damsel made her request of Mabonagrain because she wanted to keep him safe with her, secluded in their garden from the violence of the age. [Chrétien de Troyes, **Erec & Enide**, ll. 5367-6410]

MADAWG AP UTHER (Madoc, Maduc)†

Arthur's brother and the father of Eliwlod, q.v. [Spence, **Magic Arts**, p. 159]. Ronan Coghlan [**Encyclopaedia of Arthurian Legends**, p. 151] finds another possible reference to this character in the **Book Of Taliesin** and adds that one of Arthur's opponents in unidentified, presumably medieval French romances is called Madoc or Maduc.

MADERNE WELL†

North of Penzance, almost half way to the north Cornish coast, is the parish of St. Maderne,

> situate vunder the craggie hills ... nere which is a well called Maderne Well, whose fame in former ages was great; for the supposed vertue of healing, which St. Maderne had therinto infused: And manie votaries made annale pilgrimages vnto it, as they doe euen at this daye vnto the well of St. Winifride, beyounde Chester, in Denbigheshire, wherunto thowsands doe yearly make resort." [Norden]

It is a good guess that these wells had healing powers from Pagan times. The Christian saints, or at least their legends, may even have been invented or modified to Christianize the wells.

There are, of course, far too many such holy wells throughout England to itemize them all, and Maderne, although not specifically connected with Arthurian legend, is included here only as an example. Among powers sometimes connected with such wells is the quality that whichever partner, husband or wife, drinks the water soonest after the marriage ceremony will henceforth have predominance in married life. At Alternun, Cornwall, is a "bowsening pool" wherein mad folk were formerly dowsed to restore their senses. (Let those who laugh compare this remedy with our modern enlightened "shock treatments" for insanity.)

Madoc—see **MADAWG**

MADOR DE LA PORTE

This companion of the Round Table must have been one of Arthur's first knights. Malory mentions him fighting, along with Sirs Mordred and Galahantine, on the side of the King of Norgales in a tournament between him and King Bagdemagus, and "against them three [Bagdemagus] nor [his] knights might bear no strength." Lancelot, fulfilling a promise to Bagdemagus' daughter, entered the tournament and defeated all three, Mador first. Lancelot defeated Mador again some time later at the Surluse tournament.

When—according to the Vulgate account, which here varies considerably in detail from Malory's—Mador had served Arthur for forty-five years, Guenevere invited him as one of two dozen guests at a small dinner party she gave to show the world she delighted in all the knights of the Round Table, not only in Lancelot, who was absent at the time. At this dinner Mador's cousin Sir Patrise (in the Vulgate, his brother Sir Gaheris de Kareheu) fell accidental victim to poison which Sir Pinel le Savage (in the Vulgate, Sir Avarlon) meant for Gawaine. Suspicion naturally fell on the Queen.

> [Then Gawaine said,] madam, I dread me lest ye will be shamed .... This shall not so be ended, said Sir Mador de la Porte, for here have I lost a full noble knight of my blood; and therefore upon this shame and despite I will be revenged to the utterance. And there openly Sir Mador appealed the queen of the death of his cousin, Sir Patrise.

Arthur arrived, regretting that his duty to act as judge prevented him from fighting for Guenevere himself and promising Mador that she would find a champion. "My gracious lord, said Sir Mador ... though ye be our king in that degree, ye are but a knight as we are, and ye are sworn unto knighthood as well as we." According to the Vulgate, Mador resigned his allegiance to Arthur in order to fight this trial by combat. Lancelot arrived in time to champion the Queen and, for the third time in Malory's book, defeated Mador, who then asked for mercy, "released the queen of his quarrel", and was welcomed back to his place among the knights of the Round Table. The fight, however, had lasted "nigh an hour, for this Sir Mador was a strong knight, and mightily proved in many strong battles." Perhaps Mador continued to mistrust the Queen, for he joined the group that helped Mordred and Agravaine corner Lancelot with Guenevere, and was killed when Lancelot made his escape. [Malory VI, 6, 7, 18; X, 45; XVIII, 3-7; XX, 2-4; Vulgate VI]

References to Mador de la Porte in **Sir Gawaine and the Green Knight** and elsewhere suggest that in earlier romances he was much more important than we would assume from Malory alone.

FAMILY TO SIR MADOR DE LA PORTE
Brothers: Adragain, Gaheris de Kareheu
Cousin: Patrise of Ireland

Maduc—see **MADAWG**

MAGIC BOAR'S HEAD†

See under Magic Mantle, just below.

MAGIC CHESSBOARD†

Gwenbaus made this for his princess (see Forest Perilous). Lancelot later brought it to Guenevere. The chessboard had pieces of gold and silver. When anyone began to move the pieces of one side, the opposing pieces would move automatically and soon checkmate the mortal player. The board was to retain this property until the death of the most graceful and best beloved knight, who alone would never be checkmated by it. Guenevere, although an expert at chess, lost when she played on this board. Lancelot, however, won, so that the board was finally awarded to him. [Vulgate V]

A precursor to computer chess.

MAGIC GOLD HORN†

See under Magic Mantle, below.

MAGIC MANTLE

Child Ballad number 29, "The Boy and the Mantle", tells of these items:

(1) A magic mantle which will wrinkle up, change color, or both if any untrue woman wears it. The only woman at Arthur's court who can wear it is Sir Craddocke's wife, and even on her it begins to wrinkle at the toe, until she makes Full Confession: she had kissed Craddocke's mouth once before they were married. (The logical extension of this—that the mantle might have misbehaved on any woman, though she was utterly faithful to one man, if they had had relations before the knot was officially tied—does not seem to have occurred either to the balladeer or to the people in his song.)

(2) A boar's head that could only be carved by the knife of a man who was not a cuckold.

(3) A horn of red gold from which no cuckold could drink without spilling.

Of these items, the mantle definitely has pride of place. Child traces the story through French, German, Scandinavian, and other versions dating well back into the Middle Ages. It would have been nice if one of the items had been designed to test the man's faithfulness. This sounds almost like another attempt of Morgan le Fay's to convince Arthur of Guenevere's unfaithfulness, and perhaps the drinking horn of the ballad tradition is connected with Malory's tale of the drinking horn Morgan made, from which no faithless wife could drink without spilling.

MAGOUNS CASTLE

Malory identifies this as "a castle that is called Magouns, and now it is called Arundel, in Sussex." The constable of Magouns, Sir Bellangere, was cousin to Dame Anglides, who fled here with her infant son and here remained to raise him. The son was Sir Alisander le Orphelin; his father, Anglides' husband, was Prince Boudwin, slain by King Mark. [Malory X, 32-34]

MAHELOAS, BARON, LORD OF THE ISLE OF GLASS†

Listing Maheloas among the vassal lords whom Arthur summoned to court for Erec's wedding, Chrétien de Troyes describes his Isle of Glass as a place free from storm, thunder, lightning, snakes, toads, and extremes of hot and cold. This sounds to me like Avalon, and Avalon is usually identified with Glastonbury; yet further on in the same passage Chrétien names Morgan's lover Guingomar as lord of the Isle of Avalon. Possibly an example of one place—and character?—being split into two. [**Erec & Enide**, ll. 1934-1962]

MAIDENS, CASTLE OF

There may well have been two or more Castles of Maidens, and it or they are not quite like the "Castle Anthrax" which Galahad finds so full of choice damsels in the film **Monty Python and the Holy Grail**.

Perhaps the most notable account in Malory of a Castle of Maidens is that in XIII, 15-16. Seven years before the Grail Quest, Duke Lianour had held this castle. Seven wicked brothers moved in, raped his elder daughter, and murdered him and his son. When the daughter predicted the brothers would all be defeated by one knight, they decided to hold prisoner all knights and ladies who passed by. "[A]nd therefore is it called the Maidens' Castle, for they have devoured many maidens." (A "maiden", in older and broader usage, can be a virgin of either sex.) Galahad arrived and defeated all seven brothers in battle, but did not kill them. Fleeing, they ran by chance into Gawaine, Gareth, and Ywaine, who did kill them. The elder sister was dead by now, but the Duke's younger daughter was made mistress of the castle and lands. The spiritual significance (hardly anything happens during the Adventures of the Grail which is not a parable) is that the prisoners represent the good souls that were in prison (Hell or Limbo) before the time of Christ, and the seven brothers represent the seven deadly sins.

This Castle of Maidens was "a strong castle with deep ditches, and there ran beside it a fair river that hight Severn" [Malory XIII, 15]. It might be near the source of the Severn, at Llanidloes, Montgomeryshire, Wales.

Malory also mentions a Castle of Maidens in IX, 25-35, as the site of an important tournament between the King of North Wales and King Carados of Scotland. This tournament is remembered in X, 58:

> Sir, said Palomides [to Tristram, as they approached Castle Lonazep and saw the tournament set up there], meseemeth that there was as great an ordinance at the Castle of Maidens upon the rock, where ye won the prize.

This may be the same castle as that of XIII, 15-16; the tournament could have been held before the seven wicked brothers moved in. By the account of the old religious man who explained its history to Galahad, though, there would have been no reason to call it the Castle of Maidens before the time of the seven brothers.

Glennie identifies the Castle of Maidens with Edinburgh, speculating that the name may come from a house of nuns (see Dunpeledur). This contradicts both Malory's placement of the stronghold on the Severn and his tale of the seven brothers. If, however, the Castle of Maidens of the tournament is considered to be a different fortress than Duke Lianour's, then Edinburgh could accomodate it nicely, especially with Malory naming Carados of Scotland as one of the tournament's promoters and Glennie mentioning the "fortified rock" of Edinburgh.

John W. Donaldson briefly identifies the Castle of Maidens as "near Dorchester", for no reason that I can see.

See also the Castle of the Hard Rock and the Chastel as Dames.

Maidens, Isle of†—see ISLE OF MAIDENS

Maimed King—see FISHER KING, PELLAM, ARTHUR

MAIMED KNIGHT†

In one hand the Maimed Knight involuntarily grasped a sword which had penetrated his other hand. Only the best knight in the world could remove the sword. The Maimed Knight was understandably annoyed when Bors and Agravaine, meeting him, entered into an argument about whether Lancelot or Gawaine was the best knight. Naturally, it was Lancelot who finally relieved him of the sword. [Vulgate IV]

I am not sure whether this knight traveled in a litter or remained in his castle or manor; if the latter he probably was located near the marches of Stranggore.

MAINES†

Maines was one of the three sons, apparently the oldest, of King Constans of England, Arthur's grandfather. Thus, he would have been Arthur's uncle, but he was killed early, murdered by a dozen barons who wanted Vortigern for their king. Maines was survived and avenged by his brothers Uther and Pandragon. [Vulgate III]

MALAHAUT† (Malohaut?)

According to Vulgate II, the ruler of Malahaut was the King with the Hundred Knights. A town called Le Puis de Malohaut, however, was ruled by the widowed Lady of Malohaut, who became Duke Galeholt's paramour. Perhaps she acted as vice-regent for the King with the Hundred Knights. The location of this subkingdom is unknown.

Maledisant—see **BEAUVIVANTE**

MALEDISANT'S SHIELD

A great black shield, with a white hand in the midst holding a sword. The damsel Maledisant (later called Beauvivante) brought it to Arthur's court, seeking a knight to fulfill the quest of the shield's dead owner. Sir La Cote Male Taile took the quest. Malory's account leaves the quest unclear. Breuse Sans Pitie had once taken the shield from Maledisant, and Tristram had regained it for her that time. [Malory IX, 2-9]

MALGRIN

A dangerous, probably villainous knight located in the general neighborhood of the castle La Beale Regard, Sir Malgrin is mentioned in the same breath with Breuse Sans Pitie:

> Then [Mark] sent unto Queen Morgan le Fay, and to the Queen of Northgalis, praying them in his letters that they two sorceresses would set all the country in fire with ladies that were enchantresses, and by such that were dangerous knights, as Malgrin, Breuse Saunce Pité, that by no means Alisander le Orphelin should escape [Malory X, 35].

In the next chapter, Alisander meets a chatelaine who asks him to joust for her sake with her neighbor, Sir Malgrin, who "will not suffer me to be married in no manner wise for all that I can do, or any knight for my sake." Alisander and Malgrin jousted and fought on foot for

> three hours, [and] never man could say which was the better knight. ... But this Malgrin was an old roted [practiced] knight, and he was called one of the most dangerous knights of the world to do battle on foot, but on horseback there were many better.

During a lull in the fight, the felonious Malgrin told Alisander,

> Wit thou well ... for this maiden's love, of this castle, I have slain ten good knights by mishap; and by outrage and orgulité [pride] of myself I have slain ten other knights.

Alisander at last ended Malgrin's career by smiting off his head. As for the chatelaine, she asked Alisander to give her in marriage to her old sweetheart, Sir Gerine le Grose, who lived in that area. Alisander obliged. [Malory X, 36-37]

Malohaut—see also **MALAHAUT**

MALOHAUT, LADY OF†

She ruled a town called Le Puis de Malohaut, apparently in the territory of Malahaut. Since Vulgate II assigns this country to the King of the Hundred Knights, the Lady may have been his vice-regent. She was a good governor, loved by the people, and a widow.

She imprisoned Lancelot for killing the son of her seneschal, but released him on his parole so that he could attend an assembly or tournament. Probably she did not really expect him to return, but he came back without fanfare and quietly went to sleep in his cell. When the Lady found his weapons and armor battered, his horse wounded, himself wounded and asleep in his cell, she fell in love with him.

Later, however, witnessing a lovers' meeting between Lancelot and the Queen, the Lady of Malohaut set aside her own feelings and offered herself as Guenevere's confidante. Lancelot could confide in Duke Galeholt, and the Lady told Guenevere, "I believe that four can keep a secret better than three." Guenevere then tried a little matchmaking between the Lady of Malohaut and Duke Galeholt. She went about it in direct style, counseling each of them frankly to love one another, and succeeded in bringing them together so well that after Galeholt's death, the Lady of Malohaut died for love of him. [Vulgate III-IV]

Vulgate VII mentions a *Senayns li chastelains du Puj de Malohaut.* I would guess that Senayns was the widowed lady's dead husband; the name might be transferred to the lady herself.

"MALVIS"

This damsel arrived at Arthur's court "on message from the great lady Lile of Avelion", girded with a cumbersome, uncomfortable sword. She said she was looking for a knight who could draw the sword from its scabbard and thus relieve her of it, "but he must be a passing good man of his hands and of his deeds … a clean knight without villainy, and of a gentle strain of father side and mother side." Not finding such a knight at King Ryon's court, she had come on to Arthur's. Here only the impoverished prisoner Sir Balin Le Savage could draw the sword.

> Certes, said the damosel, this is a passing good knight, and the best that ever I found, and most of worship without treason, treachery, or villainy, and many marvels shall he do. Now gentle and courteous knight, give me the sword again. Nay, said Balin. … Well, said the damosel, ye are not wise to keep the sword from me, for ye shall slay with the

> sword the best friend that ye have, and the man that ye most love in the world, and the sword shall be your destruction. I shall take the adventure, said Balin … but the sword ye shall not have …. Ye shall repent it within short time, said the damosel, for I would have the sword more for your avail than for mine, for I am passing heavy for your sake; for ye will not believe that sword shall be your destruction, and that is great pity. With that the damosel departed, making great sorrow.

Meanwhile, the first English Lady of the Lake, "Nineve", arrived to claim the gift Arthur had promised her when she gave him Excalibur. She asked the head either of Balin or of "Malvis": "I take no force though I have both their heads, for he slew my brother, a good knight and a true, and that gentlewoman was causer of my father's death." Arthur refused "Nineve's" request, but Balin, learning of it, came and lopped off "Nineve's" head, to the King's chagrin. Balin explained that he had been seeking her for three years for having caused the death of his mother, that "this same lady [of the Lake] was the untruest lady living, and by enchantment and sorcery she hath been the destroyer of many good knights."

After Balin's departure, Merlin arrived. Being told all that had happened, the Mage explained:

> [T]his same damosel that here standeth [did stand?], that brought the sword unto your court, I shall tell you the cause of her coming: she was the falsest damosel that liveth. Say not so, said they. She hath a brother, [said Merlin] a passing good knight of prowess and a full true man; and this damosel loved another knight that held her to paramour, and this good knight her brother met with the knight that held her to paramour, and slew him by force of his hands. When this false damosel understood this, she went to the Lady Lile of Avelion, and besought her of help, to be avenged on her own brother. And so this Lady Lile of Avelion took her this sword that she brought with her, and told there should no man pull it out of the sheath but if he be one of the best knights of this realm, and he should be hard and full of prowess, and with that sword he should slay her brother. … Would God she had not come into this court, but she came never in fellowship of worship to do good, but always great harm.

If, in this welter of accusation and counter-accusation, we take Merlin's tale as sooth, then "Malvis" was a wicked woman. Personally, I hold Merlin's testimony suspect. By Balin's own account, which seems reliable—Merlin himself calls Balin a good knight—and by "Nineve's" own vengeful request, the dead Lady of the Lake had been wicked; but "Nineve" appears to have been a friend of Merlin himself, and a long tale of the other damsel's wickedness may have been Merlin's sagest way of taking attention off "Nineve's" wickedness and his own possible guilt by association with her. Moreover, when we look for the fulfillment of Merlin's prophecy that Balin would slay the damsel's brother with the sword, we find as about the only named candidates for her brother to be Sir Garlon and Sir Balan.

It is possible that "Malvis" was indeed the sister of both Balin and Balan; the fact that they did not recognize each other as siblings does not negate that chance, for the romances are full of such cases—one sibling leaves home while the other is still an infant, and so on (compare with Lancelot and Ector de Maris, Gawaine and Gareth). It is also possible that the damsel's brother was one of the knights killed in battle against Ryons, Nero, and Lot, or that Malory omitted the death in question completely. It is even conceivable that Sir Lanceor was "Malvis'" brother, although Balin slew him with lance rather than sword. Garlon, however, seems the likeliest knight for the brother of Merlin's tale, and Garlon's patent villainy hardly tallies with Merlin's praise of the damsel's brother. Moreover, although the damsel's praise of Balin may have been a ruse to tickle his vanity and ensure that he would keep the sword, "Malvis'" subsequent efforts to get it back from him and prevent the coming tragedy sound sincere to me. Since I can find nothing more about this damsel, unless she is to be identified with one of Malory's other ladies, the question of her guilt or innocence may perhaps be considered open. [Malory II, 1-5]

MANASSEN

While escaping from Arthur after her attempt to destroy him and Uriens, Morgan le Fay found Sir Manassen bound and about to be drowned by another knight. Manassen was of Arthur's court, but he was also the cousin of Sir Accolon, Morgan's recently killed paramour. For Accolon's sake, Morgan freed Manassen, let him drown his enemy, and directed him to tell Arthur how she had escaped him by turning herself and her knights into the likenesses of boulders, which errand Manassen carried out. [Malory IV, 15]

Mangars li Rois—see under **GUINDOEL**

MARANT (Maranz, Martans)†

Son of the King of the Hundred Knights [Vulgate V].

MARBOAR, KING (Marboac, Marboart, Narboat, etc.)

His territory was apparently on the way to Estrangor. One of his fortresses seems to have been the Castel del Molin. [Vulgate IV]

MARCHE, CASTEL DE LA†

Since King Brangoire was holding the anniversary of his coronation here, and since the Vulgate's Brangoire is Malory's King Brandegoris of Stranggore, this castle would be on the border of Stranggore [Vulgate IV].

MARCHES

The word signifies borders or border territory. We meet such characters as the Duke of the South Marches, indicating that the Marches could be political entities in themselves. Tentatively, the South Marches might parallel the eastern border of Devon, the Straight Marches follow the eastern border of Wales, and the North Marches extend along the southern border of Scotland.

MARCHES, DAMSEL OF THE†

Apparently a sovereign in her own right, this lady was a liege of Arthur's who came to her aid when Duke Galeholt invaded her territory [Vulgate III].

Marchoise, Marcoise—see MORTAISE

MARES, DAMSEL DES†

The daughter of Sir Agravadain des Vaus de Galoire, she was the victim of what seems to have been either a practical joke or a venture by Merlin into planned genetics.

Five days after the visit of Ban and Merlin, a rich knight of the neighborhood asked for the Damsel's hand in marriage. She meekly but firmly refused, confessing at last that she was with child by King Ban. Sir Agravadain requested the young lover, whose name seems to have been Leriador, to wait for two years and then try again. Instead, Leriador besieged the castle and Agravadain had to beat him off. The Damsel seems to have remained unmarried after giving birth to her son, Sir Ector de Maris, who resembled his father, King Ban.

After Sir Agravadain's death, the castle was held by his son, Ector's uncle and the Damsel's brother. The Damsel seems never to have forgot her lover, for she always kept a sapphire ring he had given her. This ring had been given him by his wife, Elaine of Benwick, who kept another one like it. Years afterwards, the Damsel des Mares was able to prove to Lancelot that her son was his half-brother by means of this ring.

The damsel left her family's castle at least once, to travel to the Royal Minster in Gaul and meet Lancelot's mother, Queen Elaine. [Vulgate III]

MARES, DES†

Kings Ban and Bors stopped here during their visit to Arthur in Britain. The castellan, Agravadain des Vaus (not to be confused with Gawaine's brother, Agravaine), had a beautiful daughter whom Merlin admired and caused to sleep with Ban, resulting in the birth of Lancelot's half-brother, Ector de Maris. [Vulgate II]

Des Mares would probably be near the sea (*mare*).

MARGANOR†

The seneschal of the King of the Hundred Knights, Sir Marganor was vanquished by Sir Ector de Maris before the castle Lestroite Marche [Vulgate III].

Margarit le Roux—see under GUINDOEL

MARGAWSE, QUEEN OF LOTHIAN AND ORKNEY (Bellicent, Morawse, Anna?, Mordads?)

One of the three daughters—seemingly the oldest—of Igraine and Gorloïs, Margawse was wedded to King Lot at the same time that her mother was wedded to Uther Pendragon, her sister Elaine to King Nentres, and her other sister, Morgan, was put to school in a nunnery. By her husband, King Lot, Margawse became the mother of Gawaine, Agravaine, Gaheris, and Gareth, and by her half-brother Arthur she became the mother of Mordred.

Although her husband was one of the chief rebels against Arthur, the Vulgate tells us that Margawse was a staunch supporter of the young High King, encouraging those of her sons who were old enough, especially Gawaine, to join Arthur's side. She herself rode down through dangerous territory to join Arthur's side in person, having several adventures on the way. Malory, however, insinuates that Lot sent his wife to Arthur's court as a spy.

> And thither came to [Arthur], King Lot's wife, of Orkney, in manner of a message, but she was sent thither to espy the court of King Arthur; and she came richly beseen, with her four sons, Gawaine, Gaheris, Agravaine, and Gareth [who must still have been a babe in arms], with many other knights and ladies. For she was a passing fair lady, therefore the king cast great love unto her, and desired to lie by her; so they were agreed .... So there she rested her a month, and at the last departed.

At this time, at least in Malory's account, she did not know Arthur was her half-brother. How she reacted to Arthur's seizure of her youngest born, Mordred, along with other lords' sons that were born at the same time, in order to destroy them, Malory does not record, though he does note it as Lot's motive for the second rebellion.

Her husband killed in this second rebellion, Margawse apparently remained north, governing Orkney and raising her youngest sons. When Gareth was old enough, she sent or allowed him to go to Arthur. After something more than a year, she followed him, arriving at Arthur's court while Gareth was absent on his first round of knightly adventures.

> And as they sat at the meat, there came in the Queen of Orkney, with ladies and knights a great number. And then Sir Gawaine, Sir Agravaine, and Gaheris arose, and went to her and saluted her upon their knees, and asked her blessing; for in fifteen year they had not seen her.

She had somehow learned how Gareth had spent his first year at court.

> Ah, brother, said the Queen unto King Arthur, and unto Sir Gawaine, and to all her sons, he did yourself great shame when ye amongst you kept my son in the kitchen and fed him like a poor hog. Fair sister, said King Arthur, ye shall right well wit I knew him not ... meseemeth ye

> might have done me to wit of his coming, and then an I had not done well to him ye might have blamed me. … Sir, said the Queen of Orkney … wit ye well that I sent him unto you right well armed and horsed, and worshipfully beseen of his body, and gold and silver plenty to spend. It may be, said the King, but thereof saw we none.

Margawse's relations with her brother and his court seem to have been cordial. Although by now middle-aged, she was still beautiful enough that Sir Lamorak, who became her paramour, was ready to defend her beauty against that of Guenevere. Lamorak being the son of Pellinore, the man who had dealt King Lot his death wound, Margawse's new affair did not please her sons. She accepted their invitation to a castle near Camelot, and there she and her lover arranged a tryst. Her son Gaheris, watching his chance, came to their bedside and struck off her head. Learning it, "the king was passing wroth, and commanded him to go out of his court." [Malory I, 2, 19; VII, 25; IX, 13; X, 24; Vulgate II]

T. H. White (who transfers her murder to Agravaine) gives her at least enough grasp of sorcery to conjure Arthur into bed with her by enchantment. I do not recall finding any indication in Malory or in the Vulgate that Margawse was an enchantress; it has been suggested, however, that, although definitely two individual characters in the sources on which I have concentrated, Morgan and Margawse originally were the same character, and became split when some scribe got confused with the case endings of a language not his own (what we would do without clumsy scribes as handy explanations I do not know). Most modern romancers put the blame for Mordred's conception entirely upon Margawse, whom they usually make aware of the incest at the time—Stewart's popular version, which for some reason changes Margawse's own parentage to make her not a legitimate daughter of Igraine and Gorloïs but a bastard of Uther, is particularly hard on her, stripping away even the shadow of self-justification for the act that other romancers allow her.

In my opinion, all this is part of the modern whitewashing of Arthur. (Notice that there is more suggestion of underlying affection than of smoldering hatred and resentment when brother and sister bicker about Gareth, as Malory records the scene.) Tennyson, unable to charge his Arthur with incest, or even adultery, on any pretext whatever, named the wife of Lot and the mother of Gawaine, Gareth, and Mordred Bellicent, perhaps to avoid any identification of her with the lusty and accidentally incestuous (but also spirited and generous) Margawse.

While Chrétien de Troyes does not mention Margawse by name (he does several times mention Morgan; if the two began as one character, she might not yet have split), he does tell us that Lot's queen and

Gawaine's mother—the woman whom later romancers were to identify as Margawse—followed her mother Queen Ygerne to the Rock of Canguin and there gave birth to a daughter, Clarissant. (Chrétien's translators Owen and Cline give notes respectively naming Ygerne's daughter Anna and Morcads.) Gawaine is astonished to hear who the queens of Canguin are, since he had believed Ygerne gone for sixty and his own mother for twenty years. [Chrétien de Troyes, **Perceval**, ca. ll. 7527-8135ff] The evidence that Canguin may be a branch of the Afterlife could facilitate combining Malory's version of Margawse's death with Chrétien's happier ending for Gawaine's mother; such a combination would make Sir Lamorak Clarissant's probable father. By the way, has anyone noticed that the two queens and princess of Canguin neatly form the venerable Trinity of Maiden, Mother, and Crone?

MARGONDES†

A leader of the Sesnes, involved in the attack on Vandaliors Castle early in Arthur's reign [Vulgate II].

MARHALT, KING OF IRELAND

Malory gives four names for Irish kings. Two, Agwisance and Anguish, I believe to be variants of a single name and to refer to the same man. The third Irish king is Ryons (Rience), also king of Norgales, etc. The fourth is Marhalt.

Marhalt was the father of Sir Marhaus and thus the father-in-law of King Anguish, who married Marhaus' sister. The king is mentioned in Malory X, 66, fighting in the Lonazep tournament, but most of the time he remains in the background, perhaps busily governing his territory.

MARHAUS (Morholt, Morolt, etc.)

This Irish knight, the son of King Marhalt, brother-in-law of King Anguish, and uncle of La Beale Isoud, was one of the most promising of the first generation of Arthur's knights, playing a substantial role in the early part of Malory's book. Gawaine and Ywaine, having left court after Morgan's attack of Arthur and Uriens, found a white shield which Marhaus had left hung to a tree, and twelve damsels defiling it on the grounds that its owner "hateth all ladies and gentlewomen." Marhaus returned, driving the damsels back into their tower and slaying the kwo knights of that tower in joust; he then recovered the muddied shield, saying, "... for her love that gave me this white shield I shall wear thee." He now jousted in friendly adventure with Gawaine. Whereas Gawaine's strength increased at noon and then gradually declined until evening, Marhaus became stronger and stronger as evening drew on; thus Marhaus defeated Gawaine. He explained that the twelve damsels who had defiled his shield were false enchantresses, but "to all good ladies and gentlewomen I owe my service as a knight ought to do." Marhaus swore friendship with Gawaine and Ywaine and the three traveled together until, in Arroy, they met the damsels "Printemps, Été, and Automne". Marhaus chose "Été" and went adventuring with her for a year.

Coming to the castle of the Duke of the South Marches, Marhaus introduced himself—perhaps a little prematurely—as a knight of King Arthur's and member of the Table Round. The Duke had sworn vengeance on that company because of Gawaine's slaying seven of his sons in battle, so he regretfully insisted that Marhaus encounter him and his remaining six sons. Marhaus defeated them all and converted them to Arthur's party. The damsel brought him next to a tournament cried by the Lady de Vawse, where he "had sometime down forty knights" and so won the prize, a gold circlet worth a thousand besants. Within a week, his damsel brought him to the territory of young Earl Fergus, where Marhaus slew the troublesome giant Taulurd. On his way back to his year's-end rendezvous with Gawaine and Ywaine, he met and smote down four other knights of Arthur's court, Sagramore le Desirous, Osanna, Dodinas le Savage, and Felot of Listinoise. Rejoining Gawaine and Ywaine, he returned with them to Arthur's court where he "was name of the bests knight living" and enrolled in the Round Table at the same time as Sir Pelleas. During Arthur's war with Lucius, Marhaus joined Lancelot, Bors, Kay, and Marrok as one of the King's personal bodyguard. He was among the knights rescued by Lancelot from Sir Turquine.

Unfortunately, when King Mark decided to stop paying his truage to King Anguish of Ireland, Marhaus fought as his brother-in-law's champion. Mark's champion was the newly-knighted, untried Tristram. Marhaus suggested, in kindly fashion, that the young knight abandon a battle he had no apparent hope of winning, but Tristram insisted on fighting.

> Thus they fought still more than half a day, and … Sir Tristram … [at the last] smote Sir Marhaus upon the helm such a buffet that it went through his helm, and through the coif of steel, and through the brain-pan, and the sword stuck so fast in the helm and in his brain-pan that Sir Tristram pulled thrice at his sword or ever he might pull it out from his head; and there Marhaus fell down on his knees, and the edge of Tristram's sword left in his brain-pan. And suddenly Sir Marhaus rose grovelling, and threw his sword and his shield from him, and so ran to his ships and fled his way … [to Tristram's shouts of] Ah! Sir Knight of the Round Table, why withdrawest thou thee? … [R]ather than I should withdraw me from thee, I had rather be hewn in an hundred pieces. Sir Marhaus answered no word but yede his way sore groaning.

Leaving his sword and shield for Tristram to appropriate, Marhaus regained his ship and was taken back to Ireland, where he died, despite all the efforts of Anguish's servants, of the piece of Tristram's sword stuck in his skull. It argues in favor of his great strength that he was able to run away at all and survive as long as he did. He almost had a Pyrrhic victory, however, for he had wounded Tristram with a poisoned spear. In a final twist of irony, when Tristram became a knight of the Round Table, his name appeared on the chair formerly occupied by Marhaus.

Marhaus' behavior in his final battle seems strange—why should such a noble champion have poisoned his spearhead? In other versions of **Tristram**, the Irish king's champion is presented as a rather less sympathetic figure from the outset. My guess is that Malory either combined two originally distinct characters or created a nobler early history for Marhaus, but needed the poisoned spear-wound to get Tristram to Ireland, so carried it over from other versions. Or perhaps Marhaus' defeat by Sir Turquine had made him over-cautious. In any case, it is a sign of Malory's storytelling skill and lasting power that he so arranged Tristram's maiden battle as to extend the reader's sympathy to both champions. [Malory IV, 17-19, 24-25, 28; V, 8; VI, 9; VIII, 4-8; X, 6]

Chrétien de Troyes knew some version of the story, without apparently caring much for it, and identified the site of Marhaus' battle with Tristram as Saint Samson's Isle, in which identification the prose **Merlin** and **Tristan** concur. [**Erec & Enide**, l. 1248 & Owen's note to same]

Mariagart, Marigart le Rox†—see under GUINDOEL

Mariales†—see under GALVOIE

MARK, KING OF CORNWALL

In Malory, the husband of La Beale Isoud and the uncle of Sir Tristram is generally painted as a scoundrel, capable of almost any ruse or treachery, both by violence—when he had the strength and advantage—and by craft, even to forging letters purportedly from the Pope, ostensibly commanding Mark himself to go on crusade, this being a ploy to put down rebellion in his own neighborhood and get Tristram away to the Holy Land. Mark's behavior toward his nephew Tristram, the son of his sister Elizabeth, is notorious—he alternately begged Tristram's help against enemies and tried to get Tristram killed or out of the country. (Shades of Saul and David! Of course, Mark did have some grounds for complaint against Tristram because of La Beale Isoud.)

Mark was "a fair speaker, and false thereunder." Lancelot called him King Fox, and it was a long time before he was compelled to swear fealty to Arthur. The knights Mark killed, both Arthur's men and his own (in rage, etc.) and presumably knights-errant and knights of other courts as well, may equal or outnumber the victims of Breuse Sans Pitie. Among Mark's victim's was his own brother, Prince Boudwin, whose popularity and success in battle Mark envied. By the murder of Boudwin, he gained the enmity of his nephew, Alisander le Orphelin; Mark eventually managed to get Alisander killed, but Alisander's son Bellangerus le Beuse finally avenged Boudwin and Alisander (and, incidentally, Mark's most famous victim, Tristram), presumably by dealing Mark his well deserved death.

Like Arthur, Mark on occasion sallied forth dressed as an ordinary knight, keeping his true identity secret—especially if he heard his companions-for-the-nonce talking against Mark of Cornwall. Faced with combat, Mark often turned poltroon—though at least once he defended himself competently in trial by combat, winning even though he was in the wrong. (Malory comments that Mark won by chance, but at least Mark had sufficient honor to show up at the battleground, having given his word to do so. See Amant.) For all his villainy, Mark fails to become a commanding figure, frequently seeming more of a butt and buffoon.

Very curiously, it was Mark who, finding Sir Lanceor and Lady Colombe dead, stopped to bury them and erect a rich tomb above them, apparently for no other motivation than kindliness and pity. In other versions of **Tristram**, earlier as well as later, Mark is shown as a more sympathetic, or at least less malicious, character. Perhaps Malory put so much emphasis on Tristram and integrated his saga so thoroughly with Arthur's in order to play up the parallel between the two great love triangles: Arthur-Guenevere-Lancelot and Mark-Isoud-Tristram. Having done so, Malory might have been constrained to make Mark as bad as possible in order to present a contrast with the comparatively good Arthur. [Malory II, 7-8; VIII, 1, 4-32; IX, 19; X, 8-15, 22, 26, 32-35, 50-51; XIX, 11]

King Mark's Family and Retainers
Wife: La Beale Isoud
Brother: Prince Boudwin
Sister: Queen Elizabeth of Lyonesse
Brother-in-law: King Meliodas
Sister-in-law: Anglides
Bastard son: Meraugis de Porlesquez
Nephews: Tristram (by Elizabeth), Alisander le Orphelin (by Boudwin)
Grand-nephew: Bellengerus le Beuse (by Alisander)
Kinsman (unspecified): Dinas
Seneschal: Dinas
Retainers: Andred (also Mark's nephew?), Amant, Bersules, Sadok, Lady Leech?
Ally?: Morgan le Fay

Spence identifies King Mark with "March, son of Mairchion" ("Horse, son of Horses"), a figure from British mythology, wherein horses held a high place, as evidenced, for instance, by the white horses on the hills of Uffington and Bratton. [**Magic Arts**, p. 160]

MARROK

I find Sir Marrok mentioned only twice in Malory, once as one of Arthur's personal bodyguard (along with the notable knights Lancelot, Bors, Kay, and Marhaus) in the war with Emperor Lucius. The second reference, however, where Marrok appears among the Round Table knights who try to heal Sir Urre, is the interesting one: "Sir Marrok, the good knight that was betrayed with his wife, for she made him seven year a wer-wolf." [Malory V, 88; XIX, 11]

I believe Marrok must be a werewolf knight whom I encountered years ago, in the retelling of an old tale which I later learned was apparently one of Marie de France's.

This knight's wife pestered him to know where he went when he left her for several days and nights of every week. At last he confessed that, through no fault of his own, he was a werewolf—here, simply a man who turns into a wolf of normal appearance, identical in body to natural wolves, and no more dangerous—probably less dangerous—to humans than they. He had to leave his clothes in a special hiding-place when he became a wolf, for if he did not have them to put on again when his wolf-time was up, he would not be able to change back into a man. This pleased his wife, who loved another knight better. She stole her husband's clothes, and he had to remain a wolf full-time for seven years. Then one day the King came hunting. The wolf seemed to appeal to him for clemency, acting like a dog or, almost, like a human. Struck with the animal's behavior, the King forbade it to be killed and had it taken back to court instead. The wolf was gentle to all humans, except two: whenever he saw his wife or her lover, he went for them savagely. This aroused the King's suspicions, and he questioned wife and lover until he had a full confession of what the woman had done and where she had hidden her husband's clothes. (I believe the wife and the lover were then executed, but cannot remember for sure.) The King and his barons recovered the clothes and laid them out on a bed in front of the wolf, but the wolf only looked at them. "He's been a wolf too long", said some of the barons. "He can no longer change back." The King realized that the wolf would naturally be reticent about changing back in full view of a sizeable audience, so he took all the men out of the chamber and had the door closed. When, about an hour later, they ventured in again, they found the knight, fully dressed, lying asleep on the bed.

MARSIL, KING OF POMITAIN

"King Marsil, that had in gift an island of Sir Galahalt [Galeholt] the haut prince; and this island had the name Pomitain." This, apparently Malory's only reference to King Marsil, comes when he is defeated by King Bagdemagus during Duke Galeholt's tournament in Surluse. [Malory X, 44]

Martans—see **MARANT**

Martorse—see **MORTAISE**

Marvels, Tower of†—see under **GALAFORT**

Maten†—see under **BLANCHE ESPINE**

MATTO LE BRUENE

> Ah, said King Mark, that is Sir Matto le Breune, that fell out of his wit because he lost his lady; for when Sir Gaheris smote down Sir Matto and won his lady of him, never since was he in his mind, and that was pity, for he was a good knight. [Malory IX, 19]

As it happens, King Mark has here mistaken Dagonet's account of a crazed Tristram for Sir Matto. From this tantalizing reference, which seems to be Malory's only mention of Sir Matto, we can at least infer that he was probably a Cornish knight and running around wild in the forests in that part of the country.

MAUDUIT†

One country, possibly in or near Cornwall (that part of the island being noted for them) was infested with giants. Arthur killed them all except a giantess and her baby son, whom he gave, along with the land, to a knight who asked for them. The baby giant was Mauduit. At fourteen, he was larger than a grown man. At fifteen, he was knighted by his foster-father. Later, he killed his parents in a fit of rage and began terrorizing the countryside. Finally he fell in love, but the lady accepted him only on condition that he swear to amend and not to leave his castle. He hung his arms in a pavilion, hoping some knight would take them and thus give him an excuse to leave his castle. The people charged twelve damsels to guard Mauduit's arms.

Ywaine came along and found an old woman beating a dwarf. At first she said she would stop if Ywaine kissed her, but then she amended the condition and make him take down Mauduit's helmet, sword, and shield. She tied the helmet and sword to the tail of her horse and made Ywaine carry the shield. Then she rode away, while the dwarf and the twelve damsels grieved. Ywaine had innocently given Mauduit the excuse to leave his castle.

Ywaine only learned the story later, from a hermit of the country. Ywaine fought and conquered a knight named Triadan and told him to go to the giant with the message that Ywaine alone was responsible and the people of the country should be spared. Mauduit's answer was to cut off Triadan's hand and go on a spree of indiscriminate slaughter. Some of the people captured Ywaine and imprisoned him in the Castel del Trespas to await Mauduit's coming. Here Lancelot, Bors, Gareth, and Bagdemagus found their comrade. Bors insisted on carrying Mauduit's shield and fighting the giant. Bors, of course, won and killed Mauduit. [Vulgate V]

MAUDUIT THE WISE†

Eighth best of Arthur's knights, according to the list Chrétien de Troyes begins in line 1691 of **Erec & Enide**. It seems highly unlikely that this Mauduit should be confused with Mauduit the wicked giant.

MEADOW, OLD AND YOUNG KNIGHTS OF THE†

See under "Portia." The old knight, rich lord of all the people we see sporting in the meadow, appears to be an elegant, prudent, and in some ways easy going personality. He swears by the faith he owes Saint Peter, which suggests some special allegiance to that apostle and might contain particular relevance if this romance is indeed a secularization of medieval afterlife stories. (Meliagrant also swears by Saint Peter; ca. l. 3470.) As Chrétien's translator D.D.R. Owen points out, the old knight's argument with his son regarding the inadvisability of fighting Lancelot foreshadows King Bademagu's similar arguments with Meliagrant in the same romance; the "Old Knight of the Meadow", unlike Bademagu, prevails upon his offspring. [Chrétien de Troyes, **Lancelot**, ll. 1661-2022 & Owen's notes to same]

MEDELANT†

Apparently either a leader of the Sesnes or a king allied with them, involved in the attack on Vandaliors Castle early in Arthur's reign [Vulgate II].

MEDGAUD† (Lindisfarne, Holy Island of Saint Cuthbert)

Site of the Abbey of the Holy Island of Saint Cuthbert, Medgaud Island is five or six miles over the sands at low tide or a mile by boat from Bamborough, Glennie's Castle Orgulous.

Medraut—see **MORDRED**

Meleagant('s)—see **MELIAGRANT('S)**

MELEHAN†

One of Mordred's two sons, probably the oldest. After Mordred's death, Melehan and his unnamed brother seized England. In a battle with

Lancelot's men on the plain of Winchester, Melehan killed Lionel but was then killed by Bors, while Lancelot slew Mordred's other son. [Vulgate VI]

MELIADOC†

As Erec's Pentecost wedding festivities wound down, a tournament was arranged to be held in about a month between Evroic and Tenebroc. Gawaine sponsored or guaranteed it on one side, Meliadoc and Meliz on the other. [Chrétien de Troyes, **Erec & Enide**, ca. l. 2131]

MELIAGRANT (Meleagant, Meliagance, Meligrance, Meliaganus, Miliagraunce, etc.)

Vulgate IV characterizes him as a proud and evil-disposed man who considered himself Lancelot's equal. Despite his faults, Meliagrant became a member of the Round Table, perhaps by virtue of being King Bagdemagus' son. He was among the knights who came with Arthur to Dame Lyonors' tournament at Castle Dangerous, where he "brake a spear upon Sir Gareth mightily and knightly." He is also recorded as fighting in Duke Galeholt's Surluse tournament, where his father Bagdemagus enlisted one Sir Sauseise to try to beat him so as to get him off the field in comparative safety.

Meliagrant's downfall was his love for Guenevere. Once, during the high days of Tristram's career, Meliagrant entered a battle with his brother of the Round Table, Lamorak, over which was the lovelier queen, Guenevere or Margawse. The quarrel was happily ended by the cool reasoning of Sir Bleoberis, who happened upon the scene with Lancelot; but Meliagrant "was a good man and of great might" and put up a fairly good defence against Lamorak while it lasted.

Finally his passion led Meliagrant into outright villainy. He ambushed the Queen and a small party of ladies, unarmed knights, squires, and yeomen while they were out a-Maying. After wounding several of Guenevere's knights, Meliagrant and his men took the Queen and all their other prisoners to Meliagrant's castle, but one child, at the Queen's behest, managed to escape and tell Lancelot. When Lancelot started after the abductor, some of Meliagrant's archers waited in hiding and shot the great knight's horse out from under him, so that he had to finish his journey in a cart. (This is one origin of the "Knight in the Cart" appellation.) Meliagrant yielded to the Queen, begging mercy, rather than fight Lancelot on the latter's arrival, and the whole group remained overnight in the castle. Lancelot, deciding to spend the night with the Queen, wounded his hands tearing out the window bars to reach her bed. In the morning, Meliagrant rather rudely opened the Queen's bedcurtains to find out why she was sleeping so late and found blood on the sheet and pillow. On this evidence, he accused her of adultery with one or more of the wounded knights. To prevent Lancelot from defending her in the trial by combat, Meliagrant set another trap.

> Then Sir Meliagrance said to Sir Launcelot: Pleaseth it you to see the estures of this castle? ... And then they went together from chamber to chamber .... So it befell upon Sir Launcelot that no peril dread, as he went with Sir Meliagraunce he trod on a trap and the board rolled, and there Sir Launcelot fell down more than ten fathom into a cave full of straw.

The damsel who acted as Lancelot's gaoler freed him in return for a kiss on the scheduled day of combat. When the fight went against Meliagrant, he tried to yield. Lancelot, seeing that the Queen wished her enemy slain, insisted on fighting to the utterance; but Meliagrant refused to rise and fight again until Lancelot offered to fight with his head and the left quarter of his body unarmed and his left hand bound behind him. Even this handicap did not help Meliagrant—Lancelot lost no time cleaving his head in two. [Malory VII, 27-28; IX, 12-13; X, 41; XIX, 1-9]

Malory puts the story of how Meliagrant abducted the Queen near the end of his work. The Vulgate puts it earlier, stretches it out and makes more of it, and differs in many details, as in the role played by Kay, but the outlines are pretty much the same. In the Vulgate, Lancelot dreads the duty of telling Bagdemagus of his son's death, but his fear is needless, for Bagdemagus, being a just man, takes it well.

One reason for the episode being so widespread in Arthurian literature, modern as well as medieval, might be its antiquity. The **Vita Sancti Gildae** by Caradoc of Lancarvan records a story, likely going back into Celtic myth, of Guenevere's abduction to Glastonbury by King Melwas of the summer land; a 12th-century carving in Modena cathedral appears to show that by Chrétien's day some version of the story had spread as far as Italy. As far as can be learned from still-extant literature, Chrétien may have been the first to use our familiar Lancelot as hero of the tale; Meliagrant would seem to have sprung from Melwas. In the process, he may have undergone the denigration that was often the lot of Pagan gods during Christianization (when they weren't turned into Christian saints instead): Meliagrant provides the one sustained, unmitigated example of pure villainy I have spotted in the works of Chrétien, who credits even Count Angrs with courage and knightly virtues "if only he hadn't been a traitor." Later writers, both medieval and modern, have done much to soften the character of a man who, in Chrétien's work, seems one of the ultimate examples of a son's rebellion against his father's ideals, perhaps for no other reason than the sake of rebellion and wickedness. (A role more commonly assigned, in Arthurian literature, to Mordred, who is absent from Chrétien's works.)

At last, Meleagant apparently succeeds in permanently alienating even Bademagu; however, this comes in the part of **Lancelot** completed, according to internal testimony, by the clerk Godefroi de Leigni. My personal impression is that Chrétien may have tired less of Lancelot and Guenevere's adultery than of Meliagrant's villainy. [Meleagant is named ca. l. 646 of **Lancelot**, but figures pretty well throughout.]

See also King Bademagu's Daughter.

MELIAGRANT'S CASTLE

> Then there was a knight that hight Meligrance, and he was son unto King Bagdemagus, and this knight had at that time a castle of the gift of King Arthur within seven miles of Westminster. [Malory XIX, 1]

Guenevere rode a-Maying with ten unarmed knights and ten ladies in the woods and fields around Westminster. Here Meliagrant waylaid them and carried them to his own castle. Later, he trapped Lancelot in his stronghold by causing him to drop "more than ten fathom into a cave full of straw." [Malory XIX, 1-7] Such trapdoors befit the castles of villainous knights.

The Vulgate account of the kidnaping of Guenevere by Meliagrant is substantially different, longer and more involved, and puts Meliagrant's castle in his father's kingdom of Gore [Vulgate IV].

See also Castle of Four Stones.

MELIAGRANT'S (Meleagant's) SENESCHAL and HIS WIFE†

In Chrétien's version of the Knight in the Cart episode, Lancelot first fights Meliagrant the day after crossing the Sword Bridge and later in order to prove Guenevere's innocence of sleeping with Kay; Bademagu gets both battles stopped in time to save his son. After the second fight, Meliagrant has Lancelot kidnaped (see "The Dwarf with a Whip") and secretly imprisoned so that he will miss their appointment to fight a third time, at Arthur's court. Meliagrant puts an unnamed seneschal of his in charge of Lancelot. Eventually news of the tournament to be held at Noauz reaches the seneschal and his people, making Lancelot so moody that the seneschal's wife, in her husband's absence, lets the prisoner out on parole in order to attend it. She even lends him her husband's new scarlet arms and fine horse. I cannot discover exactly where the seneschal goes during this time. Obviously she knows he should be gone for a while; but if he himself had gone to the tournament, why would he not have taken his own horse and arms, or at least recognized them on Lancelot? Wherever he has been, he gets home a few days before Lancelot's return. Much upset on learning what his wife has done, he reports it at once to Meliagrant, who trusts his prisoner's word but, considerably annoyed that Lancelot has been out at all, proceeds to have a strong tower built on an island for his more secure imprisonment.

I would guess the Vulgate's Roliax to be not Meliagrant's seneschal, but whatever man or men brought Lancelot his food while he was in the solitary tower. Roliax's wife might, however, have been derived from the seneschal's wife, though in Chrétien's version there seems to be no connection between her and King Bademagu's daughter, the latter finding Lancelot and enabling him to escape with no assistance but that of some careless worker who has left a pickaxe lying around outside the tower.

[Chrétien de Troyes, **Lancelot**, ll. 5435-6656]

Meliagrant's Stepsister—see BADEMAGU'S DAUGHTER

MELIANT OF LIZ†

Meliant's father was the friend and, it would seem, the liege lord of Tibaut of Tintagil. Dying, Meliant's father entrusted his young son to Tibaut to bring up, which charge Tibaut worthily carried out. While still a squire, Meliant sought the love of Tibaut's elder daughter. On her insistence, he became a knight and then, to satisfy her further demands that he prove his worth, he challenged her father Tibaut to a tournament. In her eyes, Meliant was the handsomest and best knight in this tournament; Gawaine, to please Tibaut's younger daughter, the Maid with Little Sleeves, finally entered the fighting and unhorsed Meliant at once. One can only hope that it did not destroy poor Meliant's chances for love. [Chrétien de Troyes, **Perceval**, ca. ll. 4833-5569]

One may guess that it did not, for in his first romance Chrétien had listed Meliant of Liz as the seventh best of Arthur's knights [**Erec & Enide**, ll. 1691ff.].

The similarity of their names suggests that time and the process of creative transmission turned Chrétien's Meliant of Liz into Malory's Melias de Lile.

See also Meliz.

MELIAS DE LILE

Son of the King of Denmark, Melias entered the Grail Quest as squire to King Bagdemagus, but left him at the White Abbey and went with Galahad instead. After requesting and receiving knighthood at Galahad's hands, Melias said,

> [S]ithen ye have made me a knight ye must of right grant me my first desire that is reasonable … suffer me to ride with you in this quest of the Sangreal, till that some adventure depart us.

The adventure came in about a week, when they arrived at a crossroads where was a sign warning any but good men and worthy knights from taking the road to the left, because "if thou go on the left hand thou shalt not lightly there win prowess, for thou shalt in this way be soon assayed." Melias begged of Galahad to let him take the left road. He failed the test, for when he came to a "lodge of boughs … wherein was a crown of gold", he appropriated the crown. At once another knight came and smote him down, took back the crown, and left him there until Galahad came and rescued him. Galahad brought the grievously wounded Melias to an old monk and waited three days until it became apparent that Melias would survive. The monk explained to Melias that in following the left-hand road he had acted in pride and presumption, and by taking the crown he had sinned "in covetise and in theft."

Purged, we may hope, of his excess pride, Melias became a knight of the Round Table. He went with Lancelot into exile and was made Earl of Tursaud. [Malory XIII, 9-14; XIX, 11; XX, 18]

Meligrance—see **MELIAGRANT**

KING MELIODAS OF LYONESSE

Tristram's father (according to Malory) was brother-in-law to both Mark of Cornwall and Howell of Brittany. Meliodas' imprisonment by an amorous enchantress caused the death of his first wife, Mark's sister Elizabeth, who gave birth suddenly to Tristram while searching the woods for her husband and then died of cold and exposure. Merlin released Meliodas from the enchantress on the morning after Elizabeth's death. "But the sorrow that the king made for his queen that might no tongue tell." After seven years of widowerhood, Meliodas married a daughter of Howell of Brittany—presumably an older sister of Isoud la Blanche Mains—who gave him more children. This second queen decided to get rid of Tristram so that her own offspring would inherit Lyonesse. Her first attempt to poison Tristram ended in the death of her own son, who drank the poison by mistake. She tried again, and this time Meliodas himself almost drank the poison. When she snatched it from him, he grew suspicious and, by threatening her at sword point, made her confess all. He would have burned her, but Tristram himself pleaded for her life and "made the king and her accorded. But then the king would not suffer young Tristram to abide no longer in his court" and sent him into France (perhaps to Howell's court?) under the tutorship of Gouvernail. After seven years, Tristram came home again, already well accomplished, and stayed until the age of eighteen years.

> And then the King Meliodas had great joy of Sir Tristram, and so had the queen, his wife. For ever after … because Sir Tristram saved her from the fire, she did never hate him more after, but loved him ever after, and gave Tristram many great gifts.

When Meliodas' court received news of Sir Marhaus' impending battle with Mark's champion—providing Mark could find one—to settle the truage question with the Irish king, Tristram begged his father to let him go to his uncle, be made knight at Mark's hands, and fight as his champion. After cautioning his son of Marhaus' might, Meliodas agreed. "I will well, said King Meliodas, that ye be ruled as your courage will rule you." These would seem to be Meliodas' last words to his famous son; presumably he died a natural death while Tristram was on his adventures. [Malory VIII, 1-5]

MELIOT

> Within a day or two [after interring twelve kings in St. Stephen's, Camelot] King Arthur was somewhat sick, and he let pitch his pavilion in a meadow ... and saw a knight coming even by him ... [who] passed forth to the castle of Meliot [Malory II, 12].

This knight was Herlews le Berbeus, who was slain by Sir Garlon apparently before he had reached Meliot. Arthur had sent Balin le Savage after Herlewes, and Balin's subsequent adventures with Herlews' lady to find Garlon and avenge Herlews' death took them to the "Castle of the Leprous Lady" and to Listeneise. Malory seems to tell us nothing more about Meliot Castle by that name. Nevertheless, I would like to identify it with one of a pair of castles where Balin and his brother Balan met their deaths. Malory leaves these fairly important castles unnamed.

One of them was on the mainland and the other on an island, clearly an island in a river. The lady of the mainland castle kept a custom whereby every passing knight had to joust with the knight who defended the island. The knight then defending the island was Balan, in anonymous red armor. Balin, coming to the island with a borrowed shield, kept the custom so vigorously that the two brothers mortally wounded each other in battle before learning one another's identity, and here were buried.

The lady did not know Balin's name to put it on the tomb, but Merlin came along next morning and took care of that detail. He also repommelled Balin's sword, set it in a floating marble block to drift down the river to Camelot at the right time, and left the scabbard "on this side the island" for Galahad, who should win the sword, to find. He also made a bridge of iron and steel only half a foot broad to the island, and only a good and true knight could cross this bridge. Moreover he made a bed to lie upon which brought madness, "yet Launcelot de Lake fordid that bed through his noblesse." [Malory II, 12-19, especially 17-19] I have no idea why Merlin made that bed, nor how Lancelot fordid it, unless the passage refers somehow to one of Lancelot's fits of madness. Balin's sword in its marble block floats down to Camelot for Galahad to draw it at the beginning of the Grail Adventures; Galahad is already wearing the scabbard, having picked it up on his way to court [XIII, 2-5], but Malory tells us nothing more about bed, bridge, or castle.

In Vulgate V, Gawaine tells of his adventures at the Isles Perdues, where he saw the miraculous bed of Merlin, and also the adventurous sword, by which a hermit predicted that Gawaine's best friend (Lancelot) would kill him through Mordred's fault. On this island was the force of all the enchantment in the world. Here were many damsels, and here the best of knights would find his equal in battle. This has to be where Malory placed the fatal battle of Balin and Balan. The "adventurous sword" must be Balin's Sword, which Galahad apparently sent back to his father Lancelot after the Grail Adventures.

Meliot might be the name used for the mainland castle, while the island castle could retain the Vulgate name of Isle Perdues. (Do not confuse with Duke Galeholt's castle of Isle Perdue.) Of course, since my grounds for identifying the "castle of Meliot" with this pair of castles is so slight, Meliot might be considered another castle entirely.

In any case we need a site upriver from Camelot for the castle of Balin's death. I suggest the Itchen River.

MELIOT DE LOGRES

After rescuing Nimue from Hontzlake, King Pellinore met her cousin, Sir Meliot of Logres, and his "sworn brother", Sir Brian of the Isles. Meliot was happy to see his cousin in such good hands as Pellinore's. At this time, Meliot does not seem to have been a knight of Arthur's court, but he later became a companion of the Round Table. He had earned this distinction by the time he fought and killed Sir Gilbert the Bastard, being grievously wounded himself in the process, so that Lancelot had to brave the Chapel Perilous to get the cloth needed to heal him. Meliot is named as having fought in the Winchester tournament and as trying to heal Sir Urre. He was among those knights who went with Mordred and Agravaine to trap Lancelot with the Queen, and were thus killed by the escaping Lancelot. [Malory III, 13; VI, 14-15; XVIII, 11; XIX, 11; XX, 2-4]

MELIZ†

As the festivities of Erec's Pentecost wedding wound down, a tournament was arranged to be held between Evroic and Tenebroc in about a month. Gawaine acted as its sponsor or guarantor on one side, Meliz and Meliadoc on the other. Unless "Meliz" is a name contraction for "Meliant of Liz", or unless we have here another case of postponed naming, if Chrétien has given us any earlier glimpse of either Meliz or Meliadoc, I somehow missed it despite all my pains. [Chrétien de Troyes, **Erec & Enide**, ca. l. 2131]

MENAGORMON, COUNT OF CLIVELON†

Chrétien lists him among the vassal counts whom Arthur summons to court for Erec's wedding [**Erec & Enide**, ll. 1934-1962].

MERAUGIS DE PORLESQUEZ†

A natural son of King Mark [Vulgate VII].

MERLAN LE DYABLE†

In earlier life called Merlan le Simple, he acquired the sobriquet "le dyable" ("the devil") after his coronation because he turned out to be a real rotter, cruel and treacherous. He hanged his own father on an oak in the forest. (Apparently it was Carteloise, the forest of the stag and four lions; Merlan's kingdom seems to have been somewhere in southern Scotland or northern Logres.) He was eventually killed when he insisted on fighting Lancelot before granting him hospitality in his pavilion. Although Lancelot only learned it after killing the petty monarch, he had done the country a good turn. [Vulgate V]

MERLIN (Merlin Ambrosius, Merlin Sylvester, Myrddin, etc.)

T. H. White loves him. So do Mary Stewart and Vera Chapman. Tennyson seems to admire him greatly. E. Marshall, B. F. Johnson, John Gloag, the makers of "Mr. Magoo's" version of King Arthur, and, indeed, almost all modern romancers, except Mark Twain, seem to regard the old mage with varying degrees of affection, liking, and sometimes awe; most of them are able to communicate their devotion to their readers. While reading White or Chapman, I love Merlin too. But the more I read of the medieval versions—Malory and the Vulgate—the less I understand where all these modern writers found a mage to inspire their devotion. My own personal dislike for Merlin, which probably exceeds even Mark Twain's—and which applies only to the Malorian mage, not to the Myrddin of older lore—should be taken into account by readers of these notes.

According to a tradition not found in Malory, but very likely familiar to Malory's readers, Merlin was engendered, despite all precautions, by a fiend on a woman who had been trying to remain pure. At her trial, the infant Merlin himself revealed who was his father and made a few other prophecies and revelations, at least one of them rather embarrassing to the judges. [Vulgate II] Even in Malory's account, Merlin is occasionally called a devil's son, and now and then a medieval romancer throws in a comment to the effect that, although usually regarded as beneficent, Merlin is really evil. (To use a modern and not, perhaps, strictly applicable parallel, would you trust Rosemary's baby as chief advisor to the President?) In all fairness, however, I must point out a remark in Vulgate II that, while Merlin owed his knowledge of the past to the

Devil, he owed his knowledge of the future to the Lord. Again, Vulgate II tells us that Merlin never laid his hands upon anyone, though with his power, he hardly needed to be physical! Vulgate II contains a statement that he was "treacherous and disloyal by nature" and mentions a stone at which he slew two other enchanters.

During Merlin's childhood, King Vortigern arrested him, planning to cement a new tower with his blood. Young Merlin coolly saved himself by his accurate revelations (see Vortigern's Tower). Merlin then left to study magic from Blaise, while Vortigern went on to be killed by the sons of Constans, as per Merlin's prophecy.

Outstripping his master in necromantic learning, Merlin swore never to do Blaise harm and asked him to write a book. Blaise retired into the forest of Northumberland to write down the doings of his former student. Here Merlin used to visit him from time to time.

When Constans' son, King Pandragon, was killed by the Sesnes, Merlin brought the stones of Stonehenge from Ireland to serve as his tomb. Merlin then became advisor the the new king, Pandragon's brother Uther, now surnamed Pendragon in honor of the late king. To Uther Merlin revealed the mysteries of the two holy tables—the one Christ and His disciples used at the Last Supper and the one Joseph of Arimathea and his followers set up when they came to Britain. Merlin erected the third great table, the Round Table, for Uther at Cardoel in Wales (from where it passed into the keeping of Leodegrance and thence to Arthur).

Uther conceiving a lust for the duchess Igraine of Tintagil, Merlin played his pander, magically giving Uther the appearance of the lady's husband Gorloïs, so that she lay with him unsuspecting. After the apparently coincidental death of Gorloïs, Uther married Igraine.

> Soon came Merlin unto the king, and said, Sir, ye must purvey you for the nourishing of your child. As thou wilt, said the king, be it. Well, said Merlin, I know a lord of yours in this land … and he shall have the nourishing of your child, and his name is Sir Ector … let him be sent for, for to come and speak with you …. And when the child is born let it be delivered to me at yonder privy postern unchristened …. Then when the lady was delivered, the king commanded two knights and two ladies to take the child, bound in a cloth of gold, and that ye deliver him to what poor man ye meet at the postern gate of the castle. So the child was delivered unto Merlin.

Those modern romancers who stick to some recognizable variant of this episode have exercised considerable ingenuity to explain Merlin's motives for taking Arthur and giving him to Ector with so much secrecy—not even Igraine was told where her child was taken. Tennyson came up with the most plausible explanation I've yet encountered, but he had to kill off Uther on the same night of Arthur's birth to do it.

Returning to Malory, I cannot help but wonder why and how it should have been for the good of Arthur and the kingdom to raise the heir in such secrecy. Uther married Igraine so soon after Gorloïs' death that by the rules of the milieu Arthur should have been recognized easily as Uther's legal son and heir; at any rate, the whole explanation was accepted by enough of the kingdom to give Arthur a following when Merlin finally gave it years later. Why should it not have been equally well accepted at once? Malory's Uther survived for at least two years after Arthur's birth, and after his death his widow seems to have been left unmolested, even though the realm was thrown into confusion for lack of a visible heir. If there had been a visible heir, a son known to be of Uther's marriage, would the child really have run a great risk of assassination, surrounded as he would have been by barons? Would not Igraine or some strong baron simply have been named regent until his majority? Merlin arranged the famous test of the Sword in the Stone and had Arthur crowned king on the strength of this test alone, and the sentiment of the "commons ... both rich and poor."

Under such circumstances, how blameworthy were those rebel kings and barons who refused to yield their allegiance at once to an unknown, unproven youth, the protégé of a devil's son? True, when the rebels gave Arthur their challenge, Merlin made them a bald statement, with no supporting evidence, of Arthur's birth; it seems hardly surprising that "some of them laughed him to scorn, as King Lot; and more other called him a witch." Nor had Merlin yet told Arthur himself of his parentage, which omission resulted in the incestuous begetting of Mordred on Margawse. Not until after the battle of Bedegraine—a slaughter so bloody it seems to have disgusted Merlin himself, who had helped engineer Arthur's victory by bringing the army of Ban and Bors swiftly and secretly to the place—did Merlin reveal Arthur's parentage, with some supporting evidence, to Arthur and the assembled court, in a scene that suggests a practical joke played by Merlin on Igraine to give her an additional moment of grief before restoring her to her son. In this scene Sir Ulfius, a former knight of Uther's and his companion in the abduction of Igraine at Tintagil, as well as Merlin's seeming accomplice (though perhaps unaware) in the "joke" on Igraine, himself stated that "Merlin is more to blame than" Igraine for the wars of rebellion. Perhaps the key to why Merlin wished to arrange Arthur's upbringing lies in the word "unchristened." Was Arthur ever christened, or did Ector, on receiving him, assume that Uther had seen to that point? It seems heretical to suggest it, but did Merlin wish to make of Arthur his own pawn and tool?

Merlin did considerable traveling on the Continent, most of it, one supposes, during the years when Sir Ector was raising Arthur (although some of it may also have been in the years between Vortigern's death and Pandragon's). One of his continental adventures may be found under Avenable. Surprisingly, Merlin also dabbled in Christian missionary work, converting King Flualis of Jerusalem and his wife; this royal couple had four daughters, who in turn had fifty-five sons, all good knights, and these went forth to convert the heathen; some of them reached Arthur's court. It may also have been during this period that Merlin met Viviane, fell in love with her, and taught her his crafts in return for the promise of her love.

It would be difficult and tedious to list every deed and prophecy of Merlin's; one does not envy Blaise his task. The Great Necromancer could prophesy anything—though fairly early in his career, before Arthur's birth, he decided to phrase his prophecies in obscure terms. He could apparently do anything within the scope of necromancy, except break the spell that was his own downfall. He must have made rather a pest of himself with his disguises, popping up as toddler, beggar, blind minstrel, stag, and so on, and so on, usually for no apparent reason. Indeed he seems to have had the temperament of a practical joker. Some of his prophecies may well have been more mishievous than useful. He entered the battlefield with Arthur and his armies, and does seem to have given them invaluable help, but one of Merlin's pastimes in battle was moving around the field and telling the King and his knights, every time they took a short break from doing really tremendous deeds of arms and valor, what cowards they were and how disgracefully they were carrying on. (Maybe that was Merlin's style of cheerleading.)

Merlin may not have counseled Arthur to destroy the May babies, Herod-like, but he certainly sowed the seed of that sin by telling Arthur that one of these babies would be the King's destruction, and he appears not to have lifted his voice against the mass slaughter. In all fairness, we must remember that he did warn Arthur against marrying Guenevere, foretelling her affair with Lancelot, and Arthur ignored his advice in that instance. (But did Merlin thus implant the suspicion that finally erupted in Arthur's vengeful rage?) Merlin engineered Arthur's acquisition of Excalibur, sword and sheath, but in this the mage apparently acted in unison with Malory's first British Lady of the Lake, who was later revealed, by the sincere though unfortunate Balin le Savage, to have been very wicked; it is noticeable that Merlin, when he learned of Balin's accusation, did not defend his slain cohort by denying the charge, nor rail against Balin for killing her, but only replied with a countercharge against the damsel "Malvis."

For all his foresight, Merlin had a habit of arriving just a little too late to do the most good. We know he was capable of very rapid travel, yet he let Balin lie beneath the ruins of Pellam's castle for three days before coming to rescue him, by which time Balin's damsel (Sir Herlews' lady) was dead. Later he showed up the morning after the deaths of Balin and Balan, just in time to write their names on their tomb. He delivered King Meliodas of Lyonesse from the enchantress' prison the morning after the death of Meliodas' wife—had Merlin arrived a few days earlier, the brave and devoted Elizabeth would not have died.

Although from the above Merlin would appear something of a misogynist, he could hardly have been insensitive to a beautiful face. He did not spend all his time at Arthur's court, and during one of his absences he taught Morgan le Fay necromancy in Bedingran. He later instructed Nimue in the art when she came to court, and it was she who finally rid the world of him. (In my opinion, Nimue did the world a favor.) At various times, Bagdemagus and Gawaine passed near his tomb and spoke with him; perhaps others did as well. Gawaine seems to have been the last to hear his voice (this incident is recorded under Byanne).

Malory puts the place of Merlin's imprisonment under a stone in Cornwall. I continue to find it unconvincing that the mighty Merlin could not free himself from a spell woven by one of his own students. Other, older versions of the tale have Nimue (or Viviane) retiring Merlin through affection, giving him a retreat of comfort and cheer. It is interesting that White, who loves Merlin and makes him endearing, puts him in cozy retirement in a tumulus on Bodmin Moor, Cornwall, although Nimue is not in evidence to share his society (**The Book of Merlyn**). Perhaps Merlin requested Nimue to take over the mentorship of Arthur's court for him; she does appear from time to time in this role throughout much of Malory's work. [Vulgate, chiefly vols. II & III; Malory I, 1-3, 8-25; II, 4, 8-10, 16, 19; III, 1-2; IV, 1,5; VIII, 2; XIV, 2]

In Vulgate VII, I found what appeared to be a prophecy that either Percivale or Galahad was to rescue Merlin after achieving the Grail, but nowhere else did I uncover a hint of any such deed.

Glennie calls Merlin, with Taliessin, Llywarch Hen, and Aneurin, one of the four great bards of the Arthurian Age. I have no reason to doubt this is any other Merlin than the necromancer. It was also in Glennie's book that I found the tantalizing reference to Merlin's twin sister, Ganieda.

Spence believes that Merlin's story became fused with that of Ambrosius Aurelianus, accounting for the mages's alternate names "Merlin Emrys" and "Merlin Ambrosius" [**Magic Arts**, p. 150-151].

The author of the most unexpected Arthurian novel I have yet read—a fantasy sequel to H. G. Wells' **Time Machine**—seems to have taken account of both faces of Merlin: in **Morlock Night** [DAW, ©1979], W. K. Jeter gives the reader both a good Merlin, who often prefers to call himself "Dr. Ambrose", and his evil but otherwise identical twin in appearance and powers, Dr. Merdenne.

Chrétien de Troyes alludes to Merlin exactly once, and then in a context suggesting that the mage may already have been legendary by Arthur's time: in **Erec & Enide** [ll. 6660-6712] appears the observation that in Arthur's day sterlings had been the currency throughout Britain since Merlin's time. (In **Lancelot**, ca. l. 6545, the title hero asks "God and Saint Sylvester" to curse Meliagrant for imprisoning him; it might be barely conceivable that this is a reference to Merlin under his Sylvester name, but far more likely Lancelot really means Pope Saint Sylvester, Constantine's contemporary, whose apocryphal biography made quite an impact on the medieval era [see the **New Catholic Encyclopedia**]. In any case, this passage falls in Godefroi de Leigni's part of the **Lancelot**. Readers absolutely determined to find Merlin in Chrétien's romances might also consider Igraine's Clerk, mentioned once in **Perceval**, but I think that would be an identification born of desperation.)

MERLIN, CASTEL†

Despite the name, I found no evidence to connect this stronghold with the great enchanter. Conceivably it may have been connected with the minor King Merlan le Dyable, but more likely it was in or near Galehodin's teritory (in Norgales?), perhaps being one of Galehodin's own castles. Here Ywaine left Mordred after the tournament at Peningue Castle. [Vulgate V]

MERLIN'S BED

For obscure purposes, Merlin made a bed to lie in which caused madness [Malory II, 19]. Possibly there is some confusion here with the bed in the Castle Adventurous of Carbonek, sleeping on which insured a person visions of more or less peril. See under Meliot; see also the Perilous Bed.

"MERLIN'S ROCK"

Probably somewhere in Cornwall, this is where Nimue imprisoned Merlin.

MILES OF THE LAUNDS

This promising young knight was treacherously slain by Sir Loraine le Savage while on his way to Arthur's court with his lady, Eleine, King Pellinore's daughter. When her lover died, Eleine slew herself with his sword. [Malory III, 12, 15]

Miliagraunce—see **MELIAGRANT**

MINADORAS, DUKE†

He was King Pellam's seneschal. The name is from Vulgate VII, which also, however, gives Sir Claellus as Pellam's seneschal.

MINADUS†

A Sesnes leader, involved in the Vandaliors Castle attack. He fathered Oriels and had a nephew, Herlant. [Vulgate II]

Modred—see MORDRED

MOLIN, CASTEL DEL†

Seemingly a castle of King Marboar's, whose territory was apparently on the way to Estrangore.

Two leagues from Molin was a castle of which Count Thanaguis (Tanaguin, Thangin, Thallagon) was lord. Do not confuse him with Duke Brandelis of Taningues. [Vulgate IV]

MONENNA, SAINT (Dareca)†

Saint Monenna, or Dareca, of Kilslleibeculean, Ulster, founded a church and nunnery on Dunpeledur (Edinburgh, Scotland). Glennie suggests a connection with the Castle of Maidens at Edinburgh. The saint died in 518. I assume Monenna was a woman; the "a" ending is not infallible (cf. Columba), but it was a nunnery that Monenna founded.

MONEY

The one and only time Chrétien de Troyes names Merlin is in the remark that during Arthur's day sterlings had been the currency throughout Britain since Merlin's time. [**Erec & Enide**, ca. l. 6670]

Malory mentions three units of currency: besant or bezant, pence, and pound.

Until the United Kingdom put its money on the decimal system, 12 pence equaled one shilling and 20 shillings equaled one pound. A guinea was one pound plus one shilling. A besant was a Byzantine gold coin which finally varied in value between the English sovereign and half-sovereign, or less. Silver besants were also struck, and were worth between a florin and a shilling. The English florin was issued by Edward II, and was worth six shillings or six and eightpence. The English sovereign was a gold coin minted from the time of Henry VII to that of Charles I, originally worth 22s.6d, but later worth only ten or eleven shillings.

As for the buying power of these coins, in IV, 25, Malory speaks of a "rich circlet of gold worth a thousand besants" as the prize at a tournament. Speaking of Arthur's body, the former Bishop of Canterbury says:

> But this night … came a number of ladies, and brought hither a dead corpse, and prayed me to bury him; and here they offered an hundred tapers, and they gave me an hundred besants [Malory XXI, 6].

In XXI, 8, Lancelot returns to Britain after Arthur's passing:

> [H]e made a dole, and all they that would come had as much flesh, fish, wine and ale, and every man and woman had twelve pence, come who would …. And on the morn all the priests and clerks … were there, and sang mass of Requiem; and there offered first Sir Launcelot, and he offered an hundred pound; and then the seven kings offered forty pound apiece; and also there was a thousand knights, and each of them offered a pound; and the offering dured from morn till night.

There are also these entries:

> I wot well and can make it good, said Sir Ector [to Sir Lancelot, on finding him in the Joyous Isle], it hath cost my lady, the queen, twenty thousand pound the seeking of you [Malory XI, 9].

> Madam, said Sir Launcelot … I proffered [Elaine of Astolat], for her good love that she shewed me, a thousand pound yearly to her, and to her heirs [Malory XVIII, 20].

> And so upon the morn [Elaine of Astolat] was interred richly, and Sir Launcelot offered her mass-penny [Malory XVIII, 20].

This seems to be about the extent of Malory's concern with the particulars of money.

MONTESCLAIRE†

A maiden was under siege upon the hill at Montesclaire. Whatever knight rescued her by lifting the siege would not only win high honor, but might be able to gird the Sword with the Strange Hangings on in safety, as the Loathly Damsel tells Arthur's court—without, however, going into further detail. [Chrétien de Troyes, **Perceval**, ca. ll. 4701-4713]

MONTESCLAIRE, DAMSEL OF†

What little Chrétien de Troyes tells us about her is imparted to Arthur's court by the Loathly Damsel, q.v.

Moor, Proud Knight of the—see HAUGHTY KNIGHT …

Morawse—see MARGAWSE

MORCADS†

See under Anna.

MORDRAINS, KING (Evelake)

King Evelake, or Evelac, was a pagan contemporary of Joseph of Arimathea. Joseph converted him and his brother-in-law Nascien, with their families. Evelake, now bearing the baptismal name of Mordrains, came with Joseph to Britain. Despit a warning voice, Mordrains tried to see the Grail and, not being quite good enough, was blinded and paralyzed for the attempt. Meekly accepting his punishment, he prayed to be allowed to live to see Galahad. A voice, heard only by Mordrains, Nascien, Joseph, and Josephe, promised him this favor, adding that he would be healed when Galahad visited him. He waited several centuries, praying in a monastery, for Galahad to come. Upon being healed at last by Galahad, Mordrains enjoyed a holy death. [Vulgate, chiefly I & VI; Malory XIII, 10; XIV, 4; XVII, 4, 18]

The fact that Evelake and Mordrains are the same man is not apparent in Malory, and there is one passage—XVII, 4—in which I strongly suspect Malory or his editor confused the names of Nascien and Mordrains.

MORDRAINS, ABBEY OF KING

Malory does not make it clear, but from the Vulgate we know that King Evelake and King Mordrains were the same man, Evelake being his old name and Mordrains his name as a baptized Christian. He and his brother-in-law, Nascien, were contemporaries of Joseph of Arimathea, with whom they came to Britain. Mordrains lay blind in an abbey for several hundred years, waiting for Galahad to come and restore his sight. After Galahad had done so, Mordrains died happy in his arms. [Malory XVII, 18]

I can find no good clue in Malory as to the whereabouts of this abbey, but from a comparison with Mordrains and Nascien's adventures at the Isle of Turnance and the Port of Perilous Rock, I would guess it likely to have been somewhere between Arthurian Cornwall and Avilion along the Devon-Somerset border. The Vulgate, however, places the abbey in a wood near Norgales [I, 243-244].

MORDRED (Medraut, Modred, Mordret, etc.)

At Carlion, shortly after the battle of Bedegraine and before his marriage with Guenevere, Arthur engendered Mordred in conscious adultery and unconscious incest upon his visiting half-sister, King Lot's wife Margawse. That same night, Arthur dreamed of a serpent which came forth from his side, destroyed his land and people, and fought with him to their mutual destruction. The nightmare was so vivid that Arthur had it pictured in a painting in Camelot cathedral. Some little time later, probably shortly before or shortly after Mordred's birth in Orkney, Merlin told Arthur that the child who would destroy him would be born on May Day, thus inciting Arthur to send for all noblemen's sons born about that time, put them into a leaky ship, and send them out to sea. The infant Mordred was among these children, but when the ship went down, he was cast up on shore, where "a good man found him, and nourished him till he was fourteen year old, and then he brought him to the court ...

toward the end of the Death of Arthur." Other evidence, however, suggests that the boy was somehow identified and returned to his mother to be raised and educated by her; certainly he was known to be the youngest brother of Gawaine, Agravaine, Gaheris, and Gareth. Possibly he was identified when the "good man" brought him to court at age fourteen and returned to Margawse at that time for five or six years. Meanwhile, Arthur's Herod-like trick had inspired Lot and other nobles to fresh revolt, in which Lot was killed.

Vulgate IV tells us that Mordred was knighted at the age of twenty. He was tall with fair curly hair, and would have been handsome but for a wicked expression. Only for the first two years of his knighthood did he do any good. He hated all good knights.

During those first two years, however, he seems to have been very promising. For a time he traveled adventuring with Lancelot. Together they saw the mystic stag and four lions in Carteloise Forest, and Mordred won praise from the great Du Lac for his manly endeavors. All this time, Mordred believed himself the son of King Lot.

Unfortunately, after seeing the stag and lions, Lancelot and Mordred went on toward Peningues Castle to attend a tournament. They stayed with a vavasour near the castle and went into the woods next morning to find a church or chapel at which to hear Mass. They came upon an old but vigorous priest praying at a magnificent tomb. This priest greeted Lancelot and Mordred as the two most unfortunate knights who ever lived. When they asked why, he began with Mordred. First he stripped away Mordred's belief about his parentage: Mordred was not Lot's son, but Arthur's, the serpent of Arthur's dream, who would destroy his father and do more harm in his lifetime than all his ancestors had done good, and so on, and so on.

It was rather extreme of Mordred to kill the priest, but then, all this must have been a very traumatic revelation for a young knight (no older than twenty-two) who had been winning praise until that morning. Other knights, like Lionel and Lancelot himself, did as much and more, often on less provocation, when the battle rage took them. The vavasour was greatly perturbed at the priest's death, but for Lancelot's sake said nothing. Lancelot would have found a pretext to kill Mordred, but refrained for the sake of Mordred's brother Gawaine. (Lancelot was in a shaky position to cast stones at Mordred—among the victims of Lancelot's battle rages were men whose only offense consisted in Lancelot's having made free with their pavilions without first apprising them of his presence—but this time Lancelot was annoyed because Mordred had killed the priest before he could get around to predicting Lancelot's own future. Lancelot should have been grateful for that.)

They went on to hear Mass and then to the tournament. Such was the temper of the times. That day Mordred was left in a pitiable state on the tournament field, for he would have preferred death to surrender.

The old priest's prophecy seems to me one of the most mischievous in all the cycle (tying only with Merlin's about the May baby). It formed the turning point of Mordred's career, for after this episode his evil side took the upper hand. Lancelot, on returning to court, told Guenevere of the prophecy, but did not add that Arthur was Mordred's father. Guenevere did not believe the prophecy, and so did not mention it to Arthur, who might have banished Mordred had he known of the episode.

Whether on the strength of his early promise, or because of his family connections, or because he remained a competent fighter "of his hands", Mordred became a companion of the Round Table. He seems to have retained some sense of humor; once he joined Sir Dinadan and others in playing a joke on a "Cornish knight" (King Mark): Mordred's shield was silver, with black bends. Dinadan told Mark it was Lancelot carrying this shield, after which Mordred, who was wounded, gave the shield and his armor to Dagonet, the jester, who then gave Mark a merry chase. (This same shield suggests that Mordred may have been allied, at least for a time, with Morgan le Fay.) Again, one time Mordred came upon Sir Alisander le Orphelin in a state of besottedness upon his lady love, and began leading him mockingly away, apparently for mere sport. When Percivale came to court, Mordred apparently joined Kay in mocking the young man.

More serious, he may well have been party to the scheme which culminated in Gaheris' murder of Margawse, and when the brothers tracked down Lamorak, it was Mordred who gave that knight his death wound, striking him from behind. Mordred and Agravaine also conceived a dislike for Dinadan because of the latter's friendship toward Lamorak, and during the Grail Adventures they found an opportunity to kill him.

At last Mordred and Agravaine conspired to corner Lancelot with the Queen. Mordred suvived Lancelot's escape and must have played chief witness against the lovers, thus precipitating the break between Arthur and Lancelot. When Arthur went with Gawaine to attack Lancelot in France, he left Mordred as regent and "chief ruler of all England", with governance even over Guenevere. Malory says Arthur did this because Mordred was his son, but this would seem to make Arthur surprisingly slow-witted about connecting Merlin's old prophecy and his own nightmare with Mordred, so it is my guess that Arthur may still have been unaware of the relationship and made Mordred his regent because Mordred was the last surviving brother of the King's favorite nephew Gawaine.

Left in charge, Mordred counterfeited letters telling of Arthur's death in battle. He then called a parliament to name him king, had himself crowned at Canterbury, and tried to marry Guenevere, but she tricked him and barricaded herself in the Tower of London. Mordred drove the Archbishop of Canterbury into exile for opposing him and besieged Guenevere, but withdrew on receiving word that Arthur was on his way back. Mordred tried to prevent Arthur's landing at Dover and retreated to Canterbury. The last battle was fought on Salisbury plain; Mordred was the last man left alive of all his army and allies who fought there, and at the last he was killed by Arthur—though Mordred did not return Arthur a mortal blow until he felt that he himself had his death wound.

Among Mordred's allies were the Saxons or Sesnes, who hated Arthur and wanted revenge on him. Mordred also had Irish, Scottish, and Welsh divisions in his army. He left behind two grown sons, one named Melehan and one whose name is not given. They gradually seized England after Mordred's death, but, on Lancelot's return, Bors killed Melehan and Lancelot the other son. [Vulgate II-IV; Malory I, 27; VI, 7; IX, 3, 36; X, 12, 13, 18(?), 24-25, 39, 46, 54, 58; XI, 12; XVIII, 11, 23; XX-XXI]

SIR MORDRED'S FAMILY AND ALLIES
Father: Arthur
Mother: Margawse
Half-brothers: Gawaine, Agravaine, Gaheris, Gareth
Sons: Melehan, one unnamed
Allies: Arcaus, Heliades

MOREL†

The black charger Cligés rode on the first day of the Oxford tournament. Strangely, Morel is the only one of the four—black, sorrel, tawny, and white—to whom Chrétien de Troyes seems to give a name. Yet, of the four, the white Arabian, won from the Duke of Saxony, was surely the finest and most valuable. Perhaps in Morel's case D.D.R. Owen has simply translated a name for the color as a proper noun? [**Cligés**, ca. l. 4662]

MORGAN (Morgana) LE FAY

Morgan was one of the three daughters, apparently the youngest, of Igraine and Gorloïs, and thus an elder half-sister of Arthur's. When Igraine was wed to Uther and her daughters Margawse and Elaine to Kings Lot and Nentres, Morgan was put to school in a nunnery, where, as Malory tells us, "she learned so much that she was a great clerk of necromancy." Later she was married to King Uriens of Gore, to whom she bore Ywaine le Blanchemains.

After being an early rebel, Uriens came over to Arthur and was made a companion of the Round Table. He seems to have spent much time in Arthur's court, along with his wife and son. At first Morgan and

Guenevere were friends, and Guenevere gave almost identical rings to Morgan and to Lancelot (not necessarily, one supposes, at the same time). But Morgan took Guiomar, a cousin of Guenevere's, for a lover. Finding them together, the angry Guenevere banished Guiomar. Morgan fled to Merlin, learned (or increased her earlier knowledge of) necromancy, and hated Guenevere ever afterward. This incident is recorded in Vulgate IV and may refer to the same period mentioned in Vulgate II, when Morgan met Merlin in Bedingran at the time of the knighting of Gawaine and his brothers.

Eventually returning to Arthur's court, Morgan took a new lover, Sir Accolon of Gaul, with whom she plotted the deaths of both Arthur and Uriens, planning to put Accolon and herself on the throne of Britain. The scheme was thwarted by Nimue. On learning of Accolon's death at Arthur's hands, some distance from court, Morgan attempted at least to murder her sleeping husband—surprisingly, by the natural means of a sword—but was prevented by their son Ywaine. Gaining Ywaine's promise of secrecy on her own pledge of future good behavior, she got Guenevere's permission to leave court, pretending urgent business at home. She stopped at the nunnery where Arthur lay wounded and stole the scabbard of Excalibur; the sword she could not get since he was sleeping with it. Pursued by Arthur, she threw the scabbard into a deep lake and then changed herself and her men into stones to escape capture. Their danger past, she saved Sir Manassen, a cousin of Accolon's, from enemies and sent him back to Arthur to tell how cleverly she had eluded him. She returned to Gore and garrisoned her castles in preparation for attack, nor was the precaution groundless, for Malory mentions Arthur's attempts to win back at least one castle he himself had given her in friendlier times. Soon after this return to Gore, she sent him a poisoned mantle as a pretended peace-offering, but Nimue's advice saved him from death.

One conceives that she was eventually forced to vacate Gore rather than run afoul of her husband or his deputy King Bagdemagus. She owned, acquired, or usurped more than one castle outside Gore, from which she could operate. (See La Beale Regard, Castle Chariot, and Morgan's Castle.) Her last known lover was Sir Hemison, whom she mourned deeply and buried richly when he was slain by Tristram. She also tried to make Alisander le Orphelin her paramour and, more than once, Sir Lancelot. She seems, however, to have had her lovers one at a time, taking a new one only some while after the former one was slain or otherwise lost.

With Lancelot she seems to have had an especial love-hate relationship. Malory records one instance of her kidnaping him (acting in concert with her companions at the time, the queens of Norgales, Eastland,

and the Out Isles); the Vulgate records other occasions when she got him into her power. She hated Lancelot because Guenevere loved him, and also, we may suspect, because he loved Guenevere and repulsed Morgan's own advances. Yet, whenever she captured him, she tried to get him into her own bed. As an example of one of their exchanges, after he had saved Duke Rochedon's Daughter, Morgan conjured him by what he loved best to doff his helmet. (This was probably not enchantment, but a rule of courtesy.) When he unhelmed, she said that if she had known his identity before, he would not have escaped so easily. He replied that if she were a man, he'd know how to deal with her; she responded that he would regret that comment.

For some time, probably many years, Morgan seems to have been or had the reputation of being at the heart of some network of enchantresses and villains. Once King Mark appealed to Morgan and the Queen of Norgales to set the country "in fire" with enchantresses and wicked knights like Malgrin and Breuse Sans Pitie; this suggests that there was such a network, or at least that Morgan and the Queen of Norgales wielded authority over other necromancers and wicked men. These same two are credited in Malory with putting a damsel into a scalding bath. Morgan's nephew Mordred may have served her at least for a time. Another instance of Morgan's mischief may be found under Val Sans Retour (q.v.).

After the episode of the poisoned mantle, however, Morgan's efforts against Arthur seem almost entirely directed at forcing him to recognize the love of Lancelot and Guenevere. Sir Bertilak de Hautdesert remarked to Gawaine that the affair of the Green Knight's beheading game had been staged by Morgan to shock Guenevere to death—an explanation which we may take figuratively, if not with a grain of salt; nevertheless, Morgan may well have continued to resent the fact that, after raising such a fuss about her friend's affair with Guiomar, Guenevere proceeded to enjoy a long, adulterous liaison of her own. Efforts by Morgan to reveal the adultery of Lancelot and Guenevere may be found under Morgan's Shield, Morgan's Ring, and Morgan's Drinking Horn.

In **Sir Gawaine and the Green Knight**, Morgan appears as an extremely old woman. This is curious, for here, as in Malory, she is Gawaine's aunt, and Gawaine, like Arthur and the rest of his court, is still quite young. Igraine must be granted a remarkably long period of childbearing if Morgan has naturally attained her great age in this work. I think it much more likely that, as Morgan could give Bertilak the appearance of the Green Knight, so she could give herself the appearance of any age she wished.

Eventually, Morgan retired to her castle near Tauroc, Wales, where she lived quietly for so long that Arthur and his court came to assume her dead. At last, however, Arthur chanced upon her castle while hunting, and she welcomed him warmly. On this occasion he spent a week visiting her, and the only attempt she made on his wellbeing was to show him the murals Lancelot had once painted while a prisoner in this castle, which murals revealed his relations with Guenevere. Arthur refused to believe even this evidence, but invited his half-sister to Camelot. She replied that she would never leave her castle again until the time came for her to go to Avalon.

Despite her long role as antagonist to Arthur, Guenevere, and their court, Morgan was the chief of the grieving ladies who came to bear Arthur away to Avilion after the last battle. [Vulgate II-VI; Malory I, 2; II, 11; IV, 1-14; VI, 3; VIII, 34; IX, 41-43; X, 35-38; XI, 1; XXI, 6]

MORGAN LE FAY'S FAMILY AND ALLIES
Father: Duke Gorloïs
Mother: Igraine
Sisters: Margawse, Elaine of Tintagil
Half-brother: Arthur
Husband: King Uriens
Son: Ywaine
Husband's bastard son: Yvonet li Avoutres
Brothers-in-law: King Lot (m. Margawse), King Nentres (m. Elaine)
Nephews: Gawaine, Agravaine Gaheris, Gareth, Mordred (all by Margawse); Galeshin (by Elaine)
Grandson?: Ider
Lovers: Guiomar (Guenevere's cousin), Accolon of Gaul, Hemison
Lover's (Accolon's) cousin: Manassen
Allies: Queen of Eastland?, Queen of Norgales, Queen of the Out Isles?, Queen of the Waste Lands?, Sebile, King Mark?, Breuse Sans Pitie?, Malgrin?
Protégé?: Oriolz the Dane

The fifteenth-century Catalan romance **Tirant Lo Blanc** continues this final favorable light without allusion to Morgan's villain aspect. She appears dressed in black and searching diligently for her brother; finding him, she rejoices and, in the ensuing celebration, it appears that dancing with her constitutes a signal honor for the knight she chooses as her partner. (See under Arthur.)

Spence identifies Morgan with the Morrigan, an Irish crow-goddess of war; Morgan, like Arthur, occasionally took the shape of a raven or crow. [**Magic Arts**, pp. 83, 151, 155, 160]

While never showing Morgan in person, Chrétien de Troyes refers to her rather more than to Merlin. In **Erec & Enide** [ll. 1934-1962; 4193-4228] he identifies her as Arthur's sister, mentions that Guingomar (Lord of the Isle of Avalon) is her lover, and describes a salve she made for her brother: if applied once a day, it effectively heals any wound within a week. Again, in **Yvain** [ll. 2953ff.], "Morgan the Wise" has given the lady of Noroison an ointment that cures madness. Both these preparations—assuming that they are two separate preparations—show Morgan in her beneficent aspect; I did not spot any reference in Chrétien's work to her as villain.

MORGAN'S CASTLE

In trying to dovetail Malory's evidence with that of the Vulgate, I am forced to conclude that Morgan le Fay had at least two castles. She may well have had even more, here and there about the country.

King Arthur gave Morgan a castle and later regretted his generosity, but never could win it from her again with any kind of siege engine. She sent her knights out by one, two, and three to overthrow Arthur's knights and imprison or at least strip them. This castle appears to have been not too far from Camelot, likely to the south toward Cornwall. [Malory X, 17] Were we to make it, say, Ringwood in southwest Southampton, and make Beaulieu, not far from Ringwood, the castle of La Beale Regard, it would be easy to understand why Morgan would usurp La Beale Regard. "Ringwood", indeed, would not make a bad name for the castle of a sorceress.

According to Vulgate VI, Morgan had a castle near the stronghold of Tauroc, which in turn must have been near Taneborc Castle at the entrance of Norgales. Once Arthur and his companions, lost while hunting in the woods around Tauroc, came to this Welsh castle of Morgan's. This was late in Arthur's career, and he was surprised to find his half-sister yet alive—he had presumed her dead, not having heard of her in some years. He found that her castle had silk-covered walls in the courtyard, great splendor and marvelous illumination within, and gold and silver dinner plates which he could not match even at Camelot.

Morgan had once imprisoned Lancelot in this castle, administering to him a curious powder which made him content to remain with her. He had beguiled two winters and a summer by painting his life's history, including scenes of his love for Guenevere, on the walls of his room. [Vulgate V] Morgan showed Arthur Lancelot's murals in yet another attempt to convince her brother he was being cuckolded, but he refused to believe it. Aside from this, his visit with her was amicable on both sides, and he invited her to visit court. She replied, however, that she would never return to court until she left her castle to go to Avilion. [Vulgate VI] It sounds as if the castle in the woods near Tauroc was her favorite, and that she had chosen to retire here from the world.

Morgan's Chapel†—see VAL SANS RETOUR

MORGAN'S DAMSEL

When he met her in Sir Damas' castle, masquerading as Damas' daughter, Arthur thought he recognized her as a damsel he had seen around his own court [Malory IV, 7].

Perhaps she could be identified with the damsel who brought Arthur Morgan's gift of a poisoned cloak. On Nimue's counsel, Arthur forced the maiden messenger to try the cloak on herself, despite her reluctance, and it promptly burned her to death. [Malory IV, 16]

MORGAN'S DRINKING HORN

This magical drinking horn, "harnessed with gold", could only be used in safety by ladies who were true to their husbands. If the drinker were false to her husband, all the drink would spill. Morgan le Fay (who could not herself have honestly drunk from it) sent this horn to Arthur in another attempt to publicize Guenevere's unfaithfulness, but Sir Lamorak stopped the messenger and made him take it to King Mark instead. Of a hundred ladies of Mark's court, including La Beale Isoud, only four could drink cleanly. [Malory VIII, 34] To the credit of the men, when the angered King Mark swore to burn Isoud and the other shamed ladies,

> [t]hen the barons gathered them together, and said plainly they would not have those ladies burnt for an horn made by sorcery, that came from as false a sorceress and witch as then was living. For that horn did never good, but caused strife and debate, and always in her days she had been an enemy to all true lovers. So there were many knights made their avow, an ever they met with Morgan le Fay, that they would show her short courtesy. [Malory VIII, 34]

MORGAN'S MANTLE

Morgan le Fay sent a rich mantle, set with precious stones, to Arthur, ostensibly as a peace offering. Nimue, who was perhaps also acquainted with Greek tragedy, warned Arthur not to wear it or let any of his knights wear it unless Morgan's messenger wore it first. Arthur made the damsel messenger try it on, and it immediately burned her to coals. [Malory IV, 15-16]

MORGAN'S OINTMENT(S)†

The salve which Morgan made and gave to her brother Arthur would heal any wound, even one on a joint or a nerve, within a week, if applied once every day. [Chrétien de Troyes, **Erec & Enide**, ll. 4193-4228]

Morgan gave the lady of Noroison (q.v.) a box of ointment which cured madness when rubbed into the temples of the sufferer [Chrétien, **Yvain**, ll. 2953 ff.].

These two salves might be identical, or only two of the many Morgan could probably make. I see nothing to prevent anyone from theorizing either way.

MORGAN'S POWDER†

Morgan tricked Lancelot into her castle. Putting him to sleep with drugged wine, she blew a powder into his nostrils through a silver tube, thus taking away his senses for a time. It seems to have had a curious effect. He did not lose his memory, apparently; seeing a man paint the history of Aeneas, Lancelot was inspired to paint his own life around the walls of his room. He does seem to have been quite content to remain, in effect, Morgan's prisoner for two winters and a summer. At the end of this time, a spring rose, in a garden Morgan had planted outside his window for his enjoyment, suddenly reminded him of Guenevere. So he broke the iron bars of his window, plucked the rose, armed himself, and kept on going, the spell broken. He spared Morgan on this occasion for the sake of her brother Arthur. [Vulgate V]

MORGAN'S RING†

In early days, Guenevere gave Morgan a ring which differed from the one Guenevere later gave Lancelot only in the engraving on the stone.

Kidnaping Lancelot after he had disenchanted her Val Sans Retour (q.v.), Morgan demanded the ring Guenevere had given him as a ransom. When he refused, she resorted to drugging him and exchanging rings. He did not notice the difference, and she sent his ring to court with a "confession" and apology purportedly by him, in another effort to uncover Guenevere's unfaithfulness to Arthur. Guenevere said she had given the ring to Lancelot, but honorably; Arthur said he did not believe Morgan's damsel, but, rather than lose Lancelot, he would let him love the Queen. [Vulgate IV]

MORGAN'S SHIELD

Although it was made by Morgan le Fay, I find no indication that this shield was magical in itself.

> The field was goldish, with a king and a queen therein painted, and a knight standing above them, [one foot] upon the king's head, and the other upon the queen's.

Morgan made Tristram carry this shield in the tournament at the Castle of the Hard Rock. The device signified Arthur, Guenevere, and Lancelot, although Morgan would not tell Tristram who the painted knight was. [Malory IX, 41]

Morholt, Morolt—see **MARHAUS**

MORRIS

Malory implies that the forest of Morris is in Cornwall, near Tintagil Castle. Probably Morris would stretch roughly between Tintagil and Bodmin Moor; possibly it would even take in Bodmin Moor, accommodating Dozmary Pool as the Perilous Lake of Morris. I have read the statement somewhere that Cornwall has no trees, but that is not quite true; it does have some little wooded areas, and would have had more in Arthurian times. [Malory IX, 39]

MORTAISE (Marchoise, Marcoise, Martorse, Mortoise)

In Malory VII, 24, Mortaise is put in the vicinity of Dame Lyonors' Castle Dangerous, which Gareth and Lynette reach from Caerleon. Here it seems to be a natural body of water, its passage guarded by two rascally knights whom Gareth slew. Later, in the Grail Adventures, Mortaise appears as the water beside which Lancelot was stranded for a time before boarding the ship with Galahad and the body of Percivale's sister, the water near which the Temptress told Percivale she had seen the Red Knight with the white shield, and possibly the water into which Percivale rode the demon horse before reaching the island (of Turnance?). [Malory XVII, 13; XIV, 8; XIV, 5-6]

Vulgate VI gives a fuller description, identifying Mortaise as a lake ("laigue"). After eating bread and water with a recluse, Lancelot passed the night on a high rock. The next day he came to a deep, very beautiful valley between two high rocks, before which lay Mortaise, divided in two parts by a wooded tongue of land. The wood was dense, the water very deep.

To make the Bristol Channel and Severn River the water of Mortaise, and Dundy the Isle of Turnance, should give us room to accommodate all the events Malory describes. The horseshoe bend in the Severn near Newnham might fit the Vulgate's description.

Mount Dolorous—see **KAHEDIN**

MOUNT OF ARABY, GIANT OF THE

After conquering the Giant of Saint Michael's Mount, Brittany, Arthur reminisced about the one he conquered "in the mount of Araby", who was not quite so big and fierce [Malory V, 5]. Since there seems no record, at least in Malory, of Arthur's having been out of Britain before, the "Mount of Araby" may have been in Britain—perhaps Saint Michael's Mount in Cornwall.

Mungo, Saint†—see **KENTIGERN, SAINT**

Myrddin—see **MERLIN**

NABON LE NOIRE

The lord of the Isle of Servage, he was "a great mighty giant" who hated Arthur and destroyed all of Arthur's knights who came his way. In jousting, Nabon had a trick of killing his opponent's horse. In battle, Sir Tristram slew Nabon and made Sir Segwarides lord of the isle in his place. [Malory VIII, 37-39; see also Nanowne le Petite]

NABUNAL OF MYCENE†

One of the twelve who accompanied Alexander from Greece to Britain, where Arthur knighted them all at the outset of Count Angrs' rebellion. Chrétien calls Nabunal very wise: when Alexander with thirty followers had infiltrated Windsor and pursued Angrs with his few surviving armed men to the keep, it was Nabunal who advised Alexander to have the outer approaches blocked so that the townspeople could not come to their rebel lord's help. This advice, carried out just in time, saved the day for Alexander and, thus, for Arthur. Nabunal apparently survived the fighting, but Chrétien tells us nothing more about him. [**Cligés**, ll. 102-385; 1093-ca. 2210]

Nacien—see **NASCIEN**

NANOWNE LE PETITE

All that Malory seems to tell us of this unhappy knight of Arthur's is that he was the last victim of Nabon le Noire, who put him to a shameful death, "for he was drawn limb-meal" [Malory VIII, 37].

NANTES

Chrétien de Troyes puts Nantes in Brittany among Arthur's court cities, making it the site of Erec's Yuletide coronation as king of Outre-Gales [**Erec & Enide**, ll. 6533ff.].

NANTES, BISHOP OF †

A very saintly and worthy prelate, at Arthur's behest he anointed and crowned Erec king of Outre-Gales [Chrétien de Troyes, **Erec & Enide**, ll. 6856-6887].

Nantres—see **NENTRES, KING**

Narboat—see **MARBOAR**

NASCIEN (Nacien, Seraphe)

Seraphe was the brother-in-law of King Evelake. Joseph of Arimathea converted them and their families to Christianity, giving Seraphe the baptismal name of Nascien and Evelake that of Mordrains. Nascien's wife was Flegentine, their son Celidoine, and among their descendants were the Fisher Kings, Lancelot and Galahad, and Percivale and Amide.

Mordrains, Nascien, and their families came to Britain with Joseph and Josephe. Here, forty years after Christ's Passion, Nascien successfully endured temptation by a fiend in the Port of Perilous Rock. Mordrains, meanwhile, came to the Isle of Turnance, found King Solomon's Ship, and broke King David's Sword by drawing it unworthily to slay a giant that was chasing him. Somehow killing the giant without the use of the sacred weapon, Mordrains returned to Solomon's Ship and was carried to the Port of Perilous Rock, where Nascien, fresh from his testing, miraculously repaired the sword and returned it to its sheath. They were warned by a voice to leave Solomon's Ship, and, in so doing, Mordrains received a sword wound in the right foot as punishment for drawing the sword. [Malory XVII, 4: in this passage, Nascien is credited with drawing King David's Sword and Mordrains with its mending, but, convinced that the two names have been transposed here, I have recapped the tale accordingly.]

Surviving as a holy hermit until the reign of Arthur (or perhaps returning as an apparition), Nascien filled very approximately the role in the spiritual world of the Grail Adventures that Merlin had formerly played to Arthur and his knights in the secular world: Nascien was their more or less elusive prophet, mentor, guide, and confessor. I believe he is to be identified with Malory's unnamed hermit who came to the Round Table the Whitsunday before Galahad's birth and predicted that event within the year, and with the "good old man, and … ancient, clothed all in white, and there was no knight knew from whence he came" who actually brought Galahad into Arthur's court. As Galahad succeeded in drawing Balin's sword from its floating rock, a damsel riding a white palfrey appeared on the river bank to tell Lancelot he was no longer the greatest knight of the world and to bring Arthur Nascien's message "that thee shall befall the greatest worship that ever befell king in Britain." Just before the departure of the Questers, "an old knight … and in religious clothing" came into court to give them Nascien's warning and instructions for the holy enterprise, among which was the injunction that no knight should be allowed to take along a woman. (Interesting, in light of Amide's importance to Galahad, Percivale, and Bors, and also in view of Nascien's own use of a damsel as one of his messengers.) When Galahad came to the Abbey of the Adventurous

Shield, the angelic White Knight, telling the story of the shield, mentioned Nascien's death and burial in that same abbey. Nevertheless, while in the Grail Quest Gawaine and Ector, asking for a hermit to explain their dreams, were told:

> Here is one in a little mountain, but it is so rough there may no horse go thither, and therefore ye must go upon foot; there shall ye find a poor house, and there is Nacien the hermit, which is the holiest man in this country.
>
> Then [they] rode till that they came to the rough mountain, and there they tied their horses and went on foot to the hermitage. And when they were come up they saw a poor house, and beside the chapel a little courtelage [courtyard], where Nacien the hermit gathered worts, as he which had tasted none other meat of a great while.

He explained their dreams and, finding them unworthy, gave them some harsh counsel, which they rejected. It is not unlikely that Nascien should also be identified with some of the nameless holy men who counseled other knights on this Quest, nor does it seem unlikely that, if he had indeed spent several centuries of miraculously prolonged life in Britain, he might have had more than one hermitage scattered about the island. [Vulgate, chiefly I, V, & VI; Malory, XI, 1; XIII, 3-4, 5, 8, 11; XV, 4; XVI, 2-5; XVII, 4]

According to Vulgate VII, Nascien's mother was *la bele Damoisele de la Blanche Nue* (or *Nuage*)—the lovely maiden of the white cloud. I am not completely sure, however, that this is the same Nascien. Here he appears in the thick of battle, helping sixteen other knights succor Agloval. I remember no other testimony that the hermit Nascien indulged in martial activities during Arthur's reign.

NAUNTES

> So [the eleven rebel kings] consented together to keep all the marches of Cornwall, of Wales, and of the North. So first, they put King Idres in the City of Nauntes in Britain, with four thousand men of arms, to watch both the water and the land. [Malory I, 18]

Nauntes must have been strategically important, though this seems to be the only time Malory mentions it.

There is, of course, a city names Nantes in Brittany, and Brittany is sometimes called Britain in the old books; nevertheless, the context of the passage suggests that here a city in Great Britain is meant. In present-day Merioneth County, Wales, is a point of land called Cader Idris; it is on the coast, immediately south of the inlet at Barmouth. The name Idris suggests the name of the king delegated to hold the city, making Caer Idris a candidate for "the City of Nauntes in Britain." But see Nantes. Chrétien de Troyes, himself French and apparently proud of it, saw nothing strange about Arthur holding court across the Channel in Brittany.

Neglay, Port†—see **POMEGLAY**

NENTRES (Nantres, Ventres), KING OF GARLOTH (Garlot)

Nentres married Elaine of Tintagil, by whom he sired Sir Galeshin. Nentres joined the first rebellion against Arthur, pledging 5,000 mounted men to the cause and fighting well in the battle of Bedegraine. When the kings had to suspend their rebellion because of the Saracen attack on Wandesborow Castle, Nentres was put in charge of the city of Windesan. Apparently remaining aloof from the second rebellion, Nentres eventually became a companion of the Round Table. [Malory I, 2, 8, 12-18; XIX, 11; Vulgate II]

NERIOLIS†

One of the twelve who accompanied Alexander from Greece to Britain, where Arthur knighted them all at the outset of Count Angrs' rebellion Neriolis was slain during Angrs' night sortie near the end of that rebellion. [Chrétien de Troyes, **Cligés**, ll. 102-385; 1093-ca. 2100]

NERIUS†

Among the twelve who accompanied Alexander from Greece to Britain, where Arthur knighted them all at the outset of Count Angrs' rebellion Nerius was not with Alexander's party when it penetrated Windsor and captured Angrs. Although Nerius survived the rebellion, Chrétien tells us nothing more about him. [**Cligés**, ll. 102-385; 1093-ca. 2210]

NERO

A "might man of men", Nero helped his brother King Ryons war against Leodegrance and others. Ryons captured by Balin and Balan, Nero joined battle with Arthur before Castle Terrabil. Meanwhile, Merlin came to Nero's ally, King Lot, "and held him with a tale of prophecy, till Nero and his people were destroyed." [Malory II, 9-10]

NEROVENS DE LILE

When La Cote Male Taile set out with the damsel Maledisant in her quest, Lancelot followed after, "and by the way upon a bridge there was a knight proffered Sir Launcelot to joust." After a noble sword battle, the strange knight yielded, and turned out to be Sir Nerovens de Lile, whom Lancelot himself had dubbed knight. Happily reunited, Nerovens warned Lancelot of Sir Brian de les Isles, lord of the Castle of Pendragon, who had just captured La Cote Male Taile the day before. After defeating Sir Brian, Lancelot gave Nerovens rule, under La Cote Male Taile, of Pendragon Castle and its surrounding country. Nerovens also became a companion of the Round Table. [Malory IX, 5-6, 9, 11]

Very likely Nerovens should be identified with Sir Neroneus, who accompanied Lancelot into exile and was made Earl of Pardiak {Malory XX, 18].

NIGRAMOUS, CASTLE

This was the stronghold of the sorceress Hellawes, probably located near the Chapel Perilous [Malory VI, 15]. Hellawes probably is to be identified with Helaes de la Forest Perilleuse, who appears in Vulgate VII. Although there may be many Forests Perilous (that seeming as much descriptive phrase as a proper name), for lack of a better clue Castle Nigramous and the Chapel Perilous could be placed either in the Forest Perilous of Norgales or that of southeast Wales around Dame Lyonors' Castle Dangerous. I would prefer the more southern location, in order to keep Hellawes' sphere of activity separated from Annowre's. Conversely, there might be equal rationale for making Hellawes and Annowre neighbor sorceresses.

NIMUE

At Arthur's marriage feast, Merlin bade the knights sit still around the Table, telling them they would soon see a strange and marvelous adventure. As they sat, in ran a white hart, chased by a white brachet, with thirty couple of black hounds running after. The brachet bit the hart, which then leaped and knocked over a knight. This knight got up, caught the brachet, and left the hall to mount his horse and ride away. Immediately in rode a lady on a white palfrey and

> cried aloud to King Arthur, Sir, suffer me not to have this despite, for the brachet was mine .... [W]ith this there came a knight riding all armed on a great horse, and took the lady away with him with force, and ever she cried and made great dole. When she was gone the king was glad, for she made such a noise.

But Merlin insisted that the adventures could not be dismissed so lightly. So, on the mage's advice, Gawaine was sent after the white hart, the newly knighted Tor after the knight who had stolen the brachet, and King Pellinore after the knight who had stolen the damsel. Tor came through the adventures with the most honor, for Gawaine had the mischance to slay a lady while aiming for her lord, Sir Ablamar of the Marsh, while Pellinore was so hot in his quest that he did not try to stop to help a lady with a wounded knight—only learning when he came back and found them dead that she had been his own daughter Eleine. Pellinore succeeded in the quest itself, however; he found and slew the abductor, Sir Hontzlake of Wentland, made the acquaintance of the damsel's cousin, Sir Meliot of Logurs, and his sworn brother Sir Brian of the Isles, and brought the damsel back to court. This damsel of the white brachet was Nimue.

Merlin now became besotted with Nimue, taught her magic, and took her with him on a visit to Benwick. She might already have been one of the minor damsels of the Lake; now, perhaps through Merlin's influence, she became the chief Lady of the Lake in place of the one Balin had slain (see "Nineve"). Troubled by Merlin's lecherous intentions, however, and "afeard of him because he was a devil's son", Nimue at last used the crafts he had taught her to imprison him under a great stone. (Other early versions, however, show her as putting him in comfortable retirement through genuine affection, perhaps sisterly, for him.)

Perhaps, having retired Merlin for whatever reason, Nimue felt obligated to take Arthur under her wing in Merlin's stead. Whereas Merlin's style seems to have been hovering around the court keeping more or less underfoot, Nimue apparently spent most of her time in her Lake, appearing only at need. For instance, she arrived just in time to foil Morgan's crafts and help Arthur win the fight against Sir Accolon, then quietly left again. She appeared in the Forest Perilous just in time to enlist Sir Tristram's aid and save Arthur from the sorceress Annowre. Sometimes she did not arrive as early as she might have, as in the affair of the poisoned apples; but neither had Merlin always been on time, and his tardiness had sometimes resulted in unnecessary deaths. At any rate, despite Arthur's annoyance with Nimue's noise at their first meeting, "ever she did great goodness unto King Arthur and to all his knights through her sorcery and enchantments." Despite her former opposition to Morgan, Nimue accompanied Morgan, the Queen of Norgales, and the Queen of the Waste Lands when they came in their ship to bear away the mortally wounded Arthur.

Nimue found Sir Pelleas when he was bemoaning Gawaine's betrayal of him in the matter of Dame Ettard. Falling in love with Pelleas herself, Nimue caused him to love her instead of Ettard, and Ettard to love him as hopelessly as he had originally loved her. Although she brought him to Arthur's court and may well have sponsored him when he was made a companion of the Round Table, after their marriage Nimue kept Pelleas safe from harm, presumably even in the final battles between Arthur and Mordred. (Her union with Pelleas could be reconciled with the "loving retirement" theory of what she did to Merlin. Cf. Thomas Wentworth Higginson, **Tales of Atlantis and the Enchanted Isles**, chapter VII.)

[Malory III, 5-15; IV, 1, 10, 22-23, 28; IX, 16; XVIII, 8; XXI, 6; see also The Lake]

"NINEVE" ("Niniane", "Nynyue")

The name Nimue is a clerical error for Nineve or Nynyue, and the character is named Viviane in the Old French **Merlin** (see Lady of the

Lake). For the sake of convenience, I have adopted the name "Nineve" for Malory's first British Lady of the Lake, introduced and disposed of before Nimue's appearance.

After Arthur's sword broke in combat with King Pellinore,

> No force, said Merlin, hereby is a sword that shall be yours, an I may. So they rode till they came to a lake, the which was a fair water and broad, and in the midst of the lake … an arm clothed in white samite, that held a fair sword in that hand. Lo! said Merlin, yonder is that sword that I spake of. With that they saw a damosel going upon the lake. What damosel is that? said Arthur. That is the Lady of the Lake, said Merlin; and within that lake is a rock, and therein is a fair a place as any on earth, and richly beseen; and this damosel will come to you anon, and then speak ye fair to her that she will give you that sword.

The damsel greeted Arthur and agreed to give him the sword Excalibur if he would give her a gift when she asked it. When he promised to do so, she pointed out a barge in which he could row over and take the sword and scabbard.

When, some little time afterward, Balin drew the sword of the damsel I call "Malvis", this Lady of the Lake

> came on horseback, richly beseen, and saluted King Arthur, and there asked him a gift that he promised her when she gave him the sword …. Well, said the lady, I ask the head of the knight that hath won the sword, or else the damosel's head that brought it; I take no force though I have both their heads, for he slew my brother, a good knight and a true, and that gentlewoman was causer of my father's death. Truly, said King Arthur, I may not grant neither of their heads with my worship, therefore ask what ye will else …. I will ask none other thing, said the lady. When Balin … saw the Lady of the Lake, that by her means had slain Balin's mother, and had sought her three years; and when it was told him that she asked his head of King Arthur, he went to her straight and said, Evil be you found; ye would have my head, and therefore you shall lose yours, and with his sword lightly he smote off her head before King Arthur.

Arthur was greatly displeasured and banished Balin from court, Balin still maintaining that

> this same lady was the untruest lady living, and by enchantment and sorcery she hath been the destroyer of many good knights, and she was causer that my mother was burnt, through her falsehood and treachery.

Arthur buried the lady richly, but we may probably accept Balin's accusation as accurate. This first British Lady of the Lake, if not one of Merlin's cohorts, was at least willing to work in concord with him; yet when Merlin returned to court and learned of what had happened, Malory does not record that even he made any attempt to deny Balin's charges. [Malory I, 25; II, 3-4]

"Niniane"—see **"NINEVE"**

NOAUZ†

Site of a tournament planned, by the ladies left behind during the action of the Meliagrant affair, as a sort of marriage mart to break their boredom. (See the Lady of Noauz) I should assume Noauz to be composed of castle, town, and the lands thereto pertaining, and to lie within reasonable traveling distance of Gore. [Chrétien de Troyes, **Lancelot**, ll. 5379ff.] Also, because of the name similarity, I should not be surprised if Noauz and Nohaut were the same territory.

NOAUZ, LADY OF†

While Meliagrant was holding Guenevere prisoner in Gore, the ladies and damsels of Logres, feeling blue, decided to lift their spirits by arranging a tournament, with the lady of Noauz challenging the lady of Pomelegloi (neither of whom Chrétien has mentioned before). The tournament was to be held at Noauz—I have doublechecked the passage to make sure it is she of Noauz who is named as the challenger, at least in Owen's translation. The ladies announced it well ahead of time, so as to have a good turnout; it was to serve as a sort of marriage mart, with the unwed damsels planning to accept husbands from among those knights who did well. When Guenevere was safely returned before the tournament, the ladies invited her to grace it with her presence, which she did. Alas for their wedding projects! Drawn by the presence of the queen, Lancelot attended the tournament incognito (see Meliagrant's Seneschal; also "The Loquacious Herald of Noauz") and, of course, did so splendidly—Gawaine stayed out of the second day's fighting for the pleasure of watching the unknown champion's deeds—that all the damsels fell in love with this same unknown and refused to consider having any other husband that year, so no one got married after all. [Chrétien de Troyes, **Lancelot**, ll. 5379-6078]

The name similarity makes it very tempting to identify this lady with the Vulgate's lady of Nohaut.

Noble†—see CUBELE

Nogres, Haughty Maid of—see HAUGHTY MAID OF LOGRES

NOHAUT†

Nohaut was a castle or a subkingdom. Here the Lady of Nohaut was besieged by the King of Northumberland [Vulgate III], suggesting that Nohaut was close to Northumberland.

NOHAUT, LADY OF†

She seems to have been a ruler in her own right, as well as a liege of Arthur's. When the King of Northumberland besieged her, she sent a messenger to Arthur, asking for a champion. The newly dubbed Lancelot craved to act for her. He made a side trip to rescue a damsel from a big and apparently cruel knight; this, however, turned out to be a test arranged by the Lady of Nohaut—the big knight had wanted to champion and wed her, and she had consented on condition he defeat the champion Arthur sent. (He did not.) When Lancelot arrived at Nohaut, the Lady put him to bed for fifteen days to recover from his wounds. Meanwhile, hearing no news of Lancelot at court, Kay requested the errand and was sent to Nohaut in his turn. After a quarrel between Kay and Lancelot, the Lady settled the question of which was to act for her by requesting the King of Northumberland to allow her two champions. They fought two knights of Northumberland. Lancelot, after vanquishing his opponent, offered to help Kay; Kay refused the offer and eventually succeeded in mastering his own adversary. Kay returned to court with the Lady's thanks, while Lancelot lingered awhile at Nohaut. [Vulgate III]

I strongly suspect, because of the name similarity, that the ladies of Nohaut and of Noauz should be identified with each other.

NOIRE ESPINE, DAUGHTERS OF THE LORD OF†

Chrétien gives the cause of this lord's demise as losing an argument with Death. His only survivors seem to be a pair of daughters. The elder tries to seize the entire inheritance for herself alone, at which the younger rather naively declares her intention to appeal to King Arthur. The elder secretly beats her to court and somehow enlists Gawaine as her own champion, although, as if already suspecting his maiden to be in the wrong, he makes anonymity his condition. The younger sister arrives and tries in her turn to enlist Gawaine. On his polite refusal, she can think of no other champion than the Knight with the Lion, news of whose prowess have just been brought to court by Gawaine's nephews and niece, rescued from Harpin of the Mountain. Granted the customary forty days to find her chosen champion and bring him back, the damsel falls sick on the way, leaving a friend whom I call "Secunda" to finish the search. "Secunda" proving successful, the younger damsel of Noire Espine brings Ywaine, still shrouding himself beneath his new soubriquet, back to court in the nick of time. The battle between two such obviously worthy, if unknown, champions causes all onlookers to plead with the elder daughter to yield her sister enough of the inheritance to live on, but she refuses. When Gawaine and Ywaine at last learn each other's identity and begin determinedly declaring each other the victor, Arthur shrewdly tricks the elder sister by asking, "Where is she who wishes cruelly to disinherit and beggar her sister", and pronouncing her "Here I am" a confession of guilt. Thus, Solomon-like, Arthur settles the dispute, ordering the older daughter to give the younger a fair portion and cherish her as liege-woman. [**Yvain**, ll. 4703-5107; 5808-6446]

Throughout the account, the elder sister is so consistently tagged "malevolent" and the younger shown as such a sweet thing as to make me wonder if we might have here the kind of sibling relationship Shakespeare was to repeat with Kate and Bianca.

NORGALES (North Wales, Northgalis)

To accommodate a border between Norgales and Cambenet, I would put the boundary far enough south to include most of Montgomeryshire in Norgales, following the Severn River partway. Kaleph is a castle in this subkingdom [Vulgate I].

I have not quite been able to work out the relationship and histories of the various named and unnamed kings of Norgales. As a stopgap measure, I have tried at least to gather together those characters who seem connected with this part of the country.

CONNECTED WITH NORGALES
Kings: Agrippe?, Ryons, Tradelmans, Vadalon
Queen of Norgales
King of Norgales' Daughter and her Handmaid
Lady de Vance? (desired by King Ryons)
Nero (brother of King Ryons)
Galihodin?
Retainer: Phelot

NORGALES, DAUGHTER OF THE KING OF †

Gawaine made love to her and possibly considered himself married to her, according to Vulgate III. I am not sure of which king of Norgales she was the daughter.

NORGALES, HANDMAID OF THE DAUGHTER OF THE KING OF†

Sir Sagramore is matched with her in Vulgate III.

NORGALES (Northgalis), QUEEN OF

She was one of four queens who kidnaped Lancelot and held him in Castle Chariot. The others were the Queen of Eastland, the Queen of the Isles, and Morgan le Fay.

The Queen of Norgales appears at least thrice more in association with Morgan le Fay. Trying to rouse the enchantresses and wicked knights against Alisander le Orphelin, King Mark wrote "unto Morgan le Fay, and to the Queen of Northgalis." The Queen of Norgales is credited, along with Morgan, with putting the damsel into the scalding bath. Finally, the Queen of Norgales appeared with Morgan, the Queen of the Waste Lands, and Nimue in the ship that carried Arthur away after the last battle. [Malory VI, 3-4; X, 35; XI, 1; XXI, 6]

From all of this, it seems likely that the Queen of Norgales was both Morgan's friend and associate, and the second most powerful sorceress in Britain, excluding the Lady of the Lake.

NOROISON, LADY OF, and HER DAMSELS†

The lady of Noroison and two of her damsels, while out riding in the woods, saw Ywaine asleep during his interval of running mad in the wilderness. One of the damsels approached and dismounted to study him, finally recognizing him by a scar on his face: she had seen it often, so she must have been acquainted with him earlier. She immediately understood that he could assist them in her lady's war with Count Alier.

The three women returned to their nearby castle, where the lady produced a box of ointment that Morgan had given her and entrusted it to the damsel abovementioned, with instructions to rub it just into Ywaine's temples, which would suffice to restore his sanity. (The second damsel quietly fades from the story.) Overeager, the maiden used every bit of ointment to anoint him all over his body, left clothes provided by herself and her mistress, and waited some distance away until after he had awakened in his right mind and dressed himself, when she courteously pretended to find him for the first time. (Of course, finding suitable male garments waiting ready for him in the forest may have caused a sane knight to suspect something.) While leading him back to the castle, she threw the empty ointment box into a stream so that she could tell her mistress she had lost it by accident, adding that she almost fell in after it—which would have been an even greater loss. At first enraged, and feeling almost completely sure that she could never get more of the wonderful ointment, the lady soon accepted her loss and said no more about it. Her investment paid off when Ywaine won her war against the invading Count Alier. Her people would have been glad to see Ywaine wed their lady, but when his work was done he left without explaining that he already had a wife, whose estrangement had caused his madness in the first place.

[Chrétien de Troyes, **Yvain**, ll. 2887-3340; name "Noroison" ca. l. 3290]

North Wales, Northgalis—see NORGALES

NORTHUMBERLAND

The general area we know by the same name.

NORTHUMBERLAND, FOREST OF

Here Blaise, Merlin's former teacher, settled down and wrote the chronicles of Merlin's life [Malory I, 17].

NUT†

Parent of Sir Yder [Chrétien de Troyes, **Erec & Enide**, l. 1045ff.].

"Nynyue"—see "NINEVE"

OGIER THE DANE

Brewer says that Morgan once took Ogier to Avalon, gave him a ring of youth and a crown of forgetfulness, and introduced him to King Arthur. Two hundred years later, she sent Ogier to fight the Moors in France. He routed them and then returned to Avalon. Ogier's swords were Curtana —"the cutter"—and Sauvagine; his horse was Papillon—"butterfly."

OGRINS, BROTHER†

In the earliest known version of Tristram, that of Broul, Brother Ogrins is a hermit who counsels the wandering Tristram and Yseut (Isoud) to repent of their sin. When they protest that they cannot because of having drunk the potion, he relaxes his holy rule in order to give them shelter for the night. In this version, the effects of the potion wear off after three years, and the lovers return in penitence to the hermit, who arranges a reconciliation for Isoud with Mark. Apparently a shrewd dealer for a "nonworldly" man, Ogrins buys and barters so well that Isoud can appear before Mark richly apparelled and mounted.

I have only a partial translation on hand, and do not know what happens afterwards, but there seem to be indications that Tristram and Isoud still love each other, love potion wearing off or not.

OLIVE BRANCHES

An olive branch was carried as a token that its bearer was an ambassador and messenger, and came in peace [Malory V, 1; XX, 14].

Ontzlake—see under **HONTZLAKE**

ORGUELLOUSE, EMPRISE

Duke Galeholt built this castle on a rock washed by a tributary of the Assurne River, which bordered his kingdom of Surluse. He intended it to be his place of coronation and Arthur's prison, and he never entered it in sorrow without leaving it in joy. After he became Arthur's man, however, L'Emprise Orguellouse crumbled to pieces. [Vulgate IV]

ORGULOUS, CASTLE (The Proud Castle)†

Every knight who passed by this castle was made to joust or else be taken prisoner, or at least lose his horse and harness [Malory IX, 3].

Glennie puts Castle Orgulous at Bamborough, Northumberland, on the east coast, a little south of Holy Island, near Belford but right on the coast, just on the south side of a small, squarish inlet. He gives this description:

> Occupying the whole extent of a solitary eminence, it stands among sandy downs, close by the sea, and overlooking a wide plain at the foot of the Cheviots. Nearly opposite the Castle are the Faröe Islands. [p. 64]

Castle Orgulous appears in Malory's story of La Cote Male Taile. If we assume that at the beginning of this tale, in IX, 1, Arthur is holding court at Carlisle or another northern city, I see no reason to reject Glennie's identification, exept that Malory gives Bamborough as one of two possible sites for the castle of Joyous Garde.

The Loathly Damsel is on her way to Castle Orgulous when she stops off at Carlion to scold Percivale for his failure to ask the right questions at the Grail Castle and to invite the rest of Arthur's court to adventures either at Castle Orgulous or at Montesclaire. By her account, 566 famous knights and their high-born ladies are within Castle Orgulous, ready to provide the chance for jousting and glory. Though she says it lies far from Carlion, she intends to get there, on her tawny mule, by nightfall. [Chrétien de Troyes, **Perceval**, ca. ll. 4684-4698]

ORIEL†

A Saxon warrior, involved in the attack on Vandaliors Castle [Vulgate II].

ORINGLE, COUNT OF LIMORS†

Finding Erec apparently dead of too much errant adventuring and Enide about to kill herself in despair, this Count and his men took them both back to his castle of Limors. The Count intended to bury Erec and marry Enide, making her his countess. This much seems to accord honorably with the customs of the time: so far, the Count's only fault would appear to lie in acting with so much haste. Not content to allow the new widow any interval at all for grieving, he made his chaplain perform the marriage ceremony that same evening, forcing Enide to sit with him on the dais to dine and, when she refused to make merry, actually commencing to strike her. At this point Erec woke up, saw the situation, struck down the Count, and escaped with Enide. Less fortunate than Count Galoain—although their relative degrees of guilt could be debated—the Count of Limors was left slain at his table. [Chrétien de Troyes, **Erec & Enide**, ll. 4668-4918]

ORIOLZ THE DANE†

He was the son of King Aminaduf of Denmark. The Damoiselle à la Harpe took Oriolz to heal him, but her cousin, Helaes de la Forest Perilleuse, asked him as a favor to capture Gawaine, put him in her prison, and fight with him daily—all so that she could have Gawaine as her lover. [Vulgate VII]

Could Oriolz be identified with Ogier the Dane (q.v.)?

ORKNEY

At the time of writing the first edition of this book, I suspected that "Orkney" in Arthurian lore included more than simply the Orkney Islands—that it might include all Scotland south to Lothian.

In the last pages Chrétien de Troyes wrote, he has Orkney as a city where Arthur holds court. Chrétien's Orkney lies two full traveling days (north of?) the area of Canguin and Orqueneseles, and seems to be on the mainland. This apparently puzzled Hilka, who noted that the Orkneys are islands, not a city. It would seem more or less to bear out my own earlier guess, at least as far as the place name being applied a little differently in the context of medieval Arthurian romance. [**Perceval**, ll. 8889-ca. 9165]

"ORNAGRINE"†

This unnamed damsel first appeared to Lancelot with her hair loose and a wreath of roses round her head and directed him after the knight he was then pursuing, in return for a promise that he would follow her at once whenever she required him to do so. When next she appeared, she looked seventy years old and gave Lancelot barely time to conquer a knight who was threatening to kidnap Guenevere before requiring him to follow her. Lancelot followed "Ornagrine" with his opponent's lancehead still in his side.

Since this damsel's second appearance was in the vicinity of La Fontaine aux Fees, she may have been a fairy. Certainly magic must be involved in her story somehow. She seemed to lead Lancelot, however, only into the type of adventures normally encountered by knights-errant, not into treachery or ambush. [Vulgate IV]

OROFOISE†

A country *vers Sorelois en la fin du roiaume de Norgales,* which I translate "toward Surluse near the end [tip?] of the kingdom of Norgales" [Vulgate III]. Orofoise would approximate the northern half of Shropshire.

OROFOISE, COUNTESS OF, and HER SISTER†

The Countess seems to have been a sovereign lady. When she sent her beautiful sister to Arthur seeking help, Arthur took the opportunity to go to bed with the beautiful sister. He then fought a giant on behalf of the Countess. The giant wore armor of impervious serpent hides, which must have caused Arthur a spot of trouble. [Vulgate VII]

ORQUENESELES†

Guiromelant boasts of holding this city from God, and no one else. I suspect that it is the same city to which Gawaine went, the day before meeting Guiromelant, to fetch the Haughty Maid of Logres' palfrey from its garden. Apparently lying just over the Galloway border, this was a strongly walled town, as large as Pavia, with a noble castle and a busy-looking seaport; between sea and river, it was well circled by water. [Chrétien de Troyes, **Perceval**, ca. ll. 6600-6828; 8617-8630]

ORUALE (Orvale) DE GUINDOEL†

She was a cousin of Lancelot, although she had last seen him, at the time of her rescue by Ector de Maris, when Lancelot was two months old. Oruale's mother had been a cousin of King Ban; both Oruale's parents died about two years after settling in Britain.

For Oruale's troubles at the hands of Sir Marigart, see Guindoel Castle. After rescuing her, Ector offered to be her true knight always and everywhere for Lancelot's sake; this does not, however, necessarily imply a romantic relationship. [Vulgate IV]

Osanna—see OZANA

OSSA CYLELLAUR†

He is my token "historical" military figure, a leader of the Saxons and Arthur's opponent at the battle of Badon Hill. Ossa does not appear, at least by this name, in Malory or the Vulgate, but Glennie seems to try to connect him with Gallehault (Duke Galeholt?)—a connection which need not concern us here, except as it may give grounds for making Duke Galeholt a Saxon.

OSSAISE

A knight of Surluse, he fought in Duke Galeholt's tournament and was unhorsed by Gaheris [Malory X, 48].

OUT ISLES

Somewhat arbitrarily, a good candidate for these are the Outer Hebrides.

OUT ISLES, QUEEN OF THE

With the Queen of Eastland, the Queen of Norgales, and Morgan le Fay, she kidnaped Lancelot and held him prisoner in Castle Chariot [Malory VI, 3-4]. See under Queen of Eastland.

OUTRE-GALES (Estre-Gales, Further Wales)

The kingdom of Erec's father Lac, and later of Erec himself. D.D.R. Owen hesitantly and tentatively identifies it with Strathclyde. [**Erec & Enide**, l. 1874 & Owen's note to same]

Owain—see YWAINE

OXFORD

In the plain outside Oxford, King Arthur had fortuitously arranged a four-day tournament just in time—though he could not have known it—for the debut in Britain of his Greek great-nephew Cligés. [Chrétien de Troyes, **Cligés**, ll. 4575-5062] We may perhaps assume that Oxford was another of Arthur's court cities.

OZANA (Osanna, Ozanna) LE CURE HARDY ("Ozana of the Hardy Heart")

red silver

Toward the beginning of Sir Marhaus' career, as he was returning from killing the giant Taulurd, he chanced to meet four knights of Arthur's court, Sirs Sagramore, Ozana, Dodinal le Savage, and Felot of Listeneise; Marhaus smote them down all four with one spear. Malory next mentions Sir Ozana traveling with the two Ywaines, Brandiles, Agravaine, and Mordred, all by now members of the Round Table. Dinadan meets them and cooks up with them a scheme to rout King Mark by dressing the jester Dagonet in Mordred's armor and telling Mark it is Lancelot; the scheme backfires when Mark, fleeing, meets Palomides, who refuses to be routed and instead unhorses Dagonet, Ozana, and the others. Ozana appears again at the Winchester tournament, where he is bested by Sir Lavaine.

Despite all these bestings, Ozana may well have been a good knight, most of whose history did not get into Malory's epic; a good device to show off a new knight is listing how many fine knights of established standing he can defeat. Ozana was among the knights who rode a-Maying with Guenevere when Meliagrant abducted her, and among the knights who attempted to heal Sir Urre. [Malory IV, 25; X, 11-13; XVIII, 11; XIX, 1, 11]

By his apparent choice of traveling companions, we may perhaps theorize that Ozana was more of Gawaine's faction than Lancelot's, and hence that he remained with Arthur during the split and perished in the last battle.

PALFREY BENEATH THE OAK†

Apparently belonging to Sir Greoreas' lady, this palfrey may chiefly be notable for the controversy as to whether it was *norrois* ("northern") or *noiret* ("blackish"): D.D.R. Owen prefers the first reading, Ruth Cline the second [Chrétien de Troyes, **Perceval**, ll. 6530ff., & Owen's note to 6530].

PALOMIDES (Palamides)

Sir Palomides the Saracen was the most notable of King Astlabor's three sons, the others being Sirs Safere and Segwarides, both of whom seem to have officialized their conversion to Christianity considerably before their brother.

Malory introduces Palomides in Ireland at the time when Tristram, disguised as Tramtrist, was there to be healed by La Beale Isoud. Palomides was already in love with Isoud, even "in will to be christened for her sake", and much in favor with her parents.

Isoud favored Tristram, and persuaded him to fight in rivalry to Palomides at the tournament for the Lady of the Launds. A tried and proven Palomides rode with a black shield and unhorsed, among others, many Round Table knights, including Gawaine, Kay, Sagramore, and Griflet.

Palomides might well have won the tournament but for Tristram, who defeated him and rather ungraciously, as it seems, made him swear under threat of death to forsake Isoud and to refrain from wearing armor and bearing arms for a year and a day. "Then for despite and anger Sir Palamides cut off his harness, and threw [it] away."

After the wedding of Mark and Isoud, Palomides appeared in Cornwall. (His excuse may have been to visit his brother, if Segwarides, Astlabor's son, is to be identified with the Segwarides of Mark's court.) The year being up, Palomides was back in armor, and he came in time to rescue Dame Bragwaine from a tree where two envious ladies had bound her.

Isoud, delighted at the safe restoration of her favorite handmaid, promised to grant Palomides a boon, providing it was not evil. He asked that she ride away with him as if adventuring, and Mark, hearing the whole story, agreed, planning to send Tristram to rescue her. Tristram being out hunting and not immediately available, Mark's knight Lambegus went after Palomides, who gave him a fall. During the fray, Isoud escaped and found refuge in the tower of one Sir Adtherp. Tristram came and fought furiously with Palomides before the tower, until Isoud begged Tristram to spare Palomides, lest he die unbaptized. She sent Palomides, sorely chagrined, to the court of King Arthur, rubbing in Tristram's victory over her heart by charging his rival to deliver Guenevere the message that "there be within this land but four lovers"—Lancelot and Guenevere, Tristram and Isoud.

Perhaps it was during this sojourn at Arthur's court that Palomides became a companion of the Round Table. He appears briefly in the tale of La Cote Male Taile, whom he encountered by chance while both were out adventuring. La Cote considered his unhorsing at the hands of Palomides no disgrace. Palomides may have been in pursuit of the Questing Beast when he met La Cote; he appears in this quest only a few chapters later, when Tristram and Lamorak meet him (Tristram being en route back to Cornwall from Brittany, where he has left his wife Isoud la Blanche Mains to return to his first Isoud).

Palomides' adoption of the Questing Beast is curious in light of Pellinore's old statement that this beast could never be achieved except by himself or by his next of kin; it has led at least one commentator (Keith Baines) to assume, on apparently no other grounds than this, that the Saracen Palomides was somehow next of kin to the Welsh descendant of Nascien, Pellinore. Some degree of distant cousinship is possible, dating back to some relative of Nascien's who refused to be converted by Joseph and Josephe, choosing to remain behind and father or mother a line of Saracens; I think it more likely that Palomides took on an apparently impossible quest in the effort to prove himself worthy of baptism. (Might his failure to achieve the Questing Beast have led to the vow he made sometime between his sojourn in Ireland and the Surluse tournament, not to be baptized until he had done seven true battles for Jesu's sake?) At any rate, he was so hot in the quest of the beast that he unhorsed both Tristram and Lamorak with one spear without stopping to give them swordplay, whereat Tristram, much annoyed, told Lamorak to relay the message that he—Tristram—wanted a rematch at that same well where they had just encountered.

Tristram and Palomides next encountered each other at the tournament of the Castle of Maidens, where Palomides used a black horse and a black-covered shield. Between Tristram's participation in the tournament and Lancelot's, Palomides won less honor than he had hoped. At the end of the second day's fighting, Tristram found Palomides alone in the forest in a near-suicidal rage and forcibly prevented him from harming himself, without, however, letting him know who it was that held him.

> Alas, said Sir Palomides, I may never win worship where Sir Tristram is ... and if he be away for the most part I have the gree, unless that Sir Launcelot be there or Sir Lamorak .... I would fight with [Tristram], said

> Sir Palomides, and ease my heart upon him; and yet, to say thee sooth, Sir Tristram is the gentlest knight in this world living.

Still hiding his identity, Tristram persuaded Palomides to accept lodging in his pavilion that night. After the tournament, Palomides remained so angry with Tristram for doing him out of the honors that he followed him and lost his horse in a river. Tristram, learning of this, had his rival brought to the castle of Sir Darras, where he was staying with Sir Dinadan. Unfortunately, Sir Darras learned that Tristram was blamed for slaying three of his sons at the tournament and put Tristram, Dinadan, and Palomides all three into prison, where Tristram fell sick. At first, still spurred by the old rivalry, Palomides spoke harshly to Tristram. "But when Sir Palomides saw the falling of sickness of Sir Tristram, then was he heavy for him, and comforted him in all the best wise he could." Finally, learning Tristram's identity, Darras set them free and nursed Tristram back to health.

After parting when they left Darras' castle, Tristram next met Palomides by chance in time to rescue him from Breuse Sans Pitie and nine of his knights. Palomides agreed to fight Tristram in a fortnight, when his wounds were healed, beside the tomb of Lanceor and Colombe in the meadow by Camelot. When the day came, however, Palomides was in some other lord's prison (we know little of the circumstances this time) and Tristram fought Lancelot instead, by mistake; the battle ended in a draw, after which Lancelot brought Tristram to court, where he was installed in Sir Marhaus' old seat at the Round Table.

Palomides, meanwhile, getting out of prison, returned to the pursuit of the Questing Beast. We know little of his adventures during this period, but once he rescued King Mark by striking down Brandiles, the two Ywaines, Ozana, Agravaine, and Griflet in rapid succession (in this scene, asked his identity through a squire, Palomides claimed to be "a knight-errant as they [who ask] are … and no knight of King Arthur's court", but this may simply have been a ploy to preserve his anonymity; all the participants were being very coy with their names). Shortly thereafter, he passed his mother's manor and, too hot on the Beast's trail to stop, sent her greetings and a request for food and drink. (Perhaps the entire family, or at least the [widowed?] mother and her three sons, had all come to Britain together, she settling somewhere in the southwest?) Palomides also met Lamorak outside Morgan's castle, bearing an anonymous red shield as he fought off her knights. Palomides courteously offered to help him; Lamorak took this as an insult and insisted on proving his lack of weariness by fighting Palomides. Palomides (who had a temper of his own) responded in kind, and at the end of the battle, when they learned each other's identity, they swore everlasting friendship, promising to love each other better than any other man except their respective brothers Safere and Tor. (I find no hard evidence in this scene, however, for the theory that Palomides was closely related to Pellinore, for he does not seem to recognize Lamorak as a cousin.)

Palomides next appears at the Surluse tournament, where he won much more honor than at the Castle of Maidens. In addition to the regular tournament fighting, he championed two damsels. The first "loved Sir Palomides as paramour, but the book saith she was of his kin", and she appealed for justice against one Sir Goneries "that withheld her all her lands." She seems to have been responsible for actually getting Palomides to the site of the tournament, for he was resting in a hermitage from his pursuit of the Questing Beast, and she sought him out when no other knight present would take her quarrel. He made short work of Goneries. The second damsel was King Bandes' daughter, who "heard tell that Palomides did much for damosels' sake" and enlisted him to rid her of Sir Corsabrin's unwelcome attentions. The stink that rose from Corsabrin's unchristened body put Guenevere and Duke Galeholt in mind that Palomides, still officially a Saracen, was in danger of a similarly unhallowed end, and they begged him to be baptized.

> Sir, said Palomides, I will that ye all know that into this land I came to be christened, and in my heart I am christened .... But I have made such an avow that I may not be christened till I have done seven true battles for Jesu's sake, ... and I trust God will take mine intent, for I mean truly.

Palomides also successfully defended himself against a charge of treason brought by Goneries' brother Sir Archade. The tournament lasted seven days, and Palomides won third place, after Lancelot and Lamorak.

Tristram and Palomides next met when Tristram and La Beale Isoud were living in Joyous Garde and the Questing Beast led the Saracen to the surrounding woods. As Palomides remarked, "I found never no knight in my questing of this glasting beast, but an he would joust I never refused him." But since Tristram neither identified himself nor requested a joust, and since several other knights of the Round Table and Breuse Sans Pitie also showed up in the area at this time for a general mix-and-match melee, Isoud's two lovers did not fight each other. They jousted shortly thereafter when they met by chance, without recognizing each other, on the way to the Lonazep tournament. This time Palomides, learning who had just given him a fall, appears to have made a sincere effort to bury his enmity:

> I pray you Sir Tristram, forgive me all mine evil will, and if I live I shall do you service above all other knights .... I wot not what aileth me, for

> meseemeth that ye are a good knight, and none other knight that named himself a good knight should not hate you ....

On the way to Lonazep, they found the body of King Hermance, and Palomides proved his worth by taking on himself the dead man's written request that he be avenged and his kingdom set again to rights; Tristram judged that his own primary obligation was to be at the tournament. Palomides cleared up the troubles at Hermance's Red City, so winning the people's love and gratitude that they offered him a third of their goods if he would stay with them; nevertheless, he departed and rejoined Tristram in time for the Lonazep tournament.

At first they escorted Isoud jointly and fought on the same side in the lists, but Palomides' old jealousy reasserted itself—on the first day, though he won the honors, it was not without a moment of shame when, in his overeagerness, he slew Lancelot's horse. On the second day he found Arthur ogling Isoud and (not recognizing the King) angrily struck him down; the Saracen then went over to the opposite party, Lancelot's, and changed his armor, all in an effort to fight Tristram down and perhaps do him serious mischief while feigning not to recognize him. Rebuked that evening by Isoud (who had seen all) and Tristram, Arthur and Lancelot, he wept all night after the party had separated. On the last day, beaten out of the prize again by Tristram and Lancelot, Palomides raged in the woods until the kings of Wales and Scotland found him and brought him under some sort of control. Then he stood outside Tristram's tent in the dark taunting and threatening Tristram for a time before he departed with the kings, mourning his new rift with Isoud and Tristram.

Refusing to remain with the friendly kings, Palomides found Sir Epinogris wounded. After they exchanged complaints of love, Palomides rescued and restored Epinogris' lady. In the course of this adventure, he met his brother Safere. Traveling together, they were soon captured by the men of a lord whom Palomides had slain in the fighting at Lonazep. They tried the brothers, freed Safere, and condemned Palomides, who prepared himself to meet a shameful death nobly. As he was led past Joyous Garde to Pelownes Castle for execution, both Tristram and Lancelot came to his rescue, Lancelot getting there first.

Then Palomides lived awhile in Joyous Garde, secretly tormented by the daily sight of Isoud and her love for Tristram. At last one day he went into the woods alone and made a long poem of love for Isoud. Tristram happened by and was so angered at hearing his rival sing his lady's praises that he might have killed Palomides had the Saracen not been unarmed. Once again they set a day to fight—a fortnight thence in the meadow under Joyous Garde (Palomides needed the time to recover from his lovesick weakness), but this time Tristram was wounded in a hunting accident and failed to appear. Palomides departed with Tristram's promise to come seeking him when he was whole again. Tristram won great fame that summer seeking Palomides, but failed to find him.

The end of the long rivalry did not come until shortly before the adventures of the Grail. That year, riding to the great Pentecost feast at Camelot, Tristram, unarmed but for spear and sword, met Palomides in full armor and attacked him, to the Saracen's perplexity, who could neither leave the battle without shame nor return the blows of an unarmored man without shame. At length he calmed Tristram's rage with courteous words and they were about to part peaceably when Tristram decided to give Palomides the last of the seven great battles he had vowed to do in Jesu's name before being baptized. Tristram borrowed the armor of Sir Galleron of Galway, another Round Table knight whom Palomides had jousted down just before meeting Tristram and whose response to his defeat was, "Alas … pity that so good a knight … should be unchristened." So Palomides and Tristram at last fought their long-postponed fight, hacking valiantly for more than two hours until Tristram struck Palomides' sword from his hand. They then were reconciled, and Tristram and Galleron rode with Palomides to the Suffragan of Carlisle, who baptized him while they stood his godfathers, after which all three knights rode on to Camelot.

Rather surprisingly, we hear nothing of Palomides during the Grail Adventures; Malory next mentions him as one of the guests at Guenevere's small dinner party when Sir Patrise was poisoned. The former Saracen ended in Lancelot's faction, presumably helped rescue Guenevere from the stake, and accompanied Lancelot into exile, where he was made Duke of the Provence. [Malory VIII, 9, 29-31; IX, 3, 12, 32-34, 40; X, 2, 13, 18-19, 41-88; XII, 12-14; XVIII, 3, 10, 23; XX, 5, 18]

Except in matters touching Isoud and Tristram, which were apt to drive him out of self-control, Palomides seems to have been one of the best and most courteous knights, honorable, a reliable champion, and an excellent fighter. T. H. White refers to him as "black", almost certainly using the British meaning, which includes all non-white races; I see no objection to a black Palomides in the U.S. sense.

John Erskine's novel **Tristram and Isolde, Restoring Palamede** (which probably should have been titled "Palamede and Brangain", but no doubt they thought that would sell fewer copies) gives a different but especially endearing picture of this knight.

PANDRAGON†

The second son of King Constans of England, Pandragon and his younger brother Uther burned Vortigern in his tower in revenge for Vortigern's barons' murder of their older brother Maines. Pandragon became King, but was killed by the Saxons in battle near Salisbury. Merlin erected Stonehenge as Pandragon's memorial, and Uther adopted his older brother's name in his honor. [Vulgate II]

PANTELION (Pantesileus)†

Pantelion was the master consul of Rome at the time of Arthur's war with Claudas [Vulgate V].

PARC, COUNT DEL†

He lived three leagues from Terican's (Turquine's) Hill. After Lancelot killed Turquine, the Count del Parc visited the tower and gave each former prisoner a horse. Arthur's knights returned his generosity by giving him Turquine's property. [Vulgate V] See also Turquine's Hill.

PARMENIDES†

One of the twelve who accompanied Alexander from Greece to Britain, where Arthur knighted them all at the outset of Count Angrs' rebellion. Parmenides was not among those who penetrated into Windsor with Alexander's party when it captured Angrs. Though Sir Parmenides survived that conflict, Chrétien tells us nothing more about him. [**Cligés**, ll. 102-385; 1093-ca. 2210]

Parzival—see PERCIVALE

PASE, EARL OF

This earl was uncle of the Damsel of La Beale Regard. Morgan having usurped that castle, the Damsel sent a message to her uncle requesting him to come and burn La Beale Regard with wildfire. Hating Morgan, he complied. [Malory X, 38]

His earldom would probably be within fairly easy reach of La Beale Regard.

PASS DE PERRONS†

This bad pass among sharp rocks was guarded by four knights armed as peasants, one mounted and armed in the usual knightly manner, and yet another mounted and waiting at the other end of the pass. I do not know their motivation; perhaps it was simple brigandage and robbery. No magic seems to be involved. This peril is found on the way to the "pont despee" in the land of Gore. [Vulgate IV]

PATRICK, SAINT†

Sanit Patrick's dates, 389?-461 A.D., make him a contemporary of Arthur according to the dates given by Malory and the Vulgate.

PATRIDES†

This knight of Arthur's was made Count of Flanders after Arouz was killed resisting Arthur's army on its way to battle Claudas and free Elyzabel [Vulgate V].

Either this knight or another of the same name was rescued by Percivale from the castle of Garantan, where he had been imprisoned for trying to run away with the lady of the place. [Vulgate V; this appears, however, to be a variant of the tale of the Uncourteous Lady and Sir Persides in Malory XI, 12.]

PATRISE

A knight of Ireland, cousin of Mador de la Porte, and a companion of the Round Table. One of the guests at a small dinner party of Guenevere's, Patrise was accidentally poisoned and killed by eating an apple meant for Gawaine. (The poisoner was Sir Pinel.) [Malory XVIII, 3; cf. Gaheris de Kareheu]

PEDIVERE

Sir Pedivere was chasing his wife when Lancelot found them. "Knight, fie for shame, why wilt thou slay this lady?" said Lancelot. "What hast thou to do betwixt me and my wife?" replied Pedivere. "I will slay her maugre thy head." To prevent this, Lancelot rode between them.

> Sir Launcelot, said the knight, thou dost not thy part, for this lady hath betrayed me. It is not so, said the lady, truly he saith wrong on me. And for because I love and cherish my cousin germain, he is jealous betwixt him and me; and as I shall answer to God there was never sin betwixt us.

As they were riding and talking, Pedivere called Lancelot's attention to some pretended men of arms riding after them, and lopped off the lady's head when Lancelot's back was turned. Lancelot, understandably upset, made him carry the body to Guenevere. She made him take the body to Rome and get his penance from the Pope.

> [The] Pope bade him go again unto Queen Guenever, and in Rome was his lady buried by the Pope's commandment. And after this Sir Pedivere fell to great goodness, and was an holy man and a hermit. [Malory VI, 17]

T. H. White identifies Pedivere with Bedivere. I find this identification only slightly less improbable than White's combination of Elaine of Carbonek and Elaine of Astolat—it is artistic, but I do not think it is Malory. On the other hand, there is a chance that this

Pedivere could be identified with Pedivere of the Straight Marches, serving a time at the Grail Castle between his return from Rome and his retirement into a hermitage.

PEDIVERE OF THE STRAIGHT MARCHES

When Sir Bors passed the night in the Castle Adventurous at Carbonek, a spear with a head that seemed to burn like a taper came and wounded him in the shoulder. Then a knight came and bade him arise and fight. Sir Bors "bare him backward until that he came unto a chamber door." The strange knight ducked through the door and rested in that chamber for a long time before coming out to renew the battle. In order to win, Bors had to prevent him from going into the chamber again.

This knight was Pedivere of the Straight Marches. Bors charged him to go to Arthur's court that Whitsunday. The chamber in which Pedivere refreshed himself was very likely that in which the Grail was kept. [Malory X, 4-5]

This Pedivere might be identified with Pedivere the wife-slayer and hermit, described above.

PELLAM, KING OF LISTENEISE (Pelles, The Fisher King, The Rich Fisher, King of the Waste Lands, King Pescheour, The Maimed King, etc.)

Accounts of the Fisher King are confused, perhaps hopelessly. Even Sommer seems to have had trouble getting on top of the situation. There are at least two versions in Malory alone of the Dolorous Stroke (though I do not consider them necessarily incompatible). Some versions have two or even three maimed kings, sometimes including Pellinore, contemporary with Arthur. To add to the fun, there may or may not have been an obscure connection or confusion somewhere along the line with Sir Pelleas—note the similarity of names. Reversing my technique of splitting the Lady of the Lake into three separate characters, I have attempted a simplified, but I hope acceptable, version which rolls the maimed kings into a single man. (Even in Malory, I believe that Pellam, Pelles, and King Pescheour can be considered identical, "Pescheour" being a pun on the French words for fisher and sinner. This king stays in his castle at Carbonek, guarding the Holy Grail and waiting to be healed. Malory does mention King Pellam as appearing at various tournaments, but this can be considered another Pellam, likely identical with Pellinore—who, according to Sommer, appears in some versions as an additional maimed king.)

When Joseph of Arimathea and his followers came to Britain, the Grail at first was in the keeping of Joseph's kinsman Lucans. It was

The Fisher Kings and the Kin of Pellinore

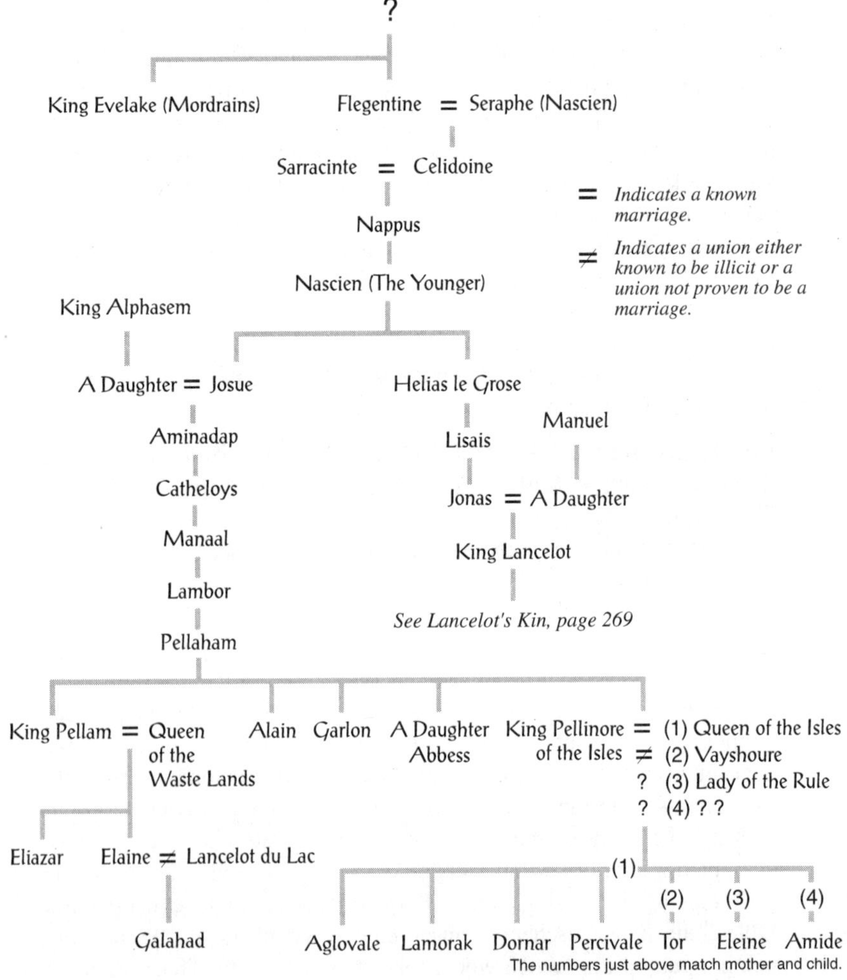

After the death of Josephe (son of Joseph of Arimathea), Helias le Grose converted King Kalafes (baptised name Alphasem) and his people. Josue, Helias' brother, married Alphasem's daughter and inherited the kingdom, which was to become The Waste Lands. At Alphasem's request, the Grail was left in his country (Castle Carbonek being built for it), and Josue started the line of Grail guardians known as the "Fisher Kings" or "Rich Fishers." ("King Petchere" is probably a play on the French words for "fisher" and "sinner", which are very similar.

given over, however, into the care of Nascien's great-great-grandson Alain (or Helias) li Gros. Alain had, at Joseph's bidding, caught a fish in a British pond. The fish was miraculously enlarged to feed all the sinners of the company (the Grail had fed those who were worthy). This incident gained for Alain and his successors the name Rich Fisher or Fisher King. While Alain's immediate descendants ended up in France to engender Lancelot du Lake, the keeping of the Grail passed over to the line of Alain's brother Josue, from whom Pellam, the last of the Fisher Kings, descended. Pellam had three known brothers: Pellinore, Alain (of Escavalon?), and Garlon (apparently the family black sheep).

In his hale days, Pellam held a feast to which no knight was admitted unless he brought his wife or his paramour. Balin le Sauvage traced Sir Garlon to this feast and there cut him down. Pellam rose, swearing that he and no man else should kill Balin in vengeance for his brother Garlon. He "caught in his hand a grim weapon" and broke Balin's sword with it, then chased Balin through the castle until they came to the chamber of the Grail. There Balin caught up the marvellous spear and smote Pellam with it, upon which both Pellam and a great part of his castle fell down, entrapping them for three days. This is Malory's first version of the Dolorous Stroke. [II, 14-15]

Later, during the Grail Quest, Dame Amide tells another version to Galahad, Percivale, and Bors: while Pellam "might ride[,] he supported much Christendom and Holy Church." One day, while out hunting, he found King Solomon's Ship and had the temerity to pull David's Sword partially from its scabbard. "So therewith entered a spear wherewith he was smitten him through both the thighs, and never sith might he be healed", until Galahad's coming. [XVII, 5]

The hunting incident might be taken to precede Garlon's death by a longer or shorter period of time, and Balin interpreted as Heaven's unwitting instrument in dealing the Dolorous Stroke, though in this particular Amide abridges the account, perhaps out of delicacy toward Balin and Garlon.

Maimed, Pellam waited in his castle until Lancelot arrived and showed his worth by rescuing the damsel from the scalding bath and slaying a dangerous dragon. The Maimed King then connived with his sorceress Dame Brisen and his daughter Elaine to bring about Galahad's begetting through trickery, fornication, and supposed adultery. Perhaps Pellam acted through inspired foresight, or perhaps he merely wanted a grandson whom he could piously educate to work his cure; it is understandable if he wanted himself and his country (which had also suffered through the Dolorous Stroke) healed as soon as possible. Pellam appears to have had the immediate supervision of Galahad's upbringing until Galahad's early adolescence, or even his middle teens. For a part of this time, having had Lancelot cured, by exposure to the Grail, from a fit of madness, Pellam set up Lancelot and Elaine to live together, without benefit of clergy, in the Joyous Isle.

Lancelot appeared at Carbonek again during the Grail Adventures, brought there by the ship with Amide's body. He had a partial vision of the Grail and fell into a twenty-four-day coma. Pellam had him nursed through this period and, when he woke, told him the sad news of Elaine's death. After Lancelot's departure, Galahad, Percivale, and Bors joined nine holy knights of other nations at Carbonek for the climactic Grail Mysteries. Neither Pellam nor his son Eliazar were permitted to remain with these knights for the great vision (though "a maid which was [Pellam's] niece" appears to have been allowed to remain—probably the Grail Bearer, or perhaps Amide, miraculously resurrected for the hour). At these mysteries, Galahad received blood from the miraculous spear with which to anoint his grandfather and cure him at last.

Some of Pellam's actions seem, to say the least, surprising for a man holding such a sacred trust as his, and it may not appear strange that, after Pellam's cure, the Grail and its accompanying relics chose to leave Carbonek forever, going with Galahad, Percivale, and Bors to Sarras and thence out of this world. Pellam, no longer guardian of the Grail, "yielded him to a place of religion of white monks, and was a full holy man." [Malory II, 14-16; XI, 2-4; XIII, 4-6; XVII, 5, 16-21]

KING PELLAM'S FAMILY AND RETAINERS
Brothers: Pellinore, Alain (of Escavalon?), Garlon
Sister: Abbess of a convent not far from Camelot
Wife?: Queen of the Waste Lands
Daughter: Elaine of Carbonek
Son: Eliazar
Grandson (by Elaine and Lancelot): Galahad
Nephews: Aglovale, Castor, Dornar, Lamorak, Percivale, Tor, Pinel le Savage?
Nieces: Amide, Eleine
Daughter's handmaid: Dame Brisen
Daughter's suitor: Bromel la Pleche
Seneschals: Claellus?, Duke Minadoras?
Retainer?: Pedivere of the Straight Marches

PELLAM'S SISTER†

She was abbess of the convent where Galahad's education was completed [Vulgate V].

PELLEAS

Malory calls Sir Pelleas one of the six knights who could defeat Gawaine. When Gawaine first met him, during the adventure of the damsels "Printemps, Été, and Automne", Pelleas was not yet a member of Arthur's court. Gawaine found him diligently pursuing his love for Ettard. At a three-day tournament in Ettard's part of the country, Pelleas had proved the best of 500 knights, winning the prize, a circlet of gold, and presenting it to Ettard as the fairest lady there (although in fact there were some fairer ones present).

> And so he chose her for his sovereign lady, and never to love other but her, but she was so proud that she had scorn of him, and said that she would never love him though he would die for her. ... And so this knight promised the Lady Ettard to follow her into this country, and never to leave her till she loved him.

He lodged by a priory, and every week she sent knights to fight him. He would defeat them all, then allow them to take him prisoner so that, when they brought him in disgrace before their lady, he would get a sight of her.

> And always she [did] him great despite, for sometimes she [made] her knights to tie him to his horse's tail, and some to bind him under the horse's belly; thus in the most shamefullest ways

that she could devise (apparently desperate, poor lady, to be rid of him) was he brought to her.

Gawaine promised Pelleas to act as a go-between:

> I will have your horse and your armour, and so will I ride unto her castle and tell her that I have slain you, and so shall I come within her to cause her to cherish me, and then shall I do my true part that ye shall not fail to have the love of her.

Gawaine managed all this except the last part—he stopped before he got around to pleading Pelleas' case. The month was May, so they went outside to take their pleasure in a pavilion. Here Pelleas found Gawaine and Ettard sleeping together, and went well-nigh mad with grief. He considered killing them, but ended by laying his naked sword "overthwart both their throats." Then he rode back to his own pavilions and announced to his knights and squires that he was going to bed and would never get up until he was dead, and when he was dead they were to take his heart between two silver dishes to Ettard.

Apparently he changed his mind about dying in bed, because Nimue met him wandering around the woods on foot. She caused an enchantment whereby Ettard fell madly in love with Pelleas, while all his love for her turned into hate. Then Nimue got Pelleas' love for herself, by enchantment or perhaps simple seduction, and married him, while Ettard died of love.

When Pentecost came, Nimue brought Pelleas to Arthur's court, where he took the prize at jousting and was elected to the Round Table, at the same time as Sir Marhaus. Nimue did not keep Pelleas completely sequestered with her in her Lake; he appears fighting in at least one tournament, riding a-Maying with Guenevere, and trying to heal Sir Urre. But Nimue "saved him that he was never slain." Probably when the Round Table was destroyed by the feud between Lancelot and Gawaine and by Mordred's rebellion, Nimue simply took Pelleas permanently into the Lake, not letting him fight at Salisbury.

One of Caxton's chapter headings calls Pelleas "King." I suspect confusion with King Pelles/Pellam. Malory tells us, immediately after describing Pelleas' election to the Round Table, that he "was one of the four that achieved the Sangreal", but we never hear any more of this; again I suspect confusion with Pelles, or possibly Percivale. Being married to Nimue, Pelleas was hardly a virgin or, like Bors, a celibate; nor was Nimue one to have taken tamely the stricture against ladies accompanying their knights in that Quest! [Malory IV, 20-28; XVIII, 23; XIX, 1, 11]

Pelles, King—see **PELLAM**

PELLINORE, KING ('The Knight with the Strange Beast')

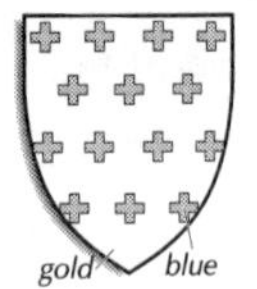

King Pellinore of the Isles earned his title, 'The Knight with the Strange Beast', for his pursuit of the Questing Beast. He was engaged in a twelve-month quest of this creature, not unlikely one of many such yearlong stints, when he first met Arthur, then in the early flush of kinghood. Having just ridden his own horse to death, Pellinore insisted on taking Arthur's, and when the young man requested to follow the Beast in the other's place, Pellinore replied, "It is in vain thy desire, for it shall never be achieved but by me, or my next kin." (Since after Pellinore's death Palomides the Saracen picked up the quest of Galtisant, it is just possible that Pellinore lied to keep Arthur from interfering.)

Before Pellinore rode off, Arthur expressed a desire to see which of them would prove better in a fair joust, to which Pellinore replied, "Well … seek me here when thou wilt, and here nigh this well thou shalt find me." Not long thereafter, Arthur got word that "one of the best knights of the world, and the strongest man of arms" had set up his pavilion by a well in the forest (possibly the same one where Pellinore had promised to give Arthur his joust) and was taking on all comers. After the young Sir Griflet begged the adventure and was defeated, Arthur himself went to fight the forest knight, who turned out to be Pellinore. After a terrific battle, Arthur's sword was broken. Rather than yield, he tried wrestling his opponent down. Adread at

Arthur's strength, Pellinore managed to unhelm him and prepared to smite off his head. Merlin arrived and told Pellinore who his adversary was, which had an opposite effect to the one desired, for now Pellinore was even more adread and would have killed Arthur to avoid reprisals. Merlin had to cast Pellinore into an enchanted sleep, whereon Arthur, mistaking it for death, blamed Merlin for slaying so good a knight. Merlin replied by revealing Pellinore's name and future good service to the High King, predicting the births of his sons Lamorak and Percivale, and adding that "he shall tell you the name of your own son, begotten of your sister, that shall be the destruction of all this realm." Malory seems not to follow up or explain this last tantalizing morsel, but it may provide an additional reason for the later enmity between Margawse's sons and Pellinore's.

Merlin took Arthur on to the Lake to receive Excalibur from "Nineve", and when Pellinore woke up, he may have sworn himself to another twelvemonth of pursuing Galtisant. Pellinore next turned up on Arthur's side during the battle with Nero, Lot, and the second rebel alliance before Castle Terrabil. In this battle Pellinore slew King Lot. He departed after the battle but soon rejoined Arthur, coming to court the day after the arrival of his own son Tor. At this time Merlin led him to the Siege Perilous and the neighboring seat (which would someday be Lancelot's) and told him, "This is your place and best ye are worthy to sit therein of any that is here." Gawaine and Gaheris, already angered by the death of their father Lot, were stirred to even greater wrath at this.

When the marriage feast of Arthur and Guenevere was enlivened by the episode of the white hart, the white brachet, and Dame Nimue, Pellinore, on Merlin's advice, was given the task of rescuing Nimue, which he accomplished, bringing her back to court. His adventure was marred, however, when in his dogged haste to find Nimue he refused to stop and help a wounded knight and his lady; they died for lack of help, and Pellinore later learned that the young woman had been his own daughter Eleine (see Eleine and Nimue). On their way back, while camped for the night, Pellinore and Nimue overheard two passing knights plot the poisoning of King Arthur; presumably Pellinore and Nimue warned the King on their return, for nothing more is heard of this plot.

Arthur called Pellinore to his assistance against the five invading kings of Denmark, Ireland, the Vale, Soleise, and Longtains, but Pellinore and his army did not arrive in time for the action. Arthur joined them three miles from the Humber after the battle and asked Pellinore's advice on the best men to fill eight vacancies in the Round Table the battle had made. Pellinore suggested four older knights,

Uriens, Hervise de Revel, the King of the Lake, and Galagars, and four young ones, Gawaine, Griflet, Kay, and for the last either Bagdemagus or Tor—"but because Sir Tor is my son I may not praise him, but else … I durst say that of his age there is not in this land a better knight." Arthur chose Tor, and presumably Bagdemagus' pique extended to Pellinore as well as to Arthur.

In the tenth year after he was knighted, Gawaine avenged his father King Lot by killing Pellinore with his own hands, and with the help of Gaheris. Malory does not describe the actual scene, mentioning it first as a thing to come and later as one that is past, but Pellinore's wife called it shameful treason.

Pellinore was the brother of Pellam the Fisher King, Alain, and Garlon. His sons in wedlock were Aglovale, Lamorak, Dornar, and Percivale. He had at least one bastard son, Tor, begotten on Vayshoure; since Tor was begotten "half by force", we may suspect that Pellinore had a degree of rash heat in his nature and may have fathered other bastards. He had two known daughters: Amide (who may have been legitimate, since her mother is unknown) and Eleine, begotten on the Lady of the Rule—apparently an extramarital liason. Pellinore seems also to have been hasty-tempered and hard to turn from his purpose once it was fixed. Nevertheless, his suggestion of Gawaine for the Round Table argues either a generous nature or an ingenuous one. Pellinore's kingdom, "the Isles", probably was off the coast of Wales. [Malory I, 19-24; II, 10-11; III, 3-5, 12-15; IV, 2-5; XI, 10; see The Isles]

KING PELLINORE'S FAMILY AND RELATIONS
Brothers: Pellam, (Alain of Escavalon?), Garlon
Wife?: La Veuve Dame de la Gaste Forest Soutaine
Paramours: Lady of the Rule, Vayshoure
Sons (in wedlock): Aglovale, Lamorak, Dornar, Percivale
Son (by Vayshoure): Tor
Daughter (by Lady of the Rule): Eleine
Daughter (by ?): Amide
Nephew?: Pinel le Savage

PELOWNES

A castle by the seaside. Takng Sir Palomides hither, his captors had to pass by Joyous Garde, where Lancelot rescued him. [Malory X, 84-85] Might it be identified with Amble, on the coast of Northumberland, a little south of Alnwick?

Pendragon—see also **PANDRAGON, UTHER PENDRAGON**

PENDRAGON

Bearing the same name as Uther Pendragon, this sounds as if it should have been a more important castle than Malory otherwise seems to indicate. The lord of Pendragon Castle at the time of Sir La Cote Male Taile was Sir Brian de les Isles, "a noble man and a great enemy unto King Arthur". Lancelot vanquished him and freed from his castle thirty of Arthur's knights, including La Cote Male Taile, and forty ladies. Lancelot made La Cote Male Taile lord of Pendragon, with Sir Nerovens de Lile his lieutenant to have rule of the castle under him. [Malory IX, 5-6, 9]

La Cote Male Taile came to Pendragon after leaving Castle Orgulous, for which I incline to accept Glennie's identification of Bamborough.

PENEVRIC†

A strong and well placed castle of Guivret the Little's, situated near the land of Count Oringle of Limors. Penevric was kept by Guivret's two sisters. [Chrétien de Troyes, **Erec & Enide**, ll. 5091-5259]

PENEVRIC, DAMSELS OF†

Two sisters of Guivret the Little, and presumably of dwarfish or small stature themselves, these delightful maidens lived at Guivret's castle of Penevric—acting as its chatelaines?—and proved their medical skill by nursing Erec back to health after his three adventurous days of virtually nonstop fighting [Chrétien de Troyes, **Erec & Enide**, ll. 5091-5236].

PENINGUE†

Surrounded by woods and fertile fields, this was one of the castles of Galehodin, the nephew of Duke Galeholt. Eventually Galehodin dubbed a wealthy and worthy burger who lived nearby and invested him with the castle. [Vulgate V] Peningue would be in Surluse, or else in Norgales near Surluse.

Pentagoel†—see **PINTADOL**

PERCARD ('The Black Knight', 'The Knight of the Black Laund')

Sir Percard was the first of four brothers who had "long time … holden war against the knights of the Round Table" and whom Gareth encountered on his way to fight Sir Ironside at Castle Dangerous. Gareth slew Percard. The other brothers, Pertolepe, Perimones, and Persant, all became knights of the Round Table, as no doubt Percard also would have, had he survived, for on learning of his death Arthur and many knights of the court called it "great pity." Percard's shield and arms, of course, were entirely black. Although Ironside was called 'The

Red Knight of the Red Launds', Percard and the other brothers do not seem to have been related to him in any way, nor involved in his siege of Castle Dangerous. [Malory VII]

PERCIVALE OF WALES (Parzival, Perceval the Welshman, Peredur, etc.)

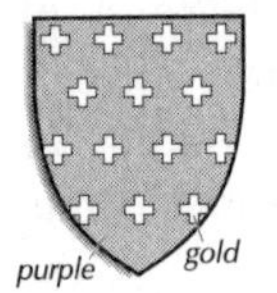

D.R.R. Owen identifies the naming of Perceval of Wales in line 1526 of Chrétien de Troyes' **Erec & Enide** as this famous knight's first documented appearance in Arthurian literature.

The following notes take into account only Chrétien de Troyes, the Vulgate, and Malory, without reference to the German or early Welsh versions, or to the various continuations of Chrétien's work except as they may have gotten into the Vulgate and Malory.

The knight's history as per Chrétien's last romance, **Perceval**:

Beneath the Welsh moutain Valbone (identified with Mount Snowdon), Percivale had been raised in ignorance of knights, organized religion, and even his own name. He was, however, good at riding his hunting horse and bringing game down with his three javelins. One day when he was about fifteen, while out in the woods he happened to meet five knights, whom he mistook for angels until the chief of them explained otherwise, adding that King Arthur, who had made him a knight, was presently at Carduel (Carlisle). Returning home, the rustic boy told his mother he had met knights, fairer than God and the angels. She fainted. On regaining consciousness, she told him his family history: his father, whose name (though she does not give it) was known throughout the islands of the sea, had been maimed with a wound through the thighs, then impoverished and driven into exile at the death of Uther Pendragon. At the time of the family's flight, the youngest son had been no more than two. His older brothers had in due time been sent, one to the king of Escavalon and the other to King Ban of Gomoret, to serve their squirehoods and be dubbed knight; both were slain in knightly combat on the way home, which caused their father to die of grief and their mother to try her best to keep her youngest at home in ignorance of all such matters.

Now, upon the lad's singleminded insistence that he, too, will be a knight, she dresses him in rough but sturdy leather clothes (perhaps the best, considering the family's history, that she has for him) and gives him advice: serve and honor all women—it is permissible to take a freely offered kiss, finger ring, or almspurse from a maiden, but nothing more; never be very long in a man's company without asking his name; converse often with gentlemen and take their advice; and pray in every church and chapel he can. So rustic has been his upbringing that he has to ask what churches and chapels are! (Yet he appears to be equally fluent in English and Welsh, translating from one language to the other and back in order to question his mother's workers on behalf of his five chance-met knights.)

Seeing him ride away, she collapses beside the drawbridge. He looks back and sees her lying as if dead, but hurries on anyway.

Next morning, he comes to a tent pitched in a field beside a stream and at first mistakes it, in its beauty, for a chapel. Going in, he finds a damsel sleeping alone. Misconstruing the spirit of his mother's advice regarding women in the way most favorable to his own inclinations, he insists on kissing her willy-nilly, seven times without pause, and might go further were it not for two things: his own inexperience, and his catching sight of an emerald ring on her finger. Appropriating the ring by force, he refreshes himself with wine and one of three venison pasties he finds in the tent, generously offering her some and seeming genuinely puzzled at her being too upset to eat. He leaves, and her sweetheart, the Haughty Knight of the Heath, shortly returns. Refusing to believe that the stranger took only kisses, and those against the damsel's will, the Haughty Knight combines her punishment with his own quest to find and slay the intruder.

Meanwhile, the youth reaches Arthur's court. The Red Knight of Quinqueroi has just thrown it into some turmoil by seizing the king's cup so recklessly that he sluiced the queen with its wine, then riding off with it. Passing him, the Welsh youth falls in love with his armor and, on seeing King Arthur, begs him for both knighthood and the red armor of that knight outside. Arthur seems quite willing, and the maiden I call "Verrine" greets the boy as the future greatest knight of all, but Kay jeers at him and strikes "Verrine." The boy, meanwhile, goes after the Red Knight and demands his armor. In reply, the Red Knight gives him a buffet with his lance, whereupon the youth kills him with a javelin cast through eye and brains. Yvonet, one of the squires from Arthur's court, has followed the youth outside and shows him how to strip the armor from the Red Knight and put it on himself, but the boy refuses to take the dead knight's silken tunic, thinking it much poorer than the coarse but sturdy clothes his mother made him. Apparently considering himself a knight simply by virtue of the armor, the boy leaves promising to come back someday, if he lives, and avenge the maid whom Kay struck.

Chrétien often makes the point in these early passages that the young man hears and understands little or not one word of what various other characters say to him; yet Percivale's own later actions and statements make it clear that some of the information filters through, if slowly and often imperfectly. The Fool Percivale may be, in more or less the Tarot sense, yet one might say there are imperfections even in his foolishness.

The boy next comes to the castle of Gornemant of Gohort, from whom he accepts a day of instructions in chivalrous combat, a night's good lodging, and certain advice before setting off again next morning; his host would like to keep him longer, but by now the youth has developed misgivings about the way he left his mother, and is anxious to return and check on her health. Gornemant formally dubs him knight (though it seems doubtful that the boy understands the significance of his act), charges him always to show mercy when a fallen adversary requests it, to help anyone in distress, and to pray often in church: in these points Gornemant either reinforces or augments the lad's mother's earlier advice, but in one other he departs from it radically and with tragic consequences: where the mother had urged asking people their names, Gornemant enjoins against talking freely.

The young knight next comes to Beaurepaire, the castle of Gornemant's niece Blancheflor; defeats both Clamadeu of the Isles and his seneschal Engygeron, who are besieging her; and wins her pledged love. Still anxious to see his mother, he leaves Beaurepaire promising to return.

Now he encounters the Fisher King's castle, where he is given Trebuchet's Sword and sees the Grail procession. More mindful of Gornemant's injunction than his mother's, he saves all his questions until morning. When morning comes, of course, it is too late: he finds himself alone in the place, and even as he exits over the drawbridge, it begins rising under him, forcing his horse to make a great leap to safety. Riding on, he finds a damsel weeping for her love, who lies in her lap freshly beheaded by the Haughty Knight of the Heath. Learning where and how the newcomer spent the night, she upbrades him for failing to ask any questions about the Grail and asks his name. Although he had never known it before, he now instinctively answers, "Perceval the Welshman", whereupon she reveals that she is his first cousin, raised with him in his mother's nursery, and that his mother is, indeed, dead. Robbed of his purpose in revisiting his home, he pursues the Haughty Knight of the Heath, defeats him, and orders him to make sure his damsel has a chance to recover from her ordeal before taking her with him to Arthur's court.

When the Haughty Knight and his damsel bring Arthur their news of Percivale, the king commands his whole court out on a search for the young knight. By chance, Percivale arrives in the vicinity and sees a goose narrowly escape from a hawk after leaving three drops of blood on the fresh snow. The blood and snow remind Percivale of his lady

Blancheflor's complexion, and he promptly loses himself in rapt contemplation of her remembered beauty, casually unhorsing both Sagramore and Kay—giving the latter a broken arm and dislocated collarbone and thus avenging the maid he struck—when they come rather rudely to see who he is. Gawaine, being ever courteous and coming when two of the drops have disappeared in the melting snow, enjoys better success and brings Percivale back to Arthur.

The whole court rejoices. On the third day of their rejoicing, the Loathly Damsel suddenly rides in, gives Percivale another scolding for his failure at the Grail Castle, and touches off a flurry of questing fever. While other knights vow to undertake this or that adventure, Percivale pledges not to pass more than a single night in any one place until he has learned the secrets of grail and bleeding lance. Here Chrétien's narrative abruptly switches to Gawaine; by the time it returns, briefly, to Percivale, he has spent five years in strange adventures, forgetful even of God. The chronology is mysterious, and may suggest either—pragmatically—that the Percivale and Gawaine narratives have been spliced together carelessly, or—mystically—that Percivale has been adventuring in some faery realm where normal time does not apply. Nevertheless, Percivale has at least remembered to send some sixty famous knights to Arthur's court after defeating them, by the Good Friday when he meets a party of penitent knights and ladies returning from making their confessions to a hermit in the woods. Percivale goes to this holy man, who turns out to be his mother's brother. The hermit instructs Percivale in his religious duties and family history: his mother is indeed dead, and it was the sin of causing her death that prevented Percivale from asking the right questions, but it is her parting prayer that has kept him safe from harm. The man served from the Grail is another of Percivale's mother's brothers, as well as father to the Fisher King, and the food served him is a single Mass wafer. Having learned all this, Percivale stays with his hermit uncle at least until Easter, which could signify that he considers his quest fulfilled.

Loose ends remain. For instance, even if Chrétien designed simply to have Percivale return and settle down with Blancheflor, there remain the mystery of the bleeding lance and the matter of Trebuchet's Sword—prophesied to break in some crucial battle, but guaranteed repairable by one man (and one man only): its maker Trebuchet. (This sword may or may not have been broken in Percivale's battle with the Haughty Knight; the authenticity of the passage is disputed. Even if broken, however, it has not been repaired.)

Chrétien had already mentioned "Perceval the Welshman" in earlier romances: **Erec & Enide** (as mentioned above), and **Cligés**, ll.

4824-4853, where the famous knight opens the third day of the Oxford tournament by jousting with, and being defeated by, young Cligés. The progression of Cligés' conquests in this episode—Sagramore the first day, Lancelot the second, Percivale the third, and Gawaine (fought to a draw) the fourth—indicates a high standing for Percivale; and his very appearance in this tournament necessitates some longer stay at Arthur's court than we find in the romance named for him. His identification as "the Welshman" may have been from the outset a sort of table-turning paradox: various verses in the **Perceval** seem to indicate that already in the late 12th century the hapless Welsh were coming in for the same sort of offensive ethnic humor we still see in the Mother Goose rhyme "Taffy Was a Welshman", and that in our own century has been applied to Polacks and Norskes.

By the time we reach Malory, Percivale's father has been identified as King Pellinore and his older brothers are Lamorak, Aglovale, Dornar, and a half-brother, Tor. Obviously, none of these was killed on the way home right after being knighted. Malory first mentions Percivale in Merlin's prophecy of his future greatness, made just before Arthur's acquisition of Excalibur. Percivale's arrival at court is described in the middle of the books of Tristram. Tristram has joined the Round Table, Arthur has supposedly reconciled his quarrel with King Mark, and the two have gone back to Cornwall together. Eight days later, Sir Aglovale brings his younger brother Percivale, acting as his squire, to Arthur's court and requests that he be made knight. Arthur dubs him the next morning, and at dinner commands him to be seated "among mean knights."

> Then was there a maiden in the queen's court that was come of high blood, and she was dumb and naver spake word. Right so she came straight into the hall, and went unto Sir Percivale, and took him by the hand and said aloud ... Arise Sir Percivale, the noble knight and God's knight, and go with me .... And there she brought him to the right side of the Siege Perilous, and said, Fair knight, take here thy siege, for that siege appertaineth to thee and to none other. Right so she departed and asked a priest. And as she was confessed and houselled then she died. Then the king and all the court made great joy of Sir Percivale.

Chrétiens's account has become much shortened and more ethereal—no mention is made of Kay's striking the prophetic damsel, but now she proceeds to a death probably symbolic in its holiness. Nevertheless, much later on, Percivale tells Persides, whom he has just rescued, to go to court and

> [a]lso tell Sir Kay the Seneschal, and to Sir Mordred, that I trust to Jesu to be of as great worthiness as either of them, for tell them I shall not forget their mocks and scorns that they did to me that day that I was

> made knight; and tell them I will never see that court till men speak more worship of me than ever men did of any of them both.

Unless Malory's editor omitted a portion of the account of Percivale's arrival at court, this passage can best be explained as an accidental carry-over from some version of Chrétien's material. In the next chapter after bringing Percivale to court, Malory describes the murder of Margawse and departure of Percivale's older brother Lamorak. This may not accurately reflect the chronology, but it provides a logical reason for Percivale to leave court—also to turn against Mordred and his brothers.

Percivale next appears in time to rescue Tristram from Mark's prison and to scold Mark. When Mark protests that Tristram is La Beale Isoud's lover, the pure and innocent Percivale refuses to believe it, gives Mark a further lecture on the shame of evil thoughts, makes him promise not to hurt Tristram (causing him to turn from overt to secret villainy), and then heads alone for his home country of Wales. A few chapters later, Percivale appears in the neighborhood of Joyous Garde, where Tristram and Isoud have taken refuge. Percivale seems to have joined Ector de Maris and Harry le Fise Lake as temporary companions in adventure; they meet Palomides, among others, and Percivale learns from the Saracen of Lamorak's death. After swoooning for grief, the young knight mourns, "Alas my good and noble brother Sir Lamorak, now shall we never meet." Apparently Percivale rode off alone in his grief, for he is not named as fighting at the Lonazep tournament, whither the other knights turn up at about this point.

When Lancelot ran away mad after Guenevere found him in bed with Elaine of Astolat, Percivale and his brother Aglovale were among the knights who joined the search for him. Aglovale and Percivale began their search by riding home to visit their mother, "that was a queen in those days." She besought them to remain with her lest she lose them as she had lost Pellinore, Lamorak, and Dornar. When they left despite her prayers, she sent a squire after them; the squire fell afoul of one Baron Goodewin, who slew him because Aglovale had slain Goodewin's brother Sir Gawdelin. Meeting the funeral party, Aglovale and Percivale went back and avenged the squire. A long time later, after much fruitless searching, the brothers lodged at Cardican Castle, and there Percivale rather inexplicably woke Aglovale's squire at midnight and made him ride secretly away with him, leaving Aglovale behind. Percivale rescued Sir Persides from the Uncourteous Lady and bade him return to court with the message to Kay and Mordred quoted above, as well as the message to Aglovale not to come seeking him, for he would never return until he had found Lancelot. (Perhaps Aglovale had determined to give up the search and ride back to court.)

Percivale eventually met Ector de Maris and they almost killed one another in a knightly battle "to the uttermost", apparently for the excellent reason of proving their strength. But Percivale prayed to Jesu and, since he was "one of the best knights of the world … in whom the very faith stood most in" and "a perfect clean maiden" (we must now forget the lusty experiments and lady love of Chrétien's Percivale), the Grail came and healed both knights, and Percivale got an imperfect "glimmering of the vessel and of the maiden that bare it." Percivale and Ector continued on together and found Lancelot living with Elaine at Joyous Isle. Percivale had a good two hours of chivalrous battle with him before they learned his identity and persuaded him to return to court.

That Pentecost, Galahad came to court and the Grail Adventures began. Percivale and Lancelot were the only Round Table knights whom Galahad did not defeat and "defoul" at his one tournament before Arthur, the day before the Questers departed. Percivale apparently began the Quest in Lancelot's company, but they encountered Galahad again near the hermitage of a female recluse; this time Galahad jousted them both down. The recluse cheered the victor so eagerly that Galahad rode away for modesty, while Lancelot rode away for shame, leaving Percivale alone with the holy woman, who turned out to be his aunt. She gave him good counsel, advising him that to find Galahad, whose fellowship he wished, he should ride to Goothe Castle and, if unsuccessful there, to Carbonek. Percivale visited King Mordrains in his abbey. He was saved from twenty attacking knights by Galahad, but Galahad rode off again before Percivale could catch up. He was given a black demon horse that would have plunged him into the roiling water had he not made the sign of the cross in time. Fasting along a rocky island, he was joined by the devil in the guise of a fair damsel, who tempted him almost to the point of making love, but again Percivale made the sign of the cross in time; the devil vanished and Percivale drove his own sword into his thigh as penance.

After these and other mystical adventures and visions, a divine or angelic messenger brought him a ship all covered in white samite to escape from the island of his temptation. When the ship came ashore on the mainland, Percivale was joined by Sir Bors de Ganis. The ship then brought them to their rendezvous with Galahad and Percivale's sister Amide. The four traveled together for a time, found King Solomon's Ship, purged the castle of Earl Hernox of its wicked occupants, and shared Eucharistic visions in Carteloise Forest. At last they came to the Castle of the Leprous Lady, where Percivale lost his sister, promising her on her deathbed to see that her last wishes were carried out. After the destruction of the castle, the three knights separated again for a while, but met once more and proceeded together to Carbonek for the climactic mysteries of the Grail.

Percivale left Carbonek with Galahad and Bors; they found their ship (with the Grail miraculously aboard) and sailed to Sarras, where they found the vessel with Amide's body and buried her before being thrown into prison by King Estorause. When they were freed and Galahad was made king for a year in Estorause's place, Percivale and Bors presumably acted as his chief counselors. Immediately after Galahad, the Grail, and Longinus' Spear were taken to Heaven, Percivale "yielded him to an hermitage out of the city, and took a religious clothing", Bors remaining with him but not taking the habit.

> Thus a year and two months lived Sir Percivale in the hermitage a full holy life, and then passed out of this world; and Bors let bury him by his sister and by Galahad in the spiritualities.

Besides supplying Percivale's age at fifteen when he received knighthood, the Vulgate reaffirms that he led a pure and chaste life and was second in holiness only to Galahad, adding that he went to Confession weekly. [Malory I, 24; X, 23, 51, 53-54, 68; XI, 10-14; XII, 7-8; XIII, 3, 17; XIV, 1-10; XVI, 17; XVII, 2-12, 19-23; Vulgate V]

PERCIVALE'S "ANGELS", THEIR FIVE KNIGHTS and THREE MAIDENS†

Percivale's mother had taught him that devils were the vilest things in existence, God and the angels the most beautiful. While out in the woods, the boy heard the crashing and clanking of a party of five knights, and at first thought that such a din meant devils: he determined to use his javelins against them. On seeing them in their shining armor, however, he changed his mind, deciding that the handsomest one must be God and the others angels. He promptly prostrated himself before them, whereupon they thought him fearful. Trying to calm his supposed fears, their leader questioned him about another party of five knights, with three damsels, which they were pursuing; the boy, on being informed they were knights and not angels, answered his interlocutor's repeated question only with questions of his own—"What is this thing? That thing?" Showing remarkable patience, the knight answered all the lad's queries—"My lance. My shield."—and so on, explaining how they were used, and eventually revealing that King Arthur had dubbed him knight and given him his arms less than five years previously. His patience was rewarded when Percivale finally told him where they were—Valbone—and took them to the harrowers and ox-drivers in his mother's oat fields, whom he questioned about the party the knights were seeking. The ox-drivers answered that they had ridden through this same pass that very day. The boy translated this information for his new idols and asked where the king who made knights could be found. The knight replied that Arthur was presently at Carlisle, after which he and his companions pursued their quarry right out of Chrétien's romance. [**Perceval**, ca. ll. 69-185]

Chrétien does not tell us who any of these thirteen were, though at some point someone seems to have found reason to identify the chief one with Ywaine. Nor does he tell us why the five Percivale met were pursuing the others—to rescue the damsels, simply to catch up with friends, or ...? I do not, however, find much evidence of emergency or hostility in their words. It might be tempting to identify them with the thirteen penitents who long afterward directed Percivale to his hermit uncle, but in this latter party the genders are reversed: ten ladies and three knights. (See Percivale's Thirteen Penitents.)

PERCIVALE'S AUNT

See under Percivale (near the end of the entry) and see also Percivale's Hermit Uncle.

PERCIVALE'S CHARCOAL BURNER†

When Percivale first struck out for King Arthur's court at Carduel (Carlisle), he asked directions of a charcoal burner whom he met driving his donkey. The charcoal burner politely gave him not only directions, but news of King Arthur's recent battle with and defeat of King Rion of the Isles. A note of Chrétien's translator Cline reminds me that this man is the one and only charcoal burner (and one of the rather few peasants with speaking parts) to be found in Chrétien's Arthurian works, and informs me that he may have been inspired by an actual charcoal burner who made it into the historical record by dint of finding and returning the young lost prince Philip-Augustus in mid-August of 1179. [**Perceval**, ll. 835-858]

Percivale's Cousin—see FISHER KING'S NIECE

PERCIVALE'S EMERALD RING†

More properly speaking, this was the ring the Haughty Knight of the Heath gave his damsel. Young Percivale, just having left home for the first time to find King Arthur's court, stole it from her in (willful?) misinterpretation of his mother's parting instruction. I cannot tell what eventually became of it; while the Haughty Knight and Percivale speak of it before they finally fight, they seem to say nothing more of it after the battle is decided. [Chrétien de Troyes, **Perceval**, ca. ll 700-723; 3877-3998]

PERCIVALE'S FATHER AND BROTHERS†(?)

In Chrétien's work, they do not seem to be King Pellinore and his sons. [**Perceval**, ca. ll. 419-488] See under Percivale.

PERCIVALE'S HERMIT UNCLE†

Directed by thirteen penitents, Percivale finds this holy man living deep in the woods. The hermit is not completely alone: he is beginning the Good Friday service together with a priest and an acolyte. Whether they live with him or have come only for the day I cannot tell, nor can I say whether the hermit is himself an ordained priest, though he seems to have pre-eminence over the undoubted priest mentioned so briefly. The hermit turns out to be Percivale's uncle on the maternal side, and the Fisher King's uncle as well, the Fisher King's father being his brother. The hermit gives Percivale confirmation of his mother's death, explains the meaning of much (not quite all) that Percivale saw at the Grail castle, and provides him with basic spiritual instruction, including a secret prayer—replete with many important names of God—not to be used except in case of dire fear. [Chrétien de Troyes, **Perceval**, ll. 6301-6518]

I see some possibility that this episode may have fulfilled Percivale's quest to Chrétien's own satisfaction. If not, then perhaps the secret prayer was to have saved Percivale when Trebuchet's Sword shattered (assuming that its shattering in his fight with the Haughty Knight is an interpolation). I might further remark that the Good Friday service does not, in modern Catholic tradition, include the Mass, nor have I yet found evidence suggesting that it might have included Mass in the 12th century; it strikes me as curious to find Chrétien calling it the Church's highest and holiest ceremony.

Could Percivale's holy uncle in Chrétien's version have become Percivale's holy aunt in Malory's?

PERCIVALE'S MOTHER†

Having seen her knightly husband maimed and impoverished, and her two older sons slain as soon as knighted, it seems only natural that she would do her best to keep her youngest son forever innocent of all knowledge of knights or any weapons except hunting javelins. He appears fluent enough, when it suits his purposes, in the language of Arthur's land as well as the language of his own home, so she has not neglected his education entirely, only selectively. When, despite her pains, he meets five knights, she yields to the inevitable and allows him to set off for court, which suggests that, though manipulative, she is neither tyrannical nor domineering. Her parting advice has been interpreted as calculated to make him appear so oafish he will soon come home again; to me, however, at least in modern translation, it seems sound knightly instruction, though he only half listens and later misinterprets some of it with results both slapstick and tragic. Probably her strangest move is keeping him in ignorance of his own name, even as she counsels him never to spend too much time with another man before asking his name. As the fifteen-year-old rides away, his mother falls in a dead faint; this, presumably, is the moment she expires of grief, which hardly sounds as if she hopes to see him return. Her fall gives him no pause at the time, but afterward "My mother told me ..." becomes his catchphrase until Gornemant advises him to stop saying it; returning to check on her obsesses him until he learns that she is indeed dead.

She was sister both to the Fisher King's father and to a holy hermit who eventually told Percivale that the sin of leaving her fallen had caused his failure at the Grail castle—a thing also told him earlier by his cousin—but her prayer had kept him alive.

[Chrétien de Troyes, **Perceval**, esp. ll. 111-634; 1570-1596; her death confirmed ca. ll. 3592-3618, also ll. 6390-6431]

PERCIVALE'S SWORD

In the pommel of Sir Percivale's sword was "a red cross and the sign of the crucifix therein." Apparently this had no special virtue other than reminding Percivale of God. [Malory XIV, 9] Percivale's sword could cut through a chain and be none the worse [Vulgate V; it would be surprising if the other noblest swords did not have this quality also].

Eventually, Percivale received Galahad's sword—apparently Balin's Sword, that Galahad had drawn from the floating block of marble at Camelot, and which he now relinquished because he had acquired King David's Sword. Percivale left his own sword at the hermitage in Carteloise Forest. This would have been the sword with the red cross in the pommel, the one known to be able to cut through chain.

Since Percivale died about a year after Galahad in Sarras, Bors could have brought back Balin's Sword for Lancelot.

See also Trebuchet's Sword.

PERCIVALE'S THIRTEEN PENITENTS†

After five years of adventuring in forgetfulness of God, Percivale met a party of three knights and ten ladies on their way back from confessing to a holy hermit. (See Percivale's Hermit Uncle.) The ladies certainly, and perhaps the knights also—the wording of the translations leaves me unsure—were barefoot, hooded, and wearing rough clothing. (D.D.R. Owen says "hair-shirts.") The knights were unarmed, for, as they told Percivale in their shock at seeing him armed, it was wrong to bear weapons on Good Friday. One of the knights gave Percivale a theological discourse which has been called more profound than the one his hermit uncle was later to give him. The group directed him to the holy man for further spiritual guidance; having just been there themselves, they had marked the path by tying branches. [Chrétien de Troyes, **Perceval**, ll. 6238-6332, & Cline's footnote to 6238] It interests me that this group of thirteen repeats the numbers but reverses the gender count of the group involved in first awakening Percivale to the existence of knights. (See Percivale's "Angels" ...)

Perdue, Isles—see **ISLE PERDUE;** see also **MELIOT**

Peredur—see **PERCIVALE**

PERILOUS BED†

No knight of Arthur's could rest in this bed without rising in shame. When Gawaine came to the castle in which it was, at the frontier of the Terre Foraine of Gore, he was further told that no one could sleep in this bed without being maimed or killed. Lancelot later stopped here for a night during his pursuit of Guenevere and her captor Meliagrant. Lancelot took the risk and slept in the bed. At midnight the house trembled, a whirlwind swept through it, and a fiery lance came in the window and advanced toward the bed with such force that it entered half a foot into the ground. Lancelot got up, cut the lance in half with his sword, and went back to bed. [Vulgate IV]

I suspect that this bed should be identified with the one that Malory tells us Merlin made. See Merlin's Bed and Castle Meliot.

PERILOUS, CASTLE

Tristram, Gouvernail, Sir Kehydius, and Dame Bragwaine were on their way by boat from Brittany to Cornwall when an extremely "contrarious wind" blew them off course to North Wales, where they came ashore near the Castle Perilous. Tristram went into the forest because "in this forest are many strange adventures, as I heard say." [Malory IX, 10] This would seem to put it near the Forest Perilous of Annowre the sorceress in North Wales [Malory IX, 16]. I would incline to put this Castle Perilous at Dyffryn or Llanbedr, above Barmouth on the coast of Merioneth County. Having blown so far, though, it would not be impossible for Tristram and party to have come ashore even farther along the coast, at, say, Llandudno or Rhyl.

Although I cannot be entirely sure, I do not think this is the same castle as Dame Lyonors' Castle Perilous, otherwise called Castle Dangerous—and not simply because I have already located that Castle Perilous in Wiltshire! For Dame Lyonors' castle, see Castle Dangerous.

PERILOUS, CHAPEL

Either this was not a Christian chapel, or it had been adapted to her own purposes by the sorceress Hellawes, Lady of the Castle Nigramous, who "ordained" the chapel to entrap Lancelot or Gawaine.

Riding in a deep forest, Lancelot followed a black brachet which was tracking a feute of blood. The brachet led him over an old, feeble bridge into an old manor, where he found the body of Sir Gilbert the Bastard, with his wife grieving for him. Leaving the manor, Lancelot met a damsel he knew, who told him that her brother, Sir Meliot de Logres, had fought and killed Sir Gilbert that day, but had been wounded himself. The bleeding could not be staunched, and Meliot could only be saved if his wounds were searched with the sword and a piece of the bloody cloth wrapping the dead knight in the Chapel Perilous. Lancelot proceeded to Chapel Perilous, on the front of which he saw many fair, rich shields hanging upside-down. Thirty armed knights barred his way, grinning and gnashing their teeth at him; when he resolutely stepped forward, they stood aside and let him pass. In the chapel, by the light of a single dim lamp, he found the body of Sir Gilbert lying covered by a cloth of silk. When Lancelot cut off a little of the cloth, the earth seemed to quake. When he came back outside, the thirty knights threatened his death if he did not lay down Sir Gilbert's sword, which he had picked up in the chapel along with the cloth. Again Lancelot passed resolutely and safely through their midst. Next he met Hellawes herself, who first threatened his death if he did not lay down the sword, then tried to get him to kiss her once. When he refused, she confessed that either to lay down the sword or to kiss her would have cost his his life. She had been in love with him for seven years and, despairing of his love, had hoped to have his dead body to kiss and fondle. She had had Sir Gawaine with her once, for a while, at which time he had fought with Sir Gilbert and cut off his left hand. (Had Hellawes been less lethal with Gawaine than with Lancelot because she did not despair of winning Gawaine's carnal love?) Proceeding from the chapel, Lancelot healed Meliot. Hellawes died. I do not know whether Sir Gilbert was Hellawes' unwilling accomplice or unwitting tool. [Malory VI, 14-15]

The Chapel Perilous would appear to have been in one of the Forests Perilous. See Castle Nigramous and Forest Perilous.

PERILOUS FORD†

This seems to lie between Queen Igraine's Canguin and Guiromelant's Orqueneseles, with an additional stretch of land on Igraine's side.

The Haughty Maid of Logres maliciously dares Gawaine to jump his horse across the Perilous Ford, saying that her dear friend the Haughty

Knight of the Rock (whom Gawaine has just defeated) has been in the habit of crossing it every day for her sake. When, thanks to Gringolet, Gawaine makes it to the other side, Guiromelant informs him that he is the first knight ever to keep his life while crossing this ford. [Chrétien de Troyes, **Perceval**, ca. ll. 8477-8602]

PERILOUS, FOREST (Forest Perdue)

In the "Forest Perilous, that was in North Wales" lived Annowre, a sorceress who loved Arthur and enticed him to her castle, later trying to kill him when he would not go to bed with her. The attempt was foiled by Sir Tristram and Nimue, and Arthur slew Annowre. [Malory IX, 16] This seems to be the forest near Castle Perilous, where Tristram had been blown ashore [Malory IX, 10]. Indeed, it is possible that Castle Perilous was Annowre's stronghold.

The Vulgate speaks of a "forest perilleuse" which seems to have been between Castle Chariot and Bedegraine. This is probably another section of Malory's Forest Perilous. Since Castle Perilous and presumably Annowre's section of the woods were near the coast, the forest must have been extensive.

Vulgate II and V give this history of the Forest Perilleuse, also called the Forest Perdue, since those who entered it were lost—temporarily, as things turned out. When Gwenbaus and King Bors were traveling to their brother King Ban at Bedingran, they found many knights and ladies dancing in a fine field in the midst of this forest. Looking on was an elderly knight, who seemed to be in charge, and a very beautiful damsel. Gwenbaus fell in love with the damsel and made up his mind to remain with her. When she wished that the dancing would go on forever, he cast a spell to oblige her, enchanting the place so that the people would go on dancing and all knights and ladies who loved or had ever loved, on coming by, would forget everything else and join the dancers until the enchantment was broken. After fourteen years, the damsel wearied of dancing and caroling, and Gwenbaus made her a magic chessboard. Eventually Gwenbaus and his damsel both died here, although the enchantment went on.

At length Sir Lancelot came to the field in the forest, where he found thirty rich pavilions. In the center of the field four large pines surrounded a chair on which rested a golden crown, the crown of Lancelot's father, King Ban, who had left it with his brother Gwenbaus. Many knights and damsels were singing and caroling around the pines. When Lancelot passed the first pavilion, his memory became blank and he joined the revelers; his squire, however, was unaffected and got away. A damsel led Lancelot to the chair and told him he must sit in it and wear the crown to see if he was their deliverer. If he was not, he would have to stay and wait with them. The damsel put the crown on Lancelot's head, saying that it was his father's crown. At that moment, Lancelot saw a statue fall and break. All the carolers recovered their memories. The spell was broken and they were freed.

There appear to have been at least two Forests Perilous, one in North Wales and another probably in southeast Wales (see Nigramous Castle). Indeed, I suspect there may have been a number of Forests Perilous, "Perilous" being the sort of adjective which might have been applied as the speaker saw fit.

PERILOUS LAKE

Despite the name, I cannot find that Malory suggests this lake to be magically dangerous. He puts it in the forest of Morris. Dozmary Pool, on a hilltop in Bodmin Moor, was long supposed to be bottomless, which would make it perilous.

The Perilous Lake is rather minor. Malory has nothing much happening here, except that Kay and Gaheris abide at it a while waiting for King Mark [Malory IX, 30].

PERILOUS ROCK, PORT OF

I find that Malory mentions this mysterious spot only once, in the Grail Adventures—and that in a flashback [XVII, 4]. Nascien, entering a ship at the isle of Turnance, was blown to "another ship where King Mordrains was, which had been tempted full evil with a fiend in the Port of Perilous Rock", all this happening forty years after Christ's Passion. If Turnance is identified with Lundy, then Morte Point, in Devonshire, west of Ilfracombe, might be a good spot for the Port of Perilous Rock, "Morte" suggesting death and therefore peril. I do not know whether the rocks are perilous there today, but even if they are not, they may have been fifteen or twenty centuries ago.

PERIMONES ('The Red Knight')

Perimones was the third of four brothers whom Gareth encountered on his way to fight Sir Ironside at Castle Dangerous. The other brothers were Percard, Persant, and Pertolepe. Perimones' shield and arms were entirely red, and care must be taken not to confuse him with Sir Ironside, who also was armed in red and called 'The Red Knight of the Red Launds.'

Perimones was lord of a white tower, "well matchecold all about, and double dyked", where he was preparing to host a tournament when Gareth passed by and he fought the young knight in at attempt to avenge his brother Percard. Perimones had at least fifty knights in his service; on being defeated he yielded them all, as well as himself, to Gareth's command. He jousted in Lyonors' tournament at Castle Dangerous and made a creditable showing, and later came to court about the time of Gareth's wedding, obtained the favor of being made Gareth's butler at the high feast of Michaelmas, and was made a member of the Round Table. Perimones was one of the knights in Guenevere's guard at the stake and was killed when Lancelot rescued her. [Malory VII, 10, 28, 35; XX, 8]

PERIS DE FOREST SAVAGE

This knight, who apparently operated near the vicinity of Sir Turquine's tower, was in the habit of haunting a fair highway in order to distress all ladies and gentlewomen, ravishing or at least robbing them.

> As Sir Turquine watched to destroy knights, so did this knight attend to destroy and distress ladies, damosels, and gentlewomen.

An unnamed damsel described his depredations to Lancelot, led the great knight to the vicinity, and then rode ahead as bait, bringing out Sir Peris so that Lancelot could kill him. [Malory VI, 10]

PERSANT OF INDE

Sir Persant earned his surname for his preference to "the colour of Inde", dark blue, which he used for his arms, armor, and shield, the trappings of his horses, the livery of his male and female attendants, and his pavilion. A goodly knight and the lord of a fair city, he was the last of four brothers whom Gareth defeated on his way to fight Sir Ironside at Castle Dangerous; the other three were Percard, Perimones, and Pertolepe. After his defeat, Persant lodged Gareth and Lynette nobly for the night and proved himself a more than hospitable host, at least by today's standards: he sent his eighteen-year-old virgin daughter to Gareth's bed with instructions to "make him no strange cheer, but good cheer, and take him in thine arms and kiss him." Persant was much impressed with Gareth's nobility when the young knight sent her back undefiled.

On Gareth's command, Persant, bringing a hundred knights, came with his surviving brothers to Arthur's court at Pentecost, where they were pardoned for the war they had long held against the knights of the Round Table. Persant fought in Lyonors' tournament at Castle Dangerous, and later came to court about the time of Gareth's wedding and obtained the favor of being Gareth's sewer-chief at the feast of Michaelmas. He was soon elected to the Round Table.

Persant appears as one of Guenevere's guests at the select dinner party where Sir Patrise was killed, and as one of ten knights to ride a-Maying with her and fall into Sir Meliagrant's ambush. He was also among the knights who tried to heal Sir Urre. He is not mentioned as being with his brothers Pertolepe and Perimones when they were killed during Guenevere's rescue from the stake; Persant may have been the oldest—the age of his daughter at the time of his meeting with Gareth suggests his maturity—and have been already retired from active service. [Malory VII, 12, 23-24, 26-28, 35; XVIII, 3; XIX, 1; XX, 8] For the possible location of his city, see under Castle Dangerous.

PERSE†

Dame Perse was an early love of Sir Ector de Maris. When Ector was late returning to her (since he was out searching for Lancelot), her dying father gave her, against her will, to Zelotes. Zelotes, however, neither married her nor permitted anyone else to marry her, but fought and killed all who approached his castle. At last Ector and his companions came by. Ector fought and killed Zelotes and was reunited with Perse. (He had found another love in the interval, but she was now dead.) Sir Lionel, seeing Perse with Ector, remarked that a woman's heart was a marvelous thing, since neither misfortune nor suffering could change its purpose. [Vulgate V, Appendix]

PERSIDES (Persedes) [of Gazewilte]†

This Sir Persides was lord of Gazewilte Castle. His lovely wife, Helaine the peerless, claimed that her beauty was superior to his bravery, so he imprisoned her until the question could be settled. She spent five years in prison, until her sister, looking for Gawaine, found Ector de Maris and fetched him instead. Ector defeated Persides and sent him and Helaine to Guenevere. [Vulgate III]

I rather doubt this knight could be identified with Malory's Persides.

PERSIDES DE BLOISE

Going to the tournament at the Castle of Maidens, Tristram lodged with old Sir Pellounes, whose castle seems to have been within sight of the Castle of Maidens. At this same time Pellounes' son, Sir Persides de Bloise, gladdened his father's heart by coming home after a two years' absence. Tristram remarked to Pellounes, "I know your son well enough for a good knight." Learning that Tristram was of Cornwall, but not his name, Persides described how he had once been in Cornwall and had jousted down ten knights before King Mark, but then Sir Tristram "overthrew me, and took my lady away from me, and that shall I never forget." He may or may not have also told Tristram of a more recent adventure, only a few days before, when he had fought and wounded Sir Mordred and would have slain him "had it not been for the love of Sir Gawaine and his brother [probably Gareth]." As they stood talking at a bay window they could watch "many knights riding to and fro toward the tournament", among whom was one whom Persides recognized with admiration as Palomides, then engaged in jousting down a baker's dozen of knights.

> Fair brother, said Sir Tristram unto Sir Persides, let us cast upon us cloaks, and let us go see the play. Not so, said Sir Persides, we will not go like knaves thither, but we will ride like men and good knights to withstand our enemies.

As a result of his honesty, Persides got a fall from Palomides. Later, in the tournament proper, he was "smitten down and almost slain" by a large party with Bleoberis and Gaheris at its head, but rescued by Tristram. Presumably Persides learned Tristram's identity and they were reconciled before the end of the tourney.

Later, Sir Percivale, searching for Lancelot, found Persides chained to a stone pillar outside the Castle of the Uncourteous Lady, rescued him, and sent him back to Arthur's court with various messages. (It is possible, however, that this was a different Persides from the one mentioned above; this Persides is identified as a knight of the Round Table, but not given the surname "de Bloise.")

Though Persides de Bloise is a minor character, his is one of the few shields that Malory describes: green with a lion of gold. [Malory IX, 27-28, 30, 32, 36; XI, 12; see "Castle of the Uncourteous Lady"]

PERTOLEPE ('The Green Knight')

Pertolepe was the second of four brothers whom Gareth encountered on his way to fight Sir Ironside at Castle Dangerous; the others were Percard, Perimones, and Persant. Pertolepe's trappings were "all in green, both his horse and his harness." On seeing Gareth in the black armor of his brother Percard, and learning that Gareth had slain Percard,

> the Green Knight rode unto a horn that was green, and it hung upon a thorn, and there he blew three deadly notes, and there came two damosels and armed him lightly. And then he took a great horse, and a green shield and a green spear.

(Although each of the four brothers is connected with a color, and although Pertolepe should not be confused with the more famous Green Knight of Gawaine's adventure, Bercilak de Hautdesert, the above passage may suggest a common origin in the roots of legend for the two.)

After his defeat, Pertolepe pledged himself and thirty knights to be at Gareth's service, lodged Gareth and Lynette for the night, and, true to Gareth's command, showed up along with his surviving brothers at Arthur's court that Pentecost. He made a good showing in Dame Lyonors' tournament at Castle Dangerous, and returned to court about the time of Gareth's wedding, bringing his thirty knights and obtaining the favor of acting as Gareth's chamberlain at the high feast of Michaelmas. Soon thereafter he was elected to the Round Table. He was among the knights killed when Lancelot rescued Guenevere from the stake. [Malory VII, 8-9, 23-28, 35; XX, 8]

Pescheour—see **PELLAM**

PESME AVANTURE†

See the various personages associated with this place as listed under its name. [Chrétien de Troyes, **Yvain**, ll. 5107-5770]

PESME AVANTURE, CAPTIVE DAMSELS OF†

There were up to 300 of them, kept hard at labor with gold thread and silks, while forced to work in rags and malnourish themselves on a sixtieth part of their earnings, the rest going to the lord of Pesme Avanture. All the while, their hearts were aching because each knight who attempted their rescue was slain by the two demons of the place. The maiden who describes their plight to Ywaine says that they have been sent here as part of the yearly ransom the young king of the Isle of Maidens pledged in return for his life, but later, after Ywaine frees them, the damsels return to their own "countries." Unless the plural is a clerical or translation slip, perhaps the king of the Isle of Maidens was not the only ruler to have been forced to pay a tribute of maidens.

All this looks very much as if Chrétien had an eye to his own time, and was protesting sweatshop conditions in the 12th-century textile industry.

[**Yvain**, ll. 5185-5808]

PESME AVANTURE, DEMONS OF†

Offspring of a human woman and a goblin (I am not sure what word D.D.R. Owen translates as "goblin", but he seems to use it and "devil" synonymously), they served—or, perhaps, ruled—the castle, lands, and lord of Pesme Avanture by fighting every knight who came, two to one. They ransomed the young king of the Isle of Maidens at the cost of an annual tribute of thirty maids, who were forced into slave labor in the textile industry. Whether or not the demons treated any other adventuring rulers in like fashion, most of their opponents they simply killed; this was called "the custom of the castle." They were giants as well as demons, dark and ugly, each one armored from shoulder to knee and armed with a light but strong round shield and a jagged, copper-covered, brassbound club of cornelwood.

On seeing Ywaine, they insisted he shut his lion in a small room, which he finally did under protest. The loyal beast broke out and got one giant down. The other turned to help his brother, and Ywaine, showing more practicality than chivalry, seized the chance to lop off his head from behind. The downed brother then owned himself vanquished; Chrétien seems to imply that the lion had wounded him mortally. [Chrétien de Troyes, **Yvain**, ll. 5256-5693]

PESME AVANTURE, LORD OF, HIS WIFE, and DAUGHTER†

What do we make of these three? To all appearances, the lord lives on or at least enjoys the wealth produced by hundred of maidens kept in wretched slave labor; yet he, his wife, and their daughter seem a happy, courteous, and completely functional family who shower visitors with lavish hospitality. True, the lord, perhaps not wishing to spoil his guest's evening and night, waits until morning, when Ywaine is about to leave, to spring the news officially that each knightly visitor must singlehandedly fight two gigantic demons and, if he manages to slay them both, he *must* marry the daughter of the house and become its new owner. The lord speaks as if it is the custom of the house that forces him to insist, against his own better nature, upon this unequal combat, which has already been the death of many a knight; but he also calls the demons his servants. Just who is master here? He acts overjoyed when Ywaine, with the lion's help, wins. He is less overjoyed when Ywaine refuses his daughter—indeed, the lord first threatens to hold him prisoner, then haughtily refuses to take his pledge to return "if possible". No pledge is necessary, the lord replies, for if the girl attracts Ywaine, he'll be back soon enough without pledging, and if she doesn't, her father thinks too highly of her to force her into any marriage.

The wife and beautiful, charming daughter presumably say something during Ywaine's visit, but their words are not recorded. Theoretically they all continue rejoicing when they see their ex-slave labor force leave with the man who has saved them.

[Chrétien de Troyes, **Yvain**, ca. ll. 5360-5770]

Pesme Avanture, Sensible Lady of—see "PRUDENTIA, DAME"

PETITE AUMOSNE†

Originally called "li Secors as poures" ("Help of the Poor"), this abbey, which was rather needy itself, was renamed La Petite Aumosne ("The Little Dole") by King Helisier, a contemporary and convert of Joseph of Arimathea, who quipped that during thirty years of holy wandering, he had received here the smallest hand-out anywhere, though it was all they had to give.

Despite its poverty, La Petite Aumosne was still around in Arthur's time, a source of religious men who could at least give traveling knights the local news.

Petite Aumosne was in the neighborhood of the castle Tertre Deuee and the "Forest of the Boiling Well", and possibly also near King Vagor's Isle Estrange [Vulgate V].

PETROINES†

This clerk held the first school at Oxford and there, also, wrote down Merlin's prophecies. From Oxford he came to Duke Galeholt's court, where he seems to have been the most prominent clerk after Helyes of Thoulouse. [Vulgate IV]

PHARIANCE (Pharien)

Malory calls Sir Phariance "a worshipful knight." When Ulfius and Brastias brought Arthur's call for support to Kings Ban and Bors, Phariance and Lionses were the two "knights of worship" sent to greet the Britons. Phariance and Lionses accompanied Ban and Bors to Britain and fought nobly in the battle of Bedegraine.

The Vulgate picks up a somewhat less flattering sequel. While a retainer of King Bors, Pharien (Phariance) killed another knight, for which Bors banished him. Phariance changed sides and became a retainer of King Claudas. Claudas loved Phariance's wife and made Phariance seneschal of Gannes for her sake. After King Bors' death, Phariance confiscated Bors' two sons, Lionel (aged twenty-one months) and young Bors (aged nine months). Phariance and his nephew Lambegues thus became the tutors of Lionel and Bors. After Seraide's rescue of the two boys from Claudas' court, Claudas threw Phariance and Lambegues into prison, but Lionses used a ruse to accomplish their rescue. Phariance and his family were brought to the French Lake, where Phariance eventually died. His wife remained with Viviane, and his sons Anguins and Tatains went on to become gallant knights. [Malory I, 10, 15, 17; Vulgate III]

PHELOT

This villainous knight was a retainer of the king of Norgales (Norgales). Lancelot met Phelot's wife hurrying after her falcon, whose lunes had got entangled in a tree. She begged Lancelot to recover the bird, lest her husband slay her for its loss. Although protesting that he was "an ill climber", Lancelot stripped to his shirt and breeches, climbed the tree, and threw down the hawk. Barely had the lady recovered it when Sir Phelot came charging out of ambush to reveal that his wife had acted on his orders in setting up a ruse to trap Lancelot up a tree without arms and armor and kill him. Lancelot killed Phelot instead, with the help of a tree branch, and left the lady in a swoon. [Malory VI, 16]

PIGNORES, KING†

An ally of the Sesnes in their attack on Vandaliors Castle [Vulgate II].

PILADES†

Always eager to be in on a fight, Sir Pilades competed in the Noauz tournament. He carried a shield made in Limoges, but not otherwise described. [Chrétien de Troyes, **Lancelot**, ll. 5824-5842]

PINABEL†

One of the twelve who accompanied Alexander from Greece to Britain, where Arthur knighted them all at the outset of Count Angrs' rebellion, Pinabel was also with Alexander's party when it penetrated Windsor to capture Angrs. Though Pinabel must have survived the episode, Chrétien tells us nothing more about him. [**Cligés**, ll. 102-385; 1093-ca. 2210]

PINEL LE SAVAGE (Avarlon)

Sir Pinel was a cousin to Sir Lamorak and a knight of the Round Table. For "pure envy and hate", Pinel tried to poison Gawaine and avenge the death of Lamorak. The poison accidentally killed Sir Patrise of Ireland instead. After lying low while Mador de la Porte impeached the Queen for Patrise's death and Lancelot fought to save her life, Pinel "fled into his country" when Nimue uncovered the truth.

This may be the same Sir Pinel mentioned as "a good man of arms" who fought on Arthur's side in the battle of Bedegraine.

In Vulgate VI, the name of this mortal enemy of Gawaine's is Sir Avarlon. As Pinel in Malory, so Avarlon in the Vulgate tries to poison Gawaine with apples at a small dinner party given by the Queen. Here, Sir Gaheris de Kareheu falls accidental victim. (Do not confuse this Gaheris with Gawaine's brother.) [Malory I, 14; XVIII, 3-8; Vulgate VI]

PINTADOL† (Pentagoel)

This castle had fallen into the power of a father and three sons who were all powerful swordsmen. Ywaine defeated them and restored Pintadol to its rightful lord, but my notes do not indicate who this rightful lord was. [Vulgate IV]

Pintadol is probably in the same general part of the country as the Dolorous Tower. I would suggest Pentire Point, across the river's mouth from Padstow, Cornwall. Norden says of Pentyre Fort: "a place dowble ditched standing vpon Pentyre hill …."

Plaine de Force—see under **PLENORIUS**

PLENORIUS AND HIS BROTHERS

Sir Plenorius and his brothers—Sirs Plaine de Force, Plaine de Amours, Pillounes, Pellogris, and Pellandris—kept a castle at the border of Surluse. They took La Cote Male Taile and King Carados of Scotland, among others, prisoner. Lancelot defeated them and rescued their prisoners, but refused to take their castle and lands.

Plenorius became a companion of the Round Table on the same Pentecost as La Cote Male Taile, "and Sir Plenorius' brethren were ever knights of King Arthur." Plaine de Force also made it to the Round

Table. Eventually Plenorius followed Lancelot into exile and was made Earl of Foise, but Malory seems not to tell us what happened to the other brothers. [Malory IX, 7-9; XIX, 11; XX, 5, 18]

PLUERE, CASTLE

Its lord was one Sir Breunor, not to be confused with Sir Breunor le Noir, who is the good La Cote Male Taile.

Here Tristram, Isoud, Governail, and Bragwaine stopped when Tristram was bringing La Beale Isoud back from Ireland to Cornwall for King Mark. They found that Sir Breunor kept this custom: whenever any knight came by with a lady, they had a beauty contest between the newcomer and Breunor's own lady. "An thy lady be fairer than mine", quoted Sir Breunor, "with thy sword smite off my lady's head; and if my lady be fairer than thine, with my sword I must strike off her head." Afterward the two knights would fight, and whichever won would kill the other and keep the castle and surviving lady. When La Beale Isoud proved the fairer, Tristram took Breunor at his word and, reasoning that the lady was as guilty as her lord, struck off her head. It is a relief to record that Tristram killed Breunor afterward in the combat, so that Breunor did not go to court and become a companion of the Round Table, as did so many former villains and enemies of Arthur after being defeated by one of Arthur's knights.

Malory makes Breunor the father of "Sir Galahad the haut prince", almost certainly Duke Galeholt, who came with the King of the Hundred Knights to avenge his father's death, but dropped the project on learning what a custom Breunor had maintained. Presumably Galeholt took the castle and disposed of it as he wished, and the custom almost certainly stopped with Breunor's death. [Malory VIII, 24-27]

There is no reference to any storm that might have blown Tristram off course on this voyage. Therefore, Pluere was probably on the coast of Cornwall or southern Wales. Leaving Ireland from Waterford Harbor would give them less open water to cross, though leaving from Cork Harbor would also have been possible. Wales may be growing overloaded with castles, and I'm not sure I like to put Pluere near Gore and Stranggore. Mark's country, on the other hand, was likely still a bit more wild and less under Arthur's influence. For Pluere, I think I would go for some site around Barnstaple Bay in present-day Devonshire.

POITIERS

In Chrétien's time, Poitiers was apparently known for its armor: Meliagrant's helmet had been made there. [**Lancelot**, ca. l. 3520]

POMEGLAY† (Port Nelgay)

A castle near the frontier of Gore [Vulgate IV].

POMELEGLOI, LADY OF†

See under the Lady of Noauz. Either or both of these ladies might have been independent heiresses or widows, as willing as anyone else to treat their tournament as a proving ground for potential husbands. There is also the chance that they were ruling castles in the absence of husband, father, or brother, who might or might not have been killed adventuring—a state of things that must have affected quite a few ladies for longish intervals of their lives, and which helps explain love affairs of married dames.

POMITAIN

Duke Galeholt gave this island as a gift to King Marsil of Pomitain [Malory X, 44]. Assuming it was one of the Long Isles, and that the Long Isles were Islay, Jura, Kintyre, and Arran, I would make Arran Pomitain. It might, of course, have been another of Galeholt's conquests entirely.

POPE

The reigning Pope took a hand (by messengers) in Arthur's affairs, as in the affairs of other kings, often enough that he must be recognized both as a force and as a character—or perhaps, since Pope follows Pope as more than one character—in the Arthurian saga. For instance, it was the Pope who ordered Arthur to be reconciled with Guenevere in the matter of 'the false Guenevere' (see Genievre, Bertholai). It was also the Pope who ordered Arthur to be reconciled with his wife after Lancelot rescued her from the stake, the Pope's command reaching them while Arthur besieged them in Joyous Garde.

Arthur met the current pontiff in person when he conquered Rome and "was crowned emperor by the pope's hand, with all the royalty that could be made, and sojourned [in Rome] a time." [Malory V, 12; XX, 13; Vulgate etc.]

"PORTIA"†

On his way to the Sword Bridge into Gore, Lancelot encountered a most beautiful lady who offered him hospitality for the night on condition that he sleep with her. Agonizing over it, but seeing no other way to pursue his quest—presumably because he needed shelter for the night—he promised to do as she asked. Her castle was spacious and well appointed, but she and Lancelot seemed to be entirely alone in it, with neither squire nor servant. This in itself signals strangeness in a milieu where privacy was not only rare but seldom sought for its own sake by anyone except the religious. Lancelot saw no one else at all until, dutifully going to her bedroom, he found her apparently about to be raped by one rough knight while two more knights and four men-at-arms stood by. Lancelot wreaked havoc upon them until the lady called them off, for they were in fact her servants and the whole thing had been staged. She and Lancelot then lay down together in a fine bed in the middle of the hall, but he kept his shirt on and she her chemise. At last, understanding his unease, she took pity and left him alone in bed. Next day she asked to go with him for some distance, if he would escort her acording to an old custom of Logres that any knight who molested an unescorted damsel was held in disgrace everywhere forever, but if she were escorted, he had only to defeat her escort in order to do as he wished with her. Knowing his own worth, Lancelot promised to keep her safe. On their way, they found a gold and ivory comb which "Portia" somehow recognized as Guenevere's. Overjoyed, Lancelot took the golden hairs from it and kept them as a cherished treasure, calmly giving the comb to "Portia" with never a thought that his lady the queen might have thanked him for its return. Farther along, they met the "Young Knight of the Meadow", who had long loved "Portia" and announced his delight at finding her under circumstances that would allow him to take her. To get better ground for fighting, however, they went on to a meadow, where the "Young Knight's" father sat on a Spanish sorrel watching his people at backgammon, chess, dice games, rounds and jigs, singing, tumbling, leaping, and wrestling—not just "frivolous" pastimes, as the author assures us. This "Old Knight of the Meadow" talked his son into postponing the combat until they had followed the lady and strange knight long enough to take his measure. Arriving at the "Church of the Tombs" and learning from its monk that Lancelot had just moved a marble slab that should have needed at least seven strongmen to budge it, thus proving his identity as the man who would free the foreign prisoners of Gore, the "Knights of the Meadow" prudently returned home. For her part, "Portia", piqued because Lancelot would not tell her his name, only that he came from King Arthur's realm, quitted him soon after they left the church. [Chrétien de Troyes, **Lancelot**, ll. 941-2023]

Chrétien's translator and commentator D.D.R. Owen remarks in a note that the episode defies any logical explanation. To me it looks crystalline: I could wish everything in the romance to be equally obvious, if I didn't suspect the work of being comedy on various levels. The neighboring knight's attentions have so wearied this lady that in order to rid herself of him she is ready to sell her body to some other champion. The apparent absence of any other people in her castle is meant to lend credence to the danger of her being raped in her own bedroom. The staged assault is a test of Lancelot's prowess. Seeing him not only superb at fighting, but ready to protect her even without his own sexual involvement, makes her willing to waive the "you must sleep with me" condition. When she asks to accompany him under the peculiar custom described above, she hopes that her unwanted suitor will try to take her away and end up decisively trounced by her new escort. The pique which finally causes her to leave Lancelot probably owes as much to the fact that this battle never occurs as to his refusal to tell her his name.

It remains possible if not probable that, in some lost source of Chrétien's, the original version of this episode constituted a further test of Lancelot's worthiness to enter the "land from which no stranger returns." For this reason, and because her castle lies near the marches of Gore, "Portia" seems to me a suitable name for this lady.

'PREMIER CONQUIS', KING†

He was one of the two allies whom Duke Galeholt loved and trusted most; the other was the King of the Hundred Knights [Vulgate III].

PRIAMUS

A Saracen knight of Tuscany, descended from Alexander, Hector, Joshua, and Macabaeus, he was the "right inheritor of Alexandria and Africa, and all the out isles." In Arthur's war against Emperor Lucius, the Saracens were allies of Rome, and Gawaine encountered and fought Sir Priamus in Italy. They wounded each other almost to death, but luckily Priamus had a balm which healed their wounds within an hour; this same balm was the only thing that could cure a wound from Priamus' sword. Priamus eagerly converted to Christianity, became a companion of the Round Table, and was made Duke of Lorraine. He was among those killed when Lancelot rescued Guenevere from the stake. [Malory V, 10-12; XX, 8]

PRIAMUS' BALM

When wounds were anointed with this balm and then washed from a vial of the four waters that came out of Paradise, the wounds healed within an hour. This worked for any wound; it was also the only way wounds from Priamus' sword could be staunched. [Malory V, 10; see Priamus' Sword.]

Lynette may have gotten this balm from Priamus and used it to heal at least one knight of her own. Since her ointment seems to have required no washing with the four waters of Paradise, however, I imagine she had her own magical healing potion.

PRIAMUS' SWORD

Only Sir Priamus' balm could staunch the bleeding of a wound made with his sword. Priamus was a Saracen whom Gawaine encountered in Italy during Arthur's war against Rome; he converted to Christianity and became a knight of the Round Table. [Malory V, especially chapter 10]

PRIDWEN†

Arthur's shield, bearing an image of the Virgin Mary [Geoffrey of Monmouth, as quoted by Miller, p. 150].

"PRINTEMPS, ÉTÉ, & AUTOMNE"

One of these damsels was sixty years old or more and wore a golden garland about her white hair; the second was thirty years old and wore a gold circlet about her head; the third was fifteen years old and wore a garland of flowers. They waited by a fountain in the forest of Arroy, and when Ywaine, Gawaine, and Marhaus came by, the damsels put themselves forward as guides for a year of adventuring. Ywaine chose the oldest, "for she hath seen much, and can best help me when I have need." Marhaus chose the thirty-year-old, and Gawaine thanked them for leaving him the youngest. Very likely these damsels were of supernatural origin in early versions of the tale or in the models from which Malory drew them, but in Malory's account they behave like ordinary women with no special powers aside from knowing their way around the territory.

"Printemps" ("spring") seems an appropriate name for the fifteen-year-old, "Été" ("summer") for the thirty-year-old, and "Automne" ("autumn") for the sixty-year-old.

"Printemps" soon grew disgruntled with Gawaine for not riding in to help Sir Pelleas right away, whether Pelleas wanted help or not, so she went off with another knight. "Été" brought Marhaus to the Duke of South Marches, whom he won for Arthur; to Lady de Vawse's tournament, where he won the prize circlet of gold; and to the lands of Earl Fergus, where he slew the giant Taulurd. "Automne" brought Ywaine to the Lady of the Rock, for whom he fought Sirs Edward and Hue of the Red Castle, so both the older damsels showed their knights good adventure. At the year's end all three knights and damsels returned to the fountain from whence they had set out, "Printemps" coming either with the knight for whom she had left Gawaine or perhaps by herself. Then the knights "departed from the damosels", who presumably settled down to await three more champions. [Malory IV, 18-28]

Proud Castle—see **ORGULOUS CASTLE**

Proud Knight (Maid) of ...—see **HAUGHTY KNIGHT (MAID) OF ...**

"PRUDENTIA, DAME"†

When Ywaine and "Secunda" come to Pesme Avanture, the townspeople anger him with taunts and insults. At length a sensible elderly lady explains that they are only trying to scare him away for his own safety, and that for their own safety none of them dare shelter him. Although her courteous advice deters him no more than the other people's taunts, he replies to her with courtesy matching her own before he, his damsel, and his lion proceed to the castle. [Chrétien de Troyes, **Yvain**, ll. 5142-ca.5180]

Puceles, Chastel as†—see **DAMES, CHASTEL AS and CASTLE OF MAIDENS**

PUIS DE MALOHAUT†

From the name, this town has to have been in the subkingdom of Malahaut. See also Malahaut, Malohaut.

Queen's Knights—see under **GUENEVERE**

QUENEDIC, SON OF KING†

Among Arthur's knights in the list Chrétien de Troyes begins in line 1691 of **Erec & Enide**.

Quinqueroi, Red Knight of—see **RED KNIGHT FROM THE FOREST OF QUINQUEROI**

QUINTAOÑA

According to Don Quixote, the honorable Lady Quintaoña was the finest cupbearer England ever had, and served as confidante and go-between for Lancelot and Guenevere [Cervantes, **Don Quixote**, Part I, Chapters 13 and 49]. Don Quixote may well have known some actual tradition from outside his own creator's head: see under Arthur.

Quintareus—see **YOUTH OF QUINTAREUS**

Raginel—see **GUINDOEL**

RAGNELL, DAME†

Arthur had fallen into the power of the Grim Baron, Gromer Somer Joure, who made him swear to return in a year and a day and either bring the correct answer to the riddle "What is it women love best?" or meet his death. While searching for the answer, Arthur met in Inglewood Forest a lady carrying a lute and riding a beautiful, richly caparisoned palfrey—but the woman herself was incredibly ugly and hideous. The Foul Ladye was Dame Ragnell, Gromer's sister (though she did not tell Arthur that), and she gave Arthur the answer to the riddle in return for his and Gawaine's promise that Gawaine would wed her. (The answer to the riddle is generally given as 'Women most desire to have power over men,' or 'To have their own will in all things.' I suspect the answer might just as well be stated, 'Women most desire exactly the same thing that men most desire.') Gromer reluctantly sparing Arthur because of Ragnell's answer to the riddle, she came along to the King's court at Carlisle, insisting on her full rights.

Though Guenevere begged her to be married secretly and privately, to spare Gawaine disgrace, Dame Ragnell calmly insisted on a full public ceremony with all the trimmings, and further set off her ugliness with a bridal dress worth three thousand gold pieces. At the marriage feast she enjoyed herself with hearty bad manners, gobbling down as much as any other six guests together. When, at last, she and Gawaine were alone in the bridal chamber, she demanded her marital rights, pointing out, "If I were beautiful, you wouldn't even have worried about whether we were married or not." When he turned to give her what she asked, he beheld one of the most beautiful women he could ever have imagined. She then explained that he could choose whether to have her beautiful at night for himself alone and ugly by day in the sight of the world, or beautiful by day and ugly by night. Stymied, or at least pretending to be, he gave the choice back to her. His generosity broke the enchantment completely—her stepmother had transformed her into an ugly hag until the best man in England married her and gave her control over his body and goods.

She remained beautiful by day and night both, and of all the wives and paramours he had in his lifetime, Gawaine loved her best. She became mother of Sir Guinglain (Gingalin) and obtained Arthur's promise of mercy for her brother. Alas, she lived only five years after her wedding. [**The Wedding of Sir Gawain and Dame Ragnell**, a Middle English metrical romance. A good prose translation and critical comments appear in Louis B. Hall's **The Knightly Tales of Sir Gawain**. Glennie mentions the Foul Ladye; Chaucer, John Gower, Howard Pyle, and no doubt many others have used the tale or a variant of it through the centuries.]

RAINDURANT†

Son of the old woman of Tergalo and a most valiant knight, he rode decked out in blue silk to be unhorsed by Erec in the tournament between Evroic and Tenebroc [Chrétien de Troyes, **Erec & Enide**, ll. 2171-2214]

RED CASTLE

Sirs Edward and Hue of the Red Castle had extorted a barony from the Lady of the Rock [Malory IV, 26]. This probably was somewhere in the marches of Wales.

RED CITY

If King Hermance's Delectable Isle is the Spurn Head peninsula in East Riding, as I think most probable, then the Red City might be Kilnsea.

RED CITY, KING OF THE†

Erec unhorsed him, along with his saddle and the reins of his bridle, in a mighty clash at the tournament between Evroic and Tenebroc [Chrétien de Troyes, **Erec & Enide**, ll. 2171-2214].

RED KNIGHT FROM THE FOREST OF QUINQUEROI†

Usually I have abbreviated this to the Red Knight of Quinqueroi, for no better reason than brevity.

As Arthur and his people are celebrating their victory over King Rion of the Isles, the Red Knight rides into the king's hall at Carlisle, seizes Arthur's gold cup so roughly that he sluices some of its wine upon Guenevere, then rides off with it, challenging Arthur either to send a champion or else surrender his lands and become the Red Knight's vassal. Young Percivale, just arriving from his home in Wales, sees the Red Knight outside, then goes in and finds Arthur in a deep funk. The king calls the Red Knight from the Forest of Quinqueroi his worst (remaining?) enemy; moreover, the wine-stained queen has retired to her room, and the king, apparently underestimating his wife, says he fears she will die of the disgrace. (Strangely, around him, his knights seem to be laughing and joking over their banquet as if oblivious to the trouble.) Finding in Arthur's words permission to take the Red Knight's armor,

Percivale promptly goes out and challenges and kills him, thereby doing Arthur a favor. [Chrétien de Troyes, **Perceval**, ca. ll. 865-1118]

One thing we might say in the Red Knight's favor: though angered by the blunt demand of a fifteen-year-old country bumpkin for his arms and armor, he strikes the boy with the butt end of his lance instead of its iron part, intent rather on teaching him a lesson than on killing him.

'Red Knight of the Red Launds'—see **IRONSIDE**

For the other "color" knights in the story of Sir Gareth, see Percard (The Black Knight), Persant of Inde (The Blue Knight—"of the colour of Inde"), Pertolepe (The Green Knight—do not confuse with Gawaine's Green Knight, Bercilak de Hautdesert), and Perimones (The Red Knight).

Rhymer's Glen† —see **DIN DREI**

Rhymer's Tower†—see **ERCILDOUNE**

Rich Fisher—see **ARTHUR, FISHER KING, PELLAM**

Rience, King—see under **RYONS**

RING

Rings may be sent from one party to another as tokens of love, distress, identification, and so on, used as signets, and so forth. Rings are perhaps the most useful pieces of jewelry for purposes of communication or of intrigue.

Rion, King of the Isles—see **RYONS**

Ritho—see under **RYONS**

ROADAN†

One of King Lac's strongholds, which Erec calls a splendid, rich fortress built in the time of Adam when he promises it and the nearby Montrevel to Enide's father [Chrétien de Troyes, **Erec & Enide**, ll. 1320-1352]. Roadan has not yet been identified with a known town. (See Montrevel.)

ROBAIS†

One of Arthur's court cities, apparently located nine days' journey from the castle of Brandigant. (Because of the possible otherworldly overtones of the Joy of the Court—see "Garden of the Joy"—I am not sure we should understand those nine days as a geographically accurate marker.) After the adventures with which he proved that marriage had not made him any less of a knight, Erec found King Arthur in Robais with 500 of his nobles, feeling distressed because he had so few at court. [**Erec & Enide**, ll. 5260-5293]

ROBERT, SAINT†

Saint Robert was an English monk. Once, at dinner, a friend gave him a piece of bread and honey. Looking out and seeing a poor man, Robert put the bread and honey on a plate and carried it to him. Next day the plate reappeared at the monastery, hovering in the air and shining bright as gold, telling the monks that the poor man whom Robert had fed was Christ Himself. To me, this sounds so much like the Holy Grail that, even though I have never yet encountered Saint Robert in any Arthurian story, I feel he nevertheless deserves to be listed here.

I found the story, complete with an illustration of the visionary dish, in the Rev. Daniel A. Lord's **Miniature Stories of the Saints**, Book Three [©1946], one of a set of four small, thin booklets I have had since childhood (when I had them all but memorized). The **New Catholic Encyclopedia** [©1967] lists several Saint Roberts, but I could find the story of the dish under none of them; I believe, however, that the one in question must be Saint Robert of Newminster, d. June 7, 1159. His feast day (June 7) matches the one Rev. Lord gives for Saint Robert, and the year of his death falls about a generation before the earliest known written Grail romance, Chrétien's **Perceval**. I suspect that the **Golden Legend** or one of the various medieval legendaries of English saints would be the best place to check for the miracle Rev. Lord describes.

Roche Dure—see HARD ROCK, CASTLE OF THE

ROCHE, LA†

Built in the time of Vortigern, this castle was held in Arthur's time by the sorceress Camille. It had a gate near the water (or moat?). This gate closed by enchantment to all strangers, at least during Camille's tenure, and beyond it, the folk of the castle could not be harmed. This did not, however, prevent Lancelot from killing them when he got into the castle; perhaps he entered by another way, or perhaps the ring given him by the French Damsel of the Lake negated Camille's magic. La Roche was located twelve Scottish leagues from Arestueil. Camille was at least half Saxon, and allied with the Saxons. [Vulgate III]

Arestueil was apparently in Scotland, but I have not discovered where. It may be Glennie's Areclutha, the area between the Firth of Clyde and the River Clyde, just below the west end of the Antonine Wall. Possibly, but not necessarily, La Roche is Malory's Castle of the Hard Rock (Roche Dure). There may also be some connection here with Malory's Lady of the Rock (see Red Castle), but I doubt it.

For an identification of Camille's castle, King's Knot is a possibility:

> [A] singular, flat-surfaced mound within a series of enclosing embankments, which would appear to be of very great antiquity; and where, "in a sport called 'Knights of the Round Table,' the Institutions of King

> Arthur were commemorated", at least, to the close of the Mediaeval Age. [Glennie, p. 42]

Stirling Castle, also called Snowdon Castle, King's Knot, or Arthur's Round Table, is at Stirling, near the mouth of the River Forth where it empties into the Firth of Forth.

ROCHEDON, DUKE, DAUGHTER OF†

In Malory, Lancelot is released from Castle Chariot by King Bagdemagus' daughter [Malory VI, 4]. In Vulgate V, this role is taken by Duke Rochedon's daughter.

Rochedon once warred with the kingdom of Sorestan. When peace was made, Rochedon's daughter, aged five years, was betrothed to the King of Sorestan's grandson, aged six. Her parents died, and the Queen of Sorestan became her guardian. When the damsel's betrothed was killed, the queen refused to let her go, insisting instead that she marry her (the queen's) brother. The damsel freed Lancelot in return for his preventing this marriage.

When Lancelot returned to Castle Chariot as agreed with Rochedon's daughter, the queen's brother slipped away rather than fight. Lancelot forced the queen to free the damsel and restore her inheritance.

ROCHESTER

The Pope charged the Bishop of Rochester to threaten interdict if Arthur did not take Guenevere back and make peace with Lancelot [Malory XX, 13]. Rochester is in Kent.

ROCHESTER, BISHOP OF

This "noble clerk ... the French book saith, it was the Bishop of Rochester" was in Rome for some reason when the Pope charged him with carrying the threat of interdict to Britain if Arthur did not take Guenevere back and make peace with Lancelot, whom he had been besieging in Joyous Garde (Malory XX, 13].

ROCK, LADY OF THE

The sixty-year-old damsel of Arroy brought Ywaine to visit this "much courteous" lady, who complained to him of Sirs Edward and Hue of the Red Castle. They had extorted a barony from her. Ywaine fought them and restored it. [Malory IV, 26-27; compare with "Printemps, Été, and Automne."]

Rock of Canguin (Chanpguin, Sanguin)—see **CANGUIN**

ROESTOC†

Lot and his sons were on their way from Logres back to Arestuel in Scotland when they met 7000 Sesnes leading 700 prisoners on the plains of Roestoc. They battled the Sesnes, at which time Gawaine won his horse Gringolet from King Clarions, though he did not kill Clarions. [Vulgate II] Since it had both plains and a ruling lady, we are probably safe in assuming Roestoc was a subkingdom.

In the sub-county of North Riding, Yorkshire, are the north York moors, which might have been the plains of Roestoc.

ROESTOC, LADY OF†

She sems to have been Roestoc's ruler. She fell in love with Gawaine and gave him a girdle and locket when he defeated Sir Segurades for her. Gawaine subsequently gave the girdle and locket to the sister of Helain de Taningues. [Vulgate III]

When Gareth conquered Sir Sornehan, it was to the Lady of Roestoc that he sent him [Vulgate V].

Vulgate VII names a *Helyes li chatelains de Roestoc*. The "li" is masculine, and Helyes appears to be one of the rebel kings, possibly killed in battle, which makes the Lady of Roestoc either his widow or his orphaned daughter.

ROEVANT†

In this forest the Damsels of Hongrefort and Glocedon caught up with Sir Bors, making it in the same part of the island as Gore and Stranggore. Here, also, the French Damsel of the Lake appointed Bors to be on a certain day. [Vulgate IV]

ROLIAX†

Sir Meliagrant made his serf Roliax Lancelot's jailer when he locked the great knight in a solitary tower surrounded by morass. Roliax had to bring food by boat, and Lancelot had to draw up the provisions in a basket. Meliagrant's stepsister, who hated him for causing her disinheritance by King Bagdemagus, was a benefactress of Roliax's wife and thus was able to help Lancelot escape. [Vulgate IV]

RON†

Arthur's spear, "long, broad in the blade and thirsty for slaughter" [Geoffrey of Monmouth, quoted by Miller, p. 150].

"ROSSIGNOL"†

Viviane, the French Damsel of the Lake, sent two unnamed maidens to help Lancelot in Britain. Eventually, mistakenly believing Lancelot to have been killed, the maiden I call "Rossignol" took the veil and became a nun in England rather than return to the Lake. [Vulgate III]

ROUND MOUNTAIN†

Site of a hermitage near Leverzep Castle.

ROUND TABLE

Our first extant knowledge of this table appears to come from Wace's **Roman De Brut** (see D.D.R. Owen's translation of the Arthurian romances of Chrétien de Troyes, 1987, note to **Erec & Enide** l. 83). Chrétien mentions the table at least [**Erec & Enide**, ca. l. 1690; **Perceval**, ca. l. 8124], but seemingly as an already established tradition.

Turning to Malory and his immediate sources, we find that Uther Pendragon gave this table to King Leodegrance, who in turn gave it, with 100 knights, to Arthur on the occasion of Arthur's marriage to Guenevere. The full complement of the Round Table was 150 knights, but presumably this included the Siege Perilous, wherein only Galahad could sit, so that the Table was completely filled only once, briefly. For practical purposes, the full complement would have been 149. Malory remarks in his colophon that "when they were whole together there was ever an hundred and forty", possibly always allowing a few seats for worthy newcomers. At least one modern romancer has considered that Merlin and Queen Guenevere were also allowed to sit in council at the Round Table; conceivably there were 140 seats for knights, with an extra ten for King, Queen, and non-knightly counselors.

The Table itself seems to have been nonmagical, although it had symbolical significance. According to the Vulgate there were three great tables: the one at which Christ and His apostles ate the Last Supper, the one at which Joseph of Arimathea and his disciples sat when they came to Britain, and the Round Table. The roundness of the Table symbolizes the world. As is fitting to complete this symbol, the Knights of the Round Table come from all parts of Christendom and heathendom [Vulgate VI]. Even baptism may not have been a prerequisite of membership; Sir Palomides seems to have been a companion of the Round Table before his baptism. See also Sieges and Siege Perilous.

"ROWSE, CASTLE DE LA"

I took the name of the castle from its lord and lady, the Duke and Duchess de la Rowse, enemies of Arthur until Gareth Beaumains conquered the Duke, who subsequently became a companion of the Round Table [Malory VII, 31-35]. The Duke's first name was Ladinas [Malory I, 17]. Their castle would have been near Dame Lyonors' Castle Dangerous.

ROWSE, DUKE AND DUCHESS DE LA

When Gareth slipped away after the tournament at his love's Castle Dangerous, he came on a stormy night to another castle, where he identified himself as one of Arthur's knights and asked for lodging. The

Duke de la Rowse was absent, but the duchess had the young man admitted, saying, "I will see that knight, and for King Arthur's sake he shall not be harbourless." She warned him, however, that her lord had "ever been against" Arthur, and so Gareth's condition for spending the night was "that wheresomever thou meet my lord, by stigh or by street, thou must yield thee to him as prisoner." Gareth agred, with the counter-stipulation that the duke would not harm him on his surrender or, if the duke seemed about to offer injury, Gareth then retained the right to fight back. This agreement reached, the duchess and her people "made him passing good cheer." Just before he left in the morning, she asked him his name, and, when he gave it as Gareth, or Beaumains, she recognized it as the name of the knight who had fought for Dame Lyonors; apparently the de la Rowses were not only neighbors of Lynette and Lyonors, but managed to keep posted on the affairs of their neighborhood.

After a few intervening adventures, Gareth chanced to meet "a goodly knight" near or on a mountain. "Abide sir knight", said the stranger, "and joust with me." Asking his name, and learning that he was the Duke de la Rowse, Gareth tried to surrender as per his promise, but the duke replied, "... make thee ready, for I will have ado with you." At the end of an hour's sore fighting, the duke yielded to Gareth and promised to take a hundred knights and go to Arthur's court at the next feast to swear homage and fealty to the King. (De la Rowse appears to have been a true sportsman, more interested in playing the game than in accumulating prisoners or holding grudges.) The duke showed up, true to his word, at Michaelmas and obtained the favor of serving Gareth's wine at that feast. At the jousting held on that feast, "King Arthur made the Duke de la Rowse a Knight of the Round Table to his life's end, and gave him great lands to spend." [Malory VII, 31-32, 35]

One Sir Ladinas de la Rouse appears fighting on the side of Arthur, Ban, and Bors in the battle of Bedegrains. This may be the French knight Ladinas introduced a few chapters earlier at the tournament held by the three kings to celebrate their alliance. Sir Ladinas of the Forest Savage appears among the Round Table knights who go a-Maying with Guenevere and fall into Meliagrant's ambush. It is tempting to identify these three Ladinases as the same knight, and to further identify them with Gareth's Duke de la Rowse, because of the "de la Rouse", even though we must then postulate that the French Sir Ladinas not only settled into a British dukedom after Bedegraine, but for some reason (perhaps because of the May babies?) shifted his alliance away from Arthur at an early period. [Malory I, 11, 17; XIX, 1]

ROYAL MINSTER†

Queen Elaine of Benwick founded this minster and convent in Benwick, France, on the hill where the French Damsel of the Lake had taken the infant Lancelot.

RULE, LADY OF THE

All I can find of her is that she was the mother of King Pellinore's daughter Eleine [Malory III, 15].

RYONS (Rience, Rion), KING of NORGALES, IRELAND, and MANY ISLES

This charming monarch had a hobby of trimming, or "purfling", his cloak with the beards of the kings he conquered. He had already shown himself antagonistic to Arthur at the time of the first kings' rebellion, but he did not join the eleven rebelling kings, pursuing instead his "great war" on Leodegrance of Cameliard. One can well imagine that he was not popular with his fellow kings of Britain, whether they opposed Arthur or not. Not long after Bedegraine, and, as it seems, about the time Arthur acquired Excalibur, Ryons sent the young king notice that his cloak was now decorated with the beards of eleven kings who had shaved their chins as part of their homage to him, and he wanted Arthur's beard to make it an even dozen. Quipping that his beard was "full young yet to make a purfle of it", Arthur conquered Ryons instead, though not without the material assistance of Balin and Balan. Acting under the guidance of Merlin, these two knights waylaid Ryons when he took time out from besieging Castle Terrabil to ride to a tryst with the Lady de Vance. Balin and Balan smote down the king, slew more than forty of his men, and routed the remnant. Ryons yielded rather than be slain, and the brothers delivered him prisoner to Arthur.

> King Arthur came then to King Rience, and said, Sir king, ye are welcome: by what adventure come ye hither? Sir, said King Rience, I came hither by an hard adventure.

This passage suggests that, with all his faults, Ryons had a streak of ironic humor and could apply it even to himself. Ryon's brother Sir Nero continued the war at Terrabil, leading ten battalions; King Lot, apparently with the rest of his royal allies of the second rebellion in his host, was on the way to join Nero, but Merlin delayed him with a ruse, so that both rebel armies were defeated and Nero, Lot, and the other kings killed in the battle. What happened to Ryons himself does not seem to be told. [Malory I, 17, 26; II, 6, 9-10]

Chrétien de Troyes mentions King Rion of the Isles, but only in passing, after Arthur and his host have beaten him in battle. [**Perceval**, ll.

850-851] In a footnote to this passage, Ruth Cline mentions that King Rion has been identified with Geoffrey of Monmouth's giant Ritho and with the giant Rithon of Wace's **Roman De Brut**. Like Malory's Ryons, Geoffrey's Ritho bedecked himself with the beards of defeated monarchs and demanded Arthur's for his collection. Chrétien does not include this detail: might he have simply used a well known episode to indicate the time of Percivale's first arrival at Arthur's court?

The Vulgate, however, tells us that Ryons was a descendant of Hercules and was killed by Arthur in single combat [Vulgate II]. The "King of Norgales" in later episodes would therefore be a different man—I think possibly Galehodin, nephew of Duke Galeholt, although I am not sufficiently confident of this to list Galehodin among the kings. Also according to the Vulgate, Tradelmant is the grandson of the King of Norgales. Tennyson seems to identify Rience of Norgales with Uriens of Gore, possibly as much for the similarity of names as for artistic purposes. Malory's Uriens of Gore, however, is listed in the first alliance of rebel kings, while Rience is off fighting Leodegrance. This is why I prefer the alternate spelling Ryons, which is a bit less like Uriens.

RYONS' MANTLE

King Ryons of North Wales, like the Giant of Saint Michael's Mount, was trimming a mantle with the beards of kings he had conquered. He already had eleven when he sent a message that he wanted Arthur's beard to complete the project. [Malory I, 26] I do not know what became of Ryons' mantle after his defeat.

RYONS' SWORD†

This was forged by Vulcan and had once belonged to Hercules, an ancestor of Ryons. Arthur won it during the battle with Ryons before Leodegrance's city of Daneblaise. [Vulgate II]

SADOK

Malory first mentions this Cornish knight as going with Sirs Tristram and Dinas to the tournament at Castle Dangerous.

Sadok was one of Mark's men, and when Mark murdered Prince Boudwin, he sent Sadok to bring back Boudwin's escaping wife Anglides and infant son Alisander. Sadok caught up with Anglides within ten miles, but let her go on condition she raise her son to avenge his father's death (which she may have intended to do anyway). Sadok returned to Mark and told him he had faithfully drowned Boudwin's son. Years later, hearing that Alisander had just been knighted, Mark realized that Sadok had betrayed his orders. Mark and some of his knights tried to kill Sadok at once, in the castle. Sadok fought and killed four knights in Mark's presence, then escaped, Tristram, Dinas, Fergus, and the other true-hearted knights about the place being in sympathy with him. Mark sent yet another "false knight" after Sadok, and Sadok slew this one, too. Then Mark sent messages to Morgan and the Queen of Norgales, enlisting their aid against Alisander—and perhaps also against Sadok.

Sadok must have either remained at large in Cornwall or secretly returned to the vicinity, for when Mark put Tristram in prison, La Beale Isoud appealed to Sadok. Sadok and two of his cousins ambushed Mark's party near Tintagil. Sadok lost one of his cousins but slew Mark's four nephews and at least one "traitor of Magouns [Castle]", then rode on to the castles of Lyonesse and Arbray, where he joined Sir Dinas and they roused the country to rebellion. Meanwhile, Percivale effected Tristram's release, and Mark tricked Dinas into disbanding the rebellion by pretending to be about to go on Crusade at the Pope's command. Mark put Tristram back in prison, Isoud appealed to Dinas and Sadok again, and this time Sadok presumably helped Dinas put Mark into prison long enough for Isoud to deliver and escape with Tristram. It is possible that Sadok and Dinas joined Tristram and Isoud at Joyous Garde.

Malory next mentions Sir Sadok and his cousin Sir Edward at the Lonazep tournament, where he calls them cousins of Sir Gawaine. (It is possible this is a different Sadok, but I think it was probably the same, for Gawaine's mother Margawse was of Cornish birth.) Sadok became a companion of the Round Table, accompanied Lancelot into exile, and was made Earl of Surlat. [Malory VII, 26-28; X, 33, 35, 50-51, 68; XIX, 11; XX, 18]

SAFERE

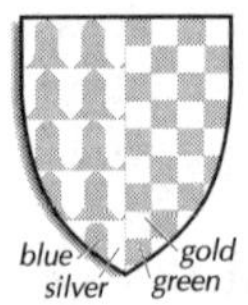

Sirs Safere and Segwarides, already christened, came with their still-unbaptized brother Palomides to the tournament at Castle Dangerous. Safere seems to appear next at a tournament given by King Carados, seemingly somewhere on the south coast, where he, Carados, and a score of other knights were struck down by young Sir Alisander le Orphelin. Safere put in another appearance at Duke Galeholt's tournament in Surluse. Between tournaments, he seems to have put in a good deal of time in errantry.

After the Lonazep tournament, somehow having acquired the shield used by Ector de Maris, Safere met, fought, and defeated one Sir Helior le Preuse and won the lady with him. Helior had just won this lady from Sir Epinogris, and Palomides arrived, to win her back for Epinogris, in time to see the fight between Helior and Safere. Palomides then fought Safere for more than an hour to win the lady; at last, admiring each other's strength, they inquired and learned each other's identities and Safere knelt to beg Palomides' forgiveness, afterward helping him escort the lady back to Epinogris. Safere then rode with Palomides for a time, but they were soon captured by men whose lord Sir Palomides had slain in the lists at Lonazep. Safere fought beside Palomides until they were defeated through weight of numbers, then spent three days in prison with him and was put on trial with him; Safere was found not guilty, while Palomides was sentenced to die.

> And when Sir Safere should be delivered there was great dole betwixt Sir Palomides and him, and many piteous complaints that Sir Safere made at his departing, there is no maker can rehearse the tenth part. ... So Sir Safere departed from his brother with the greatest dolour and sorrow that ever made knight.

He must have been equally delighted later to learn of Palomides' rescue by Lancelot.

Safere became a knight of the Round Table and continued to enjoy his tournaments, fighting at Winchester and elsewhere. He and Palomides were among Guenevere's guests at the small dinner when Patrise was poisoned. They clove to Lancelot's party when the break came and accompanied him into exile, where Safere was made Duke of Landok. [Malory VII, 26; X, 16, 36, 45, 83-84; XVIII, 3, 11, 23; XX, 17-18]

SAGRAMORE (Saigremor, Sagremor) LE DESIROUS (the Impetuous, the Hothead)

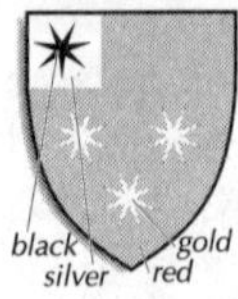

This was the name given to the knight William Bendix played to Bing Crosby's **A Connecticut Yankee in King Arthur's Court**. (In Mark Twains' novel it is Sir Kay and not Sir Sagramore who brings the Yankee to court.) The Sagramore of the romances is surely unlike William Bendix's character!

True, Sagramore does not cut all that impressive a figure in Malory. He and three other knights of Arthur's court see Lancelot riding in Kay's armor, sally out against him, and are promptly unhorsed. He goes riding in the West Country with Sir Dodinas; they meet and defeat Sir Andred, but then encounter Tristram. Sagramore scornfully remarks, "[I]t is seldom seen … that ye Cornish knights be valiant men of arms", rides against Tristram, and is again unhorsed, as is Dodinas in turn. Learning Tristram's name, they admiringly ask him to stay in their company and bid him respectful Godspeed when he rides on to rescue Segwarides' wife from Bleoberis. Sagramore and Kay chance to meet Tristram before the Castle of Maidens tournament, get into a broil when Tristram, wishing to arrive at the tournament unbruised, tries to refuse a joust, and again Sagramore is unhorsed. Once again adventuring with Dodinas, Sagramore gets it yet a third time from Tristram; Sagramore and Dodinas remount and ride after him to demand a chance for revenge, but forbear on learning that he is on his way to fight Palomides at the tomb of Lanceor and Colombe.

When Alice la Beale Pilgrim announces her intention of marrying whomever can defeat Sir Alisander le Orphelin at the ruins of La Beale Regard, Sagramore is apparently the first challenger to present himself and be defeated, whereas Alice decides to love Alisander. Sagramore is one of twenty-three knights who set out searching for Lancelot when he has gone mad on being discovered by Guenevere with Elaine of Carbonek. Lancelot unhorses Sagramore in the Winchester tournament. Sagramore is among the knights who ride a-Maying with Guenevere and fall into Meliagrant's ambush. He is one of those who try unsuccessfully to heal Sir Urre. [Malory VII, 13; VIII, 15-16; IX, 25; X, 4, 38; XI, 10; XVIII, 11; XIX, 1,11]

For all this, Sagramore seems to have been a knight of major stature among the Round Table companions, and I think it likely that Malory, unaware that his compilation/summarization/retelling would one day be the principal Arthurian sourcebook for the English-speaking world, used Sagramore's frequent unhorsing to emphasize the prowess of Lancelot, Tristram, and Alisander.

The Vulgate tells us that Sagramore was the nephew of the Emperor of Constantinople and came to Britain to join the flower of Arthur's chivalry in the first part of Arthur's reign. Sagramore "knew no limits" in a fight; however, his blood had to be up if he were to be at his fighting best. When he cooled down, he usually had a headache and a ravenous hunger. He also had an illness (epilepsy?) that manifested itself in sudden attacks, when he might think his end was near. Because of this illness, Kay gave him a second nickname besides "le Desirous": "le mort jeune" ("the dead youth"). Sagramore was rash. He was killed at last by Mordred during the last battle. [Vulgate III, V, VI]

His nickname "le Desirous" may apply to battlelust or some other trait than bed-lust (of which it would probably have taken a remarkable amount to be considered noteworthy), but Vulgate VII records the name of one of his paramours, Dame Senehauz, who gave him a daughter.

In the Idyll **Merlin and Vivien**, Tennyson applies to Sir Sagramore the story of a man who stumbles in the dark into the wrong bedroom and innocently sleeps the night through beside the woman whose room it really is, each one unaware of the other's presence until they wake in the morning. Gossip and public opinion then force them to marry, and they are happy. (Tennyson says it is a happy marriage because they are pure; a French author who retells the tale in a much later setting says they are happy because marriage is a lottery at best and they were lucky.) Arthur's court as Tennyson pictures it may have forced the parties to marry in such a situation, but I find it difficult to fit this tale of Sagramore's marriage to Arthur's court as depicted in the medieval romances.

We meet Sagramore in the works of Chrétien de Troyes: he is among Arthur's knights in the list beginning in line 1691 of **Erec & Enide**, in which romance we also see him fighting in the Tenebroc tournament [ll. 2215-2262]; he is the first of Arthur's great champions whom Cligés unhorses in the tournament near Wallingford [**Cligés**, ll. 4629-4693]; he is among the group to hear Calogrenant's story of the marvelous spring [**Yvain**, ll. 42-68]; and he figures in **Perceval** [ca. ll. 4220-4272] as the first knight to attempt bringing Percivale out of his rapt contemplation of blood-spotted snow. I regret that neither of the translations I consulted supplies the original medieval French of the soubriquet D.D.R. Owen renders as "the Impetuous" and Ruth Cline as "the Hothead"; still, I feel reasonably confident in identifying Chrétien's Sagremor with Sagramore le Desirous.

SAINT MICHAEL'S MOUNT, FRANCE

In Brittany, this hill on the tidal flats was once the haunt of a particularly repulsive giant. After slaying him, Arthur commanded Howell to build the famous church of Saint Michael's Mount. This was early in Arthur's reign, as he was setting out to conquer the Emperor of Rome. [Malory V, 5]

Do not confuse with Saint Michael's Mount, Cornwall, a similar spot east of Penzance on the south Cornish coast.

SAINT MICHAEL'S MOUNT, FRANCE, GIANT OF

One of the worst of the giants, and apparently one of the largest, he sat around naked by his fire forcing three young damsels to turn twelve babies, broached like birds on a spit, above the fire. He killed Duke Howell's wife by raping her, slitting her to the navel, which may be an indication of his size. Arthur, Kay, and Bedivere stopped to kill him and avenge the lady on their way to fight Emperor Lucius. [Malory V, 5]

According to the Vulgate, this giant wore a swordproof serpent's skin.

SAINT SAMSON'S ISLE†

According to Chrétien de Troyes, the prose **Merlin**, and the prose **Tristan**, the island where Tristram fought Marhaus. [**Erec & Enide**, l. 1248 & Owen's note to same] Presumably it lies between Britain and Ireland.

SALERNO, THREE PHYSICIANS OF†

In the Middle Ages Salerno was noted for its medical school. These three venerable graduates had the misfortune to visit Constantinople just when the Empress Fenice had secretly swallowed her nurse Thessala's potion and apparently died, in a plan to escape her wedded lord and live secretly with her lover. Examining Fenice, the chief of the three saw that she still lived. He promised, on pain of his own life, to restore her. (Whether this offer included the lives of his two companions, I cannot tell.) Demanding to be left alone with her, the three proceeded from cajolery to torture in their desperate efforts to bring her back; Thessala's potion kept her silent and immobile while they scourged her bloody and pierced her palms with molten lead. At last more than a thousand ladies, Thessala among them, peeped through a chink in the door, saw the physicians about to roast Fenice on a grill, and, outraged, broke in and killed the trio by defenestration. [Chrétien de Troyes, **Cligés**, ll. 5815-6051]

SALISBURY

The books of the Grail Adventures were kept in this city in present-day Wiltshire. Near here, also, the final battle between Arthur and Mordred took place. [Malory XVII, 23; XXI, 3] Salisbury seems to have had significance as a religious, cultural, and political center. Malory does not say that Arthur ever held court here, but it seems to me likely that he did.

SANAM, EARL

Malory seems to mention him only once, as the father of Dame Lionors (see Lyzianor). He thus became the grandfather of Arthur's bastard son Borre. Sanam may already have died, since his daughter is mentioned as the one coming to do Arthur homage after the battle of Bedegraine. [Malory I, 17]

SANDWICH

This Kentish city seems as important a port as Dover in Malory's tales. Here Arthur left for and returned from his war against the Emperor of Rome [V], and from here to Carlisle Lancelot offered to walk barefoot in penance for the war over Guenevere [XX, 16].

Sangreal—see GRAIL, HOLY

Sanguin—see CANGUIN, ROCK OF

SAPINE† (Sarpenic, Sarpetine)

A forest near the castle of Florega. Probably near Surluse; possibly near Gore. [Vulgate IV]

Saraide†—see SERAIDE

Sarpenic, Sarpetine—see SAPINE

SARRAS (Soleise?)

The Isle of Man and the Lake District work very well together as the Sarras and Waste Lands of the Grail Adventures. The Quest of Galahad and his companions ended in Sarras, and from Sarras the Grail was taken into Heaven permanently after Galahad's death. Sarras had religious and mystical associations at least from the time of Joseph of Arimathea. Vulgate I tells us that Sarras was the city from which the Saracens take their name. Evalac was the king of the island and city of Sarras when Joseph came and converted him. The island as a whole, however, does not seem to have been fully converted until Galahad's reign, if then. At the time he and his comrades arrived, Sarras was ruled by an unpleasant Pagan king named Estorause, who threw them into prison. This suggests that Sarras was a political entity as well as a mystical place, and that the secular government was unfriendly to Arthur. If Sarras is identified with Soleise, then Estorause must have succeeded the king whom Arthur and his men killed on the banks of the Humber. See also Soleise.

SAUVAGE, DAMOSEL (Dameisele)†(?)

She informed Dame Laudine, in a letter, that King Arthur intended to bring his people to the marvelous spring in Broceliande Forest. This was taken as a warning; Lunette used the information in urging Laudine to replace her newly slain husband with his slayer, Ywaine. It sounds as if the Damosel Sauvage was a spy or at least a secret friend of Laudine's, though that might be reading too much into a simple explanation of how news spread in those days. [Chrétien de Troyes, **Yvain**, ll. 1613-ca.1620]

The Damosel Savage is another name for Malory's Lynette, q.v. It could be a sort of generic tag, like "the Red Knight", etc. Or, assuming that Chrétien's Lunete became transmogrified into Malory's Lynette, someone might have misremembered to whom the name "Damosel Sauvage" actually applied.

SAUVAGE, FOREST

I have not yet come across the famous Forest Savage, or Sauvage, in my reading of Malory and the Vulgate, except as part of somebody's name: "Sir So-and-so of the Forest Sauvage." I seem to remember that T. H. White put the Forest Sauvage around Sir Ector's castle when Arthur was growing. So far I suspect that "Forest Sauvage" simply means "wild woods" and can be applied to any wooded wilderness.

See also the Wild Forest.

SAXONY, DUKE OF†

Originally, the emperor of Germany betrothed his daughter Fenice to the Duke of Saxony. When the German potentate broke his pledge in order to give her to Emperor Alis of Greece instead, the Duke of Saxony fought for her, attacking the combined armies of Greece and Germany. At last the Saxon duke agreed to formal single combat with Alis' nephew Cligés (who had slain the duke's nephew in the fighting). Seeing himself about to be defeated by the teenaged champion, the duke tried to save face by conceding early, on the pretext that it could give him no honor to defeat so young a lad, while Cligés had already won honor simply by standing up to him so long. Not even the duke's own men were fooled; yet, since the duke had, after all, had a legitimate grievance, I for one cannot help but feel some sympathy with him. [Chrétien de Troyes, **Cligés**, ll. 2669-2870, 3371-ca. 4195]

SAXONY, NEPHEW OF THE DUKE OF†

This young man served as his uncle's messenger to the court of the German emperor at Cologne, warning them that the duke would fight for Fenice. On his way out, the nephew challenged Cligés to a joust and lost. Later, by the Black Forest beside the Danube, the duke's nephew led five companions to assault Cligés and three friends as they jousted for sport near the Greek camp. In this attack the duke's nephew promptly lost his life to Cligés, but set off the one great battle between his uncle's forces and the combined armies of Greece and Germany, which led to victory for the latter. [Chrétien de Troyes, **Cligés**, ll. 2855-2955, 3395-3457ff.]

SCOTLAND

A major kingdom, Scotland probably included the territory from Hadrian's Wall northward, with nine subkingdoms: Benoye, Estrangor,

Garloth, l'Isle Estrange, the Long Isles, Lothian, the North Marches, Orkney, and Pomitain.

Chrétien de Troyes mentions that Arthur swelled his army with reinforcements drawn from Scotland. [Cligés, ca. l. 1482]

SCOTTEWATRE

Medieval name for the Firth of Forth [D.D.R. Owen, note to Chrétien's **Perceval**, l. 3675]. See Cotoatre.

Seavenshale—see SEVEN SHIELDS

SEBILE (Sebille?)†

According to Vulgate V, Sebile and Morgan were the two women most proficient in magic after the Damsel of the Lake. Instead of Malory's Queens of Gore (Morgan), Norgales, Eastland, and the Out Isles, the Vulgate account of Lancelot's kidnaping has Morgan, Sebile, and the Queen of Sorestan as the abductresses. I believe the Queens of Eastland and Sorestan are probably identical; thus Sebile may be the Queen either of Norgales or the Out Isles. Possibly, since Malory names Ryons as king of "Northgalis and Many Isles", the Queens of Norgales and the "Out Isles" were originally one and the same character, and Malory or some scribe between him and the older versions mistakenly split her in two. See also Sebille.

SEBILLE (Sebile?)†

Vulgate VII has a Sebille who seems, as nearly as I can make it out, to be the pagan queen of Sarmenie, and who may have had an affair with Sagremor (Sagramore), who was her prisoner for a while and through whom she was converted and baptized. A knight called Le Noir Chevalier Fae appears as either her consort or her enemy—I suspect the former, but could not be quite sure from the text. Sebille seems to have jouneyed to Britain with a company of knights armed in black, and she may possibly have been a warrior queen. See also Sebile.

"SECUNDA"†

Having decided that only the Knight with the Lion could champion her cause against her greedy elder sister, and being given the customary forty days to find him, the younger daughter of the late lord of Noire Espine began her quest. Pausing at a friend's home, she fell sick of grief and worry. So another damsel set out to find the knight for her. This is the maiden whom I arbitrarily call "Secunda." Though Chrétien does not give her a name, he shows her as plucky and resourceful as any knight on quest; she succeeds in locating Ywaine and his lion, visits Pesme Avanture with him, and brings him back in time for the recovered younger daughter of Noire Espine to get him to Arthur's court on the appointed day.

Considering that "Secunda" appears to be, not so much herself the friend of the damsel who needs help, as the friend or handmaid of a friend, her role in this story, though comparatively short, speaks volumes to me of the solidarity of sisterhood (using modern feminist terminology) in Chrétien's world. "Secunda" alone would be enough to give the lie to our curiously distorted idea of passive feminity in Arthurian romance. [**Yvain**, ll. 4821-5839]

SEGWARIDES (Segurades?)

Vulgate III has a Sir Segurades whom Gawaine fought and defeated on behalf of the Lady of Roestoc. Malory may have two different Sirs Segwarides, but I am going on the theory that Palomides' brother Segwarides, who was already christened by the time of Dame Lyonors' tournament at Castle Dangerous, to which he came with his brothers, is the same Segwarides who appears in Cornwall, apparently having settled there in time to become embroiled with Tristram.

After first meeting La Beale Isoud in Ireland, Tristram returned to Cornwall. Before being sent back to Ireland to bring Isoud to Mark, and thus before drinking the love potion with her, the great knight had an affair with Sir Segwarides' wife. Mark also was in love with this lady, and ambushed Tristram on his way to her one night. Tristram left Mark and his two helpers in sorry state, but was wounded himself and left some of his blood in his paramour's bed. Finding it, Segwarides threatened his wife until she told him who her lover was. Segwarides pursued Tristram, was defeated (of course), and did not dare meddle with the great knight thereafter, "for he that hath a privy hurt is loath to have a shame outward."

After Segwarides' recovery, but still before Isoud's coming to Cornwall, Bleoberis de Ganis rode into Mark's court one day and asked a boon. When Mark granted it, Bleoberis rode off with Segwarides' wife. When Segwarides got wind of it, he set off after Bleoberis and was wounded severely in the fight. Then Tristram followed and fought Bleoberis until they decided to let the lady choose between them. She said that she would not return to Tristram, since he had not come to save her at once but had let her husband chase Bleoberis first. She begged Bleoberis to take her to the abbey where Segwarides lay wounded and Bleoberis obliged. So husband and wife were reconciled, at least outwardly, and the news of Tristram's battle with Bleoberis "pleased Sir Segwarides right well."

Much later, after Tristram's marriage, when he, Isoud la Blanche Mains, and Kehydius were blown ashore near the Isle of Servage, Segwarides turned up again, traveling in the forest with an unnamed damsel. Segwarides greeted Tristram with the words:

> I know you for Sir Tristram de Liones, the man in the world that I have most cause to hate, because ye departed the love between me and my wife; but as for that, I will never hate a noble knight for a light lady; and therefore, I pray you, be my friend, and I will be yours unto my power; for wit ye well ye are hard bestead in this valley, and we shall have enough to do either of us to succour other.

This is a masterpiece of reasoning. "And then Sir Segwarides brought Sir Tristram to a lady thereby that was born in Cornwall", possibly the same damsel mentioned earlier as riding with Segwarides, "and she told him all the perils of that valley." It was the valley of the wicked Sir Nabon le Noire, and after killing him Tristram made Segwarides lord of the Isle of Servage.

Sir Segwarides turned up yet again, in company with the King of the Hundred Knights, riding by Joyous Garde when Tristram was living there with Isoud. Tristram and his friends were preparing for the Lonazep tournament and, in some apparently lighthearted jousting, Segwarides unhorsed Gareth before, as it seems, joining the merry group in Joyous Garde. (If there are indeed two knights of this name in Malory, the Segwarides who unhorsed Gareth before Joyous Garde would probably be Palomides' brother as distinct from the Segwarides of Cornwall.)

Segwarides was almost certainly a companion of the Round Table, like his brothers Palomides and Safere. He was killed during Lancelot's rescue of the Queen from the stake, which is interesting, since both Palomides and Safere clove to Lancelot's party. [Malory VII, 26; VIII, 13-18, 38-39; X, 16, 60; XX, 8]

SEGWARIDES' WIFE

Before the arrival of La Beale Isoud, Bleoberis de Ganis chose her as the loveliest lady at King Mark's court. She was an early paramour of Tristram's and also attracted the amorous devotion of Mark, but eventually chose to return to her husband. If their reconciliation lasted, she would presumably have become lady of the Isle of Servage when Segwarides became its lord. [Malory VIII, 13-18, 38-39; see Segwarides]

In his excellent novel **Tristram and Isolde: Restoring Palamede**, Erskine names this lady Phenice.

SELISES

Nephew of the King of the Hundred Knights, and "a good man of arms", Sir Selises fought in the Lonazep tournament. He may be identical with the Sir Selises of the Dolorous Tower whom Malory lists among the Round Table knights that tried to heal Sir Urre and who followed Lancelot into exile and was made Earl of Masauke. [Malory X, 67; XIX, 11; XX, 18]

The connection of Selises with the Dolorous Tower is not explained. In the Vulgate, Sir Carados' Dolorous Tower was given to Sir Melians li Gai.

Seloude—see **CELIBE**

SEMIRAMIS and HIS COMPANION†

They fought together in the Noauz tournament. Both rode dappled horses and carried identical shields: gold with sable lions. [Chrétien de Troyes, **Lancelot**, ll. 5783-5823] As far as I can see, any resemblance between Sir Semiramis and the legendary queen of Assyria is purely coincidental. Maybe Chrétien just knew the name and liked it.

SENEHAUZ†

The paramour of an apparently very minor knight named Blios, Senehauz was rescued by Sir Sagramore, who promptly engendered a daughter on her. The daughter resembled Sagramore more closely than a picture, and was sent to court to be raised by Guenevere. The daughter's name does not seem to be given, but she might have been called Senehauz after her mother. [Vulgate VII]

SENTRAILLE DE LUSHON

Sentraille was one of Tristram's knights. After Tristram had escaped the judgment of Mark and Andred by leaping out of a chapel on the sea cliffs down to the rocks below, Sentraille helped Gouvernail and Sir Lambegus pull him up again. Sentraille became a companion of the Round Table. [Malory VIII, 35; XIX, 11]

SEQUENCE†

Apparently yet another sword of Arthur's, which he used only in mortal combat. Lancelot used it in battle before the castle of La Roche, when Arthur was Camille's prisoner there. [Vulgate III]. Could it have been the sword Arthur pulled from the stone and anvil?

SERAIDE (Saraide)†

One of the maidens of Viviane, the French Damsel of the Lake, Seraide seems to have held a high place in the Damsel's service. Her grasp of magic, while doubtless far short of Viviane's, Nimue's, or Morgan's, was practical and useful.

At Viviane's instructions, Seraide went to rescue young Lionel and Bors from the court of King Claudas. Claudas resisted giving the children up, and during the fray the two boys mortally wounded Claudas' son Dorin. Seraide, throwing herself between the children and Claudas, received a grievous wound in her own right cheek from the king's sword. Through a magical ruse, however, she did escape with the boys to the Lake, where their cousin Lancelot treated them as equals. Seraide became Sir Lionel's lady in particular and acted as mentor and friend to all four kinsmen—Lionel, Bors, Lancelot, and the British-born Ector de Maris.

After Duke Galeholt's death, Seraide took his sword to Bors. When Lancelot found Galeholt's tomb, it was Seraide who kept him from killing himself in grief and told him that Viviane commanded him to take Galeholt's body to Joyous Garde. [Vulgate III, IV]

Seraphe—see **NASCIEN**

SERVAGE, ISLE OF

In Book VIII, 37, Malory calls it an isle. In VIII, 38 he calls it also a valley and places it in Wales.

SERVANUS, SAINT†

Young Saint Kentigern was put under the discipline of Servanus at the monastery of Culross [Glennie].

SERVAUSE LE BREUSE

Malory seems to mention this companion of the Round Table only once, among the would-be healers of Sir Urre. The single mention, however, describes an interesting peculiarity:

> Sir Servause le Breuse, that was called a passing strong knight, for as the book saith, the chief Lady of the Lake feasted Sir Lancelot and Servause le Breuse, and when she had feasted them both at sundry times she prayed them to give her a boon. And they granted it her. And then she prayed Sir Servause that he would promise her never to do battle against Sir Launcelot du Lake, and in same wise she prayed Sir Launcelot never to do battle against Sir Servause, and so either promised her. For the French book saith, that Sir Servause had never courage nor lust to do battle against no man, but if it were against giants, and against dragons, and wild beasts. [Malory XIX, 11]

SEVEN SHIELDS, CASTLE OF THE† (Seavenshale, Sewing Shields)

Seven Shields was Sir Walter Scott's choice for the name of this, another site beneath which Arthur and his knights are said to lie sleeping.

It is in Northumberland, on or almost on the Wall, apparently on the northernside; Seven Shields is perhaps ten miles west and slightly north of Hexham on the river Tyne.

SHIELD

You can have all sorts of fun with shields. You can trade them and seem to be somebody else, cover them and get into fights anonymously, or, if you are a damsel, show up at court with one and ask for a knight to finish the dead original owner's quest. You can make veiled innuendoes on shields which you give knights to carry unsuspectingly.

Lancelot left his own shield with Elaine of Astolat while he borrowed her brother's; she nurtured her love for Lancelot while caring for his shield, found out from Gawaine (who recognized the device) the identity of her hero, and eventually died of love. A shield can even be used as an offensive weapon to finish a fight successfully after your sword has been lost or broken. The uses of shields are limited only by imagination.

Not infrequently, knights refer to having received their shields as gifts from their ladies. A young knight bore a blank shield until he had earned the right to a coat of arms.

See also the Appendix, Coats of Arms.

SHIP

Magical or mystical ships figure very largely in the Adventures of the Grail. The pattern is that an unmanned ship comes ashore, you find it and get in, and it takes you somewhere, usually to a physical and/or mystical adventure. It can be quite dangerous.

Chief of the holy ships is Solomon's ship. The vessels need not, however, be holy or mystical. In Malory IV, Morgan le Fay apparently sends a similarly mysterious ship to entrap Arthur. The ships need not even be magical. In Malory X, 59, Tristram and Palomides find "a rich vessel hilled over with red silk" in which lies the body of the murdered King Hermance, with a letter in his hand telling his story and asking for an avenger. Here there seems to be no magic, simply human device. Rembember also the barget in which, at her own dying request, the body of Elaine of Astolat is placed to go to Camelot; her barge, however, is steered and rowed by a bargeman. [Malory XVIII, 19-20]

At the dying request of Percivale's saintly sister Amide, Galahad and his companions put her body into a barge covered with black silk and set it adrift on the sea, to meet them again in Sarras at the end of the Grail Adventures. Lancelot, finding and entering this ship, "felt the most sweetness that ever he felt, and he was fulfilled with all thing [sic] that he thought on or desired." The Lord fed him as the Israelites were fed with manna, and he stayed with the ship for many months, during which time he was joined for half a year by his son Galahad. Occasionally they left the vessel for a time to adventure on land. About a month after Galahad quit the ship for good, it brought Lancelot to Carbonek, leaving him there to his own Grail visions while it proceeded on to Sarras with Amide's body, which had apparently remained fresh and sweet in the best tradition of saint's bodies. [Malory XVII, 11, 13-14, 21]

SHOREHAM

Chrétien names this as the place from which Sir Alexander embarked on his return to Greece. Since he here took his leave of Arthur's entire court, Shoreham might have been another of Arthur's court cities. [**Cligés**, ll. 2419-2456] Collier's **World Atlas and Gazetteer** [©1942] lists no Shoreham anywhere except one in Addison County, Vermont; I should guess, however, that settlers brought the name to Vermont from England.

"SHREWD DAMSEL AT THE WINDOW"†

When Lancelot first fought Meliagrant in Gore, the queen's champion was still suffering so much from the wounds he had sustained crossing the Sword Bridge that Meliagrant actually began at one point to get the upper hand. A shrewd damsel who was at the window of the keep watching the battle with Guenevere, Bademagu, and others asked the Queen for her champion's name, learned it, and used it to call down to him and draw his attention to the fact that Guenevere was looking on. She then had to call down a second time in order to get him to return his attention from Guenevere to Meliagrant, but after that Lancelot pulled himself together and soon had Meliagrant on the run. [Chrétien de Troyes, **Lancelot**, ll. 3638ff.]

This damsel seems to be one of the foreign prisoners in Gore, or I would feel tempted to identify her with King Bademagu's daughter.

See also "Elinor."

SIEGE

Sieges—the seats at the Round Table—had a magical property. The name of its proper occupant appeared in letters of gold on the back of each chair, seemingly whenever he was near enough to come in and take his seat. Nevertheless, when a knight was known dead, his successor was chosen by natural means—appointed by the King on the advice of counselors, or possibly elected. There must have been a waiting list of candidates.

Ideally, companions of the Table should not fight each other, except "for love" or at tournaments. There are, however, numerous instances of Table knights killing their comrades in battle, frequently through the careless but common habit of fighting first, with a strange or a covered shield, and then of identifying yourself to your opponent, or checking to learn his identity after the damage has been done. There seems also to have been some rivalry, especially in the early days of Arthur's court, between the companions of the Round Table and an auxiliary company of Arthur's warriors known as the Queen's Knights. Also, of course, there was inevitable jealousy and friction between personalities. Lancelot and Gawaine themselves, for instance, were dear friends; but some of their respective followers were capable of vicious bloodshed in the argument of which of the two great knights was the greater.

The Knights of the Round Table repeated their vows every Pentecost.

SIEGE PERILOUS

If you want to get rid of someone, make him vow to sit in this, the forbidden seat at the Round Table. The Siege Perilous would also be useful to suicide with the maximum dramatic effect. Nobody but Galahad could sit in this chair, and anyone else who tried it was devoured by a column of fire. In the Vulgate, one knight, Sir Brumant l'Orguilleus, came all the way from France to sit in the Siege Perilous. He knew he had made a silly, boastful vow, and wept all the way to the Siege, but a vow was a vow. Lancelot, sitting in the chair next to the Siege Perilous, did not move away when the fire descended, and was not even singed by the holocaust that devoured Brumant.

The Siege Perilous was to be filled by Galahad 454 winters after the Passion of Our Lord [Malory XIII, 2]. This gives us a date for the era of Malory's Arthur.

SIGN OF THE CROSS

This, of course, is a gesture rather than a tangible object. It is a prayer made with the right hand. (I imagine the left would do if the right were lost or disabled.) It is natural and available to all—at least to all Christians—yet its effects can be remarkable in the field of mystical temptation. It is readily available and very efficacious in dispelling fiends and breaking diabolic delusions. (See, e.g., Malory XIV, 6, 9; possibly XVI, 12)

SILVER LEG, MAN WITH THE†

As the Ferryman of Canguin led Gawaine into the castle proper, they passed a one-legged man sitting on a bunch of rushes (Owen's translation) or gladioli (Cline's) at the foot of the stairs. His missing limb had been replaced with one either made of or coated with silver, decorated with bands of gold and jewels. He sat silently whittling on an ashwood stick. After passing him, the ferryman told Gawaine that this one-legged man enjoyed a rich income from his various great properties, and that Gawaine would have heard some disturbing things had the ferryman not been present when they encountered him. This curious silver-legged man plays no further role in what Chrétien left us, but he has clearly provided delightful fodder for Chrétien scholars. Is he an otherworldly figure? The shadow of an old Pagan god? Does his missing leg somehow connect him with the maimed Fisher King? Might some old scribal error or mistranslation even have transferred the silver, gold, and jewels to his artificial leg from a chessboard he originally had? [**Perceval**, ca. ll. 7649-7675 & Owen's & Cline's notes]

"Silver Pipe, Fountain of the"—see "FOUNTAIN OF THE SILVER PIPE"

SILVER SHIELDS, THREE†

These shields were marked with one, two, and three red bands respectively. The French Damsel of the Lake sent them to Lancelot when he was conquering La Dolorous Garde. The shields were to renew, double, and treble his strength when he used them. [Vulgate III]

SILVER TABLE

In Carbonek, the Grail rested on a silver table. Sometimes it also traveled on this table [cf. Malory XIII, 18, and XVII, 21].

SLEEPING POTION

Morgan le Fay gave Sir Alisander a drink which put him into wakeless slumber for three days and three nights. During this time the enchantress could transport him to the castle La Beale Regard. [Malory X, 37]

Small Sleeves, Maiden with the—see **LITTLE SLEEVES, MAID WITH**

Snowden, Mount—see **VALBONE**

SOLEISE (Sarras?)

Malory seems to mention Soleise only once, listing it with Denmark, Ireland, the Vale, and the Isle of Longtains [IV, 2]. The inclusion of Denmark and Ireland suggests that the other three were also outside the larger British Isle. The kings of these five countries united to war against Arthur, who defeated and killed them beside the Humber River. The Isle of Man is enough outside Great Britain to count as "foreign", and is in a good position for alliance with Ireland; hence, it might make a good Soleise. See also Sarras.

SOLOMON'S SHIP

When King Solomon learned through a vision that his descendant (Galahad) would be a marvelously good and pure knight, he and his wife made a ship for this descendant to find. The wife, although called an "evil" woman, first advised making this ship and seems to have done most of the planning. The ship was fashioned of the best and most durable wood, covered with rot-proof silk, and stocked with wonderful items:

King David's sword.

A marvelous scabbard for the sword.

Girdles of hemp for the sword and scabbard.

Three spindles: one white, one red, one green.

A great rich bed, covered with silk, to hold all the above.

A purse containing a writ to explain the origin of everything.

The night after the ship was completed, an angel came to sprinkle it with water from a silver vessel and write words on the sword hilt and ship. The words written on the ship were:

> Thou man that wilt enter within me, beware that thou be full within the faith, for I ne am but Faith and Belief.

Or, according to another version:

> Thou man, which shall enter into this ship, beware thou be in steadfast belief, for I am Faith, and therefore beware how thou enterest, for an thou fail I shall not help thee.

(Malory gives both versions, one in XVII, 2 and one in XVII, 7.)

Solomon beheld the angel in a dream-vision. On awakening and reading the words on the ship, he himself feared to enter in, and so the vessel was shoved into the sea to move rapidly away of itself.

KING DAVID'S SWORD

Following his wife's advice, Solomon had his father David's sword repommelled with a rich pommel subtly made. The pommel was of stone, with "all manner of colours that any man might find, and everych of the colours had divers virtues." One scale of the haft was a rib of a serpent "which was conversant in Calidone, and is called the Serpent of the fiend." The virtue of this bone is that the hand that handles it will never be weary nor hurt. The Vulgate names the serpent Papagustes and says its virtue is to guard the bearer from excessive heat. The other scale of the haft was a rib of a fish called Ertanax—Orteniaus in the Vulgate—which lived in the Euphrates. Whoever handled the bones of Ertanax would never be weary and, while handling it, would think only of the task before him at the time; as the Vulgate explains this, he would forget everythink except the purpose for which he drew the sword. On the sword were the words:

> Let see who shall assay to draw me out of my sheath, but if he be more hardier than any other; and who that draweth me, wit ye well that he shall never fail of shame of his body, or to be wounded to the death.

Attempting to draw the sword had brought grief to various men through the ages, and Galahad would not have tried it had not Amide assured him the sword was meant for him. Amide gave the name of the sword as The Sword with the Strange Girdles.

THE SCABBARD

It was made of serpent's skin, and written on it in gold and silver were the words:

> He which shall wield me ought to be more harder than any other, if he bear me as truly as me ought to be borne. For the body of him which I ought to hang by, he shall not be shamed in no place while he is girt with this girdle, nor never none be so hardy to do away this girdle; for

> it ought not be done away but by the hands of a maid, and a maid all the days of her life, both in will and in deed. And if she break her virginity she shall die the most villainous death that ever died any woman.

On the other side, which was red as blood, was written in letters black as coal:

> He that shall praise me most, most shall he find me to blame at a great need; and to whom I should be most debonair shall I be most felon, and that shall be at one time.

This last referred to the adventure of Nascien, some time before Galahad and his companions found the ship. Nascien had drawn the sword to defend himself against a giant, but the sword broke. Later Nascien met his brother-in-law Mordrains, who mended the sword. (So says Malory, but I much suspect that in this passage Malory got the names of Nascien and Mordrains reversed, so that Mordrains was the one who drew the sword, and Nascien the one who mended it.) Amide named this scabbard Mover of Blood "for no man that hath blood in him shall never see the one part of the sheath which was made of the Tree of Life." In the Vulgate, the scabbard is named Memory of Blood, which seems to make slightly more sense.

HEMP GIRDLES

Solomon's wife provided hemp girdles because she had no worthy materials to sustain so high a sword. The hemp girdles were to be replaced by a worthy maiden damsel, as mentioned in the writing on the scabbard. When Amide had learned the adventure that was ordained for her, she cut off her hair and wove it, along with golden threads, into a girdle, set with gems and a golden buckle. She carried this girdle with her in a box until her time came to use it for girding David's Sword to Galahad's side.

THE SPINDLES

When Adam and Eve were driven from Paradise, Eve carried along the branch on which the forbidden fruit was hung, and planted it, "for she had no coffer to keep it in." It grew into a tree that remained white as snow as long as Eve remained a virgin, but when God bade Adam "know his wife fleshly as nature required" and they lay together begetting children under this same tree, its wood turned green. (Despite the premium put upon virginity in these legends, the Original Sin in this Medieval version can hardly have been sex!) Later Cain slew Abel under the tree's branches, and its wood became red. When Solomon's wife made a carpenter take enough wood from the tree to make the spindles, the tree bled on being cut. Using the natural colors of the wood, the carpenter was able to fashion a white, a green, and a red spindle.

(How were all three colors preserved? At first glance, it seems as if they should only have been able to make red spindles. Yet once, walking in the woods in winter, I really did find a kind of triple-trunked bush with one slim trunk that looked red, one green, and one whitish, growing from a single base. The likeliest explanation to the problem of the spindles, however, was suggested by my mother: each time only the outer layer of the tree changed color, and so grew until the next color change, so that the inner rings remained white, the middle green, and the outermost red.)

I do not know why spindles, in preference to anything else, were made from this tree. Perhaps in another version the spindles had something to do with the making of the new girdle by the pure damsel. The Vulgate tells us that they were arranged in, apparently, an "H" shape, the upright spindles white and red, the horizontal one green. [Perhaps symbolizing the "yoke of Christ?"]

THE BED and THE PURSE

They seem purely utilitarian. [Malory XVII, 2-7; Vulgate VI]

Solomon's would appear to be the same ship that picks up Galahad and his two companions again three days after they leave Carbonek and takes them to Sarras. This time, when they come on board, they find the Grail, covered with red samite, standing there on its silver table. [Malory XVII, 21]

SOREDAMORS†

According to Chrétien de Troyes, Soredamors was Gawaine's sister, Alexander's wife, and the mother of Cligés. We first meet her as Guenevere's handmaiden on the ship carrying Arthur, his queen, and Alexander across the Channel for a royal visit to Brittany. Although her name means "gilded over with love", Soredamors had always scorned that emotion until meeting Alexander. Then each fell desperately in love with the other but, afraid to reveal their hearts, both suffered in secret, giving their author opportunity to describe their yearnings and soliloquies at great and quite possibly satirical length, until Guenevere shrewdly brought them face to face and advised them to speak up. This interview took place immediately after Alexander had captured the rebel Count Angrs of Windsor, so the marriage was celebrated at once along with the victory. Soredamors was pregnant with Cligés five months later. He was apparently her only child. She returned to Greece with her husband and son on the death of the old emperor, Alexander's father. For some years Alexander was emperor in all but title; he died of a sickness while their son was still a boy, and Soredamors soon succumbed to a broken heart. [Chrétien de Troyes, **Cligés**, ll. 441-2621]

I have yet to find Gawaine given a sister in any later romance. It seems curious that so few, if any, later romancers followed Chrétien in this, but much of **Cligés** is only peripherally an Arthurian romance, which may help explain Soredamors' disappearance from the cast.

Sorelois—see SURLUSE

SORESTAN (Eastland)

According to the Vulgate, Sorestan borders Norgales "par evers" Sorelois (Surluse). I do not know whether this means Sorestan was between Surluse and Norgales, or Surluse between Sorestan and Norgales, or both Surluse and Sorestan bordering Norgales; I think the last is the most likely, and suggest Sorestan be approximately the rest of Chester excluding the peninsula proposed for Surluse.

In Vulgate V, Morgan, Sebile, and the Queen of Sorestan kidnap Lancelot. This seems to be the episode Malory gives in Book VI, 3-4, although Malory has four queens: Morgan and the Queens of Norgales (Norgales), Eastland, and the Out Isles. It seems likely that the Queen of Sorestan should be identified with the Queen of Eastland, and, thus, that Malory's Eastland is the Sorestan of the Vulgate.

Malory's Eastland, on the other hand, might for convenience's sake be considered separately from Sorestan. Using this theory, Lincolnshire might be called Eastland. Or the name might be given to the easternmost bulge of the island, including Norfolk, Suffolk, and Essex (which name, of course, derives from "East Sex"). Eastland might, indeed, include all the counties listed as raised by Mordred in Malory XXI, 26: Kent, Southsex, Surrey, Estsex, Southfolk, and Northfolk, which would all be sub-subkingdoms.

Sorestan, Queen of—see EASTLAND, QUEEN OF

SORHAUTE

Malory mentions this in I, 18: "a city that hight Sorhaute, the which city was within King Uriens' [land]." This would put it in Gore. The Vulgate, however, seems to put Sorhaute in Sorelois (Surluse), Duke Galeholt's favorite subkingdom [Vulgate IV]. Malory may be mistaken about placing it in Uriens' hands, or he or his immediate source may have confused the name Sorhaute or a variant thereof with Gohorru, the capital of Gore. I would put Sorhaute in Surluse.

SORIONDES†

A nephew of Maaglant, this Saxon warrior was involved in the attack on Vandaliors Castle [Vulgate II].

SORNEGRIEU†

A leader of the Sesnes involved in the attack on Vandaliors Castle [Vulgate II].

SORRY NAG†

The poor, wretched packhorse which Gawaine appropriates from the ugly squire for Greoreas and then is forced to ride himself reminds me so irresistibly of Don Quixote's Rosinante that I cannot help but wonder if some image of Gawaine sitting on this unbudgeable nag to meet Greoreas' nephew could conceivably have echoed its way down four centuries to tickle Cervantes' funny bone [Chrétien de Troyes, **Perceval**, ll. 6983-7359].

SOUTH MARCHES

Almost certainly the marches of Arthurian Cornwall. Putting them east of Avilion would give Cornwall proper more territory and help fill in more of the central region. Or they might simply be the area south of Avilion to the sea, forming a sort of pass from Logres to Cornwall.

SOUTH MARCHES, DUKE OF THE

This duke had at least thirteen sons. Gawaine slew seven, for which cause the duke and his remaining six sons were Arthur's sworn enemies. Therefore, when Sir Marhaus arrived with the damsel "Été" and introduced himself—perhaps a trifle prematurely—as a knight of the Round Table, the duke gave him hospitality for the night but informed him regretfully that on the morn he would have to battle his host and his host's six sons. Marhaus defeated them all and sent them to Arthur's court that Whitsuntide, where they were all reconciled to the King. [Malory IV, 24-25]

Mark Twain makes amusing use of this family and their history in chapters 14, 15, and 19 of **A Connecticut Yankee in King Arthur's Court**.

SOUTHAMPTON

Chrétien mentions this as the port where Alexander and his companions came ashore when they arrived in Britain from their Greek homeland [**Cligés**, ll. 27—305].

Spear of Vengeance—see **LONGINUS' SPEAR**

SPIRITUAL PALACE†

At the Spiritual Palace of Sarras, Christ consecrated Joseph, son of Joseph of Arimathea, as His first bishop (of Britain?). It was for this reason that Galahad and his companions were directed to take the Grail to Sarras. [Vulgate VI]

STAG, WHITE†

Chrétien de Troyes tells us of the custom of hunting the white stag, and how whoever can kill it must kiss the fairest maid in the court [**Erec & Enide**, ll. 27-125]. This custom seems already to have fallen into disuse, for Arthur wishes to revive it, despite Gawaine's prudent advice that choosing the fairest maid can only cause trouble, since every knight thinks his lady the fairest. By "maiden", I think we must understand virgin or at least unmarried woman, since nobody ever thinks of solving the problem by naming the Queen as fairest. D.D.R. Owen, in the notes to his translation of Chrétien, identifies the White Stag as otherworldly in origin. It may have gotten into Malory as the white hart whose appearance with a white brachet and sixty black hounds marked Nimue's coming to court. (See Nimue.)

STONE CIRCLE

If Stonehenge could be called a pre-Christian cathedral, this small antiquity near Land's End might be called a pre-Christian chapel, and is included as an example of such. If you drew a line from Newlyn or Mousehole to Saint Just, westernmost Cornwall, the Stone Circle would be in just about the middle of the land thus marked off. I visited this one several years ago. I had a devil of a time finding it—had to go through a cow field or two—and have had a devil of a time relocating what I think to be the same one on my Ordnance Survey map of Land's End. The antiquity had been cleared out during the early part of our century, and apparently not since. The stones, as I recall, were each one about as tall as a person, and the circle perhaps as large in area as a good-sized living room; it was a very regular circle, in a good state of preservation, much overgrown with weeds and nettles.

STONEHENGE

According to a tradition which I did not find in Malory, but which is recorded in Vulgate II, Merlin brought Stonehenge from Ireland to Salisbury Plain, moving the stones by magic in order to make them a funerary monument for kings slain in battle. This gives us a lovely magical act, but takes away the grandest of the purely Pagan religious centers. I personally would prefer to keep the magical ability of such mighty necromancers as Merlin to move huge stones, but omit its application to Stonehenge, saving the famous place as Britain's major Pagan (whether Druidical or pre-Druidical) religious center.

Examples of the numerous smaller stone antiquities to be found throughout Britain, Brittany, and so on which might be considered pagan "chapels" are the Hurlers, the Nine Sisters, the Stone Circle near Land's End, Plouhinec, and many others not included here.

The Druids, of course, are supposed to have used oak groves, which suggests they did not erect many permanent structures. Some of the forests with "perilous" or "magical" properties originally may have been Druid holy places. Modern archaeologists believe that Stonehenge far antedates the Druids.

STONY CROSS, CHAPEL OF THE

After leaving the hermitage of the Queen of the Waste Lands, Lancelot rode at random (Malory does not specify for how long) into a wild forest, where

> at the last he came to a stony cross which departed two ways in waste land; and by the cross was a stone that was of marble, but it was so dark that Sir Launcelot might not wit what it was.

Looking around, he saw an old chapel. The door was "waste and broken", but within the chapel was a fair altar, richly arrayed with cloth of silk and a silver candlestick holding six candles. Lancelot found no way, however, to get inside, so he returned and slept by the cross. In the night, when he was between sleep and waking, he saw a knight borne to the chapel on a litter. The Grail arrived on a silver table and healed the sick knight. Afterward, concluding that Lancelot must be in some deadly sin because he had slept through the miracle, the newly healed knight took Lancelot's helm, sword, and horse. Lancelot then heard a voice speaking to him in symbols. Waking, he found a hermitage on a high hill, where the hermit (Nascien?) expounded the vision. [Malory XIII, 17-20]

My guess is that this chapel was either in or near Listeneise. Cross Fell, near the joining of Durham, Cumberland, and Northumberland counties, might be a good place to put it.

STONY PASSAGE†

This rocky passage was so narrow that only a single horse could get through it at a time. It lay in the marches of Gore, across one of the ways to the Sword Bridge, and was guarded by at least one knight, a number of men-at-arms, and a wooden tower with a lookout constantly posted. Although told that a longer way around to the Sword Bridge would be safer, Lancelot insisted on taking the shorter way, guided by two sons, one knighted, of his host of the evening before—the family were British prisoners in Gore. When they reached the Stony Passage, its guardian knight's lance broke and the men-at-arms, aiming their axes, deliberately missed Lancelot and his horse, as if wanting him to pass. Perhaps they too were foreign prisoners, pressed into unwilling service and eager for the man who would release them. [Chrétien de Troyes, **Lancelot**, ll. 2170-2266]

STRAIGHT MARCHES

These would seem to be either the marches between Wales and Logres or those between Logres and Scotland. A nice cordon might be made of Staffordshire, Worcestershire, and Herefordshire or a part thereof, between the sub-kingdoms immediately east of Wales and the sub-kingdoms of Arroy (Warwickshire) and Leicester.

'Strange Beast, Knight with the'—see PELLINORE

STRANGGORE

Identification of Stranggore as the Swansea peninsula to the east of Pembroke, at the western end of Glamorganshire, Wales, is arbitrary but very handy to the kingdom of Gore.

SUGALES†

I find this name in the Vulgate, although not in Malory. It would, of course, simply be southern Wales.

SURLUSE (Sorelois)

At its border is a fair village with a strong bridge guarded by knights who must be defeated if a person would gain admittance [Malory IX, 7]. Vulgate III amplifies this description. Surluse was bordered on one side by the sea and on the other, toward Arthur's realm, by the Assurne River. It was a delightful and fertile country with many rivers and splendid woods. In earlier days it had had many passages, but King Gloier, Duke Galeholt's predecessor, had limited the passages to two, each one barred by a strong tower, a knight, and ten armed sergeants. These bridges were the Pont Norgalois and the Pont Irois. Any knight defeated while trying to cross either bridge had to stay and help guard it. Galeholt, who conquered Gloier and won Surluse, seemingly maintained these two passages.

I cannot find any Assurne River; perhaps it is too small for my maps. The name of the Pont Norgalois suggests Norgales. In Volume V, the Vulgate says that Sorestan borders Norgales "par devers" Surluse. There is a longish, squarish peninsula in Cheshire, between the inlets of the rivers Dee and Mersey, which is far and away my personal favorite for Surluse.

SWORD

If a book is not handy to swear an oath upon, a knight can always use the cross formed by the handle of his sword [cf. Malory IX, 39]. I do not know whether such an oath is less binding than one sworn on a book.

SWORD BEARER†

The squire who brought Trebuchet's Sword to the Fisher King, along with the message that the Fisher King's niece had sent it and that she would be greatly pleased if it were passed along to a suitable champion who would use it well, strikes me as a responsible enough character to merit individual inclusion here. In a sense, his errand can be said to herald the Grail procession. I am not sure whose squire he was, the Fisher King's or the niece's, but he was quite well informed. [Chrétien de Troyes, **Perceval**, ca. ll. 3130-3157]

SWORD BRIDGE†

The more perilous of the two bridges into Gore, it was like a sharp sword. No man before Lancelot had ever succeeded in crossing it. Chrétien's description rather clearly equates it with the "pont despee" of the Vulgate.

Chrétien compares the water racing beneath the Sword Bridge with the Devil's river: black, thunderous, turgid, deep, and ready to swallow anything that might fall into it. (By contrast, the river at the Water Bridge must have been calm and quiet.) The Sword Bridge itself consisted of one great, gleaming sword, as long as two lances, nailed at each end to a treetrunk. On the far side, two lions or leopards waited, tied to a stone slab. Ignoring all warnings, Lancelot stripped the armor from his hands, legs, and feet so as to get a better purchase on the metal with his bare hands, feet and knees, shrewdly preferring cuts to a plunge into the river. Once on the other side, he found the lions gone and, using his ring, proved that they were mere delusory enchantment. [Chrétien de Troyes, **Lancelot**, ll. 648-713; 3021-3150] For a curious parallel in American Indian myth, see under Gore.

SWORD WITH THE STRANGE BALDRIC (Hangings)†

The only thing Chrétien tells us about this weapon is that, according to the Loathly Damsel, the knight who rescues the maiden of Montesclaire may win the right to gird it on safely. [**Perceval**, ca. ll. 4706-4713]

See also Trebuchet's Sword.

SYCAMORE, HEATH OF THE†

This lay near one of Arthur's court cities, but I can find nothing in Chrétien's—or, more accurately, his continuator Godefroi de Leigni's—surrounding text to tell me which one. I should guess Carlisle, since that city, rather than Camelot, seems to be Arthur's principal seat in the early tales.

Beside the keep (wherever it was) there spread a heath called the most beautiful outside Ireland. Through it a clear stream flowed swiftly over a pebbled bed bright as silver and through a channel of pure gold, running down across the heath and through a valley between two woods. Over the stream grew a great, wide-spreading sycamore planted in the time of Abel. The grass that bordered the area was green throughout the year.

On this lovely field Lancelot fought his last fight with Meliagrant, to the latter's extinction. Well, it sounds as pretty a place as any in which to die, and quite possibly closer than most of Arthur's own properties to the other world.

[Chrétien de Troyes & Godefroi de Leigni, **Lancelot**, ll. 6987-7031]

TALEBRE† (Conlotebre, Conlouzebre, Zelegebres)

Arthur summoned the barons of Carmelide (Cameliard) to this city when he acknowledged Genievre, alias "the false Guenevere", as his queen [Vulgate IV]. Presumably it would have been in or near Cameliard.

TALIESSIN†

Glennie lists him as one of the four great bards of the Arthurian age, the others being Llywarch Hen, Aneurin, and Merlin. (Glennie puts the Arthurian age in the sixth century, while Malory and the Vulgate put it in the fifth.)

"Taliessin is our fullest throat of song," says Arthur in Tennyson's idyll **The Holy Grail**.

TALL KNIGHT IN THE PALFREY'S GARDEN†

When the Haughty Maid of Logres sent Gawaine across the river into the garden for her little piebald palfrey, he found a tall knight sitting there beneath an olive tree, quietly looking on. This knight warned Gawaine that every previous knight who had taken the palfrey had lost his head for his pains. Not that the tall knight would himself lift a finger to fight Gawaine—which might have surprised medieval audiences as much as modern readers. No, for all his size and knighthood, he simply acted as a sort of human warning sign. [Chrétien de Troyes, **Perceval**, ca. ll. 6783-6818]

TANEBORC† (Baillon)

A strong castle at the entrance of Norgales, this may have been one of Arthur's own fortresses. It was, at least, a place at which he stayed sometimes, perhaps even a court city. Here, three days after holding court at Cardiff, at a time when he was preparing for war against King Claudas, Arthur received intelligence of Claudas' own preparations across the Channel. At Taneborc, also, Arthur held at least one tournament, after which he and Guenevere spent the night at his castle of Tauroc. [Vulgate V, VI]

TANINGUES (Tranurgor)

By the name, this would seem to be another "Gore" dukedom, with Brandelis as its duke.

Since Sagramore set out from Camelot Forest and encountered Duke Brandelis after several other pavilions and adventures, I would guess Taningues to be in the southern part of the island, possibly one of the promontories on the coast of Southampton or Sussex. I propose the peninsula at the southwest end of Sussex between Chichester and Arundel. Since Arundel is Malory's Magouns Castle, the Taningues border would be south of it. [Vulgate IV]

Additionally, a squire, Helain de Taningues, held a castle in the neighborhood of Taningues. If Taningues is identified as the peninsula at the western end of Sussex, then the castle might be Chichester (Roman name Noviomagu).

TANTALIS†

Empress of Greece and Constantinople, mother of Alexander and Alis, and grandmother of Cligés. All Chrétien really tells us about Tantalis, however, are her name and her great sadness when her older son Alexander left for Britain. We do not know whether she predeceased her husband the old emperor, or survived him to see Alexander's return and to lend the help of a medieval dowager empress in raising her grandson. [Chrétien de Troyes, **Cligés**, ll. 45, ca. 220]

TARN WADLING† (Tarn Wathelyne) [in Inglewood Forest]

Arthur met the Grim Baron of Castle Hewin here [Glennie, p. 72]. Inglewood is in Cumberland, south of Carlisle.

TAULAS (Tauleas) AND TAULURD

These two giants were brothers. Taulas is stated as living in Cornwall. He was a small enough giant to ride a horse. For seven years Taulas kept to his castle for fear of Tristram. One day, hearing that Tristram was dead, he came out to attack Sir Dinant. Tristram was not dead, however, only wandering around mad, and at the instigation of nearby herdsmen he came to kill the giant. [Malory IV, 25; IX, 20]

Taulurd was so large that no horse could carry him. He was a wily fighter who destroyed the lands of Earl Fergus and imprisoned ladies and knights in his own castle. Sir Marhaus killed him by driving him into the water and stoning him to death. Since Fergus later became Tristram's man, I think it probable that Taulurd lived in or near Cornwall. [Malory IV, 25]

TAULAS OF THE DESERT†

Since a Taulas is among Arthur's knights in the list Chrétien de Troyes begins in line 1691 of **Erec & Enide**, and since Chrétien tells us that he never tired of arms, I seriously doubt that he should be identified with Malory's apparently wicked giant Taulas, who spent seven years hiding in his own castle. In **Lancelot**, however, lines 5824-5842, Chrétien mentions a Taulas of the Desert fighting in the Noauz tournament, carrying a fine shield which came from Lyons on the Rhone and had been presented to him for some notable service, but which is not otherwise described. I feel confident enough that this

Taulas is the same knight listed in **Erec & Enide** to combine them in one entry here.

Tauleas—see **TAULAS AND TAULURD**

TAUROC†

This stronghold of Arthur's must have been handy to Taneborc Castle, at the entrance to Norgales. Morgan le Fay had a castle in the woods around Tauroc.

"Between Mold and Denbigh is Moel Arthur, an ancient British for, defended by two ditches of great length" [Glennie, p. 7]. Mold and Denbigh are in Denbigh County, north Wales. I vote to identify Moel Arthur with Tauroc.

TENEBROC†

Chrétien's name for Edinburgh [**Erec & Enide**, l. 2131, & Owen's note to same].

TENT, DAMSEL OF THE†

The unfortunate sweetheart of the Haughty Knight of the Heath, q.v.

TERGALO, OLD WOMAN OF†

Mother of the valiant knight Raindurant, who was unhorsed by Erec at the tournament between Evroic and Tenebroc [Chrétien de Troyes, **Erec & Enide**, ll. 2171-2214]. That Raindurant's father is not named may suggest that his mother held some independence, even authority. At the least, fame or notoriety.

Terican—see **TURQUINE**

Terican's Hill†—see **TURQUINE'S HILL**

TERRABIL

This was a second castle of the Duke of Tintagil, ten miles from Tintagil. It had "many issues and posterns out." This was where Gorloïs was slain the same night Uther begat Arthur on Igraine in the sister castle of Tintagil. Arthur later battled and defeated the armies of King Ryons' brother Nero and King Lot in the field before Terrabil, where Lot met his death. [Malory I, 1, 3; II, 10]

When I visited Tintagil in the late 1960's, neither the official guide nor anyone else I questioned had ever heard of Terrabil. John W. Donaldson places it near St. Kew, Cornwall, about midway between Camelford and Padstow. This seems more plausible than a few of Donaldson's other place identifications, especially since Mee, in **The King's England: Cornwall**, notes prehistoric earthworks and rumors of Arthurian castles. The best clue I have yet found, however, appears in the Survey of Cornwall. Carew identifies Terrabil as adjacent to the town of Launceston, and says that it was from the regard of the castle's triple walls that men so named it. The site appears to be a little farther than ten miles from Tintagil—although not, I think above twenty miles, and miles might have been longer in Malory's day, or Arthur's. Having visited the ruins of grand, dour old Launceston Castle, I also believe it to be the bones of Terrabil.

Terre Foraine—see **FOREIGN LAND**

Tertre as Caitis†—see **DRUAS' HILL**

Tertre Deuee†—see **DEUEE, TERTRE**

THENEW†

She was the daughter of King Lothus and mother of Saint Kentigern. See under Kentigern.

THESSALA†

Fenice's nurse was named Thessala after the country of her birth. Chrétien de Troyes assures us that Thessaly was a land of traditional charms and devilish enchantments; Thessala was certainly adept at brews. Not only could she cure diseases and heal wounds of all kinds, she also knew how to prepare a potion that, when Emperor Alis drank it on his wedding night, caused him ever afterward to fall asleep and dream so convincingly of enjoying his wife that he believed he was doing so in fact, while she lay untouched beside him. Later, Thessala made Fenice a potion that caused her to seem dead long enough for Cligés to spirit her away. During Fenice's shammed illness preparatory to this ruse, Thessala also showed plain old human cunning in fooling the doctors by substituting the urine of a woman who really was mortally sick for that of her mistress. [Chrétien de Troyes, **Cligés**, ll. 3002-3371, ca. 5365ff.]

THOAS†

He was a young knight when he fought in the Noauz tournament. His shield was made in London and bore two swallows in flight. [Chrétien de Troyes, **Lancelot**, ll. 5824-5842] Any firm identification with King Thoas of Ireland looks to me unlikely, especially considering that Chrétien also has the (unnamed) King of Ireland's son fighting in the same tournament.

THOAS, KING OF IRELAND†

Apparently a Saxon king, Thoas was involved in the attack on Valdaliors Castle. He was eventually killed by Gawaine when he tried to invade England with other Saxons. [Vulgate II]

THOMAS THE RHYMER† (Thomas of Ercildoune)

This famous visitor to the land of Faery lived in the thirteenth century. Glennie tells us that many traditions connect him with Arthur, as

> the unwilling, and too quickly vanishing guide of those adventurous spirits who have entered the mysterious Halls beneath the Eildons, and attempted to achieve the re-awakening of Arthur ... only to be cast forth.

The tradition recorded in Malory has Arthur lying not beneath the Eildons, but in Avilion (Glastonbury). Different spatial relationships, however, may hold in Faery than here on the surface.

THREE MARYS' OINTMENT†

According to Chrétien's translator D.D.R. Owen, this was the ointment which Mary Magdalene, Mary Salome, and Mary the mother of James procured to anoint the body of Christ. In **Mary Magdalen, Myth and Metaphor** [New York, Harcourt Brace, ©1993], Susan Haskins quotes the apocryphal Gospel of Philip as identifying the three Marys who walked always with the Lord as being His mother, either her sister or His—there seems to be some confusion of pronouns in the translation of this pseudo-Gospel passage—and Mary Magdalen. The Gospel of Philip is a Gnostic text, among those found at Nag Hammadi; might this particular tradition have survived into Chrétien's milieu? In any case, whoever the Marys were, their ointment obviously had excellent curative powers, for King Bademagu offered it for the wounds Lancelot sustained from crossing the Sword Bridge. As Owen points out, Bademagu's having this (rather than, say, one of Morgan's preparations) reinforces the echo of the Harrowing of Hell. [Chrétien de Troyes, **Lancelot**, l. 3374 & Owen's note to same]

TIBAUT (Tiebaut) OF TINTAGEL†

Tibaut raised his deceased lord's son Meliant de Liz to the age of knighthood, at which time Sir Meliant challenged him to a tournament in order to win his elder daughter. At first Tibaut seems to have been reluctant to let the tournament actually proceed, but the chance arrival of one (or, it was first thought, two) of Arthur's champions inspired Tibaut's vavasour Garin to urge his lord to let his own knights leave Tintagil and fight at their pleasure. Garin seemed to assume that Arthur's knight(s) would enter on the town's side—I am not sure why, unless Tibaut was one of Arthur's avowed allies or leigemen. When Arthur's knight (Gawaine, though they did not know his identity) abstained all day from the tourney, Tibaut listened to his elder daughter and was about to arrest the stranger as a merchant illegally disguised in order to avoid tolls; Garin explained that the stranger, now his guest, was honorably saving himself for trial by combat. At Garin's home,

Tibaut found his younger daughter, the Maid with Little Sleeves, pleading with the strange knight to fight next day for her sake. Sounding much like a modern parent, Tibaut tried to make her stop pestering Garin's guest; the later showed his true fatherly affection by having a fine sleeve of crimson samite made especially for her to give her knight as a token, meanwhile scolding her elder sister for slapping and otherwise mistreating her. [Chrétien de Troyes, **Perceval**, ca. ll. 4835-5464]

TIBAUT'S ELDER DAUGHTER†

Loved by Meliant of Liz, she insisted that he prove his worth by doing great feats of chivalry in a tournament against her father. There seems nothing in this to outrage medieval sensibilities. (Compare her plan with that described under the Lady of Noauz.) She explained that she set a high price upon her love because paying for a thing made it sweeter—a sentiment hardly unknown even in our day! It is her treatment of her younger sister, the Maid with Little Sleeves, that gives us our first pause in considering how good Meliant's choice might be. The elder sister can hardly be faulted for seeing her own would-be lover as the best and handsomest knight present; when she slaps her little sister's face and pulls her hair for opining that a better man is in sight, even their attendant damsels act shocked, finally intervening to rescue the child. Again, the elder sister seems maliciously eager to seize upon some ladies' theory—that her sister's knight is a merchant in masquerade—as a reason for their father to arrest him. No doubt some longstanding sibling rivalry exists between the two sisters, but to try to have a stranger, even a shady merchant, arrested on a hanging offense carries sibling rivalry rather far. [Chrétien de Troyes, **Perceval**, ca. ll. 4849-5560]

Tibise—see **CELIBE**

Tiebaut—see **TIBAUT**

TINTAGIL

Naturally, this dukedom is composed of the territory around Tintagil Castle, possibly including more or less the whole northern half of present-day Cornwall.

Chrétien de Troyes mentions Tintagil as one of Arthur's places for holding court; it was in Tintagil that Erec, still with Arthur's court, heard the news of King Lac's death [**Erec & Enide**, ll. 6510-6532]. Assuming that Tibaut of Tintagil, q.v., was one of Arthur's vassals, his residency there would be quite compatible with Arthur's use of it as a court city.

TINTAGIL CASTLE

This famous castle on the north coast of Cornwall still bears its name on modern maps. Here Uther Pendragon begat Arthur on Igraine. The castle later was taken over by a pair of wicked giants whom Lancelot finally slew. Still later, it became one of Mark's strongholds. [Malory I, 3; VI, 11; IX, 39]

TINTAGIL, THE GIANTS OF

Two unnamed giants took over Tintagil, apparently between the tenure of Gorloïs and that of Mark. As a hobby, these giants took up collecting ladies and damsels as their prisoners. Lancelot killed the pesky pair. [Malory VI, 11]

Tirre—see under **LAVAINE**

TOMBS, CHURCH OF THE†

On his way with "Portia" to Gore's Sword Bridge, Lancelot came to a pleasantly situated church with a walled cemetery. Leaving the damsel to watch the horses, he went in and prayed. On his way out, he met an aged monk who showed him the cemetery, which held splendid but still empty tombs inscribed for the men who would eventually lie there: Gawaine, Louis, Ywaine, etc. Most magnificent of all was a new marble sarcophagus with a lid that would require seven strong men to lift it, as the monk assured the knight—only he who was destined to free the foreign prisoners of Gore could lift it unaided. Lancelot promptly lifted it unaided, asked who was to lie here, and received the logical enough reply that it was eventually to entomb the man who freed the prisoners of Gore. [Chrétien de Troyes, **Lancelot**, ll. 1841-1992]

I assume that this church eventually became the abbies listed under Abbey of the Adventurous Shield and Abbey of the Burning Tomb. I am not, however, prepared to argue that Chrétien's version is the original.

"Tombs, Monk of the"†—see **"TOMBS, CHURCH OF THE"**

TOR (Tor le Fise Aries, Tor le Fise de Vayshoure)

Forthwithal there came a poor man into the court, and brought with him a fair young man of eighteen years of age riding upon a lean mare .... Anon as he came before the king, he saluted him and said: O King Arthur ... it was told me that at this time of your marriage ye would give any man the gift that he would ask, out except that were unreasonable .... Sir I ask nothing else but that ye will make my son here a knight. It is a great thing thou askest of me, said the king. What is thy name? ... Sir, my name is Aries the cowherd. Whether cometh this of thee or of thy son? said the king. Nay, sir, said Aries, this desire cometh of my son and not of me, for I ... have thirteen sons, and all they will fall to what labour I put them, and will be right glad to do labour, but this child will not labour for me, for anything that my wife or I may do, but always he will be shooting or

> casting darts, and glad for to see battles and to behold knights, and always day and night he desireth of me to be made a knight. What is thy name? said the king unto the young man. Sir, my name is Tor. The king beheld him fast, and saw he was passingly well-visaged and passingly well made of his years.

Arthur told Aries to fetch the other sons for comparison,

> and all were shaped much like the poor man. But Tor was not like none of them all in shape nor in countenance, for he was much more than any of them. Now, said King Arthur unto the cowherd, where is the sword he shall be made knight withal? It is here, said Tor. Take it out of the sheath, said the king, and require me to make you a knight.

Thus Tor became a knight of Arthur's court promptly for the asking. Only after he was dubbed did Merlin reveal him to be the bastard son of King Pellinore, begotten on the cowherd's wife before her marriage. Coming of such paternal blood, Merlin predicted, Tor would make a fine knight. (Rumours of Tor's birth may have persisted, however, for although he is sometimes surnamed "le Fise de Vayshoure"—"the son of Vayshoure", surely after his mother—he is also sometimes called "le Fise Aries" after the cowherd.)

Tor's original request had also included a place at the Round Table: no bashful lad, Tor. This distinction did not come, however, until after he had proved himself at least twice. The first time was in the quest of the white brachet (see under Nimue). Beginning his maiden adventure, Tor jousted down Sir Felot of Langduk and Sir Petipase of Winchelsea, who had insisted on fighting him, and sent them to court. (Sir Petipase, at least, became one of Arthur's knights and was killed trying to help Mordred and Agravaine corner Lancelot with the Queen.) The dwarf who had served Felot and Petipase requested becoming Tor's dwarf instead, and brought him to a pavilion where he found the white brachet with an unnamed lady. Tor reappropriated the brachet, and was overtaken next day by Abelleus. As they fought for the brachet, a lady of the neighborhood rode up to tell Tor that Abelleus was a villain who had killed her brother before her eyes, "and I kneeled half an hour afore him in the mire for to save my brother's life", wherefore she required Tor to dispose of the scoundrel. He did, afterward lodging with the lady and her husband, "a passing fair old knight", who courteously put their house "always at [Tor's] commandment." When Tor returned to court and told his adventures, Arthur—on Merlin's advice—rewarded him with an earldom of lands, although his seat at the Round Table had to wait until after the war with the invading kings of Denmark, Ireland, the Vale, Soleise, and Longtains had left eight vacancies at the Table, which Arthur refilled according to Pellinore's advice. After naming Uriens, Hervise de Revel, the King of the Lake, Galagars, Gawaine, Griflet, and

Kay, Pellinore modestly gave Arthur a choice of either Tor or Bagdemagus for the eighth seat.

> But because Sir Tor is my son I may not praise him, but else, an he were not my son, I durst say that of his age there is not in this land a better knight than he is, nor of better conditions and loath to do any wrong, and loath to take any wrong. By my head, said Arthur, he is a passing good knight as any … for I have seen him proved, but he saith little and he doth much more, for I know none in all this court an he were as well born on his mother's side as he is on your side, that is like him of prowess and of might: and therefore I will have him at this time, and leave Sir Bagdemagus till another time.

Tor makes a brief appearance in the rambling adventures of Sir Tristram. He jousts down Sir Kay in sport, then joins Kay, Tristram, and Brandiles at their lodging, where Tristram sits silent and anonymous while the other three tell "Cornish knight" jokes; on the morrow, Tristram jousts down Brandiles and Tor and snubs Kay before revealing his identity. A little farther on Malory describes a visit of King Mark to Sir Tor's castle, but Tor himself is not in residence at the time and his lieutenant Sir Berluse is the one who grudgingly carries out the duties of host to the unloved king.

Tor was killed during Lancelot's rescue of Guenevere from the stake. Tor's half-brothers were Lamorak, Aglovale, Dornar, and Percivale; his known half-sisters were Amide and Eleine. [Malory III, 4-5, 9-11; IV, 5; IX, 15; X, 9; XX, 8]

Chrétien de Troyes names Tor the son of King Ars among the prominent knights of Arthur's court [**Erec & Enide**, ca. l. 1527.].

TORIN†

One of the twelve who accompanied Alexander from Greece to Britain, where Arthur knighted them all at the outset of Count Angrs' rebellion. Although Chrétien calls Torin "mighty", he did not happen to be with the party that infiltrated Windsor and captured Angrs. Sir Torin survived the rebellion, but Chrétien tells us no more about him. [**Cligés**, ll. 102-385; 1093-ca. 2210]

Perhaps I owe it to myself to point out that I did not read **Cligés** until 1995, and any resemblance between Sir Torin and my own character Torin the Toymaker is both purely nominal and purely coincidental.

TOWER OF LONDON

You may have heard that William the Conqueror put this up. Don't believe it! Malory tells us that Guenevere barricaded herself in the Tower of London to escape Mordred, so it had to have been around in Arthur's time. [Malory XXI, 1]

Seriously, there was a tower here at least from Roman times.

Tower of Marvels†—see under **GALAFORT**

TRADELMANS, KING OF NORGALES†

Tradelmans would seem to be the grandson of King Ryons, whom he apparently succeeded. The brother of Tradelmans was Sir Belinans, whose son was Sir Dodinas. [Vulgate II]

Possibly Tradelmans should be identified with Cradelmas.

Tranurgor—see **TANINGUES**

TREBES†

This apparently was the major castle of King Ban, in France. Near Trebes was Bois en Val, site of the "Lake" where the Damsel of the Lake raised Lancelot. [Vulgate III]

Malory identifies Benwick, King Ban's country, as Beaune or Bayonne [XX, 18]. There is a city of Bayonne on the coast at the southwesternmost part of modern France, just north of the Pyrenees. Perhaps eighty miles east of Bayonne is a city called Tarbes. Could Tarbes derive from Trebes?

TREBUCHET†

The forger of the sword that the Fisher King gave Percivale. This was the last of only three swords Trebuchet was to forge in his life. Trebuchet alone had foreknowledge of the perilous occasion on which this splendid weapon would break, and he alone would be able to mend it. The context suggests that he may have had some personal acquaintance with the Fisher King's niece, who sent the sword to her uncle. Despite his name, which sounds both Cornish and French, Trebuchet lived near Cotoatre, identified with the Firth of Forth. [Chrétien de Troyes, **Perceval**, ca. ll. 3138-3156; 3675ff.]

TREBUCHET'S SWORD†

Trebuchet forged this as one of only three swords he was ever to make in his life: this sounds like a deliberate decision on his part, since he apparently survived the making of the last sword by some time. Why the fact of his making so few swords should enhance their value puzzles me, but perhaps I am too steeped in the idea that long experience and practice produces the best work; perhaps Trebuchet had honed his skill on other types of smithery. In any case, this remarkable and guaranteed-unique sword was notably light for its size and strength. It seems to have had but a single flaw: it was predestined to break on one occasion, and only one, but on that occasion its wielder's life would be at stake. Its shattering, however, would not necessarily result in the bearer's death (though it would clearly test his survival skills).

How the Fisher King's niece obtained the sword from its maker is not told, but she sent it to her uncle with the request that he pass it on to a worthy recipient. Percivale having just arrived, and not yet having failed to ask the right questions about the Grail, the Fisher King presented it to him. Next day, seeing him wearing it, the niece explained to him how, when it broke, he would be able to get it repaired—but only by carrying the pieces back to Trebuchet at Cotoatre. There is a possibility that the sword broke during Percivale's fight with the Haughty Knight of the Heath, but the authenticity of this passage lies under serious question.

This sword's pommel was gold and its sheath bore Venetian embroidery—trappings worthy of a mystical, magical blade with only that one tiny defect. Its baldric being worth a fortune makes me wonder if there could be any connection between this weapon and the Sword with the Strange Baldric mentioned later in the same romance. [Chrétien de Troyes, **Perceval**, ca. ll. 3130-3189; 3654-3690; 3926 ff.]

TRESPAS, CASTEL DEL†

Here Ywaine was imprisoned until the rampaging giant Mauduit should come to fight him [Vulgate V]. Probably it was not too far from the Castle de la Blanche Espine.

If Warbelow Barrow were identified with Blanche Espine, then the Castel del Trespas might be Arthur's Hall.

Arthur's Hall is in Cornwall, about midway between Camelford and Bodmin. Glennie mentions it as a "little entrenchment" not far from Camelford. Norden amplifies the description:

> It is a square plott about 60 foote longe and about 35 foote broad, situate on a playne Mountayne, wrowghte some 3 foote into the grounde; and by reason of the depression of the place, ther standeth a stange or Poole of water, the place sett rounde about with flatt stones...

Camelford is about a third of the way from Tintagil to Launceston, or some three to four miles.

TREVERAIN, COUNT OF†

Chrétien lists him among the vassals whom Arthur summoned to court for Erec's wedding, adding that he brought with him 100 knights [**Erec & Enide**, ll. 1934-1962]. By the 18th and 19th centuries, the prefix "Tre-" was considered to mark a native of Cornwall.

TRISTRAM (Tristran, Tristan, etc.) OF LYONESSE

The story of Tristram and Isolde has its own vast, rich body of material, and the Tristram cycle often seems independent of, though coexistent with, the Arthurian cycle. Although the Vulgate and other pre-Malory treatments sometimes refer to Arthur and Tristram as contemporaries, Malory's is the earliest version I have yet found to attempt a true integration of the two cycles. Malory's may also remain the best such integration, even though his books of Tristram are perhaps that portion of **Le Morte D'Arthur** where modern readers are likeliest to bog down. (I believe that this may have been Malory's intent—that, in addition to using the Tristram-Isoud-Mark triangle as counterpoint to the Lancelot-Guenevere-Arthur one, Malory may have aimed to use the tale of Tristram as a vehicle for showing the disintegration of the original ideals of the Round Table into more or less aimless, wandering, sometimes ridiculous adventures and petty or bitter feuds. Be that as it may, Malory himself seems to have wearied of the business and cut it off short well before he got to the actual scene of Tristram's death.)

Hal Foster managed a consistent integration of Tristram into **Prince Valiant** before the time came to kill Tristram off, but the major modern romances I have read generally seem to concentrate on either Tristram or on Arthur—Tennyson, for instance, uses Tristram in **The Last Tournament**, but does not seem to like him very much; T. H. White seems to use him sparingly and grudgingly; Catherine Christian, although making Palomides a major character in **The Pendragon**, divorces him from the Tristram affair, which she brushes off with a brief mention as a rather sordid business of very little use to anyone but harpers; Erskine, on the other hand, chose to keep Arthur's court out of his version of **Tristran and Isolde**, even though he had already done a novel about Galahad, Lancelot, and Guenevere; and so on.

For the above reasons, and also because I, personally, have a great deal of difficulty trying to generate the interest in Tristram and his cycle that I feel for Arthur and his, I confine the present entry to Malory's version, disregarding all the other and better Tristram romances.

The son of King Meliodas and Queen Elizabeth of Lyonesse, Tristram was born in an unhappy hour—his father had been kidnaped by an amourous enchantress and his mother, giving birth while out searching for her husband, died of exposure. When Tristram was a child, his stepmother tried to poison him so that her own sons would inherit Lyonesse; when she was caught, Tristram showed a forgiving and compassionate nature by pleading for her life. Meliodas granted his request, but, apparently a bit annoyed with his son, sent the boy into France for seven years under the tutorship of Gouvernail, who later became Tristram's loyal and competent squire. It was probably during this period that Tristram attracted the affection of King Faramon's daughter, who gave him a brachet and later died for love; the attachment may have been unsolicited, but I tend to suspect Tristram of some youthful trifling in the art of dalliance—he seems to have been of quite an amorous nature.

> And there was Tristram more than seven years. And then when he well could speak the language, and had learned all that he might learn in that country, then he came home to his father, King Meliodas, again. And so Tristram learned to be an harper passing all other, that there was none such called in no country, and so on harping and on instruments of music he applied him in his youth for to learn.
>
> And after, as he grew in might and strength, he laboured ever in hunting and in hawking, so that never gentleman more ... And ... he began good measures of blowing of beasts of venery, and beasts of chase, and all manner of vermin, and all these terms we have yet of hawking and hunting. And therefore the book of venery, of hawking, and hunting, is called the book of Sir Tristram.

All this in addition to becoming the only fighting man of the time (except Galahad) who could conceivably have been able to beat Lancelot in a fair passage of arms (except during the spiritual adventures of the Grail)! Tristram sounds rather like what later centuries would call "Renaissance man," and "every estate loved him, where that he went." (Administration, however, does not seem to have been among his many talents; he rarely if ever appears to have returned home to see how his own inheritance of Lyonesse was getting along.)

When Tristram was about eighteen, he fought and mortally wounded Sir Marhaus in a single combat to free his uncle, King Mark of Cornwall, from paying truage to King Anguish of Ireland. Since Marhaus had used a poisoned spear, however, Tristram sickened of his own wounds, until at least, by the advice of a wise woman, Mark sent him into Ireland to be healed. Here, under the name Tramtrist, he met, was healed by, and probably began to fall in love with La Beale Isoud, whom he taught to harp. He also seems to have met Palomides for the first time—and not in the friendliest situation—and he developed a friendship with Isoud's father Anguish that survived even Isoud's mother's discovery that Tristram was the man who had killer her brother Marhaus. Tristram and Isoud exchanged rings before he fled Ireland, but, on arriving back in Cornwall, Tristram got his father's permission to stay in Mark's court (even though "largely King Melodias and his queen departed of their lands and goods to Sir Tristram"), where he eventually entered a rivalry with Mark for the love of Sir Segwarides' wife. Finally Mark, whose initial love of his nephew had turned to dislike, sent him into Ireland to bring back La Beale Isoud to be queen of Cornwall. On the return voyage, Tristram and Isoud accidentally shared a love potion meant for Isoud and Mark.

The important details of the love of Tristram and La Beale Isoud are given under her name. Eventually banished from Cornwall for ten years, Tristram went to Logres, where he fought at the Castle of Maidens tournament and was imprisoned for a time, along with

Palomides and Dinadan, by one Sir Darras. On his release, he chanced to visit a castle of Morgan le Fay's. She gave him a shield depicting Arthur, Guenevere, "and a knight who holdeth them both in bondage", refused to tell him that knight's name, and made him promise to bear the shield at the tournament at the Castle of the Hard Rock. Her lover Sir Hemison, jealous of her attentions to Tristram, pursued the departing champion of Cornwall and was killed.

Tristram distinguished himself at the Hard Rock tournament, smiting down Arthur himself in defense of Morgan's shield. After the tournament, Tristram rode by the stronghold of Breuse Sans Pitie in time to save Palomides from Breuse and his men. Tristram and Palomides separated after setting a day to meet again and settle their old rivalry in a meadow near Camelot. Palomides missed the appointment, but Lancelot happened to ride by Lanceor and Colombe's tomb, clad all in white and bearing a covered shield; Tristram mistook Lancelot for Palomides, and the two greatest knights and "best lovers" of their generation battled each other as Merlin had prophesied years before that they would beside that tomb. The bout ended in a draw, each champion surrendering to the other on learning his identity, and Lancelot brought Tristram to court, where he was installed as a member of the Round Table, getting Sir Marhaus' old chair.

The rest of Tristram's story as given by Malory can be found under La Beale Isoud. See also these many entries: Agwisance, Andred, Blamore de Ganis, Bleoberis de Ganis, Bragwaine, Breunor, Eliot, Queen Elizabeth of Lyonesse, King Faramon of France & Daughter, Fergus, Gouvernail, Hemison, Isoud La Blanche Mains, Kehydius, Lambegus, Lady Leech of Cornwall, King Melodias of Lyonesse, Brother Ogrins, Palomides, Persides de Bloise, Sagramore le Desirous, Segwarides, Segwarides' Wife. [Malory II, 8; IV, 28; VII, 35; VIII-X; XII; XIX, 11]

I am guessing that the "Tristan who never laughed" listed by Chrétien de Troyes among Arthur's knights [**Erec & Enide**, ll. 1691-1750] is identical with the famous Tristram, whose story Chrétien knew without, apparently, approving of its lovers.

SIR TRISTRAM'S FAMILY AND RETAINERS
Father: King Meliodas of Lyonesse
Mother: Queen Elizabeth
Uncle (maternal): King Mark
Stepmother's father: Hoel
Father-in-law: Hoel
Wife: Isoud la Blanche Mains
Lover: La Beale Isoud
Early lover: Sir Segwarides' Wife

Brother-in-law: Kehydius
Teacher and squire: Gouvernail
Mentor: Brother Ogrins
Ally: Dinas
Knights and protégés: Fergus, Lambegus, Segwarides, Sentraille de Lushon
Squire: Hebes le Renoumes
Would-be lover: King Faramon's Daughter

Tristram's Stepmother—see under MELIODAS, KING OF LYONESSE

Tubelle†—see CUBELE

TURNANCE

Malory seems to name this site only once, as an island where Nascien spent eight days, some forty years after Christ's Passion [Malory XVII, 4]. I surmise, however, that it may be the same island where Percivale spent some time during the Grail Adventures [Malory XIV, 6-10]. If so, it is a likely place to experience visions and temptations when one is questing for the Grail. Turnance figures more extensively in the Vulgate account.

I would suggest identifying it with Lundy Island in the Bristol Channel. See also Mortaise and the Port of Perilous Rock.

TURQUINE (Terican)

While seeking Lancelot and adventures, Sir Ector de Maris asked a forester if there were any of the latter nearby.

> Sir, said the forester … within this mile, is a strong manor, and well dyked, and by that manor, on the left hand, there is a fair ford for horses to drink of, and over that ford there groweth a fair tree, and thereon hang many fair shields that wielded sometime good knights, and at the hole of the tree hangeth a basin of copper and latten [brass], and strike upon that basin with the butt of thy spear thrice, and soon after that thou shalt hear new tidings, [or] else hast thou the fairest grace that many a year had ever knight that passed through this forest.

Ector thanked the forester and followed his instructions. Forth came Sir Turquine and bade Ector make ready.

Ector began well, striking Turquine such "a great buffet that his horse turned twice about." Turquine, being a strong knight of great prowess, quickly turned the tables and took Ector prisoner back to his own hall. In honor of Ector's having put up the best fight of any opponent in twelve years, Turquine offered to give him his life in exhange for Ector's promise to remain his prisoner for said life's duration. When Ector refused these terms, Turquine had him stripped and beaten with thorns before throwing him into the deep dungeon with the other prisoners, "three score and four", including some of the Round Table.

Sir Lancelot was guided in his turn to Turquine by a damsel who remarked that she knew of no one else who might conquer the villainous knight. After a battle of two hours, Turquine, much impressed by Lancelot's prowess, asked his name, offering him friendship and the free release of all the prisoners on condition that the stranger was not the one knight whom Turquine hated above all others. Lancelot asked which was the hated knight.

> Faithfully, said Sir Turquine, his name is Sir Launcelot du Lake, for he slew my brother, Sir Carados, at the dolorous tower, that was one of the best knights alive; and therefore ... may I once meet with him, the one of us shall make an end of other, I make mine avow. And for Sir Launcelot's sake I have slain an hundred good knights, and as many I have maimed all utterly that they might never after help themselves, and many have died in prison, and yet have I three score and four.

Lancelot announced who he was. "Ah", said Turquine, "Lancelot, thou art unto me most welcome that ever was knight, for we shall never depart till the one of us be dead." It seems almost superfluous to report that Turquine was the one who was left dead. [Malory VI, 2, 7-9]

Sommer standardizes Turquine's name as Terican in the Vulgate, where the tale differs in a few details. See also Carados of the Dolorous Tower.

TURQUINE'S (Terican's) HILL†

Turquine (Terican in the Vulgate) was the brother of Sir Carados, but in the Vulgate it appears that he did not help keep the Dolorous Tower. Instead, he had his own collection point for vanquished opponents on the hill named for him. Near this hill was a fountain running through a silver tube onto a marble slab and thence into a leaden vessel. The fountain was overshadowed by three pines on which hung the shields, helmets, and lances of the knights Terican had conquered. When Sir Ector de Maris arrived, there were sixty shields, including twenty-four belonging to knights of Arthur. Also near or more likely on the hill was a stronghold where Terican kept his prisoners. After Lancelot killed Terican, Arthur's knights gave the property to one Count del Parc. [Vulgate V]

The fountain with the silver pipe sounds suspiciously similar to that fountain near which Morgan caused Sir Accolon to awake [Malory IV, 8]. See "Fountain of the Silver Pipe." This fountain was near the castle of Sir Damas, which was two days' journey from Camelot—all of which may help to locate Turquine's Hill and his brother's Dolorous Tower.

> Between Castle Cary and Yeovil, on the escarpment of the oolite, abutting on the plain which extends to Ilchester, is Cadbury, 'a hill of a mile

> compass at the top, four trenches encircling it, and twixt every of them an earthen wall; the content of it, within about twenty acres full of ruins and reliques of old buildings .... In the fourth ditch is a spring called King Arthur's Well. [Glennie, p. 10]

Cadbury is considered a candidate for Camelot, but it sounds to me like a fine site for Turquine's Hill, with King Arthur's Well as the "Fountain of the Silver Pipe." Yeovil appears to be right on the southern border of Somersetshire and Dorsetshire, which might put it in the Arthurian South Marches.

UGLY BRAVE†

Sixth best of Arthur's knights, according to the list Chrétien de Troyes begins in line 1691 of **Erec & Enide**. I regret being unable to give the original French of this interesting appellation, English translations of which may vary.

Ugly Maid—see **LOATHLY DAMSEL**

UGLY SQUIRE†

He had a long chest, short neck, stiff red hair in tangles, and a face that must have been hirsute as any beast's, what with bushy forked beard, twisted mustache, and eyebrows so thick they covered his forehead and nose. As Gawaine ministered to the wounded Greoreas at the Galloway border, this squire rode by on a wretched packhorse, for which Greoreas asked. When Gawaine went to request it, the squire proved as surly as he was ugly, actually goading the normally courteous Gawaine into giving him a slap that knocked him out of the saddle. The squire threatened the knight with dire consequences, but Greoreas assured Gawaine that the fellow never said a civil word to anyone. It might be suggested, however, that the squire's threat came true when Greoreas stole Gringolet, leaving Gawaine the sorry nag. [Chrétien de Troyes, **Perceval**, ca. ll. 6982-7048]

ULBAWES (Ulbause), EARL

This earl of Surluse fought Duke Chaleins of Clarance at Duke Galeholt's tournament, "and either of them smote other down." Ulbawes became a knight of the Round Table. [Malory X, 48; XIX, 11]

ULFIN

Sir Ulfin was a hermit living on the way to Castle Carbonek. Galahad lodged with him one night during the Grail Adventures. Percivale's sister Amide found Galahad here and led him to the ship where Bors and Percival were waiting. [Malory XVII, 1-2]

Ulfin might well be identified with Sir Ulfius.

ULFIUS

The noble knight Sir Ulfius became Uther Pendragon's confidant in the matter of Uther's love for Igraine. It was Ulfius who conceived the idea of fetching Merlin to help the king consummate his desire. When Merlin gave Uther the likeness of Igraine's husband and himself the likeness of Gorloïs' knight Jordanus, he gave Ulfius the likeness of Sir Brastias, another of the Duke's men. After Duke Gorloïs' death became commonly known, Ulfius arranged the treaty and forwarded the marriage between Uther and Igraine.

Some years later, the newly crowned Arthur made Ulfius his chamberlain. Ulfius served Arthur well during the first rebellion of the kings. The last Malory seems to tell us of Ulfius, at least as an active knight, is when he impeached Igraine of treason for not coming forward to testify to Arthur's identity; this, however, may have been a "staged" rather than a serious accusation. Like many other knights, Ulfius may have retired to a religious life; the similarity of names suggests he should be identified with the hermit Ulfin mentioned in the Grail Adventures. [Malory I, 1-21; XVII, 1]

Ulfius may well have been a companion of the Round Table when Uther had it. The service Malory records Ulfius as doing for Arthur comes before the young king received his father's Table from Leodegrance; Ulfius may have retired or died before Arthur's marriage, but if the old knight did remain long enough in Arthur's court, he would surely have been reinstated or elected to the Round Table.

UNCOURTEOUS LADY, CASTLE OF THE

A knight who accepted the hospitality of this castle would do well to keep his sword handy at all times.

> And so Sir Percivale ... came upon a bridge of stone, and there he found a knight that was bound with a chain fast about the waist unto a pillar of stone .... said that knight: I am a knight of the Table Round, and my name is Sir Persides; and thus by adventure I came this way, and here I lodged in this castle at the bridge foot, and therein dwelleth an uncourteous lady; and because she proffered me to be her paramour, and I refused her, she set her men upon me suddenly or ever I might come to my weapon; and thus they bound me, and here I wot well I shall die but if some man of worship break my bands. [Malory XI, 12]

Percivale broke his bonds, despite the efforts of an armed knight who came riding out of the castle onto the bridge to prevent him. He then made the Uncourteous Lady, who stood in the tower watching them, deliver up all of Persides' servants, and threatened to stay around and fordo her evil customs. Deciding, however, that his present business (looking for Lancelot) was more pressing, he left her alone and spent the night at Persides' castle, which must have been nearby.

The castle of the Uncourteous Lady was in the vicinity of Cardican Castle.

From Vulgate V, it appears that the name of this castle may be Garantan. The Vulgate account, however, differs enough from Malory's to make me uncertain.

URIENS (Urien), KING OF GORE

The husband of Morgan le Fay and the father of two sons named Ywaine, Uriens was among the allied kings—probably one of the ringleaders—in the first rebellion against the young Arthur. He fought in the battle of Bedegraine and afterward hosted his fellow rebels in his city of Sorhaute. He did not join the second rebellion, however, and was reconciled with Arthur, either between the two rebellions or when he came with his wife Morgan to the rich funeral Arthur gave Lot and the other kings who died in battle before Castle Terrabil. On the advice of King Pellinore, Uriens was made a companion of the Round Table after the decisive battle on the Humber against the invading kings of Denmark, Ireland, the Vale, Soleise, and Longtains.

Uriens went hunting with Arthur and Sir Accolon of Gaul on the expedition that led into Morgan's engineered attempt on Arthur's life, but, after the three hunters had fallen asleep aboard the mysterious boat, Uriens woke up next morning in his wife's arms, abed in Camelot. After the failure of her attempt on Arthur's life, Morgan attempted to salvage something by killing her husband, at least, with his sword as he slept, but their son, Ywaine le Blanchemains, prevented her. Although Ywaine promised to keep the secret, on condition his mother try no such thing again, the incident seems to have marked a permanent separation between Uriens and his wife; Morgan shortly thereafter left court and it appears likely that the royal couple never met again. Uriens remained faithfully with Arthur, being listed among those who attempted to heal Sir Urre. [Malory I, 2, 8, 15, 18; II, 2; IV, 4, 6, 13; XIX, 11]

In Chrétien's works, Gore is the land of King Bademagu—here, a monarch of quasimystical proportions—but Uriens is clearly identified as Ywaine's father [E.g., **Yvain**, ca. l. 1020, ca. l. 1818; **Perceval**, l. 8149ff.]. Like his son, Uriens appears originally to have been a real person who lived in the kingdom of Rheged, in southern Scotland and northern England, in the sixth century. [See, e.g., Owen's note to **Yvain**, l. 56; Cline's to **Perceval**, l. 8149]

URRE OF HUNGARY

Urre was a "good knight in the land of Hungary … and he was an adventurous knight, and in all places where he might hear of any deeds of worship there would he be." In Spain he slew an earl's son, Sir Alphegus, in tournament. In the fight Urre himself received seven great wounds, three on the head, four on the body and left hand. (Might he have been a left-hander?) Alphegus' mother, a sorceress, enchanted Urre so that his wounds would never heal until searched (probed, or touched) by the best knight of the world. Urre's mother took him in a horse litter, and, with his sister Felelolie and a page to take care of the horses, they searched seven years through "all lands christened" for the best knight of the world, coming at last to Arthur's court. Urre submitted to being handled by every knight of the Round Table then on hand—a hundred and ten of them—before Lancelot returned from an adventure and healed him.

Soon thereafter Urre was made a knight of the Round Table, and his sister married Sir Lavaine, who was elected to the Table at the same time.

> And this Sir Urre would never go from Sir Launcelot, but he and Sir Lavaine awaited evermore upon him; and they were in all the court accounted for good knights, and full desirous in arms; and many noble deeds they did, for they would have no rest, but ever sought adventures.

Urre accompanied Lancelot into exile and was made Earl of Estrake. [Malory XIX, 10-13; XX, 18]

UTHER PENDRAGON (Uter Pandragon, Utherpendragon)

Constans, King of Britain, had three sons: Maines, Pandragon, and Uther. After Constans' death, a number of barons murdered Maines in order to put Constans' seneschal Vortigern on the throne. Pandragon and Uther dispatched Vortigern and Pandragon became king, but was killed in battle with the Saxons. Uther took the kingship in his turn, adopting his elder brother's name and having Merlin bring the stones of Stonehenge to serve as Pandragon's memorial. [Vulgate II]

Here Malory takes up Uther's story.

> It befell in the days of Uther Pendragon, when he was king of all England, and so reigned, that there was a mighty duke in Cornwall that held war against him long time .... And so by means King Uther sent for this duke, charging him to bring his wife with him, for she was called a fair lady.

It is not clear to me whether Uther's summons was meant, at least ostensibly, to patch up a truce, or whether the war of this paragraph refers to what happens next. Duke Gorloïs and his wife Igraine departed suddenly and secretly when Igraine learned that Uther had amorous intentions on her. By the advice of his privy council, Uther tried summoning them back and, when they refused, gave Gorloïs plain, fair warning, "and bade him be ready and stuff him and garnish him, for within forty days he would fetch him out of the biggest castle that he hath." This, at least, seems open and honest. Gorloïs apparently put up a good fight, holding the siege at a standstill. "Then for pure anger and for great love of fair Igraine the king Uther fell sick." (It sounds to me like a fit of pouting impatience.) Uther's knight Ulfius fetched Merlin, who worked his magic to enable Uther to have his way with Igraine, she believing him her husband. That same night Gorloïs was killed in a sortie, after which the barons sued for peace, and Ulfius proposed that Uther wed Igraine. "And anon, like a lusty knight", which he was, Uther assented and, having made an unintentionally dishonest woman of Igraine, proceeded to make an honest one of her, doubtless leaving her very little choice in the matter. It hardly seems farfetched to suppose that Uther had a hand in arranging the marriages of Igraine's daughters also, Margawse to King Lot, Elaine to King Nentres, and Morgan (after a nunnery education) to King Uriens.

Meanwhile, apparently a bit of a joker, Uther was saving up the good news of who was the father of Igraine's next child. She, poor lady, having learned that her first husband was killed before the hour when she had thought he had come to her, "waxed daily greater and greater", all the while "marvell[ing] who that might be that lay with her in likeness of her lord" but saying nothing—very likely supposing it to have been a demon, like the one that had fathered Merlin. After about half a year, Uther finally sprang his little surprise, asking her to tell him "by the faith she owed to him", whose child was growing within her. She was "sore abashed", as well she might be—she must have hoped he would accept it as Gorloïs' child, or perhaps his own—and now his question showed he suspected something. At last, on his promise of loving her better for knowing the truth, she confessed all that she knew. Having dragged it from her, he graciously revealed his side of the incident, and that he himself, disguised by Merlin, had fathered the child. "Then the queen made great joy when she knew who was the father of her child." (A human seducer, however treacherous, must have seemed preferable to a demon.) Uther did not leave her long to rejoice, however: at the child Arthur's birth, he delivered it unchristened to Merlin, as per the mage's instructions; and, although Uther knew where Merlin was taking the child, he neglected to tell Igraine—it is not recorded that he consulted her at all before taking her son. (And he had burned so with love of her!)

Within two years Uther fell seriously ill. His enemies were making inroads on his kingdom, so he took Merlin's advice and had himself carried to battle in a horse-litter to Saint Albans, where his army met a "great host of the North." Whether inspired by the great deeds of Sir Ulfius and Sir Brastias, or by the presence of their king with the army, Uther's men prevailed. The king returned to London with great rejoicing, but soon fell so sick that he lay speechless for three days and nights. At last Merlin promised the barons he would make the king to speak.

> So on the morn all the barons with Merlin came to-fore the king; then Merlin said aloud unto King Uther, Sir shall your son Arthur be king after your days ...? Then Uther Pendragon turned him, and said in hearing of them all, I give him God's blessing and mine, and bid him pray for my soul, and righteously and worshipfully that he claim the crown, upon forfeiture of my blessing; and therwith he yielded up the ghost, and then was he interred as longed to a king. Wherefore the queen, fair Igraine, made great sorrow, and all the barons.

I must confess that Igraine's sorrow rather surprises me. Perhaps he had turned into a decent husband after all, but it seems to me more likely that she made public show of mourning, while her private grief was more for being left protectorless in unsettled times and for the knowledge of what he had done with her son having apparently been lost with him than for love of Uther himself. Nevertheless, where his lusts were concerned, Uther seems to have been a strong and brave king and, not impossibly, a decent administrator of the public weal. [Malory I, 1-4]

Chrétien de Troyes shows Arthur referring to his father Pendragon as a just emperor and king [**Erec & Enide**, ca. l. 1818]. Uther Pendragon is again named as Arthur's father in **Yvain**, ca. l. 655.

Spence tentatively identifies Uther with the Celtic god Beli; both were said to have been buried at Salisbury Plain [**Magic Arts**, p. 15].

Uwaine—see **YWAINE**

VADALON†

King Vadalon was brother to the King of Norgales (probably not Ryons) and eventually might have been king of Norgales in his turn [Vulgate IV; see under King Agrippe's Daughter].

A brave but cruel knight named Vadalon received Sir Ector de Maris' seat at the Round Table after Lancelot and his supporters left Arthur [Vulgate VI]. I do not know whether this knight should be identified with the King Vadalon who banded Agrippe's daughter, but I think it not improbable. King Vadalon could also be called "cruel", and, while I have not discovered whether or not Sir Bors encountered King Vadalon during the year he was pledged to carry the shield Agrippe's daughter gave him, or what the outcome of that fight—if it ever took place—might have been, it would as neatly fit the patten of such events if Bors conquered and converted Vadalon and brought him to Arthur as a faithful vassal, eventually to be given a place at the Round Table, as it would if Bors conquered and killed King Vadalon.

VAGON

Vagon is the name of a city, of a castle, and of the old lord thereof. It seems to have been the knights' first stop after leaving Camelot on the Quest of the Holy Grail. [Malory XIII, 8] It might be identified with Alton or with Basingstoke.

VAGOR, KING†

Vagor's son, Marabron, charged Sir Lionel with treason. The wife of Marabron's brother had played on Lionel the same sort of trick Potiphar's wife played on Joseph (Genesis 39), forcing Lionel to kill the husband in self-defense. King Vagor held Lionel prisoner in his castle. Lancelot arrived and championed Lionel, fighting Marabron and forcing him to retract the charge. [Vulgate V; see L'Isle Estrange.]

VAL SANS RETOUR† (Val des Faux Amants)

Apparently Morgan's Chapel stood at the entrance to this beautiful valley, located between Escalon li Tenebreux and the Dolorous Tower.

Twenty years before Lancelot defeated Carados of the Dolorous Tower, Morgan le Fay found her faithless lover in this valley with her rival. She spellcast the valley so that no knight could get out, although all other folk could come and go at will. Only a knight who had always been true in love could deliver the trapped knights.

Sir Galeshin's adventures will serve as an example. He came first to a low gate, where he dismounted. He then passed through a large hall to a vault guarded by two pairs of chained dragons, which attacked only knight, and from which Galeshin's sword rebounded as from an anvil. (Perhaps this gate and hall were Morgan's Chapel.) Next he came to a narrow plank spanning a deep water, where two knights knocked him in. Four men rescued him from the water, took his sword, shield, and helmet, and led him in to meet his fellow prisoners, who included three other companions of the Round Table.

Lancelot, coming through on his way to the Dolorous Tower, slew the dragons and crossed the plank through strategem. Once over, he looked at his ring, which had the power to dispel enchantments, and the plank with its guarding knights vanished. Lancelot then cut down several apparently real defenders, chasing one down the hall stairs, through a garden, over an enchanted stream, through another large hall, and into the pavilion where Morgan lay asleep. Lancelot slew the refugee and apologized to the enchantress for entering her chamber. Thus did Lancelot break the spell and free the prisoners, including Morgan's faithless lover. In return, however, Morgan kidnaped Lancelot while he slept and imprisoned him, although she let him out for awhile on his parole so that he could kill Sir Carados. [Vulgate IV]

VALBONE†

Round this Welsh mountain and its passes Percivale spent his childhood years. In talking with the first knights he ever met, he pointed out his mother's workers tending her fields of oats. Valbone has been identified with Mount Snowden. [Chrétien de Troyes, **Perceval**, ca. ll. 295-327, & Cline's note to 298]

VAMBIERES†

A very strong city, apparently near the city or castle of Clarence [Vulgate].

VANCE, LADY DE

All I can find of her is that King Ryons desired to lie with her, which was his undoing; Balin and Balan ambushed him on the way to her and brought him prisoner to Arthur. Ryons had sent twenty of his knights on ahead to "warn" her of his coming, but whether she was willing or not I cannot say. [Malory II, 9]

VANDALIORS†

According to Malory the rebel kings had to leave off warring with Arthur because the Saracens were besieging their castle of Wandesborow. In the Vulgate, however, the rebel kings were called away from their war with Arthur because the Sesnes, or Saxons, were attacking Vandaliors, in Cornwall (Cornuaille).

Vandaliors sounds as if it could be a variant of Wandesborow, which see, and Malory might have confused the Sesnes with the Saracens in this passage. Nevertheless, I would like to consider Wandesborow and Vandaliors as two separate strongholds. Vandaliors I would put on Mount's Bay, Cornwall, either at Penzance or at the Lizard Head. Since Penzance had not in earlier times the prominence it enjoys today, Lizard Head might be better. Just a little north of Lizard Head up the west coast is Goon-goofe, of which Norden tells us:

> A mountayne by the sea side ... [its name] signifying the hill of bloude. There are auntiente markes of martiall actes, as trenches of Defence, and hills of Burialls.

Vanora—see **GUENEVERE**

VAWSE, LADY DE

All I can find about her is that she held a tournament at which the prize was a rich circlet of gold worth a thousand besants; Sir Marhaus won the prize while adventuring with the damsel "Été" (see "Printemps, Été, & Automne"). Lady de Vawse must have lived within two days' ride of the South Marches. [Malory IV, 25]

It is tempting to postulate a scribe's or printer's error somewhere along the line and identify her with Lady de Vance.

VAYSHOURE

I got the name of Aries' wife by process of elimination, since in Malory IX, 15, Sir Tor is called "le Fise de Vayshoure"—the son of Vayshoure.

When Aries the cowherd brought his supposed son Tor to Arthur, the King asked to see Aries' wife.

> Anon the wife was fetched, which was a fair housewife, and there she answered Merlin full womanly, and there she told the king and Merlin that when she was a maid, and went to milk kine, there met with her a stern knight [Pellinore], and half by force he had my maidenhead, and at that time he begat my son Tor, and he took away from me my greyhound that I had that time with me, and said that he would keep the greyhound for my love. Ah, said the cowherd, I weened not his, but I may believe it well, for he [Tor] had never no tatches of me. Sir, said Tor unto Merlin, dishonour not my mother. Sir, said Merlin, it is more for your worship than hurt, for your father is a good man and a king, and he may right well advance you and your mother, for ye were begotten or ever she was wedded. That is truth, said the wife. It is the less grief unto me, said the cowherd. [Malory III, 3]

Ventres—see **NENTRES, KING**

"VERRINE"

This high-born damsel of Guenevere's court was mute until the arrival of Sir Percival, when at last she spoke. Greeting him, she led him to his seat at the left of the Siege Perilous and predicted his future greatness. She also predicted her own death, which took place four days later; she was buried in the cathedral at Cardiff. From the circumstances of the miracle, I assume she had led a holy life. [Malory X, 23; Vulgate V; see also under Percivale]

In Chrétien's version of the Percivale story, while the damsel who laughs is one of the queen's maids, I find no hard evidence that she had been speechless for six years—only that she had not laughed. Ruth Cline cites a suggestion that there may have been something of the geis about this not laughing; it remains a marvel that the courtly maid could look at the young backwoods simpleton and immediately recognize the future greatest knight of all. Nor can I find any indication of her premature death: in Chrétien, she returns Percivale's greeting with a smile as well as laughter, making her seem livelier and merrier than in subsequent versions. Nor does she even lead Percivale to his Round Table seat: Kay, angry because she has stated her opinion of the bumpkin's future greatness aloud for everyone to hear, knocks her down with a slap and kicks the court fool into the fire for siding with her, while Percivale simply takes off to defeat the Red Knight of Quinqueroi … though he does eventually return and avenge the maid. [**Perceval**, ll. 1034-1066; ca. 1200; 1239-1274; & here & there to 4477; ca. 4575; 4579-4602]

This maid and the fool (whom I doubt to be Dagonet) are almost always glimpsed in the same passages. I see no romantic tension in this, but neither do I see anything absolutely precluding such an interpretation.

Vertiger—see VORTIGERN

VEUVE DAME DE LA GASTE FOREST SOUTAINE†

According to Vulgate VII, she was the mother of Sir Agloval.

At one time, and in some versions, King Pellinore seems to have been identical with King Pelles/Pellam, the Maimed King, etc. Sommer appears to have been more or less on top in differentiating Pellinore and Pellam. I incline to accept "La Veuve Dame …" as the nearest thing I have yet uncovered to a name for Pellinore's wife and the mother of his sons in wedlock. In Vulgate VII, she appears to be ruling over a number of subjects, and this is not incompatible with the standard tale of Percivale and his mother.

VIVIANE (Vivien)†

The chief French Lady of the Lake—see also Lady of the Lake, Nimue, and "Nineve."

Viviane's father, Dyonas, was a vavasour of high lineage who long served the Duke of Burgoyne and married the Duke's daughter. The goddess Diane of the Woods, who used to visit Dyonas, promised him that his first child would be coveted by one of the wisest of men. Merlin met Dyonas' daughter Viviane at a fountain when she was twelve years old, and she promised to give him her love when he had taught her his crafts. According to this Vulgate account, Viviane was the woman who imprisoned Merlin.

When Queen Elaine of Benwick left her tiny son Galahad on a hill in sight of their conquered city, in order to rush to her dying husband, Viviane seized the opportunity to take the child. She renamed him Lancelot and raised him in her own rich city, disguised to mundane eyes beneath the appearance of a lake—hence "Lancelot of the Lake." Later, Viviane sent one of her chief damsels, Seraide, to rescue Lancelot's cousins Lionel and Bors from King Claudas and bring them, also, to the Lake.

When Lancelot was eighteen, Viviane yielded to his request, coached him in the requirements of knighthood, equipped him, and brought him and his cousins to Arthur's court. Viviane continued to act as Lancelot's guardian, through personal visits to Britain and through subordinate damsels whom she sent in her place.

She came to La Roche while Arthur was Camille's prisoner there and completed the matchmaking between Lancelot and Guenevere, counseling the Queen to love Lancelot with all her heart. Viviane then returned home, remarking, "I am anxious not to displease him who loves me, well knowing that a lover can only be happy when the object of his love is near." [Vulgate III, p. 419]

When Sir Bors and Viviane visited each other during Arthur's war with Claudas, Bors invested in Viviane's husband with the Chastel del Cor, apparently in France [Vulgate II-V].

According to the Vulgate, the Damsels of the Lake owed their knowledge of magic—apparently all of it—to Merlin. Tennyson makes Vivien a votary of the old pagan sun worship. He also makes her definitely evil, but this accords ill with the roles both of Nimue in Malory and Viviane in the Vulgate—moreover, in order to do it, he divorces Viviane from the beneficent Lady of the Lake and makes them two separate characters. Though Viviane has against her the imprisonment of Merlin, the kidnaping of Lancelot (though it may be said to have had good results), and the promotion of the affair between Lancelot and Guenevere (but she was not the only go-between in the case), she still seems to be shown in a good light, as a generally beneficent enchantress.

VIVIANE'S FAMILY AND RELATIONS
Adopted son: Lancelot
Protégés: Lionel, Sir Bors de Ganis
Cousin: Lunette
Damsels: "Rossignol", Seraide
Lover: Merlin

VORTIGERN† (Vertiger)

Vortigern was seneschal to King Constans of Britain, Arthur's grandfather. After the death of Constans, twelve barons who wanted Vortigern for their king murdered Constans' eldest son, Maines. Vortigern gained the kingship and allied himself to the Saxons. In fear of Constans' remaining sons, Pandragon and Uther, Vortigern tried to build himself a tower, but did not succeed until after the child Merlin had shown him a pair of dragons in a great water beneath the tower's proposed foundations, and made a very unfavorable prophecy about what the dragons symbolized for Vortigern. True to Merlin's prediction, Pandragon and Uther killed Vortigern and burned his tower. [Vulgate II] See also Vortigern's Tower.

VORTIGERN'S (Vertiger's) TOWER†

According to a tradition not found in Malory, this tower kept falling down. Vortigern's astrologers told him that to stand the masonry required the blood of a fatherless child. Vortigern found the young Merlin, who had been engendered by a devil and thus could be considered fatherless, but Merlin saved himself by making explanations and predictions which were found true. According to Merlin's statement, a lake was discovered beneath the tower. There a red dragon (symbolizing Vortigern) and a white dragon (symbolizing Pandragon and Uther, the two sons of King Constans, whom Vortigern had murdered to gain his power) fought to the death. The white dragon killed the red, but soon afterward died itself. The sons of Constans burned Vortigern's Tower after they killed him.

Clues in the Vulgate led me to believe that Vortigern's Tower was near Winchester. Because of the name, Din Guortigern, mentioned by Nennius and identified by one Mr. Pearson as on the Teviot River, is another contender. [Glennie, p. xxv]

WADE

Sir Wade must have been a great and famous knight in his day, judging from the company in which Dame Lynette puts him, even though this is the one reference I find to Wade in Malory. Rebuking Gareth Beaumains, Lynette says: "wert thou as wight as ever was Wade or Launcelot, Tristram or the good knight Sir Lamorak." [Malory VII, 9]

WALES

A major kingdom in legend and history. Monmouthshire is sometimes included in Wales. For purposes of Arthurian romancing, it seems to me that the entire north-south border might be moved east a little, through about the middle of Herford and Shropshire. Subkingdoms of Wales include Cambenet, Escavalon, Gore, Isle of Servage, the Isles, Norgales, Orofoise, Sorestan, the Straight Marches (?), Stranggore, Sugales, and Surluse.

Chrétien names Wales as one of the kingdoms from which Arthur drew reinforcements for his army. [**Cligés**, ca. l. 1482]

WALLINGFORD

The place where Cligés spent his first fortnight or so in Britain. Near Wallingford, also, stayed most of the knights attending the Oxford tournament. [Chrétien de Troyes, **Cligés**, ll. 4575-ca. 4635] Collier's **World Atlas and Gazetteer** [©1942] lists no Wallingford in the British Isles, but it does list three in the U.S.A.—in Connecticut, Pennsylvania, and Vermont (Rutland County); see note under Shoreham.

Wander—see GUENEVERE

WANDESBOROW

The eleven rebel kings had to leave off warring with Arthur for a time after the battle of Bedegraine when they learned that the Saracens had landed and were besieging their castle of Wandesborow [Malory I, 17-18].

The root "wand", as I recall, means "white." There is a Whitehaven in Cumberland and a Whitby in Yorkshire. Glennie lists a Caer Vandwy and identifies it as Cramond, near Leith, on the Firth of Forth, Scotland. Whitehaven seems too near King Pellam's territory if that is identified with the Lake District. I would prefer to identify Wandesborow with Caer Vandwy.

It may well be, of course, that Wandesborow and Vandaliors, which see, should be considered identical, in which case the Cornish site would be taken. It does not seem impossible, though, that the rebel kings were simultaneously or coincidentally attacked by two different foreign enemies at two different strongholds.

WASTE LANDS

Grail territory. See Listeneise and Carbonek Castle.

Waste Lands, King of the—see PELLAM, KING OF LISTENEISE

WASTE LANDS, QUEEN OF THE

While on the Grail Quest, Galahad encountered Lancelot and Percivale in a "waste forest", before the hermitage of a female recluse. When Galahad had unhorsed Lancelot and Percivale, the recluse hailed him, saying, "An yonder two knights had known thee as well as I do they would not have encountered with thee." At this, Galahad departed hastily, lest she reveal his identity. Lancelot also rode off on his own, but Percivale, returning to the hermitess, learned that she was his aunt.

> For some called me sometime the Queen of the Waste Lands, and I was called the queen of most riches in the world; and it pleased me never my riches so much as doth my poverty.

She revealed to Percivale that his mother had died, explained to him certain matters concerning the significance of the Round Table and the Sangreal, and counseled him to find Galahad again, beginning at Goothe Castle, "where he hath a cousin-germain, and there may ye be lodged this night." Goothe must have been in the vicinity of the queen's hermitage. If unsuccessful in getting news of Galahad at Goothe, Percivale was to ride on straight to Carbonek.

Lancelot also, later in the Grail Quest, received sound counsel and advice, as well as dinner, from a recluse. Lancelot's recluse might have been the Queen of the Waste Lands again, or she might have been an entirely different holy woman. She seems to have lived in a deep valley, near a mountain difficult of ascent, with a river in the vicinity—I would hazard a guess that the site might conceivably be somewhere in the Cotswolds, Gloucestershire.

Presumably the Queen of the Waste Lands who comes with Morgan, Nimue, and the Queen of Norgales to carry Arthur away after the last battle is the same Queen of the Waste Lands who appears in the Grail Adventures. If so, the presence of a Christian mystic and holy woman with two queens who have generally, up to now, been characterized as wicked enchantresses is very interesting. [Malory XIII, 17; XIV, 1-2; XV, 5-6; XXI, 5-6]

From Malory alone, the Queen of the Waste Lands appears to have been Pellam's wife, the couple living apart for greater purity. Tennyson, though skimming over Elaine of Carbonek and giving his own unsympathetic interpretation of Pellam, seems obliquely to second this theory in the Idyll **Balin and Balan**: "Pellam ... hath pushed aside his faithful wife." The Vulgate, however, makes her the widow of a man killed in an earlier war—possibly King Lambor, Pellam's grandfather. This would make her Percivale's great-great-aunt and quite a venerable, aged dame. Here too she has a son, Dables (Orabiax, Dyabel, etc.) who goes to Pellam to be knighted. [Vulgate VI]

There may also be some connection or confusion between the Queen of the Waste Lands and la Veuve Dame de la Gaste Forest Soutaine.

Watch, Knights of the—see GUARD, KNIGHTS OF THE

WATER BRIDGE†

The less hazardous of the two crossings into Gore, the Water Bridge was so called because it ran under the surface, with as much water above it as below. Chrétien describes it as only a foot and a half wide, and equally thick. It rather clearly equates with the Vulgate's "pont desouz ewe."

Having traveled some way together in pursuit of Meliagrant and Guenevere, Lancelot and Gawaine learned of the two bridges from the "Damsel of the Crossroads." Pressed by Lancelot to choose first, Gawaine finally declared for the underwater bridge. Even though, like Lancelot, he left his horse and more cumbersome arms on the other side, he was to fall in. Chrétien does not detail Gawaine's adventures on his way to the Water Bridge, saying only that they had been many, hard, and perilous. While they may also have consumed an inordinate number of days, the length of time Lancelot had already spent on the Gore side of the bridges before Gawaine was found creates the impression that the latter knight must have bobbed about in the water for quite a while before his rescue. His apparent long survival in the water may give further evidence of the otherworldly nature of Bademagu's Gore. [Chrétien de Troyes, **Lancelot**, ll. 648-713; 5125-5160]

Weeping Castle—see CASTLE PLUERE

WESTMINSTER

The name West Minster dates at least from 875 A.D. in a charter of King Offa. Since Malory uses the name, it seems more than fair for us to use it. The monastery was built on Thornea, a small island formed by outlets of the Tyburn and a ditch. The Thames was the eastern boundary. The monastery already existed at the time of the charter (perhaps on an old Pagan holy site?). Canute or a predecessor established a royal palace here, and Edward the Confessor built a new church and monastery. The town grew up around the religious establishments. In Arthur's England, London would not yet have engulfed Westminster.

WHIP, DWARF WITH A†

As Lancelot, during his adventures in Gore, led a rescue party to the Water Bridge in search of Gawaine, they were met by a dwarf riding a great hunting horse and carrying a whip to control it. The dwarf asked for Lancelot, promising to lead him to an excellent place, for his own profit, and bring him back shortly—provided he came alone. Lancelot trustingly did so and ended up being held prisoner in an isolated tower, guarded by Meliagrant's seneschal and his wife.

Those who had been with Lancelot later described the dwarf as stunted, hunchbacked, and grimacing; their memories of his appearance might, of course, have been colored by realization of his treachery. In any event, he would presumably have been either one of Meliagrant's servants or else acting for pay. [Chrétien de Troyes, **Lancelot**, ll. 5064-5125; 5161-5198]

White Abbey—see ABBEY OF THE ADVENTUROUS SHIELD and ABBEY OF THE BURNING TOMB

WILD FOREST

Percivale's name for his boyhood homeland, as he calls it when leaving Blancheflor to return home and check on his mother [Chrétien de Troyes, **Perceval**, ca. ll. 2955-2958]. See also Forest Sauvage.

WILDFIRE

Used in military actions to burn ships, castles, and so on [Malory X, 32, 38].

WINCHESTER

Malory twice identifies it as Camelot, q.v.

Chrétien de Troyes, however, who elsewhere gave us our first named record of Camelot, cites Winchester under its own name as among Arthur's court cities. Leaving Southampton on a May daybreak, and following the direct route, Alexander and his Greek companions arrived in Winchester before six a.m. to find Arthur. [**Cligés,** ll. 270-305]

WINDESAN (Windesant)

When King Idres was put in the city of Nauntes, King Nentes was put into Windesan with 4,000 knights to watch by water and by land [Malory I, 18]. Nentres being king of Garloth, the city of Windesan likely was in or was near his own territory, which probably was in the north, possibly East Lothian. For Windesan I suggest Berwick on Tweed. Glennie (who, however, identifies Berwick with Joyous Garde) describes it as crowning ... the northern heights at the mouth of the Tweed, looking eastward on the sea, that dashes up to high caverned cliffs, and commanding westward the vale of the beautiful river, here flowing between steep braes, shadowy with trees, or bright with corn and pasture ...." [p. 63]

WINDESORES†

Its lord was Sinados [Vulgate III]. It may be identical with Wandesborow, Vandaliors, or both. Perhaps more likely, it may be a variant spelling for Windsor. Norden lists a Windesore which is a mile or two inland from New Quay, on the north coast of Cornwall, "the howse of Mr. Windesore, situate amonge the minerall hills."

WINDSOR

Malory tosses in the name in XVIII, 2. Windsor Castle was founded by William I on the site of an earlier fortress.

Windsor Forest is around Windsor Castle. In **The Merry Wives of Windsor**, Shakespeare preserves for facetious purposes the tradition of Herne the Hunter, who haunts this woods; Ainsworth, in **Windsor Castle**, one of his better historical romances, uses Herne for more genuinely ghostly effects.

According to Chrétien de Troyes, Windsor was the city of Count Angrs, who, serving Arthur as regent (probably fairly early in the latter's reign), executed a major rebellion, for which he was eventually executed in his turn. Preparing for his revolt, Angrs fortified his castle of Windsor well, on its high hill with the Thames flowing beneath: he gave it triple walls and moats, palisades and ditches, until Arthur might have had the devil's own time capturing it, had Sir Alexander not defeated Angrs with a bold ruse. [**Cligés**, ll. 1236 ff.]

WINE

In Arthur's day, wine was an uncommon beverage in England [Vulgate VI]. This could explain how easy it seems to be to get a person to drink drugged wine.

The wine of Beaune, or Bayonne, France, must have been prized: "some men call it Bayonne, and some men call it Beaune, where the wine of Beaune is" [Malory XX, 18; cf. Benwick].

WONDROUS BED†

Crafted by Igraine's clerk to test the worth of adventuresome knights, this bed waited in the middle of Canguin's brightly floored hall, being the first thing one saw on entering through the ivory and ebony doors. The bed had silver cords; all the rest of it was gold, with a brilliant carbuncle in each of its four posts. It stood on dogs carved with grotesque faces, the dogs in turn resting on castors that allowed the light touch of a finger to send the bed rolling from one colorfully painted marble wall to another. It was spread with a heavy silk coverlet, and at each intersection of the cords hung a bell.

To sit upon this bed was perilous indeed, but no warning the ferryman of Canguin could give had any power to prevent Gawaine from essaying the adventure. The knight waited only until the boatman, choosing to spare himself the coming sights, had left the room. As soon as our hero sat, the hall resounded with the alarm of ringing bells and screeching bedcords. The clear glass windows opened to let in a cloud of bolts and arrows, more than seven hundred of which struck Gawaine's shield, some of them wounding him. When the windows closed again, he began to pull the missiles from his shield, but was interrupted by the opening of the door to admit a fierce lion, which plunged its claws into his shield as if into wax. He had to stop its attack by using his sword to strike off its head and the two feet in his shield: the paws were still hanging there next day, to prove the truth of his tale when he recounted it to Guiromelant.

The conquest of the lion ended the trial, along with the marvels (or at least the perilous ones), of the place, marking Gawaine as the long-awaited lord of the Rock of Canguin. He had not expected this lordship and, on learning that it entailed an obligation never again to leave the castle, naturally fell into a depression, one so severe that the ferryman soon persuaded Queen Igraine to relax the residency requirement a bit. [Chrétien de Troyes, **Perceval**, ca. ll. 7679-8038; 8339-8349]

Compare the "Deadly Bed."

YDER†

Chrétien names this king as among Arthur's allies and advisors [**Erec & Enide**, l. 311ff.]. We meet him again fighting in the Noauz tournament, where his shield is identified by a stag emerging from a gate [Chrétien, **Lancelot**, ca. ll. 5820-5823].

Do not confuse him with Yder son of Nut, but cf. Ider and King Idres.

YDER OF THE DOLOROUS MOUNT†(?)

Chrétien de Troyes would appear to mention three Yders in **Erec & Enide**. I doubt that Yder of the Dolorous Mount, named among Arthur's knights in the list beginning in line 1691, should be identified with Yder the son of Nut. I see more chance that he and King Yder are the same, and that the exigencies of Chrétien's original verse account for the differences in nomenclature.

YDER THE SON OF NUT†(?)

Sir Yder was riding along one day with his damsel and his dwarf when they passed Queen Guenevere, her maiden, and Erec on their way to join Arthur's hunt for the White Stag. Yder allowed his dwarf to insult and strike first Guenevere's maiden and then Erec when they approached to invite the knight and lady to see the Queen. After obtaining Guenevere's permission to pursue the strangers, Erec followed Yder to Lalut, where Erec met his future bride Enide and for the sake of her beauty fought Yder, defeated him, and sent him with his damsel and dwarf to Arthur's court to give himself up to the Queen and tell his story. Yder had previously won the prize sparrow-hawk for his own damsel two years in a row, so either he was no mean champion or his damsel was so beautiful that nobody cared to challenge her right until the local maid Enide found a knight. Guenevere freed Yder at once on condition that he remain constantly at court, which he gladly did, becoming a member of the Queen's company. Presumably, his dwarf and damsel stayed with him. His arms were blazoned gold and azure. [Chrétien de Troyes, **Erec & Enide**, ll. 125-1143]

Yder the son of Nut can probably be identified with Malory's Ider, Idrus, or both. See also Ider.

Ygerne, Ygerne's Clerk, etc.—see **IGRAINE, IGRAINE'S CLERK, etc.**

Ygraine—see **IGRAINE**

YON, KING†

Yon appears to have been a subking in Gaul, captured by Bagdemagus during Athur's war against Claudas. Bagdemagus added Yon's contingent to his own, and Yon himself seems not only to have gone over to Arthur's side, but to have distinguished himself as one of the best leaders on that side. [Vulgate V]

King Yon later turns up in Arthur's court, among the barons. After Lancelot was discovered with Guenevere, when Arthur commanded his barons to sentence the Queen without delay, Yon reminded him that it was not the custom to pass any judgments after the hour of Nonne (about mid-afternoon).

Yon was killed in the last battle with Mordred's forces [Vulgate VI].

Might Yon conceivably be identified with Yonec, the title character in one of the works of Marie de France?

YORK

Malory tells us that Arthur held a parliament here [V, 3], sufficient grounds for assuming he also held court at York, the traditional great city of the north. York is inland on the Ouse River, which flows into the Humber.

Youth in the Crimson Mantle—see under **IGRAINE'S SQUIRE**

YOUTH OF QUINTAREUS†

Among Arthur's knights in the list Chrétien de Troyes begins in line 1691 of **Erec & Enide**.

YOUTH WITH THE GOLDEN RING†

Among Arthur's knights in the list Chrétien de Troyes begins in line 1691 of **Erec & Enide**. I regret being unable to give the original French of his appellation, which may vary with the English translation.

Yseult, Ysolde—see **ISOUD**

YVAINE (Ewain, Owain, Uwain, Yvain, Yvonet, etc.)

Vulgate VII, p. 240, gives a list of six different knights with this name. Chrétien de Troyes gives the name Yvain four times in the list of Arthur's knights beginning line 1691 of **Erec & Enide**: Yvain son of Uriens, Yvain of Loenel, Yvain the Bastard, and Yvain of Cavaliot.

The only two I include here are the sons of King Uriens. His legitimate son, by Queen Morgan, is given under Ywaine.

Chrétien's "Yvain the Bastard" would probably be the one I originally listed as Yvonet li Avoutres; Chrétien mentions him again in **Perceval**, ca. ll. 8149-8162. It seems to me simplest to leave him entered here as Yvonet le Avoutres and risk confusion with the squire(s?) Yvonet of Chrétien's **Perceval**.

YVONET†

We meet this courtly squire early in Chrétien's **Perceval**: when Percivale first arrives at Arthur's court, Yvonet, holding a knife in his hand (he has obviously just been carving meat for the banquet), comes forward and points the king out to him. As Percivale leaves to challenge the Red Knight of Quinqueroi, Yvonet follows him, eager to learn the outcome at first hand and bring the news back to court. Going alone (which may suggest he has slipped out secretly) and following paths he knows, he apparently arrives in time to witness the battle. Watching Percivale drag the Red Knight's body around trying to get the armor off, Yvonet enjoys a laugh (presumably good-humored) at his inexpertise, then helps him with the arms and armor, afterward carrying Arthur's cup and Percivale's message (about returning to avenge "Verrine") back to court along with word of how the fight went.

Much later in the same romance, when Gawaine sets forth to answer Guigambresil's challenge, he takes seven squires along with him. Chrétien makes the point that, although many fellow knights offer to lend him good horses and pieces of equipment, he takes only what is his own; presumably this includes the squires. We learn in line 5664 that Yvonet is one of them, not improbably the principal one. They accompany Gawaine as far as Escavalon, but, after undertaking the quest of the bleeding lance, he sends them home. They are mournful, but obedient.

D.D.R. Owen remarks in a note that these two Yvonets are not necessarily the same character; I have failed to find any reason to suppose them different, unless it is the theory that Gawaine's adventures were originally meant to form a separate romance from Percivale's—and not even that would preclude the same squire Yvonet from appearing in both. Chrétien leaves so many key characters unnamed or very tardily named, that when he drops one in ready-named, I cannot help but suspect a figure already established in the chivalric literature of his time. Or even, perhaps, a living person known to the original target audience? Whatever the case, this Yvonet cannot be either of Uriens' sons, for they are both already knights, as Gawaine later explains to Queen Igraine.

[**Perceval**, ll. 915; ca.1067-1274; 4798-4806; 5664-5674; 6206-6213; Owen's note to 915; & Cline's to 916]

YVONET LI AVOUTRES (Uwaine Les Adventurous; Uwaine Les Avoutres, Yvain the Bastard, etc.)

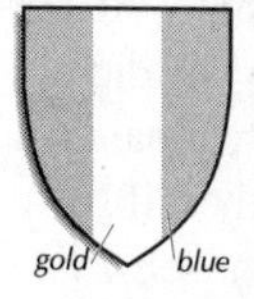

King Uriens of Gore had two sons of the same name: Yvonet le Grand by Arthur's half-sister Morgan, and Yvonet li Avoutres by the wife of Uriens' seneschal (Vulgate II). To try to keep things a little less confusing, I have used the more common present-day variant spelling Ywaine for the legitimate son, Le Grand (also called Le Blanchemains, etc.), and reserved the variant Yvonet for Li Avoutres.

Malory uses both brothers, but does not explain their birth history, which may lead to confusion. Both appear together on at least two occasions, once at the tournament at Castle Dangerous and once in company with Sirs Brandiles, Ozana, Agravaine, and Mordred in one of the interminable mix-and-match adventures that largely make up Malory's books of Tristram. Yvonet, or Uwaine les Avoutres as Malory calls him, was killed by Gawaine, ironically, while they were both on the Grail Quest. Happening to meet, they indulged in a joust, and by misadventure Yvonet was mortally wounded. Gawaine got him to an abbey, where he was unarmed and given the Sacrament.

> Then Gawaine asked him what he was ... I am, said he, of King Arthur's court, and was a fellow of the Round Table, and we were brethren sworn together; and now Sir Gawaine, thou hast slain me, and my name is Uwaine les Avoutres, that sometime was son unto King Uriens, and was in quest of the Sangreal; and now forgive it thee God, for it shall ever be said that the one sworn brother hath slain the other. [Malory VII, 27+; X, 11; XVI, 2]

Chrétien de Troyes lists Yvain the Bastard among Arthur's good knights in the list beginning line 1691 of **Erec & Enide**. He mentions him again in **Perceval**, ca. lines 8149-8162, when Queen Igraine asks Gawaine about King Uriens and his sons, and Gawaine tells her about both Yvains; the second is called "the Bastard" and has beaten every knight he has ever fought. Both Yvains are considered extremely courteous, brave, and intelligent—aside from his own personal friendship for the first (legitimate) one, Gawaine seems to place them on a level.

YWAINE (Ewain, Ewain Le Blanchemains, Owain, Owen, Uwain, Uwaine, Yvain, Yvonet Le Grand, Le Chevalier Au Lion, Knight with the Lion, etc.)

Ywaine was the son of King Uriens and Queen Morgan of Gore, half-brother to Yvonet li Avoutres (see above), cousin and close friend to Gawaine. He may have come to Arthur's court as early as the funeral of Lot and the other kings of the second rebellion, along with his parents, who attended that funeral.

At Camelot, Ywaine found his mother about to slay his sleeping father. He prevented her, exclaiming, "Ah … men saith that Merlin was begotten of a devil, but I may say an earthly devil bare me." At her pleading, he agreed not to speak of her attempt on condition she did not try it again. She proceeded to leave court, steal the scabbard of Excalibur, and attempt to destroy Arthur by sending him the gift of a poisoned cloak. It would not be surprising if Ywaine felt himself freed of his promise not to reveal her attempt on Uriens' life, but the tale seems to imply that he kept the secret, at least for the time; after the poisoned cloak incident, both Morgan's husband and son were suspected of being in her counsel. Arthur quickly dismissed his suspicion against Uriens, but banished Ywaine from court, which must have been hard on the young knight. Gawaine remarked, "Whoso banisheth my cousin-germain shall banish me", and went with Ywaine. They met Sir Marhaus and shortly thereafter found the damsels "Printemps, Été, and Automne" in Arroy Forest. Ywaine chose "Automne" for his guide, saying, "I am the youngest and most weakest [of us three knights] … therefore I will have the eldest damosel, for she hath seen much, and can best help me when I have need."

Traveling with her, he distinguished himself, winning a tournament near the Welsh marches and gaining back for the Lady of the Rock a barony that Sirs Edward and Hue of the Red Castle had extorted from her. At the end of a twelvemonth, after meeting again with their damsels at the appointed place in Arroy, Ywaine, Gawaine, and Marhaus were found by a messenger of Arthur's. The King must have realized his error in banishing Ywaine almost at once, for he had been seeking his nephews nearly a year. They returned to court, taking Marhaus with them. It may have been at this time that Ywaine was made a member of the Round Table, though Malory only mentions that Marhaus and Pelleas were so honored at the next feast. [Malory I, 2; II, 11; IV, 13, 16-19, 26-28]

Chrétien de Troyes devoted what I consider the best of his finished romances to Ywaine; its relationship to the **Mabinogion** tale **Owen and Lunet**—which is based on the other, or whether both spring from some lost original—remains, as far as I can tell, under dispute. Chrétien recounts how, while the court was at Carlisle, Ywaine's cousin Sir Calogrenant told a small group including Ywaine, Kay, Gawaine, Dodinel, Sagramore, and Guenevere about his adventures seven years earlier at a marvelous spring in Broceliande Forest: using a conveniently placed basin to dip water from this spring onto a nearby rock caused a terrific storm to arise and, after the storm, a knight to appear and chastise the impudent person who had poured the water. Learning this story, Arthur decided to take his court and see the place for himself. Ywaine, however, secretly slipped away and got there well ahead of them, tried his own luck at storm-making, and killed the spring's champion (Esclados the Red) in fair combat. This left Esclados the Red's widow, Dame Laudine, without a protector for herself, her castle, or the spring. Ywaine fell in love with Laudine and, with the assistance of her damsel Lunette, who gave him good advice and a magic ring of invisibility, eventually won her and became guardian of the magic spring in time to carry out his new duties when Arthur, arriving with his court, poured water on the rock. Not recognizing the fully armored Ywaine, Kay took the fight for Arthur and was promptly defeated. There followed a happy reunion and welcome for Arthur and his people at Laudine's castle. Unfortunately, Gawaine persuaded Ywaine that he should spend a year adventuring and tourneying, lest folk say his marriage had made him soft. Laudine gave her husband a magic ring to keep him safe and let him go on the condition that he return in exactly a year. He let the months get away from him and stayed away too long, whereon Laudine sent a damsel (not Lunette) to demand the ring back and forbade him ever to see him again.

Ywaine promptly went mad with grief and ran amok in the wild forest, augmenting his diet of raw meat with bread from a hermit, until the lady of Noroison and two of her damsels found him asleep; one of them recognized him by a scar on his face. They healed him with a salve that Morgan the Wise had given the lady, whose war against Count Alier Ywaine then won. Refusing her offer of marriage, he wandered away and rescued a lion from a serpent.

The lion became his grateful companion for life. Under the name of the Knight with the Lion, Ywaine embarked on a series of adventures, always fighting for the good, in contrast to his earlier year's adventures of tourneying for the mere glory of it. Among other deeds, he saved a sister of Gawaine and her family (see "Alteria") from the wicked giant Harpin of the Mountain, and rescued Lunette from an accusation of treachery by fighting for her in trial by combat. With the damsel I call "Secunda", he visited Pesme Avanture and righted the injustice there by slaying two demons with the assistance of his lion. Eventually, still incognito, he arrived at Arthur's court to champion the younger daughter of the lord of Noire Espine in an inheritance dispute with her sister. Unknown to Ywaine, Gawaine was championing the elder sister, so there resulted one of those grand battles, so beloved of the romancers, between two great and evenly matched knights who are really dear friends or relatives that do not recognize each other in their armor. Fortunately for Gawaine, this time the lion was successfully kept out of the fight, so it ended happily: on finally learning each other's identity, each hero swore himself vanquished by the other, and Arthur settled the case between the two sisters with a Solomon-like judgment. After time in the infirmary to heal, Ywaine, with his lion, returned to Broceliande, where Lunette effected a reconciliation between husband and wife.

Without attempting to summarize Ywaine's adventures as recorded in the Vulgate, we return to Malory. While Tristram, Palomides, and Dinadan were languishing in Sir Darras' prison after the Castle of Maidens tournament, Ywaine le Blanchemains (I have not yet discovered why Malory gives Morgan's son this appellation), seemingly having joined a general search for Tristram and quite possibly suspecting Mark of further treachery, appeared before Mark's castle and issued a challenge to "all the knights of Cornwall." Only Andred was willing to encounter him, to Andred's immediate unhorsing and wounding. At Mark's insistence, Sir Dinas the Seneschal jousted with Ywaine and was overthrown. Then Sir Gaheris, who happened to be visiting Mark, rode out, but Ywaine recognized his shield and refused to have ado with a brother of the Round Table. As Ywaine rode away, Mark rode after and dealt him a treacherous and serious blow from behind. Fortunately, Sir Kay happened along in time to get Ywaine to the Abbey of the Black Cross to be healed. [Malory IX, 38]

Ywaine fades out of Malory's account after this episode; he is mentioned with his half-brother and namesake [X, 11], and after that, perplexingly, there is little or nothing. Possibly by XVI Malory himself had the Ywaines confused and considered this Ywaine—rather than his half-brother Les Avoutres—to have been the one who was killed during the Grail Quest and was therefore out of the story. In Vulgate VI we learn that the deaths of Gawaine, his brothers, and Kay, and the rift between Arthur and Lancelot with his supporters, have left Ywaine as Arthur's remaining mainstay. Ywaine is killed by Mordred in the last battle.

Ywaine's coat of arms presumably includes a lion.

Whether or not Arthur is an historical figure, Ywaine and his father Uriens seem to be based on men who actually lived in the sixth century in Rheged (northern England and southern Scotland). [See, for instance, D.D.R. Owen's note to Chrétien's **Yvain**, l. 56] Need I observe that what these men became in the romances surely bears very little resemblance to what they were in life?

The adventures of a knight named Owayne in Saint Patrick's Purgatory, another very popular focus of romance from at least as early as the 12th century, make me wonder why Ywaine seems to have missed getting into the Grail cycle in any major way.

YWAINE'S HERMIT†

When Ywaine ran mad because he had lost his wife's love by staying away from her too long, he seized bow and arrows from a serving-lad and lived in the woods on raw meat alone until he happened upon the hut of a poor hermit. This man reacted with both fear and charity, fleeing into his house but setting out a pitcher of pure water and some of his own very coarse barley bread. Maddened though he was, Ywaine promptly fell into the habit of returning to the hermit's house every day and leaving a slain beast in return for his bread and water. The good man probably ate the meat and certainly sold the skins and bought better bread. He sounds like a practical fellow, and may have been a bit sorry when Ywaine was found and restored to sanity. D.D.R. Owen points to a comparison with Tristram's Ogrine (Brother Ogrins). [Chrétien de Troyes, **Yvain**, ll. 2802-2917]

YWAINE'S (Yvain's) LION†

D.D.R. Owen suggests that this noble beast may have been derived from the lion befriended by Androcles. It seems remarkably humanesque in its intelligence: even though Ywaine must sever a piece of its tail in saving it from the serpent, it remains his loyal helper for life; at one point, supposing Ywaine dead, it almost kills itself by deliberately running on Ywaine's sword.

The lion's size looks a little problematical. Early on their first night together, it kills a deer and finishes off the whole creature except for Ywaine's single piece of loin. Later, when the lion has been wounded in battle with Laudine's seneschal and his brothers, Ywaine lines his shield with bracken and moss, lays the beast on it at length, and carries him on his horse, which may more nearly suggest the size of a large hound.

It has apparently recovered completely by the time Ywaine must battle the giant demons of Pesme Avanture: at their insistence, he shuts it away in a small room, but, driven frantic by the sounds of fighting, it breaks out and accounts for one of the pair, enabling Ywaine to finish the other. Ywaine and the lion make a formidable fighting team. It is as well for Gawaine, even if it does seem a bit convenient for the author of the romance, that Ywaine and the younger daughter of the lord of Noire Espine have the foresight to slip away and leave the loyal beast where they have spent the night, so that the man can fight this one battle alone, the lion catching up only after it is finished. [Chrétien de Troyes, **Yvain**, ll. 3341 on]

YWAINE'S SQUIRE†

When Ywaine made up his mind to slip away and reach the marvelous spring in Broceliande Forest without first seeking his sovereign's permission, he relied on a trusty squire to help him keep his departure secret. Though Ywaine did not take him with him, and though he accompanied his instructions with a mild threat (for form's sake?), he is described as concealing nothing from this squire. The relationship looks deep and filled with mutual respect; one feels surprised to see so little of the squire, who disappears from the story after this one episode. [Chrétien de Troyes, **Yvain**, ll. 723-ca.760]

Zelegbres—see **TALEBRE**

King Arthur's Britain
ORKNEY
THE OUT ISLES
THE LONG ISLES
SCOTLAND
Pomitain
ESTRANGOR
BENOYE
LOTHIAN
Abercurnig
Wandesborow
Castle of Maidens
GARLOTH
Windesan
NOHAUT
Castle Orgulous
La Joyous (Dolorous) Garde
Perlownes
Lonazep
Campacorentin Forest
NORTH MARCH
Castle of the Leprous Lady
Carteloise Forest
Cartreloise
L'Isle Estrange
Northumberland Forest
NORTHUMBERLAND
Carlisle
Celibe Forest
THE WASTELANDS
Goothe
Carbonek
Castle of Bliant
Castle Blank
LISTENEISE
Chapel of the Conjuration
Chapel of the Stony Cross
AMANS
Forest Sauvage?
York
SARRAS

RISH SEA
RTH SEA
AND
ENGLISH CHANNEL
York
Abbey of Beale Adventure
CAMELIARD
Carohaise
ROESTOC
Forest Sauvage?
SURLUSE
Sorhaute
Sapine Forest
SORESTAN
Lincoln
Bedegraine Forest
Bedegraine Castle
EASTLANDS
Leister
THE ISLES
Tauroc
Teneborc
Kynke Kenadonne
OROFOISE
NORGALES
Perilous Forest
Morgan's Castle
Castle Perilous
Chapel Desolate
Nauntes
Isle of Servage
WALES
CAMBENET
Hautdesert
Green Chapel
Red Castle
Wroxeter
Abblasoure
Castle of Maidens
Castle Chariot
STRAIGHT MARCHES
NORFOLK
Venta
Forest Sauvage?
SUFFOLK
Arroy Forest
Bresquehan Forest
Perilous Forest
Cardican
Landoine Forest
SUGALES
GORE
Abbey of the Burning Tomb
Roevant Forest
STRANGGORE
Hereford
ARROY
LEISTER
Gloucester
Colchester
Gloevant Forest
ESCAVALON
Pass Perilous
Cirencester
Oxford
LOGRES
Windsor Forest
ESSEX
Galhom
Carleon
Inde
London
Windsor
Cardif
Castle Dangerous
Fountain of the Silver Pipe (Turquine's Hill)
Castle of Sir Damas
LAMBETH
Bath
Silchester
VAGON
Rochester
Canterbury
Sandwich
Turnance
Port of the Perilous Bay
Castle de la Rowse
Astolat
Castle Pluere
Beale-Valet
Glastonbury
Almesbury
Meloit & Isles Perdue
SURREY
KENT
Dover
AVILION
Salisbury
Camelot
TANINGUES
The Weald
SUSSEX
TINTAGIL
Dolorous Tower (La Beale Garde)
Morgan's Castle
Camelot Forest
SOUTHMARCH
La Beale Regard
Arundel
Chichester
Tintagil
Morris Forest
Black Chapel
Exeter
Dorchester
Abbey of the Black Cross
The Perilous Lake
Terrabil
CORNWALL
Lyonesse Castle
Castle Ganis
Arbray
LYONESSE
Vandoliers

APPENDICES

A Tentative Chronology of Arthur's Reign

The era of Arthur, according to the Vulgate and Malory, is the first half of the fifth century after Christ. Galahad arrived at Arthur's court in the year 454 A.D. [Vulgate VI; Malory XIII, 2].

By long usage, characters of the sixth century, especially saints and poets, may be incorporated into Arthurian adventure. Certain personages from earlier centuries may also appear: Nascien the hermit and King Mordrains, contemporaries of Joseph of Arimathea, both miraculously survived into Arthur's time, and Joseph himself appears in visions. Other saints and angels could surely appear in visions as well. I have never yet encountered the Wandering Jew in Arthurian legend, but see no reason why he should not appear in Arthur's world.

Christ himself appears in the form of an old holy man. Vulgate VI strongly suggests that the old man who arrives by boat to explain Percivale's visions on the island during the Grail Quest is "the bread of life from heaven," i.e., Christ. [Vulgate VI, p. 82; cf. Malory XIV, 7]

The Devil likewise appears in person. He may take the form of a venerable holy man to interpret falsely someone's vision or experiences, a beautiful woman to tempt a knight's chastity, or even a horse to try to drown its rider. According to Nascien, it was the Devil who entered into Guenevere and made her desire Lancelot, because that was the only way the evil one could get a hold on the great knight [Vulgate VI]. I also found one named demon, Aselaphes, who killed King Tholomer lest Josephe convert him [Vulgate I, p. 76]. This was long before Arthur's time, but devils are immortal. Nearer home, a devil is credited with fathering Merlin.

In arranging this chronology, I generally gave more weight to the Vulgate than to Malory, since the Vulgate seems to me more internally consistent.

Dates marked *ca.* have been computed. Dates not so marked are known from Malory or from the Vulgate—but I have found only two known dates, 435 A.D. and 454 A.D. Events left undated I theorize to have fallen between the dated events, probably in the approximate order listed. Parenthesized events are in especially tentative placement.

The numbers in brackets give book and chapter of Malory. Events not found in Malory are marked with a dagger; they are from the Vulgate unless otherwise noted.

ca. 410 A.D.

- Arthur crowned [I, 7].[1]
- First rebellion of British kings [I, 8-18].

- (Sagramore arrives in Britain.†)
- Alliance with Ban and Bors [I, 8-18].[2]
- Merlin meets Viviane, aged 15 [I, 8-18].†
- Battle of Bedegraine [I, 8-18].
- Arthur engenders Borre (Lohot) on Lyzianor [I, 8-18].
- Ban and Bors help Arthur save Leodegrance from Ryons [I, 8-18].
- Gwenbaus settles down with his princess in Forest Perilleuse.†
- Margawse and her sons visit Arthur in Caerleon. Arthur engenders Mordred and has nightmare of serpent. [I, 19]
- Arthur reunited with his mother [I, 21].
- Arthur fights Pellinore and gains Excalibur [I, 23-25].
- (Mark of Cornwall murders his brother, Prince Boudwin [X, 32-33].)

ca. 413 A.D.

- Mordred's birth. The drowning of the May babies. [I, 27]
- The death of "Nineve", the first British Lady of the Lake [II].
- The final defeat of King Ryons [II].
- The second rebellion of British kings, under Lot, and the death of Lot [II].
- Lot's sons established at Arthur's court [II].
- Balin deals Pellam the Dolorous Stroke [II].
- The tale of Balin and Balan [II].
- The marriage of Arthur and installation of the Round Table at Arthur's court [III, 1-2].
- The first attempt of Genievre to supplant Guenevere.†
- Pellinore rescues Nimue and brings her to court [III, 5, 12-15].
- Morgan leaves Arthur's court the first time, meets Merlin in Bedingran and studies with him.†
- The invasion of the five kings and the battle at the Humber [IV, 2-4].
- Gawaine wins Gringolet.†
- Arthur and the surviving kings of the former rebellions, now allied, defeat the Saxons.†
- (The affair of Sir Gawaine and the Green Knight.†)
- Merlin and Nimue visit Ban and Elaine in Benwick [IV, 1].
- Nimue becomes chief British Lady of the Lake, imprisons Merlin in Cornwall [IV, 1].
- Morgan attempts to kill Arthur and Uriens and put her lover Accolon and herself on the throne; she permanently leaves Arthur's court when the attempt fails [IV, 6-16].
- Claudas defeats Ban and Bors. Viviane appropriates the infant Lancelot. Claudas and one of his men visit Arthur's court as spies for a year.†

ca. 415 A.D.

- (Morgan enchants the Val des Faux Amants.†)
- Arthur's first war with Rome. Death of Emperor Lucius in battle. Arthur crowned emperor in Rome. [V][3]
- Seraide rescues the young Lionel and Bors from Claudas, brings them to live with Lancelot in the French Lake.†
- (Tristram defeats Marhaus and begins his own career [VIII, 4-7].)

ca. 428 A.D.

- Viviane brings Lancelot, aged 18, and his cousins to Arthur's court.†
- Lancelot wins Dolorous/Joyous Garde.†
- Duke Galeholt tries to conquer Arthur.†
- Nascien visits Arthur's court, perhaps for the first but not for the last time.†
- Lancelot wins Galeholt's allegiance for Arthur.†
- Lancelot and Guenevere, Galeholt and the Lady of Malohaut, pledge their love at Carlisle.†
- (The tale of La Cote Male Taile [IX, 1-9].)
- Lancelot, still an unattached knight-errant, leaves court again. A search is started for him.†
- The defeat of Camille and the Saxons at La Roche. Lancelot officially joins Arthur's court, confirms his love with Guenevere.†
- (The tale of Gareth Beaumains [VII].)
- (The murder of Margawse [X, 24].)[4]
- (The Surluse tournament [X, 40-49].)[4]
- (The murder of Lamorak [X, 54].)[4]

ca. 430 to 432 A.D.

- Genievre's second attempt to supplant Guenevere succeeds for about two years, during which time Guenevere lives with Lancelot in Surluse.†
- Carados of the Dolorous Tower captures Gawaine (after the feast celebrating Lancelot and Guenevere's return†).
- On the way to save Gawaine, Lancelot passes through Morgan's Val des Faux Amants and she persuades him that Guenevere no longer loves him; he therefore avoids court and goes mad.†
- Lancelot kills Carados, rescues Gawaine [VIII, 28].
- Deaths of Duke Galeholt and the Lady of Malohaut.†
- Meliagrant kidnaps Guenevere; Lancelot eventually rescues her [XIX, 1-9].
- Bors helps King Agrippe's daughter.†
- Bors engenders Helin le Blank on King Bradegoris' daughter [cf. XII, 9; XVI, 6].
- (The Castle of Maidens tournament [IX, 27-35].)
- (The Castle of the Hard Rock tournament [IX, 41-44; X, 1].)
- Lancelot follows the damsel "Ornagrine" to adventure; Mordred, about twenty years old and newly knighted, joins the search for Lancelot.†
- Guenevere sends Elyzabel to France to enlist Vivianc's aid in finding Lancelot; Claudas imprisons Elyzabel before she can reach Viviane.†
- Lancelot falls sick, meets and is nursed by Amable.†

ca. 433 A.D.

- Lionel finds Lancelot; Lionel is captured by Turquine while Lancelot is kidnaped by Morgan and her cohorts [VI, 1-4].
- Freed from Morgan's Castle Chariot, Lancelot visits Carbonek, engenders Galahad on Pellam's daughter Elaine [XI, 1-3].
- Lancelot frees the knights and ladies in Gwenbaus' Forest Perilous.†

- Lancelot kills Turquine, frees Lionel and the other prisoners [VI, 7-9].
- Morgan captures Lancelot again, holds him two winters and a summer. He paints murals of his life and love.†
- (Gawaine and his brothers kill King Pellinore [XI, 10].)
- Escaping from Morgan, Lancelot meets Mordred; they travel together until, before the Peningues tournament, Mordred learns the truth of his birth and the prophecy of his future. The turning point of Mordred's career.†
- Bors visits Carbonek and its Adventurous Palace [XI, 4-6].
- (Alisander le Orphelin marries Alice la Beale Pilgrim [X, 39].)
- Lancelot saves Kay and then takes his armor [VI, 11-13].

435 A.D.

- Lancelot returns to Arthur's court at Camelot [VI, 18; the date is known from Vulgate V].
- Whitsunday: Brumant l'Orguilleus dies in the Siege Perilous.†
- (The battle of Lancelot and Tristram; Tristram becomes a knight of the Round Table [X, 5-6].)
- (The Lonazep tournament [X, 56-58, 65-80].)
- Learning of Elyzabel's imprisonment, Guenevere and† Arthur war on and finally defeat Claudas [XI, 6].
- Elaine of Carbonek visits Arthur's court for the feast celebrating the victory over Claudas. Lancelot goes mad. [XI, 7-10; XII, 1-3]

ca. 446 or 449 A.D.

- Percivale, aged about 15, comes to court [X, 23].
- Lancelot is cured of his madness at Carbonek, takes the name Le Chevaler Mal Fet, and lives with Elaine two to four years in Joyous Isle [XII, 4-6].
- Tristram and La Beale Isoud live at Joyous Garde [XII, 11].[5]

ca. 451 or 454 A.D.

- Ector and Percivale find Lancelot and persuade him to return to court. Galahad comes also, and stays in a convent near Camelot[6] [XII, 7-10].
- Palomides is baptized [XII, 14].

454 A.D.

- Galahad comes to Camelot. The start of the Grail Quest—officially, this would last at least a year, but many knights were gone far longer, and some never returned. Bors must have been gone at least four years. [XIII-XVII; the date is known both from Malory and the Vulgate]
- (Mark kills Tristram [cf. XIX, 11].)

ca. 461 A.D.

- The attempt on Gawaine's life with a poisoned apple is made [XVIII, 1-8].
- The Winchester tournament and the Elaine of Astolat affair occur [XVIII, 9-20].[7]
- Arthur visits Morgan in her castle, but Lancelot's murals fail to convince him of the affair between Lancelot and Guenevere.†
- Sir Urre is healed [XIX, 10-13].

- Lancelot and Guenevere are surprised [XX, 1-8].
- Arthur and Gawaine besiege Lancelot in Joyous Garde [XX, 10-13].
- Lancelot is banished [XX, 14-18].
- Arthur and Gawaine besiege Lancelot in France [XX, 19-22].
- The Romans take advantage of the situation and attack Arthur in France. The second war with Rome ends less successfully for Arthur. Kay dies in battle.†

ca. 465 A.D.

- The last battle and the passing of Arthur [XXI, 1-6].

[1]*This date is computed from the following evidence: the Vulgate puts Turquine's capture of Lionel in the twenty-third year of Arthur's reign; the return of Lancelot to Arthur's court, after killing Turquine and subsequently spending a year and a half as Morgan's prisoner, is the year 435.*

[2]*According to the Vulgate, Arthur goes to France for a time to help Ban and Bors against Claudas before they cross to Britain to help Arthur win the battle of Bedegraine.*

[3]*Though Malory has Lancelot fighting in this campaign, I had enough trouble trying to fit in such other adventures as the various tournaments and the tale of Gareth Beaumains in the time the Vulgate allows for Lancelot's being with the rest of Arthur's company.*

[4]*An alternative dating for these three sequential events would be in the probable interval between Lancelot's return from Joyous Isle and Galahad's arrival in Camelot, ca. 451-454 A.D. Such dating must assume that Malory either invented and embroidered his account in ignorance of Duke Galeholt's death, or had Galeholt confused with his heir and successor.*

[5]*"[K]ept not [Tristram] with him La Beale Isoud near three year in Joyous Garde?" [Malory XX, 6]*

[6]*Galahad may have spent up to three years in the holy retreat before coming on to Camelot.*

[7]*Arthur remarks just before the Winchester tournament, "[T]his year ye saw not such a noble fellowship together except at Whitsuntide when Galahad departed from the court" [Malory XVIII, 8].*

Just after the Winchester tournament, Gawaine tells Elaine of Astolat (when he sees Lancelot's shield), "I have known that noble knight this four-and-twenty year" [Malory XVIII, 14]. But this would put Lancelot's arrival in Britain in about the year 437—an impossibility according to the Vulgate account, for the date of 435 for Lancelot's return to court is one of the two definite dates I have found. Either Malory condenses by five to seven years, or Lancelot has only been carrying this particular coat of arms for twenty-four years, or twenty-four is used as a common time approximation like a dozen, a score, or the Biblical forty. Perhaps Gawaine is vain enough to knock off a few years from his and Lancelot's true ages.

Arthurian Classes and Roles

Children

Guenevere was once reduced to using a child of her chamber as a messenger. The child, probably a page, was in her Maying party when it was ambushed and captured by Meliagrant and his men. Guenevere called the child, who was "swiftly horsed", and slipped him her ring and a message for Lancelot. Escaping from the group even while Meliagrant was getting it back to his castle, the child proved himself a very reliable and competent messenger. [Malory XIX, 3]

This is about the only thing I have found relative to children in general, at least older than infancy. There is, of course, the episode of the May babies [Malory I, 27], the tale of Arthur's own birth, and incidents in the childhood years of certain characters, like Bors and Lionel, who came to prominence as adults. There is the evidence that a number of characters—Merlin, Percivale, Galahad, Viviane, Elaine of Astolat, Arthur himself—became prominent in their early teens, only a few years removed from the age we consider childhood. It may be worth noting that our sentimental emphasis on childhood as a semi-sacred state of being and children as innocent little angels to be coddled and envied seems to be a much later development, perhaps largely a product of this and the last century. Arthurian children may well have been treated with more practical regard for their capabilities, given responsibility earlier, and less carefully shielded from "sex and violence"—and this may have led to their seeming invisibility in the romances.

At the same time, some careers seem to have lasted much longer in the romances than we might think likely, with our common idea that medieval people were considered aged by fifty. For instance, think of the Vulgate's testimony that Mador de la Porte had served Arthur forty-five years and was still hale and hearty enough to give Lancelot a good fight in Guenevere's trial by combat. Contrary to the popular modern picture, the testimony of Malory and the Vulgate indicates that Guenevere must have been somewhat older than Lancelot—sort of an Elizabeth-Essex love, in a way; Morgawse must have been considerably older than her lover Lamorak. Literary convention may have expanded these great character's ages and youths, of course. Also, I have long believed that we commonly misinterpret the statistics of "average life expectancy" in other centuries—I suspect that life expectancy was short because of high mortality among infants, children, and youths, not because a person was "old" at age thirty—that a member of the upper classes, with a reasonaably good diet and a reasonably good balance of work, exercise, and rest, could look forward to as strong and sound a "three-score and ten" or longer as we moderns, barring plague and accident. Whatever the historical truth, however, the impression I draw from the medieval Arthurian romances is of a society in which age differences and generation gaps were not nearly so important as we have made them today.

Clerks

I confess I do not know whether to classify clerks as holy folk, magicians, neither, or both. Clerks were very likely clerics or clergy, but this does not necessarily imply personal holiness. In historical times, a man's entering the lower orders of the clergy did not preclude his later taking a wife. Possibly Arthurian clerks included persons who were not officially clergy but who specialized in reading and writing. Notice, however, that the knights and ladies of Arthurian romance are frequently, perhaps generally, literate; it comes as a shock to learn that King Claudas cannot read [Vulgate V]. Nevertheless, several different manuscript styles had developed, each with specified official uses—writers and polished calligraphers being different entities, clerks therefore would fill important roles at even generally literate courts in the days before printing.

As well as keeping written records, clerks seem to have made sure that etiquette was upheld. They also conducted investigations into the future by searching dreams and visions [Vulgate V].

Dwarves

Dwarves appear everywhere, usually as servants. They often seem to fill a role similar to that of squires, but, presumably, with no chance of becoming knights. Occasionally, as in the Vulgate, we read of the daughter or niece of a dwarf becoming the lover of a knight. I theorize that dwarves may have been members of an earlier, conquered race, the folk who are supposed to have gone into the caves and burrows as their land was engulfed by successive waves of Celts, Angles, and so on, the folk who according to one theory became the "fairies" of folklore—Sutcliff's "little dark people." There are also tales, however, of traders called Comprachicos or Comprapequeños who bought children and surgically made them into misshapen dwarves, apparently for resale.

An indication of one dwarf's size is found in Malory VII, 19:

> And then when [Sir Gringamore] saw Sir Beaumains fast asleep, he came stilly stalking behind the dwarf, and plucked him fast under his arm, and so he rode away with him as fast as ever he might unto his own castle.

A dwarf of Morgan's is described as having "a great mouth and a flat nose" [Malory IV, 8]. I wonder if the term "dwarf" might not have become at least partially synonymous with a certain type of servant, so that not all "dwarves" were actually members of a dwarvish race or mutilated children.

Whether a dwarf could serve as a physical bodyguard is doubtful, but dwarves may show considerable intelligence and resourcefulness. Dame Elyzabel once traveled from Britain to Gaul on a fairly dangerous mission with a squire and a dwarf as—seemingly—her only companions.

As an example of master-dwarf relationships, Gareth and his damsel came to a pavilion. The master was gone, but the dwarf was ready to welcome them provisionally on his master's permission. When the master came back, however, he began beating his dwarf for extending even this much courtesy unauthorized. Gareth thrashed the master and made him beg his dwarf's pardon. The dwarf forgave his master on condition he would never lay hands on him again and would bear him no grudge. [Vulgate V]

For all their importance as a class, I do not remember one dwarf who is given a name. The only one I have included is Gareth's dwarf.

Giants

The size of giants varies. The Giant of Saint Michael's Mount was probably the biggest, if we take the fact the he split Hoel's wife to the navel while forcing her as indicative of his size—a regular ogre of the "Jack the Giant Killer" tradition. Hargodabrans, the Saxon, was fifteen feet tall. Galapas' size may perhaps be judged by Arthur's remark after cutting off his legs to the knees: "Now art thou better of a size to deal with than thou were." Some giants were small enough to ride horseback, like Nabon le Noire and Taulas. Taulas' brother Taulurd, however, was too big for any horse. Carados of the Dolorous Tower is said to have been "made like a giant"; this may mean simply that he was an especially large man. If it means that he was in every sense a "giant", then the same should be said of his brother Sir Turquine. Lucius' bodyguard was fifty giants reputedly engendered of fiends. Chances seem good that the giants were or were considered a race apart; the smaller ones at least, though, seem to have been capable of interbreeding with humans. Duke Galeholt was said to be the son of a "beautiful giantess." (Of course, Galeholt is also the reputed son of the wicked Sir Breunor of Castle Pluere.)

There may, perhaps, have been more than one species of giant. It is even possible that at one time the giants had been equated with the Saxons, though I would not care to make too much of that theory at this time. As the Bible says somewhere, "There were giants in the earth in those days …."

Hermits, Monks, Nuns

We read of "white monks", "black monks", and so on. Since no Rome-authorized orders were yet established, the older British Christianity must have had its own traditions and garb.

As terms, "friar" and "monk" are not interchangeable. Monks settle down in a monastic community—geographical stability is a condition of their "contemplative" vocation. Friars travel about imparting the Gospel—they have "active" vocations. Friars, like the Crusades, are an Arthurian anachronism, for the preaching orders of friars developed much later than the earlier monastic orders. A "convent" applies to houses of monks or of nuns.

Hermits are distinct from friars and monks. The image of hermits, living alone and in poverty, does not seem incompatible with Arthurian tradition, but Malory states a different picture:

> For in those days it was not the guise of hermits as is nowadays, for there were none hermits [then] but that they had been men of worship and of prowess; and those hermits held great household, and refreshed people ... in distress [XVIII, 3].

Maybe anyone could become a hermit without even leaving home, by devoting himself or herself to prayers, piety, and hospitality. An old, retired knight might be both a vavasour and a hermit at once; many anchorites might not have bothered to obtain special authorization from the British Church.

"I will take me to penance," says Lancelot at the end of his knightly career, "and pray while my life lasteth, if I may find any hermit, either gray or white, that will receive me" [Malory XXI, 10]. There was and is a type of religious settlement in which the members, instead of living the common life of a monastery, come together for Mass and some of their prayers, and otherwise live alone in their separate little dwellings. I would guess that the hermitage of the former Archbishop of Canterbury, where Lancelot and so many of his former brothers of the Round Table ended up, became a settlement of this type.

Messengers Pursuivants

> And ... Tristram met with pursuivants, and they told him that there was made a great cry of tournament between King Carados of Scotland and the King of North Wales, and either should joust against other at the Castle of Maidens; and these pursuivants sought all the country after the good knights, and in especial King Carados let make seeking for Sir Launcelot du Lake, and the King of Northgalis let seek after Sir Tristram de Liones. [Malory IX, 25]

For less official messengers, almost anyone can be used—damsels, dwarves, clerks, squires, minstrels, even, at need, children. Hermits and monks, of course, would have been exempt from being pressed into messenger service except in the very gravest emergency. I do not recall one knight ever using another knight for the mere and sole purpose of a messenger, but knights did give each other messages and news to take back to court. Kings could surely have used knights for messengers; likely, however, a non-combatant would have had a certain ambassadorial immunity as messenger which a knight would not want to have.

Ambassadorial immunity did not always work. At the advice of Nimue, Arthur made Morgan's damsel wear a cloak that Morgan had sent as a gift to Arthur; the cloak burned the messenger to coals—Nimue must have suspected some such outcome when she made her suggestion [Malory IV, 16]. When Guenevere sent her cousin Dame Elyzabel to France to summon Viviane, Claudas held Elyzabel, her squire, and her dwarf in prison until Guenevere realized the errand was taking far too long; eventually, Arthur had to go to war against Claudas to gain Elyzabel's release.

Minstrels

> When the harper [Eliot] had sung his song [Dinadan's lay against Mark] to the end King Mark was wonderly wroth, and said: Thou harper, how durst thou be so bold on thy head to sing this song afore me. Sir, said Eliot, wit you well I am a minstrel, and I must do as I am commanded of these lords that I bear the arms of. And sir, wit you well that Sir Dinadan, a knight of the Table Round, made this song, and made me to sing it afore you. Thou sayest well, said King Mark, and because thou art a minstrel thou shalt go quit, but I charge thee hie thee fast out of my sight. [Malory X, 31]

Sorcerers, Necromancers, Enchantresses

Probably people who simply knew the natural properties of various herbs were considered sorcerors and sorceresses, as well as folk who knew the more "supernatural" branches of necromancy. The Latin *veneficium* means both "poisoning" and "sorcery."

Any woman, or at least any beautiful woman, like Guenevere or Isoud la Blanche Mains, might have a touch of the enchantress about her. Possibly the twelve damsels of the tower, who had such mutual animosity for Sir Marhaus and whom he characterized as "sorceresses and enchanters many of them", come under this classification—though Marhaus claimed that they could make a knight, be he ever so good of body and full of prowess, "a stark coward to have the better of him", they certainly are not shown doing anything to justify this supposed power; Marhaus' distinction between them and "good ladies and gentlewomen" may be merely the distinction between amorous temptresses and modest dames. [Malory IV, 17-18]

Squires

We notice two types of squires: young men completing their education, for whom squirehood is a step to knighthood, and older men who have apparently made squiring their lifetime career. One example of an older squire who seems to have had no intention of ever advancing to knighthood is Tristram's gentleman tutor and servant Gouvernail. Sir Gawaine's Eliezer seems to me another example. Beric, Prince Valiant's squire in the early years of Hal Foster's strip, appears to be a faithful modern interpretation of this type of squire. Such squires were much more than servants to their knights—they were also friends, battle companions at need, sometimes even mentors.

Generally, in the Arthurian romances, squires accompany their knights or ladies; we seldom see squires striking out on their own until after they are dubbed knight. The dubbing, however, can be performed by a squire's own knight or any other knight on very short notice and anywhere, even the battlefield.

Vulgate III says that "a squire must not strike a knight" [I, 372]. Nevertheless, "gentlemen and yeomen" could help knights attack other knights [cf. Malory X, 84]. Intermediary ground appears between temporary squires and lifelong squires—men who, for some reason, delayed being knighted. Quite possibly whether or not a squire was allowed to strike a knight depended on the squire's birth and degree of nobility and also on the circumstances of the fight. At least one squire, Helain de Taningues, became lord of a castle before being dubbed. True, his folk did not much like it, but he had promised his mother not to let anyone dub him except Sir Gawaine. [Vulgate III]

Venturing outside the Arthurian romances for further examples, in Charles Kingsley's novel **Hereward the Wake**, Hereward, a contemporary of William the Conqueror, remained a squire for a long while, but attached himself to no knight and fought as freely, in tournament and elsewhere, as a knight—he remarked that he wanted to show the world that an English squire was as good as a Norman knight. Suffolk, the English commander at Orleans when Joan of Arc raised the seige of that city, is said to have dubbed the French squire Guillaume Regnault a knight before surrendering to him, refusing to be captured by anyone under the rank of knight. (Mark Twain, transferring the tradition to a lesser English officer, gives a short and effective dramatization of the incident in his **Personal Recollections of Joan of Arc**.)

Surgeons, Leeches

There do seem to have been males who made a definite profession and livelihood of the healing arts. Women and hermits could be and frequently were surgeons and healers also, sometimes notable ones, like both the Isouds and the Lady Leech of Cornwall. I doubt, however, that a woman, unless she was a village herbwoman or wise woman of the peasantry, could have made a profession of it in the sense of earning her livelihood thereby; and a hermit should not have needed to heal for material payment. The opinion of a good female healer seems nevertheless to have been considered as good as the opinion of a professional male medic. Doubtless it would have been, if not necessary, at least very, very handy for women—indeed, for anyone—to have some knowledge of healing and nursing, as well as of first aid. One never knew when the need might arise. For instance, Lancelot fell sick one time of drinking from a fountain that had been infected by poisonous serpents; Amable used a combination of medicine and sweating therapy to cure him [Vulgate V].

> And them that were hurt [Arthur] let the surgeons do search their hurts and wounds and commanded to spare no salves nor medicines till they were whole. [Malory V, 8]
>
> And when [Marhaus'] head was searched a piece of Sir Tristram's sword was found therein, and might never be had out of his head for no surgeons, and so he died of Sir Tristram's sword; and that piece of the sword the queen, his sister, kept it for ever with her, for she thought to be revenged as she might. [Malory VIII, 8]
>
> Then the king for great favour made Tristram to be put in his daughter's [La Beale Isoud's] ward and keeping, because she was a noble surgeon. And when she had searched him she found in the bottom of his wound that therein was poison, and so she healed him within a while. [Malory VIII, 9]
>
> So upon a day, by the assent of Sir Launcelot, Sir Bors, and Sir Lavaine, they made the hermit to seek in woods for divers herbs, and so Sir Launcelot made fair Elaine to gather herbs for him to make him a bain [bath]. In the meanwhile Sir Launcelot made him to arm him at all pieces ... and ... strained himself so straitly...that the button of his wound brast both within and without; and therewithal the blood came out so fiercely that. ... he fell down on the one side [of his horse] to the earth like a dead corpse ....
>
> With this came the holy hermit, Sir Baudwin of Brittany, and when he found Sir Launcelot in that plight he said but little, but wit ye well he was wroth; and then he bade them: Let us have him in. And so they all bare him unto the hermitage, and unarmed him, and laid him in his bed; and evermore his wound bled piteously, but he stirred no limb of him. Then the knight-hermit put a thing in his nose and a little deal of water in his mouth. And then Sir Launcelot waked of his swoon, and then the hermit staunched his bleeding. [Malory XVIII, 17]

There came to be a difference between doctors and surgeons; in **Gil Blas**, Le Sage displays mistrust, not to say contempt, for doctors, but respect for surgeons. I do not sense such a clear distinction in the Arthurian romances, but possibly the beginnings of the division may be visible in the two types of treatment: cleaning and bandaging, and using herbs and other medicinal preparations. The latter type of treatment would have required the same type of knowledge as that needed by a poisoner, so that healing may have been considered akin to sorcery when practiced by anyone other than surgeons and holy hermits.

Varlets

A varlet was a man or boy acting as a servant, a groom, or as other attendant to a military leader. By extension the word came to mean anyone of a knavish or rascally disposition. Though varlet seems a popular insult word in today's pseudoarchaic dialogue, the first definition is the one we want in reading such passages as this:

> So Sir Tristram had three squires, and La Beale Isoud had three gentlewomen, and both the queen and they were richly apparelled; and other people had they none ... but varlets to bear their shields and their spears [Malory X, 65].

Vavasours

According to the Oxford English Dictionary, a feudal tenant ranking immediately below a baron. According to D.D.R. Owen's glossary to his translation of Chrétien de Troyes (1987), a lesser vassal or the vassal of another vassal. Vavasours turn up frequently in the romances, usually as older, possibly impoverished, but very respectable knights with beautiful daughters, eager and ambitious sons, or both. One gets the impression that the two most popular roles for knights who survived to a ripe old retirement age were hermit and vavasour.

Women

The Arthurian milieu is predominantly a man's world, yet the picture I draw from Malory and the Vulgate is considerably better for women than most modern interpretations and impressions seem to credit it for being—and I do not mean in regard to chivalrous courtesy (which can so easily degenerate into patronizing) and the Round Table aim of succoring all ladies and damsels. The touchstone is whether the authors treat their female characters as intelligent and responsible adults. I find that Malory is fair to his women in this regard, the Vulgate even fairer. This attitude carries over into the fictional setting, so that women have much more freedom of movement and right to property than we usually think of when we picture the High Middle Ages.

Women, it has been conjectured, made up the bulk of the readership for these romances, and this may account for the place they hold therein as characters. It may also account in part for the rarity with which female characters are given names—perhaps the female readers, or the authors who wrote for them, may have felt it easier for real people to identify with nameless than with named characters.

When the knights of the Leprous Lady wished to bleed Percivale's sister, Percivale protested that "a maid in what[ever] place she cometh is free" [Malory XVII, 10]. This was clearly the ideal rather than the general rule, even in the context of Malory's romance; in the context of the real world of Malory's time it may have been mere wishful thinking, the literary daydreams of female readers. Nevertheless, in the romances themselves, we often meet female characters riding the countryside as freely as knights—sometimes, despite their lack of arms and armor to defend themselves, the ladies even ride with very few attendants. Thus Guenevere's cousin Elyzabel sets off with a squire and a dwarf to carry a message from Arthur's court to the French Damsel of the Lake across the Channel—and would probably complete her mission, despite the perils of the road, had it not been for King Claudas' suspicious nature when she stops at his court.

The Damsel of La Beale Regard demonstrates some skill in the donning of armor and use of weapons. Sommer remarks in a footnote in Vulgate VIII that a certain passage implies that the ladies traveling with Sir Griflet assist him (to cross a lake, I think). They next appear to give material aid in rescuing a knight, though after he is mounted they then seem to stand back and simply watch. In Vulgate IV, when Lancelot sits down to watch a tournament between the Castle aux Dames and the Castle aux Pucelles, a damsel comes by and asks for his shield, since he obviously has no use for it. The evidence of Sir Griflet's ladies is textually dubious, and that of the damsel asking for Lancelot's shield seems to be a broad hint that he should get into the fight rather than a suggestion that she will if he will not. Nevertheless, the total impression created by these and similar instances is a doubt as to whether the women of the romances were really as unfamiliar with weapons as are the standard "damsels in distress" of our much later tales.

When Arthur and his party chanced upon Morgan's castle in the woods around Tauroc and learned that the porter must speak with his mistress about whether to admit them, Sir Sagramore "wondered that there was no master" [Vulgate VI]. Although we meet an occasional example in the Vulgate of a castle which cannot be inherited by the lord's daughter, we find many more castles and even small countries which appear to be under the governance of ladies rather than knights. In view of this pattern, Sagramore's surprise seems strange. Perhaps the fact that Sagramore had come from the East had something to do with his surprise.

It was customary for high-born damsels to wait on their parents' guests at table [Vulgate VI]. In the light of the cases of young knights, high court officials, and even of kings serving at table, I interpret the maidens' duty of serving not as a sign of female subservience, but as a courtly means of finishing their education while including them, to some measure, in society and giving them a chance to hear the guests' news.

The Damsel of Hongrefort bore responsibility for her own actions and for seeking penance and forgiveness. King Agrippe's daughter made a vow and embarked on a quest at least as painful as any knight's. Women appear as skillful surgeons, wise and holy hermitesses, and messengers, as well as highly competent (if evil) enchantresses. They are clever, resourceful, capable of handling livestock and serving as squires. In sum, the women of the medieval romances—whether these were colored by memories of woman's place in old Celtic society or by the wishes of female readers—are very far from the retiring, stay-at-home, rather helpless creatures who appear to have become popular in Victorian retellings.

Blood Feuds

Side by side with the more official legal processes, the right of men to avenge their kinsfolk's deaths seems to have been more or less recognized and approved, at least by custom. Thus, Dame Anglides can give her son Alisander his father's bloody doublet and charge him as a duty to avenge the murder on his uncle Mark, La Cote Male Taile can appear at Arthur's court wearing his father's bloody coat and proclaiming his intention to wear it until his father is avenged, and Alisander's son Bellangere can at last avenge the deaths of both Alisander and Boudwin, all without a word of either legal or moral censure—indeed, with more than a hint of praise. [Malory X, 34; IX, 1; XIX, 11]

The important requirement seems to have been that such killings for revenge be done in the manner of fair and honorable combat; a revenge killing done from ambush, or perpetrated by a number of men acting against one, were spoken of with outrage and contempt. It must also have helped if the person slain out of revenge was generally disliked; Mark's eventual death at Bellangere's hands seems to merit praise, while Pellinore's death at the hands of Lot's sons merits censure, even though both are merely mentioned, not described, in Malory's text [XIX, 11; XI, 10]. Mark was a recognized scoundrel, Pellinore was famed as a noble knight. Mark was also killed in revenge for treasons that would be considered murders today as well as in Arthur's time, Pellinore in revenge for a killing done in plain battle. This suggests that personal revenge may have been an accepted way of getting at your enemy when legal means failed or were unavailable for any reason.

Probably the most notable blood feuds were the one between the sons of Lot and the family of Pellinore, which started early in Arthur's reign when Pellinore killed Lot in battle and which eventually resulted in the deaths of Pellinore, Margawse, Lamorak, possibly Dornar, and Patrise (who died of poison which a kinsman of Lamorak's meant for Gawaine); and the one between Gawaine and Lancelot, which rose in the very twilight of Arthur's reign, when Lancelot killed Gareth and Gaheris by accident in rescuing Guenevere from the stake. It may have been such feuds as this that gave rise to the old saw,

> [T]here is hard battle thereas kin and friends do battle either against another, there may be no mercy but mortal war,

even though Lancelot cites the proverb, not in reference to blood feuds, but in reference to the wounds his kinsmen have inflicted on him in the Winchester tournament, through failing to recognize him as Lancelot. [Malory XVIII, 16]

We can understand murder and violent death giving rise to such vendettas; it is more surprising to find that mere jealousy almost started at least one such bloodletting.

> Sir Tristram achieved many great battles, wherethrough all the noise fell to Sir Tristram, and it ceased of Sir Launcelot; and therefore Sir Launcelot's brethren and his kinsmen would have slain Sir Tristram because of his fame. But when Sir Launcelot wist how his kinsmen were set, he said to them openly: Wit you well, that an the envy of you all be so hardy to wait upon my lord Sir Tristram, with any hurt, shame, or villainy, as I am true knight I shall slay the best of you with mine own hands. Alas, fie for shame, should ye for his noble deeds await upon him to slay him. [Malory X, 88]

Considering the magnitude of the personalities involved, we breathe a sigh of relief that Lancelot nipped this affair in the bud.

As kinship and friendship was at the heart of these feuds, so, conversely, the parties involved might be protected from further reprisal by other kinships and friendships. Thus the position of Gawaine and his brothers as favorite nephews of Arthur enabled them for years to carry on their feud with Pellinore's family with no more than moral interference from other noble knights who disapproved of the way they were handling it. For instance, Tristram once met Agravaine and Gaheris, told them, "[Y]e be called the greatest destroyers and murderers of good knights that be now in this realm," but refrained from chastizing them bodily for the death of Sir Lamorak: "Well … for King Arthur's sake I shall let you pass as at this time." [Malory X, 55]

Coats of Arms

Recognizing knights by their coats of arms was tricky. Tragic as the outcome could be when knights did not carry their own shields, especially in a social milieu where the rule seemed to be to interact first and ask names later, if at all, the practice of bearing somebody else's shield remained popular. A knight might borrow the shield of a friend or help himself to the shield of a defeated foe. Lancelot was especially fond of using an anonymous or a borrowed shield. On one occasion, he saved Kay from attackers, then got up early in the morning while Kay was still asleep and took Kay's arms. Kay, riding back to Camelot with Lancelot's shield perforce, arrived unmolested, since knights had already learned better than to meddle with Lancelot; Lancelot, meanwhile, being mistaken for the unpopular Kay, took the chance to leave a trail of unhorsed opponents behind him.

For anonymity, a knight could carry a plain-colored shield (white, black, green, red, and so on), or cover his shield, or even apparently do both at once! Anonymous shields seem to have been very popular with villainous knights. Blank shields, usually white but sometimes red (according to Vulgate VI), and presumably any other tincture, were carried by young knights in their first year of knighthood, before they had earned the right to bear a device. Thus, when established knights disguised themselves with blank shields of any color, they would seem to have been disguising their skill and experience as well as their identities. A knight like Lancelot would do this in order to attract more attackers and thus win greater honor; a knight like Breuse Sans Pitie would do it in order to trick potential victims into a false sense of security.

Plain white shields were also used by the Queen's Knights, a sort of secondary company (secondary, that is, to the Round Table) of Arhur's court.

Because it was such common practice to use an anonymous or borrowed shield, knights sometimes resorted to other devices in order to identify themselves. In one tournament, the companions of the Round Table wore round leather badges so as to know each other. Guenevere finally insisted Lancelot start wearing her favor in tournaments so that his relatives would know him and not gang up on him as they had done with almost fatal result to the great knight at Winchester.

Cultural Heritage

Arthur's court and contemporaries had their own adventures to talk about, but only as these took place. What other material did their minstrels and storytellers use for an evening's entertainment; what other knights and heroes of history, legend, and literature did Arthur's people have to feed their imagination?

Perhaps foremost, there were the heroes of the Old and New Testaments and of the Grail history: John the Hircanian, Judas and Symon Maccabeus, David and Solomon, Joseph of Arimathea, and so on. The basic tales of the Biblical characters seem to have been recognizable (use a Bible with the dozen or so books which the Protestant tradition considers apocryphal and the Catholic tradition inspired), but other material had gotten mixed into the legends as well; besides such non-Biblical information as that found in Malory and the Vulgate (as, for instance, in Amide's tale of King Solomon's Ship), Arthurian folk might have retold such tales as can be found in **The Lost Books of the Bible** and **The Forgotten Books of Eden**. The Grail tradition as Arthurian characters were most likely to have known it can probably best be examined in Volume I of the Vulgate, Lestoire del Saint Graal. In addition, Arthurian folk surely would have had tales of early Christian saints and martyrs of the Roman and British martyrologies and the beginnings of **The Golden Legend** (a collection of saints' lives set down by Jacobus de Voragine in the thirteenth century), as well as others remembered chiefly in local oral tradition.

For secular figures, they had the history and legends of classical antiquity. **Sir Gawaine and the Green Knight** begins by referring to the Trojan War, Aeneas, Romulus, and others (in the Middle Ages, folks tended to sympathize with the Trojans rather than the Greeks). Seeing an artist paint the history of Aeneas gave Lancelot, while a prisoner in Morgan's castle, the inspiration for muralizing his own exploits [Vulgate V]. Very occasionally, as in the tale of Viviane's birth, we see a hint that the deities of classical and other non-Christian mythology may have been considered real, whether or not diabolic [Vulgate II]. Closer to Arthur's time were the heroes of early British history.

> I have understood that Belinus and Brenius, kings of Britain, have had the empire in their hands many days, and also Constantine the son of Heleine, which is an open evidence that we owe no tribute to Rome. [Malory V, 1; Arthur speaking]

The Heleine of this passage would be the same Saint Helena credited with finding the True Cross. A chronicle of early British history may be found in Spenser's **Faerie Queen**, Book II, Canto X—Spenser's version of Arthurian adventure is probably irreconcilable with Malory's, but, in a well annotated edition (like that edited by Thomas P. Roche, Jr., Penguin Books, 1978) his list of British rulers from Brute to Uther may be helpful to those who wish to go more deeply into the subject. There are other accounts.

Palomides, his brothers, and Priamus might have brought Eastern lore and legends to Arthur's England, if they still wanted to talk about such "pagan" things when they had determined to be Christened. Similarly, Urre of Hungary could have brought bits of Eastern European lore, and so on. As Arthur's Round Table drew knights from distant lands and became a symbol of the world, so Arthur's court may well have enjoyed a much wider range of culture and literature than we usually associate with the period.

Distances and Travel Time

Thirty English miles could be covered in four days—see Vulgate VI, p. 262, where Lancelot and Ector, four days before Lancelot must be at Camelot to fight for the Queen, pass the night at Alphin castle, thirty English miles from Camelot. (I suspect, however, that, at need, thirty English miles could be covered in a much shorter time than four days.)

Also according to the Vulgate [VI, p. 264], Arthur and his army reached Joyous Garde on the second day after leaving Camelot, after one overnight stop. The Vulgate, however, makes Camelot distinct from Winchester (in flat contradiction to Malory). Nevertheless, Camelot appears reasonably near Winchester even in the Vulgate. Thus, from the vicinity of Winchester to the Humber, the distance could be covered in less than two days. Even allowing for the fact that this may have been a forced march, such speed makes identification of one site by its distance according to days' travel from another exceedingly chancy.

Sir Persant's city was seven miles from Castle Dangerous. Gareth offered to be finished with Persant "within two hours after noon … [a]nd then shall we come to the siege [of Castle Dangerous] by daylight." Gareth presumably meant that he would also have time to fight the besieging champion by daylight. The season was late spring or early summer—a few days after Whitsuntide, so that the days would have been fairly long. As it turned out, Gareth and Lynette stopped for the night with Persant, but Gareth's statement may help indicate normal traveling time on horseback.

Six miles was considered a reasonable distance to travel to hear Mass. Presumably, traveling six miles for this purpose was permissible on a Saturday or Sunday, even though other travel was frowned upon on the Sabbath. Gawaine was once admonished by a friar for riding late on Saturday; the knight swore not to do so again unless it was unavoidable. [Vulgate IV, p. 148]

> Then … on foot they yede [traveled] from Glastonbury to Almesbury, the which is little more than thirty mile. And thither they came within two days, for they were weak and feeble to go [Malory XXI, 11].

Normal traveling time on horseback from Georgia to New Orleans (550 miles) was 13 1/2 days in the middle of the nineteenth century. A horse named Paddy, ridden by Sam Dale with a vital message, is cited for covering the distance in 7 1/2 days, cutting six days from the normal travel time. On the other hand, in a feature article printed in the **Chicago Sun-Times**, April 12, 1978, Dennis Waite describes trying to hike from Llanberis, Wales, to the summit of Mount Snowden, three and a half miles on a dirt road. Waite's landlady claimed the walk was "two hours up and one hour back", but an English couple Waite's party met as the Americans finally turned back in discouragement said the walk, round-trip, took a full day. Obviously, time spent in traveling from place to place in the Arthurian landscape depends on type of terrain—forested, mountainous, and so on—as well as on type of locomotion (horse, mule, wagon, foot) and availability of roads (many of the old Roman roads, like the famous Watling Street, would naturally have been available to Arthurian travelers).

When it was necessary or desired, messengers and pursuivants could carry news quite rapidly—as we think of news as spreading in those days. Gareth defeated Ironside and raised the siege of Castle Dangerous shortly after Pentecost. There followed a few extra adventures which must have taken up to a week. Arthur and Lyonors then decided to have a tournament at Castle Dangerous at Assumption, in mid-August.

> And so the cry was made in England, Wales, and Scotland, Ireland, Cornwall, and in all the Out Isles, and in Brittany and in many countriess; that at the feast of our Lady the Assumption next coming, men should come to the Castle [Dangerous] beside the Isle of Avilion[:] ... And two months was to the day that the tournament should be.

Two months for the messengers to cover all that area and still leave the interested knights in time to see to their preparations (though they seem to have kept ready for knightly adventure throughout the warm seasons) and travel to Lyonors' castle from those distant countries!

One further note: romance accounts of time spent in travel need not always be taken literally or seriously. Harris, commenting on a passage in Chrétien's **Yvain**, theorizes that Chrétien may have been poking fun at the speed of characters' travel in old romances. [Dell ed. of **Yvain**, New York, 1963, p. 151]

Holding Court

When Uther Pendragon held court, the clerks would not allow any knight to take his seat unless he had a face wound. This custom was discontinued in Arthur's time, when Lancelot, Duke Galeholt, and Ector de Maris became companions of the Round Table; it was replaced by the custom that no companion could take his seat on high festivals unless he had conquered a knight the week before. Ywaine, at least, found the custom irksome. [Vulgate V] So, most likely, did Kay and other knights.

Also, at the first court Arthur held after his marriage, on the fifteenth of August (Assumption), he made his famous vow never to sit down to dinner until some adventure was reported to him [Vulgate II, p. 319-320].

Arthur held five courts annually at which he wore his crown: at the feasts of Easter, Ascension, Whitsuntide (Pentecost), All Saints, and Christmas. Easter was the highest festival, Whitsuntide—the renewal of Easter joy—the most joyful. [Vulgate III, p. 107-108]

At the Pentecost court of Galahad's arrival, the Queen and her ladies appear to be dining apart from the King and his men. Other scenes, however, show men and women as dining together, those of highest rank taking the highest seats on the dais. (See, for instance, Sir **Gawaine and the Green Knight**.) Serving at table seems to have been an honor—sometimes, at least, for the servers as well as those served. Clearly, the higher-ranking were those who served you, the more were you honored—on the Pentecost of the Grail, Malory records that young knights (probably as opposed to squires or pages) served at table [XIII, 3]; when Arthur feasted Kings Ban and Bors at All Hallowmass, near the beginning of his reign, Sir Kay the seneschal, Sir Lucas the butler, and Sir Griflet served, or at least "had the rule of all the service that served the kings" [I, 10]; according to Vulgate IV, four kings and other high barons served at Arthur's table on the Pentecost of Galahad's arrival (perhaps Malory's serving knights served at the lesser tables). In the tale of Gareth Beaumains, the various knights he has conquered during his adventures show up and as honors beg to serve as his chief butler, sewer-chief, wine-server, and so on at the feast.

Individual Combats and Courtesy

> By the way as [Sir Dinadan] rode he saw where stood an errant knight, and made him ready for to joust. Not so, said Dinadan, for I have no will to joust. With me shall ye joust, said the knight, or that ye pass this way. Whether ask ye jousts, [said Dinadan] by love or by hate? The knight answered: Wit ye well I ask it for love and not for hate. It may well be so, said Sir Dinadan, but ye proffer me hard love when ye will joust with me with a sharp spear. [Dinadan then proposed that they meet at Arthur's court and have the joust there.] ... Well, said the knight, sith ye will not joust with me, I pray you tell me your name.

Learning it, the strange knight said he knew Dinadan for a good knight and agreed to call off the joust entirely. [Malory X, 20]

A trial of arms seems to have been almost as common a method for two knights, meeting by chance, to greet each other as a hello and a handshake. The perplexing rule, which seems standard, of jousting first and asking names afterward could lead to tragedy, especially when knights so often traveled with strange, blank, or covered shields rather than their own; nevertheless, it seems to be an outgrowth of a more general precept of etiquette that frowned on exchanging names too quickly. For instance, Sir Bercilak and his people welcomed Gawaine into their castle, unarmed him, offered him a choice of indoor apparel, assigned him a chamber and servants, and brought him to supper, all before asking him—by hints and subtle, delicate questions—his identity and court of origin; Gawaine did not ask his host's name until after the beheading contest, when host and Green Knight were revealed as one and the same. [**Sir Gawaine and the Green Knight**]

Sir Lamorak, adventuring anonymously, outjousted and unhorsed both Palomides and Dinadan, "but their horses he would not suffer his squires to meddle with ... because they were knights-errant" [Malory X, 18]. This, however, may have been more Lamorak's generosity than common practice. Strictly speaking, the arms and steeds of the defeated knights probably always belonged by right to the victorious opponent, but in friendly encounters the victors, especially when Round Table companions or otherwise notable for honor and courtesy, seem generally to have waived their claim. The defeated combatant also seemed to owe his service and allegiance to his conqueror; this rule seems always to have been applied when the victor was of Arthur's court and could thus gain his opponent's allegiance for the King.

At the castle of Sir Tor le Fise Aries, the lieutenant of the castle, Sir Berluse, recognized King Mark as the man who had killed his father and would have killed Berluse himself. But

> for the love of my lord [Tor] of this castle I will neither hurt you nor harm you, nor none of your fellowship [said Berluse]. But wit you well, when

> ye are past this lodging I shall hurt you an I may, for ye slew my father traitorly. But first for the love of my lord, Sir Tor, and for the love of Sir Lamorak, the honourable knight that here is lodged, ye shall have none ill lodging. [Malory X, 9]

It appears that castles and the rules of hospitality could serve as well as a church for sanctuary.

Kingdoms and Dukedoms

Major Kingdoms of Great Britain

In Book VII, 26, Malory indicates that the major divisions of Britain were England (or Logres), Wales, Scotland, Cornwall, Ireland, the Out Isles, and Brittany. Later, in VIII, 1, he tells us:

> And at that time King Arthur reigned, and he was whole king of England, Wales, and Scotland, and of many other realms; howbeit there were many kings ... for in Wales were two kings, and in the north were many kings; and in Cornwall and in the west were two kings; also in Ireland were two or three kings, and all were under the obeissance of King Arthur. So was the King of France, and the King of Brittany, and all the lordships unto Rome.

(This was after Arthur's war against and defeat of the Emperor Lucius.)

The difference between a "kingdom" and a "dukedom" seems marginal. We find dukes hobnobbing with kings, apparently as political and military equals; we also find some kings owing homage to other kings, as when King Anguish of Ireland demands tribute from King Mark of Cornwall. We meet kings whose territory seems to consist of a city, as well as kings who appear, like Lerner and Loewe's Pellinore, to have misplaced and even forgotten the names of their kingdoms. "Duke" Galeholt the Haut Prince gives an island to Marsil, who becomes "King" thereof. On the whole, I receive the impression that the principal distinction between a king and a duke lies in the title, and that a dukedom qualifies as a subkingdom. Similarly, there probably is not too much social descent to holdings clearly labeled as earldoms. Any knight could become lord of at least one castle and the surrounding territory, and rulers awarded lands and titles to their knights, even though the knights might continue to spend most of their time at court or on quest.

We may perhaps assume, in the lack of other evidence, that a number of Britain's kingdoms and dukedoms might have had pretty much the same boundaries and in many cases the same rulers before Arthur's high kingship as after he came to the throne.

In XXI, 26, speaking of the army Mordred raised against Arthur, Malory lists Kent, Southsex, Surrey, Estsex, Southfolk, and Northfolk. Since these are recognizably the names of modern counties, and since, in consulting a modern map of England, we find we can stick "Duke of" in front of most county names and produce familiar titles of history and romance, I suspect that subkingdoms could be formed by following modern county lines. This may not be accurate according to the newer schools of Arthurian realism, but I believe it would be quite compatible with the anachronistic spirit of Malorian romance.

Virtually all castles had villages and territories attached, and sometimes the dividing line between a castle and a subkingdom seems rather fine.

Subkingdoms are listed alphabetically. Tentative identifications according to place names on modern maps will be found as individual entries. Virtually all identifications are questionable.

The subkingdoms are: King Amans' Land, Arroy, Avilion, Benoye, Cambenet, Cameliard, Clarance, the Delectable Isle, Escavalon, Estrangor, the Foreign Land, Garboth, Gore, l'Isle Estrange, the Isles, Leicester, Listeneise, the Long Isles, Lothian, Lyonesse, Malahaut, Nohaut, Norgales, North Marches, Northumberland, Orkney, Orofoise, Pomitain, Roestoc, Isle of Servage, Sorestan, South Marches, Straight Marches, Stranggore, Sugales, Surluse or Sorelois, Taningues, and Tintagil.

Since Britain was covered with forest in the old days, wherever you move on a map of Arthurian Britain, you will not be far from the nearest forest. Some of the less obviously magical or mystical forests which I found given definite names in Malory or the Vulgate include Arroy, Bedegrain, Bresquehan†, Campacorentin†, Celibe†, Gloevant†, Landoine†, Morris, Roevant†, Sapine†, and Windsor.

Foreign Kingdoms

This far from exhaustive list concentrates on the countries named by Malory. The close-at-hand kingdoms and subkingdoms include: France [Gaul], with Benwick [or Benoye, or Benoyc, with its city of the same name], Brittany or Little Britain, Burgoyne, Champayne, Guienne; Flanders, with its port city of Barflete; Ireland, with Galway; the Out Isles; and Sarras.

More distant nations mentioned by Malory are: Almaine [Germany], Denmark, the Holy Land, Hungary, Italy, Lombardy, Isle of Longtains [the Shetland Islands?], Rome, Sessoin [Saxony], Spain [Saracens or Moors were here], Tuscany, Vale [the Faeroës Islands], and Wentland [Prussia?].

In Book V, chapter 2, Malory gives a list of the countries to which the Roman Emperor Lucius sent messengers for help in his war against Arthur: Ambage, Arrage, Alexandria, India, Armenia ("whereas the river of Euphrates runneth into Asia"), Africa, Europe the Large, Ertayne and Elamye, Araby, Egypt, Damascus, Damietta and Cayer, Cappadocia, Tarsus, Turkey, Pontus and Pamphylia, Syria and Galatia, Greece, Cyprus, Macedonia, Calabria, Cateland, and Portugal ("with many thousands of Spaniards")—all these being subject to or allied with Rome.

Knighthood and Knight-errantry

When Lancelot was eighteen years old and itching to become a knight, Viviane told him these qualifications for the order:

> At the beginning all men were equals; but when envy and covetousness grew, when force triumphed over right, it became necessary to appoint defenders for the weak against the strong. They were called knights. The strongest, ablest, and best were selected for this purpose. A knight must be merciful, kind-hearted, liberal, just, and fearless. Shame must be harder for him to bear than death. He is a defender of the Holy Church. In those early days nobody, unless he was a knight, mounted a horse. The arms a knight carries are designed for special purposes. As the shield covers the knight, he must protect the Holy Church from robbers and infidels. As the hauberk guards the knight's body, he must safeguard the Holy Church. The helmet shields the knight's head; the knight must shield the Holy Church from all who attempt to injure her. As the fear of the lance-head drives back the unarmed, the fear of the knight must prevent all evil-doers from approaching the Holy Church. The double-edged sword, the most honourable weapon, is used to kill by stabbing and to strike right and left. Its two edges signify that the knight is the servant of God and the people. The sword's point is the symbol of obedience. All people must obey the knight. The horse which carries the knight signifies the people. The people enjoy the knight's protection; they must provide him with the necessities for an honourable life. As the knight guides his horse, he must lead the people. He must defend the clergy, the widows, orphans, the tithes, and alms. The Church must maintain the knight spiritually. The knight must posess two hearts, one soft as wax, the other hard as diamond [or, lodestone]. Inexorable towards the wicked, the knight must be merciful towards the good. He must have no pity for the evil-doer, and not be hard towards those claiming pity and compassion. Such are some of the obligations of a knight. A knight who fails to fulfil them disgraces himself in this world and loses his place in heaven.

As examples of worthy knights, the Damsel of the Lake then cited John the Hircanian, Judas Maccabeus and his brother Symon, and King David—all in the Old Testament time when the Israelites fought their enemies; and, after the Passion of Christ, Joseph of Arimathea, his son King Galahad, and their descendants King Pelles of Listenois and his brother Alain le Gros. [Vulgate III, p. 111-117]

Helin le Blank, Galahad, and Percivale were all dubbed knights at age fifteen [Malory XII, 9; Vulgate V; Vulgate VI, however, says that Galahad was eighteen.]. Lancelot, as appears above, was dubbed in his late teens. I believe that age twenty-one was usual in historical practice for a young man who had come up through the standard education of page, squire, and bachelor; I suspect that fifteen was unusually young even in romance and legend, and is mentioned as showing that the youth was a prodigy.

Young knights were often put to the worse in jousting, for fighting on horseback required experience. Because of their youthful strength and agility, they were good on foot. Thus, older knights might seek to gain glory by jousting with younger, but then refuse to fight the younger knights on foot. Sir Mordred (probably still in his earlier promise, before his wickedness came to the surface) explains this to the damsel Maledisant:

> [La Cote Male Taile] is a good knight, and I doubt not but he shall prove a noble knight; but as yet he may not yet sit sure on horseback, for he that shall be a good horseman it must come of usage and exercise. But when he cometh to the strokes of his sword he is then noble and mighty, and that saw Sir Bleoberis and Sir Palomides, for wit ye well they are wily men of arms, and anon they know when they see a young knight by his riding, how they are sure to give him a fall from his horse or a great buffet. But for the most part they will not light on foot with young knights, for they are wight and strongly armed. For in likewise Sir Launcelot du Lake, when he was first made knight, he was often put to the worse upon horseback, but ever upon foot he recovered his renown, and slew and defoiled many knights of the Round Table. And therefore the rebukes that Sir Launcelot did unto many knights causeth them that be men of prowess to beware; for often I have seen the old proved knights rebuked and slain by them that were but young beginners. [Malory IX, 4]

Malory also remarks that the knight "was never formed that all times might stand, but sometimes he was put to the worse by mal-fortune; and at sometime the worse knight put the better knight to a rebuke" [IX, 12].

Sir Dinadan, after egging King Mark on to fight Lamorak, rails at Mark for being bested:

> Then Sir Dinadan mocked King Mark and said: Ye are not able to match a good knight. As for that, said King Mark, at the first time I jousted with this knight ye refused him. Think ye that it is a shame to me? said Sir Dinadan: nay sir, it is ever worship to a knight to refuse that thing that he may not attain, therefore your worship had been much more to have refused him as I did; for I warn you plainly he is able to beat such five as ye and I be; for ye knights of Cornwall are no men of worship as other knights are. And because ye are no men of worship ye hate all men of worship, for never was bred in your country such a[nother] knight as is Sir Tristram. [Malory X, 8]

Dinadan was never a man to fight needlessly, and his opinion as to the glory of refusing single combat with a better knight may be strictly a personal excuse rather than a widespread sentiment. As for the latter part of his statement, similar gratuitous expressions occur so often in Malory's work (despite the fact that the Cornish knights who appear as characters seem no worse as a body than any other group of knights) that I believe "Cornish knight" jokes must have been to Malory's generation what "Polack" jokes are to ours; perhaps every generation has its butt for such jokes, whether it be the Cornish knight, the Irishman, the moron, the Pole, the Italian, or the mother-in-law.

Weapons might be poisoned. Sir Marhaus carried a venomed spear into battle with Tristram. It did not save Marhaus, but Tristram could not be healed of the wound until he went into Ireland, where the venom had come from, and was cared for by La Beale Isoud. (Does this suggest a bit of sorcery in the preparation of the venom?) Marhaus had been accounted a noble knight and had been a member of the Round Table, and I recall no censure of him for carrying a poisoned weapon, even though this trick might have been a holdover from an earlier version of the Tristram tale in which Marhaus lacked the noble history he has in Malory. [Malory VIII, 8, etc.]

Lancelot remarked, after Meliagrant's archers had shot his horse from ambush, "... it is an old saw, A good man is never in danger but when he is in the danger of a coward" [Malory XIX, 4]. Another point to remember is that "when men be hot in deeds of arms oft they hurt their friends as well as their foes." Again, Lancelot is talking, and he certainly ought to know! [Malory IX, 36]

Simply being wounded need not keep a good knight down. King Mark needed Tristram to fight the Saxon captain Elias, but Tristram was lying abed, sorely wounded from the previous day's battle. At Mark's plea, Tristram agreed to get up and fight again, "for as yet my wounds be green, and they will be sorer a seven night than they be now; and therefore ... I will do battle to-morn [against Elias]." Tristram won. [Malory X, 30]

Knights of the Round Table

A question mark after the name of a knight in the Round Table list indicates that he is pretty well established as having been of Arthur's court for at least a time and his known stature or some other evidence suggests he would have been a companion of the Table. The parenthesized word (late) after a companion's name indicates that he only became a member of the Round Table on the eve of Arthur's downfall—Gaheres took Gareth's seat, Helyan Lancelot's, Bellinor that of Bors de Ganis, and Vadalon that of Ector de Maris after the split between Arthur and Lancelot, even though Lancelot, Bors, and Ector were still alive.

These lists do not reflect Arthur's court at any given moment. For instance, Tristram only became a member of the court and companion of the Round Table some time after Marhaus' death at Tristram's own hands. (Tristram took Marhaus' seat.) Even those knights alive at the same time would rarely if ever have all been present at court at once. Knights, Round Table and otherwise, were continually leaving on missions, quests, and other adventures. Lancelot had a habit of going off incognito without telling anyone ahead of time, while some knights, like Tristram, Pelleas, and Galahad, seem to have spent hardly any of their lives at Arthur's court.

I have not attempted a complete list of all known knights of the Round Table, but only those actually to be found in the entries. Some, however, only appear in the notes for other characters; for instance, the King of the Lake and Sir Galagars are found in the notes for Sir Griflet, Sir Plaine de Force in those for Sir Plenorius. I have left off the titles "King" and "Duke" except where they seemed necessary for identification. The relative importance of these characters is unjudged.

Knights of the Round Table

Aglovale
Agravaine
Agwisance
Bagdemagus
Baudwin of Britain?
Bedivere
Bellengerus le Beuse
Belleus
Belliance le Orgulus
Bellinor (late)
Blamore de Ganis
Bleoberis de Ganis
Borre (Lohot)
Bors de Ganis
Brandiles
Brastias?
Cador of Cornwall[1]
King Carados of Scotland[1]
Chaleins[2]
Clariance of Northumberland
Colgrevance
Constantine
La Cote Male Taile (Sir Breunor le Noir)
Dinadan
Dinas
Dodinas le Savage
Dornar
Ector de Maris
Edward of Orkney
Epinegris
Florence
Gaheres (late)
Gaheris
Galagars
Galahad
Duke Galeholt
Galeshin[2]
Galihodin
Galleron
Gareth
Gawaine
Geraint (Erec)
Gingalin
Griflet
Grummore Grummursum
Harry le Fise Lake
Hebes le Renoumes
Helin le Blank
Helyan of Ireland (late)
Hermind
Hervise de Revel
Ironside
Kainus le Strange
Karados of Estrangor[1]
Kay
King of the Hundred Knights
King of the Lake
Lambegus
Lamorak
Lancelot
Lavaine
Lionel
Lovel
Lucan the Butler
Mador de la Porte
Marhaus
Marrok
Meliagrance
Melias de Lile
Meliot de Logres
Mordred
Nentres of Garloth
Nerovens de Lile
Ozanna le Cure Hardy
Palomides
Patrise
Pelleas
Pellinore
Percivale
Perimones
Persant
Pertolepe
Pinel le Savage
Plaine de Force
Plenorius
Priamus
Sadok?
Safere
Sagramore
Segwarides?
Sentraille de Lushon
Servause le Breuse
Tor
Tristram
Ulbawes
Ulfius?
Uriens of Gore
Urre of Hungary
Vadalon (late)
Yvonet li Avoutres
Ywaine

[1] *It is possible that Karados of Estrangor is the same man as either Cador of Cornwall or Carados of Scotland.*

[2] *It is possible that Chaleins and Galeshin are the same man.*

Magical Acts

In this section, I have not tried to include the making of a number of magical items; these are described instead as entries. Nor have I attempted to itemize the various prophecies and disguises of Merlin. Merlin can seemingly appear in any guise from toddler to old beggar, prophesy anything about anybody, and probably look into everybody's past as well. His prophecies, however, are often mysterious and veiled.

I do not recall that any necromancer except Merlin utters prophecies, not even Morgan or Nimue, who learned necromancy from him. Many holy people expound symbolic happenings and visions and utter prophecies, but these come under the classification of mystical and religious experience rather than of magic as such.

It seems to me that prophecies may do more harm than good. According to the Vulgate, Mordred was doing reasonably well during his first two years of knighthood. Then he met a priest who seized the opportunity to tell him that he was not the son of Lot, but of Arthur; that he was a serpent who would devour his father; that he would do more harm than all his ancestors had done good; and so on, and so on. Mordred's moral disintegration appears to date from this experience. Might things have been different had that priest kept his mouth shut?

It is not always easy to determine whether a given act is really "magical" as we would understand the term, or simply performed with the aid of natural herbs and drugs, persuasion, or other human skill of a high degree.

With the exceptions of Merlin's various disguises and prophecies, the various magical items, and the prophecies and other supernatural deeds that would come under the heading of religious experience, I have tried to give all the specific magical acts performed in the books of Malory and the Vulgate, in sufficient detail for as much understanding of the processes and uses of the magic as possible. I have also tried to indicate in the descriptions which acts might have been done with "natural" techniques like drugs. Rather than attempting to classify them, I have given them in the order I found them. Magical Acts numbers 1-21 are taken from Malory; numbers 22-34 are drawn from the Vulgate. No attempt has been made to fit these two sublists into chronological order. For that matter, Malory's work, at least as set up by Caxton, is not always internally consistent in its chronology. It may be of interest, however, to note that, if the mystic Adventures of the Grail are left out of consideration, as here, then most of the forthright magic seems to be found in the earlier adventures.

Magical Acts Selected from Malory

1. To enable Uther to lie with Igraine, Merlin gave Uther the appearance of Igraine's husband, Uther's knight Ulfius the appearance of the Duke's knight Brastias, and himself the appearance of the Duke's knight Jordanus. This seems a clear-cut case of shape-changing, rather than mere natural disguise. [Malory I, 2]

2. Merlin brought the host of Kings Ban and Bors, ten thousand men on horseback, to Dover and

   > northward, the priviest way that could be thought, unto the forest of Bedegraine, and there in a valley he lodged them secretly.
   >
   > Then rode Merlin unto Arthur and the two kings, and told them how he had sped; whereof they had great marvel, that man on earth might speed so soon, and go and come. [Malory I, 11]

   This might have been no more than excellent generalship and an extremely good horse and knowledge of the roads. Merlin being the author of these deeds, however, it looks more like casting some sort of screen of invisibility over the army and traveling by supernatural means.

3. Merlin cast a spell on King Pellinore which put him to sleep for three hours. This was at Pellinore's first meeting with Arthur, when Pellinore, learning whom he had just felled in battle, was about to slay Arthur for dread of royal revenge. Merlin thus enabled Arthur to escape without injury to Pellinore, although the sleep was so deep that Arthur at first blamed Merlin for having killed Pellinore. [Malory I, 24]

   Under the circumstances, Merlin would hardly have had time to use drugs.

4. Merlin made Arthur invisible to Pellinore and thus prevented a battle. (Pellinore was not yet one of Arthur's friends and advisors.) [Malory I, 25]

5. On the tomb of Lanceor and Colombe, Merlin wrote in letters of gold the names of the two best knights in the world, Lancelot and Tristram, neither of whom had yet appeared, but who would one day fight at this same tomb. [Malory II, 8]

6. Arthur buried the bodies of twelve rebel kings in the Church of Saint Stephen's in Camelot. (These included King Lot, but were not an identical group with the first eleven rebel kings.) Each of their effigies, made of latten (brass) and copper gilt with gold, held a wax taper that burned night and day, and above them stood a figure of Arthur holding a drawn sword. Merlin made these effigies "by his subtle craft" and told Arthur that the tapers would burn until Merlin's own death, and that shortly thereafter would come the Adventures of the Grail. [Malory II, 11]

By his "death" Merlin presumably meant his imprisonment; in fact the Grail adventures would seem to come quite some time after that event. Perhaps the great mage was speaking on a "brevity of human life compared with the age of the world" scale.

7. Sir Garlon went around invisible, killing knights at will [Malory II, 12-14].
8. Merlin saved Balin after Pellam's castle had fallen on him because of the Dolorous Stroke. Apparently, to do this Merlin had to move a deal of stone by magical means. [Malory II, 16]
9. Merlin "let write" Balin's name and history in letters of gold on his tomb; the lady who had buried Balin had not known his name [Malory II, 18-19].
10. Because Nimue seems to have acquired a bad reputation for the following deed, which reputation I am not sure she entirely deserves, I give it in Malory's words.

> ... Merlin fell in a dotage on the damosel that King Pellinore brought to court, and she was one of the damosels of the lake, that hight Nimue. But Merlin would let her have no rest, but always he would be with her. And ever she made Merlin good cheer till she had learned of him all manner thing that she desired; and he was assotted upon her, that he might not be from her. So on a time he told King Arthur that he should not dure long, but for all his crafts he should be put in the earth quick.
>
> Ah, said the king, since ye know of your adventure, purvey for it, and put away by your crafts that misadventure. Nay, said Merlin, it will not be; so he departed from the king. And within a while the Damosel of the Lake departed, and Merlin went with her evermore wheresomever she went. And ofttimes Merlin would have had her privily away by his subtle crafts; then she made him to swear that he should never do none enchantment upon her if he would have his will. And so he sware; so she and Merlin went over the sea unto the land of Benwick [where Merlin prophesied Lancelot's greatness to Lancelot's mother Queen Elaine] .... And so, soon after, the lady and Merlin departed, and by the way Merlin showed her many wonders, and came into Cornwall. And always Merlin lay about the lady to have her maidenhood, and she was ever passing weary of him, and fain would have been delivered of him, for she was afeard of him because he was a devil's son, and she could not beskift him by no mean. And so on a time it happed that Merlin showed to her in a rock whereas was a great wonder, and wrought by enchantment, that went under a great stone. So by her subtle working she made Merlin to go under that stone to let her wit of the marvels there; but she wrought so there for him that he came never out for all the craft he could do. And so she departed and left Merlin. [Malory IV, 1]

11. Arthur, King Uriens, and Sir Accolon were out hunting when they came to the shore and "a little ship, all apparelled with silk ... came right unto them and landed on the sands." Seeing nobody aboard, the trio got in. Suddenly a hundred torches lit the ship and twelve fair damsels came out to welcome the men inside, serve them fine supper, and lead them each to separate bedchambers. In the morning

Uriens woke up back in Camelot, two days' journey away, in the arms of his wife Morgan (who apparently engineered the episode). Arthur woke up in a dark prison full of woeful knights; to free them and himself, the king had to fight on behalf of the evil Sir Damas against the champion of the good Sir Ontzlake. Accolon woke on the edge of a deep well, and there Morgan's dwarf found him and brought him to Sir Ontzlake's manor to be Ontzlake's champion. [Malory IV, 6-9; see also Fountain of the Silver Pipe.

12. Tied in with 11 above, Morgan le Fay counterfeited Excalibur and its scabbard so that she could give the originals to Sir Accolon, her lover. Arthur, fighting Accolon, did not realize the substitution until he found himself bleeding and the false Excalibur breaking in his hands. Nimue, apparently through her magical craft, found out about all this, came to the place, and by enchantments struck Excalibur out of Accolon's hand, Arthur recovering it. Arthur was then able to tear the magic scabbard from Accolon's side and so win the fight. [Malory II, 11; XV, 8-11]

13. Morgan, escaping with forty mounted knights of hers after her attempt to kill Arthur as described above in numbers 11 and 12,

> rode into a valley where many great stones were, and when she saw she must be overtaken, she shaped herself, horse and man, by enchantment unto a great marble stone.

On this same trip she threw the scabbard of Excalibur into a lake, and later rescued Sir Manassen from a knight who would have drowned him; both these last were natural acts. [Malory IV, 14-15]

14. Twelve damsels and two knights dwelt in a turret, near a place where Sir Marhaus was staying for at least a time. They were sorceresses and enchantresses who could make a knight, be he never so good of body and full of prowess, "a stark coward to have no better of him." I cannot find out how they did this. [Malory IV, 17-18]

15. Pelleas loved Ettard and Ettard hated Pelleas. Nimue cast Pelleas into an enchanted sleep for two hours, brought Ettard to where he lay, and through her power reversed the affections, so that Ettard died of love for Pelleas while he left her and married Nimue, with whom he lived happily ever after. [Malory IV, 20-23] I could not find whether, while turning Pelleas' love for Ettard into hate, Nimue also used magic to win his affections for herself, or whether she won him by natural means alone. Ever afterward, Nimue kept Pelleas from fighting Lancelot "by her means." This may refer to more magic, or to loving persuasion.

16. Dame Lynette, through her subtle crafts, kept her sister and Sir Gareth honest before their marriage. When Lyonors went down to Gareth, who was sleeping in the hall, Lynette sent a great, grisly knight of her own to attack Gareth in his bed. Lynette's knight wounded Gareth in the thing and Gareth lopped off his opponent's head; Lynette came in, anointed the head with an ointment, and

stuck it back on the neck in the sight of all, healing her knight. Ten days later, Gareth, healing naturally, appointed a night to try it again with Lyonors. When Lynette sent down her knight this time, Gareth not only beheaded him, but hacked the head into a hundred gobbets and threw them out the window into the ditches of the castle. Lynette calmly fetched them up, pieced them together, and restored her knight again. Gareth did not heal this time until Lynette healed him. Apparently, Gareth and Lyonors now decided to wait until they were married. [Malory VII, 22-23, 26]

17. An unnamed lady loved King Meliodas, Tristram's father. One day when he rode hunting, "by an enchantment" he followed a hart to an old castle "and there anon he was taken prisoner by the lady that loved him." Merlin at last rescued him in an unstated way. [Malory VIII, 1-2]

18. Morgan le Fay, developing a passion for Sir Alisander le Orphelin, first inflamed his wounds with one ointment, then healed them with another, apparently to trick him into a greater gratitude [Malory X, 37]. This sounds like a simple case of herbal lore.

19. Morgan le Fay and the Queen of Northgalis put a damsel into a bath of scalding water, where she remained for five years until Sir Lancelot took her hand and led her out. Other knights had tried, but this was another case where only the best knight would do. [Malory XI, 1]

    Although Malory charges the scalding bath to Morgan and her cohort, in the Vulgate the damsel tells those who come to attempt her rescue that she is being punished for sin. Since the tower where she suffers is in or near Carbonek (or Corbin), I incline to the mystical-righteous interpretation and, despite Malory's charge, absolve Morgan and the Queen of Northgalis, except perhaps as instruments of Heaven.

    When Gawaine dipped his arm into the water, he thought his hand had been burned off. Only magic or miracle could enable the damsel to survive her long wait in such water.

20. When Lancelot first came to Carbonek, Dame Brisen, who was "one of the greatest enchantresses that was at that time in the world living," was requested by King Pellam to help bring about a coupling between his daughter and the great knight, in order to produce Galahad. Dame Brisen had Lancelot receive "a ring from Queen Guenever like as it had come from her" as a token for a tryst. After arriving at the specified castle and taking those folk for the people normally around the Queen, he accepts a cup full of wine, "and anon as he had drunken that wine he was so assotted and mad that he might make no delay", and bedded Elaine as though she were Guenevere.

The wine might have contained a simple aphrodisiac; the mistaking of Elaine's knights for the Queen's and even of Elaine for Guenevere might have been accomplished simply through suggestion, darkness, and muddling Lancelot's head with wine and herbs. The messenger with the ring like Guenevere's is less easy to dismiss. It sounds as if Malory should have told us that Brisen "made one to come to Sir Lancelot [in the likeness of one] that he knew well"—that Brisen, in short, did much the same kind of thing Merlin had done earlier to get Uther into Igraine's bed.

(There is no evidence that Brisen learned any craft from Merlin.)

Later, Elaine and Brisen visited Camelot. Learning by her crafts that Lancelot and the Queen had made a date to spend the night together, Brisen pretended to be Guenevere's messenger and brought Lancelot to Elaine's room, next door to the Queen's, where again he slept with Elaine, believing her to be Guenevere. When Guenevere found them this time, her wrath and jealousy drove him to a fit of madness. This later incident may have been a case of natural intrigue and deceit. [Malory XI, 7-8]

21. Sir Pinel le Savage tried to poison Gawaine with apples, Gawaine's favorite fruit, at a small dinner given by Guenevere. Sir Patrise of Ireland, a cousin of Mador de la Porte, ate an apple first and died. Guenevere was accused and Lancelot saved her from execution by fighting Mador; not until Nimue came and applied her crafts to the problem was the truth of the murder disclosed. [Malory XVIII, 3-8, especially 8]

    One wonders why the Damsel of the Lake did not show up earlier and save Guenevere the agony of being mistakenly accused. Either Nimue's crafts did not tell her what was going on so quickly as they had in the affair of the false Excalibur (see Magical Act 12), or, perhaps, she was too busy with Pelleas at the moment to check up on the court.

The events of obviously mystical origin—the miracles either of God or of the Devil, which are especially prevalent in the Grail Adventures—would probably be beyond the reach of a simple necromancer, even one as great as Merlin or Morgan. A saintly person who performs such acts does so by the grace and power of God.

Perhaps Malory's most memorable example of the Devil's craft comes in Book XIV, chapters 5 and 6. Sir Percivale, during the Grail Adventures, lost his horse and accepted another from a strange lady. The steed was black and Percivale "marvelled that it was so great and so well apparelled." Trustingly and unthinkingly, Percivale leaped up on its back, and

> within an hour and less [the horse] bare him four days' journey thence, until he came to a rough water the which roared, and his horse would have borne him into it. And when Sir Percivale came nigh the brim, and

> saw the water so boistous, he doubted to overpass it. And then he made a sign of the cross in his forehead. When the fiend felt him so charged he shook off Sir Percivale, and he went into the water crying and roaring, making great sorrow, and it seemed unto him that the water brent.

The devil also takes the shape of a beautiful lady to tempt a knight's chastity, or of a holy man to expound some vision falsely [cf. Malory XIV, 8-10; XVI, 11].

Magical Acts Selected from the Vulgate

22. Merlin brought the stones of Stonehenge from Ireland to their present site as a tomb for King Pandragon. (Pandragon was Uther's brother, from whom Uther took his second name. They were both sons of King Constans of England.) [Vulgate II]

23. At first, Merlin was not averse to prophesying in plain language. But a certain foolish baron, trying to catch him up, came to him on three separate occasions to ask, "How will I die?" The first time, Merlin told him that he would break his neck; the second time, that he would hang himself; the third time, that he would drown. These seemingly irreconcilable prophecies were all fulfilled when the baron had a freak accident. He was thrown from his horse on the bank of a river in such a way that his neck was broken; the reins were wrapped around his neck, hanging him; and his head and shoulders were under the water of the river.

    It was apparently this incident which made Merlin decide to stop prophesying plainly and only prophesy obscurely [Vulgate II].

24. Disguised as an old man, Merlin brought Gawaine from Camelot to Dover to help Sagramore and his companions, who had landed at Dover only to be beset by the Sesnes. [Vulgate II]

25. Just before battle, Merlin ignited the tents of the rebel barons [Vulgate II].

26. Arthur was fighting the Sesnes for Leodegrance. The porter, apparently not wanting his side to issue forth to fight the foe and perhaps be defeated, refused to open the gate. Merlin opened it by his craft. It reclosed afterward of itself. Merlin carried Arthur's dragon standard during this battle, and the dragon on the banner spat fire. Toward the end of the battle, Merlin produced first a storm, then a fog to stop the Sesnes. That night, Arthur and his men, still finishing off the foe, were able to see by the fire the dragon standard spat. [Vulgate II]

27. Merlin traveled from Rome to his old master Blaise in Northumberland in twenty-four hours [Vulgate II].

28. On first meeting Viviane, Merlin produced a phantom castle, knights and ladies, and an orchard which remained after the other things had vanished [Vulgate II].

29. Merlin began Viviane's instruction by teaching her how to produce a river [Vulgate II].
30. While in France helping Kings Ban and Bors against King Claudas, Merlin blew a horn and made a fiery cloud appear in the sky as the signal for battle [Vulgate II].
31. When Merlin was escorting Ban and Bors back from Britain to their own kingdom, they stopped for a night at the Castle des Mares. Since Ban greatly admired the daughter of the castellan, Sir Agravadain, Merlin cast a spell between her and Ban so that they lay together without any sense of shame. Merlin broke the spell after leading the damsel back to her own room, but she was still left loving Ban (who had a wife back home) better than any other man. The damsel gave birth to a child resembling King Ban. This child was Sir Ector de Maris, Lancelot's half-brother. The incident also resulted, incidentally, in warfare between Sir Agravadain and his daughter's lover.
32. When Seraide went to the court of King Claudas to rescue young Lionel and Bors, she had to give them the appearance of greyhounds. At the same time, two real greyhounds took on the appearance of the boys. When Seraide had gotten the boys safely away and given them back their own appearance, the enchanted greyhounds, which Claudas had imprisoned, also regained their real shapes. [Vulgate III]
33. A clerk of Cologne had found that Duke Galeholt must pass a bridge of forty-five planks, which indicated his term of life; but they did not know whether this meant years, months, or days. To find out, Helyes of Thoulouse went alone with Galeholt into the chapel. Helyes got charcoal from the porter of the chapel, closed the door, and drew four groups of forty-five lines each on the wall, each group smaller than the preceding one. These groups indicated years, months, weeks, and days. Helyes gave Galeholt the pyx and he himself took the jeweled cross from the altar. Then Helyes read from his book until he was exhausted and feverishly excited. He began to read again, the chapel darkened, and a fearful voice was heard. The two men, each clutching his holy talisman, fell to the floor. The earth quaked, the chapel seemed to turn round, and an arm clothed in an ample sleeve and holding a fiery sword appeared through the closed door. It went straight to Helyes and Galeholt, but could not hurt them because of the cross and the pyx. At last the arm went to the wall, effaced 41 1/4 of the largest marks, and vanished. Thus Helyes understood that the forty-five planks were forty-five years, the complete sum of Galeholt's life from birth to death, and that the Duke had only three and three-quarters years remaining. Helyes told him, however, that he could prolong his life by keeping his friend Lancelot with him. (Galeholt refused to take advantage of Lancelot's friendship by abridging his freedom to go where he would.) [Vulgate IV]

Malory records a somewhat reminiscent conjuring up of a demon. [Book XV, 1-2; see Chapel of the Demon] The incident in Malory, however, is not only milder and apparently fraught with less danger to the holy man who does the conjuring, but seems more clearly a case of religion than magic. Helyes' summoning of the arm, although it has its religious elements, seems more nearly a case of necromancy.

34. In an effort to make Lancelot forget Guenevere, Morgan, with the help of strong drugs, caused him to have strange dreams. She so contrived matters that on awakening he would find himself in the same surroundings he had seen in his dreams, thus convincing him the dreams were real. (This argues a control over someone else's dreams that science fiction hardly dares describe today.) [Vulgate IV]

Names

Chrétien and Malory's characters commonly put off name introductions until long after we moderns would do it. Possibly the apparent reluctance of Arthurian characters to ask and give each other their names was an outgrowth of the primitive idea that knowing a man or woman's name gave you power over him or her. If so, reluctance to give enemies the clue to your name by carrying your own shield for them to recognize might have led to the frequent practice of covering your shield or using an unemblazoned one. Whatever the reason, the shyness of the characters about their names seems to have carried over into the attitudes of the romancers themselves. The romancers often seem more conscientious about naming their knights and kings than about naming their ladies, squires, hermits, and so on; Chrétien, however, apparently calls many even of Arthur's chief knights by tags and soubriquets rather than by proper names in our sense. He also explains, when about a third of the way through Enide's story he finally tells us her christened name, that her married status now makes this proper and that before the wedding none of the other characters knew her name, any more than the reader did. Chrétien's practice is far from consistent—he names Fenice, heroine (or antiheroine) of his next romance, at once, well before her marriage; he gives no reason that I could find for withholding the proper names of both of Enide's (married) parents until almost the end of the story. He frequently makes a point of characters not knowing one another's names; it is not the reader alone who labors under this handicap. Julian Harris says that Chrétien did this to arouse readers' curiosity. [Introd. to **Yvain**, NY, 1969, p. 27] Consider, also, the interesting case of Chrétien's **Perceval**, who seems not even to know his own name until suddenly it comes to him through some instinct or inspiration.

In our era it is considered good practice to attach names to most characters as quickly as possible, thus giving readers a handle on them. Whereas in reading such novelists as Fielding, Dickens, Dostoevsky, Heyer, and James Jones we may find ourselves floundering in a sea of names and trying desperately to make sure we attach them to the right characters, in reading the medieval romances we face the opposite problem and often learn a great deal about characters before we know what to call them. Perhaps the medieval way was no more confusing, after all. Unfortunately, by the time we reach the prose Vulgate, numerous characters—not always minor—remain unnamed permanently, perhaps through carrying the postponed-naming device too far, perhaps through later copyists missing the name when it finally did appear, buried in the text, without benefit of our modern system of capitalization.

It is logical that this system would lead to situations in which a character's name was lost and a later author or scribe would assign a new name. Still later, another reworker of the material might find the character under both names and take him or her for two different characters with similar stories. Meanwhile, other romancers, feeling the need to name some character, were doubtless appropriating names from other major or minor characters, somewhat as Vera Chapman, one of the very best recent Arthurian romancers, has appropriated the name of Bagdemagus—who has become a rather minor character to our century—for the name of a villain who bears virtually no resemblance to the Bagdemagus of the Vulgate. Here I will leave this particular tangle of names and characters—a hopeless or a glorious tangle, depending on how keen you are on scholarly and literary mysteries.

Despite the great number of nameless characters, the romances provide us with an overwhelming number of proper names, most of them very strange-sounding to our ears and twisting to our tongues. The names to be found in the "Who's Who" of the present work reflect a melting pot of the sources of Arthurian legend and romance. Here are Roman and Classical names: Lucius, Alisander (from Alexander), Colombe, Belleus; names of Hebrew origin: Joseph, Eliazar; Welsh names: Gawaine, Ywaine, Guenevere, Cei (Kay); French names: Brumant l'Orguilleus, Floree, Beauvivante; even some solid British names of a more or less modern sound: Ironside. Many of the names, of course, are still in common use today—some, no doubt, as a result of their prominence in Arthurian lore, like Gareth, Lancelot, Gavin, possibly even Arthur; but some, I think, would have remained in use even had there been no popular body of Arthurian lore, like Elaine, Mark, Elizabeth, Hue (Hugh), Edward. (That Kay and Florence are common names today is probably a complete coincidence.) The name of Lancelot's virgin lover, Amable, is not, perhaps, a common name in our generation; indeed, I found it only in the appendix to Volume V of the Vulgate—elsewhere she is one of the nameless damsels. But the name seems to have been popular until our own century. It appears, for instance, in Ainsworth's excellent melodramatic Victorian historical novel **Old Saint Paul's**, set during the London plague and fire of the latter seventeenth century, and in other period novels.

There remain a good many especially strange-sounding names, largely from the Vulgate—names which, though from a French source, do not seem quite French. Though a knowledge of modern French can enable a reader to get at least the sense of much of the Vulgate, it must be remembered that there were other dialects in that geographical area besides the one which became modern French. *Langue d'oïl* romancers who transferred their tales from the Breton, *langue d'oc*, and other dialects would probably have carried the proper names over almost unchanged. Thymadeuc (in the Morbihan), Guenael, Vacandard, Fastrad of Gaviamex, Senanque, Vezelay—these are names that would hardly have sounded out of place among the Arthurian sites and characters in this volume; I found them in Thomas Merton's book about Cistercian life, **The Waters of Siloe**, and some, at least, must have originated in a French dialect other than the *langue d'oïl*. Alazaïs, Grazide, Vuissane—easily as strange to our eyes and ears as most of the proper names in Malory and the Vulgate—I found in an article about a fourteenth-century cleric in Occitan-speaking France, totally unrelated to Arthurian studies.

One further point: finding names for characters must have been as common a problem among medieval as among modern storytellers. (That, indeed, may have been another reason why they left so many characters unnamed.) It is entirely possible that some Arthurian names sounded as strange, awkward, contrived, even unsatisfactory to medieval readers—even, perhaps, to the very storytellers who had devised them in desperation—as they sound to us.

It seems rather popular in modern Arthurian novels to refer to Arthur's own name as outlandish. Perhaps there is a scholarly basis for this; perhaps it is simply another instance of heightening the sense of difference between eras by referring to a common name in our century as an uncommon name in the past—I have also found the name Thomas so treated. The surprise that characters express in such novels, however—their puzzlement as to where such a name as "Arthur" could have come from—has never convinced me. "Arthur" seems such a logical development from "Uther", and I cannot remember any similar surprise among characters over Uther's name.

Prophecies

According to a hermit's interpretation, one of the visions Gawaine had in Carbonek foretold Gawaine's own death. Gawaine consoled himself (very sensibly, in my opinion) with the reflection that prophecies were uncertain. [Vulgate V]

Merlin's prophecies all apparently came true, though some were notably obscure and thus open to various interpretations. They must not all have come true during Arthur's own time, for prophecies attributed to the great mage continued to circulate during the historical Middle Ages. [See also *Magical Acts* on page 528.]

At least some prophecies seem to have been "of God", especially those concerning the Grail. Others, apparently, were discovered through necromancy. The question, of course, is how far a prophecy—even a competent, truthful one—predicts an absolute and unchangeable future and how far it helps create the circumstances it predicts. Personally, I not only question the value of prophecies, but think some of them were mischievous, dangerous, and pernicious. It is a pity that Mordred, when confronted with a devastating prophecy at an impressionable age, did not show his brother Gawaine's healthy skepticism: the end of Arthur's story might have been very different.

Questing and Errantry

A quest generally lasted only a year and a day, apparently whether accomplished or not. For this we have Gawaine's authority. [Vulgate V, p. 270]

The pattern of errantry seems to have been that you helped whomever first requested it of you, without bothering to investigate which side was more nearly in the right—unless, of course, one of the parties was a lady, in which case you generally helped her against the male involved. This system could result in the reversal of justice. Once a wronged husband reprimanded Gawaine for the practice of Arthur's knights of taking the woman's part automatically without first hearing both sides [Vulgate V, appendix]. Another time, Gareth, Gaheris, and Agravaine entered a dispute on the right side and were winning it when Lancelot and Lionel came along, entered on the wrong side without taking time to investigate and weigh the merits of both sides, and won for the wrong side [Vulgate V].

It was considered disgraceful for a knight to ride in a cart, or "chariot." Lancelot turned this into honor as Le Chavaler du Chariot.

> For ... because of despite that knights and ladies called him the knight that rode in the chariot like as if he were judged to the gallows, therefore in despite of all them that named him so, he was carried in a chariot a twelvemonth ... [and] he never in a twelvemonth came on horseback. And ... he did that twelvemonth more than forty battles. [Malory XIX, 13; the first trip in a cart had been to Meliagrant's castle to save Guenevere after Meliagrant's archers killed Lancelot's horse from ambush.]

Lancelot's quest in a cart may not have been quite as offbeat as it sounds. After a tournament of King Brangoire's, the twelve best knights of the tourney gave "gifts" to Brangoire's daughter, which gifts consisted of extravagant promises of what they were going to do. The gifts varied from simply silly to needlessly bloodthirsty. The most sensible of the lot was probably the young knight who swore not to joust for a year except with his right leg on the neck of his horse; all he had to do, once he sobered up, was to refrain from jousting at all. One of the worst was he who promised to cut off the heads of all the knights he conquered and send them to the princess. Yet another gallant promised to kiss every damsel he found with a knight; Lancelot encountered him, defeated him for trying to kiss the damsel Lancelot was escorting, and scolded him for foolishness. [Vulgate IV]

Nevertheless, one sometimes receives the impression that almost anything can be forgiven and overlooked if the perpetrator claims it was done to fulfil a vow or promise, especially one made because of a woman. Sir Ironside, while besieging Castle Dangerous, hanged nearly forty knights by the neck shamefully from trees. He did it because once he had loved a lady whose brother had been killed by (she said) either Lancelot or Gawaine; she had made Ironside promise by the faith of his knighthood "to labour daily in arms" until he met one of those twain, and to put all he overcame in the meantime to a shameful death. Ironside was not only forgiven, but made a knight of the Round Table. [Malory VII]

In the mischievous Middle English metrical romance **The Avowynge of King Arthur**, Arthur vows to slay a notorious wild boar singlehandedly before the next day. He then commands his companions each to make his own vow. Gawaine vows to keep vigil all night at Tarn Wadling; Kay vows to ride about the woods until day and fight to the death anyone who tries to block his way; Bawdewyn (Baldwin) vows never to be jealous of his wife or any other lady, never to dread death, and to give any comer good hospitality.

Relations between Knights and Ladies

Far too much has been written elsewhere on the subject of courtly love, how far it was sensual and how far platonic, for me to attempt to answer the question here. I have, however, culled some relevant passages from Malory:

> [The Damsel said] ... almighty Jesu preserve you ... for the curteist knight thou art, and meekest unto all ladies and gentlewomen, that now liveth. But one thing, sir knight, methinketh ye lack, ye that are a knight wifeless, that [y]e will not love some maiden or gentlewoman, for I could never hear say that ever ye loved any of no matter degree, and that is great pity; but it is noised that ye love Queen Guenever, and that she hath been ordained by enchantment that ye shall never love none other but her ... wherefore many in this land, of high estate and low, make great sorrow.
>
> Fair damosel, said Sir Launcelot, I may not warn people to speak of me what it pleaseth them; but for to be a wedded man, I think it not; for then I must couch with her, and leave arms and tournaments, battles, and adventures; and as for to say for to take my pleasaunce with paramours, that will I refuse in principal for dread of God; for knights that be adventurous or lecherous shall not be happy nor fortunate unto the wars, for other they shall be overcome with a simpler knight than they be themselves, other else they shall by unhap and their cursedness slay better men than they be themselves. And so who that useth paramours shall be unhappy, and all thing is unhappy that is about them. [VI, 10]
>
> La Beale Isoud made a letter unto Queen Guenever, complaining her of the untruth of Sir Tristram, and how he had wedded the king's daughter of Brittany. Queen Guenever sent her another letter, and bade her be of good cheer, for she should have joy after sorrow, for Sir Tristram was so noble a knight called that by crafts of sorcery ladies would make such noble men to wed them. But in the end, Queen Guenever said, it shall be thus, that he shall hate her, and love you better than ever he did to-fore. [VIII, 37]
>
> Then Sir Dinadan told Sir Tristram his name, but Sir Tristram would not tell him his name, wherefore Sir Dinadan was wroth. For such a foolish knight as ye are, said Sir Dinadan, I saw but late this day lying by a well, and he fared as he slept; and there he lay like a fool grinning, and would not speak, and his shield lay by him, and his horse stood by him; and well I wot he was a lover. Ah, fair sir, said Sir Tristram, are ye not a lover? Mary, fie on that craft! said Sir Dinadan. That is evil said, said Sir Tristram, for a knight may never be of prowess but if he be a lover. [X, 55]
>
> And when Sir Launcelot heard [of the death of Elaine of Astolat] he said: ... God knoweth I was never causer of her death by my willing ... but that she was both fair and good, and much I was beholden unto her, but she loved me out of measure. Ye might have shewed her, said

> the queen, some bounty and gentleness that might have preserved her life. Madam, said Sir Launcelot, she would none other ways be answered but that she would be my wife, outher else my paramour; and of these two I would not grant her, but I proffered her, for her good love that she shewed me, a thousand pound yearly to her, and to her heirs, and to wed in any manner knight that she could find best to love in her heart. For madam, said Sir Launcelot, I love not to be constrained to love; for love must arise of the heart, and not by no constraint. That is truth, said the king, and many knight's love is free in himself, and never will be bounden, for where he is bounden he looseth himself. [XVIII, 20]

> For like as herbs and trees bring forth fruit and flourish in May, in like wise every lusty heart that is in any manner a lover, springeth and flourisheth in lusty deeds. For it giveth unto all lovers courage, that lusty month of May .... For then all herbs and trees renew a man and a woman, and likewise lovers call again to their mind old gentleness and old service, and many kind deeds that were forgotten by negligence. For like as winter rasure doth alway arase and deface green summer, so fareth it by unstable love in man and woman. For in many persons there is no stability; for we may see all day, for a little blast of winter's rasure, anon we shall deface and lay apart true love for little or nought .... [T]his is no wisdom nor stability, but it is feebleness of nature and great disworship, whosomever useth this. Therefore ... let every man of worship flourish his heart in this world, first unto God, and next unto the joy of them that he promised his faith unto; for there was never worshipful man or worshipful woman, but they loved one better than another; and worship in arms may never be foiled, but first reserve the honour to God, and secondly the quarrel must come of thy lady: and such love I call virtuous love.

> But nowadays men can not love seven night but they must have all their desires: that love may not endure by reason; for where they be soon accorded and hasty heat, soon it cooleth. ... But the old love was not so; men and women could love together seven years, and no licours lusts were between them, and then was love, truth, and faithfulness: and lo, in likewise was used love in King Arthur's days. ... [T]herefore all ye that be lovers call unto your remembrance the month of May, like as did Queen Guenever, for whom I make here a little mention, that while she lived she was a true lover, and therefore she had a good end. [XVIII, 25]

Passages could be pulled out of Malory to argue that there was no "sensual" love between Lancelot and Guenevere; but, on the whole, the bulk of evidence points to a full, carnal affair. Passing on to lesser lovers, extramarital affairs, whether dignified under the heading of courtly love or not, appear to have been common, as evidenced by the tests of the Magic Mantle and Morgan's Drinking Horn. No doubt this was only to be expected in an age when women were married off for other reasons than their own choice and love and when, moreover, a lady's husband was liable to be killed in any tournament or chance joust, and a lover or two on the side might provide a reserve husband and protector with the minimum loss of time. We should also remember that, though the women were more likely to receive the censure, they were not always primarily to blame. There was, for instance, the curious request of Sir Bleoberis de Ganis, a knight of the Round Table, who rode into King Mark's court and asked that Mark should give him whatever gift he desired.

> When the king heard him ask so, he marvelled of his asking, but because he was a knight of the Round Table, and of a great reknown, King Mark granted him his whole asking. Then, said Sir Bleoberis, I will have the fairest lady in your court that me list to choose. I may not say nay, said King Mark; now choose at your adventure. And so Sir Bleoberis did choose Sir Segwarides' wife, and took her by the hand, and so went his way with her [on horseback]. [Malory VIII, 15]

It is possible that Bleoberis and other knights in similar episodes in the Vulgate were chiefly interested in winning glory by defeating the men who came after them to rescue the lady, but the business has a suspicious look, especially when such incidents as that concerning Lancelot's cousin Iblis and Sir Gaheris are added. On the other hand, by a sort of triple standard, while an unfaithful wife or hasty maiden might lay herself open to more official censure and marital retribution than an erring husband, there seems also to have been an undercurrent of popular admiration for many such women. Guenevere and La Beale Isoud may have risked death for having their lovers, but they also gain the old romancers' sympathy and praise. If Pellinore is not scolded by the other characters for engendering Tor "half by force", neither is Tor's mother upbraided for the episode; indeed, there is a hint that she profited by it when Tor was knighted. Surely "it was not then as it is now", for while all this sexual passion was accepted and to some extent sanctioned, purity and virginity were at the same time admired, even in the male—not, as sometimes today, considered the only sexual depravity; chastity was a sign of virtue, not psychological sickness.

Perhaps both views of courtly love are correct—it has room for both fleshly and spiritual affairs. Sir Galahad and Percivale's sister Amide exemplify courtly love in its most spiritual aspect, with no fleshly interludes. Lancelot had a strictly platonic arrangement with the damsel Amable, who, like Elaine of Astolat, fell hopelessly in love with him, but who, unlike Elaine, refused to let it kill her. Instead, she ingeniously proposed that, if she remained a virgin for Lancelot's love, he could love her as a virgin and his other lady as a paramour, and so love them both without dishonor. The scheme worked admirably. (Malory, however, does not record this affair.)

Whenever a knight succored, or even met, a lady or damsel, he usually offered to be her true knight forever and in all places. Obviously, such a vow cannot always indicate a courtly love affair.

Dinadan's comments in the third passage cited above are not without reason. There was a curious phenomenon liable to affect any true lover, from Lancelot on down. Sometimes, looking up in the middle of a fight or at another time and seeing his lady watching him, the knight would go into a sort of trance or stupor, contemplating her beauty and virtue, his love for her, or whatever. In this state, the lover was witless and helpless. Anyone who came along could take his horse's reins and lead him anywhere, push him into the river, and so on. It is fortunate that this fit never struck Lancelot when he was championing Guenevere in trial by combat. A good friend might bring the afflicted party out of his trance by a solid thwack with the flat of a sword, as the Damsel of La Beale Regard once did Sir Alisander; on the whole, the thing really must have been enough to make thinkers like Dinadan shy away from becoming lovers. (Percivale, in a similar lover's meditation, nevertheless jousted as well as ever—but Percivale's abstraction was called forth merely by blood and snow that reminded him of his love's complexion, not by the presence of his love herself.)

Once Sir Lamorak met Sir Meliagrant and they promptly started fighting to prove which of their ladies—Margawse or Guenevere respectively—was the most beautiful woman in the land. Lancelot came along, rode between them, and asked why two of Arthur's knights were fighting one another. On learning the cause of the quarrel, Lancelot was ready to fight Lamorak himself in defense of Guenevere's superior beauty. Lamorak explained, "[E]very man thinketh his own lady fairest." Bleoberis, a neutral party, agreed, saying to Lancelot, "I have a lady, and me thinketh that she is the fairest lady of the world. Were this a great reason that ye should be wroth with me for such language?" Thus they all made up and parted friends, though one wonders why Lamorak and Bleoberis did not speak so reasonably and peaceably when it was a mere matter of Lamorak against Meliagrant. [Malory IX, 13-14] Notice that this is a case in which a knight, Meliagrant, loves as his lady a woman who does not reciprocate; though Meliagrant was later to attempt to force his love by kidnaping Guenevere, in this particular quarrel it is possible that Meliagrant is more nearly an example of pure courtly devotion than is Lamorak, who may well already have been enjoying Margawse's favors.

Dates and Time

The Arthurian year uses the major feasts of the Christian church as chief reference points. Not all these feasts have been constant, either in date or in importance, through the centuries; indeed, the historical fifth and sixth centuries were times of two separate traditions for fixing the date of Easter in the Western church. At one point, the controversy led half of one monarch's court to celebrate Easter while the other half was still in Lenten mourning. I think we may probably assume, however, that to Malory's Arthur, Advent (the beginning of the liturgical year, lasting from about a month before Christmas until Christmas), Christmas, Epiphany, Lent, Easter, Ascension, and Pentecost (Whitsunday) fell about where they fall today in relation to each other and the seasons—Easter and the seasons and feasts counting from its placement (Lent, Ascension, Pentecost) being movable, of course.

Feasts of the saints and even of Mary may be more subject to change than the greater feasts given above. In the seventeenth century, for instance, St. Joseph's Day fell on March 17; today March 17 goes to St. Patrick and St. Joseph has been moved to March 19. From various references in the romances, however, I am confident that Assumption fell then when it falls now, and I am also reasonably confident that feasts like All Saints, which appear to have been timed with a view to replacing or Christianizing older Pagan holy days, also remain about where they were in Malory's time. Here, then, are a few modern dates for various feasts of Mary and the saints which may come in handy in finding our place on the Arthurian calendar:

March 25: Annunciation (Commemorates the angel Gabriel's appearance to Mary. Sometimes called "Lady Day." At one time considered the start of a new year.)
June 24: St. John the Baptist
July 22: St. Mary Magdalen
August 15: Assumption (Celebrates the taking of Mary's body into Heaven.)
September 29: St. Michael the Archangel ("Michaelmas")
November 1: All Saints
November 11: St. Martin ("Martinmas")
December 26: St. Stephen

Hours of the Day

Arthurian people spoke of what o'clock it was.

> [A]nd so the queen lay long in her bed until it was nine of the clock.
>
> Then Sir Meliagrance went to the queen's chamber, and found her ladies there ready clothed. Jesu mercy, said Sir Meliagrance, what aileth you, madam, that ye sleep thus long? [Malory XIX, 6]

> Sir, said Sir Bors, I shall do my pain, and or it be seven of the clock I shall wit of such as ye have said before, who will hold with you. [Malory XX, 5]

More common, however, may have been the system of dividing up the day by the liturgical hours of the Church. In practice, the times of reciting these hours is adapted to other demands of monks and nuns' days, such as field work. Also, the entire period between one "hour" and the next may be referred to by the name of the earlier hour. Here is more or less how the liturgical hours divide the day:

Prime: 6:00 a.m.

Terce or **Underne**: 9:00 a.m.

Sext: Noon

None: Midafternoon, 2:30 or 3:00 p.m.

Vespers: Late afternoon or early evening

Compline: Bedtime (I am not sure whether this hour had as yet developed in Arthurian times.)

Matins and Lauds: Frequently recited together. Traditionally, Matins should begin in the middle of the night, a few hours after midnight; in monasteries and convents where the full Office is chanted, Matins and Lauds may go on till dawn in the seasons of longer days. Matins, however, has come to apply in popular parlance to dawn and early morning: "The birds were saying their Matins."

Tournaments and Jousting

Tournaments were obviously rough. At that of Winchester, Lancelot

> gave Sir Bors such a buffet that he made him bow his head passing low; and therewithal he raced off his helm, and might have slain him ... and in the same wise he served Sir Ector and Sir Lionel. For as the book saith he might have slain them, but when he saw their visages his heart might not serve him thereto, but left them there. [Malory XVIII, 11]

I should hope his heart might not serve—they were his close kinsmen! Still, it is hardly surprising that we often read in the romances of knights (usually minor characters) having been slain in tournament.

Sometimes tournaments seem to fill the function, more or less, of wars fought between two kings by appointment. A peculiarity of most tournaments, however, seems to have been that a knight could enter on the side that seemed weaker, even against his own sovereign, in order to win greater glory for himself. If, during the melee, it seemed that his chosen side was winning too easily (possibly because of his own efforts), he could honorably change sides. This appears to have been a recognized means of enhancing one's glory as a fighter; the greatest knights of the Round Table indulged in it. (One conjures up visions of football-players-errant, probably mostly backs, traveling around from game to game entering each contest under the above rules of side-choosing and side-changing.)

At one tournament, Lancelot struck Bors, saddle and all, to the ground. Gawaine, watching this, remarked that Bors was "unhorsed, but not dishonoured" [Vulgate VI, p. 212]. Apparently, if you went down in a joust because your saddle (or presumably—by extension—your horse) failed, you lost no honor. I rather doubt that this rule held true in the failing of lances, for it often seems the usual outcome of a joust that Sir X's lance breaks but Sir Y's lance holds, in which case Sir Y almost automatically bears Sir X to the earth.

Heralds to announce combatants and to cry "Lesses les aler" ("*Lessez-les aller*"—"Let them go!") and "knights parters of the field" are mentioned in the combat between Lancelot and Meliagrant [Malory XIX, 9]. Though this was a trial by combat, heralds and knights parters must have been found also at tournaments. In this particular combat, the knights parters took off half of Lancelot's armor and bound his left hand behind his back as the conditions upon which Meliagrant agreed to continue the battle—this must have been a rather unusual duty for the knights parters. When Palomides kept his appointment to fight Tristram one time that Tristram failed to appear, the Saracen knight brought with him four knights of Arthur's court and three sergeants-of-arms to "bear record of the battle .... And the one sergeant brought in his helm, the other his spear, the third his sword." [Malory X, 88] Though this was a single combat of the type that may have given rise to the duel of later centuries, sergeants-of-arms would surely also have served at tournaments.

Killing horses in battle seems to have been considered all right in warfare (as, presumably, against Saxons) but it was understandably frowned upon in "friendly" fighting such as that of tournaments. At the Lonazep tournament,

> Sir Palomides rushed unto Sir Launcelot, and thought to have put him to a shame; and with his sword he smote his horse's neck that Sir Launcelot rode upon, and then Sir Launcelot fell to the earth. Then was the cry huge and great: See how Sir Palomides the Saracen hath smitten down Sir Launcelot's horse. Right then were there many knights wroth with Sir Palomides because he had done that deed; therefore many knights held there against that it was unknightly done in a tournament to kill an horse wilfully, but that it had been done in plain battle, life for life. [Malory X, 70]

The incident is perplexing in that Palomides generally seems a more courteous knight. Perhaps, as a Saracen, he retained memories of Arthur's knights slaying horses in plain battle with his own people and did not quite as yet understand the tournament distinction. Or possibly the killing of horses in the lists was prohibited by an unwritten rather than an official rule.

Arthur's World According to Chrétien

Watch closely now: Chrétien tells us that according to a custom established in Logres before Lancelot's day, if a knight met a damsel traveling alone, raping her would cause him to be disgraced in all courts forever; but if she were traveling with a knight, the new knight had only to defeat her escort in combat, after which he could have his will of her without reproach. Even as Lerner and Loewe's "Camelot" line about virgins traveling unmolested echoes through our minds, we should perhaps remind ourselves that Chrétien was writing about what he and his audience already regarded as a mythical, even semimystical distant past, and probably not treating it with as much respect as some would like to believe. I even scent some possibility that Chrétien may have invented the above custom in order to facilitate his plot. [**Lancelot**, ll. 1293-1337]

Among other customs Chrétien records of Arthur's times, some of which we can recognize from other and frequently later sources, and which may or may not apply to Chrétien's own contemporary milieu, we find Arthur's guarantee of safe conduct for virgins when journeying through his land [**Perceval**, ca. ll. 7120-7131]; the forty days' grace period to find a champion for one's cause in trial by combat [**Yvain**, ca. l. 4800]; and Arthur's refusal to dine on high feast-days before hearing some news [**Perceval**, ca. ll. 2821-2825]. Knights were exempt from taxes or tolls which traveling merchants had to pay; a merchant who disguised himself as a knight in order to take advantage of the exemption courted the thief's death of hanging [**Perceval**, ll. 5060-5090]. In tournament, a knight defeated, or "taken prisoner", was bound to keep faith by seeking his conqueror out within the year [**Cligés**, ll. 4727-4759]. Once taken prisoner, a knight could no longer participate in the tournament. Knights who had "taken the cross" as crusaders could not participate in any tournament—though this seems an anachronism, since the Crusades surely postdated even Chrétien's Arthurian "in those days." A knight might also take at least a temporary vow of peace for such reasons as to observe the Truce of God or to save himself for judicial combat. [**Perceval**, l. 5058 & Owen's note to same] Not limited to tournament usage was the custom of surrendering "as you were when defeated": thus, Clamadeu of the Isles had to travel to Arthur's court and deliver himself up still wearing exactly the gear he had worn when Percivale defeated him [**Perceval**, ca. ll. 2722-2747].

While Chrétien more than once includes passages regarding the supposed inferiority of women, I should guess these passages to reflect—even satirize—the misogyny of his era rather than his own attitude.

Satire and parody, sometimes hard to recognize even in their own day, can become very tricky indeed to distinguish from serious opinion centuries after their specific original targets have been forgotten and the language itself changed. Nevertheless, I would contend that nobody who created the vital, active female characters Chrétien left us can truly have subscribed to misogyny. For instance, in addition to all the examples found in the entries for various of his women characters, at least three times (not counting uses made of Morgan's ointments) he shows women instrumental in the healing of wounds: in **Perceval** [ca. ll. 4340-4345], two maids assist their physician-teacher in treating Kay's broken arm and dislocated collarbone; in **Yvain** [4691ff.] and **Erec & Enide** [5091-5235] the ladies nurse and doctor on their own.

Before Percivale leaves home, his mother counsels him about the importance of quickly learning the names of his companions; it later transpires that he would have been wiser to follow the spirit of her advice than Gornemant's caution against speaking too much [**Perceval**, ca. ll. 558-562; 3192-3358, etc.]. Her words strike a curious note, for not only does she seem never to have told her son *his own* name, but her author, Chrétien himself, often left his own characters nameless, or delayed giving their names until—possibly—after their deaths! (In **Erec & Enide**, ll. 2025-ca. 2035, he explains that it is not customary to call women by their true names until they are married. He does not apply this rule with any consistency—cf. the case of Fenice; nor does it seem to explain male characters long left unnamed.)

A good description of the process of packing up the royal court can be found in **Perceval**, lines 4144-4161. Although in this case Arthur is taking his entire company on a search for the young Welsh knight, they would be following the same routine they knew by the long practice of attending their monarch on his regular progress through various court cities of his realm.

In **Yvain**, Chrétien tells his readers that one league of "our" country equals two leagues of "that" country. "Our" country here would be Chrétien's own area of France, while "that" country would probably be Arthur's Britain. There might, however, be some chance of "that country" being the Other World, which throughout Chrétien's works never seems very far from Logres, even though otherworldly pockets, whether of Faery or of the Afterlife (if, indeed, there is a sharp distinction) may not be overtly identified as such.

Chrétien: an Initial Impression

Chrétien de Troyes wrote in the French of the late twelth century and in verse. Translations of his work into modern English verse seem even scarcer than prose versions. So, preferring translations that approximate as closely as possible the form and style of any original, I put off reading Chrétien for years.

When Greg proposed expanding **The King Arthur Companion** by combing Chrétien's Arthurian romances as I had earlier combed Malory and the Vulgate, and even loaned me his copy of D.D.R. Owen's recent translation for the work, I found myself in a world with a charm that survives even transference into the prose of an alien culture eight centuries removed from its author. If I have had to suspend my other projects for half a year, Chrétien has repaid me munificently.

Not that I feel equally delighted with Owen's translation. By his own admission, Owen intended it in part as a legitimate pony for students simultaneously tackling Chrétien's work in the original. Therefore, he wished to make it as literal as possible, even reproducing most of Chrétien's sudden changes in verb tense. The most accurate word-for-word translation of any work is not necessarily the one that best recaptures its spirit; the usefulness of Owen's version even as a pony must be severely limited, at least in the Everyman edition of 1987, by the way in which it is printed as straight prose, with verse numbers only at the beginning of each paragraph, the paragraph division being Owen's (although the stinginess of verse numeration could be the editor's). On the surface, this version of Chrétien's romances reads very much like a rather clumsy modernization of Malory. I suspect that the incessant shifts back and forth between past and historical present tense, which can seriously annoy the reader of modern English, were scarcely even noticed by the original audience: even in our own century, such shifts remain common in certain non-English literatures.

I happen to possess a nineteenth-century copy of **Cligés** in the original French, with editorial matter in German; I tried to read the text, but could sense only its sprightly and musical charm, without being able to follow the story at all. It was not until I reached Chrétien's last romance, and turned to a lucky acquisition from my own backlog—Ruth Harwood Cline's translation into modern English verse—that I enjoyed a taste of what I had only been able to sense from **Cligés** in the original language. While preparing my **Companion** entries for **Perceval**, I have continually consulted Cline's version along with Owen's, and found a few scholarly differences; they rarely if ever jolt one's understanding of the text in any important way. I can but wish that I had a complete set of Chrétien's romances in verse translations by Ruth Harwood Cline or someone equally skillful. (True, she insists on the "guh-WANE" pronunciation of Gawain's name; but, as Bret Maverick observed somewhere, it's hard to buck the whole stampede.)

Yet verse enjoyed a popularity among readers of Chrétien's day that it does not enjoy in our own time. Perhaps the best way to translate the spirit of his romances for us moderns would be to make them into comic books or animated cartoon features. Time and again, I found myself best able to make sense of a scene by visualizing it as something out of a 1940s movie cartoon; much or most of Chrétien's **Lancelot** seems to me a glorious cross between an extended dream sequence and a classic Bugs Bunny escapade.

Such graphics would need to be done in a style balanced between the purely whimsical and the quasirealistic, capable of melting from the outrageously comic to the more or less serious and back again at a moment's notice. Puns and topical allusions relevant to our own milieu should replace those relevant to Chrétien's—advertising slogans, for example, might be used instead of proverbs no longer in everybody's mouth; caricatures of famous twentieth-century individuals (either real or ficitional) could replace allusions accessible nowadays, if at all, only to scholars, letting us glimpse, say, Prince Valiant in lieu of Ignaures or Droes d'Aves.

While felicity of wordplay disappears as language changes, and satire loses its punch as its targets fade from current affairs into footnotes in scholarly tomes (until ancient satire risks being mistaken for a serious presentation of the very thing the author was refuting!), situational humor remains. I cannot shake the feeling that to read and interpret Chrétien's Arthurian romances solemnly may well be analogous to sitting snug in the twenty-eighth century trying to piece together deep philosophical theological meanings and an accurate historical understanding of twentieth-century life out of the collected works of P.G. Wodehouse.

This is not by any means to state that comedy never rests on deep foundations nor yields seeds of serious thought. Every Gilbert & Sullivan opera has, mixed into the giddy fun, moments of serious dramatic interest, occasionally verging on the tragic. All my life, I have heard much about the importance of comic relief in serious drama and tragedy, but little or nothing about dramatic or even tragic relief in comedy; yet the latter must certainly hold as much importance as the former. We like to cry or tremble—provided we can do it safely and vicariously—as much as we like to laugh, and we like to think, solve puzzles, and seek out symbolisms as much as we like to laugh, cry, or tremble. I have found

Chrétien's romances primarily comical, yet with an inescapable underpinning of sentiment (not sentimentality) and even mysticism.

Take, for example, all these apparent pockets and outbranches of the Otherworld, from King Evrain's Brandigant, to King Bademagu's Gorre, to Queen Ygerne's Rock of Canguin, that seem to dot Chrétien's fictional landscape more thickly than lost civilizations in Tarzan's Africa. Is it Faeryland, or the Christian Afterlife, or some blend of both that Chrétien's characters continually encounter? If Gorre and Canguin are indeed outposts of Heaven, one regrets that Chrétien could not come and go as easily as his characters, so that he could have left us his own ending of **Perceval** and perhaps **Lancelot**.

In the process of getting preliminary impressions of Chrétien's works, I have also gotten some preliminary impression of Chrétien scholarship in relation to general Arthurian studies; this latter is a very strange impression indeed. Granted, it is based on a mere smattering of books and footnote references to other books, yet the picture these give me seems uncomfortably consistent. I get the idea that people who study Chrétien have as little truck as possible with people who study the later Arthurian romances, and vice versa. Just for instance: D.D.R. Owen seems unacquainted with the scarcely obscure tradition that has Gawaine wielding Excalibur, and both Owen and Cline give us footnotes that identify Ygerne's daughter (Gawaine's mother) with no apparent awareness of her name in the Vulgate and Malorian cycles, where she is far from an unimportant figure. Meanwhile, such a voluminous Arthurian student as John Mathews can state in **The Elements of the Arthurian Tradition** [©1989] that every important version of the Arthurian cycle since Geoffrey of Monmouth has featured Merlin!

I can better understand this attitude in the Chrétien people, for I find that Chrétien's world is, indeed, worth exploring in its own right and for its own sake. Why scholars of the other Arthurian traditions should largely ignore or downplay Chrétien's work seems more difficult to comprehend.

The Chrétien people credit him with actually creating the Arthurian romance as we know it. As of this writing, the only evidence I have seen to throw doubt on this accreditation is my reading of Chrétien's romances themselves: beginning with the earliest one, **Erec & Enide**, much in them strikes me as parody, and I find it difficult to imagine how or why any author could simultaneously create a genre and parody it. This might, however, be explained with the theory that the genre Chrétien spoofed was that of the *chansons de geste*. That would mean that Arthurian romance was born as a joke and soon started taking itself far too seriously. I can see how this thought, even if subconscious, might offend many grave Arthurian scholars; perhaps their attitude (assuming I read it correctly) is not so incomprehensible, after all.

Among my books is an undistinguished 1901 printing of Tennyson's **Idylls** with a quaintly dated introduction by Eugene Parsons, remarkable for giving about as many reasons not to bother with the book as to read it, and beginning with the *cons*. Parsons felt that such medieval romances as the **Morte D'arthur** were "wearisome reading", the taste for which was "on the decline in this matter-of-fact scientific age." Putting this 1901 opinion together with my own small observation of Arthurian literature in the twentieth century, I find it hard to avoid the conclusion that we largely owe both the resurgence of Arthurian interest and its prevailing present-day emphasis to the two World Wars. To some degree, King Arthur seems to have become a symbol of the English spirit during the darkest war years. I should guess this to be why the "Last Light against the Heathen Darkness" or "Cosmic Good Standing against Cosmic Evil" school has become so very prominent in Arthurian writing.

If I remember aright, it was German scholars of the nineteenth century who kicked off the present round of Chrétien studies. This might work against him among our own century's English and English-speaking Arthurianites, especially in measure as they remember battling descendants of some of the German scholars' fellow countrymen and women. (Let me emphasize the word "some." German blood flows in my own veins, a heritage from my mother's side of the family.) If I am not too far off the mark, then today's Arthurian fiction and nonfiction, in the English-speaking world, may show some probably unconscious feeling that the *German* rediscovery of a twelfth-century *French* romancer automatically relegates that romancer's work to secondary or negligible importance. Arthur was British; hence, his roots *must* be British, and the French poet's work a mere versifying of British originals—and never mind the close connection in Chrétien's day between the two sides of the Channel.

More than once, I have found the **Mabinogion** matter-of-factly listed as the main source of the earliest known Arthurian material. I myself accepted this without question ... right up until last winter, when it finally penetrated my historical consciousness that the great Welsh collection as we have it today was actually first written down about a century *after* Chrétien's death! This gives Chrétien scholars room to argue that the **Mabinogion**'s authors took three of their tales from Chrétien, rather than the other way around. (The all-British school, of course, has to maintain that the **Mabinogion** stories were already ancient and venerable, presumably pretty well word for word, by the time they were committed to parchment.) Between these two schools stands the opinion I find most rational: that both Chrétien and the **Mabinogion** author(s) drew from a common source, lost to us.

There still exists a pre-Chrétien and Lancelot-less Welsh version of Guenevere's abduction by an Otherworldly ruler. Alas, this is not one of the three stories named as common to Chrétien and the **Mabinogion** — they are EREC (alias GEREINT), **Yvain** (OWAIN), and **Perceval** (PEREDUR). The story of Guenevere's abduction does, however, lend strength to the Lost Common Source theory. At the same time, I conceive that much in Chrétien's treatments could have worked its way back across the Channel and influenced the Welsh treatments as we have them. A lot of literary cross-fertilizing can happen within the generations of a century, especially in an era without copyright restrictions.

It is easy enough, when dealing with authors of eight centuries ago, to raise the assumption of lost originals for anything one does not want such authors to have invented. The Lost Original theory can never be *dis*proved, thanks to the number of volumes known to have disappeared in burned libraries and other mishaps ... but there always remains the hope that some new discovery will take place to *prove* it.

Nevertheless, as nearly as I can make out pending the discovery of such theoretical lost originals, Chrétien may well have given us the traditional characterizations of Kay (who plays a more or less featured supporting role in all Chrétien's Arthurian romances except **Cligés**, even getting a longish and physically flattering portrait in **Perceval**—and who was to remain remarkably unchanged right through Malory's time into the present); Gawaine (who, while much degenerated, still remains recognizable in Malory and was to reappear more or less á la Chrétien, except with black hair, in Hal Foster's **Prince Valiant**); Lancelot; Ywaine; probably Guenevere; Percivale; and Gawaine's horse Gringolet. I say characterizations: of course, many if not all these characters existed already in tales of Britain's King Arthur, but Chrétien may have been the one to put that distinctive stamp on their personalities. To him we may even owe a certain saucy and self-sufficient type of damsel who reappears in various characters through later romances. He seems to have given us the very name "Camelot", though I question this because for him it was no more than one of Arthur's many court cities, of which Caerleon actually seems the most prominent. He may have been the first to put the Grail into the Arthurian saga: he himself mentions taking its story from another book, but I suspect that this kind of claim could sometimes amount to a mere literary device, as it rather often does now; even assuming that this source existed, who is to say that it mixed Arthur into the Grail story?

On the other hand, while Chrétien several times mentions Morgan, her Malorian nemesis Merlin is conspicuously absent from his surviving work, as is Mordred. While he names Gawaine's father and three full brothers pretty much as Malory was to name them, he also shows Gawaine as having a number of sisters who seem to have vanished completely from the cycle by the time it reached Malory. While the events of his **Lancelot** and the titular part of his **Perceval** were to be retold by romancer after romancer down into our own times, his other plots, even those that reappear in the **Mabinogion**, seem pretty well to have faded out. Ywaine and Erec-Gereint remain as characters, but their adventures as Chrétien told them do not; Tennyson picked Gereint's tale up once more, but presumably from the **Mabinogion**. All this would seem to suggest that Chrétien really was not quite so influential as all that, and bring us back to the Lost Original Source theory. I want to be as fair as possible.

On internal evidence alone, I do not think that Chrétien invented Lancelot. (He could not even have known that someday this name would form a built-in English pun—"lance-a-lot"—though that knowledge almost certainly have delighted him.) Chrétien first names Lancelot in **Erec**, as Arthur's third-best knight, in which role he reappears for the sole purpose of being unhorsed by young Cligés to show off the latter's prowess. These romances are dated as of earlier composition than the one in which Chrétien featured Lancelot as hero. It strikes me as highly unlikely that any fictioneer would make up an entity, assign him such a prominent place in the roll call, and then use him in such bit parts as Lancelot plays in **Erec** and **Cligés**. It makes poor dramatic sense now, and in this point I can hardly believe literary composition has changed so very much. Therefore, I think Chrétien was reusing a knight who already existed, probably in fiction, probably as one of Arthur's best.

Coghlan and Matthews, citing Loomis, suggest this was a mythic Welsh knight named Llwch Lleminawc, but without adducing much further evidence than the fact that both characters have "l" in their names. I should like to know more about the twelfth-century Swiss romance **Lanzalet**.

That Chrétien could indeed sprinkle his romances with cameo appearances of or allusions to heroes known to his audience from other presumably popular romances is apparent from the cases of Tristran, Ignaures, and Duke Laudunet. I suspect that such cases abound in Chrétien's supporting casts and lists of knights, but the songs and stories about them have disappeared, perhaps forever. Lancelot's may well be such a case.

Turning from what Chrétien de Troyes may or may not have given us to what he all but indisputably *did*, we have either five or six Arthurian romances, three of them presumed complete from his pen:

Erec & Enide (dated ca. 1170)
Cligés (ca. 1176)
Lancelot, or **The Knight of the Cart** (ca. 1177)
Yvain, or **The Knight with the Lion** (ca. 1177)
Perceval, or **The Story of the Grail** (ca. 1182)

Yvain alone, with its atypically modern-sounding opening and sure touch throughout, should have been enough to establish its author's reputation down to our time.

Perceval, as we have it, includes enough material about Gawaine to fuel the theory that his adventures originally formed a second unfinished romance, which someone worked into Percivale's story after Chrétien's death. The alternative theory has it that Chrétien meant all along to counterbalance Percivale's story with Gawaine's and that, aside from being incomplete, what we have is as nearly what Chrétien intended as centuries of ms. to ms. transmission have left it.

D.D.R. Owen rather clearly subscribes to the Separate Unfinished Romances theory, Ruth Harwood Cline to the As Chrétien Designed It one. Much can be said in favor of either theory, and I intend here neither to summarize the arguments I have so far seen, nor to commit myself irrevocably either way. Emotionally, I prefer the As Chrétien Designed It theory. This may in part result from my enjoying Cline's translation so much more than Owen's; still, Cline points out enough plot parallels to raise in my mind the spectral idea that, if Chrétien had indeed been working on two separate pieces, his mind might have been slipping into repetitive patterns. This seems to me a worse slippage than the chronology problems raised if the two plots were meant from the first to comprise a unified whole: these time discrepancies could result from the rush of inspired composition; the author himself might have smoothed them away had he been granted life and leisure for revision.

Of course, Chrétien might have meant **Perceval** and **Gawain** as companion pieces, like **Lancelot** and **Yvain**. Dare I suggest that he might actually have considered **Perceval** as good as finished? Percivale's quest reaches a possible conclusion of sorts: obviously, not one that satisfied generations of continuators, but one that would satisfy me, anyway. Gawaine's tale inescapably and unarguably breaks off unfinished.

Internal evidence marks **Lancelot** (on my initial impression, probably the weakest of the canon) and **Yvain** (which I think easily the best) as companion pieces: time and again in **Yvain** someone (usually Gawaine) is unavailable to do something important (usually save somebody's life) because of being away in Gorre just when he is needed.

Owen appeals to the theory that Chrétien was too moral a man to approve the adulterous theme of **Lancelot**, which the fancy of a patroness had forced him to tackle, and that this could explain why he finally turned it over to someone else to finish. This theory does not satisfy me at all.

Lancelot ends with the statement by Godefroi de Leigni (a clerk apparently unknown to history save through this single chance) that, "I have finished Chrétien's romance; I had his own permission to do so; I wrote it from the point where Lancelot is walled in." **Yvain** ends with the statement, by Chrétien, that, "This is all there is of the story; you will never read any more unless it is added by some mendacious hand." What happened here? In light of such an accusatory-sounding statement at the end of **Yvain**, can we really accept it on faith, as Owen seems to, that Godefroi had Chrétien's permission to finish **Lancelot**; or can we interpret Godefroi's statement, again as Owen seems to, as meaning that Godefroi followed some plot outline given him by Chrétien?

For the sake of argument, let me accept that Godefroi finished **Lancelot** in accordance with Chrétien's own wishes and plot outline. In that scenario, by the point at which Godefroi testifies to taking over, the adulterous action is finished and done with, and all that remains is a bit of mopping up. That means that Chrétien plowed through the part he presumably found most distasteful and then cut himself out of any chance of punishing the adulterers, if only just a little. Strange, if distaste for adulterous love were really the reason he stopped work on **Lancelot**.

Consider **Cligés**, in which the titular hero and his lady miss being adulterers in the full sense of the word only by the merest technicality: Fenice has used her nurse's sorcery to cheat her legal husband out of any except imaginary relations with her, while she saves herself for Cligés. I am a firm believer in striving to recapture the mindsets of other cultures, but, in my opinion, to say that Chrétien, as a learned and moral man, could ease his conscience about Cligés and Fenice with such a technical argument and then in the next romance suffer moral outrage at the Lancelot-Guenevere affair is to assume a far greater difference in mindset than the rest of Chrétien's work displays, or than the rest of **Cligés** itself displays, for that matter. To argue that Fenice and Cligs are punished in advance, she with the agonies inflicted on her as a direct result of her ruse of feigning death, he by the fear that she will not survive, would be to ignore the fact that a certain amount of suffering is the all but inevitable lot of all heroes and heroines, no matter how virtuous, en route to the ending, no matter how happy, of any action story.

Consider, however, how Fenice, the woman whose deep dread of becoming known as another Isolde drives her to subterfuge and secrecy, becomes instead the notorious example who causes all future emperors of Constantinople to distrust their wives. Is not the most obvious explanation of this ironic conclusion the idea that Chrétien meant to show this adultery (in all but the most technical sense) bringing about its own punishment after all?

From beginning to end, **Cligés** is a work of moral ambiguities. Many of its "good guys" seem virtually indistinguishable from its "bad guys." Sometimes, indeed, as in the case of Sir Bertrand, the functional antagonists seem far more admirable than the nominal protagonists. But, if **Cligés** is the most obvious and outstanding example, the rest of Chrétien's world partakes of this same moral ambiguity. Over and over, we find good people involved in blameworthy actions and bad people softened by description of some virtue, explanation of motive, or change of heart. Aside from a very occasional stereotypical ogre or monster whose role lasts only long enough to describe his defeat, Chrétien's world is refreshingly free from the Unredeemed Evil vs. All-Pure Good mentality too often associated with Arthurian saga, at least nowadays. Chrétien gives us portraits of people in whom faults and virtues blend.

The single sustained exception I found—the one example of an unredeemedly villainous villain whose role continues throughout the romance—is **Lancelot**'s nemesis, Meliagrant. If Chrétien stopped work on **Lancelot** for any reason other than eagerness to begin work on that jewel of romances **Yvain**, I think it must have been less out of distaste for Lancelot and Guenevere, than out of boredom with Meliagrant.

At the point when Godefroi testifies that he took over, Meliagrant has twice fought Lancelot and twice had his life saved only by dint of his father Bademagu's intervention. A third combat has been scheduled, this one to take place at Arthur's rather than Bademagu's court. Meleagant will fight to prove his charge that Guenevere committed adultery with Sir Kay. Lancelot—or, in Lancelot's absence, his good friend Gawain—will champion the queen's innocence. But Meliagrant has secretly and treacherously imprisoned Lancelot.

In Godefroi's conclusion, Meleagant and Bademagu have a falling-out that permanently costs the son his father's affection. A damsel introduced far earlier, when Lancelot generously did her the favor of beheading her unwanted suitor, suddenly turns out to be Bademagu's daughter. Like Blondel looking for Richard the Lion-Heart, she goes in search of Lancelot, finds him, and enables him to get to Arthur's court in time to fight and kill Meleagant.

Bademagu has already, in Chrétien's part of the tale, forgiven Meliagrant worse sins than the one that causes the fatal rupture. This supposedly final rift between father and son strikes me as too convenient to Godefroi's purpose, too great a change in Bademagu's essential character, to ring true. I wonder if the following ending might have been more to Chrétien's taste, more in keeping with the general tenor of his opus: Lancelot does not get out of captivity in time to fight for his queen. That is their punishment for adultery. Gawaine, who, although already showing amorous tendencies in his own right, remains totally innocent of any knowledge of the adultery, is the one to fight Meliagrant and save Guenevere. This makes up for Gawaine's earlier failure to cross the Water Bridge into Gorre, and reinforces the place he still retains at this stage of Arthur's greatest knight. Bademagu once again pleads for his wayward son, so that, when the battle is obviously won in Guenevere's favor, Arthur passes judgment, sparing Meleagant's life while, probably, banishing him forever from Logres.

There remains in my mind the nattering notion that Godefroi de Leigni may himself be a fiction: that, feeling unsatisfied with how **Lancelot** had turned out, but not wanting to spend any further time with it, either because his patroness wanted it with no more delay or because he wanted to turn to **Yvain** a.s.a.p., Chrétien cobbled Godefroi up as an excuse for an ending he himself didn't much care for. On the face of it, this looks unlikely: would not Chrétien's patroness have known whether or not Godefroi existed? Still, such literary pretexts and devices have been used often enough to render me as cautious about accepting Godefroi de Leigni's actual existence, as I am about accepting books known only through an author's reference to them. Both Godefroi de Leigni and the book from which Chrétien testifies drawing the story of the Grail may all be part of Chrétien's joke—and the joke be on us, for taking it all so seriously!

Even as I began reading Chrétien's romances, two comic-book series were hitting the stands: a four-part continuation of Hal Foster's **Prince Valiant**, carrying the hero's story past Arthur's final battle; and a three-part story of how **Goofy King Arthur** came to the throne, featuring Goofy as Arthur (surely the most unexpected bit of casting since Daffy Duck played the part in the TV special *A Connecticut Rabbit*), Pete as Sir Kay, and Mickey Mouse himself—graduated from his role as the Sorcerer's Apprentice?—as Merlin. Both series were distributed at least in part by Marvel Comics. Some copies of the latter, however, bear the Gladstone logo, being found in that company's "Donald and Mickey", nos. 28-30. Through correspondence with John Clark, editor of the Bruce Hamilton Company Gladstone Disney Comic Line, I learned that **Goofy King Arthur** was one of a "Goofy through history" series, written by Greg Crosby and Cal Howard, and drawn in Argentina by the Jaime Diaz Studio in the late 1970s, but only appearing in the U.S.A. in 1995. The **Prince Valiant** saga is credited to Charles Vess, Elaine Lee, John Ridgway, Curtis Woodbridge, and John Workman, and was published by Marvel beginning in December 1994, on quality paper and with volume titles rather temerariously appropriated from those of T. H. White's **Once And Future King**.

These two works represent to me the twin extremes of Arthurian literature. It seems appropriate that the comic one should be about Arthur's coming, the serious one about his passing and its consequences. I found the **Prince Valiant** continuation eminently satisfying; at the same time, it is almost relentlessly grim. My study of Chrétien's works throws the Disney offering into an interesting perspective: while many readers might legitimately deplore it as a degenerate parody of the Matter of Britain, **Goofy King Arthur** looks to me far the closer of the two graphic novellas to the style and spirit in which Arthurian romance began. Assuming Chrétien to have been indeed the parent of the knightly romance, it seems to have been born in just such a spirit of fun as it was to expire, four centuries later, with **Don Quixote**. I cannot help but picture Chrétien de Troyes and Miguel de Cervantes, brought together through the magic of time warps and universal translators, enjoying each other's company with many a slapstick anecdote and good chuckle.

Bibliographical Note

I had intended to attempt a longish bibliography of all the titles in my personal Arthurian collection plus a few more for which I have the necessary information. It seems that every month at least one or two new Arthurian titles are published, besides the older ones that are constantly coming to my attention, so I decided to list here only those volumes that remained constantly at my elbow. The other sources, those I used less frequently, are (I hope) sufficiently identified where cited. Anything like a comprehensive bibliography of Arthurian books and Arthurian-related material would probably be an effort at least as long as the whole of this present book.

Malory, Sir Thomas. **Le Morte d'Arthur: The Book of King Arthur and His Knights of the Round Table**.

There are many editions of this work. My copy has the imprint New Hyde Park, N.Y.: University Books, ©1961; being a one-volume reprint of A.W. Pollard's version as printed in 1920 for the Medici Society. The index is so faulty that I demand it share the blame with me for any mistakes and overlooked references I have made! I do not claim this is the best edition of Malory ever printed, nor even the best presently in print; it had the great advantage of being the one I had ready to hand, and a personal copy suitable for hard use. It also has book and chapter divisions labeled as originating with Caxton, which facilitates making references.

A superb edition of Malory for the reader who would like to sample the flavor of the original is **Arthur Pendragon of Britain: A Romantic Narrative** by Sir Thomas Malory as edited from **Le Morte d'Arthur** by John W. Donaldson, illustrated by Andrew Wyeth. New York: G.P. Putnam's Sons [©1943].

Donaldson went on the principle that Malory *would* have edited and improved his work if he had had the chance—so Donaldson attempted to do it for him, cut the length of the book roughly in half, and succeeded admirably in making a coherent narrative of the books of Tristram ... but kept Malory's own language, with a minimum of minor verbal changes (aside from the cuts) everywhere except in the Grail Adventures. I was far from satisfied with the way Donaldson handled the Grail Adventures; the condensing of Tristram's adventures unfortunately cut out most of the episodes where Palomides shows to best advantage and only left those where he shows to worst; and Donaldson's apparent unawareness of the looseness with which terms of relationship were used led him to change Bors de Ganis from Lancelot's cousin to his nephew. With these cautions, I recommend

Donaldson's version very highly indeed. I do not recommend Keith Baines' retelling in modern prose, however.

The Vulgate Version of the Arthurian Romances. Edited from manuscripts in the British Museum by H. Oskar Sommer. Washington: The Carnegie Institution of Washington, 1909-1916. 8 v. (Vol. VIII is an index; vol. VII is a fragmentary romance supplementary to rather than continuing the cycle as presented in the first six volumes.)

The text of this is in medieval French, so I do not pretend I combed every page. But Sommer provided what seems to be a pretty complete summary in English glosses on every page of the first six volumes, and even from these the riches of the Vulgate version are obvious. Quotations identified as from the Vulgate are quotations of Sommer's English summary unless otherwise identified or in French. Names drawn from the Vulgate are generally in Sommer's standardizations. The AMS press appears to be making some gesture toward keeping the Vulgate in print at a typically outrageous scholarly price, but I have not yet at the time of revising this handbook been able to obtain the volumes and have had to depend on the notes made some time ago now, which were done, of necessity, in haste and may not always be perfectly reliable.

For Chrétien, I have used the most recent Everyman Classics edition: Chrétien de Troyes, **Arthurian Romances**, tr. with an introd. and notes by D.R.R. Owen; London and Melbourne: Dent, Everyman's Library [©1987]. This is a prose translation, with paragraphing by the translator and a line number only at the beginning of each paragraph, which makes it difficult to cite by exact line. Therefore, I have either given inclusive line numbers from the beginning of one paragraph to the beginning of another, or used "ca." if I felt brave enough to attempt an educated guess. Only when I found material at the very beginning or end of a paragraph, or when Owen's note pinpointed the line, have I ventured to cite an exact line number. Sometimes, when a citation would have involved too many lines, I have contented myself with giving merely the title of the romance in question.

Owen avows that his translation is primarily meant as an aid to students reading Chrétien's original Old French. No doubt it was because he expected his serious readers to have a copy of the original text at hand that he neglected to repeat the original versions of names and soubriquets in his own volume. I keenly regret this absence, which leaves me, for instance, able only to guess that the Do named as Girflet's parent is indeed "Dieu" and that Sagremor the Impetuous is indeed our old friend Sagramore le Desirous—not to mention such intriguing figures as the Handsome Coward and the Ugly Brave.

For Chrétien's **Perceval**, I have used Ruth Harwood Cline's sprightly translation into modern English verse (New York, etc.: Pergamon Press [©1983]) side by side with Owen's prose version. This enabled me to use a little more exactness about verse numbers in Chrétien's last romance; however, since Cline could not always render her translation 100% line for line, I have been generous with the "ca." in my citations.

The introduction and notes to my Dell edition of **Yvain** have been of as much use as the text: **Yvain, ou Le Chavalier au Lion**, [by] Chrétien de Troyes; translated into modern French by André Mary; introduction and notes by Julian Harris. New York: Dell Publishing Co., ©1963 (The Laurel Language Library; Germaine Bree, General Editor, French Series).

The Middle English metrical romances constitute a fourth rich source of Arthurian story more or less compatible with Malory and the Vulgate. The most famous and almost certainly the best of these romances is, of course, **Sir Gawaine and the Green Knight**, published in many, many editions, translations both verse and prose, and new versions over the last century or so. My favorite translation is that of John Gardner (in **The Complete Works of the Gawaine-Poet: In a Modern English Version with a Critical Introduction** by John Gardner, Woodcuts by Fritz Kredel. Chicago & London: University of Chicago Press, ©1965. Currently available in paperback). A number of other metrical romances are currently available in modern English prose translations in **The Knightly Tales of Sir Gawain**, with introductions and translations by Louis B. Hall (Chicago: Nelson-Hall, ©1976). This volume includes **Sir Gawaine and the Carl of Carlisle**, **The Green Knight** (an alternate version to the famous one mentioned above), **The Adventures at Tarn Wadling**, **Gologros and Gawain**, **An Adventure of Sir Gawain; The Avowing of King Arthur, Sir Gawain, Sir Kay, and Baldwin of Britain;** and **The Wedding of Sir Gawain and Dame Ragnell**.

Also constantly at my side was:

Glennie, John S. Stuart. **Arthurian Localities: Their Historical Origin, Chief Country, and Fingalian Relations ...** Edinburgh: Edmonton and Douglas, 1869, vi, 140 p. map.

The chief difficulty in using Glennie was that he wanted to put almost *all* Arthurian sites in southern Scotland and northernmost England. Also, his references to characters are often more tantalizing than enlightening.

After using the Edinburgh edition in a library, I acquired another copy, printed in **Merlin, or The Early History of King Arthur: A Prose Romance (about 1450-1460 A.D.)**, edited ... by Henry B.

Wheatley; Part [i.e., vol.] III. London: Early English Text Society, ca. 1869; reprinted 1938 by Kegan Paul, Trench, Trübner & Co. for the Society. This printing has the work paginated in lower-case Roman numerals, [xvii] to cxlvi; the numerals do not coincide with the Arabic pagination of the Edinburgh edition. Where I have cited Glennie with Arabic page numbers, the reference is to the Edinburgh ed. and drawn from my notes; where I have used Roman numerals, the reference is to the EETS publication.

It is popular to slight Alfred, Lord Tennyson's **Idylls of the King** nowadays; the only faults I find with these **Idylls** are Tennyson's treatment of Guenevere and his Victorianizing of Arthurian morality and mores. Otherwise, I think Tennyson's is a lovely version, and I have been favorably impressed with his scholarship. My best copy of **Idylls** is the Heritage Press edition of 1939, with illustrations in sepia and white by Robert Ball. Tennyson's **Idylls** are probably absolutely the latest literary rendition which I would ever be tempted to use as an "authority."

For geographical work, I used:

Collier's World Atlas and Gazetteer. New York, P. F. Collier & Son Corp., ©1942. Having been the family atlas for as long as I can remember, this shared with the University Books edition of Malory the great advantage of being ever-available.

Norden, John. **A Topographical and Historical Description of Cornwall**. London: Printed by W. Pearson ... 1728. Reprinted 1966 [by] Frank Graham, Newcastle Upon Tyne. Norden probably made his Survey of Cornwall in 1584, according to Graham's preface. The book makes one's mouth water for a description of the rest of Britain in the same style.

I also kept handy, in addition to the **Oxford English Dictionary** (The Compact Edition, complete text reproduced micrographically, Oxford University Press, 1971) and other dictionaries and standard reference works:

Brewer, E. Cobham. **The Reader's Handbook of Famous Names in Fiction, Allusions, References, Proverbs, Plots, Stories, and Poems**. A new ed., revised throughout and greatly enlarged. Philadelphia: Lippincott, 1899. Republished by Gale Research Company, Detroit, 1966. 2 v.

I confess that I am likelier to get around to reading new Arthurian novels before new books of Arthurian research. My favorite modern literary treatments so far are Rosemary Sutcliff's **Sword at Sunset**, Edison Marshall's **The Pagan King**, Vera Chapman's **Three Damosels** trilogy (**The King's Damosel, The Green Knight, King Arthur's Daughter**), John Erskine's **Tristran and Isolde** (though this one is not really "Arthurian" in that Arthur and his court do not appear), Mark Twain's **A Connecticut Yankee in King Arthur's Court**, Tennyson's **Idylls**, and T. H. White's **The Once and Future King**, which got me hooked on this whole field—if, indeed, Hal Foster's **Prince Valiant** had not already done it. Nor can I close without mentioning the film **Monty Python and the Holy Grail**, which may be to our generation what **Connecticut Yankee** was to Twain's, and which should be seen whenever possible as an antidote to taking the Arthurian legend too seriously. The present work was already in print when I obtained Thomas Berger's 1978 novel **Arthur Rex**, surely one of the grandest Arthurians of our century, although, like rare wine and fine cheese, it may be best savored slowly, in small portions.

The conviction grew greater and greater in me while working on this project that in style and spirit Hal Foster may be the closest heir to the medieval romancers that our modern era has produced. The comic strip of our day is perhaps the most popular of "literary" mediums, as the presentations of minstrels would have been in the Middle Ages. Foster's technique of making up his own hero and inserting him into the already-existing body of Arthurian material is almost surely what many of the medieval romancers must have done through the centuries; had Foster lived before Malory, Val, Aleta, Arn, and others might well have gotten into Malory and thence into the present handbook.

In preparing the second edition, I regret that time allowed me to read only two chapters of Lewis Spence's interesting book **The Magic Arts in Celtic Britain**, cited in my text as **Magic Arts**. (Reprint ed. NY: Dorset Press [1992]; original publisher and date not given, but latest date in Spence's bibliographical list is 1944.) In chapter XII, "The Cultus of Arthur", Spence expounds the theory that the Matter of Britain preserves an ancient religion in which Arthur was a hero-god, the savior who would deliver Britain from the Saxon invader and who was central to a cult that developed as Rome was abandoning the island. In chapter XIII, "The Mystery of the Grail", he identifies the Holy Grail with the Cauldron of Annwn of older Celtic mythology. With the Grail, I found Spence on solid ground. His theory about Arthur as god failed, however, to convince me. The documentary evidence may exist that Arthur played so large a role in British awareness as early as the sixth century C.E., but I have not yet encountered it. Nor can I consider the **Mabinogion** such evidence: it may well embody stories that were hoary when Chrétien wrote, but we cannot know this, if our earliest written copy of the Welsh tales dates from about a century after Chrétien. Much interfusing can happen in a century! Especially when we consider the ties between Britain and Brittany at this period, and the geographical proximity of Wales to the more Normanized east of the island. Were Arthur and his knights the old Celtic gods, or did someone identify them with the old gods in those generations between Chrétien and the extant written versions of the Welsh tales? As nearly as I have yet discovered, by the time the earliest known Arthurian romances were written down, the Saxon invaders against whom the hero-god Arthur was once purportedly invoked had not only interbred with the earlier Britons to become the island nation's common stock, but had in their turn suffered defeat by and were beginning to assimilate the new Norman invaders. Though I must reread the Victorians to be sure, I cannot remember actually meeting the idea of Arthur as the Last Light against the Savage Darkness in any earlier source than Spence's own study—assuming Spence to have written during World War II, as his bibliographical list suggests. I thus find in his work support for my own theory that this view of Arthur has been born of a perceived need of our own times. Of course, in similar and obviously sincere fashion Spence found in his reading support for his theories; to me it looks like one more new belief system determinedly finding or forging ancient roots for itself.

Before reading Spence, I would have credited filmmaker John Boorman with the happy inspiration of identifying Arthur with the Maimed King and thus making magnificent dramatic sense of the Grail Quest. But no: here is the same identification recorded in Spence's pages. Now, when I find Merlin willingly taken by the Great Dragon in the **Prince Valiant** sequel to Arthur's passing, I feel unwilling even to guess whether the comic-book team borrowed this earth serpent from Boorman's movie **Excalibur** or whether it goes back to some common source as yet unknown to me. This incertitude, in a case of contemporary Arthurian literature ... and can we feel surprised about confusion when dealing with the medieval works?

Whether or not the religious aspect propounded by Spence is truly ancient, it appears to be alive today. In presenting it as a living religious system, John Mathews, author of **The Elements of the Arthurian Tradition** (Shaftesbury, Dorset; Rockport, Mass.; & Brisbane, Queensland: Element [Books Limited, ©1989]), does not even list Spence in his bibliography, an omission suggesting to me that the movement is rather widespread. As for myself, while claiming the right to dip into such publications, as respectfully as into those of any other religion (after all, Mathews has done me the honor of listing the 1983 edition of this **Companion** in his bibliography), I wish to make it clear that with me Arthurianism is a literary enthusiasm and a semischolarly hobby, nothing more.

PHYLLIS ANN KARR

has written many recent works of fiction, including *My Lady Quixote*, *Lady Susan*, *Frostflower and Thorn*, *Meadowsong*, *Perola*, *The Elopement*, *Wildraith's Last Battle*, and *Frostflower and Windbourne*. Of special interest to readers of this book is her Arthurian murder mystery, *Idylls of the Queen*. A freelance writer, the author was born in a Navy hospital in Oakland, California, and was raised in the northwest tip of Indiana. She currently resides with her husband in Bayfield County, Wisconsin, a long county with a single traffic light.

PENDRAGON™ FICTION

Percivale and the Presence of God

by Jim Hunter

The young Percival of Arthurian legend. Freely adapted from Malory and Chrétien de Troyes, the story tells of Percival's dual quest for Arthur and the Grail, and of the strange loss that follows. — "One thrills time and again at [Hunter's] use of words."–*Daily Telegraph.* "Percival considers in turn the evidence for something outside his realistic world of mud and murder: conscience, sexuality, love, altruism."–*Times Literary Supplement.* "[Hunter's] best book so far."–*Guardian.*

The Bear of Britain

by Edward Frankland

A daring and brilliant effort to recreate the historical Arthur, set amid the savage confusion of the Dark Ages. Frankland's portrait of Arthur bears the stamp of truth. Not the Arthur of Geoffrey, of Malory, or of Tennyson, Frankland's Arthur is a tough Celtic warrior, the last native monarch of the British peoples as they struggle against the Saxon invaders.